W9-BBT-342

ENCYCLOPEDIA OF AFRICAN AMERICAN HISTORY 1896 TO THE PRESENT

FROM THE AGE OF SEGREGATION TO THE TWENTY-FIRST CENTURY

About the Encyclopedia

The editorial board and Oxford University Press have developed two encyclopedias of African American history and culture. The purpose of the two sets is to provide a comprehensive view of the wealth of information about and scholarship on African Americans from 1619 to the present in what began as a collection of European colonies, but which became the United States of America.

Encyclopedia of African American History, 1619–1895:
From the Colonial Period to the Age of Frederick Douglass
(Published in 2006)

Encyclopedia of African American History, 1896 to the Present:
From the Age of Segregation to the Twenty-first Century

ENCYCLOPEDIA OF AFRICAN AMERICAN HISTORY 1896 TO THE PRESENT

FROM THE AGE OF SEGREGATION TO THE TWENTY-FIRST CENTURY

Editor in Chief

Paul Finkelman

VOLUME 1

A–C

OXFORD
UNIVERSITY PRESS
2009

OXFORD
UNIVERSITY PRESS

Oxford University Press, Inc., publishes works that further
Oxford University's objective of excellence
in research, scholarship, and education.

Oxford New York
Auckland Cape Town Dar es Salaam Hong Kong Karachi
Kuala Lumpur Madrid Melbourne Mexico City Nairobi
New Delhi Shanghai Taipei Toronto

With offices in
Argentina Austria Brazil Chile Czech Republic France Greece
Guatemala Hungary Italy Japan Poland Portugal Singapore
South Korea Switzerland Thailand Turkey Ukraine Vietnam

Published by Oxford University Press, Inc.
198 Madison Avenue, New York, New York, 10016
www.oup.com

The Library of Congress Cataloging-in-Publication Data

Encyclopedia of African American history, 1896 to the present : from the age of segregation to the twenty-first century /
editor in chief, Paul Finkelman.
p. cm.
Includes bibliographical references and index.
ISBN 978-0-19-516779-5 (set : alk. paper)
1. African Americans—History—Encyclopedias. 2. African Americans—History—1877–1964—Encyclopedias.
3. African Americans—History—1964—Encyclopedias. 4. African Americans—Biography—Encyclopedias.
I. Finkelman, Paul, 1949–
E185.E5453 2009
973'.0496073—dc22
2008034263

3 5 7 9 8 6 4

Printed in the United States of America on acid-free paper

EDITORIAL AND PRODUCTION STAFF

ACQUIRING EDITOR

Ralph Carlson

DEVELOPMENT EDITORS

Anthony Aiello Timothy H. Sachs

PRODUCTION EDITORS

Georgia S. Maas Nancy B. Tan

EDITORIAL ASSISTANTS

Stephen Alsa Christina Carroll Alex K. Rich Holly Seabury Shona Sequeira

EDP COORDINATOR

Chad Zimmerman

PRODUCTION ASSISTANTS

Luba Patlakh Byron Wright

COPYEDITORS

Heidi Yerkes
Sylvia J. Cannizzaro Joe Clements Gretchen Gordon Jean F. Kaplan
Peter Letzelter-Smith Katherine H. Maas
Robin Perlow Mary Hawkins Sachs

PROOFREADERS

Katharyn Dunham Mary Flower Carol Holmes Mary-Lou Pilkinton

ART RESEARCH

Hilary Mac Austin

INDEX PREPARED BY

Katharyn Dunham, ParaGraphs

COMPOSITOR

SPi

MANUFACTURING CONTROLLER

Genieve Shaw

COVER DESIGN

Nora Wertz

EXECUTIVE EDITOR

Stephen Wagley

PUBLISHER

Casper Grathwohl

For John Hope Franklin

A mentor, a role model, and a friend

Contents

List of Entries

VOLUME 3

VOLUME 4

Introduction

In 2006, Oxford University Press published the three-volume *Encyclopedia of African American History, 1619–1895.* Now, the five-volume *Encyclopedia of African American History, 1896 to the Present* begins where that set left off: it completes the comprehensive survey of African American history with nearly 1,250 entries that reflect the trauma, tragedy, hope, and accomplishments of black culture and life since 1896. The previous set began with the emergence of slavery near the beginning of the colonial period and ended with the death of Frederick Douglass, the massive disfranchisement of African Americans following the end of Reconstruction, and the emergence of Booker T. Washington as the most prominent black man in the nation. The new set begins in 1896—the year in which the U.S. Supreme Court decided *Plessy v. Ferguson*, giving its stamp of approval to the emerging de jure segregation in the American South—and ends in our own time, an age in which two African Americans in a row have served as U.S. secretary of state and a third has been elected president of the United States.

These five volumes chronicle an astounding history, from segregation to integration at the highest levels of American society. They also chronicle the incomplete nature of this transformation, placing in historical context the continued discrimination against African Americans and the grim disparities in wealth, access to health care, and life chances between blacks and whites in modern America. The entries in this Encyclopedia chronicle heroism and determination, success and failure, cultural innovation, and social change that have affected blacks and whites over the course of our history. In 1903 the great black intellectual W. E. B. Du Bois predicted that the problem of the twentieth century would be the problem of "the color line." These volumes underscore the continuing accuracy of his prediction.

This new set begins in the mid-1890s, a watershed period for African Americans. In 1895 Frederick Douglass died. Since the 1840s this independent newspaper editor, politician and officeholder, adviser to presidents, and successful orator had been the de facto spokesman of an entire race. His autobiography, which went through three incarnations, inspired Americans, black and white, for half a century.

The passing of Douglass—an uncompromising, fearless black man who never flinched in his opposition to slavery, racism, and discrimination—marked the end of an era. In 1896, the year after Douglass died, the Supreme Court in *Plessy v. Ferguson* upheld the right of the states formally to segregate African Americans. The Court's decision signaled that the federal courts would no longer attempt to protect the promise of equality found in the amendments added to the Constitution after the Civil War. By the end of the nineteenth century, the legal and political conditions for blacks had worsened. The Supreme Court gave implicit approval to the disfranchisement of southern blacks in *Williams v. Mississippi* in 1898, and in the same year the national government turned a blind eye to the massive use of force, violence, and intimidation that led to a virtual coup d'état in Wilmington, North Carolina, where black elected officials were forced to resign their offices to avoid being murdered. In 1901 Representative George H. White of North Carolina left office, the last of two generations of post–Civil War blacks to serve in Congress. More than seven decades passed before southern blacks again had a major voice in the national legislature.

At Atlanta's Cotton States and International Exposition in September 1895, seven months after the death of Douglass, Booker T. Washington gave his most famous speech. Known derisively as the Atlanta Compromise, this speech was not the surrender of a black leader, but it did reflect a realistic understanding that segregation was the way of the near future, and it recognized that, at least in the South, blacks faced a diminishing role in politics and social life. With about 90 percent of all blacks living in the former slave states, Washington believed that African Americans faced a grim future and that simply protecting the lives and livelihoods of blacks must be the central mission of any leader. With rural poverty on the rise and lynching a constant threat, Washington sought to provide some security and safety for blacks until the time was ripe to regain political rights and greater economic opportunity.

Washington was the most important African American of his age, and he was the most influential black man among whites. But as the five volumes of the new Encyclopedia show, other African Americans, in the North as well as in the South, struggled to make a place for themselves in American society. In education, culture, law, business, politics, and sports, black people created space for themselves and struggled to achieve a measure of equality. The NAACP emerged early in the twentieth century as a voice for civil rights, with a litigation staff ready to fight in the courts to force the United States to live up to the promises of the Constitution. In the Spanish-American War and World War I, black soldiers proved their mettle and gained fame and even grudging respect from the majority-white culture that preferred simply to segregate blacks and forget about them. In the Harlem Renaissance black writers, artists, musicians, and performers fundamentally altered the very nature of American cultural life. In the boxing ring Jack Johnson and Joe Louis challenged the absurdities of racism, while more quietly, but just as profoundly, scholars and scientists such as W. E. B. Du Bois, Carter G. Woodson, and Charles Drew demonstrated—to anyone who cared to notice—that black intellectual accomplishment disproved, over and over again, racist assumptions about inequality.

World War I, the Great Depression, and World War II profoundly altered the demography of race, as millions of southern blacks moved north and west, seeking better lives. They encountered racism and discrimination, but they also found more economic opportunity, access to better education, and the chance to participate in politics. By the end of World War II northern blacks had two seats in Congress, and hundreds more sat in state legislatures and on city councils. Returning veterans from World War II were unwilling to accept second-class status, and political, legal, economic, social, and cultural conditions were right for change. Significantly, only a year after the war ended, the Brooklyn Dodgers signed Jackie Robinson, a former U.S. Army lieutenant and star college athlete, to play baseball in a previously all-white league. His teammate on the UCLA football team, Kenny Washington, helped integrate professional football at about the same time.

Civil rights activists and lawyers, aided by some sympathetic northern politicians, soon pushed for an end to segregation. The Supreme Court decision in *Brown v. Board of Education* in 1954 did not end all racism or segregation in the nation. It did not even lead to a system of integrated schools. But it did send a signal to millions of southern blacks that at least one branch of the national government was ready to support a struggle for equality. The struggle was carried out on many levels. In the streets Martin Luther King Jr. and others led countless demonstrations—often in the face of brutal suppression by angry white mobs or policemen who considered "law and order" to mean beating unarmed civil rights marchers. In the courts lawyers and judges grappled with how to reshape American law from endorsing segregation to banning it. Political leaders, responding to the courage of civil rights demonstrators and the brutality of southern officials and police, finally acted. Presidents Eisenhower, Kennedy, and Johnson sent federal marshals and federal troops to enforce court orders and to protect civil rights demonstrators. Congress passed three major civil rights laws—in 1964, 1965, and 1968—that finally broke the back of segregation. The costs were high, including the deaths of King, Medgar Evers, and many others whose names and stories find their place in these volumes. The formal end to segregation did not end racism or discrimination. Nor did it produce social, political, or economic equality. Urban riots and radical politics, also chronicled here, illustrate the failure of laws or of the massive changes in politics to create a truly equal America.

African American history is not, of course, just about politics, law, or discrimination. Culture, art, music, literature, play, work, family, and faith more regularly affect people in their day-to-day lives. The five volumes of the new Encyclopedia provide an analysis of cultural figures from the jazz and blues musicians of a century ago to the hip-hop artists of today, from Paul Robeson's impact on white and black culture in the 1920s and 1930s to Oprah's impact in the twenty-first century, and from James Baldwin to Maya Angelou.

This Encyclopedia goes to press in the wake of the 2008 presidential election. The election marks a new phase in African American history—and American history. Indeed, with this election America is now forever changed. This is the only way to understand the spectacular rise of Barack Obama.

When Obama was born in 1961, as this Encyclopedia teaches us, segregation was still legal in a third of the nation. The majority of blacks lived in the South, where few could vote; almost none went to integrated schools; and they were barred from public facilities, restaurants, hotels, theaters, amusement parks, public parks, and just about everything else. No black person had ever served on the Supreme Court, in a president's cabinet, or as the elected governor of a state. None had been in the Senate since Reconstruction. None had served as the mayor of a major city. Nor had any ever been the chairman of the Joint Chiefs of Staff. Except for some meaningless third parties, none had ever even considered running for President.

When Obama was born, the bloodiest battles of the civil rights movement were yet to be fought and the civil rights martyrs who would define the decade—including and especially Medgar Evers and Martin Luther King Jr.—were still alive. So too were the three young men who would be murdered attempting to register voters in Philadelphia, Mississippi—Michael Schwerner, Andrew Goodman, and James Chaney—and the four young girls who would be blown up in the Sixteenth Street Baptist Church in Birmingham, Alabama. In 1961 Viola Liuzzo was busy raising her children in Detroit. She would later be murdered at Selma.

Barack Obama was born into an America that was a deeply segregated place. His black father and white mother's marriage was not legal in about eighteen different states. Anyone predicting that the son of this union would one day be president would have risked being committed to a mental hospital. The idea of a black president was not just remote, it was impossible to conceive. Only in a science fiction story about an alternative universe could the parents of the baby Barack Obama have thought he would one day be president of the Harvard Law Review, a member of the U.S. Senate, and eventually the primary resident of the White House.

In the sweep of American history, the election of 2008 seemed like a welcome to an alternative universe.

An Obama presidency will not end racism. It may in fact lead to some increase in overt racist talk, as those who don't like his policies will blame them on race. But in other ways, an Obama presidency will change the nature of race relations. Whites who said they would never vote for a black man, in the end, did just that. The Republican Party, which played the race card so effectively with Willie Horton in 1988, was unable to do so this time. During the campaign, supporters of Republican candidate John McCain offered up offensive and nasty racist characterizations of Obama, including distributing handbills that looked like food stamps with Obama on them. In a last desperate effort the McCain campaign focused on Obama's former preacher, the Reverend Jeremiah Wright, who was notorious for his harsh and often seemingly unpatriotic rhetoric denouncing racism. Obama had successfully distanced himself from Wright, and in the political world of 2008 a radical minister is no Willie Horton. No one seemed to be much affected by the effort, as white voters supported Obama at about the same level they had supported white Democratic candidates in recent years.

Even as he became the first black president, Obama transcended race. His earliest support did not come from the black community, but from upper-middle-class Americans of all races, who were charmed by his intelligence and thoughtfulness and anxious to find a new political leader in the new century. Obama campaigned on economics, foreign policy, health care, and jobs. He rarely spoke of inequality or civil rights, not because he is not concerned about them, but because he understood that the central issues of the election—jobs, the economy, health care, and the Iraq War—transcended race. Thus, Obama campaigned on issues that affect all Americans, without regard to race, geography, or class.

Indeed, in the end Obama is not America's first black president—he is America's first president who happens to be black. The difference is huge, and it suggests the beginning of a new chapter in African American history.

Whether focusing on politics, economics, business, law, or culture, the entries in the new Encyclopedia provide information to readers while reminding them of the importance of race to the development of American history. In the end the new Encyclopedia chronicles American history, reminding us that the history of America has always been, in large part, the history of race and race relations. In the *Encyclopedia of African American History, 1896 to the Present*, we offer both a history of African Americans and a way of seeing that history as it is intertwined with all of American history.

Using the Encyclopedia. There are nearly 1,250 entries in the *Encyclopedia of African American History, 1896 to the Present*, arranged in alphabetical order letter by letter. The contributors have sought to write in clear language with a minimum of technical vocabulary. There are approximately as many biographies as there are topical entries, and the Encyclopedia includes entries on each of the fifty states and on each of the U.S. presidential administrations in the period. In selecting the subjects for the biographical entries, we made every effort to include a representative group of individuals—most of them black and a few of them white—who have had a significant impact on African American history and culture. There are far more important figures in African American history than could be included in these volumes; many more biographies are available in the eight-volume *African American National Biography*, edited by Henry Louis Gates Jr. and Evelyn Brooks Higginbotham.

Composite entries in the Encyclopedia gather together discussions of similar or related topics under one headword. For example, under the headword "Desegregation and Integration" the reader will find five subentries: an overview entry followed by individual entries on desegregation and integration in the armed forces, higher education, public education, and professional athletics. A headnote listing the various subentries introduces each composite entry.

To guide readers from one article to related discussions elsewhere in the Encyclopedia, end-references appear at the end of most articles. A selective bibliography at the end of each article directs the reader who wishes to pursue a topic in greater detail to primary sources, to the most useful works in English, and to the most important scholarly works in any language. Blind entries direct the user from an alternate form of an entry term to the entry itself. For example, the blind entry "Unions, Labor" tells the reader to look under "Organized Labor." The Encyclopedia includes approximately 450 illustrations.

Volume 5 of the Encyclopedia contains the thematic outline, the directory of contributors, and the index. Readers interested in finding all the articles on a particular subject—for example, on Politics and Government, or on Literature—may consult the thematic outline, which shows how articles relate to one another and to the overall design of the Encyclopedia. The comprehensive index lists all the topics covered in the Encyclopedia, including those that are not headwords themselves. Volume 5 also includes a chronology, a year-by-year account of important events from 1896 to 2008.

Acknowledgments. This project, comprising both the earlier encyclopedia from 1619 to 1895 and the new encyclopedia from 1896 to the present, has evolved and grown over seven years. It was always a group effort. My coeditors—Diane Barnes, Graham Hodges, Gerald Horne, and Cary Wintz—worked tirelessly to plan and complete the two encyclopedias. Two publishers at Oxford sponsored the project: the project began under Karen Day and was completed under Casper Grathwohl. Both Karen and Casper are dedicated to the highest values of scholarship and knowledge. Casper's leadership allowed for the expansion of the project from six stand-alone volumes to two encyclopedias totaling eight volumes. Tim DeWerff and Stephen Wagley both supervised the development of this undertaking. The publication of these eight volumes caps off two decades of my collaborations with Stephen, whose intelligence, sense of humor, friendship, and great judgment make the hardest jobs run smoothly. The other all-stars of the Oxford team were my two development editors, Tony Aiello and Tim Sachs. I am greatly indebted to them for their dedication, hard work, creativity, and good humor. Most of all, I value their friendship.

Authors rely on countless specialists who work behind the scenes to turn our raw texts into books that are both attractive and readable. In that light I thank Georgia Maas for her work as production editor, the many copyeditors and proofreaders she managed, and Hilary Mac Austin for researching the stunning images in these volumes.

Dedication. We have dedicated the Encyclopedia to John Hope Franklin, the dean of African American history. John Hope was one of my advisers and teachers when I was in graduate school. Three decades later he remains a close friend, mentor, and role model. Although this dedication is personal, it is also professional. Since the publication of his first book more than sixty-five years ago, John Hope has been a relentless advocate for history and a tireless scholar of the African American experience. All of us who write and do research in this field owe him an enormous debt. He is without peer in his scholarship on the many ways in which African Americans have shaped the history of the United States. At age ninety-three John Hope continues to write and speak out on issues of public concern and on the importance of history to overcome the racism of our past. We hope these volumes will enable all who use them to understand our history better so that we can make our future better.

Paul Finkelman
Albany, New York
November 2008

ENCYCLOPEDIA OF AFRICAN AMERICAN HISTORY 1896 TO THE PRESENT

FROM THE AGE OF SEGREGATION TO THE TWENTY-FIRST CENTURY

AARON, HANK (b. 5 February 1934), baseball player, baseball executive, civil rights advocate, and businessman. Henry Louis "Hank" Aaron was born and raised in Mobile, Alabama, the son of Herbert and Estella Aaron. He was a member of the second generation of black baseball players to enter the major leagues following Jackie Robinson's breaking of the color line in professional baseball in 1947. Aaron began playing for the Milwaukee Braves in 1954; at about the same time Willie Mays joined the New York Giants and Ernie Banks joined the Chicago Cubs. They were among the last black players who began their careers in the Negro Leagues. In 1974 Aaron broke Babe Ruth's lifetime home run record of 714. When he retired from baseball in 1976 after twenty-three seasons, Aaron held the career records for most home runs (755), most runs batted in (2,297), most total bases (6,856), and most extra-base hits (1,477); was second in total at bats (12,364) and runs scored (2,174); was third in games played (3,298) and hits (3,771); and was eighth in career doubles.

Aaron's consistency as a batter hitting for both average and power over a long career is unmatched. In twenty consecutive seasons he hit twenty or more home runs; he also had twenty consecutive seasons in which he had more than one hundred hits per season. His consistency in home runs surpassed Ruth's record of sixteen seasons of twenty or more home runs and also outpaced his contemporaries, such as Eddie Mathew, Willie Mays, and Barry Bonds (fifteen seasons each), Reggie Jackson (thirteen seasons), Frank Robinson (twelve seasons), and Mickey Mantle (eleven seasons). In the early twenty-first century Aaron was also the only player to have hit thirty or more home runs in fifteen seasons. Thirty years after he retired, this record remained. His record of more than one hundred hits in twenty consecutive seasons tied him with Ty Cobb for second place behind Pete Rose (twenty-one seasons). In the spring of 1959 *Newsweek* asserted that Aaron had "become the best hitter in baseball" (quoted in Aaron and Wheeler, p. 163). This assessment remained accurate for another decade. In 1982 Aaron was elected to the Baseball Hall of Fame with 97.8 percent of the ballots, second only to Cobb.

Youth. Aaron was born in a section of Mobile known as Down the Bay. When he was eight his family moved to Toulminville, just outside the city limits. His father had steady wartime work in the shipyards as a boilermaker's assistant and was able to save enough money to buy two lots for $110 and hire carpenters for another $100 to build a six-room house. Most of the materials came from a house that had recently been torn down. With their own home and no rent and no mortgage, the Aarons were unusual among black Alabamans at this time. His father later opened a tavern, the Black Cat Inn, in Toulminville. Although cash poor, by the standards of black Alabama the Aarons were well-off, even though most white Americans would have seen them as impoverished. The fact that Estella Aaron was never employed outside the home when Hank was growing up—she was never a maid, cook, or laundress for white families in Mobile—is one measure of Herbert Aaron's hard work, frugality, and modest economic success.

Throughout his childhood Hank constantly played baseball or some version of it, even hitting bottle caps with broomsticks and making baseballs out of tin cans. By age sixteen he was skipping school to play pool and whenever possible baseball. He was eventually expelled from school and was soon playing semipro baseball for the Mobile Black Bears as a teenager on a team of men. In 1951 he was getting at least $10 a game for the Bears when the team's coach Ed Scott urged the Indianapolis Clowns of the Negro Leagues to look at Aaron. In the spring of 1952 Aaron joined the Clowns for $200 a month, an enormous sum for a black teenager in the deeply segregated South. The owner of the Clowns soon contacted the Boston Braves, telling them of the "18-year-old shortstop batting cleanup for us" (Aaron and Wheeler, p. 43). By the end of May the Clowns had dealt Aaron to the Braves, who paid him $350 a month and gave the Clowns $10,000. At the time Aaron was only eighteen, and his father had to sign the contract.

Aaron spent the rest of the summer playing for a Braves farm team in Eau Claire, Wisconsin. This was a shocking change for Aaron, who had never played with—or

Hank Aaron. A jubilant Hank Aaron after his 715th career home run in a game against the Los Angeles Dodgers in Atlanta Stadium, 8 April 1974. Photograph by Bob Daugherty. AP IMAGES

against—white players. The trip to Eau Claire was his first in an airplane. Wisconsin was dramatically different from Alabama. As he wrote in his autobiography, "Eau Claire was not a hateful place for a black person—nothing like the South—but we didn't exactly blend in" (Aaron and Wheeler, p. 55). Aaron was able to eat in restaurants and stay in hotels with whites. But he also experienced people staring at him, almost in disbelief—"looking at me," he wrote, "as though I were some kind of strange creature" (Aaron and Wheeler, p. 55). Aside from two other ballplayers, there was only one other African American in the city. Aaron and the other black players met white people there who had never even seen a black person. Perhaps the most dramatic change in his cultural circumstances, he rented a room in a house owned by a white family and sat on the family's front porch holding hands with their daughter. In Mobile such an act might have led to a lynching. Three years after Aaron went to Eau Claire, after all, the fourteen-year-old Emmett Till was tortured and murdered merely for whistling at a white woman in Money, Mississippi. Despite his relative social freedom and a salary that surpassed anything he could find in Alabama, Aaron contemplated quitting shortly after he arrived because living in a small town in Wisconsin was "almost like being in a foreign country" (Aaron and Wheeler, p. 59).

Aaron won the Rookie of the Year Award in Eau Claire. The next year, 1953, he played in Florida for Jacksonville in the South Atlantic League, known as the Sally League. Aaron and two others, Horace Garner and Felix Mantilla, integrated the league. These players did not face the national press and pressure that Robinson had encountered when he integrated the minor leagues in 1946 and the majors in 1947. But they faced potentially more dangerous conditions: fans threw rocks at them and sent them death threats. At one game in Montgomery the FBI had agents sitting in the stands. The president of the Sally League went to numerous Jacksonville games, mostly to monitor the treatment of Aaron, who was clearly the league's up-and-coming star and therefore the player most likely to face violence.

Major Leagues. In 1954 Aaron joined the Milwaukee Braves, leading them to the World Series in 1957 with an eleventh-inning home run on the last day of the season. His teammates carried him off the field on their shoulders. The Braves won the series in seven games and returned in 1958, when they lost in seven games. Never again did Aaron play in a World Series. However, he continued year after year to be the most consistent offensive player in the game. In 1966 the Braves moved to Atlanta, becoming the first baseball team to play in the Old South. Although segregation was no longer legal, Aaron felt some discomfort playing in a city where overt racism—and especially the use of overtly racist language by fans and critics—was still rampant. While in Atlanta, Aaron divorced his wife, whom he had met while playing in the Sally League, and in 1974 he married Billye Williams, a local television talk show host and the widow of a Morehouse University professor and civil rights activist. Aaron's engagement and marriage brought him into increasing contact with the local and national civil rights community.

By the time he met Williams, Aaron was closing in on Ruth's lifetime home run record. In 1969 he passed Mantle for the third most home runs in a career at 537. The next year he became the only player to have three thousand hits in a career and hit more than five hundred home runs. In 1971 he became the third player to hit more than six hundred home runs. In the next season he passed Mays in lifetime home runs. As the 1973 season began, Aaron was just forty-one home runs away from tying Ruth's lifetime home run record of 714, which was arguably the most famous and iconic record in American sports. During the season Aaron received an enormous amount of hate mail, with some people threatening to kill him if he broke Ruth's record. All these hate letters were racially motivated, and they almost always had the word "nigger" in them. By the end of the season Aaron had full-time police protection. The stress on him was enormous but appeared not to affect his playing skills: he hit forty home runs, the eighth time in his career that he hit forty or more in one season.

Aaron hit number 714 to tie the record in his first at bat in the first game of the next season. The game was played on the anniversary of the assassination of Dr. Martin Luther King Jr., and reflecting his increasing interest in civil rights, Aaron successfully convinced the home team Cincinnati Reds to observe a moment of silence before the game. That day he also announced the creation of the Hank Aaron Scholarship Fund. He broke the record a few days later in the first home game of the season in Atlanta. Although numerous celebrities and dignitaries flew in for the game, the commissioner of baseball Bowie Kuhn was noticeably absent. By this time Aaron was increasingly critical of Major League Baseball for its failure to promote blacks from the field to managerial positions, either on the field or in the front office. By September, Aaron was openly critical of the Braves for not offering him either a position in their executive offices or as manager of the team when they fired their manager at the end of the season. Happily for Aaron, he was traded to the newly created Milwaukee Brewers, where he played in 1975 and 1976. He then returned to the Braves, which had been bought by the media magnate Ted Turner. Aaron was hired as a vice president.

Following his retirement as a player, Aaron became openly critical of baseball for its failure to promote more than a handful of black players to the positions of power and decision-making. Unlike many former professional athletes, he openly spoke out about civil rights, racism, and the need for gender and racial equity in sports.

Legacy. In 1982, the first year that he was eligible, Aaron was elected to the National Baseball Hall of Fame. This honor capped a spectacular career. In 1957 and 1963 he led the league in home runs and runs batted in (RBIs). He led the league in home runs in 1957 (44), 1963 (44), 1966 (44), and 1967 (39). He led the league in batting average in 1956 (.328) and 1959 (.355). He was named the Sports Illustrated Player of the Year in 1956 and won the Most Valuable Player Award in 1957. He was chosen for the All-Star Team every year from 1955 to 1975 and in 1959 became the first player unanimously chosen by all the other players to play on the All-Star Team.

Aaron's unanimous election to the All-Star Team illustrates an oddity of his career. Fellow players recognized him as one of the greatest athletes in the game. He came to spring training already in excellent shape. He was not a prude and drank a beer on occasion, but he avoided the self-destructive drinking and womanizing of many players. He prepared for his craft and was a relentless competitor with stunning talent and an incredible work ethic. Thus Mantle asserted shortly after Aaron retired: "As far as I'm concerned, Aaron is the best ball player of my era. . . . He is to baseball of the last 15 years what Joe DiMaggio was before him" (*Baseball Almanac*, Aaron biography).

But despite the respect and admiration, Aaron did not achieve the superstar status of such contemporaries as Mantle, Mays, Sandy Koufax, Roberto Clemente, Pete Rose, or his own teammate Warren Spahn. This was in part because of his personality. He was quiet, circumspect, and workmanlike. His playing came with an ease and smoothness that professionals understood to be the result of hard work, great conditioning, careful study of his opponents, and incredible talent. Fans saw only a smoothly functioning player—perhaps the best all-around player of his era—who was always at the top of the leading statistical measure of hitting, hitting for power, fielding, and base running. He never had spectacular seasons, as did Mantle or Koufax. Indeed the most remarkable aspect of his career may be that he hit 755 home runs but never hit more than 47 in any one season. He lacked the spirit of Mays, the boyish good looks and charm of Mantle, or the charisma of Clemente and Koufax.

But year in and year out Aaron was the best and most consistent hitter and fielder in the game. For most of his career he played in the smallest media market of professional baseball, out of the limelight. Unlike the Dodgers, Cubs, or Yankees, the Milwaukee Braves—and in his last two years the Milwaukee Brewers—had almost no national constituency. Atlanta was a bigger market, but not much bigger in the late 1960s and early 1970s when Aaron played there. Thus it was only when he began to approach Ruth's record, in 1972, that Aaron gained the media attention that his skills and accomplishments had merited all along.

Outside baseball Aaron became the successful owner of a car dealership, served on various civil and corporate boards, and took an increasingly active role in civil rights causes, working with both the NAACP and the Reverend Jesse Jackson's various programs. In 1982 Aaron received the Presidential Medal of Freedom, the nation's highest civilian award.

[*See also* Baseball; Bonds, Barry; *and* Sports, *subentry* Professional Sports.]

Bibliography

Aaron, Hank, with Lonnie Wheeler. *I Had a Hammer: The Hank Aaron Story*. New York: HarperCollins, 1991.

Stanton, Tom. *Hank Aaron and the Home Run That Changed America*. New York: W. Morrow, 2004.

Tolan, Sandy. *Me and Hank: A Boy and His Hero, Twenty-five Years Later*. New York: Free Press, 2000.

—Paul Finkelman

ABERNATHY, RALPH DAVID (b. 11 March 1926; d. 17 April 1990), minister, civil rights activist, and close adviser to Martin Luther King Jr. An Alabama native, Abernathy was one of twelve children born to successful farmers who had managed to rise from sharecropping to owning a five-hundred-acre farm. Abernathy's father was a deacon in a local church, and from a young age Abernathy wanted to join the ministry. He became an ordained Baptist minister in 1948. In 1950 he received a BS in mathematics from Alabama State University. He began what became a career in political activism while in college by leading demonstrations to protest the poor quality of food in the campus cafeteria and the lack of heat and hot water in campus housing. While in college he became interested in sociology, and he earned an MA in the subject from Atlanta University in 1951.

Abernathy became pastor of the First Baptist Church in Montgomery, Alabama, in 1951. Three years later Martin Luther King Jr. accepted the position of pastor at the nearby Dexter Avenue Baptist Church, and Abernathy and King began a friendship and collaboration that lasted until King's death. In 1955, after Rosa Parks refused to give up her seat on a city bus to a white passenger, the two men helped found the Montgomery Improvement Association (MIA). The MIA helped coordinate and sustain the Montgomery bus boycott, which some local women had already begun. After a year of protest the boycott was successful, and public transportation in Montgomery was desegregated. This success gave momentum to civil rights protesters throughout the South. However, Abernathy's involvement in the movement meant that he was often the victim of white intimidation and reprisals. For example, in 1957 both his home and his church were firebombed. Although his family remained unharmed, the church was destroyed.

King, Abernathy, and other black southern ministers founded the Southern Christian Leadership Conference (SCLC) in 1957 to facilitate nonviolent activism. King was the organization's first president, and Abernathy served initially as secretary-treasurer. The organization moved its headquarters to Atlanta in 1960. Following this relocation, Abernathy became pastor of Atlanta's West Hunter Street Baptist Church in 1961. In addition to his duties as pastor, Abernathy continued to work for the SCLC, leading sit-ins, marches, and rallies throughout the South.

During the civil rights movement, King and Abernathy were jailed together seventeen times. These experiences further solidified their friendship and mutual respect. At King's request, Abernathy became vice president of the SCLC and King's heir apparent.

After King's assassination in April 1968, Abernathy became president of the SCLC. Under Abernathy's leadership the SCLC continued the Poor People's Campaign, which had been in the planning stages at King's death. The campaign began on 13 May 1968. At Abernathy's urging, fifty thousand poor and homeless people built a shantytown near the Lincoln Memorial in Washington, D.C., to draw attention to their poverty. After the protesters refused to leave, the police forcedly disassembled the shantytown on 24 June, and Abernathy was jailed for twenty days on charges of unlawful assembly.

Throughout his tenure as president of the SCLC, Abernathy continued to advocate on behalf of the poor, to protest against the Vietnam War, and to hold voter registration drives throughout the South. However, Abernathy resigned from the SCLC in 1977 amid allegations of financial mismanagement. By then the once-great civil rights organization was in decline. The fate of the SCLC was shared by many other civil rights organizations that also struggled to redefine themselves after some of the most tangible goals of the civil rights movement had been met.

After leaving the SCLC, Abernathy ran unsuccessfully for the U.S. congressional seat for Georgia vacated by the African American Andrew Young. Abernathy then founded the Foundation for Economic Enterprises Development (FEED), which focused on the economic growth of the African American community. He also served as pastor at the West Hunter Street Baptist Church until 1990.

From time to time Abernathy became the source of controversy. In 1978 he publicly criticized a script of a docudrama about King's civil rights activities, claiming that it did not give adequate credit to other leaders of the movement. Coretta Scott King, the slain leader's widow, publicly disagreed with Abernathy, claiming that the film was an accurate representation of King's work.

Abernathy created a furor among many members of the black community in 1980 when he endorsed the conservative Republican Ronald Reagan for president. He did so claiming that Reagan would appoint blacks to important posts in his administration. Abernathy's decision to support Reagan further alienated him from Coretta Scott King and other former friends. Abernathy later expressed disappointment at Reagan's poor record on civil rights issues and declined to endorse Reagan when he ran for reelection in 1984.

During the 1980s Abernathy was a founder and vice president of the American Freedom Coalition, a group devoted to uniting conservatives around common goals. Among other things the group promoted anticommunism and opposed abortion rights for women.

In 1989 Abernathy published his autobiography *And the Walls Came Tumbling Down*, which once again generated controversy, this time because of Abernathy's references to King's extramarital affairs. Some of Abernathy's colleagues accused him of betraying King, a charge that Abernathy emphatically denied. Abernathy claimed that he did not reveal any information that had not already become public. Furthermore, although he disapproved of King's behavior, Abernathy said that he understood that being away from home so frequently contributed to King's temptation toward infidelity.

Abernathy received numerous awards and honorary degrees. A major highway in Atlanta is named in his honor. He died of a heart attack in Atlanta in 1990. Despite his long and varied career, Abernathy continues to be widely admired for his participation in the civil rights movement in the 1950s and 1960s.

[*See also* Civil Rights Movement; Conservatism and Conservatives, Black; King, Coretta Scott; King, Martin Luther, Jr.; Montgomery Bus Boycott; Poor People's Campaign; Reagan, Ronald, Administration of; *and* Southern Christian Leadership Conference.]

BIBLIOGRAPHY

Abernathy, Ralph David. *And the Walls Came Tumbling Down: An Autobiography*. New York: Harper and Row, 1989.

Branch, Taylor. *Parting the Waters: America in the King Years, 1954–63*. New York: Simon & Schuster, 1989.

Garrow, David J. *Bearing the Cross: Martin Luther King, Jr., and the Southern Christian Leadership Conference*. New York: William Morrow, 1986.

—JENNIFER JENSEN WALLACH

ABU-JAMAL, MUMIA (b. 24 April 1954), radical prison journalist and author. Mumia Abu-Jamal was born Wesley Cook in Philadelphia, Pennsylvania. As a teenager in the 1960s he was attracted to the Black Panther Party (BPP). Cook—christened "Mumia" by one of his high school teachers—helped form the BPP's Philadelphia chapter in spring 1969 and became the chapter's lieutenant of information. He wrote articles for the *Black Panther*, the party's national newspaper, and traveled to several cities to perform BPP work. He left the party in the fall of 1970 because of the split between Eldridge Cleaver and Huey Newton.

After attending Goddard College in Plainfield, Vermont, Cook, now calling himself Mumia Abu-Jamal—the surname is Arabic for "father of Jamal," Jamal being his firstborn—returned to Philadelphia and began a radio broadcasting career in the early 1970s. Abu-Jamal was part of the first generation of black journalists to become professional newscasters for local and national black commercial radio. He worked for affiliates of the National Black Network and the Mutual Black Network, two black-oriented radio news networks. His early career crested when he joined WUHY (now WHYY), a National Public Radio (NPR) affiliate. As one of the nation's few black NPR regional correspondents, Abu-Jamal reported for both *91 Report*, the affiliate's weekday newsmagazine, and *All Things Considered*, the network's national daily afternoon newsmagazine. But he eventually alienated mainstream broadcasters because of his on-air sympathy for the MOVE organization, a radical, mostly black back-to-nature group based in Philadelphia. As a result, Abu-Jamal began driving a borrowed cab and engaging in sporadic radio freelancing.

Mumia Abu-Jamal. The imprisoned journalist Mumia Abu-Jamal, 1995. REUTERS

In the early morning of 9 December 1981, Abu-Jamal, while driving a cab, was drawn into a confrontation between Daniel Faulkner, a white Philadelphia police officer, and Abu-Jamal's brother, William. Both Abu-Jamal and Faulkner were shot. Faulkner died at the scene, and Abu-Jamal was tried for Faulkner's murder. The case and trial were sources of great controversy. His detractors argued that the evidence of his guilt was overwhelming (for instance, Abu-Jamal's gun was at the scene), while his supporters charged that his lawyer was incompetent, the judge was biased in favor of the police, and the sentencing hearing overemphasized his teenage years spent with the BPP. Abu-Jamal—who was not allowed to continue representing himself at his trial because he wanted to replace his court-appointed defense attorney with the MOVE founder John Africa—was convicted of first-degree murder and given the death penalty. As of 2008 his case was still under appeal.

Abu-Jamal has had several clashes, both legal and philosophical, with prison officials and with noncommercial radio over his right to continue to speak and write as a paid journalist and author. In May 1994, NPR contracted him to do a series of recorded commentaries on prison life for *All Things Considered* but, amid public controversy, decided not to air them just days before their scheduled broadcast. The following year Abu-Jamal was placed in the death-row equivalent of solitary confinement for publishing *Live from Death Row*, his first book, because prison authorities argued that the book constituted proof of Abu-Jamal's involvement in entrepreneurship in defiance of regulations. State prison authorities banned outsiders from using any recording equipment in state prisons in 1996, shortly after Home Box Office aired the sympathetic documentary *Mumia Abu-Jamal: A Case of Reasonable Doubt?* that included an on-camera interview with Abu-Jamal.

In February 1997 the left-leaning Pacifica Radio's national weekday newsmagazine *Democracy Now!* lost a dozen affiliates in Pennsylvania: the relay radio station in Philadelphia canceled its contract with the newscast because commentary from Abu-Jamal was part of the program's lineup. In August 1999 prison authorities, believing once again that Abu-Jamal was violating regulations, yanked the wires of Abu-Jamal's telephone out of its wall when he began doing live commentaries on Pacifica Radio's *Democracy Now!* He was eventually allowed to resume his broadcasts.

Although still incarcerated, in the early twenty-first century Abu-Jamal continued to be a prolific writer and an international cause célèbre—his plight attracted considerable attention overseas. He has written a pamphlet, five nonfiction books that include *Live from Death Row* (1995) and *Death Blossoms: Reflections from a Prisoner of Conscience* (1997), and hundreds of commentaries that have been aired on the Pacifica Radio network and published on the Internet and in black newspapers and leftist radical journals.

[*See also* Black Panther Party; Criminal Justice; *and* Prisoners' Rights and Reform Movements.]

BIBLIOGRAPHY

Abu-Jamal, Mumia. *All Things Censored*. Edited by Noelle Hanrahan. New York: Seven Stories Press, 2000. A collection of his best essays from *Live from Death Row* and *Death Blossoms*, as well as previously unpublished material.

Bisson, Terry. *On a Move: The Story of Mumia Abu-Jamal*. New York: Litmus Books, 2000.

Lindorff, Dave. *Killing Time: An Investigation into the Death Row Case of Mumia Abu-Jamal*. Monroe, Me.: Common Courage Press, 2003.

Williams, Daniel R. *Executing Justice: An Inside Account of the Case of Mumia Abu-Jamal*. New York: St. Martin's Press, 2001.

—TODD STEVEN BURROUGHS

ABYSSINIAN BAPTIST CHURCH. The African American members of the First Baptist Church in New York City withdrew their membership in 1808 when they were subjected to racially segregated seating. With Ethiopian merchants they organized their own church, called "Abyssinian" after the merchants' nation of origin. The church was located at 44 Anthony Street, and the Reverend Vanvelser was its first pastor. Abyssinian numbered three hundred members in 1827 when slavery ended in New York. The Reverends William Spellman, Robert D. Wynn, and Charles Satchell Morris served as pastors during the church's early history. By 1902 the church was a renowned place of worship with more than sixteen hundred members.

The appointment of the Reverend Adam Clayton Powell Sr. in 1908 ushered in a new era of the church's history. His pastorate was devoted to spiritual and financial development. In 1920 he acquired property in Harlem and then oversaw the building of the church's Gothic and Tudor structure with stained-glass windows and a marble pulpit. The congregation moved to its new quarters—located on West 138th Street—in 1923 and was still there in the twenty-first century. When Powell retired in 1937, the church had more than seven thousand members, operated a residence for the elderly, and supported a mission in West Africa.

Powell's son, the charismatic Adam Clayton Powell Jr., brought even greater growth during his pastorate from 1937 to 1971. The congregation grew to ten thousand members, and Powell Jr. linked the Christian message of social justice to the civil rights movement. Powell Jr., a highly skilled politician, served eleven terms in the U.S. House of Representatives, starting in 1945. As the

Abyssinian Baptist Church. Senator Hillary Rodham Clinton speaks at the Abyssinian Baptist Church on West 138th Street in New York City, 20 January 2008. Photograph by Elise Amendola. AP Images

chairman of the Committee on Education and Labor from 1961, he helped pass more than fifty public laws that benefited all Americans. Outspoken and controversial, Powell Jr. led a relentless struggle for racial equality. Meanwhile the church provided both spiritual guidance and social welfare programs to its members and the community. Powell Jr. retired from Abyssinian in 1971; he had been excluded from his congressional seat in 1967 following allegations of misappropriating committee funds. He died in 1972.

The Reverend Samuel DeWitt Proctor, a distinguished teacher and public servant, succeeded Adam Clayton Powell Jr. A stirring orator, Proctor brought a high degree of prestige to the Abyssinian pulpit. His students included the Reverend Martin Luther King Jr. and the Reverend Jesse Jackson. During his tenure Abyssinian remained an uncompromised force in the fight for social justice. Proctor retired in 1989 and died in 1997.

Under the leadership of the Reverend Calvin O. Butts III since 1989, the church has become a viable economic force in the Harlem community. The Abyssinian Development Corporation, a nonprofit organization created in 1989, brought a supermarket and more than one hundred housing units to the community. Service programs offered by the church include youth AIDS prevention, academic enrichment, and athletic programs. Like his predecessors, Butts continues to use Christian activism to fight racial discrimination. The problems of police brutality, negative billboard advertising, and negative rap lyrics are issues of importance to Butts. He has led the Abyssinian Baptist Church into the twenty-first century committed to the Christian commands to spread the gospel, feed the hungry, shelter the homeless, clothe the naked, and give hope to the hopeless.

[*See also* Baptist Church, African Americans and; *and biographical entries on figures mentioned in this article*.]

Bibliography

Gore, Bob. *We've Come This Far: The Abyssinian Baptist Church*. New York: Stewart, Tabori & Chang, 2001. A photographic journal with attractive black-and-white photographs that supplement written church history.

Haskins, James S. *Adam Clayton Powell: Portrait of a Marching Black*. New York: Dial, 1974.

—Kerima M. Lewis

ACTORS AND ACTRESSES. The first image of an African American in film occurred in 1903 with the silent movie *Uncle Tom's Cabin*. The twelve-minute-long movie, though, starred a white actor in blackface as the title character. For African American actors and actresses, the opportunity to appear in films, and subsequently in television and serious theater productions, took a while to develop. During the late nineteenth and early twentieth centuries, the white actors who portrayed black characters, such as those who performed in D. W. Griffith's *The Birth of a Nation* in 1915, established several derogatory characters. Over the next century, black actors and actresses found themselves working against these stereotypes.

The practice of excluding African Americans from performing began during the post–Civil War period and extended to all forms of acting. In Wild West shows and circuses, black actors and actresses were almost nonexistent. The African Americans who appeared usually performed only as comedic characters, acting out white racial views. Some exceptions existed. Bill Pickett, the African American cowboy who pioneered the sport of steer wrestling, performed as the premier act in the Ranch Wild

West Show and other shows throughout the United States, Canada, Mexico, and South America during the early 1900s. Pickett's experience failed to correspond to that of most African Americans, especially considering the small minority of people in America who participated in ranching and rodeos.

The primary venue of performing for African American actors and actresses following the Civil War was in minstrel shows. Minstrel shows occurred throughout the 1800s and were a popular form of entertainment. The performances included comic skits, variety acts, dancing, musical acts, and singing. The characters in these shows were always African Americans who presented the African American race in a derogatory fashion. The three-act format of the shows always began with the actors dancing onto stage, where they sang songs and told jokes. The second act included a wide array of possible performances, the most popular of which included a mock-political speech full of puns that sought to show the perceived ignorance of African Americans while also denigrating efforts at civil rights. The final act of the performance consisted of either a musical skit that praised pre–Civil War plantation life or a humorous mocking of a popular play. Both types of performance included lots of physical humor and slapstick jokes. The most important aspect of the minstrel shows, though, centered on the fact that the actors presenting the demeaning stereotypes of African Americans were white actors with their hands and faces painted black.

By the late 1860s and 1870s, African American actors also became minstrels, but they also painted their faces black to conform to the white audiences' preferences at the time. Some of the first black actors to perform in minstrel shows, William Henry Lane and Thomas Dilward, began to perform during the 1840s and 1850s. In the period after 1865, African American minstrels followed the same racial stereotypes as their white counterparts, mainly because the predominantly white audiences expected as much.

Several all–African American minstrel troupes achieved national success during the 1860s and 1870s. One of the first prominent groups, Brooker and Clayton's Georgia Minstrels, performed throughout the North. Another group, Sam Hague's Slave Troupe of Georgia Minstrels, toured England in 1866. By the 1870s, white businessmen purchased many of the black minstrel shows. In 1872, for example, Charles Callender bought Hague's show, renamed it Callender's Georgia Minstrels, and turned the group into the most popular minstrel show in America. At the same time, several prominent individual African American performers, including Billy Kirsands, James Bland, and Wallace King, reached levels of national prominence among minstrels.

While black minstrel performers never received pay equal to that of their white counterparts, the shows did expose many white audiences to African American culture, especially music, for the first time. Throughout the last two decades of the nineteenth century, African American performers in minstrel shows began to drop the painting of their faces, and the shows featured more African American music and themes. Religion came to be a common part of shows, as did jubilee singing. By the end of the century, the African American minstrel shows took on a polished, more formal atmosphere. In the end, the most important legacy of the minstrel shows involved the fact that, despite the racist overtones, they provided African American actors their first significant access to theaters and show business.

Roles in the First Half of the Twentieth Century. The roles offered to African American actors and actresses in the theater during the first half of the twentieth century presented the same problems as those faced by minstrel actors. African American characters existed in supporting roles in plays, usually comedic in nature. The characters, written by white playwrights, most often used patronizing images of blacks in order to appeal to the white audiences' racial beliefs.

For African American drama groups, the only opportunity to perform involved vaudeville skits and ragtime revues. During the late 1800s and early 1900s, African American–owned theaters began to appear throughout the country. The first black-owned theater, the Pekin Theater, opened in Chicago in 1905, giving African American actors, actresses, and audiences an opportunity to experience more dramatic roles.

In the early twentieth century, African Americans began to play black characters in the movies at the same time that black actors and actresses received roles in theater productions. The characters for African Americans, though, were all created to portray the racist assumption that blacks were inferior to whites. The African American characters only existed as faithful servants, superstitious and ignorant rural folks, lazy and immoral workers, or violent males. All of the stereotypes also attributed an almost childlike mental ability to African Americans.

During the first two decades of the twentieth century, black actors and actresses found themselves cast in supporting roles that fit within the existing stereotypes. Furthermore, just as in minstrel shows, filmmakers used these stereotypes as comic relief, with the most well-known black actors and actresses becoming famous as sources of audience humor. Several early actors who fell under this model appeared in the *Our Gang* series of comedic short films produced by Hal Roach.

Beginning in 1922, Roach's *Our Gang* films sought to show the humorous element existing in childhood. In pursuing this goal, Roach used three black actors and characters as a focus of the audience's humor. The role of the first character, Farina, played by the eighteen-month-old Allen Hoskins, consisted of him crying at points where the director found the gag most humorous, and his hair, which was in tight pigtails, standing straight up when Farina was frightened.

Farina proved so popular with audiences that Roach added two more African American boys to the series. Matthew "Stymie" Beard appeared in the films with a shaved head and wearing a derby hat and colorful zoot suits. The third character, William "Buckwheat" Thomas, dressed in the same gingham outfits and had the same braided hair as Farina. One factor that proved interesting about the *Our Gang* series was that the young African American actors interacted with their white counterparts in an environment of near equality. No racial hierarchy or prejudice existed among the children, even though the characters of Farina, Stymie, and Buckwheat followed traditional racial stereotypes.

The equal status of the African American child actors and the white child actors in *Our Gang* failed to correspond with the roles for adult actors and actresses of the period. At the same time as the advent of sound in motion pictures, African American actors and actresses found themselves forced to adopt the stereotypes supported by white studio executives, directors, and writers. In *Hearts in Dixie*, produced in 1929, an almost all–African American cast portrayed slaves happily living, singing, and dancing on a southern plantation before the Civil War. The leading black actor and actress in the cast were Clarence Muse and Mildred Washington. The African American actor who attracted the most audience interest in the show, though, was a young dancer named Stepin Fetchit. Operating in a comedic jester role, Fetchit's dancing and antics proved so entertaining that the second half of the movie focused entirely on his character.

Fetchit used the popularity he garnered in *Hearts in Dixie* to carry himself to national fame during the 1930s as a dancing, singing, and comic sidekick to many white stars, including Will Rogers and Shirley Temple. During the 1930s, Fetchit was probably the best known and most successful African American actor in America.

Other African American actors and actresses during the 1930s and 1940s found themselves relegated to demeaning sidekick and servant roles. Bill "Bojangles" Robinson danced as Shirley Temple's servant. Louise Beavers played maids or housekeepers. Eddie "Rochester" Anderson and Butterfly McQueen played butlers and maids. Hattie McDaniel became most famous for her portrayal of the O'Hara family's slave in *Gone with the Wind*. Ironically, McDaniel's performance in *Gone with the Wind* won her the Academy Award for Best Supporting Actress in 1939, making her the first African American to receive an Oscar.

African Americans as Owners and Producers. During the period of the 1920s and 1930s, some African American actors, actresses, and directors began to make their own movies, depicting topics and themes strictly for black audiences. These films, along with plays produced at the African American–owned theaters, focused on ideas of social justice and persecution. Black filmmakers and theater directors sought to portray African American life realistically, as well as to refute the derogatory stereotypes of blacks presented by most Hollywood movies.

One African American actor, Noble Johnson, started his own motion picture company in 1916. His company, the Lincoln Motion Picture Company, the first black-owned movie studio, included African American actors and actresses, directors, and crew members. The Lincoln Company showed its movies in black churches and schools and segregated movie theaters.

Another African American film producer was Oscar Micheaux. A novelist, Micheaux became involved in movies over issues concerning the transition of his books into films. Micheaux's movies gave black actors and actresses another venue in which to express their dramatic acting talents.

African Americans in the theater experienced the same struggles as those in other venues. Black-owned theaters featured prominent actors such as Paul Robeson and Charles Sidney Gilpin. Gilpin became one of the first African American actors to star in a major dramatic role in a prominent white theater when he starred in Eugene O'Neill's play *The Emperor Jones* in 1920. Robeson later performed the role, in 1924.

Robeson acted mainly in England, where more opportunities existed for African Americans. In 1928, Robeson returned to America and filled the role of Joe in *Show Boat*. Two years later, in England, he played Othello in the Shakespeare play by the same name. When *Othello* later came to America, Robeson became the first African American to play the title character on Broadway.

For black actors and actresses, the Harlem Renaissance of the 1920s provided expanded opportunities, especially in the theater. African American playwrights such as Willis Richardson and Angelina Weld Grimké (1805–1879) wrote plays that looked at black issues and celebrated African American culture. At the same time, black colleges and high schools began theater programs, which, along with black community theaters, gave thousands of African American actors and actresses experience and exposure.

Stage and Film Actress. Angela Bassett in the role of Lady Macbeth at the Public Theater, New York City. Production under the direction of George C. Wolfe, 1998. PHOTOFEST

As America entered the 1950s, the roles for African Americans in movies changed with the racial climate of the time. Roles as maids and servants continued as the main form of employment for black actors and actresses; prominent African American entertainers appeared in movies, and they always managed to sing a popular song. Big band leaders and jazz singers such as Cab Calloway and Duke Ellington appeared with their bands in numerous films. Since many of the black entertainers already possessed national reputations for their nightclub acts, white writers wrote nightclub scenes into their movies for them to appeal to audience interest. One actress who prospered under this format was Lena Horne. Horne's biggest role came in the 1943 movie *Stormy Weather*, which featured an all-black cast. Unfortunately for Horne and the other black entertainers, for the most part their musical numbers existed outside the movies' plots. As a result, the white directors could easily cut their scenes if the movie ran too long.

A Midcentury Shift in Portrayal. As America underwent major changes in the 1950s and 1960s because of the civil rights movement, Hollywood movies began to examine racial issues. The subject matter for films featuring African Americans became more substantial, as did the roles offered black actors and actresses. African Americans now played heroes, not just sidekicks. As a result, several African American actors and actresses became national stars. Actors such as Woody Strode and Harry Belafonte and actresses such as Eartha Kitt enjoyed careers that spanned decades. Furthermore, with black actors and actresses in more serious roles, African American performances began to receive critical accolades. Dorothy Dandridge became an international symbol of beauty at the same time that she also received an Oscar nomination for Best Actress in 1954 for her role in the film *Carmen Jones*.

Sidney Poitier established himself as the most acclaimed African American actor of the last half of the twentieth century. In 1964, Poitier became the first African American to win the Academy Award for Best Actor for his work in *Lilies of the Field*. Poitier went on to costar with several of the most successful white actors of the time, including Rod Steiger, Spencer Tracy, and Katharine Hepburn. Poitier's success opened opportunities for other black actors.

During the 1970s, the roles for African American actors and actresses changed again. The decade saw more African American directors making movies for black audiences that reflected current emotions. In 1971, Gordon Parks directed Richard Roundtree as the title character in the movie *Shaft*. In the film, Roundtree played a private detective who presented a powerful hero image for African Americans. The success of *Shaft* led to numerous other African American movies that featured black action stars such as Jim Brown, Fred Williamson, and Jim Kelly.

The black theater experience after World War II followed the same pattern as the movies, with African American characters acting in plays but never holding more than supporting roles. This began to change in the late 1960s and 1970s with the Black Arts Movement. More African Americans created their own dramatic groups. One prominent group was the National Black Theater, started by Barbara Ann Teer. Lorraine Hansberry, who wrote *A Raisin in the Sun*, became the first African American woman to write a play for Broadway. Other prominent black playwrights who wrote for African American actors and audiences were August Wilson and Maya Angelou. Actors and actresses brought the same type of powerful character that appeared in the 1970s black action movies to Broadway. For example, in 1969 James Earl Jones won a Tony Award for Best Actor for his work in *The Great White Hope*.

The Dynamics of Television as a Medium. Television provided a new medium for African American actors and actresses during the last half of the twentieth century. The earliest television shows already existed as radio shows, and they simply switched to the new media platform. These programs, such as *Amos 'n' Andy* and *Beulah*, brought existing audiences with them, along with existing racial stereotypes. While the shows portrayed derogatory views of African Americans, the appearance of black actors and actresses in the lead roles proved significant, especially since the radio programs usually had employed a white actor to portray the African American characters. As a result, in 1950, *Beulah*, which starred Ethel Waters, McDaniel, and Beavers all at different times in the title role during the show's four-year run, became the first television program to star an African American actress.

Throughout the 1960s, African American actors and actresses found their roles on television shows limited to supporting characters; they continued to play maids and servants to white characters. A few exceptions existed. In the 1956–1957 television season, Nat King Cole starred in his own weekly variety show. A decade later, Bill Cosby starred opposite Robert Culp in the action-adventure series *I Spy*, while Diahann Carroll portrayed the title character in *Julia*.

Similarly to the changes in motion pictures and theater, the 1970s presented black actors and actresses with more opportunities in television. *The Jeffersons*, *Good Times*, *What's Happening*, *That's My Mama*, and *Sanford and Son* all focused on African American families. The African Americans in the shows, such as Redd Foxx, Jimmie Walker, and Sherman Helmsley, all became national stars. The most important television event of the 1970s, though, involved the twelve-hour miniseries *Roots*. Based on the book by Alex Haley, *Roots* featured dozens of prominent black actors and actresses, attracted over 130 million viewers, and presented an honest and unflinching portrayal of African American history, including the Atlantic slave trade, slavery, and racial segregation in America.

Building on the success of *Roots* and the African American movies of the 1970s, black actors and actresses in the 1980s and 1990s reached new levels of success. The comedian Richard Pryor became one of the top-paid actors in Hollywood. Eddie Murphy's movies, including the *Beverly Hills Cop* and the *48 Hrs.* series, were international blockbusters. Numerous television shows appeared that starred African American actors and actresses.

One particularly significant show in the 1980s and 1990s was *The Cosby Show*. Based on the comedy of Bill Cosby, the show portrayed an upper-middle-class African American family. Cosby's show focused on African

Hollywood Actor. Forest Whitaker arrives for the *Vanity Fair* Oscar party at Morton's in West Hollywood, 2007. Photograph by Chris Pizzello. Reuters

American culture and on issues important to all families, not just to African Americans. *The Cosby Show* proved such a success that it raised the other shows in NBC's Thursday night lineup to the Top Ten in ratings.

During the last decades of the twentieth century, African American actors and actresses received more critical acclaim for their work than ever before. Before 1980, only two African Americans won academy awards for acting. After 1980, eleven Oscars went to black actors and actresses. Louis Gossett Jr., Denzel Washington, Cuba Gooding Jr., and Morgan Freeman all won Oscars as Best Supporting Actor. Whoopi Goldberg and Jennifer Hudson won for Best Supporting Actress, while Halle Berry became the first African American to win Best Actress. Best Actor awards went to Denzel Washington, Jamie Foxx, and Forest Whitaker. Furthermore, in 2002 the Academy of Motion Pictures presented Poitier with the Lifetime Achievement award. Numerous other black actors and actresses received nominations for awards, too.

As the world enters the twenty-first century, African American actors and actresses still face stereotypes and prejudice, but the future looks optimistic. Gone are the racist ideas of the minstrel shows and early dramas. Television networks and movie companies produce shows specifically for African American audiences. As a result, the potential for young black actors and actresses to portray serious characters exists.

[*See also Birth of a Nation, The*; Black Arts Movement; Blaxploitation Films; *Emperor Jones, The*; Entertainment Industry and African Americans; Film and Filmmakers; Film and Television Depictions of African Americans; Harlem Renaissance; Jazz; Minstrel Tradition; *Roots*; Television; *and biographical entries on figures mentioned in this article.*]

BIBLIOGRAPHY

Bogle, Donald. *Toms, Coons, Mulattoes, Mammies, and Bucks: An Interpretive History of Blacks in American Films*. 3d ed. New York: Continuum, 1994. An outstanding study of the types of roles offered to African American actors and actresses.

Guerrero, Ed. *Framing Blackness: The African American Image in Film*. Philadelphia: Temple University Press, 1993. A scholarly study of the role of films in creating the racial identity of African Americans.

Hill, Errol G., and James V. Hatch. *A History of African American Theatre*. Cambridge, U.K., and New York: Cambridge University Press, 2003. An excellent examination of the history of black theater and African American theater companies.

MacDonald, J. Fred. *Blacks and White TV: African Americans in Television since 1948*. New York: Wadsworth, 1992. An in-depth look at African Americans in television, including the early stereotypes and the recent increase in roles and opportunities.

Toll, Robert C. *Blacking Up: The Minstrel Show in Nineteenth Century America*. New York: Oxford University Press, 1974. A good history of minstrel shows in America.

—ROB FINK

ADOPTION. Adoption traditionally refers to the legal act of permanently placing a child under the age of eighteen with a family other than the child's birth parents. Often, in the United States, these children are taken from the foster care system. There are various obstacles to the adoption of foster children, specifically black children. Among them is the lack of communication between foster care and adoption agencies, the fact that there are fewer black social workers than there are black foster children, and the understaffing of foster care agencies.

Difficulties in the foster care system affect the growth and decline of adoption rates. For example, in 1967 a study conducted in Washington, D.C., concluded that it was harder for black women to give their children up for adoption than white women because many of the women were young and lived in low-income neighborhoods. Between 1969 and 1971, the United Black Fund and the United Givers Fund in D.C., through the Stern Community Law Firm, gave free legal assistance to those who wanted to adopt children. Perhaps because of this initiative, adoption rates rose in D.C. between these years. The 1973 *Roe v. Wade* Supreme Court legalization of abortion resulted in a broad decline in the number of white babies to be adopted; while the numbers of black children eligible for adoption did decrease, the decrease was not as significant.

Transracial adoption, the adoption of children from a particular "race" by members of another "race," has had a long history in the United States. There are documented instances of whites adopting black children as early as 1948 in Minnesota. The National Association of Black Social Workers (NABSW) has been integral to the debate about the efficacy of whites adopting black children. In 1972, the NABSW issued a report stating that it better served the interests of black children to be adopted by black families. Subsequently, in 1973, the Child Welfare League of America issued a response to the NABSW, saying that it was preferable to place children with members of their own "race."

The NABSW also responded negatively to the Multiethnic Placement Act of 1994, amended in 1996, which prohibits agencies receiving federal funding from considering ethnic, cultural, and racial background in the placement of children for adoption. The NABSW claimed that the act put black children at a disadvantage.

The 2000 U.S. census requested information about adoption for the first time. In 2004 the Child Welfare League reported that 45,000 black children were waiting to be adopted from foster care and of the 26 percent of black children who were adopted from foster care, about 4,200 were adopted transracially, nearly all by whites.

Some well-known adoptees by black families include Les Brown, the motivational speaker and author; Daunte

Culpepper, the football quarterback; Tommy Davidson, the actor and comedian; Bo Diddley, the singer, songwriter, and guitarist; and Nicole Richie, the celebrity socialite and adopted daughter of the singer-songwriter Lionel Richie.

[*See also* Identity.]

BIBLIOGRAPHY

Clemetson, Lynette, and Ron Nixon. "Overcoming Adoption's Racial Barriers." *New York Times*, 17 August 2006. Addresses transracial adoption and includes interviews with people on both sides of the debate.

Day, Dawn. *The Adoption of Black Children: Counteracting Institutional Discrimination*. Lexington, Mass.: Lexington Books, 1979. Excellent sociological study of black adoption in the United States before 1980, especially concerning the D.C.–Maryland–Virginia area. This source also includes a comprehensive bibliography related to the topic of black adoption.

—QRESCENT MALI MASON

AFFIRMATIVE ACTION. Affirmative action, a legal and social policy intended to foster equal opportunity in America, accelerated during the political and social ferment in the 1960s as a highly controversial concept and array of programs developed in response to the accumulated and lingering inequality that especially afflicted African Americans.

In a sense, affirmative action can be said to have begun when the idea was put forth in the post–Civil War era that formerly enslaved individuals should be accorded "forty acres and a mule," that is, given compensation for their years of deprivation in the form of help in starting a new life. Or it could be argued that the executive order issued by President Franklin D. Roosevelt on the eve of World War II, which called for steering government contracts away from businesses that chose to discriminate racially, gave rise to a form of affirmative action, in that these businesses often felt constrained to take aggressive measures to increase their employment of African Americans in order to continue receiving contracts.

The Legacy of the Past. Despite these precedents, affirmative action generally is associated with the rise of the modern civil rights movement. In the historic 1954 *Brown v. Board of Education* decision, the U.S. Supreme Court legally abolished the mythology of "separate but equal" derived from the 1896 *Plessy v. Ferguson* decision. When the Court reversed that precedent, the question that emerged was whether there could be true "equal protection" as "guaranteed" in the Fourteenth Amendment of the United States Constitution if the inherited economic, political, legal, educational, and social inequality from centuries of slavery and a century of post–Civil War inequality imposed by various Jim Crow laws and practices was not mitigated.

With the rise of the civil rights movement in the 1950s, leading civil rights advocates such as Martin Luther King Jr. argued that it was not enough simply to outlaw future discrimination when centuries of slavery, brutality, and discrimination had forged a legacy of profound economic, political, intellectual, and social poverty and powerlessness. Such leaders argued that more affirmative remedies were required to create a foundation for effective equal opportunity. In combination with the legal strategies of Charles Hamilton Houston and Thurgood Marshall at the NAACP Legal Defense and Educational Fund, social and political pressure and mass mobilization led to the implementation of a new approach to racial discrimination and inequality—broadly encapsulated as "affirmative action."

Until the passage of various civil rights statutes in the mid-1960s, the focus of legislation and constitutional provisions had been on abolishing discrimination by making it illegal. In 1964 the first official usage of the term "affirmative action" came in Title VII of the Civil Rights Act of 1964. The statute reads as follows:

> If the court finds that the respondent has intentionally engaged in or is intentionally engaging in an unlawful employment practice charged in the complaint, the court may enjoin the respondent from engaging in such unlawful employment practice, and order such *affirmative action* [italics added] as may be appropriate, which may include, but is not limited to, reinstatement or hiring of employees, with or without back pay (payable by the employer, employment agency, or labor organization, as the case may be, responsible for the unlawful employment practice), or any other equitable relief as the court deems appropriate.

In 1965 President Lyndon Baines Johnson signed Executive Order 11246 requiring federal contractors to "take affirmative action to ensure that applicants are employed, and that employees are treated during employment, without regard to their race, creed, color, or national origin." In 1967 in response to the rise of the women's movement's use of voting and public campaigns for equality, President Johnson expanded the executive order to benefit women.

In any event, the United States Supreme Court subsequently upheld the principle of affirmative action, starting with *Griggs v. Duke Power Company* in 1971. After persistent political attacks against affirmative action, along with a conservative political backlash against many of the 1960s civil rights gains, in the 1979 case of *Regents of the University of California v. Bakke* the Court held that affirmative action could not take the form of racial quotas and could not create separate standards for evaluating

Rally for Affirmative Action. Anti-*Bakke* protest outside the New York federal courthouse, 29 July 1978. Photograph by Bettye Lane. © Bettye Lane

students. Subsequent cases further limited the availability and forms of affirmative action to the point where many advocates felt that affirmative action was marginalized and rendered almost moot.

Affirmative Action and Women. The history of affirmative action relative to gender issues has had a similar trajectory. By some measures, women of various ethnicities have been the major beneficiaries historically of affirmative action, although routinely affirmative action has been seen as a program devoted exclusively to the uplift of African Americans. The rise of the women's movement and feminism in the 1960s presented the need to address socioeconomic and political inequalities between men and women in the United States. Long before affirmative action policy took hold, an Equal Rights Amendment to the U.S. Constitution was drafted in the aftermath of World War I as a follow-up to the constitutional amendment guaranteeing women's voting rights.

The ERA, as it came to be known, was designed to outlaw discrimination and inequality on the basis of gender. By the 1970s, although a majority of states had ratified the ERA, the number still fell short of the three-fourths required, so the ERA was never passed. At the same time the unequal treatment of women in education, employment, economics, law, and politics was brought to the forefront of national consciousness through the work of feminist leaders such as Gloria Steinem, Betty Friedan, and the African American Shirley Chisholm. While the push to ratify the ERA stalled, affirmative action became increasingly involved in addressing gender inequality in employment and education. In many other countries, affirmative action principles have been applied to balance electoral slates by gender in order to achieve equal representation of women in various branches of government.

The greater success of feminism in mitigating much of the inequality in some arenas has often been contrasted with the lack of similar progress on a mass scale relative to race and national origin. This has placed a strain on the alliance between the civil rights and women's movements at a time when the concepts and programs emerging from the affirmative action paradigm were coming under increasing attack from mainstream institutions and organized sectors of society.

A similar conflict arose in the historic relationship between the Jewish American and African American communities. Though many Jews were strong supporters of the civil rights movement in the 1950s and 1960s, a number of Jewish leaders opposed affirmative action proposals, deeming them to be racial quotas and therefore akin to the quotas that once limited the number of Jewish people admitted into universities and other institutions. This opposition occurred in the face of an adamant challenge by a number of Jewish women—particularly on university faculties—who argued that affirmative action was essential to knocking down the barriers that had limited their opportunities.

The Late Twentieth Century and the Future. Over the decades since the first official affirmative action policy was enunciated, social, political, and legal debate has been heated and polarized regarding the validity and necessity of this approach to remedy past discrimination and lingering social and institutional inequalities. A political and social backlash triggered by so-called angry white men, including right-wing pundits and individuals associated with conservative think tanks, called into question the reason for, the fairness of, and the effectiveness of such an affirmative action strategy. The growing conservative movement of the 1980s caused affirmative action increasingly to be attacked as "reverse discrimination" and as being harmful to both minority and majority populations.

Critics pointed to advances in racial integration and the improved social and economic conditions of many African Americans as proof that affirmative action was no longer needed. Further, they argued, continuing inequality is a result of innate deficits of character, culture, or intellect—not discrimination. Hence the "culture of poverty" argument—or the idea that it was not racism but the "culture" of African Americans that was hindering their rise—gained ascendance.

Conversely, defenders of affirmative action have argued that affirmative action is a fundamental reason for racial progress and advancement for women. Moreover, advocates contend that continuing inequality is a result of a failure of government and civil society to apply affirmative action thoroughly and vigorously, thus reflecting the continuation of historically rooted inequality throughout the nation's institutions. Rejecting the claim that the United States is, or ever was, a color-blind meritocracy that rewards anyone who has ability and who gives sufficient effort, civil rights advocates pointed to past and continuing discriminatory practices as de facto pro-white affirmative action, exemplified by legacy admissions in many private universities that benefit the children of alumni.

Economic and political leaders in the United States have found themselves on both sides of the debate as to the benefits of affirmative action, with arguments being made relative to the effectiveness and equity of diversity in building a unified and prosperous society. Arenas such as the military and sports have benefited from advances resulting from various forms of affirmative action, and leaders of the related institutions have become advocates of the need for such policies. Thus advocates of the policies that have led to the increase in numbers of African American professional athletes and coaches often contrast the current situation with that of the past, when those who were obviously qualified were systematically barred. They argue that the increase in minority numbers not only has created more opportunities for African Americans and enriched sports but also has highlighted the fact that previously unqualified whites were obtaining posts undeservedly—which sheds light on why there might be so much staunch opposition to affirmative action in other fields.

Many of the leading public figures advancing various arguments against affirmative action, nonetheless, are African American and Latino Americans: they include Ward Connerly, a former regent of the University of California; Thomas Sowell, a conservative economist; Linda Chavez, a former director of the U.S. Commission on Civil Rights; and the U.S. Supreme Court justice Clarence Thomas. Connerly has led highly visible and successful attacks on affirmative action policy in the states of California, Michigan, and Washington. He spearheaded Proposition 209 in California, which passed as a ballot proposition in 1996 with 54 percent of the vote and thereby led to amending the state constitution to prohibit affirmative action by preventing the use of race, gender, or ethnicity in public institutions for the purposes of hiring or admission into public universities. Proposition 209 was upheld in federal court on appeal. Since 209 passed, the admission of African American and Latino American students into the state's public universities has dropped by more than half. Following California's lead, by 2000 the percentage of U.S. universities with affirmative action recruitment programs dropped from 90 percent to 65 percent, with private universities dropping to 50 percent.

A similar ballot proposal (Proposal 2) passed in Michigan in 2006 with 58 percent of the vote, which matched the vote for a similar proposal in the state of Washington in 1998. At the same time, affirmative action was the central issue in two key U.S. Supreme Court cases coming out of Michigan in 2003: *Gratz v. Bollinger* and *Grutter v. Bollinger*. The Court upheld affirmative action policies that used race, ethnicity, or gender as a factor in deciding university admissions, but it overturned a policy that gave alleged direct preferences in admissions based on those criteria.

Civil rights advocates point out that the vast majority of African Americans and Latino Americans, who were intended as the initial beneficiaries of affirmative action policies, still languish in inferior socioeconomic and political circumstances in society. Data shows that health, education, employment, housing, and voting rights discrimination persists and that this discrimination limits the life opportunities of individuals from these groups. Failure to diversify police and law enforcement agencies is connected, according to these advocates, to the persistence of racially discriminatory policing (racial profiling) and to a situation in which dramatically disparate numbers of African Americans and Latinos (compared to whites) are incarcerated in greater and greater numbers. The Harvard University Law School professor Charles Ogletree explored debates within the civil rights community as to whether the successful push for legal equality was effective or even strategically beneficial in his 2004 book *All Deliberate Speed: Reflections on the First Half Century of "Brown v. Board of Education."*

Some liberal analysts argue that the problem with affirmative action is that it places too much focus on racial and ethnic identity and not enough on class. They argue that affirmative action and the subsequent diversity initiatives reinforce racial concepts without eliminating the underlying inequality that impacts racial groups as a class or subclass in society. Proposals from this corner focus on providing assistance in various forms to economically disadvantaged people regardless of racial identity.

Corporate and political institutions have benefited from the partial elimination of racial barriers with the rise of minority elites who play visible and strategic roles without—according to their critics—empowering their broader communities or threatening the broader socioeconomic balance of wealth and power in society. African American and Hispanic chief executive officers, chief financial officers, secretaries of state, attorneys general, judges, mayors, and other high-ranking business and civic professionals give the appearance of equal opportunity while the vast majority of the minority groups they ostensibly represent still live in inferior socioeconomic conditions.

Outside the United States, various affirmative action proposals have been instituted to address the inferior status or position of minority groups (as in France, China, and Belgium), as well as of groups that are economically or socially oppressed despite their majority numbers (as in South Africa, Malaysia, and India). The results of such programs have received the same mixed reviews that they have in the United States, and it is unclear that long-term, ingrained institutional social inequality has been eliminated anywhere as a result of any version of such programs. It is also not clear that affirmative action policies anywhere in the world have ever been fully implemented on a broad enough scale or with a long enough timetable to address the problems that they targeted.

Conservative and fascist movements, together with a resurgence of racial violence, have arisen in the United States as well as in several European countries in reaction to affirmative action programs. The rise of hate crimes and hate groups in the United States has been documented by the Southern Poverty Law Center and connected to the backlash against affirmative action over several decades.

Some minority group leaders and institutions have revived the call for reparations or self-help principles or both as representing alternative approaches to the problem of persistent inequality and injustice in the United States—for example, some people advocate offering compensation to the descendants of enslaved Africans for their ancestors' unpaid labor over the centuries. A number of initiatives have also arisen to encourage private institutions such as corporations and foundations to develop programs supporting the educational and social opportunities of African Americans and Latino Americans without running afoul of legal restrictions against affirmative action. It is clear, as the U.S. Supreme Court justice Sandra Day O'Connor stated in her majority opinion in *Grutter v. Bollinger*, that the issue of affirmative action will continue to be revisited in the coming decades to determine whether the inequities of the past persist and require some form of legal and public solution.

[*See also* Civil Rights Act of 1964; Civil Rights Movement; Conservatism and Conservatives, Black; Discrimination; Education; Equal Employment Opportunity Commission; Poverty, Culture of; Public Assistance; Racism; Reparations; *and biographical entries on figures mentioned in this article*.]

BIBLIOGRAPHY

Anderson, Terry H. *The Pursuit of Fairness: A History of Affirmative Action*. New York: Oxford University Press, 2005.

Ball, Howard. *The "Bakke" Case: Race, Education, and Affirmative Action*. Lawrence: University Press of Kansas, 2000.

Beckwith, Francis J., and Todd E. Jones, eds. *Affirmative Action: Social Justice or Reverse Discrimination?* Amherst, N.Y.: Prometheus Books, 1997.

Carter, Stephen L. *Reflections of an Affirmative Action Baby*. New York: Basic Books, 1991.

Chávez, Lydia. *The Color Bind: California's Battle to End Affirmative Action*. Berkeley: University of California Press, 1998.

Crosby, Faye J. *Affirmative Action Is Dead: Long Live Affirmative Action*. New Haven, Conn.: Yale University Press, 2004.

Curry, George E., ed., with Cornel West. *The Affirmative Action Debate*. Reading, Mass.: Addison-Wesley, 1996.

Eastland, Terry. *Ending Affirmative Action: The Case for Colorblind Justice*. New York: Basic Books, 1997.

Horne, Gerald. *Reversing Discrimination: The Case for Affirmative Action*. New York: International Publishers, 1992.

Katznelson, Ira. *When Affirmative Action Was White: An Untold History of Racial Inequality in Twentieth-Century America*. New York: W. W. Norton, 2006.

Lynch, Frederick R. *Invisible Victims: White Males and the Crisis of Affirmative Action*. New York: Greenwood Press, 1989.

Moore, Jamillah. *Race and College Admissions: A Case for Affirmative Action*. Jefferson, N.C.: McFarland, 2005.

Ogletree, Charles, Jr. *All Deliberate Speed: Reflections on the First Half Century of "Brown v. Board of Education."* New York: W. W. Norton, 2004.

Orfield, Gary, and Edward Miller, eds. *Chilling Admissions: The Affirmative Action Crisis and the Search for Alternatives*. Cambridge, Mass.: Civil Rights Project, Harvard University, 1998.

Skrentny, John David. *The Ironies of Affirmative Action: Politics, Culture, and Justice in America*. Chicago: University of Chicago Press, 1996.

—JOSEPH WILSON
—DAVID ADDAMS

AFRICA, IDEA OF. Africa has meant many different things to many different people. The word "Africa" may have come from a Greek word meaning "without cold" or from a Latin reference to the "land of the Afri," probably a Berber tribe. There is also a similar Latin word meaning "warm." Whatever the origin of the word itself, "Africa" has certain meanings for African Americans and other meanings for white Americans. Within each of these groups, of course, there are many subdivisions, ranging along the entire spectrum of political and cultural opinions.

For some time, it was common for Europeans and white Americans to refer to Africa as the Dark Continent, with a derogatory connotation. The word "Africa" carried with it the meaning of lack of civilization, intellect, and sophistication. As Dorothy Hammond and Alta Jablow observe in *The Myth of Africa*, the West defined Africa as that which the West was not. Thus if the West embodied civilization, then Africa was savage and primitive. The leap from this premise was that without the West's help, Africa could never attain civilization. In this view colonialism was good for Africa, and the West was involved not in exploitation but in a civilizing mission.

Hammond and Jablow scoured the Western writing on Africa from the sixteenth through the twentieth centuries. Despite the great volume and variety of writing, they perceived one central theme: namely, the battle between civilized and savage. Moreover, the Western literary image of Africa was a myth, one of fantasy about a people who never existed.

To support this overriding myth, the West created other myths, such as the myth of primitivism. This myth states that Africa is and always has been backward and has contributed nothing to world civilization, the arts, or technology. Another myth is that Africa has no history and indeed has never had political freedom or democracy. In sum, in this view nothing good has ever come out of Africa.

Black Nationalism. If the popular idea of Africa for whites has been that of the romantic Dark Continent filled with savages who are childlike and require care, for African Americans the idea of Africa has been more complicated. From at least the 1700s, black nationalism has put forward a different image of Africa. Generally, this image has been one of a place where creativity and freedom can flourish—a place to which members of the African diaspora can return to reclaim their rightful heritage.

In this image, Africa is the motherland, a sacred and mythical place. It also has a sacred, romantic, and mythologized history in which it is a place of peace and harmony. War was absent, as was slavery and conflict of any kind. Africa became the antithesis of the agony and struggle that blacks faced in the New World. It was a place where Africans, not whites, ruled, and therefore it was certain to be a place of justice for African peoples.

Africa was, then, a refuge from racism and slavery. Of course, this image was inaccurate, but it helped argue for the dignity and humanity of African peoples. Additionally, there were strong contradictions within the black-nationalist ideology. Indeed, the terms of the discussion were often responses to white racism, and thus they were determined by whites. Often black nationalists presented Africa as Europe with dark-skinned people. These nationalists sought to prove that all that Europeans thought good in Europe was also to be found in Africa. There were some exceptions, but generally the arguments were set to prove that if Europe had something, then so did Africa, and probably Africa had had it before Europe had.

However, there were people who did seek to discover alternative realities, to look for what African structures, ideologies, and history might have to offer as guidelines. Some of these people were scholars under the influence of the Columbia University anthropologist Franz Boas. The dancer Katherine Dunham, for example, studied anthropology at Northwestern University but met Franz Boas and Zora Neale Hurston, his student. Certainly, Dunham was aware of Franziska Boas, his daughter, who was also a dancer and worked along the same lines that she did.

Dunham conducted studies in Haiti and became integrated into its culture, living there half her life and becoming a Vodun priestess. Under the influence of the Northwestern University anthropologist Melville Herskovits—himself a student of Franz Boas's—she noted the manner in which African culture became integrated with Western culture. She studied dance in the same way that Hurston studied folklore and the adaptation that African Americans made of African themes to American life. The creative, integrative process of people and their experiences was stressed over the static preconceived ideas of ideologues of any type.

Race and Africa: The Twentieth Century. In a commencement address that W. E. B. Du Bois invited him to give at Atlanta University in 1906, Franz Boas laid down an argument that could be heard throughout the twentieth century, although many did not realize that the argument was Boas's. He began by rejecting the view that any weaknesses of the "American Negro" are "racially inherent." He also rejected the view that the advances coming directly out of Africa, such as fire and stone tools, are inferior to other technological advances. Any alleged current inferiorities of African Americans cannot have come from ancestors who made such great advances. Indeed, if one adds the political advances made in Africa, including the empires of Ghana, Mali, and Songhai, then one must wonder at the charges that racists level at Africans and African Americans.

Boas then moved on to the circumstances under which people brought Africans to the Americas—that is, to the brutality of force and the curse of slavery. He warned the students not to expect those in power to extend help or sympathy. Oppressors do not generally aid those whom they oppress nor extend understanding or sympathy to them. He urged the students to chart their own course and not be discouraged by the distortions of those in power.

Pan-African Movements and the Harlem Renaissance. The New Negro movement of the 1920s and 1930s, which became the Harlem Renaissance, was related to the Pan-African movements of Edward Blyden and Marcus Garvey. Africa became a symbol of what was and would again be the best in African American life and culture, and of all that was good in African American life. Instead of being ashamed of Africa, people began to praise things African—African art, music, poetry.

There was an emphasis on the oneness of Africans in Africa and the diaspora. In music, for example, Duke Ellington began to stress the significance and artistic quality of what came to be called jazz, which he connected to the spirit and rhythm descended from African music. Ellington stressed the positive in black American life and wrote tone poems and concert music in a jazz vein, although he never liked the term "jazz" because there were too many types of music under that heading and because he did not like categories or pigeonholes for music. As soon as he had the power to do so, Ellington shed the "jungle music" label and the cotton-field motif and donned a tuxedo, and had his band members dress in a similar fashion. As the years progressed he absorbed more rhythms and harmonies from African music into his own.

The Pan-African Congresses continued to inspire black artists through emphasizing the unity of the black experience and the need to unite to shake off the shackles of colonialism and segregation. There was, therefore, the consciousness of a need to tell a common story and through telling it to seek to improve the future. Blyden, Du Bois, and Garvey, among others, helped instill "race pride" among artists and others. Africa became a powerful symbol of that pride and of what one could achieve.

African Independence and Civil Rights. The 1960s witnessed great change throughout the African continent as country after country gained its independence from colonial rule. The African independence movement coincided with the American civil rights movement and inspired it as well. As the frustration of the civil rights movement began to mount, the ideas championed by Marcus Garvey—race pride aggressively embraced and black separatism—began to take hold among many African Americans. Some African Americans went to Africa: W. E. B. Du Bois went to Ghana, others went to Ethiopia and elsewhere, seeking acceptance and an immersion in African culture. The motherland was seen as providing nourishment for their souls and as allowing them to become complete human beings.

Black-nationalist beliefs, though complex, can be stated rather simply: the need for total separation of black society from white society, of African Americans from Euroamericans, and pride for the race. This racial pride is based upon Pan-Africanism. Because slavery and slave practice merged peoples of different backgrounds, African Americans were forced to find a unity within ethnic and cultural diversity, to forge a new identity and culture from the mixture of the old ones, a syncretic identity.

Assessment. "Africa" has served as a powerful idea among both black Americans and white Americans. Among whites and some blacks the meanings have been mostly derogatory and negative, symbolizing all that is the opposite of civilization and order. At times, however, these negative meanings have been—ironically—attractive. There has been a romanticization of the primitive and a glorification of it and its power to unleash ur-instincts. Getting down and "funky" while shedding the prohibitions and restrictions of civilized life has an appeal. No matter that most African life is ordered, civilized, and under great restriction, the view of the "sexy Negro" has proved powerful in Western literature.

On the other hand, Africa has had a positive meaning among many African Americans. It has been the focus of black liberation and Black Power ideologies, a place that stands for freedom and equality. Race pride and separatism, in one sense or another, have informed this meaning. The Pan-African movement, the Harlem Renaissance, and the civil rights and African liberation movements have drawn on this vision of Africa for inspiration.

[*See also* Black Nationalism; Black Power Movement; Pan-Africanism; *and biographical entries on figures mentioned in this article*.]

BIBLIOGRAPHY

Alex-Assensoh, Yvette M., and Lawrence J. Hanks, eds. *Black and Multiracial Politics in America*. New York: New York University Press, 2000.

Carmichael, Stokely, and Charles V. Hamilton. *Black Power: The Politics of Liberation in America*. New York: Random House, 1967.

Gates, Henry Louis, Jr. "The Trope of a New Negro and the Reconstruction of the Image of the Black." *Representations* 24 (Fall 1988): 129–155.

Hammond, Dorothy, and Alta Jablow. *The Myth of Africa*. New York: Library of Social Science, 1977. Originally published in 1970 as *The Africa That Never Was*.
Mudimbe, V. Y. *The Invention of Africa: Gnosis, Philosophy, and the Order of Knowledge*. Bloomington: Indiana University Press, 1988.
Walker, Corey D. B. "Improvised Africans: The Myth and Meaning of Africa in Nineteenth Century African American Thought." *West Africa Review* 2, no. 2 (2001).

—FRANK A. SALAMONE

AFRICAN BLOOD BROTHERHOOD. The African Blood Brotherhood for African Liberation and Redemption (ABB) was a Marxist communist and black nationalist organization that emerged in response to the violent race riots of the Red Summer of 1919. Founded in 1919 in Harlem by Cyril V. Briggs, a West Indian immigrant, the organization was structured as a secret fraternal society for men and women of African descent; it espoused armed self defense. Its objectives were racial equality, a liberated and unified black race, the cultivation of racial self-respect, organized opposition to the Ku Klux Klan, industrial development, education of the black masses, higher wages and improved working conditions for African American workers, and cooperation with other "dark" races and class-conscious white workers. Because the organization and the actions of its members were to be kept secret, much of the ABB's early activities are not documented. The ABB gained publicity only when it became associated with Marcus Garvey and the Universal Negro Improvement Association (UNIA) and when the ABB became involved with the race riot in Tulsa, Oklahoma, in May 1921. At its peak the ABB's membership included as many as fifty thousand people, and the group counted one hundred and fifty branches throughout the United States and the West Indies.

Complete with its own rituals, passwords, signs, oaths, and initiation ceremony, the ABB allegedly drew its name from a symbolic blood-sharing ceremony executed by a number of African ethnic groups; however, members of the organization chose to emphasize the significance of their name as being rooted in their purpose. Inspired by the Irish Republican Brotherhood, a nationalist organization that emerged out of and influenced the Fenian movement, the ABB's Supreme Council formed an anti-imperialist group made up of individuals of African blood for the purpose of liberating Africa and people of African descent from white oppression. The governing structure gave the council the power to determine all policy, and the members were ordered into degrees that represented their level within the organization.

Briggs served as the executive head of the ABB and of the council. Many of the council members were also West Indian immigrants. Richard B. Moore of Barbados served as the educational director; W. A. Domingo of Jamaica served as the director of publicity and propaganda; Otto Huiswood of Suriname served as the national organizer; Grace Campbell, who had Jamaican roots, served as the director of consumers' cooperatives; William H. Jones served as the physical director; Theo Burrell served as the secretary; and Ben Burrell served as the director of historical research. The Harlem Renaissance writer Claude McKay and the political activists Harry Haywood and Lovett Fort-Whiteman also played significant roles in the ABB's development.

Briggs entered the United States in 1905 and worked as a journalist for numerous publications and newspapers, including the *Colored American Review*, the mouthpiece of the black business community in Harlem, and the *Amsterdam News*. In 1919, after being fired from his editorship of the *Amsterdam News* for his radical views regarding a separate black nation within the United States, Briggs turned his full attention to the *Crusader*, which he had already launched in September 1918. Initially the *Crusader* served as the organ of the Hamitic League of the World, a nationalist group founded by George Wells Parker that also advocated race consciousness, but soon the *Crusader* began to function as the official organ of the ABB. In addition to publishing political editorials, the *Crusader* reported on business ventures, theater, and sports and literary events. Briggs ceased its publication in 1922, though he continued to maintain the Crusader News Agency.

During this period, Briggs's political shift to the Left led to his adoption of communism by 1920. The black Left, already focused on anticolonial struggles in Africa and recognizing the limits of the League of Nations, was naturally attracted to the anticolonial stance of the Soviet Union. Disillusioned with American socialists and their lack of racial consciousness, Briggs showed his support for the Russian Bolsheviks in the October 1919 issue of the *Crusader*. It was also in that issue that the first reference to the ABB was made. At the very end of this issue Briggs announced the organization and invited blacks willing to go the limit to inquire about the group. Membership was to be by enlistment only, and there were no membership fees. It was not until February 1920 that readers of the *Crusader* were allowed some insight into the organization; the paper printed a full-page recruitment advertisement for the ABB, though still it conveyed scant information. Briggs did reveal that the council expected its instructions to be perceived as law and its suggestions to be thoughtfully considered by members. The advertisement included a list of sixteen suggestions.

The ABB's involvement in the Tulsa riot in 1921 brought the organization further public attention. A race riot ensued following the arrest and attempted lynching of the nineteen-year-old Dick Rowland, an African American man in Tulsa accused of assaulting a white woman. The riot ended with the deaths of hundreds of African Americans. The inability to get antilynching legislation passed in the Senate indicated to the ABB's council that the use of armed force was necessary to defend black communities against the violence perpetrated by whites. The Tulsa authorities publicly blamed the ABB for inciting the riot, but Briggs responded in a formal statement printed in the *New York Times* that neither the ABB nor its Tulsa branch could claim to be aggressors in the riot, and that the blacks who gathered to prevent a lynching were in fact the ones who were acting in defense of law and order. He advertised that the ABB was interested in assisting blacks in organizing for self defense, and he went on to invite blacks to a mass meeting to discuss a plan of action. In the riot's aftermath the ABB experienced a surge in membership and at the same time attracted the attention of the Justice Department and the Federal Bureau of Investigation (FBI), which then kept the group under surveillance.

The ABB's ideological differences with Marcus Garvey and the UNIA also brought the group a measure of publicity. At first Briggs endorsed the UNIA, but Garvey saw racial solidarity as the only means for progress, and Briggs's focus on aligning people of African descent with the communist movement antagonized Garvey. Like A. Philip Randolph and his group of *Messenger* writers, the ABB saw racism as an offshoot of capitalism and viewed Marxism as the solution to the race problem. Still, Garvey and Briggs became bitter rivals; Garvey arrogantly dismissed Briggs, and Briggs responded in kind. From late 1921 to 1922, Briggs in his editorials publicly accused Garvey of fraud, questioned his loyalties, and suggested his involvement with the Ku Klux Klan.

The ABB also attempted to create a cooperative economic arrangement, and a council member was assigned to the consumers' cooperative project. Briggs imagined a conglomerate of twenty-five cooperative stores built in cities with significant black populations; the shares for the stores would be sold only to members of the organization. Moore headed the cooperative project in 1921, but by 1923 his title had shifted to that of educational director. No evidence shows the ABB to have succeeded with the cooperative project, though there was much talk about the ABB owning a wholesale store. By 1923 the ABB, in addition to its revolutionary politics, also functioned as a mutual aid society, providing its members with a sickness and death benefit. The success of this venture is questionable because the organization disbanded within the year.

By the end of 1923 the ABB had ceased to function as an independent political organization, and it merged with the Workers' Party of America. The party offered to finance the ABB on the condition that the party control the activities of the ABB. The council agreed to the merger for a number of reasons. Most members of the council were also members of the Workers' Party, attracted as they were to the Bolshevik Revolution and what it represented: an anti-imperialist socialist stance without racism or colonial influence. The group was also struggling with financial difficulties brought on by the recession of the early 1920s and worsened by the ABB's small membership and by the demise of the *Crusader*. In addition the vendetta against Garvey, publicized in the *Crusader*, alienated many members and supporters of the organization.

Despite its brief existence the ABB left a profound legacy of black radicalism, activism, political efficacy, and agency. The organization's ideology and program merged black nationalism with black Bolshevism and Marxism, and this unique ideology greatly influenced the African American social and political thought of its period. The council managed to join the Comintern, the international arm of Russia's Communist Party, an organization that appeared to take the socalled Negro question seriously. Lenin himself drafted his "Theses on the National and Colonial Questions," which clearly positioned Russia's Communist Party and the Comintern as anti-imperialists, anticolonial, and anti–bourgeois democracy. With help in drafting from members of the ABB, the party also produced a resolution on the Negro question. Members of the council helped form the American Negro Labor Congress. Finally, the ABB must be viewed as a precursor of the radical nationalist groups that emerged from the radical political climate of the 1960s and 1970s.

[*See also* American Negro Labor Congress; Black Nationalism; Briggs, Cyril; Communism and African Americans; Garvey, Marcus; Tulsa Riot; Union of Soviet Socialist Republics; *and* Universal Negro Improvement Association.]

Bibliography

Cruse, Harold. *The Crisis of the Negro Intellectual*. New York: William Morrow, 1967.

Dawson, Michael C. *Black Visions: The Roots of Contemporary African-American Political Ideologies*. Chicago: University of Chicago Press, 2001.

James, Winston. *Holding Aloft the Banner of Ethiopia: Caribbean Radicalism in Early TwentiethCentury America*. New York: Verso, 1998.

Moore, Richard B. *Richard B. Moore, Caribbean Militant in Harlem: Collected Writings 1920–1972*. Edited by Joyce Moore Turner and W. Burghardt Turner. Bloomington: Indiana University Press, 1992.

Vincent, Theodore G. *Black Power and the Garvey Movement (1970)*. Baltimore: Black Classic Press, 2006.

—Rochell Isaac

AFRICAN DIASPORA. The African diaspora is the movement of people of African descent to other parts of the world; participants in the diaspora are diasporans. Struggle and resistance and the impulse to freedom inform the African diasporan memory, religion, and culture. The transatlantic African diaspora began in the fifteenth century. Earlier, Africans had moved individually and voluntarily to the Middle East, Europe, and Asia; their descendants merged with the dominant population, and only their DNA showed their African ancestry. The 1 to 11 million northern and eastern Africans taken by the Arab slave trade to Islamic countries in Asia and the Middle East intermarried, blended, and left only their DNA as physical evidence. The transatlantic slave trade relocated 10 to 12 million Africans, too many for the white populations of the Americas to absorb, particularly given the nature of the slavery and the assumptions underlying it.

The Atlantic Diaspora. The success of the transatlantic slave trade required cooperative Africans. Europeans gave Africans firearms, textiles from India, cowrie shells from Indonesia, and tobacco from the Americas. In return, Africa gave Europe gold, ivory, and—most significantly—slaves. The trek to the point of departure and the Middle Passage cost lives. Perhaps a third of the newly enslaved died in Africa. Another 18 to 20 percent died on overcrowded and unsanitary slave ships. Africans in the transatlantic diaspora were not commonly household workers or concubines or warriors or artisans, as was the case in the Islamic slavery. Males outnumbered females two to one, the reverse of the Islamic ratio. The slaves entered a racist and protocapitalist environment, again unlike the Arab trade. And it brought blacks into a white society numerically too small to absorb it. Of the 10 to 12 million Africans shipped during the slave trade era, 645,000 went to British North America, and another 1.8 million went to other British colonies, primarily in the West Indies.

In 2000, African Americans were 12.1 percent of the U.S. population. They resided primarily in urban areas or in the South. Blacks composed the vast majority of the Caribbean population by the eighteenth century. Natives had died out, and Europeans had settled only in small numbers. By the time Britain abolished the slave trade in 1807, slaves were 80 percent of the population of St. Domingue and Jamaica. In Brazil, slaves were 35 percent, and another third of the population were free people of color. In the southern colonies of British North America, the slave trade ended earlier than elsewhere. Without new Africans, the Creoles, persons of mixed African and European ancestry, quickly predominated. By 1850 less than 1 percent of U.S. slaves were born in Africa. U.S. slaves had much less cultural reinforcement than did blacks in Latin America and the Caribbean, where new Africans continued to arrive. Brazil outlawed the trade only in the 1880s.

The diaspora meant loss of family, friends, village, and community. But the loss was not total. Although scholars disagree about the extent, their consensus is that the Middle Passage failed to destroy African culture totally and that the field hand, mineworker, street vendor, servant, and artisan all preserved at least some of their heritage. Africans came to their new world with language, traditional arts, beliefs, and memories of Africa. Also, although the Europeans established a hierarchy based on color, and slaves made the same distinctions as masters did, in at least some instances the nobility and religious leaders taken captive held their positions of authority even in slave society. In some cases tribal groupings persisted in the Americas, and slave risings in Brazil and the Caribbean were sometimes by one specific group or another, but more commonly the various African groups—and their cultural survivals—intermingled in the Americas.

Religion is an example of cultural blending. The slaves did not bring one African religion to the Americas. Rather, they brought many varieties because the slaves included many varieties of Africans—Yoruba, Akan, Ewe, Dahomean, Hausa, and many more. They lost their traditional religious leaders, and they mingled cultures and memories of Africa. The African religion withstood Christianizing masters and overseers and slave churches. Where the slave trade persisted, the slave population was overwhelmingly greater in number than that of whites. The result was a Creole religion incorporating elements of the various religions brought to the Caribbean and North and South America. The divergence developed under slavery continued through the modern era. Specific practices such as spirit possession, Santeria and *Espiritismo*, differ in Cuba and Puerto Rico and in the Cuban diaspora in Europe. The religion of the diaspora is not European or African but African American.

The Post–Civil War Period. After blacks were emancipated, they had to deal with freedom. They had to define political, spiritual, and social expectations, goals, and context for their lives. During the years from the Civil War to World War I, slave testimonies and other black writings expressed their hopes and their struggles. They were not yet open about the truth of slave experience, especially not to whites, who quickly accepted the myth of the "Lost Cause," with its antebellum plantations and happy slaves. Blacks turned their attention to developing their own society and culture beside the white one.

The rejection by blacks of white institutions indicated that their slave experience was not as whites chose to believe. Most black Christians, regardless of nation, preferred to worship in their own churches or in denominations such as Pentecostalism that had black origins and no history of discrimination or domination by whites. The church also provided a venue for political activism and cultural autonomy. After the Civil War, the freedmen quickly removed from the Baptists, the Methodists, and other white denominations. They established their own churches and their own denominations such as African Methodist Episcopal and National Baptist. They preserved some of the white ceremony, but under a white veneer was a vibrant black religion incorporating Bantu or Mande, Gullah or Yoruba mysticism and magic.

Black cooking, black music (jazz, blues, gospel from the late nineteenth century), black speech, black art—all resembled white forms but had a black flavor, a twist, a different set of spices. Language evolved from pidgin and Gullah to Ebonics and ghetto, not because of difficulty learning English but as survivals of the African cultural influence. Gullah, for instance, had influences from up to ten African languages as well as from Native American and European languages.

The Century Turns. The black middle class arose from the educational and urban employment opportunities that emerged after the Civil War. As Reconstruction gave way to debt peonage, sharecropping, and the gradual loss of civil rights, segregation became the norm and then, by the turn of the century, the law, under the Jim Crow legislation. Blacks developed their own separate churches, lodges, newspapers, and schools, and a black middle class began to develop. The "respectable" middle class emphasized "racial uplift." Uplift meant improving the black masses, instilling race pride, and forcing the world to acknowledge black worth. The educator Booker T. Washington and his "Tuskegee Machine" represented racial uplift in a segregated environment.

Even as Washington ceded to white demands for segregation in his "Atlanta Compromise" of 1896, the old "Sambo," or "mudsill," gave way to the New Negro. During the final decades of the nineteenth century, the intellectual and abolitionist leader Frederick Douglass died, and the scholar W. E. B. Du Bois and others began to challenge Washington's accommodationism. The New Negro stood up for his rights and demanded recognition of African and African American culture on their own merits, not as copies of white society.

The Intellectuals. The rise of an educated black middle class produced an intellectual elite that rejected second-class status. The turn-of-the-century Niagara Movement and the NAACP made Du Bois a spokesperson for the New Negro in the new century. Black history by black historians emerged in the final quarter of the nineteenth century. The American Negro Academy, founded in 1897, had as founding members the poet Paul Laurence Dunbar, Du Bois, the Presbyterian minister Francis J. Grimké, and other prominent black scholars and intellectuals. The historian Carter G. Woodson established the Association for the Study of Negro Life and History to promote black self-esteem and reduce white prejudice. Woodson's association published the *Journal of Negro History*, textbooks, and volumes of black scholarship. In 1926, Woodson also inaugurated Negro History Week.

Afrocentrism. Both racial uplift and the New Negro incorporated black pride, whose most effective and enduring expression was Afrocentrism. Afrocentrism contends that any analysis of African culture and behavior must rest on African ideals, not European ones. Its roots in black nationalism date to Martin R. Delany and Edward W. Blyden late in the nineteenth century. Initially it stressed black contributions to Old World cultures, and its religious aspect included the Moorish Science Temple. Later the Nation of Islam continued the pattern of developing a cosmology and worldview that differed from those of whites.

Afrocentrism rejects linear history for the more traditional circular history. In its religious form it values intuition, cooperation, and integration with a spiritual world populated by gods and ghosts. A major religious form is Ethiopianism, which arose before the American Revolution and thus predates secular Pan-Africanism. Ethiopianism speaks of the spiritual and secular liberation of blacks wherever they might be. Ethiopianism in the Caribbean, Europe, and Africa is the faith of Rastafarians.

Ethiopianism peaked in the 1930s when diasporans protested the Italian invasion of Ethiopia as an attack on Ras Tafari (later the emperor Haile Selassie), the black king who symbolized black pride and independence. U.S. blacks tried to enlist in the Ethiopian fight; Trinidad, home of the newly created calypso, produced songs that spread the black perspective on the Ethiopian conflict around the world by means of black sailors. The singer and songwriter Bob Marley continued the musical message of a simplified Rastafarianism, black protest, and the black experience through 1970s reggae.

The Crisis and the *Journal of Negro History* stressed the contributions of Africans to human history in compensating for the prevailing white view that blacks had provided nothing. Other influences on Afrocentrism were Ethiopianism and Pan-Africanism. DuBois constructed a Pan-Africanism based on West African tradition and organized conferences from 1917 through 1927. Marcus Garvey, the founder of the Universal Negro Improvement Association, was a major Pan-Africanist. In France and French Africa, the African-centered movement of the poet and political leader Léopold Sédar Senghor went by the name

Négritude. With the rise of African independence and nationalism in the 1960s and the African American civil rights movement, Pan-Africanism became primarily an African movement under the leadership of the Ghanaian political leader Kwame Nkrumah. Afrocentrism popularized African cuisine, clothing, and other cultural trappings, and the commercialization of these elements quickly ensued.

Aside from reggae, the migration of Trinidadians, Antiguans, Jamaicans, and other West Indians has spread Rastafarianism to North American and European cities, where new adherents make pilgrimages to Jamaica to explore the roots of the movement.

Epitomizing the Afrocentric movement was Garvey's concept of "Africa for the Africans at home and abroad." Garvey had founded his own movement in Jamaica, then spread the word through the Caribbean and Central and North America. Garvey and other Pan-Africanists saw a free Africa as essential to freedom for diasporans. Garvey's movement was integral to the Harlem Renaissance.

The Harlem Renaissance. Harlem changed from a white to a black community during the Great Migration. The Great Migration brought hundreds of thousands of rural southern blacks into the urban North, particularly Harlem, to take defense jobs during World War I. The Harlem Renaissance culminated the New Negro movement (or New Negro Renaissance or Negro Renaissance) that began in repudiation of Washington and black middle-class conservatism and erupted as blacks defended themselves against the violence of the Red Summer in 1919. By the 1910s many middle-class blacks supported the move for racial equality that had begun in the 1880s. Harlem housed a substantial population of the new socially aware and educated middle class. This middle class made Harlem the nation's black political and cultural center.

From the beginning of the 1920s into the early 1930s, the Harlem Renaissance was the cultural and intellectual peak aspect of the New Negro movement. It was also the first instance in which American publishers and the reading public took black literature seriously and noticed that blacks had a culture of value. Predominantly a literary movement, the renaissance also produced new black music, theater, art, and politics. Black culture had begun to flower before the turn of the century with the musical works of the composers and performers Bob Cole, J. Rosamond Johnson, and others. The Great Migration brought jazz and blues from the South to the Midwest and Harlem. Writers who paved the way for the renaissance included James Weldon Johnson and Charles W. Chesnutt. Dunbar was also important. By the end of the war, Johnson and the writer Claude McKay were dealing with the Harlem Renaissance themes of black life and the struggle for black identity in their writing. Works of the 1920s included McKay's 1922 book of poetry, *Harlem Shadows*; Jean Toomer's 1923 collection of sketches, poetry, and drama, *Cane*; and Jessie Redmon Fauset's 1924 novel, *There Is Confusion*.

In March 1924 the National Urban League's Charles S. Johnson introduced the new talent to New York's white literary leaders. A Harlem issue of the sociological journal *Survey Graphic* in 1925 and the white novelist Carl Van Vechten's 1926 *Nigger Heaven* (popular but offensive to many blacks) made Harlem fashionable for both white and black New Yorkers. Nationally, there arose a passion for black literature and music. In 1926 the black-produced literary magazine *Fire!!* gave outlet to new writers, including Zora Neale Hurston, Langston Hughes, and Wallace Thurman.

The Harlem Renaissance expressed black humanity and dignity despite poverty and racism. Art was a means of reestablishing African American knowledge of Africa while the New Negro fought the postwar repression at home. Awareness brought ambivalence, as in the poet Countée Cullen's "Heritage": Is Africa the ideal home or is it a savage wilderness? Hughes, on the other hand, in his poetry defined Africa as the diasporans' source of life and energy. The Great Depression ended the renaissance, but the emphasis on humanity and dignity and the power of black cultural influences continued.

In the 1930s African Americans began to look both to communism and to their history of fighting injustice. The flirtation with communism attracted only a small portion of blacks; the mainstream remained attracted to American nationalism and a struggle within the system. The impact of the historian Herbert Aptheker's *American Negro Slave Revolts*, published in 1943, carried through into the civil rights movement of the 1960s, particularly the Black Power militancy that followed the activism of the Southern Christian Leadership Conference. The 1960s were the last decade in which African Americans reached to Africa in a show of solidarity. After that, there were Africans and Afro-Caribbeans in the United States, and friction arose between the immigrants and the natives.

West Indian Immigration. From the late nineteenth century until the 1930s, the United States frequently intervened militarily in the Caribbean. American businesspeople invested heavily in the occupied or formerly occupied nations. U.S. labor recruitment in the first two decades of the twentieth century induced Puerto Ricans and others to labor in agriculture in Hawaii and the South and West. During World War I, with European immigration slowed, 100,000 Caribbean workers came to the United States. Between the 1920s and 1940s immigration slowed, and blacks who were long established in the United States took jobs formerly taken by immigrants. When immigration resumed after World War II, Puerto Ricans were the overwhelming majority of Caribbean immigrants until the Cuban Revolution of 1959. Since then, migrants from Haiti, Jamaica, the Dominican Republic, and other Caribbean islands have displaced blacks and Puerto Ricans as low-paid urban workers.

The New Diaspora. In the 1960s and 1970s Africans abroad were eager to bring their American or European education back home to build the nation. But war, poverty, and other problems shifted the migration from temporary to permanent. Between 1960 and 1975 Africa lost 27,000 skilled people, and between 1975 and 1984 another 40,000 left the continent. Between 1990 and 2003 annual departures averaged 20,000. African immigration grew more than fourfold between 1961 and 1980; between 1981 and 2000, it grew from 109,733 to 531,832.

In the early twenty-first century, the United States had over 600,000 Africans. They came from Nigeria, Ghana, Ethiopia, Eritrea, Egypt, Sierra Leone, Somalia, and South Africa, Angola, Cape Verde, Mozambique, Equatorial Guinea, Kenya, and Cameroon. In 2000 they were 6 percent of the total immigrant population and almost 5 percent of the black population. Over half, 57 percent, immigrated between 1990 and 2000. African-born immigrants were 1.6 percent of the black population.

As did other immigrants, Africans initially gathered in an urban area before dispersing to the suburbs. Africans moved to the traditional New York, Washington, Atlanta, Houston, Chicago, and Los Angeles, but in the early twenty-first century they increasingly headed for smaller cities in Maine, Iowa, Ohio, and Nebraska, even in the Dakotas. They worked as cab drivers, cooks, security guards, and as professionals. The new African immigrants were the most educated group in the United States, with 37 percent holding at least a bachelor's degree, compared to a native-born 23 percent. Nigerians had achieved a higher percentage of graduate-level degrees than any other immigrant group; the 2006 American Community Survey counted 17 percent with master's degrees and 4 percent with Ph.D.'s, compared with native percentages of 8 and 1 percent respectively. Professors, doctors, and lawyers came for opportunity that their home countries could not provide. Their average yearly income in 1999 was $40,000. In 1993 there were over 21,000 Nigerian physicians in the United States despite a Nigerian health care system that suffered a critical shortage of doctors.

Diasporan African organizations included the All African Peoples Organization in Omaha, Nebraska; the Nigerian-American Chamber of Commerce in Miami; the Tristate (Ohio, Indiana, and Kentucky) Cameroon Family; the Nigerian Women Eagles Club in Cincinnati, Ohio; and the African Heritage, Inc., in Wisconsin.

Africans remitted to their home communities, but their focus was the United States. Efforts to shift their focus included the Digital Diaspora Network Africa, established in 2002. Leaders of technology firms, nonprofits, and UN agencies sought to reverse the brain drain; to develop the brain trust by persuading diasporans to use the Internet to make their skills available at home. The DDNA also sought to convince the thousands of doctors, engineers, and other technical and professional Africans to return to Africa.

The Old Diasporans vs. the New. Africans and West Indians learned the hard way that to white Americans an African looks just like an African American. They were stereotyped as drug-dealing criminals, lazy and on welfare. They suffered harassment, intimidation, and occasionally murder by police—in 1999, New York City police killed the Guinean immigrant Amadou Diallo. West Indians lacked the African American history of political activism. Africans and West Indians sought symbolic recognition and access to decision-making bodies but they did not seek reform or redistribution. African American activists have long sought reform, a change in the way the socioeconomic structure works, and redistribution, taking part of America's wealth from those who have (generally whites) and giving it to those who have not (disproportionately black.) Afro-Caribbean immigrants wanted but could not have the traditional European immigrant's route to success—hard work, group solidarity, and acceptance on merit into the mainstream. European immigrant groups "whitened" over time and entered the mainstream; African diasporans were often regarded by the dominant society as black and second class regardless of their accomplishments. And the old European immigrant concentration in an ethnic neighborhood has given way to dispersion of immigrants through multiethnic suburbs and the absence of the ethnic institutions that promoted old immigrant group solidarity.

In case after case of discrimination and violence against African or Afro-Caribbean immigrants, the protest and demonstration leaders were African Americans, not immigrants. African Americans often resented immigrants who took their jobs and the affirmative action slots in universities and elsewhere that they struggled to gain. Africans and West Indians faced hostility by African Americans, who might have regarded Africans as being to blame for selling their ancestors into slavery or who might have resented what they perceived as an African attitude of superiority. Black Americans had made strides politically, economically, and socially. The African American community had a strong middle class, better educated and wealthier than ever before, with an annual purchasing power over $450 million per year. The second group of diasporans took advantage of the progress that African Americans had earned, and black Americans resented that.

[*See also* Afrocentrism; Black Nationalism; Black Studies; Caribbean, The; Genealogy; Harlem Renaissance; Immigration to the United States, Black; Pan-Africanism; Religious Communities and Practices; *and biographical entries on figures mentioned in this article.*]

BIBLIOGRAPHY

Austin, Algernon. *Achieving Blackness: Race, Black Nationalism, and Afrocentrism in the Twentieth Century*. New York: New York University Press, 2006.

Azevedo, Mario Joaquim, ed. *Africana Studies: A Survey of Africa and the African Diaspora*. 3d ed. Durham, N.C.: Carolina Academic Press, 2005.

French, Scot. *The Rebellious Slave: Nat Turner in American Memory*. Boston: Houghton Mifflin, 2004.

Harris, Joseph E., ed. *Global Dimensions of the African Diaspora*. 2d ed. Washington, D.C.: Howard University Press, 1993.

Hutchinson, George. *The Harlem Renaissance in Black and White*. Cambridge, Mass.: Belknap Press of Harvard University Press, 1995.

Irele, F. Abiola. *The African Imagination: Literature in Africa and the Black Diaspora*. New York: Oxford University Press, 2001.

Okpewho, Isidore, Carole Boyce Davies, and Ali Alamin Mazrui, eds. *The African Diaspora: African Origins and New World Identities*. Bloomington: Indiana University Press, 1999.

Rogers, Reuel R. *Afro-Caribbean Immigrants and the Politics of Incorporation Ethnicity, Exception, or Exit*. New York: Cambridge University Press, 2006.

Walters, Ronald W. *Pan Africanism in the African Diaspora: An Analysis of Modern Afrocentric Political Movements*. Detroit, Mich.: Wayne State University Press, 1993.

—JOHN H. BARNHILL

AFRICAN LIBERATION SUPPORT COMMITTEE.

AFRICAN LIBERATION SUPPORT COMMITTEE. The urban uprisings of the late 1960s in the United States brought together black intellectuals and the urban masses, producing a new generation of militant organizations. The 1970s witnessed a resurgence of Pan-Africanism in the Black Power movement. A key group dedicated to the civil rights movement in the United States and the liberation struggle in Africa, the African Liberation Support Committee (ALSC), was a united front of black nationalist, Pan-Africanist, and Marxist groups.

At a 1963 meeting, the Organization of African Unity (OAU) declared 25 May African Liberation Day (ALD). In 1971, the African American educator Owusu Saduakai (Howard Fuller) led a delegation of black nationalists to Africa. They met with leaders of the fight against Portuguese colonialism in Angola, Guinea-Bissau, and Mozambique. Upon the group's return, Saduakai announced the establishment of the African Liberation Day Coordinating Committee, whose purpose was to generate support among black Americans for anticolonial African liberation struggles. This became the African Liberation Support Committee. In addition to Sadaukai, ALSC leaders included the poet Amiri Baraka (LeRoi Jones) and the activist Maulana Karenga (Ron Everett). At a January 1972 meeting, the ALSC made plans to celebrate African Liberation Day in the United States. ALD would be celebrated on the Saturday closest to 25 May, the day chosen by the OAU to demonstrate solidarity with the African liberation movements. On 27 May 1972, thirty thousand people participated in a march and rally in Washington, D.C. Twenty thousand more demonstrated in other cities. The following year, on 26 May 1973, ALD demonstrations were held in over thirty cities in the United States, Canada, and the Caribbean. Over one hundred thousand people participated and over $40,000 was raised, to be divided among various African liberation groups. At the third annual ALD demonstration, held on 25 May 1974, ten thousand blacks attended rallies in support of African liberation and against U.S. imperialism and racism (ALSC figures); though the numbers at rallies grew smaller, thousands of activists joined annual ALD marches for the rest of the 1970s.

The ALSC program sought to raise money for liberation groups; conduct educational programs and distribute literature on racism, colonialism, and imperialism; aid the black community at home; and support annual ALD demonstrations. Although the program was unanimously adopted at a 1973 steering committee meeting, by 1974 the ALSC began a period of crisis. Previous ideological differences had been minimized for the larger cause of black unity. Over time those who defined themselves as Marxists—and were often influenced by China—came to challenge the nationalists. By 1975 the committee fractured over (for example) whether race or class provided the best analysis for understanding the black condition. Various nationalists and Pan-Africanists left the ALSC. The bitterness of the debates polarized relations between the two camps, and in 1975 the ALSC national headquarters closed.

The ASLC was for the 1970s what the Paul Robeson and W. E. B. Du Bois–led Council on African Affairs had been in the 1937–1955 period. Although functioning for only a few years, the ALSC produced important research and disseminated a large amount of educational material. It provided money, supplies, and direct links to African revolutionaries. Most important, it increased the anti-imperialist awareness of African Americans through its African Liberation Day observances.

[*See also* Pan-Africanism *and biographical entries on figures mentioned in this article.*]

BIBLIOGRAPHY

Walters, Ronald W. *Pan Africanism in the African Diaspora: An Analysis of Modern Afrocentric Political Movements*. Detroit: Wayne State University Press, 1997. Chapter 2 is "The Pan African Movement in the United States." Ronald Walters was briefly a member of the executive committee of the African Liberation Support Committee.

Woodward, Komozi. *A Nation within a Nation: Amiri Baraka (LeRoi Jones) and Black Power Politics*. Chapel Hill and London: University of North Carolina Press, 1999. Chapter 5 positions the African Liberation Support Committee in the larger Black Power movement. The book contains an extensive bibliography.

—PETER BRUSH

AFRO-AMERICAN COUNCIL. The Afro-American Council was one of the earliest national African American political organizations in the United States. The council was essentially a rebirth of the Afro-American League, which existed from 1890 to 1893. The purpose of the Afro-American League, and later the Afro-American Council, was to provide a national forum for African Americans, to respond to the growing level of white violence against blacks in the southern United States, and to fight increasing legal segregation.

In its initial existence as the Afro-American League, the organization advocated five principal goals or points of protest: to fight the suppression of black suffrage in the southern United States, to fight legal and social support for lynching, to equalize funding for white and black schools, to end the system of chain gangs in the South—which were used to provide cheap labor to white business owners—and to remove discrimination in railroad travel and hotel accommodations. The founder of the Afro-American League was T. Thomas Fortune, the editor of the *New York Age*. He attempted to form a national organization that was to be financially supported by a number of state and local chapters. After an initial convention in January 1890, the support for the league soon ended because of limited financial support, an inability to maintain African American support, and divisions among African American leaders on the direction of national protest.

By September 1898 the rise in the number of lynchings throughout the southern United States had brought renewed interest in a national black organization to fight for equality and civil rights. In Rochester, New York, the Afro-American Council was created using the platform and organization of the failed league. The Afro-American Council was organized in a number of subunits, called bureaus, that represented the council's primary concerns: antilynching, business, education, and literature. A number of black leaders, such as W. E. B. Du Bois and Ida B. Wells-Barnett, served as heads of the different bureaus. Bishop Alexander Walters of the African Methodist Episcopal Zion Church was elected the first president of the council and served until 1902. The council also elected a vice president to support the work of the president.

Besides Walters, T. Thomas Fortune and Booker T. Washington became the council's main supporters. Washington was increasingly being seen as the leader of the Negro community by the white political leadership. Washington's involvement in the council exposed the growing conflict within the national African American political leadership. His support for economic self-determination for the Negro people drew support from the white leadership but threw him into conflict with those black leaders who supported more radical methods to equalize the races within America.

One such leader was William Monroe Trotter, who was the editor of the *Boston Guardian*. Trotter advocated a stronger response from the African American community, bringing pressure to bear upon the white political leaders in order to rein in the lawlessness of southern communities toward their black neighbors. Trotter—and others, among them Du Bois—increasingly fell into the anti-Washington camp within the council. They sought to remove Washington from the council and to erase Washington's influence on African American leadership at the national level. Trotter used his newspaper to strike out against the growing power of Booker T. Washington and his dreams of racial economic self-determination.

During the council's second national convention in Chicago in November 1899, the conflict between the two camps intensified to the point that the convention consisted of resolutions being filed either to condemn or to support Booker T. Washington. Du Bois continued to support the work of the anti-Washington coalition, but publicly he at first remained unassociated with them. A year later Washington called a meeting in Boston of the National Negro Leadership League just prior to the council's convention in Indianapolis, hoping to undercut his opponents' base of support. Later, in 1902, Washington had one of his strongest supporters, the Afro-American League founder T. Thomas Fortune, elected president of the Afro-American Council, and a slate of Washington supporters were made bureau officers. Trotter argued that Fortune was only a puppet and that the real power in the council was still Washington.

Trotter attempted to curb Washington's power within the council at the next convention, at Louisville, Kentucky, in 1903, where Fortune was reelected as the council's president. Trotter and his supporters, known as "Trotterites," mounted strong attacks against Washington and his supporters through a series of resolutions on the convention floor, each of which was downed by the shouts of Washington's supporters. With his support within the council plain, Washington worked to minimize Trotter and his supporters and used the council to advance his theories of economic self-determination. The council also attempted to challenge the South's denying blacks the vote but was rebuffed by the U.S. Supreme Court.

As with the defunct league, money troubles soon began to affect the council. Fortune resigned his presidency in 1904, citing his inability to raise capital and the apathy of the African American population. In 1905 Bishop Walters again assumed the presidency of the council. Also in 1905 a number of African American leaders including Du Bois and Trotter, dissatisfied with the council, met in Canada near Niagara Falls to fashion a more radical political movement. The resulting Niagara Movement pulled supporters away from the council and served to weaken the council further. Walters attempted to steer the council away from Washington's influence but was unsuccessful. A proposed alliance of the council, the Niagara Movement, the American Negro Academy, and the National Negro American Political League failed to materialize, and the council began to fall apart. The council became effectively dissolved in 1909 when its members left to join the National Association for the Advancement of Colored People (NAACP), founded in 1909, and the National Urban League, founded in 1910.

[*See also* National Association for the Advancement of Colored People; National Urban League; Niagara Movement; Washington–Du Bois Conflict; and *biographical entries on figures mentioned in this article*.]

BIBLIOGRAPHY

Fox, Stephen *The Guardian of Boston: William Monroe Trotter*. New York: Athenaeum, 1970.

Harlan, Louis R. *Booker T. Washington: The Wizard of Tuskegee, 1901–1915*. New York: Oxford University Press, 1983.

Thornbrough, Emma Lou. "The National Afro-American League, 1887–1908." *Journal of Southern History* 27, no. 4 (November 1961): 494-512.

Wolters, Raymond. *Du Bois and His Rivals* Columbia: University of Missouri Press, 2002.

—WILLIAM H. BROWN

AFROCENTRISM. Afrocentricity is a concept that blossomed in the late twentieth century and was derived from the intellectual movement with the same name. Although Molefi Asante, the former chairman of the Department of African American Studies at Temple University—the first doctoral-degree-granting department of its kind—is most closely identified with Afrocentricity, the Afrocentricity movement is also closely identified with Maulana Karenga, the founder of Kwanzaa, a widely observed African American cultural holiday that occurs in late December. Afrocentricity is an intellectual outgrowth of a number of concepts: black nationalism, most commonly associated with Marcus Garvey of the Universal Negro Improvement Association, Malcolm X, and Elijah Muhammad's and Louis Farrakhan's Nation of Islam; Négritude, the cultural ideology of "Blackness" originated by the Senegalese president Léopold Sédar Senghor; Pan-Africanism, with its goal of promoting the political and economic unity of Africa and people of African descent, an idea first articulated by Henry Sylvester Williams, a lawyer from Trinidad active in the early twentieth century, W. E. B. Du Bois, Kwame Nkrumah, and others; and Kawaida, the ideological underpinnings of Karenga's movement for the cultural and spiritual unity and mobilization of people of African descent, which also gave rise to the Kwanzaa celebration.

Though these latter concepts emerged and intertwined in the twentieth-century crucible of political struggle by national and intellectual leaders striving to chart a path for the decolonization of Africa and the quest for self-determination and human rights for the peoples of the African diaspora, Afrocentricity is essentially an intellectual phenomenon that asserts the need to analyze historical and social data and experience from the perspective of the African—that is, the need to place Africa and Africans at the center of analysis and perspective. Asante positions Afrocentricity against Eurocentrism as an intellectual antidote or mental correction of a historical error in perspective and policy. Asante posits that Afrocentricity is an intellectually superior methodology because it is more conceptually and cosmologically inclusive, decentralized, and integral in opposition to the European perspective (especially European imperialism). As Asante has articulated it, Eurocentrism has been the dominant perspective—particularly in North America—and thus Afrocentricity is meant to rectify this imbalance.

Asante characterizes Eurocentrism as having created a false, fragmented, and dichotomous hierarchy of truth and reality through philosophy, history, and scientific concepts that insist on the centrality of their truth (with "history" being defined as "his story," meaning the story of the European); Eurocentrism positions itself as guardian of truth over others in the intellectual, spiritual, and political realms. Afrocentricity methodologically places the African perspective(s) at the center of a perception and analysis of the experience of Africans around the world. Part of the reason for this approach is to remedy the glut of European perspectives that have defined and obfuscated the experience of Africa and people of African descent since the height of the European domination of African and world affairs through colonialism, transatlantic slavery, and postcolonial globalization.

Afrocentricity begins with a fundamental recognition and promotion of the African origins of human civilization in the Nile Valley cultures of the various empires and dynasties that existed in the region of the African continent now known as Egypt and Ethiopia. Afrocentricity also gives a significant place in global history and culture to other African civilizations and societies (Yoruba, Zulu, Masai, Great Zimbabwe, and so forth) and is subscribed to by an array of African and African American (North and South American, Caribbean) intellectuals, as well as by intellectuals of African ancestry based in Europe. Afrocentrism has also led to the revision of much of history—for instance, the reclaiming of the Christian messiah, Jesus of Nazareth, as an African deity (or a black deity with roots in African civilization), as well as the claiming of Islam as an African-originated religion. Some thinkers who identify with Afrocentricity argue that, based on geographic or phenotypic evidence, other world religions such as Judaism, Buddhism, or Hinduism can be identified has having African (or black) origins or aspects.

At the center of all of this analysis are claims and arguments from several centuries of literature and scholarship that present both new historical artifacts and data or new interpretations of established evidence and literature, not to mention archaeological and prosopographical explorations. The central principle of this body of work is that the original scholarship and literature was both biased and incomplete, and thus what is required is revisiting the assumptions of historical research and analysis, as well as searching for more complete records and accounts of history. Though history has always been open for critique and revision, the basis for this perspective remains controversial among certain scholars.

The controversy revolves, in part, around both the need for and the best method of developing methodologies, academic programs, and departments to study Africana, African Americans, and the African diaspora. Afrocentrism has been attacked by some scholars and advocates as racist, irrelevant, and intellectually flawed or fraudulent. Mary Lefkowitz's *Not Out of Africa* (1996) is the widest-ranging and best-known critique. So far, Afrocentrism has failed to create an internationally accredited institution of higher education, or one subscribed to by a critical mass of the African diaspora or its intellectual elite.

This leaves—according to the critical point of view—the Islamic universities or madrassas of fifteenth- and sixteenth-century Timbuktu in Mali as the last African-originated intellectual institutions in history, preceded by Greek centers of knowledge and learning, including those in Alexandria, Egypt. Both of these sets of institutions have their origins in the literary traditions of external civilizations—to the extent that one views Islam and Greece as external to Africa—in contrast to the oral tradition of most well-known African civilizations.

Afrocentrism began to evolve from the twentieth-century scholarship of Asante, Karenga, Du Bois, Martin Bernal, John Henrik Clarke, Cheikh Anta Diop, Chancellor Williams, George James, J. A. Rogers, Ivan Van Sertima, and Yosef Ben-Jochannan. Though not all of these scholars are properly or even exclusively called Afrocentrists, their perspective and findings have to a greater or lesser degree contributed to a critique of Eurocentric scholarship and historical analysis and have laid the foundation for a countercultural scholarship and worldview.

Afrocentrism also has a smaller and more recent branch of scholarship that traces the African genetic roots of humanity as evidence of the African origins of human civilization. Although scientists now generally agree that the oldest human beings and human communities existed in Africa, the "civilization conveyor belt" theory that human migration out of Africa took an "African civilization" per se around the world has not been universally accepted. Civilizations, according to this dissenting view, are seen as having a polycentric and uneven process of development throughout human history, with no single source as the precise and exact origin. In sum, though viewed as controversial by some, Afrocentrism is best seen as a response to a kind of unthinking Eurocentrism and as a corrective to a pervasive racism that has dominated intellectual life at least since the rise of the African slave trade.

[*See also* Black Nationalism; Historiography; Kwanzaa; Nation of Islam; Pan-Africanism; *and biographical entries on figures mentioned in this article*.]

BIBLIOGRAPHY

Asante, Molefi Kete. *The Afrocentric Idea*. Rev. ed. Philadelphia: Temple University Press, 1998.

Asante, Molefi Kete. *Kemet, Afrocentricity, and Knowledge*. Trenton, N.J.: Africa World Press, 1990.

Bernal, Martin. "The Afrocentric Interpretation of History: Martin Bernal Replies to Mary Lefkowitz." *Journal of Blacks in Higher Education* 11 (Spring 1996): 86–94.

Van Dyk, Sandra. "Molefi Kete Asante's Theory of Afrocentricity: The Development of a Theory of Cultural Location." PhD diss., Temple University, 1998.

Winters, Clyde Ahmad. "Afrocentrism: A Valid Frame of Reference." *Journal of Black Studies* 25, no. 2 (1994): 170–190.

—JOSEPH WILSON
—DAVID ADDAMS

AGRICULTURE AND AGRICULTURAL LABOR.

The history of African Americans in the United States is intimately intertwined with the history of American agriculture. From the colonial era to the early nineteenth century, the labor of African Americans—enslaved ones, specifically—powered American agribusiness, producing crops such as cotton, tobacco, rice, and sugar. Although emancipation ended African Americans' legal bondage as agricultural laborers, African Americans remained a significant portion of the Americans who made their living by agricultural labor. U.S. census statistics from 1900 through 1954 show that during that time African Americans constituted an average of 28.7 percent of the nation's farm operators. Between 1954 and 1959, the percentage of African American farmers dropped by nearly 9 points. Since 1959 the number of African American farmers—then 265,261—has continued to dwindle until in the early twenty-first century there were only about 15,000 African American farmers remaining, which is less than 0.2 percent of all American farmers.

Sharecropping and Peonage. It was within the South that African American farmers made their most significant impact. In 1900 African Americans constituted a major portion of the farming population in the states of the former Confederacy, especially in the states of the Deep South. One-third of the farmers in Georgia and Florida were African American, and more than 42 percent in Alabama were African American; African American farmers constituted a bare majority of farmers in Louisiana and a clear majority in South Carolina and Mississippi. Around the perimeter of the former Confederacy, African American farmers constituted up to one-quarter of farmers.

Cotton Production. A woman transfers cotton on the farm of Jesse Middleton Hunt in Jones County, Georgia, 1900. VANISHING GEORGIA COLLECTION, GEORGIA ARCHIVES

Though the presence of African Americans on the farm remained significant, by 1900 it was clear that African Americans in the South had made little progress toward farm ownership. Indeed, there was an inverse relationship between the percentage of African Americans in the farming population and the level of farm ownership. Within the South, West Virginia census data shows that nearly two-thirds of its African American farmers owned their farms. In Virginia, 50 percent of African American farmers owned their farms, and nearly 50 percent of African American farmers in Maryland owned their farms. In Florida, more than 40 percent of African American farmers owned their farms. Kentucky, Delaware, and Missouri each had at least one-third owners among all black farm operators. In North Carolina, Texas, Arkansas, and Tennessee, between 20 and 26 percent of African American farmers owned the land they tilled. However, from Louisiana to South Carolina, low percentages of black farm ownership existed, from 11.53 percent in Georgia to 18.15 percent in South Carolina.

Where African Americans lived and farmed outside the South, and the percentage of farm owners was substantially higher, this apparently higher figure was offset by the small number of African American farmers. Indeed in many southern states with low rates of farm ownership among African Americans, the number of owners was actually higher than in the states outside the South. Between 1896 and 1920 many African Americans were able to rise into the ranks of farm owners as the price for cotton crops rose with demand. After 1920 there was a general decline in African American ownership throughout the South.

The majority of African American farmers were sharecroppers—not out of choice, but out of necessity. For a number of reasons the freed generation's expectation that they would be given land of their own—"forty acres and a mule," the symbolic phrase stemming from a Union field order seeming to grant land and livestock—to embark on lives as independent yeoman farmers did not materialize. Many former slaves expected that the lands that they would receive were those on which they had formerly toiled as bound laborers. When former masters abandoned these holdings as the Union army advanced, freed African Americans began to farm the land in their own interest. To their dismay and frustration, when the planters returned they expected the return of their land, and government officials sided with the landowners—over the objections of the blacks, who believed they held "sweat equity" in the land.

The federal government's solution to African Americans' thirst for land was to enact the Southern Homestead Act in 1866. This law opened federal lands in Alabama, Louisiana, Arkansas, Florida, and Mississippi for settlement not only by African Americans but by landless whites as well. A homesteader could settle eighty acres and pay five dollars to register the patent, compared to 160 acres and a registration fee of ten dollars in the Southern Homestead Act of 1862. The 1866 plan had intended to put land ownership within the reach of former slaves, but its framers clearly did not think through the logistical problems or human consequences of the law. Most African Americans left slavery with no material resources: no horses, no wagons, and no money. All of these things were needed to help them move to one of the states covered by the act, to build homes, and to survive until their farms could be established. Further, this emigration would mean that those who chose to move would leave behind familial and community connections. About four thousand blacks filed land patents between 1866 and 1869. The program was plagued by corruption, and the lands available were of poor quality. In 1876 the law was repealed.

Staple-crop farming remained the mainstay of the southern economy in the decades after the Civil War. With the reconfiscation of the lands that former slaves had squatted on, the former slaves had to make pragmatic decisions about their economic futures. Even before the war ended, federal officials with the Freedmen's Bureau had encouraged and coerced former slaves to enter into labor contracts with landowning whites, which provided the whites with the ability to have their crops cultivated for them and provided the former slaves with shelter and some minimal means of sustenance.

Over time, this evolved into the system called sharecropping. By the end of the nineteenth century, as the statistics show, this nonowner farming system dominated the African American farm experience. The crop-lien arrangement, in which the "cropper's" interest in the crop was mortgaged to secure working capital for farm and home provisions, became the cornerstone of a system that resulted in virtual servitude for many African Americans. How the crop was divided—"shared"—varied according to what each party brought to the table. African Americans who owned farm stock or implements were able to strike deals with their employers for a greater share of the crop than were those whose farm implements and personal supplies such as food and clothing were furnished by their landlord, or by local merchants who provided credit advances.

This system was fraught with corruption. It exploited the illiteracy of many farmers, and it thrived on institutionalized racism. Often the contract stipulated that every available inch of ground be planted in a staple crop and that the gross receipts resulting from the sale of the crop would be used to settle the farmer's debts before any profit was realized. It also meant that rather than being able to feed and provide for their families from the fruits of their own labor, these farmers were forced to rely on store-bought goods. African Americans signed contracts that included obtaining advances at usurious rates of interest. Once the crops were harvested and the accounts settled, many sharecroppers found themselves still indebted to their landlords.

Unlettered African Americans, even if they had a good sense for numbers, did not stand a chance against the often padded ledgers of their creditors. An African American farmer was fortunate if he broke even. However, far too many farmers found themselves rolling over debt against future profits in the hope that they would break even at a future time. The result for many was a new version of slavery—peonage—caused by the fact that black farmers could not move to another location in search of better opportunities because of their indebtedness. By the end of the century, peonage laws made the grip of white landlords even tighter.

Cash tenants fared somewhat better. These tenants paid a flat rate to rent the land they farmed, and they had complete autonomy to decide what type and amount of crops they would plant. A third category of laborers who did not own farms was wage laborers who worked as day laborers. As late as 1940 these laborers constituted a third or more of nontenant African American farmers in all the southern states except Kentucky, Oklahoma, Tennessee, Texas, and West Virginia.

At the end of the nineteenth century, African Americans produced more than 4 million bales of cotton, which accounted for 39 percent of all cotton production. The 90 million pounds of tobacco produced on African American farms constituted 10 percent of all tobacco production. Cotton was the leading crop produced by African American farmers. In every region of the South, black farmers devoted more acreage to cotton than to any other crop. African Americans planted 14,087,998 acres in corn in 1899. The acreage in corn increased by about 660,000 acres between 1899 and 1909 to 14.75 million acres. Over the same period, cotton acreage, which was 19,312,514 acres in 1899, exploded by nearly half a million acres to 24.1 million in 1909.

Agrarian Societies and Land-Grant Colleges. In the late nineteenth century, agrarian movements strove to maintain farmers' relevance in American society even as industrial capitalism and urbanization gained ascendancy. Within that framework, African American farmers worked hard to uplift themselves economically and to develop viable autonomous communities. African American farmers had joined with other farming groups that had been dispossessed by late-nineteenth-century industrialization by establishing the Colored Farmers Alliance. By the middle of the 1890s the power of this organization had collapsed, along with that of the other progressive organizations with which they collaborated. However, on the local level, new organizations sprang up to encourage mutual cooperation and support. In 1890 the educator Robert Lloyd Smith, formerly an aide to the first Tuskegee Institute principal Booker T. Washington and an advocate of Washington's philosophy of black self-help through industrial education, developed the Farmers Improvement Society of Texas (FIST). The organization served as a vehicle for Smith successfully to seek office as a Texas legislator in 1894 and 1896. By 1906, with the participation of African Americans in Texas politics at an end, the cooperative focused its resources on collective support that allowed its members to acquire farms and the credit needed for independent operations. FIST was so successful that it expanded its operations to Oklahoma and Arkansas.

In addition to grassroots efforts to improve the conditions of African American agriculture, in the late nineteenth century a new phenomenon, the drive for scientific agriculture, emerged. This augured mixed possibilities for African American farmers. Within the black community, diversified farming was encouraged through the black land-grant

Agricultural Labor. Hamper of beans being transported to a packinghouse in order to be processed and shipped, Belle Glade, Florida, 1947. Florida Photographic Collection, State Library and Archives of Florida

colleges. Tuskegee, in particular, pioneered the promotion of diversified agriculture among African Americans through its summer short courses and institutes. Washington and his staff promoted agriculture practices that would allow African American farmers to work their way out of debt and toward farm ownership. With the financial support of northern white philanthropists, Washington developed a program of farmers' institutes. These institutes were attended by better-off farmers not only from Macon County, where the school was located, but also from across Alabama and outside the state. Tuskegee's courses and their graduates, who served on the faculties of other black colleges in the South or started colleges of their own, had a far-reaching impact.

As land-grant colleges for African Americans in other states were created in the wake of the Morrill Act of 1890, which financially supported both black and white agricultural and industrial education, these schools began to hold their own institutes. These new institutes were most successful in providing education to farm owners, because those who farmed the land of others lacked the autonomy to implement new farming approaches without the permission of the owner of the land. For landlords, the cash nexus dictated that staple-crop production—in many cases cotton production—was most profitable. The sharecropping system, established as a compromise between land and labor during Reconstruction, had locked the South in a cycle of retrograde agriculture that continued well into the twentieth century.

Generally the efforts to encourage progressive farming among African Americans were not met with notable support in the states where most of them lived and worked until the trifecta of the onslaught of the boll weevil, a decline in cotton prices, and an increase in opportunities for industrial employment, especially outside the South, led to the abandonment of the farm by a significant number of African American farmers. The boll-weevil infestation devastated southern agriculture and, in the process, the economic prospects of many African American farmers. Even as the pest swept its way from Texas northward in every direction, landowners showed a continued passion for cotton production to feed the nation's expanding textile industry and responded to the pest, as the data shows, by attempting to "outplant" it.

Cotton was not the only crop of significance that African Americans farmed. In tobacco-growing areas, tenancy rates were as high as two-thirds in some states. Boom-and-bust cycles in tobacco paralleled those in cotton, and by the early 1920s the price per pound was less than twenty-five cents.

The early crisis in cotton production led many southern states to see the utility of investing in a new program of farm improvement, the cooperative extension service. The service was established in 1915 as a result of the Smith-Lever Act. Under the program, local men and women were hired to provide rural people with instruction in improved farming and homemaking methods. In the states where most African Americans lived, the program was met with a mixture of enthusiasm and suspicion from whites and blacks alike. Some whites were skeptical that African American farmers had the aptitude to put scientific practices into place. Others were concerned about the interposition of the federal government between landowners and laborers. White political leaders were most concerned about the social ramifications of using African Americans as extension agents because their status as federal employees seemed out of order in an increasingly segregated South. Although there had been successful African American agents, such as Thomas Campbell and John Pierce, in programs that antedated Smith-Lever, in some states the white leadership had a strong desire to limit the benefits that African Americans received. Some in the African American community initially perceived extension programs as another method by which white landowners intended to extract wealth from their labor. This sentiment was probably more prevalent among laborers than among African American landowners.

The political impediments to employment were the greatest difficulty to be overcome. Supporters of African American land-grant colleges attempted to have Smith-Lever funds divided so that African American colleges would receive a direct appropriation. After a racially charged debate in which southern senators insisted that African Americans lacked the capacity to carry out scientific agriculture, the amendments to divide the fund failed. Subsequently, southern states hired African American workers, albeit at much lower numbers and at a much slower rate of expansion than they did in their white men and women's programs. Nationally a total of 63 black men and women were hired as agents in 1915. By 1929 a total of 329 served as agents in the South. The number of agents fluctuated according to economic and social conditions, and therefore the growth of the program was uneven. Generally the number of African American agents increased by about two hundred agents per decade through the early 1950s. The majority of African American agents served African American landowners; as a result the number of agents was not sufficient to serve most of the African American population. Some states opposed the employment of African American men and women as agents of the federal government. There was fear that white landowners would object to the entire program if it appeared that a black agent rather than the landlord were the source of authority over the tenant. However, as the labor crisis in southern agriculture escalated during the 1920s, support for extension work developed in areas where African Americans constituted a significant percentage of the population.

As envisioned for whites, the extension program was a capitalist enterprise. However, many historians have argued that its benefits accrued most to farmers who were already prosperous. For African Americans the scope of the program was limited, perhaps in part because even black landowners were rarely prosperous. A live-at-home program was developed and delivered to African American farmers. Its emphasis was on subsistence farming. In those areas where tenants received farm services, farm ownership was not part of the calculus of this program. In addition, some white landowners preferred plantation projects in which white agents provided agricultural instruction to tenants under the landlord's watchful eye to having African American agents serve their workers.

These programs failed to end the African Americans' exodus from the farm. The decrease of African American farmers in the South during the 1920s was nearly 5 percent. Owners and managers experienced the greatest decline in acreage farmed during that period. Ironically, all the former Confederate and border states, with the exception of South Carolina and Georgia, experienced a net increase in African American tenants during the 1920s. In the next decade the demographic landscape of the rural South was totally transformed by the flight of African Americans from the farm. Between 1930 and 1940 the number of black farm operators dropped by 23 percent nationally, with the percentage of part owners and tenants declining by one-fourth.

The Great Depression. The Great Depression had a transformative role on African Americans in agriculture as a result of economic conditions nationally and of the change in federal agricultural policy. Agriculture was among the first of the economic sectors to be affected by the Depression. Southern agriculture was particularly hard-hit. Cotton produced in 1925 and 1926 had earned farmers 20.19 cents per pound. In 1929 the price was 16.78 cents per pound, and by 1930 the price had fallen to 9.46 cents per pound. The Depression years quickly revealed the lie of southern paternalism in the relation between planter and tenant. In economic hard times, southern landlords saw to the needs of their own families before those of their tenants.

The federal government attempted to stave off the economic impact of falling prices by the creation of the Agricultural Marketing Act in 1929. A year later the federal government created the Cotton Stabilization Board to buy cotton held by private cotton cooperatives. Cotton growers were encouraged to curtail the creation of surpluses, but success was limited. Economic conditions became acute and adversely affected the rural presence of African Americans after 1930. Most important were the implementation of federal farm policies that encouraged white landowners to break their dependency on African American farm laborers.

In 1933 the administration of Franklin D. Roosevelt took steps to intervene directly in reducing the production of cotton. The Agricultural Adjustment Act of 1933 (AAA) offered direct payments to farmers to reduce the amount of acres planted in cotton. More than any other government measure, this led to the demographic collapse of the African American presence in southern agriculture, where African Americans had historically made their most significant impact. Under the AAA, 10.5 million acres were removed from cotton production, and direct cash payments of $116 million were made to farmers. The AAA instituted price supports for cotton and tobacco as well, but none of these policies was as draconian and as wide ranging in its effect as the cotton reduction program.

Southern legislative delegations used their leverage in the House of Representatives and the Senate to ensure that federal largesse came with as few strings attached as possible. As a result they were able to limit the African American benefit from these programs and control the opportunities for material improvement of their labor force, while the New Deal allowed those southerners who were most affluent in land to profit. Despite federal efforts to ensure that disbursement of federal funds was shared between landlords and tenants in a manner proportionate to the manner in which they split their crops, this was rarely the case. Landlords used tenants' share of any federal proceeds to settle outstanding debts owed to them by their tenants. Some landlords even plowed under the acreage of their tenants and dismissed the tenants, keeping all payments for themselves.

The AAA did little more for African Americans in the professions. During the 1920s and 1930s the federal extension service for African Americans had slowly shrunk because the pattern of hiring agents in southern states typically mirrored hiring patterns nationally, with the majority of funding diverted toward services for whites. However, in ancillary programs such as resettlement, African Americans were hired to be the face of the federal government. Special agents, including Jennie Booth Moton, the wife of Robert Russa Moton, the second principal of Tuskegee, were hired for public relations campaigns to encourage African Americans to support federal agricultural programs. Even with such public relations activities, African American farmers fared worse under federal programs.

The manner in which federal assistance was provided locally had a more far-reaching effect than publicity visits. The federal extension service was assigned the primary responsibility for enlisting farmers for loans. The South's segregated extension service replicated the racial hierarchy of southern society generally. As an institution, the black extension service lacked the necessary structure or autonomous power to ensure significant participation by African American farmers. Not every county in the South employed African American agents. Within the structure of the extension service itself, there was racial hierarchy—formal in some states and informal in others. The employment status of African American extension workers was tenuous at best. The federal extension service abdicated any oversight regarding the employment of African American agents. These factors combined to make it extremely difficult for African American farmers to participate in the program because white extension agents were given charge of distributing the application forms.

An incident from a seed loan program in South Carolina in 1931 suggests the difficulties that African American agents had in securing loan opportunities for clients. African American farmers had reported not being able to secure loans whether or not there was an extension agent in the county. African American farmers in Aiken County were promised an equal share of applications. They were asked to leave the room while applications were distributed to the white agents, and subsequently few African American farmers received application forms. Richland County's industrious African American agent, James E. Dickson, had farmers arrive early at the white agent's office to get application forms. After twelve African American farmers received applications, the remaining African American farmers were told by the white agent that there were no more loan forms. Though the agent promised to call when new forms arrived, he never did. The response to a complaint on these matters by the state's white director of extension work was: "It must not be said that we are discriminating against any class of farmers."

African American laborers did not take these slights passively. Emigration was the clearest expression of their dissatisfaction with their mistreatment. Those who wanted to remain in the South resorted to radical means. In 1934 the Southern Tenant Farmers Union was organized in Arkansas. African Americans in Alabama became involved with the Communist Party. Through these groups, African Americans organized to fight for fair treatment under New Deal programs.

As the economic crisis deepened, the federal government responded to the marginalization of poor farmers—of whom African Americans were a significant part—by attempting to help them become self-sufficient. The Rural Rehabilitation Division (RRD), created within the Federal Emergency Relief Administration, was the first attempt by the Roosevelt administration to transform landless farmers into yeomen. The Resettlement Administration was superseded by the RRD in 1935 to purchase land and resell it to farmers and help them establish cooperatives to sell their goods. This bureaucracy was established as a response to a study on tenancy commissioned by Roosevelt. The RRD was folded into the Farm Security Administration (FSA) two years later.

The success of these projects in creating a class of landowners was less than stellar. The bureaucracy was unable to address the extent of the need for farms. The FSA and its successor, the Farmers' Home Administration, made a total of 47,104 loans to tenants who wanted to purchase land; in 1945 this left about three times that number unassisted. The success of the program in creating a class of African American farmers is uncertain, although it likely ameliorated some of the worst suffering of the group. Though more than 600,000 loans were made over the years 1934 through 1941, in the years from 1938 to 1941 only slightly more than 8,000 of these loans were for farm purchases. However, the FSA was perhaps one of the more successful programs for small farmers, which is what most African American farmers were. The FSA had made loans in the amount of $516 million by 1943. The FSA ended in 1946, apparently a victim of conservative agricultural interests. From the Southern Homestead Act, through Smith-Lever and various other extension acts, to New Deal plow-under policies, to programs such as the FSA, there is the recurrent theme of using the power of the government in support of advanced agriculture, which was synonymous with the mechanized operations of white farmers.

World War II and After. During the years of World War II, both the federal government and the states took a special interest in encouraging agricultural production among African American farmers. The U.S. Department of Agriculture (USDA) even issued publications celebrating the role of the "Negro" in agriculture and the vital role of African Americans farmers in producing for the war. Yet during the next decade the number of black-operated farms began a decline from which it has not recovered. More than half a million African Americans—10.39 percent of all farmers—made their living from farming in 1950. By the end of the decade that number had been halved, and the percentage of farms operated by African Americans had dropped by more than 3 percent. In absolute numbers, the decline was astonishing: from 272,541 farmers in 1959 to 87,393 in 1969, 37,351 in 1978, 22,954 in 1987, and 18,816 in 1997. In that year one-third of the farms owned by African Americans were between 10 and 39 acres, and another third were between 50 and 139 acres. Farms of between 1 and 9 acres were the third largest category of farm ownership. Only 752 farms were 500 acres or larger. Farm tenants, formerly the largest category of African American farmers, accounted for only 1,891 of all African American farmers and farmed only 221,432 of the 2.5 million acres farmed by African Americans.

The role of mechanization and chemical herbicides and their intersection with the civil rights movement contributed to the decline from 1940 onward. In essence, technological innovation and social restructuring combined to end the fragmented plantation system of agriculture. The most significant shift toward mechanization began after World War II. The use of tractors rather than draft animals allowed landowners to enlarge their holdings; this led to a decline in the need for sharecroppers. Some farmers moved away from cotton agriculture. Those who continued to grow the crop achieved economies of scale by using tractors and mechanical cotton pickers to replace human, mostly African American, labor. Mechanization also enabled these farmers to pursue mixed agricultural production. Although mechanical cotton pickers had been manufactured and sold as early as 1941, it was not until the 1950s that the machines' use drastically affected the number of African American farmers. By the 1960s, mechanization was used in other agricultural enterprises, including the production of tobacco. An example of the impact of commercial herbicides is what happened in the Mississippi Delta. There the employment of unskilled labor dropped 72 percent in the three years after the introduction of herbicides.

Mechanization had repercussions other than economies of scale. Nan Woodruff documents the connection among New Deal policy, the activity of the Southern Tenant Farmers' Union in the 1940s, and mechanization in the delta states. Planters hoped to adopt technological innovation and still preserve the paternalistic racial patterns traditional to the region, but this was an endeavor destined to fail. As African Americans' pursuit of civil rights escalated, farms became centers of conflict between the landed and the laboring classes. For example, in 1962 the sharecropper Fannie Lou Hamer, who subsequently became a civil rights organizer and a founder of the Mississippi Freedom Democratic Party, was evicted from the plantation where she and her husband lived and worked because she tried to register to vote.

The politics of the civil rights years affected not only African American farmers but also the African American agricultural professionals who served them. These agents sought employment equity for themselves and improved access to federal resources for their clients with little success. Indeed, the 1950s marked the beginning of a precipitous decline in the number of African American extension personnel in the southern states, where the greatest number had been employed, although at the same time opportunities for employment opened up in branches of the USDA in which African Americans had not been previously employed. In 1986 African American agents successfully sued for and won equal employment rights in *Bazemore v. Friday*.

In 1981 the administration of Ronald Reagan disbanded the civil rights division of the USDA, which contributed to an increasingly dire plight for African American farmers. In the early twenty-first century, African American participation in federal programs both as employees and as clients was still marginal.

Between 1997 and 2002 the number of African American farmers grew by at least ten thousand. African Americans farm in every state. In the states of the former Confederacy, which built their economies with African American labor for two and a half centuries, the number of African American farmers increased, with Mississippi leading the way. Only South Carolina, North Carolina, and Tennessee experienced a decline in the number of African American farmers during those years.

African American farmers have protested against the USDA, whose policies have marginalized African American and other small farmers, and they have sought legal redress as well: in the 1999 class-action lawsuit *Pigford v. Glickman*, African American farmers sued the USDA, alleging a pattern of discrimination. The plaintiffs in the suit contended that the USDA loan policies ensnared African American farmers in a cycle of debt that led to financial distress and in some cases to land loss. Bureaucracy at both the state and federal level has made it difficult for African American farmers to obtain adequate redress under the *Glickman* ruling. For example, those seeking redress are confronted by bureaucratic red tape that requires them to document any discrimination.

The position of African American farmers remains precarious. As of 2003, 40 percent of applications for monetary compensation under the simplest terms of the settlement had been denied—although there has been a steady decline in the percentage denied, to 36 percent in 2005 and 31 percent in 2008. The original timeline, which Secretary of Agriculture Ann Veneman in the USDA appeal *Pigford v. Veneman* sought to enforce, has been the greatest obstacle. The case was active in the early twenty-first century as *Pigford v. Schafer*. The plight of African American farmers has become part of the political landscape: in 2004, Congress held hearings on the notice aspect of the original *Pigford* ruling. The African American Farmers Benefits Relief Act, which would extend the time to file claims, remained in subcommittee in May 2008.

African American farmers continue to feel economically insecure. The Kentucky farmer Harry Terril Young filed a lawsuit against the USDA in 2006 and against the FSA in 2007 to stop the foreclosure sale of his farm. The 2006 lawsuit has been dismissed. The family farm as an American institution is on a decline from which it will likely never recover, as agribusinesses have reshaped the landscape of agricultural production. It is certainly unlikely that, as a group, African American farmers will ever again play the dominant economic role that they played in southern agriculture for centuries.

[*See also* Farmers and Land Ownership; Peonage; *and* Sharecropping.]

BIBLIOGRAPHY

Daniel, Pete. *The Shadow of Slavery: Peonage in the South, 1901–1969*. London and New York: Oxford University Press, 1973.

Harris, Carmen V. " 'The Extension Service Is Not an Integration Agency': The Idea of Race in the Federal Cooperative Extension Service." *Agricultural History* 82, no. 2 (Spring 2008): 193–219.

Hurt, R. Douglas, ed. *African American Life in the Rural South, 1900–1950*. Columbia: University of Missouri Press, 2003.

Lanza, Michael L. *Agrarianism and Reconstruction Politics: The Southern Homestead Act*. Baton Rouge: Louisiana State University Press, 1990.

Nieman, Donald G. *From Slavery to Sharecropping: White Land and Black Labor in the Rural South, 1865–1900*. New York: Garland, 1994.

Reynolds, Bruce J. "Black Farmers in America, 1865–2000: The Pursuit of Independent Farming and the Role of Cooperatives." *RBS Research Report* 194 (2002).

Schor, Joel. "Black Farmers/Farms: The Search for Equity." *Agriculture and Human Values* 13, no. 3 (June 1996): 48–63.

Schweninger, Loren. "A Vanishing Breed: Black Farm Owners in the South, 1651–1982." *Agricultural History* 63, no. 3 (Summer 1989): 41–60.

—CARMEN V. HARRIS

AIDS. Scientists have debated the origins of the human immunodeficiency virus (HIV) and the acquired immunodeficiency syndrome (AIDS) since they first recognized them in 1981 when clusters of homosexual men in California and New York were found to have suppressed immune systems. Since then HIV has become pandemic, affecting all segments of the population in every corner of the globe. Scientists believe that the disease originated in Cameroon, where a related virus called simian immunodeficiency virus (SIV) has been found in chimpanzees. The theory is that SIV jumped from chimpanzees to humans sometime in the twentieth century. A retrospective study of preserved blood samples done in 1998 confirmed that the earliest known case of HIV was in a Congolese man who died in 1959.

AIDS was first labeled gay-related immune deficiency (GRID) by the U.S. government's Centers for Disease Control and Prevention (CDC). The earliest studies in the United States focused on a small subpopulation of gay men in Los Angeles, San Francisco, and New York City who seemed to be suffering from suppressed immune systems coupled with opportunistic infections such as pneumonia, thrush, and, especially, Kaposi's sarcoma. HIV causes progressive suppression of the immune system in infected individuals. When a person's immune system is suppressed enough to become susceptible to opportunistic infections, the person is said to have AIDS. HIV is transmitted through bodily fluids such as blood and semen. The most likely means of becoming infected by such bodily fluids is through sexual intercourse or the use of intravenous drugs, the latter activity functioning as a risk factor because of the frequent practice among drug abusers of sharing unsterilized needles. The virus can also be transmitted through exposure to tainted blood products or, during gestation or birth, from mother to child.

Initial Scare. During the initial scare created by the mysterious and lethal nature of the disease, people feared transmission through drinking cups, saliva, toilet seats, or other casual contact. All these sources have proven extremely unlikely. During the early 1980s, urban centers such as New York, Los Angeles, and San Francisco were the loci of AIDS diagnoses. Soon thereafter, news of the diagnosis of the infection in Haitian immigrants challenged the prevailing notion that AIDS was a disease of urban, mostly white, male homosexual communities. The reports of an outbreak of this disease among Haitians in Miami and in other U.S. cities led to the inaccurate labeling of Haitians as another risk group. The American public's reaction was to decry illegal immigration from Haiti, framing the disease—falsely—as a foreign threat from an alleged unhygienic, depraved, and racially stigmatized source. In fact, the more likely problem was the crushing poverty of the island's inhabitants, which forced many Haitians to participate in the sex-tourism industry. Though not identifying themselves as homosexual, many Haitian men had sex with foreign men for money, and then in turn infected their heterosexual partners. At one point scientists theorized that Haiti was a possible place of origin of the disease, but researchers now believe that AIDS was introduced to Haiti in the late 1970s by tourists.

The AIDS crisis and the U.S. government's initial apathetic response spurred the creation of grassroots activist organizations created to care for the sick, educate the public, and change public policy. Founded in 1981, the Gay Men's Health Crisis (GMHC) was one of the first service organizations to respond to the AIDS panic. The organization, still active in the early twenty-first century, devotes its energies to community education, preventive measures, and providing assistance to the sick. Central to its mission is an effort to fight homophobia in the United States, a way of thinking that, it posits, has detrimentally affected the nation's ability to cope with and fight the disease. In 1987 Larry Kramer, a cofounder of the GMHC, feeling that the GMHC had become politically impotent, founded the AIDS Coalition to Unleash Power (ACT UP). ACT UP focuses on direct political action such as public demonstrations and civil disobedience.

Although the media, especially the entertainment industry, continued to push for greater attention to and education about AIDS, most mainstream Americans continued to associate the disease with stigma or even moral failure. Some claimed that AIDS was God's retribution for homosexual promiscuity, a "gay plague" to purge the sinful from the nation. Ronald Reagan's administration, dependent on the so-called religious right for much of its political sway, hesitated to take any steps that could be interpreted as supportive of homosexuality. By connecting AIDS to gay men, to intravenous drug users, or to illegal immigrants, Americans hoped to put a barrier between the threat to "others" and their sense of their own safety and security. This view ignored the facts of transmission, which increasingly included vehicles such as heterosexual intercourse and mother-child perinatal development.

Media coverage of HIV-positive celebrities further diversified the image of the AIDS patient in America. Max Robinson, the first black national network-news anchor, died of the disease in 1988. The tennis player Arthur Ashe was diagnosed in 1988 and became an advocate for AIDS education worldwide. And in November 1991 the professional basketball star Magic Johnson announced that he had tested positive for HIV. As perhaps the most famous person living with the virus, Johnson served as an important spokesperson for HIV and AIDS awareness, especially in African American communities. He created the Magic Johnson Foundation, which works to educate and raise the visibility of AIDS-related issues in inner cities.

Twenty-first Century. In the early twenty-first century the CDC reported that about half of new AIDS cases in the United States were among African Americans. This includes a large contingent infected through heterosexual activity. The CDC also reported dramatic increases in cases among Latino and Native American populations. AIDS has become the number one cause of death among African American women aged twenty-five to thirty-four, among the top three causes of death for African American men aged twenty-five to fifty-four, and among the top four causes of death for African American women aged twenty-five to fifty-four.

Many factors contribute to the higher rates of infection and progression of HIV in African American, Latino, and Native American communities. The continued disparities between economic classes limit minority access to health information, health care, and health insurance. African Americans and people in other minority groups are less likely to have taken an HIV test; by not knowing their status, they may unknowingly persist in high-risk behaviors that lead to more infections. Because of low testing rates across all populations, the threat of unknown transmission of HIV continues. The high rate of incarceration of people in minority groups also exacerbates the problem: HIV rates among the incarcerated are in many cases six times those of the general public, and ongoing drug

AIDS Protest. ACT-UP AIDS protest at City Hall Plaza, New York City, 2 May 1988. Photograph by Bettye Lane. © Bettye Lane

use and sexual contact within prison walls facilitates transmission of the virus.

Conspiracy fears continue to retard attempts to control or treat AIDS. Occurring on the heels of the exposure of the Tuskegee syphilis experiment, in which the United States Public Health Service studied but did not treat black men in Alabama for more than forty years, it is perhaps not surprising that many African Americans interpret AIDS information with reservations and doubt. Some people believe that AIDS was invented by the U.S. government to use as biological warfare against homosexuals and African Americans. Many hold that the government is holding back information or even a cure from the poorest elements of the population, in effect using AIDS as a tool of genocide. Other populations also are suspicious of the sudden onset of the infection, of its tendency to center in some geographic regions—such as sub-Saharan Africa, with its high percentage of people who are black and live in poverty—and in some populations—such as gay and minority populations—and of the government's initially slow response to the crisis.

With the advent of the availability of more effective drug therapy in the developed world, the meaning of an HIV diagnosis has shifted from a death sentence to a chronic medical condition, with the progression to AIDS occurring later in the course of the disease and with a significantly lengthened life expectancy for an infected person. In response, the media and public opinion have tended to shift the rhetoric on AIDS, now framing it as a global, rather than an American, problem. Americans tend to consider AIDS to be an issue in the Caribbean and in sub-Saharan Africa. However, the rates of HIV infection continue to increase among minority and underserved populations in the United States, and HIV and AIDS continue to present a major cost to the American public in terms of both financial expenditure and human suffering.

[*See also* Health and Medicine; Homosexuality and Transgenderism; Latinos and Black Latinos; Sexuality; Tuskegee Experiment; *and biographical entries on figures mentioned in this article*.]

BIBLIOGRAPHY

Centers for Disease Control and Prevention. "Fact Sheet: HIV/AIDS among African Americans." Revised June 2007. http://www.cdc.gov/hiv/topics/aa/resources/factsheets/aa.htm.

Cohen, Cathy J. *The Boundaries of Blackness: AIDS and the Breakdown of Black Politics*. Chicago: University of Chicago Press, 1999.

Grmek, Mirko D. *History of AIDS: Emergence and Origin of a Modern Pandemic*. Translated by Russell C. Maulitz and Jacalyn Duffin. Princeton, N.J.: Princeton University Press, 1990.

Hunter, Susan S. *AIDS in America*. New York: Palgrave Macmillan, 2006.

Jones, James H. *Bad Blood: The Tuskegee Syphilis Experiment*. Rev. ed. New York: Free Press, 1993.

—COURTNEY Q. SHAH

AILEY, ALVIN. (b. 5 January 1931; d. 1 December 1989), choreographer and dancer. Born in Rogers, Texas, Alvin Ailey was raised in a single-parent home headed by his mother, Lula Elizabeth Cooper. Ailey and his mother earned money by picking cotton and doing domestic work for local families. In 1942 Ailey moved to Los Angeles; he attended George Washington Carver Junior High School and Jefferson High School, where he developed an interest in music and literature. After graduation he went on to study literature at the University of California at Los Angeles.

Ailey's dance training began in 1949 when a friend, Carmen DeLavallade, introduced him to Lester Horton, founder of the Lester Horton Dance Theater. Horton was one of the few dance instructors who accepted black students, and he became Ailey's first dance coach. When Horton died in 1953, Ailey became the director of the company. The following year Ailey moved to New York City, where he joined DeLavallade in the Broadway dance production *House of Flowers*. While appearing in other stage performances, Ailey continued his studies under Martha Graham, Charles Weidman, Doris Humphrey, Hanya Holm, and Karel Shook.

In 1958 Ailey founded his own dance company, the Alvin Ailey American Dance Theater. Against the backdrop of the burgeoning civil rights movement, Ailey performed dances that celebrated the strength, vibrancy, and sorrow of black people. Ailey's choreography blended the techniques of modern dance, jazz, and ballet. It also drew upon elements of African American culture and Ailey's childhood experiences. A bar in Texas named the Dewdrop Inn and the Mount Olive Baptist Church that he attended as a boy inspired two of his major pieces, *Blues Suite* (1958) and *Revelations* (1960). The Alvin Ailey American Dance Theater infused modern dance with the "blood memories" of African American history. *Revelations*, the Alvin Ailey American Dance Theater's most celebrated production, is performed to a soundtrack of African American spirituals. It explores the evolution of black music and dance from its African origins and examines the role of religious faith in black life.

Ailey stopped dancing in 1965 and cut back on his work as a choreographer during the 1970s in order to spend time raising money for his growing company. The company toured the United States and abroad so extensively that between 1958 and 1989 it had performed for an estimated 15 million people in forty-eight states and forty-five countries on six continents. During that time Ailey received the NAACP's prestigious Spingarn Medal (1976) and the Samuel H. Scripps American Dance Festival Award (1987). In addition to creating more than fifty dances for his own company, Ailey choreographed for the American Ballet Theater, the London Festival Ballet, the Robert Joffrey Ballet, the Paris Opera Ballet, and the Royal Danish Ballet.

In 1989, at the age of fifty-eight, Alvin Ailey died after a painful struggle with AIDS-related complications. Under the artistic direction of the former principal dancer Judith Jamison, in the twenty-first century the Alvin Ailey American Dance Theater continues to devote itself to both the performance of modern dance classics and the encouragement of young artists.

[*See also* Alvin Ailey American Dance Theater; Choreographers; Dance; *and* Jamison, Judith.]

BIBLIOGRAPHY

Ailey, Alvin, and A. Peter Bailey. *Revelations: The Autobiography of Alvin Ailey*. Secaucus, N.J.: Carol Publishing Group, 1995.

Dunning, Jennifer. *Alvin Ailey: A Life in Dance*. Reading, Mass.: Addison-Wesley, 1996.

—CANDACE CARDWELL

ALABAMA. In 1819 Alabama was the twenty-second state admitted to the Union. Alabama has long been a hub of the African American struggle for civil rights. After the Civil War, the formerly enslaved faced intimidation at the polls despite the assurances of the Alabama supreme court chief justice Elisha Woolsey Peck that the rights promised them in Alabama's 1868 constitution would be enforced. Robert Jefferson Norrell opens his book *Reaping the Whirlwind* with an account of how the African American Republican state legislator James Alston saw his house fired upon twice; he left Tuskegee in 1870 (pp. 3–4). Even under these hostile circumstances, however, the African Americans Benjamin Turner, James Rapier, and Jeremiah Haralson served in the U.S. House of Representatives during the 1870s.

When Democrats regained control of Alabama's legislature and governorship in 1874, public schools were separate but far from equal. As Horace Mann Bond demonstrated in *Negro Education in Alabama*, in 1887 white public schools received more state funding per student than African American public schools did. The disparity widened when a state educational apportionment act in 1891 allowed local school boards to disburse state funds between white and black schools according to their own discretion in a "just and equitable" manner. Bond found that in Wilcox County, for example, where African Americans constituted more than five-sixths of students, expenditures per student for black schools barely changed from 1890 to 1930, while expenditures per student for white schools increased more than seventeenfold.

Because African Americans were perceived by powerful white industrialists and cotton planters—the "Big Mule Alliance" that dominated the state politically—as a cheap labor force, black schools that received state funding were intended to provide industrial education or teacher training. Alabama State Teacher's College (now Alabama State University) was originally established in Montgomery in 1866 as the private Lincoln Normal School. Hoping to encourage African Americans to stay in Macon County, the white state legislators and newspaper owners Arthur Brooks and Colonel Wilbur Foster sponsored legislation for Tuskegee Institute's founding in 1881. Booker T. Washington, who was educated at the premier southern industrial school for African Americans, the Hampton Institute in Virginia, became Tuskegee's first superintendent. Although Tuskegee received state funds, Washington and his successor Robert Moton raised most of its revenues privately, ensuring considerable autonomy.

Washington firmly believed in the value of an industrial education, stating in his Atlanta Exposition Address of 1895 that African Americans should pursue economic advancement before political agitation. Nevertheless, Washington openly criticized the 1891 school funding bill, and Moton successfully campaigned for black doctors and nurses to be allowed to operate a Veterans Administration hospital built on Tuskegee's campus in the 1920s in the face of threats received from local whites. The Huntsville Normal School (now Alabama A&M University) first opened in 1875 with a state appropriation for teacher training. It became the State Normal and Industrial School at Huntsville in 1878, and then received federal support after the Morrill Land Grant Act was fully extended to former Confederate states in 1890.

Alabama's predominantly white political establishment sought to prevent blacks from improving their economic status by keeping them out of political power. In the 1890s Alabamans elected two members of the short-lived Populist Party to Congress; their platform united blacks and poor whites who believed that the crop-lien system in sharecropping, high interest rates, and corporate influence on government precluded individual economic advancement. After the Populists disintegrated—a result of their abortive fusion with the Democrats in support of the presidential candidate William Jennings Bryan in 1896—Alabama's Democratic leadership produced the constitution of 1901 to prevent future challenges. The constitution instituted poll taxes and subjectively administered literacy tests: prospective voters were required to read and interpret parts of the U.S. Constitution, which in practice meant that white citizens were asked relatively simple questions while black citizens were required to perform sophisticated analyses of Alabama's political system. Alabama had approximately eighty thousand African American voters before these changes were put into place and scarcely one thousand black voters afterward.

The new constitution also prohibited the legislature from legalizing interracial marriages. Although it was not enforced in the late twentieth century, this provision was not repealed until a 2000 referendum. In 1896 the U.S. Supreme Court decision in *Plessy v. Ferguson* stated that separate facilities were legal so long as they were equal; the segregation of public institutions, perhaps most notably schools, continued.

With African Americans thus disfranchised and discriminated against, lynching became more frequent. The Tuskegee Institute began to maintain statistics on lynching, and between 1882 and 1968, 299 cases of African American lynchings were reported in Alabama; allegations of sexual violence against white women were the leading excuse for this vigilante injustice across the South.

The case of the Scottsboro Boys was one of the most egregious examples of injustice toward African Americans in the era of segregation. In March 1931 two white teenage girls who were caught stowing away on a freight train accused nine black males, aged thirteen to nineteen, of rape. Within fifteen days all of the accused had been tried, convicted, and—with the exception of the youngest, who received a prison sentence—sentenced to death. The case gained national attention when the NAACP and the Communist Party's International Labor Defense intervened to appeal the hasty convictions. The *Richmond Times-Dispatch* editor Virginius Dabney and other white liberals championed the boys' cause. In 1933 one of the accusers, Ruby Bates, testified that the rapes never happened. The U.S. Supreme Court in its *Powell v. Alabama* decision in 1932 ruled that the defendants had been deprived of proper counsel and ordered new trials. Charges against four of the defendants were not dropped until 1937; the others were reconvicted and sentenced to lengthy prison terms. Not until 1950 was the last of the Scottsboro Boys released on parole.

Post–World War II Activism. The struggle against European fascism in World War II inspired African Americans to crusade for greater rights at home. The Tuskegee Institute was selected as a site where African American pilots were trained. Although the NAACP president Walter White was disappointed that integrated pilot training did not occur, the Tuskegee Airmen and the approximately three thousand other African American military personnel in Tuskegee showed great solidarity. Colonel Noel Parrish, the white director of training, did away with Jim Crow signs at the base and integrated the officers' mess.

Around Tuskegee there emerged an African American middle class of faculty and professionals who pushed for more civil rights. Charles Gomillion, a professor of political science, sued Macon County officials over an outlandish 1957 gerrymandering of the city boundary intended to exclude blacks from voting in municipal elections. Gomillion spearheaded a successful boycott of white-owned businesses until voter registration was available equally to both blacks and whites. The U.S. Supreme Court ruled the state legislature's gerrymander unconstitutional in 1961 in *Gomillion v. Lightfoot*.

In Montgomery, Rosa Parks was arrested on 1 December 1955 for violating a segregation ordinance by not yielding her bus seat to a white passenger, prompting a yearlong African American boycott of city buses. Local African American leaders enlisted the young Reverend Martin Luther King Jr., then pastor of Montgomery's Dexter Avenue Baptist Church, to organize the boycott. King's youth and status as a newcomer in Montgomery meant that he had neither made enemies among nor accepted favors from city fathers. In December 1956 the U.S. Supreme Court struck down the segregation ordinance, catapulting King to national prominence. The next year he established the Southern Christian Leadership Conference (SCLC), a regional organization devoted to supporting nonviolent protests based on the Montgomery model.

Organizations like the SCLC were vital to the struggle for civil rights, as segregationist whites undertook a strategy of massive resistance to desegregation decisions issued by federal courts. Two years before the Montgomery decision, in 1954 the U.S. Supreme Court desegregated public schools nationwide with its *Brown v. Board of Education* decision. Some whites kept children home or organized private academies, such as the Macon Academy, to circumvent the ruling. Earlier Supreme Court rulings (among them *Sweatt v. Painter* and *McLaurin v. Oklahoma*, both 1950) mandated desegregation of higher education facilities; in 1956 Autherine Lucy gained admission to the University of Alabama at Tuscaloosa. Her attendance sparked riots by the local White Citizens' Council, and the university suspended Lucy, ostensibly for her own safety. After she criticized the university's trustees for failing to ensure her safe attendance, Lucy was expelled for insubordination. The chief editor of the *Tuscaloosa News* Buford Boone won a Pulitzer Prize for his editorial "What a Price for Peace," which lamented the apparent success of massive resistance. Lucy eventually returned to the university in more progressive times, earning her master's degree in elementary education in 1992.

Massive resistance apparently triumphed again in 1956 when the state attorney general, and soon to be governor, John Patterson gained a state court injunction against the NAACP's activities. With the NAACP outlawed, alternative groups like the SCLC and the Reverend Fred Shuttlesworth's Alabama Christian Movement for Human Rights—which challenged segregation in Birmingham so vigorously that Shuttlesworth's rectory was bombed in 1956—became especially necessary.

The 1960s. The Congress of Racial Equality (CORE) and the Student Nonviolent Coordinating Committee (SNCC) were two other organizations that rose to prominence in the 1960s. CORE led Freedom Rides in 1961, taking buses across the South to test the federally mandated desegregation of interstate travel facilities. White supremacists attacked and burned one bus near Anniston, Alabama; in Birmingham the segregationist police commissioner Eugene "Bull" Connor personally drove a few arrested riders across the border to Tennessee. Another angry mob physically threatened the remaining Freedom Riders as they met with King in his Montgomery church.

King decided to confront segregation with the SCLC's resources in Birmingham, which he called "the most racist city in America." There Connor kept the police and fire departments lily-white, while parks, swimming pools, and department store lunch counters remained inaccessible to African Americans. Leading department stores patronized by African Americans had no African American employees. The protests appeared doomed in late April 1963 when demonstrators, including King and Shuttlesworth, were arrested peacefully under a state court injunction against marches; fines and court costs mounted. While incarcerated, King wrote his "Letter from Birmingham Jail," admonishing several prominent local white clergymen that justice should be an ultimate goal. When African American public school students began marching en masse in early May, Connor ordered attacks on them with fire hoses and dogs. National television coverage of this response inspired President John F. Kennedy to call for the legislation that became the Civil Rights Act of 1964. King won promises from the Birmingham Chamber of Commerce to hire African Americans and end the segregation of store facilities.

The March on Washington in August 1963, where King delivered his famous "I Have a Dream" speech, celebrated the Birmingham triumph, but the September bombing of Birmingham's Sixteenth Street Baptist Church made it painfully clear that there was still much work to be done. Not until 1977 was the white supremacist Robert Chambliss convicted of the crime and sentenced to life in prison. Shortly after the turn of the millennium, he was joined in prison by his coconspirators Thomas Blanton and Bobby Frank Cherry.

Also in 1963 Governor George Wallace made his "stand in the schoolhouse door" at the University of Alabama, pandering to his segregationist constituency as Vivian Malone and James Hood made their second attempt to integrate the university with federal support. Wallace yielded to their military and Justice Department escorts, not wishing to incite deadly riots like those that accompanied James Meredith's integration of Ole Miss in 1962. Auburn University was integrated the following year, and Harold Franklin was the first black student to enroll there.

The last great confrontation between organized African Americans and segregationists occurred in March 1965 when King chose to confront black disfranchisement in Dallas County. As late as 1965 only 13 percent of African Americans eligible to vote were registered. King believed that Sheriff James Clark was potentially as volatile as Connor had been, and he planned a march from the county seat at Selma to Montgomery in order to publicize the need for federal voting rights legislation. Young activists from SNCC marched to the Edmund Pettus Bridge outside Selma. There on 7 March, later known as "Bloody Sunday," Clark's deputies beat and teargassed nearly six hundred marchers. Two weeks later King proceeded with his march from Selma to Montgomery; more than thirty-two hundred people marched, and twenty-five thousand people rallied in Montgomery on 25 March. The murder of Viola Liuzzo, a Detroit housewife who volunteered to drive marchers back to Selma, by Ku Klux Klansmen moved President Lyndon B. Johnson to call for the Voting Rights Act of 1965.

In the aftermath of the voting rights legislation, by 1974 African American mayors were elected in eight Alabama towns with combined populations of approximately sixty-one thousand. Roosevelt City and Prichard faced high unemployment because of downturns in the steel industry; according to Kenneth Colburn in *Southern Black Mayors*, four of these towns experienced budgetary deficits, including Tuskegee, where Johnny Ford was elected mayor in 1972. African American political influence grew until by 2007 fifty-three municipalities, with constituencies totaling more than eight hundred thousand, had African American mayors. The state's largest city, Birmingham, was one of those municipalities; there fifty thousand African Americans registered to vote in 1966, the same year that the police department was integrated. The former zoology professor and city councilman Richard Arrington was elected as the city's first African American mayor in 1979. Earl Hilliard became Alabama's sole African American member of the U.S. House of Representatives, serving a district that included Birmingham and a large part of central Alabama from 1993 to 2003. He was succeeded by another African American, Artur Davis.

According to Nahfiza Ahmed, the Non-Partisan Voters League, a local, predominantly middle-class civil rights group established after the state injunction against the NAACP, successfully sued in the mid-1960s to desegregate Mobile's public schools and university and to integrate the Alabama National Guard and the local bus

Selma-to-Montgomery March. Mississippi highway patrolmen look on as marchers arrive in Montgomery, Alabama, 25 March 1965. BIRMINGHAM NEWS/POLARIS

terminal. Another group of professional African Americans, frustrated by local businesses' discriminatory hiring practices, formed the Neighborhood Organization Workers (NOW) in 1966. NOW organized a boycott of white businesses in 1968 and threatened to "burn Mobile down" in 1969 unless downtown businesses hired more African American salespeople, according to Ahmed. In 1970 three of the group's members were indicted for murder, destroying NOW's credibility.

After the 1960s: Lingering Disparities. Although the decades since the 1960s have been relatively uneventful, racial inequalities have persisted in Alabama well into the twenty-first century.

In 1990 one source of lingering racism was exposed and excised when Birmingham's Shoal Creek Country Club hosted the PGA Championship and a club official boasted about discriminatory acceptance policies. Mayor Arrington helped arrange the businessman Louis Willie's admission as Shoal Creek's first African American member in order to stall public outcry and the loss of television sponsors.

Even though more than 25 percent of Alabama's population was African American, in 2006 the black student population of the University of Alabama and Auburn University was 11 percent and 8.2 percent, respectively. The University of Alabama also struggled with de facto segregation in fraternities and sororities since its president, Dr. Robert Witt, brought attention to the issue in 2003. Traditionally black public institutions, on the other hand, primarily enrolled students of color, with white students making up a minority on their campuses. For 2007–2008 Alabama State University had a nonblack student population of 11 percent and offered diversity scholarships. Roughly 13 percent of Alabama A&M's student population in 2005 was nonblack. Alabama, despite great strides during the 1950s and 1960s, is still a work in progress.

[*See also* Alabama State University; Birmingham Campaign; Civil Rights; Civil Rights, White Responses and Resistance to; Civil Rights Act of 1964; Civil Rights Movement; Desegregation and Integration; Dexter Avenue Baptist Church; King, Martin Luther, Jr.; Montgomery Bus Boycott; Montgomery Conference; Scottsboro Incident; Sixteenth Street Baptist Church; Tuskegee Institute; *and* Washington, Booker T.]

BIBLIOGRAPHY

"Address of the Colored Convention to the People of Alabama, 1867." In *Reading the American Past: Selected Historical Documents*, edited by Michael Johnson. 2d ed. Boston: St. Martin's Press, 2002.

Ahmed, Nahfiza. "The Neighborhood Organization Workers of Mobile, Alabama: Black Power Politics and Local Civil Rights Activism in the Deep South." *Southern Historian* 20 (1999): 25–40.

Bond, Horace Mann. *Negro Education in Alabama: A Study in Cotton and Steel* (1939). Tuscaloosa: University of Alabama Press, 1994.

Colburn, Kenneth S. *Southern Black Mayors: Local Problems and Federal Responses*. 2d ed. Washington, D.C.: Joint Center for Political Studies, 1974.

Egerton, John. *Speak Now against the Day: The Generation before the Civil Rights Movement in the South*. New York: Knopf, 1994.

Eskew, Glenn T. *But for Birmingham: The Local and National Movements in the Civil Rights Struggle*. Chapel Hill: University of North Carolina Press, 1997.

Hughes, William Hardin, and Frederick D. Patterson, eds. *Robert Russa Moton of Hampton and Tuskegee*. Chapel Hill: University of North Carolina Press, 1956.

Menard, Meghan. "Closing the Divide: Racial Issues within Greek System Produce Heated Discussion." *The Crimson White*, 1 February 2007.

Norrell, Robert Jefferson. *Reaping the Whirlwind: The Civil Rights Movement in Tuskegee* (1985). Chapel Hill: University of North Carolina Press, 1998.

Permaloff, Anne, and Carl Grafton. *Political Power in Alabama: The More Things Change....* Athens, Ga.: University of Georgia Press, 1995.

—WESLEY BORUCKI

ALABAMA STATE UNIVERSITY. Like most historically black colleges and universities in the United States, Alabama State University was created in the wake of the Civil War. In 1865, a convalescing Union soldier from the North began to educate former slaves outside Marion, the county seat of Perry County, in the racially divided and often violent Black Belt subregion of Alabama. The following year, the soldier contacted the Congregationalist-headed American Missionary Association (AMA), whose leaders wanted to found black common schools in several Southern states. Consequently, AMA officials sent an agent and minister from New York named Thomas Steward to the Alabama Black Belt.

Reverend Steward arrived in Perry County in January 1867. By this time, several leading blacks and a handful of prominent whites in the county had already tried to erect a black common school in Marion. Following their lead, Steward created a small school in a partly finished Methodist church, and the Lincoln School of Marion was begun. Steward was the principal, and nine ex-slaves—James Childs, Alexander Curtis, Nicholas Dale, John Freeman, David Harris, Thomas Lee, Nathan Levert, Joey Pinch, and Thomas Speed—were the trustees.

The "Marion Nine" incorporated the Lincoln School in July 1867. Two years later, state legislators made Lincoln Alabama's only black normal school (meaning that its principal mission was to educate aspiring teachers), but the legislators did not allocate state funds until 1870. In January of that year, Principal Steward, who had been elected to the state legislature in 1868, convinced other state legislators to provide buildings and money for the Lincoln Normal School (LNS), and LNS became a legitimate, state-sponsored institution.

Lincoln's prominence grew during the early 1870s. In 1874, as conservative Democrats regained control of most statewide political offices, ending Reconstruction in Alabama, LNS became the Alabama State Lincoln Normal School and University (ASLNSU). Unbeknown to anyone at the time, and most individuals since, ASLNSU was the first state-sponsored liberal arts institution for the higher education of blacks in United States history. In 1887, a conflict between ASLNSU students and a group of cadets attending an all-white military academy in Marion prompted some of the town's leading white conservatives to pressure state lawmakers to close ASLNSU. The same year, a suspicious fire destroyed ASLNSU's primary building. Prodded by the conservatives, Alabama legislators decreed that henceforward not one of the university's buildings could be used to educate blacks and that a state-sponsored black university could be located anywhere in the state except Marion. After much debate and politicking, ASLNSU's higher-education department was relocated to Montgomery. The primary and high-school departments remained in Marion under the school's original name.

In 1899, the name of ASLNSU was changed to the Normal School for Colored Students (NSCS); William B. Paterson, a white man from Scotland, headed the institution. Following Paterson's death in 1915, his immediate successors, black men John W. Beverly—the school's first black instructor and president—and George W. Trenholm broadened the mission of NSCS to include commerce and home economics as well as teacher education. In addition, NSCS became a junior college. The next president, Harper C. Trenholm, was even more successful than his predecessors. Under the younger Trenholm, NSCS became a four-year university in 1928. The following year, the name of NSCS was changed to the Alabama State Teachers College (ASTC), which in 1931 conferred its first baccalaureate degree in teacher education. A graduate program was begun in 1940, and ASTC awarded its first graduate degree in 1943. The same year, satellite campuses were established in Birmingham and in Mobile.

The following two decades were pivotal ones for the college, whose name was changed to the Alabama State College (ASC) in 1954. The same year, the U.S. Supreme Court delivered its landmark *Brown v. Board of Education* ruling, declaring that segregated educational facilities were unconstitutional. Because staunchly conservative white Alabama lawmakers opposed the ruling, it had little effect on ASC. Unable to attend the University of Alabama,

Auburn University, or any other predominantly white college or university in large number until the early 1970s, the vast majority of black Alabamians pursuing higher education continued to attend ASC or one of the state's other historically black colleges and universities, whose students, employees, and graduates played key roles in the modern civil rights movement. However, only one of these black schools produced individuals who participated in every major battle of the movement: ASC.

On 1 December 1955, ASC alumna Rosa Parks was arrested for refusing to give up her seat on a city bus. The same day, two ASC students helped ASC English professor and Women's Political Council President Jo Ann Robinson duplicate thousands of leaflets advertising a proposed boycott of city buses. Once the boycott began, Robinson's colleague, Thelma Glass—an ASC English, geography, and history professor, and one-time secretary of the council—helped create the handbills that were distributed throughout the city to publicize boycott activities. Rufus A. Lewis, a former ASC football coach and Montgomery Improvement Association leader, helped organize the carpool system that facilitated the boycott. Fred Gray, an ASC alumnus, was the first attorney of Martin Luther King Jr., whose wife, Coretta, was a 1949 alumna of the Lincoln High School in Marion. Gray also was the lead attorney in a series of landmark civil-rights cases. One case, *Browder v. Gayle* (1956), helped integrate Montgomery city buses; another, *Gomillion v. Lightfoot* (1960), set the precedent for the one-man, one-voice concept.

Numerous other ASC students, employees, graduates, and supporters—Ralph Abernathy, Inez Baskin, Mary F. Burks, James Haskins, Bernard LaFayette, Benard Lee, Edgar D. Nixon, Mr. and Mrs. James Pierce, Dr. Lawrence Reddick, Fred D. Reese, Fred Shuttlesworth, Reverend B. J. Simms, Dr. and Mrs. H. Councill Trenholm, Jr., Dr. Norman Walton—played pivotal roles in the modern Civil Rights movement. Though noble, their up-front and behind-the-scenes activism had an adverse effect on the college. Throughout the late 1950s, white lawmakers decreased ASC's funding. As a consequence, the college in 1961 lost its accreditation by the Southern Association on Colleges and Schools.

Alabama State College was reaccredited in 1966. Three years later, the college was renamed Alabama State University (ASU). In 1995, a remedial decree from a higher-education desegregation case called *Knight v. Alabama* transformed ASU into a comprehensive regional institution that today offers forty-seven degree programs, including three at the doctoral level, to more than five thousand students of all ethnic and racial backgrounds from forty-two states and seven countries. The university is accredited by several associations, charters in excess of seventy student organizations, operates WVAS-FM, an eighty-thousand-watt public radio station, and competes in a variety of collegiate and intercollegiate sports. Although the university's curricula and degree programs have expanded tremendously since the nineteenth century, many students still attend ASU to become teachers. In 2004 the university produced more African American educators than any other college or university in the nation.

[*See also* Education; Historically Black Colleges and Universities; *and* Montgomery Bus Boycott.]

BIBLIOGRAPHY

Bailey, Richard. *Neither Carpetbaggers nor Scalawags: Black Officeholders in the Reconstruction of Alabama, 1867–1878.* 3d ed. Montgomery, Al.: R. Bailey Publishers, 1995.

Fairclough, Adam. *Better Day Coming: Blacks and Equality, 1890–2000.* New York: Viking, 2001.

Gaillard, Frye. *Cradle of Freedom: Alabama and the Movement that Changed America.* Tuscaloosa: University of Alabama Press, 2004.

Robinson, Jo Ann. *The Montgomery Bus Boycott and the Women Who Started It: The Memoir of Jo Ann Gibson Robinson.* Knoxville: University of Tennessee Press, 1987.

Sherer, Robert G. *Black Education in Alabama, 1865–1901.* Tuscaloosa: University of Alabama Press, 1997.

Williams, Juan and Dwayne Ashley. *I'll Find a Way or Make One: A Tribute to Historically Black Colleges and Universities.* New York: Amistad, 2004.

—BERTIS ENGLISH

ALASKA. The United States' northernmost state has always had a low black population, one of the lowest in the United States. The 2000 U.S. Census lists Alaska as having 21,787 black residents who make up 3.5 percent of its population. This is likely as much an effect of geographical boundaries as societal forces. After the Civil War, blacks migrated to Alaska in search of new economic opportunities; they became seafarers and worked in the whaling and fur industries and were better able to find meaningful work than many of those who stayed in the American South. The Alaska Gold Rush in the 1890s brought many from the contiguous United States to Alaska, African Americans among them, and many stayed—some for profit and some for adventure's sake.

President Franklin D. Roosevelt authorized the building of the Alaska Highway in February 1942, and more than three thousand black engineers worked on the Alaska Highway during World War II. Units were strictly segregated, and the effects of racism were felt by many black workers. Today, the highway has numerous memorials to veterans, including the Black Veterans Memorial Bridge, which was dedicated in 1993. Black battalions were assigned to the Aleutian Islands during the Aleutian Campaign, and even today the military continues to play an important role in bringing blacks to Alaska. There is a strong correlation between the number of personnel assigned to Alaska's military instillations and the number of blacks in the population at large.

Anchorage (260,283 residents, 5.8 percent of whom are black) and Fairbanks (30,224, 11.2 percent black), have the highest black populations in Alaska; in several of Alaska's bigger cities, the number of black residents is only in the double digits. That being said, metropolitan areas have higher populations of blacks than Alaska's more rural areas, a trend common across the United States. Race relations in Alaska have always been relatively healthy; there have been several discrimination issues surrounding the state's many military bases, but ultimately Alaska has not exhibited the degree of racial tensions that many other states have.

James C. Hayes, the former mayor of Fairbanks (1992–2001), was Alaska's first black mayor. Hayes graduated from the University of Alaska-Fairbanks and began a political career on the local school board. He also served as an assistant pastor in a local church and is the father of two children. Blacks are more appreciated as a significant culture force in Alaska than ever before, both as a result of Mayor Hayes's political success and because of the actions of George T. Harper, president and cofounder of the Blacks in Alaska History Project. The Blacks in Alaska History Project was incorporated as a nonprofit in 1995; the archives are located at the University of Alaska-Anchorage. The purpose of the project is to document the many contributions of African Americans to Alaska by maintaining photographs, documents, and other historical artifacts and by sponsoring exhibits and lectures.

BIBLIOGRAPHY

George T. Harper Papers. Blacks in Alaska History Project. The University of Alaska-Anchorage Special Collections Department. The UAA Archives and Special Collections Department holds these papers, which are an excellent source of information on blacks in Alaska.

"James C. Hayes: Alaska's First Black Mayor—Mayor of Fairbanks." *Ebony*, October 1993. This article gives an excellent overview of Mayor Hayes, his political career, and other information.

NICK J. SCIULLO

ALBANY MOVEMENT. The Albany Movement began in Georgia in the fall of 1961 and ended in the summer of 1962. It was considered one of the first mass movements in the twentieth-century civil rights movement whose goal was to desegregate an entire community; the authorities jailed more than one thousand African Americans in Albany, Georgia, and its surrounding counties. In December 1961 Martin Luther King Jr. was drawn into the movement as hundreds of black protesters, including King, were arrested in one week. Eight months later King left Albany, having admitted that he had failed to accomplish the movement's goals. As part of the history of the civil rights movement, Albany was a significant lesson King learned and later applied successfully in Birmingham, Alabama.

Albany's Past. As in many southern towns and cities, Albany's civil rights movement started during Reconstruction, when politically active black men elected other African Americans to local and state offices. By the early-twentieth-century Jim Crow era, fewer than thirty African Americans were registered to vote in Albany. At the end of World War I (1918), the war veteran C. W. King founded a local branch of the National Association for the Advancement of Colored People (NAACP) in Albany. After having been dormant, it was reignited beginning in the 1940s. The desire to garner control of their lives led middle-class blacks to organize voter registration drives. This resounding activism resulted in blacks petitioning local governments to make needed improvements to the infrastructure of African American neighborhoods. The son of C. W. King, C. B. King, carried on this activism by entering law school and then using his talents on behalf of other blacks in the segregated courtrooms in southwest Georgia.

The Albany Movement, Martin Luther King Jr., and SNCC. Albany witnessed the historical intersection of local efforts with those of three young Student Nonviolent Coordinating Committee (SNCC) workers—Charles Sherrod, Cordell Reagon, and Charles Jones—whose focus in Albany was to conduct a voter registration drive. These SNCC workers encouraged students and others to challenge traditional policies on segregation. From the outset, they faced strong opposition and resistance from whites and conservative blacks. This division within the black community plagued their efforts for two years, but blacks rose above these divisions at important moments.

In mid-November 1961 black improvement organizations formed the Albany Movement and selected William G. Anderson, a young black osteopath, as its president. Mass meetings were called, marches were formed, and by mid-December, more than five hundred marchers and protesters were jailed. Leaders who were not in jail gathered in a private home following the mass meetings. After two consecutive days of mass arrests, the strain was evident: of the three hundred still in jail, each leader knew at least a dozen who desperately needed to be released in order to keep jobs, to keep their sanity, or to maintain the cohesion of their families. Unfortunately, the monies used for the two hundred released on $100 cash bonds each had used up all of the available money in black Albany. No one knew how to get the prisoners out. Under this constant pressure, the Albany Movement politics broke down as

James Forman, SNCC executive director and organizer, spoke against inviting King to Albany, saying that they already had a strong "people's movement" that could be weakened by King. On another front, a boycott of the downtown merchants as well as the city bus system was supported by the Albany Movement's demands; unfortunately, the leaders were unsure how to arrange alternative transportation in light of the money shortage. Many of them confessed that because of their lack of experience, they were not sure how to work effectively in the business of protest. Dr. Anderson, seconded by Bernard Lee, suggested asking Martin Luther King Jr. and the Southern Christian Leadership Conference (SCLC) to help keep the momentum going and to secure greater publicity. Against SNCC wishes, a telegram was immediately sent and King responded. At the mass meetings of Albany's Shiloh Baptist and Mount Zion Baptist Churches, King admonished parishioners to keep moving together. Afterward, the leaders felt that King's presence would soon produce some kind of settlement, which would make another march unnecessary. Later that night, Anderson sent a telegram to Albany's mayor, Asa Kelley, who with other city officials took offense at Anderson's conduct and addressed a letter not to Anderson but to Marion Page, the movement's secretary. The mayor summoned reporters and announced that Albany was breaking off negotiations. Finding "no common ground," some 150 marchers agreed to follow King to City Hall.

Even though King and others were arrested and jailed, King believed that city officials had agreed to make certain concessions. However, once King accepted bail, he discovered that white leadership had refused to consider any of the movement's demands. King returned to Albany the following summer for sentencing on the convictions related to the December marches. He and his fellow civil rights leader Ralph Abernathy chose jail rather than paying the fine. King, believing that thousands would join him, pledged to remain in jail as long as necessary to force change in Albany's segregation policies, and his SCLC staff remained in the city. But King had an equally forceful opponent in maintaining segregation in the Albany police chief Laurie Pritchett, who ordered his officers to avoid violence, at least when TV cameras and reporters were present. Pritchett was prepared for the thousands of marchers and had them arrested and hauled off to jail. In the end, King ran out of marchers and ran into the failing mental health of Anderson and the in-fighting of SNCC members. King was considered ineffective in bringing about any real changes in Albany.

Bernice Johnson Reagon. Among the black civil rights leaders who emerged at this time was Bernice Johnson (b. 4 October 1942), who was a music student at Albany State College when she began participating in demonstrations sponsored by SNCC. As a singer and activist in the Albany Movement, she saw the power of song pull together sections of the black community at a time when other means of communication were ineffective. Johnson, who would marry Cordell Reagon in 1963, formed the SNCC Freedom Singers with Reagon, Rutha Harris, and Charles Neblett. The group traveled the country teaching freedom songs of the movement and songs learned in the churches of Johnson's youth. She would go on to form Sweet Honey in the Rock, an a cappella ensemble of African American women singers.

Legacy. From King's perspective the Albany Movement was a failure, but blacks in Albany disagreed. SNCC was successful in registering voters not only in Albany but also in nearby Americus and Moultrie, and African Americans in other southwest Georgia towns and counties were moved to challenge their local white power structures. The civil rights movement went through several changes in Albany once the segregation laws were challenged and overturned. In the late 1960s and 1970s leaders turned to school integration, and King used the lessons he learned in Albany to help in the real challenge of Birmingham, Alabama.

[*See also* Birmingham Campaign; Civil Rights Movement; Civil Rights, White Responses and Resistance to; Forman, James; Georgia; *and* King, Martin Luther, Jr.]

BIBLIOGRAPHY

Branch, Taylor. *Parting the Waters: America in the King Years 1954–63*. New York: Simon & Schuster, 1988. Definitive text detailing Martin Luther King Jr.'s relationship with the civil rights movement in the years between 1954 and 1963.

"Georgia Encyclopedia." http://www.georgiaencyclopedia.org/nge/Article.jsp?id=h-2521&h1=y. Biographical information on Bernice Johnson Reagon's life, career, and involvement with the SNCC Freedom Singers as well as the formation of the a cappella ensemble of African American women called Sweet Honey in the Rock.

Washington, James Melvin, ed. *A Testament of Hope: The Essential Writings of Martin Luther King, Jr.* San Francisco: Harper & Row, 1986. Writings, speeches, and interviews of Martin Luther King Jr.

—TIA GAFFORD

ALCORN STATE UNIVERSITY. Originally founded as an institution to educate "Negro males," Alcorn State University eventually evolved to become the primary coed institution of higher education for black students in the state of Mississippi. Named to honor the governor at the time of its founding, James L. Alcorn, the university is located in Lorman, Mississippi. Established on 13 May 1871 through the Morrill Land Grant Act of 1862 and an act by the Mississippi state legislature, Alcorn holds the distinctions of being the oldest land-grant university in Mississippi and the oldest historically black land-grant university in the United States. During its long history Alcorn has undergone three name changes: originally it was Alcorn University, in 1878 it became Alcorn Agricultural and Mechanical College, and then in 1974 it became Alcorn State University.

Alcorn occupies the site where Oakland College originally existed. Oakland, founded in 1828, was a Presbyterian school devoted to the education of white men. With the advent of the Civil War, Oakland closed its doors to allow its students to enlist in the Confederate army. After the Civil War ended the college remained closed, and the state eventually purchased the site to establish a school of higher education for its black citizens. Initially Alcorn admitted only male students, but in 1895 it allowed females. Hiram R. Revels, the first black senator in U.S. history, was Alcorn's first president. He resigned his Senate seat to assume the presidency in 1871. Revels, along with subsequent Alcorn presidents, sought to improve conditions and curriculum for the institution in an attempt to answer the needs of Mississippi's black students.

Like most historically black colleges and universities (HBCUs) at that time, Alcorn functioned more as the equivalent of a modern high school and a trade school. This type of curriculum can be partially attributed to the Morrill Act of 1890, which advocated withholding congressional funds from states that did not provide educational opportunities of higher learning to their black citizens. Essentially, Morrill 1890 reinforced and perpetuated the "separate but equal" doctrine later allowed in *Plessy v. Ferguson* (1896). States such as Mississippi used Morrill 1890 funds to support segregated education until its legal demise through *Brown v. Board of Education* (1954), in which the Supreme Court ruled such systems unconstitutional. Mississippi promoted the labor trades and basic education for black students particularly through Morrill tenets and the discriminatory practices of the time.

Alcorn, like its fellow HBCUs, addressed the need to educate black people in the post–Civil War United States. These HBCUs were underfunded by their respective states and offered a rudimentary education, yet they provided the bulk of higher education for black students seeking college degrees. Most were established under austere conditions with meager resources, and Alcorn fits this profile. In 1871 Alcorn's student body totaled 179 and its faculty eight, and its teaching curriculum was in traditional trades combined with college-level courses. Jim Crow laws and other discriminatory practices prevented HBCUs such as Alcorn from educating black youth for the professions or in preparation for graduate schools.

Historically, despite its curriculum, Alcorn was a major source of teachers for black public schools. As the times changed, Alcorn and its curriculum did, too, addressing these educational deficiencies to become a full-fledged university. By the early twenty-first century Alcorn's curriculum offered numerous disciplines of study, including an extensive variety of bachelor's and master's degree programs. The upgraded curriculum is a testament to Alcorn's efforts throughout its history to obtain university status, yet also prepare students professionally.

The university has benefited from a financial settlement from a college desegregation lawsuit initiated by the late Jake Ayers Sr. In 1975 Ayers filed the lawsuit against the state of Mississippi because of inequitable funding for Mississippi's three historically black universities. After numerous appeals, the case was settled in 2004 with the stipulation that Mississippi HBCUs were required to desegregate their student bodies in order to receive the award money. Alcorn aggressively recruited white students throughout the United States and internationally, which helped them to reach the goal mandated by the Ayers lawsuit agreement. For its desegregation efforts, in 2005 Alcorn received $1.7 million in an endowment. The university has earmarked the endowment's interest money for improvements in its academic programs and construction of new campus buildings.

From its humble beginning of three buildings on 225 acres to its eighty buildings on 1,700 acres and thousands of graduates—including the civil rights leader Medgar Evers, the actor Michael Clarke Duncan, and the National Football League quarterback Steve McNair—Alcorn has evolved as an HBCU committed to educating all types of students as it strives to meet their educational needs in the twenty-first century and beyond.

[*See also* Higher Education; Historically Black Colleges and Universities; *and* Mississippi.]

BIBLIOGRAPHY

Posey, Josephine McCann. *Against Great Odds: The History of Alcorn State University*. Jackson: University Press of Mississippi, 1994. The quintessential work on the history of Alcorn State University.

—ALEXIS D. MCCOY

ALI, MUHAMMAD (b. 17 January 1942), boxer, civil rights activist. Perhaps one of the most recognized people in the world, Muhammad Ali was born Cassius Marcellus Clay Jr. to Cassius Marcellus Clay Sr. and Odessa (Grady) Clay in Louisville, Kentucky. He was named in honor of his father and the white Kentucky abolitionist Cassius M. Clay. Clay attended the all-black Central High School in Louisville, Kentucky, graduating 376th out of a senior class of 391. Ali has been married four times: to Sonji Roi,

Kalilah Tolona (formerly Belinda Boyd), Veronica Porsche, and Yolanda Ali. He has been married to Yolanda since 1986, and has seven daughters and two sons, including Laila Ali, a boxer in her own right.

Early Career. Clay was the most dominant heavyweight boxer of the 1960s and 1970s, successfully defending the heavyweight title nineteen times. Clay's boxing career began inauspiciously at the age of twelve when the theft of his bicycle and his desire to "whup whoever stole it" led him to seek boxing instruction from Joe E. Martin, an Irish American policeman. He trained at Columbia Gym and soon appeared on television in the amateur boxing show *Tomorrow's Champions*. Lacking the power of many heavyweight fighters, he developed a unique style that allowed him to dance around his opponents in the ring. As an amateur Clay fought in 167 bouts, winning 161, including six Kentucky Golden Glove titles, two National Golden Glove tournaments, two national Amateur Athletic Union (AAU) titles, and an Olympic gold medal as a light heavyweight in Rome. By 1960, Clay was managed by a local group of wealthy whites called the Louisville Sponsoring Group, who placed him with the veteran trainer Angelo Dundee.

Clay found that no matter their achievements African Americans were not insulated from racial discrimination. Although Louisville hosted a parade in his honor, Clay was denied service at a segregated diner while wearing his gold medal upon returning to the city. By his own account, he went to a bridge and threw his Olympic medal into the Ohio River in response, saying "I went all the way to Italy to represent my country, won a gold medal, and now I come back to America and can't even get served at a five-and-dime store . . . . That gold medal didn't mean a thing to me if my black brothers and sisters were treated wrong in a country I was supposed to represent." Whether accurate or not, his account served to direct public attention to the realities of racial segregation in his hometown and in the nation as a whole. In any case, he was presented with a replacement medal at the 1996 Summer Olympic Games in Atlanta, Georgia, where he lit the torch at the opening ceremonies. By the time he turned professional, the "Louisville Lip" was known as a brash, cocky, and extremely vocal fighter. No other black athlete since Jack Johnson had been so outspoken, and in the context of the civil rights era, the impact of Clay's words and actions extended far beyond the bounds of his profession.

In October 1960 Clay won his first professional bout, defeating Tunney Hunsaker in a six-round decision. He won his next eighteen fights, often accurately predicting the round in which he would knock out his opponent. As a boxer Clay mixed heavyweight size, dazzling speed, a vicious left jab, agile footwork, and furious combinations with a flair for self-promotion to create a compound toxic for his opponents. Using the boxing ring as a public stage, in rhymed verse Clay masterfully utilized African American traditions of "signifying" and "playing the dozens" as an integral part of his strategy. For instance, in the period before his first championship fight he famously proclaimed he would, "Float like a butterfly and sting like a bee . . . your hands can't hit what your eyes can't see." On 25 February 1964 Clay won the heavyweight championship, defeating Sonny Liston in one of the most astonishing victories in boxing history. In his own words, he "shook up the world!"

Conversion to Islam. In a press conference the following morning, Clay announced he was a member of the Nation of Islam, and officially changed his name to Muhammad Ali, as was custom within the Nation of Islam. Muhammad means "one who is worthy of praise" and Ali means the "fourth rightly guided caliph." Although his declaration surprised many, his association with the Nation dated to 1961 through relationships with Muslim ministers such as Malcolm X and Jeremiah Shabazz; many of Ali's biographers suspect he converted to Islam as early as 1962. Perhaps the Nation of Islam offered Ali, like many African Americans, a strong spiritual basis for racial and gender identity as well as a militant stance on injustice. Given the popular perception of the Nation of Islam as subversive, dangerous, and "anti-white," had Ali announced his conversion before 1964, his announcement would have been met with considerable controversy. Indeed, with the notable exception of the sports announcer Howard Cosell, few journalists accepted his new name, often continuing to refer to Ali as Clay. In 1975 Ali converted to Sunni Islam, and later to Sufism.

Within the boxing ring Ali easily defended his championship, defeating nine opponents including Sonny Liston and Floyd Patterson. In 1964 Ali failed the U.S. Armed Forces qualifying examination because of his poor writing and spelling. However, in 1966 he was reclassified as 1A, fit for draft and induction, after the test was revised. He was stripped of his title in 1967, after his requests for military draft deferment and exemption from service as a conscientious objector were denied. Ali explained, "I have searched my conscience and I find I cannot be true to my belief in my religion by accepting such a call." Adamantly, Ali proclaimed, "Keep asking me, no matter how long/On the war in Vietnam I sing this song/I ain't got no quarrel with them Viet Cong . . . . They never called me nigger." Not only did Ali refuse to fight for religious reasons, but as he told a *Sports Illustrated* reporter, "Why should they ask me to put on a uniform and go ten thousand miles from home and drop bombs and bullets on brown people in Vietnam while so-called Negro people in Louisville are treated like dogs?" The New York State Athletic Commission and the World Boxing Association revoked Ali's boxing license and awarded his title to Joe Frazier within minutes of his refusal to "take one step forward." The governor of Maine argued that Ali "should be held in utter contempt by every patriotic American." Ali was found guilty of resisting the draft and sentenced to five years in prison and fined ten thousand dollars. Ali's principled opposition to war, even as the United States became more deeply involved in Vietnam, provoked both hatred and admiration. While Ali's critics portrayed him as anti-American, his challenge to traditional authority and the notion that African Americans should be subservient and respectful of white authority made him a cultural hero.

During his absence from the ring he supported himself by opening a restaurant chain called "Champburger," speaking at universities across the nation, and even starring in the Broadway musical *Big Time Buck White*. After more than three years, Ali resumed fighting, although the Supreme Court did not officially reverse his conviction until October 1970 after finding that the Federal Bureau of Investigation (FBI) illegally wiretapped his telephone.After a pair of knockout victories, Ali challenged "Smokin'" Joe Frazier for the heavyweight championship in what was called "The Fight of the Century." On 8 March 1971 he lost to Frazier in a fifteen-round bout, suffering the first loss of his career. Ali suffered his second career loss and a broken jaw at the hands of Ken Norton in 1973.

Notable Fights. By 1974 George Foreman was the heavyweight champion. After Ali defeated Frazier in a rematch, the fight promoter Don King arranged for an Ali-Foreman match with each participant receiving a purse of five

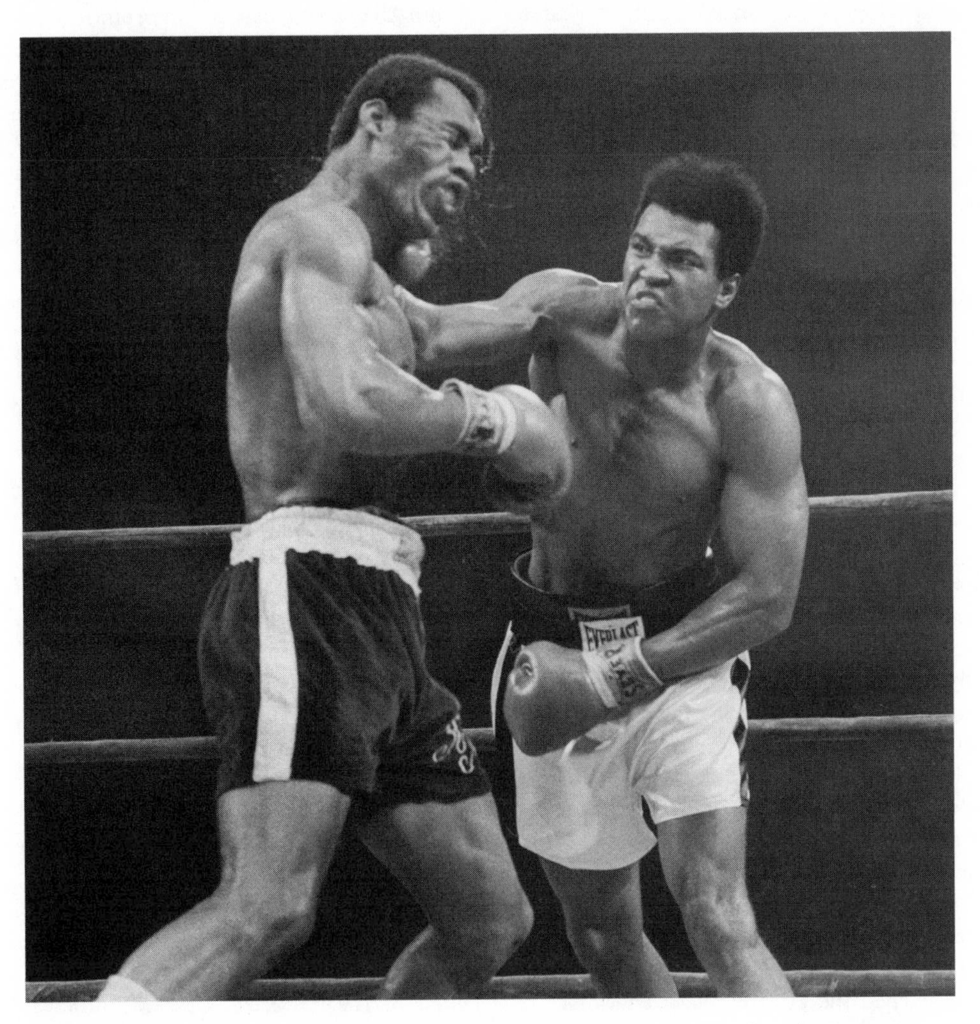

Ali vs. Norton. Muhammad Ali fights Ken Norton in a twelve-round rematch at the Forum in Inglewood, California, 10 September 1973. AP IMAGES

million dollars. Dubbed the "Rumble in the Jungle," the fight was held on 30 October 1974, in Kinshasa, Zaire (now the Democratic Republic of the Congo). Though most boxing analysts viewed Foreman as invincible, Ali defeated him using an innovative defensive tactic he labeled the "rope-a-dope," which involved resting on the ropes of the boxing ring, shielding one's face and body, while allowing the opponent to tire himself out by punching at this seemingly inviting target. Ali defended his title ten times over the next four years, most famously defeating Joe Frazier in a match billed as the "Thrilla in Manila" on 1 October 1975. Many boxing aficionados consider this match in the Philippines to be the greatest heavyweight boxing match in history. After fourteen brutal rounds Ali said, "It was the closest thing to death that I could feel." In 1978 Ali lost the title to Leon Spinks but regained the title in the same year, defeating Spinks in a fifteen-round decision to become the only boxer to win the heavyweight championship three times. Ali retired from boxing on 27 June 1979, but returned within a year to challenge Larry Holmes for the championship. Ali was knocked out in the eleventh round, suffering 125 punches in the ninth and tenth rounds alone. Ali retired permanently in 1981 after losing in ten rounds to Trevor Berbick.

Not only did Ali extend his long reach within the ring, but as indicated by his stance against racial inequality and the Vietnam War, his influence outside the ring is substantial as well. His willingness to box in places like Kinshasa, Manila, and Kuala Lumpur also reflects his larger concerns with the wellbeing of people of color throughout the world. Ali has been instrumental in the effort to feed the world's hungry, personally delivering medical supplies and food to Morocco, Mexico, Ivory Coast, and Indonesia. During the first Gulf War he traveled to Iraq to secure the release of fifteen U.S. hostages, and more recently he went to Afghanistan as a United Nations (UN) "Messenger of Peace." He has also made goodwill missions to North Korea and Cuba. Ali is no less active domestically, participating in countless philanthropic organizations, including the Make-A-Wish-Foundation and the Special Olympics. He has also advocated boxing reform, lending his name to the Boxing Reform Act, and raised funds for the Muhammad Ali Parkinson Research Center. Through his activism he has met with numerous dignitaries, including Queen Elizabeth II, Pope John Paul II, and Nelson Mandela upon his release from prison in South Africa for opposing apartheid. Ali has received many awards celebrating his achievements. In 1978, Walnut Street, the center of Louisville's black community prior to urban renewal, was renamed Muhammad Ali Boulevard. Most notably, he earned the Presidential Medal of Freedom and the Otto Hahn Peace Medal in Gold from the United Nations Association of Germany in 2005.

Parkinson's Syndrome. Perhaps the greatest challenge of Ali's life followed his boxing career, as he developed Parkinson's syndrome, a neurological condition that left his mental faculties intact but caused tremors, loss of balance, confusion, and slurred speech. Of his illness, Ali was quoted as saying, "I've got Parkinson's syndrome. I'm in no pain . . ." A number of doctors maintain that Ali's condition is in fact "Pugilistic Parkinsonism," a product of the numerous blows he suffered to the head during his boxing career, prompting some health organizations to petition for the abolition of boxing. Yet, according to his wife, Yolanda, "Muhammad knows he has this illness for a reason. It's not by chance. Parkinson's disease has made him a more spiritual person." Though slowed by his illness, Ali remains active, traveling for the majority of the year making public appearances and advocating poverty relief, education, and tolerance.

In 2005 the $60 million nonprofit Muhammad Ali Center opened in Louisville, Kentucky. It exhibits memorabilia from Ali's boxing career and promotes the ideals that characterize the life of Muhammad Ali by focusing on "core themes of peace, social responsibility, respect and personal growth." Ultimately Ali created a legacy that transcended boxing, achieving recognition as a symbol of black pride and racial consciousness epitomizing the courage to stand on principle and challenge injustice. Ali became a hero to millions throughout the world promoting unity, justice, and peace. Ali's own words best characterize his life; quite simply, he is "The Greatest."

[*See also* Boxing; Johnson, Jack; Nation of Islam; *and* Olympics.]

BIBLIOGRAPHY

Gast, Leon. *When We Were Kings*. New York: PolyGram Video, 1997.

Hauser, Thomas. *Muhammad Ali: His Life and Times*. New York: Simon & Schuster, 1991.

Marqusee, Mike. *Redemption Song: Muhammad Ali and the Spirit of the Sixties*. London and New York: Verso, 1999.

Remnick, David. *King of the World: Muhammad Ali and the Rise of an American Hero*. New York: Random House, 1998.

—LUTHER ADAMS

ALVIN AILEY AMERICAN DANCE THEATER.

The Alvin Ailey American Dance Theater, founded in 1958 by Alvin Ailey, is an internationally renowned modern dance company emphasizing Western and Afrocentric concert dance. Ailey was born in Rogers, Texas, in 1931. While attending the University of California at Los Angeles (UCLA), he received formal training in the Lester Horton technique, which was inspired by Horton's knowledge of the cultures of Native Americans, Asians, and the African diaspora. The Horton company stressed theatrical components, including storytelling, music, and stage design. After Horton's death in 1953, Ailey served as artistic director until 1954, when he moved to New York City to study dance with Charles Weidman, Hanya Holm, Martha Graham, and Doris Humphrey. In March 1958, Ailey formed his own company. Over the years the company has enjoyed financial support from many sources, including the U.S. Department of State and the Rockefeller Foundation. The company was first in residence in 1960 at the Clark Center for the Performing Arts in Manhattan, and in 1969 it moved to the Brooklyn Academy of Music, where Ailey established a school of dance. In 1971 Ailey's company became resident at New York's City Center, where it performs every holiday season.

The rise of Ailey's company coincided with the civil rights and Black Power movements of the 1960s and 1970s. These movements not only emphasized the need for African Americans to receive equal protection and opportunities under the law, but also encouraged African Americans to take pride in the culture of the African diaspora. Much of Ailey's choreography embodied this emphasis. During his lifetime Ailey choreographed seventy-nine ballets, many of which were inspired by his memories of Texas, as well as his knowledge of gospel, spiritual, and blues music. His work incorporates modern dance, ballet, jazz, and Africanist aesthetics. The ballet *Blues Suite* (1958), for instance, set in a music hall, may seem to reassert stereotypes of the hypersexualized black body; but upon further examination it is able to convey the music hall as an escape from social, economic, and political inequalities suffered by African Americans during the Great Depression. It thereby transforms the meaning of blues music and dance from its oversexualized image and brings out its political implications. *Revelations* (1960), Ailey's most acclaimed work, uses African American spirituals and explores several aspects of Christianity, including baptism by water. Ailey's multicultural aesthetic is also embodied in the company's touring history, which includes performing in Africa, Asia, Russia, and the United States.

Alvin Ailey. The dancers Marilyn Banks and Masazumi Chaya pose with Alvin Ailey, 1980. Photograph by Marty Reichenthal. AP IMAGES

After Ailey's death in 1989, the dancer and choreographer Judith Jamison, who had danced with the company from 1965 to 1980, took over as artistic director, as Ailey had requested. Under Jamison's leadership the company performed both works by Ailey and new ballets. In the early twenty-first century the company had performed over two hundred ballets by more than seventy choreographers. In 1998 the company created a joint BFA program with Fordham University that provides students with a combination of a liberal arts education and dance training. More than half a century old, the Alvin Ailey American Dance Theater has enjoyed undeniable accomplishment, having performed in forty-eight states, seventy-one countries, and six continents for an estimated 21 million people.

[*See also* Ailey, Alvin; Choreographers; Dance; *and* Jamison, Judith.]

BIBLIOGRAPHY

Ailey, Alvin, and A. Peter Bailey. *Revelations: The Autobiography of Alvin Ailey*. Secaucus, N.J.: Carol Publishing, 1995.

DeFrantz, Thomas. *Dancing Revelations: Alvin Ailey's Embodiment of African American Culture*. New York: Oxford University Press, 2004.

Jamison, Judith, and Howard Kaplan. *Dancing Spirit: An Autobiography*. New York: Doubleday, 1993.

—JACQUELINE M. JONES

AME CHURCH. The long and illustrious history of the African Methodist Episcopal (AME) Church dates back to the eighteenth century. The founder Richard Allen, a former slave who had been able to purchase his freedom

AME Church. The general officers of the AME Church from 1896 to 1900. PHOTOGRAPHS AND PRINTS DIVISION, SCHOMBURG CENTER FOR RESEARCH IN BLACK CULTURE, THE NEW YORK PUBLIC LIBRARY, ASTOR, LENOX AND TILDEN FOUNDATIONS

and was an ordained Methodist minister, was assigned to Saint George's Methodist Episcopal Church in Philadelphia, where he was allowed to preach to blacks. When in November 1787 several black church members, including Absalom Jones, were pulled from their knees while praying, all the black worshippers left Saint George's to form a church of their own. The Bethel African Methodist Episcopal Church was established in Philadelphia in 1793 and opened in July 1794. In 1816, Richard Allen united black Methodist congregations from the greater Philadelphia area, founding the African Methodist Episcopal Church; he was elected the first bishop during the new church's first General Conference. The Book of Discipline, Articles of Religion, and the General Rules of the Methodist Episcopal Church were also adopted at the conference. Church publishing endeavors included the establishment of the *Christian Recorder* in 1852 and the *AME Church Review* in 1884. Involved in the struggle to dismantle slavery, AME churches served as way stations on the Underground Railroad.

The church membership grew to more than four hundred thousand by 1880. Because the uplift of African Americans through education remained an important focus, the church founded several colleges for black students: Wilberforce University in Wilberforce, Ohio, in 1856; Edward Waters College in Jacksonville, Florida, in 1866; Paul Quinn College in Austin, Texas, in 1872; Daniel Payne College in Birmingham, Alabama, in 1880; Morris Brown College in Atlanta in 1881; Kittrell College in Kittrell, North Carolina, in 1886; and Shorter College in North Little Rock, Arkansas, in 1886. The policy of having an all-male clergy prohibited the ordination of women in the church until 1960. The first woman bishop, Vashti Murphy McKenzie, was elected and consecrated in 2000.

The twentieth century brought social, economic, and political upheaval to the African American community. Large numbers of southern blacks migrated north to escape racial violence, discrimination, and disfranchisement. Many who arrived in the urban areas found their way to AME churches. Working within a framework of a social gospel, ministers like Bishop Reverdy C. Ransom of Chicago headed churches that offered general education, job training, health care, and housing programs. The AME Church was involved in ending poverty and discrimination long before the civil rights movement began in the 1960s.

The civil rights era was one of collective political action that joined churches of all denominations in the struggle for justice. AME ministers led marches and recruited members of their congregations for planned demonstrations. They also encouraged their members to attend meetings and give money to support boycotts such as the bus boycott in Montgomery, Alabama, in 1954. Rosa Parks belonged to AME congregations in Alabama and Detroit, Michigan. The response of AME Church members to the civil rights movement was tremendous. Brown Chapel AME in Selma, Alabama, became an important base during the voting rights campaign in 1965. Some churches were attacked; Mount Zion AME in Longdale, Mississippi, for example, was bombed in June 1964.

Bishop John H. Adams led a successful boycott of Seattle public schools in 1966. Other AME Church members have included Reverend Oliver Brown, chief plaintiff in *Brown v. Board of Education* (1954), and Daisy Bates, a leader in the efforts to desegregate the Little Rock public schools. The March on Washington in 1963 was the brainchild of A. Philip Randolph, a lifelong member of the AME Church. Roy Wilkins, executive director of the NAACP, was also a member of the AME Church. Stephanie Wilson, a NASA mission specialist with the space shuttle *Discovery*, is also a member of the church.

The AME Church and the NAACP shared a cooperative relationship for many years. Members of the church helped found the NAACP in 1910, and the doors of AME churches were always open for NAACP branches. Working in partnership, both organizations served as a training ground for black political leadership. Together the AME Church and the NAACP have provided opportunities for thousands of black Americans to find the dignity and respect denied them by the white community.

The AME Church also had influence in the black theology movement of the late 1960s. James Cone, called the father of liberation theology for his pioneering views on black liberation theology, explained that the adoption of a black Christ as a religious symbol was a liberating concept for African American churches. This African American scholar has authored numerous works and is an AME Church member. Bishop John D. Bright was one of four AME ministers who signed the first statement disseminated by the National Conference of Black Churchmen in the 1960s, calling on black churches to do more in meeting the economic, social, and religious needs of the black community.

AME churches remain committed to the economic empowerment of the African American community. Under the leadership of the former congressman Reverend Floyd Flake, the Greater Allen AME Cathedral in Jamaica, Queens, New York, completed a multimillion-dollar economic revitalization project that includes low-income housing, a nursing home, a private Christian school, and thriving small businesses. Saint James AME Church played an integral part in the revitalization of Newark, New Jersey, with its $55 million housing development project. The Bridge Street AME Church in Brooklyn, New York, offers a private Christian school, a credit union, and small-business counseling services to its members. The Renaissance Venture Capital Fund and Commercial Loan Program of the First AME Church in Los Angeles funded more than two hundred small businesses and created more than two hundred new home owners. Grant AME Church in the Watts neighborhood of Los Angeles is participating with the city of Los Angeles to complete a $10 million mixed-use commercial and retail project in the Watts community. Bethel AME Church provides the inner-city Baltimore community with an outreach center, a substance abuse and AIDS ministry, and a private Christian school.

The governing body of the AME Church is the General Conference, which meets on a quadrennial basis. The General Conference elects and consecrates the bishops of the church. The AME Church is divided into eighteen episcopal districts. Districts one through thirteen oversee the United States, Canada, and Bermuda; the remaining districts oversee the foreign missions in Jamaica, Haiti, the Dominican Republic, the Virgin Islands, the Windward Islands, Guyana, Suriname, and twenty African countries. The church is a member of the National Council of Churches and the World Council of Churches. In 2000 there were six thousand churches with a membership of more than two million in the United States.

[*See also* AME Zion Church; Black Church; *and* Religion.]

BIBLIOGRAPHY

Dodson, Jualynne E. *Engendering Church: Women, Power, and the AME Church*. Lanham, Md.: Rowman & Littlefield, 2002. Good overview of the historical role of women in the AME Church.

Gregg, Howard D. *History of the African Methodist Episcopal Church: The Black Church in Action*. Nashville, Tenn.: AMEC, 1980. Church history written by a former editor of the *AME Church Review*.

Pinn, Anthony B. *The Black Church in the Post–Civil Rights Era*. Maryknoll, N.Y.: Orbis Books, 2002. A good discussion of the contemporary issues confronting all black churches.

—KERIMA M. LEWIS

AME CHURCH REVIEW. The *African Methodist Episcopal Church Review* (*AME Church Review*) has the distinction of being the oldest magazine owned and published by African Americans. The denomination's first periodical, the *African Methodist Episcopal Church Magazine*, appeared in September 1841. The General Conference that met in Baltimore, Maryland, in 1884 changed the name of this periodical to the *AME Church Review*. The AME Church saw a need for a scholarly magazine to complement its *Christian Recorder*, which had been published as a weekly newspaper since 1852. Headquarters for the magazine was set up in Philadelphia, and Bishop Benjamin Tucker Tanner was appointed the first editor-manager.

As a quarterly magazine the *Review* was not limited to the news and business of the AME Church but provided thought-provoking, intellectual, and scholarly articles. The first issue of the *AME Church Review* appeared in July 1884 with the lead article, "Thoughts about the Past, the Present, and the Future of the African M. E. Church," written by Daniel Payne, an AME bishop. Other articles appearing in this first issue were on New Testament Greek, black contributions to science, art, and literature, and the Haitian Revolution.

The early publications of the *Review* covered the fields of art, politics, civics, education, and sociology. The magazine not only provided a forum for promising black authors but also served as an educational vehicle for the clergy and laity of the church. In 1889 the second editor, Bishop L. J. Coppin, explained that the purpose of this national journal was "to give to the world the best thoughts of the race, irrespective of religious persuasion or political opinion." In line with the church's long history of protesting racial bigotry, the *Review* sought to engage a broader American dialogue on human rights and other pressing issues of day.

Throughout the years of its publication the *Review* has lived up to its ambitious goals of high editorial standards. From the post-Reconstruction era to World War I, the magazine attracted such distinguished contributors as Frederick Douglass, W. E. B. Du Bois, Booker T. Washington, and Ida B. Wells. These contributors addressed issues of national importance including civil rights, education, the relationship of women to the ministry, and the benefits of a social gospel and socialism. Other articles published during this period discussed the unfinished work of Reconstruction and the importance of African American participation in national politics. AME ministers who served in the capacity of editor-manager during the first hundred years of publication included Professor H. T. Kealing, Bishop R. C. Ransom, J. G. Robinson, H. D. Gregg, J. S. Brookens, G. A. Singleton, Ben H. Hill, and Dr. W. D. Johnson. Each of these editors was a brilliant, college-educated man who made his own important contributions to the historical and theological scholarship of the magazine.

The articles written during the early twentieth century ranged from the need for improved educational opportunities and the political situation of African Americans to the exclusion of women from the AME pastorate and the importance of the church's missions in Africa. Articles of a theological perspective not only challenged the biblical interpretation that African Americans were descendants of Ham but also examined the validity of the theory of evolution. The articles written during this period were of the highest intellectual caliber and were part of the AME vision of equality between blacks and whites. Topics covered during the World War II period reviewed American imperialism and the progress of African Americans since the ending of slavery. Another article discussed the church's role in providing social services as a means to improving the socioeconomic opportunities of African Americans.

The *Review* continued to focus on the social, political, and economic condition of African Americans through the latter part of the twentieth century. A recurring debate through the years concerned the merger of the AME and AME Zion denominations. The ordination of women also remained a recurring theme until Vashti Murphy McKenzie was ordained an AME bishop in 2000. The *Review* continued to provide its readers with articles on the history of African Americans and the history of AME Church. In addition, theological articles discussed subjects related to the denomination's Christian beliefs and such issues as black liberation theology. The topics of a more contemporary focus have ranged from Haitian immigration, the HIV/AIDS crisis, and the 11 September 2001 terrorist attacks to the Million Man and Million Woman marches and the Iraq war. The editor-publisher since 1988, the Reverend Dennis C. Dickerson, also serves as the denomination's church historian.

[*See also* AME Church *and biographical entries on figures mentioned in this article*.]

BIBLIOGRAPHY

Angell, Stephen W., and Anthony B. Pinn, eds. *Social Protest Thought in the African Methodist Episcopal Church, 1862–1939*. Knoxville: University of Tennessee Press, 2000. A well-written overview of the early history of the *AME Church Review*.

Williams, Gilbert Anthony. *The Christian Recorder, Newspaper of the AME Church: History of a Forum for Ideas, 1854–1902*. Jefferson, N.C.: McFarland, 1996. A good secondary source focusing on the *Recorder*.

—KERIMA M. LEWIS

AMENIA CONFERENCES. [*This entry consists of two subentries, on the conferences of 1916 and 1933.*]

Amenia Conference of 1916

After the death of Booker T. Washington in November 1915, the person who had sparred with him most intensely, W. E. B. Du Bois, promoted a conference of black leaders and representative white men and women to attempt conciliation and a bridging of the gaps that had grown between the accommodationist and activist camps, particularly after the founding of the National Association for the Advancement of Colored People (NAACP) in 1909. The time had come for leaders of differing opinions to have an open and honest discussion and to decide which principles ought to guide the growing civil rights movement. Joel Elias Spingarn, then chairman of the NAACP Board of Directors, offered to host this select gathering at his Troutbeck estate in Amenia, Dutchess County, New York, 85 miles (137 kilometers) north of New York City.

Invitations were issued to some two hundred people for 24–26 August 1916. The conference was to be informal throughout, although a subject, a presiding leader, and a noncontroversial discussion leader were designated for each of the sessions. The conference was described as having the approval and support of the NAACP, but the organization took neither authority nor responsibility for the proceedings and none of the participants was expected to be committed to the association's program or principles. Attendees were guests of Spingarn from their arrival at the Amenia train station, were housed in a tent colony on the shore of Troutbeck's three-acre pond, were fed at a commissariat and mess tent, and were strongly urged to bring swimsuits. The newly hired NAACP secretary Roy Nash skillfully completed the organizational tasks of making sure that tents, cots, blankets, and towels were in place well before the conference.

In his eighteen-page leaflet "The Amenia Conference: An Historic Negro Gathering," Du Bois credits the bucolic setting, the excellent food, and the informality of the events for the participants' congeniality and productivity. He describes swimming, rowing, hiking, sitting on the hillside, picking flowers, and singing. Humor and closeness made pretensions evaporate. Du Bois's refusal to put himself forward as a leader also contributed to freedom of expression. Sessions concentrated on education, industry, politics, civil and legal discrimination, social discrimination, and a working plan for the future. Discussion leaders included the Atlanta University president John Hope, the African Methodist Episcopal Zion Church bishop Alexander Walters, the journalist Frederick Randolph Moore, the activist Mary Church Terrell, the Morgan College dean William Pickens, and the poet and novelist James Weldon Johnson.

In his original guest list, Du Bois had classified people as "Niagara Movement Man," "Washington Man," or "?" Spingarn ran the list by Robert Moton—who had succeeded Washington as principal at the Tuskegee Institute—and others, as a result of which several names were added. Of the fifty-five who ultimately attended, the numbers of those historically supportive of Du Bois and of those historically supportive of Booker T. Washington were nearly equal.

In his leaflet, Du Bois listed people by region. Those from the South included Washington's conservative former secretary Emmett J. Scott, the educator Lucy Laney, and the politician James Carroll Napier. Attendees from the West included the politician Francis H. Warren of Detroit, the dentist Charles E. Bentley and the lawyer George W. Ellis of Chicago, and the author Charles W. Chesnutt of Cleveland, Ohio. From the East came the National Association of Colored Women leader Mary B. Talbert, the educator Kelly Miller, the dramatist Thomas Montgomery Gregory, the NAACP's Washington, D.C., member Neval Thomas, the social worker and peace activist Alphaeus Hunton, the lawyers William H. Lewis and George W. Crawford, and Garnet Waller, a founder of the Niagara Movement. Daily guests included such prominent black and white people as the governor of New York, Charles A. Whitman; C. W. Anderson, a Washington stalwart and Collector of Internal Revenue; Congressman William S. Bennett; the editor Oswald Garrison Villard; and the lawyer and suffragist Inez Milholland Boissevain.

Principles agreed upon by the conference attendees included the desirability of all kinds of education for African Americans; the need for complete political freedom; the need for organization and practical planning among leaders; the eschewing of factions and suspicions; respect for the methods of those working in various sections of the country, especially the South; the privacy of the process and the desirability of widespread discussion of the resolutions of the conference; and the beneficial prospect of similar annual private and informal discussions. Goals were agreed upon, but there was no consensus on how these goals ought to be reached.

The Amenia Conference of 1916 was not open to the public; reporters were not allowed, and guests were assured that their names would not be published without their consent. However, with so much agreement on core principles, the group voted to make these principles known. Accordingly, Frederick Moore published a report of the recommendations in the *New York Age* on 14 September 1916, describing the conference as the birth of a new spirit of unity; James Weldon Johnson wrote of the meetings in his *Age* column. Du Bois's leaflet did not appear until 1925, when he indicated that the immediate pressures of the U.S. entry into World War I the year after the conference had interfered with some of its potential positive outcomes.

One outcome that is credited to the interactions at Amenia was the hiring in December 1916 of James Weldon Johnson, formerly a Washington man, by the NAACP. The impression that Johnson made on Spingarn at Amenia also convinced those such as Mary White Ovington who had previously suspected Johnson of being too conservative. Working together on the successful conference also brought Spingarn and Du Bois closer. In this way, perhaps the most significant outcome of the 1916 Amenia Conference was that it brought the NAACP into prominence, as seen especially in its activities such as the Dyer anti-lynching campaign after World War I.

[*See also* National Association for the Advancement of Colored People; Washington–Du Bois Conflict; *and biographical entries on figures mentioned in this article*.]

BIBLIOGRAPHY

Du Bois, W. E. B. "The Amenia Conference: An Historic Gathering." Amenia, N.Y.: Troutbeck Press, 1925. Reprinted in *W. E. B. Du Bois: A Reader*, edited by David Levering Lewis. New York: Henry Holt, 1995. Two hundred copies of this leaflet were printed for private distribution, but copies or microfilms of it are available at sixteen libraries nationally and in various archives such as the Mary Church Terrell Papers at the Library of Congress.

Kellogg, Charles Flint. *NAACP: A History of the National Association for the Advancement of Colored People*. Vol. 1: *1909–1920*. Baltimore: Johns Hopkins Press, 1967. Kellogg describes the conference in the context of the first ten years of the NAACP, concluding that the conference enabled leaders to fight more successfully and confidently during the war years. Kellogg also credits the conference and Spingarn's impressions with the later hiring of James Weldon Johnson.

Lewis, David Levering. *W. E. B. Du Bois: Biography of a Race, 1868–1919*. New York: Henry Holt, 1993. This thorough and lively biography presents considerable detail about the planning and outcome of the 1916 Amenia Conference. Lewis describes results as less genuine unity, more "cosmetic harmony and pragmatic tolerance" (p. 521).

Ross, Barbara Joyce. *J. E. Spingarn and the Rise of the NAACP, 1911–1939*. New York: Atheneum, 1972. Concentrating on Spingarn's role, Ross argues that his planning of Amenia with Du Bois was in service of Spingarn's dream of bringing Booker T. Washington's supporters closer to the NAACP.

—CAROLYN WEDIN

Amenia Conference of 1933

The Amenia Conference of 1933 got its name from the Upstate New York town near Troutbeck, the country estate of Joel Elias Spingarn, a wealthy Jewish intellectual and chairman of the board of directors of the NAACP, which he had helped to found in 1909. In 1916 Spingarn for the first time had invited a group of black and white racial reformers to Amenia in order to discuss the future strategy of the NAACP. At the onset of the Great Depression the association again faced serious external and internal challenges; the black community was facing economic disaster, and many young black activists embraced socialist and communist ideas, viewing the plight of African Americans primarily as a matter of class rather than of race.

As early as 1932 the NAACP's annual conference passed resolutions calling for a new economic program for black America that would involve the redistribution of wealth, higher taxes for the rich, and social security programs for American workers regardless of race and color. The young reformers, however, wanted to go further and transform the NAACP into some kind of interracial labor organization. They called for a new leadership and for loosening the association's ties to white patronage.

In August 1933, Spingarn invited a group of some forty, mostly young black activists to Amenia, including such future luminaries as Ralph Johnson Bunche, Abram Harris Jr., Charles Hamilton Houston, Frances Williams, and E. Franklin Frazier. Among the older participants were W. E. B. Du Bois, the editor of the NAACP magazine *The Crisis*; the NAACP secretary Walter White; the NAACP cofounder Mary White Ovington; and of course Spingarn himself.

The young vanguard vigorously argued in favor of weaning the association away from the black and white elites and of getting closer to the black masses, employing a heavy dose of radical Marxist rhetoric. They remained aware, however, that class solidarity between black and white workers still had a long way to go. On the other hand, the older leaders wished to preserve the character of the NAACP as foremost an organization fighting racial discrimination and segregation. Apart from passing a number of resolutions emphasizing the economic underpinnings of the race question, the most important outcome of the 1933 Amenia Conference was the formation of a new committee to work out the future plan and program of the NAACP. Its recommendations, which were adopted in 1935 by the NAACP annual convention, remained, however, firmly within the reformist approach of the NAACP and did not effect significant organizational changes.

W. E. B. Du Bois was disappointed by the outcome of the Amenia Conference because he had hoped that the emphasis on economic issues would lead to a new program of racial solidarity and self-help, which he had advocated for some time. Instead he found himself caught between the economic determinism of the young Marxists on the one hand and the traditional liberalism of the NAACP leadership on the other. In January 1934, Du Bois published an editorial in *The Crisis* in which he distinguished between voluntary and discriminatory segregation and called for autonomous black economic institutions. The editorial sparked a major controversy and led to Du Bois's resignation from *The Crisis* and the NAACP.

[*See also* Communism and African Americans; National Association for the Advancement of Colored People; *and biographical entries on figures mentioned in this article*.]

BIBLIOGRAPHY

Berg, Manfred. *The Ticket to Freedom: The NAACP and the Struggle for Black Political Integration*. Gainesville: University Press of Florida, 2005. A comprehensive political history of the NAACP focusing on the period from 1909 to 1970.

Du Bois, W. E. B. *Dusk of Dawn: An Essay toward an Autobiography of a Race Concept* (1940). New Brunswick, N.J.: Transaction, 1984. Du Bois's memoirs from his childhood to 1940.

Ross, Barbara Joyce. *J. E. Spingarn and the Rise of the NAACP, 1911–1939*. New York: Atheneum, 1972. A biographical account of Spingarn's role in the history of the NAACP.

—Manfred Berg

AMERICAN COLONIZATION SOCIETY. Founded in December 1816, the American Colonization Society (ACS) was the first national organization to take on the problem of slavery in the United States. The ACS proposed an expatriation scheme to rid the nation of slavery and of free African Americans. The prominent founders Charles Fenton Mercer, Henry Clay, Daniel Webster, and others secured federal funding and in 1822 founded the colony of Liberia on Africa's west coast as the destination for America's blacks.

Even before the founding of the ACS, the colonization of African Americans was an issue that divided both whites and blacks. Some African Americans supported colonization, arguing that free blacks would never be fully included in the white-dominated society of the United States. Others argued just as forcibly that blacks were entitled to full rights as American citizens and should remain to fight on behalf of their race.

The ACS drew initial support from several elements in the white community, initially attracting those who believed that slavery was a mortal sin alongside southerners determined to rid the country of the menace of a growing population of free blacks. After 1831, and especially following the Nat Turner rebellion in Virginia, antislavery activists such as William Lloyd Garrison withdrew from the ACS and vehemently condemned the group's mission and actions. Nevertheless, throughout the nineteenth century the organization survived and continued to support the expatriation of African Americans. Liberia became an independent nation in 1847, with one of those expatriates, a black boatman from Virginia named Joseph Jenkins Roberts, serving as its first president. By 1867 some thirteen thousand emigrants were sent to Liberia under the auspices of the ACS.

Following the emancipation of American slaves in 1865, the role of the ACS became less clear. ACS leaders continued to argue that colonization was even more important because African Americans were not fit for citizenship in the United States. The organization purchased a new ship and instigated a new campaign to convince blacks to settle in Liberia. Spokesmen for the ACS warned that the end of slavery was merely the beginning of the problem facing African Americans in the United States. Most African Americans ignored the pleas of colonizationists, but some two thousand blacks did emigrate to Liberia between 1867 and 1871.

When Democrats regained control of the South at the end of Reconstruction, black interest in colonization increased. Unfortunately, the demand for emigration drained the funds of the ACS, and the organization was nearly bankrupt by the mid-1870s. In the 1880s and 1890s the ACS sent fewer and fewer blacks to Africa, with the last group of émigrés departing in 1904. After that date the ACS functioned more as a Liberian aid society, focusing on education and missionary efforts, until its dissolution in 1964. In 1913 and again in 1964 the ACS donated its records to the Library of Congress, where they are available for the use of scholars and students.

[*See also* Expatriates *and* Liberia.]

Bibliography

Burin, Eric. *Slavery and the Peculiar Solution: A History of the American Colonization Society*. Gainesville: University Press of Florida, 2005.

Staudenraus, P. J. *The African Colonization Movement, 1816–1865*. New York: Columbia University Press, 1961.

—L. Diane Barnes

AMERICAN DILEMMA, AN. *An American Dilemma: The Negro Problem and Modern Democracy*, the Swedish social scientist Gunnar Myrdal's study of race relations in the United States, had remarkable influence after it appeared in 1944. The Supreme Court, for example, cited Myrdal's work with approval in the 1954 *Brown v. Board of Education* decision. Within the national government, social engineers crafted ameliorative, race-based policy from *Dilemma*'s prescriptions. For decades American liberals found its optimism congenial to much of their thinking. The word "dilemma" became linguistic coin of the realm, a liberal shorthand for America whenever cast in racial relief. The study helped create what many scholars came to call a "liberal orthodoxy" on race among social scientists, a perspective that dominated American social thought from the end of World War II until the mid-1960s.

The Carnegie Foundation sponsored and funded the study. The original proposal for a comprehensive study of the so-called Negro problem came in 1935 from a Carnegie board member, Newton D. Baker, and it won the support of the foundation's president Frederick Keppel. Baker's proposal departed from the traditional focus of the foundation's race-relations work, black education in the South—a legacy of Andrew Carnegie's admiration for Booker T. Washington. The times demanded it. Amid an economic depression that had devastated countless African American communities, the Negro problem seemed more acute than ever before.

After considering various candidates to undertake the study, Keppel decided on Gunnar Myrdal, who accepted in 1938. The Carnegie president believed that as a European from a non-imperial power, Myrdal would remain relatively free of the bias and emotionalism that usually accompanied studies of race relations in the United States. Myrdal proved an inspired choice, both because of his experience with public policy in Sweden and, ironically, because of his rejection of the putatively "value free" social science then in vogue in the United States, which often masked racially conservative assumptions.

Myrdal employed an army of researchers, white and black, to help him with his project. He especially courted African American scholars. He sought advice from W. E. B. Du Bois and the Howard University philosopher Alain Locke; also from Howard he picked up significant contributions from the political scientist Ralph Johnson Bunche and the sociologist E. Franklin Frazier. From Fisk University, Myrdal got the participation of the sociologist Charles S. Johnson, whose students conducted fieldwork for the study.

Perhaps the influence of *An American Dilemma* befitted the physical immensity of the final product, which comprised 1,483 pages altogether. A direct, elegantly presented thesis framed its numerous details. The great dilemma that plagued American democracy was a white moral problem. Whites' "creed"—such universally held American values as democracy, liberty, and equality of opportunity—clashed with their workaday practice of racial prejudice. Not limited to purely psychological dissonance, this basic dilemma struck sour notes that resonated throughout American society and its institutions. The disconnect between American creed and American practice demanded resolution; it goaded whites to live up to their ideals. Such contradictions would not long withstand increasing black militancy and international pressure.

Perhaps too optimistically, Myrdal believed that with the right information and proper education, whites would eventually resolve the dilemma; despite their often willful myopia, they wanted "to be rational and just" (p. 1023). The creed was powerful; it would win out over prejudice. Controversially Myrdal also concluded that African American culture, as a "pathological" variant of white culture, on the whole lacked the necessary resources to combat the problem.

After *An American Dilemma* appeared, several critics gushed that the Swede was a worthy successor to the nineteenth-century Frenchman Alexis de Tocqueville as an acute foreign observer of Americans. For its time *Dilemma* was a courageous and uncompromising work. Du Bois, quoting extended passages of Myrdal's work for his own review, deemed it clear-eyed and unrivaled in its coverage of the subject. E. Franklin Frazier praised its balance and sharp judgment. Others were less enthusiastic. Some white southern reviewers hashed out familiar arguments, particularly the inability of outsiders to understand the peculiarities of their region. Marxists objected to the centrality of ideas, rather than material conditions, in much of Myrdal's analysis.

The most prescient contemporary criticism of *Dilemma* emerged some two decades later. Ralph Ellison's review, originally drafted in 1944, appeared in his book of essays *Shadow and Act* in 1964. Ellison, though recognizing the importance of the study, questioned Myrdal's dismissal of black culture as merely a pathological variant of white culture. After the mid-1960s this brand of criticism, buoyed by a new generation of more racially conscious and culturally nationalist scholars, made *An American Dilemma* seem out of touch with trends in social science. Nonetheless, the study marked a critical moment in the evolution of Americans' ideas about race and democracy, and it brought an unprecedented amount of attention to the problem of racism in the United States.

[*See also* Carnegie Corporation; Racism; Social Sciences and Civil Rights; *and biographical entries on figures mentioned in this article.*]

BIBLIOGRAPHY

Jackson, Walter A. *Gunnar Myrdal and America's Conscience: Social Engineering and Racial Liberalism, 1938–1987*. Chapel Hill: University of North Carolina Press, 1990. In addition to a wealth of analysis and biographical material, treats the making of *Dilemma* and the intricacies of Myrdal's relationship with the Carnegie Foundation.

King, Richard H. *Race, Culture, and the Intellectuals, 1940–1970*. Baltimore, Md.: Johns Hopkins University Press, 2004. Offers an extended treatment of Myrdal and *Dilemma*, placing the thinker and the work amid transatlantic streams of racial thought in social science and beyond.

Myrdal, Gunnar, with the assistance of Richard Sterner and Arnold Rose. *An American Dilemma: The Negro Problem and Modern Democracy*. 2 vols. New York and London: Harper & Brothers, 1944.

Southern, David W. *Gunnar Myrdal and Black-White Relations: The Use and Abuse of "An American Dilemma," 1944–1969*. Baton Rouge: Louisiana State University Press, 1987. The most detailed treatment available of the reception and influence of *An American Dilemma*.

—PETER A. KURYLA

AMERICAN NEGRO ACADEMY. The American Negro Academy (ANA), the first major learned society of African Americans, was founded on 5 March 1897 in Washington, D.C. The ANA's constitution described the ANA as "an organization of authors, scholars, artists, and those distinguished in other walks of life; men of African descent, for the promotion of Letters, Science, and Art."

The purpose of the group was to advance the race by strengthening and encouraging its intellectual life through strengthening and encouraging its leaders. During the same period, white Americans were also founding learned, professional, and ethnic historical societies, but often these societies excluded people of African descent. So the ANA provided African Americans their own society.

The ANA's cofounder and first president, Alexander Crummell, was its driving force. When he founded the ANA, Crummell was a seventy-eight-year-old Episcopal clergyman, writer, educator, and missionary, and the unsurpassed black intellectual of the nineteenth century. He had been raised and educated on New York City's Lower East Side. Denied a theological education at the General Seminary of the Episcopal Church in New York City, Crummell moved to England, where he received a bachelor's degree from Queens' College, Cambridge, in 1853. Crummell spent from the early 1850s to 1874 in England and Liberia. After he returned to the United States he helped found and then was rector of Saint Luke's Episcopal Church in Washington, D.C., Washington's first independent black Episcopal church.

Crummell believed that "a race was . . . to be considered civilized only when it produced a sophisticated and regenerative culture of its own." In his judgment American blacks lacked civilization. The only way for the race to earn respect in American society was to change this, to gain civilization and avoid being despised and repulsed and remaining in poverty and drudgery. These were the reasons behind his founding the ANA.

The ANA's membership included some of the most important leaders in the black community. Francis James Grimké was a Presbyterian minister who trained at Lincoln University in Pennsylvania and the Princeton Theological Seminary. W. E. B. Du Bois was in 1897 a professor of history and sociology at Atlanta University. William H. Crogman was a professor of classics at Clark Atlanta University. William S. Scarborough, a classics scholar, was on the faculty of Wilberforce University in Ohio. John W. Cromwell was an attorney, politician, and founder and editor of the *People's Advocate*, a black newspaper published in Washington, D.C., from 1876.

During its thirty-one-year existence the ANA drew many of the most accomplished and creative black intellectuals in the United States. Some of the members achieved their greatest accomplishments after the turn of the century. John Hope became president of Morehouse College in 1906 and of the Atlanta University Center when it was created in 1929. Alain Locke, a writer and critic, was a key figure in the Harlem Renaissance. The historian Carter G. Woodson founded the Association for the Study of Negro Life and History (later called the Association for the Study of African American Life and History) in 1915. James Weldon Johnson became a well-known poet, writer, and civil rights leader.

Unfortunately the ANA remained relatively small. Its activities and goals appealed only to a small group of blacks who wanted to operate as a think tank. Even though there were black women with similar interests, the academy stayed all male. The organization failed to achieve many of its goals. However, throughout the thirty-one years that the organization existed, it published twenty-two papers and a total of thirty-one articles. The longest one was thirty-eight pages. Some articles were not scholarly.

The ANA was never able to fund a permanent home or maintain its collection of "valuable data and the works of Negro authors": books, pictures, and other materials related to black American and African history (Moss, p. 292). The failure of the academy meant the loss of a place to keep those items that had been archived. Some items were returned to donors or kept by one or more of the members. The greater society, both blacks and whites, largely ignored the writings of the academy. Because the ANA could never secure enough money to publish the works of its members on a regular basis or have them published by white journals, whites consciously or unconsciously rejected the ANA's validity as a learned society and its members' claims to be intellectuals.

In the black community the papers that the academy occasionally published had no effect because most blacks did not purchase or read them. The papers were well written and thought provoking, but most blacks were simply trying to make a living, taking care of their families, and trying to minimize violent contacts with whites. The ANA's analyses of these people's problems, plus the solutions and responses suggested, would have been difficult for them to understand or would have seemed irrelevant—and actually implementing some of the solutions would have been dangerous. The practical, conservative race-building and economic strategies of Booker T. Washington were much more appealing and easily understood.

Nevertheless, the ANA did have limited success. A small group of thoughtful blacks and whites reacted positively to several of the papers, and some of the country's foremost libraries and institutions of higher learning requested copies. This greatly encouraged the members of the academy in their pursuit of being taken seriously as intellectuals.

Although the ANA did not achieve all that it set out to do, considering the many forces during the early twentieth century that discouraged the efforts of educated blacks to make valuable contributions to the scholarly body of knowledge, it is amazing that the organization managed to exist for as long as it did.

[*See also* Association for the Study of African American Life and History; Clark Atlanta University; Harlem Renaissance; Historians; Intellectuals; Morehouse College; Talented Tenth; Wilberforce University; *and biographical entries on figures mentioned in this article*.]

BIBLIOGRAPHY

Blaxton, Reginald G. "The American Negro Academy: Black Excellence 100 Years Ago." *American Visions* 12, no. 1 (1997): 17–20.

Moss, Alfred A., Jr. *The American Negro Academy: Voice of the Talented Tenth*. Baton Rouge: Louisiana State University Press, 1981.

—JOY A. MCDONALD

AMERICAN NEGRO LABOR CONGRESS. The year 1925 was pivotal for the African American labor movement: three major unions for African Americans began: the American Negro Labor Congress, the Trade Union Committee for Organizing Negro Workers, and the Brotherhood of Sleeping Car Porters. African Americans had been ignored or excluded by mainstream labor organizations such as the American Federation of Labor, so these new organizations attempted to address the needs of African American laborers. One of the organizations, the American Negro Labor Congress (ANLC), was organized by the American Communist Party to address the social and economic concerns of African Americans. The ANLC also hoped to exploit concerns such as racism and racial discrimination to launch a major workers' union in the nation. Although the ANLC began with much fanfare and publicity, it was never able to rally the masses of African American workers and was criticized by most African American leaders of the period.

In late October 1925 the ANLC was organized in Chicago. The primary national organizer was Lovett Fort-Whiteman, an African American Communist who had studied both at Tuskegee and in Moscow. The ANLC promoted a platform that urged unity among African American laborers, racial equality, the destruction of the Ku Klux Klan, and the end of racial segregation in the United States. Fort-Whiteman held a special contempt for the American Federation of Labor and its leader William Green; he singled out both of them as segregationist and racist. Given its platform and its militancy, the ANLC soon came under the close scrutiny of the Federal Bureau of Investigation (FBI). The ANLC was viewed as a front for the Communist Party, and the FBI infiltrated it and filed regular reports about its activities.

Despite its agenda of racial unity and race consciousness, the ANLC never attracted large numbers of African Americans to its cause. Fort-Whiteman, having lived abroad for several years, was out of touch with the African American community. He was more interested in class consciousness than in race. In a 1925 *Time* magazine interview he stated that "the Negro people were of no importance as a race." Rather he focused on African Americans' power as an industrial class. Also, Fort-Whiteman was somewhat of a self-promoter who felt threatened when those around him offered suggestions on how to increase African American participation in the organization. Thus the organization made few inroads into the African American community and organized only a few local units. Because of its poor showing in Chicago, the organization moved to New York in 1928. By this time it was already under new leadership. Another Communist, Richard Moore, led the organization until its demise in 1930. Fort-Whiteman left the United States for the Soviet Union in 1930, and he later was killed in the Stalinist purges.

The response of most African American leaders to the ANLC was decidedly negative. Asa Philip Randolph, the socialist leader who founded and led the Brotherhood of Sleeping Car Porters, argued that the ANLC could never understand the problems of African American workers because its Communist leadership was foreign and did not understand the situation of African Americans. The National Urban League was also critical of the ANLC and suggested that it be ignored. Marcus Garvey, founder and head of the United Negro Improvement Association (UNIA), rejected the ANLC because he felt that no Communist-affiliated organization would ever put African American needs first. Only W. E. B. Du Bois provided a dissenting opinion. He hailed the founding of the ANLC as "significant." Du Bois wanted action and not talk. He felt that no American organization would put race at the top of its agenda, and he hoped that the ANLC would address racial issues.

By 1930 the ANLC had also been condemned by the African American press for being inspired by Communism. Only the organization's official paper, the *Negro Champion*, which was subsidized by the Communist Party, continued functioning. The League of Struggle for Negro Rights superseded the ANLC in 1930. The ANLC never met its goal of uniting the African American labor movement with the Communist Party of the United States.

[*See also* Brotherhood of Sleeping Car Porters; Communism and African Americans; Organized Labor; *and biographial entries on figures mentioned in this article*.]

BIBLIOGRAPHY

Foner, Philip S. *History of the Labor Movement in the United States*. 4 vols. New York: International Publishers, 1972–1975.

Harris, William H. *The Harder We Run: Black Workers since the Civil War*. New York: Oxford University Press, 1982. Contains an excellent overview of black workers from the Civil War through the 1970s, as well as some information about reactions to the ANLC.

Harris, William H. *Keeping the Faith: A. Philip Randolph, Milton P. Webster, and the Brotherhood of Sleeping Car Porters, 1925–37*. Urbana: University of Illinois Press, 1977. Gives the reaction of Randolph to Communists and the ANLC.

Wesley, Charles H. "Organized Labor and the Negro." *Journal of Negro Education* 8 (July 1939): 449–461. Provides good information on the role of African Americans in the U.S. labor movement.

—Jeffrey E. Page

AME ZION CHURCH. When Methodism arrived in New York State in 1766, it welcomed blacks into its Christian fellowship. As the Methodist Church expanded it became increasingly discriminatory toward African Americans. After years of ill treatment, in 1796 the 155 black members of the John Street Methodist Episcopal Church in New York City formed a separate church. Although incorporated in 1821 under the name African Methodist Episcopal Church in America, the church was never affiliated with the denomination of the same name organized in 1816 by Richard Allen in Philadelphia. Zion was the name of the New York denomination's first chapel, built in 1801. The AME Zion Church adhered to the doctrines of the Methodist Episcopal Church and adopted an episcopal form of government.

The AME Zion denomination grew as churches were added in Connecticut, New Jersey, and Pennsylvania. Their affiliation with the Methodist Episcopal Church ended when James Varick was ordained the first bishop of the AME Zion Church in 1822. The name "Zion" was added to the denominational title in 1848 to distinguish the church from the AME Church. The church became known as a "freedom church" for assisting slaves to escape to the North. Abolitionists who were members of the Zion church included Harriet Tubman, Frederick Douglass, and Sojourner Truth. Several AME Zion churches served as Underground Railroad stations.

In 1864 Mother AME Zion Church, the original Zion Chapel, moved from 152 Church Street in lower Manhattan to West Tenth and Bleecker Streets in Greenwich Village. After the end of the Civil War, large numbers of former slaves joined the denomination when Bishop James W. Hood organized missions throughout the South. Also established were schools for children and uneducated adults. The church's publishing company, the Book Concern, published the *Star of Zion* newspaper from 1876 and the *AME Zion Quarterly Review* from 1890. Tuskegee Institute in Alabama had its origins in the AME Zion Church. By the 1880s the church had expanded westward to Missouri, Wyoming, Oregon, California, and Nevada. When Bishop Hood made Julia Foote a deacon in 1894, the church became the first African American denomination to ordain women. In 1896 Booker T. Washington gave the keynote address at the church's centennial celebration, which took place at its new location, 127 West Eighty-ninth Street in New York.

The twentieth century ushered in a period of turmoil for the denomination. The membership of Mother Zion declined when several pastors were assigned in succession during a ten-year period. Despite hard times, between 1900 and 1904, AME Zion Church raised $2 million for the economic advancement of the African American community. Mother Zion moved uptown to 127 West Eighty-ninth Street in 1904. Beginning in 1910, Bishop Alexander Walters organized missions in West Africa, South America, and the West Indies. Bishop Walters was an influential AME Zion minister who helped found the NAACP in 1910 and was an early vice president of the organization. By 1906 the denomination numbered 184,542 members in 2,197 churches in the United States.

World War I was a time of racial tension and economic difficulties throughout the United States. Thousands of blacks came north to fill war-related jobs. Many of the newly arrived affiliated with the AME Zion Church. In 1914, Mother Zion moved to 151 West 136th Street, and in 1925 the church moved again, into a newly constructed neo-Gothic church building at 140 West 137th Street; it remained there in the twenty-first century. The move to the Harlem community brought a period of renewal for Mother Zion as the church began to gain prominence as a leading religious and social institution. Membership of the AME Zion denomination numbered 700,000 by 1916.

The second wave of the denomination's expansion began in the 1940s with the Second Great Migration. As the country recovered from the economic hardships of the Depression, there was a resurgence of racial violence. This social unrest required the church to rethink its social responsibilities to the black community. The 1944 General Conference did not support U.S. participation in World War II. Mother Zion served as a platform for the political activism of nationally known African Americans including Langston Hughes, W. E. B. Du Bois, and Paul Robeson. Membership at Mother Zion grew to six thousand during the pastorate of Robeson's brother, Dr. Benjamin C. Robeson, from 1936 to 1963. The 150-year celebration held in 1946 included congratulatory speeches from Mary McLeod Bethune and Adam Clayton Powell Jr. President Harry S. Truman received a delegation from the AME Zion Church during that year.

AME Zion churches played pivotal roles in the organization of the bus boycott in Montgomery, Alabama, in 1954. Following the *Brown v. Board of Education* decision in 1954, the church participated in the struggle to desegregate public schools in the South. Zion members marched from Selma to Montgomery in 1965. Prominent church members include the pathologist and educator

AME Zion Church Congregation. The congregation of Bush Chapel AME Zion Church in Barrow County, Georgia, gathers on Easter Sunday, 1920. VANISHING GEORGIA COLLECTION, GEORGIA ARCHIVES

Dr. Solomon C. Fuller, the sculptor Selma Burke, the New York attorney Ruth Whitehead Whaley, and the president of Atlanta University, Rufus Early Clement. The church's commitment to the economic development of the black community was furthered when Bishop Herbert Bell Shaw was elected chairman of the National Conference of Black Churchmen (NCBC) in 1967.

The establishment of nursing homes, health-care centers, and educational facilities by the AME Zion Church brought improved socioeconomic opportunities to the black community. Each year summer and recreational camps are held on several church-owned properties. During the 1970s the AME Zion Church completed several housing projects with federal government funding in New York, North Carolina, and Michigan. In 1972, Mother Zion completed the building of the James Varick Community Center in Harlem. The center offers a day care, recreational programs, mental health services, and relocation services for the homeless. AME Zion educational institutions include Livingstone College and Hood Theological Seminary (1879), both in Salisbury, North Carolina; Clinton Junior College (1894) in Rock Hill, South Carolina; and Lomax-Hannon Junior College (1893) in Greenville, Alabama. Foreign missions are maintained in Liberia, Sierra Leone, Belize, Honduras, and Haiti; the church also sponsors training schools and educational centers in Africa. In 1999 the church had more than 2 million members in 6,200 churches.

[*See also* AME Church; Black Church; *and* Religion.]

BIBLIOGRAPHY

Edwards, Cornell, and Diane Chappelle, eds. *An Epic of the People: Mother AME Zion Church*. New York: Mother AME Zion Church, 2001. A photographic journal completed by the Historical Committee of Mother Zion Church.

Pinn, Anthony B. *The Black Church in the Post–Civil Rights Era*. Maryknoll, N.Y.: Orbis Books, 2002. A good discussion of the contemporary issues confronting all black churches.

Walls, William J. *The African Methodist Episcopal Zion Church: Reality of the Black Church*. Charlotte, N.C.: AME Zion Publishing House, 1974. A detailed history of the church, written by one of its bishops.

—Kerima M. Lewis

AMOS 'N' ANDY. *Amos 'n' Andy*, both the radio show and the television show that followed, is a name that conjures up racial stereotypes. *Amos 'n' Andy* was one of the twentieth century's most popular and controversial comedy shows depicting black characters.

The show was the creation of two enterprising white actors and musicians, Freeman F. Gosden and Charles J. Correll. In 1925 Gosden and Correll debuted as musicians on WGN radio in Chicago. After discussions with station management regarding a new radio show, the pair suggested a blackface minstrel show in which they would play black characters. The original names of the characters were Sam and Henry; *Sam 'n' Henry* debuted on 12 January 1926. The show used stereotypical representations of black speech and black urban life.

Sam 'n' Henry ran on WGN for two years and was quite successful. Some critics such as Mel Watkins suggest that the characters Sam and Henry owed much to material borrowed from prominent black comedic acts in contemporary Chicago. The show became so popular that Gosden and Correll suggested that it be recorded and that the rights to rebroadcast the shows then be sold to other radio stations throughout the country—a concept that is now known as syndication. WGN did not like the idea, so Gosden and Correll quit the station and eventually went to WMAQ, a rival station, where the renamed *Amos 'n' Andy* show—WGN continued to own the rights to the name *Sam 'n' Henry*—first aired on 19 March 1928. Using the syndication network of the *Chicago Daily News*, the parent company of WMAQ, Gosden and Correll succeeding in distributing their show to interested stations, with each episode airing simultaneously nationwide. Though the names of the characters had changed, little else had; Sam (Godsden) and Henry (Correll) were now reborn as Amos Jones and Andrew Hogg Brown.

Cast of *Amos 'n' Andy*. Alvin Childress as Amos Jones (*left*), Tim Moore as George "Kingfish" Stevens (*center*), and Spencer Williams as Andrew Hogg Brown (*right*) of the *Amos 'n' Andy* show (CBS), 1951–1953. CBS/Photofest

Amos 'n' Andy was the most popular of the minstrel-style shows common on radio during the 1920s and 1930s, a genre that included such shows as the *Burnt Cork Review*, the *Sealy Air Minstrels*, *George and Rufus*, *Aunt Jemima*, and *Plantation Party*. These shows featured blackface acts such as Honey Boy and Sassafras and Molasses 'n' January (*Showboat*), Moonshine and Sawdust (the *Gulf Show*), Buck and Wheat (*Aunt Jemima*), and Watermelon and Cantaloupe (*Corn Cob Pipe Club*).

For the program's entire run as a nightly radio serial, Gosden and Correll portrayed all the male roles. At first Amos Jones and Andy Brown worked on a Georgia farm not far from Atlanta, and during the episodes of the first week they made plans to travel north to Chicago. With four ham-and-cheese sandwiches and twenty-four dollars, they bought train tickets and headed for Chicago, where they lived in a State Street roominghouse and experienced some rough times before launching their own business, the Fresh Air Taxi Company.

With the advent of commercial success and a national audience, the serial's central characters—Amos, Andy, and George "Kingfish" Stevens—relocated from Chicago to Harlem. Other characters included John Augustus "Brother" Crawford, an industrious but long-suffering family man; Henry Van Porter, a social-climbing real estate broker and insurance salesman; Frederick Montgomery Gwindell, a hard-charging newspaperman; Ruby (Taylor) Jones, Amos's fiancée and later wife; William Lewis Taylor, her well-spoken, college-educated father; and Lightnin', a slow-moving, "Stepin Fetchit"–type character. The show was an incredible national success, listened to by both whites and blacks. Based on the popularity of the show, Correll and Gosden starred in an Amos and Andy film in 1930, *Check and Double Check*, in blackface. In 1943 the radio program went from a fifteen-minute CBS weekday dramatic serial to an NBC half-hour weekly comedy. At this point some African American comedy professionals were brought in to fill out the cast.

The show's caricatures of African American life and its perpetuation of racist stereotypes led to national protests by outraged African Americans. Leading the protest efforts against the show were the African Methodist Episcopal bishop W. J. Walls, the publisher of the *Pittsburgh Courier* Robert Vann, and the scholar Benjamin Brawley. In the December 1930 issue of *Abbott's Monthly*, Bishop Walls wrote an article that sharply criticized the show. From the pages of the *Pittsburgh Courier*, Vann began a petition to get the program pulled from the air, with a stated goal of a million signatures.

CBS Television bought the rights to *Amos 'n' Andy* in 1948, and the show was produced from 1951 to 1953 with seventy-eight filmed episodes. Although Gosden and Correll wanted to play the title roles themselves, the producers were able to convince them to use black actors to play the black characters on television. So the TV series did use African American actors in the main roles, although the actors were instructed to keep their voices and speech patterns as close to Gosden and Correll's as possible. Amos was played by Alvin Childress, Andy by Spencer Williams, and Kingfish by Tim Moore. Many of the shows were devoted to Kingfish as head of the Mystic Knights of Sea Lodge. Ernestine Wade played Sapphire, Kingfish's wife. Ramona Smith, Sapphire's mother, was played by Amanda Randolph, and Lightnin' was played by Horace Stewart.

Shortly after the television program debuted in 1951, the NAACP mounted a formal protest, including publishing an article entitled "Why the *Amos 'n' Andy* Show Should Be Taken Off the Air." Pressure from the organization helped to force the show's cancellation at the end of the 1953 season. However, the show remained in syndication until 1966 when CBS, under continued pressure from the NAACP and other civil rights groups, finally canceled it again.

[*See also* Broadcast Industry, African Americans in the; Film and Television Depictions of African Americans; Minstrel Tradition; Radio; Stereotypes of African Americans; *and* Television.]

BIBLIOGRAPHY

Ely, Melvin Patrick. *The Adventures of Amos 'n' Andy: A Social History of an American Phenomenon*. New York: Free Press, 1991. A thorough discussion of both the radio show and the television program, with detailed discussion of the controversies surrounding them.

McLeod, Elizabeth. *The Original Amos 'n' Andy: Freeman Gosden, Charles Correll, and the 1928–1943 Radio Serial*. Jefferson, N.C.: McFarland, 2005. Principally a sympathetic discussion of the origins and impact of the *Amos 'n' Andy* radio show.

Watkins, Mel. *On the Real Side: Laughing, Lying, and Signifying—The Underground Tradition of African-American Humor That Transformed American Culture, from Slavery to Richard Pryor*. New York: Simon & Schuster, 1994. Offers a historical look at *Amos 'n' Andy*, focusing on the show as an example of "racial ventriloquy."

—FRANK E. DOBSON JR.

AMSTERDAM NEWS. In 1909—the same year that W. E. B. Du Bois helped found the NAACP and that the African American Matthew Henson went with Robert Peary on what became the first successful journey to the North Pole—James Henry Anderson from South Carolina established the *New York Amsterdam News*. Anderson was born soon after the Civil War. At the age of twelve he left South Carolina, a runaway who worked an assortment of jobs, finally settling in New York City. He came up with the idea of establishing a newspaper aimed directly at the needs of an African American audience. This was a brave move on his part: at the time, there were only about fifty such newspapers in the entire country.

Anderson's small investment led to the *Amsterdam News*, a newspaper that grew to have a strong influence in the black community. He named the newspaper after his own neighborhood in Harlem, and he used his wife's dressmaker's table to lay out the newspaper. At first the *Amsterdam News* cost two cents an issue and had six pages of news; it came out once a week and stuck to city news—mainly news that concerned the black community.

In 1910 Anderson took in a partner, Edward A. Warren. When Warren died in 1921, his widow and daughter took over the newspaper's money interests. In 1926, five years before his death, Anderson left the *Amsterdam News*, selling his shares to the Warrens. Anderson spent his remaining years as a leading citizen, taking an interest in various community affairs, including serving as a Boy Scout commissioner.

Growth and a Period of Problems. The *Amsterdam News* continued its growth under the Warrens. In 1930 the *Amsterdam News* became a member of the Audit Bureau of Circulation, the second black newspaper to do so. A Brooklyn office opened in 1932. However, the Great Depression and labor problems began to hit the newspaper. Workers demanded more money, and in 1935 they went on strike and ultimately unionized; thus the *News* became unionized because black workers went on strike against black owners. The *News* was the first totally unionized black newspaper in the United States.

The strike and its aftermath forced the Warrens into bankruptcy and compelled them to sell the newspaper for only $5,000, a bargain even during the Depression. Following the sale the newspaper resumed its prosperous growth. The new owners, Drs. C. B. Powell and Phillip M. H. Savory, guided the newspaper into national prominence, and it had great influence. The newspaper earlier had influence in the Republican Party; during the 1930s it switched to the Democrats and supported Franklin D. Roosevelt and his New Deal. The newspaper also forged an alliance between Jews and African Americans.

During World War II the *Amsterdam News* continued to champion the cause of black Americans, this time of those in the military. It united with other newspapers in African American communities in endorsing the "Double V" campaign—a campaign for double victory, in the fight for democratic rights both at home and around the world. That African Americans did not have democratic rights at home even as they fought for democratic rights abroad was an irony that the newspaper's writers exploited to great effect.

The Civil Rights Period. By the middle of the twentieth century the *Amsterdam News* had become the largest black newspaper in the United States and a prominent champion of the civil rights movement. The *News* was a consistent supporter of Martin Luther King Jr.'s nonviolent program and of his leadership of the movement. That support, however, did not hinder the *Amsterdam News* from noting the black community's rising support for Elijah Muhammad and Malcolm X.

Savory died in 1965, leaving Powell alone as publisher. In April 1971, Powell sold his newspaper to a group consisting of the Manhattan Borough president Percy Sutton, the financier Clarence Jones, and Wilbert A. Tatum. The $5,000 investment had grown to $2.3 million. During the 1970s the *Amsterdam News* became more militant, but by the end of the decade it had resumed a more moderate position; it also went from a broadsheet format to a tabloid format.

In 1983 the *Amsterdam News* faced another strike. The next year it had a new publisher, Wilbert Tatum. Tatum led the newspaper back to more controversial stands, and it involved itself deeply in local matters.

Significance of the *Amsterdam News*. Many prominent African Americans have written for the *Amsterdam News*, from W. E. B. Du Bois through Adam Clayton Powell Jr., and including Roy Wilkins and Malcolm X. These writers have added much to the authenticity of the *Amsterdam News* and have exhibited the range of opinions within the black community. Indeed, Marvel Cooke, a prominent journalist and civil rights activist during the Harlem Renaissance, was a staff writer for the *Amsterdam News*, and she was the paper's first woman news reporter.

After Wilbert Tatum's death in 1982, his daughter Elinor began to run the *Amsterdam News*. Elinor Tatum brought the newspaper into the twenty-first century and has made use of online technology to continue the paper's legacy and broaden its reach. She still adheres to Anderson's goal of serving the needs of the black community and being its voice.

[*See also* Black-Jewish Relations; Black Press; Harlem; Journalism, Print and Broadcast; *and* New York City.]

BIBLIOGRAPHY

Brandt, Nat. *Harlem at War: The Black Experience in WWII*. Syracuse, N.Y.: Syracuse University Press, 1996.

Greenberg, Cheryl Lynn. *"Or Does It Explode?": Black Harlem in the Great Depression*. New York: Oxford University Press, 1991.

Jacobs, Ronald N. *Race, Media, and the Crisis of Civil Society: From Watts to Rodney King*. New York: Cambridge University Press, 2000.

Krenn, Michael L. *Black Diplomacy: African Americans and the State Department, 1945–1969*. Armonk, N.Y.: M. E. Sharpe, 1999.

Trotta, Liz. "Combative Publisher Revels in Controversy." *Washington Times*, 20 January 1998.

—FRANK A. SALAMONE

ANDERSON, CHARLES WILLIAM (b. 28 April 1866; d. 28 January 1938), internal revenue collector and Republican politician. Charles Anderson was the black Karl Rove of his day; he was Booker T. Washington's most trusted confidante and an activist in Washington's cause from his location in New York City. There is some dispute as to whether Anderson was born in Oxford, Ohio, or in Tennessee, as census records seem to suggest. Though for the most part self-educated, he did attend public schools in Oxford and Middleton, Ohio, as well as Spencerian Business College in Cleveland and the Berlitz School of Languages in Worcester, Massachusetts. Moving to New York City in 1886, he immediately became involved in Republican politics, stumping in the Negro wards. In 1890 he became president of the Young Men's Colored Republican Club of New York County, and by 1895 he was considered a "prominent" black New Yorker by the *Times*, which reported him among members of the Douglass Club, which tested the Civil Rights Act of 1895 by organizing groups of blacks to visit twenty restaurants, hotels, and bathhouses. After gaining admission to seventeen of the facilities, Anderson threatened lawsuits against two restaurants which did not admit them (O'Neil's and Thorgeson's). Since this activity aroused the objection of the Booker T. Washington forces from Tuskegee Institute, one wonders if this is when the first contact was made between them. It is not clear that Anderson followed through on the lawsuits.

Anderson received his first patronage position as gauger in a district office of the Internal Revenue Service in 1890. He would remain in public office, except for a few months in 1915, until retiring in 1934, the most recognized black politician in New York. James Weldon Johnson, who gained fame as a writer and as the NAACP executive secretary in the 1920s, first met Anderson in about 1899, most likely at New York City's Hotel Marshall, when Johnson and his brother Rosamond first came to New York City to try out the musical comedy business. In his autobiography, *Along This Way* (1933), Johnson describes his friend as smart, cultured, and perceptive, a gifted leader, with excellent oratorical skills. Anderson preferred his cultured discussions with a glass of champagne in his hand and sprinkled his speeches with Shakespearean allusions.

In the summer of 1904, Anderson came to Johnson with what he called a "strange request." President Theodore Roosevelt's campaign for reelection was just beginning, and Anderson dropped in the Cole and Johnson Brothers studio to reveal his plans for a "Colored Republican Club" on West Fifty-third Street, in a three-story-plus-basement across from the Marshall. It would be furnished in "good style," complete with billiard and pool rooms, an assembly room, a lounge and card rooms, and committee rooms. Money had already been provided, and Anderson prevailed upon Johnson to be treasurer and chair the house committee. After a grand opening, with universal surprise at the elegance of the appointments, membership increased, assisted by Johnson bringing in weekly performers from the Marshall.

Anderson's payoff in his effective activities for President Roosevelt was an appointment in March 1905 as collector of internal revenue for the Second District of New York City, which included Wall Street. It was a "personal" appointment, the *Times* reported, with little the senators could or would do to stop it, thought there was some "ugly talk." Folks who knew Charlie Anderson were surprised, said the *Times*, since they thought he was happy with the twenty-five-hundred-dollar job he held through the New York State Republicans as inspector of racing for the Racing Commission—at least judging by the number of horse races he bet on all over the state. But this new job was a sinecure, the article ended, and would give Anderson plenty of time to continue his political and social activities.

And indeed, Anderson did appear to have a lot of time in the next decade, to be Booker T. Washington's eyes and ears and nose and all-around dirty trickster in New York City. It was Anderson who arranged for a reporter to castigate the interracial Cosmopolitan Club Dinner of 1908 and again in 1912. It was Anderson who infiltrated the early meetings of the NAACP and reported back to Washington just who was meeting with "the enemy." It was Anderson who brought James Weldon Johnson to Fred Moore at the *Age* as an editorial writer (when Johnson returned from abroad from the political appointments he had received from Roosevelt via Anderson and Washington), effectively keeping this rising star from the W. E. B. Du Bois NAACP camp just a little bit longer.

It must be said that, by all accounts, Anderson did his collector's job very conscientiously, fairly, and efficiently, so much so that he was the last of the Republican appointees to be removed under the Democratic president Woodrow Wilson. He moved on to become New York's supervising agent of the agriculture department, from 1915 to 1922, when President Warren Harding returned him to his post as collector of internal revenue, this time for the Third District, New York City, a post he held until retirement in 1934, when his wife, Emma Anderson, died.

Anderson seems to have lost his touch and some of his enthusiasm for the game after the death of Booker T. Washington in 1915. A. Philip Randolph, in the Socialist *Messenger*, in July 1919, wrote that men like Anderson were "of the old school who make much over what they style as 'playing the game of politics,' which in other words simply means getting next to 'campaign slush funds' and landing a rubber stamp job. Their positions rest upon their ability to echo the will of the masters through flamboyant oratory and their unquestioning obedience to the Republican machine."

Anderson and Fred Moore of the *Age* had long competed both openly and secretly—including Anderson's keeping Washington fully informed about Moore's activities when "the Wizard of Tuskegee" was alive. In 1922, with a change of leadership in the Negro Business League, additional stress was put on the organization by the unexpected bankruptcy of Charles W. Anderson, the league's treasurer. He had also misappropriated league funds, Fred Moore wrote, leaving situations "so entangled that it will take more than a Philadelphia lawyer to straighten them out." Emmett Scott, who was leaving the organization's presidency, is the person who disclosed Anderson's misuse of $2,104.11 of league funds.

Anderson died on 28 January 1938 in his home at 156 West 132nd Street, of pneumonia, after a three-year illness. Three hundred people attended his brief Episcopal funeral, and "many members of his race now active in public life paid tribute," wrote the *Times*. He was buried in Woodlawn Cemetery.

[*See also* Moore, Fred R.; National Negro Business League; *and* Republican Party.]

BIBLIOGRAPHY

Burrows, John H. *The Necessity of Myth: A History of the National Negro Business League, 1900–1945*. Auburn, Ala.: Hickory Hill Press, 1988. This book documents the way in which the Gospel of Wealth was a big part of the Negro Business League; it also discusses Anderson's bankruptcy in the 1920s and his misuse of league funds.

Johnson, James Weldon. *Along This Way*. New York: Viking, 1933. Johnson speaks highly of Anderson from their early meetings, between 1904 and 1912, and then Anderson "my good friend" disappears from the book.

Levy, Eugene. *James Weldon Johnson: Black Leader, Black Voice*. Chicago: University of Chicago Press, 1973. This book states Anderson's essence very nicely, in calling him "the quintessential politician," a minor but significant part of the wedge President Roosevelt constructed between "rival New York Republican factions."

—CAROLYN WEDIN

ANDERSON, EDDIE (b. 18 September 1905; d. 28 February 1977), actor and comedian. Anderson's character Rochester, the manservant in the Jack Benny radio shows and films of the 1930s and 1940s and later on the *Jack Benny Show* on network television, brought him fame and fortune and made him a household name in mid-twentieth-century America. During the 1930s and later, most African American screen actors and actresses who took roles in white-produced Hollywood films were depicted in subservient or demeaning parts. Anderson, however, was the independent, hilariously witty favorite loved by audiences across the nation. His unique ability to stir his audience with humor and sympathy made him the highest-paid black actor of his time. Though his role as a manservant was superficially subservient, he was in fact saucy, sarcastic, ironic, and anything but subservient. His trademark answer to his boss, "Yes, Mister Benny," was delivered in a tone that let viewers know that Rochester was equally as powerful as his employer in their shared life.

Edmund Lincoln Anderson was born in Oakland, California. Growing up in a family of circus performers and entertainers, he learned show business from a young age. His father, known as "Big Ed" Anderson in the circus, was a minstrel player, and his mother Ella Anderson was a tightrope walker. Eddie, his brother Cornelius Anderson, and a friend formed an act called the Three Black Aces.

Anderson's first major screen role was playing the character known as Noah in the 1936 movie *The Green Pastures*. His character in an all-black cast portrayed a comic yet pitiable black manservant, a Hollywood role that traditionally depicted subservience and submission. But the character Anderson played in Benny's television shows and films was different from previous black character roles. Anderson costarred with Benny as the manservant who was an equal to his boss in crafty and humorous ways. Rochester always got the last laugh. He comically exposed his boss's goofs or mishaps while, most important, creating a scenario in which the humor was not about color but about human idiosyncrasies and behaviors. Benny's television show was one of the first to elevate an African American actor because of his or her talents as an actor. Anderson was responsible for much of Benny's success.

Anderson's biggest parts came during the 1940s in some of Hollywood's most liberal black feature films, such as *Cabin in the Sky* (1943), which had an all-black cast. For the first time in Hollywood the black man was given a sense of sexuality, heroism, individuality, and human character. In *Cabin in the Sky* the married Little Joe Jackson, played by Anderson, is seen chasing after the beautiful Lena Horne. When Petunia, Anderson's wife, declares that she is leaving him for good, the audience is sympathetic and emotionally moved. Anderson's more than forty films include *What Price Hollywood?* (1932), *It Happened in New Orleans* (1936), *Three Men on a Horse* (1936), *Topper Double Bill* (1937), *Gone with the Wind* (1939), *Honolulu* (1939), *Kiss the Boys Goodbye* (1941), *Birth of the Blues* (1941), *Topper Returns* (1941), *Tales of Manhattan* (1942), *Stormy Weather* (1943), *Brewster's Millions* (1945), *I Love a Bandleader* (1945), and *The Show-off* (1946). His talent gave rise to the acceptance of other African American actors and actresses and paved the way for their success. America loved Rochester, tuning in each week and waiting to see what he would do next. A few years after the *Jack Benny Show* ended in the 1960s, Anderson died at the age of seventy-two.

[*See also* Actors and Actresses; Comedians; Film and Television Depictions of African Americans; *and* Stereotypes of African Americans.]

BIBLIOGRAPHY

Bogle, Donald. *Prime Time Blues: African Americans on Network Television*. New York: Farrar, Straus & Giroux, 2001.

Bogle, Donald. *Toms, Coons, Mulattoes, Mammies, and Bucks: An Interpretive History of Blacks in American Films*. 3d ed. New York: Continuum, 1994.

—MARIA STILSON

ANDERSON, MARIAN (b. 27 February 1897; d. 8 April 1993), opera singer. Marian Anderson was born on 27 February 1897 in South Philadelphia, Pennsylvania, the first of three daughters born to Anna and John Anderson. Nicknamed the "baby contralto" for her lush, deep voice when she sang in local churches as a child, Anderson fought hard to foster her career in Europe and the United States, and in the process she became an advocate for civil rights in the United States.

When Anderson was twelve years old her father died from a head injury sustained while working at Philadelphia's Reading Terminal Market. He was thirty-four years old, and his death left his widow, Anna, with three young daughters to raise. They moved in with Marian's paternal grandparents. Anna had been a teacher before she married Marian's father, but she was not credentialed in Pennsylvania. To keep her family together, Anna took in laundry and worked as a cleaning woman for a local department store. Marian and her sisters did odd jobs to help with the family's finances.

Anderson loved music and sang in both the junior and senior choirs at the Union Baptist Church in Philadelphia, where her family worshipped. Singing came naturally to her, and she sang often in public. She found a mentor in Roland Hayes, a renowned African American classical singer who garnered an international reputation and regularly appeared at her church. He encouraged Anderson

Marian Anderson. The singer Marian Anderson with Kurt Johnen, Berlin, 1931. THE WALTER J. AND LEONORE ANNENBERG RARE BOOK AND MANUSCRIPT LIBRARY, UNIVERSITY OF PENNSYLVANIA

to take formal voice lessons. Church members donated money to pay for the lessons, and Anderson applied to a local school. The experience was her first with race discrimination. She was abruptly told that the school did not accept African Americans. She studied instead with Mary Saunders Patterson, a well-known singer who lived several blocks from the Anderson family, and when Patterson felt that Anderson had outgrown her, Anderson studied with Agnes Reifsnyder, a white vocal coach who did not discriminate against talented African American students.

Anderson's first contact with the Jim Crow laws of the South came in 1917 when she was invited to sing at the Georgia Industrial State College in Savannah. When they changed trains in Washington, D.C., Anderson and her mother were steered toward the back of the train to the coaches reserved for African Americans. The filth of the coach, both inside and out, and the poor air quality made a lasting impression on Anderson.

Anderson spent years honing her singing career. She sang at New York City's Town Hall in 1924 to stinging reviews. Though critics liked her voice, they suggested that she needed to work on her technique. The experience hurt, but Anderson worked in earnest to develop as a vocalist. She won a contest sponsored by the National Music League in 1925 and then studied with vocal coaches in the United States and Europe, learning her repertoire and the nuances of the foreign languages necessary to be a top classical singer. Anderson first sang at Carnegie Hall in 1928 and performed highly regarded concerts throughout Europe in the 1930s.

Anderson became a symbol of the struggle for civil rights in the United States in 1939 when the Daughters of the American Revolution (DAR) refused a request from Howard University to host a concert featuring Anderson in front of an integrated audience at Constitution Hall in Washington, D.C. The hall was home to both the Washington Opera Company and the National Symphony Orchestra and was part of the DAR's national headquarters. Anderson had sung often in Washington, D.C. After returning from a triumphant European tour in 1936, Howard University's concert hall was deemed too small to hold Anderson's fans. The university tried several locations between 1936 and 1939, but each time the demand for tickets outstripped the hall's capacity. Constitution Hall was the one hall in Washington, D.C., whose acoustics and four-thousand-seat capacity compared to the concert halls in which Anderson routinely sang.

The DAR, however, had instituted a "white artists only" policy in 1932. The university had applied before for permission to host Anderson at Constitution Hall and had been denied. This time Howard officials did not back down. V. D. Johnston, the university's treasurer, wrote an open letter published in the *Washington Times-Herald* decrying the DAR's decision. The *Times-Herald* responded with an op-ed piece on why it was important to allow Anderson to sing at Constitution Hall. In reaction a powerful group of supporters, including First Lady Eleanor Roosevelt, the executive secretary of the NAACP Walter White, and the secretary of the interior Harold Ickes worked to gather public support to pressure the DAR to reconsider its decision.

After also being turned down by a local school board to host a concert at Armstrong High School, Anderson's manager Sol Hurok, White, and Ickes arranged for Anderson to perform a free public concert on Easter Sunday, 9 April 1939, at five o'clock in front of the Lincoln Memorial. Seventy-five thousand people showed up to hear her sing. Neither Anderson nor the people who heard her ever forgot the experience. To the end of her life people would approach Anderson to tell her that they had heard her Easter concert and how much it had meant to them to hear her glorious voice.

Anderson married her high school sweetheart, Orpheus Fisher, in 1943 and retired in 1965. Her career included many firsts. In the 1930s she was the first African American to perform in Scandinavia. She was the first African American to perform with the New York Metropolitan Opera, when in 1955 she sang the role of Ulrica in Guiseppe Verdi's *Un ballo in maschera* (A Masked Ball). She went on to become the first African American permanent member of the Metropolitan Opera company.

Anderson's work was global beyond her singing career. She became a United Nations goodwill ambassador and in 1958 was officially named a delegate to the United Nations. In 1963 Anderson was one of the first recipients of the Presidential Medal of Freedom. She died in Portland, Oregon, at the home of her nephew, James DePriest, on 8 April 1993 at the age of ninety-six. Anderson is buried at Eden Cemetery in Collingdale, Pennsylvania.

[*See also* Music; Price, Leontyne; *and* Roosevelt, Eleanor, and African Americans.]

BIBLIOGRAPHY

Anderson, Marian. *My Lord, What a Morning: An Autobiography*. Music in American Life Series. Urbana: University of Illinois Press, 2002.

Anderson, Marian, with the Victory Symphony Orchestra. *The Lady from Philadelphia*. Wadhurst, U.K.: Pearl, 1993. Compact disc.

Freedman, Russell. *The Voice That Challenged a Nation: Marian Anderson and the Struggle for Equal Rights*. New York: Clarion Books, 2004.

Keiler, Allan. *Marian Anderson: A Singer's Journey*. Music in American Life Series. Urbana: University of Illinois Press, 2002.

—SUSAN EDWARDS

ANGELOU, MAYA (b. 4 April 1928), author and performer. Born Marguerite Ann Johnson in St. Louis, Missouri, to Bailey Johnson and Vivian Baxter Johnson, Angelou was given her shortened first name, Maya, by her brother Bailey. She later modified the name of her first husband, Tosh Angelos, to whom she was married from 1952 to 1955, to form her last name. Her parents divorced soon after her birth, and in 1930 she and her brother were sent to Stamps, Arkansas, where they were raised for most of the next ten years by their paternal grandmother, Anne Henderson (or "Momma"). After Angelou's graduation with honors in 1940 from Lafayette County Training School, she and her brother were put on a train for San Francisco, where they were to live with their recently remarried mother. In 1944 the unmarried sixteen-year-old Angelou gave birth to her only child, Clyde Johnson, later Guy Johnson, three weeks after her high school graduation.

Autobiographies. Angelou's life to this point became the subject of her first publication, the superbly written and honest *I Know Why the Caged Bird Sings* (1970), its title taken from the poem by Paul Laurence Dunbar. The book is dedicated to "My Son, Guy Johnson, and all the Strong Black Birds of Promise Who Defy the Odds and Gods and Sing Their Songs" and in it she thanks her mother and brother, the Harlem Writers' Guild, and many individuals. The honesty of Angelou's narration, especially of her seduction and rape by her mother's boyfriend and her decision as a teenager to have sex for the experience, which resulted in her pregnancy, has frequently put the book on censorship lists but also repeatedly on lists of best books for young adults and best of the best books for young adults. Valérie Baisnée, in *Gendered Resistance* (1997), looking at four women's autobiographies, praises Angelou's "ability to use the writer's voice to speak for social injustice mixed

Conference Speaker. Maya Angelou at the National Women's Conference, 1977. Photograph by Bettye Lane. © BETTYE LANE

with a resistance to the class, gender, and race ideologies that restrict the writer's autonomy" (p. 90).

In the years after Guy's birth, Angelou tried out many jobs and men, worked as the first black woman on a cable car and in a house of prostitution, and was tempted by narcotics. These events are narrated in the second volume of her autobiography, *Gather Together in My Name*, published in 1974. This book she dedicated to Bailey Johnson and other "real brothers" including James Baldwin. In the following volume, *Singin' and Swingin' and Gettin' Merry like Christmas* (1976), she has married Angelos and begun performing at the Purple Onion nightclub. The center of the book is the 1954 tour of Europe and Africa with a traveling theater company performing *Porgy and Bess* (in which Angelou played Ruby), under the auspices of the U.S. State Department.

In 1955 Angelou and her son moved to New York City, where she had no trouble meeting artists and writers, many through the Harlem Writer's Guild, and finding work, performing off-Broadway in *Calypso Heat Wave* and Jean Genet's *The Blacks*. She produced *Cabaret for Freedom* with Godfrey Cambridge and, at the request of Martin Luther King Jr., became the northern coordinator for the Southern Christian Leadership Conference (SCLC). These events form the core of *Heart of a Woman*, published in 1981. This book is dedicated to her grandson Colin Ashanti Murphy-Johnson with "special thanks to a few of the many sister/friends whose love encourages me to spell my name: WOMAN," followed by a list of fourteen, including the author Paule Marshall.

Within the space of two years, 1960–1962, Angelou met the South African freedom fighter Vusumzi Make, and she and her son moved to Cairo, Egypt, with him, then Angelou left Make (sources differ on whether they were officially married or not, though Angelou says they were) and moved with Guy to Ghana, where again she had no trouble marketing her talents and skills. She became a feature editor for the *African Review*, wrote articles for the *Ghanaian Times* and the Ghanaian Broadcasting Company, and worked as an administrative assistant at the University of Ghana. The Ghana experience became the center of the fifth volume of her autobiography, *All God's Children Need Traveling Shoes*, serialized in *Essence* magazine then published in book form in 1986. This book is dedicated to "Julian and Malcolm and all the fallen ones who were passionately and earnestly looking for a home." The title page is followed by "swing low, sweet chariot, coming for to carry me home."

The sixth volume of Angelou's autobiography did not appear until 2002. It covers the years 1964–1968, when she returned to the United States, and the intensities of the civil rights movement, including the assassinations of Malcolm X (whom Angelou first met in Ghana) in 1965 and of Martin Luther King Jr. (who was killed on her birthday) in 1968. This book, *A Song Flung up to Heaven*, is dedicated to her great-grandchildren Caylin Nicole Johnson and Brandon Bailey Johnson and "my entire family wherever and whoever you are." Angelou thanks "seven of my living teachers," including Andrew Young. In this relatively short volume, Angelou writes right before the end: "I thought about black women and wondered how we got to be the way we were. . . . We had come so far from where we started. . . . I thought if I wrote a book, I would have to examine the quality in the human spirit that continues to rise despite the slings and arrows of outrageous fortune" (Angelou, *Collected Autobiographies*, p. 1166).

One can also consider Angelou's delightful *Hallelujah! The Welcome Table: A Lifetime of Memories with Recipes* (2004) an autobiography. She intersperses life stories with recipes and photographs from her very social home and heart, such as the chapters "Assurance of Caramel Cake," "Momma's Grandbabies Love Cracklin' Cracklin'," "Potato Salad Towers Over Difficulties," and "Recipes from Another County."

Other Writings. Angelou's vast writing and publishing production beyond the six or seven autobiographies is all the more amazing because she says she does not write in her spacious redbrick colonial home or on a computer, but instead rents a hotel room, where she has a thesaurus, a Bible, a dictionary, a pack of cards, and yellow legal pads (on which she composes with a pen). She has published collections of essays, including *Wouldn't Take Nothing for My Journey Now* (1993) and *Even the Stars Look Lonesome* (1997); children's books, including *Life Doesn't Frighten Me* (1993), *My Painted House, My Friendly Chicken, and Me* (1994), *Kofi and His Magic* (1996), and four volumes of *Maya's World* (2004) on children in Lapland, Italy, France, and Hawaii; plays and screenplays; short stories; recordings; and spoken word albums.

But most popular with readers and audiences, if not with literary critics, are her poems, published in six collections between *Just Give Me a Cool Drink of Water Fore I Diiie* (1971), which was nominated for a Pulitzer Prize, and *I Shall Not Be Moved* (1990); a volume of her collected poems was issued in 1994. Most people are at least aware of Angelou as the poet of "On the Pulse of Morning" (1993), written and read at the request of the forty-second president of the United States Bill Clinton at his inauguration on 20 January 1993. After that event Angelou became a popular presenter of poems for special occasions, including "A Brave and Startling Truth" at the fiftieth anniversary of the United Nations on 26 June 1995; "From a Black Woman to a Black Man" at the Million Man March on 16 October 1995; and "Amazing Peace" at the National Christmas Tree Ceremony at the White House on 1 December 2005.

Other Work and Honors. Angelou also continued to perform in as well as write and direct a large number of television programs and films, including documentaries and feature films, and she performed in classic plays, such as Bertold Brecht's *Mother Courage* and Jean Anouilh's *Medea*. She received an Emmy nomination for her depiction of Nyo Boto, or Grandmother, in the 1977 miniseries of Alex Haley's *Roots*; her poems were featured, and she made a short appearance, in the 1993 Janet Jackson and John Singleton movie *Poetic Justice*; she appeared as Anna in *How to Make an American Quilt* (1995); and she directed *Down in the Delta* (1998).

It is not possible to list here even a fraction of the honorary degrees, woman of the year, and other awards Angelou accumulated, the many commissions and councils and boards she served on, or the distinguished visiting professor posts and writer in residence positions she held. In 1981 she became the first Reynold's Professor of American Studies at Wake Forest University in Winston-Salem, North Carolina, a lifetime appointment. She is an admired performer on the lecture circuit, giving of herself unstintingly in these presentations. Joanne Braxton, in *Modern American Women Writers* (1993), describes Angelou's lectures and readings as almost "hypnotic"—she "performs, lectures, scolds, and teaches" (p. 7). Angelou is an exceptionally talented, skilled, and accessible author, speaker, and performer.

[*See also* Actors and Actresses; Literature; *Roots*; *and* Southern Christian Leadership Conference.]

BIBLIOGRAPHY

Angelou, Maya. *The Collected Autobiographies of Maya Angelou*. New York: Modern Library, 2004. Includes the full texts of the six autobiographies.

Angelou, Maya. *The Complete Collected Poems of Maya Angelou*. New York: Random House, 1994. Thirty-eight poems from *Just Give Me a Cool Drink of Water Fore I Diiie*, thirty-six from *O Pray My Wings Are Gonna Fit Me Well*, thirty-two from *And Still I Rise*, twenty-eight from *Shaker, Why Don't You Sing*, thirty-two from *I Shall Not Be Moved*, and "On the pulse of Morning" from the Clinton inauguration.

Angelou, Maya. *Hallelujah! The Welcome Table: A Lifetime of Memories with Recipes*. New York: Random House, 2004.

Baisnée, Valérie. *Gendered Resistance: The Autobiographies of Simone de Beauvoir, Maya Angelou, Janet Frame, and Marguerite Duras*. Amsterdam and Atlanta: Rodopi, 1997.

Braxton, Joanne. "Maya Angelou." In *Modern American Women Writers*, edited by Elaine Showalter, Lea Baechler, and A. Walton Litz, pp. 1–7. New York: Collier, 1993.

Burr, Zofia. "Maya Angelou on the Inaugural Stage." In *Of Women, Poetry, and Power: Strategies of Address in Dickinson, Miles, Brooks, Lorde, and Angelou*, pp. 180–194. Urbana: University of Illinois Press, 2002. Delves into the Clinton inauguration poem in response to critics who say that Angelou's poetry is weakened by its performance nature and popularity. Excellent in going into her sources for writing the poem.

Elliot, Jeffrey M., ed. *Conversations with Maya Angelou*. Jackson: University Press of Mississippi, 1989. Over thirty interviews, including those with Bill Moyers and *Black Scholar*. Chronologically arranged; index.

Kite, L. Patricia. *Maya Angelou*. Minneapolis, Minn.: Lerner, 1999. Of the many books for junior high or high school readers, this is one of the better biographical books, with emphasis on Angelou's successful battling of the challenges of poverty, race discrimination, and single motherhood, and with good supplementary materials, including pictures of historical events. Sources; notes; extensive bibliography; index; many photos.

Landrum, Gene N. "Maya Angelou—Assertive; Author, Actress, Educator." In *Profiles of Black Success: Thirteen Creative Geniuses Who Changed the World*, pp. 109–125. Amherst, N.Y.: Prometheus, 1997. Angelou is one of three women discussed, along with Shirley Chisholm and Oprah Winfrey. Exceptional detailed biographical look at Angelou's strengths.

—CAROLYN WEDIN

ANNA T. JEANES FUND. Anna T. Jeanes was born 7 April 1822, the youngest of a large family of Quakers, or Religious Society of Friends. Six siblings, including Anna, lived long lives, but only one married, and none had children, so without cousins, nieces, nephews, or children of her own, Anna Jeanes was left in 1894 with a fortune largely from a brother's holdings in coal.

Jeanes had a keen sense of humor, a musical laugh, painting talent, a love of stories, and an independent spirit. She published books on world religions and of her own poetry, and she also endowed and planned the four-story, comfortable Friends' Boarding Home at Germantown, Pennsylvania, where she lived simply.

She died at age eighty-five; her will was filed in Philadelphia on 30 September 1907. She instructed that she be cremated, and she left money to encourage cremation for others. Her bequests included money to homes for aged and infirm colored persons, destitute colored children, blind men, and widows and single women; to various hospitals and soup societies, including the Friends' hospital for "cancerous, nervous and disabling ailments"; to Friends' Freeman Schools; to a firemen's pension fund; and to Swarthmore College (on the condition that they discontinue intercollegiate athletics).

But the major portion of her estate became the fund bearing her name, as her will read, "trusting, and believing, in the practicable and far-reaching good, that may result from the moral and elevating influence of Rural Schools for Negros in the South taught by reputable teachers." She appointed Booker T. Washington of Tuskegee Institute and Hollis Burke Frissell of Hampton, Virginia, as trustees of an endowment fund in perpetuity of one million dollars, with power to appoint a board, for a single purpose: community, country, or rural schools in the southern United States "for the purpose of rudimentary education." She was precise: the money was not to go to large schools.

The description of the elderly, minute Jeanes, weighing about seventy-five pounds, laying down the law to Washington and Frissell and George Foster Peabody—eminent figures among her choice of members for the General Education Board—dangling a million-dollar bequest before them, is priceless. They tried to argue her out of designating only certain government securities for investment, but she would not budge. Thus over the decades, the Anna T. Jeanes Fund suffered less from economic vagaries than did most other endowments. Signing the papers, she said, "Thee does not need to thank me. It is I who needs to thank thee, and I didn't do it to save my soul from hell, either!"

So after her death, the money was there, and the will was specific. She had also chosen William Howard Taft and Andrew Carnegie to be board members. Where to begin? Their early agreement was to study the general education situation, work with approval and cooperation of local public school officials, and provide "effective training for rural life among the Southern Negroes." James Hardy Dillard, a professor of Latin and the dean at Tulane University, trained in law also, was hired as the fund's first president in 1908; he held the post until his retirement in 1932, assisted by B. C. Caldwell of Louisiana as field director.

Washington, Frissell, Taft, and Carnegie all died in office as trustees (1916; 1918; 1930; 1920), as did original trustees Walter Hines Page (1919) and Robert Curtis Ogden (1914). From the original board, still alive and on the board in 1933 were George Foster Peabody, Robert Russa Moton, James C. Napier, James Hardy Dillard, Robert Lloyd Smith, and Samuel Chiles Mitchel. Later appointees included Emmett Julian Scott and Arthur Davis Wright. Washington was chair of the Executive Committee until his death, then Frissell was until his death, and then Robert Moton.

Virginia Estelle Randolph of Mountain Road School in Henrico County, Virginia, became the first Jeanes teacher, at age eighteen. Jackson Davis, as county superintendent, thought she could visit and help other schools as well, "a leader by being a servant of all." By 1909–1910, 129 Jeanes teachers were at work in 130 counties in thirteen southern states; by 1913–1914, there were 118 in 119 counties, twenty-nine men and eighty-nine women. Most of them were experienced teachers, about half educated at Hampton or Tuskegee or similar schools, and their reported activities were as varied as the needs in rural communities. "Industrial work" (sewing, darning, cooking, agriculture, gardening, blacksmithing, carpentry, and making chair seats, hammocks, and shuck mats) is first mentioned in reports to the fund, but soon there was also instruction in drawing and singing, building and repairing schools, and creating shelves, washing areas, and pumps. Health lectures were made to students and families, and improvement leagues and mothers' clubs were organized; concerts were arranged for fund-raising. Jeanes teachers or, as they came to be called, supervising teachers, often walked from place to place, carrying needed materials. By 1911, Dillard issued some guidance—keep in touch with school officials, he told them; assist in organizing people in the community; cooperate with ministers; introduce simple industrial work; encourage orderliness, promptness, cleanliness. All in all, the Jeanes Fund supported a kind of nascent domestic peace corps, and the goal was "Progress by Cooperation."

In 1909, the fund spent $14,759 on teacher's salaries, with no information about public monies included in the report. At its height of expenditure, in 1926, the fund spent $120,013 on those salaries, but the public contribution was by then $142,089. By 1932, the fund was down to $88,264 for salaries and the public up to $173,411. Questions arose as cooperation with public school officials led to increasing public school monies—how should Jeanes Fund money be spent? The board ventured increasingly into funding school buildings, longer school terms, and summer terms, especially in cooperation with the Slater Fund, which Dillard also headed. And cooperation with other philanthropies, particularly the Phelps-Stokes Fund, led, particularly under Thomas Jesse Jones's leadership of that fund, into model Jeanes schools and teachers being set up in Liberia and Kenya and other international locations, and exchanges with African teachers and administrators. In the late 1930s, several funds, including the Anna T. Jeanes Fund, merged to form the Southern Education Foundation. The Jeanes programs continued until the desegregation of the 1960s.

Over time the emphasis of the teaching changed from industrial to academic, with corresponding training. By 1933–1934, half of the 17 men, 177 married or widowed women, and 109 unmarried women who were Jeanes supervising teachers had training in academic curricula. Emphasis also changed to more supervisory roles rather than teaching. The impact of the Jeanes Fund, through Jeanes teachers especially, is as difficult to quantify or estimate as is any kind of teaching. But anecdotal evidence, as well as studies done using that evidence, suggests a large positive legacy.

[*See also* Peabody Education Fund; Phelps-Stokes Fund; Philanthropy; Quakers; *and* Slater Fund.]

BIBLIOGRAPHY

Brawley, Benjamin Griffith. *Doctor Dillard of the Jeanes Fund.* With an introduction by Anson Phelps Stokes. 1930. Reprint, Freeport, N.Y.: Books for Libraries Press, 1971. Dillard was of slave-holding ancestry, and his movement first into teaching and then into race relations with the Jeanes and Slater funds makes for an intriguing story.

Fairclough, Adam. *Teaching Equality: Black Schools in the Age of Jim Crow*. Athens and London: University of Georgia Press, 2001. This short book's three chapters, or lectures, "Liberation or Collaboration? Black Teachers in the Era of White Supremacy," "Robert R. Moton and the Travail of the Black College President," and "Black Teachers and the Civil Rights Movement" take the positive tack that even when black education leaders were seemingly giving in to a prevailing white power context, they were acting effectively more as double agents than as traitors.

Jones, Lance George Edward. *The Jeanes Teacher in the United States, 1908–1933: An Account of Twenty-five Years' Experience in the Supervision of Negro Rural Schools*. Chapel Hill: University of North Carolina Press, 1937. This is a nicely written book, with a mix of generalization and individual experience, that includes reports from Jeanes teachers.

Littlefield, Valinda W. "'To Do the Next Needed Thing': Jeanes Teachers in the Southern United States 1908–1934." In *Telling Women's Lives*, edited by Kathleen Weiler and Sue Middleton. Philadelphia: Open University Press, 1999. In this collection of women's stories from England, Wales, New Zealand, and Portugal, Littlefield's American story of the Jeanes teachers, who "gradually altered the lives of an oppressed group," is inspiring.

—CAROLYN WEDIN

ANTIAPARTHEID. The term "antiapartheid" describes the concept of opposition to the racially oppressive apartheid government in South Africa—from the passage of the first apartheid laws in 1948 to the abolition of apartheid in 1994—and the global movement that developed to express and act on that opposition. Apartheid was a social and political structure of racial hierarchy and segregation imposed by the brutal military and police state dictatorship of a minority white government in a predominantly black nation. Black South Africans had struggled against the European colonization of their land by the British Empire and against the military and economic domination of the native people by white settlers of Dutch and British origin from the outset in the seventeenth century. Nevertheless, the promulgation of apartheid—or the doctrine of "apartness" in the language of the Afrikaaners, or descendants of the Dutch settlers—was an acceleration of a preexisting racism that had commenced virtually from the arrival of European settlers at the southern tip of Africa in 1652. Fundamentally, apartheid was a racist system of managing labor: Africans were basically deemed not to be citizens of the land in which they were born and had to carry "passbooks"—or passports—to enter certain neighborhoods or to work at certain sites.

The imposition of apartheid laws and systematic racial separation in 1948 coalesced African and global opposition to the South African minority government at a time when the rest of the world was beginning to embark on a process of decolonization and the dismantling of racially discriminatory political and legal systems. The antiapartheid movement began to gather momentum and global support in 1960 after a massacre of apartheid protesters in Sharpeville, South Africa, drew international attention to the fascist nature and Nazi-like tendencies of the South African government. In 1962 one of the leading South African leaders of the antiapartheid movement, Nelson Mandela (b. 1918), was sentenced to life imprisonment for his political activities.

Mandela's status among a growing cadre of political prisoners and detainees galvanized indigenous and global opposition to the South African government; the opposition was primarily led by recently decolonized independent African and Asian nations with the support of the Soviet Union and other socialist and social-democratic nations. Apartheid was declared a "crime against . . . mankind" by the United Nations in 1970, and a vote calling for South Africa's expulsion from the United Nations was put forward in 1974. The expulsion was blocked by vetoes from the United States, the United Kingdom, and France.

In 1976 the brutal murder of hundreds of students protesting apartheid in the South African township of Soweto as a historical policy continuum dating from the 1960 Sharpeville massacre sparked a global call for the withdrawal by countries and corporations of all economic, military, and diplomatic ties. Among other things, these students were protesting attempts to teach them in Afrikaans, which they perceived as a way to tie them more closely to their oppressors. Growing protests throughout the world demanded economic divestment from the South African economy. Citizen, labor, student, religious, and investor campaigns threatening boycotts and embarrassment led many companies and nations to withdraw from economic and diplomatic relations with South Africa over the next eighteen years years.

For example, at campuses across the United States students protested vigorously when it was ascertained that the endowment—or investment portfolio—of their college or university had holdings in corporations that had investments in apartheid South Africa. Religious denominations acted similarly. At the docks, longshoremen refused to unload cargo from ships that hailed from apartheid South Africa. Scores of local antiapartheid organizations formed in the United States. The Harlem-based South African Freedom Day Coalition held demonstrations and orchestrated mass arrests at the South African consulate in New York. In Washington, D.C., beginning in the fall of 1984, TransAfrica—a lobbying organization designed to influence U.S. foreign policy toward Africa and the Caribbean and headed by Randall Robinson—orchestrated similar demonstrations at the South African Embassy. Demonstrations of various sorts unfolded at various apartheid-related sites across the nation.

Antiapartheid Protest. A young activist at a New York City antiapartheid protest. Photograph by Lydia Ann Douglas.

In response to the political pressure and potential for consumer boycotts, many U.S. corporations attempted to distance themselves from the apartheid regime by subscribing to the "Sullivan principles," a set of human rights standards for business operations within South Africa that was developed by Leon Sullivan, an influential African American minister from Philadelphia who was also a member of the General Motors board of directors.

International scrutiny and pressure heightened further after the South African government murdered Stephen Biko, a leader of the 1976 protests against apartheid, while he was in police custody. In condemnation, international bodies including the International Olympic Committee and the Commonwealth of Nations (formerly the British Commonwealth) expelled the South African government from membership, exacerbating the regime's isolation. By 1977 the United Nations Security Council imposed a mandatory arms embargo against South Africa.

In 1978 the United Nations dramatized the internationalization of antiapartheid sentiment when it gave awards to seven important world figures in recognition of their contribution to the international campaign against apartheid:

- The Reverend Canon L. John Collins (1905–1982) of the United Kingdom
- Michael Manley (1924–1997) of Jamaica
- General Murtala Muhammad (1938–1976) of Nigeria
- Gamal Abdel Nasser (1918–1970) of Egypt
- Jawaharlal Nehru (1889–1964) of India
- Olof Palme (1927–1986) of Sweden
- Paul Robeson (1898–1976) of the United States

This was followed in 1982 by a similar resolution recognizing the antiapartheid contributions of other world leaders:

- President Houari Boumedienne (1932–1978) of Algeria
- Romesh Chandra of India
- Jeanne Martin-Ciss (b. 1926) of Guinea
- The Most Reverend Trevor Huddleston (1913–1998) of the United Kingdom
- The Reverend Dr. Martin Luther King Jr. (1929–1968) of the United States
- Jan Nico Scholten (b. 1932) of the Netherlands

By 1985 the UN Security Council had passed a nonbinding resolution urging the United Nations member states to adopt stringent economic sanctions against South Africa.

In 1990—as the global antiapartheid campaign reached a crescendo of resistance, fomenting broad-based international pressure targeting the apartheid government—political bans against black political parties in South Africa were revoked and Nelson Mandela was released from prison along with other political prisoners. Continued pressure from within and outside the country forced the South African government to make more concessions on the path to dismantling apartheid. In 1993 Nelson Mandela addressed the United Nations Special Committee against Apartheid, speaking as the president of the African National Congress (ANC) of South Africa and calling for the lifting of economic sanctions against South Africa in recognition of the progress toward the abolition of apartheid. The United Nations voted to withdraw such sanctions, including an oil embargo.

In 1994, under the impetus of the ANC and other revolutionary organizations, South Africa adopted a new constitution abolishing apartheid and held democratic elections that resulted in the election of Nelson Mandela as president of the new government. The international antiapartheid movement was consequently disbanded. Nonetheless the underlying economic conditions of racial inequality in South Africa persist, even as the legalized forms of apartheid have been dismantled.

[*See also* Civil Rights, International, *and biographical entries on figures mentioned in this article*.]

BIBLIOGRAPHY

Clark, Nancy L., and William H. Worger. *South Africa: The Rise and Fall of Apartheid*. London: Longman, 2004.

Limb, Peter. *The ANC and Black Workers in South Africa, 1912–1992: An Annotated Bibliography*. London: Hans Zell, 1993.

Mandela, Nelson. *Long Walk to Freedom: The Autobiography of Nelson Mandela*. London: Little, Brown, 1994.

Thompson, Leonard. *A History of South Africa*. 3d ed. New Haven, Conn.: Yale University Press, 2001.

—JOSEPH WILSON
—DAVID ADDAMS

ANTICOMMUNISM AND CIVIL RIGHTS. Anticommunism was frequently deployed to discredit the aims, objectives, and methods of the civil rights movement. Opponents of civil rights claimed that movement members and organizations had Communist affiliations in the hopes of tarnishing reputations and straining alliances. Although a feature of the domestic political landscape since the Red Scare following World War I, anticommunism became a truly powerful force only in the late 1940s, intensifying as the Cold War progressed.

The fact remains, however, that the Communist Party—founded in the United States shortly after the conclusion of World War I—attracted a significant number of African American intellectuals in particular. This list included W. E. B. Du Bois, who joined the party in 1961 just before becoming an expatriate in Ghana, and his spouse, Shirley Graham Du Bois. Paul Robeson, the famed artist and activist, evidently was not a member of the party but like many others—for example, the celebrated writer Langston Hughes—cooperated with Communists on more than one occasion. One of the central reasons why the party was subjected to so much hostility was that from its inception it was closely associated with the Soviet Union, which was viewed widely as a major antagonist of the United States.

In their attempts to discredit the civil rights movement, opponents of civil rights often neglected the distinctions between liberal causes and the activities of the Communist Party. In a 1963 session of the U.S. Senate, for example, the Georgia governor Ross Barnett alleged that

Anticommunist Propaganda. A billboard along the march from Selma to Montgomery accuses Martin Luther King Jr. of being a Communist. The photograph actually shows King at a meeting of the Highlander Folk School in Monteagle, Tennessee, which trained union organizers and civil rights demonstrators. Photograph by Spider Martin.

Martin Luther King Jr. was a Communist by citing his presence at a 1957 celebration at the Highlander Folk School, a labor and civil rights education center started in 1938 in Monteagle, Tennessee. Barnett produced a photograph depicting King, the civil rights activist Rosa Parks, the Highlander director Myles Horton, and several other members of the civil rights and labor movement communities attending a lecture at the school. Only one person in the photo, Abner Berry, was actually connected to the Communist Party. Georgia officials later placed the photograph on billboards throughout the South with the caption "Martin Luther King at Communist Training School" in the hopes of rousing popular anticommunist sentiment against the civil rights leader.

The Black Left and Civil Rights. This is not to say that civil rights leaders did not have connections with the political Left. Many prominent civil rights leaders—including Bayard Rustin and Jack O'Dell, close aides to King; Ella Baker, founder of the Student Nonviolent Coordinating Committee (SNCC); and A. Philip Randolph, a principal organizer of the 1963 March on Washington and longtime union leader—were involved at one time or another with the labor movement's left wing, which counted many Communists among its ranks. Rustin, in fact, had even been a member of the Young Communist League from 1936 to 1941. Like many other African Americans during the Great Depression, he was attracted to the Communist movement because of its vocal advocacy of black civil rights and radical economic change. He left the Communist Party in the early 1940s and remained suspicious of its aims for the rest of his life, but many other African Americans remained attracted to the Communist movement, including O'Dell, who was a party member during the 1950s.

The Communist Party was active in the arena of civil rights during the postwar period through the Civil Rights Congress (CRC), a left-wing protest organization begun in 1946. The CRC tackled many civil rights and civil liberties issues from school desegregation to combating Jim Crow in public accommodations to defending Communists convicted under the Smith Act. In late 1954 the Subversive Activities Control Board, a government organization established pursuant to the McCarran Internal Security Act of 1950 to investigate the Communist Party, placed the CRC on its list of "Communist front" organizations. This move served to destroy the embattled organization by straining already tenuous alliances with the civil rights mainstream.

Anticommunism and the End of the New Deal. In 1938 the Texas Democrat Martin Dies was authorized by the House of Representatives to form what became the special House Committee on Un-American Activities (HUAC) to investigate "un-American propaganda." HUAC was particularly concerned with Communist propaganda among African Americans. Dies feared that blacks, especially in the South, would become attracted to the Communist Party. He labeled the National Negro Congress (NNC), a left-wing civil rights organization, as particularly suspect. By 1940 pressure from the Dies Committee strained the NNC's affiliation with the Congress of Industrial Organizations (CIO), a powerful confederation of unions in the United States and Canada, ending their cooperation and wounding the NNC severely. Sensing the changing political mood, the African American labor leader A. Philip Randolph, the NNC's president from 1936 to 1940, broke with the congress, claiming: "Negroes cannot afford to add the handicap of being 'black' to the handicap of being 'red.' " He would remain an anticommunist for the rest of his career and made a point of barring party members from participating in future protests that he helped orchestrate.

Through HUAC, Dies used anticommunism to rally conservatives against Franklin D. Roosevelt's New Deal. The Fair Employment Practices Committee (FEPC), a federal watchdog agency initiated by Executive Order 8802 in 1941 to investigate racial discrimination in the defense industry, was a particular target for southern conservatives. The committee's formation marked a considerable milestone in civil rights history by making businesses accountable for discrimination and by raising wages for black workers—despite problems of compliance and enforcement, especially in the South. Many southern conservatives were incensed over Roosevelt's attempt to curb racism and assailed the FEPC as "communistic."

The FEPC remained a mainstay of the civil rights agenda well into the 1950s, but it was eventually abandoned in the face of growing anticommunist pressure. President Harry S. Truman let a bill for a permanent FEPC founder in Congress in 1948 despite its central place among his civil rights promises.

Anticommunism and Civil Rights. The conflation of civil rights activism and Communism was strategic. Appeals to anticommunism—more so than appeals to overt racism—were a more powerful weapon against antiracism advocates. Thus by branding individuals committed to the black freedom struggle as "subversive," white politicians in the South could in a single stroke discredit local movements for social change and gain valuable allies north of the Mason-Dixon Line who were similarly concerned with supposed incursions by the Kremlin.

Until the late 1940s mainstream black activists resisted anticommunism actively because they equated it with the viewpoint of racist politicians. Southern congressmen who opposed civil rights legislation, such as John E. Rankin and James Eastland of Mississippi and John S. Wood of Georgia, were active anticommunists as well as vehement segregationists. Soon, however, the NAACP and other civil rights organizations were openly preaching anticommunism, as they proved unable to resist the resurgence of this philosophy that accompanied the conclusion of World War II. "Far from being sincere about doing something for Negro rights," the NAACP official Roy Wilkins wrote in the introduction to a 1951 pamphlet *The Communist Party—Enemy of Negro Equality*, "the Communists use the Negro merely as a pawn in the Soviet campaign against the United States and the western world." At the 1950 national convention, NAACP officials passed a resolution granting the board of directors the power to expel suspected Communists, beginning an internal purge that consumed the organization for many years.

Despite these efforts, segregationists still branded the NAACP as "Communist dominated." During the 1950s state governments across the South formed commissions to investigate the NAACP's Communist affiliations. The organization was banned in Alabama for failing to produce a membership list, which the state had hoped to use to target local activists. And Senator Eastland claimed that the antisegregation decision in the seminal NAACP-led Supreme Court case *Brown v. Board of Education* (1954) indicated Communist domination of the nation's highest court.

Cold War Politics. The political currency of anticommunism increased dramatically with the onset of the Cold War. In March 1947 the Truman administration imposed loyalty oaths for federal employees. Three months later Congress passed the Labor Management Relations Act, commonly referred to as the Taft-Hartley Act, which, in addition to restricting labor organizing, required all union leaders to sign affidavits renouncing any connection to the Communist Party or to any other group "advocating the overthrow of the government." The same year also bore witness to the blacklisting of numerous artists and writers in the entertainment industry. And beginning in 1948, the Alger Hiss case, which concerned a State Department official accused of espionage, raised public concern about Soviet infiltration of the government.

The election of 1948 marked a sea change in the intertwined histories of anticommunism and civil rights. The Democratic Party, which had been in power for sixteen years under Roosevelt and Truman, was fractured over the issue of civil rights. The right wing, especially in the South, left the party to form the States' Rights Democrats, commonly referred to as the "Dixiecrats." They ran the segregationist U.S. senator Strom Thurmond of South Carolina as their presidential candidate. The left wing, led by Henry A. Wallace, Roosevelt's vice president from 1941 to 1945, broke away to form the Progressive Party.

The Wallace campaign attacked the Truman administration's position on civil rights. Fearing that he would lose important black votes, Truman adopted the strongest civil rights plank since Reconstruction. At the same time, Truman and other centrist Democrats focused on the Communist Party's support of the Progressive campaign. They furiously Red-baited the campaign—alleging that the Progressive Party was little more than a front for Moscow—in order to scare potential voters back into the Democratic fold. "Cold War liberalism," a political ideology supportive of civil rights yet staunchly anticommunist, was solidified in the election of 1948 and would define the tenor of U.S. politics for decades to come.

International Context. Anticommunism cannot be understood as merely a domestic phenomenon. Events like the detonation of the first Soviet atomic bomb and the establishment of the People's Republic of China, both of which occurred in 1949, encouraged fears that World War III lay on the horizon. Within this context Communism was constructed as the greatest threat to the United States and Western civilization. American Communists, who were seen as domestic representatives of the Soviet Union, inevitably became anathema.

However, the United States was also the subject of scrutiny. Postwar racial violence, especially the persecution of black servicemen, was decried in the international press as evidence of the disparity between the image and the reality of American democracy. Soviet propaganda often played on the theme of racial inequality and violence in the United States, further perturbing officials and frustrating their attempts to keep up an image of racial progressiveness abroad.

Outspoken black members of the Left joined in condemning U.S. racism. W. E. B. Du Bois, William L. Patterson, and Paul Robeson were censured for attacking American racism while abroad, and they were even denied passports by the State Department. This action was especially harmful to Robeson, a renowned singer and actor who relied on his foreign audience after he was blacklisted at major venues in the United States for his political views.

Even less politically notorious African Americans, such as the entertainer Josephine Baker, were also considered security risks and monitored while abroad. Baker used the stage as a platform to denounce Jim Crow discrimination in the United States at several international events during the 1950s. Although she had made similar claims while touring in North America, the State Department took interest only when she was preparing to go abroad.

The Federal Bureau of Investigation (FBI) tried unsuccessfully to uncover any leftist connections that could be used to discredit her.

Government Surveillance. Government agencies often associated civil rights activity and Communism. J. Edgar Hoover, director of the FBI from 1924 (effectively from 1923) to 1972, had been drawing connections between black activism and Communist subversion since the Red Scare of 1919, when federal agents imprisoned and deported many suspected radicals. His belief that civil rights activism was fundamentally subversive dictated a great deal of the FBI's surveillance activities during his tenure of nearly half a century.

Hoover's activities intensified during the civil rights struggles of the early 1960s. The FBI's Counter Intelligence Program, or COINTELPRO, which began in 1956 to monitor and disrupt the activities of the Communist Party, also focused on civil rights activists. FBI agents used the program's extralegal powers to monitor and attempt to blackmail Martin Luther King Jr. and his Southern Christian Leadership Conference (SCLC) from 1962 until King's death in 1968. In *Racial Matters*, the historian Kenneth O'Reilly asserts that by discrediting such a central figure as King, Hoover and FBI agents "hoped to make a public case about the basically un-American nature of the civil rights movement" (p. 139). The bureau also kept close tabs on SNCC, the Congress of Racial Equality, and other protest organizations. From 1967 to the mid-1970s COINTELPRO also ran an especially effective campaign against the Black Panthers—which, too, had been linked to Communism—a radical black nationalist organization that grew in part out of SNCC and frustrations with the pace of civil rights progress.

[*See also* Civil Rights Movement; COINTELPRO; Cold War; Communism and African Americans; Federal Bureau of Investigation; McCarthyism; National Negro Congress; Union of Soviet Socialist Republics; *and biographical entries on figures mentioned in this article*.]

BIBLIOGRAPHY

Biondi, Martha. *To Stand and Fight: The Struggle for Civil Rights in Postwar New York City*. Cambridge, Mass.: Harvard University Press, 2003. Chapters 7 and 8 focus on the effects of anticommunism on civil rights struggles in New York and the nation.

Borstelmann, Thomas. *The Cold War and the Color Line: American Race Relations in the Global Arena*. Cambridge, Mass.: Harvard University Press, 2001. Places civil rights struggles and ideas about race within the global context.

Branch, Taylor. *Parting the Waters: America in the King Years, 1954–63*. New York: Simon & Schuster, 1988. Chapters 15 and 22 cover the Red-baiting of Martin Luther King Jr. and his staff.

D'Emilio, John. *Lost Prophet: The Life and Times of Bayard Rustin*. New York: Free Press, 2003.

Dudziak, Mary. *Cold War Civil Rights: Race and the Image of American Democracy*. Princeton, N.J.: Princeton University Press, 2000. Argues that the U.S. government passed civil rights legislation because of international pressures.

Fosl, Catherine. *Subversive Southerner: Anne Braden and the Struggle for Racial Justice in the Cold War South*. New York: Palgrave Macmillan, 2002. An excellent biography of an important civil rights activist that explores the effect of the Cold War on her life.

Kornweibel, Theodore. *"Seeing Red": Federal Campaigns against Black Militancy, 1919–1925*. Bloomington: Indiana University Press, 1998. Best account of early government anticommunism directed at African American protest organizations.

Lewis, George. *The White South and the Red Menace: Segregationists, Anticommunism, and Massive Resistance, 1945–1965*. Gainesville: University Press of Florida, 2004. Examines the role of anticommunism in segregationist thought, emphasizing the role of anticommunism as an ideology around which northern and southern conservatives could coalesce.

O'Reilly, Kenneth. *Racial Matters: The FBI's Secret File on Black America, 1960–1972*. New York: Free Press; London: Collier Macmillan, 1989. Best treatment of the FBI's surveillance of civil rights organizations.

Ransby, Barbara. *Ella Baker and the Black Freedom Movement: A Radical Democratic Vision*. Chapel Hill: University of North Carolina Press, 2003. Discusses Baker's complicated position as a member of the anti-Stalinist Left.

Woods, Jeff. *Black Struggle, Red Scare: Segregation and Anti-Communism in the South, 1948–1968*. Baton Rouge: Louisiana State University Press, 2004. Very similar in scope and argument to Lewis, but pays more attention to the civil rights struggle.

—ORION A. TEAL

ANTILYNCHING CAMPAIGN. The antilynching movement peaked in the years between the 1890s and the 1930s. It coincided with the increase in lynching that followed the end of Reconstruction in 1877. During the height of the campaign African Americans from all regions of the country, but particularly the South and the Midwest, actively attempted to quell the epidemic of lynching. They used various tactics. Early in the movement African Americans approached various political leaders to take up their cause. When this proved ineffective, they drafted appeals for state and national legislatures to investigate lynching and to pass antilynching bills. Women's groups constituted a large portion of the antilynching movement throughout its existence, and they tended to focus on education rather than legislation. Although eclipsed by more general civil rights concerns in the 1940s and after, lynching remained a major concern of African American activists throughout the twentieth century.

Lynching and Early Calls against It. Although lynching had existed since the colonial period, it became more prevalent in the years following Reconstruction. Slavery

Antilynching Protest. Members of the NAACP New York City Youth Council picket for antilynching legislation outside the Strand Theatre in Times Square, New York City, 1937. PRINTS AND PHOTOGRAPHS DIVISION, LIBRARY OF CONGRESS

had regulated the behavior of African Americans in the South before the Civil War, and after Reconstruction southern whites used lynching to police the boundaries of white-supremacist southern society. Southern whites argued that lynching increased after Reconstruction as a result of what they claimed was a new problem: an epidemic of black men raping white women. Southern whites argued that before the Civil War the institution of slavery had prevented such crimes from occurring. Once slavery was abolished, they claimed, they did not have adequate control over the supposedly barbaric inclinations of African American men, who could attack white women with little fear of recourse. During and after Reconstruction, therefore, the Ku Klux Klan, citizens' vigilante groups, and paramilitary groups funded by state and local governments lynched African American men on the pretense that they were meting out the appropriate punishment for rapists.

Southern whites' contention that lynching occurred only to punish black rapists was engraved into the public consciousness through repetition. Southern newspapers repeatedly insisted that lynching occurred to punish black men who raped white women. When the southern press admitted that the victim of lynching had been punished for a crime other than rape, it stated that the victim had transgressed racial boundaries in some other manner. According to this ideology, going outside the boundaries of one's position in the racial hierarchy in any respect deserved punishment by lynching, because if one transgression was allowed to go unpunished, it could—and would—lead to the ultimate transgression: the rape of a white woman.

Statistics indicate that more often than not rape, or even charges of sexual assault, was not the cause for lynching. In most cases African Americans were lynched for acting in a way that whites considered an affront to white supremacy: refusing to step off the sidewalk when a white woman passed, looking a white man directly in the eye, and complaining about poor wages were among the offenses that led to lynching. Frequently lynching was tied to fears about African Americans' economic independence. Black men who were self-sufficient or who owned their own businesses frequently became the targets of lynch mobs.

Between the 1880s and the 1930s most politically active African Americans viewed lynching as the greatest impediment to achieving equality. Lynching was the most tangible example of African Americans' subordinate position in the United States, and the fact that lynching spread throughout the country in the late nineteenth century evidenced the extent of African Americans' subjugation. Although African Americans discussed the problem of lynching throughout Reconstruction, the call of the activist leader Frederick Douglass in 1883 for African Americans to organize in response to the increase in lynching set the antilynching movement in motion.

The early period of the antilynching movement was characterized by the meeting of black conventions. These conventions usually occurred in response to a specific incident. Although they sometimes increased membership in the movement, they made few concrete gains with respect to halting or decreasing the frequency of lynching. In response to Douglass's invocation, African Americans in Texas, South Carolina, and Arkansas all held conventions in 1883 focused on the problem of lynching. Characteristic of the convention movement, the Arkansas convention concentrated on trying to get the Republican Party to take up the antilynching issue as a defense of African American civil rights more generally. Their plea fell on deaf ears because the Republican Party was in the process of distancing itself from African American issues in an effort to thwart Democratic inroads among northern voters. The last major convention of the period was held in Frankfort, Kentucky, in 1885. The convention drew up a resolution asking the state legislature to appoint a committee to investigate the rise in lynching. The legislature never created such a committee.

National Support. In the 1890s the antilynching movement gained national support. It was championed by two national organizations: the Afro-American League (AAL) and the National Equal Rights Council (NERC). At its inception the AAL expressed radical ideas, including the creation of a distinct African American nation. Its greatest accomplishment was the 1890 submission of a petition to the U.S. Congress to investigate the epidemic of lynching. The petition was never read on the floor of the House, however, and the AAL decreased its emphasis on the problem of lynching in the years that followed. Ultimately the Afro-American Council—the successor of the AAL—was co-opted by the black elite and did not develop a mass base. The NERC, formed following an 1893 Cincinnati convention, accomplished the first legislative gain of the antilynching movement. Under the NERC's lobby, in 1896 the Ohio legislature passed the first antilynching law, which made mob violence and execution without trial a crime. The NERC was short-lived as an institution, however, and had virtually disappeared by the turn of the century.

Far more significant was the contribution of Ida B. Wells (later Wells-Barnett) to the antilynching campaign. When three of her friends were lynched in her hometown of Memphis, Tennessee, in 1892, Wells denounced the crimes in her newspaper the *Free Speech and Headlight*. In response to her editorializing on lynching, white rioters burned her newspaper office and threatened her life. After living for a time in Brooklyn, New York, while writing for the *New York Age*, Wells toured Great Britain twice, hoping to bring some of the same sort of pressure to bear on the U.S. government that Douglass had through his abolitionist speaking tours decades earlier. She lived briefly in California and then traveled to Chicago, where she continued her antilynching activism.

Wells had partnered with Douglass to protest the exclusion of African American history from the World's Columbian Exposition held in Chicago in 1893. Although relegated to the sideshow-style midway, Douglass and Wells distributed both antilynching pamphlets and a pamphlet titled *Reasons Why the Colored American Is Not in the World's Columbian Exposition*. Following the Columbian Exposition, Wells settled in Chicago, and in 1895 she married the Chicago attorney, newspaperman, and widower Ferdinand L. Barnett. While raising his two children and their four, she continued to write about lynching in both the black and white press. She harnessed the power of preexisting black women's clubs and founded new women's groups that raised money for pamphleteering and other antilynching publicity.

Wells's most original contribution to the antilynching campaign was her critique of southern manhood. In her 1892 pamphlet *Southern Horrors: Lynch Law in All Its Phases* and in her public speeches, Wells argued that white men's insistence that they lynched black men for raping white women hinted at their own insecurity about the consensual unions between white women and black men. Wells suggested that the emphasis on black men as rapists revealed white men's masculine insecurities and demonstrated their inability to control white women. Wells also laid some of the blame for the continued epidemic of lynching on white women, who she claimed let their black lovers be lynched rather than owning to their willingness to enter interracial relationships. Although her challenges to southern white manhood did little to alter the frequency of lynching, Wells recruited many supporters to the antilynching movement, particularly women, both black and white.

The establishment of the NAACP in 1909 also contributed significantly to the antilynching campaign. In 1916 the NAACP created an antilynching committee to focus on pushing legislative action and increasing public awareness. To this end the committee published *Thirty Years of Lynching in the United States, 1889–1918 in 1919*, which included statistics on the number of lynchings that had occurred in those years. The committee continued to spread awareness about lynching in 1922 by printing lynching statistics under the heading "The Shame of America" in full-page advertisements in both the *New York Times* and the *Atlanta Constitution*.

In 1919 the NAACP rallied behind the Dyer Antilynching Bill, which had been introduced to Congress by Congressman Leonidas C. Dyer of Missouri. The bill would have punished local, county, and state authorities who did not deter and punish lynching. It was endorsed by President Warren G. Harding and passed by the House of Representatives in 1922, but it was filibustered by Democrats in the Senate. Little progress was made between the defeat of the Dyer Bill and the introduction of the Costigan-Wagner Bill, the brainchild of the NAACP executive secretary Walter White, who through his fiction and nonfiction books addressing the many social facets of lynching, his association with members of the Harlem Renaissance, and his antilynching activism was an important figure in the effort to end lynching. The Costigan-Wagner Bill was brought before Congress and was defeated in the House by southern Democrats in 1935. President Franklin D. Roosevelt refused to support the bill.

Following the failure of Costigan-Wagner, most African American political groups concentrated on a broader spectrum of civil rights issues rather than on lynching in particular. At the same time, however, the antilynching torch was taken up by a white women's group in the South. In 1930 Jessie Daniel Ames founded the Association of Southern Women for the Prevention of Lynching (ASWPL). Ames called for white women to organize in an effort to use their influence on southern society to deter lynching. Although active in a variety of integrated organizations, Ames argued that the ASWPL should have an exclusively white membership. As a white female organization, Ames believed, the ASWPL would be particularly successful at convincing people that the pretense for lynching—black men raping white women—was a myth. The group used statistics to demonstrate that the primary charge brought against individuals who were lynched was rarely sexual assault. Furthermore, even when rape was the initial accusation, lynch mobs rarely offered evidence or produced the supposedly assaulted white woman. The ASWPL succeeded in getting numerous police officers, officials, and citizens to pledge their opposition to lynching. By the time that the ASWPL disbanded in 1942, lynching throughout the United States had decreased substantially.

Later Activism. Although lynching was a less central issue for African Americans in the early years of the Cold War, antilynching activism continued. In 1946 the singer, actor, and political activist Paul Robeson founded the American Crusade against Lynching (ACAL). Like Wells, Robeson tried to pressure the federal government to enact antilynching measures by publicizing abroad the frequency of lynching in the United States. Unlike Wells, however, Robeson was forced to contend with the Cold War mentality of the 1940s, in the context of which his criticisms made him appear to be a potential subversive and Communist threat. Both Robeson and the ACAL were investigated by the FBI.

In the 1950s, issues of political equality eclipsed the antilynching movement as the civil rights movement gained strength. With increased national and international scrutiny focused on the South, lynching took a pronounced turn. Although many white southerners retaliated against civil rights activists with violence, lynching began to take place secretively. In the politically charged civil rights era, lynchings were investigated by the FBI. The best known of these investigations was that into the murders of James E. Chaney, Michael Schwerner, and Andrew Goodman in Mississippi in 1964. Local authorities and civilians could no longer expect to enact vigilantism before large crowds without facing punishment. Yet by the early twenty-first century no national antilynching bill had been enacted. The closest that Congress had come to passing an antilynching bill was the formal apology issued by the Senate on 13 June 2005 for failing to pass antilynching legislation in the past.

Just as African Americans in the late nineteenth century saw lynching as their greatest obstacle to overcome because of its symbolism, in the twentieth and early twenty-first centuries lynching was used to symbolize the oppression endured by African Americans for hundreds of years. Lynching and opposition to lynching frequently appeared in popular culture, particularly following the civil rights era. The 1939 song "Strange Fruit" recorded by the singer Billie Holiday was one of the earliest acknowledgments of lynching in popular culture. Harper Lee's novel *To Kill a Mockingbird* (1960), though not ostensibly focused on lynching, attacked its chief justification, demonstrating that the charge that black men rape white women was frequently a ruse. A series of documentaries examined lynching; they included *The Untold Story of Emmett Louis Till* and PBS's *Strange Fruit*. In 2000 *Without Sanctuary: Lynching Photography in America*, a book based on an exhibit of the same name, was published. It featured postcards made from photographs taken at lynchings.

[*See also* Douglass, Frederick, in American Memory; Dyer Antilynching Bill; Hose, Sam, Lynching of; Lynching and Mob Violence; Robeson, Paul; Till, Emmett, Lynching of; Violence against African Americans; Wells-Barnett, Ida B.; *and* Women's Clubs.]

BIBLIOGRAPHY

Beck, E. M., and Stewart E. Tolnay. *A Festival of Violence: An Analysis of Southern Lynchings, 1882–1930.* Urbana: University of Illinois Press, 1995. Provides an overview of the history of lynching in the United States, with particular emphasis on the nineteenth century and the Southeast; concludes with a discussion of the Great Migration and its effects on lynching in the South.

Metress, Christopher, ed. *The Lynching of Emmett Till: A Documentary Narrative.* Charlottesville: University of Virginia Press, 2002. An expansive collection of primary-source documents pertaining to the Emmett Till case; includes press reports of the trial, trial records, and more recent analyses of the case.

Royster, Jacqueline Jones, ed. *Southern Horrors and Other Writings: The Anti-Lynching Campaign of Ida B. Wells, 1892–1900.* Boston: Bedford Books, 1997. Contains the author's notes on historical background, Wells's role in the antilynching crusade, and documents written by Wells.

Schechter, Patricia A. *Ida B. Wells-Barnett and American Reform, 1880–1930.* Chapel Hill: University of North Carolina Press, 2001. A biography of Wells that contains an extensive discussion of her involvement in the antilynching campaign. Helps fit Wells's antilynching activism into the context of her political activism more generally.

—G. MEHERA GERARDO

ANTI-SEMITISM. *See* Black-Jewish Relations.

ANTIWAR MOVEMENT, VIETNAM. The Vietnam War coincided with struggles for civil rights and economic equality in the United States. Many African Americans who spoke out against the war did so because they believed that it diverted funds and attention from domestic social programs. Others considered it a racist war, both because of the disproportionate number of black soldiers placed in combat units and because the war consisted of an attack on an Asian nation by the powerful, white-controlled United States. Black servicemen and servicewomen united to speak out against racism and sexism in the military, viewing the Vietnam War as an extension of civil rights injustices that African Americans endured at home. Throughout the course of the war, prominent African American leaders and organizations, including Martin Luther King Jr. and the Student Nonviolent Coordinating Committee (SNCC), publicly opposed the war and encouraged other African Americans to join them.

In the early years of his presidency, Lyndon B. Johnson launched his War on Poverty, a variety of social programs designed to alleviate poverty and inequality, especially in inner cities. In 1964, Johnson introduced the Economic Opportunity Act, which created programs such as Head Start, the Job Corps, Volunteers in Service to America, and Upward Bound. He asked Congress for $1 billion in 1964 and $2 billion over the next two years to fund antipoverty programs. Even before becoming president, Johnson had worked closely with African Americans as the head of President John F. Kennedy's Committee on Equal Employment Opportunities. When Johnson assumed the presidency he made eradicating poverty at all levels of American society one of his primary goals.

Yet the Vietnam War soon edged out domestic issues as Johnson's main concern, causing a rift between the president and King, who had supported Johnson. King and other African American leaders had debated about taking a stand against the Vietnam War; many feared that such a position would harm civil rights efforts that relied on government support. In 1967, King issued his "Declaration of Independence from the War in Vietnam," in which he expressed his disappointment that U.S. officials had neglected the War on Poverty in favor of the conflict in Vietnam. He argued that the military sent African American men overseas to fight for liberties that they did not enjoy at home. He criticized the effects of the war on the Vietnamese, and he stated that the war undermined ideals of independence and democracy.

A year before King spoke out against the war, the Student Nonviolent Coordinating Committee issued a position paper entitled "On Vietnam." In it SNCC accused the U.S. government of lying about its concern for the freedom of the Vietnamese just as it lied about its desire to grant equality to African Americans. The paper compared the murders of civil rights activists to the deaths of Vietnamese civilians and blamed the U.S. government for both. SNCC also encouraged African American men to avoid the draft and instead engage in the fight for freedom at home. The group demanded that civil rights activism count as an alternative to military service. In its manifesto "The Basis of Black Power," also from 1966, SNCC members rejected the American ideology that led to war in Vietnam, political control in Africa and Latin America, and slavery. As a result of SNCC's outspoken opposition to the Vietnam War, FBI agents spied on the group's members and later monitored the activities of the Black Panthers, the organization most commonly associated with Black Power ideology.

Perhaps the most famous African American to refuse the draft was Muhammad Ali. He tried to claim status as a conscientious objector on the basis of his membership in the Nation of Islam, but the draft board denied his request on the ground that Muslims did not oppose all wars. The board also accused Ali of insincerity in his religious claims. Refusing to serve in the military, Ali was convicted of draft evasion in 1967 and was stripped of his heavyweight championship. He was sentenced to five years in prison, but the Supreme Court eventually overturned his conviction on a technicality.

As troops expressed opposition to the war, especially in the years after 1968 and the Tet Offensive, some black GIs rejected military sexism and connected degradation of women with the oppression of African Americans as a whole. Some black soldiers called on all African American men to renounce sexism and view black women as equals, at home and on base. Writing in antiwar newspapers, they called for solidarity between black servicemen and servicewomen against sexism and racism in the armed forces. In July 1970 authorities at the Great Lakes Naval Training Center in Illinois jailed four African American members of the navy's Women Accepted for Volunteer Emergency Service (WAVES) after they protested the alleged assault of another black WAVE member. As a show of solidarity, about seventy-five black sailors surrounded the building where the WAVE members were held.

In June 1971 the army discharged six black members of the Women's Army Corps (WAC) who had participated in civil rights demonstrations at Fort Meade, Maryland. Of the base's thirteen thousand residents that year, about 23 percent were African American. The women belonged to Brothers and Sisters for Equality, a group of black GIs and WACs that sought to bring attention to military racism. The six WACs were among nearly one hundred service people who had participated in a civil rights march around the base that ended in the detainment of twenty-two men and women. In November 1971 military police arrested 138 African American servicemen and servicewomen stationed at Fort McClellan, Alabama, after a weekend of protests against racism on base. The events at Fort Meade, the Great Lakes Naval Training Center, and Fort McClellan illustrate ways in which black servicemen and servicewomen united against discrimination in the military.

Antiwar Activism. An anti–Vietnam War demonstrator, Washington, D.C. Photograph by Bettye Lane. © Bettye Lane

Black women on the home front experienced the Vietnam War through their husbands, sons, and brothers, and the conflict caused some women to organize in protest against its attack on their families. Black Women Enraged, a Harlem group founded to oppose the draft, criticized not only the Department of Defense and the armed forces, but also the women's sons, brothers, and husbands for not refusing to fight a war waged by whites. Members of Black Women Enraged were not necessarily pacifists, but they demanded that black men ignore the calls for their military service and instead stay home and fight in the battles for civil rights.

The Black Women's Organization against War and Racism, a group based in Berkeley, California, also encouraged black men to refuse to go to Vietnam. For the members of Black Women Enraged and the Black Women's Organization against War and Racism, "real" men stayed in the community to fight poverty and racism. Such men did not blindly obey a military that represented a system that oppressed them. The Black and Third World Women's Alliance took the argument one step further, calling on black women to assert themselves in the social wars at home, just as women in North Vietnam took up arms in the fight against the United States and the government of South Vietnam. In all three groups the women's activism exposed the racism and sexism of the Vietnam War, offered alternative social structures, and highlighted the limits and failures of American ideas about masculine power and race.

A maternal sense of duty to protect young men motivated Diane Nash to travel to North Vietnam in December 1966 with three other women. Nash, one of the founders of SNCC and a prominent civil rights activist, decided to make the trip after she saw a photograph of a Vietnamese woman holding a wounded child in her arms. Nash was the only African American in the group, which spent eleven days as guests of the North Vietnamese government. The Vietnamese Women's Union paid for a portion of the American women's airfare to Hanoi. During the trip Nash and her companions met with members of the Women's Union of South Vietnam, members of the South Vietnamese Youth for Liberation, Catholic priests sympathetic to North Vietnam, various government officials, and Ho Chi Minh, the president of North Vietnam. Nash called the Vietnam War a war of economic and racial exploitation, and she called on young black Americans to think before entering into or supporting a war against a people of color.

Beginning in 1965 with the riot in the Watts neighborhood of Los Angeles, U.S. cities erupted in the flames of battles for civil liberties and economic justice. In 1967, racially motivated riots erupted in Detroit, Newark, Buffalo, and Plainfield, New Jersey, showcasing the seriousness of racial tensions and the desperation of cities that the U.S. government had neglected in favor of the Vietnam War. Some African Americans questioned the logic behind sending troops and financial support to a war nearly eight thousand miles away when violence and poverty plagued the streets of urban neighborhoods in the United States. The conditions motivated some African Americans to speak out against the war—through public protests, draft evasion, and resistance within the military. In the minds of some black antiwar activists, the Vietnam War symbolized an extension overseas of American racism.

[*See also* Civil Rights; Johnson, Lyndon B., Administration of; Military, Racism in; Racism; Student Nonviolent Coordinating Committee; Vietnam War; *and* War on Poverty.]

BIBLIOGRAPHY

Bloom, Alexander, and Wini Breines, eds. *"Takin' It to the Streets": A Sixties Reader*. 2d ed. New York: Oxford University Press, 2003.

Gill, Gerald. "From Maternal Pacifism to Revolutionary Solidarity: African-American Women's Opposition to the Vietnam War." *Sights on the Sixties*, edited by Barbara L. Tischler, pp. 177–195. New Brunswick, N.J.: Rutgers University Press, 1992.

Latty, Yvonne, ed. *We Were There: Voices of African American Veterans, from World War II to the War in Iraq*. New York: Amistad, 2004.

Moser, Richard R. *The New Winter Soldiers: GI and Veteran Dissent during the Vietnam Era*. New Brunswick, N.J.: Rutgers University Press, 1996.

Moss, George Donelson. *Vietnam: An American Ordeal*. 5th ed. Upper Saddle River, N.J.: Pearson Prentice Hall, 2006.

Nash, Diane. "Journey to North Vietnam." *Freedomways* 7, no. 2 (Spring 1967): 118–128.

Terry, Wallace, ed. *Bloods: An Oral History of the Vietnam War*. New York: Random House, 1984. The personal narratives of black veterans of the war.

—HEATHER MARIE STUR

APOLLO THEATER. Inheriting the hopes and dreams of the fading Harlem Renaissance, New York's famed Apollo Theater opened at 253 West 125th Street between Seventh Avenue (now Adam Clayton Powell Boulevard) and Eighth Avenue (now Frederick Douglass Boulevard) in January 1934, becoming the first theater on 125th Street, the commercial center of Harlem, to provide live performances to black Harlem. Built in 1913, the Apollo's building had previously been occupied by two entertainment companies that had practiced "segregation without signs," the exclusionary racial policies that motivated the fierce "Buy Black" campaign begun on 125th Street in the spring of 1934.

Besting the Lincoln and the historic Lafayette theaters, both located north of 125th Street where racial barriers had already fallen, the Apollo emerged as the victor in a frantic struggle for audiences in a Depression-ridden Harlem where nearly 50 percent of the population was on the unemployment rolls. In the eyes of one of the managers, the theater was never an architectural gem; however, in an example of beauty residing in the eyes of the beholder, Harlemites found ultimate glamour in the red velvet stage curtain and red velvet seats that comprised the orchestra, two balconies, and box seats for the theater's seventeen hundred guests. Its fortunes linked to the politics of race and space in Harlem and to the community's abiding love of entertainment, the Apollo opened on a note of racial pride that would continue throughout its history.

For most of the first four decades of its existence, the new theater was managed by the Jewish entrepreneur Frank Schiffman and his two sons, Bobby and Jack. Schiffman and his partner, Leo Brecher, veterans of the entertainment business in Harlem, took over the theater in 1935 following the sudden death of Sydney Cohen, the theater's first owner. The talent Cohen brought from the beloved Lafayette to help jumpstart the Apollo secured the new theater's survival by introducing the Harlem Amateur Night, a concept borrowed from the Lafayette that became the Apollo's signature program. A precursor of *American Idol*, the Apollo's Amateur Night was hosted by the popular entertainer Ralph Cooper, and it was broadcast live on national radio. Held on Wednesdays in the late evening, the contest became an immediate success with the audience's avid music lovers, characterized as the toughest audience in the nation, who took great pride in helping to propel the careers of the talented unknowns bravely appearing on the Apollo's stage and touching the Tree of Hope.

Cut from a tree in front of the Lafayette, the Tree of Hope was believed to carry magical powers bestowing luck and blessings on the amateur performers in their bid for the chance to win twenty-five dollars and a week's engagement at the theater. Moreover, because it was attended by promoters, agents, talent scouts, and producers, Amateur Night opened avenues for contracts, attesting that winners were indeed in a place "where stars are born and legends are made." Lessening the

Apollo Theater. Marquee at the Apollo Theater, New York City, c. 1946–1948. Photograph by William P. Gottlieb. © William P. Gottlieb; www.jazzphotos.com

embarrassment of the losers and contributing to the fun-laden evenings, a comedic "executioner," dressed in ragtag clothing and hoisting an antic pistol, ran underperformers off the stage to the wild cheering and boos of the talent-loving, fun-loving Apollo audience. During the first quarter of the theater's history, well over fifteen thousand contestants competed on the Apollo stage. Amateur Night boosted the careers of Ella Fitzgerald, Sarah Vaughan, Billy Eckstine, Pearl Bailey, Gladys Knight, James Brown, Luther Vandross, Gloria Lynn, Dionne Warwick, Stephanie Mills, and Stevie Wonder.

By carrying the contests across the country, the radio broadcasts gave the Apollo a national reputation not only for creating new stars but also for featuring the best talent in the country. Indeed, the Apollo's successive and successful waves of entertainers and musical innovations constitute a chronology of black music, covering blues and swing bands in the 1930s, bebop in the 1940s, rhythm and blues and rock and roll in the 1950s, gospel and soul in the 1960s, Motown revues in the 1970s, and rap and hip hop in the 1980s and 1990s. Virtually every major star has performed at the Apollo. A short list of performers includes Bessie Smith, Billie Holiday, Duke Ellington, Count Basie, Earl Hines, Cab Calloway, Lionel Hampton, Dizzy Gillepsie, Charlie Parker, Nat King Cole, Dinah Washington, the Ink Spots, the Mills Brothers, Little Esther, Michael Jackson, Aretha Franklin, Mary J. Blige, and Sean "P. Diddy" Combs. The comedians Butterbeans and Susie, Dewey "Pigmeat" Markham, Moms Mabley, Clinton "Dusty" Fletcher, Nipsey Russell, Flip Wilson, and Bill Cosby as well as dancing greats such as the Nicholas Brothers, Bill "Bojangles" Robinson, Bill Bailey, Sammy Davis Jr., and Honi Coles were Apollo favorites, with Coles becoming production manager in the 1960s.

Throughout its history, the Apollo has brought white musicians to its stage, starting with the big bands of Benny Goodman, Charlie Barnet, and Woody Herman. Charlie Ventura, George Shearing, and Buddy Rich appeared at the Apollo, as did Bobby Darin, Jerry Lee Lewis, and Buddy Holly and the jazz greats Dave Brubeck, Herbie Mann, and Stan Getz. Whites comprised a sizable portion of the audience, and the white celebrities Mae West, Joan Crawford, Milton Berle, Jack Benny, Jackie Gleason, and Marilyn Monroe were Amateur Night fans.

Heralded by the opening of the Apollo in 1934, the four decades that followed were known as Harlem's heyday, a period that witnessed the development and then the deterioration of black Harlem. Housing and entertainment opportunities made possible by the civil rights movement of the 1960s drew many middle-class residents away from Harlem. Businesses damaged in the 1968 Harlem riots remained closed; unemployment and poverty increased; entertainers found a smaller audience uptown and more lucrative venues downtown. Closed by the Schiffman family in 1976 because of its dwindling income and a resurgence of race and space politics around the issue of black ownership of Harlem, the theater reopened in 1981 under black leadership spearheaded by Percy Sutton, an attorney, businessman, and former president of the borough of Manhattan. In 1983 city, state, and national landmark status was bestowed on the theater, which, newly refurbished, reopened in 1985 with a three-hour "Motown Salutes the Apollo" NBC television special hosted by Bill Cosby. Amateur Night at the Apollo, again hosted by Cooper, returned and regained its popularity, but it failed to keep the Apollo in financial health. In 1991 yet another reorganization produced the Apollo Theater Foundation, a nonprofit corporation, to save the indebted theater.

In the early twenty-first century the Apollo is run by the foundation, which is supported by Time Warner. The foundation is chaired by Time Warner's Richard D. Parsons, and its members include luminaries such as the musician and producer Quincy Jones and the publisher Edward T. Lewis, the founder of *Essence* magazine. The Apollo operates in a rapidly gentrifying Harlem that is experiencing intense residential and commercial construction activity accompanied by escalating rental and real estate purchase prices that are bringing in new residents and driving a new Harlem exodus. The former president Bill Clinton has an office on 125th Street, a street that also plays host to Starbucks, H&M, Blockbuster, Staples, and other national corporations. The Apollo started a renovation in 2001 that restored the exterior. In 2010 the theater is scheduled to close for nine months for the construction of an addition that will include a gallery, an educational and community center, additional seats, and a café. Its fortunes still linked to the politics of race and space in Harlem, the new Apollo will find itself at the center of an increasingly gentrified Harlem made possible by the recent passing of a controversial rezoning plan designed to encourage the further development of new business on 125th Street, a cyclical return to the race and space wars that gave the theater birth.

[*See also* Blues; Gospel Music; Harlem; Harlem Renaissance; Jazz; Music; Soul Music; *and biographical entries on of figures mentioned in this article*.]

BIBLIOGRAPHY

Cooper, Ralph, and Steve Dougherty. *Amateur Night at the Apollo: Ralph Cooper Presents Five Decades of Great Entertainment*. New York: HarperCollins, 1990.

Fox, Ted. *Showtime at the Apollo*. Rev. ed. New York: Mill Road Enterprises, 2003.

Garland, Phyl. *The Sound of Soul*. Chicago: Henry Regnery Co., 1969.

Greenberg, Cheryl Lynn. *Or Does It Explode?: Black Harlem in the Great Depression*. New York: Oxford University Press, 1991.

Schiffman, Jack. *Harlem Heyday: A Pictorial History of Modern Black Show Business and the Apollo Theatre*. Buffalo, N.Y.: Prometheus, 1984.

Schiffman, Jack. *Uptown: The Story of Harlem's Apollo Theatre*. New York: Cowles, 1971.

—ONITA ESTES-HICKS

APTHEKER, HERBERT (b. 31 July 31 1915; d. 17 March 2003), one of the most prolific white scholars of African American history in the twentieth century. Herbert Aptheker was born in Brooklyn, New York, in 1915 and was educated at Columbia University in the 1930s, where he took an undergraduate degree in geology and an MA and a PhD in history. His first important publication, *American Negro Slave Revolts* (1943), was based on his doctoral dissertation and challenged the prevailing wisdom that slaves were largely passive victims of white masters. In part an outgrowth of Aptheker's master's thesis on Nat Turner, *American Negro Slave Revolts* immediately became a controversial work and has remained so since. He was befriended by the influential African American historian Carter G. Woodson and the legendary black intellectual W. E. B. Du Bois, both of whom encouraged his interest in Negro history. Aptheker's other writings include a seven-volume *Documentary History of the Negro People in the United States* (1951–1994), *Afro-American History: The Modern Era* (1971), and *Anti-Racism in U. S. History* (1992).

Aptheker was a political activist whose scholarship often reflected his Marxist principles. He joined the Communist Party in 1939 and remained its chief American theoretical defender until he resigned his membership in 1991. In addition to his scholarship, Aptheker wrote for and edited several Marxist publications and worked as the executive director of the American Institute for Marxist Studies. He served in the U.S. Army during World War II but was forcibly and dishonorably discharged in 1950 for his radical writings. Aptheker led a controversial delegation to Hanoi in 1965 to protest the Vietnam War and, at one point, was described by the FBI as "the most dangerous communist in the United States." Perhaps owing to his outspoken leftist convictions, he struggled to find a full-time faculty appointment, settling instead for many adjunct positions, some of which were at prestigious institutions like Yale, the University of California, and Stanford.

Aptheker first met W. E. B. Du Bois in the late 1940s and shared an office with him while Aptheker worked on the early volumes of his *Documentary History*. They were drawn together in part by their shared devotion to black history and in part by their political radicalism. By 1948 both Du Bois and Aptheker had a growing sense of political alienation, which helped them forge a close and lasting friendship. Aptheker's recollection is that in one of those early sessions Du Bois asked him to edit his correspondence, a task at which Aptheker labored for much of the rest of his career. He produced three volumes of Du Bois's letters and several other editions of his unpublished writings. When Du Bois became a communist and moved to Ghana in 1961, Aptheker became the de facto custodian of the Du Bois papers, which ultimately were given to the University of Massachusetts (Amherst) Library.

In the last years of his life, Aptheker assisted in the editing and publication of the Martin Luther King papers at Stanford University. He died in Mountain View, California, on 17 March 2003.

[*See also* Du Bois, W. E. B.]

BIBLIOGRAPHY

Carson, Clayborne. "Herbert Aptheker." *OAH* [Organization of American Historians] *Newsletter*, May 2003. This laudatory and sympathetic obituary by a prominent African American historian is useful for establishing the main events of Aptheker's long career.

Kelley, Robin D. G. "Afterword." *Journal of American History* 77, no. 1 (June 2000): 168–171. This brief tribute to Aptheker is generally reflective of his reputation among politically active historians.

Shapiro, Herbert, ed. *African American History and Radical Historiography: Essays in Honor of Herbert Aptheker*. Minneapolis, Minn. MEP, 1998. Essays by several well-known activist historians.

—CHARLES ORSON COOK

ARCHITECTS AND ARCHITECTURE. From the ground up, African Americans have always contributed to the design and construction of buildings in America. Sadly, the participation of blacks in architecture has been one not wanting of ability, but wanting of opportunity. African American slaves created much of the built environment in colonial America. Slaves were often skilled artisans who widely contributed to the construction of much of the plantation South. Even in the northern states, African Americans did construction work, although few had the opportunity to design and supervise construction projects. Blacks found few outlets in construction after the Civil War. As industrialization expanded, blacks were excluded from trade unions, and recessions eliminated most economic opportunities for African Americans. Only with the beginnings of education for African Americans did the professional field of architecture hold any promise for blacks, and even that was limited. After Massachusetts Institute of Technology (MIT) established the first architecture curriculum in the United States in 1868, Hampton Institute offered education in the building trades for young blacks, and Tuskegee Institute soon followed suit under Booker T. Washington. Although Washington and Tuskegee deserve much of the credit for the rise of blacks in the architecture profession, it would be well into the twentieth century before African American contributions to architecture would be recognized. Despite these strides forward, many black architects in the twenty-first century are still limited to the technical side of architecture, not the design field.

Booker T. Washington recruited the MIT-educated architect Robert R. Taylor (1868–1942) to head Tuskegee's Mechanical Industries Department in 1893. Remaining at the school until 1933, Taylor educated numerous prominent African American architects and was responsible for many buildings on the institution's campus, including Butler Chapel and Washington's private residence, "The Oaks." Also on Tuskegee's faculty was Wallace Rayfield, an 1899 graduate of Columbia University who spent eight years at the school. Leaving over an anticipated but disputed raise, Rayfield practiced in Birmingham, where he designed homes but was particularly active in the design of churches, including the Sixteenth Street Church, so prominent as a civil rights landmark in the city.

One of Taylor's first protégées at Tuskegee was John A. Lankford, who later established one of the first African American practices in Washington, D.C. Lankford was involved in education for black architects at Shaw University in Raleigh, North Carolina, and at Howard University but is most renowned for his architectural designs, especially churches. Big Bethel African Methodist Episcopal Church on Atlanta's historic Auburn Avenue (1924) is among his more prominent commissions. He was the first licensed black architect in both the District and Virginia, and he worked for several federal government agencies on architectural and engineering assignments. Still another architect with Tuskegee ties was William Pittman, who studied at Tuskegee and at Drexel Institute, taught at Tuskegee, and joined Lankford's Washington office in

1905. The following year he opened his own office and won a competition for the Negro Building for Jamestown, Virginia's tercentennial. Pittman oversaw the construction of the building, making him the first African American contracted for a federal building. He designed several institutional buildings in Washington and, after 1912, in Texas.

Vertner Tandy was a 1909 Cornell University graduate who was also on the Tuskegee faculty and later was the first African American architect in New York State. Tandy briefly was in partnership with George Washington Foster Jr., a black architect who studied at Cooper Union and worked in the New York firm of Daniel Burnham (whose practice was based in Chicago), where Foster probably worked on the design of the Flatiron Building. Tandy and Foster's best-known design was the Saint Philip's Protestant Episcopal Church in Harlem (1910–1911).

The most prominent of the post–Tuskegee era black architects were Julian Francis Abele and Paul Revere Williams. Abele graduated in architecture from the University of Pennsylvania in 1902 and was a junior architect working for Horace Trumbauer in Philadelphia. His works included Harvard's Widener Library (1915), the Philadelphia Museum of Art (1926), and nearly fifty buildings on the campus of Duke University from 1925 to 1940.

Public Housing Architect. The architect and engineer Hilyard R. Robinson works on plans and specifications for one of two war-housing projects at Ypsilanti, Michigan. In addition to public-housing projects, Robinson designed buildings at Howard University, Hampton Institute, and the Tuskegee Army Air Field, home of the Tuskegee Airmen. Photograph by Roger Smith. PHOTOGRAPHS AND PRINTS DIVISION, SCHOMBURG CENTER FOR RESEARCH IN BLACK CULTURE, THE NEW YORK PUBLIC LIBRARY, ASTOR, LENOX AND TILDEN FOUNDATIONS

Williams attended the University of Southern California's School of Architecture and studied at the Beaux-Arts Institute in New York. He returned to Los Angeles and opened his own office in 1923. Best remembered as the architect to the stars, Williams designed homes for Hollywood celebrities such as Betty Grable, Frank Sinatra, Cary Grant, and William Holden among others. But Williams was far more influential as an architect of larger structures, as his designs included churches, schools, public housing, and numerous other buildings; his commissions read like a who's who of American architects.

World War II opened an entirely new arena for African American architects—federal contracts. In 1942, the Nashville firm of McKissack and McKissack was granted the $4.2 million contact for Tuskegee Air Force base, home to the famed Tuskegee Airmen. A California firm begun by Williams gained a $39 million contract for a naval base in Long Beach. Following the war, the GI Bill provided educational funding for black veterans to attend schools such as Howard, Hampton, and Tuskegee that were training a new generation of architects. Howard's School of Architecture received landmark accreditation in 1949. A series of Supreme Court cases culminating in *Brown v. Board of Education* (1954) eventually opened previously all-white universities, where blacks enrolled in architecture programs. Scholarships were funded by the Ford Foundation, and the American Institute of Architects also supported minority education. Since the mid-twentieth century, African American architects such as Harvey Gantt, Max Bond, Robert T. Coles, Donald Stull, David Lee, Roberta Washington, and Norma Sklarek have risen to the top of the architecture profession. Despite these and other successes by black architects, inequities in architectural commissions and opportunities still exist.

Accepted architectural styles most often dictate design and construction, but one style directly attributed to African Americans is notable. The shotgun house (so named because one could fire a shotgun through the house without hitting anyone) is attributed to free blacks in New Orleans in the early nineteenth century. Constructed as one room wide and two or more rooms deep, the shotgun house spread among black communities across the South, and hundreds have been purchased by developers for contemporary housing alternatives.

In 1989, Robert Coles lamented the numbers of African American architects, a dearth of minority-owned firms, and declining enrollment among blacks in architecture schools. Black architects, Coles concluded, are an endangered species.

[*See also* Higher Education; Sixteenth Street Baptist Church; *and entries on institutions of higher education mentioned in this article*.]

BIBLIOGRAPHY

Travis, Jack. *African American Architects in Current Practice*. Princeton, N.J.: Princeton Architectural Press, 1991. Biographical dictionary of African American architects.

Wilson, Dreck S., ed. *African American Architects: A Biographical Dictionary, 1865–1945*. New York: Routledge, 2004. Historical biographical dictionary of African American architects.

—BOYD CHILDRESS

ARIZONA. African Americans in Arizona have a long history of community building and organizing to better their social, economic, and political status. By 1896, people of African descent had resided in what is currently the state of Arizona for at least 368 years. Beginning in 1528 with the arrival of the Moroccan Esteban de Dorantes, the first of many Spanish-speaking blacks, people of African descent have been a critical component of this diverse region. Many of the English-speaking blacks who moved to the territory by 1880 worked to integrate themselves, directly and indirectly, into the area's fledgling economic and political culture. Moreover, African American cowboys, like the legendary Nat Love, later drove cattle through Arizona. The 9th and 10th cavalries, or "buffalo soldiers," served the U.S. government by protecting settlers and subduing Mexican revolutionaries, indigenous Americans, outlaw gunfighters, and cattle thieves. In addition, black women including Elizabeth Hudson Smith and Arya Hackett established influential and prosperous businesses despite racial and gender discrimination in Wickenburg, Arizona, and Phoenix, Arizona, respectively.

African Americans began to migrate to Arizona by 1900 in larger numbers, and although the black population remained relatively small, it constituted nearly 3 percent of the total population (11,134) of Phoenix, the state's capital city. African Americans also forged communities within smaller Arizona towns such as Flagstaff, McNairy, Miami, Mobile, Randolph, and Yuma. By 1920, the lives of most African American Arizonans would unfold in their state's largest, most urbanized cities, Phoenix and Tucson. This migration, prompted by the cotton industry, entrepreneurial opportunities, and promises of a freer life, gave rise to an energetic black Arizona population that chafed under Jim Crow segregation and southern racial etiquette. By 1926, the Arizona legislature passed a school segregation law and designated "interracial" marriages unlawful, while chapters of the Ku Klux Klan were organized around the state, reflecting local bigotry. Furthermore, the meticulously constructed Phoenician residential Palmcroft District, and its white homeowners, created and maintained restrictive covenants limiting the sale of Palmcroft real estate to whites only by 1926.

African Americans' subordinate position was exacerbated by the Great Depression and discriminatory New Deal "relief" programs. African Americans in Arizona, however, resisted their marginalization. They formed protest organizations such as the NAACP, the National Urban League (NUL), and the Universal Negro Improvement Association (UNIA). In 1931, in Phoenix, James L. Davis, Sidney Scott, H. D. Simpson, and other activists, created the Phoenix Protection League (PPL) to combat racial employment discrimination in Phoenix. All organized African American acts, community building, and resistance were driven by Arizona's black churches and black women's associations, such as the Arizona Federation of Colored Women's Clubs, which owned and operated many of the halls in which black people could assemble.

By the 1940s, the state's more fluid race relations and black Arizonans' determination to secure greater opportunities led to the creation of closely knit black communities throughout Arizona. The impact of America's involvement in World War II on African Americans in Arizona, and throughout the nation, is complex. On the one hand, the war ended the Great Depression, launched a new wave of black migration to the state, and ushered in a period of unprecedented progress in black employment, mobility, and professional activism. On the other hand, America's crusade in the name of freedom and democracy in World War II failed to reach millions of its black citizens at home, and Arizona was no exception. White supremacy and racial discrimination flourished in Arizona during the war. African Americans joined the armed services to fight America's fascist enemies, while resisting white supremacy and their own subordinate status. Black people responded to the challenge of white supremacy and the lack of opportunity by migrating in large numbers to western states including Arizona, taking advantage of career opportunities created by war mobilization. During this time, black people established and restructured protest organizations, which formed the backbone of the modern civil rights movement.

Between 1946 and 1970, African Americans, such as Opal Ellis, Lincoln Ragsdale, Eugene Grigsby, George Brooks, Cloves Campbell Sr., and their multiracial allies in Arizona such as Herbert Finn, William Mahoney, and Manuel Pena, waged a battle for civil rights in the state. Roused by years of racial discrimination, World War II, and America's promise of democracy, they were sustained by a swelling African American population. They were also buoyed by the burgeoning postwar liberalism of a number of white western leaders. Armed with their experiences, hope, and passion, and aided by sympathetic white Phoenicians, black Arizonans led the way in securing victories for racial justice in the state, sometimes in advance of national milestones in civil rights. For example, Arizona's activists won a major victory against de jure segregation when Arizona Superior Court Judge Fred Struckmeyer, in *Robert B. Phillips, Jr., et al. v. Phoenix Union High Schools and College District, et al., no. 72909*, outlawed school segregation in high schools and colleges throughout Arizona in 1953, almost one full year before the *Brown v. Board of Education* decision in 1954.

For generations, Jim Crow and racial discrimination, and the struggle to destroy them, inspired black solidarity in Arizona. Black Arizonans, like their counterparts throughout the United States, were never a homogeneous group, but acute oppression compelled them to conceal many of their ideological differences. By 1971, however, African Americans in Arizona, having won the legal battle against segregation and white supremacy, began to publicly disagree on social, economic, and political issues. Conflicts between the expanding black middle class and dispossessed African Americans locked into decaying inner cities broadened. Disputes among the proponents of integration, assimilation, and black nationalism surged. Chief among the warring factions that emerged were a band of black neoconservatives and the black liberal establishment. By the 1970s and 1980s, blacks in Arizona, like African Americans elsewhere, embraced myriad strategies to obtain and maintain socioeconomic equality. Regardless of the various philosophies that were bandied about, however, at issue was still the progress and stability of the black community in an era that witnessed surging black opportunities on the one hand, and expanding black poverty and social dislocation on the other.

Between 1991 and the present, African Americans in Arizona continued to build on the gains they had made since the civil rights movement; they effectively broke down additional extralegal and political barriers to black socioeconomic equality. In 1992, for example, black activists led a successful effort to create the first voter-approved Martin Luther King Jr. holiday in the United States. By the mid-1990s, however, African Americans in Arizona had accepted the fact that the legacy of white supremacy and lingering racial inequality remained as barriers between many blacks and upward mobility. Due in large part to the successes of the civil rights movement, the largest black middle class in the nation's history emerged, and Arizona became home to a critical mass of them. At the same time, however, many black people continued to live at or below the poverty line in the state, as a result of historic and persistent racial discrimination. Nevertheless, during the 1990s African Americans in Arizona became increasingly active: calling attention to racial intolerance and inequality, cultivating political power and representation, helping to fuel the state's interest in diversity, supporting and enhancing black entrepreneurship, and continuing to preserve, enhance, and champion African American culture and community.

[*See also* Jim Crow Laws.]

BIBLIOGRAPHY

Harris, Richard E. *The First 100 Years: A History of Arizona Blacks*. Apache Junction, Ariz.: Relmo, 1983.

Luckingham, Bradford. *Minorities in Phoenix: A Profile of Mexican American, Chinese American, and African American Communities, 1860–1992*. Tucson: University of Arizona Press, 1994.

Rothschild, Mary Aickin, and Pamela Claire Hronek. *Doing What the Day Brought: An Oral History of Arizona Women*. Tucson: University of Arizona Press, 1992.

Taylor, Quintard. *In Search of the Racial Frontier: African Americans in the American West, 1528–1990*. New York: W. W. Norton, 1998.

Whitaker, Matthew C. *Race Work: The Rise of Civil Rights in the Urban West*. Lincoln: University of Nebraska Press, 2005.

—MATTHEW C. WHITAKER

ARKANSAS. Afro-Arkansans, like other black southerners, clearly benefited from the dramatic political and social changes of the Reconstruction era. Arkansas blacks, usually as Republicans, participated in the Constitutional Conventions of 1868 and 1874, and Negroes served in both houses of the state legislature until the last few years of the nineteenth century despite the fact that conservative white Democrats controlled the politics of the state after 1874. Moreover, a threefold increase in the state's black population from 1869–1890 meant that an important segment of the electorate up until the 1890s was African American. Sixteen of the state's counties and at least two important towns were majority black. The late nineteenth century also produced a small but growing urban black middle class, and a Reconstruction-inspired common-school law held out the promise of free (albeit segregated) public education—including a state normal school—for Arkansas Negroes. Bishop Henry M. Turner of the African Methodist Episcopal Church voiced the hope, if not quite the reality, of many when he observed in 1889 that "Arkansas is destined to be the great Negro state of the country. . . . This is the state for colored men who wish to live by their merits."

Disfranchisement and Segregation. By 1890, however, forces were at work that would erode much of Bishop Turner's optimism about the status of African Americans in Arkansas and throughout the South. The most immediate cause of change was political. Although conservative white Democrats had allowed a measure of black political autonomy in the 1870s and 1880s, the strength of rural populism among whites and blacks threatened to unseat political elites in both major parties. Beginning in 1888, the Arkansas legislature legalized suffrage restrictions that substantially lowered the number of registered black voters. The poll tax of 1893 was particularly effective in eliminating black and poor white voters. In 1906, the Arkansas Democratic Party abandoned its traditional convention system of nominating candidates in favor of primary elections, which were open only to white voters. This so-called white primary completed the process of disfranchisement of Arkansas Negroes with devastating results. By 1895 there were no black representatives in the state legislature, and the number of registered African American voters had fallen drastically. A handful of federal appointees to minor local offices remained, but their influence on state politics was increasingly marginalized. Partly in response to these conditions, Arkansas had a vigorous back-to-Africa movement in the late nineteenth century.

Moreover, the 1890s and the first decade of the twentieth century witnessed an increasingly rigid system of de jure racial segregation. Even before the Supreme Court case of *Plessy v. Ferguson* (1896), the Arkansas legislature moved to segregate blacks and whites on railroad cars, and in 1903 similar racial separation became required on municipal trolleys. Within a decade, state prisons, hospitals, and schools became a part of the Jim Crow system, too. Local communities added still another layer of segregation, with innumerable ordinances that discouraged interracial contact in theaters, ballparks, restaurants, and other public venues. The poet and novelist Maya Angelou captured the pervasiveness of racial separation in the 1930s by remembering that in her Arkansas childhood "segregation was so complete that most Black children didn't really know what whites looked like."

The emergence of a Jim Crow system was also accompanied by heightened racial tension and violence. From the 1880s through the 1920s, more than two hundred blacks were lynched in Arkansas. Not infrequently, lynchings were carried out with either the tacit approval of authorities, or, in some cases, the active assistance of law enforcement officials or local elites. Lynchings were sometimes public events, which attracted large crowds, and they seldom resulted in the arrest or conviction of the perpetrators. Lynch mobs, like the one in a notorious Little Rock example in 1927, sometimes saw themselves as the protectors of white womanhood, but the statistical evidence indicates that less than a third of black victims were accused of rape. A few white officials publicly opposed lynching, but it remained an extreme, though not uncommon, feature of racial life in Arkansas until the 1930s.

An attempt to "cleanse" some communities of black residents was also an irregular, but not unknown, practice in the early twentieth century. The rice farming community of Lonoke, just east of Little Rock, intimidated many Negroes into leaving town hastily in the late 1890s, and an equally egregious instance occurred several years later in Sheridan, Arkansas. Perhaps the most dramatic example, however, happened in Harrison, in northern Arkansas, when two riots—one in 1905 and another in 1909—had the practical effect of eliminating virtually the entire black population of Boone County. Isolated incidents of forcing blacks to abandon entire towns, the notorious "sundown towns," have been documented as late as the 1970s. In the eastern Arkansas delta region, where most of the state's Negro population lived, race relations were particularly strained. The rural community of Elaine, for example, was the scene of one of the bloodiest race riots in United States history in 1919, when local whites, aided by the state militia, killed an estimated several hundred black Arkansans who were accused of fomenting a race war in Phillips County. Similarly, in 1934, the organizing efforts of the Southern Tenant Farmer's Union among eastern Arkansas blacks was met with open threats of organized violence from local conservative whites.

Despite these hostile conditions, however, Arkansas Negroes found ways to build and maintain productive lives and lasting communities. This was particularly true in urban areas like Little Rock and Pine Bluff, where an active, black middle class emerged. Little Rock's growth was in inverse proportion to the decline of the state's agricultural economy. Railroad development in the late nineteenth century and federal expenditures during World War I were important factors in accelerating the city's industrial development. Its population in 1870 was approximately twelve thousand, but by the end of the nineteenth century that number had tripled. After a brief setback in the 1930s, the City of Roses boasted a population of almost ninety thousand just prior to World II. Of that number, fully 25 percent were black. By the 1930s, the city had a thriving black downtown, "Little Rock's Harlem," which was the home of businesses, fraternal orders, nightclubs, and restaurants. In addition, the Little Rock metropolitan area was the home to three black colleges, scores of black churches, and local chapters of the National Association for the Advancement of Colored People (NAACP) and the Urban League. Pine Bluff experienced a less dramatic growth, but its black community included some of the most influential Negroes in the state, and it would supply more than its share of activists.

World War II was a pivotal point for Afro-Arkansans. For one thing, it accelerated the state's industrial development and hastened the decline of its agricultural economy. The result was a spectacular case of rural depopulation. In Arkansas and the South generally, blacks had been moving out of the state in significant numbers since the Great Migration of the World War I era. But, between 1940 and 1960, a total of 850,000 persons (about 44 percent of the population) left the state. African Americans were overrepresented among those who fled Arkansas in those years; their overall proportion of the population declined from 27 percent to 19 percent. Meanwhile, Little Rock's black community grew by almost ten thousand, making African Americans about one-third of the capital city's total population. Other towns and cities reported similar increases. Not surprisingly, these urban centers later became the home of increasing protests against racial discrimination.

In the late 1920s, John Marshall Robinson, a black Little Rock physician, founded the Arkansas Negro Democratic Association (ANDA). Composed of businessmen, attorneys, and other professionals, the ANDA became an early advocate for voting rights reform, and in Pine Bluff the Committee on Negro Organizations (CNO), led by the attorney William Harold Flowers, became a powerful voice for racial justice in the 1940s. In addition, the Arkansas Council on Human Relations (ACHR), a biracial group supported by moderate whites, worked successfully throughout the 1950s and beyond with subtle, though notable success. Thus, local organizations, usually in urban areas, were poised to change race relations forever in Arkansas. Most visible among those were Arkansas chapters of the NAACP, which were evolving into increasingly strident sources of political and social change.

The Civil Rights Movement and After. The most spectacular episodes of NAACP activism came in public secondary education in the 1950s. Early school desegregation took place quietly and peacefully in two Arkansas towns and in another (Hoxie) with controversy, but the attempt to desegregate Little Rock's Central High School in 1957 brought the state's black activists as well as their white opponents to national attention. Daisy Gaston Bates, the state NAACP president, was foremost among those demanding school desegregation in Little Rock, even before the 1954 *Brown v. Board of Education* Supreme Court decision. Daisy Bates and her husband, L. C. Bates, pressed their cause over the objections of many in the black community and most whites in the pages of their newspaper, *Arkansas State Press,* as well as through the NAACP. It was Bates who organized the nine Negro students—the "Little Rock Nine"—who attempted to enroll in Central High School in September 1957, and it was she who counseled and comforted those teenagers through the difficult months of 1957 and 1958. For a time, Daisy Bates was Arkansas's most famous African American, who appeared to single-handedly challenge the segregationist governor Orval Faubus's attempt to block the integration of Central High School. Her victory, won with the reluctant support of President Dwight Eisenhower and federal troops, was short-lived—Governor Faubus closed the high schools in Little Rock (including Central) the following year—but her example supplied a good deal of courage and inspiration to others seeking change.

National civil rights groups had a more mixed record of success in Arkansas. The Congress on Racial Equality's (CORE) 1961 Freedom Rides were effectively undermined by local courts, and, about the same time, student-led sit-in demonstrations in Little Rock never achieved universal support, even in the black community. School desegregation in the 1960s also met determined resistance in the form of "freedom of choice" programs adopted by many local school districts. The Student Nonviolent Coordinating Committee (SNCC) was more successful, especially in registering voters in the heavily populated black counties of eastern Arkansas. In fact, SNCC's organizing activities were a key factor in electing the moderate Republican, Winthrop Rockefeller, as governor in 1966. Clearly, de jure segregation was virtually extinguished by the late 1960s, but significant pockets of white resistance persisted in many of the state's localities. Still, schools, including the state university, were, ostensibly at least, biracial by the end of the 1960s, and, thanks largely to the Lyndon Johnson administration's War on Poverty, many smaller communities had organized efforts to help poor blacks. Many of those initiatives created a new generation of black activists in small-town and rural Arkansas.

By 1972, there were almost a hundred elected black officials in Arkansas—the second highest of any southern state—and hundreds more served alongside whites as salaried public employees. Moreover, by 1976, 94 percent of Arkansas's black eligible voters were registered, effectively making the Democratic Party the vehicle for political civil rights in the state. Arkansas African Americans were instrumental in electing Bill Clinton governor in the 1980s and president a decade later. Arkansas remains one of the few remaining bastions of the Democratic Party in statewide elections, thanks in large part to black voters.

[*See also* Little Rock, Arkansas, *and entries on people and organizations mentioned in this article*.]

BIBLIOGRAPHY

Gordon, Fon Louise. *Cast and Class: The Black Experience in Arkansas, 1890–1920*. Athens: University of Georgia Press, 1995. A short, but invaluable account of the establishment of segregation in Arkansas.

Graves, John William. *Town and Country: Race Relations in an Urban-Rural Context, Arkansas, 1865–1905*. Fayetteville: University of Arkansas Press, 1990. Details the divergence of rural and urban interests.

Jacoway, Elizabeth. *Turn Away Thy Son: The Crisis That Shocked the Nation*. New York: Free Press, 2007. A somewhat controversial installment in the growing literature on the Little Rock crisis and, as of its publication, the definitive account. The author spares few in this skeptical treatment of the Central High School incident. Her portrait of Orval Faubus is more generous than most.

Kirk, John A. *Redefining the Color Line: Black Activism in Little Rock, Arkansas, 1940–1970*. Gainesville: University Press of Florida, 2002. Excellent for understanding the climate of racial change in a southern city.

—Charles Orson Cook

ARMSTRONG, LOUIS (b. 4 August 1901; d. 6 July 1971), jazz cornet player, trumpeter, and vocalist. Louis Armstrong's musical style and charismatic personality transformed jazz from a "raucous" and "vulgar" regional form of dance music into an internationally beloved popular art form. Also known as "Satchel-mouth" and "Pops," Armstrong first gained renown as an innovative cornet player and trumpeter whose creative energy helped bring about the movement of jazz into swing in the 1920s. But he also achieved fame as a vocalist whose distinctive style, including some specific features identified as "Afro-American," influenced scores of jazz singers and thus played a significant role in shaping popular music of the twentieth century.

Background and Early Career. Armstrong was born into a poor family in New Orleans, Louisiana, and grew up in a tough neighborhood of the "Back-of-Town" area. Before his father, William Armstrong, permanently abandoned the family, his mother, Mary Armstrong ("Mayann"), temporarily turned over the upbringing of Louis and his younger sister, Beatrice ("Mama Lucy") Armstrong Collins, to their grandmother, Josephine Armstrong. His grandmother used Chinaberry switches to teach Louis some early lessons in discipline; but she also taught him something about slavery days, Vodun, Congo Square (now Louis Armstrong Park), and African musical traditions. Later, his performances revealed such Vodun influences as scatting, growling, and the exaggerated facial expressions common among members of spasm bands in Storyville, the red light district of New Orleans. At age five, he was reunited with Mayann, his mother, with whom he finally was able to form a loving and trusting relationship. From Mayann, he gained his lifelong obsession with food and with the purgatives she derived from a combination of southern and African sources. Despite a legacy from some of his elders of "slavery, malice, jealousy, and hate dividing the races," Louis gained from his mother her uncanny ability to find the good in almost everyone (Bergreen, p. 27). He received his only formal education by attending the Fisk School for Boys, located near his home, through the fifth grade.

Even as a small child, Louis developed a fascination with the emerging jazz music played by Joe "King" Oliver and others at such nearby joints as the racy and raucous Funky Butt Hall. He bought his first cornet with money loaned to him by the Karnoffskys, a neighboring family of Russian-Jewish immigrants, for whom he worked as a coal delivery boy in Storyville. At age eleven, the self-taught amateur cornet player joined a street quartet of "Back-of-Town" boys soon good enough to draw the attention of Bunk Johnson, one of the three trumpeter "kings" of early New Orleans jazz. Johnson may have responded to young Louis's incessant pleas "to learn him how to play" by providing some rudimentary but important instruction; more likely, however, Joe "Buddy" Petit played a larger role (Bergreen, p. 63). During much of the next fifteen months, Louis received musical training of a more formal nature as a member of the band in the New Orleans Home for Colored Waifs, where he was sent for juvenile delinquency after firing his "step-father's" pistol into the air during a 1912 New Year's Eve celebration.

By 1914, Armstrong had acquired the skills necessary to become a fledgling member of the local fraternity of honky-tonk and parade musicians before the closing of Storyville in 1917 set the stage for the great jazz diaspora. When Oliver left New Orleans for Chicago in 1918, Armstrong took Oliver's place in Kid Ory's band, then regarded as the best "hot jazz" band in New Orleans. He was also hired as second trumpet in the popular Tuxedo Brass Band. An early marriage in 1918 to Daisy Parker, a skinny prostitute (at the Brick House) who wore artificial hips to bolster her figure, ended in 1922 owing to the combination of their dalliances, his devotion to the cornet, and her habit of relying on a razor to settle their differences, but not before the couple had unofficially adopted Clarence Hatfield, the son of a cousin who died following childbirth.

During a time when he also hauled coal and briefly but unsuccessfully tried his hand at pimping, Armstrong's early career included stints at Henry Matranga's place, Pete Lala's joint, Henry Ponce's raunchy honky-tonk, and the Brick House, along with a variety of local parade bands and Fate Marable's orchestra on the *Dixie Belle*, a New Orleans riverboat. For several years following World War I—beginning only a few months after the Original Dixieland Jazz Band's recording of "Tiger Rag" had started a national jazz sensation—Armstrong traveled seasonally with Marable's orchestra up and down the Mississippi River. He later described his experience with Marable as essential to his development as a musician. By 1921 Armstrong was experimenting with the notion of his

Louis Armstrong. Jazz musician Louis Armstrong, 1953. New York World–Telegram and the Sun Newspaper Photograph Collection, Prints and Photographs Division, Library of Congress

cornet leading the group but without interrupting the overall flow of the music—the prototype of the modern jazz solo.

The World's Greatest Trumpet Player. In 1922 Armstrong accepted King Oliver's famous invitation to join his Creole Jazz Band in Chicago. By the fall of that year, Armstrong—who soon hit two hundred high C's in a much-storied cutting contest (one of many contests in which instrumentalists challenged each other)—had become the new phenomenon on the Chicago scene. A new era in jazz music had begun to take shape through the inspired stylizations delivered by Armstrong. He made his first recordings in 1923 with Oliver's band, the most influential "hot jazz" band in Chicago, when the city was an emerging center of jazz music. The appearance of such recordings had a profound impact on jazz because now performers could hear repeatedly and imitate accurately the stylizations of creative musicians such as Armstrong. Originally, Armstrong had been eager to work with Oliver—who served as both mentor and father figure; and in the process he had met and married his second wife, Lil Hardin Armstrong, the pianist in Oliver's band. By early 1925, however, Armstrong had succumbed to Lil's urgings to seek more prominent billing, and so he quit Oliver's group. Armstrong and Oliver parted amicably before Armstrong moved to New York City to join the Fletcher Henderson Orchestra, the leading African American group of the time and a factor in the rise of swing music. Armstrong's introduction to New York City came at precisely the same time that the Harlem Renaissance was becoming a nationally recognized phenomenon. Soon Armstrong switched to the trumpet in order to blend better with the other musicians in Henderson's group. Armstrong's innovations in this period served as harmonic and rhythmic harbingers of jazz trends over the next several decades. At the time, Armstrong may have come close to achieving the journalist Heywood Broun's expectations for a "supremely great negro artist" who could embody the spirit of the Harlem Renaissance.

After returning to Chicago late in 1925, Armstrong began recording under his own name with his renowned Hot Five and Hot Seven. Armstrong's early years with his Hot Five and Hot Seven groups produced his best recorded performances, distinguished by cornet and trumpet improvisations that set jazz standards for the time. Among the common features of Armstrong's virtuosity are joyous and original melodies, creative leaps, and subtle or driving rhythms. The originality of his pieces is heightened by Armstrong's playing techniques, developed through constant practice. His unique skills contributed greatly to the emergence of the trumpet as a solo instrument in jazz. Among the recorded hits of this period were "Muggles" (referring to marijuana, for which Armstrong had a lifelong fondness), "West End Blues" (which set the jazz standard for decades due to Armstrong's improvisational trumpet introduction), and "Weatherbird" (featuring the famous 1928 duet with Earl Hines). The 1926 Hot Five recording of "Heebie Jeebies" featured the first recorded example of Armstrong's scat singing; and the huge popular response made the group the best known jazz band in the nation.

The Great "Satchmo." Following a brief return to Harlem in 1929 and a musical part in the show *Hot Chocolates*, Armstrong moved briefly to Los Angeles in 1930 (where he was arrested for possession of marijuana); but by 1931 he had returned to Chicago and recorded successfully despite the downturn of the Depression era. He soon began touring Europe and thus his fame grew internationally. Over the next thirty years, he lived primarily on the road as he performed more than three hundred engagements annually. Armstrong's fame derived largely from his artistry, but his popularity also stemmed from his natural good humor and his lifetime dedication to pleasing his audiences. Just watching an Armstrong performance could be an exhilarating experience. His joyful spirit radiated through the audience as he bowed backward and pointed his trumpet skyward while blasting out high C's. As he wiped away sweat with his trademark handkerchief, Satchmo (as he had come to be known) flashed the famous toothy grin that symbolized the happiness his music brought both him and his audience. After spending many years on the road, he settled (or at least bought a home) in Queens, New York, in 1943 with his fourth wife, Lucille, whom he had wed in 1942.

When big band bookings fell off in the late 1940s, Armstrong's longtime manager Joe Glaser disbanded the sixteen-piece orchestra and began booking a six-piece group called the All Stars. Armstrong made numerous recordings with the All Stars during a period when he also appeared in more than thirty motion pictures. A while later he made some amazing recordings with Duke Ellington. In 1964 he recorded "Hello Dolly!" his best-selling record, which became number one on the hit chart and made Armstrong, at sixty-four, the oldest person ever to accomplish this feat. Failing health finally limited his appearances, but he still maintained a hectic tour schedule until only a few years before his death. In his later years, critics and colleagues noted that sometimes he seemed to be playing by rote but during other gigs he often astonished his band with his energetic performances; he continued to play until only weeks before he died in 1971 of a heart attack at age sixty-nine.

"Ambassador Satch" and King of the Zulus. By the 1960s, "Ambassador Satch" had toured Africa, Europe, and Asia with tremendous success under U.S. State Department auspices. During the Central High crisis (Little Rock) of 1957, however, he canceled a State Department tour of the USSR, saying: "The way they are treating my people in the South, the government can go to hell" (Bergreen, p. 471). Indeed, Armstrong never dismissed the racism and bigotry that he and other blacks had suffered. While talking extensively about race in America, he made it clear that he knew—as expressed in one of his recordings—what it meant to be "Black and Blue." As a protest against segregation in New Orleans, he refused to perform there for many years until after passage of the Civil Rights Act. And when the Selma-to-Montgomery marchers were attacked in 1965, he proclaimed: "They would beat Jesus if he was black and marched" (Bergreen, p. 319). Some critics still labeled him an Uncle Tom and criticized him for playing before segregated audiences, appearing in a grass skirt as "King of the Zulus," and using other racist caricatures during his performances. "Of course Pops Toms," said Billie Holiday in his defense, "but he Toms from the heart" (Bergreen, p. 246). And his accepting the Mardi Gras title of "King of the Zulus," bestowed on Armstrong in 1949 by the leading black Carnival Krewe, was simply his acknowledgment of a local honor; for generations, the traditional grass skirt and blackface makeup of the Zulus had been used to satirize white southern racist attitudes. Late in his career, however, the "Satchmo" nickname and Armstrong's warm southern personality, coupled with his natural love of entertaining and his obvious efforts to please his audience, resulted in a public persona—the grin, the clowning, the handkerchief—that seemed affected and even somewhat of a racist caricature.

Lip damage caused by Armstrong's high-pressure playing technique is clearly visible in pictures from the mid-1920s. Because the damage prevented him from playing at times, he began to sing more purposefully to fill time during performances. He put the trumpet aside temporarily before changing his embouchure in order to continue playing, but as a result singing had become a greater part of his performances. Long before "Hello Dolly!" he had achieved a hit with his playing and scat singing in "Heebie Jeebies." While some critics may overreach by crediting Armstrong with the invention of jazz singing, Armstrong's influence on Harry "Bing" Crosby and others is particularly important to the subsequent development of popular music. Crosby admired and copied Armstrong and other African American artists, as is evident on such early Crosby recordings as the 1931 hit "Just One More Chance." As a result, Crosby has been credited with weaving into the fabric of popular music "an Afro-American concept of song as a lyrical extension of speech."

Armstrong was without peer as a performer-writer; his autobiographical musings focused on his early years in New Orleans and his life during the jazz age. Armstrong's writings (most of which he expected to be published posthumously) included many ribald jokes and intimate personal reminiscences. Overall they should be valued as both an account of the lives of poor blacks in New Orleans at the turn of the twentieth century, and a collection of proverbs—"the fruit of a lifetime's experience as a black man and black musician in twentieth-century America."

Among Armstrong's best-known popular hits were "Stardust," "What a Wonderful World," "When the Saints Go Marching In," "Dream a Little Dream of Me," "Ain't Misbehavin'," and "Stompin' at the Savoy." Many years after his death, Armstrong's recordings remain popular, and his music is more widely available a generation after his death than at any time during his lifetime. "Melancholy Blues" as recorded by Armstrong and the Hot Seven was included on the Voyager Golden Record sent into outer space to represent the greatest musical achievements of humankind.

[*See also* Jazz *and* New Orleans.]

BIBLIOGRAPHY

Armstrong, Louis. *Louis Armstrong, in His Own Words: Selected Writings*. Edited by Thomas Brothers. New York: Oxford University Press, 1999.

Armstrong, Louis. *Satchmo: My Life in New Orleans*. New York: Prentice-Hall, 1954.

Bergreen, Laurence. *Louis Armstrong: An Extravagant Life*. New York: Broadway, 1997.

Collier, James. *Louis Armstrong: An American Genius*. New York: Oxford University Press, 1983.

—KARL RODABAUGH

ASANTE, MOLEFI (b. 14 August 1942), scholar. One of the foremost contemporary scholars in the field of African American studies, Asante was born Arthur Lee Smith Jr. in Valdosta, Georgia, one of sixteen children of Arthur Lee Smith and Lillie Smith. In 1964 he graduated cum laude from Oklahoma Christian University with a BA in communications. The next year he earned his MA, also in communications, from Pepperdine University. Three years later, in 1968, he earned his PhD in communications from the University of California, Los Angeles (UCLA).

After spending a year at Purdue University, Asante returned to UCLA as a faculty member. With the 1969 publication of his first major work, *Rhetoric of Black Revolution*, he was named director of the university's Center for Afro-American Studies. He helped create the African American Library at UCLA and helped establish its MA program in Afro-American studies. In 1971 he founded and served as editor of the *Journal of Black Studies*, dealing with many aspects of the black experience. He adopted the name Molefi Kete Asante while visiting the University of Ghana in 1973. That same year, at the age of thirty, he was appointed a full professor and chair of the communications department at the State University of New York at Buffalo. During his tenure at Buffalo, Asante published many books and articles dealing with transracial communication. In 1977 he made the transition from the communications department to the department of black studies, where he also served as chair.

In 1980 Asante released the work that defined a great part of his career, *Afrocentricity*. The book outlines the concept of Afrocentricity, a term coined by Asante, which attempts to recenter knowledge in an African rather than a European context. Asante argued that his purpose in writing this book was to provide "agency" to African Americans who had been, as a people, disoriented because of a negatively biased conception of their own history. He expanded upon this idea in two further works, *The Afrocentric Idea* (1987) and *Kemet, Afrocentricity, and Knowledge* (1990). His works sparked great controversy; competing scholars deemed the theory an exaggeration of African contributions to history and an assertion of black superiority.

In 1984 Asante was appointed chair of the African American studies department at Temple University. At Temple he founded the first PhD program for African American studies. Throughout all the controversy surrounding his work, Asante continued to be a prolific author, publishing more than sixty books and three hundred articles on various topics. He served as a visiting professor at Florida State University, Howard University, and the University of Zimbabwe, where he trained a group of journalists after that country's independence movement. Though disputes with faculty caused him to resign as chair, he continued to teach and publish at Temple University. Other notable releases include *The History of Africa* (2007) and *An Afrocentric Manifesto* (2007).

[*See also* Africa, Idea of; Afrocentrism; *and* Educators and Academics.]

BIBLIOGRAPHY

Jackson, Ronald L., II, and Sonja M. Brown Givens. *Black Pioneers in Communication Research*. New York: Sage, 2006. Includes a profile of Asante focusing on his work in communications.

Turner, Diane D. "An Oral History Interview: Molefi Kete Asante." *Journal of Black Studies* 32, no. 6 (July 2002): 711–734.

—DANIEL DOUGLAS

ASHE, ARTHUR (b. 10 July 1943; d. 6 February 1993), tennis player, activist, broadcast journalist, and humanitarian. Born in Richmond, Virginia, Arthur Robert Ashe Jr. was the son of Arthur and Mattie Ashe. Arthur experienced a traumatic loss at age six when his mother died suddenly. He turned inward and toward books and learning. An excellent student, he graduated first in his high school class. Given his appetite for books, success as a student was likely; however, given his physical stature, his success as a tennis player was a surprise. Though physically small, the skills he honed on the public recreational courts, maintained by his father, helped mold him into a top player.

Coming of age in segregated Richmond, Virginia, shaped Ashe's early tennis experiences and informed his political consciousness. He was not allowed to compete on the city's best courts or in the city's top tournaments. To improve his game he moved from Richmond to Saint Louis in 1960. The skills he sharpened made him good enough to earn a tennis scholarship to the University of California, Los Angeles (UCLA).

As a standout college player, Ashe was selected for Davis Cup play in 1963, making him the first African American picked to play for the U.S. team. Before graduating from UCLA with a bachelor of science degree in business administration in 1966, Ashe further distinguished himself as an athlete with individual and team National Collegiate Athletic Association championships in 1965. After UCLA, Ashe became a first lieutenant during his tenure in the U.S. Army from 1966 to 1968. He also served as captain of the Davis Cup team in 1966 and 1967.

In 1968 against the backdrop of the assassinations of Martin Luther King Jr. and Robert Kennedy, urban rioting, and, in sports, the Mexico City Olympics protest, Ashe became the first black male to win the U.S. Open. Thus at a critical historical moment Ashe emerged as a national symbol of hope.

In 1969 Ashe helped found the Association of Tennis Professionals, a union of sorts that enabled tennis players to earn a living as professional athletes. Later that same year he became the first African American ranked as the number one American tennis player.

Ashe used his status and visibility to apply for a visa to play in the South African Open, then a significant tournament ranked only a tier below the prestigious Grand Slam events. Ashe knew that his visa would be denied because of the country's apartheid government, which systematically discriminated against those of African descent. When his visa was rejected, Ashe called for South Africa's expulsion from the International Lawn Tennis Federation and from Davis Cup play, and he gained significant support. His actions drew attention to the injustices of South Africa's political system before this had become a significant political issue for many Americans. In 1973 when South Africa granted Ashe a visa after denying him three times, he became the first black person to play in the South African Open. This was a controversial first because of an international boycott of the country. Contrary to popular opinion, however, Ashe negotiated with the South African government to facilitate the desegregation of Johannesburg's Ellis Park for his matches. With Tom Okker as his partner, Ashe won the doubles match and earned the admiration of many South African fans.

In 1975 Ashe became the first black man to win Wimbledon, beating Jimmy Connors. Long admired for his integrity and grace under pressure, Ashe was further distinguished because his quiet, calm demeanor was so starkly different from those of Connors and John McEnroe, the biggest male tennis stars of the era.

Arthur Ashe. The men's singles champion Arthur Ashe after his victory over Jimmy Connors at Wimbledon, 5 July 1975. AP Images

After his historic Wimbledon victory, Ashe, along with the musician and actor Harry Belafonte, founded Artists and Athletes against Apartheid, which encouraged entertainers and athletes to respect the United Nations sanctions against South Africa. The organization's influence kept economic pressure on the South African government and contributed to its demise. When Nelson Mandela was released from Robben Island Prison in 1990, Ashe, for his efforts, was one of the first people that Mandela wanted to meet. The two met in 1992.

Ashe retired from tennis after suffering a heart attack in 1979, though he remained active in the sport as the Davis Cup team captain. Ashe also further immersed himself in scholarship. In 1983 he lectured at Yale University under a Kiphuth Fellowship. He refused a teaching post at Yale and chose instead Florida Memorial College in order to teach black students at a historically black school. Finding a dearth of scholarship on the black athlete in the United States, he personally funded research into the subject. *A Hard Road to Glory: A History of the African-American Athlete* (1988), a three-volume work, was the result of his investment. The work was well received, and PBS used it as the basis for a television special that eventually won an Emmy.

With Ashe's second heart attack in 1983, he received a blood transfusion that led to his contracting HIV. After Ashe underwent brain surgery in 1988, doctors confirmed that he had AIDS. HIV and AIDS prevention were then added to the list of social programs and political causes that Ashe championed. The Arthur Ashe Foundation for the Defeat of AIDS raises money to fund research and treatment for AIDS patients in the United States and beyond. Ashe continued to fight other political battles as well. In 1992 he was arrested for his part in a protest against the poor treatment of Haitian immigrants and U.S. policy on Haiti.

The 1968 U.S. Open and 1975 Wimbledon championship titles that Arthur Ashe earned distinguished him as an athlete. The sincerity of his fight against the ugliness of injustice revealed his poised fearlessness. Ashe's ability to apply tactical skills, discipline, and courage learned from years of athletic training to the urgent problems of his day made him a much-admired citizen long after his death in 1993 from complications from AIDS. In honor of Ashe, in 1997 the U.S. Tennis Association dedicated its largest stadium in his name. His hometown of Richmond also acknowledged his legacy by erecting a statue in his honor on Monument Avenue, a historic location otherwise populated by Confederate war heroes.

[*See also* AIDS; Antiapartheid; Haiti; *and* Sports.]

BIBLIOGRAPHY

ArthurAshe.org. http://www.arthurashe.org. This is an excellent source for video footage of Ashe discussing his life and work.

Ashe, Arthur, and Arnold Rampersad. *Days of Grace: A Memoir*. New York: Alfred A. Knopf, 1993.

Official Web site of Arthur Ashe. "Arthur Ashe Biography." http://www.cmgworldwide.com/sports/ashe/about/bio.htm. This is an excellent source for its listing of Ashe's numerous awards and achievements.

—MICHELLE S. HITE

ASSOCIATED NEGRO PRESS. The most prominent black print news service of the first half of the twentieth century, the Associated Negro Press (ANP) was created by Claude Barnett, a former advertisement representative for the *Chicago Defender*. The ANP served the nation's black weekly newspapers, providing news briefs, feature articles, and opinion pieces. Barnett founded the Associated Negro Press in Chicago in 1919. It became the most prominent national wire service for black newspapers until the National Newspaper Publishers Association established its wire service in 1944. The ANP lasted until the late 1960s.

After a stint in the Chicago post office—which included a part-time job selling photographic portraits of black people—Barnett joined the *Defender*. He traveled the country for the *Defender* in 1918 to get news and advertising representatives, talking to many black newspaper editors. Barnett resigned from the *Defender* and started his own agency, the Associated Negro Press, in 1919. The vast majority of his clients were black weekly newspapers. Barnett charged newspapers different prices according to their sizes and the grades of news. In turn, newspapers were supposed to provide news from their regions. The ANP also supplied news to businesses, individuals, and schools.

Barnett recruited a legion of volunteer journalists and part-time (and, later, full-time) reporters and correspondents in various cities, including New York, Philadelphia, Columbia, South Carolina, and seven other cities. He also had correspondents in Nigeria, Ghana, Haiti, Ethiopia, India, Kenya, Jamaica, London, Tokyo, and Moscow. Journalists who later went on to significant careers in the black press, like Enoch Waters at the *Chicago Defender* and Roy Wilkins, a young managing editor at the *Kansas City Call*, got their start at the ANP.

During its tenure, the ANP—which established offices in New York City and Washington, D.C.—had a succession of editors, including Nahum Daniel Brascher, Percival L. Prattis, Frank Marshall Davis, and Charlene Harston. Its Washington correspondents included Alvin E. White, Ernest Johnson, and Alice A. Dunnigan, who became the first black female accredited correspondent to cover Congress.

A variety of news and information sources served the growing black press in the 1920s and 1930s. Barnett was so successful that at least forty-eight competitors attempted to copy his methods between 1919 and 1949. The press offices of the NAACP and the Tuskegee Institute served as fonts of information for the black press. These offices kept up weekly information about desegregation court cases and lynchings.

In 1928 the ANP interviewed Oscar De Priest, the first African American to win a congressional seat in the twentieth century, after his victory. Barnett often used his contacts to get ANP interviews with prominent elected officials, including John Nance Garner, Franklin Delano Roosevelt's vice president from 1933 to 1941, in the late 1930s.

In the 1930s Barnett employed writers who were specialists in their beats: education, radio, music, and sports, among other topics. Its columnists that decade included Kelly Miller, dean of arts and sciences of Howard University; the Harlem writer Langston Hughes; and Mary Church Terrell, founding president of the National Association of Colored Women. Between 1935 and 1937 the ANP got $2,500 in grants from the Rosenwald Fund. Barnett used part of the money to set up a salary for a regular Washington correspondent. One of the ANP's regular contributors was John Spivak, a white reporter who covered the Scottsboro Boys case, the internationally known frame-up of nine black youths accused of raping two white women.

The ANP peaked in 1935 with 235 clients, but it had limited influence in terms of journalism, civil rights, politics, economics, and social policy. The real editorial power was held by local newspapers. The publishers of those newspapers—led by the *Pittsburgh Courier*, the *Defender*, and the *Baltimore Afro-American*, all three of which had national editions by the 1930s—had limited interest in or commitment to the ANP. In 1940 African American newspapers came together in Chicago to form the National Newspaper Publishers Association (NNPA), a national trade organization for black newspapers, thus creating a national news service of their own. By 1945 the NNPA News Service had an office in Washington, D.C.

The growth of the NNPA News Service, the explosion of black magazines such as *Ebony* and *Jet*, the start of the modern civil rights movement, and Barnett's desire to expand to Africa all contributed to the demise of the ANP. The ANP had only thirty-seven clients in 1958. In 1960 Barnett formed the World News Service to serve newspapers in Africa. Barnett sent the world service news by airmail from Chicago. When Barnett retired, selling the ANP in 1964, its client list totaled seventy-five black newspapers, two radio stations, two magazines, two hundred African newspapers, and other nonmedia institutions.

The ANP was sold to Alfred Duckett, a New York City public relations executive. It moved to New York, but it had faded by 1970. Many black entrepreneurs, journalists, and activists tried to create a news service serving black print, but only the NNPA News Service lasted, and by the early 1990s, even it existed only as a press release and columnist service.

[*See also* Black Press; Civil Rights and the Media; Journalism, Print and Broadcast; *and* National Newspaper Publishers Association.]

Bibliography

Burroughs, Todd Steven. "Drums in the Global Village: Toward an Ideological History of Black Media." PhD diss., University of Maryland, College Park, 2001.

Hogan, Lawrence D. *A Black National News Service: The Associated Negro Press and Claude Barnett, 1919–1945*. Rutherford, N.J.: Farleigh Dickinson University Press, 1984.

Kobre, Sidney, and Reva H. Kobre. *A Gallery of Black Journalists Who Advanced Their Race and Our Nation*. Hampton, Va.: United Brothers and Sisters Communications Systems, 1993. A popular history of black journalism, featuring profiles of black journalists and black periodicals.

Wilson, Clint C., II, and Armistead Pride. *A History of the Black Press*. Washington, D.C.: Howard University Press, 1997.

Wolseley, Roland E. *The Black Press, U.S.A.* 2d ed. Ames: Iowa State University Press, 1990. A scholarly study of black periodicals.

—Todd Steven Burroughs

ASSOCIATION FOR THE STUDY OF AFRICAN AMERICAN LIFE AND HISTORY. The Association for the Study of African American Life and History (ASALH) is the world's oldest learned society dedicated to the promotion, research, preservation, interpretation, and dissemination of information about the life, history, and culture of Africans, African Americans, and the African diaspora. Founded in Chicago on 8 September 1915 as the Association for the Study of Negro Life and History by Carter G. Woodson (1875–1950) and four other people, the association was incorporated under the laws of the District of Columbia on 3 October 1915. Its stated purposes were to collect sociological and historical data, to publish books on Negro life and history, to promote the study of the Negro through clubs and schools, and to bring about harmony between the races by interpreting the one to the other.

In the beginning the association had very little moral or financial support, and its longevity must be ascribed to the vision, initiative, self-sacrifice, and persistence of Woodson. Woodson, the son of slaves, had a PhD in history from Harvard University, but he gave up a teaching position and devoted his time and energies to directing the association. In 1916, to clarify his vision, he borrowed money to publish the first issue of the *Journal of Negro History*. Its scholarly articles and documents attracted the attention of academics, who responded with subscriptions. However, there was little support for the journal outside academia. Woodson sought financial help from as many as two hundred philanthropists, but his letters yielded a mere fourteen dollars. The only substantial support from outside the black community came from Julius Rosenwald, who was so impressed by a sample copy of the journal that he promised Woodson a hundred dollars a quarter to underwrite its publication. The journal, now named the *Journal of African American History*, still publishes peer-reviewed, scholarly historical articles, rare documents, book reviews, and notes, and may be found in all reputable libraries.

In 1926 Woodson and the association inaugurated Negro History Week. He established this celebration during the second week in February—a week during which the birthdays of Frederick Douglass and Abraham Lincoln fell—not to play up grievances but to bring to the forefront of the nation's consciousness the contributions made by African Americans to the building of the nation. Woodson believed that a focus on black achievements not only would stimulate self-pride and self-improvement among Negroes but also would secure for the race the same consideration that is given to white achievement in the curricula of schools and colleges. During the United States bicentennial observance in 1976 the association expanded the celebration to include the entire month of February; the association sets the theme for Black History Month and publishes products suitable for classroom use that promote the theme.

The hunger for curricular materials to teach Negro history during the designated week was so great that in 1937 Woodson and the association launched another publication geared toward enhancing teaching and learning in black history among elementary and secondary educators. The *Negro History Bulletin*, today called the *Black History Bulletin*, publishes articles on all aspects of black history that are grounded in educational theory and supported by practice. Twice a year the *Bulletin* gives teachers fresh perspectives on the current Black History Month theme through lesson plans, suggestions for classroom activities, copies of primary sources, and other Black History Month products published by the association. Much of this material was at first published by the association's publishing arm, Associated Publishers, founded by Carter G. Woodson in 1922 to publish books on black history. Woodson's classic study *The Mis-Education of the Negro* was published in 1933, and several other texts on the history of African Americans were published over the years. However, the publishing firm operated at a loss for years and was eventually sold.

Woodson died in 1950, and since then the ASALH has been led by committed presidents, most of whom are practicing academics and who serve three-year terms. The president is assisted by an executive council, elected by the members, and an advisory board of scholars, businesspeople, and laypeople. The association's headquarters are in Washington, D.C.

The ASALH continues the work and legacy of its founder, Carter G. Woodson, as it strives to be the nexus of the ivory tower and the global public. The association is organized around a network of national and international branches whose diverse membership is designed to promote the knowledge of African and African American history, and the history of Africans in the diaspora, through a program of education, research, and publishing. Its membership includes scholars and laypeople, and its mission still revolves around promoting a fundamental truth to the world: people of African descent are makers of history.

[*See also Journal of Negro History*; Negro History Week/Month; *and* Woodson, Carter G.]

BIBLIOGRAPHY

Hine, Darlene Clark, William C. Hine, and Stanley Harrold. *The African-American Odyssey*. Upper Saddle River, N.J.: Prentice Hall, 2000.

Quarles, Benjamin. *The Negro in the Making of America*. New York: Collier, 1964.

Woodson, Carter G. *African Background Outlined*. Washington, D.C.: Association for the Study of Negro Life and History, 1936.

Woodson, Carter G. *The Mis-Education of the Negro*. Washington, D.C.: Associated Publishers, 1933.

—ANNETTE PALMER

ASTRONAUTS. African Americans have always played an important part in the U.S. space program. Robert Henry Lawrence Jr. was the first African American astronaut, although he never went on a space mission. Lawrence was an air force test pilot and among the first people named to the U.S. Air Force manned orbiting laboratory program, a precursor to the space shuttle program developed in the 1960s by the National Aeronautics and Space Administration (NASA). Lawrence died in an airplane accident in 1967, and NASA did not recruit another African American astronaut for more than ten years.

In 1978 three African American men were selected by NASA for the astronaut training program: Guion S. Bluford Jr., Frederick Gregory, and Ronald E. McNair. Bluford became the first African American to fly in space in 1983, and he took part in four missions, totaling more than 688 hours in space, before retiring from NASA in 1993. McNair took part in two missions aboard the space shuttle *Challenger*. In 1984 on mission 44-B he played a key role in the development of the shuttle's remote manipulator arm, testing it for use in retrieving damaged satellite equipment. In 1986 McNair was again to fly aboard

Astronaut Guion S. Bluford Jr. On 30 August 1983 Guion S. Bluford Jr. became the first African American to venture into space. NASA

Challenger; this time he was scheduled to use the remote manipulator arm to release a satellite that would photograph Halley's Comet. On that mission, however, a technical problem caused *Challenger* to disintegrate a minute and a half after launching on 28 January 1986, and McNair was killed along with the rest of the shuttle crew. In 1992 Mae Jemison became the first African American female astronaut to fly in space, as a crew member aboard the space shuttle *Endeavour*.

African American astronauts have also been active in the space program at the administrative level. Isaac T. Gillam IV managed NASA's Delta program, charged with the launch of weather and communications satellites into orbit. Gillam became the first African American to lead a NASA research center when he directed NASA's Dryden Flight Research Center in Edwards, California, a facility for testing space shuttles. Charles F. Bolden Jr., a space shuttle pilot on four flights from 1986 to 1994 logging more than 680 hours in space, served as deputy administrator of NASA from 1992 to 1994.

[*See also* Space Program, U.S., African Americans in, *and* Technology and Engineering.]

BIBLIOGRAPHY

Burns, Khephra, and William Miles. *Black Stars in Orbit: NASA's African-American Astronauts*. San Diego, Calif.: Harcourt Brace, 1995.

Gubert, Betty Kaplan, Miriam Sawyer, and Caroline M. Fannin. *Distinguished African Americans in Aviation and Space Science*. Westport, Conn.: Oryx Press, 2002.

Hardesty, Von. *Black Wings: Courageous Stories of African Americans in Aviation and Space History*. New York: Harper Collins, 2008.

—COURTNEY L. YOUNG

ATLANTA. In 1900, Atlanta was the forty-third largest city in the United States with a population of almost ninety thousand, 40 percent of which was African American. Three southern cities at the time were larger than Atlanta—the river cities of New Orleans, Louisville, and Memphis. Over the course of the twentieth century, Atlanta's explosive growth—first as a railroad crossroads and later as an air and automobile/trucking center—outpaced that of its regional rivals as it became the ninth-largest metropolitan area and the unofficial center of the civil rights movement in the United States.

Living in the city in 1900 was W. E. B. Du Bois, a professor at Atlanta University who had come in 1897 to undertake the scientific study of the American Negro. From 1898 to 1914, Du Bois edited the Atlanta University Publications, annual assessments of African American life and institutions. In 1903, he published a series of reflective essays, *The Souls of Black Folk*, in which he predicted correctly that the problem of the twentieth century would be the problem of the color line. He also dubbed Booker T. Washington's address eight years earlier at the 1895 opening of Atlanta's Cotton States and International Exposition the "Atlanta Compromise." Washington's address had been enthusiastically received by a mostly white (and segregated audience), but Du Bois criticized Washington's address for recommending Negro submission in the face of white domination. Du Bois argued that Washington's approach to race relations abandoned political and judicial recourse by blacks to the abrogation of their civil rights and discouraged black youth from pursuing the opportunity of higher education.

Du Bois saw in Atlanta what happened when African Americans abandoned politics and rejected higher education. In April 1899, while he was walking downtown, Du Bois observed human knuckles in a grocery store window—they were the knuckles of Sam Hose, put there by whites who had traveled to the nearby town of Newnan to witness the torture, killing, and mutilation of the

Atlanta Community. African Americans and houses in Atlanta, Georgia, 1936. Photograph by Walker Evans. Farm Security Administration–Office of War Information Photograph Collection, Prints and Photographs Division, Library of Congress

accused felon. This example of white savagery enacted on blacks (because they lacked recourse to political and judicial institutions) motivated Du Bois to work toward guaranteeing basic civil rights for African Americans.

Teaching and living among young African Americans, Du Bois experienced firsthand the value of a liberal arts education. He also worked with other professionals in Atlanta, including John Hope (1868–1936), a professor at Atlanta Baptist College (now Morehouse College), who became its first black president in 1906, and Alonzo Herndon (1858–1927), a black barber who parlayed a successful chain of shops catering to a white clientele into a fortune in real estate and life insurance. Du Bois, Hope, and Herndon all traveled to Niagara Falls in July 1905 for a meeting to discuss civil rights that led to the founding of the National Association for the Advancement of Colored People (NAACP) because their rise into the professions in Atlanta had not saved them from subjugation to the color line.

The Atlanta Race Riot. Repression of African Americans in Atlanta led to the 1906 Race Riot, during which white mobs roamed the downtown attacking and murdering African Americans who were traveling on trolleys or by foot and by destroying black-owned businesses, including Herndon's barber shop. Du Bois responded with the "Litany of Atlanta," written on "the Day of Death, 1906" and published 11 October in the *Independent*: "A city lay in travail, God our Lord, and from her loins sprang twin Murder and Black Hate. Red was the midnight; clang, crack, and cry of death and fury filled the air and trembled underneath the stars where church spires pointed silently to Thee" (656–657). The riot, which had been provoked by sensational articles in the white press and a race-baiting gubernatorial campaign, was followed by the additional repression of civil and human rights. Jim Crow laws passed by the state legislature in 1891 requiring streetcar segregation, once sporadically implemented, were now rigidly enforced, and the 1907 general assembly passed an amendment to the state constitution that set up registration barriers and reduced registered black voters in the state from 25 percent to 4 percent of previously eligible males. Although blacks constituted 40 percent of Atlanta's population, there were no black elected officials, judges, jury members, policemen, or legislative representatives. The city's principal centers of government—the Capitol,

Atlanta City Hall, and Fulton County Court House—were segregated facilities.

In 1920 Atlanta's population topped 200,000, 31 percent of which was black. The Chamber of Commerce sought to attract regional headquarters of national corporations to Atlanta with an advertising campaign in the *Saturday Evening Post* in the mid-1920s. The city was becoming known as the headquarters of the Coca-Cola Company, whose franchised bottlers were spreading across the country. The Ku Klux Klan was another franchising operation revived in Atlanta in 1915 at the time of the showing of D. W. Griffith's *The Birth of a Nation*, a fictionalized account of the post–Civil War terrorist organization. Like Coca Cola and other corporations, its national and regional offices were located in several downtown skyscrapers. The revived Klan set up local "klaverns" throughout the nation, and its chapters in Atlanta and Georgia played important roles in local and state government into the 1970s.

Auburn Avenue. In response to the hostile environment, African Americans began to cluster their businesses and social clubs within areas of the city with large black residential populations. By 1940, Auburn Avenue had become the center of black business and social life. Historic churches like Big Bethel AME (1891), Wheat Street Baptist (1920–1923), and Ebenezer Baptist (1922) lined the avenue, along with office buildings—the Rucker Building (1904), the Odd Fellows Building (1912), the Herndon Building (1924), and the Prince Hall Masons Building (1937)—which housed black professionals, insurance companies, and social service and civic organizations. On the city's west side, Atlanta University Center was formed in 1929 to unite Clark College, Morris Brown College, and Gammon Theological Seminary with Atlanta University, Morehouse College and Spelman College. These institutions stimulated the growth of nearby neighborhoods and a commercial district of movie theaters, restaurants, and storefront offices along Hunter Street (now Martin Luther King Jr. Boulevard).

Black-White Negotiations. The religious, educational, and professional leaders in Atlanta's black neighborhoods served both as advocates for the civil and political rights of African Americans and as negotiators with the white power structure of Atlanta when it served white interests to respond to black needs. The whites-only Democratic primary was the principal barrier to effective black

Atlanta, 1954. Theatergoers outside the colored entrance to the Roxy Theatre. Special Collections and Archives, Pullen Library, Georgia State University

political influence because it determined the winner of the general election. In a 1921 bond referendum that required an affirmative vote in the general election, white business leaders gained black support with a promise to build the first public black high school in the city. After the referendum passed, the African American banker and developer Heman Perry (1873–1929) worked with the city to provide land for the school and also the first public park for African Americans, attractive elements of the Washington Park subdivision that he was developing just west of the Atlanta University Center.

The nexus of colleges, businesses, and civic associations served as an incubator for several generations of leaders who laid the ground work for the civil rights movement of the 1960s and 1970s. John Wesley Dobbs (1882–1961), the grand master of the Prince Hall Masons and the grandfather of Maynard Jackson (the city's first African American mayor), founded the Atlanta Civil and Political League to promote African American voting in 1936. A Democrat, he joined with the Republican A. T. Walden (1885–1965) to form the nonpartisan Atlanta Negro Voters League in 1949 to expand black voter registration in response to the outlawing of the whites-only Democratic primary in 1946.

The late 1940s and 1950s were a time of advancement for African Americans in Atlanta—their voting strength made them a force in mayoral and Board of Aldermen elections. Mayor William Hartsfield (1890–1971), a segregationist who (like other white politicians) had depended on the vote of a white electorate, became an accommodationist when he saw that he could attract black voters to his base. He subsequently hired the first black policemen in 1948 and had the city install street lights on Auburn Avenue. The array of African American leaders in Atlanta in mid-century included college presidents such as Benjamin Mays (1894–1984), ministers such as William Holmes Borders (1905–1993) and Martin Luther King Sr. (1899–1984), entrepreneurs such as the banker Jesse Blayton, Sr. (1897–1977), and the insurance executive Norris Bumstead Herndon (1897–1977). The milieu of Auburn Avenue and the Atlanta University Center incubated a new generation of race leaders who actively challenged the color line, the most famous of whom is Martin Luther King Jr. (1929–1968).

Martin Luther King Jr. Dr. King grew up on Auburn Avenue near Ebenezer Baptist Church where his father and grandfather were pastors, attended Washington High School and Morehouse College, and left the city for advanced theological education. He returned to Atlanta early in 1960 after his successful leadership of the Montgomery Bus Boycott. The Atlanta to which he returned was still a relatively small city of less than half a million, but, coupled with its burgeoning suburban counties, its metropolitan population exceeded a million and catapulted the city to the top twenty-five largest in the United States. The Chamber of Commerce, which was promoting the city in national magazines with a "Forward Atlanta" campaign, was seeking to attract corporate headquarters of national firms. Martin Luther King Jr. came to head the Southern Christian Leadership Conference (SCLC), which was headquartered in the Prince Hall Mason's Building on Auburn Avenue. King also served as assistant pastor to his father at the nearby Ebenezer Baptist Church.

After the February 1960 Greensboro lunch counter sit-in, students from Morehouse College, Spelman College, and the other Atlanta University Center institutions, led by Lonnie King (b. 1936), Julian Bond (b. 1940), and Marian Wright Edelman (b. 1939), organized a coordinated series of sit-ins at the cafeterias of the Capitol, Atlanta City Hall, Fulton County Court House, and other public facilities. The students preceded their demonstrations with the publication of a full-page ad in the 9 March 1960 *Atlanta Constitution* of "An Appeal for Human Rights," declaring that "[We do] not intend to wait placidly for those rights which are already legally and morally ours to be meted out to us one at a time," and that they could no longer "tolerate, in a nation professing democracy... the discriminatory conditions under which the Negro [was] living... in Atlanta, Georgia—supposedly one of the most progressive cities in the South" (p. 13).

The Atlanta University Center presidents and the ministers at the city's leading black churches were surprised by the student demonstrations; African American community leaders had been making slow progress in their negotiations with white political and business leaders. To attract national attention to their efforts and put additional pressure on the white power structure and the old-guard black leaders, the students recruited Martin Luther King Jr. to participate in a restaurant sit-in at Rich's, the city's leading department store, on 19 October 1960. The demonstration had its intended effect; Dr. King was arrested and then sent to the state prison at Reidsville on a charge that he had violated the terms of his probation (the result of an earlier traffic offense). King's plight attracted national attention when John F. Kennedy called Coretta Scott King to offer sympathy, and his campaign worked with white state and city politicians to have King released.

Under pressure from the federal courts and demonstrations by the new generation of student leaders, white leaders negotiated the desegregation of the Atlanta public schools in August 1961; many downtown lunch counters followed suit in September. This was an important step for Atlanta, since it happened peacefully with full cooperation of the black and white leadership in the city, and stood in contrast with the violent demonstrations that accompanied desegregation in other southern cities. However, this token school desegregation involved only nine black students in four high schools, and many restaurants and hotels in Atlanta continued to maintain the color line.

"A City Too Busy to Hate." While the struggle to dismantle the color line in Atlanta continued during the 1960s, the relative willingness of white civic and political leaders in the city to mediate this process attracted national attention. Atlanta mayor Ivan Allen (1911–2003), who in 1962—early in his tenure as mayor—erected a barricade on Payton Road to thwart the expansion of a black suburban neighborhood into a white area, came to see that the federal government could be a positive force for change in Atlanta. He was the only Southern mayor to testify before Congress in favor of the 1964 Civil Rights Act. In their efforts to attract corporate offices, the city's chamber of commerce touted Atlanta as the "city too busy to hate" in order to gain comparative advantage over its regional rivals where violent white protests caught the headlines.

There was a major disconnect between the relatively moderate politics in Atlanta City Hall and the defiant segregationist activities in the Capitol across the street. The 1956 general assembly added the Confederate Battle Emblem to the Georgia flag as a sign of its resistance to federal rulings requiring desegregation. But federal court rulings were having their effect; Georgia was forced to reapportion its legislative seats, paving the way for the 1962 election of Leroy Johnson (b. 1928) from Atlanta to the state senate and leading to the desegregation of the Capitol. In the city, the increase in the number of black residents contributed to the election of Q. V. Williamson to the Atlanta Board of Aldermen in 1965.

Black Political Base. The turmoil in the 1960s led to dramatic demographic changes in Atlanta as school desegregation began and African Americans were elected to public office. Although the total population of the City of Atlanta grew between 1960 and 1970 to just under 500,000, the white population decreased by 50,000 and the black population increased by 120,000. By 1970, at 48 percent of the population, whites were a minority in the city. Those whites who fled Atlanta could be found alongside thousands of migrants from the Northeast and the Midwest in the burgeoning suburban counties surrounding the central city. The concentration of black voting districts in the core of the metropolitan region created a base for black political advancement. In 1972, Andrew Young (b. 1932), a civil rights veteran and an aide to Martin Luther King Jr., was elected to represent Georgia's Fifth District in Congress. The following year, Maynard Jackson (1938–2003) was elected the city's first African American mayor.

The white population of the city dropped by another 120,000 thousand in the 1970s, as the new black political leadership forged a working relationship with the business community. Under the forceful leadership of Mayor Maynard Jackson, the two major public works projects of the decade—the construction of Hartsfield-Jackson International Airport and the Metropolitan Atlanta Rapid Transit Authority's rail-transit system—were opened to black- and female-owned businesses. The effort to attract big-league teams to Atlanta in the mid-1960s brought integrated sports with the Atlanta Braves, the Atlanta Hawks, and the Atlanta Falcons. Not only did these teams serve to enhance Atlanta's national image, they also promoted African American sports heroes like Hank Aaron (b. 1934), who broke Babe Ruth's home-run record in Atlanta Fulton County Stadium in 1974 and became part of the Atlanta civic and business establishment after his sports career ended.

Post–Civil Rights Atlanta. The overwhelmingly white suburban counties surrounding Atlanta experienced rapid growth in the late twentieth century. But by the 1990s, the population of these counties had changed, as both blacks and nonwhite immigrants settled in suburban subdivisions and apartment complexes. By 2000, DeKalb and Clayton counties were majority black; Fulton County, which includes the city of Atlanta, was 44 percent African American; and Cobb and Gwinnett counties were 19 percent and 13 percent black, respectively. As the African American populations increased in the suburban counties, blacks began to be elected to public office. In 1978, Michael Lomax (b. 1947) was elected the first black chair of the Fulton County Commission. In 2000, Vernon Jones (b. 1960) was elected the black CEO of DeKalb County.

The signature event in Atlanta in the 1990s was the 1996 Centennial Olympic Games brought to Atlanta by Billy Payne (b. 1947) and Mayor Andrew Young. The city updated its "City Too Busy to Hate" image, promoting itself as the civil rights capital of the nation, touting the successful struggle to end segregation. The King birth home became an important part of the city's tourist promotion after Congressman John Lewis (b. 1940) succeeded in garnering Congressional support for the creation of the Martin Luther King National Historic Site on Auburn Avenue. National corporations funded Coretta Scott King's memorial to her slain husband, the King Center, where the King tomb rested above a reflecting pool. Other tourist sites related to the city's segregated past were reinterpreted to fit into a biracial promotional image. The Margaret Mitchell House, where *Gone with the Wind* (with its racist stereotypes) was penned, established a biracial board that heralded Margaret Mitchell's subsidies to black medical students. Stone Mountain, with its Confederate memorial carving of President Jefferson Davis and Generals Robert E. Lee and Stonewall Jackson and its history as the site of the cross burning that revived the KKK in 1915, was transformed into a recreational attraction in majority-black DeKalb county with a spectacular nighttime laser-fireworks show that played on the mountain face and boomed an integrated medley of rhythm and blues and country songs.

In 2000, Atlanta boasted a population of over 5.2 million and claimed the ninth spot among the largest American metropolitan areas. De jure segregation had ended as African Americans were guaranteed access to public accommodations, had taken seats as elected representatives, were hired for city and county positions, and had relocated into all areas of the metropolis. However, patterns of segregation were still visible in neighborhoods, churches, and schools. A map of Atlanta's racial demography in 2000 revealed a central core that was heavily black south, southeast, and southwest of the downtown and extending into the suburban counties. As predicted by Du Bois, the color line was the problem of the twentieth century, and its residual effects in Atlanta continued into the twenty-first century.

[*See also* Atlanta Exposition Address (Atlanta Compromise); Atlanta Riot; Atlanta University; *Birth of a Nation, The*; Du Bois, W. E. B.; Georgia; Hose, Sam, Lynching of; Jackson, Maynard; King, Martin Luther, Jr.; King, Martin Luther, Sr.; *and* Young, Andrew.]

BIBLIOGRAPHY

Allen, Frederick. *Atlanta Rising: The Invention of an International City 1946–1996*. Atlanta: Longstreet Press, 1996. A journalistic account of Atlanta's growth focusing on the white power structure.

Ambrose, Andy. *Atlanta: An Illustrated History*. Athens, Ga.: Hill Street Press, 2003. An overview of Atlanta history with an emphasis of the evolving patterns of race relations.

Bayor, Ronald H. *Race and the Shaping of Twentieth-Century Atlanta*. Chapel Hill: University of North Carolina Press, 1996. Traces the indelible mark of racial bias through the century.

Ferguson, Karen. *Black Politics in New Deal Atlanta*. Chapel Hill: University of North Carolina Press, 2002. Examines the divide between the conservative African American elite leadership that emerged in the 1930s and 40s and the radical students of the 1960s.

Godshalk, David F. *Veiled Visions: The 1906 Atlanta Race Riot and the Reshaping of American Race Relations*. Chapel Hill: University of North Carolina Press, 2005. A detailed account of the Atlanta Race Riot and its differing narratives for black and white Atlanta.

Hunter, Tera W. *To 'Joy My Freedom: Southern Black Women's Lives and Labors after the Civil War*. Cambridge, Mass.: Harvard University Press, 1997. Chapters 3–10 examine the lives of black domestic workers in Atlanta in the late nineteenth and early twentieth centuries.

Keating, Larry. *Atlanta: Race, Class and Urban Expansion*. Philadelphia: Temple University Press, 2001. Examines public and private developments that have maintained race and class segregation as metropolitan Atlanta has spilled into surrounding counties.

Kruse, Kevin M. *White Flight: Atlanta and the Making of Modern Conservatism*. Princeton, N.J.: Princeton University Press, 2005. Argues that the demographic changes brought about by white suburban flight in Atlanta contributed to the modern conservative movement.

Kuhn, Clifford M., Harlon E. Joye, and E. Bernard West. *Living Atlanta: An Oral History of the City, 1914–1948*. Athens: University of Georgia Press, 1990. Oral histories by black and white, prominent and ordinary Atlantans, of life in a segregated city before World War II.

Lewis, David Levering. *W. E. B. Du Bois: Biography of a Race, 1868–1919*. New York: Henry Holt, 1993. Chapters 8–14 detail the Atlanta experiences of Du Bois.

Pomerantz, Gary M. *Where Peachtree Meets Sweet Auburn: The Saga of Two Families and the Making of Atlanta*. New York: Scribner, 1996. Parts IV–VII are a masterful interweaving narrative of the histories of the family of 1960s Mayor Ivan Allen Jr. and John Wesley Dobbs, whose grandson Maynard Jackson became the city's first African American mayor.

—TIMOTHY J. CRIMMINS

ATLANTA EXPOSITION ADDRESS (ATLANTA COMPROMISE). The Atlanta Exposition Address, a speech by the former slave and educator-administrator Booker T. Washington that was delivered on 18 September 1895 during the opening of the Cotton States and International Exposition (CSIE) in Atlanta, Georgia, remains one of the most notable and controversial speeches in United States history. For the previous fourteen years, Washington had served as the principal of the all-black Tuskegee Institute in Macon County, Alabama. Washington had accepted the position after several whites, including his mentor, Samuel Armstrong, the president of Hampton Institute in Virginia, had turned down the offer. In fact, it was Armstrong who recommended Washington, a distinguished Hampton graduate whom the paternalistic Armstrong truly respected. Having seen Washington arrive at Hampton with ragged clothes and practically no money, sweep floors as an entrance exam, perform manual labor throughout his matriculation, yet still graduate at the top of his class, Armstrong believed that Washington illustrated how productive, ethical, self-reliant, and hardworking it was possible for black people to be if they received industrial and vocational, as opposed to only classical, educations.

Black Education and Southern Politics. Armstrong was fond of saying that blacks needed the education of the hand, head, and heart that manual instruction and stern, Christian-based discipline could provide. Washington concurred. One of the saddest sights that he ever saw as a free man, he said, was a three-hundred-dollar rosewood piano in a school located in the heart of Alabama's predominantly black Cotton Belt subregion of the state (also called the Black Belt because much of the soil there is dark); Tuskegee was located on the northeastern edge of this subregion. Many adult blacks who lived near the school did not own land. Others lived in rented, one-room cabins and were deeply indebted to local merchants who had supplied tools and other necessities on credit. Not one black had a bank account, but nearly every black was proud of the school's piano and the classical education that students received.

A purely classical education was folly during the late nineteenth century, argued Washington. The Second Industrial Revolution had begun, and a combined academic, industrial, and vocational education would help prepare "ordinary" blacks to become excellent wage earners. By following the Hampton-Tuskegee model, "extraordinary" blacks would acquire the practical experience that had helped some of the nation's most successful white businesspersons excel. Keenly aware that the white business establishment had not opened many doors for aspiring black entrepreneurs, especially in the South, Washington developed a plan whereby educated, industrious, law-abiding blacks could create economic opportunities for themselves. For Washington, a strong black economic presence would dovetail into a stronger black political presence because business and politics were inseparable, an idea that numerous Gilded Age business-political relationships seemed to validate.

At the time of Washington's address, American politics was controlled by white Democrats who were determined to undo completely what they called the radicalization of the nation, and what others called Reconstruction. In the South, where the majority of black citizens lived, leading Democrats had been in the process of implementing strategies—literacy tests, poll taxes, grandfather clauses—to check black political progress since the 1870s, when Democrats (and opportunistic white Republicans) began to dismantle Reconstruction and restore conservative white rule. Oftentimes, the Democrats' psychological and extralegal strategies were more effective than their legal ones. By convincing poor-to-middle-class whites that Reconstruction had placed the "bottom rail on top," the Democrats were able to unite white persons of various and sometimes divergent backgrounds. Together, they constituted an almost solid Democratic voting block throughout the postbellum South. Even in places where blacks equaled or outnumbered whites, such as Tuskegee, discriminatory registration criteria, intimidation, and voting fraud helped ensure that Democrats would occupy many local and, in the case of Alabama, all statewide offices during the Restoration era. As a consequence, blacks would remain disfranchised.

By 1895, the socioeconomic and political realities of the South were hardly what Henry Grady, the former editor of the *Atlanta Constitution*, and other promoters of the New South had hypothesized. According to Grady, the South had emerged from the Civil War new and unadulterated. Rather than being a region where independent farming and racial solidarity were the cornerstones of society, the postwar South was a bastion of biracial cooperation in which industry and commerce could thrive unimpeded by labor unions. Land was fertile and cheap, waterways were abundant, and immigrants were welcomed. The fact that the South led the nation in postbellum lynching and other racially and politically motivated acts of violence and that academic education lagged behind the North were absent from Grady's New South vision. Therefore, northern businesses and capital could be moved below the Mason-Dixon Line without investors having to worry about being hamstrung by "Old South" social, political, or economic ills.

Grady delivered his most famous New South speech to the New England Society of New York (now the New England Society in the City of New York) in 1886. Seven years later, the World's Columbian Exposition was held in Chicago. The exposition showcased the type of technologies Grady had hoped would become commonplace in the South. The exposition also proved that prejudice and discrimination were not limited to the South. The exposition's organizers—all white men of considerable political, business, and academic distinction—did not invite a single black speaker, and they segregated black vendors and attractions. The dearth of blackness infuriated prominent blacks such as Ida B. Wells-Barnett, who had relocated to Chicago after being chased out of Tennessee for protesting race-based violence, and Frederick Douglass, the most powerful black person in the United States. Though Douglass was a featured attraction at the "White City," as the exposition was called, he spent most of his time denouncing the absence of blacks. Thousands of "common" blacks showed their frustration by boycotting the exposition.

Black Visibility and Participation. The southern organizers of the CSIE were determined to make wiser decisions than had their northern predecessors. To better the chance of receiving assistance from the federal government, in the spring of 1895 the CSIE organizers asked a few black southerners to join approximately twenty-five of Georgia's most influential white men in appearing before Congress to solicit help for the CSIE. Because of Washington's success at Tuskegee and his general demeanor, he received an invitation. Speaking last, Washington criticized black disfranchisement but declared that blacks should not rely solely on the vote to better their plight. In addition to the ballot, blacks needed character, industry, intelligence, property, skills, and thrift to succeed in life.

Any race whose members lacked these characteristics would ultimately fail, avowed Washington, before reiterating the need for congressional assistance. By supporting the CSIE, the congressmen could provide the South and the nation something of lasting value, concluded Washington.

Congress responded favorably. With the requisite financial backing, the CSIE organizers began to assemble a program. They decided that one exhibit would be devoted to highlighting the progress of emancipated blacks, some of whom would construct the building in which the exhibit would be housed. Washington was asked to head the venture but declined because of previous obligations at Tuskegee.

As the CSIE neared, the organizers continued to discuss black participation. Concerned that the planned black exhibition would stoke the flames of racial and political inequality that were burning in the segregated, or Jim Crow, South, the CSIE board of directors decided to allow a black man to give an opening-day address. Because Douglass had died in February 1895 and Wells and other candidates were considered too controversial to represent the so-called New South, the board members turned to Washington, who, as it turned out, in less than ten minutes delivered one of the greatest speeches in American history.

Washington began by thanking the CSIE organizers for including black persons in the planning process. He reported that their actions would do more to help cement positive relations among blacks and whites than any other occurrence since emancipation. Next, Washington discussed the overall progress of nineteenth-century blacks. Slavery, he implied, had made the vast majority of blacks unaware that land ownership and financial accumulation were as important to individual and collective growth as holding political office. Therefore, when freedom came, most blacks had wanted to become politicians rather than skilled laborers, landowners, or merchants. Washington then uttered some of the most memorable words of his speech. A lost ship whose captain and crew were in dire need of water spotted a friendly vessel. The persons aboard the latter vessel told the former four times to cast down their buckets where they were before the captain of the lost ship heeded the advice.

Blacks, Washington said, needed to cast down their buckets where they were—the South—rather than relocating to other parts of the nation and the world, as colonization proponents and white supremacists had encouraged blacks to do. Though segregated and often violent, the South still provided blacks the best opportunity to excel in agriculture, commerce, industry, and the professions, proclaimed Washington. Freed blacks' greatest danger, he alleged, was forgetting that most blacks would always be common laborers and not men of letters. Nor should blacks regret this fact, explained Washington. No people, he said, could thrive until they realized that tilling fields was as dignified as writing poems.

Washington had similar advice for southern whites. Rather than looking to foreigners for laborers, the whites needed to employ blacks, millions of whom had remained peaceful at a time when causing mayhem would have been relatively easy. Though he was not specific, Washington obviously meant the Civil War, when many male whites had been on the battlefield. Following the war, most blacks had remained peaceful as they tilled fields, cleared forests, built railroads and cities, and shunned unions. With the proper educational support, respect, and financial incentives, patient and understanding blacks, Washington was certain, would help grow a truly new, progressive South whose unified citizens would march hand in hand into the twentieth century. Continued racial antagonism would only retard the South's progress. Washington concluded this part of his address with a memorable line regarding equality. In purely social areas, blacks and whites could be as separate as the fingers; but in areas essential to mutual progress, they could be as united as the hand.

Contrary to the opinion of some commentators, Washington was not delusional. He knew there were sizeable social, political, and economic obstacles that southern blacks and whites would continue to face. However, Washington was confident that with the help of the North and of God, the South could be as successful as the CSIE. Appealing to common white sentiment while expressing a tautology, Washington deemed complete social and political equality folly. And in keeping with his belief that blacks who were able to produce essential goods less expensively than their competitors produced such goods, Washington told his listeners that no economically viable people could be disfranchised for long. Washington conceded that civil rights were important, but being able to utilize these rights was even more important and was impossible without governmental safeguards, which southern states and the southern-controlled U.S. Supreme Court had begun to retract.

Responses to the Address. Initially, Washington's speech was praised highly. Black America, it seemed, had found an able successor to Douglass. White philanthropists and businessmen began to donate money to Washington, who used it to attract more capable black educators to Tuskegee and to fight southern Jim Crow. W. E. B. Du Bois, ultimately one of Washington's most recognized critics, described the address as a speech fitly spoken and contemplated joining the Tuskegee faculty.

Only later, after several personal bouts with Washington, would Du Bois refer to the 1895 address in Atlanta as a compromise and condemn Washington's "Tuskegee Machine" as largely self-serving and antithetical to black progress.

Today, people remain as divided about Washington's speech as they do about Washington himself. Part of this division can be attributed to an unfamiliarity with the historic context in which the speech was given, and another part to the frequent subtleties that Washington employed in the speech. A number of people have based their opinion of the speech on the words of Du Bois and other critics rather than analyzing the speech themselves. The speech's defenders, by contrast, have contended that many critics, including Du Bois, had no significant first-hand experience with late-nineteenth-century southern politics or culture and were therefore unqualified to express opinions about the speech's fitness. Other defenders have recognized Washington as being an immeasurably shrewd individual whose devotion to the betterment of the Tuskegee institution that he had headed since 1881 caused him to soften his words on southern Jim Crow. Whatever the case may be, it is certain that Washington's Atlanta Exposition Address placed him in the national spotlight and solidified his place among the nation's greatest black speechmakers.

[*See also* Du Bois, W. E. B., *subentry* Life and Career; Education; Educators and Academics; Hampton Institute; Jim Crow Laws; New South; Tuskegee Institute; Voting Rights; Washington, Booker T.; Washington–Du Bois Conflict; *and* Wells-Barnett, Ida B.]

BIBLIOGRAPHY

Anderson, James D. *The Education of Blacks in the South, 1860–1935*. Chapel Hill: University of North Carolina Press, 1988.

Bond, Horace Mann. *The Education of the Negro in the American Social Order*. New York: Octagon Books, 1966.

Du Bois, W. E. B. *The Souls of Black Folk*. Edited by Brent Hayes Edwards. Oxford and New York: Oxford University Press, 2007. First published in 1903.

Harlan, Louis R. *Booker T. Washington: The Making of a Black Leader, 1856–1901*. New York: Oxford University Press, 1972.

Harlan, Louis R. *Booker T. Washington: The Wizard of Tuskegee, 1901–1915*. New York: Oxford University Press, 1983.

Harlan, Louis R., ed. *The Booker T. Washington Papers*. Urbana: University of Illinois Press, 1989.

Harris, Thomas E. *Analysis of the Clash over Issues between Booker T. Washington and W. E. B. Du Bois*. New York: Garland, 1981.

Meier, August. *Negro Thought in America, 1880–1915: Racial Ideologies in the Age of Booker T. Washington*. Ann Arbor: University of Michigan Press, 1969.

Moore, Jacqueline M. *Booker T. Washington, W. E. B. Du Bois, and the Struggle for Racial Uplift*. Wilmington, Del.: Scholarly Resources, 2003.

Washington, Booker T. *Up From Slavery*. Edited by William L. Andrews. Oxford and New York: Oxford University Press, 1995. First published in 1901.

West, Michael Rudolph. *The Education of Booker T. Washington: American Democracy and the Idea of Race Relations*. New York: Columbia University Press, 2006.

—BERTIS ENGLISH

ATLANTA LIFE INSURANCE COMPANY. By 2008, Atlanta Life Financial Group was the largest black-owned insurance company in the United States. In 1905 Alonzo F. Herndon, a prominent businessman, founded Atlanta Life, which was one of America's first black-owned insurance companies. Its history reflects the history of African American entrepreneurship and the climb from slavery to freedom; it illustrates a record of business success among African Americans during the period of segregation and discrimination.

African American insurance companies had their origins shortly after the Civil War as newly emancipated slaves relied on mutual aid activities set up by churches and fraternal organizations to provide basic insurance services—especially burial funds and some support during emergencies. As churches and fraternal orders increased their financial strength, they also expanded their social services. Some black fraternal orders established trusts that provided even greater financial advancement through the creation of banks, timber businesses, newspapers, retail emporiums, and finally mortgage and insurance companies. One of the latter was Atlanta Mutual, which later became Atlanta Life.

Herndon was born into slavery on a Georgia plantation in 1858. Moving to Atlanta at age twenty-four, Herndon began a barbershop with a partner, an entrepreneurial venture that soon led to the purchase of several more barbershops including the elaborate Crystal Palace in 1904 at 66 Peachtree Street. The next year, 1905, marked the turning point for the successful entrepreneur. He acquired several church insurance associations, and the Atlanta Benevolent Association. He merged these into Atlanta Mutual, capitalized with $5,000 and headquartered in the Rucker Building on Auburn Avenue.

Initially the corporation functioned as a mutual assessment association in which policyholders (more than twenty-three thousand by 2009) paid premiums for a policy that offered modest death benefits. In 1922 Atlanta Mutual, renamed Atlanta Life, transformed itself into a legal reserve company backed by $100,000 in stock, most of which was owned by Herndon. This enabled the company to expand rapidly. Two years later the company had offices in more than a dozen states, including Florida, Tennessee, Kentucky, Missouri, Kansas, and Texas.

Herndon died in 1927 at the age of sixty-seven, leaving the company to his son Norris Herndon, who headed the company for more than forty-five years. Educated at Atlanta University and Harvard, he followed a conservative business model, effectively guiding the company through the Great Depression and into the postwar period. The company's assets increased to $54 million in 1960, and over $175 million by the time he retired in 1973. Norris Herndon also supported the civil rights movement in the 1960s through contributions from the Herndon Foundation and by providing other services to the movement including providing employment for civil rights workers who lost their jobs because of their political activities.

Following Norris Herndon's retirement in 1973, the company continued to prosper through a succession of chief executives. In 2001 the company restructured itself as a financial services company, Atlanta Life Financial Group. It provided a vast array of financial support services both to individuals and to other institutions and individuals. Atlanta Life represents both the success and potential of African American business enterprises. At its beginning in the early years of the twentieth century it reflected the ideals of racial self-help that characterized the teachings of Booker T. Washington in the era of segregation. In the 1950s and 1960s it used its financial power to actively underwrite the struggle for equal rights. Throughout, it was a model corporation, carefully maintaining its financial strength and providing service to its clients by paying claims promptly.

[*See also* Entrepreneurship.]

Bibliography

Henderson, Alexa Benson. *Atlanta Life Insurance Company: Guardian of Black Economic Dignity*. Tuscaloosa: University of Alabama Press, 1990.

Henderson, Alexa Benson. "Atlanta Life Insurance Company." In *The New Georgia Encyclopedia*. http://www.georgiaencyclopedia.org/.

Ingham, John N., and Lynne B. Feldman. *African-American Business Leaders: A Biographical Dictionary*. Westport, Conn.: Greenwood Press, 1994.

Merritt, Carole. *The Herndons: An Atlanta Family*. Athens: University of Georgia Press, 2002.

—Maria Stilson
—Cary D. Wintz

ATLANTA RIOT. On 22–24 September 1906, white mobs killed dozens of blacks, wounded many others, and caused considerable property damage across the city of Atlanta. This race riot was the result of racial tensions, political rage, and dramatized newspaper reports of black men assaulting white women.

By the early twentieth century, Atlanta was a center of regional commerce. The booming economy brought people from the South and other parts of the United States to the Atlanta area. The city's population soared almost 70 percent between 1900 and 1910. The rapid growth and prosperity rekindled racial and class tensions; competition for a limited number of jobs resulted in new tensions between blacks and poor whites. Georgia's 1906 gubernatorial campaign heightened these tensions by promoting the ideas that black prosperity took jobs from white men and that blacks gained social advances at the expense of whites. Newspapers ran dramatized reports of attempted rapes by black men against defenseless white women and warned white men to protect their wives and daughters from sex-crazed black men.

Hoke Smith and Clark Howell were both political leaders in Atlanta and candidates for governor in 1906. Smith was supported by the reform wing of the Democratic Party, while Howell was allied with conservative Democrats. Smith used the *Atlanta Journal*—which he had formerly owned—as a political platform, while Howell, publisher of the rival *Constitution*, did the same with his newspaper. Howell directed his campaign at the segment of whites who resented the success of black business owners in Atlanta, while Smith preached the necessity of keeping black men in a subordinate position. Allowing black men to own businesses, become prosperous, and vote, both Smith and Howell argued, would make the black men feel equal to whites and lead them to feel "worthy" of white women. Goaded by the threat of "Negro domination," white business leaders joined forces to gain economic and social control of black businesses. Howell believed that the white primary and the poll tax were enough to limit black voting and claimed that Smith was not the separationist that he boasted himself to be, charging Smith with cooperating with black political leaders.

The working class was fed propaganda through the newspapers that Howell and Smith controlled. Sensational stories, meant to encourage the mobs, were printed about fictional sexual assaults by black men on white women. Other articles supported or encouraged lynching, lawlessness, and mob violence.

On the afternoon of 22 September 1906, Atlanta newspapers reported four alleged assaults on white women (none of which was ever proved). As shocking details circulated, white boys and men, fearing for the safety of their wives and daughters, gathered. City leaders, including Mayor James G. Woodward, failed to calm the growing crowd. By early evening the deadliest riot in the city's history had begun. For more than five hours mobs of more than ten thousand white men roamed the streets, killing at least sixteen black men, terrorizing others, and destroying the property of those in their path. The mobs attacked black business owners and entered streetcars, beating black men and women along the way and killing at least three men. The police attempted unsuccessfully to control the mobs. The militia was called in around midnight but was unable to restrain the mobs until a heavy rain drove them indoors.

On Sunday, 23 September, white police and militia patrolled the streets, while blacks, fearing the mobs' return, secretly armed themselves. While the black community worked to defend their homes, vigilante groups continued to raid black neighborhoods.

On Monday, 24 September, a group of heavily armed blacks held a meeting in Brownsville. Fulton County police, fearing retaliation, appeared at the meeting, and a shootout ensued, during which one police officer was killed. Three companies of the local militia were sent to Brownsville, where they seized weapons and arrested more than 250 black men. On Monday and Tuesday white officials, businessmen, and clergy called for an end to the violence. Black leaders were called in to conduct negotiations for racial reconciliation. Newspaper accounts give different tallies of the killed, ranging from twenty to forty black men.

The two most prominent black leaders of the day, Booker T. Washington and W. E. B. Du Bois, interpreted the riot and its aftermath in very different ways. Du Bois, who was teaching in Atlanta, witnessed firsthand the riot and its frightening aftermath. He joined with black men in the role of protector and defender and armed himself with a double-barreled shotgun. The riot forced Du Bois to reconsider his focus on the Talented Tenth and to push instead for radical justice. Washington, on the other hand, had rushed to Atlanta and urged the city's black community to exercise self-control. He reminded blacks that the disharmony in Atlanta was the exception, not the rule; blacks should shun violence and retaliation and focus on reconciliation.

The men and women who were attacked had followed Washington's advice. Du Bois acknowledged that the attacks resulted from the prodding of politicians, newspapers, and white supremacists, and his point of view changed to encompass support for defensive violence. Du Bois, despite threats, continued to expose racial injustices and push for civil rights agitation; Washington, whose gospel of nonviolent demonstration would not find a home until the civil rights movement of the 1960s, found himself secluded from his former supporters.

In 2006 the Coalition to Remember the 1906 Atlanta Race Riot held a series of events to promote public awareness of this episode in Atlanta's history. The coalition's intent was to restore the memory of the 1906 riot, as well as to encourage reconsolidation within the community.

[*See also* Atlanta; Du Bois, W. E. B.; Lynching and Mob Violence; Riots and Rebellions; Violence against African Americans; *and* Washington, Booker T.]

BIBLIOGRAPHY

Bauerlein, Mark. *Negrophobia: A Race Riot in Atlanta*. San Francisco: Encounter Books, 2001.

Cohen, William. *At Freedom's Edge: Black Mobility and the Southern White Quest for Racial Control 1861–1915*. Baton Rouge: Louisiana State University Press, 1991.

Godshalk, David Fort. *Veiled Vision: The 1906 Atlanta Race Riot and the Reshaping of American Race Relations*. Chapel Hill: University of North Carolina Press, 2005.

Myrdal, Gunner. *An American Dilemma: The Negro Problem and Modern Democracy* (1944). New Brunswick, N.J.: Transaction, 1996.

Wolters, Raymond. *Du Bois and His Rivals*. Columbia: University of Missouri Press, 2002.

—PAULA COCHRAN

ATLANTA UNIVERSITY. Ever since it enrolled its first class in 1865, Atlanta University has been an important force in African American graduate-level education. It continues to be a major force today as Clark Atlanta University, created in 1988 from the consolidation of Clark College (established 1869) and Atlanta University. It enrolls about four thousand undergraduate students and twelve hundred graduate students and has about three hundred faculty members.

Atlanta University has had a number of distinguished students and professors over the years. None, however, was more distinguished than W. E. B. Du Bois. Du Bois taught at Atlanta on two occasions. The first was from 1897 and 1910, when he was professor of economics and history. When Du Bois arrived at Atlanta in 1897 he was the only African American on the faculty. His second tenure was from 1934 to 1944, when he served as chair of the sociology department. While teaching at Atlanta, Du Bois launched his famous series of studies on African American life, which was a continuation of work he did in Philadelphia in 1896–1897 that culminated in *The Philadelphia Negro* (1899). The Atlanta University studies constituted the first long-term sociological investigation of African Americans in the United States.

Du Bois left Atlanta University in 1910 to work full-time with the National Association for the Advancement of Colored People (NAACP), which he helped found in 1909. He began the NAACP's journal *The Crisis* in 1910 and he began the journal *Phylon* in 1940.

Growth. The American Missionary Association founded Atlanta University in 1865, and the Freedman's Bureau provided aid in later years. Atlanta University was the first university to give graduate degrees predominantly to African Americans; it began offering bachelor's degrees by the end of the 1870s.

The university continued to expand into the 1920s and beyond. The reputation of its faculty and the quality of its alumni aided that expansion, as did its service to the African American community in providing teachers and librarians to public schools in the South. In 1929 the university affiliated with Spelman and Morehouse, two historically black undergraduate colleges. Clark College affiliated in the 1930s. Initially focused on liberal arts, Atlanta University opened various professional schools in the 1940s: one for library service (1941), one for education (1944), and one for business administration (1946). In 1947 the Atlanta School of Social Work (as of 2001, the Whitney M. Young Jr. School of Social Work) was integrated into the university. In 1994 the university added the School of International Affairs and Development.

In 1957 the Atlanta University Center was created through the more formal union of Atlanta University, Clark, Morehouse, Morris Brown, and Spelman colleges, and Gammon Theological Seminary. Morehouse School of Medicine joined later. The Atlanta University Center is the largest consortium of historically black institutions in the United States. Students may attend classes in any of the member schools.

Atlanta University Students. The future executive secretary of the NAACP, Walter White, and fellow teammates on the varsity debate team, Atlanta University, 1916. Yale Collection of American Literature, Beinecke Rare Book and Manuscript Library, Yale University

Significant Faculty and Alumni. In addition to Du Bois, a number of other intellectuals contributed to the reputation of Atlanta University. Hale Woodruff, the prominent artist, began an art exhibition series that led to the great African American art collection at Atlanta. Dennis Kimbro, author of *Think and Grow Rich: A Black Choice* (1991), was a faculty member, as was J. Ernest Wilkins, the mathematician and physicist. Horace Mann Bond, Virginia Lacy Jones, Whitney M. Young Jr., and Henry C. McBay were also faculty members. The alumnus James Weldon Johnson became a prominent Harlem Renaissance novelist, statesman, and composer. The first African American West Point graduate, Henry O. Flipper, was an alumnus, as was the civil rights leader Ralph Abernathy. A number of entertainers have graduated from Atlanta, including the rappers DJ Drama and Bobby Creekwater. Other graduates include Otis Johnson, the mayor of Savannah, and Dorothy Yancy, president of Johnson C. Smith University.

Although he was neither a faculty member nor an alumnus, the Columbia University anthropologist Franz Boas played a large role in the intellectual development of Atlanta University and the future thought of African Americans such as W. E. B. Du Bois. Du Bois, a close friend, invited Boas to give the 1906 commencement address at Atlanta. Boas took the opportunity to express his views on the racial equality of human beings and the importance of African history to the world.

John Hope (1868–1936) also contributed a great deal to the cultural and intellectual tradition at Atlanta University. Hope was born in Augusta, Georgia, and taught at Brown University, Roger Williams University, and Atlanta Baptist College, which became Morehouse College; in 1906 he became the first African American president of Atlanta Baptist. Hope's training was in political science, and his inclination was to be a political activist for civil rights. When Morehouse and Spelman merged with Atlanta University in 1929, Hope was the unanimous choice to head the new entity as its president. He remained president until his death in 1936.

Clark Atlanta University was formed in 1988. As of 2003 it had 4,900 students and 298 faculty members. It is the only part of the Atlanta University System that confers graduate degrees and has become a world-famous, world-class university, sponsoring prestigious journals, publishing esteemed books, and supporting respected lecture series.

[*See also* Clark Atlanta University; Morehouse College; Spelman College; *and biographical entries on figures mentioned in this article*.]

BIBLIOGRAPHY

Adams, Myron W. *A History of Atlanta University*. Atlanta: Atlanta University Press, 1930.

Bacote, Clarence A. *The Story of Atlanta University: A Century of Service, 1865–1965*. Atlanta: Atlanta University, 1969.

Dittmer, John. *Black Georgia in the Progressive Era, 1900–1920*. Urbana: University of Illinois Press, 1977.

Lewis, David Levering. *W. E. B. Du Bois: Biography of a Race, 1868–1919*. New York: H. Holt, 1993.

—FRANK A. SALAMONE

ATLANTA WORLD. As the first African American newspaper in the United States to achieve success as a daily, the *Atlanta Daily World* stands apart from other black American papers. Founded in 1928 by then twenty-six-year-old William Alexander Scott II, the *Atlanta World* was the second black-owned newspaper in the city. Its competition, the *Atlanta Independent*, ceased operation in 1933. Scott envisioned a newspaper published by blacks for blacks, the voice of the black middle class, advocating due process and a lack of militancy. Circulation expanded rapidly among the city's ninety thousand African Americans. Scott was able to attract advertising from local businesses including Coca-Cola; Sears, Roebuck, and Company; and Rich's, Atlanta's largest family-owned department store. In 1931 the Scott family established a small chain of African American papers, including the *Chattanooga Tribune* and *Memphis World*, which would grow to the fifty-paper Southern (later Scott) Newspaper Syndicate. By 1932, the *Atlanta World* had reinvented itself as a daily paper—the *Atlanta Daily World*. Two years later in 1934, Scott, in a crime that went unsolved, was murdered outside his home.

Cornelius Adolphus Scott succeeded his older brother, beginning a career that ran sixty-three years. Following on the success of his brother, Scott continued a nonmilitant policy, yet supported voting rights and voter registration for blacks, editorializing against the poll tax in 1944, which was repealed the next year. Under Scott, the *World* integrated the congressional press galleries and was the first African American newspaper to cover President Franklin D. Roosevelt's news conferences. Scott and the *World* supported the Atlanta Negro Voters League and fair employment practices in hiring, and opposed the Klan and segregation. From 1946 to 1948, the paper pushed the city's police department to employ black officers, and eight were hired in 1948. Scott and the reporter Bob Johnson (of the Johnson publishing family) led an effort to keep Auburn Avenue—Atlanta's historically black business community where *World* offices were housed—out of the city's urban renewal plan, preserving the black business district.

Much like Atlanta's own Martin Luther King Jr.'s approach to race matters, the *World* assumed a cautious, less confrontational stance on racial and civil rights issues such as busing, and opposed student sit-ins, more concerned about participating students' safety. As a result of the *World*'s conservative policy, two more radical black newspapers sprang up in 1960 and 1966, yet neither challenged the role of the *World* as the voice of black business interests in Atlanta.

Following the national trend in newspaper circulation, the *Atlanta Daily World* cut back to a four-day schedule in 1970 with a circulation slightly exceeding thirty thousand. In 2002 circulation was eighteen thousand and the paper went online. Circulation has continued a gradual decline. In 1997 Scott retired, ending a remarkable career in journalism and publishing. On 28 April 1997 his great-niece and William Alexander Scott II's granddaughter, Alexis Scott Reeves, formerly with the *Atlanta Journal Constitution*, took over the role as publisher.

[*See also* Atlanta *and* Journalism, Print and Broadcast.]

BIBLIOGRAPHY

Odom-Hinman, Maria E. *The Cautious Crusader: How the Atlanta Daily World Covered the Struggle for African American Rights from 1945 to 1985*. PhD diss., University of Maryland, 2005. History of the *Atlanta Daily World* with an emphasis on the civil rights era.

Pomerantz, Gary. *Where Peachtree Meets Sweet Auburn: The Saga of Two Families and the Making of Atlanta*. New York: Scribner, 1996. History of Atlanta in the twentieth century with an emphasis on race relations and the city's growth.

—BOYD CHILDRESS

ATTORNEYS. *See* Legal Profession.

B

BAKER, ELLA (b. 13 December 1903; d. 13 December 1986), civil rights activist who was instrumental in founding the Student Nonviolent Coordinating Committee (SNCC). Ella Josephine Baker grew up in Littleton, North Carolina, listening to her grandparents' stories about slavery and their struggle to support themselves and their families after Emancipation. Her maternal grandparents were farmers who had managed to acquire their own land, whereas her paternal grandparents, like many former slaves, were landless tenant farmers. Baker's parents, Blake and Georgianna Ross Baker, met in secondary school and were determined to use their educations to establish better lives for themselves and their children. Blake Baker worked as a waiter on a steamship, a job that required frequent travel away from his wife and three children. Before her marriage in 1896, Georgianna Baker worked as a schoolteacher. Later she worked as a housewife, occasionally taking in boarders to earn extra income, and she was actively involved in the local Baptist church. She saw participation in church activities as a way to aid the less fortunate, and her commitment to social activism had a strong influence on her elder daughter.

Activism. The Bakers were strong advocates of formal education. In 1918 Ella Baker entered Shaw University, a Baptist boarding school and college in Raleigh, North Carolina. She earned a BA in sociology in 1927 and was valedictorian of her class. While in college she began what was to become a long career in social activism, leading, for example, a somewhat unlikely campaign against the school's conservative dress code, which forbade female students from wearing silk stockings.

After graduation Baker moved to Harlem, where she quickly helped found and later became national director of the Young Negroes' Cooperative League (YNCL), an organization that hoped to increase black economic power by pooling resources and by establishing cooperatively owned stores. Like many other black intellectuals at this time, Baker was increasingly drawn to the socialist movement. This orientation encouraged her to adopt a more internationalist perspective and to see problems like racism and poverty within a multinational framework. She was reputedly sympathetic to the Lovestonites, socialists who thought that the United States would follow its own unique path to socialism and need not follow the Bolshevik model of revolution. Baker's growing Pan-Africanist views led to a stint as a reporter for the *West Indian News*. In 1935 she also participated in protests against the Italian occupation of Ethiopia under Benito Mussolini.

Baker also worked for the Workers' Education Project (WEP), a Works Progress Administration program designed to educate workers in basic skills and to educate them about various topics of particular concern to working-class individuals. Baker participated in literacy and consumer education programs and was deeply troubled to observe firsthand the devastating impact that the Great Depression had on the already precarious financial positions of many African Americans. In 1935 she coauthored an article with Marvel Cooke, published in November in *The Crisis*, titled "The Bronx Slave Market," in which she publicized the plight of chronically underemployed and exploited black domestic workers who sometimes were forced to resort to prostitution in order to make a living.

In 1941 Baker married T. J. Roberts. They had met at Shaw University and had maintained a long-distance friendship ever since. Baker was intensely private on the subject of her romantic life, refusing to answer questions about her husband or her marriage. She made what was an unusual decision for the time when she chose not to take her husband's last name. Many of her professional associates did not even know that she was married. Furthermore her decision to marry did not alter her dedication to her career, and she often worked at jobs that required frequent travel. The marriage ended in divorce in 1958.

In 1938 Baker began working for the NAACP, first as a field secretary and later as the director of branches. In that capacity she traveled throughout the South raising funds and recruiting members. Baker was away from New York for as much as half of each year. During her extensive travels she built relationships and developed a familiarity with the southern political situation that served her well in future years as she continued her participation in the southern freedom struggle.

Baker's approach to activism emphasized grassroots organizing and differed from that of the NAACP, which

Ella Baker. SNCC founder Ella Baker, 1980. Photograph by Bettye Lane. © Bettye Lane

fought discrimination primarily through a centralized mechanism. The NAACP concentrated its energies on fighting discrimination through the legal system, which meant that highly trained legal professionals often assumed more prominent roles in the organization than did the mass of less educated people whom the organization sought to represent. These differences—in both philosophies and leadership styles—sometimes led to tension between Baker and the largely male leadership of the organization. She resigned from her position as national branch director in 1946 partially because of her frustration over bureaucracy within the NAACP and her belief that the venerable organization had lost touch with the ordinary people whose needs she thought should be driving the struggle for civil rights.

She also gave up her NAACP position because of family obligations. Her travel schedule became impractical after she volunteered to raise her eight-year-old niece Jacqueline. However, Baker remained active as a volunteer, and in 1952 she was elected the first female director of the New York City branch of the NAACP. As branch president she played a large role in the fight to desegregate New York City public schools.

Baker briefly flirted with becoming involved with electoral politics. She became a member of the Liberal Party, which had close ties to the labor movement and advocated racial integration, a commitment made visible in its decision to run black candidates for office. Baker ran unsuccessfully for a position on the New York City Council as a candidate for the Liberal Party in both 1951 and 1953.

In 1956 Baker, along with Stanley Levison and Bayard Rustin, founded In Friendship, a group designed to raise money for the growing civil rights movement in the South. The group raised funds to support the Montgomery bus boycott and to aid individuals who had suffered economic reprisals because of their civil rights activities. The organization ceased to exist in 1957 after the founding of the Southern Christian Leadership Conference (SCLC), which was designed to help coordinate the southern civil rights movement.

Levison and Rustin were both close advisers of the SCLC president Martin Luther King Jr. At their urging, King in 1958 invited Baker to move to Atlanta to work for the organization. Initially she directed the Crusade for Citizenship program, which initiated voter registration drives throughout the South. She also ran the Atlanta headquarters of the SCLC and served briefly as executive director, an unusual accomplishment for a woman working in an organization dominated by male clergy. While employed by the SCLC, Baker was faced with frustrations similar to those she had experienced while working for the NAACP a decade earlier. Baker disagreed with the way the SCLC was dominated by King, a single charismatic leader.

Instead, she continued to favor a decentralized structure and a greater dependency on grassroots leadership. She repeatedly claimed that "strong people don't need a strong leader" (quoted in, e.g., James, p. 83).

Not only was Baker uncomfortable with the management style of the male leadership of the SCLC, but many of the men in the organization found the presence of a strong female staff member unsettling as well, especially at a time when women were encouraged to stay in the background behind more visible male leaders. Because Baker challenged traditional gender roles, her brief tenure as executive director led to some tension within the SCLC.

SNCC. In 1960 a series of student-led sit-ins at lunch counters across the South inspired young people throughout the country to think more proactively about how they could influence the struggle for civil rights. On Easter weekend in 1960 Baker sponsored a meeting of sit-in leaders and sympathizers at her alma mater, Shaw University. This South-wide Youth Leadership Conference was designed as a forum to discuss ways to capitalize on the momentum of the student-led protests. Many within the SCLC hoped that Baker would encourage the students to form a youth branch of the SCLC. Instead she encouraged the students to found their own independent organization, to form their own agenda, and not to meekly take orders from more established groups. This stance led her to leave the SCLC, and in 1960 she became an adviser to the newly founded Student Nonviolent Coordinating Committee (SNCC). This new group was structured around democratic principles and was dedicated to grassroots politics and empowerment of local people—principles that Baker had long held dear but had found lacking in both the NAACP and the SCLC.

In 1960, to support herself financially while serving as an adviser to SNCC, Baker took a job with the Young Women's Christian Association. She was influential in organizing the Mississippi Freedom Democratic Party (MFDP), which attempted to unseat the all-white Mississippi delegation to the 1964 Democratic National Convention. Baker was the keynote speaker at the new party's 1964 convention, and she went to Washington, D.C., to set up a national office for the party. The MFDP helped publicize discriminatory practices within the Democratic Party and the problem of black disfranchisement in the South. Although the MFDP was unsuccessful in its initial ambitious goal, the MFDP's efforts encouraged the Democratic Party to adopt a more racially inclusive agenda. Furthermore the organization's ability to inspire the black electorate encouraged more African Americans to become involved in the political process, particularly after the Voting Rights Act of 1965 ended black disfranchisement in the South. While serving as an adviser for SNCC, Baker was also a consultant for the Southern Conference Educational Fund, which sought to increase white support for the civil rights movement.

Baker remained politically engaged long after the 1960s, and her activism extended beyond the southern freedom struggle. In 1972 she traveled the country as part of the Free Angela campaign, demanding the release of Angela Davis from prison. Baker also became vice chair of the Mass Party Organizing Committee, a socialist organization, in 1972. She actively opposed apartheid in South Africa and was an adviser to the African National Congress. She also supported the Puerto Rican Solidarity Committee, speaking out in favor of Puerto Rican independence.

Some of Baker's admirers called her *fundi*, a Swahili word for a learned person who passes her or his knowledge on to other people. Considering her five decades of activism and participation in a variety of organizations, this title seems apt. Baker's beliefs about the nature of effective leadership led her to see her role as an adviser and organizer rather than as a solitary visionary leader. This approach earned her the grateful admiration of many civil rights activists—both the paid staff of national organizations and the local people who formed the backbone of the struggle. However, her enormous contribution to the philosophical foundations of the civil rights movement—especially of SNCC—have often been minimized or unjustly overlooked in mainstream histories of the period.

Baker died in New York City on her eighty-third birthday. Her biographer Barbara Ransby observed that the overflow crowd at Baker's funeral at Harlem's Abyssinian Baptist Church was remarkably diverse in terms of race, age, and political persuasion. The eclectic gathering reflected how far-reaching her influence was and how widely inspirational her belief in participatory democracy could be. The Ella Baker Center for Human Rights, founded in Oakland, California, in 1996, hopes to carry on her legacy by championing the rights and harnessing the abilities of everyday people.

[*See also* Civil Rights Movement; Mississippi Freedom Democratic Party; National Association for the Advancement of Colored People; Southern Christian Leadership Conference; *and* Student Nonviolent Coordinating Committee.]

BIBLIOGRAPHY

Giddings, Paula. *When and Where I Enter: The Impact of Black Women on Race and Sex in America*. New York: W. Morrow, 1984.

Grant, Joanne. *Ella Baker: Freedom Bound*. New York: John Wiley and Sons, 1998. In addition to this biography, Grant also produced a television documentary about Baker's life, *"Fundi": The Story of Ella Baker* (1981).

James, Joy. *Transcending the Talented Tenth: Black Leaders and American Intellectuals*. New York: Routledge, 1997.

Ransby, Barbara. *Ella Baker and the Black Freedom Movement: A Radical Democratic Vision*. Chapel Hill: University of North Carolina Press, 2003. Chronicles Baker's involvement with various social-activist organizations, explains her political philosophy, and puts her accomplishments in the context of the broader civil rights movement.

—JENNIFER JENSEN WALLACH

BAKER, GEORGE. *See* Divine, Father.

BAKER, JOSEPHINE (b. 3 June 1906; d. 12 April 1975), singer and dancer. Josephine Baker was born Freda Josephine McDonald in a poor black neighborhood in Saint Louis, Missouri. Her mother, Carrie MacDonald, was twenty-one years old at the time and worked as a laundry woman. Her father, Eddie Carson, a vaudeville drummer, left his wife a year after Josephine was born. Josephine thus grew up fatherless and in poverty. When she was eight years old, her mother hired her out to a white woman as a maid. From then on, Josephine was on her own in life. An ambitious and optimistic child, she learned to dance in the back streets of Saint Louis. She went to the zoo, watched kangaroos, camels, and giraffes, and imitated their movements. She wanted to be a great dancer and live a glamorous life. At the age of twelve, she dropped out of school, and at thirteen, her professional life began, when she left Saint Louis to travel around the South with a troupe called the Dixie Steppers. That same year, 1919, she married a steelworker, Willie Wells. The marriage lasted only a few months. In 1921 she married for the second time, to Willie Baker, and she took his last name. In 1922 she left the Dixie Steppers, as well as her husband, and moved to New York City to perform on Broadway.

As a chorus girl in *Shuffle Along*, a musical comedy written by Eubie Blake and Noble Sissle, Josephine Baker began to enchant Broadway audiences who came to see the play and also the funny chorus girl who clowned, crossed her eyes, and danced in a way that no one else did at the time. Soon she built a reputation of her own and became a box office draw. After *Shuffle Along* closed, she performed in *The Chocolate Dandies*, another show written by Sissle and Blake. The year was 1924, and it marked a pivotal point in Baker's career. From the point of view of white audiences, Josephine Baker was the "real colored thing," the authentic black female. They were enchanted by her primitive and sensual movements. Such a reception of Baker's art certainly fit the general ethos of the times: during the period of the Harlem Renaissance, many black artists used primitive and sensual images and music to celebrate African American culture, and their work was celebrated by the white cultural elite.

In 1925 Baker went to Paris to dance in the Revue Nègre at the Théâtre des Champs-Élysées. This was the peak of the Jazz Age in France, and the sensational revue exploded on the stage. Baker, nineteen years old at the time, captivated the French audience with her talent and beauty. This was the beginning of a love relationship between the young black star and the Parisians, a relationship that would last until her death. Baker clowned, sang, and tap danced. It was particularly the *danse sauvage* (savage dance), invented by the choreographer Jacques Charles,

Josephine Baker. Postcard of Josephine Baker for *La Vénus noire*. YALE COLLECTION OF AMERICAN LITERATURE, BEINECKE RARE BOOK AND MANUSCRIPT LIBRARY, YALE UNIVERSITY

that enchanted the audiences. As she danced, she was bare-breasted, wearing only a bikini of feathers and a necklace of feathers. Her wild dance, fast and improvisational, combined moves of the belly dance with those from African tribal dances. With this dance, Baker became the first modern sex symbol of the twentieth century. During the 1920s, Baker became a magic name in Europe not only because of her primitive, erotic appeal, sexiness, and talent but also because of the fame generated by her flamboyant lifestyle. Embodying the unrestrained joy of the Jazz Age and representing African eccentricity, Baker became known as the "Ebony Venus," admired by artists and leftist intellectuals including E. E. Cummings, Ernest Hemingway, Luigi Pirandello, Jean Cocteau, and Pablo Picasso. She inspired artwork by Alexander Calder and Georges Rouault, as well as the poster artist Paul Colin, who created a portfolio called *Le tumulte noir,* which immortalized Baker with the image showing her in her banana skirt. Josephine Baker put her stamp on the entertainment and cultural scene of France in the 1920s and 1930s. She opened her own Paris nightclub (Chez Josephine), sang, performed in casinos, and made films. Finding more acceptance as a black performer in France than in the United States, she became a French citizen upon marrying her third husband, Jean Lion, in 1937.

With World War II, a new phase started in Baker's life. She served as a Red Cross nurse in Belgium, and upon Germany's occupation of France, she worked for the French Resistance as an underground courier. She also sang for French troops posted along the German frontier. (In 1961, she received the French Legion of Honor medal for her humanitarian efforts and contributions to the French cause during the war.) After the war, Baker married for the fourth time, to Jo Buillon, a French jazz bandleader, and she began to adopt babies from different cultures, races, and religions. She called them her Rainbow Tribe and presented her family as a model of brotherhood among children coming from very different backgrounds. She housed them at her three-hundred-acre estate, Les Milandes.

In the 1950s and 1960s Baker made frequent visits to the United States not only as an artist but also as a human rights activist for the African American cause. Challenging the separate-but-equal ideology, she refused to perform to segregated audiences. She often stated that race relations injured American democracy, and she participated in the civil rights march in Washington, D.C., in 1963. When Baker died in 1975 at the age of sixty-nine, she was a legendary star, a war hero, a civil rights activist, and the mother of twelve children.

[*See also* Dance; Entertainment Industry and African Americans; France; *and* Harlem Renaissance.]

BIBLIOGRAPHY

Baker, Jean-Claude, and Chris Chase. *Josephine: The Hungry Heart.* New York: Random House, 1993.

Haney, Lynn. *Naked at the Feast: A Biography of Josephine Baker.* New York: Dodd, Mead, 1981.

Papich, Stephen. *Remembering Josephine.* Indianapolis: Bobbs-Merrill, 1976.

—ASLI TEKINAY

BAKER, RAY STANNARD (b. 17 April 1870; d. 12 July 1946), journalist. Born in Lansing, Michigan, Ray Stannard Baker was the son of Joseph and Alice Stannard Baker. Joseph moved the family to Saint Croix Falls, Wisconsin, in 1875 where he worked as a real estate and utility agent. Ray dabbled in literary, agricultural, and scientific studies at Michigan Agricultural College (now Michigan State University) before turning his attention to the law. He studied at the University of Michigan Law School for only one semester, however, before becoming interested in prose writing. In 1893 he became a reporter for the *Chicago Record* newspaper. When the Panic of 1893 gripped Chicago, Baker saw levels of poverty, unemployment, and unrest beyond what he had ever seen before, and he was drawn to the experiences of the poor whom he found in soup kitchens, jails, and flophouses. Baker gained further sympathy for the common man when he covered the labor leader Jacob Coxey's march with an "army" of unemployed men toward Washington, D.C., for public works legislation and when he covered the Pullman strike.

Baker began his career as a muckraker (a journalist who exposes society's wrongs) by documenting class disparities. In 1897, *McClure's Magazine* hired Baker; during his tenure at *McClure's* he achieved fame by uncovering labor union corruption. Baker sympathized with workers who did not belong to the United Mine Workers during the anthracite coal strike of 1902. Baker found such animosity toward nonunion scabs that those who wanted to cross picket lines were often unable to work. One nonunion miner was killed. By reporting such intimidation, Baker argued that large unions did not always protect rank-and-file laborers.

Baker and his *McClure's* colleagues Ida Tarbell and Lincoln Steffens purchased the *American Magazine* in 1906. Baker had already covered four lynchings for *McClure's,* and the subject jelled with his interest in union lawlessness. He began his investigations by studying Atlanta's 1906 race riot, interviewing leaders such as Booker T. Washington and W. E. B. Du Bois. Baker's first article on the South appeared in April 1907, but more popular were his articles devoted to the North that appeared in 1908. That year Baker combined his articles from the *American* and *McClure's* into the critically acclaimed volume *Following the Color Line*.

Baker strove for journalistic objectivity in *Following the Color Line*, claiming that he wrote "not as a Northerner, nor as a Southerner, but as an American" (p. xv). Baker held a naive optimism toward Progressive southern politicians like Governor James Vardaman of Mississippi and Senator Ben Tillman of South Carolina. Although they were racists, they empowered common whites against the old aristocracy, and blacks could imbibe this democratic spirit. Still, Baker captured the hopelessness of southern black sharecroppers who were beginning to migrate to northern cities for better jobs. The hostility of northern whites to these new arrivals hastened the growth of black enclaves. Both the North and the South were "undemocratic," but blacks were culpable, too (p. 267). Baker blamed the 1904 and 1906 riots in Springfield, Ohio, on ignorant whites and a morally delinquent African American "underclass." The 1904 riot began after a black transient, Richard Dixon, raped and murdered a white woman. Baker blamed Springfield's black community for allowing prostitution and vote selling, activities that inspired the contempt of their white neighbors.

Baker supported Booker T. Washington's advocacy of industrial education for African American advancement. Acknowledging that unequal educational opportunities had limited blacks' entry into skilled trades, Baker argued that skilled training would foster occupational diversity; blacks could then serve their race without threatening white laborers. Baker agreed with Washington's emphasis on personal responsibility before rights, criticizing young northern blacks who confused "liberty for license" with their "bumptiousness" (p. 125). He dismissed the *Boston Guardian* editor William Monroe Trotter, a critic of Washington, as needlessly "violent and bitter" (p. 225).

Baker believed that Americans both white and black needed to change their behavior in order to bring about an end to racial discord. Certain leaders, such as Judge Paul Speake of Huntsville, Alabama, and the acting Alabama governor Russell Cunningham, showed courage by prosecuting leaders of a 1904 Huntsville mob for murder. Jurors acquitted these lynchers, but Baker cited Speake's subsequent reelection as judge as an example of courageous leadership's rewards.

By the mid-1910s Baker had endorsed Du Bois's confrontational approach toward civil rights. Woodrow Wilson's failure to challenge segregation in the South by appointing African Americans to federal positions—even in the Post Office—growing interracial bitterness nationwide over jobs, and what Baker saw as overall white indifference to racism left Baker frustrated with gradualist approaches. In 1915 Baker became an honorary president of the NAACP, and in 1919 he was Wilson's press secretary at Versailles. His main study thereafter was Woodrow Wilson's life, publishing *Woodrow Wilson and World Settlement* in 1922 and his eight-volume *Woodrow Wilson: Life and Letters* between 1927 and 1939. Baker died in Amherst, Massachusetts.

[*See also* Black Press; Industrial Education Movement; Journalism, Print and Broadcast; Organized Labor; Washington, Booker T; *and* Wilson, Woodrow, Administration of.]

BIBLIOGRAPHY

Baker, Ray Stannard. *Following the Color Line: American Negro Citizenship in the Progressive Era* (1908). Edited by Dewey W. Grantham Jr. New York: Harper & Row, 1964.

Bannister, Robert C. *Ray Stannard Baker: The Mind and Thought of a Progressive*. New Haven, Conn.: Yale University Press, 1966. Covers Baker's journalistic and historical studies in depth throughout his life. Particularly insightful is chapter 7, in which Bannister addresses the time period of *Following the Color Line* and describes Baker's conception of a "New Democracy" for the twentieth century.

Fitzpatrick, Ellen F., ed. *Muckraking: Three Landmark Articles*. Boston: Bedford Books of St. Martin's Press, 1994. Includes Baker's exposure of the intimidation of nonunion miners during the anthracite coal strike of 1902; Fitzpatrick's introduction describes the historical factors that led to Baker's sympathy with the common man.

Semonche, John E. *Ray Stannard Baker: A Quest for Democracy in Modern America, 1870–1918*. Chapel Hill: University of North Carolina Press, 1969. Primarily addresses Baker's muckraking career and thought through his writings on World War I, and chapter 7 is devoted to Baker's writings under his pseudonym "David Grayson."

—WESLEY BORUCKI

BALDWIN, JAMES (b. 2 August 1924; d. 1 December 1987), writer and civil rights activist. James Arthur Baldwin was born James Arthur Jones in Harlem Hospital in New York City to Emma Berdis Jones. He was adopted by Jones's husband David Baldwin, a Baptist preacher and factory worker, in 1927.

By the time of his death Baldwin had become a kind of prophetic spokesperson—as both artist and activist—for black life and black history in America, a strong critic of the country he loved. This he accomplished with considerable reflective time spent outside the country, especially in France and Turkey; with wide-ranging artistic and literary contacts; and with a consummate skill in several literary genres, especially the essay, the novel, and the play.

Home life for "Jimmy" was hectic and demanding. He moved frequently between crowded apartments in Harlem with his overworked mother, his angry stepfather, David Baldwin's mother and oldest son, and eight brothers and sisters, the youngest born on the same day his stepfather died, 29 July 1943. Early on Baldwin took refuge in books

James Baldwin. A 1960s photo of the writer James Baldwin with the musician Nina Simone. PHOTOGRAPHS AND PRINTS DIVISION, SCHOMBURG CENTER FOR RESEARCH IN BLACK CULTURE, THE NEW YORK PUBLIC LIBRARY, ASTOR, LENOX AND TILDEN FOUNDATIONS

and reading; school (Frederick Douglass Junior High and De Witt Clinton High School); church (he was converted and preached for three years at Fireside Pentecostal Assembly); and theater, to which he was introduced by teachers.

Core Ideas. After he did factory work for a time following high school, Baldwin's thirty-three years of writing, publishing, giving speeches and interviews, and teaching can be seen as a kind of incremental repetition of some core ideas. As the older brother, he became accustomed to, as he said, telling people what to do and spanking them. He believed black history was central to American history and that it was necessary for individuals and groups to face up to that history and learn how to use it. In his essay "Fifth Avenue, Uptown: A Letter from Harlem," collected in *Nobody Knows My Name* in 1961, he said, "It is a terrible, an inexorable, law that one cannot deny the humanity of another, without diminishing one's own: in the face of one's victim, one sees oneself" (*Nobody Knows My Name*, p. 71). Baldwin believed our suffering is our bridge to one another, that integration is not the same thing as assimilation, and that change is difficult for all.

To Baldwin, overarching ideologies were suspect, oversimplified. "The multiple truths about a people," he said, "are revealed by that people's artists. ... Societies are never able to examine, to overhaul themselves; this effort must be made by that yeast which every society cunningly and unfailingly secretes. This ferment, this disturbance, is the responsibility, and the necessity, of writers" ("As Much Truth as One Can Bear," p. 38). Over and over the word that reappears in Baldwin's self-concept is "witness"—not just an observer but a participant and testifier, bringing forth "a possibility which we will not live to see" (Mead and Baldwin, p. 201).

Writings. Baldwin was an excellent prose stylist, effectively employing apt metaphors, fitting images, parallelism in phrasing and sentence structure, allusions to the King James version of the Bible—and more. But it is his honesty and courage in using these skills and knowledge to reflect on his own experience that generates, develops, and sustains his ideas. A prime example is the essay that catapulted him to national prominence when it appeared in the *New Yorker* on 17 November 1962, "Letter from a Region in My Mind," collected in *The Fire Next Time* (1963) as "Down at the Cross: Letter." It opens with teenagers on the avenue in Harlem "at the beginning of our burning time." He flees to the church, his "gimmick," until he discovers it is "a mask for hatred and self-hatred and despair." This transitions into his adult encounter with Elijah Muhammad, the leader of the Black Muslims, and the two theses of "washing whiter than snow" and "the white man is the devil," create the synthesis of his conclusion: we must learn from the past and have honesty, love, and integration. Otherwise we have the warning of the Old Testament, in the words of a slave song: "God gave Noah the rainbow sign, No more water, the fire next time!"

Baldwin published many reviews and essays, including attacks on his mentor Richard Wright: "Everybody's Protest Novel" in *Zero* (spring 1949) and *Partisan Review* (June 1949) and "Many Thousands Gone" in *Partisan Review* (November–December 1951), both collected in *Notes of a Native Son* (1955). Baldwin debuted as a fiction writer in 1953 with the autobiographical novel *Go Tell It on the Mountain*, in which the experience of conversion of the fourteen-year-old John Grimes in a storefront Pentecostal church frames the stories in turn of his aunt, his stepfather, and his mother. "I'm ready.... I'm coming. I'm on my way," the book concludes aptly for both protagonist and author.

Baldwin's second novel, *Giovanni's Room* (1956), and his third, the best-selling *Another Country* (1962), use sexuality as metaphor for identity, the first centering on a white, gay American protagonist in France and his Italian lover, the next on multiple black and white, gay and straight, married and unmarried, male and female musicians and writers in New York City. Both books convey the necessity of seeing the "darker side" of life, whether through homosexual or heterosexual experience, interracial interactions, music, writing, or death.

Tell Me How Long the Train's Been Gone (1968) is the first-person remembering of an actor, Leo Proudhammer, after he suffers a heart attack. A new militancy is suggested with some ambiguity at the end of the book, when the protagonist seems for a time to adopt the beliefs of a young radical, Christopher. *If Beale Street Could Talk* (1974) attempts a first-person narration by a nineteen-year-old, uneducated, unmarried, pregnant black female, Clementine Rivers or "Tish." The two novels explore American society, writ large and complicated in the former and intimate and simplified, from the perspective of a single family, in the latter.

Baldwin's final and longest novel is his 1979 *Just above My Head*, the title, from the song of that name, suggesting affirmation and even joy. The book centers on brothers, opening with the death of the "Soul Emperor" Arthur Montana, a famed gospel singer, and continuing in the narration of his brother Hall, who had been Arthur's manager. Hall reconstructs civil rights history with Arthur in a quartet traveling through the South, and the book uses music as the metaphor linking art and life. Baldwin does something of the same thing in his oft-anthologized long short story "Sonny's Blues," collected in *Going to Meet the Man* (1965). There too the older brother tells the younger brother's story.

Theater and Dramatizations. From the early 1950s Baldwin used "the *communion* which is the theatre" ("Notes for *The Amen Corner*") to convey his thinking, beginning with the play *The Amen Corner*, using his Pentecostal Church and music experience. First staged by Owen Dodson's Howard University Players in May 1955, the play ran for forty-eight performances at the Barrymore Theater in New York in 1965 and toured Europe and Israel. In 1985–1986 *The Amen Corner* ran for seven months in London.

Baldwin's best and most well-known drama came out of his travels in the American Deep South, where he made his first trip in 1957; the murder of the young black man Emmett Till in Mississippi in 1955; and the assassination of the National Association for the Advancement of Colored People (NAACP) leader, and Baldwin's friend, Medgar Wylie Evers also in Mississippi in 1963. *Blues for Mister Charlie* (1964) is dedicated to Evers. Essentially posing the question of the efficacy of nonviolent protest versus the Malcolm X "by any means necessary" mode of action, Baldwin seems to weigh the two equally, with the Reverend Meridian Henry, a leader of nonviolent protests, at the conclusion saying, "You know, for us, it all began with the Bible and the gun," and when asked what he has done with the gun, he replies that it is in his pulpit, under the Bible, "like the pilgrims of old."

This sounds shockingly militant to a white audience. Black audiences Baldwin shocks by creating a rounded character in his white killer, Lyle Britten, and this is what gives this expressionistic play its thought-provoking power on both sides. Essentially, as an artist and a prophet, Baldwin can understand an event like the Till murder only if he can see the murderer as fully human and all of us humans capable of doing what any one person does. "We have the duty to try to understand this wretched man," he writes in his notes to the play. "For we, the American people, have created him, he is our servant. ... It is we who have locked him in the prison of his color." *Blues for Mister Charlie* ran from 23 April to 29 August 1964 at the ANTA Theater in New York City, directed by Burgess Meredith and starring Pat Hingle, Al Freeman Jr., Diana Sands, and Rip Torn.

One Day, When I Was Lost: A Scenario Based on Alex Haley's "The Autobiography of Malcolm X" (1973) was published some years after Baldwin walked out of a

Columbia Pictures contract to do a screenplay, and in his *No Name in the Street* (1972) he describes that experience. Baldwin's novel *Go Tell It on the Mountain* was dramatized on public television's American Playhouse in January 1985. His long essay on the movies, *The Devil Finds Work*, was published in 1976. A short documentary, *James Baldwin from Another Place*, was made in Istanbul in 1970 by Sedat Pakay, and *I Heard It through the Grapevine*, a record of Baldwin's travels through the South in 1980, was released for television in 1982 by Dick Fontaine and Pat Hartley. Baldwin tried his hand at directing at least once, a Turkish production of John Herbert's *Fortune and Men's Eyes* in Istanbul in 1969.

Critiques and Recognition. Baldwin wore himself out essentially, giving of himself through his writing, speaking, and teaching, including his last post in the Afro-American Studies Department at the University of Massachusetts, Amherst, and he was repeatedly hospitalized throughout his adulthood. Critical reception of his writing has sought to reconcile the voice of the artist with the voice of the activist, heard so often during the civil rights movement. Some have thought that his critical reception has been fairer in Europe than in the United States, where he was attacked among other things for his homosexuality, most notoriously by Eldridge Cleaver in *Soul on Ice* in 1968. Baldwin appeared on the cover of *Time* magazine (17 May 1963) and was the recipient of numerous awards, including an honorary doctorate from the University of Nice, France; the literary award the Socialist Rights of Man; and commander in the French Legion of Honor, awarded by President François Mitterand on 19 June 1986.

In 1971 Baldwin purchased a large house and ten acres of land in the south of France at Saint-Paul de Vence, a place where he could retreat and rest and entertain his numerous friends and large family. It was there, in early 1987, that tests revealed the cancer of the esophagus that killed him by the end of the year. He died in his bed with his brother David and long-term friends Lucien Happersberger and Bernard Hassell at his side on 1 December. His funeral service at the Episcopal Cathedral of Saint John the Divine, in New York City, following viewings in Saint-Paul de Vence and Harlem, was attended by over five thousand people. He was eulogized by Toni Morrison, Maya Angelou, Amiri Baraka, and others and buried on 8 December at Ferncliff Cemetery, Hartsdale, New York.

[*See also* Evers, Medgar Wylie; Homosexuality and Transgenderism; Literature; Sexuality; *and* Till, Emmett, Lynching of.]

BIBLIOGRAPHY

Baldwin, James. "As Much Truth as One Can Bear." *New York Times Book Review*, 14 January 1962.

Baldwin, James. *Blues for Mister Charlie*. New York: Dial, 1964.

Baldwin, James. *Collected Essays*. New York: Library of America, 1998. Selected by Toni Morrison. Chronology; notes, including biblical citations and translations from the French.

Baldwin, James. *Early Novels and Stories*. New York: Library of America, 1998. Selected by Toni Morrison. Chronology; notes including biblical citations and translations from the French.

Baldwin, James. *The Fire Next Time*. New York: Dial, 1963.

Baldwin, James. *Go Tell It on the Mountain*. New York: Knopf, 1953.

Baldwin, James. *Nobody Knows My Name*. New York: Dial, 1961.

Baldwin, James. "Notes for *The Amen Corner*." In *The Amen Corner: A Play*, pp. xi–xvii. New York: Vintage International, 1998. First published 1968 by Dial Press.

Balfour, Lawrie. *The Evidence of Things Not Said: James Baldwin and the Promise of American Democracy*. Ithaca, N.Y.: Cornell University Press, 2001. Chapters cover the difficulty of a national dialogue on race, an extension of W. E. B. Du Bois's double consciousness to Baldwin's writing on democracy and difference, American racial images, the presumptions of innocence, and the problems of language. Notes; bibliography of the extensive number of Baldwin works cited and others; index.

Bobia, Rosa. *The Critical Reception of James Baldwin in France*. New York: Lang, 1997. Includes essays on the African American presence in France and Baldwin's reception, notes, and a bibliography of French material on Baldwin, such as reviews, interviews, periodical and newspaper articles, radio and television programs, dissertations, and chapters in books.

McBride, Dwight A., ed. *James Baldwin Now*. New York: New York University Press, 1999. McBride examines cultural studies in the academy on Baldwin in many subject areas, not just literary. The sections are "Baldwin and Race," "Baldwin and Sexuality," "Baldwin and the Transatlantic," "Baldwin and Inter-textuality," and "Baldwin and the Literary." Select bibliography of works by and on Baldwin; index.

Mead, Margaret, and James Baldwin. *A Rap on Race*. Philadelphia: Lippincott, 1971.

Scott, Lynn Orilla. *Witness to the Journey: James Baldwin's Later Fiction*. East Lansing: Michigan State University Press, 2002. Valuable in its discussion of the often neglected later novels and in its overview of the decline and resurgence in Baldwin studies. Scott centers on three themes in the late fiction: the family's role, the price of success, and race and sex in America. Coda; notes; works cited; index.

Standley, Fred L., and Louis H. Pratt, eds. *Conversations with James Baldwin*. Jackson: University Press of Mississippi, 1989. Twenty-seven interviews from 1961 to just a few weeks before Baldwin's death, including the last formal conversation with him by Quincy Troupe. Introduction; chronology; index.

Weatherby, W. J. *James Baldwin: Artist on Fire*. New York: Fine, 1989. Based on many interviews and more informal and intimate than the two standard biographies, this book, by a friend of Baldwin, is full of details about love affairs, drinking, and smoking but also about Baldwin's relationships with other writers, black and white, his family, and his close friends, including the months before his death. Source notes; index; acknowledgments.

—CAROLYN WEDIN

BALTIMORE. From 1896 to the early twenty-first century, African Americans in Baltimore, Maryland, faced many of the same challenges as other African Americans throughout the United States. Nevertheless,

African American Baltimoreans coalesced into a strong, vibrant community that beat down much of the bigotry and racial prejudice that surrounded them.

In the final decade of the nineteenth century, the city of Baltimore was an unusual combination of northern industrial interests and southern (often bigoted) traditions. African Americans made up 15 percent of the population of the city in 1890, and they made their presence felt. In 1890, Harry Sythe Cummings, a black who graduated from the Maryland Law School before segregation denied entry to African Americans, was elected councilman from the Eleventh Ward. He was followed in 1895 by Dr. J. Marcus Cargill, who was also elected to city council.

The African American community was led by a strong class of professionals—the physicians, educators, dentists, pharmacists, and salesmen who inhabited "old west" Baltimore. In 1892 the Reverend W. M. Alexander established the *Baltimore Afro-American* newspaper, which was still published in the early twenty-first century. A group of African American physicians—William T. Carr, J. Marcus Cargill, and William H. Thompson—established the Provident Hospital for African Americans in Baltimore in 1894. African American educators established the Maryland Progressive State Colored Teachers Association in 1886, which in part spurred the increase in the number of black schools from ten to twenty-seven; meanwhile, the number of African American children enrolled in school increased from 900 to 9,300 between 1867 and 1900. Despite these efforts by African American educators, in 1890 more than one-third of the African American population over the age of ten was illiterate, Baltimore's schools were segregated, only 35 of the 210 teachers in the African American schools were African American themselves, and the school buildings for African Americans were often unhealthy.

Early Twentieth-Century Migration. In the early 1900s the growing number of African American migrants from the Eastern Shore of Maryland and other southern states fed the growing racial tension as these new residents of the city competed with foreign immigrants for the lowest-paid—yet labor-intensive—jobs. The presence of these new city-dwellers spurred whites to attempt to disfranchise them. In 1903, 1905, and 1908, ballot issues that would have deprived both African Americans and recent European immigrants of the right to vote were supported by most of Maryland, but in Baltimore these attempts were overwhelmingly defeated by a coalition of the Colored Law and Order League, the Foreign Born Voters League, and other progressive groups. Subsequent efforts in 1911 and 1913 to establish other segregation practices were equally unsuccessful.

In 1910 the Baltimore City Council enacted its first ordinance establishing racially segregated neighborhoods, but the ordinance was voided by a local court. The city then enacted a second ordinance, which was again challenged in court. In 1913 the Maryland Court of Appeals, the highest court in the state, in its decision in *State v. Gurry*, voided the second ordinance. The city then adopted a third ordinance that was based on an ordinance passed in Louisville, Kentucky. In *Buchanan v. Warley* (1917), the U.S. Supreme Court found the Louisville ordinance—and hence the Baltimore ordinance—to be unconstitutional. Despite these judicial proclamations striking down government-sponsored housing segregation, private actions, such as restrictive covenants, established and maintained segregated housing in Baltimore and throughout the nation until the U.S. Supreme Court held in *Shelley v. Kraemer* (1948) that such covenants are not enforceable.

The increasing number of African Americans in Baltimore also strained the limited pool of available housing. In the first decade of the twentieth century, the population of African American professionals had moved into northwest Baltimore. These were predominantly young, literate, and healthy. They lived in the area of Pennsylvania Avenue and Dolphin Street. Their numbers increased markedly from 8 percent to 60 percent of the population of the Seventh Ward between 1900 and 1910.

Social-improvement groups arose in the early twentieth century. An NAACP chapter—now the second oldest in the nation—was established in the city in 1912, and later a chapter of Marcus Garvey's Universal Negro Improvement Association was established. An African American YMCA was built on Druid Hill Avenue. The area of Pennsylvania Avenue below Dolphin Street became Baltimore's Harlem. The district became a mecca of theaters and clubs that offered minstrels, ragtime, and the emerging new sound of jazz, performed by the likes of Eubie Blake, a native son of Baltimore. The city was home to several other noted artists, such as Eleanora Fagan, better known as Billie Holiday, who was born in the city in 1915.

New Wave of Migration. In the 1930s a new wave of migration to Baltimore from the Eastern Shore and southern Maryland again increased the black population, so that by the mid-1930s, 17 percent of the population of Baltimore was African American. This included approximately 5,500 teachers, doctors, nurses, lawyers, and other professionals; however, 40 percent of the African Americans relied upon public support, compared to 13 percent of the white population.

The most prominent African American lawyer in Baltimore at this time was Thurgood Marshall, the future associate justice of the U.S. Supreme Court. A native Baltimorean, Marshall earned his law degree at Howard University Law School under the tutelage of Charles Hamilton Houston and later followed Houston into the

NAACP. Marshall litigated several cases involving both Baltimore and the state of Maryland. Of particular significance is *Pearson v. Murray* (1936). In this case the young Marshall and his mentor, Houston, were able to convince the Maryland Court of Appeals, the state's highest court, to order the integration of the University of Maryland School of Law. This must have especially pleased Marshall, who had been denied entrance to the law school because of his race.

The desegregation of the public schools in Baltimore predated such action on the national level. In 1952 the Baltimore school board decided that it was too expensive to maintain two sets of "separate but equal" high schools that could provide specialized education to students. Approximately one dozen black students were admitted to the previously all-white Polytechnic High School. Subsequently, responding to the U.S. Supreme Court's *Brown v. Board of Education* decision in 1954, the city school board ordered "desegregation in compliance with the law," and 1,800 of the 57,000 African American students in Baltimore city public schools transferred into previously all-white schools. This action, however, was not without reaction. Between 1954 and 1970, white children left the Baltimore city public schools to attend all-white suburban and private schools. By 1978 more than two-thirds of the students in the Baltimore public schools were black.

During the 1960s the city split into two parts: one white and one black. By 1968 the population of Baltimore was approximately 60 percent African American. The tension that was inherent in this situation was ignited in spring 1968 by the assassination of Martin Luther King Jr. King was killed in Memphis, Tennessee, on Thursday, 4 April; by the following day riots had spread through eastern Baltimore, and the governor declared martial law in the city. More than five thousand national guardsmen poured into the city, but to little avail. On 7 April, President Lyndon Johnson provided the city with an additional five thousand regular U.S. Army troops. By the next day, Monday, 8 April, the federal and state soldiers, along with the city police, had isolated the riots to the African American neighborhoods, but it required nearly a year to quiet the tension and dissatisfaction that permeated these neighborhoods.

After the Riots. The riots nearly destroyed the city. Fearing further violence, the federal government expanded existing antipoverty programs and established new ones. Low-income housing was constructed primarily in existing African American neighborhoods. Eighteen high-rise apartment buildings for low-income people were constructed in western Baltimore, such as Lexington Terrace, whose buildings rose fourteen stories and contained seven hundred apartments. The success of these antipoverty programs of the 1960s and thereafter remains questionable. In 1990 the median annual household income for African American families in the Lexington Terrace complex was only $5,000. By 2000 the high-rise public-housing buildings had disappeared from the landscape of western Baltimore, but the African American population remained in the smaller apartment buildings and single-family residences that had replaced the high rises.

During the 1930s and 1940s, African Americans had no role in city government, but as they began to populate the Democratic Party, they began to take control of their destiny. In 1971, Clarence "Du" Burns was elected to the Baltimore City Council for the Second District. By 1986 he had risen to president of the council, and in 1987 he became mayor when Mayor William D. Schaefer resigned to become governor of Maryland. Burns, however, lost the 1987 Democratic primary election to Kurt Schmoke, another African American, who went on to become the first African American elected to the office of mayor. Schmoke was reelected twice and served as mayor until 1999.

In 1987 the story began to repeat itself. In that year Sheila Dixon was elected as a councilperson from the Fourth District. In 1999 she was elected president of the council, and in 2007 she became mayor upon the resignation of Martin O'Malley, who became governor. She was the third African American and the first woman to serve as mayor of Baltimore. The African American presence on the city council has also increased since the 1980s. A series of redistricting actions in 1991 and 2004 resulted in African Americans holding eight seats in the fourteen-member council.

[*See also Baltimore Afro-American*; Black Migration; Immigrants and African Americans; Maryland; *and* Riots and Rebellions of the 1960s.]

BIBLIOGRAPHY

Brugger, Robert J. *Maryland: A Middle Temperament, 1634–1980*. Baltimore: Johns Hopkins University Press, 1988. A lengthy and thorough history of the state of Maryland from its colonial roots to 1980, with numerous references to the African American experience.

Olesker, Michael. *Baltimore: If You Live Here, You're Home*. Baltimore: Johns Hopkins University Press, 1995. A collection of essays on life in the city of Baltimore.

Olson, Sherry H. *Baltimore: The Building of an American City*. Baltimore: Johns Hopkins University Press, 1980. A short history of the city of Baltimore, with an emphasis on the twentieth century.

—THOMAS E. CARNEY

BALTIMORE AFRO-AMERICAN. The *Baltimore Afro-American*, first published in 1893, was the second-oldest African American newspaper in the United States at the beginning of the twenty-first century and has been owned and operated by John H. Murphy Sr. and his descendants for most of its history. Throughout the years it pressed for racial reform on the local, national, and international levels. In its early years it campaigned for and fostered the development of an African American middle class as it fought to open positions in local, state, and federal governments to African Americans.

The first edition of the *Afro-American* appeared on 13 August 1893. The paper went bankrupt in 1896, and in 1897 it came into the hands of Murphy, who controlled the paper until his death in 1922. Murphy, a former slave and a Civil War veteran, had previously managed the *Afro-American*'s printing department. In this period the paper's circulation included not only Baltimore but also Washington, D.C., Philadelphia, and New York, where news bureaus were established. The early growth of the newspaper certainly resulted from the sensationalism that drove its headlines—it covered contemporary sex scandals and crime stories—but the soul of the paper remained its editorial page.

In the early twentieth century and thereafter the newspaper served as a primary advocate for educational opportunities for African Americans. It demanded equal facilities for African American students and equal opportunity and equal pay for the African Americans working in the schools. Murphy believed that education was key to the goals of freedom and equality in the segregated society of the time. These goals were extended to the opportunities in the federal and state governments.

Nevertheless the *Afro-American* through the beginning of the twentieth century accepted the segregated state of American and Baltimore societies. The paper's position changed in the 1920s and 1930s. Its editorials then called for equal opportunity within a desegregated society. In the late 1930s the *Afro-American*'s editorials encouraged the local and state NAACP chapters to pursue a litigation strategy to establish equality in education. The NAACP's action culminated in the Maryland legislature's providing funding to equalize the salaries of white and African American teachers. In the late 1940s the newspaper published a series of articles on overcrowding and the decrepit conditions of Baltimore's African American schools that led to the construction of five new elementary schools and a new vocational high school.

Since the Civil War, African Americans had supported the Republican Party, which had been their champion and advocate from the late 1850s into the Reconstruction period. In 1924, however, dissatisfied with the failure of Presidents Theodore Roosevelt, William Howard Taft, Warren G. Harding, and Calvin Coolidge to support African Americans, the paper endorsed Robert La Follette, the progressive senator from Wisconsin. From 1928 through 1940 the paper endorsed the Democratic candidates for president, Alfred E. Smith and Franklin D. Roosevelt. But faced with Roosevelt's failure to open up federal jobs to African Americans, the paper in 1941 supported the protest march called by A. Philip Randolph to encourage Roosevelt to act on discrimination in the federal government. On the eve of the march Roosevelt relented and signed Executive Order 8802, which established the Fair Employment Practices Commission. Four years later, however, the newspaper's efforts to have the commission made permanent failed.

Under the editorship of Carl Murphy, the *Afro-American* expanded its focus. In one series of articles and editorials, the paper highlighted the unrest on campuses of historically African American universities. This coverage helped lead to the appointment of African American presidents at such universities as Howard and Fisk. News stories, editorials, and monetary support by the paper eventually led to the desegregation of the graduate schools at the University of Maryland.

On the local level the *Afro-American* was unrelenting as it pressed for equality. In the 1940s the newspaper supported the local NAACP chapter's lawsuit against the Enoch Pratt Free Library to force the admission of African Americans into the library school. Ultimately the U.S. Circuit Court of Appeals, in *Kerr et al. v. Enoch Pratt Free Library of Baltimore City et al.* (1945), found the denial of admission unconstitutional. This suit fell in line with the paper's efforts to open up the professions, in this case the profession of librarian, to African Americans.

Under Carl Murphy the *Afro-American* also sought to reinforce the integrity of the African American community in Baltimore. In his editorials Murphy supported middle-class values and argued that strong African American families were the foundation for a strong African American community. In furtherance of Murphy's campaign for a better Baltimore, the newspaper in 1932 sponsored a cooking school to teach practical home economics to young mothers. In 1935 the paper sponsored the Clean Block Campaign, a children's campaign that cleaned up the streets in African American neighborhoods.

When World War II came, the paper called for African American support for the war effort while simultaneously chiding the government for its refusal to use African American soldiers and sailors in combat roles. The paper carried stories of the war from its correspondents in Europe as well as stories by African American servicemen who recounted the racist insults inflicted upon them in and around military camps in the South.

In the second half of twentieth century the *Afro-American* became a vehement supporter of the modern civil rights movement as it rallied its readers to join in the agitation for desegregation and equal opportunity. The paper also became a firm supporter of the Democratic Party, except for a short flirtation with President Dwight D. Eisenhower in the mid-1950s and Governor Spiro T. Agnew in the 1960s. On both occasions the paper soon regretted giving its support to the Republican candidate.

The end of the twentieth century held the greatest changes for the *Afro-American*. In 1932 the newspaper's circulation stood at 45,000; by 1945 the circulation had risen to 235,000. The increase in circulation generated increased advertising revenue so that, even though the circulation leveled off, the gross income of the newspaper rose to $1.5 million by 1949. The paper remained in the hands of the Murphy family. When Carl Murphy died in 1967, the management of the paper passed to the next generation of Murphys, who faced a new set of challenges. By 1980 the circulation had declined, and African American reporters now found work in the mass media. The management of the paper, acting in response to the declining revenue, closed its offices in Philadelphia and Richmond and modernized its printing operations.

[*See also* Baltimore; Black Press; Journalism, Print and Broadcast; *and* Maryland.]

BIBLIOGRAPHY

Brugger, Robert J. *Maryland: A Middle Temperament, 1634–1980*. Baltimore: Johns Hopkins University Press, 1988. Includes a description of the role of the *Afro-American* in the twentieth century.

Dann, Martin E. *The Black Press, 1827–1890: The Quest for National Identity*. New York: Putnam, 1971. Includes references to the founding of the *Afro-American*.

Farrar, Hayward. *The Baltimore Afro-American, 1892–1950*. Westport, Conn.: Greenwood, 1998. The only history of the paper; carefully recounts its changing roles throughout its history.

—THOMAS E. CARNEY

BAMBARA, TONI CADE (b. 25 March 1939; d. 9 December 1995), author, activist, essayist, film critic, and educator. Bambara was born in New York City and raised in and around the New York–New Jersey area. Her given name was Miltona Mirkin Cade, which she shortened to Toni at age five. As an adult she added Bambara to her signature after discovering that one of her grandmothers had used the name in her sketchbooks. In 1970 she had her name legally changed to Toni Cade Bambara. Her mother, Helen Brent Henderson Cade Brehon, to whom Bambara's first novel, *The Salt Eaters* (1980) is dedicated, encouraged her love of learning and her appreciation for oral history. After earning a Bachelor of Arts degree in theater arts from Queens College in 1959, she became a social worker with the Colony Settlement House in Brooklyn while studying for her MA in English, which she completed in 1965.

Considering her role as a cultural critic, an intellectual, and a champion for disfranchised people of color in the United States and abroad, Bambara's oeuvre reflects her commitment to the black poor and working class, who are often portrayed stereotypically in American literature and culture. Her work consistently reflects a dual commitment to facilitating social justice and promoting artistry. As such, Bambara's writing explores the role of community in deflecting the debilitating effects racism, sexism, and classism have on people of color as they struggle daily to maintain their dignity. Bambara's lifework was informed both by her professional understanding of sociological frameworks and by her lived experience of preserving and showcasing stories of blacks, whose lives,

Toni Cade Bambara, c. 1971. Photograph by Chester Higgins.

she felt, could be both enriched and expressed through good literature.

Bambara was a prolific writer whose intense political and cultural involvement in African American life led her to edit *The Black Woman: An Anthology* (1970). This important book was the first collection featuring black women authors and activists, many of whom subsequently gained fame, including Nikki Giovanni, Alice Walker, and Audre Lorde. Released to critical acclaim, Bambara's first solo collection of short stories, *Gorilla, My Love* (1972), reflected her keen sense of voice and characterization, especially as expressed by preadolescent black female protagonists.

In 1974 Bambara and her daughter Karma moved to Atlanta, Georgia, where Bambara continued her work as a grassroots organizer, taught and lectured extensively, and built productive creative communities for writers of color. She founded the Southern Collective of African American Writers and the First World Writers, two groups that fostered intellectual and interpersonal exchange among African American writers. In the mid-1970s Bambara broadened the international scope of her work with extensive travel opportunities. In particular her visits to Cuba in 1973 and to V ietnam in 1975 had a powerful impact on her story collection, *The Sea Birds Are Still Alive* (1977).

In her mid-career, Bambara passionately explored the medium of film, becoming an influential critic and champion of black independent cinema. In the 1980s she frequently traveled to Philadelphia, Pennsylvania, where she learned cinematography from Louis Massiah, the founder and director of the Scribe Video Center. Bambara collaborated on two documentary projects, *The Bombing of Osage Avenue* (1986) and *W. E. B. Du Bois: A Biography in Four Voices* (1995). Three of her short stories, "Gorilla, My Love," "Medley," and "Witchbird," have been adapted to film, while others (especially "Raymond's Run" and "The Lesson") are widely anthologized.

[*See also* Literature.]

BIBLIOGRAPHY

Bambara, Toni Cade. *Deep Sightings and Rescue Missions: Fiction, Essays, and Conversations*. New York: Pantheon, 1996. Edited by Toni Morrison, this definitive collection gathers Bambara's previously unpublished short stories along with film criticism and interviews.

—AISHA X. L. FRANCIS

BANKS, ERNIE (b. 31 January 1931), baseball player. One of the most successful major league baseball players never to play on a championship team, Banks earned a reputation during his nineteen-year tenure with the Chicago Cubs as one of the most solid, dependable players in the game. He was known for his affable, optimistic attitude, epitomized by his well-known catchphrase: "It's a beautiful day for a ballgame. Let's play two!"

Banks was born in Dallas, Texas, to a poor family. In his autobiography, *Mr. Cub* (1971), he relates the story that, when he was a child, a boy from his neighborhood stole a chicken that had been intended for the Banks family's Thanksgiving dinner. Banks's mother had killed the chicken herself, and Banks had to wrestle the boy for the bird in a nearby basement apartment to reclaim the family's dinner.

Banks began playing softball in high school, where he first played shortstop, the position he excelled at during the first half of his major league career. One summer while Banks was playing in Dallas, he caught the eye of Bill Blair, a scout for the Negro League team the Detroit Colts. Blair introduced Banks to Johnny Carter, the Colts' owner, who offered Banks a tryout for the team. In his first tryout game Banks hit a home run, and he was offered a spot on the team.

After two seasons with the Colts, Banks was recruited by the Kansas City Monarchs, one of the best-known Negro League teams. The Monarchs offered Banks $300 per month, an astounding salary for the young player. At the end of his first season with the Monarchs, he was offered a chance to play for Jackie Robinson's All-Stars, a team of well-known African American players who toured the United States playing games against the Negro League's Indianapolis Clowns. The experience offered Banks the opportunity to learn from the legendary Robinson, who frequently gave him tips to help his playing techniques.

In 1952 Banks's career was interrupted when, at the age of nineteen, he was drafted into the army. He played successfully for his battalion's softball team and was noticed by baseball scouts attending the games. In the years after Robinson's success as the first black player in the major leagues, many teams began recruiting African Americans, and Banks received letters of interest from the Cleveland Indians and the Brooklyn Dodgers. His tour in the army ended in 1953, and he returned to the Kansas City Monarchs. The Chicago Cubs soon purchased Banks's contract from the Monarchs, and on 17 September 1953 he began the first of nineteen seasons with the team.

Banks was well liked on the team and had strong relationships with the Cubs' management and players alike. While traveling with the team, however, he frequently encountered the bigotry and segregation prevalent in the United States at the time. In *Mr. Cub*, Banks relates that while on the road he and Gene Baker, the Cubs' only other black player at the time, had to stay in different hotels, eat at different restaurants, and spend their time in different neighborhoods than their fellow white players. Despite such encounters with racism, Banks felt it was not the job of sports players to make political commentary and thus focused all of his interviews and public appearances on discussing baseball.

Banks's playing was exemplary. In 1955 he hit five grand slams, setting a major league record that lasted for over twenty years. He was awarded the National League's Most Valuable Player Award in 1958 and 1959. In 1970 he became the ninth major league layer to hit five hundred home runs.

Toward the end of his career, Banks's playing weakened slightly. In 1962 he was moved from shortstop to first base owing to a knee injury. By the late 1960s the Cubs' manager Leo Durocher was hesitant to include Banks in the team's starting lineup, though he met a harsh reaction from fans whenever he failed to do so. Banks retired in 1971 with 512 career home runs and 1,636 runs batted in. Between 1956 and 1961 he had played in 717 consecutive games, one of the longest streaks in baseball.

Ernie Banks. National Baseball Hall of Fame inductee Ernie Banks. NATIONAL BASEBALL HALL OF FAME, COOPERSTOWN, N.Y.

Banks was inducted into the Baseball Hall of Fame in 1977 and worked through much of the 1970s as a coach with the Cubs. His number 14 was the first to be retired by the team. He founded the Ernie Banks Live Above and Beyond Foundation, which helps underprivileged children and strives to end racial prejudice and discrimination.

[*See also* Baseball.]

BIBLIOGRAPHY

Banks, Ernie, and Jim Enright. *Mr. Cub*. Chicago: Follett, 1971.

Pietrusza, David, Matthew Silverman, and Michael Gershman, eds. *Baseball: The Biographical Encyclopedia*. Kingston, N.Y.: Total Sports Illustrated, 2000.

—RONALD ENICLERICO

BANKS, TYRA (b. 4 December 1973), model and talk show host. Tyra Lynne Banks was born in Los Angeles to Carolyn London, a medical photographer and business manager, and Donald Banks, a computer consultant. Her parents divorced when she was six, but their relationship remained friendly, and both parents helped manage her career. Banks attended Immaculate Heart High School, an all-girls Catholic school. She was teased, as she recalled, for being a "tall beanpole freak all the girls would laugh at" and remembered this being "a really unhappy time" (Allan). She was accepted to Loyola Marymount University in Los Angeles. Weeks before school started, she was "discovered" and began modeling at age seventeen. She said that she "didn't leave [for Paris] thinking [she] was going to be some big fashion model" and "just wanted to make money for college" (Lenord). Her first week in Paris, in 1991, she booked twenty-five shows, unprecedented for a first timer.

The cutthroat modeling industry did not take kindly to a newcomer, particularly a black one. Naomi Campbell had Banks banned from a Chanel show and tried to force her out of their shared agency, Elite Model Management. Echoing Iman twenty years earlier, Banks said that "back then there were 10 top models... but there was an unwritten rule that only one of them could be black. And Naomi was that one black girl" (Allan). This forced competition was a large part of Banks's decision to quit haute couture modeling and begin accepting more mainstream, commercial jobs. In 2006 she invited Campbell onto her talk show, *The Tyra Banks Show*, and the women candidly discussed those years. Campbell offered an apology, and Banks made it clear that "the press had cast Naomi and [me] as rivals before we ever met each other" (Allan).

Despite these challenges, Banks launched a successful modeling career, working for dozens of designers as well as for product advertisements. Her biggest advertising success was landing a CoverGirl Cosmetics contract, only the second black woman to do so and one of only three black models by the early twenty-first century. Subsequent black CoverGirl models have been celebrities or winners of *America's Next Top Model*, of which CoverGirl is the major sponsor.

Banks has been on the covers of almost all the major women's and fashion magazines. She was the first black model on the covers of *GQ*, the *Victoria's Secret* catalog, and the *Sports Illustrated* swimsuit issue (with Valeria Mazza, who is Argentinean), all in 1996. In 1997 she made a solo appearance on the cover of the *Sports Illustrated* swimsuit issue, the first black woman to do so. By the early twenty-first century one other black woman, Beyoncé Knowles, who is not primarily a model, had appeared on the cover.

Ten years after her iconic appearance, Banks re-created the *Sports Illustrated* photo shoot in the same bikini and appeared on the cover of *People* magazine in a one-piece bathing suit with the headline "You Call *This* Fat?" responding to critics who had noticed the approximately thirty pounds she had gained. In her interview with *People* she wondered, "So when they say that my body is 'ugly' and 'disgusting,' what does that make those [my young fans] feel like?" ("Cover Story"). Two years earlier on her show she had put on a fat suit, transforming herself into a 350-pound woman, and used the experience to talk to viewers about how obesity "seemed like the last form of open discrimination that's okay" (Associated Press). In a further effort to send the message that women's bodies do not need to be "enhanced," either with extreme dieting or plastic surgery, Banks in 2005 had a sonogram on her talk show to prove that she never had breast implants.

In addition to being named Supermodel of the Year, Banks was ranked in "the Time 100" twice (2006 and 2007). As of the early twenty-first century she was one of only seven women and five black people to rank repeatedly; the other blacks were Nelson Mandela, Barack Obama, Condoleezza Rice, and Oprah Winfrey. Her two television shows, *America's Next Top Model* (begun in 2003) and *The Tyra Banks Show* (begun in 2005), were almost immediate hits and both were nominated for NAACP Image Awards; *America's Next Top Model* was also nominated for GLAAD Media Awards. *The Tyra Banks Show* also won several Daytime Emmy Awards.

America's Next Top Model is known for being open to different types of women. Banks made it clear that she would not tolerate prejudice and discrimination. The show has had at least three openly gay contestants and several who came out after their appearances. There have also been a number of black contestants and black or biracial winners. Several of the models have been plus-size, including the winner of Cycle 10, Whitney Thompson.

In the 1990s Banks was referred to as "the next Naomi." Subsequently she was called the next Oprah, in part due to her extensive philanthropic work. Banks's attempts to change the images of what a healthy woman, a black woman, and a model look like are only a small part of what she does. Her biggest effort has been creating the TZONE Foundation, which provides grants to women-run organizations for women, the goal being to "support women and girls by increasing awareness of the needs, aspirations and accomplishments of outstanding women-led organizations" (http://www.tzonefoundation.org).

Banks was the subject of the cover story in the *New York Times Magazine* on 1 June 2008. The story, titled "Banksable," discussed her repertoire of smiles and fashion career but focused on her "brand" and her skills in arenas beyond modeling. Leslie Moonves, president and CEO of the CBS Corporation, complimented her unanticipated "drive [and] creative ability" (p. 41). The article acknowledged criticisms of Banks and her shows, including the charge that *America's Next Top Model* is unrealistic and does not actually lead to stardom. Moonves's statement was reinforced by the account of the reporter, Lynn Hirschberg, who observed both the kindness Banks demonstrated for strangers and the brutal honesty, even anger, she showed for *Top Model* contestants.

The "Banksable" article was characteristic of the media's coverage of Banks at that time: it made note of her modeling career and the problems she experienced breaking out of the model mold, then moved on to discuss her transformation to a successful businesswoman and media icon, including a comparison to Oprah Winfrey. Media portrayals of Banks have almost uniformly portrayed her as an uncompromising figure.

[*See also* Models.]

Bibliography

Allan, Hawa. "When Tyra Met Naomi." *Bitch*, 29 February 2008. http://bitchmagazine.org/article/when-tyra-met-naomi.

Associated Press. "Tyra Banks dons fat suit to understand obesity." 2 November 2005. http://www.msnbc.msn.com/id/9900379/

Blakeley, Kiri. "Tyra Banks on It." *Forbes*, 3 July 2006.

Hirschberg, Lynn. "Banksable." *The New York Times Magazine*, 1 June 2008.

Lenord, Peter. "Celebrity Interview—Tyra Banks." *H! Society*, 18 November 2005.

"Tyra Banks Speaks Out about Her Weight." *People*, 24 January 2007.

Wolf, Naomi. "The Time 100: Heroes and Pioneers; Tyra Banks." *Time*, 14 May 2007.

—Abigail Finkelman

BANKS, AFRICAN AMERICAN–OWNED. Wealth has often acted as a means of empowerment and equality among African Americans when many realized that even with their pennies earned they could amass small fortunes and ultimately hold economic power. From 1888 to 1934, 134 black-owned banks were established, and they funded many black businesses. But then the Great Depression forced many of these banks to shut their doors. According to the Federal Reserve, by the early twenty-first century roughly thirty-two black-owned banks existed across America.

Community and church organizations played a significant role in the beginning of banks. Black churches had assets in real estate, and often this was the only monetary asset of the community. The donations that churches collected weekly helped to establish the first black-owned banks. In time these banks flourished, leading the way to the growth and development of black business with millions of dollars of transactions.

The first African American–owned bank was the Savings Bank of the Grand Fountain, United Order of the True Reformers, in Richmond, Virginia. Chartered by the Virginia legislature in 1888, the bank opened one year later on 3 April 1889. This bank was an extension of the United Order of the True Reformers, a fraternal organization founded in 1881 by William Washington Browne.

Another early black-owned bank was the Capital Savings Bank of Washington, D.C., which opened for business on 17 October 1888 and closed in 1902. The building that was once the headquarters for the bank was given National Historic Landmark status in 1975. Another early bank, the Saint Luke Penny Savings Bank, opened in 1903. It was founded by an African American woman, Maggie Walker, in Richmond, Virginia. This bank was geared toward small investors, including women. The Saint Luke Penny Savings Bank eventually merged with two other black-owned banks in Richmond to form the Consolidated Bank and Trust, which by the early twenty-first century was the oldest existing African American–owned and operated bank in America. Still based in Richmond, the bank had several branches in Virginia.

The 1920s was the golden era of growth and development for black-owned businesses. By 1932 more than 100,000 individual black-owned businesses were in operation. However, the Great Depression greatly affected black businesses and banks, and by 1940 many of them were forced to close because the banks had to call in loans that most could not afford to pay. Banks were further indebted when people needed to withdraw savings in order to survive. Ultimately the Depression crippled many black-owned banks, forcing them to close their doors for good.

One bank, the Citizens and Southern Bank and Trust Company, was able to survive the Depression. This bank was founded in Philadelphia in 1921 by Major Richard R. Wright (1855–1947), a military officer, entrepreneur, and president for thirty years of the Georgia State Industrial College in Savannah. At the time, the Citizens and Southern Bank and Trust Company was the only African American–owned bank in the North. The bank withstood the Depression and continued to prosper for many years after, being sold in 1957 with assets totaling $5.5 million.

Independence Federal Savings Bank was founded in Washington, D.C., in 1968 by leaders of the black community, such as William Fitzgerald III, who championed the bank's mission to provide services to minorities, women, small businesses, and home buyers. With more than $160 million in assets by the early twenty-first century, this bank remained one of the largest black-owned banks in the United States. However, it has had its fair share of turbulence, including the Washington Teachers Union scandal in which more than $5 million dollars was embezzled, and six board members (including two of Fitzgerald's heirs) resigned.

Emma C. Chappell founded the United Bank of Philadelphia in 1992. At the time the bank was the only African American–owned full-service bank serving the minority community of Philadelphia. Chappell worked tirelessly to get the bank off the ground, and ultimately support from the community made the bank possible. United Bank has been deemed "the bank the people built." This bank has an unusual organization, being structured on a grassroots foundation. Collectively, three thousand people invested $3.3 million, which represents more than half the capitalization amount required by the state's department of banking.

United Bank, once named bank of the year by the U.S. Small Business Administration, by the early twenty-first century held assets of $150 million and $7.7 million in Tier 1 capital. In 1999, United Bank reported a net loss of $1.2 million with the Securities and Exchange Commission, and in 2000 the Federal Reserve forced Chappell to relinquish control as president and chief executive officer (CEO) and take a director's seat. Evelyn F. Smalls was appointed as the new president and CEO, and Brenda M. Hudson-Nelson as executive vice president and chief financial officer—both were African American women.

Online banking is also becoming more prominent in black communities. OneUnited Bank, which calls itself the first black-owned Internet bank, is an online bank with offices in Boston, Los Angeles, and Miami. This bank offers full services online and thus allows customers to manage their finances anywhere. OneUnited Bank was established by combining black-owned banks across America that shared the same vision of helping and uniting the community. Every year from 2004 to 2007,

OneUnited was awarded the Bank Enterprise Award by the U.S. Department of Treasury for its community-development lending.

[*See also* Black Capitalism; Entrepreneurship; Fraternal Organizations, African American; *and* Insurance Companies, African American–Owned.]

BIBLIOGRAPHY

Branch, Muriel Miller, and Dorothy Marie Rice. *Pennies to Dollars: The Story of Maggie Lena Walker*. North Haven, Conn.: Shoe String Press, 1997.

Brown, Carolyn M. "A Bank Grows in Philly." *Black Enterprise*, June 1995.

Coles, Flournoy A., Jr. "Financial Institutions and Black Entrepreneurship." *Journal of Black Studies* 3, no. 3 (March 1973): 329–349.

Dingle, Derek T. *Black Enterprise Titans of the B.E. 100s: Black CEOs Who Redefined and Conquered American Business*. New York: Wiley, 1999.

Hammond, Theresa A. *A White-Collar Profession: African American Certified Public Accountants since 1921*. Chapel Hill: University of North Carolina Press, 2007.

Wade, Marcia A. "Takeover of Independence Bank." *Black Enterprise*, September 2002.

—LAURA CRKOVSKI

BAPTIST CHURCH, AFRICAN AMERICANS AND. In many respects the final decades of the nineteenth century were the golden years of the African American Baptist experience. For a brief time at the close of the nineteenth century and in the early years of the twentieth century, the several divisions of the African American Baptist church came together to form a single convention, before once again dividing into several conventions by the late twentieth century.

Many African American Baptists during this period also collaborated with white Baptist congregations and conventions to advance educational opportunities for African Americans. Primarily with the support of the American Baptist Home Mission Society, African American Baptists founded such institutions of higher learning as Morehouse College and Spelman College. During this period the nation experienced the Great Migration of African Americans out of the South into the North and within the South to cities. The southern African Americans had grown up in a rural culture, and most were unacquainted with an urban way of life. The African American Baptist church sought to urbanize these people. Women were most responsible for this effort: in 1900 African American Baptist women established their first convention, which worked to provide various social assistance programs. This experience strengthened African American women's leadership and organizational skills, which in turn fostered the establishment and growth of African American women's clubs.

The Institutional Church. The modern African American Baptist movement began at the end of the nineteenth century. Prior to 1895, African American Baptist congregations were organized into three different conventions: the Foreign Mission Baptist Convention (founded in 1880), the American National Baptist Convention (1886), and the National Baptist Education Convention (1893). In September 1895 more than five hundred representatives of the three conventions met in Atlanta and merged into the National Baptist Convention, U.S.A. (NBCUSA).

Unity among Baptists was fragile. In 1897 the Foreign Mission of the NBCUSA decided to move its headquarters from Richmond, Virginia, to Louisville, Kentucky. The publishing decisions of the NBCUSA's board also jeopardized existing relations with the white Baptist organizations. In 1897 these decisions prompted a number of members loyal to the Richmond headquarters to separate and establish a new convention, the Lott Carey Foreign Mission Convention. A few years later, in 1905, the NBCUSA and the Lott Carey convention effected a reconciliation on paper; nevertheless the two conventions continued to operate separately, although many members continued to hold dual memberships in the two conventions, even into the twenty-first century.

A second schism occurred in 1915 and was also related to publishing. At the end of the nineteenth century, the NBCUSA established its own publishing board, which was initially placed under the direction of the Home Mission Board, headed by R. H. Boyd. Boyd constructed a publishing facility on land that he owned in Tennessee and incorporated the publishing entity. When the NBCUSA attempted to exert more control over the publishing entity, Boyd and his supporters separated and became the core of a new convention, the National Baptist Convention of America (NBCA), which was established in 1915. Since then the new convention, the NBCA, has been headed by a succession of presidents; the publishing arm of the convention, however, has remained the domain of the Boyd family.

In the 1960s the NBCUSA splintered again. The Reverend Joseph H. Jackson dominated the convention, which was very conservative and favored a gradualist approach to the challenges of segregation and discrimination. Rejecting Jackson's domination, a number of members, in particular those who were active in the civil rights movement, established their own convention, the Progressive National Baptist Convention, in 1961.

Education. This history of disruptions in the African American Baptist experience in the twentieth century belies the importance of African American Baptists. By 1990 African American membership in the African

American–dominated Baptist conventions exceeded 12 million, making the Baptist Church the largest African American religion in the United States.

In the years after the Civil War many groups, including the African American Baptists, became concerned and involved with providing educational opportunities for the newly freed slaves. The African American Baptists established two of the most prominent historically black institutions of higher learning. Originally founded in 1867 as the Augusta Institute by the Reverend William Jefferson White, an Augusta Baptist minister, and the Reverend Richard C. Coulter, a former slave, the institution moved to Atlanta and in 1913 was renamed Morehouse College. Its purpose was to educate African American men in the areas of education and ministry, but John Hope—the college's first African American president, from 1906—worked very hard to establish the school as a first-class academic institution. As a result of his efforts the college is often called the Harvard of the South, and its alumni include such notable African Americans as Martin Luther King Jr., Spike Lee, and Edwin Moses.

The second institution was founded in 1881 and named the Atlanta Baptist Female Seminary. Its name was changed in the late 1880s to Spelman College in honor of Laura Spelman, wife of John D. Rockefeller, who had endowed the college with a sizable gift. Like Morehouse College, Spelman College is now recognized as a prominent women's college and includes among its alumnae the actress Keisha Knight Pulliam, the writer Alice Walker, and Alberta Williams King, the mother of Martin Luther King Jr.

Social Assistance. Another important aspect of the African American Baptist experience in the twentieth century was the rise of the Women's Convention. The convention originally developed in 1900 as an auxiliary to the NBCUSA, but it quickly exerted its own independence and did not suffer from the schism of 1915. The convention grew quickly, and by 1907 it had more than a million members. The convention firmly and quickly established its own agenda. In its early years the convention provided support for missionary activities, as well as tuition assistance for African students in the United States. The convention also supported secular activities and groups that advocated for African Americans and women, such as the National Association of Colored Women. The Women's Convention campaigned for improved housing conditions and condemned child labor. In 1909 it established the first school for black women owned by black women, the National Training School for Women and Girls, which was much like Booker T. Washington's Tuskegee Institute. The convention's efforts were guided by Nannie Helen Burroughs.

After 1910 the focus of both the NBCUSA and the Women's Convention turned upon the many African American migrants who were then pouring into such major urban areas as Birmingham, Atlanta, Richmond, Chicago, Detroit, Cleveland, and New York. Many African American Baptist churches became the center of social services for the new city dwellers, providing such services as kindergartens, sewing and cooking classes for women, penny-savings banks, and settlement houses. The African American Baptist church also sought to blend the rural and urban cultures through the use of music. Southern music and other worship practices such as summer camps and camp meetings were thus integrated into the northern experience.

The major issue facing African Americans in the twentieth century was segregation, set in place by Jim Crow laws and validated by the Supreme Court in *Plessy v. Ferguson* in 1896. Nearly fifty years later the Reverend Sandy F. Ray, an African American Baptist minister, called upon his fellow Americans, as well as fellow Baptists, to work to realize the dream of equality for all. In 1948 a meeting of African American Baptists in Birmingham, Alabama, echoing Ray's statement, called on all Christians to work to end segregation. These early calls for the end of segregation are evidence of the beginning of the modern civil rights movement and of the African American Baptist church's commitment to ending segregation.

The African American Baptist church could not, however, agree upon a strategy to attain the goal. Some, most notably Joseph H. Jackson, the president of the NBCUSA, advocated a gradualist strategy, reminiscent of the earlier efforts of Booker T. Washington. Jackson, who presided over the NBCUSA from 1953 to 1982, refused to support the efforts of King, who advocated a strategy of civil disobedience. In 1963 many African American Baptist ministers, including Jesse Jackson, Benjamin Hooks, and William H. Gray III, joined King in the Progressive National Baptist Convention, which supported the King strategy.

Nevertheless many African American Baptists vigorously supported ending segregation. All the African American Baptist conventions supported the National Association for the Advancement of Colored People (NAACP) and, eventually, King's Southern Christian Leadership Conference, founded in 1957. After 1983 even the NBCUSA, under the leadership of the Reverend T. J. Jemison, joined in the support of King's strategy, resulting in a unified African American Baptist effort to end segregation.

[*See also* Abyssinian Baptist Church; Black Church; Dexter Avenue Baptist Church; Great Migration; Hooks, Benjamin; King, Martin Luther, Jr., Philosophy of; Morehouse College; National Association of Colored Women;

National Baptist Convention; National Baptist Publishing Board; Progressive National Baptist Convention; Religion; Sixteenth Street Baptist Church; Southern Christian Leadership Conference; Spelman College; Washington, Booker T.; *and* Women's Clubs.]

BIBLIOGRAPHY

Fitts, Leroy. *A History of Black Baptists*. Nashville, Tenn.: Broadman Press, 1985. Provides a history of the African American experience in the Baptist Church from the colonial period to the twentieth century.

Higginbotham, Evelyn Brooks. *Righteous Discontent: The Women's Movement in the Black Baptist Church, 1880–1920*. Cambridge, Mass.: Harvard University Press, 1993. A rare gender- and race-based study that fills in the holes in the history of the African American church.

Leonard, Bill J. *Baptists in America*. New York: Columbia University Press, 2005. Carefully notes the role of African Americans in the church.

Lincoln, C. Eric, and Lawrence H. Mamiya. *The Black Church in the African American Experience*. Durham, N.C.: Duke University Press, 1990. A comprehensive study of the African American church that discusses the black Baptist church at length.

—THOMAS E. CARNEY

BARAKA, AMIRI (b. 7 October 1934), playwright, poet, writer, and one of the leaders of the black revolt of the 1960s. Imamu Amiri Baraka was born Everett Leroy Jones during the Great Depression in Newark, New Jersey. He is credited as one of the most outspoken advocates of a black cultural and political revival in the 1960s. He attended Barringer High School and Rutgers University, where he pursued philosophy and religious studies, before enrolling in Howard University in Washington, D.C. It was then that he changed his name to LeRoi Jones. Baraka graduated from Howard University in 1953, and in 1954 he joined the U.S. Air Force, in which he served for three years. When an anonymous tipster suggested that he was a communist sympathizer, Baraka's belongings were searched for subversive literature. Because some of his books were deemed socialist, Baraka was discharged from the military. Shortly thereafter he moved to Greenwich Village and enrolled in Columbia University to study comparative literature. He also began attending the New School for Social Research.

While in New York, Baraka became involved in the current art circle that included Beat poets such as Charles Olson and Allen Ginsberg. During his Beat period (1957–1962) Baraka began writing his poetry and drama. In 1958 he married Hettie Jones, who was Jewish; the couple had two children. In 1958, with Hettie, Baraka founded the avant-garde literary magazine *Yugen*. That same year Baraka also founded Totem Press, becoming one of the most influential editors of the Beat movement, publishing not-yet-known works by Ginsberg and Jack Kerouac. In 1958 Baraka published his first play, *A Good Girl Is Hard to Find*.

In 1960, at the invitation of Richard Gibson, a black journalist who was living in Paris, Baraka visited Cuba. Greatly influenced by the Cuban Revolution, Baraka became increasingly preoccupied with the potential for a black revolution. In 1961 an underground press that published work by Ginsberg and Kerouac published Baraka's anthology of poetry *Preface to a Twenty Volume Suicide Note*, which contained the first inklings of Baraka's future interest in black emancipation and his mistrust of white America. The anthology was followed by the collection *The Dead Lecturer* (1964).

In 1963 Baraka published *Blues People: Negro Music in White America*, and a year later four of Baraka's plays were produced: *The Baptism*, *The Toilet*, *The Slave*, and *The Dutchman*. *The Dutchman*, the sadomasochistic tale of a casual encounter between a crude white woman and a

Amiri Baraka. Amiri Baraka, at the time the New Jersey poet laureate, defends a poem he wrote that implied that Israel knew in advance of plans for the September 11 terrorist attacks, October 2002. Photograph by Mike Derer. AP IMAGES

preppy black man, premiered at the Cherry Lane Theatre on 24 March 1964 and won a *Village Voice* Obie Award for best Off-Broadway play. Written in the spirit of Antonin Artaud's theater of cruelty, the play challenged the audience's stereotypes and defined Baraka as a precursor of the militant black theater. In 1966 *The Dutchman* was made into a movie directed by Anthony Harvey and starred Shirley Knight and Al Freeman Jr.

In 1965, after the assassination of the black Muslim leader Malcolm X, Baraka moved to Harlem. There he founded the Black Arts Repertory Theater School, which quickly became an influential breeding ground for talented black artists and writers. Although the theater itself was short-lived, the Harlem Black Arts Movement that followed it inspired the development of a national Black Arts Movement and the rise of over eight hundred other black theaters and art centers in the United States. They included the Free Southern Theater in New Orleans; the Concept East Theater and Broadsides Press in Detroit, led by Dudley Randall; the Afro-Arts Theater and the Organization of Black American Culture in Chicago, led by Gwendolyn Brooks; and the National Black Theatre in Harlem, led by Barbara Ann Teer. Also in 1965 Baraka and Jones divorced, and a year later Baraka married Sylvia Robinson, an African American who later took the name Amina Baraka. At that time Baraka gave up his English name and began to call himself Amiri Baraka.

The years 1965–1974 marked Baraka's turn to black nationalism. As a political and cultural activist, he rose to national prominence during the modern Black Convention movement, which began in 1966 with the Black Arts Convention in Detroit and the National Black Power Conference in Washington, D.C. Under Baraka's leadership, factions of the Black Arts and Black Power movements merged, fostering the politics of black cultural nationalism that began to define the modern Black Convention movement.

In 1968 Baraka founded the Black Community Development and Defense Organization. He also became secretary general of the National Black Political Assembly and chairman of the Congress of African People. Baraka's goal was to develop a number of organizations that focused on the formation of black nationality. He helped form many organizations, among them the United Brothers, the Committee for a Unified NewArk, the NewArk Student Federation, and Unity and Struggle, and assisted a few jihad publications. In the 1970s the local organizations emerged into the national spotlight, forming the Congress of African People, the African Liberation Support Committee, the National Black Assembly, and the Black Women's United Front.

The Black Power movement was marked by unrest and urban uprisings, which included the 1965 Watts and 1967 New Jersey uprisings. After the assassination of Martin Luther King Jr. on 4 April 1968, approximately 200 urban uprisings occurred in 172 cities, followed by 500 racial confrontations in 1969. The climate of these years forged African Americans' need for self-determination and a new black consciousness. Baraka was at the forefront of these events, teaching at San Francisco State University and watching closely the development of the Black Panther organization, founded in Oakland in 1966. Baraka's writing became increasingly militant, depicting violence against women, whites, gays, and Jews. What some saw as an expression of the historically oppressed black voice, others viewed as homophobia, sexism, and anti-Semitism.

In 1974, however, Baraka distanced himself from black nationalism and became a Marxist, arguing against the imperialist tendencies of the United States and its allies in the North Atlantic and for the liberation of what came to be called the Third World. In 1979 he became a lecturer at the State University of New York–Stony Brook in the Department of African Studies. Although he officially denounced his former anti-Semitic remarks, he continued to refer to himself as an anti-Zionist. In 1983 Baraka and his wife Amina edited *Confirmation: An Anthology of African-American Women*, which won an American Book Award from the Before Columbus Foundation. In 1984 Baraka published *The Autobiography of LeRoi Jones*. That same year he became a full professor at Stony Brook.

In 1987, with Maya Angelou and Toni Morrison, Baraka was invited to speak at the ceremony commemorating the late writer James Baldwin. Also that year Baraka, collaborating again with Amina, published *The Music: Reflections on Jazz and Blues*. Baraka's list of awards includes a Guggenheim Fellowship, a National Endowment for the Arts grant, the PEN/Faulkner Award, the Rockefeller Foundation Award for Drama, the Langston Hughes Award from the City College of New York, and a Lifetime Achievement Award from the Before Columbus Foundation.

After the attacks of 11 September 2001, Baraka wrote "Somebody Blew Up America," a poem in which he suggested that the George W. Bush administration and Israel were complicit in the plot. The Anti-Defamation League denounced the poem as anti-Semitic, and the controversy cost Baraka his position as poet laureate of New Jersey. Nevertheless, he has been credited with inspiring a new generation of black poets and writers and with opening previously unavailable publishing opportunities.

[*See also* Black Arts Movement; Black Nationalism; *and* Literature.]

BIBLIOGRAPHY

Baraka, Imamu Amiri. *Afrikan Revolution: A Poem*. Newark, N.J.: Jihad, 1973.

Baraka, Imamu Amiri. *Four Black Revolutionary Plays: All Praises to the Black Man*. Indianapolis, Ind.: Bobbs-Merrill, 1969.

Benston, Kimberly W. *Baraka: The Renegade and the Mask*. New Haven, Conn.: Yale University Press, 1976.

Brown, Lloyd W. *Amiri Baraka*. Boston: Twayne, 1980.

Elam, Harry J., Jr. *Taking It to the Streets: The Social Protest Theater of Luis Valdez and Amiri Baraka*. Ann Arbor: University of Michigan Press, 1997.

Harris, William J. *The Poetry and Poetics of Amiri Baraka: The Jazz Aesthetic*. Columbia: University of Missouri Press, 1985.

Hudson, Theodore R. *From LeRoi Jones to Amiri Baraka: The Literary Works*. Durham, N.C.: Duke University Press, 1973.

Woodard, Komozi. *A Nation within a Nation: Amiri Baraka (LeRoi Jones) and Black Power Politics*. Chapel Hill: University of North Carolina Press, 1999.

—Magda Romanska

BARBERSHOPS. When the movie *Barbershop* hit theaters in 2002, it offered audiences and critics a rare glimpse into the lives and conversations of ordinary black men and women. Though the movie was not a documentary, the tenor of the discussions it projected, as well as the topics debated, offered a realistic portrait of what some scholars have considered to be the everyday talk of African Americans. Indeed, one particular character's garrulous rant about the foibles of revered figures such as the activists Rosa Parks, Martin Luther King Jr., and Jesse Jackson led to vigorous protests from the minister and activist Al Sharpton and Jackson himself, though others argued that if one were not free to speak his mind in a barbershop, where could he speak freely?

Barbershops have a long history in African American communities as businesses and spaces where black men have gathered to speak openly—both comically and seriously—about issues ranging from politics to sports to relationships to whites. Though they are spaces open to the public, barbershops share with fraternal orders a sense of privacy and seclusion because women and whites are allowed only under certain circumstances. The mere presence of a woman or a white often changes the nature of the dialogue that occurs. Yet barbershops are also more democratic spaces than such private, self-selecting organizations as fraternal orders because virtually all black men are allowed inside—for a cut, a conversation, an argument, or merely, as the historian Craig Marberry has observed, "the hum of men among men."

Historically, barbershops and the men who own them have been some of the key institutions and figures in the African American community. During the antebellum period, wealthier free blacks often ran barbershops that served both a white and a black clientele, particularly in northern cities. In the South, black barbers could shave whites because barbering was seen as a servile occupation. These practices were not without problems, as one incident recorded by a black newspaper shows: the newspaper related how an African American in antebellum New York was refused a shave by a black barber because the barber had just used his tools on a white man who was still lingering in the shop. Estimates suggest that before the Civil War barbershops constituted one-tenth of the businesses owned by African Americans. In 1854, to cite just one example, San Francisco boasted sixteen black-owned barbershops.

Following the Civil War and into the late nineteenth century, the practice of shaving whites gave way to more segregated practices. In the North this was the result of increased numbers of immigrants from European countries, while in the South the legal separation of the races resulted in black businessmen turning inward and developing an African American clientele. Exclusion from the broader society, though not desired, conferred on barbershops a place of significance second only, perhaps, to African American churches. As tensions heightened because of the migration of southern blacks northward during and after World War I, barbers such as Robert Horton routinely read and discussed the *Chicago Defender* with his patrons, or made plans to organize expeditions. During the civil rights movement, strategic plans relating to marches, protests, and the like were often fleshed out in such spaces.

What the sociologists St. Clair Drake and Horace Cayton observed more than sixty years ago still holds true: the barbershop, the beauty shop, and the funeral home serving African Americans remained firmly in the hands of African Americans. That all of these businesses also touch upon or treat the body in some way signals their importance as cultural institutions. All involve intimate acts in which the particular meaning that is invested in the body—from the texture of one's hair to the laying on of hands in preparing the body and soul for passage to the next world—cannot be reduced to the social construction of race.

Even in the early twenty-first century one of the most important rites in a young African American boy's life is his first haircut at the barbershop. As if to highlight that this is where a great deal of male socialization does or can take place, in the early twenty-first century an organization called Boys Booked on Barbershops started to stock barbershops with books for the young to read while waiting for a turn in the chair. Those African American men who move to a new city and ask for advice on where they can get their hair cut are often given that and much more: the possibility of a community that takes shape in, and because of, the shop. Perhaps what is most important about barbershops is that they bring together a cross section of men whose views and opinions are heard, challenged, and weighed seriously by others—when they are so seldom heard or sought out by the public at large.

Given his past history as a grassroots organizer, it should not be surprising that the 2008 presidential candidate Barack Obama invested many of his resources and much of his energy early in the campaign seeking to get support for his nomination by establishing contacts with local barbershops in states such as South Carolina—and by taking his turn in the chair.

[*See also* Entrepreneurship *and* Hair and Beauty Culture.]

BIBLIOGRAPHY

Drake, St. Clair, and Horace R. Cayton. *Black Metropolis: A Study of Negro Life in a Northern City*. New York: Harcourt, Brace, 1945.

Harris-Lacewell, Melissa. *Barbershops, Bibles, and BET: Everyday Talk and Black Political Thought*. Princeton, N.J.: Princeton University Press, 2004.

Marberry, Craig. *Cuttin' Up: Wit and Wisdom from Black Barber Shops*. New York: Doubleday, 2005.

—JILL DUPONT

BARNETT, FERDINAND L. (b. c. 1859; d. 11 March 1936), attorney and journalist. Ferdinand Lee Barnett was born in Nashville, Tennessee, in 1859. His father, born a slave, purchased his freedom and worked much of his life as a blacksmith. The family moved to Canada soon after Ferdinand was born and then to Chicago in 1869. Barnett was educated in Chicago schools, graduating from high school in 1874 with high honors. After teaching in the South for two years, he returned to Chicago and attended Chicago College of Law, later affiliated with Northwestern Law School.

Barnett graduated from law school and was admitted to the Illinois bar in 1878. Rather than immediately practicing law, he founded the *Conservator*, Chicago's first African American newspaper. The *Conservator* was a radical voice for justice and racial solidarity as means to equal rights for African Americans. The *Conservator* also drew national attention to Barnett. He served as Chicago's delegate to the National Conference of Colored Men of the United States held 6–9 May 1879 in Nashville. In a passionate speech, Barnett urged the audience to put aside differences and come together for the betterment of the race. According to him, the path to racial progress lay in political and economic unity coupled with education. Predating similar arguments forwarded by Booker T. Washington and W. E. B. Du Bois, he insisted that educators needed to take an active role in uplifting poor, southern, and other less fortunate African Americans for the benefit of the entire race.

Barnett edited and wrote for the weekly *Conservator* for five years before opening a law practice. In 1892, he partnered with another prominent African American attorney, S. Laing Williams, but the two later split over Williams's close affiliation with Booker T. Washington. Barnett consistently opposed Washington's politics and favored more overt action. For example, when repeated requests to include African Americans in the World Columbian Exposition were denied and Chicago hosted the event in 1893 without any mention of African American contributions to American culture and wealth, Barnett coauthored a pamphlet with Frederick Douglass and Ida B. Wells entitled *The Reason Why the Colored American Is Not in the World's Columbian Exposition—The Afro-American's Contribution to Columbian Literature*. The eighty-one-page tract forcefully laid out the discrimination African Americans faced in American society. Barnett was one of very few editors of African American newspapers across the country to support the idea, financing and producing the pamphlet himself. Not only did he write sections, he also helped to distribute ten thousand copies at the Exposition. The work also marked the beginning of his long personal and professional relationship with Ida B. Wells.

In late June 1895, Barnett married Wells, who remained in Chicago after the Columbian Exposition. Even large white newspapers including the *Chicago Tribune* and the *New York Times* covered this wedding of two prominent African Americans. Barnett had been married before; his first wife, Molly Graham Barnett, was the first African American woman to graduate from the University of Illinois. She died in 1888 when their two children, Ferdinand L. Barnett, Jr., and Albert Graham Barnett were four and two years old. Barnett and Wells had four children together: Charles Aked, named in honor of the English antilynching crusader, was born in 1896; Herman Kohlsaat followed in 1897 and was named after the *Chicago Inter-Ocean* owner and supporter of *Conservator*; two daughters, Ida B. Wells Jr., and Alfreda M. were born in 1901 and 1904. The family lived together on Chicago's South Side until Wells died in 1931.

Barnett's law practice and status in Chicago's white and expanding African American communities grew. In 1896, he became the first African American assistant state's attorney in Illinois, appointed by the newly elected state's attorney (and future governor) Charles S. Deneen. While Barnett's experience qualified him for the position, he owed his selection to the African American Cook County Commissioner Edward H. Wright, who delayed appropriations for Deneen's office until Barnett was chosen. Barnett worked in the state's attorney's office for fourteen years. In his distinguished career there, he served in the juvenile court, in state antitrust cases, and was in charge of habeas corpus and extradition proceedings. Many of his cases reached the Illinois Supreme Court, where he achieved a great record of success.

Active in national and local Republican politics, Barnett's participation in the Republican presidential campaign in 1896 put him in line for his assistant state's attorney post. In 1904, his consistent support earned him the leadership of the Chicago branch of the Republican Party's Negro Bureau over Booker T. Washington's choice, his former law partner S. Laing Williams. Barnett's reputation and service earned him the party's nomination for judge in the new municipal court in Chicago, the first African American candidate in Chicago for a position on the bench. Put forward by the Deneen faction over the strong objections of most white Republicans, Barnett did not enjoy GOP support in a year of Republican successes. Initial results indicated that Barnett had won the close election, but after a recount, Barnett lost by 304 votes in an election in which over 200,000 votes had been cast. Reflecting both Chicago demographics and racism and the lack of party and institutional support, Barnett received more than twenty thousand fewer votes than any other Republican candidate. He was the lone African American on the ticket and the only Republican municipal judge candidate out of twenty-seven to lose.

Barnett worked for the state's attorneys until 1910, when he returned to full-time private practice. His legal work focused on advocating for African American rights. He represented African Americans in employment discrimination cases, and often worked on criminal cases pro bono. Barnett remained active in local and national politics. He always placed the advancement of the race above party politics and, like many other African Americans, supported the Democratic Party in the 1920s and 1930s. He died in his South Side home at the age of 77. Now remembered primarily as Ida B. Wells' husband, Ferdinand L. Barnett was, in the words of *Chicago Defender*, "one of the foremost citizens Chicago has ever had," an unflappable fighter for African American equality.

[*See also:* Chicago; *Chicago Defender*; *and* Wells-Barnett, Ida B.]

BIBLIOGRAPHY

"Ferdinand Lee Barnett" *The Broad Ax*. 10 November 1906: 1. This front-page article is the best source for Barnett's early life and his time as an assistant state's attorney, even though it prematurely declares Barnett the winner of the 1906 judicial election. Little secondary literature exists that directly examines Barnett's life and career, but he was a fixture in local newspapers, including the *Chicago Tribune, Chicago Daily News*, and especially the *Chicago Defender*. A full run of the *Conservator* does not exist, although some years are available.

Gosnell, Harold F. *Negro Politicians: The Rise of Negro Politics in Chicago*. Chicago: University of Chicago Press, 1935. Barnett's forays into local politics, including the disputed 1906 municipal judge election, are covered in this book.

Ida B. Wells Papers. Special Collections Research Center. Joseph Regenstein Library. University of Chicago. Papers. The Ida B. Wells Papers contain correspondence between Ferdinand L. Barnett and his wife, as well as a scrapbook containing most of his newspaper articles.

Spear, Allen H. *Black Chicago: The Making of a Negro Ghetto, 1890–1920*. Chicago: University of Chicago Press, 1967. Along with brief biographical and professional information, Barnett's intellectual and political views about race advancement are discussed here.

Wells-Barnett, Ida B. *Crusade for Justice: The Autobiography of Ida B. Wells*. Edited by Alfreda M. Duster. Chicago: University of Chicago Press, 1970. More personal information is sprinkled throughout this book, along with details about some of the legal work Barnett did for Wells in the struggle against lynching.

—DAVID A. SPATZ

BARRY, MARION (b. 6 March 1936), civil rights activist, mayor, and city councilman. For more than two decades Marion Barry as a political leader of Washington, D.C., epitomized all that is good and bad about the politics of the urban South.

Born in Itta Bena, Mississippi, to a father who was a sharecropper and a mother who was a domestic, Marion Shepilov Barry was raised near Memphis, Tennessee, and experienced the twin hardships of poverty and segregation in the post–World War II South. He graduated from Booker T. Washington High School in 1954 and went on to earn a bachelor's degree at Memphis's LeMoyne College in 1958 and a master's degree in chemistry at Fisk University in Nashville in 1960. While a college student Barry led a well-publicized effort to force a white LeMoyne College trustee to retract disparaging remarks that he made about blacks during a Memphis bus-desegregation campaign.

Increasingly involved in the civil rights movement, Barry arrived in Washington, D.C., in 1963–1964 as an organizer for the Student Nonviolent Coordinating Committee. An able civil rights agitator, in the early 1970s Barry won a place on the District of Columbia's school board and used this position as a springboard for improved desegregated public schools in the District. He also became actively involved in the D.C. home rule movement, to obtain independence for the District from federal congressional control; with this accomplished in 1974, Barry was elected to Washington's first city council. In 1978, vowing to cut government waste and provide housing for the city's poor, Barry defeated the incumbent mayor Walter Washington and the city council president Sterling Tucker in a three-way race for the mayor's post.

As the second mayor of Washington, D.C., from 1979 to 1991, and as the fourth mayor, from 1995 to 1999, Marion Barry dominated civic life in the federal capital. Barry helped to rebuild the District's downtown and was a booster for a city that historically had been known as "Congress's segregated plaything." Barry also made

Washington a model in terms of creating programs to help the poor and the elderly.

Unfortunately Barry's accomplishments were overshadowed by an aura of political chicanery, sexual peccadilloes, and drug use. In 1990 he was convicted on a charge of cocaine use and served six months in a federal prison. The mercurial politico returned to public life after his release from prison, being elected to the city council in 1992, and then he successfully ran for mayor in 1994. In the late 1990s the city changed. Whites, Hispanics, and Asians moved to the District, and a new breed of African American reformers worked to defeat the Barry machine. Still, Barry remained a force in local politics and was elected to the city council from Ward 8 in 2004.

[*See also* Washington, D.C.]

BIBLIOGRAPHY

Agronsky, Jonathan I. Z. *Marion Barry: The Politics of Race*. Latham, N.Y.: British American, 1991. A journalist's account of Barry's years in Washington.

Barras, Jonetta Rose. *The Last of the Black Emperors: The Hollow Comeback of Marion Barry in the New Age of Black Leaders*. Baltimore: Bancroft Press, 1998. A well-written and insightful analysis of Barry's political career.

—JOHN R. WENNERSTEN

BARTHÉ, RICHMOND (b. 28 January 1901; d. 5 March 1989), artist. Barthé's stylistic sculptures of the African American captured the human passion and genuine character, culture, and ethnic identity of the race. His sensitivity in his work revealed a glimpse into the life and spirit of the African American during an era of oppression and persecution. Barthé's unique ability to expose the vulnerability of his subjects brought him wide recognition in the art world and the social circles of the early and mid-twentieth century.

Born in Bay Saint Louis, Mississippi, Barthé grew up on the coastal bay, an area populated by wealthy New Orleans families. His father, Richmond Barthé Sr., died at the age of twenty-two, when Barthé was only a few months old. Barthé's mother, Marie Clementine Robateau Barthé, left a single mother, raised him while working as a seamstress. When Barthé was six she married his godfather, William Franklin, a workingman and a cornet player in local bands.

As a child Barthé spent his time drawing and painting. His natural talent and personality led to an introduction to the wealthy Pond family in New Orleans. Mrs. Pond took him in and was directly responsible for Barthé's well-known disposition of grace and style. Her introductions to influential people in New Orleans led to further exposure and enabled Barthé to develop his talent as a painter.

Barthé's art career formally started at the age of twenty-three, when the Reverend Jack Kane, pastor of the Blessed Sacrament Church, recognized his talent and sent him to the Art Institute of Chicago. At the institute Barthé met influential painters such as Archibald J. Motley Jr., who was later recognized for his paintings of black life in Chicago's Bronzeville and his portraiture of beautiful women of mixed ancestry and race. One of the most significant influences on Barthé's work came from Charles Schroeder, a professor at the institute. Under Schroeder's instruction Barthé studied anatomy and figure construction. Schroeder was directly responsible for Barthé's turn to sculpture, the medium upon which he built his career.

Though Barthé's sculptures of male nudes became a recognized symbol of his work, he was careful to display a sexually conservative role in the public's eye. His close relationship with Alain Locke, the famous African American philosopher, was publicly recognized as a professional association. Locke was an influential academic advocate of the New Negro movement and included many of Barthé's works in his pictorial survey *The Negro in Art: A Pictorial Record of the Negro Artist and of the Negro Theme in Art* (1940). Locke was known as a promoter of young African American artists. As an admirer and collector of Barthé's work, Locke was careful to protect his own public identity while privately advocating same-sex relationships. His personal connection with Barthé remained private.

Barthé is best known for his 1930s sculptures reflecting the racial and political tensions in the United States. Among his most famous works are *Mother and Son* (1939), a sculpture of an African American woman holding her lifeless son's body after he was lynched; *African Dancer* (1933); *Feral Benga* (1935); and *Life Mask of Rose McClendon* (1932), a mask of one of the first African American women to become a theatrical star.

Barthé exhibited in New York's well-known museums and galleries, such as the Caz-Delba Gallery at Rockefeller Center, the Whitney Museum of American Art, and the Arden Galleries. His works have also been exhibited throughout Europe, and many are in private collections all over the world.

Because of the social and political content of Barthé's work, it was highly publicized during the 1940s antisegregation movements by interracial groups, government officials, and local radio. During the 1960s civil rights movement recognition of Barthé continued to grow. In honor of Barthé's contributions to African American culture, the mayor of Saint Louis presented him with the keys to the city, universities invited Barthé to be a guest speaker, and the press and television called upon him for interviews.

Barthé spent his final years sculpting in Pasadena, California. After his death, friends, including the actor

James Garner, raised funds to create the Barthé Historical Society, directed by Lee Brown of the California Institue of Technology.

[*See also* Homosexuality and Transgenderism; Locke, Alain; Motley, Archibald J., Jr.; New Negro; *and* Visual Arts.]

BIBLIOGRAPHY

Bearden, Romare, and Harry Henderson. *A History of African-American Artists*. New York: Pantheon Books, 1993.

Vendryes, Margaret Rose. "Casting *Feral Benga*: A Biography of Richmond Barthé's Signature Work." Anyone Can Fly Foundation. http://www.artsnet.org/anyonecanfly/library/Vendryes_on_Barthe.html.

—MARIA STILSON

BASEBALL. [*This entry includes two subentries, on the Negro Leagues and on integrated professional baseball.*]

Negro Leagues

When Jackie Robinson took the field for the Brooklyn Dodgers in 1947, his appearance marked the beginning of what many African Americans hoped was only the first in a series of social breakthroughs. What could be more telling of a race's ability and potential, after all, than success achieved on the level playing fields of America's national pastime? It is difficult to overstate the significance of Robinson's triumphant rookie year, a season in which he was scrutinized and tested both on and off the baseball diamond. Decades later his feat is remembered and recounted as part of a string of civil rights accomplishments leading up to—and beyond—the 1954 *Brown v. Board of Education* decision that declared segregation in public schools unconstitutional.

Robinson's successful desegregation of Major League Baseball also signaled the beginning of the end for Negro League baseball, perhaps the most successful and vibrant of the black institutions that emerged when African Americans were excluded from a variety of arenas in the first half of the twentieth century. Before Robinson could even dream of the opportunity that he seized following World War II, the foundation for his achievement lay in the rugged hands of players like Quincy Troupe, who once lamented that he came along "twenty years too soon," or in the elegance of Buck O'Neil, who insisted he was "right on time." It is the wistfulness and buoyancy embodied in these statements that testify to the mixed legacy of the Negro Leagues—the hopes that were never fulfilled, and a livelihood that was prized by many who struggled against a discriminatory society.

Early Years. Indeed, Trouppe and O'Neil represent only a slim if well-known slice of time in the history of black baseball, which had many different incarnations before the post-Depression era. It is the post-Depression era that is best remembered, perhaps because its stars loomed larger and brighter in an era of greater visibility and press coverage: Josh Gibson, Buck Leonard, Cool Papa Bell, and the irrepressible Satchel Paige, to name just a few. But their accomplishments, like Robinson's, were built on a foundation that had been established by players like Solomon White, Dave Malarcher, Bud Fowler, Rube Foster, and Moses Fleetwood Walker, little-known names from an obscure era of professional and semiprofessional baseball, both black and white.

If, as many have suggested, the fortunes of African Americans in baseball were an accurate reflection of their status within society generally, then it is not surprising that nineteenth-century baseball teams and leagues were not governed by the strict racial codes that emerged during the course of the early twentieth century. This is not to say that discrimination did not exist, only that general patterns of exclusion did not stop Bud Fowler from joining the minor league team in Lynn, Massachusetts, in 1878, becoming the first African American to play professional baseball. Nor did it stop Moses Fleetwood Walker from earning distinction in 1884 as the first black to play alongside whites in the major leagues as a member of the Toledo entry in the American Association. Although estimates of their numbers vary, no fewer than thirteen African Americans—and perhaps as many as thirty-three—played on major and minor league professional teams in the latter part of the nineteenth century. Black clubs also played in white associations of semiprofessional and minor league teams and occasionally competed against major league teams.

But as early as 1885 when the Brooklyn-based Cuban Giants—who were neither Cuban nor giants, smirked a writer for the *New York Sun*—became the first of several clubs to emerge and form leagues of African American or "colored" teams, a tradition of black-only baseball teams was born. In the late nineteenth and early twentieth centuries the Cuban Giants were joined by such teams as the Page Fence Giants of Adrian, Michigan, the Philadelphia Giants, the Cuban X Giants, the Saint Paul Gophers in Minnesota, the Pittsburgh Keystones, the Chicago Unions, and the Chicago Union Giants (later called the Leland Giants and Chicago American Giants). Solomon White, an infielder for the Philadelphia Giants—along with the pitcher Rube Foster, on a team that won an astounding 133 of 154 games in 1904—later estimated that there were as many as nine black semiprofessional teams in the Philadelphia area alone in the early 1900s. As the

Negro League Game. Umpire Peter Strauch calls player Larry Doby of the Newark Eagles safe after Doby slides into home plate, manned by Philadelphia Stars catcher Bill Cash. Strauch's call caused an outfield riot, 1946. Photographs and Prints Division, Schomburg Center for Research in Black Culture, The New York Public Library, Astor, Lenox and Tilden Foundations

professional baseball leagues closed their doors to African Americans by 1898, these early teams formed the nucleus of a growing and vibrant baseball scene in black communities.

Many of these teams were located in cities along the East Coast and in the Midwest where there were significant African American populations, but attendance in the early years was always spotty, if not downright disappointing. Until the Brooklyn Royal Giants were created by two black co-owners in 1904, most of these teams were financed by whites more interested in their own pocketbooks than in the well-being of their players. Schedules and games were often improvised with very little advance notice for fans or players, and the players often jumped from team to team seeking better wages. The names and locations of clubs often changed just as quickly, making it difficult to establish team rivalries or hometown loyalties. Until World War I most teams barnstormed throughout the North—and to a lesser degree the South—where they picked up followers and sometimes recruited new players.

Rube Foster and the NNL. The transience and fragility of black baseball can be gleaned from the career of Rube Foster, by all accounts an extraordinary pitcher for a number of teams. From a young age Foster's entire life revolved around baseball: at age eighteen in 1897 he shrugged off his father's disapproval and joined a Texas barnstorming team, the Waco Yellow Jackets. He was discovered in Texas and brought to Chicago by Frank Leland in 1902 to become part of the Chicago Union Giants. Mirroring the moves of other players at this time, he jumped Chicago for a white semipro team in Otsego, Michigan, and later the Cuban X Giants in Zanesville, Ohio. In 1903 he pitched the X Giants to the so-called colored championship against the Philadelphia Giants; the following year he delivered a title to Philadelphia after picking up both wins in the three-game championship against the Cuban X Giants. Foster also played alongside the future heavyweight champion Jack Johnson, who played first base on that 1904 team.

In 1907 he rejoined Frank Leland, hoping for a better salary. The two fought over finances until Leland relented

Negro League Founder. Rube Foster, a powerful pitcher and the founder of the first Negro National League, stands second from right. SPNB Collection/Los Angeles Public Library

and allowed Foster to do the booking for the Leland Giants and secure a larger percentage of the gate for his fellow players, who were chronically underpaid. Foster organized barnstorming tours against white semipro teams throughout the Midwest and developed rivalries with a number of similar teams in Chicago, then emerging as a hothouse of baseball. Foster also pitched and lost to the Chicago Cubs on three different occasions during his career with the Giants, and ultimately he took over as manager of Leland's team in 1910. During that season his team won 123 games and lost only six. In 1911 he became co-owner with the white businessman John Schorling of the newly christened Chicago American Giants.

Though a number of African American leagues were attempted throughout this early period, it was not until blacks began migrating north in ever-increasing numbers that these efforts began to pay off. Still, it was Foster's business acumen, promotional savvy, and foresight that propelled black baseball forward into its first dynamic and profitable era. As he organized tours in California during the winter months, he expanded black baseball's reach, aided by accounts in the *Chicago Defender*, the most widely circulated black newspaper of the day. Foster also reinstituted the East-West Colored Championship, a popular one-game affair pitting an East Coast team against a club from the Midwest.

As Foster drew accolades from Chicago's black community, new teams were formed in Indianapolis, Saint Louis, and Kansas City. By 1919 Foster and his Chicago American Giants had become major—and profitable—powers in the world of black baseball. With the critical mass necessary to support a number of black teams, Foster forged the Negro National League (NNL), composed of outfits from the Midwest, in 1920. A complementary association, the Eastern Colored League, was formed in 1923, and the two leagues instituted an annual series—modeled on the Major Leagues' World Series—that pitted the best of each league against each other in a clash for African American baseball supremacy.

The 1920s and early 1930s witnessed a period of growth and expansion of black baseball in southern states generally, and in cities such as Birmingham, Alabama, and Memphis, Tennessee, specifically. In the North, Pittsburgh became a hotbed of baseball activity, with teams ranging from the industrial to the semiprofessional to the two jewels of Negro League baseball: the Homestead Grays and the Pittsburgh Crawfords. Black newspapers in major northern cities promoted upcoming contests, published box scores, and monitored the fortunes of their local teams, thus tightening the connection between baseball clubs and the communities in which they played. Patterns that had existed since the turn of the century—such as winter baseball in Florida, other southern states, and the Caribbean—became routine. In places such as Cuba, players competed and lived free of the racial prejudice that they confronted in the United States—even in the North and East—and formed friendships with white Major Leaguers who were often teammates.

The Dominican Republic, Mexico, and Venezuela also served as winter destinations for black players, some of whom never returned after experiencing a freer life in Latin America. One of those who regularly traveled to Mexico, Willie Wells, declared that he felt like he was truly a man during his winter sojourns.

Decline and Disappearance. Though escalating player salaries, infighting, the demise of the Eastern Colored League in 1928, and the tragic death of Rube Foster in 1930 all undermined the teams' prosperity, the onset of the Depression initiated a downward spiral from which the NNL could not recover. The owner of the Pittsburgh Crawfords, Gus Greenlee, helped to reorganize the NNL in the early 1930s using the wealth he had amassed as a numbers banker who ran an illegal lottery. He and other such men were some of the only sources available to keep Negro League baseball solvent, which they did with mixed success—and the assistance of white booking agents—throughout the 1930s. Though the morality and volatility of some of the owners remained a constant source of concern, most blacks agreed that black baseball teams were critical in holding African American communities together. Effa Manley, the wife of the numbers man Abe Manley—and the only woman to head a franchise, the Newark Eagles—best exemplified what baseball made possible by attracting crowds through her financial drives for the NAACP and the "Don't Buy Where You Can't Work" campaign. The profits of such owners, however, often came at the expense of their players' salaries, forcing emerging and recognizable stars such Satchel Paige, Josh Gibson, Cool Papa Bell, Judy Johnson, and Buck Leonard to use what leverage they had in parlaying their services to other Negro League or Latin American teams.

Most players did not have that option, nor did they have name recognition outside the black communities in which they played. Despite the charisma and talent of Paige, Gibson, and Bell, even the best players rarely entered the white consciousness. Few whites ever took in a Negro League game, though it was common for black players to attend Major League games. Negro League players took pride in the way they played the game, executing what Rube Foster once called "intelligent" baseball: bunting, stealing, deploying the hit and run, moving runners along, even stealing home. What seemed daring to observers of Jackie Robinson's larceny on the base paths was routine to most Negro Leaguers. Those who later made it to the Major Leagues, including Satchel Paige, were also surprised and disappointed that Major Leaguers did not seem to enjoy talking about baseball as much as he and his fellow barnstormers did, and they missed spending long bus rides and hours at the ballpark examining the mysteries of the game they loved.

It was also during the 1930s and 1940s that white spectators received a distorted image of African American ballplayers from comedic teams such as the Indianapolis Clowns, the Zulu Cannibal Giants, and the Tennessee Rats, some of whose antics made it into a 1970s film *Bingo Long and His Traveling All Stars*, which purported to depict Negro League baseball. For all the carnival showmanship of such teams—which drew large white crowds—for most players, baseball was a good job to have during a difficult period despite the arduous travel, playing several games in a day, and experiencing the indignities that came with traveling in southern cities.

With the U.S. entrance into World War II and the interracial groundwork that had been laid in the Dominican Republic and Cuba, professional baseball prepared for integration. As many authors have suggested, Jackie Robinson was not necessarily the best of the black players available, but his wartime service, education at UCLA, and talent made him the right choice. His successful rookie season encouraged other teams to sign players, though the transformation was slow: in 1951 only six teams were integrated.

Integration hastened the decline of the Negro Leagues because fans increasingly spent their incomes on Major League games or stayed home to follow games on the radio or television. As profits continued to dwindle, some teams resorted to gimmicks like signing women such as Toni Stone and Mamie "Peanut" Johnson, talented and proud players who could not save the declining fortunes and fan base of African American baseball. By 1961 the Negro Leagues were officially defunct.

The history and legacy of the Negro Leagues are commemorated in the Negro Leagues Baseball Museum, founded in 1990 in Kansas City, Kansas, and in the thirty-five players elected to the National Baseball Hall of Fame. These include owners such as Effa Manley and Cumberland Posey and players such as Josh Gibson and Cool Papa Bell, who spent his entire, brilliant career in the

Negro Leagues. In 1946 Bell—then forty-three—was batting .441 and chasing the Negro League batting title alongside Monte Irvin. Over the last few days of the season, Bell removed himself from the lineup. Because he did not have enough plate appearances to qualify for the batting crown, the younger Irvin took the title with an average of .389. Asked later why he had disqualified himself, Bell observed that it was time for the younger players to be noticed so that they could receive opportunities to play in the Major Leagues. Perhaps no better testament to Bell's unselfishness can be found than in the fact that Irvin—as well as transitional players such as Hank Aaron, Willie Mays, and Ernie Banks—is also enshrined in the Baseball Hall of Fame.

[*See also* Desegregation and Integration, *subentry* Professional Athletics; Sports, *subentry* Professional Sports; *and biographical entries on figures mentioned in this article*.]

BIBLIOGRAPHY

Heaphy, Leslie, ed. *Black Baseball and Chicago: Essays on the Players, Teams, and Games of the Negro League's Most Important City*. Jefferson, N.C.: McFarland, 2006. Includes appendices with detailed rosters and timelines.

Hogan, Lawrence. *Shades of Glory: The Negro Leagues and the Story of African-American Baseball*. Washington, D.C.: National Geographic Society, 2006. A series of essays in narrative form authored by Hogan and other contributors in rough chronological order, detailing the history of Negro League baseball from the nineteenth century until the last franchise was sold in 1984. Well written and accessible, this is probably the fullest account of African American baseball.

Kirwin, Bill, ed. *Out of the Shadows: African American Baseball from the Cuban Giants to Jackie Robinson*. Lincoln: University of Nebraska Press, 2005. A series of essays on baseball teams and players before and after integration; notable entries include pieces on the Cuban Giants, Effa Manley, Mamie "Peanut" Johnson, Don Newcombe, and Dick Allen.

Lanctot, Neil. *Negro League Baseball: The Rise and Ruin of a Black Institution*. Philadelphia: University of Pennsylvania Press, 2004. A massive history of Negro League baseball from the Depression through the post-integration era, focusing primarily on the business and financial aspects of various teams, individual owners, and the league itself.

Peterson, Robert. *Only the Ball Was White: A History of Legendary Black Players and All-Black Professional Teams*. New York: Oxford University Press, 1970. Has a nice balance between league history and individual players; the essay on Rube Foster is particularly helpful, and rosters, statistics, league standings, and box scores are included in the appendices.

Rogosin, Donn. *Invisible Men: Life in Baseball's Negro Leagues*. Lincoln: University of Nebraska Press, 1983. Based on many oral histories.

Tygiel, Jules. *Baseball's Great Experiment: Jackie Robinson and His Legacy*. New York: Oxford University Press, 1983. Arguably the best account of how Jackie Robinson integrated baseball, from the perspective of Robinson, Branch Rickey, black sportswriters, and opponents of integration.

—JILL DUPONT

Integrated Professional Baseball

Baseball has often been called America's pastime, yet African Americans were long excluded from the game. When Jackie Robinson broke baseball's color line in 1947, he expected to blaze a path for blacks to enter both the player and supervisory ranks in baseball. Black athletes such as Willie Mays, Hank Aaron, Reggie Jackson, and Barry Bonds did became the most dominating players of their eras, but by the early twenty-first century African American players and fans had decreased sharply in number. Only a handful of blacks had cracked the managerial ranks, and off-field personnel were overwhelmingly white.

Major League Baseball never formally banned blacks from playing. The ban—which began in the 1880s—was just a matter of custom, albeit a firmly entrenched one. Since the early days of the Negro Leagues, sportswriters for African American newspapers had condemned Major League Baseball for keeping black ballplayers out of the game. Most of the black players in the Negro Leagues also barnstormed around the nation, playing exhibition games. Often when they faced the white-only teams of Major Leaguers they defeated them.

By the 1930s the attacks on segregated baseball had grown very strong, but the Major League Baseball commissioner and former judge Kenesaw Mountain Landis wanted blacks to remain in their own league. In 1942 when the flamboyant showman Bill Veeck announced his intention to buy the Philadelphia Phillies and break the color line by hiring the best talent available, including black players, Landis—according to Veeck's later account—blocked the sale. Despite shortages of white players during World War II, no blacks were invited to join Major League teams. When Landis died in 1944, Happy Chandler succeeded him. A former U.S. senator from Kentucky, Chandler did not appear to be a pathbreaker for integration. However, Chandler argued that if blacks could fight against Germany and Japan, then they could fight for a Major League team. Branch Rickey, seeking to improve his woeful team, signed Jackie Robinson in August 1945, less than a year after Landis's death.

The Early Stars. On 15 April 1947, Robinson became the first African American to play Major League Baseball when he joined the National League's Brooklyn Dodgers; he had played in the Negro Leagues with the Kansas City Monarchs in 1945 and in the minor leagues with a Dodgers affiliate in 1946. Some Negro League players thought that Robinson was the wrong man to break the color line because he was not a good enough player. They worried that he would fail, thereby giving credence to the notion that blacks were not good enough to compete against whites. However, in ten seasons with the Dodgers,

Robinson batted .311 overall, was named National League Rookie of the Year in 1947, and was named National League Most Valuable Player in 1949. An infielder who played both first and second base, Robinson was named to the All-Star team six times, and while he was on the team the Dodgers won six National League pennants and in 1955 won the World Series—the team's only World Series while in Brooklyn. Robinson achieved all these triumphs while white, racist players waited for him on the base paths with sharpened spikes, pitchers threw at his head to test him, and racist insults flew at him from both opposing fans and players. Hate mail excoriating the Dodgers for hiring Robinson, plus letters attacking him personally, piled up in the team offices. Although Robinson never publicly reacted to the hatred, the stress gave him stomach pains for the duration of his career and may have shortened his life—he died at age fifty-three.

Robinson opened the floodgates, and soon a host of other black players jumped from the Negro Leagues to the Major Leagues. Roy Campanella, perhaps the greatest all-around catcher in the history of baseball, became the second black player signed by the Brooklyn Dodgers. After integrating two minor league teams, he joined the Major Leagues in 1948. The pitcher Don Newcombe, the third black player signed by the Dodgers, had played in the Negro Leagues with the Newark Eagles and joined the Major Leagues in 1949. He became the first star black pitcher in the National League with the Dodgers, and when the Cy Young Award was created in 1956, he was the first recipient.

Larry Doby also played for the Newark Eagles before becoming the first African American player in the American League: Bill Veeck hired him to play for the Cleveland Indians in 1947. An outfielder who was a seven-time All-Star for Cleveland and led the league in home runs twice, Doby later served as the second black manager in the Major Leagues when he helmed the Chicago White Sox for part of the 1978 season.

Satchel Paige, who spent his prime years in the Negro Leagues, became the first African American pitcher in the American League and the first to pitch in a World Series. He joined the Cleveland Indians in 1948 and also played with the Saint Louis Browns and the Kansas City Athletics. He served as a player-coach with the Atlanta Braves for the 1969 season, mostly as a goodwill gesture that enabled Paige to earn a big-league pension.

Ernie Banks, nicknamed "Mr. Cub," was from 1953 the first black player with the Chicago Cubs and became the longtime face of the franchise because he played with the Cubs until 1971. Banks, a shortstop and first baseman, rarely made a fielding error, and he hit more than five hundred home runs in his career.

By the time Banks entered the Major Leagues, many teams had still failed to integrate. One such team was the New York Yankees, the royalty of Major League Baseball, even though the franchise was located only a few miles from Harlem in one direction and from the Brooklyn Dodgers in the other. The Yankee owners George Weiss, Del Webb, and Dan Topping claimed that they did not hire African Americans because they could not find any player good enough for the team. This argument found few supporters, partly because no team had more scouts and resources than the Yankees did. In April 1952 protesters picketed Yankee Stadium to push the process of integration. When asked why the Yankees did not have any black players, Jackie Robinson attacked the Yankee management on television for being prejudiced.

The catcher Elston Howard finally integrated the Yankees in 1955, serving as a replacement for the perennial All-Star Yogi Berra. Howard alternated between catcher and outfielder, unable to break into the ranks of the regular players. Although Howard did not complain, other black players saw racism in his treatment, especially because he received comparatively little publicity in New York, the biggest media market in the world. Howard eventually in 1963 became the first African American to be named Most Valuable Player in the American League. The Boston Red Sox were the last team to integrate, in 1959.

Although the Major League teams slowly integrated, Jim Crow ruled at spring training. Small Florida towns that hosted Major League clubs did not welcome black players in hotels or restaurants. On one occasion Howard and his fellow Yankee Hector Lopez were not permitted to stay with the team at the hotel in Fort Myers. Instead they slept in a black-owned funeral home with five dead bodies. African American players eventually filed a grievance with the Players Association over separate and unequal treatment.

The Black Superstars. When the best baseball players are named, Willie Mays and Hank Aaron are always on the list. An All-Star more than twenty times, Mays became the first African American superstar of the 1950s, playing with the New York and San Francisco Giants. Mays broke into professional baseball with the Birmingham Black Barons. In 1950 when it became apparent to Major League officials that the Negro Leagues were dying and that blacks could thrive in the Major Leagues, teams began courting Mays. He signed with the Giants because they paid Birmingham $14,000 for his contract—other teams offered no more than $7,500 and paid Mays $6,000. In twenty-two seasons, Mays batted .302, hit 660 home runs, and drove in 1,903 runs. In 1979, his first year of eligibility, Mays was elected to the Hall of Fame with 94.6 percent of the vote.

Meanwhile, after a brief stay with the Indianapolis Clowns of the Negro Leagues and in the minor leagues, Hank Aaron joined the Milwaukee Braves in 1954. He broke Babe Ruth's all-time home run record in 1974 with the Atlanta Braves. In the city that billed itself as "too busy to hate," Aaron received hate mail as he approached Ruth's record. He used the letters as sources of inspiration, determining to break the record for himself, for Jackie Robinson, and for all black people. In twenty-three Major League seasons and 3,298 games, Aaron compiled a .305 batting average, hitting 755 home runs and driving in 2,297 runs.

In the early 2000s the San Francisco Giants outfielder Barry Bonds set records for bases on balls in a season and intentional walks because teams refused to let him hit. The records indicate Bonds's dominance of the game. Yet one of the best players baseball has ever seen has been dogged by questions about steroid use. In 2007, Bonds broke Aaron's home run record to little acclaim and much controversy. Widely regarded as an embarrassment to baseball, Bonds could not find a team to hire him in 2008, though his batting skills still appeared quite strong. Effectively he had been banned from baseball, even though white players who admitted using steroids continued to have careers on the field. Bonds has denied knowingly using steroids, despite a 2008 federal indictment.

Bill White, 1996. Bill White, president of the National League from 1989 to 1994, was the first black president of one of Major League Baseball's leagues. Photograph by Chris O'Meara. AP Images

The Managerial Ranks and Front Offices. It took more than two decades for blacks to move from playing in the Major Leagues to making executive decisions. Elston Howard became the first black coach in the American League when he joined the Yankees as first-base coach in 1969. Poor health prompted Howard to move into the Yankees front office in 1980. Upon Howard's death later that year, at only age fifty-one, his wife attributed his early demise to stress over racism and at not being able to break into the managerial ranks. In 1968 Monte Irvin, a star hitter in the Negro Leagues who was once projected to be the first African American in the Major League, became the first African American to join the commissioner's office. A skilled mediator, he worked for seventeen years as a troubleshooter under William Eckert and then Bowie Kuhn.

Frank Robinson, who won the Most Valuable Player award in both the American (1966) and National (1961) leagues, became the first black manager in 1975, with the Cleveland Indians. Unlike many managers, especially those who were star players, Robinson has had a long career. He has worked for the San Francisco Giants, the Baltimore Orioles, and the Montreal Expos/Washington Nationals. Other African American managers have included Larry Doby, Maury Wills, Willie Randolph, and Dusty Baker. The number of blacks in key front-office positions has remained fairly low, however.

Declining Popularity. By the first decade of the twenty-first century, the number of African Americans playing and watching professional baseball had dwindled to an all-time low. In the 1970s African Americans constituted more than 27 percent of all players. In the 2006 season the number of black baseball players had declined to 8.4 percent. In 2007 the Houston Astros and the Atlanta Braves, both teams that play in heavily black cities, had no black players on their opening-day rosters. The high-profile New York Yankees and Boston Red Sox had one each. The African American star pitcher C. C. Sabathia of the Cleveland Indians, the only black player on his team's opening-day roster in 2007, described the situation as a crisis.

The gulf between African Americans and baseball is deep. Blacks constituted about 12.5 percent of the U.S. population in 1997, yet less than 3 percent of the players at the highest competitive levels of youth baseball and 3 percent of NCAA Division I baseball players were African American. Blacks constituted less than 5 percent of fans at some Major League baseball parks. A July 1998 survey by the Kansas City Royals showed that only 3.2 percent of those in the stands were African American. In contrast, in Jackie Robinson's era black youths played baseball in great numbers, and the black community strongly supported black players at every professional level. This loss of interest has been linked to the decline of the Negro Leagues. As Negro League players finished their Major League careers and their numbers dwindled, the numbers of black fans also began dwindling.

The place that baseball once held in the lives of young African Americans has been taken by basketball and football. The abundance of black role models in basketball, the perception of basketball's great influence on social mobility, and basketball's image as a form of expression and empowerment all mean that basketball is likely to keep its hold on black youth. Basketball and football players are portrayed in the media as living the lives that black youth would like to emulate. Baseball players do not receive the same level of attention, and the sport is often seen as slow and boring. In essence, baseball lost the marketing war.

Whereas basketball is suited to urban America, baseball requires impoverished areas to provide enough green space for a baseball diamond that also has a lot of maintenance costs. The game requires gloves, balls, and bats, while basketball requires only blacktop and a basketball hoop. In 2002 youth baseball coaches in six states attributed the lack of racial diversity on their teams to the paucity of baseball facilities in black neighborhoods, the cost of playing baseball, and the lack of both parental and community support. Basketball has become an integral part of black culture, while baseball is seen by young blacks and their parents as a white or Latino sport. In a January 2007 poll, only 7 percent of African Americans named baseball as their favorite sport. Without a strong base of fans and a large pool of up-and-coming players, black participation in baseball is likely to fade away.

To prevent this, Major League Baseball has taken several steps. In 2006 the commissioner Bud Selig created the Civil Rights Game, an exhibition to be played each March in Memphis, Tennessee, around the time when the civil rights leader Martin Luther King Jr. was assassinated. The league is also working to boost the number of black children playing the game by working with Little League Baseball, the National Urban League, and the Boys and Girls Clubs. In 1992 it began Reviving Baseball in Inner Cities (RBI), a program designed to encourage academic achievement and participation in baseball in more than two hundred urban areas in the United States. Nearly half of the more than 120,000 youths participating in RBI are African American, and graduates include Jimmy Rollins of the Philadelphia Phillies and Carl Crawford of the Tampa Bay Rays. In 2006, Major League Baseball opened a $10 million Urban Youth Academy in Compton, California. Featuring ten acres of ball fields and a 12,500-square-foot clubhouse, the academy is a prototype for similar facilities that are planned in Washington, D.C., Boston, Houston, Miami, and Philadelphia.

To address the shortage of blacks in the front offices, the league offers two-year executive apprenticeship programs. Under the Diverse Business Partners Program, the league is requesting teams to work with minority-owned and women-owned businesses whenever possible. Some of the businesses have purchased season tickets, thereby bringing blacks back into the seats and perhaps helping to create a black fan base.

[*See also* Black Coaches Association; Sports, *subentry* Professional Sports; *and biographical entries on figures mentioned in this article*.]

BIBLIOGRAPHY

Davis, Yusuf. "Where Are the African-American Baseball Players? The Numbers Continue to Decline." *Ebony*, May 2007, pp. 172–175.

Dewey, Donald. *The 10th Man: The Fan in Baseball History*. New York: Carroll & Graf, 2004.

Freedman, Lew. *African American Pioneers of Baseball: A Biographical Encyclopedia*. Westport, Conn.: Greenwood Press, 2007.

Lamb, Chris. *Blackout: The Untold Story of Jackie Robinson's First Spring Training*. Lincoln: University of Nebraska Press, 2004.

Ogden, David C., and Michael L. Hilt. "Collective Identity and Basketball: An Explanation for the Decreasing Number of African-Americans on America's Baseball Diamonds." *Journal of Leisure Research* 35, no. 2 (2003): 213–227.

Rielly, Edward J. *Baseball and American Culture: Across the Diamond*. New York: Haworth Press, 2003.

Tygiel, Jules. *Baseball's Great Experiment: Jackie Robinson and His Legacy*. Rev. ed. New York: Oxford University Press, 1997.

—CARYN E. NEUMANN

BASIE, COUNT (b. 21 August 1904; d. 26 April 1984), orchestra leader. William "Count" Basie was born in Red Bank, New Jersey, in 1904. Although he received some formal musical training, much of Basie's skill as a musician was the result of self-teaching and apprenticeship to some of the leading jazz musicians of the early 1920s. After working with Fats Waller in New York City and playing the organ in Harlem movie houses, Basie went on the road with Gonzelle White and her jazz band in 1927. Stranded in Kansas City, Missouri, as a result of poor decisions by White and several promoters, Basie became a mainstay of the local jazz scene there. He played piano for some of Kansas City's leading dance bands before joining the Oklahoma Blue Devils in the early 1930s.

Basie was subsequently recruited by Bennie Moten (who gave him the nickname "No Count" as a joke about Basie's alleged financial irresponsibility), and it was with the Moten orchestra that Basie developed his signature style. Moten and other Kansas City bands favored a riff-driven, four-beat swing style that tended to use the piano as a part of the rhythm section. While the East Coast dance bands favored lush and complicated arrangements, Moten and the Kansas City "territorial" bands featured much more improvisation and a style that came to be known as "jump" blues. In the early 1930s Moten took his band to Camden, New Jersey, for recording sessions, and the music met with surprising success. After Moten's death in 1935, Basie took the reins of Moten's band

Count Basie. In New York City, between 1946 and 1948. Photograph by William Gottlieb. © WILLIAM P. GOTTLIEB; WWW.JAZZPHOTOS.COM

and augmented it with sidemen such as Lester Young and Buster Smith from Kansas City. The Count Basie Orchestra became one of the more storied bands of the swing era. Building the band's reputation in a series of "battle of the bands" shows with Chick Webb at the Savoy Ballroom in Harlem, the success of the Basie band was paralleled only by that of Duke Ellington and some of the major white touring bands such as Benny Goodman's.

Throughout the 1930s and 1940s the Basie band toured the country frequently. Adding vocalists such as Jimmie Rushing and Billie Holiday, the band broadened its repertoire but still favored the "jump" blues style. In 1937 the band recorded "One O'clock Jump." Originally an improvisation on a riff borrowed from a Don Redman recording, the tune became Basie's theme song and, arguably, the piece most emblematic of the Count Basie style, with its four-beat rhythm, minimalist piano playing, and exuberant horn solos. Popular with black and white audiences alike, the band weathered some controversy in the late 1930s and 1940s by playing the left-wing Popular Front benefit concerts. In 1943 Basie also became the first black bandleader to play the Lincoln Hotel ballroom, a popular site in New York for dance concerts.

Throughout the 1950s and 1960s, despite the difficulties he encountered in keeping a large band financially viable, Basie led several versions of his orchestra and continued to record and tour extensively. The later versions of the orchestra featured vocalists and musicians such as Jimmy Witherspoon, Joe Williams, Illinois Jacquet, and Thad Jones. Basie died in 1984.

[*See also* Jazz; Music; *and biographical entries on figures mentioned in this article*.]

BIBLIOGRAPHY

Erenberg, Lewis A. *Swingin' the Dream: Big Band Jazz and the Rebirth of American Culture*. Chicago: University of Chicago Press, 1998.

Giddins, Gary. *Visions of Jazz: The First Century*. New York: Oxford University Press, 1998.
Oliphant, Dave. *The Early Swing Era: 1930–1941*. Westport, Conn.: Greenwood, 2002.

—WILLIAM CARNEY

BASKETBALL. Officials at the International Young Men's Christian Training School (now Springfield College) in Massachusetts asked Dr. James Naismith, a physical education teacher, to come up with an indoor activity for winter that would reduce rowdy behavior among its students, as well as keep them in shape during the winter. As a result, in 1891 Naismith created basketball as an indoor sport. It did not take long for basketball to become popular. Although it is not known exactly when African Americans began playing basketball, it is probable that the sport had already reached many black communities in the early 1900s, especially in the YMCAs, YWCAs, and athletic clubs in the North. Several blacks—most notably Dr. Edwin B. Henderson, the chief of physical education in the District of Columbia for what was then called the Colored School Division—were active at the turn of the twentieth century in making basketball a sport and leisure activity for black youths. Henderson attended a training session on basketball at Harvard University in 1904. He returned to Washington and introduced the sport at the local black Twelfth Street YMCA and adopted it as part of the interscholastic athletic program in the "colored" schools.

Amateur Competition. Henderson also played a pivotal role in organizing black athletic clubs in the District of Columbia and instituting regional play in basketball among black clubs along the East Coast, primarily in New York, Newark, Philadelphia, Baltimore, and Washington, D.C. Around the same time that Henderson was laying the foundation for competitive basketball among black youths in schools and athletic clubs, blacks in several other northern cities began to organize club teams outside the YMCA and YWCA. Sports enthusiasts created the Smart Set Club (SSC) around 1905 and introduced basketball as a competitive sport for men and women. However, sexism limited the participation of black women to only a few club teams. The SSC joined other clubs to form the Olympian Athletic League in New York. In 1907 African American basketball players representing the SSC and the Crescent City Athletic

Basketball Championship. Sisters Paula and Pam McGee after USC's win over Tennessee in the NCAA championship game, 1 April 1984. Photograph by Paul Chinn. HERALD EXAMINER COLLECTION/ LOS ANGELES PUBLIC LIBRARY

Club from Washington, D.C., participated in what was probably the first formal basketball game among black athletes involving the two cities.

Like track and field and other sports, basketball did not spread rapidly among black youths in the South. There were some social reasons for this relating to the structure of southern society. First, young blacks in the South lived primarily in rural areas and spent most of their time engaged in agricultural endeavors. This left little time for basketball or other leisure activities. Also, the segregated black schools existed on threadbare funding, leaving little money for athletic equipment or the construction of indoor gymnasiums. Further, there were fewer blacks in the South who had the resources to support athletic club teams. Fortunately YMCAs and YWCAs provided facilities for young black men and women to compete in team basketball and other sports. However, cities and towns in the South where there were black colleges fared better in establishing sports programs for African Americans.

Howard University, Hampton Institute, Virginia Union University, and several other black colleges began playing basketball around 1909. Howard's teams consisted of experienced athletes who had played basketball at the Twelfth Street YMCA in Washington. Consequently Howard had an advantage over many of its opponents and developed one of the most successful black collegiate basketball programs of the time. In 1912 Shaw University in North Carolina joined Howard, Lincoln University of Pennsylvania, and Virginia Union to form the Colored (later Central) Intercollegiate Athletic Association (CIAA), the first black college conference for competitive sports. Other conferences emerged in the 1920s, including the Southwest Athletic Conference (SWAC) and the Southern Intercollegiate Athletic Conference (SIAC). Morgan State College joined the CIAA in the 1920s and under the guidance of the legendary coach Eddie Hurt became the dominant black college basketball team until the late 1930s.

While black colleges were expanding their participation in basketball despite inferior facilities and limited resources, some black athletes played basketball on white college teams, mainly in the Northeast and Midwest, but faced considerable opposition from segregationists. Among these pioneers were Wilbur Woods at the University of Nebraska (1907–1910), Cumberland Posey at Penn State University (1909), Paul Robeson at Rutgers University (1915–1918), and Charles Richard Drew, who was a star player for Amherst College (1923–1925). In the late 1930s and early 1940s Jack Roosevelt "Jackie" Robinson and Wilmeth Sidat-Singh made significant contributions to the basketball programs at the University of California, Los Angeles (UCLA) and Syracuse University, respectively, but black basketball players did not make a significant impact at white colleges until the 1950s.

Professional Competition. Soon after Naismith created basketball, many entrepreneurs, including African Americans, established professional basketball teams and leagues. They quickly recognized basketball as a sport that had a potentially large fan base and that therefore was ripe for profit-making business ventures. Because segregation and racism prevented black athletes from playing on white professional teams, blacks created teams of their own. Posey, a former star on the Penn State University basketball team, was the most successful of these. Posey first formed a professional club team called Monticello that was mildly successful. He then established the Loendi Big Five in Pittsburgh, which featured some of the best black basketball talent available. Loendi dominated black basketball and probably would have done equally as well against the best white teams if not for segregation. Posey's teams ruled the world of black basketball until the advent of the Harlem Renaissance (the Rens) and the Harlem Globetrotters.

African American basketball players began playing in professional leagues in 1923 when Robert Douglas created the all-black Spartan Braves basketball team in New York. Douglas, in what proved to be a shrewd and bold move, signed a contract with the owners of the Renaissance Casino and Ballroom in Harlem that allowed his team the permanent use of the ballroom for its games. The deal allowed Douglas to take advantage of the large crowds that frequented the ballroom and the various jazz establishments and nightclubs in Harlem. In return he changed the name of the team to the Harlem Renaissance. By associating his basketball team with the New Negro movement in Harlem, Douglas made his business venture seem progressive and supportive of the struggle for equal rights.

The Harlem Rens attracted some of the best black basketball players in the country, including James "Pappy" Ricks, Clarence "Fats" Jenkins, Charles "Tarzan" Cooper, William "Pops" Gates, Eyre "Bruiser" Saitch, Zack Clayton, and others. The team was popular and made money, and in addition, Douglas offered his players full-salary contracts for the entire season rather than pay per game as had been the tradition. Within a short time the Harlem Rens became the best black basketball team in the country, challenged only by the Harlem Globetrotters. From the mid-1920s into the 1940s the Rens took on all challengers and comported themselves well against semipro, professional, and college teams, both black and white. The Rens' schedules included competitive games against the all-white Boston Celtics, which piqued the interest of many basketball fans. The Rens won as many games as they lost to the Celtics, and, in fact, they beat the Celtics in what was deemed the world championship of professional basketball in 1932. In 1939 the *Chicago Herald-American* newspaper sponsored a basketball tournament that it called the first World Professional Basketball Tournament, and the Rens were among the twelve teams invited to participate. The Rens beat the all-white Oshkosh All-Stars of the segregated National Basketball League—a forerunner of the National Basketball Association (NBA)—to win the title.

The only other black basketball team to scale the heights that the Rens reached was the Harlem Globe Trotters (later Globetrotters). Contrary to popular belief, the Harlem Globetrotters did not originate in Harlem at all but rather on the south side of Chicago. Like that of the Harlem Rens, the founding of the Globetrotters was closely connected to a famous ballroom. I. J. Faggen, the builder of the Savoy Ballroom in New York, constructed another and more fabulous Savoy Ballroom in Chicago in 1927, and as an added attraction he signed a contract with the Savoy Big Five, the best club basketball team in Chicago, to play exhibition basketball games to complement ballroom dancing. During its inaugural season at the ballroom in 1928, the Savoy Big Five played before overflow crowds and defeated a collection of outstanding basketball teams that included teams from Howard University, Fisk University, and several other black colleges. In addition, their win over Loendi of Pittsburgh indicated that the Savoy Big Five was as good as any basketball team in the country.

The success of the Savoy Big Five was short-lived as a result of internal strife over salaries. Several members left the squad and formed an alternative team, which they named the Globe Trotters. In 1928, under Tommy Brookins's leadership, the Globe Trotters toured southern Illinois and Indiana. At some point Abe Saperstein, a local Jewish American athletic coach and sports enthusiast, gained control of the team. There are numerous contradictions, myths, and distortions about Saperstein's early affiliation with the Globe Trotters. Apparently Saperstein, forever the opportunist, had been a road and booking manager for Brookins's Globe Trotters when he decided to form a second Globe Trotter team to play in other areas of the Midwest. When Brookins finally confronted him about the matter, Saperstein attempted to convince Brookins that he had acted in the best interest of everyone. Apparently, at some point Brookins decided to pursue other interests, disbanded his version of the Globe Trotters, persuaded Saperstein to take several of his players, and essentially handed him the team on the proverbial silver platter.

Those who saw the Globetrotters play later remembered the comedic antics of Inman Jackson, Meadowlark Lemon, Reece "Goose" Tatum, and others. Include the remarkable ball handling and dribbling skills of Marques Haynes and Curly Neal and one was left with the memory of an exciting, entertaining, and memorable event. The score, or who won the game, was irrelevant. The Globetrotters' comedy routines made the average fan forget that the Trotters were excellent and legitimate basketball players or that it was a serious basketball team in the beginning.

In the ten years after he assumed control of the Trotters in 1929, Saperstein, using his considerable booking and marketing skills, took the Globetrotters on endless tours of the Midwest and mountain states using more and more comedy routines. However, he continued to challenge the Harlem Rens to play for the "colored" basketball championship. Saperstein's prayer was answered when in 1939 the Hearst Newspaper Syndicate allocated a $10,000 prize to sponsor a World Professional Basketball Tournament in Chicago that would include the best black and white basketball teams. The Harlem Renaissance and the Harlem Globetrotters were among the twelve teams invited. The Rens defeated the Globetrotters in the semifinals. The two teams met in the finals the following year, and the Trotters avenged their loss to the Rens.

The victory marked the beginning of the Globetrotters' reign not only as the best black basketball team but also, arguably, as the best basketball team in the world. Unfortunately it also marked the decline of the Rens, who for almost twenty years had been the kings of the basketball world. In 1950 the Globetrotters made their first European tour en route to becoming one of the best-known sports teams in the world. However, except for playing, and often beating, collections of the best college players in the country, comedic entertainment became the Trotters' forte, some of which occasionally appeared tawdry, stereotypical, and in the minstrel tradition. Saperstein had his critics in the African American community during the years of the civil rights movement, including those who believed that he used his influence to prevent integration in the nascent National Basketball Association so as not to lose his player base. Most African Americans, however, viewed the Globetrotters' comedy as humane, entertaining, and inclusive.

Integration. William Garrett enrolled at Indiana University in 1947 and became the first African American to play basketball in the Big Ten conference, where he earned All-American honors in 1951. In 1948 Don Barksdale, an All-American forward on the UCLA basketball team, became the first African American basketball player selected to the United States Olympic basketball squad. In addition, Barksdale was the first black to make an impact on the basketball program of a major white college after World War II. Despite the success of Garrett and Barksdale, there was no rush to recruit black basketball players at white colleges even after the University of San Francisco won national basketball titles in 1955 and 1956, thanks largely to the black players William "Bill"

Russell and K. C. Jones. The African Americans on white college teams during this time continued to endure physical threats and discrimination in hotels and restaurants when they traveled with their white teammates.

Russell, Jones, the ill-fated Maurice Stokes (who died prematurely), Hal Greer, Elgin Baylor, Guy Rodgers, the three-time All-American Oscar Robertson, and Wilton "Wilt" Chamberlain, the most dominating seven-foot basketball player ever, all entered the NBA in the 1950s and early 1960s after successful tenures at white colleges. Their success on the basketball court translated into an economic benefit for the colleges: as the money for the television rights to broadcast college games increased tremendously, a successful athletic program could enrich the coffers of major white colleges by millions of dollars. In this environment the recruitment of outstanding black athletes was imminent, except in the South, where entrenched segregation remained.

When Congress passed the Civil Rights Act of 1964, most white colleges in the South still had not begun to integrate their sports programs. Furthermore, the white colleges outside the South that were actively recruiting black basketball players were hesitant about having too many blacks on their teams. The 1963 National Collegiate Athletic Association (NCAA) basketball championship, in which Loyola University of Chicago defeated the heavily favored University of Cincinnati, was something of a milestone in that Loyola had four blacks in its starting lineup and Cincinnati had three. The 1966 NCAA final provided an even more dramatic racial contrast when Don Haskins, the coach of tiny Texas Western College, started five African Americans against the lily-white University of Kentucky basketball team. That the racial overtones of the game were so visibly pervasive was unfortunate, because Texas Western's victory over mighty Kentucky was truly one of the great upsets in modern sports. Kentucky's coach Adolph Rupp was a basketball icon, but he was also a captive of southern convention in racial matters and did not recruit a black player until 1972.

Style. As basketball became popular among black youths, the fast-paced, expressive style of the basketball played on the playgrounds and at YMCAs in black urban communities differed significantly from the more conservative style played in white communities, for example in Indiana and West Virginia, where basketball among white youths became akin to a second religion. The style was reflected in the play of the Harlem Rens in the 1920s, which may best be described as up-tempo and improvisational. However, the rules that governed basketball at the time slowed the game down considerably, making an up-tempo game impossible. Nonetheless the style continued in black communities but evolved and changed. The African American basketball players who entered white colleges and the NBA in the 1950s and 1960s popularized this style of basketball.

For fans and players one of the most exciting plays is the dunk shot—another element of modern basketball that may have originated on the playgrounds of African American communities. Stories abound about legendary dunkers like the Harlem Globetrotter great "Jumping" Jackie Jackson, who showcased his talent at Rucker Park in New York, the most famous basketball playground in America. However, creative dunkers like Jackson could be found on almost any black playground. Russell, Chamberlain, Walt Bellamy, Nate Thurmond, and Kareem Abdul Jabbar (Lew Alcindor), most of whom honed their skills on playgrounds, were so tall and athletic that dunking seemed almost unfair to some. In fact, the governing committee of the NCAA, in a move directed at Alcindor during his tenure at UCLA, banned the dunk in college basketball from 1967 to 1976. Ironically, shorter players like Gus Johnson, Connie Hawkins, Dominique Wilkins, Julius "Dr. J" Erving, and Michael Jordan brought the dunk shot to the status of high art.

It was not until the 1990s that the contemporary manifestation of playground basketball became known as "street" or "blacktop" basketball. References to street basketball were pervasive among players, sportscasters, and fans as if it were new. What they were really talking about was the fast-paced, inventive, expressive, in-your-face basketball played in urban black neighborhoods that had been a significant and influential part of sports culture for years. Several companies even produced commercials advertising athletic shoes and other products using the jargon and sights and sounds of urban, black America. Basketball players, young and old, black and white, male and female, emulated this style of basketball on playgrounds, in middle schools, in high schools, in colleges, and on the professional level. The assumption that street basketball was a recent phenomenon was laughable to old-timers who had played basketball or watched the game change dramatically over the years.

It is difficult to pinpoint the origin of modern street basketball, but one possibility involves a game, with many different versions, that black youngsters, both rural and urban, played on playgrounds. The purpose of the game—called "Horse," "Chump," or other names—was to create and make a very difficult basketball shot, which your opponents then had to replicate in every detail including dribbling and body motions. If an opponent did not duplicate, he received a letter for each unduplicated shot until the letters spelled the name of the game being played, and the player was eliminated. The elimination continued until only one player was left as the winner. Whatever the version, the game resulted in some very creative basketball that some believe laid the foundation for the way athletes play modern basketball. In fact, some of those same old-timers also scoff at historians' suggestion that Hank Luisetti, the white Stanford University basketball star (1934–1936), invented the jump shot—a shot that revolutionized basketball—claiming to have seen black youths employ the jump shot on the playgrounds before Luisetti popularized it.

Fancy, sleight-of-hand, jitterbug dribbling—one significant component of modern, urban basketball—appears to have a specific origin, but in an unlikely place. Marques Haynes of Sand Springs, Oklahoma, spent much of his early youth dribbling a ball of some kind and became extremely proficient in doing so. However, even though he was the star of Langston University's basketball team in 1942, few people knew about Haynes's unbelievable dribbling skills until the championship basketball game of the Southwest Conference Tournament in Baton Rouge, Louisiana, in 1945 that matched two powerful black colleges, Langston and Southern. With Langston having an insurmountable lead in the final minutes of the championship game, Haynes put on the most incredible display of dribbling and ball handling ever seen in a basketball game before or since. He dribbled the ball between his legs, behind his back, lying on his back, and lying on his side. The entire exasperated Southern University team chased the jitterbug-dribbling Haynes without success, much to the delight of twenty-five hundred screaming fans. Eventually, with the time clock winding down to zero, Haynes streaked to the basket, made a layup shot, and just continued running into the locker room.

Following the game against Southern University, Langston defeated the mighty Harlem Globetrotters, and after graduating in 1946 Haynes spent the greater part of his basketball career as the Globetrotters' own ball-handling genius. In the process he toured the world and became the most emulated of all the Globetrotters. Every young basketball player who saw him, white or black, wanted to be like Marques. The overwhelming consensus of those who saw Haynes in his prime is that no one before or since could control the basketball the way he did. Contemporary high school, college, and professional basketball players who believe that they are dribbling like Bob Cousy, Oscar Robertson, Guy Rodgers, Magic Johnson, Isaiah Thomas, Pete Maravich, or Nate Archibald are actually emulating Haynes.

Changes. The changes in basketball since the 1970s have been especially important for African American players. Although women had played basketball from its inception, sexism prevented women's basketball from getting popular support until Congress passed Title IX of the Education Amendments Act of 1972, which stipulated that colleges and universities that received federal funds had to provide sports programs for women. This gave the three-time All-American Cheryl Miller, who attended the University of Southern California, and other black female athletes an opportunity to compete in collegiate basketball. The International Olympic Committee inaugurated women's basketball in 1976, and numerous black females have played in the Olympics since then. Furthermore, the superstars Cynthia Cooper, Nikki McCray, Sheryl Swoopes, Tina Thompson, and other black players have helped to popularize women's professional basketball since the inauguration of the Women's National Basketball Association in 1996.

Magic Johnson of the Los Angeles Lakers and Michael Jordan of the Chicago Bulls, among others, represented the public face of professional basketball from the mid-1980s into the 1990s, and they were excellent ambassadors as the popularity of the sport continued to grow and as player salaries spiraled upward to millions of dollars. Johnson's flashy style as—arguably—the best passer ever, his ebullient personality, and his knowledge, love, and respect for the game made him a fan favorite. Jordan's domination in winning ten scoring titles, leading Chicago to six NBA titles, and his creative dunking ability made him the preeminent player of his time and, maybe, of all time. In addition his popularity led to commercial endorsements that far exceeded his salary as a basketball player and opened the door for other African American athletes to endorse products. In addition Jordan and Johnson helped to popularize a style of basketball internationally that originated and evolved in black urban communities.

The dominance of blacks in basketball coincided with the civil rights movement and resulted in more opportunities for blacks as coaches in college and professional basketball and related occupations. In 1984 John Thompson of Georgetown University became the first African American basketball coach to lead a team to the national title. Bill Russell and Lenny Wilkins are among a number of black coaches who have achieved success in professional basketball, while Wes Unseld and Wayne Embry are typical of blacks gaining entrance to management positions. It is not unusual to find African Americans like Phil Chenier, Walt Frazier, Kenny Smith, Cheryl Miller, and others working as analysts on broadcasts of basketball games in both national and local television and radio markets. Some blacks, like Manny Jackson, the owner of the Harlem Globetrotters, are also seeking to become owners of professional basketball teams. These advances in basketball would have been unimaginable in the 1950s.

[*See also* Harlem Globetrotters; Sports, College and Amateur; Sports, Professional; *and biographical entries on figures mentioned in this article*.]

BIBLIOGRAPHY

Ashe, Arthur R., Jr. *A Hard Road to Glory, Basketball: The African-American Athlete in Basketball*. New York: Amistad, 1993. Includes a valuable reference section.

Green, Ben. *Spinning the Globe: The Rise, Fall, and Return to Greatness of the Harlem Globetrotters*. New York: Amistad, 2005. An informative, well-written, and well-researched account.

Mallozzi, Vincent M. *Asphalt Gods: An Oral History of the Rucker Tournament*. New York: Doubleday, 2003. An informative narrative about the most famous street basketball playground and tournament in America; lacks an analysis of its social significance.

—DONALD ROE

BASQUIAT, JEAN-MICHEL (b. 22 December 1960; d. 12 August 1988), painter. Basquiat was born to a Puerto Rican mother, Matilde Basquiat, and a Haitian father, Gérard Jean-Baptiste Basquiat, who was a former Haitian minister of the interior. Basquiat's mother encouraged his interest in all forms of the visual arts. He attended a Catholic high school but dropped out a year before his graduation and moved from Brooklyn to Manhattan. There he lived with various friends and supported himself by selling small, postcard-size art and T-shirts.

When Basquiat was only seventeen he started partnering with his friend Al Diaz in lower Manhattan to graffiti dilapidated buildings and subway trains with images and poems, signing the artwork "SAMO," which represented "same ole shit." The graffiti often included cryptic sayings, such as "plush safe he think; SAMO," "SAMO is an escape clause," and "SAMO does not cause cancer in laboratory animals." Within a year this graffiti garnered considerable interest. The *Village Voice* published an article on the graffiti, and soon thereafter Basquiat included "SAMO IS DEAD" on one building. Basquiat became a local celebrity in a short time. He was featured often on the New York local cable access show hosted by the writer Glenn O'Brien. Basquiat was also involved in music, playing with more than one band, most notably the band Gray.

Basquiat was included in his first group show in New York in 1980, and the next year the poet and art critic Rene Ricard wrote an article on him for *Art Forum* magazine. The article made Basquiat internationally known, and he became of great interest to the art community. In 1982 he was included in the largest biennial in the United States, the Whitney Biennial, which was a guarantee of substantial attention and consideration as a serious

Collaborative Art. The artists Andy Warhol and Jean-Michel Basquiat stand before some of their collaborative art pieces at the Tony Shafrazi Gallery in New York City, 1985. Photograph by Richard Drew. AP IMAGES

visual artist. He was now a part of the official art world. His works appeared with other notable artists, including Keith Haring and Julian Schnabel, and he quickly developed a strong following of wealthy art collectors, who purchased his works from top New York galleries. Basquiat's mistrust of gallery owners led him to change his gallery affiliation frequently. He was considered a part of the Neo-Expressionist movement, has been called a member of the hip-hop culture, and was considered a postmodern "primitive" due to his ethnic heritage.

In 1982, when Basquiat was twenty-two years old, the art critic Roberta Smith reviewed his art in the *Village Voice*. She was less than impressed with his graffiti-style work. She commented that the artist had "absorbed every trick in contemporary painting's book" and she clearly did not see him as particularly original or innovative. She admitted that it was hard to dislike his works but also that they seemed a bit too tame and well put together. In other words, the works were not as original as they appeared, they were "too put together to be as raw as they pretend."

In the same year Basquiat began dating the then unknown performer Madonna and also began a friendship with Andy Warhol. The mid-1980s were deeply troubled for Basquiat. He developed an interest in drugs, which led to a heroin addiction. In 1985 he appeared on the cover of the *New York Times Magazine*; he had come of age. With this major article, Basquiat began exhibiting his works in Europe as well. He was at the pinnacle of his career.

Basquiat is known for his graphically inspired, graffiti-style art, which includes doodles, words, images, masklike faces, and bright colors. He made constant references to African American life and notable African Americans in his work, critiquing the urban culture of his time. He collaborated with Warhol on several occasions. After Warhol's death in 1987, Basquiat's life seemed to spiral even more out of control. He died of a heroin overdose in 1988 at the age of twenty-seven. He is considered a major artist of his generation. There have been numerous retrospectives of his work, including a show that traveled to the Brooklyn Museum and the Los Angeles Museum of Contemporary Art in 2005 and the Museum of Fine Art in Houston in 2006.

[*See also* Visual Arts.]

BIBLIOGRAPHY

Marshall, Richard, et al. *Jean-Michel Basquiat: Works on Paper*. New York: Tony Shafrazi Gallery, 1999. Published in conjunction with the exhibition "Jean-Michel Basquiat: Works on Paper" shown at the Galerie Enrico Navarra, Paris.

Marshall, Richard, ed. *Jean-Michel Basquiat*. New York: Harry N. Abrams, 1992. Published in conjunction with the exhibition "Jean-Michel Basquiat" shown at the Whitney Museum of American Art.

Patton, Sharon F. *African-American Art*. Oxford and New York: Oxford University Press, 1998. See pp. 238–239.

Smith, Roberta. "Jean-Michel Basquiat and the Contemporary Art Scene." *Village Voice*, 23 March 1982.

—AMY HELENE KIRSCHKE

BASS, CHARLOTTA (b.?; d. 12 April 1969), journalist, editor, business owner, civil rights leader, community activist, feminist, and political candidate. In 1952, she became the first African American woman to run for the vice presidency of the United States. There are conflicting reports about Bass's date and place of birth and scant information about her life prior to coming to Los Angeles. Some sources report that she was born as early as 1874/1875, while others estimate the year of her birth was somewhere in the vicinity of 1879/1880. Likewise, the place of her birth is open to speculation and some references are made to Sumter, South Carolina, while other sources indicate Little Compton, Rhode Island. The historian Gerald Gill points out that Bass played no small role in complicating the facts around the actual date and place of her birth.

The historical record, however, indicates her birth name was Charlotta Amanda Spears, that she came to Los Angeles in 1910, and that health issues prompted her migration. She attended Brown University, Columbia University, and the University of California. Starting in 1910, through the avenue of journalism, Bass became actively involved in the affairs of the Los Angeles African American community. She was initially hired to sell subscriptions for *The Eagle*, which was the oldest active African American newspaper in California, at a wage of five dollars per week. After migrating from Texas, John J. Neimore had started the newspaper in 1879, and Bass's arrival was a welcome addition. Bass rapidly moved to become the paper's reporter, managing editor, business manager, publisher, and finally owner in 1912. After an extended illness, Neimore died in 1912, and the paper was taken over by Captain G. W. Hawkins. Bass acquired the paper in turn, and she assumed the full responsibilities of its operation in the same year. After assuming ownership of the paper, Bass changed its name to the *California Eagle* and around this time (1913) she recruited the former Topeka, Kansas, newspaperman Joseph Blackburn Bass as her editor and later publisher. Charlotta A. Spears married Joseph Blackburn Bass in 1914 and they remained a vital newspaper team, public advocates for the African American community as well as husband and wife until Joseph's death in November 1934.

In its early days, the *California Eagle* was stalwartly Republican in its orientation. In their role as journalists qua political activists, Charlotta and Joseph Bass supported Frederick M. Roberts in his successful 1918 bid to become the first African American elected to the California State Assembly. Given Charlotta's feminist commitments, she not only supported African American Republican candidates but also white women who held progressive views on race and gender. Consequently, Charlotta Bass endorsed the white Republican Estelle Lawton Lindsey in her 1917 campaign for City Council of Los Angeles and Lindsey gained a seat on the council.

Nevertheless, the political scope of Bass's activities exceeded the boundaries of electoral politics. Ever conscious of the significance of Africa and Pan-Africanism for African Americans, Bass was crucially involved in the Paris (1919) Pan-African Congress. Led by W. E. B. Du Bois, this conference provoked United States government concern over African Americans lending support to African independence movements and their ancillary critiques of colonialism in Africa. Bass managed to make it to Paris despite the fact that the United States government tried to disrupt the travel plans of African Americans wanting to attend. She later served on the conference committee that promoted its agenda through propaganda and education.

Charlotta Bass was a unique figure in Pan-African history, able not only to support Du Bois's Pan-Africanist efforts but also actively engaged in working with Marcus Garvey's Universal Negro Improvement Association (UNIA). Du Bois and Garvey were bitter rivals and as a result the members of their respective organizations were often at odds. Bass, on the other hand, was not only the co-founder of the Los Angeles chapter of the UNIA; she also assumed the role of "lady president" of the L.A. branch.

Charlotta Bass's commitment to advancing the cause of African American liberation grew over the decades and expanded well beyond World War II. Among the many organizations in which she was actively engaged were: NAACP, the International Labour Defense, Council on African Affairs, Civil Rights Congress, Sojourners for Truth and Justice, National Negro Congress, Los Angeles Negro Victory Committee, and the California Independent Progressive Party.

The post–World War II period signaled Bass's transition to a more leftist political viewpoint that accentuated the critique of bourgeois politics, and she decided to run for district seat on the city council in 1945. Bass gained huge support from the African American community and forced a run-off vote with the incumbent. Although she lost in the run-off, Bass became more committed to criticism of the political status quo. A supporter of Henry Wallace and the Progressive Party campaign of 1948, Bass became a Progressive Party candidate in 1950, running for the 14th Congressional District Seat in California. Although she lost her bid for office, her commitment to the Progressive Party cause grew especially in light of the escalation of racial discrimination in the United States and the Korean War abroad. Consequently, Bass joined the Progressive presidential candidate Vincent Hallinan as his vice presidential partner in 1952. With the campaign slogan, "Win or Lose—We Win," Bass proved to be a strong campaigner and charismatic public speaker who gave voice to myriad domestic and foreign concerns. She condemned the Korean War, called for peace with the Soviet Union, advocated for the recognition of the People's Republic of China, and promoted support for the independence of Africa. Collectively, Bass's proposals offered a new perspective on U.S. foreign policy that stood in stark contrast to the political platforms of both the Republicans and Democrats. Bass was quick to point out the connection between racism in the domestic sphere and the ways in which imperialism and war abroad restricted women's rights. After selling the *California Eagle* in 1951, she continued with political and community activities until her health began to deteriorate in the 1960s. The FBI considered Bass a threat and continued its surveillance even after she had a stroke in 1967. Bass died on 12 April 1969.

[*See also* Du Bois, W. E. B.; Journalism, Print and Broadcast; *and* Politics and Politicians.]

BIBLIOGRAPHY

Freer, Regina. "L. A. Race Woman: Charlotta Bass and the Complexities of Black Political Development in Los Angeles." *American Quarterly* 56, no. 3 (September 2004): 607–682. This article does a fine job of locating the political thinking and activity of Bass within the framework of African American politics in Los Angeles over a broad historical period.

Gill, Gerald. "From Progressive Republican to Independent Progressive: The Political Career of Charlotta A. Bass." In *African American Women and the Vote, 1837–1955*, edited by Ann D. Gordon. pp. 156–171. Amherst: University of Massachusetts Press, 1997. This essay offers not only extensive empirical detail but also analytical insights very important to understanding Bass's political thinking over several decades. The essay is a continuation of Gill's pioneering article on Bass "Win or Lose—We Win: The 1952 Vice-Presidential Campaign of Charlotta A. Bass." In *The Afro-American Woman: Struggles and Images*, edited by Sharon Harley and Roslyn Terborg-Penn. Port Washington, N.Y.: Kennikat Press, 1978.

—JOHN H. MCCLENDON III

BASSETT, ANGELA (b. 16 August 1958), television, stage, and film actor. The Oscar-nominated actor Angela Bassett has managed to attain success while maintaining personal integrity and social conscience. Although her principles have cost her some measure of fame, she has appeared in more than forty television movies and films.

Bassett was born in New York City and was raised in Saint Petersburg, Florida. Her mother, a civil servant, raised Angela and her sister to value hard work and education. After an eleventh-grade Upward Bound trip to see a James Earl Jones performance, Bassett took up acting and was awarded a scholarship to Yale University. In 1980 she earned a bachelor's degree in African American studies, and she earned an MFA from the Yale School of Drama in 1983.

Bassett's screen career began in 1985, and *F/X* (1986) marked her feature-film debut. She gained recognition in *Boyz in the Hood* (1991) and as Betty Shabazz in Spike Lee's *Malcolm X* (1992). In *What's Love Got to Do With It?* (1993), Bassett portrayed Tina Turner, for which she won a Golden Globe and an NAACP Image Award and was nominated for an Academy Award.

In 1995 Bassett appeared in five films, including an adaptation of Terry McMillan's best-selling novel *Waiting to Exhale*, and in 1998 she was in McMillan's *How Stella Got Her Groove Back*. In 2002 Bassett was nominated for an Emmy for her role as Rosa Parks in *The Rosa Parks Story* on CBS, which she also produced. In 2006 Bassett again played opposite Laurence Fishburne (costar of *What's Love Got to Do With It?*) in *Akeelah and the Bee*.

On 12 October 1997 Bassett married the actor Courtney Vance, a 1986 graduate of the Yale School of Drama. In 2007 the couple wrote a very engaging and personal dual autobiography, *Friends: A Love Story*. The book details each actor's struggle for balance and reveals the personal side of Bassett, including her religious grounding and her struggle to have children. The couple had twins by a surrogate and wrote the book to celebrate their ten-year anniversary.

[*See also* Actors and Actresses; Film and Filmmakers; *and* Film and Television Depictions of African Americans.]

BIBLIOGRAPHY

Fitzgerald, Dawn. *Angela Bassett*. Philadelphia: Chelsea House Publishers, 2002.

—STEPHANIE Y. EVANS

BATES, DAISY LEE (b. 11 November 1913; d. 4 November 1999), one of the twentieth-century South's most consistent and effective civil rights leaders, perhaps best remembered for her role in the desegregation of Little Rock, Arkansas, Central High School in 1957–1958. Her name has become synonymous with racial integration, and her memoir *The Long Shadow of Little Rock* (1962) has emerged as one of the standard texts on the subject.

Although accounts vary, she was born Daisy Lee Gaston, probably in 1913, in Huttig, Arkansas, a small mill town in the southeastern part of the state near the border with Louisiana. Her childhood memories are dotted with several episodes of racial discrimination, but her recollection that she grew up with foster parents because her mother had died while resisting the assault of white rapists (her father subsequently left town and her life) left an indelible and horrific mark on her psyche. Though her recollections have never been confirmed, it is clear that coming of age in the world of unchallenged white supremacy helped mold her world view.

In 1942 she married L. C. Bates, an older insurance salesman and sometime journalist, after a lengthy courtship. She joined her new husband in Little Rock and helped him in publishing the *Arkansas State Press*; the first issue appeared in May 1941. The *State Press* became an outspoken advocate of civil rights, with particular emphasis on the rights of returning black World War II veterans who were often the victims of violence and police brutality in Little Rock. The paper also championed the cause of equal pay for black teachers and the abolition of the white primary. In addition, Daisy Bates quickly established herself as a militant voice within the National Association for the Advancement of Colored People (NAACP) and even sought to establish a Pulaski County branch of that organization, which attempted to overshadow the more conservative leadership of the Little Rock chapter. In part because of her outspoken demeanor, Bates became the president of the Arkansas NAACP in 1952 and promptly took up negotiations with the Little Rock school board to desegregate the city's schools. She even contemplated a lawsuit against the board, but the national office of the NAACP persuaded her to abandon those plans until the Supreme Court could hand down a decision in *Brown v. Board of Education* (1954).

Although the Little Rock school board was among the first in the South to indicate a willingness to comply with the *Brown* decision, it soon began to equivocate on its initial plans. It moved back its schedule to open schools to children of both races by several years while a new desegregated high school could be built. By 1956, Bates had grown restive over the delays; working with a young Pine Bluff, Arkansas, attorney named Wiley Branton, she assembled a lawsuit that would force immediate desegregation. The result was that the federal courts ordered Little Rock Central High School to be integrated beginning in September 1957.

The sitting governor, Francis Cherry, announced his intentions to comply with the law, but he was defeated in 1956 by a segregationist, Orval Faubus, who had campaigned to resist federal interference with race relations in Arkansas. Bates, however, was determined to push ahead in the case, and she helped select nine students (the "Little Rock Nine") who, in 1957, would be the first blacks to attend Central High and for whom she became an adviser and proctor. Governor Faubus initially used the state national guard to keep the black students from attending Central High, but eventually he yielded to federal authorities, who used regular army troops to stabilize conditions and break the color line at the previously all-white high school. The Little Rock Nine became the victims of relentless threats and countless insults from many of their white classmates and from conservative white elements in Little Rock at large. Bates and her husband also bore much of the hatred of local segregationists, including several white ministers. Bates's memoir recounts how she and her husband kept loaded weapons at the ready to repel what they feared might be an assault on their home.

The Little Rock Nine did actually attend Central High School, and almost all of them graduated. But Bates and her husband lost their newspaper in 1959, when advertising revenues dried up in the wake of their activism. L. C. Bates took a post with the NAACP, and Daisy Bates spent the better part of the next two years writing her famous memoir; it was published in 1962. She worked for a time for the Democratic National Committee, and she participated in the antipoverty programs of the Lyndon Johnson administration in Washington, D.C., but she suffered a stroke in 1965, forcing her return to Arkansas. L. C. Bates died in 1980, but Daisy Bates revived their newspaper under new management and ownership in 1984 and once more took up the cause of racial justice. That same year the University of Arkansas awarded her an honorary doctor of laws degree. She died in Little Rock in 1999 after several years of declining health.

[*See also* Arkansas; Civil Rights Movement; Desegregation and Integration; *and* Little Rock, Arkansas.]

Bibliography

Bates, Daisy Gaston. *The Long Shadow of Little Rock*. New York: David McKay, 1962. Daisy Bates's classic memoir and a standard in the literature of the civil rights movement.

Kirk, John A. *Redefining the Color Line: Black Activism in Little Rock, Arkansas, 1940–1970*. Gainesville: University Press of Florida, 2002. Excellent for understanding the climate of racial change in a southern city.

Stockley, Grif. *Daisy Bates: Civil Rights Crusader from Arkansas*. Jackson: University Press of Mississippi, 2005. The best full-length scholarly account of Bates and her career in print.

—Charles Orson Cook

BEARDEN, ROMARE (b. 2 September 1911; d. 12 March 1988), painter, printmaker, and collage artist. Romare Howard Bearden was born in Charlotte, North Carolina, on 12 September 1911, to Richard Howard and Bessye Bearden. Although he only spent two years in North Carolina, his grandparents conveyed a sense of history and connection to the South, a connection that was reflected in his work throughout his career. Most of his childhood and adult life were spent in New York. He moved to New York in 1914, and then to Harlem in 1920. His mother, Bessye, was elected to the New York City school board in 1922; education was of paramount importance in his family. Bearden had an expansive, diverse career and is considered one of the finest American artists of the twentieth century. He had an interest in political, social, and cultural issues, including the visual arts, music, and literature. He was particularly interested in African American history and dealt directly with issues of race and prejudice, as well as African American memory, history, and culture. His career of more than thirty years as a New York City social worker provided endless material for his art, which was created during the evenings and on weekends. Bearden was deeply committed throughout his career to the aid and support of emerging artists in the humanities, not limited to the visual arts.

Romare Bearden began college at Lincoln University and then transferred to Boston University, finally

Romare Bearden, 1975. Photograph by Chester Higgins.

completing his education degree at New York University. At both BU and NYU, Bearden studied art and contributed cartoons to the universities' journals, including the humor magazine *Beanpot* at BU, where he served as art director, and NYU's *The Medley*, where he served as art director and lead cartoonist. Some of his NYU cartoons appeared in a more political context, in the NAACP's *Crisis* magazine. In these cartoons, Bearden addressed issues of unemployment, racism, and even lynching. In 1931 Bearden met the African American cartoonist Elmer Simms, who had a profound effect on his career. Simms was the first black cartoonist to work at several white publications, including the *New Yorker* and the *Saturday Evening Post*.

The Art Students League in New York provided Bearden with a stimulating environment, a place for him to work with the German expatriate artist George Grosz. He also studied briefly at the Sorbonne in Paris. Bearden was greatly influenced by the cartoonist William Gropper, a political satirist whose work appeared in several journals, including *The New Masses* and *Daily Worker*. In 1935, Bearden became a weekly editorial cartoonist for the *Baltimore Afro-American*, where he illustrated for two years; some of these cartoons were reprinted in the *Crisis* magazine. These early cartoons established Bearden's life-long interest in social realism and social commentary through art. Bearden used cartoons to highlight the injustice and inequality of Depression-era America, and his work serves as a reminder of the potential for politically charged art to provide a "magnifying glass" for society's problems and contradictions.

In 1935 Bearden attended an artists' meeting led by the sculptor Augusta Savage; the group, which would become the Harlem Artists Guild, inspired him to spend his free time creating art. He found inspiration in artists of the past, including the artists Giotto and Duccio, as well as modern masters such as Cézanne, Matisse, and Picasso. He was also inspired by Japanese prints, Chinese painting, and traditional African art, especially West African masks. Bearden was offered his first solo exhibition in Harlem in 1940 at a gallery at 306 West 141st Street, followed by a one-man show at the G Space Gallery in Washington, D.C., in 1944. He was included in a group show at the Apollo Theatre in Harlem in 1941, along with other notable artists including William Henry Johnson, Joseph Delaney, and Eldzier Cortor. Bearden remained friends with an elite group of artists and literati, including Langston Hughes, James Baldwin, Stuart Davis, Duke Ellington, Ralph Ellison, Joan Miró, George Grosz, Alvin Ailey, and Jacob Lawrence.

After experimenting with abstraction, Bearden became best known for his collages, which he developed in his apartment in New York by cutting up old magazines. These collages were some of the most poignant studies of African American identity and collective memory in the visual arts. Bearden used symbols from his background in Mecklenburg County, North Carolina, a brief childhood stint in Pittsburgh, and years in Harlem. He often included railroads, musical instruments, overalls, and icons of rural life in his pieces. He was following in the tradition of William Henry Johnson, Horace Pippin, and Jacob Lawrence. Images of the South, learned from his grandparents, were a major part of his constructions. He also designed sets and programs for his wife Nanette Rohan Bearden's dance company, The Contemporary Dance Theatre, as well as costumes and sets for the famed Alvin Ailey American Dance Theater. Bearden had married Nanette Rohan in 1954; her family was from St. Martin, in the Caribbean. The two eventually established a second home on the island of St. Martin; the tropical landscapes of island life appeared in his later works.

In 1963, inspired by the Harlem Renaissance movement from which he had once distanced himself, Bearden and thirteen other artists formed the Spiral Group, reexamining the role of the artist during the civil rights era. It was at this time that Bearden developed his collage-style "Projections," in which he worked from photographs and cut magazines, creating works consciously alluding to African American culture, including jazz, folk music, religion, magic, recreation, and rural and urban life. Bearden took images from the past and reworked them, creating a unique composition that recalled the past masters of art, reinterpreting them in an African American vocabulary of memory and identity. In 1964, Bearden was appointed the first art director of the Harlem Cultural Council, an organization created to support the arts in Harlem. The organization was incorporated in 1965. Jazz was a lifelong influence on the art of Bearden, and he supported jazz musicians through his work on the Council. The Council helped create the Jazzmobile and Dancemobile, both offshoots of the Harlem Cultural Council, designed to bring visiting artists in jazz and dance to the streets of Harlem.

Bearden's *Three Folk Musicians* of 1967 typifies his mixture of his past, bringing together various memories of Charlotte, North Carolina, Pittsburgh, and Harlem. Here he was emphasizing African American life with roots in the rural South without referring to any specific memory or moment. The collage-based, Cubism-inspired piece surely reflects knowledge of Picasso's *Three Musicians* of 1921, a Synthetic Cubist piece that appears to be collage, but is an oil painting. Now Bearden, nodding to Picasso, brought an African American folk aesthetic to his work, placing his figures in overalls, recalling the African masks that also inspired Picasso. Bearden, in contrast to Picasso, claims a cultural memory of Africa.

Bearden began working with prints regularly in the 1970s and 1980s. His *Morning*, in 1975, was a collage that he turned into a limited edition of silkscreen prints. In this work he shows a mother lovingly leaning down to kiss a child—the faces recall masks of the Dan society of the Ivory Coast, an image that recalls the influence of both African art and the artist Aaron Douglas. The image includes a still life, a rocking chair, and a potbellied stove, all placing the African American family in the genre of traditional American life. The collage (and subsequent print) recall both Cubism and the art of Matisse.

Bearden authored several books, including *A History of African American Artists: From 1792 to the Present*, co-authored with Harry Henderson and published posthumously in 1993. His work is contained in major collections internationally, including the Metropolitan Museum of Art, the Whitney Museum of American Art, the Philadelphia Museum of Art, the Museum of Fine Arts in Boston, and The Studio Museum in Harlem. He had several retrospectives while still a working artist as well as posthumous retrospectives, most notably at the National Gallery of Art, Washington, D.C. (2003). His awards are many, including the Mayor's Award of Honor for Art and Culture in New York City in 1984 and the National Medal of Arts, presented by President Ronald Reagan in 1987. On 12 March 1988, Romare Bearden died of cancer. His memorial service was held at the Cathedral of Saint John the Divine in New York, and a memorial exhibition was hung at the cathedral as part of a celebration of his life. Several Harlem notables spoke at the service, including the author Ralph Ellison. Shortly thereafter, his widow accepted a Lifetime Achievement Award for Bearden from the Studio Museum in Harlem. Bearden's long career, from political cartooning, to abstraction, to collage, to prints, included a depth of understanding of African American collective history and identity, both in the rural South and urban North.

[*See also* Harlem Renaissance *and* Visual Arts.]

BIBLIOGRAPHY

Braff, Phylllis. "Romare Bearden's Images of the Black Experience, in Prints." *New York Times*, 11 February 1996.

Fine, Ruth. *The Art of Romare Bearden*. Washington: National Gallery of Art, 2003.

Gips, Terry. *Narratives of African American Art and Identity: The David C. Driskell Collection*. San Francisco: Pomegranate Press, 1998.

Glazer, Lee Stephens. "Signifying Identity: Art and Race in Romare Bearden's Projections." *The Art Bulletin* 76, no. 3 (September, 1994): 411–426.

Schwartzman, Myron, and August Wilson. *Romare Bearden: His Life and Art*. New York: Harry Abrams, 1990.

—AMY HELENE KIRSCHKE

BELAFONTE, HARRY (b. 1 March 1927), singer, actor, activist, and humanitarian. Harold George Belafonte was born in New York City to Harold George Belafonte Sr., a native of Martinique, and Melvine Love Belafonte, who was from Jamaica. Melvine Belafonte moved her family back to Jamaica in 1935 after rioting broke out in Harlem. Young Harry lived in the Blue Mountains, Saint Anne's Bay, and Kingston before returning to Harlem in 1940. Belafonte, who suffered from dyslexia, dropped out of school in the ninth grade and joined the U.S. Navy in 1944.

The seeds of Belafonte's humanitarian, social, and political activism began to bloom during his military service. His experiences performing the servile jobs assigned to enlisted blacks were eye-opening. His stint on active duty further shaped his views on freedom and eventually found expression in his music and his causes. While in the navy he met a group of African American men, people he later described as intellectuals. He spent time with them, listening and learning. One gave him a copy of W. E. B. Du Bois's book *Color and Democracy*, which Belafonte struggled to read. He returned from the war fully expecting that the democracy for which he and others had fought would be used to improve the plight of African Americans. He became angry and disillusioned as he realized that the issues for which he fought did not apply to him.

Acting and Music. Belafonte left the navy in 1948. Around the same time he saw a play at the American Negro Theater and fell in love with acting. For the next year he performed in several productions staged by the American Negro Theater, making his acting debut in *Juno and the Paycock*. It was there that he met Sidney Poitier, a fellow performer with roots outside of the United States—in his case, the Bahamas—with whom he enjoyed a complex friendship. While starring in various plays at the American Negro Theater, Belafonte also met Paul Robeson, who complimented him on one of his performances. Belafonte was humbled by the attention of Robeson, who became a close friend, mentor, and hero.

Belafonte believed that acting was his calling; however, it was music, or more specifically calypso, that catapulted him to fame. A friend convinced him to perform at the Royal Roost jazz tavern's amateur night. He ended up with a full-time gig and a recording contract with RCA. Belafonte began his unintended musical career singing jazz, then switched to pop songs. His repertoire included an original composition entitled "Recognition." In 1950 the winds of social change could be heard in the lyrics of folk music. Belafonte, newly reinvented as a folk singer, opened his act at the Village Vanguard in 1951. He began singing calypso music, successfully introducing it to mainstream audiences in the United States.

Community Activist. Harry Belafonte attends a rent hike demonstration, New York City, 1980. Photograph by Bettye Lane. © BETTYE LANE

Belafonte released his first album, *Calypso*, in 1956; it sold more than 1.5 million copies. He became the first African American to have a record achieve platinum status. Two of his signature tunes, the "Banana Boat Song" and "Jamaica Farewell," ignited the craze for calypso. His music career, which continued into the early twenty-first century, included African American spirituals, blues, and ballads. Ironically, as he gained fame singing calypso, his right to interpret that music was challenged. Calypso originated in Trinidad, not Jamaica, and purists argued that that distinction disqualified Belafonte. Their music was often bawdy and raunchy, celebrating male domination over and brutality toward women. Belafonte's lyrics demythologized and humanized Afro-Caribbean people.

Belafonte appeared as the school principal in his first major film, the all-black *Bright Road* (1953), along with Dorothy Dandridge. The same year John Murray Anderson cast Belafonte in his Broadway production *John Murray Anderson's Almanac*. Belafonte, the only African American performer in the cast, won the 1954 Tony Award for Best Featured Actor in a Musical and was one of two recipients of the 1954 Theatre World Award.

Belafonte and Dandridge teamed up again in 1954 for the movie *Carmen Jones*, another all-black production based on Georges Bizet's opera *Carmen*. Belafonte's character, Joe, was a young army officer engaged to be married. When Carmen, played by Dandridge, is arrested and placed in Joe's custody, she seduces him, with tragic results. Belafonte, suave and good-looking, and Dandridge, sultry and sensual as Carmen, lit up the screen with their chemistry. The theater director George C. Wolfe described their performances as highly suggestive and declared them two of the most beautiful people in the world. While critics were not persuaded, many African Americans were thrilled.

During the mid- to late 1950s Belafonte was possibly the most popular entertainer in the United States. The "King of Calypso," as he was often called, had outsold Elvis Presley and Frank Sinatra, both of whom were big stars in their own right. In 1957 *Look* magazine gushingly anointed Belafonte the first black matinee idol in America's entertainment history. His television credits include the Emmy Award–winning show *Tonight with Harry Belafonte*, a program he produced in 1960. Although that show was popular with viewers and Belafonte had an agreement to produce and host four more programs, he found his hands tied by policies that limited his involvement. He refused to agree to changes the sponsor wanted, and the remaining shows were canceled.

As his celebrity grew, Belafonte chose to address issues of race and racism in his music and his movies, notably in the films *Island in the Sun* (1957) and *Odds Against Tomorrow* (1959). He turned down scripts for *Porgy and Bess*, *Lilies of the Field*, and *To Sir, with Love* because he felt they were demeaning.

Political Activism. While the media fawned over him, Belafonte stepped into the fledgling civil rights movement. He met Martin Luther King Jr. in 1956 during the Montgomery bus boycott. Though somewhat leery of black clergy, Belafonte forged a lasting friendship with King that extended to Coretta Scott King and their children. Belafonte was one of King's most trusted confidants and advisers.

Belafonte embraced the civil rights movement as a necessary tool to achieve democracy and equality for African Americans, lending his physical presence, talent, time, and money to advance the cause. There was literally no aspect of the movement in which he was not involved. He provided the seed money for the newly organized Student Nonviolent Coordinating Committee. He raised money for the Freedom Rides, bailed student protestors out of jail, and paid King's bail when he was imprisoned in Birmingham. Belafonte helped organize the March on Washington and supported voter registration drives. He was subjected to intense pressure during the latter stages of the McCarthy era due to his involvement in the civil rights movement. When asked how he felt about it, Belafonte replied that it meant he was doing something right.

Belafonte's concern for the plight of people of color led to his involvement in the fight for sanctions against South Africa and independence for African and Caribbean nations struggling under the oppression of colonialism. He corresponded with Nelson Mandela during the latter's twenty-seven-year incarceration.

Belafonte came up with the idea for a fund-raiser to address the famine in Ethiopia. The result was the Grammy Award–winning song *We Are the World*, which was performed at a Live Aid concert and later released as an album in 1985.

Belafonte's social, political, and humanitarian efforts also have continued into the early twenty-first century, and he has been frequently honored for his work. He was appointed an international goodwill ambassador by UNICEF in 1987 and was a Kennedy Center honoree in 1989. AFRICARE gave him the Bishop John T. Walker Distinguished Humanitarian Service Award in 2002, the John F. Kennedy Library conferred its Distinguished American Award on him in 2002, and the Global Exchange presented him with its Human Rights Domestic Award in 2004. Awarded the Black Entertainment Television's Humanitarian Award in 2006, Belafonte dedicated it to Nelson Mandela.

Continuing to entertain and advocate, Belafonte released *The Long Road to Freedom: An Anthology of Black Music*, a history of black America in music, in 2001. He was diagnosed with prostate cancer in 1995 and became a spokesperson for early detection, using his celebrity to help promote a public awareness campaign aimed at African American men.

Belafonte's political activism often generated controversy. He is a vocal critic of U.S. foreign policy and President George W. Bush and an outspoken opponent of the war in Iraq. During an interview in October 2002 he characterized the secretaries of state Colin Powell and Condoleezza Rice as house slaves. He called President Bush a terrorist and likened Homeland Security to the gestapo. In January 2006 Belafonte led a delegation to Venezuela to meet with Venezuelan president Hugo Chavez.

Throughout his career Belafonte has stressed that his activism is as much a part of his artistry as his music; he remains unapologetic and undeterred. During an interview on the popular syndicated radio program *Democracy Now*, he called President Bush, Secretary of State Rice, Secretary of Defense Donald Rumsfeld, Vice President Dick Cheney, and Attorney General Alberto Gonzalez terrorists. He endeavors to foster a clear understanding of the role U.S. foreign policy plays in fomenting unrest, war, and poverty around the world.

[*See also* Actors and Actresses; Civil Rights, International; Iraq War; King, Martin Luther, Jr.; Music; Robeson, Paul; *and* Theater.]

BIBLIOGRAPHY

Belafonte, Harry. "Harry Belafonte on Bush, Iraq, Hurricane Katrina, and Having His Conversations with Martin Luther King Wiretapped by the FBI." *Democracy Now*, interview by Amy Goodman, 30 January 2006. http://www.democracynow.org/shows/2006/1.

Gates, Henry Louis, Jr. *Thirteen Ways of Looking at a Black Man*. New York: Random House, 1997. A collection of previously published essays on thirteen prominent African American men, including Belafonte.

—THERESA W. BENNETT-WILKES

BELL, COOL PAPA (b. 17 May 1903; d. 7 March 1991), Hall of Fame Negro League baseball player. The son of a farmer from Starkville, Mississippi, and the grandson of a Native American, James "Cool Papa" Bell was considered the fastest man ever to play baseball. The legends concerning his quickness prove almost Herculean in the retelling, with numerous accounts of Bell scoring in games from first base on bunts by his teammates. Bell also stole 175 bases over 200 games.

Bell began his baseball career in his hometown of Starkville, competing in local pick-up games with older youths and adults on the local sandlots. As Bell entered his teens, he found himself forced to move to Saint Louis to live with a brother because in 1920 Starkville possessed neither an African American high school nor any job opportunities for young black men.

In Saint Louis, Bell attended high school for two years while working in a packing plant. He also played baseball for a local semi-professional team. Bell soon attracted attention from the local Negro League team, the Saint Louis Stars, and signed a contract for ninety dollars a month. By 1924, he was the team's regular centerfielder.

Bell's career in professional African American baseball lasted over twenty-eight years. The bulk of his tenure was spent with three prominent teams, the Saint Louis Stars, the Pittsburgh Crawfords, and the Homestead Grays. All three teams won multiple Negro League world championships.

The combination of good bat control and incredible running speed allowed Bell to post a high batting average every season. He never batted below .300 in Negro League baseball, posting personal records of .362 with the Saint Louis Stars in 1926, .362 with the Pittsburgh Crawfords in 1933, and .396 with the Homestead Grays in 1946. Bell also won the Triple Crown while competing with Tampico of the Mexican League in 1940, batting .437 with twelve homeruns and seventy-nine runs batted in.

In 1937, Bell was a part of the famous team of Negro League all-stars put together by Satchel Paige to compete in the Dominican Republic. The dictator Raphael Trujillo sought to maintain power in the Caribbean country and believed a championship baseball team would help accomplish his goal. Trujillo paid Paige to assemble a team. Bell, along with numerous other African American stars, jumped at the high salaries offered by Trujillo. Upon arriving in the Dominican Republic, the players discovered that Trujillo had assigned armed guards to ensure that his team focused only on baseball. Bell played his part and batted .318 as the team won the championship and Trujillo maintained power.

Bell finished his career as a player and manager for a couple of minor league black teams. In 1951, the Saint Louis Browns of the American League offered Bell a contract. Well past his prime, Bell declined, but he

Baseball Teammates. Pittsburgh Crawfords outfielders Sammy Bankhead, Cool Papa Bell, and Sammy Crutchfield, c. 1930s. PHOTOGRAPHS AND PRINTS DIVISION, SCHOMBURG CENTER FOR RESEARCH IN BLACK CULTURE, THE NEW YORK PUBLIC LIBRARY, ASTOR, LENOX AND TILDEN FOUNDATIONS

accepted a part-time job as a scout. He held this position until the team moved in 1954. After baseball, he worked as a custodian and night security officer for the Saint Louis City Hall. In 1974, Bell was elected to the National Baseball Hall of Fame. Bell died in his home on Dickson Street in Saint Louis, Missouri; he was eighty-seven years old. The city renamed Dickson Street "James 'Cool Papa' Bell Avenue" after his death.

[*See also* Baseball.]

BIBLIOGRAPHY

Peterson, Robert. *Only the Ball Was White: A History of Legendary Black Players and All-Black Professional Teams*. New York: Oxford University Press, 1992. One of the first and best studies of Negro League baseball.

Ribowsky, Mark. *A Complete History of the Negro Leagues: 1884–1955*. Secaucus, N.J.: Carol Publishing Group, 1995. One of the most comprehensive studies of the Negro Leagues.

Riley, James A. *The Biographical Encyclopedia of the Negro Baseball Leagues*. New York: Carroll & Graff, 2002. An outstanding reference tool on Negro League baseball players and teams.

—ROB FINK

BELL, DERRICK (b. 6 November 1930), law professor, writer, and theoretical pioneer in critical race theory, narrative scholarship, and the economic-determinist approach to race history. As a student and professor of law, Derrick Bell pioneered critical race theory as a tool to explain and challenge the centrality of an apparently immutable racism that permeates every aspect of U.S. society. Bell sees this amorphous yet unremitting racism as essential to the maintenance of the U.S. socioeconomic order. His perspective derives from his personal experience coming of age in an era marked by global struggles for liberation. In his essay "Great Expectations" he vividly describes the effect of government policies on black Americans:

> If the nation's policies towards blacks were revised to require weekly, random round-ups of several hundred blacks who were then taken to a secluded place and shot, that policy would be more dramatic, but hardly different in result, than the policies now in effect, which most of us feel powerless to change. (p. 806)

After high school, Bell—born Derrick A. Bell Jr. in Pittsburgh, Pennsylvania—attended Duquesne University in western Pennsylvania. There he joined the Reserve Officer Training Corps (ROTC), and following his graduation in 1952 he went to Korea as part of the U.S. Air Force. He returned in 1954 and enrolled at the University of Pittsburgh Law School, where he earned his degree in 1957. Having distinguished himself there, Bell accepted a position in the Civil Rights Division of the U.S. Justice Department. When he refused to relinquish his membership in the NAACP he was implicitly encouraged to leave the department and did so in 1959.

At the invitation of Thurgood Marshall, Bell joined the NAACP Legal Defense and Educational Fund, where he oversaw three hundred school desegregation cases. In 1969 Bell accepted a position as the first black member of Harvard University's law school, where in 1971 he became the first tenured African American. While on sabbatical leave from Harvard in 1981, Bell accepted a position as dean of the law school at the University of Oregon; he resigned this position in 1985 when the university prevented him from hiring an Asian American woman. He returned to Harvard but resigned his position in 1992 over the school's evident inability to hire a black woman to the faculty.

Bell has authored numerous books and articles, notably *Faces at the Bottom of the Well: The Permanence of Racism* (1992), which remains a mainstay among law school texts, and *Silent Covenants: "Brown v. Board of Education" and the Unfulfilled Hopes for Racial Reform* (2004). Since 1991 Bell has been a visiting professor at New York University School of Law, and in the early twenty-first century he remained among the most sought-after spokespersons concerning issues of race, law, and social justice.

[*See also* Educators and Academics; Legal Profession; Race, Theories of; *and* Racism.]

BIBLIOGRAPHY

Bell, Derrick. *The Derrick Bell Reader*. Edited by Richard Delgado and Jean Stefancic. New York: New York University Press, 2005. The most comprehensive collection of Bell's work, spanning his intellectual career.

Bell, Derrick. "Great Expectations: Defining the Divide between Blacks and Jews" (1994). In *Strangers and Neighbors: Relations between Blacks and Jews in the United States*, edited by Maurianne Adams and John H. Bracey, pp. 802–812. Amherst: University of Massachusetts Press, 1999. A brilliant and brief overview of Bell's politics and perspectives, usually applied to law, directed here toward the specifics of the relationship betweens Jews and people of African descent.

—JARED A. BALL

BELTON, SHARON SAYLES (b. 13 May 1951), politician and human relations advocate. In November 1993 Sayles Belton made history as the first African American and first female elected mayor of Minneapolis, Minnesota. A native of Minneapolis, she was born Sharon Sayles, the daughter of Bill Sayles, the city's first African American car salesman, and Marian Sayles. After her parents divorced, Sayles Belton lived briefly with her mother. Marian Sayles moved to Cleveland, and Sayles Belton then lived with her father and stepmother. During her high school years she volunteered as a candy striper, that is, a nurse's assistant, an experience that exposed her to human suffering.

Sayles Belton attended Macalester College in Saint Paul, Minnesota. She continued to do volunteer work, registering African Americans to vote in Jackson, Mississippi. She became pregnant during her senior year, and her daughter was born with brain damage. Unmarried and unemployed, Sayles Belton dropped out of school and was briefly on public assistance. She eventually got a job as a parole officer, and with the help and support of her family, she completed her college education while remaining active in the community.

Sayles Belton's political career began to take shape during her years as a parole officer. She actively worked to provide support systems for abused women and children. She cofounded the Harriet Tubman Shelter for Battered Women in 1978, the first refuge of its kind in Minneapolis. She was also a cofounder of the National Coalition against Sexual Assault and was elected its president in 1981 (the coalition is now defunct). She served as director of the Minnesota Program for Victims of Sexual Assault in 1983. During her tenure, twenty-six rape crisis centers were opened.

In 1984 Sayles Belton became the first African American elected to the Minneapolis City Council. In 1989 she was elected president of the council, a position she held until her election as mayor. Sayles Belton served as mayor of Minneapolis, a city that is almost 80 percent white, from 1994 to 2001. She focused her energies on reducing crime, expanding the city's economy by recruiting new businesses, and providing housing and job training for low-income families. During her years on the council Sayles Belton earned a reputation as a consensus builder and bridge builder as well as a good listener. She was defeated in her bid for a third term in 2001.

Sayles Belton was the 1997 recipient of the Rosa Parks Award, given by the American Association for Affirmative Action. The National Bar Association honored her with the Gertrude E. Rush Distinguished Service Award in 1998. In 2002 she received the Joan and Walter Mondale Award for Public Service and a doctor of humane letters from Walden University.

Sayles Belton is a senior fellow at the Roy Wilkins Center for Human Relations and Social Justice, a division of the Hubert H. Humphrey Institute of Public Affairs at the University of Minnesota, Minneapolis. Her areas of expertise include women's issues, family and children's issues, antiracism initiatives, police-community relations, community and neighborhood development, public policy development, and public leadership.

[*See also* Minnesota; Public Assistance; *and* Women.]

BIBLIOGRAPHY

Biography Resource Center. Sharon Sayles Belton. Biographical sketch, career assessment and list of articles on Sayles Belton. http://galenet.galegroup.com.

Carey, Charles W., Jr. *African-American Political Leaders*. New York: Facts on File, 2004. African-American History Online. Biographical sketch. http://www.fofweb.com.

—THERESA W. BENNETT-WILKES

BENEVOLENT SOCIETIES. Throughout its history the black community in the United States has been faced with the daunting task of improving the economic and social status of its members in a society pervaded by racism. Black Americans, like other groups in American society, were determined to solve this problem by taking matters into their own hands. In developing self-help programs they both used already existing agencies, such as schools and churches, and also established new ones, such as mutual aid societies and business leagues. From Reconstruction to the 1930s, black churches, fraternal orders, and mutual aid societies were a chief resource that ensured the social, economic, and academic endurance of many black families.

Throughout the nineteenth century churches had been an important venue for the social and cultural life of African Americans. Pressured by an increasingly progressive membership, many churches started to spawn agencies of self-help around the turn of the century. Not only did churches promote education through Bible reading and literary societies, but their members also established missions in the slums, worked in jails, and ran orphanages and homes for the elderly. Black churches started to serve their communities by opening nurseries, music schools, and schools for domestic training, or by establishing employment bureaus, homes for working girls, and women's welfare leagues. During the Progressive Era these institutions of black benevolence contributed greatly to improving the conditions in urban communities.

The rapid growth of fraternal orders and benefit associations also attested to the black struggle for social self-sufficiency. The leaders of these groups advocated a gospel of money and morality, education and family, racial solidarity and self-help. Thus African Americans joined lodges and orders such as the Masons and the Odd Fellows and organizations such as the Knights of Pythias and the Knights of Tabor in considerable numbers. Black women became members of the Household of Ruth—the women's auxiliary of the Odd Fellows—the Sisters of Pythias, or the Order of the Eastern Star, which was open to both women and men. These secret orders and others, such as the Ancient Sons of Israel, the International Order of Good Samaritans, and the Independent

Order of Saint Luke, provided not only the venues for social intercourse often denied to African Americans but also cash benefits to members for family burial expenses, insurance against sickness and death, and aid to the widows and orphans of deceased members.

Large and nationally prominent black fraternal orders like the United Order of True Reformers went beyond this. The members of the True Reformers pooled their funds to buy real estate, a farm, and a hotel, and they established an insurance fund to provide for the support of widows and the education of orphans of their deceased members. In 1889 the order founded the first black chartered bank in the United States, the True Reformers' Savings Bank of Richmond, Virginia. By 1907 the deposits of this bank amounted to $1 million, but the bank collapsed three years later. Like many fraternal orders the True Reformers dissolved during the Great Depression. Others, like the Black Elks, operated into the twenty-first century.

Often the meeting halls of black fraternal orders also functioned as the center of black business operations and as cultural venues for concerts, plays, carnival balls, dances, and other social events. They were also intended to exhibit the skills of African American architects and craftsmen. True Reformer Hall in Washington, D.C., for example, was a stately five-story building that housed retail space, offices, a dance hall, and an armory for Washington's black National Guard unit.

Mutual benefit societies also existed outside the secret orders. In the South many such societies were started at Emancipation, when African Americans had no health or burial insurance. Organizations like the Young Mutual Society of Augusta, Georgia, founded in 1886, or the Beneficial Association of Petersburg, Virginia, founded in 1893, remained relatively small and local; other black self-help organizations like the Workers Mutual Aid Association of Virginia, founded in 1894, boasted a membership of more than four thousand at the turn of the century. Typically these organizations imposed high weekly dues but served as important business training grounds.

Many black insurance companies had their roots in mutual aid societies. Both the National Benefit Life Insurance Company in Washington, D.C., and the North Carolina Mutual Life Insurance Company were founded by former members of the True Reformers. These businesses were founded for economic, rather than social, purposes, and they flourished because many white companies were reluctant to insure African Americans. On the other hand, most banks that were closely connected to black fraternal orders or churches were rather short-lived because they rarely developed the trading volume necessary to sustain such an enterprise.

Black college fraternities and sororities started to form early in the twentieth century. Among the most important fraternities are Alpha Phi Alpha, established in 1906 at Cornell University; Kappa Alpha Psi, established in 1911 at Indiana University in Bloomington; Omega Psi Phi, established in 1911 at Howard University; and Phi Beta Sigma, established in 1914 at Howard University. Among the most important black sororities are Alpha Kappa Alpha, established in 1908 at Howard University; Delta Sigma Theta, established in 1913 at Howard University; and Zeta Phi Beta, established in 1920 at Howard University.

Founded originally for ethnic fellowship, by the middle of the twentieth century these and other black Greek fraternities started to work for numerous social and philanthropic causes. Their members marched against lynching and segregation, participated in sit-ins, raised scholarship funds, and contributed money and volunteer hours to such groups as the NAACP, the National Urban League, the United Negro College Fund, and the Leadership Conference on Civil Rights. Many black leaders past and present have belonged to a black fraternity or sorority, among them Mary Church Terrell, W. E. B. Du Bois, Jesse Owens, Marian Anderson, Rosa Parks, Daisy Bates, Martin Luther King Jr., Thurgood Marshall, Adam Clayton Powell Jr., Andrew Young, Sharon Pratt Kelly, and Toni Morrison.

By the early twenty-first century the principle of black self-help was epitomized in the work of historically black orders and fraternities, as well as new nonprofit organizations like Links, the Circle Brotherhood Association, and the National Organization of Concerned Black Men, which were all committed to better education, health, and economic opportunities for the African American community.

[*See also* Banks, African American–Owned; Fraternal Organizations, African American; Fraternities, University and College; Insurance Companies, African American–Owned; *and biographical entries on figures mentioned in this article*.]

BIBLIOGRAPHY

Brown, Tamara L., Gregory S. Parks, and Clarenda M. Phillips, eds. *African American Fraternities and Sororities: The Legacy and the Vision*. Lexington: University Press of Kentucky, 2005. A collection of original essays offering a comprehensive overview of the historical, cultural, political, and social circumstances that led to the creation of black Greek-letter organizations.

Fahey, David M. *The Black Lodge in White America: "True Reformer" Browne and His Economic Strategy*. Lanham, Md.: University Press of America, 1994. A biography of William Washington Browne, the founder of the United Order of True Reformers.

Franklin, John Hope, and Alfred A. Moss Jr. *From Slavery to Freedom: A History of African Americans*. 8th ed. New York: Alfred A. Knopf,

2000. The chapter "Philanthropy and Self-Help" provides the historical context for the emergence of black self-help organizations.

Weare, Walter B. *Black Business in the New South: A Social History of the North Carolina Mutual Life Insurance Company*. Urbana: University of Illinois Press, 1973.

—Anja Schüler

BENGA, OTA (b. 1881[?]; d. 21 March 1916), African "Pygmy" who was put on display at the Bronx Zoo. In 1904, the white missionary Samuel Phillips Verner brought Ota Benga, whose freedom he had purchased with a bribe to Belgian Congo officials, and seven other Congolese Pygmies to the Saint Louis World's Fair as part of an ethnological exhibit of primitive peoples, which included, among others, the Native American Apache chief Geronimo. Verner's agreement with the World's Fair required him to bring several Africans and as much of their village intact as possible. He actually brought fewer tribesmen than his contract required and many fewer artifacts, but the exhibit was one of the most popular attractions at the fair. The Africans were the objects of constant public attention, and they also drew the interest of professional and academic ethnologists, who measured the physical and mental characteristics of the Pygmies, concluding that they were inferior in virtually every way to Anglo Americans.

By the time of the Saint Louis World's Fair, Verner had served several years as a Presbyterian missionary in Africa. He quickly had discovered that white American audiences had a fascination with African peoples and artifacts, and he aggressively pursued the World's Fair to subsidize his African contingent. His efforts paid off with a contract of $8,500 for salary and expenses. Thereafter, Verner continued to press museums (including the Smithsonian), and ultimately the Bronx Zoo, to either hire him as an expert or purchase his private collection of Africana. Verner returned his exhibited Pygmies to the Congo, but Benga, whose village had previously been destroyed and his family killed, elected to stay with his missionary companion, even though it meant living in the United States.

When Ota Benga arrived in New York in 1906 for his second visit to the United States, Verner had already approached the New York Museum of Natural History, the Smithsonian, and the Bronx Zoo about the possibility of selling either his African expertise, his personal collection of Africana, or both. In early August 1906, he left Benga with the director of the American Museum of Natural History in New York while he traveled alone to the Smithsonian in Washington, D.C., to press his case. For the next few weeks, Ota Benga was a literal guest at the museum, where he ate, slept, and wandered about, virtually at will. But he soon grew restive, and Verner, now facing imminent bankruptcy, was forced to return to New York, dispose of his collection, and find a new home for Benga. The Museum of Natural History, eager to be rid of both Verner and Benga, had contacted the New York Zoological Garden (more popularly called the Bronx Zoo) and its director, William Temple Hornaday, about the possibility of transferring Benga and Verner's artifacts to his institution.

Hornaday was fascinated with the potential of an exhibit featuring a primitive man. He reasoned, accurately as it turned out, that such an attraction would significantly increase attendance at the zoo and place the Zoological Garden on the scientific and entertainment map. After several days of allowing Benga free access to the grounds of the zoo, Hornaday persuaded his African guest to make his home in the primate house, mostly in the company of a Southeast Asian orangutan. He also wrote an article in the zoo's newsletter announcing the acquisition of Ota Benga and the opening of a new exhibit where Benga could be seen by zoo patrons. The public responded with enthusiasm rivaling that at the Saint Louis World's Fair two years earlier. Ota Benga's first day in front of crowds was 8 September 1906. Hornaday had given him a bow and arrow with which to entertain the spectators and a ball of twine to show his skill in weaving. He was dressed in street clothes—although without shoes—and occasionally sipped a bottle of soda. The sign on his cage gave his height at 4 feet 11 inches, his weight as 103 pounds, and his age as 23. This same sign announced that Benga would be "exhibited each afternoon during September." On the second day, the orangutan and Benga wrestled and played games, and, by that time, Director Hornaday had added a parrot and assorted bones to the exhibit in an apparent attempt to lend a note of African authenticity. An estimated forty thousand people per day came to see Ota Benga at the Bronx Zoo; he was a smash hit.

But he was also at the center of raging controversy. Almost immediately a group of African American ministers denounced the exhibit as degrading and insulting to black people. As the Reverend James Gordon, the superintendent of the Howard Colored Orphan Asylum in Brooklyn put it, "our race is depressed enough without exhibiting one of us with apes . . . We think we are worthy of being considered human beings with souls." R. MacArthur of the Calvary Baptist Church complained that "the person responsible for this exhibit degrades himself as much as he does the African." The New York mayor George McClellan refused to meet with the outraged clergymen, but their protest led to the scrapping of the exhibition after a few days. On 27 September 1906, Ota Benga left the zoo and entered Gordon's orphanage, where he stayed for much of the next four years. But Benga was considerably older than the other orphans—he had been married with children in the Congo—and Gordon was never comfortable with Benga's close contact with the girls in the orphanage. After at least one sexual encounter with one of these girls, Gordon had Benga transferred to the orphanage's farm on Long Island, but this too proved unsatisfactory. Gordon eventually provided for a permanent home for Ota Benga at the Lynchburg Baptist Seminary in Virginia, where he learned some English and converted to Christianity. He was employed briefly at a local tobacco factory and later at several odd jobs, and for a time he attempted to acculturate himself into southern society. He had little success, and he experienced frequent cultural frustration outside the seminary grounds. On 21 March 1916, Ota Benga took his own life with a stolen pistol. Meanwhile, Verner, who had managed to elude bankruptcy through business interests in Panama, returned to the United States in 1922 to become a superintendent of schools in North Carolina.

[*See also* Eugenics Movement.]

BIBLIOGRAPHY

Bradford, Phillips Verner, and Harvey Blume. *Ota: The Pygmy in the Zoo*. New York: St. Martin's Press, 1992. This peculiar volume, part family history and part history of American fascination with Africa at the turn of the twentieth century, is the only full-length study of the Ota Benga episode. The title is misleading; most of the book is actually about Samuel Phillips Verner, the eccentric Presbyterian missionary who brought Benga and other Africans to the United States.

Lindfors, Bernth, ed. *Africans on Stage: Studies in Ethnological Show Business*. Bloomington and Indianapolis: Indiana University Press, 1999. Lindfors has assembled a volume of separately authored essays that make it painfully clear that the Ota Benga story was not an isolated event. Unfortunately, the piece about Benga is more about P. T. Barnum than about Ota Benga.

—CHARLES ORSON COOK

BENNETT, GWENDOLYN (b. 8 July 1902; d. 30 May 1981), poet, artist, illustrator, teacher, and journalist. (Some of her works appear under Gwendolyn Bennett Jackson and Gwendolyn Bennett Crosscup.) Bennett was the daughter of Joshua R. Bennett and Mayme F. Abernathy, teachers on a Nevada Native American reservation. She was born in Giddings, Texas, and later lived in Pennsylvania, Florida, and New York. When Bennett's parents divorced, she moved to New York with her stepmother and father. She was married to Alfred Jackson, a physician (1928) and then to Richard Crosscup, a teacher (1941). She had no children.

As an African American poet, artist, illustrator, teacher, and journalist, Bennett contributed significantly to the Harlem Renaissance (an African American artistic movement) and to U.S. history and culture. She attended fine arts classes at Columbia University (1921), at Pratt Institute (1924), and in France (1925). She taught watercolor, crafts, and design at Howard University in Washington, D.C., and at Tennessee State University. She also won awards, including a Delta Sigma Theta Sorority Fellowship (1925) and a Barnes Foundation Fellowship (1928). While Bennett was still an undergraduate, her poem "Nocturne" was published in *The Crisis* (November 1923) and "Heritage" was accepted by *Opportunity* (December 1923). She was also the author of "The Ebony Flute," a literary column in *Opportunity*. Bennett has no collected volume of her verse, but her other works appeared in *Palms*, *Gypsy*, William Stanley Braithwaite's *Anthology of Magazine Verse* (1927), *Yearbook of American Poetry* (1927), and *The Book of American Negro Poetry* (1931). She also published two short stories: "Wedding Day" in *Fire!!* (1926) and "Tokens" in Charles S. Johnson's *Ebony and Topaz* (1927).

Most of Bennett's works, especially "Heritage" and "To a Dark Girl," illustrate her pride in the African tradition and African American history and culture. The poems demonstrate her consciousness of the political, social, and economic inequalities around her. Other themes in her poems deal with nature, love, death, and romance. Through her writing and activities, she facilitated the formation of the Black Arts Movement in the 1960s and 1970s.

She also influenced her well-known colleagues, such as the painter Aaron Douglas and the writers Langston Hughes and Countée Cullen. She was determined to preserve the cultural and social integrity of black artists and worked tirelessly on behalf of the Harlem Artists Guild, the National Negro Congress, the Artists Union, and the Negro People's Theater. She served on the board of directors of the Negro Playwrights Company. In the 1940s she gave a series of lectures on African American arts at the School for Democracy. Subsequently, she was suspended from the Harlem Community Art Center by the U.S. House Un-American Activities Committee (HUAC) for sympathizing with leftist ideas. She then co-founded the George Carver Community School, but it was closed in 1947, after the HUAC accused it too of communist biases. She retired in the late 1960s and moved with her husband to Kutztown, Pennsylvania, where she opened an antiques store. She died in 1981 of heart disease.

[*See also* Black Arts Movement *and* Harlem Renaissance.]

BIBLIOGRAPHY

Benbow-Pfalzgraf, Taryn, ed. *American Women Writers: A Critical Reference Guide: From Colonial Times to the Present*. 2d ed., vol. 1. Detroit: St. James Press, 2000. Recounts the life and works of American women from colonial days to the present.

Contemporary Black Biography. Vol. 59. Thomson Gale, 2007. Reproduced in *Biography Resource Center*. Farmington Hills,

Mich.: Gale, 2008. http://galenet.galegroup.com/servlet/BioRC Profiles internationally known individuals active in a wide variety of fields.

Garraty, John A., and Mark C. Carnes, eds. *American National Biography*, vol. 2, New York: Oxford University Press, 1999. A source of historical American biography, it offers portraits of men and women whose lives have shaped the nation. All figures included in the *ANB* died before 1996.

Riggs, Thomas, ed. *St. James Guide to Black Artists*. Detroit: St. James Press, 1997. Compiles information on artists of African descent. Its main focus is on twentieth-century artists, but it also includes a few selected nineteenth-century artists. Most of the artists are of African American origin, but the rest are from Africa, the Caribbean, and other parts of the diaspora.

—MAUD C. MUNDAVA

BENNETT, LERONE (b. 17 October 1928), author, editor at *Ebony* magazine for more than fifty years, and popular historian of African American history. Lerone Bennett Jr. was born in Clarksdale, Mississippi, on 17 October 1928 to Lerone Bennett Sr. and Alma Reed. He grew up in Jackson, Mississippi, and graduated from Morehouse College in Georgia in 1949. He became a journalist for the *Atlanta Daily World* that same year. Four years later he joined *Jet* in Chicago as associate editor, and the next year he moved to *Ebony* as associate editor. He moved up the editorial ranks at *Ebony*, becoming senior editor in 1958. In 1987 he became executive editor. While at *Ebony*, Bennett also continued to write, and the magazine published his articles on African American history.

Bennett collected his early articles for his first book, *Before the* Mayflower: *A History of the Negro in America, 1619–1962* (1962); it has since gone through many editions. This book became a popular book of history: it helped a large audience discover that African Americans do have a history and that this history has shaped current conditions in the community. Bennett continued writing widely on the role of African Americans in American history, producing a number of books on the African American experience, including *What Manner of Man: A Biography of Martin Luther King, Jr.* (1964), *Pioneers in Protest* (1968), *The Shaping of Black America* (1975), and *Wade in the Water: Great Moments in Black History* (1979).

Bennett's reception as a popular historian has been great, and he has received numerous honors for his work. These include the Literature Award of the Academy of Arts and Letters, the Book of the Year Award from Capital Press Club, and the Patron Saints Award from the Society of Midland Authors. Additionally, many groups have called upon him to advise them on African American issues, including the National Advisory Commission on Civil Disorders.

Bennett's reception as a serious historian, however, has not been so universal. Professional historians have taken issue with many of his writings. Indeed, although professional historians have differed with Bennett on other issues, his views of Lincoln as a white supremacist have come under particular attack. Lucas Morel writes in his scathing review of Bennett's *Forced into Glory: Abraham Lincoln's White Dream* (2000): "Bennett's exercise in exasperation over Lincoln as the Great Emancipator displays his woeful ignorance about the principles and practices of American self-government."

Eric Foner's review of this book was more temperate, though he, too, had serious differences with Bennett. Foner notes that Bennett is "not an academic historian," but that his books are "popular history at its best," reaching a broad audience. Noting Bennett's accomplishments and the role that he played in alerting people to problems with Lincoln's sainted image, Foner argues that Bennett does not understand how Lincoln could be both one who shared the racist ideas of his time and one who also opposed slavery. Although Lincoln was neither an abolitionist nor a Radical Republican and held typical mid-nineteenth-century racist views, he was also a person who demonstrated significant moral growth. As Foner concluded, "If America ever hopes to resolve its racial dilemmas, we need to repudiate the worst of Lincoln, while embracing the best."

[*See also Ebony*; *Jet*; *and* Lincoln, Abraham, in African American Memory.]

BIBLIOGRAPHY

Foner, Eric. Review of *Forced into Glory: Abraham Lincoln's White Dream*, by Lerone Bennett Jr. *Los Angeles Times Book Review*, 9 April 2000. http://www.ericfoner.com/reviews/040900latimes.html.

McCain, Robert Stacy. "Black Historian Documents Lincoln's Racism." *Washington Times*, 26 May 2000.

Morel, Lucas E. "Forced into Gory Lincoln Revisionism." *Claremont Review of Books*, Fall 2000. http://www.claremont.org/publications/crb/id.749/article_detail.asp.

—FRANK A. SALAMONE

BERRY, CHUCK (b. 18 October 1926), rock-and-roll pioneer. Chuck Berry is truly the father of rock and roll. His vibrant songwriting, innovative guitar playing, and live performances inspired legions of followers, and he was the single most important figure in defining a new genre that mixed country and rhythm and blues.

Charles Edward Anderson Berry was born to Henry William Berry Sr., a carpenter, and Martha Bell Banks, a housewife, in Saint Louis, Missouri, in 1926. The family belonged to a Baptist church, and Berry's earliest memories were of his parents singing gospel songs around the house. His first try at show business, singing "Confessin' the Blues" to a friend's guitar accompaniment at a high school talent show, inspired him to play guitar.

While still in high school in Saint Louis he left for a trip to California with two friends. When their money ran low, they robbed a few small businesses and were arrested after stealing a car. After pleading guilty and cooperating with the police, Berry was sentenced to the maximum of ten years. He spent three years in Algoa prison and was released in 1947 at the age of twenty-one.

He married Themetta Suggs on 28 October 1948. They raised a family while he held jobs as an autoworker, janitor, and hairstylist, as well as working for his father as a carpenter.

In 1952 he joined the Sir John Trio as guitarist and performed blues, country-and-western, and Nat King Cole tunes in the clubs of East Saint Louis. In order to distinguish himself he started to develop his physical stage act, making gestures and facial expressions to emphasize lyrics.

During a trip to Chicago in 1955 he met his idol, the legendary bluesman Muddy Waters, after a nightclub performance. Waters referred him to the Chess Records label. After playing some of his homemade recordings for Leonard Chess, Chuck Berry was signed to a contract and set for a recording session on 21 May 1955.

In the session Chess rejected his song title "Ida Red" as sounding too country and renamed it "Maybellene." Consistent with the payola practices of the day, the disc jockey Alan Freed's name was added to the song's composer credits, which secured the airplay that got the song exposed to white audiences. Set to a hopped-up country beat, "Maybellene" contained a ripping guitar solo that epitomized the sound of a new generation. It became a Top Ten Billboard hit that launched Berry's career and helped usher in a new era in popular music.

Berry became an energetic entertainer noted for his squatting trademark "duck walk." His song lyrics were well-written odes to universal teenage themes of dancing, fast cars, and school, while his music contained an instantly recognizable lead guitar style that alternated with propulsive piano. The sound broke down racial barriers as he became one of the first black performers to appeal to white teenagers.

The across-the-board appeal of "Maybellene" catapulted Berry into the spotlight and put him in demand across the country. Freed used him for his rock-and-roll shows at the Brooklyn Paramount and Fox theaters, where Berry played mainly to white audiences. Appearances followed in the movies *Rock, Rock, Rock* (1956) and *Go, Johnny, Go!* (1959) and on television shows such as Dick Clark's *American Bandstand.* During his peak years of 1955 to 1959, Berry churned out the hit records "Roll Over Beethoven," "Reelin' and Rockin'," "Sweet Little Sixteen," and "Johnny B. Goode," which would become rock-and-roll standards.

Chuck Berry. Rock-and-roll guitarist Chuck Berry at the Chicago Blues Festival, 2001. Photograph by Michael Jackson.

Like others of his era Berry was shorted on songwriting royalties and swindled by unscrupulous managers and concert promoters, but the experience served him well as he took over the business aspects of his career. He invested his earnings in real estate in Saint Louis, opening Club Bandstand in 1958 (where black and white teenagers were permitted to dance together), and he later built an amusement park.

The racial prejudices of the pre–civil rights era soon ensnared him. After a concert in Meridian, Mississippi, in 1959, Berry was charged with disturbing the peace because a white girl kissed him during the show. He reversed on appeal a 1960 conviction for violations of the Mann Act, a law that prohibited transporting minors across state lines for immoral purposes, but he was convicted of similar charges in 1961. Sentenced to three years in federal prison, he served less than two, spending his time getting his high school diploma and writing songs that would later become hits.

By the time he was released in 1963, British bands had started their invasion of the U.S. market. This phenomenon breathed new life into his career, as early Rolling Stones and Beatles albums contained versions of his songs. The Beach Boys reworked his songs into hits of their own, while Berry hit the charts again with "Nadine," "No Particular Place to Go," and "You Never Can Tell."

Throughout the 1960s and into the 1970s Berry continued his constant worldwide touring, using different pickup bands in each city. This practice caused his reputation to suffer, as audiences complained about sloppy performances. In 1971 he hit the charts again with the novelty song "My Ding-a-Ling," but by 1979 he spent three months in jail for tax evasion. In the 1980s Berry released his autobiography, was inducted into the Rock and Roll Hall of Fame, and was the subject of a full-length movie, *Hail! Hail! Rock 'n' Roll*. The 1987 film was based on a sixtieth-birthday concert of his hits performed at the Fox Theatre in Saint Louis, a place that had once denied him admittance because of his skin color.

Berry's estate was raided in 1990 by the U.S. Drug Enforcement Administration; although drugs and pornographic films were seized, the charges were later dismissed.

His song lyrics are the language of rock and roll, and his electric guitar playing provided the basic encyclopedia of rock guitar licks. A legend of American music, Chuck Berry's music put the beat into rock and roll.

[*See also* Music.]

BIBLIOGRAPHY

Berry, Chuck. *Chuck Berry: The Autobiography*. New York: Harmony Books, 1987.

Gillett, Charlie. *Sound of the City: The Rise of Rock and Roll*. 2d ed. New York: Da Capo Press, 1996. The standard volume for the history of rock and roll.

Pegg, Bruce. *Brown Eyed Handsome Man: The Life and Hard Times of Chuck Berry*. New York: Routledge, 2002.

Rolling Stone Magazine, eds. *The Rolling Stone Interviews: 1967–1980*. New York: St. Martin's Press, 1989.

—TIMOTHY J. O'BRIEN

BERRY, HALLE (b. 14 August 1966), actor. Halle Berry was born in Cleveland, Ohio, to Jerome Berry, an African American hospital attendant, and Judith Hawkins Berry, a white psychiatric nurse. Leaving an abusive relationship, Judith Berry moved Halle and her older sister Heidi to the Cleveland suburb of Bedford where, despite many racist attitudes, Halle flourished in high school.

In 1985 Berry won the Miss Teen All American pageant, in 1986 she was first runner-up in the Miss USA pageant, and also in 1986 she represented the United States in the Miss World competition in London. After her pageants she enrolled in Cleveland's Cuyahoga Community College to study broadcast journalism. She moved to Chicago and then to Manhattan, where she managed to get small roles in several television programs.

Berry first gained widespread recognition as Vivian, a crack addict, in Spike Lee's *Jungle Fever* (1991), and she won roles in *The Last Boy Scout* (1991), *Boomerang* (1992), and *The Flintstones* (1994). In *Losing Isaiah* (1995), Berry played Khaila, an illiterate drug addict who abandons her child in a garbage can. Critics charged Berry with exacerbating the problem of stereotyping black women as prostitutes and drug addicts in the television and film industry. She answered by capturing major roles in *Executive Decision* (1996), *BAPS* (1997), *Bulworth* (1998), and the television miniseries *The Wedding* (1998). In 1999 she starred in the HBO movie *Introducing Dorothy Dandridge*, for which she won a Golden Globe Award, a Screen Actors Guild Award, an NAACP Image Award, and an Emmy.

By 2000 Berry had gained marked success and had also overcome many obstacles in her personal life. She had been through abusive relationships, including one in which a man had beaten her so mercilessly that she lost part of her hearing in her left ear. In 1993 she met and married the Atlanta Braves outfielder David Justice, but after a rocky relationship the couple divorced in 1996. With much privacy, Berry married Eric Benét, a jazz musician, in 2001. They divorced in 2004, after which Berry stated that she would never marry again.

In February 2000, Berry was involved in a hit-and-run accident that erupted into a tabloid scandal. However, Berry worked through the controversy and was featured as Storm in *X-Men* (2000), the major motion picture adapted from the Marvel Comics series. In 2001 she co-starred with John Travolta as Ginger in the action movie *Swordfish*, for which Berry earned $2.5 million. She filmed a topless scene but defended her nudity as an opportunity for a black actress to play a major role that had been traditionally off-limits.

In March 2002, at the seventy-fourth Academy Awards, Berry made history when she became the first African American woman to win an Oscar for best actress. Her performance in *Monster's Ball* also garnered the Screen Actors Guild Award, the National Board of Review Award, the Silver Berlin Bear at the Berlin Film Festival, and a nomination for a Golden Globe. Though her role was again controversial, in her Oscar acceptance speech she hailed the award as a victory for black women like Dorothy Dandridge, Lena Horne, and Diahann Carroll, who had come before her.

Halle Berry. The first African American woman to win an Oscar for best actress, Halle Berry accepts the award for her work in the film *Monster's Ball* at the Academy Awards in Los Angeles, 2002. Photograph by Kevork Djansezian. AP Images

Diagnosed with diabetes in 1989, Berry became a philanthropist for the Juvenile Diabetes Research Foundation, and she also supports the National Breast Cancer Coalition. She has a multimillion-dollar contract with Revlon and commands millions of dollars per movie. In 2002 she played Jinx in the James Bond movie *Die Another Day* and in 2004 starred as the coveted lead of *Catwoman*. Though she has thus far stuck to her vow never to remarry, in September 2007, at the age of forty-one, she announced her pregnancy with her boyfriend Gabriel Aubry.

[*See also* Actors and Actresses *and* Film and Television Depictions of African Americans.]

Bibliography

Farley, Christopher John. *Introducing Halle Berry: A Biography*. New York: Pocket Books, 2002.

Kenyatta, Kelly. *Red Hot Halle: The Story of an American Best Actress*. Chicago: W. H. Kelly, 2003.

—Stephanie Y. Evans

BERRY, MARY F. (b. 17 February 1938), civil rights activist, historian, and legal scholar. Mary Frances Berry was born in Nashville, Tennessee, one of three children of George and Frances Berry. Like many African Americans, Berry experienced racial segregation as well as poverty while growing up in the South. As children she and her older brother George were placed in an orphanage during a period of economic crisis.

At Nashville's segregated Pearl High School, Berry was encouraged by the educator Minerva Hawkins to apply herself seriously to her studies. After graduation Berry attended Fisk University and then transferred to Howard University, where she earned a BA in philosophy in 1961 and an MA in history in 1962. She continued her studies at the University of Michigan, where she earned a PhD in U.S. and constitutional history and a doctorate of jurisprudence.

As a scholar, Berry's numerous publications include *Black Resistance, White Law* (1971) and *Long Memory* (coauthored with John Blassingame, 1982); as an administrator she served as director of Afro-American studies at the University of Maryland. At the University of Colorado she became the first African American woman to hold the position of provost at a major research university. Berry taught history at numerous institutions including Howard University and the University of Pennsylvania, where she has been the Geraldine R. Segal Professor of American Social Thought and History.

Berry's career has demonstrated an enduring commitment to civil rights activism. She served as assistant secretary for education in the U.S. Department of Health, Education, and Welfare under President Jimmy Carter, who in 1980 appointed her to the U.S. Commission on Civil Rights. In 1984 President Ronald Reagan attempted to remove Berry from the civil rights commission because of their divergent political views; Berry went to court and successfully checked Reagan's attempt to unseat her. She became the first African American woman to act as the civil rights commission's chair after her appointment by President Bill Clinton in 1993. As a founding member of the Free South Africa Movement, she protested apartheid in South Africa. Berry's life stands as a testament to the philosophy of W. E. B. Du Bois, that the pursuit of knowledge must be wedded to activism.

[*See also* Antiapartheid; Historians; *and* Intellectuals.]

Bibliography

Berry, Mary F. *Black Resistance, White Law: A History of Constitutional Racism in America*. New York: Appleton-Century Crofts, 1971. Reprint, New York: Penguin, 1994.

Berry, Mary F. *The Pig Farmer's Daughter and Other Tales of American Justice: Episodes of Racism and Sexism in the Courts from 1865 to the Present*. New York: Alfred A. Knopf, 1999.

Berry, Mary F., and John W. Blassingame. *Long Memory: The Black Experience in America*. New York: Oxford University Press, 1982.
Meier, August, and Elliott Rudwick. *Black History and the Historical Profession, 1915–1980*. Urbana: University of Illinois Press, 1986.

—LUTHER ADAMS

BETHUNE, MARY MCLEOD (b. 10 July 1875; d. 18 May 1955), educator, feminist, and civil rights leader. Born near Maysville, South Carolina, Mary McLeod was the fifteenth of seventeen children born to two former slaves, Sam McLeod and Patsy (McIntosh). Most of her brothers and sisters had been born into slavery. The family was poor, but the McLeods farmed their own land. Patsy McLeod continued to work for her former owner, while her husband grew cotton and rice with the help of their children. As a young girl, Mary was known as an expert cotton picker who at the age of nine could pick 250 pounds per day. She also helped her mother deliver laundry to white families.

McLeod recognized early in life that the ability to read and write was central to improving the lives of African Americans. In the mid-1880s the Mission Board of the Presbyterian Church opened a school in Maysville for the children of former slaves, and Mary McLeod walked the five miles into town every day to attend; in her free time she taught her parents and siblings. She excelled as a student in the one-room schoolhouse and received a scholarship to attend Scotia Seminary (now Barber-Scotia College) near Concord, North Carolina, from 1888 to 1894.

After her graduation McLeod was awarded a scholarship to Dwight Moody's Institute for Home and Foreign Missions in Chicago; she was the only African American student there at the time. Her dream of going to Africa as a missionary proved impossible, and she instead returned to Maysville to become the assistant of her former teacher, Emma Jane Wilson, at the Presbyterian Mission School. Shortly thereafter McLeod received a one-year appointment to the Haines Normal and Industrial Institute in Augusta, Georgia; at Haines she not only gained experience in teaching a wide range of courses in a predominantly female setting but also organized a Sabbath school and helped set up a city hospital.

Early Educational Endeavors. In 1897 the Presbyterian Board assigned McLeod to Kendell Institute in Sumpter, South Carolina, where she continued to teach and serve the community. In Sumpter she met and married the former schoolteacher Albertus Bethune and subsequently moved to Savannah, Georgia, where she gave birth to their son, Albertus McLeod Bethune, in 1899. Also in 1899 Mary McLeod Bethune was offered the opportunity to start a school in Palatka, Florida, where she spent the next five years teaching and doing community service. She also sold life insurance because her teacher's salary could not meet the living expenses of her family.

In 1904 she opened the Daytona Literary and Industrial School for Training Negro Girls in Daytona, Florida, with five pupils. Bethune kept her school solvent by charging tuition (fifty cents per week) for those who could afford it, taking in boarders, selling chicken dinners and pies, and soliciting funds from northern philanthropists and wealthy Florida tourists. The school expanded rapidly and enrolled 250 students only two years after its creation. In 1907 it moved into a permanent facility and ultimately grew to a thirty-two-acre campus with fourteen buildings and four hundred students.

Also in 1907 Bethune's marriage failed, and the couple separated. Bethune remained president of her institution until 1942, when bad health forced her to resign. In 1923 her school merged with the Cookman Institute, a Methodist school for black boys, to become Bethune-Cookman College, a move that ensured the financial health of the institution. Bethune was a gifted teacher guided by deep religious beliefs, a remarkable community leader with deft organizational skills, a brilliant speaker, and as untiring a fund-raiser as Booker T. Washington.

Both Bethune and Washington held educational philosophies based on Christian virtue and focused on teacher education, industrial and domestic training, and good manners. This philosophy proved to be a divisive issue among black leaders and remained so for many years. Bethune, however, was not opposed to higher education for blacks, and during the New Deal she became the only black person to control financial resources that supported black college students.

A National Leader. In the second decade of the twentieth century Mary McLeod Bethune emerged as an African American leader, first locally, then nationally. In Daytona she worked on a number of community issues, most notably the effort to keep the county dry. In 1912 she joined the Equal Suffrage League, a member organization of the National Association of Colored Women's Clubs, and associated with leaders of Daytona's most influential white women's association, the Palmetto Club.

After women were enfranchised in 1920, in a door-to-door fund-raising effort Bethune collected money to help people pay the poll taxes, a form of direct per capita taxation that effectively disfranchised much of the cash-poor rural population of the South—and thereby most blacks. She also taught classes to prepare Daytona blacks for the literacy test. Her voter drives resulted in a confrontation with the Ku Klux Klan, from which she emerged as a black civil rights leader known beyond her community.

School for Girls. Mary McLeod Bethune with girls from the Daytona Literary and Industrial School for Training Negro Girls, c. 1905. FLORIDA PHOTOGRAPHIC COLLECTION, STATE LIBRARY AND ARCHIVES OF FLORIDA

As the president of the Florida State Federation of Colored Women's Clubs, Bethune coordinated the activities of black women's clubs throughout the Southeast to fight against school segregation and for improved health-care facilities for black children, and she founded a rehabilitation home for delinquent black girls. In 1920 she was the only southern woman elected to the National Urban League's executive board. She also served on the Interracial Council and as president of the National Association of Teachers in Colored Schools.

In 1924 Bethune became the eighth president of the National Association of Colored Women's Clubs; during her four-year tenure the association acquired its national headquarters in Washington, D.C. Throughout her life Bethune was active in a number of national civil rights organizations, including the National Association for the Advancement of Colored People (NAACP), which awarded her its Spingarn Medal for Distinguished Services in 1935 and named her vice president in 1940. Bethune also served as vice president of the Commission on Interracial Cooperation and the National Urban League; in 1938 she was a cofounder of the Southern Conference for Human Welfare (SCHW), and she later worked for the Southern Conference Educational Fund, which the SCHW had set up.

In time Bethune was able to work for black education on a national level. She was soon considered an expert on black educational institutions. In 1928 she attended the Child Welfare Conference convened by President Calvin Coolidge, and she continued this work while on the National Commission for Child Welfare during President Herbert Hoover's administration. She also served as an adviser on black education and racial affairs to the Coolidge administration and later served on the Hoover Commission on Home Building and Home Ownership. Her growing involvement in these national commissions, as well as her reputation in the black women's club movement, facilitated her contacts with influential politicians both black and white, a circle that eventually included Eleanor and Franklin D. Roosevelt.

New Deal Politics. Mary McLeod Bethune received special support from Eleanor Roosevelt, who facilitated Bethune's appointment to federal agencies and helped her to raise funds for her college. Bethune also became acquainted with President Roosevelt, although she may have exaggerated the closeness of that relationship. As an eminent educator and feminist, Bethune became a member of the Federal Council on Negro Affairs—often referred to as President Roosevelt's "Black Cabinet"—an informal but influential group of black policy advisers.

During the Roosevelt administration Bethune received a number of federal appointments, first to the Planning Committee of the Office of Education of Negroes, and in

1936 to a more prominent position as director of the Division of Negro Affairs in the National Youth Administration (NYA), making Bethune the first black woman to head a federal agency; she headed the division until the NYA was abolished in 1943. As an NYA official she worked to resolve the problems that black youths had to contend with, problems that often resulted from discrimination and racism and were compounded by the Depression.

Though many of Bethune's public statements as NYA director revealed a moderate approach to race relations, her work consistently strove for equal representation of blacks in the NYA. Although the agency tacitly accepted racial separation in its programs, it did appoint black state and local supervisors (albeit with inequitable salaries) in districts with large black populations to ensure that young blacks profited from training and student work programs. Much of Bethune's success relied on her relationships with black and white administrators as well as with local communities. Like many other black leaders of the time, Bethune only rarely advanced desegregation policies in these federal programs, but she insisted on equal (if separate) consideration for blacks in NYA programs and demanded that national NYA officials overrule southern administrators.

Besides insisting on black supervisors for black projects, she also insisted on black participation in the policy making of the NYA and on training for blacks that went beyond menial jobs—all concepts that often met with resistance in southern states. As head of the Division of Negro Affairs, Bethune traveled frequently and visited black NYA programs in every state, programs that were often cosponsored by other black community agencies like the YMCA, high schools and colleges, and local branches of the Urban League.

In 1937 Bethune organized the federally sponsored National Conference on the Problems of the Negro and Negro Youth, considered the most important black meeting on civil rights. This put her firmly in the middle of the black consensus. The meeting addressed the most pivotal issues of the black community at the time and called for equal protection, improved health care and housing, adequate opportunities for education, and the end of discriminatory employment in federal projects. In 1941 Bethune joined A. Philip Randolph's March on Washington Movement.

She also continued her feminist work, founding the National Council of Negro Women (NCNW) in 1935 and presiding over the organization for fourteen years. The NCNW functioned as a clearinghouse for information concerning the activities of black women and dedicated itself to outlawing the poll tax, to eliminating lynching, to integrating the armed forces and government housing, and to developing public health programs. It also established ties with international institutions and with people around the world. In the 1930s and 1940s the NCNW approached a status comparable to that of other women's organizations in the nation's capital.

Activism during and after World War II. During World War II, Bethune continued to serve her country while at the same time opposing racism and racist policies. In 1942 she lobbied for the admission of black women into the Women's Army Auxiliary Corps (WAAC), and two years later she became the national commander of the Women's Army for National Defense, a newly founded all-black women's organization.

In 1945 Bethune was appointed as one of the black consultants to the constituent assembly of the United Nations in San Francisco, as a representative not of the NCWC, whose application had been turned down by the State Department, but of the NAACP. Together with W. E. B. Du Bois and Walter White, she supported the demands of African and Asian people for independence.

Bethune's childhood dream of visiting Africa was fulfilled in 1949 when she represented her nation at the inauguration of Liberia's president William V. S. Tubman. In the same year she became the first woman to receive Haiti's highest award, the Medal of Honor and Merit, an honor followed by the Star of Africa from the Republic of Liberia in 1952. In 1951 she served on President Harry S. Truman's Committee of Twelve for National Defense.

Bethune continued to work with a number of civic organizations, among them the Association of American Colleges and the League of Women Voters. At the same time, she was targeted for alleged connections to the Communist Party; the allegation was later ridiculed by Eleanor Roosevelt in her daily syndicated newspaper column "My Day." Bethune, too, authored syndicated newspaper columns, beginning in the 1930s when she reported on her NYA work in the *Pittsburgh Courier*. Starting in 1948 she contributed regularly to the *Chicago Defender*, covering domestic and foreign issues such as the political developments in Liberia and Haiti and the landmark Supreme Court decision in *Brown v. Board of Education* (1954).

It was important to Bethune—who had served as a trustee of Frederick Douglass's home in Washington, D.C.—that African Americans build and control viable autonomous institutions. In 1953 she established the Mary McLeod Bethune Foundation, a charitable and educational enterprise created to preserve her papers, establish scholarships for her school, and advance interracial goodwill. She envisioned interracial conferences with women of all classes and religious beliefs and hoped that her foundation would inspire young people to strive for racial equality and economic opportunity. Eleanor Roosevelt spoke at the gala dedication.

Mary McLeod Bethune, 1950s. Florida Photographic Collection, State Library and Archives of Florida

At the same time, Bethune had started to write her autobiography—which was never completed. Her papers can be found in the national headquarters of the two women's organizations that she headed, as well as in the National Archives, but the principal collection is with the Bethune Foundation at Bethune-Cookman College. Apart from diaries and personal correspondence, her papers consist primarily of NYA documents and records of the college. Bethune's former residence houses the collections and was designated a National Historic Landmark by the National Park Service in 1975.

Mary McLeod Bethune, the child of former slaves, lived to see the 1954 Supreme Court decision in *Brown v. Board of Education* that declared the "separate but equal" doctrine unconstitutional. In her weekly *Chicago Defender* column Bethune commented on *Brown*:

> There can be no divided democracy, no class-government, no half-free country, under the constitution. Therefore, there can be no discrimination, no segregation, no separation of some citizens from the rights that belong to all .... We are on our way. But these are the frontiers which we must conquer .... We must gain full equality in education, ... in the franchise, ... in economic opportunity, and full equality in the abundance of life.

Bethune died of a heart attack in Daytona Beach, Florida. Her legacy is one of interracial cooperation and the belief that what blacks in the United States needed most was increased educational and economic opportunity. Her life and work connected the social reform efforts of the post-Reconstruction era to the political protests that formed after World War II. She was the first African American—as well as the first woman—to be honored with a statue on public land in Washington, D.C., when the Mary McLeod Bethune Memorial was unveiled in 1974.

[*See also* Bethune-Cookman College; Black Cabinets; Education; Industrial Education Movement; National Association for the Advancement of Colored People; National Council of Negro Women; National Urban League; Roosevelt, Eleanor, and African Americans; Roosevelt, Franklin D., Administration of; Women; *and* Women's Clubs.]

Bibliography

Bennett, Carolyn LaBelle. *Annotated Bibliography of Mary McLeod Bethune's "Chicago Defender" Columns, 1948–1955*. Lewiston, N.Y.: Edwin Mellen Press, 2001.

Bethune, Mary McLeod. *Mary McLeod Bethune, Building a Better World: Essays and Selected Documents*. Edited by Audrey Thomas McCluskey and Elaine M. Smith. Bloomington: Indiana University Press, 1999.

Hanson, Joyce Ann. *Mary McLeod Bethune and Black Women's Political Activism*. Columbia: University Press of Missouri, 2003. The most comprehensive study of Bethune's life; examines her work and provides an understanding of the centrality of black women to the political fight for social, economic, and racial justice.

Holt, Rackham. *Mary McLeod Bethune: A Biography*. Garden City, N.Y.: Doubleday, 1964. A somewhat dated but still useful biography.

Ross, B. Joyce. "Mary McLeod Bethune and the National Youth Administration: A Case Study of Power Relationships in the Black Cabinet of Franklin D. Roosevelt." In *Black Leaders of the Twentieth Century*, edited by John Hope Franklin and August Meier, pp. 191–220. Urbana: University of Illinois Press, 1982. An in-depth look at Bethune's work for the Roosevelt administration.

Smith, Elaine M. "Bethune, Mary McLeod." In *Black Women in America*, edited by Darlene Clarke Hine, 2d ed., pp. 94–104. New York: Oxford University Press, 2005.

—Anja Schüler

BETHUNE-COOKMAN COLLEGE. Mary McLeod Bethune, a child of former slaves and a visionary educator, political adviser, and civil rights leader, opened the Daytona Educational and Industrial Training School for Negro Girls in October 1904 in a small, two-story house she rented for eleven dollars a month in Daytona Beach, Florida. A graduate of Maysville Presbyterian Mission School, Scotia Seminary, and the Moody Bible Institute, Bethune wanted to use her own education to serve society. The school she founded reflected Bethune's belief that education for African American girls had been ignored in the United States, and that universal education was the foundation of a democracy.

Five girls who each paid fifty cents a week and Bethune's own son made up the school's first student body. Students who could not afford to pay helped clean and repair the school. They used overturned boxes and crates for desks and chairs, charcoal for pencils, and crushed elderberries for ink. Bethune served as administrator, teacher, and custodian. To raise funds she and her students sold homemade pies and ice cream to area construction workers. Bethune also supported adults who wanted an education by offering night classes in a variety of subjects such as civics and civil rights. On Sundays the school offered lessons in African and African American history.

Bethune's school for girls became a coeducational high school in 1923 by merging with Cookman Institute of Jacksonville, Florida. In 1924 Bethune-Cookman affiliated itself with the Methodist Church. The school became Bethune-Cookman Junior College in 1931. Bethune retired from the presidency in 1941, by which time the Florida legislature had approved Bethune-Cookman College as a four-year baccalaureate degree–granting institution that offered both teacher training and a liberal arts education.

James A. Colston served as president from 1942 to 1946, at which time Bethune took over again for one year. Richard V. Moore Sr. became president in 1947, and it was under his leadership that the college was accredited by the Southern Association of Colleges and Schools (1970) and joined the United Negro College Fund. The fourth president of the college was Oswald P. Bronson, a Bethune-Cookman alumnus who served from 1975 to 2004. Under Bronson's leadership both the physical plant and major offerings increased.

Bethune-Cookman's motto is "Enter to learn; depart to serve," and its mission is to serve, in the Christian tradition, the educational, social, and cultural needs of its students. The university seeks as well to develop in its students the desire and capacity for continuous intellectual and professional growth, leadership, and service to others.

Trudie Kibbe Reed became the university's fifth president and its second female president in 2004, and Bethune-Cookman College officially became a university in 2007. The university's main campus has seven historic buildings among thirty-six situated on seventy acres in Daytona Beach. Its continuing-education division operates sites in Bradenton, Fort Pierce, Sanford, and West Palm Beach. In the early twenty-first century, nearly three thousand students from more than thirty-five nations were enrolled in six degree-granting schools: business, teacher education, arts and humanities, nursing, social sciences, and science, engineering, and mathematics. Students may choose from among thirty-seven majors. The student-to-faculty ratio is 18:1. Bethune-Cookman offers a variety of extracurricular activities for its students, ranging from its world-famous Marching Wildcats band, also known as The Pride, and its 14 Karat Gold dancers to its gospel choir, Greek-letter society, intramural sports clubs, and honor society.

Shortly after she opened her school, Bethune sought funding from local and national donors to ensure its sustained viability. Bethune-Cookman's first major donor was the industrialist James M. Gamble, owner of the Proctor and Gamble Company. He served as chair of the college's board of trustees until his death. The university's foundation is housed in Bethune's house, located on the main campus and listed in the National Register of Historic Places. In 2008 Bethune-Cookman's endowment had reached nearly $43 million.

Part of the university's legacy is advocacy for civil rights. Bethune herself founded the school in the segregated South and worked for voting rights, even in the face of threats from the Ku Klux Klan. She opened a hospital on-site for the college's students because they were not afforded treatment at the local segregated hospital. Buoyed by the support of its approximately thirteen thousand alumni who have graduated since 1941, Bethune-Cookman University has strived to carry out the legacy of faith, service, and scholarship set forth by its founder, Mary McLeod Bethune.

[*See also* Bethune, Mary McLeod, *and* Historically Black Colleges and Universities.]

BIBLIOGRAPHY

Bethune, Mary McLeod. *Mary McLeod Bethune, Building a Better World: Essays and Selected Documents*. Edited by Audrey Thomas McCluskey and Elaine M. Smith. Bloomington: Indiana University Press, 2002.

Flemming, Sheila Y. *Bethune-Cookman College, 1904–1994: The Answered Prayer to a Dream*. Virginia Beach, Va.: Donning, 1995.

Roebuck, Julian B., and Komanduri S. Murty. *Historically Black Colleges and Universities: Their Place in American Higher Education*. Westport, Conn.: Praeger, 1993.

—SUSAN EDWARDS

BEYONCÉ (b. 4 September 1981), singer and actress. Beyoncé Giselle Knowles—or, as she is also known, Beyoncé—was born to Mathew and Tina Knowles in Houston, Texas. Her father sold medical scanners, and her mother ran a hair salon. With LaTavia Roberson and Kelly Rowland, Beyoncé was recruited by two Houston businessmen to form a preteen rhythm-and-blues group under the name Girl's Tyme, which the businessmen managed. In 1992 the group appeared on a nationally syndicated televised talent competition, *Star Search*, and lost doing a rap song.

Shortly thereafter Beyoncé's father took over as her manager. He added LeToya Luckett to the group, creating a rhythm-and-blues quartet that they named the Dolls. The Dolls began to perform in concerts starring artists such as Nas. In 1997 they changed their name to Destiny's Child, and they signed with the Columbia recording label. Their first recording, "Killing Time," appeared on the soundtrack for the film *Men in Black* in 1997. The next year their first single, "No, No, No," hit number three on the Billboard charts, and their debut, eponymous album sold more than a million copies. In 1998, after touring the United States and Europe, the group won three of nine categories at the fourth annual Soul Train Lady of Soul Awards, and in 1999 the group ranked in the top forty Billboard album charts forty-seven out of fifty-two weeks for their album *The Writing's on the Wall*. In the same year the group contributed a song each to the films *Why Do Fools Fall in Love?* and *Life*, and in 2000 they recorded a song for the movie *Romeo Must Die*. Finally, in 2001 Beyoncé contributed a single to the film *Down to Earth*. In early 2000 the NAACP honored Destiny's Child with an Image Award. In March 2000 the group broke up, and all four women went their own way successfully.

In 2001 Beyoncé made her acting debut. That year she appeared as Carmen Brown in the MTV production *Carmen: A Hip Hopera*. In 2002 she starred in *Austin Powers: Goldmember*. In 2006 she was the costar with Steve Martin of the remake of *The Pink Panther*. In 2003 she recorded her first solo album, *Dangerously in Love*, and sold 1.4 million copies. She also won five Grammy awards for that album.

In 2005 Beyoncé and her mother collaborated to create the fashion clothing company the House of Dereon, named after Beyoncé's grandmother. The company specializes in urban and couture styles that retail at prices between one hundred dollars and three hundred dollars.

Beyoncé released her second solo album, *B'Day*, in 2006. In 2006 she also starred in the film *Dreamgirls*, playing Deena Jones and singing the Academy Award–nominated song "Listen." In 2007 she became the first woman to win the International Artist Award of Excellence at the American Music Awards. On 4 April 2008 she married her boyfriend of six years, Jay-Z, at his New York City apartment. They sold photographs of the wedding to the *Chicago Sun-Times* and donated the money they received to Darfur relief and to a New York City children's sports program supported by Jay-Z.

[*See also* Actors and Actresses; Hip Hop; Jay-Z; Music; *and* Rhythm and Blues.]

BIBLIOGRAPHY

Farley, Christopher John. "Call of the Child." *Time*, 15 January 2001.

Norment, Lynn. "Destiny's Child: The Growing Pains of Fame." *Ebony*, September 2000.

—SCOTT SHEIDLOWER

BIGGERS, JOHN (b. 13 April 1924; d. 25 January 2001), artist. Originally from Gastonia, North Carolina, Biggers grew up in the segregated South, the youngest of seven children. His childhood was marred by tragedy, with the deaths of his sister and his father, both from diabetes. John attempted to help his mother in any way he could, often helping with the laundry she took in to support the family. These images eventually appeared in his work.

With the sole responsibility of raising her large family, Biggers's mother decided to send the two youngest boys to Lincoln Academy. This was an important development in John's interest in African culture. The principal of the school had served as a missionary in West Africa and was determined to instill a respect and an understanding of African culture in his students. Biggers had the unusual experience of learning in detail about African culture, an interest that grew as he developed as an artist. In 1941 he entered Hampton Institute (later known as Hampton University), where he met fellow artists Charles White and Elizabeth Catlett. Biggers's studies were interrupted when he was drafted into the U.S. Navy during World War II.

Upon his return Biggers enrolled in Pennsylvania State University in 1946, where he earned a BS and an MS in 1948 and finally a PhD in 1954. At Pennsylvania State he studied with Viktor Lowenfeld, who had included Biggers's work in prior exhibitions. Lowenfeld had served as the director of African art at the Vienna Museum für Volkerkunde until he fled from the Nazis. He encouraged Biggers to explore the culture of Africa in depth, to explore the artistic, religious, and cultural symbols of the continent. Biggers ultimately used much of this symbolism in his murals.

In 1949, while still working on his doctorate, Biggers moved to Houston, where he joined the faculty as founding chair of the art department at Texas Southern University (at that time known as Texas State University for Negroes). Biggers remained active on the faculty until he retired in 1983. He encouraged his art students to paint their own lives and experiences, much as he had.

Biggers had a successful career in Texas too, although he faced the realities of segregation. He won two purchase prizes in the 1950s from the Houston Museum of Fine Arts and the Dallas Museum of Art, but as a black artist he was not allowed to attend the artists' receptions. In 1957 he won a United Nations Educational, Scientific, and Cultural Organization (UNESCO) grant, a life-altering experience that sent him to West Africa. This trip changed the way he saw the world and dramatically altered his art. He recognized the originality of African art and how it connected to modernism in art as well. Biggers's book *Ananse: The Web of Life in Africa* (1962) resulted from this trip. He wrote that he was inspired to include woman as a primary focus in his works: "The African woman, in her divine creative capacity, motivated within me a desire to paint murals on creation from a matriarchal point of view; whereas the European artist had been motivated to paint creation from a patriarchal point of view" (Biggers, p. 35).

Biggers's work evolved from a critique of the injustices faced by black Americans to a more symbolic study of the strength, beauty, and resiliency of African Americans. He created twenty-seven public murals and countless canvases. His murals were his greatest legacy, and they created a great deal of private symbolism. He was especially interested in woman as a symbol in his work, paying homage to the wit and strength of both African and African American women. He had seen firsthand the hard work and struggle of his mother, and he was horrified by the second-class treatment women received. He hoped to illuminate some of those injustices and honor women as equal partners in the struggle and celebration of life. His murals include shotgun houses, quilts, pots, kettles, and washboards, which recall both the domestic and the spiritual lives of Africans and African Americans. His shotgun houses are a form of architecture typical in southern black life with roots in Africa, and they appear in many of his late works, including *Quilting Party* (1981).

Biggers had many one-man shows, including a major retrospective of his work that traveled to seven museums, including the Museum of Fine Arts in Boston; the Hampton University Museum in Hampton, Virginia; and the Museum of Fine Arts in Houston, Texas. He continued to work until his death from complications from diabetes.

[*See also* Visual Arts.]

BIBLIOGRAPHY

Biggers, John. *Ananse: The Web of Life in Africa*. Austin: University of Texas Press, 1962.

Theisen, Olive Jensen. *A Life on Paper: The Drawings and Lithographs of John Thomas Biggers*. Denton: University of North Texas Press, 2006.

Wardlaw, Alvia J. *The Art of John Biggers*. New York: Harry N. Abrams, 1995.

—Amy Helene Kirschke

BIGGIE SMALLS. *See* Notorious B.I.G.

BING, DAVE (b. 24 November 1943), basketball player. David Bing was born and raised in Washington, D.C., where he attended Spingarn High School. He starred on the Spingarn basketball team, earning All-Metro honors and in 1962 being named a *Parade* All-American. That success drew the attention of the University of Michigan and the University of California at Los Angeles, but Bing instead chose to attend Syracuse University, reasoning that he would be more successful at a basketball program with a lower profile. He was correct. In three of his four seasons at Syracuse, Bing led the team in scoring, averaging more than twenty points a game. In his senior year (1966) Bing averaged 28.4 points a game—fifth highest in the country—and was named an All-American. Meanwhile he turned the perennially struggling Syracuse into a winning program. Professional scouts noticed, and in 1966 the Detroit Pistons drafted Bing in the first round of the National Basketball Association (NBA) draft, the second overall pick behind Cazzie Russell. In his first professional season Bing averaged twenty points a game and earned the NBA's Rookie of the Year award. The following season he averaged 27.1 points a game to lead the NBA in scoring, the first guard to do so in twenty years.

In 1969 the American Basketball Association planned on placing a team in Washington, D.C., and lured by the opportunity to earn a larger paycheck and to return to his hometown, Bing signed a contract with the new franchise. When it settled in Norfolk, Virginia, rather than Washington, however, Bing decided to stay with the Pistons. He was a team leader and a consistent scorer, but he missed the first part of the 1971–1972 season after an eye injury left his eyesight permanently impaired. He returned in late December 1971 and continued to play and succeed through the first half of the decade.

Still, Bing wanted an opportunity to play in his hometown. By the mid-1970s the NBA had a franchise in the nation's capital, the Washington Bullets, and in 1975 the Pistons granted Bing's request to be traded. Though he made the 1976 All-Star team—as he did six other seasons—the most productive years of his career were complete. Bing spent two years in Washington, then one year with the Boston Celtics before retiring after the 1977–1978 season. Overall Bing averaged 20.3 points and 6 assists per game.

During his career Bing maintained an active interest in business. He worked for various Detroit corporations during off-seasons. He read consistently on road trips, and in 1980 he put that new knowledge to work, returning to Detroit to form Bing Steel, a supplier for the car industry. His success led to further manufacturing acquisitions, and by the 1990s the Bing Group had become one of the largest black-owned industrial corporations in the nation. Bing used his success to better his community. In 1989 Detroit planned to eliminate sports programs in public high schools. Bing spearheaded a campaign that raised the money to save local high school sports. His success in business and civic life led the NBA to award him the Schick Achievement Award for post-basketball success in 1990. He remained active in Detroit housing and education projects.

In 1983 Bing's number 21 was the first to be retired by the Pistons. In 1990 he was elected to the Naismith Memorial Basketball Hall of Fame, and in 1996 the NBA named him one of the Fifty Greatest Players in NBA history.

[*See also* Basketball *and* Entrepreneurship.]

BIBLIOGRAPHY

Addy, Steve. *The Detroit Pistons: Four Decades of Motor City Memories*. Champaign, Ill.: Sports Publishing, 1997.

Howell, Dave. "Detroit Pistons Legend Dave Bing." http://www.nba.com/pistons/history/dave_bing_profile.html.

Waters, Mike. *Legends of Syracuse Basketball*. Champaign, Ill.: Sports Publishing, 2004.

—THOMAS AIELLO

BIRMINGHAM CAMPAIGN. The Birmingham Campaign, waged throughout 1963 and 1964, represented one of the turning points in the long-term success of the American civil rights movement. The shocking scenes of civil rights demonstrators, many of them young children, being attacked by water hoses and police attack dogs helped galvanize national public opinion against the forces of segregation and added support to the passage and implementation of the Civil Rights Act of 1964.

Background. In the early 1960s Birmingham's status as the largest segregated city in the United States made it a tempting target for civil rights forces. Founded by real estate developers and businessmen in 1871, by the twentieth century the city had gained prominence as an iron- and steel-manufacturing center. Known as the "Magic City" and the "Pittsburgh of the South," by then it was a bustling city with over 38,000 inhabitants. Many residents were African American or European immigrants who worked in the city's numerous factories and processing centers.

As early as the 1880s, Birmingham's city leaders promoted an elaborate system of segregation designed to exclude local blacks from voting booths and classrooms, restaurants, and parks usually reserved for whites. African Americans responded by seeking solidarity within their own neighborhoods and forming their own schools, businesses, churches, and civic organizations.

For much of its early history Birmingham residents remained aware that their city's crippling legacy of racism existed side by side with its economic progress. At Birmingham's 1921 jubilee celebration, then U.S. president Warren G. Harding urged city leaders, "Let the black man vote when he is fit to vote; prohibit the white man voting when he is unfit to vote." Nevertheless, segregation remained an entrenched part of Birmingham life for the next forty years. In addition to segregation laws and inflexible social customs, local whites used violence and intimidation to maintain the racial status quo. Birmingham soon gained the infamous nickname of "Bombingham" because of the over fifty bombings that took place there between 1947 and 1963 aimed at Birmingham's African American community.

On 17 May 1954, Earl Warren, the chief justice of the U.S. Supreme Court, handed down the landmark decision *Brown v. Board of Education*. The *Brown* decision declared segregation in public schools, and by extension all public facilities, to be inherently unconstitutional. Many southern whites condemned *Brown* and began to consider ways to defend segregation. For example, in 1956 the Alabama legislature passed a School Placement Law. The act granted headmasters wide latitude to admit or bar students from their schools, allowed school boards to close public schools, and denied any state responsibility for mandatory education.

Long frustrated by ambivalent authorities and encouraged by the success of the Montgomery bus boycott of 1955, local civil rights activists finally formulated plans to challenge Birmingham's segregation. In Montgomery, on 1 December 1955 the seamstress and civil rights activist Rosa Parks had defied local laws by refusing to give up her seat to a white passenger on a city bus. Following her arrest, the twenty-six-year-old Reverend Martin Luther King Jr., the pastor of the Dexter Avenue Baptist Church, and the local leader of the National Association for the Advancement of Colored People (NAACP) Edgar Daniel Nixon formed the Montgomery Improvement Association (MIA). The MIA launched a yearlong boycott of the city's segregated bus system. In December 1956 a federal district court struck down Alabama's segregated busing laws. The boycott helped to secure the international reputation of King, who went on to form the Southern Christian Leadership Conference (SCLC) in 1957 to launch civil rights campaigns across the nation.

In June 1956 the Alabama legislature outlawed the NAACP in Alabama for its role in the bus boycott. The same month, Fred L. Shuttlesworth, the pastor of the Bethel Baptist Church in Birmingham, organized the Alabama Christian Movement for Human Rights

(ACMHR) to challenge segregation in the Magic City. In December the ACMHR launched protests against Birmingham's segregated bus facilities, demanded that city authorities hire black police officers, and attempted to desegregate local high schools. Local whites responded by castrating the African American judge Edward Aaron and attacking Shuttlesworth and his wife as they attempted to enroll their daughter at the predominantly white Phillips High School. As he had done in Little Rock, Arkansas, in 1957, President Dwight D. Eisenhower dispatched federal troops to maintain order in Birmingham's schools.

In the following year Shuttlesworth launched several lawsuits in the federal district court against Birmingham's segregated public schools, parks, and swimming pools. These lawsuits represented an attempt to overload the federal court system with civil rights litigation. However, this strategy encountered resistance when the Supreme Court ruled in *Shuttlesworth et al. v. Birmingham Board of Education* in 1957 that Alabama's 1956 School Placement Law, strictly construed, did not create discriminated school facilities in Birmingham.

Despite large pro-segregationist rallies held throughout Birmingham, civil rights activity continued to grow over the next two years. In February 1960 students from the historically black Miles College risked police intimidation to protest Birmingham's system of segregation by holding a prayer vigil in Kelly Ingram Park opposite the Sixteenth Street Baptist Church. The protesters gathered to support the Freedom Riders, black and white college students who challenged segregated busing laws throughout the South. The ACMHR also sheltered a group of Freedom Riders attacked by a white mob at Birmingham's Greyhound bus station in May 1961.

Birmingham's civil rights community scored another victory on 24 October 1961, when the federal district court judge Hobart Grooms declared Birmingham's segregated parks unconstitutional. However, the pro-segregationist city commissioners Bull Connor, James Morgan, and J. T. Waggoner overcame opposition from moderate white city business leaders and closed the city's parks on 15 January 1962. During the following night three African American churches in Birmingham were bombed.

Civil rights activity in Birmingham continued to blossom over the next two years. In January 1962, a Miles student, Frank Dukes, and his fellow classmates launched a "Selective Buying Campaign" to boycott local businesses that practiced segregation. Three months later, in April, the ACMHR and the SCLC hosted a joint conference in Birmingham entitled "Ways and Means to Integrate the South." The SCLC also hosted its annual meeting in Birmingham the following September. However, on 15 December 1962, Shuttlesworth's church was bombed.

The Campaign of 1963. As early as the time of the Ways and Means conference in the spring of 1962, Shuttlesworth and the ACMHR had urged the SCLC and other civil rights organizations to join forces for an all-out push against segregation in Birmingham. King readily agreed to such a move. In November 1961, King and the SCLC had joined members of the Student Nonviolent Coordinating Committee (SNCC) in protesting segregated bus facilities in Albany, Georgia. However, local white officials had used a minimum of violence against the protesters and had pledged to desegregate local bus lines if the protesters would call off future demonstrations. When the Albany authorities later refused to honor their word, King and his followers realized they had lost precious time and resources. A victory in Birmingham, the most segregated city in the nation, might restore the momentum of the civil rights movement.

King and other leaders of the SCLC, such as Ralph David Abernathy and Wyatt Tee Walker, arrived in Birmingham in March 1963. SNCC members soon arrived as well. Shuttlesworth and Walker jointly planned Project C, which would "confront" segregationist forces in Birmingham with a series of coordinated boycotts, protests, and mass arrests. Project C started on 3 April 1963 when sixty-five demonstrators conducted sit-ins at the downtown Woolworth's and Loveman's lunch counters, resulting in twenty-one arrests. Three days later Shuttlesworth and Walker led a group of protestors to City Hall to urge the dismantling of Birmingham's segregation ordinances. Police intercepted the demonstrators, who knelt in prayer before being arrested. However, on the following day, Palm Sunday, over a thousand demonstrators had gathered outside Saint Paul Methodist Church for another march when local authorities arrested them for conducting a public march without a permit. Three days later the Alabama circuit court judge W. A. Jenkins enjoined any further protests in Birmingham. Nevertheless, on 12 April, Good Friday, King, Shuttlesworth, and Abernathy led fifty protesters who had gathered for another march in violation of the court order and were promptly arrested. While serving an eight-day sentence in solitary confinement at the Birmingham jail, King wrote his famous "Letter from Birmingham Jail" in response to claims from local clergymen who condemned the demonstrations as untimely and counterproductive.

King's arrest created a national media sensation and prompted further protests. On 14 April, Easter Sunday, police stopped a crowd of over a thousand demonstrators marching on the city jail and arrested thirty-two leaders. Three days later the Reverend Henry Crawford and fifteen female protesters were likewise taken into custody for attempting another demonstration. However, such protests rapidly lost momentum following King's release from prison on April 20. Realizing the need to keep up momentum, King authorized the use of children in future protests.

On 2 May 1963, known as "D-Day," hundreds of school children gathered at the Sixteenth Street Baptist Church to march on City Hall. Police arrested over six hundred students and carted many off to jail in the same buses that normally took them to school. The following day more children assembled at the church to demonstrate. Connor ordered police and fire officials to turn back marchers in Kelly Ingram Park with fire hoses and attack dogs. Angry onlookers retaliated by throwing bricks and rocks at the police. Such violent scenes were televised nationally and helped to turn national public opinion against Birmingham's city leaders. Despite the extent of the brutality, the demonstrations continued for the next eight days, resulting in the arrest of over two thousand protesters.

Hoping to end the violence, King, the U.S. department of justice envoy Burke Marshall, and several white business and city officials worked behind the scenes to broker a compromise. On 10 May King agreed to call off demonstrations in return for a plan to desegregate gradually Birmingham's public facilities and to release all demonstrators. However, on the night of 11 May two bombs exploded, one at the home of King's brother, A. D. King, and another at the headquarters for the SCLC, the A. G. Gaston Motel. Although no fatalities occurred, the bombings sparked riots throughout downtown Birmingham. The next morning the Alabama National Guard arrived to occupy Birmingham and quell any further violence.

On 11 June 1963, President John F. Kennedy addressed the nation on the subject of civil rights, prompted in large part by the recent events in Birmingham. Kennedy warned, "The events in Birmingham and elsewhere have so increased the cries for equality that no city or state or legislative body can prudently choose to ignore them." Feeling the eyes of the nation upon them, a newly appointed Birmingham city government quickly repealed all of the city's segregation ordinances on 23 July.

Yet events in Birmingham continued to grow worse. In early September, local whites wielding Confederate battle flags protested the integration of public high schools. On 15 September 1963 a bomb exploded at the Sixteenth Street Baptist Church, center of much civil rights activity over the past several years. Four young girls, Addie May Collins, Denise McNair, Carole Robertson, and Cynthia Wesley, were killed in the blast. This attack led to several incidents of violence throughout the city during which a black man and a thirteen-year-old black boy were also killed.

On 18 September, King stood before a crowd of over eight hundred mourners to deliver a eulogy at the funeral for the victims of the Sixteenth Street Baptist Church bombing. National media attention generated by the bombing, combined with Kennedy's assassination on 22 November 1963, helped shift the public mood toward support for the passage of the federal Civil Rights Act of 1964.

Violent Reaction to Demonstrations. Youths pummeled by water from a fire hose during a Children's Crusade demonstration in Birmingham, Alabama, May 1963. BIRMINGHAM NEWS/POLARIS

The Aftermath. Despite the intense efforts of civil rights protesters in Birmingham, the steps toward social reform taken by the local whites were often slow and grudging. In July 1964, Ollie McClung, the proprietor of Ollie's Barbeque in Birmingham, challenged the Civil Rights Act of 1964, which mandated the desegregation of restaurants and motels that catered to out-of-state clients. On 14 December 1964 the Supreme Court ruled in *Katzenbach v. McClung* that Congress wielded broad constitutional authority to desegregate any private businesses that touched on interstate commerce.

Although initially excluded from city politics, in the late 1960s and 1970s a new generation of enfranchised black voters began to make their political presence felt. In 1979, Dr. Richard Arrington, a former Miles biology professor and a city council member, became Birmingham's first African American mayor, a post he held for the next twenty years. Under Arrington's leadership, Birmingham took tentative steps to deal with its racist past. In 1978, 1986, and 1988, Birmingham officials erected statues of King and other civil rights legends in Kelly Ingram Park. In 1982, Arrington also led efforts to place Birmingham's traditionally African American Fourth Avenue business district on the National Register of Historic Places. A decade later, local business and civic leaders created the Birmingham Civil Rights Institute, a museum, archives, and community center designed to preserve the city's civil rights heritage.

[*See also* Abernathy, Ralph David; Alabama; *Brown v. Board of Education;* Civil Rights Act of 1964; Civil Rights Movement; Desegregation and Integration, *subentry* Public Education; Eisenhower, Dwight D., Administration of; Freedom Rides; Kennedy, John F., Administration of; King, Martin Luther, Jr.; King, Martin Luther, Jr., Philosophy of; Montgomery Bus Boycott; National Association for the Advancement of Colored People; Nixon, Edgar Daniel; Parks, Rosa; Segregation; Shuttlesworth, Fred L.; Sixteenth Street Baptist Church; Southern Christian Leadership Conference; Student Nonviolent Coordinating Committee; *and* Walker, Wyatt Tee.]

BIBLIOGRAPHY

Bass, S. Jonathan. *Blessed Are the Peacemakers: Martin Luther King Jr., Eight White Religious Leaders, and the "Letter from Birmingham Jail."* Baton Rouge: Louisiana State University Press, 2001. An in-depth examination of the debate between Martin Luther King Jr. and local white ministers over the civil rights movement.

Connerly, Charles E. *"The Most Segregated City in America": City Planning and Civil Rights in Birmingham, 1920–1980*. Charlottesville: University of Virginia Press, 2005. Examines the ways in which city leaders planned Birmingham to reinforce a system of segregation.

Eskew, Glenn T. *But for Birmingham: The Local and National Movements in the Civil Rights Struggle*. Chapel Hill: University of North Carolina Press, 1997. An in-depth examination of the Birmingham civil rights campaign, placed within the context of the national civil rights movement.

Garrow, David J., ed. *Birmingham, Alabama, 1956–1963: The Black Struggle for Civil Rights*. Brooklyn, N.Y.: Carlson, 1989. Represents a solid portrayal of the Birmingham civil rights campaign, with particular emphasis on Birmingham's African American community.

Huntley, Horace, and David Montgomery, eds. *Black Workers' Struggle for Equality in Birmingham*. Urbana: University of Illinois Press, 2004. Examines the role of labor unions and workers in the Birmingham civil rights campaign.

Kelley, Robin D. G. *Race Rebels: Culture, Politics, and the Black Working Class*. New York: Free Press, 1994. An insightful account of the nature and meaning of black resistance in Birmingham both before and during the civil rights campaign of 1963.

McWhorter, Diane. *Carry Me Home; Birmingham, Alabama: The Climactic Battle of the Civil Rights Revolution*. New York: Simon and Schuster, 2001. A Pulitzer Prize–winning account of the Birmingham campaign, seen as the decisive battle for the civil rights movement.

Thornton, J. Mills, III. *Dividing Lines: Municipal Politics and the Struggle for Civil Rights in Montgomery, Birmingham, and Selma*. Tuscaloosa: University of Alabama Press, 2002. Compares nonviolence strategies of Martin Luther King Jr. in three American cities.

—THOMAS H. COX

BIRMINGHAM CHURCH BOMBING. *See* Civil Rights, White Responses and Resistance to.

BIRTH OF A NATION, THE. Since its highly publicized, successful, and controversial opening in 1915, the twelve-reel, feature-length D. W. Griffith film *The Birth of a Nation* has presented enduring questions of how to deal with a filmic work of art that is so bad because it is so good, so dangerous because it is so convincing. Seemingly able to inform and sway audiences on its historic topic—the South in the Civil War of 1861–1865 and the period of Reconstruction that followed—*The Birth of a Nation* has reached millions of people with a particular slant on race relations and American history, a bias difficult to access and more difficult still to eradicate.

Griffith and His Movie. Griffith made his enduring name as a director—as well as a fortune—with this film. Born and raised in Kentucky on exaggerated tales of his father in the Civil War, Griffith was sympathetic to the story presented by the rabid racist Thomas Dixon Jr. in his novels *The Leopard's Spots* (1902) and *The Clansman* (1905), and in the play (also titled *The Clansman*) based upon them. These works posited the white-robed, cross-burning Ku Klux Klan as the Reconstruction-era saviors of the white South from the political and social power of the newly freed black slaves after the Civil War.

Griffith had already used several such stories in short films made for the Biograph Company, which distributed hundreds of movies in this vein between 1911 and 1915. Then in 1914, in a profit-sharing deal that made Dixon wealthy as well, Griffith seized the opportunity to buy the rights to *The Clansman* and filmed the movie, called *The Birth of a Nation*, in the California countryside during a few short months. Ablaze with creative inspiration, Griffith refused to commit a script to paper and swore the actors to secrecy.

The first part of *The Birth of a Nation*, not taken from Dixon, presents a southern family, the Camerons—happy and kind to slaves, who are devoted to them in return—in a pleasant plantation setting that was all too soon torn asunder by the Civil War. A northern family, the Stonemans, are friends of the Camerons until the war divides them—Philip Stoneman has fallen in love with Margaret Cameron, and her brother Ben has fallen in love with Philip's sister Elsie. Much of Griffith's inventive skill in filming and editing the first part of the movie is spent on the war itself, ending in the assassination of President Abraham Lincoln, scenes that strove for perfect historical accuracy. Skillfully interspersing the personal with the panoramic, the tale of the Camerons and the Stonemans develops with such touching scenes as Mrs. Stoneman visiting the hospitalized Ben Cameron in Washington, D.C., and a tearful plea to President Lincoln for the young Confederate's life.

With the death of Abraham Lincoln comes the end of any possible reconciliation between northerners and the white South, according to Griffith, leading to the excesses of black power egged on by evil white northerners in the second part of the movie: Reconstruction. Here Griffith adopts Dixon's ideology more fully, depicting the blacks in the South Carolina legislature and on the streets as so ignorant and vicious that the audience is moved to cheer on the Klan as the only possible response to such oppression. Adding fuel to the fire is the recurring image of white women in sexual peril: Gus, a black renegade, lusts after young Flora Cameron, and Elsie Stoneman receives a proposal of marriage from Silas Lynch, the mulatto who works for her father, a leader of the radical faction in the Reconstruction Senate. By the time Ben Cameron, "the Little Colonel," hits upon the idea for a racist secret society while watching two black children scared away by white kids who are under a white sheet, the unwitting viewing audience has been convinced of the justice and rightness of the Ku Klux Klan's cause.

Though Griffith did not invent the various film techniques that make *The Birth of a Nation* so powerful—the split screen, crosscutting, dramatic lighting, close-ups—he certainly showed how these techniques could work together with a romantic plot (the white fellows ultimately get the white girls) and action to draw in and hold an audience. Thomas Dixon convinced his friend and former classmate Woodrow Wilson to show the movie at the White House—very likely the first film ever shown there—after which Wilson, historian and president of the United States, is purported to have tearfully said, "It is like writing history with Lightning. And my only regret is that it is all so terribly true." Not surprisingly, innumerable students and fans of the film then and since have all too often failed to recognize *The Birth of a Nation*'s racial bias and have taken its depictions for history.

Film Poster. Publicity for D. W. Griffith's *The Birth of a Nation* (1915). Billy Rose Theatre Division, The New York Public Library for the Performing Arts, Astor, Lenox and Tilden Foundations

Counteractions to *The Birth of a Nation*. From the very first, those who perceived the pernicious racial bias of *The Birth of a Nation* have protested in various ways, often to prevent its being shown at all. In 1994, for example, the British Board of Film Classification forbade its being released in video version in the United Kingdom because of its racism. Protests, or counteractions, can be divided into two categories: attempts to get the film banned or cut by various means, including mass demonstrations and the distribution of countermaterial, and fighting film with film.

Much of the early protest action was carried on by the NAACP, particularly the first big demonstrations and hearings in New York and Boston. The NAACP first lobbied the National Board of Censorship in Motion Pictures to cut certain scenes, but it was unsuccessful. After hearings in Boston and other locations, some scenes believed to be conducive to violence were cut from some showings; on occasion, so much was cut that the resulting film left the audience considerably confused about the plot. A prime candidate for censorship was the sequence in which the ignorant, brutal Gus (played, as were all the major black roles, by an actor in blackface) pursues young Flora Cameron through a forest. With much of the pursuit eliminated, audiences were sometimes left wondering why Flora threw herself over a cliff.

In its mass demonstration in New York City on 30 March 1915, just after the film's opening at the Liberty Theatre, the NAACP waylaid any potential sensationalizing of white women and black men marching together by making the event all male. (Likewise in 1917, after the riots in East Saint Louis, Illinois, the precaution was taken of allowing only blacks to march.) In 1915 the group of five hundred made its way to the office of Mayor John P. Mitchel only to discover that an ally of Booker T. Washington, Charles Anderson, had gotten there first, and Anderson's Tuskegee group got credit for the mayor's order to eliminate objectionable scenes.

A valuable counterargument to racist caricatures of blacks was the NAACP's research into the real story of South Carolina's postwar legislature and the publication of its findings. The truth contrasted greatly with Griffith's depiction of barefoot, chicken-chomping legislators: the real-life legislators had passed progressive bills that funded public schools and care of the elderly. Informative pamphlets and flyers handed out at theaters encouraged viewers to think twice about what the movie showed them. A short story based on an actual event in Alabama, "The White Brute," by the NAACP board member Mary White Ovington, was also duplicated by the thousands and given to patrons entering the theaters. In this narrative a young Negro bride is taken from her husband and raped by white men as the couple wait in a train station to travel to their new home (the story is reprinted in *Black and White Sat Down Together: The Reminiscences of an NAACP Founder*).

The counteractive movement of fighting film with film continued into the early twenty-first century, arguably with greater success. Protesters recognized early on that any form of censorship is less likely to be effective than a compelling film that tells a different side of the same story. A young screenwriter from the Universal Film Company, Elaine Sterne, wrote a story called "Lincoln's Dream" as a response to *The Birth of a Nation*, read it to various NAACP chapters, and inspired them to raise money for its production. When they failed to come up with the necessary funds, a shorter version was eventually made under the title *Birth of a Race* (1918), but by the time enough money had been raised for its release, *Birth of a Race* had been watered down beyond recognition. Oscar Micheaux's 1919 film *Within Our Gates* was another response to *The Birth of a Nation*, dramatizing a lynching of innocent blacks as well as the attempted rape of a black woman by a wealthy white man.

D. W. Griffith seemed to be genuinely astonished by the objections raised to *The Birth of a Nation* and maintained that stance until his death in 1948. Scholars disagree on the extent to which the biased racial views of the film can be blamed on Griffith rather than Dixon, author of the original source material. What is certain is that it was Griffith who created a work of art that has been the inspiration for many varied responses, both to the film as a film and to the film as an embodiment of an outdated and regressive racial philosophy.

[*See also Birth of a Race, The; Clansman, The;* Dixon, Thomas, Jr.; Film and Filmmakers; Film and Television Depictions of African Americans; Ku Klux Klan; *and* National Association for the Advancement of Colored People.]

Bibliography

Aitken, Roy E. *The Birth of a Nation Story*. Middleburg, Va.: William W. Denlinger, 1965. Describes the making of the film from the sympathetic and unquestioning point of view of Roy and Harry Aitken, who had raised the money for the production.

Bogle, Donald. *Toms, Coons, Mulattoes, Mammies, and Bucks: An Interpretive History of Blacks in American Films*. 3d ed. New York: Continuum, 1994. Historical overview of American feature films up to the 1980s; describes *The Birth of a Nation* as introducing the "final mythic type, the brutal black buck" and indelibly using the other types (p. 13).

Cripps, Thomas. *Slow Fade to Black: The Negro in American Film, 1900–1942*. New York: Oxford University Press, 1977. A solid social history of the film and its predecessors, though it seems to have an undertone of bias against the NAACP.

Lang, Robert, ed. *The Birth of a Nation: D. W. Griffith, Director*. New Brunswick, N.J.: Rutgers University Press, 1994. A comprehensive collection of materials.

Leab, Daniel. *From Sambo to Superspade: The Black Experience in Motion Pictures*. Boston: Houghton Mifflin, 1975.

Luker, Ralph E., ed. *Black and White Sat Down Together: The Reminiscences of an NAACP Founder*. New York: Feminist Press, 1995.

Schickel, Richard. *D. W. Griffith: An American Life*. New York: Simon & Schuster, 1984. Schickel finds few parallels to Griffith in the history of art; Griffith is the "product of, and perhaps ultimately the victim of, our particular history, our particular spirit—the best of it and the worst of it" (p. 13). Schickel's main sources are the repository for Griffith's personal papers at the Museum of Modern Art Film Library in New York City, the memories of those who knew and worked with him, and the Griffith Corporation scrapbooks.

—CAROLYN WEDIN

BIRTH OF A RACE, THE. *The Birth of a Race* (1918) was the much-heralded and widely anticipated African American cinematic response to the brutally racist images in D. W. Griffith's popular film *The Birth of a Nation* (1915). *The Birth of a Nation* and other films such as *The Nigger* (1917) and *Colored Villainy* (1917) generated a quick and angry response among urban blacks and became the focal point for a nascent movement among African American civic groups to create their own vision of the Negro in American life.

Having rejected early attempts to persuade whites to censor films with blatantly racist images, such leaders as W. E. B. Du Bois and May Childs Nerney of the NAACP and Booker T. Washington and Emmett J. Scott of the Tuskegee Institute struggled with what would be the most appropriate response to Griffith's film. Among the possibilities they considered were film versions of Washington's 1901 autobiography *Up from Slavery* or perhaps a cinematic version of Harriet Beecher Stowe's 1852 best-selling novel *Uncle Tom's Cabin*. It was Emmett J. Scott, Washington's confidant and private secretary at Tuskegee, who made the initial contacts with Hollywood filmmakers to produce a story of universal Negro progress that he hoped would effectively counter Griffith's interpretation of the African American past.

The project was hamstrung from the beginning. After an abortive attempt to produce "Lincoln's Dream," a film that would appeal to white audiences and that would capture the progress and sufferings of American Negroes, the NAACP contingent gave up on the project. Du Bois himself announced plans to create his own dramatic pageant of black history, but it never came to pass. Meanwhile Scott pressed on with his hope that he could produce a film with a black cast and crew that would be loosely based on *Up from Slavery*, but he never could find sufficient financing or even interest for an all-black film in the white-dominated world of Hollywood.

The final version of *The Birth of a Race*, which premiered in Chicago in late 1918, bore scant resemblance to the aspirations of any of the black planners. In an attempt to attract white audiences, African American actors and themes were missing from all but a few scenes. Moreover the American entry into World War I in 1917 helped change the entire focus of the film from black progress to the general triumph of American idealism. In fact the story line of the final product was actually about the moral dilemma facing a German American family at the outbreak of the war. George Smitt, the German American character on whom the moral debate centers, ultimately makes the right choice and fights with the Americans. But before he does, the film takes the viewer through a mélange of flashback images, building the case from Jesus Christ through Abraham Lincoln of the superiority of American national idealism. But the critics were not impressed; reviews ranged from lukewarm to devastating.

To be sure, there are glimmers in some scenes of what might have been the first great cinematic story of black culture and progress. One particular scene late in the film portrays two farmers, one white, the other black, who leave their plows to take up arms against the Kaiser in the cause of liberty, presumably for blacks as well as whites. And the scenes featuring Lincoln and the Civil War have at least the promise of a story that might have featured more black actors and a film that could have gone a long way toward neutralizing the bestial images of black people presented in *The Birth of a Nation*.

[*See also Birth of a Nation, The;* Film and Filmmakers; Film and Television Depictions of African Americans; *and biographical entries on figures mentioned in this article*.]

BIBLIOGRAPHY

Bernardi, Daniel, ed. *The Birth of Whiteness: Race and the Emergence of U.S. Cinema*. New Brunswick, N.J.: Rutgers University Press, 1966. An excellent overview of race in the cinema, including the story of *Birth of a Race*.

Cripps, Thomas. "The *Birth of a Race* Company: An Early Stride toward a Black Cinema." *Journal of Negro History* 59, no. 1 (January 1974): 28–37. Perhaps the most detailed account of the abortive attempt to establish a black cinema.

—CHARLES ORSON COOK

BISEXUALITY. *See* Homosexuality and Transgenderism.

BLACK ARTS MOVEMENT. The Black Arts Movement was a loosely affiliated group of politically motivated activist poets, painters, musicians, dramatists, and other artists working in American urban centers, beginning roughly in 1965 and losing momentum by the mid-1970s. It is considered to be the artistic arm of the Black Power movement. Though African American fiction and visual art expressed a similar radicalism and appeared under the scope of Black Arts, the movement's emphasis on performative expression gave precedence to vernacular poetry and the dramatic arts.

Inception. The poet LeRoi Jones is generally credited with developing what would become the Black Arts Movement. Though Malcolm X was killed by black assassins, Jones and other black artists and activists interpreted the murder as a plot engineered by agents of the rich and powerful. In response to his death in late February 1965 and to the broader culture of racial violence throughout the mid-1960s, Jones left his wife, a white woman named Hettie Cohen Jones, and moved from the Lower East Side of Manhattan to Harlem, where he founded the Black Arts Repertory Theatre/School. Later that year, he would leave Harlem for his hometown of Newark, New Jersey, where he established a black cultural center called Spirit House. In 1967, Jones changed his name to Imamu Amiri Baraka.

While the assassination of Malcolm X provided the immediate catalyst for the radicalization of the work of Baraka and others, it was one of many political and artistic influences that went into creating the Black Arts aesthetic. The political unrest resulting from the fight against apartheid in South Africa looked very similar to the Watts riots and other violent demonstrations in the United States, and, in response, many activist writers modeled their own creations on the rhetoric, philosophy, or cultural cues of similarly oppressed black nations.

More immediately, the Black Arts Movement was fostered by a series of black writing groups that came before it in the early 1960s. In 1960, On Guard for Freedom, a similarly political black literary group, developed in Manhattan and included Jones, Tom Dent, Walter Bowe, and Calvin Hicks, all later associated with Black Arts. In 1962, members of that group would join with Askia M. Touré, Brenda Walcott, Calvin C. Hernton, David Henderson, and others to form the Umbra Workshop. Umbra attempted to combine radical race politics with a distinct literary voice but ultimately collapsed because of internal dissent over the primacy of activism or literary pursuit. The Black Arts Movement would solve this inherent paradox by making activism the functional outgrowth of poetic discourse. Politics—specifically anger over the state of race relations in the United States—was the aesthetic.

Spread. Although the movement had a decidedly New York genesis, it spread quickly throughout America's urban centers. Chicago's Third World Press published many of the poets associated with the Black Arts Movement. The city's Organization of Black American Culture sponsored a variety of authors and artists and housed a significant public mural project. The Kuumba Theatre Company provided a venue to stage black activist drama. In Detroit, Broadside Press and Lotus Press published both new and established black poets. Broadside was founded in 1965 and published hundreds of poets by the end of its first decade. It was also in Detroit where Ron Milner and Woodie King—the leading playwright and theatrical producer, respectively, of the Black Arts Movement—created the dramatic group Black Arts Midwest. In Cleveland, Karamu House, a neighborhood center and black theater, led Ohio's Black Arts endeavors (though its origins preceded the 1960s upsurge). In Indianapolis, the television program *The Black Experience*, produced by the poet Mari Evans, served as a spotlight for black social and cultural issues.

In Los Angeles, a variety of theater groups, including the Inner City Repertory Company and the Performing Arts Society of Los Angeles, fostered the Black Arts aesthetic, and Black Arts West dominated in San Francisco. California's *Black Dialogue*, first published in 1964, was the first major literary publication of the Black Arts Movement, followed soon by *Soulbook*, published that same year. Dingane Joe Goncalves, the poetry editor of *Black Dialogue*, saw a need for a publication specifically dedicated to the genre and in response created the *Journal of Black Poetry*, which would publish more than five hundred poets and continue through summer 1975. In 1969, Nathan Hare and Robert Chrisman published *Black Scholar*, which quickly became the premier journal of African American studies and theory. Though the California-based publication was only tangentially related to the Black Arts Movement—it was a more scholarly publication that did not emphasize performative poetry or dramatic arts—the politicized publishing culture bred by the Black Arts Movement created the opportunity for its birth.

The movement also reached the South. Tom Dent and Kalamu ya Salaam of New Orleans developed the Free Southern Theatre, from which grew BLKARTSOUTH. The Southern Black Cultural Alliance helped develop theater projects in southern urban centers such as Miami and Houston. The authors John O'Neal, Gilbert Moses, and Jerry Ward also contributed to the southern outgrowth of Black Arts.

Dissolution. Back in Chicago, perhaps the most significant Black Arts publication was *Black World*, published by John H. Johnson. Its publication serves to highlight some of the inherent contradictions within the Black Arts Movement. *Black World* began as *Negro Digest*, Johnson's mimic of *Reader's Digest*. But its editor, Hoyt Fuller, envisioned the publication as a forum for black literature and expression. In 1970, that transition was codified with the magazine's name change. Still, Johnson publications generally tended to be staunchly against overt militancy. Sister publications *Ebony* and *Jet* emphasized examples of black middle- and upper-class success rather than working-class struggles. Similarly, Jones's move to Harlem to create the Black Arts Repertory Theatre/School—an organization devoted to the production of material unequivocally opposed to the mainstream—was funded by a prestigious 1965 Guggenheim Fellowship.

This funding discrepancy was sometimes mirrored by a contradiction in content. Gil Scott-Heron received critical and popular acclaim for his poetry about racial unrest. Perhaps his most famous work, "The Revolution Will Not Be Televised," denigrated the mainstream mass media, but the poem reached the audience it did because of significant mainstream radio play.

Of course, those content contradictions were not always present. Writers of the Black Arts Movement published their own periodicals, pamphlets, and anthologies as a specific reaction against a lack of mainstream interest in their work. And that lack of interest came largely because of the confrontational, often shocking nature of Black Arts poetry and drama. Black Arts poets sought to eliminate any vestiges of white mainstream literary sensibilities by attacking those sensibilities at their core. Jones wrote in 1965 that "we want poems that kill." Larry Neal's 1968 essay on the theory behind the Black Arts aesthetic noted that the movement was the "spiritual sister of the Black Power concept." Nikki Giovanni's "The True Import of Present Dialogue: Black vs. Negro" made rhythmic play from the notions of killing "niggers," "white men," "blond heads," and "Jews." Shock value was deemed necessary to wake purportedly tired minds, but the shocking nature of some of the Black Arts work has stained its historical reputation.

So too has the at times racist, sexist, homophobic, and anti-Semitic nature of some of the Black Arts poetry. Some of the work celebrated violence. Some of the work celebrated black masculinity as a counter to historical dehumanization. Still, the movement did foster the development of numerous women writers. The playwright and poet Ntozake Shange, along with the poets Jayne Cortez, Sonia Sanchez, Audre Lorde, and June Jordan, used the direct, vernacular, political presentation of the typical Black Arts aesthetic to examine the intersections of gender and race in the Black Power struggle.

Though the Black Arts Movement did not fall to such contradictions, they certainly played a role in its dissolution. A principal reason for the movement's dissipation was a move by Amiri Baraka and other activists and authors away from Pan-African nationalism in favor of Marxism, which alienated many in the movement and took most of the new communists in different aesthetic directions. A second reason for the breakup was co-option by the mainstream. Black Arts authors became famous. Baraka, Giovanni, and Scott-Heron had an economic drawing power outside of the cloistered community of black activists. In 1976, Shange had a play produced on Broadway. That same year, Johnson stopped publishing *Black World* in the face of an advertising backlash over pro-Palestinian articles in the magazine. Broadside Press did not disappear in 1976, but its budget decreased and its prolific publishing record slowed dramatically. The Black Arts Movement was slowing down.

While it produced a strong compendium of poetry and drama that serves as a vital link in the evolutionary chain of African American literature, the Black Arts Movement also left a legacy for later generations. Its emphasis on speech and performance as sources of literary power influenced the development of rap and hip-hop music in the late twentieth century, as well as making space for the rise of spoken-word and performance poetry, which has developed an audience and artist base beyond the bounds of race.

[*See also* Baraka, Amiri; Black Power Movement; Giovanni, Nikki; King, Woodie; Milner, Ron; Neal, Larry; *and* Scott-Heron, Gil.]

BIBLIOGRAPHY

Clarke, Cheryl. *"After Mecca": Women Poets and the Black Arts Movement*. New Brunswick, N.J.: Rutgers University Press, 2005.

Collins, Lisa Gail, and Margo Natalie Crawford, eds. *New Thoughts on the Black Arts Movement*. New Brunswick, N.J.: Rutgers University Press, 2006.

Jones, LeRoi, and Larry Neal, eds. *Black Fire: An Anthology of Afro-American Writing*. New York: William Morrow & Co., 1968.

Neal, Larry. "The Black Arts Movement." *Drama Review* 12 (Summer 1968): 29–39.

Smethurst, James Edward. *The Black Arts Movement: Literary Nationalism in the 1960s and 1970s*. Chapel Hill: University of North Carolina Press, 2005.

—THOMAS AIELLO

BLACK CABINETS. The advisory relationship between African Americans and their president underwent significant change during the twentieth century. In 1901 Booker T. Washington slipped out of the nation's capital on a midnight train after a historic meeting at the White House with President Theodore Roosevelt, so sensitive were they to the politics of the Jim Crow South. Yet by the end of the century the nation welcomed Colin Powell's nomination as secretary of state with great enthusiasm. This transformation owed much to the growth of black political power. Indeed, the growth of black political power forced President Franklin D. Roosevelt to make room for black advisers deep within the executive branch of government, a group later known as the Black Cabinet. These blacks created a bridge for greater African American participation in the policymaking process.

Before William McKinley's assassination in 1901, presidents had made only sporadic efforts to seek advice from African American leaders. Upon taking office, Theodore Roosevelt decided to reach out to the most influential black leader of his era, the Tuskegee principal Booker T. Washington. The president was far more interested in black votes than in civil rights, but he wished to reward Washington's moderate views on race issues. In a historic move, Roosevelt invited Washington to dine with him at the White House in October 1901 to discuss federal patronage appointments in the South. When news leaked that the president had shared his dinner table with a black man, criticism from southern newspapers was swift and violent. Undeterred, the Tuskegee educator maintained his role as a discreet unofficial adviser, corresponding with Roosevelt and select members of his cabinet on southern patronage matters. One of the cabinet members whom Washington corresponded with was the 1904–1908 secretary of war William Howard Taft; they continued to correspond when Taft became president in 1908.

During the 1920s Robert Russa Moton became the new Tuskegee principal and continued his predecessor's role of advising presidents on patronage issues. Indeed, he helped block President Herbert Hoover's controversial nominee to the Supreme Court, John J. Parker, whose racist views made him an unacceptable choice. Though White House interest in civil rights remained stagnant, presidents Warren G. Harding, Hoover, and Calvin Coolidge did nominate a series of blacks to ambassadorial posts for political patronage purposes; the posts were in a limited number of locations, generally only in Africa and the Caribbean. In 1921, for example, Harding named Solomon Porter Hood as minister to Liberia. Coolidge replaced Hood with another African American, William Francis, and Hoover later dispatched Charles Mitchell. In 1921 Henry Ossian Flipper became special assistant to Secretary of the Interior Albert Fall without the assistance of patronage. Flipper, the first black graduate of the U.S. Military Academy at West Point, was a valuable counselor on the Mexican Revolution and southwestern matters, having traveled extensively through those regions as a mining engineer. While the 1920s roared, these modest appointments prepared public opinion for greater black participation in the White House bureaucracy.

Franklin Roosevelt's Black Cabinet. Franklin Roosevelt's tacit endorsement of an unofficial Black Cabinet marked a significant turning point in the African American advisory relationship with the presidency. Although Roosevelt placed national recovery and later the war effort ahead of civil rights, throughout his New Deal recovery programs he saw little political harm in allowing African Americans to staff offices related to so-called Negro affairs. This was a symbolic reward for black support at the polls in 1932. In 1933 journalists began using the terms "Black Cabinet" and "Black Brain Trust" to describe this new group of black employees of the federal government. They came from a rich variety of backgrounds but shared a few common qualities: they were highly qualified, nonpolitical, and committed to improving blacks' rights. These blacks made up an unofficial group that, with one exception, did not have direct access to Roosevelt. Rather, these third-tier bureaucrats privately coordinated their efforts to serve the long-range interests of blacks in the fields of housing, education, and fair employment practices.

A government culture less than enthusiastic about these black employees' existence made progress difficult. Nonetheless, they found a welcome home in the Department of the Interior, serving in such New Deal programs as the Civilian Conservation Corps and the National Youth Administration. More than two hundred blacks served in the federal government during Roosevelt's time in office, but scholars generally agree that only about fifteen formed an inner circle and were truly influential. Of these, two emerged as leaders: Robert C. Weaver and Mary McLeod Bethune.

In October 1933 Robert Weaver became assistant to Clark Foreman, special adviser for the Department of the Interior on Negro affairs. The twenty-six-year-old native of Washington, D.C., was the first African American to earn a PhD in economics from Harvard, and in 1934 he assumed Foreman's position and then quickly emerged as a leader within the Black Cabinet. On the surface Weaver had a modest leadership style and a passion for anonymity. Consequently he was often criticized by the black community for being an ineffective civil rights leader—overly compromising and subservient to whites. His closest associates, however, knew better. Weaver hosted weekly gatherings at his home on California Street, where poker mixed with all-night discussions about how best to advance equal opportunities for blacks. His counsel became highly sought, and although he did not have direct access to the Oval Office, he was able to lobby the president indirectly through Secretary Harold Ickes, the media, and his fellow Black Cabineteer Mary McLeod Bethune. During his ten-year tenure with the Roosevelt administration, Weaver emerged as the architect for equal employment opportunities within the Department of the Interior, developed studies on black housing and labor difficulties, and helped desegregate lunchrooms in government buildings throughout Washington.

The most influential member of Roosevelt's Black Cabinet was Mary McLeod Bethune, a charismatic Florida college president with a long history of civil rights activism. During the 1920s, Bethune attended several national youth conferences with Eleanor Roosevelt. After the Roosevelts went to Washington in 1933, the first lady nominated Bethune first to the Planning Committee of the Office of Education of Negroes and then, in 1936, to head the Negro division of the National Youth Administration. Bethune was the first black woman to head a federal agency, and she did so until the National Youth Administration was shut down in 1943.

As Mrs. Roosevelt's regular companion, Bethune was the only member of the Black Cabinet with access to the First Family. Indeed, her ability to see the president on short notice was a well-known fact around the Georgetown parlor circuit. "Ma" Bethune—she had been born in 1875, so she was sixty years old by 1935—initiated the first Black Cabinet meeting at her home in 1934 and thereafter worked closely with Weaver and his young associates. From time to time they called upon her to lobby key officials; this often took the form of lectures spiced with liberal doses of shame and flattery. Throughout her years of service to the Roosevelts, Bethune remained a respected champion of the needs of black youth.

During the war years, Black Cabineteers made slow progress advancing civil rights from within the confines of a federal bureaucracy whose priorities lay elsewhere. The work was frustrating, and critics were quick to downplay accomplishments. During one meeting in 1942, General Henry H. "Hap" Arnold told the Black Cabineteer Truman Gibson that blacks would never be welcome in the U.S. Army Air Corps. Rather than argue with the general over the military's segregationist policies, Gibson took the news to Bethune. "Ma" took the story directly to Eleanor Roosevelt, and before long pressure from the White House led to the formation of the Tuskegee Airmen. Some saw this as a victory, though critics noted that black and white pilots would still fight the nation's enemies in segregated squadrons. But the formation of the Tuskegee Airmen was typical of the incremental approach adopted by the original Black Cabineteers, achieving what was possible in the moment, hoping that it would form a stepping-stone in the years ahead.

Robert C. Weaver, 1964. Robert Weaver, the first black to earn a PhD in economics from Harvard University, was an influential young leader in President Franklin Roosevelt's "Black Cabinet." Weaver became the first official black cabinet secretary when President Lyndon Johnson appointed him the first secretary of the Department of Housing and Urban Development in 1966. Photograph by Yoichi Okamoto. LYNDON B. JOHNSON LIBRARY, NATIONAL ARCHIVES

Historians agree that Roosevelt's Black Cabinet dissolved during World War II as frustrations over government priorities led to a slow series of resignations. Although the term "Black Cabinet" faded from use during the postwar years, presidents continued to appoint and consult blacks at a modest rate. Truman Gibson, for example, remained a part-time consultant to President Harry S. Truman as his administration studied the feasibility of military desegregation. In 1954 President Dwight D. Eisenhower made the Chicago lawyer Jesse Ernest Wilkins Sr. the assistant secretary of labor. Indeed, Wilkins became the first black to represent his department at a presidential cabinet meeting that same year.

Official Cabinet Members. During these early Cold War years, support for the appointment of blacks to the official cabinet grew thanks to the groundwork laid by Roosevelt's Black Cabinet and the momentum generated by the civil rights movement. In 1961 President John F. Kennedy took a step that his predecessors had avoided: he sent a black nominee to Capitol Hill for a confirmation hearing. Kennedy wanted the former Black Cabineteer Robert Weaver to lead the Housing and Home Finance Agency, promising to make him the first black cabinet secretary once Congress approved of the new Department of Housing and Urban Development. Lyndon B. Johnson honored his slain predecessor's wish in 1966, and Weaver became the new department's first secretary, serving until the end of 1968.

During the late twentieth century, other African Americans followed Weaver's footsteps into the official presidential cabinet. In 1993 President Bill Clinton made good on his campaign promise to diversify his cabinet by appointing four blacks, three more than any previous administration. Perhaps more significant, Clinton assigned some of these nominees to departments with responsibilities far broader than the welfare of the black community. One notable selection was Hazel O'Leary as secretary of energy: she was both the first woman and the first African American to hold the position. She earned praise for declassifying documents detailing government radiation experiments on humans and blocked a Republican Congress from downsizing her department. Similarly, Ron Brown became the first African American to serve as secretary of commerce. Under his leadership the Commerce Department was reorganized, and he encouraged all Americans to participate in the global economy.

In 2000 President George W. Bush chose Colin Powell for the most coveted cabinet post in the land: secretary of state. The nomination of Powell reflected the century-long transformation in the advisory relationship between blacks and their president, from the unofficial to the official, from limited patronage consultations to policymaker, and from domestic policy advisers to foreign policy advisers. Powell's confirmation hearing before a receptive Senate underscored the extent to which walls had been torn down. Indeed, it had been a long road since that historic evening when Booker T. Washington bid farewell to his presidential host, then slipped away on a midnight train.

[*See also* Black Politics; Politics and Politicians; *and entries on people and presidential administrations mentioned in this article*.]

BIBLIOGRAPHY

Brown, Tracey. *The Life and Times of Ron Brown*. New York: William Morrow, 1998. A useful account of Brown's work as secretary of commerce during the Clinton administration.

Brundage, W. Fitzhugh, ed. *Booker T. Washington and Black Progress: "Up from Slavery" 100 Years Later*. Gainesville: University Press of Florida, 2003. A collection of essays that challenge the orthodox interpretation that Washington was an apologist for segregation and disfranchisement.

Gibson, Truman K., Jr., with Steve Huntley. *Knocking Down Barriers: My Fight for Black America*. Evanston, Ill.: Northwestern University Press, 2005. Offers an excellent account of the challenges Gibson faced working within the War Department.

Morris, Edmund. *Theodore Rex*. New York: Random House, 2001. Includes a useful look at Booker T. Washington from Theodore Roosevelt's perspective.

Riley, Russell. *The Presidency and the Politics of Racial Inequality: Nation-Keeping from 1831 to 1965*. New York: Columbia University Press, 1999. An indispensable scholarly analysis of the limits of presidential power as it facilitated and hindered the rise of black political power; contains a particularly useful bibliography of secondary sources.

—BRIAN CLANCY

BLACK CAPITALISM. Economic deprivation has plagued the post-Emancipation African American experience. Throughout U.S. history some critical observers have argued that independent business ownership and entrepreneurship by blacks is the solution to African American economic disfranchisement. In 1968 the presidential candidate Richard Nixon made what he called "black capitalism" the centerpiece of his civil rights platform. "Black capitalism" became a phrase used to categorize a broad range of intellectual postulates, government programs, and mentorship initiatives designed to engender the development and control of industries by African Americans.

Within African American communities, segregated business operations had long operated parallel to white business operations. Certain religious communities, like African American Muslims, specifically enjoined their members to build stores and factories as alternative vendors. Black capitalism in these enclaves was a function of separatist racial ideologies; the people argued that purchases made in white-owned businesses served white interests and white domination.

Black capitalism became a federal aspiration, though, as a response to the de facto segregation that persisted beyond legal desegregation. These governmental efforts were focused on incorporating black entrepreneurs into the national economy. Between 1965 and 1967 the Office of Federal Contract Compliance (OFCC) attempted slowly to respond to civil rights protestors and their demands for economic desegregation. Under the direction of President Lyndon Johnson, the OFCC crafted policies endorsing tentative goals for minority hires, initially requiring bidders on government contracts to submit affirmative action plans for minority employment. These tentative policies eventually cohered into the Philadelphia Plan, which was Johnson's overarching timetable to garner minority bids for government construction work. Many government officials perceived these timetables as quota mandates, and in 1968 the U.S. comptroller general Elmer B. Staats ruled that the Philadelphia Plan violated the Civil Rights Act of 1964.

The Vietnam War conscription significantly reduced the number of skilled construction workers. By the late 1960s the cost of new housing had soared, and, combined with the advocacy of the newly formed National Afro-American Builders Corporation, this led to the rebirth of the Philadelphia Plan. Under the auspices of the OFCC, Labor Secretary for Wages and Standards Arthur A. Fletcher, one of the highest-ranking African Americans in the Nixon administration, redrafted the Philadelphia Plan, requiring that federal contractors employ a certain percentage of minorities. Rather than establish precise quotas, however, Fletcher created numerical "ranges" for employment of African Americans. For example, 5 to 9 percent of iron workers on federal projects were to be black in 1970, with ranges increasing each year thereafter.

Alongside the hiring timetables designed by Fletcher and the OFCC, Nixon also created the Office of Minority Business Enterprise (OMBE) in 1969 to serve as the federal coordinator and information clearinghouse for minority-owned businesses. The OMBE provided guidance to minority business owners in their efforts to secure bonds, loans, and financing, as well as providing managerial and technical assistance to nascent entrepreneurs. Black capitalism thus emerged in the 1970s as a combined effort to enforce fair employment practices, to encourage the development of minority business, and to promote black economic self-improvement. For instance, Project OWN encouraged commercial banks to lend to black enterprise. "The laws have caught up with our conscience," Nixon announced in his first inaugural address. "What remains is to give life to what is in the law" (quoted in Randolph and Weems, p. 57). The focus of Nixon's initiatives was the provision of loan assistance and preferential procurement of federal contracts for black business owners.

The impact of this federal intervention was immediately evident in many markets. For example, in 1970 only fourteen radio stations were owned by African Americans. By 1989 the practices of the OMBE and the Small Business Administration (SBA) had raised that number to 170 radio stations and 13 television stations. Although this number still represented only 2 percent of the broadcasting industry, it signaled a significant shift, the result of active efforts to ease licensing processes and capital acquisition. The OMBE and the SBA pressed other government agencies, such as the Federal Communications Commission (FCC), to alter their policies in adherence to black capitalism. The FCC instituted a sale policy that permitted broadcasters in danger of losing their licenses to sell them to minority persons or groups; such sales ensured three years of tax deferment on capital gains to the seller.

The heyday of federally mandated black capitalism was short lived. In 1989 the Supreme Court held in *Croson v. Richmond* that minority set-aside contracts violated the constitutional rights of certain contractors. Within months the number of contracts awarded to African American contractors decreased sharply. Since then, several local governments have conducted studies to provide a legal basis to reinstate minority contract programs. The encouragement of black ownership of business remains the priority of advocates of black capitalism, who see industry ownership and control as a prime means for enlarging the capital base of African American communities and curbing their rising unemployment rates.

[*See also* Affirmative Action; Entrepreneurship; National Negro Business League; *and* Nixon, Richard, Administration of.]

Bibliography

Bates, Timothy. "Government as Financial Intermediary for Minority Entrepreneurs: An Evaluation." *Journal of Business* 48, no. 4 (October 1975): 541–557.

Kotlowski, Dean J. "Richard Nixon and the Origins of Affirmative Action." *Historian* 60, no. 3 (Spring 1998): 523–541.

Randolph, Lewis A., and Robert E. Weems. "The Ideological Origins of Richard M. Nixon's 'Black Capitalism' Initiative." *Review of Black Political Economy* 29, no. 1 (June 2001): 49–61.

—Kathryn Lofton

BLACK CHURCH. By the end of the nineteenth century African Americans had cut a wide swath across the American religious spectrum. Indeed, African American churches had become a major part of the mainline American Christian tradition and continued to expand their presence throughout the twentieth century. As a result of demographic changes in the African American population, their churches became part of the geographical landscape throughout the United States. Challenged by the rise of new theological and social issues, African American churches and their leadership became major forces in the political, religious, and social history of the country.

Mainline Christian African American Churches. An endemic problem for voluntary organizations—and the Baptist conventions are voluntary organizations—is instability. In the latter half of the nineteenth century the black Baptists went through several conventions, and the problem of instability continued into the twentieth century. By the 1880s two denominations had the greatest numbers of African Americans: the Baptists and the Methodists. In 1895 the African American Baptists formed the National Baptist Convention, U.S.A. (NBC-USA), through the merger of the Baptist Foreign Mission Convention of the United States and the American National Baptist Convention. The rise of the NBC-USA coincided with the enactment of Jim Crow laws throughout the south and with the U.S. Supreme Court decision in *Plessy v. Ferguson* (1896) that made segregation the law of the land. Under the leadership of the Reverend E. C. Morris, the first president of the convention, the NBC-USA became an advocate for its black members in the area of education by supporting numerous primary and secondary schools, as well as colleges. In 1909 it formally adopted the self-help policy advocated by Booker T. Washington. It also supported the newly established National Association for the Advancement of Colored People (NAACP) and began to campaign for African Americans' right to vote and serve on juries.

In 1952, with the election of the Reverend J. H. Jackson as president of the convention, the NBC-USA took on a conservative policy that rejected the philosophy of civil disobedience and nonviolent opposition to segregation—the philosophy advocated by emerging civil rights leaders such as Martin Luther King Jr. This policy was not reversed until the election of the Reverend Dr. Theodore J. Jemison as president of the convention in 1982. Jemison acted immediately to reconfirm the convention's earlier role as an advocate for black Americans' rights by initiating a nationwide voter registration program.

Despite its inconsistent commitment to the rights of blacks, the NBC-USA has grown. In 1915 the convention reported a membership of approximately 3 million in more than 20,000 affiliated churches. By 1989 membership had soared to nearly 7.5 million in 30,000 affiliated churches, making the NBC-USA the largest single black religious denomination in the United States.

In 1897 a faction within the NBC-USA broke away to establish the Lott Carey Foreign Missionary Convention. The separation was the result of the appointment of new leaders in the convention who moved the headquarters of the Foreign Mission Board from Richmond, Virginia, to Louisville, Kentucky. The new leaders also established a new publishing policy that some longtime members viewed as undercutting their relationships with white Baptists. The seceding group was composed of representatives from the mid-Atlantic states who were better educated and more socially accomplished than other members. In 1905 the NBC-USA and the Lott Carey Convention were able to reconcile some of their differences, but the two groups continue to operate separately, although many officers and members belong to both groups. In the twentieth century the splits continued. Another group, under the leadership of the Reverend R. H. Boyd, who had served as the secretary of the publishing board of the NBC-USA, broke away in 1915 and took the name of National Baptist Convention of America (NBCA). The split was the result of a conflict that arose between Boyd and the Reverend E. C. Morris, who served as president of the NBC-USA from 1895 to 1923. The conflict, over control of the publishing board, raged from 1905 until 1915, when Boyd won out in a civil lawsuit. The National Baptist Publishing Board became the foundation for the NBCA. The primary work of the NBCA has been in publishing, but it has also worked hard in the same areas as the NBC-USA, such as education. It also has a long, continuing commitment to civil rights—for example it supported an early antilynching program—and urban issues. The first president of the NBCA was the Reverend E. P. Jones. By 1989 the group had grown to 2.4 million members.

The issue of control of the National Baptist Publishing Board has been a source of continuing conflict. The Boyd family maintained control of these operations from 1905 until 1988, when they and their supporters broke with the NBCA to form the National Missionary Baptist Convention of America.

The Progressive National Baptist Convention (PNBC), also known as the Progressive Baptist Alliance, broke from the NBC-USA as a result of the efforts of the Reverend J. H. Jackson to maintain his control over the convention. The dispute began in 1960 and culminated in 1961 with the removal of Martin Luther King Sr., Martin Luther King Jr., and others from their respective offices in the NBC-USA. The new convention was formally established at a meeting at the Zion Baptist Church in Cincinnati, Ohio, under the leadership of the Reverend L. Venchael Booth, who served as the chairman of the Volunteer Committee for the Formation of a New National Baptist Convention. The following year, the Reverend T. M. Chambers was elected the first president of the fledgling convention. Reflecting the character of its founding members, the PNBC immediately acted to support the civil rights efforts of the 1960s (including the Black Power movement) and was one of the earliest groups to oppose, formally and vehemently, the Vietnam War. By 1970 several white Baptist churches had formed dual associations with the PNBC; conversely, some PNBC congregations have established memberships in white Baptist conventions. The PNBC remains the smallest of the three black Baptist conventions.

African Americans are also spread across the spectrum of Methodist denominations in the United States. The African Methodist Episcopal Church (AME), established in 1816, had 450,000 members by 1896. Its growth in the second half of the nineteenth century and in the twentieth century occurred primarily in America in the north and west, and overseas in Africa and the Caribbean. This denomination has, since its origin, been committed to social action that focuses on the poor and underprivileged.

African American Churches on the Edge. At the beginning of the twentieth century the African American church was greatly affected by two external forces. The first was the impact of the Holiness and Pentecostal movements upon African Americans. The founder and earliest exponent of Holiness thought was a Methodist woman, Phoebe Worrell Palmer, who lived in New York City. In 1835 she began holding a weekly "Tuesday Meeting for the Promotion of Holiness." She focused on the Holy Spirit as the font of enlightenment and power. Her efforts resulted initially in the Church of the Nazarene and later in the

African Methodist Episcopal Church. Women attend a Youth League event outside the First AME Church, 1918. Shades of L.A. Archives/Los Angeles Public Library

development of a similar school of thought called Pentecostalism, which by 1990 was the fastest-growing segment of American Christianity. Palmer's thoughts took on an institutional form in the 1880s when members of the Methodist church established the National Camp Meeting Association for the Promotion of Holiness. Other Holiness groups developed within the Methodist and Baptist churches.

By the 1890s, however, many blacks and whites within the Holiness movement withdrew from the Methodist and Baptist churches. In 1906 many adherents of Holiness thought were attracted to the Azusa Street Revival in Los Angeles, California. William J. Seymour, a black Holiness preacher, established the revival, formally known as the Apostolic Faith Gospel Movement. Seymour had studied under Charles F. Parnham, the founder of the Pentecostal movement. Like Parnham, Seymour taught that true conversion was followed by a "baptism of the Holy Spirit," which in turn led to perfect holiness. Services at the revival were marked by speaking in tongues and the healing of the sick. The movement itself was marked by true egalitarianism: women and men preached, and the congregation welcomed whites, blacks, and Hispanics.

A disciple of Seymour's, Charles H. Mason, returned to his home in Memphis and, along with Charles Jones, established a church called the Church of God in Christ. The two differed over dogma, however—Jones rejected the notion of speaking in tongues—and the church split. Mason and his followers continued under the name of the Church of God in Christ, and eventually became the largest black Pentecostal denomination. Jones established the Church of Christ (Holiness). These churches have been disparagingly referred to as "holy rollers" because of the emotional nature of the church service, which supposedly causes fervent worshippers to roll on the floor and which incorporates the use of such secular musical instruments as the guitar, piano, and drums into a style of music that has become known as black gospel music.

The second twentieth-century force that affected the African American church was the Great Migration, a massive movement—beginning in the early twentieth century—of African Americans out of the South and into the West and (primarily) the North. At its peak, between 1940 and 1970, 4.4 million blacks left their homes in the South in search of opportunities in the industrially developing cities of the North. Many of these itinerant blacks found their new environs unfriendly and uncomfortable. In particular many missed the warmth and support of their churches, but they lacked the funds to build new churches in the crowded cities that they now inhabited.

As a result, black churches came to occupy vacant storefronts and warehouses, such as the Azusa Street Mission. The African American search for religious solace in the cities also gave rise to cults that were founded upon the personalities of single individuals. Such was the Universal Peace Mission Movement of Father Divine, a movement that dominated the African American religious experience during the first half of the twentieth century. It was founded by Father Major Jealous Divine, who was born George Baker in Georgia around 1880. Father Divine's community began quietly in the 1920s, when he provided housing for a number of his black followers. As the number of those followers grew, they came to include both blacks and whites. The movement came to prominence in the early 1930s when Father Divine was arrested for disturbing the peace. Only days after he sentenced Father Divine to jail, the judge, who had previously been in robust health, died, and Father Divine claimed responsibility. Soon after Divine and his followers moved to Harlem.

Father Divine's movement was a hodgepodge of religious traditions. His premise was that all men are equal before God and therefore have the same rights: the rights to life, liberty, and happiness. Father Divine had a clear International Modesty Code that prohibited tobacco, alcohol, and contact between the sexes. Even married couples who were members of the movement were required to live apart.

Unlike other cultlike religious organizations, none of the Peace Mission's assets were titled in Father Divine's name; rather, each group of believers incorporated their church and affiliated it with Father Divine's movement. The movement experienced its greatest growth during Father Divine's lifetime. After his death in 1965, the Peace Mission maintained churches in Philadelphia, the Bronx, Newark, Los Angeles, and Sacramento.

Similar to Father Divine's Universal Peace Mission, the United House of Prayer for All People was established by Charles Manuel Grace. "Sweet Daddy," as his followers called him, was born in the Cape Verde Islands and moved to Massachusetts, where he worked as a railroad short-order cook, a salesman, and a grocer. In 1919 he established his first United House of Prayer in Wareham, Massachusetts. Subsequently other churches were founded in Charlotte, North Carolina, in Washington, D.C., and in other locations along the east coast of the United States. The church followed the Pentecostal tradition, emphasizing sanctification, purification through a holy life, and the presence of the Holy Spirit. The church drew its membership primarily from the economically depressed ghettos of the growing cities.

Following the African American tradition, the ceremonies of the United House of Prayer were marked by song, dance, and hand clapping, with the Pentecostal touch of speaking in tongues. Unlike other African American churches, however, Sweet Daddy's House of Prayer had no social programs or agenda. The church did carry on an extensive business in a number of products, including soap, toothpaste, and cookies—all of which were marketed under the name "Daddy Grace." The church and its founder suffered a major collapse in 1970 when the Internal Revenue Service seized most of Grace's properties to pay an alleged $5,966,000 in back taxes.

Growth of an Alternate Religious Tradition. In the twentieth century the black church became the initial arena for the pursuit of African American identity, independence, equality, and complete freedom. The best-known experiment in this respect was carried out by Marcus Mosiah Garvey, a native of Jamaica who organized the Universal Negro Improvement Association (UNIA) in Jamaica in 1914. The purpose of the organization was to bring all people of African descent together. Greatly impressed by the work of Booker T. Washington to educate and train blacks in the United States, Garvey came to the United States in 1916 to convince Washington to train blacks to become missionaries in Africa. But these

Charles Manuel "Sweet Daddy" Grace, c. 1930. Photograph by Addison Scurlock. Scurlock Studio Records, Archives Center, National Museum of American History, Smithsonian Institution

missionaries would not try to save souls or convert the Africans to Christian religions; rather, Garvey envisioned that they would provide technical training to the Africans. Unfortunately Washington had died by the time Garvey arrived. Garvey thereupon decided to remain and establish branches of his organization in the United States. The movement was popular with the black communities and quickly caught on.

The religious tradition of the UNIA borrowed heavily from the Catholic Church. It characterized Jesus Christ as the "Black Savior" and the Virgin Mary as the "Black Madonna." Many within the black communities flocked to Garvey's "Liberty Halls," where they proclaimed their belief "in God, the Creator, ... Jesus Christ, His Son," and "Marcus Garvey, the leader of the Negro peoples of the world."

The success of Garvey's message of African unity tied to religion upset many in both the black and white communities. Partially as a result of an FBI investigation, Garvey was convicted of mail fraud and sentenced to prison. In 1927, having served two years, he was deported. The loss of Garvey's presence and leadership resulted in the collapse of UNIA; however, his ideas of Pan-Africanism tied to religion would survive.

The search for freedom and equality was not limited to a Christian context. Almost since the arrival of the first African slaves in Jamestown, African Americans had metaphorically compared themselves to the Old Testament Jews. In 1896 William S. Crowdy, a black man from Lawrence, Kansas, began to preach a new version of Judaism in which he argued that blacks were part of the lost tribes of Israel. To advance his beliefs, he founded the Church of God and Saints of Christ. This merger of Jewish and black identity was repeated in the 1920s when Wentworth A. Matthew brought together a congregation of black Jews in Harlem known as the Commandment Keepers Congregation of the Living God. Matthew rejected the emotionally charged Christianity of the African American churches in favor of strict discipline and morality that would enhance the image of African Americans. Crowdy's and Matthew's breaks with Christianity would not be the only such deviations in the twentieth century.

At about the same time that Crowdy and Matthew were preaching a convergence of blacks and Judaism, Timothy Drew, a black railroad worker from North Carolina, was changing his name to Noble Drew Ali. In 1913 he established the first Moorish Science Temple in Newark, New Jersey. He published the beliefs of his church in a sixty-page pamphlet entitled "The Holy Koran," which should not be confused with the Qu'ran of orthodox Islam because there is no similarity in the doctrines set out in the two. Drew built his belief system on recent black history. He argued that just as Saint John the Baptist had been the herald for Jesus Christ, so Marcus Garvey was the herald of Noble Drew Ali. Noble Drew established the headquarters of the Moorish Science Temple in Chicago and established other temples in several cities. After his death in 1929 the efforts of his followers were stymied by the rise of a second black church founded upon the Muslim tradition—the Nation of Islam.

Little is known about the life of Wallace D. Fard before his appearance as an itinerant peddler in Detroit in 1930. Fard preached to his customers that blacks were part of the "lost-found tribe of Shabazz" and that salvation depended upon the development of "knowledge of self." To provide a foundation for his Nation of Islam, he developed a creation story: in the beginning all men were created black, but an evil "Dr. Yakub" created a race of white devils whom he was unable to control. The white devils multiplied and took control of the world, which Allah permitted, but at the end of the allotted time—at the end of the world—the Nation of Islam would return to its proper place as ruler. For this reason, rather than seeking integration, which was the goal of many during the years of Jim Crow, blacks must separate themselves from the white race and prepare for the new age, during which the Nation of Islam would prevail. In 1934 Fard was arrested for disturbing the peace and ordered by the police to leave Detroit. By this time he had established two congregations, one in Detroit and one in Chicago, and several educational programs. He left his church in the hands of Elijah Poole, whom he renamed Elijah Muhammad. Fard then simply disappeared. Some believe that he was murdered.

Elijah Muhammad taught that Fard was the incarnation of Allah and that he had returned to Heaven to prepare for the end of the world. Muhammad also argued that he was the messenger of Fard/Allah. Under his leadership, which lasted until 1975, the Nation of Islam experienced substantial growth. By 1960 its membership exceeded 100,000. Much of this growth was the result of the work of Malcolm X, formerly known as Malcolm Little. Malcolm was the son of a Baptist minister who had been a supporter of Marcus Garvey. He grew up always on the edge of trouble, and by 1950 he was in prison. There he began to read the writings of Elijah Muhammad and became a fervent convert to the Nation of Islam. Upon his release, he formally joined the Nation of Islam and began to work tirelessly to spread its word and increase its membership. He was a staunch critic of those blacks who had accepted Christianity—"the white man's religion." He dedicated himself to the tenets of Islam as he understood them, which included strict discipline and dietary regulations. He also helped to establish a number of remarkably successful rehabilitation programs within the Nation of Islam to address the needs of those who had been released from prison, drug addicts, and alcoholics. The turning point for Elijah Muhammad, Malcolm X, and the Nation of Islam occurred with a falling out between Muhammad and Malcolm after Malcolm returned from his hajj. While on the hajj—the pilgrimage to Mecca that is required of all able orthodox Muslims—Malcolm was shocked to find that Islam attracted and included followers from all races, including whites. For him this revelation struck at the very foundations of the Nation of Islam. Upon his return to the United States he broke with the Nation of Islam and established his own church, The Muslim Mosque, Inc., and proclaimed a message of Pan-Africanism. He became a confirmed and active critic of the Nation of Islam, which was the reason that he was assassinated in 1964.

The apparent successor to Elijah Muhammad as the leader of the Nation of Islam was his son, Warith Deen Muhammad. Warith however had been estranged from his father for some time. The estrangement was possibly the result of Warith's personal experiences with Islam, for he had learned Arabic, visited Mecca, and become a serious student of orthodox Islam. Prior to Muhammad's death in 1975 he and Warith reconciled, and upon Muhammad's death Warith assumed the leadership of the Nation of Islam. In 1985 Warith attempted to disband the Nation of Islam and led most of its followers into orthodox Islam. A small number of the followers of the Nation of Islam, led by Minister Louis Farrakhan, retained the name and the teachings of Elijah Muhammad. Despite the efforts of Farrakhan, including the One Million Man March of October 1995, it is estimated that membership in the Nation of Islam is only about 20,000 nationally. Warith's decision to lead the Nation of Islam into orthodox Islam hints at an important context that is seldom discussed. There had been since the 1920s a moderate-sized orthodox Muslim community in the United States, and it grew steadily: by the late 1990s it was estimated at 5 million people, with approximately 2 million of those being African Americans. This movement is marked by racial equality and inclusiveness. It also represents a serious movement away from what is perceived of as the Christian-centeredness of African American society.

The Black Church and the Civil Rights Movement. The greatest battle for the African American churches in the twentieth century was for racial equality and freedom. The Civil War and its accompanying Thirteenth, Fourteenth, and Fifteenth amendments ended the formal institution of slavery and professed to offer blacks freedom, but the reality of life was much different. Soon after the end of Reconstruction in 1877, most southern states rushed to enact Jim Crow laws that in a real sense reestablished slavery. Blacks were banned from white restaurants, places of entertainment, and public accommodation. They were required to ride segregated streetcars and, later, buses, and were required to use only specified water fountains and bathrooms. Any attempt by blacks to exercise their rights to vote or sit on juries was met with harassment and often death. Such treatment made freedom only a word and, in a practical sense, condemned most blacks to a life of poverty. The overwhelming nature of this problem—the condemnation of an entire people to the status of second-class citizenry—became a social issue that the African American churches in the twentieth century could not avoid. But not all decided to address it in the same way.

In 1909 a biracial group that included the great W. E. B. Du Bois established the National Association for the Advancement of Colored People (NAACP). This was a direct response to Jim Crow. Many African American churches, including the AME, the AME Zion, and the Baptists, responded to this effort by supporting both the NAACP and the newly formed National Urban League. They also established their own programs to foster the education and the development of skills among their black members.

The role of black churches in the lives of their members reached its pinnacle in the late 1950s. Some historians have marked this period as the transition from the Negro church to the black church, and the person most responsible for this transition was the Reverend Martin Luther King Jr., for it was he who made the church aware of its power to effect social change. King became pastor of the Dexter Street Baptist Church in Montgomery, Alabama, in 1954. He helped establish the Montgomery Improvement Association, which supported the Montgomery Bus Boycott of 1955–1956. This action marked the beginning of the aggressive involvement of the black churches in the fledgling civil rights movement. Much has been made of King's adoption—and the black church's endorsement—of Gandhi's philosophy of nonviolence. In truth King's philosophy is better understood as the merger of religion and resistance, as a philosophy of challenge and religious fervor in which the proponents of civil rights challenged the Jim Crow establishment while singing black spirituals whose roots often reached back to the slave cultures of the pre–Civil War period.

In 1957 more than sixty black ministers met at Ebenezer Baptist Church in Atlanta, Georgia, to set up the Southern Christian Leadership Conference (SCLC); they elected Martin Luther King Jr. to be their first president. But these actions were not well received in all black churches. Dr. Joseph H. Jackson, the much-revered and longtime president of the National Baptist Convention, was critical of his younger brothers and their actions. He sought to steer the convention into a nonconfrontational posture that would be acceptable to white-dominated

Jefferson Baptist Church Congregation. Putnam County, Georgia, 1941. Photograph by Irving Rusinow. DEPARTMENT OF AGRICULTURE, NATIONAL ARCHIVES AND RECORDS ADMINISTRATION

denominations. As a result the more liberal and often younger members of the convention, such as Martin Luther King Jr. and his father Martin Luther King Sr., left the NBC to form the Progressive Baptist Alliance. This period was marked by the rise of a new black clergy who would lead the black church into the twenty-first century, such as Ralph Abernathy, who would succeed King as president of the SCLC, and Wyatt Walker, who was the executive director of SCLC from 1960 to 1964.

Of particular importance is Leon H. Sullivan. Sullivan was born in West Virginia and served as an assistant pastor under the Reverend Adam Clayton Powell at the Abyssinian Baptist Church in New York City. Eventually he became pastor of the poor Zion Baptist Church in northern Philadelphia. Sullivan helped establish the Philadelphia Four Hundred, a group of black ministers who promoted "selected patronage" to force the end of segregation and aid in the employment of blacks. Under this program, ministers would advise their congregations not to buy at those businesses that refused or failed to employ blacks. Later Sullivan founded the Opportunity Industrialization Centers in Philadelphia and other cities. The purpose of the centers was to educate and train blacks so they would be prepared to work in new jobs as the jobs became available. Sullivan subsequently took his battle for equal employment and rights for blacks to the international stage. He joined the board of directors of General Motors in 1971, becoming the first black to sit on the board of a major American corporation. From this position he championed the cause of freeing Nelson Mandela and ending apartheid in South Africa.

The presence of black churches in the civil rights movement was not limited to the South. In 1966 black clergy from such white-dominated denominations as the Presbyterian, Episcopalian, and Congregationalist churches met in New York City to form the National Council of Black Churchmen. The group issued a statement, entitled "Black Power," in the same year. Because this statement coincided with similar rhetoric by the Black Panthers and the Nation of Islam, it unsettled many white and black clergy. The statement however was nothing more than a call for Christian justice and equality for blacks.

The assassination of the Reverend Martin Luther King Jr. in 1968 had a serious impact on the black church's role in the civil rights movement, principally because it deprived both the church and the movement of King's leadership. King's death did not end the church's involvement, however: individuals, such as the Reverend Leon

Sullivan, and congregations, such as the Ebenezer Baptist Church in Atlanta, continued and continue to play an active role in advancing and protecting the rights and interests of African Americans.

The Black Church and the Black Community at the End of the Millennium. By the 1980s the black church had arrived at a destiny driven by two major elements in its history. The liberation tradition that originated almost two centuries earlier with Denmark Vesey and Gabriel Prosser had continued through Frederick Douglass, Harriet Tubman, and Sojourner Truth, to reach its pinnacle with Reverend Martin Luther King Jr. and the civil rights movement. There was also a long history of self-help that began with the Free African Society, established by Richard Allen and Absalom Jones in 1787, the mutual aid societies that spread throughout the northern states prior to the Civil War and reached their peak with the NAACP and the National Urban League.

These two threads in the black church experience converged in the 1980s, as black ministers dedicated themselves and their churches to the development of a positive black consciousness and identity. In 1976 the Reverend Floyd H. Flake was appointed the minister of Allen AME Church in Jamaica, Queens, New York. This was a middle-class congregation of 1,400 members. Over the next ten years, Reverend Flake and his congregation worked to remake their community. The church raised millions of dollars, erected buildings, and established a number of nonprofit corporations to provide educational programs for the young and social service programs for the elderly. Such activities were not unique. Other black churches throughout the country carried on similar activities: Shiloh Baptist Church of Washington, D.C., Abyssinian Baptist Church of Harlem, and Ward AME Church of Los Angeles.

This growth of self-awareness also occurred in the American Catholic Church. Between 1945 and 1975 the number of black Catholics grew from 296,988 to 916,854. As of 2008 there were more than 2 million. In 1970 the National Office of Black Catholics was established under the direction of Father Joseph M. Davis, S.M., and in 1980 the Institute for Black Catholic Studies was established at Xavier University of Louisiana in New Orleans. Both of these worked to establish a black identity in the American Catholic Church by developing a strong African American ministry and worship ceremonies that could relate to the history and culture of blacks, such as the use of drumming and African music. In 1984 the ten black Catholic bishops in the United States called upon black Catholics to contribute their history to aid in the development of the American Catholic Church at large. Finally, in 1987, after a lapse of ninety years, the African American Catholic Congress met again for the purpose of emphasizing the role of blacks in the history of the American Catholic Church.

Even as many observers grieved over the secularization of American society and the decline of religion in America, in 1996 the largest gathering of black men in American history took place in Washington, D.C., under the direction of the Reverend Louis Farrakhan of the Nation of Islam. Many other religious and civil black leaders were critical of Farrakhan and his so-called Million Man March; nevertheless the great number of black men who participated in this event did reflect the strong sense of church that continued to exist in the black community. In 1938 the U.S. Census estimated that 5.7 million blacks out of a total black population of 12.8 million were church members; nearly fifty years later the Yearbook of American and Canadian Churches estimated that black church membership exceeded 17 million. Such numbers and the expansive list of social programs carried on under the auspices of the black church clearly indicates that as the twenty-first century begins, the black church remains an important institution in the black community.

[*See also* AME Church; Baptist Church, African Americans and; Divine, Father; Farrakhan, Louis; Flake, Floyd; Garvey, Marcus; King, Martin Luther, Jr.; Muhammad, Elijah; Nation of Islam; Religion; Religious Communities and Practices; Southern Christian Leadership Conference.]

BIBLIOGRAPHY

Frazier, E. Franklin, and C. Eric Lincoln. *The Negro Church in America/The Black Church Since Frazier*. New York: Schocken, 1974. Frazier's concise and insightful look at the black church in America since the coming of the first slaves, with an essay by Lincoln on the black church since the civil rights movement.

Hudson, Winthrop S., and John Corrigan. *Religion in America*. 6th ed. Upper Saddle River, N.J.: Prentice Hall, 1999. Skillfully places black churches within the context of American religion.

Lincoln, C. Eric, and Lawrence H. Mamiya. *The Black Church in the African American Experience*. Durham, N.C.: Duke University Press, 1990. A history of the black church with a sociological emphasis.

Noll, Mark A. *The Old Religion in a New World: The History of North American Christianity*. Grand Rapids, Mich.: William B. Eerdmans, 2002. The most recent and complete look at the black church in the context of American history.

Raboteau, Albert J. *Canaan Land: A Religious History of African Americans*. New York: Oxford University Press, 2001. An insightful look at black religion by one of the most respected African American religious historians.

THOMAS E. CARNEY

BLACK COACHES ASSOCIATION. The Black Coaches Association (BCA) is a nonprofit organization that aims to address the disparity between the high percentage of minority professional and collegiate athletes and the low percentage of minority coaches. Formed in 1988, the Black Coaches Association began as a group of assistant basketball and football coaches who wanted to address the dramatic dearth of minority coaches in head coaching positions. Although the BCA initially focused on supporting African American coaches, it subsequently expanded its mission to include all minority ethnic groups. In May 2007 the BCA officially changed its name to the Black Coaches and Administrators to better reflect its membership.

In both basketball and football a substantial proportion of the athletes at the collegiate and professional level belong to racial minorities; on many teams minority players outnumber white players. In 2002, for example, minority players—mostly African Americans—accounted for approximately 70 percent of the National Football League.

Coaches often start out as athletes. It follows logically that, given the large proportion of minority players in these sports, a sizable proportion of the coaches in football and basketball programs would also come from minority groups. Historically, however, most coaches have been white, and this trend continues to prevail, especially in the sport of college football, where in the 2006 season minority coaches held the top coaching job at only eleven of the more than two hundred Division 1A and 1AA schools (excluding historically black institutions).

One of the BCA's most successful awareness campaigns is its issuance of an annual "Hiring Report Card" that examines the hiring process used by Division 1A and 1AA schools when they select a new head coach for their football programs. The BCA issued its first Hiring Report Card to coincide with the 2003–2004 football season. Each Hiring Report Card examines five areas of the hiring process: the communications between schools and the BCA, the percentage of minority members in hiring and search committees, the percentage of on-campus interviews that went to minority candidates, the length of the hiring process, and the presence of, and documented adherence to, affirmative action policies at the school. The Hiring Report Cards have generated media interest in major sports and news outlets—with coverage in *Sports Illustrated*, on *ESPN*, and in the Associated Press—thus drawing attention to the issue.

In addition to its Hiring Report Cards, the Black Coaches Association has successfully raised both funds and awareness for its cause by sponsoring a college basketball tournament and a college football game. The football game, known as the BCA Classic, ran from 1997 to 2004. The preseason basketball tournament of the same name began in 1994, and the tournament's success has led the organizers to expand it, incorporating more teams into the existing tournament and adding a second event, the BCA Invitational.

A milestone of sorts for the BCA was reached in early 2007 when the championship game for the National Football League, the Super Bowl, featured two African American coaches: the winning coach, Tony Dungy of the Indianapolis Colts, and Lovie Smith of the losing Chicago Bears. Nevertheless, the disparity that brought the BCA into being some decades ago persists.

[*See also* Sports.]

BIBLIOGRAPHY

Black Coaches and Administrators Web site. http://www.bcasports.org. The official site of the BCA; includes archive copies of previous "Hiring Report Cards" and general information about the group, membership, and events.

Thomas, Ron. *They Cleared the Lane: The NBA's Black Pioneers*. Lincoln: University of Nebraska Press, 2002. Chapter 16 discusses the dearth of black coaches in the National Basketball Association and describes the careers of several black coaches in the NBA.

—JEFFREY WOMACK

BLACK COLLEGES AND UNIVERSITIES. *See* Historically Black Colleges and Universities.

BLACK ENTERTAINMENT TELEVISION. Robert L. Johnson is the black entrepreneur responsible for Black Entertainment Television (BET). Johnson was born in Hickory, Mississippi, on 8 April 1946, the ninth of ten children. He went on to receive his bachelor's degree from the University of Illinois at Urbana-Champaign (UIUC) in 1968. It was at UIUC that Johnson became a member of Kappa Alpha Psi Fraternity and met Sheila Crump, who later became his wife. Johnson completed graduate studies at Princeton University, earning his master's degree in public administration in 1972.

In 1976 Johnson joined the National Cable Television Association (NCTA). At this time, Johnson more closely considered an idea he had to start a channel that focused its programming on African Americans. At an NCTA convention, he met Bob Rosencrans, the chief of UA/Columbia Cablevision. Johnson inquired about using a two-hour block of programming time on Friday nights on Rosencrans's cable network. Rosencrans agreed to let Johnson use this time free of charge. On 8 August 1979 Johnson put out a press release announcing that Black Entertainment Television (BET) was to debut in January 1980. Having quit his job and taken out a $15,000 loan from a Washington bank, Johnson asked the NCTA to

Launch of BET.com. Black Entertainment Television chairman and founder Robert Johnson announces the launch of a Web site targeted to blacks, 12 August 1999. The Web site initiative, led by BET Holdings with support from the NAACP, the United Negro College Fund, and a group of top media companies, aimed to narrow the "digital divide"—the significantly lower use of the Internet by blacks. Photograph by Diane Bondareff. AP IMAGES

give him a $15,000 consulting contract. He incorporated the company for $42 on 13 September 1979.

In November of the same year, Johnson scheduled a meeting with the chief executive at TeleCommunications Incorporated (TCI), John Malone. By the end of the meeting, Malone agreed to buy 20 percent ($180,000) of Johnson's company and loan him the other 80 percent ($320,000). Johnson readily accepted this offer, and BET became TCI's first investment in programming. BET aired for the first time on 25 January 1980, broadcasting a movie titled *A Visit to Chief's Son*. The initial launch reached 3.8 million subscribers across the United States. Through continued expansions and added programs, BET grew to launch its own twenty-four-hour network on 1 October 1983.

In 1991 BET was listed on the New York Stock Exchange, becoming the first black-controlled company to do so. Johnson bought back all BET stock that was publicly traded in 1998. Subsequently, he sold BET to Viacom (the public media conglomerate responsible for other television networks like MTV and Comedy Central and the film production company DreamWorks) for $3 billion on 3 November 2000. With this move, Johnson became one of a handful of billionaires of African ancestry in the world.

In the years since its inception, BET has received much criticism about its content. Critics focus on BET's predominantly hip-hop video-laden programming that reinforces negative stereotypes of the black community, including a focus on materialism and hyper-masculinity. Most recently, in 2004, students at Spelman College, a historically black women's institution, criticized BET for the content aired on its *BET: Uncut* television program, which featured highly sexualized videos with little censorship. *BET: Uncut* was removed from BET programming in 2006. Due to dissatisfaction with what some critics termed "Black Exploitation Television," other black-focused television networks, including TV One and the Black Family Channel, have become increasingly popular and strong competitors for BET's audience.

[*See also* Blaxploitation Films; Entertainment Industry and African Americans; Film and Television Depictions of African Americans; *and* Television.]

BIBLIOGRAPHY

Jackson, David Earl, Marie Dutton Brown, and Linda Tarrant-Reid. *Celebrating Twenty Years: Black Star Power*. Washington, D.C.: BET Books, 2000. This short book recounts the history of BET from its own perspective.

Pulley, Brett. *The Billion Dollar BET: Robert Johnson and the Inside Story of Black Entertainment Television*. Hoboken, N.J.: John Wiley & Sons, 2004. This is one of the first biographies of Robert Johnson that chronicles his career achievements, specifically his involvement with BET.

Ross, Janell. "It's Raw. It's Raunchy. Why Are Women Fed Up with Hip-Hop?" *News & Observer*, 1 January 2006. This article highlights criticisms against the misogynistic nature of BET's programming and hip hop as a genre.

—QRESCENT MALI MASON

BLACK-JEWISH RELATIONS. Black-Jewish relations represent a richly layered chapter in twentieth-century U.S. history and, depending upon the area of activity or the time period involved, convey distinctive lessons not just for Jews or blacks but for all Americans with commitments to fair play, social justice, and human rights at home and abroad. The active engagement of Jewish Americans in civil rights struggles on behalf of blacks—from the establishment of the NAACP in 1909 to the freedom riders and other civil rights events and actions in the 1960s—is an inspiring narrative of interethnic cooperation.

At the same time, the participation of blacks and Jews in the labor movement and the Communist Party USA during the 1930s and 1940s has since the 1960s produced multiple ambivalent readings of motive and attitudes on both sides. And at least since the 1990s an exasperating level of open conflict and ugliness has emerged between the two groups—as demonstrated in heated exchanges within the academy and between organizations such as the Nation of Islam (NOI) and the Anti-Defamation League (ADL), as well as in the responses from the two sides to the 1991 Crown Heights riot in Brooklyn, New York.

In her 2006 book *Troubling the Waters*, Cheryl Lynn Greenberg views the history of black-Jewish relations as a microhistory of American liberalism (p. 8). Greenberg argues persuasively that Jews and blacks have had "different but overlapping goals and interests which converged in a particular historical moment" and that their divergent visions, always marked by "low-level tensions and occasional sharp disagreement," have weakened "the alliance as external realities changed" (p. 1).

Even though the earliest Jewish-black interaction materialized mostly in the urban North around the turn of the twentieth century, the Jewish and black presences in the United States can be traced back to earlier centuries. A Portuguese-speaking Jew, Abraão de Lucena, appears to have arrived in New Amsterdam (Dutch New York) from Amsterdam in 1654; he later settled in Georgia. But the arrival of African slaves in Jamestown, Virginia, in 1619 predates the immigration of any significant number of Jews to the United States by at least a century. Prior to the American Revolution, approximately two thousand Jews, predominantly from Spain and Portugal, lived in the British colonies. During the Civil War, in which Jews fought on both sides, there were fewer than two hundred thousand Jews in the United States—less than 1 percent of the population.

Throughout the nineteenth century, however, the Jewish population steadily increased, and after 1880 an additional 2 million Jews arrived from East Europe and settled mostly north of the Mason-Dixon Line. Because 90 percent of African Americans still lived in the South in 1880, there was minimal interaction between the two groups. The few Jews who lived in the South either owned slaves or otherwise accepted the "peculiar institution" by their silence. And Jews in the North rarely spoke out against slavery, their attitudes barely distinguishable from those of other Euro-Americans.

Migration to the Urban North. Around the turn of the twentieth century, with greater economic opportunities in the industrialized North, blacks embarked on massive migrations north, where they converged in cities and hoped to fill an increased demand for laborers. In moving from the South to the North during the Great Migration (1910–1930), southern blacks faced many obstacles, even if—unlike East European immigrants—they did not have to board a steamer to cross an ocean, learn a new language, or cope with the scrutiny of officials at Ellis Island. Then between 1940 and 1960 roughly 3 million blacks left the South, twice as many as had left during the Great Migration. And yet as the fiction of writers like Abraham Cahan, Anzia Yezierska, Mary Antin, Henry Roth, Rudolph Fisher, Wallace Thurman, and William Attaway reflects, blacks who moved from the rural South to northern cities during the early years of the twentieth century experienced a change in lifestyle, culture, and social expectations that was no less dramatic or traumatic than the changes that new Jewish and other immigrants from Europe experienced.

As demonstrated powerfully by two 1941 works—Richard Wright's *12 Million Black Voices* and Jacob Lawrence's sixty-painting series *The Migration of the Negro*—African Americans often moved to the North for the same reasons that immigrants came to the United States: to escape poverty or persecution or both and to seek better lives for themselves and their children. The move to the North represented for most blacks a second emancipation, just as many immigrants viewed their Americanization with awe and gratitude despite the discrimination they faced. The two vast and concurrent migrations of African Americans and European Jews into northern cities meant that these two groups were entangled throughout the twentieth century.

For centuries African Americans have felt a kindred connection to the Old Testament Jewish experience in Egypt. Just as the Israelites endured slavery under the pharaoh in Egypt, the ancestors of African Americans were brought against their will to the New World and sold into bondage. Since their days in slavery blacks have identified with the Jewish experience and have drawn parallels between the Jews' escape from Egypt led by Moses—as depicted in the book of Exodus in the Bible—and their own release from slavery and their migration north to greater freedom and opportunity. Blacks routinely referred to the Exodus story in their spirituals such as "Go Down, Moses," relating the sufferings of the Jews to their own despair as they beseeched their Lord for a Moses who would liberate them. Before and since emancipation, black sermons have often employed metaphors of the Promised Land to envision an America without racism. But until the twentieth century this fascination with biblical Jews had no opportunity to translate itself into interaction with real-life Jews.

Once the two groups began to interact in the urban North, however, African and Jewish Americans found many reasons to commiserate with each other, given their shared histories of being oppressed and marginalized. Unlike the German-speaking Jews who lived relatively solvent lives, most of the East European Jews who immigrated to the United States in the early twentieth century were financially impoverished and were part of the lower working class. Similarly, blacks who had also migrated north with the hope of improved social freedom and economic stability found themselves subject to continued racial discrimination and living in poverty-stricken ghettos. Rarely welcomed as tenants in white neighborhoods, Jews were forced into the slums alongside blacks. As a result these urban ghettos became the setting of both early cooperation and early conflict between Jewish and African Americans.

Interwar Civil Rights and Labor Organizations. Under a cloud of racial and ethnic prejudice, American Jews and blacks found common ground for cooperation. The massive wave of Jewish immigrants from Russia and East Europe who arrived in the early twentieth century brought with them progressive ideas about socialism, communism, and the power of labor unions. The Jewish community quickly rallied to establish organizations to defend Jewish interests: the American Jewish Committee in 1906, the Anti-Defamation League of B'nai B'rith in 1913, and finally the American Jewish Congress in 1918.

At around the same time, blacks, too, established organizations to defend their interests: for instance, the National Association of Colored Women (NACW) in 1896, the National Urban League (NUL) in 1910, and Marcus Garvey's Universal Negro Improvement Association (UNIA) in 1914. Jews and blacks came together most prominently in 1909 to help establish the National Association for the Advancement of Colored People (NAACP), the longest-surviving civil rights organization for blacks. Joel Elias Spingarn was a founder and from 1930 to his death in 1939 served as president, as did Kivie Kaplan from 1966 to 1975. Jack Greenberg served as the director-counsel of the NAACP Legal Defense and Educational Fund from 1961 to 1984, and Herbert Hill served as the NAACP's head of labor relations from 1951 to 1977.

During the 1920s Jewish writers such as Fannie Hurst, Waldo Frank, and Victor Calverton played an important role in supporting the work of young African American writers, even as Carl Van Vechten persuaded Alfred and Blanche Knopf to publish the fiction and poetry of Harlem Renaissance writers such as Langston Hughes, Nella Larsen, Rudolph Fisher, and the NAACP secretary Walter White. Along with other literary radicals, Jewish scholars shaped new thinking on democracy and cultural pluralism in the early years of the twentieth century, and they continued to challenge racial constructs in social science scholarship in later decades.

Jews formed some of the most active and forceful labor unions in New York and beyond, advocating worker solidarity through picket signs printed in Yiddish and Hebrew and promoting a theme of brotherhood without the distinction of race or religion. These predominantly Jewish unions were among the first to make titled positions available to black workers. They also sought to encourage a more personal interaction between black children and Jewish children through racially mixed summer camps. The steadfast determination and intensity of Jewish activism in socialist groups foreshadowed the later heavy Jewish involvement in the Communist Party during the 1930s. The Communist Party's emphasis on class struggle held understandable appeal for both blacks and Jews. In an effort to unite the minority working classes, activists recruited heavily in the Harlem area of New York City. Because many of the Communist organizers in Harlem were Jewish, their efforts during the 1920s and 1930s brought many Jews and blacks together in significant ways to further their common cause. Such attempts to support and advance the Communist movement in Harlem continued into the 1940s.

Within these mixed communities, despite some undercurrent of tensions and differences, there existed considerable consensus and common purpose. Most blacks found their Jewish colleagues in the movement to be kind, compassionate, and supportive of their political and economic causes. Jews performed multiple roles beyond that of party activists and organizers—for example, as backers of the NAACP and labor union officials. In addition, Jews were often the only people who employed blacks or extended them credit. The cordial and reciprocal alliance that formed between the Jewish and black community, while economically advantageous, also stemmed from a mutual understanding and empathy for their similar plights.

In the first half of the twentieth century, simultaneous collaboration and conflict distinguished communities made up of both blacks and Jews. Despite efforts to achieve equality, the cultural gulf that divided these subcommunities, both physically and psychologically, inevitably surfaced. Often disparities were perceived, particularly by blacks, as thinly veiled if not open forms of prejudice and oppression. Jews were commonly merchants and landlords, as well as teachers and administrators in public schools in black neighborhoods. These positions afforded them direct contact with blacks, often on a daily basis, and yielded more control and authority over blacks than other whites had.

Although Jews served a vital and distinct purpose in the community, the inherent advantage of white skin, combined with Jews' better socioeconomic living conditions—which were apparent on a daily basis—reawakened black feelings of white oppression and served to incite anti-Jewish sentiments. The seemingly reciprocal yet actually one-sided arrangement that had formed proved to be a highly volatile contradiction that remained at the heart of the relationship between blacks and Jews for the remainder of the century.

Despite the discrimination they faced in many areas of life, Jewish Americans must have been aware of the privileges that their white skin sometimes gave—privileges never given to black Americans. Yet out of an affirmative respect for their own history of persecution, Jews as a group for the most part have resisted the temptation of surrendering fully to a white American identity. Still, in *The Crisis of the Negro Intellectual* (1967), Harold Cruse questions the motives behind Jews' involvement in black causes. Accusing the Jews of serving agendas, Cruse attempts to explain why the false Jewish friends were purged from the increasingly black nationalist struggles for identity and self-determination.

The Leo Frank Incident and the Harlem Riots. In 1913 black and Jewish populations clashed in a particularly infamous incident that served to devastate both communities as it gained national notoriety. Thirteen-year-old Mary Phagan, a young white girl who worked at a pencil factory in Atlanta, Georgia, was found murdered. Leo Frank, a Jewish man who supervised the factory, was accused and later convicted of the crime based on testimony given by Jim Conley, an African American man who worked as a janitor at the factory. It was during Frank's trial that the Anti-Defamation League was established. At the trial Conley testified that he served as a lookout for Frank, who at times used his supervisory position to prey sexually on both young girls and boys. Frank was convicted and sentenced to die, but in summer 1915 the governor of Georgia, unconvinced of Frank's guilt, commuted his sentence to life in prison. Shortly after, a mob of nearly thirty armed men forced their way into the prison and kidnapped Frank, whom they drove to a lynching site more than two hundred miles away and killed.

The Frank incident pitted blacks against Jews. Blacks alleged that Conley had been exploited by Frank, while Jews contended that Conley had wrongly accused Frank of being a pervert. The repercussions of the Frank trial grew more ominous when the lynch mob reconvened that year to revive the presence of the Ku Klux Klan (KKK) in the United States. The Klan had essentially been extinct since the passage of the Civil Rights Act of 1871, also known as the Ku Klux Klan Act. The reemergence of the KKK, notorious for its racist and anti-Semitic views, struck a chord of terror among both blacks and Jews.

In March 1935 a series of riots took place in Harlem, whose flourishing Jewish community of 178,000 in 1917 had been reduced to only 5,000 by 1930. The riots took place in reaction to the spread of a false report that a Puerto Rican teenager, Lino Rivera, had been beaten to death for shoplifting a ten-cent penknife at the Kress Five and Ten Store. In actuality an employee had caught the boy stealing and threatened to beat him, resulting in a scuffle in which Rivera bit the employee's hand. Coincidentally a hearse was parked nearby when an ambulance drove up to treat the employee's wound. Although the store manager had called the police, who later released the boy, rumors spread quickly that the boy had been brutally beaten and killed by white police. Organizers from the Young Communist League, along with members of a more radical African American group known as the Young Liberators, arranged demonstrations that quickly turned violent.

According to Winston McDowell, these riots had been preceded for three years by a jobs campaign for Depression-ridden black workers by the Harlem elite, as well as by demagogues such as the black Muslim Sufi Abdul Hamid, who had arrived in Harlem after some success in a jobs campaign in Chicago. In 1931 whites and Jews owned 83 percent of the business establishments in Harlem. Of these 1,916 establishments, only 24 percent employed blacks—usually in low-paying positions—and 59 percent refused to hire blacks at all. Hamid, who denied vehemently that he was an anti-Semite, undoubtedly incited poor blacks against Jewish and white businesses in Harlem. Although the riots caused several deaths, along with property damage of at least $200 at each of more than six hundred stores, the stores owned by two Jewish businessmen, Morris Weinstein and Samuel S. Leibowitz, who were active in the black community as "joint sufferers" were completely spared by the mobs.

The 1935 riots—and again the August 1943 riots—reflected the inconsistencies and bitterness felt by the black community, whose employment rate, public housing, health, and social well-being were disproportionately below those of white Americans, including Jewish Americans. Although resentments over social and political inequities continued to inflame tensions between blacks and Euro-American Jews, the civil rights organizations that had been established after World War I continued to grow in strength and influence. Their belief that a combined effort was essential in order to fight racism and anti-Semitism resulted in later collaborative efforts on both local and national scales.

March to Full Civil Rights. In 1942 the Congress of Racial Equality (CORE) was formed in Chicago by whites, Jews, and blacks under the leadership of George Houser, James Farmer, Bernice Fisher, and Bayard Rustin to organize sit-ins against segregation. The tenets of CORE were rooted in Henry David Thoreau's philosophy of civil disobedience and Mohandas K. Gandhi's teachings of nonviolent resistance. In early 1947 the group planned a two-week expedition through Virginia, North Carolina, Tennessee, and Kentucky. Eight Jewish men and eight black men representing CORE embarked on what they called the Journey of Reconciliation for the purpose of testing the Supreme Court's 1946 decision that had declared segregated seating of interstate passengers unconstitutional. The men were stopped and arrested several times. The journey ultimately ended in North Carolina, where the Jews were given stiff sentences for their role in inciting blacks to defy the state's Jim Crow laws, and the blacks, including Rustin, were forced to work on a chain gang.

More than a decade later CORE resurrected the legacy of the Journey of Reconciliation as it again sought to test Supreme Court mandates against segregated interstate transportation and terminals. Farmer renewed the spirit of the Journey of Reconciliation under the new name Freedom Ride. The freedom riders were groups of black and white activists, both men and women, who boarded buses headed south. The white, mostly Jewish passengers took seats in the back, while blacks sat in front. The same strategy was employed when entering restrooms in the terminals. Both blacks and whites used the areas designated off-limits to their race.

The freedom riders left Washington, D.C., on 4 May 1961 and intended to arrive in New Orleans on 17 May, marking the seventh anniversary of the *Brown v. Board of Education* decision that had declared segregation in public schools unconstitutional. The Freedom Ride, which had split into two groups in Alabama, met with shocking violence and failed to reach its destination. Between a third and a half of those who participated in the Freedom Rides were Jews. Many of the activists suffered horrific beatings and were jailed throughout the summer.

In 1961 when President John F. Kennedy appointed the director-counsel of the NAACP Legal Defense and Educational Fund Thurgood Marshall to the U.S. Court of Appeals for the Second Circuit, Jack Greenberg, a white Jewish lawyer who had worked for the fund and under Marshall since 1949, was chosen to replace him. The appointment was not without significance. By the 1960s the alliance that had formed between African and Jewish Americans had achieved measurable success through the joint efforts of organizations such as the NAACP and Jewish groups such as the American Jewish Committee and local Jewish community relations councils. Jewish donations accounted for a primary source of funding for the nation's two largest African American organizations, the NAACP and the National Urban League. Greenberg effectively and profitably directed the NAACP Legal Defense Fund until 1984, symbolizing the deep underlying commitment and cooperation that existed between blacks and Jews in the civil rights movement.

Earlier, in 1958, as described in Melissa Fay Greene's book *The Temple Bombing*, an Atlanta synagogue was bombed because its rabbi was an outspoken champion of integration. Another central figure in the civil rights movement was Stanley Levison, a Jewish businessman who served as a top aide and literary agent to Martin Luther King Jr. Levison was active as a fund-raiser and publicizer in King's Southern Christian Leadership Conference (SCLC).

March on Washington and the Freedom Summer. For the next several years the civil rights movement played out on a national stage. On 28 August 1963, Martin Luther King Jr. delivered his legendary "I Have a Dream" speech on the steps of the Lincoln Memorial. Approximately 200,000 people were in attendance, 80 percent of whom were African American and 20 percent a mix of whites, Jews, and others. The following year Congress passed the Civil Rights Act, and President Lyndon B. Johnson signed it into law on 2 July 1964.

The year 1964 also saw the advent of the Mississippi Summer Project, otherwise known as the Freedom Summer, beginning in June. Its goal was to register as many African Americans as possible to vote. The Freedom

Black-Jewish Relations. Rabbi Abraham Heschel presents the Judaism and World Peace award to the Reverend Dr. Martin Luther King Jr., 1965. NEW YORK WORLD–TELEGRAM AND THE SUN NEWSPAPER PHOTOGRAPH COLLECTION, PRINTS AND PHOTOGRAPHS DIVISION, LIBRARY OF CONGRESS

Summer was staffed mostly by young, white volunteers, many of whom were college students from the North and many of whom were Jewish Americans. On 21 June three young activists—James Chaney, a black CORE organizer from Mississippi, and two Jews from New York, the CORE organizer Michael Schwerner and the summer volunteer Andrew Goodman—were apparently abducted by two carloads of Ku Klux Klan members after having investigated a church burning in Neshoba County, a Klan stronghold. The men shot Schwerner and Goodman and then shot Chaney, after chain-whipping and mutilating him. The bodies of the three young men were discovered nearly two months later buried in an earthen dam.

The Freedom Summer activists, subjected to horrendous racist and anti-Semitic violence, thus exemplified the joint and valiant efforts of both blacks and Jews to challenge and end discrimination. The murders of Schwerner, Goodman, and Chaney have inspired at least three films: the 1975 TV docudrama *Attack on Terror: The FBI vs. the Ku Klux Klan*, the 1988 film *Mississippi Burning* directed by Alan Parker, and the 1990 TV movie *Murder in Mississippi*.

Black Power and Nation of Islam. Originally founded in Oakland, California, in 1966 and based on black nationalism, the Black Panther Party focused on defending African Americans against police brutality. Its leaders, like its philosophies, changed over the years, with constituents often opposing the views of party leaders. In 1968 Stokely Carmichael, the former head of the Student Nonviolent Coordinating Committee (SNCC), was named the party's prime minister. Carmichael was opposed to allowing whites and Jews to join the organization, convinced that they were unable to identify with the black struggle. The party's cofounder, Bobby Seale, sought to re-form the party into an instrument of social justice for everyone regardless of race or ethnicity. Eventually the Black Panthers denounced black nationalism as a form of "black racism" and focused instead on more ethnically inclusive social reform.

The founding of the Black Power movement—of which the Black Panthers were initially a part—represented a significant turning point in the black-Jewish alliance. The militant approaches of the Black Panthers put them at odds with Jews, who had achieved substantial strides through nonviolent, collaborative efforts and who felt threatened by strong militant tactics, particularly after the destruction witnessed during the Watts Riot in 1965. Although blacks and Jews had by the late 1960s developed significant differences regarding the methods of civil activism, Jews had also begun contemplating their own cultural identity, concerned as they were about the depletion of Jewishness through assimilation into whiteness. For example, in 1977 in an essay that introduced his landmark anthology *Jewish-American Stories*, Irving Howe declared that Jewish American fiction as a distinctive literary category was dead, or in any case that it had "moved past its high point" (quoted in Shapiro, p. vii). The growing need for internal reflection on the challenges of Jewish American identity, coupled with the opposing philosophies of activism, served further to estrange the Jewish and African American communities.

There were other local and national incidents and issues that contributed in the late 1960s and the 1970s to the unraveling of the close relationship between blacks and Jews. In 1968, for instance, a progressive move was initiated to overhaul the education of poor black students in the Ocean Hill–Brownsville school district in New York City. The Board of Education relinquished much of its control to parents, and the community promptly reassigned more than a dozen teachers. A heated battle ensued between the community and the predominantly white Jewish educators who were represented by the United

Federation of Teachers. In this racially divisive episode the union eventually won in court, but the city refused to uphold the decision, leading to a series of strikes by the teachers that effectively closed 85 percent of New York City's schools.

Then in the 1974 (*DeFunis v. Odegaard*) and 1978 (*University of California Regents v. Bakke*) affirmative action cases, black and Jewish organizations had for the first time taken opposite positions regarding a civil rights issue. In August 1979 the Jewish community was accused by black leaders of engineering the resignation of Andrew Young, an African American and the U.S. ambassador to the United Nations, after he met with a leader of the Palestine Liberation Organization even though U.S. policy forbade such contacts. Many Jews and others were angered in early 1984 when it was revealed that the Reverend Jesse Jackson, in a conversation with a black reporter for the *Washington Post*, referred to Jews as "Hymies" and to New York City as "Hymietown." Louis Farrakhan, the leader of the Nation of Islam, defended Jackson stridently, and since 1984 attacks by Farrakhan on Israel and Judaism have not helped matters.

In 1991 there were clashes between the Hasidic community and their West Indian neighbors in Crown Heights, Brooklyn, that threw a pall over black-Jewish relations. In the same year inflammatory attacks were exchanged between Leonard Jeffries, an Afrocentric black scholar at City College of the City University of New York, and his conservative Jewish colleague Michael Levin. In 1992 Henry Louis Gates Jr.'s attempt to confront black anti-Semitism in a *New York Times* op-ed piece was seen as one-sided because it did not raise the issue of Jewish antiblack racism. As a result of these and many other such incidents that sparked accusations of, from blacks, racism and, from Jews, anti-Semitism, many considered the alliance between African and Jewish Americans to have been irreparably damaged.

Looking Forward. It is worth noting, however, that although the traditionally close working relationship between African American and Jewish Americans is for all practical purposes a phenomenon of the past, issues of social justice remain important to both groups. The two communities both continue to play a cooperative role in the larger social justice and human rights movements. For example, organizations such as Jewish Funds for Justice have made a particular effort to reach out to black church leaders and have partnered successfully on community-organizing efforts in places such as Columbus, Ohio, and Boston.

In addition a growing number of people of color are part of some Jewish congregations, and some black Jewish congregations exist, too, including a vibrant one in Cairo, Illinois. Chabad-Lubavitch of Harlem, the only surviving synagogue in Harlem, is a living congregation for City College students and others. For Eric Sundquist, the author of *Strangers in the Land: Blacks, Jews, Post-Holocaust America* (2005), "the black-Jewish question is intrinsic to and inextricable from any understanding of American culture and cultural politics in the post-war

Protest. Crown Heights protest, Brooklyn, July 1978. Photograph by Bettye Lane. © Bettye Lane

decades." According to Sundquist, in playing a formative role in music, literature, and intellectual debate, both blacks and Jews have had a "tense but creative relationship with the mainstream" and tell "an archetypal American story of the vicissitudes of pluralism" (p. 12).

[*See also* Civil Rights Movement; Crown Heights Riot; Frank, Leo; Immigrants and African Americans; Jews, Black; Mississippi Freedom Summer; National Association for the Advancement of Colored People; Nation of Islam; Spingarn, Joel Elias; *and* Whiteness.]

BIBLIOGRAPHY

Franklin, V. P., et al., ed. *African Americans and Jews in the Twentieth Century: Studies in Convergence and Conflict*. Columbia: University of Missouri Press, 1998.

Gates, Henry Louis, Jr. "Black Demagogues and Pseudo-Scholars." *New York Times*, 20 July 1992.

Greenberg, Cheryl Lynn. *Troubling the Waters: Black-Jewish Relations in the American Century*. Princeton, N.J.: Princeton University Press, 2006.

Greene, Melissa Fay. *The Temple Bombing*. Reading, Mass.: Addison-Wesley, 1996.

McDowell, Winston. "Race and Ethnicity during the Harlem Jobs Campaign, 1932–1935." *Journal of Negro History* 69, no. 3/4 (Summer–Autumn 1984): 134–146.

Oney, Steve. *And the Dead Shall Rise: The Murder of Mary Phagan and the Lynching of Leo Frank*. New York: Pantheon, 2003.

Salzman, Jack, with Adina Back and Gretchen Sullivan Sorin, eds. *Bridges and Boundaries: African Americans and American Jews*. New York: George Braziller, 1992.

Shapiro, Gerald, ed. *American Jewish Fiction: A Century of Stories*. Lincoln: University of Nebraska Press, 1998.

Sundquist, Eric J. *Strangers in the Land: Blacks, Jews, Post-Holocaust America*. Cambridge, Mass.: Belknap Press of Harvard University Press, 2005.

—AMRITJIT SINGH

BLACK LIBERATION ARMY. The Black Liberation Army (BLA) defined itself as a politico-military organization engaged in armed struggle against the U.S. government. Operating from about 1971 to 1981, the BLA used tactics including bombings, robberies, and prison breaks. Although not all its members were Marxists, the BLA considered itself the embryonic form of the people's army of the black nation in America. It compared itself to the National Liberation Front, or Vietcong, of Vietnam. The BLA credited Malcolm X for its ideology and claimed to be the inheritor of Malcolm's legacy.

The Black Panther Party (BPP) was the largest, most important revolutionary organization of the black liberation movement of the 1960s and 1970s. By 1968, because of government repression, some Panther leaders saw the need for a guerrilla army that would serve as a vanguard revolutionary force. According to this concept the force would be the Black Liberation Army. It would be clandestine, and members' identities would be kept secret. By 1971, police repression forced an ideological split in the BPP between members who wanted to move away from the policy of armed struggle and those who wanted to emphasize it. Panthers who wanted to emphasize armed struggle, along with black militants from other organizations, filled the ranks of the BLA. Police estimated that the group had about one hundred active members.

The purpose of the BLA was to defend, organize, and fight for black people militarily against internal and external enemies. Internal enemies included thieves and drug sellers who preyed on the black community. In some cases drug dealers were killed and their facilities raided. The primary external enemy was the police; many black Americans lived in fear of brutality at their hands. Beginning in 1971 the BLA attacked and killed police officers in New York, San Francisco, and Atlanta. The BLA's claims of responsibility led to a vigorous police counterinsurgency campaign. By 1975, police claimed that most BLA members were dead, jailed, or awaiting trial. That year the BLA created a coordinating committee (BLA-CC) to provide centralized leadership and expand the movement's political base. It published a newsletter that circulated in prisons. Politically, it embraced a nationalist perspective that supported the New Afrikan independence movement.

In 1973 the BLA leader Assata Shakur was arrested after a shootout with troopers on the New Jersey Turnpike. Between 1973 and 1977 she was tried seven times for various crimes, including robbery, kidnapping, and murder. Finally convicted of murder and other crimes in 1977 by an all-white jury, Shakur was sentenced to life in prison. In November 1979 three armed members of the Black Liberation Army effected Shakur's escape from a New Jersey prison. In spite of the efforts of state and federal police and their Joint Terrorist Task Force, Shakur remained a fugitive, eventually obtaining political asylum in Cuba.

Between 1976 and 1981 the BLA and its supporters, including white supporters, staged several "expropriations" or robberies to acquire funds in order to defend blacks against what the BLA saw as right-wing white-supremacist groups that included U.S. military and police forces. A botched 1981 armored-car holdup in New York was the last Panther-BLA expropriation action. Police and prosecutors redoubled their efforts to capture and bring BLA activists and their supporters to trial. By the early 1980s, both the Black Panther Party and the Black Liberation Army had been disbanded.

[*See also* Black Nationalism; Black Panther Party; Radicalism; *and* Shakur, Assata.]

BIBLIOGRAPHY

Austin, Curtis J. *Up against the Wall: Violence in the Making and Unmaking of the Black Panther Party*. Fayetteville: University of Arkansas Press, 2006. Chapter 9, "The Rift," describes the relationship between the Black Liberation Army and the Black Panther Party.

Umoja, Akinyele O. "The Black Liberation Army and the Radical Legacy of the Black Panther Party." In *Black Power in the Belly of the Beast*, edited by Judson L. Jeffries, pp. 224–251. Urbana: University of Illinois Press, 2006.

—PETER BRUSH

BLACK MIGRATION. Major movements of the black population within the United States began with the importations of the slave trade and continued with the movements of runaway slaves. After they were emancipated, many blacks moved to the North and West to find economic opportunities; some, disappointed, returned to the South. Blacks have also migrated to the United States from other countries, notably those in Africa and the Caribbean.

Runaway Slaves. Runaway slaves formed an important component of black migration before the Civil War. Runaways often took advantage of times of political disturbance to make their escape. During the American Revolution, thousands of runaways took advantage of British proclamations that offered enslaved men freedom if they fought for the king. At the end of the war, the British sent a number of those who had enlisted into slavery in the West Indies. The War of 1812 offered similar opportunities, with British commanders recruiting slaves to occupy New Orleans in order to break the morale of southern American soldiers.

In the period leading up to the Civil War, runaways most often set their sights on the North or Canada—journeys that could take up to a year to complete. The majority of runaways were soon recaptured, since, thanks to laws such as the Fugitive Slave Act of 1850, slave owners in the United States retained the right to recover their "property," even in the North. The autobiographies of some runaways, such as Frederick Douglass, reveal an ongoing anxiety about the possibility of recapture, as well as a regret that friends and family were left behind in slavery. Runaways often entered Canada to escape the reaches of the Fugitive Slave Act.

The majority of successful runaways were young men who had not yet begun a family. Women were less likely to flee, since most already had children to care for by their late teens. Only rarely did entire family groups escape.

In slave-owner advertisements, fugitive slaves are often described as intelligent—thus they were more likely to feel the humiliation of slavery and more able to navigate an escape. One of the most well-known examples of such ingenuity is Henry "Box" Brown. After his owner sold Brown's wife and children, Brown mailed himself in a wooden box to an abolitionist in Philadelphia. He described his journey in his autobiography, *Narrative of the Life of Henry Box Brown, Written by Himself*. Such autobiographies, which detailed the cruelties of slavery, were influential in promoting the abolitionist movement.

Other runaways never left the South. Instead, they fled from plantations to cities, such as Washington, D.C., or New Orleans, where they could impersonate bondspeople or free blacks and obtain employment as laborers or household servants. After establishing themselves in a city, they often provided assistance to new runaways, forming part of the Underground Railroad.

Other runaways fled into isolated backcountry areas or Indian territory, forming "Maroon" communities of former slaves. One of the largest of these was located in the Great Dismal Swamp between Virginia and North Carolina, where by the nineteenth century, several thousand escaped slaves lived. Maroons usually had little education, and thus could not obtain employment in cities, unlike literate escaped slaves. Many had assaulted their owners or overseers before escaping, and they often lived through raids on surrounding farms.

The outbreak of the Civil War led to the most dramatic incidence of runaways, with tens of thousands of slaves making their way to Union army lines. Though free, they were confined to camps without adequate shelter or supplies—with the exception of the black men who, beginning in 1862, were allowed to enlist in the army.

The Great Migrations. In 1900 almost 90 percent of all blacks in America lived in the rural South. In the early twentieth century many blacks began to move to northern cities in a period known as the "Great Migration." By the 1960s, more than 5 million blacks had left the South. The largest shift occurred when about 500,000 blacks, mostly agricultural workers, moved to the North and Midwest during World War I, when labor shortages caused factories to change their former policies of barring black employees. During the Great Depression, migration slowed as jobs disappeared, but the labor shortage caused by World War II led to another mass movement, referred to as the "Second Great Migration."

Blacks moved to the North in search of better job opportunities in the industrial North where, though they were paid less than white workers, they earned far more than they could in the South. Northern factories sent agents to the South who recruited young men, advancing them their railway fare. Other blacks came to the North by so-called step migration, stopping along the way to earn money for the next fare.

The developed North also offered better schools and other social services than did the South, which was still slowly recovering from the Civil War. The North also held out the chance of political enfranchisement—by 1910, most southern blacks had lost the ability to vote because of Jim Crow laws. Blacks also hoped to escape the worsening state of race relations in the South marked by the rise of the Ku Klux Klan and the growing number of incidents of lynch-mob violence. Many blacks registered to vote upon arrival in the North, leading to the election of black candidates. For example, Oscar De Priest became Chicago's first black councilman in 1915, and in 1928 he was the first black elected to Congress in the twentieth century.

The same desires also prompted a move to cities for those who remained in the South, with the majority of black southerners becoming urban dwellers in the twentieth century. The invasion of the boll weevil, which began to devastate the South's cotton crop in 1898, meant that rural agricultural jobs could no longer be blacks' main source of employment.

White attitudes toward the newly arrived southerners were not always welcoming. Violence against blacks and race riots were common, especially following World War I, when veterans returned to find their jobs filled by blacks who were willing to work for lower wages. Tensions also ran high with the millions of recent European immigrants who also moved to the North to find wartime jobs.

Whites-only union regulations or company policies barred most blacks from obtaining better-paying positions. War-related inflation meant that the price of food and lodging greatly increased during the early twentieth century, with the result that many migrant families fell below the poverty level despite the higher northern wages. For that reason, many black women began to work outside the home, at first as domestic laborers and then in wartime factories.

Migrants concentrated in areas offering inexpensive housing. Whites then moved out of these areas, leading to the creation of black ghettos. There, the black mortality rate was much higher than that of whites because of overcrowding and a shortage of access to medical care in segregated hospitals. However, "white flight" also had benefits: by the 1960s, blacks were the political majority in some cities.

Some black leaders were skeptical of migration. Both Douglass and Booker T. Washington urged blacks not to abandon the South. Other black leaders in the North encouraged blacks to move. The newspaperman Robert Abbott wrote about the job opportunities of the North in the black newspaper the *Chicago Defender* and gave copies to black railway porters to give to southern travelers.

Chicago's black population grew greatly (148 percent between 1910 and 1920), as did that of other industrial centers such as Detroit (611 percent), Pittsburgh (500 percent), and New York (66 percent). The migrants established hundreds of new churches, often in small storefronts with pastors who were themselves migrant laborers. Migrant pride also found an outlet in new religious movements; the most influential was the Nation of Islam, established in Detroit in 1931. The black-nationalist movement also drew from migrants' determination to improve their lives and a willingness to compete with whites to do so. Migration also meant that rhythm and blues and other forms of music developed in the South were popularized in the North.

Western Migrations. After the Civil War, blacks joined the movement of white settlers into America's western territories, whose black population grew to 1.7 million by 1950. They were attracted by the territories' cheap land and freedom from the new Jim Crow laws, which restricted the political and social opportunities of blacks in the South.

Many black settlers were attracted to Kansas because of the state's proximity and its long abolitionist tradition. Benjamin "Pap" Singleton's 1874 circular "The Advantage of Living in a Free State" caused a "Kansas Fever," with at least ten thousand blacks, called Exodusters, moving to Kansas by 1890. The reactions of white Kansans were mixed: some celebrated the blacks' desire to obtain freedom, while others feared that the settlers, mostly poor, would become dependent on the state.

The Oklahoma Territory, like Kansas, was another major destination for black migration. In the 1890s the federal government opened vast tracts of land in the territory for settlement, allowing blacks to create new towns in which they could escape from racism and hold political office. The black settlers became farmers, with black landownership in Oklahoma and Kansas peaking around 1900. By 1910, following several years of crop failures and, in 1907, the disfranchisement of black voters when Oklahoma gained statehood, many blacks sold their land and moved back to cities.

Similar all-black communities were founded in the late nineteenth century in Nebraska, the Dakota Territory, and California; the majority also failed in the early twentieth century. Today, most blacks continue to live in the cities of the West instead of in rural areas.

Western cities such as Denver or San Francisco offered blacks few economic opportunities in the early twentieth century, but they were the sites of the formation of black community life—and also for the growth of tension with other groups. For example, in 1903 the Southern Pacific

Railroad Company doubled the black population of Los Angeles by bringing in two thousand black laborers to substitute for striking Hispanic construction workers; the rivalry this created is still present in the city.

The last major influx of blacks to the West was during World War II, when many blacks moved for the higher pay offered in shipyards and aircraft factories in California, Oregon, and Washington. After the war, some moved away when these defense industry jobs evaporated—Portland, Oregon, had lost half of its black population by 1947—but in other cities, blacks had gained enough of a presence in integrated unions that in the 1950s they steadily began to enter the middle-class workforce.

Return to the South. The South itself has long been the site of internal migration. After Emancipation, the majority of blacks worked as agricultural laborers in rural areas. When the boll weevil caused the crash of the cotton market in the late nineteenth century, many blacks who did not take part in the migration north or west began to move to urban areas within the South.

Beginning in the 1960s, the number of blacks moving to the South became greater than the number leaving. Many were dissatisfied with the increasing unemployment, deteriorating conditions, and crime of northern cities. Blacks who had moved north in the Great Migration wanted to reunite with their families and retire in their childhood towns, making the black move to the South largely a return migration. Others saw opportunity in the South's lower cost of living and developing economy. Manufacturers were moving to the South, attracted by cheaper labor and tax breaks.

Many college-educated blacks moved to the South, seeing promise in the era's Supreme Court decisions and federal government actions, which began to strike down Jim Crow laws. Northern-educated blacks were active in protesting remaining forms of segregation in the South, and many obtained political office.

Also, the North and West had failed to be the havens migrating blacks had hoped. Incidents such as the riots in the Watts neighborhood of Los Angeles in 1965 had shown blacks that the South was not the only site of racial violence.

Africa. Even before the Civil War, freed blacks thought of Africa as an escape from America's racism, political disfranchisement, and lack of economic opportunities. In 1815 the first known black emigration to Africa took place when Paul Cuffee sailed with thirty-eight companions to Sierra Leone. The controversial and white-managed American Colonization Society, founded in 1816, established settlements in Liberia, transporting around 1,500 emigrants in the nineteenth century. The emigrants' continued use of English and their attempts to convert Liberians to Christianity made them unpopular.

Not until the early twentieth century, with Marcus Garvey's founding of the Universal Negro Improvement Association, did the idea of emigration to Africa have widespread appeal. Garvey's back-to-Africa campaign was popular with black laborers, who accepted his claim that blacks would never attain full social equality in America. Garvey was unsuccessful in organizing colonizing trips, but his message inspired others to emigrate on their own. Once there, these migrants also faced conflicts with native Africans.

The number of voluntary migrants from Africa to America has surpassed the numbers of those forced to make the journey by the slave trade, but in the early twenty-first century Africans still represented a small portion of black immigrants. They sought job opportunities or escape from political oppression, as did the thousands of refugees from the Marxist regimes of Ethiopia and Eritrea in the 1980s. Most African immigrants lived in cities, where many gravitated to neighborhoods populated by their countrymen. Almost half of African immigrants had college degrees, meaning that African countries experienced a "brain drain" from their departure, though immigrants' remittances constituted an appreciable part of their home countries' economy.

The Caribbean. Many blacks moved from the Caribbean in the nineteenth and twentieth centuries. The largest group was migrants from the Spanish-speaking Caribbean: Puerto Rico, Cuba, and the Dominican Republic. Some left for political reasons. Many others sought economic opportunities in America as the sugarcane industry of the Caribbean collapsed. Unskilled Caribbean laborers found jobs in South America, while those who moved to the United States were generally more literate and skilled. Their primary destinations were South Florida and New York City, and they formed a large part of these areas' black middle class and established many social, political, and economic organizations. The labor shortages of World War II led to an influx of Caribbean migrant workers, many of whom remained in America.

Beginning in the 1960s, a number of migrants and their descendants began to return to the Caribbean, dissatisfied with living conditions and job opportunities in the United States. The large population of English-speaking islanders has forced a reevaluation of Spanish-speaking Caribbean cultural identity. Caribbean migrants also have had large impacts on American culture such as popular music, which Caribbean music such as reggae has influenced.

Caribbean migrants' use of Spanish has also impacted the relations of Hispanics and blacks in America.

[*See also* African Diaspora; American Colonization Society; Caribbean, The; Great Migration; Great Migration, Second; *and* Universal Negro Improvement Association.]

BIBLIOGRAPHY

Arthur, John A. *Invisible Sojourners: African Immigrant Diaspora in the United States*. Westport, Conn.: Praeger, 2000.

de Graaf, Lawrence B., Kevin Mulroy, and Quintard Taylor, eds. *Seeking El Dorado: African Americans in California*. Seattle: University of Washington Press, 2001.

Franklin, John Hope, and Loren Schweninger. *Runaway Slaves: Rebels on the Plantation*. New York: Oxford University Press, 1999.

Hamilton, Kenneth W. *Black Towns and Profit: Promotion and Development in the Trans-Appalachian West, 1877–1915*. Urbana: University of Illinois Press, 1991.

Harrison, Alferdteen, ed. *Black Exodus: The Great Migration from the American South*. Jackson: University Press of Mississippi, 1991.

Kasinitz, Philip. *Caribbean New York: Black Immigrants and the Politics of Race*. Ithaca, N.Y.: Cornell University Press, 1992.

Leaming, Hugo Prosper. *Hidden Americans: Maroons of Virginia and the Carolinas*. New York: Garland Publishing, 1995.

Painter, Nell Irvin. *Exodusters: Black Migration to Kansas After Reconstruction*. Lawrence: University Press of Kansas, 1986.

Sagás, Ernesto, and Sintia E. Molina, eds. *Dominican Migration: Transnational Perspectives*. Gainesville: University Press of Florida, 2004.

Smith, James Wesley. *Sojourners in Search of Freedom: The Settlement of Liberia by Black Americans*. Lanham, Md.: University Press of America, 1987.

Stack, Carol B. *Call to Home: African Americans Reclaim the Rural South*. New York: Basic Books, 1996.

—ERIN L. THOMPSON

BLACK NATIONALISM. Black nationalism is the belief system that endorses the creation of a black nation-state. It also supports the establishment of black-controlled institutions to meet the political, social, educational, economic, and spiritual needs of black people, independent of nonblacks. Celebration of African ancestry and territorial separatism are essential components of black nationalism. Though not fully developed into a cogent system of beliefs, the impulse of black nationalism finds its earliest expression in the resistance of enslaved Africans to the Atlantic slave trade from the sixteenth century. Various groups of Africans, who felt no particular organic connection as "black" people, were forced into a new racialized identity in a brutal and dehumanizing process of enslavement. The transportation and forced amalgamation of hundreds of different African nationalities resulted in Creolized communities in the Americas; enslaved Africans revolted and established new societies, which functioned autonomously on the outskirts of colonial towns and cities. These were locked in conflict with colonial authorities, which sought their destruction and the reenslavement of their inhabitants. Known by various names, including cimarrones, Maroons, and, in the United States, outliers, these groups were largely subsistence farmers who sometimes raided white farms, liberated enslaved Africans, and intermixed with indigenous peoples. Largely by default these societies embraced the fundamental tenets of black nationalism: armed self-defense, self-determination, and territorial separatism. Communities of outliers were found in Louisiana, Virginia, and Florida, among other places; none were so large or powerful, though, as the Maroons in Jamaica or Palmares in Brazil. Maroons participated in the successful insurrection against enslavers in the Haitian Revolution (1794–1803), which resulted in the first black republic in the western hemisphere. The most successful group of outliers in the United States was the group of escaped Africans who insinuated themselves into the Seminole nation in Florida; after a series of wars with the U.S. military in the early nineteenth century, many of these Africans remained in Florida rather than be enslaved or removed to Indian Territory.

The first organized expressions of black nationalism found among free blacks in the American colonies developed in the late eighteenth century. By the Revolutionary era African Americans were developing relatively large free communities in American cities. Denied access to white churches, schools, and social organizations, black people created their own organizations. Though the principle of self-determination is clearly present in these efforts, it would not be correct to call these efforts nationalistic; like those of Africans who escaped slavery into autonomous communities, they were by default black controlled. Most African Americans expressed little desire to establish a black nation-state or move to Africa, and opposition to racial integration was not expressed by the organized black leadership of the era.

Paul Cuffe, a wealthy black shipbuilder in early nineteenth-century Massachusetts, endorsed the belief that many black people would enjoy a better life in Africa than in the United States. This was the earliest organized expression of emigrationism in the country. Working with the white supremacist American Colonization Society (ACS), Cuffe helped send African Americans to Africa. Many whites who funded the ACS believed that free black people were dangerous to the stability of the country, that free blacks could encourage unrest among slaves, or that free blacks were simply not wanted among whites.

Increasingly, legislation preventing black people from voting, attending schools, getting jobs or housing, or enjoying basic protections of the law fomented cynicism among African Americans. In 1829 David Walker published his *Appeal*, which implied that black armed resistance could destroy white America if white supremacy did not end. The *Appeal* also suggested that America could be the most powerful nation on earth if whites and blacks were united in brotherhood; it was not nationalistic in the strict sense. It was however an early written expression of a core nationalist belief in black self-defense and racial pride. Two years later an enslaved Baptist minister in Southampton County, Virginia, led the best-known slave insurrection in U.S. history. "Prophet" Nat Turner galvanized enslaved people around the belief that God spoke to him through visions of good black spirits engaged in battle against evil white ones. According to Turner, God wanted "His people" freed from bondage against the "Serpent" enslaver. Though an iconic act of resistance to slavery, this revolt was organized around an inchoate form of religious black nationalism. It was not until Martin R. Delany, in the 1850s, that a mature, explicit endorsement of black nationalism is found among the written work of African Americans.

A journalist for the abolitionist Frederick Douglass's *North Star*, Delany broke with Douglass over the issue of emigration. Born free in Virginia, he had experienced bitter racism and grown intolerant of the belief that whites could be collectively convinced to be fair and just. Unable to entertain emigration to mostly white Canada, Delany recommended South or Central America as possible homes for African Americans in his 1852 book *The Condition, Elevation, Emigration, and Destiny of the Colored People of the United States*. Delany later insisted that black people create a nation in Africa, one separate from the auspices of the white-controlled ACS. He visited Africa in 1859, establishing a treaty with local leaders in what is now Nigeria. Not only did Delany support a black nation-state as essential to black liberation but he also extolled the first explicit celebration of cultural nationalism found among African American leaders. Upon his return to the United States he donned African garb in an attempt to refute racist assumptions of African savagery, and claimed deep pride in being of African ancestry, speaking of knowledge of a rich African history systematically denied by white supremacists. His return from Africa coincided with the beginning in 1861 of the U.S. Civil War, which convinced Delany to reconsider his nationalist politics in hope that the war could result in the abolition of slavery. He enlisted in the Union army, becoming a major and the highest-ranked black person in the armed forces. Following the Civil War, the decline of Reconstruction in the 1870s, and the rise of new white supremacist laws, Delany once again endorsed black nationalism, even working in alliance with whites who insisted on removing black people from the country.

What marked Delany as different from many of his contemporaries was his celebration of black pride and black self-determination and his deep distrust of white people. Despite the latter, he embraced white America's ideas of culture and religion. On the one hand he stressed that the historic glory of Africa had been denied by Europeans to reinforce white supremacy; on the other he insisted that it was necessary for African Americans to "regenerate" Africa "morally, religiously, socially, politically, and commercially," instilling Western values.

There were other emigrationists who intersected with Delany on fundamental issues. Most black nationalists deep into the twentieth century insisted that Africans in the diaspora had crucial skills—or were simply "civilized"—and had a duty to establish links with their "despoiled" people in Africa. The late nineteenth-century black nationalists Alexander Crummell and Edward Wilmont Blyden argued that Africans were incapable of producing the technology necessary to develop without values and resources from the West; in fact it was necessary to evoke a cultural rebirth in Africa.

Pan-Africanism. By the turn of the twentieth century a new expression of black self-determination was developing under the term "Pan-Africanism." Not as concerned with moving blacks in the diaspora back to Africa, it was originally focused on resisting racial subjugation where black people lived. In 1900 the Trinidadian Henry Sylvester Williams organized a Pan-African Conference in London, which assembled representatives from the three independent black states of Haiti, Ethiopia, and Liberia, as well as colonized countries and the United States. Among the participants from the United States was W. E. B. Du Bois, an emerging activist and scholar. Pan-Africanism, as articulated by its earliest exponents, was not nationalist but insisted on worldwide liberation of black people and the international solidarity of people of African descent. The fusion of Pan-Africanism's international politics and black nationalism's territorial separatism would be found in the Universal Negro Improvement Association, which emerged in the 1920s as the largest mass movement of black people.

Marcus Garvey established the Universal Negro Improvement Association (UNIA) in 1914 in Jamaica. The UNIA was incorporated in the United States in 1918, two years after its founder immigrated. Espousing a mix of militant black nationalism and self-reliance, Garvey created a massive organization headquartered in Harlem but extending to forty-one countries and including millions of members. His aim to "civilize the backward tribes of Africa" was yet another example of the nineteenth-century nationalist civilizing mission. Like his predecessors he was a Christian, but the Christianity he endorsed replaced European-looking images of divinities in churches and homes with African ones. The African Orthodox Church, headed by Archbishop

George Alexander McGuire, affiliated with the UNIA, and advocated a black God for black people.

Garvey's efforts appealed to huge numbers of black people. The UNIA's grocery stores, apartment buildings, and cleaners; the highly militarized African Legion and Black Cross Nurses; and the most widely read black newspaper in history, the *Negro World*, made the UNIA highly visible and attractive to many. Its adoption of the red, black, and green tricolor flag in 1920 introduced what has remained the iconic expression of black nationalism, influencing the formation of flags for emerging African countries in the 1960s. The UNIA employed and celebrated the history and sanctity of black life in ways people had never seen; it also provided important psychological space in which to vent at the pressing force of white supremacy. Garvey articulated the distrust many blacks had of white-controlled institutions, warning against involvement with any whites who appeared to be friends of blacks. Though he did not believe in innate racial difference, he held that the white liberal was just as prone to join a lynch mob as was a Georgia Klansman.

Many African American leaders joined with radicals such as black communists to denounce Garvey for allowing Klan members to speak at UNIA meetings, where they encouraged blacks to leave the white man's country. With the support of Du Bois and others, the federal government arrested Garvey on mail fraud charges and sentenced him to prison in 1925. He was released and deported in 1927. The African Blood Brotherhood (ABB), founded by leftist black nationalists in Harlem after World War I, was a product of the "New Negro" defiance of the era and the general radical politics that circulated in New York City. Created in 1919 by Cyril Briggs, a communist and journalist, the ABB was composed of men from throughout the United States, many of whom had served in the war. Many others were Caribbean-born radicals who flirted with the UNIA and/or the Communist Party. They embraced self-defense and were sensitive to the need to collaborate with radicalized whites. Members of the Brotherhood considered their semiclandestine, paramilitary organization the "Pan-African Army" of the black world. Membership ranged from three to five thousand at its height. Briggs's monthly magazine, *The Crusader*, became the official organ of the ABB and reached a peak circulation of 33,000. The group had fifty branches, including those in Chicago, Baltimore, Oklahoma, West Virginia, Africa, and the West Indies. The ABB utilized a Marxist class analysis that emphasized working-class consciousness. This was in fact the first significant fusion of Marxism, black nationalism, and Pan-Africanism. While its rhetoric regarding mass culture is largely unknown, it is clear that the ABB did not denounce black folk culture in the same ways as most nationalists. Heightening class consciousness, mobilizing workers, and establishing alliances with radicalized whites and "small oppressed nations" were the chief concerns of the ABB. Furthermore, it embraced notions of uplift, military efficiency, and other ideals celebrated by nationalists.

A number of local black nationalist organizations functioned in various capacities in the years before World War I through the emergence in the 1950s of the modern civil rights movement. Noble Drew Ali established the Moorish Science Temple of America (MSTA) in 1913. The MSTA insisted that people of African descent in America were properly "Moors," not to be called colored, Negro, black, or African. Though not adherents of any orthodox form of Islam, MSTA members considered themselves Muslims, and attached "El" or "Bey" to their surnames to represent their proper identity. Ali insisted that Marcus Garvey was an ideological kindred spirit. Spreading from Newark to Pittsburgh, Detroit, and Chicago, the organization required "clean living" among its members. Black people were to view themselves as central to their own spiritual world: God spoke to them specifically as a people. Moreover, when anthropomorphized, benevolent divinities took the form of black people. A number of other nationalists found inspiration in the UNIA; few however would be national in scope. Harlem, the former headquarters of the UNIA, became a hotbed of black nationalist activity in the years following the 1927 deportation of Marcus Garvey. The former UNIA member Carlos Cooks established the African Nationalist Pioneer Movement and organized "Buy Black" campaigns in New York, boycotts, and preparation for armed defense against white terrorists. Eddie "Porkchop" Davis, Audrey "Queen Mother" Moore, Charles Kenyatta, Major Thornhill, Oba O. Adefumi, Robert Harris and others were some of the many local nationalists in New York from the 1940s through the 1960s.

The Civil Rights Movement and Black Nationalism. By the mid-1950s the modern civil rights movement had introduced a new language and practice of mass mobilization of African Americans. The challenge for nationalists to successfully appeal to the mass of African Americans remained the same in some regards, while drastically changing in others. In fact it was the rise of the civil rights movement that proved to be the greatest recruiting tool for the Nation of Islam (NOI or the Nation), which had functioned with relatively small temples in midwestern and northeastern cities until the late 1950s.

Formed by a mysterious itinerant peddler, W. D. Fard Muhammad, in Detroit in 1930, the Nation built on the legacies of the UNIA and the MSTA by developing various institutions, including businesses, farms, and schools. Like the UNIA, it extolled territorial separatism, racial pride, and religious nationalism. Like the MSTA, it insisted on a spiritual renewal and a new identity as Muslims, complete with new names. Unlike either earlier organization however, the NOI insisted on the absolute devilry of whites.

Led by Elijah Muhammad from 1934 until his death in 1975, the Nation of Islam called for a complete separation from white people and the establishment of an independent black nation-state in either North America or Africa. Whites were genetic mutants who were evil by design and could not be expected to be fair, just, or anything other than evil. They had inhabited caves in the Caucasus Mountains, where they lived on all fours and developed amorous relations with canines. In fact dogs are the "closest relatives to the white man"; that is why modern whites refer to the dog as their "best friend." The Nation had done what no major national organization had: formulated a belief system that systematically undermined white supremacy by declaring whiteness a biological, innate evil. It openly ridiculed whites as inferior, crude, vicious, and beastlike. Calling whites "pale things," "dogs," "crackers," and "devils," black nationalists had taken a bold turn to meet some of the deep psychological consequences of being black in a virulently antiblack country. They had taken whites off their pedestal, while building up black people. Moreover the Nation was distinct from other nationalist groups in its position on integration: it supported integration with Asians, Native Americans, and all other people of color, who were considered "black." In essence this was not integration but unification with a community of black people who had been divided by a common enemy.

By 1959 Malcolm X, the prominent national spokesman for the Nation, was teaching audiences that the proper term for the people was "black." A Negro was one who was ignorant, shiftless, deaf, dumb, and "blind." The most interviewed black person in America in 1962, Malcolm X with his militancy and vitriol could not be ignored by white or black people. Even civil rights activists were affected, some moving closer to black nationalism.

At the center of this ideological evolution was the Student Nonviolent Coordinating Committee (SNCC). Founded in 1960 SNCC was closely affiliated with the older Southern Christian Leadership Conference (SCLC), led by Martin Luther King Jr. The most prominent leader of the civil rights movement, King was an adamant proponent of its notion of nonviolence and racial reconciliation. By 1966 a new variant of black nationalism was developing among activists, which became known as the Black Power movement. The term "Black Power" meant different things to different people; fundamentally, it demanded the empowerment of black people, politically, socially, and economically. Although it did not require territorial separatism as had the UNIA or NOI, it insisted on black pride, self-determination, self-defense, and dignity. Like Pan-Africanism, Black Power was not synonymous with black nationalism, but complemented it.

It was at a 1966 march led by the Congress for Racial Equality, the SCLC, and SNCC, that the fissure between the traditional civil rights language and the ideas of Black Power was crystallized. The SNCC chairman Stokely Carmichael told a crowd of supporters that black people should stand up and demand Black Power throughout the state and country. The following night Willie Ricks, a leading SNCC organizer, reiterated Carmichael's demand when he galvanized the crowd and, in his typical charismatic fashion, declared that black people must demand Black Power.

The popularization of the phrase Black Power created considerable trepidation among mainstream civil rights activists; to many it implied antiwhite violence that would tear the movement asunder. King tried in vain to dissuade the crowd from using what he considered divisive words. For him the call for Black Power was "unfortunate because it tends to give the impression of black nationalism."

Black militants and nationalists throughout the country however, frustrated by what they considered the tragic failure of nonviolent integration and by continued racist aggression, welcomed the call for Black Power. For King, black nationalism and Black Power were part and parcel of a "nihilistic philosophy born out of the conviction that the Negro can't win. It is, at bottom, the view that American society is so hopelessly corrupt and enmeshed in evil that there is no possibility of salvation from within." Carmichael however asserted that Black Power was the proper articulation of the needs of the masses of black people. "Black power," he explained, "is a call for black people to begin to define their own goals, to lead their own organizations and to support those organizations. It is a call to reject the racist institutions and values of this society." The Lowndes County, Alabama, Freedom Organization (LCFO) was a true manifestation of this idea, he claimed. Its symbol, the Black Panther, gave the group its nickname, the Black Panther Party.

Across the nation, scores of organizations emerged that viewed themselves as Black Power groups. Several adopted the LCFO name, Black Panther Party. There were independent organizations with this name in New York, Chicago, Los Angeles, Oakland, and San Francisco. There were the Organization Us in Los Angeles, the Congress of African People in Newark, the Republic of New Africa and the Dodge Revolutionary Union Movement of black workers in Michigan. Other nationalist groups included the Shrine of the Black Madonna, formed by the Reverend Albert Cleage in Detroit, the African Descendents Nationalist

The Reverend Albert B. Cleage Jr. Addressing the crowd at the March on Detroit, 23 June 1963. VIRTUAL MOTOR CITY COLLECTION, WALTER P. REUTHER LIBRARY, WAYNE STATE UNIVERSITY

Independence Party, formed in Philadelphia, and the Afro-American Association, formed by Donald Freeman in the California Bay Area.

Black Power also precipitated an unprecedented expression of black art, scholarship, political activism, professional organization, and intellectual discourse. Poets, writers, and other intellectuals, such as Larry Neal, Robert Chrisman, Askia Touré, Sonia Sanchez, Haki Madhubuti, Amiri Baraka, Robert L. Allen, John Henrik Clark, James Turner, and Nikki Giovanni, constructed new intellectual interrogations of race and America. The Organization Us founder and leading cultural nationalist Maulana Karenga developed a new celebration, Kwanzaa. Advocates on college campuses demanded black studies programs, black cultural centers, and the hiring of black faculty and staff by white universities long hostile to hiring people of color. In music James Brown, Curtis Mayfield, Donald Byrd, and the Last Poets demonstrated the musical contours of Black Power. Black professionals with unprecedented access to white professional associations chose to develop new black associations rather than concentrate their activities solely in majority white groups. Between 1968 and 1975 dozens of professional groups such as those of sociologists, political scientists, social workers, journalists, police officers, and engineers were formed. Fashion and language were altered by Black Power. Stemming from the Nation of Islam's rejection of the word "Negro" and the embrace of "black", the Black Power movement helped retire the term "Negro" in the Anglophone world as a reference to people of African descent.

International connections with Black Power were many and complex. Julian Mayfield joined the expatriate community of African Americans in Ghana (which had included Du Bois and his wife) and worked as a communications aide to the Ghanaian president Kwame Nkrumah from 1962 to 1966. Though he worked in Ghana before the Black Power movement, Mayfield remained connected to the African American community and embraced the new slogan as it spread through the black world. From 1971 to 1975 Mayfield worked as an adviser to Forbes Burnham, the prime minister of Guyana, home to the Black Power radical Walter Rodney. Newly independent countries in the Caribbean struggled over the direction of Black Power, which tended to lean toward leftist, anti-imperialist, and anticapitalist politics. In Trinidad, Jamaica, and Barbados political elites attempted to marginalize Black Power advocates. Rodney was assassinated in Guyana after he was banned from Jamaica, where he had been a professor. In South Africa the antiapartheid student leader Steve Biko was similarly affected by the slogan. He was killed by police in 1977. As in these countries black radicals witnessed considerable state repression in the United States. But no group experienced the same international attention or level of state repression as the Black Panther Party of Oakland, California.

The Black Panther Party began as a nationalist organization in 1966, but by late 1968 it had adopted a Marxist-Leninist ideological framework that considered racial or ethnic nationalism problematic; nationalism that did not consider connections with class was an effort to bolster bourgeois control of economic markets, while maintaining class oppression. The BPP, a self-described revolutionary nationalist organization, called for a United Nations–supervised plebiscite so black people could vote on whether to separate from the United States, and identified the three evils of capitalism, imperialism, and racism as universal enemies for revolutionaries. But, the Panthers reasoned, until capitalism was destroyed race and its consequences were very real. It was imperative therefore for black people to work in black communities for black self-determination. Though there were no white members, some Latino and Asian members were active in the BPP from its earliest years.

The Panthers created a revolutionary nationalism that was highly derivative but also suffused with the social criticism and intellectual contributions of its cofounders Huey Newton and Bobby Seale and others like Eldridge Cleaver, their minister of information. The Party created a series of survival programs, including free breakfast, food giveaways, and free medical care to poor black communities. Between 1968 and 1970 the Panthers also had a series of shootouts and police raids. J. Edgar Hoover, the notorious director of the FBI, called the Panthers the "greatest threat to national security" and unleashed a massive campaign to disrupt the party, as well as other black nationalist groups, resulting in over twenty dead BPP members.

By 1975 the Black Power movement in its most activist form was in retreat. Organizations like the Nation of Islam, Congress of African People, Black Panther Party, Republic of New Afrika, and Organization Us were in decline. Many leaders had been jailed, killed, or exiled. Throughout the 1970s a growing black middle class, the rise of publicly elected black officials, and a decrease in the most explicit manifestations of white supremacy converged to create hopeful times for many black people. The increase in poverty, illicit drug trade, and spiraling crime rates of the late 1980s however precipitated renewed sense of alarm among many African Americans.

The Nation of Islam, under the leadership of Louis Farrakhan, tapped into the new mood of cynicism and anger. Farrakhan spoke to black audiences across the country about the need for black people to live responsible lives free of drugs, alcohol, gambling, welfare, or unhealthy diets. His message of personal responsibility and industriousness resonated with classic black nationalist values; these were not particularly different from African American core cultural values, making his appeal powerful. And unlike political conservatives who had begun to coopt the idea of "personal responsibility," the Nation offered a vitriolic attack on the institutionalized nature of white supremacy. Calling whites devils and other racial pejoratives, the Nation generated considerable hostility from the mainstream media and black intellectuals alike. But the organization grew in visibility and resources as the attacks against it increased. The NOI provided security for high-crime housing projects nationwide, reducing crime precipitously in most cases. A longtime supporter of capitalist enterprise, the Nation expanded its business empire, employing many poor and working-class people, while also looking outward in entirely new ways. In fact it endorsed voting for the first time when Jesse Jackson ran for the presidential nomination of the Democratic Party in 1984. Despite the accusations that the organization was racist, sexist, and homophobic, it continued to expand its appeal, culminating in the organization of the largest gathering of black people in history, the Million Man March in 1995. In 1998 the Nation became the only known Muslim body in the world to allow women to serve as imams or ministers. During the civil war in Yugoslavia Farrakhan publicly recognized white Muslims; he officiated at white-black marriages at the Million Family March in 2000, and offered support for gay participants at the 2005 Millions More March, demonstrating that he was ideologically dynamic and willing to insist on "black unity."

The landscape of the United States is indelibly marked by the many and varied efforts of black nationalists. The legacies of Black Power are ubiquitous. The National Black United Front, Prisoners of Conscious Committee, and New Afrikan Peoples Organization are some of many black nationalist groups that maintain grassroots campaigns. From reparations for the descendants of former slaves to attention to the poor and the prison-industrial complex, nationalists' concerns often intersect with those of other groups, giving them continued visibility and a voice to a large segment of the black community.

[*See also* Africa, Idea of; Black Panther Party; Black Power Movement; Black Radical Congress; Black Towns; Congress of African People; Nation of Islam; Republic of New Afrika; Universal Negro Improvement Association; *and biographical entries on figures mentioned in this article.*]

BIBLIOGRAPHY

Bush, Rod. *We Are Not What We Seem: Black Nationalism and Class Struggle in the American Century*. New York: New York University Press, 1999.

Churchill, Ward, and Jim Vander Wall. *Agents of Repression: The FBI's Secret Wars Against the Black Panther Party and the American Indian Movement*. Boston: South End, 1988.

Essien-Udom, E. U. *Black Nationalism: The Search for an Identity in America*. Chicago: University of Chicago Press, 1962.

Martin, Tony. *Race First: The Ideological and Organizational Struggles of Marcus Garvey and the Universal Negro Improvement Association*. Westport, Conn.: Greenwood, 1976.

Moses, Wilson J. *The Golden Age of Black Nationalism, 1850–1925*. Hamden, Conn.: Archon, 1978.

Ogbar, Jeffrey O. G. *Black Power: Radical Politics and African American Identity*. Baltimore: Johns Hopkins University Press, 2004.

Smethurst, James Edward. *The Black Arts Movement: Literary Nationalism in the 1960s and 1970s*. Chapel Hill: University of North Carolina Press, 2005.

Van Deburg, William L. *New Day in Babylon: The Black Power Movement and American Culture, 1965–1975*. Chicago: University of Chicago Press, 1992.

—Jeffrey O. G. Ogbar

BLACK PANTHER PARTY. The Black Panther Party (BPP) was one of the most prominent and notorious organizations of black power to emerge during the 1960s. It successfully organized thousands of militant blacks committed to improving the social conditions of their communities. The Panthers' founders, Huey P. Newton and Bobby Seale, were initially inspired by the work of the Student Nonviolent Coordinating Committee (SNCC) in conjunction with activists from rural Alabama who formed the Lowndes County Freedom Organization (LCFO). But Newton and Seale, attracted also to the revolutionary rhetoric and black nationalistic ideals of Malcolm X, adopted the black panther as a symbol and formed the Black Panther Party for Self-Defense in October 1966 in Oakland, California, after they were unsuccessful in their efforts to influence the politics of existing campus organizations. Newton was a former street criminal who had gone on to study at Oakland's Merritt College, and Seale was a former soldier, sheet-metal worker, and part-time comedian who also attended Merritt College.

Upon reading the works of Mao Zedong and Che Guevara, Newton and Seale decided to form an armed, militantly nationalistic self-defense organization whose objective was to protect the black communities by ending police brutality. Seale became the chairman of the group. David Hilliard was brought into the BPP by Newton in 1967 and quickly became chief of staff. Later—with Newton in jail and the party's minister of information, Eldridge Cleaver, in exile—Hilliard assumed the position of party chairman. Hilliard achieved fame during an antiwar rally in 1969 when he denounced President Richard Nixon and called for his death. Hilliard was eventually arrested, but the case dissolved a few months after his arrest.

Wearing black leather jackets and berets and carrying shotguns and other handguns in full view, the Black Panthers were a notorious symbol of black revolutionary fervor. The BPP also denounced the civil rights movement and argued that only violent revolution could eliminate racism and black oppression. They called for armed self-defense, urging blacks across the United States to engage in direct confrontation with police as a means to accelerate the revolutionary struggle.

The BPP was officially founded when Newton and Seale drafted a ten-point platform calling for the political autonomy of all black communities. The ten-point program also included demands for political freedom, black control of black communities, full employment, an end to white economic exploitation, better housing, better education, health services, fair trials, exemption of black men from military service, and an end to police brutality. The BPP stressed black cultural pride and promoted education and other "Survival Programs" (community-based programs), such as free breakfasts for children; free health clinics including testing for sickle cell anemia, blood drives, vision tests, vaccines, nutrition classes and hygiene workshops; an accredited elementary school in Oakland; grocery giveaways; shoe and clothing drives; transportation and other services for senior citizens; free busing; and at times, free legal aid programs. Party members worked to instill racial pride, they lectured and wrote about black history, and they launched drug education programs in the communities. As the organization grew in numbers, however, it repudiated much of its early nationalism in favor of a Marxist-Leninist approach that envisioned socialist revolution as the means of achieving black power. Maoist ideology also became an integral part of the party's political discourse.

State and federal campaigns of repression—including infiltration for surveillance purposes, the use of deadly force, harassment campaigns of arrest and incarceration, and the exploitation of political differences—as well as internal conflict within the organization eventually led to the BPP's demise. The party suffered from divisive debates over the correct revolutionary line for black liberation, the role of armed struggle versus electoral politics, and the question of alliances with whites. It was divided over how best to relate with other black organizations. The BPP also failed adequately to address the problem of gender equality. For the most part, the organization, unable to create programs that promoted equality between the sexes, insisted on maintaining male privileges that reinforced traditional gender roles. By the 1970s women outnumbered men in the party and had made significant impacts in its programs, but many of those women eventually left the BPP because men held fast to the ideas of male privilege. Arguing that gender inequality went against the idea of black liberation, many women members decided to form their own auxiliary BPPs. Internal disputes remained unabated. In 1969, after establishing more than thirty chapters and gaining a widespread following, the BPP had a membership estimated at between ten thousand and thirty thousand. By the mid-1970s,

Party Rally. Black Panthers on the speakers' stage for a "Free Huey" rally in front of the Federal Building in San Francisco, May Day, 1969. Photograph by Ilka Hartmann. © ILKA HARTMANN

however, the organization had only about one thousand members.

The entire period of the BPP's existence was marked by severe police repression. Panthers alarmed white Americans when they took up arms and patrolled the streets to monitor police. Following a shoot-out between Newton and police officers in 1967, practically all BPP leadership was on the run from law enforcement officials. In 1968, the Federal Bureau of Investigation under J. Edgar Hoover directed the Bureau's counterinsurgency program known as COINTELPRO, which used tactics of surveillance and infiltration, to exploit and create dissension within the Black Panthers and other radical groups in hopes of crippling them. Seale became a particular target of FBI persecution, and he was arrested and charged with conspiring to riot during the 1968 Democratic Party convention in Chicago. Between 1968 and 1971, more than three hundred Black Panthers were jailed, forced into hiding, exiled, or killed in the course of law enforcement campaigns against the organization.

On 22 August 1989, Huey Newton—who had for years been battling problems with alcohol and drug abuse and frequent run-ins with the law—was shot and killed in Oakland during an aborted drug deal. Seale survived his ordeal with the FBI, and in 1973 he ran for mayor of Oakland but was defeated by a narrow margin. Although the BPP was officially dismantled in 1982, it had actually begun to break up by the early 1970s. It continued, however, to serve as the symbolic reference point for black militancy. At its best, the Black Panther Party offers an historical example of brave activists willing to die for the people and provides black Americans with a sense of pride and honor.

[*See also* Black Nationalism; Black Power Movement; COINTELPRO; Student Nonviolent Coordinating Committee; *and biographical entries on figures mentioned in this article*.]

BIBLIOGRAPHY

Foner, Philip S., ed. *The Black Panthers Speak*. Philadelphia: Lippincott, 1970.

Hine, Darline C., William C. Hine, and Stanley Harrold. *African Americans: A Concise History*. Upper Saddle River, N.J.: Pearson, 2004.

Taylor, Quintard. *In Search of the Racial Frontier: African Americans in the American West, 1528–1990*. New York: W. W. Norton, 1998.

West, Thomas R., and James W. Mooney, eds. *To Redeem a Nation: A History and Anthology of the Civil Rights Movement*. St. James, N.Y.: Brandywine Press, 1993.

Williams, Michael W., ed. *The African American Encyclopedia*. Vol. 1. New York: Marshall Cavendish, 1993.

—JESSE J. ESPARZA

BLACK POLITICS. In the decades following Reconstruction, African Americans continued to push for an expansion of their democratic rights, despite facing increasing political marginalization and economic hardship. Growing debt, low commodity prices, and low wages kept most African Americans dependent upon large landowners. By the late 1870s most former slaves had become sharecroppers, indebted to local landlords and merchants on whom they relied for supplies, credit, and land on which to farm. Even though many black men and women had secured land after Emancipation, this usually consisted of small plots—making it difficult for them to compete with cash crops in a global marketplace. Brazil, Egypt, and India for instance, had become major cotton-producing nations, pulling down prices and requiring farmers in the Cotton Belt to grow ever larger harvests in order to make a profit.

The collapse of Reconstruction in the late 1870s came with the reassertion of the Democratic Party in the South—then home to over 90 percent of African Americans in the nation. Forcibly removed from offices, African Americans and their remaining southern white Republican allies were left to defend themselves against the old plantation class as the leaders of the two major parties negotiated what later became known as the Compromise of 1877. In that year the national Republican Party, in a bargain with the Democratic Party over contested Electoral College votes in Florida, South Carolina, Louisiana, and Oregon, took the U.S. presidency in exchange for Congressional assurances that the last federal troops in the South would be withdrawn—definitively ending Reconstruction.

With few exceptions, notably North Carolina's Second Congressional District (one of several Republican strongholds in the South), the Southern Democracy—the planters, white-dominated courts, law enforcement, and paramilitary forces affiliated with the Democratic Party—had retaken control. African Americans sustained a significant legal blow in 1883, when the U.S. Supreme Court declared the Civil Rights Law of 1875 unconstitutional. Through a series of court cases the Supreme Court weakened the Fourteenth Amendment's guarantee of black citizenship, narrowing federal protection of the right to vote among African American men twenty-one or more years old, as guaranteed by the Fifteenth Amendment. Black voter participation plummeted as a consequence: in South Carolina it fell from 96 to 26 percent between 1876 and 1888; in Georgia black voting fell from 53 to 18 percent during the same period.

Black farmers, sharecroppers, and agrarian workers responded to the stripping of their political rights by organizing their communities to act. Tens of thousands of southern African Americans migrated west; for instance, in the Exoduster Movement between 1877 and 1881, seventy thousand men, women, and children left the South and settled in Kansas. Other African Americans challenged the Democratic Party by joining white independents and running third-party and independent-Republican fusion campaigns; still others recommitted themselves to building community-based institutions of mutual support and education.

Independent black-white electoral coalitions—such as those formed in the Virginia Readjustment Party, the Texas Greenback Labor Party, and the Mississippi Republican-Greenback fusion in the late 1870s and early 1880s—mostly ended in defeat. The electoral failures in the years following Reconstruction, economic instability, and the erosion of civil and political rights led many African Americans to shun electoral politics altogether and focus instead on strengthening their own local communities. African Americans spread public schools; hundreds of Baptist and African Methodist Episcopalian churches were established in the countryside, as were benevolent societies and fraternal orders such as the black Freemasons and the Order of Mosaic Templars. The networks these institutions created in turn lay the base for the emergence of a broad, black-led agrarian movement for political and economic reform.

Black Populism. By the mid-1880s African Americans had established a series of agrarian and labor organizations that included the Colored Wheels in Arkansas, the Cooperative Workers of America in South Carolina, the Knights of Labor in North Carolina, and the Colored Farmers Alliance in Texas. Fed by overlapping membership in the black churches, fraternal orders, and mutual aid groups, these rural organizations formed the nexus of black populism. The movement took electoral form in the early 1890s through the founding and subsequent development of the People's Party and through fusion efforts with the Republican Party, which commanded the loyalty of most African Americans. Leading black populists included the Reverend Walter A. Pattillo, state lecturer for the North Carolina Colored Alliance, and John B. Rayner, known as the "silver-tongued orator of the colored race," who served on the People's Party's state executive committee in Texas. Few black women held official leadership positions but several women did serve in such capacities, including Lutie A. Lytle and Fanny "the Queen" Glass.

The Southern Democracy responded to the rise of black populism with a vengeance; their response included propaganda warning of a "second Reconstruction," legal maneuverings to disfranchise African American voters, manipulation of votes at the polls, and escalating violence. The white press fueled fear among its readers of "Negro rule" to create divisions among black and white independents. Lynchings, often organized as public spectacles advertised ahead of time, soared in number, as did attacks on and assassinations of independent political leaders, black and white. Throughout the 1890s more than a hundred lynchings were reported annually, with a chilling effect on political efforts to challenge the Democratic Party.

Democrats responded to the growth of independent politics by legally disfranchising African Americans by rewriting state constitutions, beginning in Mississippi in 1890, followed by South Carolina in 1895 and Louisiana in 1898. African American electoral participation fell dramatically as a result of grandfather clauses stating that only those whose grandfathers could vote prior to the Civil War were eligible to vote, poll taxes (a fee charged to cast a ballot), white primaries in which African Americans were excluded from the first round of voting, and other discriminatory laws.

In the midst of local and state-based attacks on African American voting rights came the 1896 Supreme Court ruling in *Plessy v. Ferguson*, which sanctioned segregation, not only providing its legal justification but also placing the imprimatur of the nation's highest court on the policy. The Court's majority decision supported the practice of having separate public facilities for black and white people (in this case, railway carriages in Louisiana). With the backing of the Supreme Court it was only a matter of time before Jim Crow—the legal disfranchisement and segregation of African Americans, primarily in the South—took hold. By the turn of the century most public facilities were segregated along racial lines and most African Americans were disfranchised in the South, as were tens of thousands of poor whites unable to pay poll taxes.

The Southern Democracy had succeeded in crushing the political threat posed by black and white populists in the 1890s; now it even had the backing of the federal government to help ensure against future threats that independents would come together at the ballot box. Many African Americans expressed their reluctance to engage in the electoral process, fully aware of the repercussions for challenging the Southern Democracy. It was in this context that Booker T. Washington, and the philosophy of accommodation that became attached to his name, gained prominence.

Washington and Du Bois. Booker T. Washington (1856–1915), a former slave from Virginia, led the Tuskegee Institute in Alabama from the early 1880s through the turn of the century. He became the nation's best-known black leader, taking the exalted place of Frederick Douglass, who died in 1895. That year, at the Atlanta Cotton States and International Exposition, Washington publicly supported segregation in combination with industrial education for African Americans. As he put it, "In all things that are purely social, we can be as separate as the fingers, yet one as the hand in all things essential to mutual progress." His views were generally embraced by southern white leaders (and his programs funded by northern white businessmen) since they largely posed no political threat to the established order, serving instead as a counterweight to black leadership that demanded the full rights and prerogatives of citizenship for African Americans.

While preaching accommodation and a rejection of black political participation, Washington backed candidates for public office through his "Tuskegee Machine," the name given to his considerable political and economic influence. Moreover he privately financed legal cases against electoral discrimination. For instance he challenged grandfather clauses enacted in Louisiana and Alabama. Washington, with his focus on economic self-help and industrial education, is often contrasted with W. E. B. Du Bois (1868–1963), who spoke out against Jim Crow and urged African Americans to take direct political action. In practice however their political differences were less obvious than has usually been claimed.

As Southern Democrats consolidated Jim Crow through state constitutional amendments and municipal codes, Du Bois, a middle-class, Harvard-trained historian who grew up in the North, became one of Washington's most vocal critics. Du Bois deplored Washington's urging accommodation over political action, despite having initially praised him for his extraordinary personal success in rising out of slavery. Du Bois, who would come to be regarded as the twentieth century's most influential African American before Martin Luther King Jr., grew increasingly militant in his call to halt the erosion of black civil and political rights.

A new generation of black leaders, many of whom took their cues from Du Bois, began to emerge. These leaders, most of whom eventually established themselves in northern cities, included the suffragist Ida B. Wells-Barnett, most famous for her antilynching journalism; William Monroe Trotter, the fiercely independent advocate for black civil rights; Cyril Briggs, founder of the African Blood Brotherhood and later a Communist Party leader; Marcus Garvey, the eminent black nationalist who led the Universal Negro Improvement Association (UNIA); and A. Philip Randolph, the socialist labor organizer who headed the Brotherhood of Sleeping Car Porters (BSCP). Fueling the growth of black political action—broadly defined—in the North was the massive demographic shift under way as African Americans moved out of the rural South to urban centers in the North.

The Great Migration. In the early twentieth century African Americans migrated out of the South in the hundreds of thousands, then millions. In what became known as the Great Migration they moved to Chicago, Philadelphia, New York, and other thriving northern cities. Black migration out of the South, driven by economic depression coupled with Jim Crow (and later with the increasing use of the mechanical cotton picker), accelerated with the advent of World War I as factory jobs were opened to black workers. Although economic incentives and greater political freedom drew substantial numbers of southerners to the North, the vast majority of African Americans remained in the South.

In the North, Du Bois organized a small group of black men and women in 1905, dubbed the Niagara Movement. They renounced Washington's accommodation policies and demanded—as Du Bois put it—"full manhood suffrage." Their short-lived organization established thirty local branches, enrolling African Americans who began to speak out on civil and political rights. The Niagara Movement's most valuable contribution lay in serving as the immediate forerunner of the NAACP, established in 1909, which became the preeminent civil rights organization of the twentieth century. Through its numerous legal campaigns, the NAACP helped to erode Jim Crow by challenging the constitutionality of local and state laws in the South.

While legal challenges to Jim Crow were under way, many black leaders, chiefly Du Bois, argued that the participation of more than 400,000 black soldiers in the armed forces during World War I, and their wartime sacrifices, had entitled African Americans to first-class citizenship. Such demands, and the manner in which they were made, inspired the "New Negro"—African Americans, especially younger ones—to assert themselves. Centered on Harlem, this new political energy was enhanced by Garvey, a Jamaican immigrant whose UNIA would come to include four million or more members, with chapters across the United States, in the Caribbean, Central and South America, England, and Africa.

In the years following World War I, Garvey commanded the largest following of black people in the nation's history up to that time. His arguments for economic self-sufficiency and his articulation and projection of black pride through black nationalism reinvigorated the African American community. This was at a time when lynching of black men and women continued unabated, and "race riots" led to the death of dozens of African Americans at the hands of white mobs (East Saint Louis in 1917, Chicago in 1919, and Tulsa in 1921). Garvey, who sharply criticized Du Bois and the integrated NAACP for its elitist leadership, brought life and dignity to millions of poor and working-class African Americans. Long after he was deported in 1927 on trumped-up charges of mail fraud, Garveyism served as an inspiration to black people throughout the African diaspora.

By the late 1920s more than two million African Americans had moved north. In 1900 only 22.7 percent of African Americans were living in urban centers, but by 1950 this had increased to 61.7 percent. The influx of southern African Americans into cities such as Chicago and New York in the early part of the century led to greater black political influence in those places. One sign of this development was the 1928 election of the Chicago-based Republican Oscar DePriest to Congress, making him the first African American to enter the U.S. House of Representatives since the North Carolina Republican George H. White's departure from Congress a quarter of a century earlier.

From Republican to Democratic Identity. Although most African Americans identified themselves as Republicans, the Great Depression of the 1930s saw a significant shift in party identification among black voters toward the Democratic Party. Mass social action during the early years of the Depression in response to the deepening economic crisis (including black unemployment reaching 60 percent) took organizational form in the Sharecroppers Union, Southern Tenant Farmers Association, and Congress of Industrial Organizations. Social discontent fueled support for a number of third parties, which African Americans joined and helped to lead—the Socialist Party under the grassroots leadership of Frank Crosswaith, the Communist Party (which ran African American James Ford for U.S. vice president in 1932, 1936, and 1940), and the American Labor Party (which helped to elect the popular Harlem minister Adam Clayton Powell Jr. to Congress from New York).

Threatened by unrest and by growing support for independent parties and labor organizations, Democrats and Republicans were forced to make certain concessions to poor and working people. In 1935 President Franklin D. Roosevelt, a northern Democrat, worked with Congress to enact laws that gave labor unions the right to organize, limited the workday to eight hours, established a minimum wage, and guaranteed Social Security and unemployment insurance. (First Lady Eleanor Roosevelt would also encourage the organization of a "Black Cabinet," which included the educator Mary McLeod Bethune.) The African American electorate consequently broke with the party of Abraham Lincoln and began to support Democrats in the North; the southern branch of the Democratic Party however remained explicitly white supremacist. The 1934 congressional elections would see the first wave of black support for the Democratic Party; by the 1936 presidential election most African Americans were casting their votes for Roosevelt and his party. Together with organized labor, black voters would form the backbone of the "New Deal coalition," which sustained the Democratic Party for the next seventy-five years.

Federal relief programs under the New Deal provided jobs, financial aid, and government-financed housing to many African Americans, but the programs also hurt rural black families and individual workers. The Agricultural Adjustment Administration aided large-scale farm owners, virtually all of whom were white, while ignoring the plight of sharecroppers and agrarian workers. Many of the latter were fired when farm production was reduced as government subsidies helped to stabilize commodity prices. Likewise the Social Security Act provided for industrial workers, albeit unevenly (initially, women did not receive any retirement benefits) but denied financial assistance to the farmers, sharecroppers, and domestic workers who comprised over 65 percent of all black workers. Jim Crow, often portrayed as a strictly southern phenomenon, was nevertheless rampant in the North: African Americans continued to earn lower wages, pay higher rent, earn fewer promotions, and face greater restrictions to higher education than did their white counterparts.

With the rise of third parties in the 1930s, the Democratic and Republican parties closed ranks by instituting a series of local ballot access laws to make it more difficult for independents to compete in the electoral arena. Onerous petitioning requirements were passed, as were filing fees and other measures that structurally discriminated against independent candidates and third parties. In 1931 Florida abolished all means for independent candidates and new parties to get on the ballot; in 1937 California raised the signature requirement for new party petitions from 1 percent of the last gubernatorial vote to 10 percent. But even as growing numbers of black voters flowed into the Democratic Party, African Americans supported and fielded independent and third-party candidacies.

Political Independence. Du Bois was briefly a member of the Socialist Party and throughout most of his life actively supported independent electoral options for the black community. In 1950 he ran for the U.S. Senate on the Progressive Party line in New York; two years earlier Paul Robeson—the black All-American football player, actor, attorney, and progressive leader—had been considered for the vice-presidential spot on the Progressive Party ticket with Henry Wallace. (Wallace's candidacy in 1948 spurred an independent presidential run to the right of the Democratic Party by the Dixiecrat segregationist Strom Thurmond, marking a shift among southern white voters away from the Democratic Party and, in years to come, toward the Republican Party.)

A number of African Americans who rose to top leadership positions within the burgeoning modern civil rights movement affiliated with third parties. Ella Baker, who had served as field secretary for the NAACP from 1938 to 1946, ran for New York City Council on the Liberal Party ticket in 1953. However, the attack on political independents following World War II spurred by Wisconsin Senator Joseph McCarthy's anticommunist Red Scare forced many progressives underground and out of the electoral arena. Despite efforts to isolate and suppress voices of dissent, the modern civil rights movement gained traction.

One year after the landmark Supreme Court decision in *Brown v. Board of Education* (overturning *Plessy v. Ferguson*), the Montgomery bus boycott in Alabama sparked a decade of intense and broad-based civil rights activism. This included sit-ins, marches, petitioning, further boycotts, and the creation of a number of independent organizations—from the Montgomery Improvement Association to the Student Nonviolent Coordinating Committee. By the mid-1960s the civil rights movement (also known as the Black Freedom movement) succeeded in dismantling Jim Crow. Tens of thousands of African Americans, mobilized by King and dozens of lesser-known leaders, including Ella Baker and Edgar D. Nixon, pushed for the restoration of civil and voting rights. Federal intervention into the South, along with passage of the Civil Rights Act of 1964 and the Voting Rights Acts of 1965 signed by President Lyndon B. Johnson, would however help to ensure African-American loyalty to the Democratic Party for the remainder of the twentieth century. By the 1960s a convoluted maze of state election laws had also been concocted to keep independents off the ballot. Still, in 1964 the Mississippi Freedom Democratic Party (MFDP), principally under the leadership of black women—Fannie Lou Hamer, Annie Devine, and Victoria Gray—arose to challenge the seating of the "regular" (whites only) state Democratic Party at the national nominating convention in Atlantic City, New Jersey. The MFDP delegates, who held a nationally televised protest outside the main convention hall, were eventually awarded two at-large seats—but without voting rights. They rejected the offer; the Democratic Party would in coming years rewrite its delegate apportionment rules to include women and other minorities. Some viewed this as a positive move, while others saw it as a way to appease dissidents by keeping the particular selection of such delegates in the hands of top-level partisan operators.

As the "War on Poverty" at home was overshadowed by the bipartisan escalation of the American war in Vietnam, the late 1960s saw a flowering of independent parties. Rooted in a combination of the antiwar, civil rights, and early Black Power movements were California's Peace and Freedom Party, the Wisconsin Alliance, the Chicano La Raza Unida in the Southwest, the Puerto Rican Young Lords in Chicago and New York, and most notably, the Black Panther Party, which began organizing in Oakland, California, but soon had a significant presence in every major northern city. In 1968 the Peace and Freedom Party ran the Black Panther minister of information Eldridge Cleaver for U.S. president. Cleaver however was wounded in a shoot-out with Oakland police and, facing criminal charges, fled the country.

King, who was considering an independent presidential run just before his assassination in 1968, and Malcolm X, in his "the ballot or the bullet" speech a few years earlier, recognized that growing African American dependence on the Democratic Party was a central and problematic issue that needed to be worked out as part of a broader strategy for the empowerment of the black community. Malcolm said, "I'm not trying to knock out the Democrats for the Republicans. We'll get to them in a minute. But it is true; you put the Democrats first and the Democrats put you last." A strategy to begin developing new alliances and electoral options however would need to be pursued by a new generation of African Americans; the radicalism of the 1960s was being undercut by Democratic (and Republican) co-optation and reactionary law enforcement, expressed in increased police attacks and the covert activities (later disclosed) of the FBI's counterintelligence program, COINTELPRO.

The Gary Convention and Black Empowerment. Since the late 1960s, there has been ongoing disagreement and debate among African Americans over which political direction black voters should take. In March of 1972, at the height of the Black Power movement, and the same year that the voting age was lowered to eighteen by the Twenty-sixth Amendment, a National Black Political Convention was held in Gary, Indiana. African Americans from across the country met to discuss the state of black politics and possible future directions. Organized by Gary's mayor Richard Hatcher, Congressman Charles Diggs of Detroit, and the New Jersey-based activist Amiri Baraka, the convention debated whether it was more advantageous to increase the number of African Americans elected to office through the Democratic Party or to build a political alternative. Among the seven thousand delegates and observers in attendance, younger participants favored an independent political strategy. However, the convention adjourned still divided on the issue of which electoral path to pursue, and the Democratic Party reform option prevailed by default.

Since the Gary convention several approaches to black political empowerment have been put forth. Black-led reform of the Democratic Party was advocated by the Reverend Jesse Jackson throughout the 1980s and 1990s. In the same vein, in 2005 William Fletcher called for a "Neo-Rainbow" movement "to move the party to the left," despite the party's ongoing shift to the right. The formation of an all-black party was proposed by Ron Daniels and the National Black Political Party in 1980, by Joseph Mack and the Black Nationalist United African Party in 1990, and by New York City Councilman Charles Barron in 2004. The Reverend Al Sharpton created an eclectic approach—he ran in the Democratic Party's presidential primary in 2004 but years earlier had supported the black nationalist Joseph Mack and promised, but then declined, to run for state office on the pro-socialist New Alliance Party line. A final approach—independent and fusion politics—has been promoted by Lenora Fulani since the 1980s. This approach has entailed supporting independent and pro-reform major party candidates who agree to back measures that help to democratize the electoral process while simultaneously creating a multiracial, multi-ideological electoral base to give political independents greater visibility and leverage.

In reaction to the strategy that came out of the Gary convention to reform the Democratic Party, black nationalists such as Ron Daniels launched an effort to establish an all-black political party in 1976. Building on the networks created by the National Black Political Assembly, they held a convention in Philadelphia in 1980 at which approximately 1,500 delegates formed the National Black Independent Political Party. Lecturers were dispatched around the country to help build the party, but as quickly as their efforts were initiated, they ended. With the election of Ronald Reagan in 1980, most abandoned the project and rejoined the Democratic Party in a "united front against fascism." With mounting frustration and deepening poverty in the black community, some saw the 1983 victory in Chicago of Harold Washington's insurgent independent mayoral candidacy as a model for reforming the Democratic Party in a more progressive direction. The hope was to replicate the success of the Washington model nationwide. An apparent opportunity came the following year, when Jesse Jackson decided to seek the Democratic Party's presidential nomination.

Running as an insurgent Democrat, Jackson spoke passionately about the twin issues of poverty and injustice in the nation. Millions of people were inspired by his candidacy, which garnered more than 3.5 million votes in the primaries. Just as significant as the number of votes was the incipient rebellion against both major parties expressed by Jackson's candidacy. A survey conducted by the University of Michigan's Institute for Social Research that year revealed that 57 percent of the people who voted for Jackson in the primary said they would have supported him in the general election had he decided to run as an independent—which he did not do. Four years later Jackson ran again, this time with a much stronger national organization and fundraising base than in his first run (he raised over $21 million, compared to $11 million the first time). He garnered twice as many votes in the 1988 Democratic primaries, but he was again denied the party's nomination; the national convention in Atlanta would hold out little promise of a leftward shift in the party's political trajectory.

Among those who encouraged Jackson to break with the Democratic Party was Lenora Fulani, then emerging as a national advocate for black political independence. Toward this end her 1988 independent presidential campaign promoted a strategy of "two roads are better than one." She urged her supporters to vote for Jackson in the Democratic primary and then—in the probable event that he did not receive the party's nomination—to vote for her as a third-party candidate in the general election. After gathering nearly 1.5 million signatures (nearly forty times the number required by the major party candidates), she became the first woman and first African American presidential candidate to get on the ballot in all fifty states and the District of Columbia. (In 1969 Shirley Chisholm had become the first African American women elected to Congress; she subsequently ran for U.S. president as a Democrat, but was never nominated and therefore did not appear on the ballot.)

In 1992 the white billionaire H. Ross Perot called on Fulani's legal team for counsel as he initiated his independent presidential bid, centered on a critique of the two major parties. A CBS News poll in May of that year showed that at least 12 percent of African Americans said they supported Perot's independent candidacy, compared with 22 percent support among all voters. Despite bipartisan attacks, ridicule, and disparagement, 7 percent of African Americans voted for Perot at the ballot box (nearly 800,000 votes). Perot received an unprecedented 19 percent of the overall vote (nearly 20 million votes). Never before had so many Americans voted for an independent candidate. The winner that year was the Democrat and Arkansas governor Bill Clinton. He was later called the "first black president," despite following his Republican predecessors by rolling back, or altogether ending, a number of gains won by the civil rights movement (including affirmative action, low-income housing, and welfare) while boosting corporate dividends and engaging in overseas military ventures.

In the wake of the 1992 election, black and white independents around the country sought to create new political alliances that could challenge not only the bipartisan establishment but also ideologically driven politics. Out of these efforts, in 1994 a new national party—the Patriot Party—was formed, bringing together independents from across the political spectrum. Dr. Jessie Fields, a black physician from Harlem who had been active in third-party politics since the late 1980s, was elected vice chair of the new party. The party effectively served as a transitional organization, acting as a bridge between the millions of Perot supporters and preexisting elements of the independent movement that became the Reform Party, a key element of which was the Fulani-organized Black Reformers Network.

On the heels of the Million Man March, organized by the Nation of Islam's minister Louis Farrakhan, the Democratic Party—whose leading lights by then included Congressmen Kweisi Mfume of Maryland and Charles B. Rangel of New York, and Carol Moseley Braun of Illinois, the first black woman elected to the U.S. Senate—began to show itself susceptible. During the 1997 gubernatorial race in Virginia, for instance, black voter turnout was markedly down. The Democrat, Donald Beyer, polled 80 percent of the vote among African Americans and lost to Republican Jim Gilmore. This was a notable departure from the usual 95 percent black support that traditionally went to Democrats. Former Democratic governor Doug Wilder (the state's first and only black governor) refused to endorse Beyer, instead remaining neutral.

Perhaps the clearest expression of black voters' disaffection from the Democratic Party in recent years came during the mayoral cycle in New York City in 2005, when the white billionaire Michael Bloomberg—running on both the Republican and Independence Party lines in a fusion bid—received 47 percent of the African American vote (up from his 30 percent support among African Americans in his 2001 run for office). Bloomberg had initially received the Independence nomination after promising to create a charter revision commission to explore revising the city's election laws in favor of nonpartisan municipal elections.

Black Politics in the Twenty-first Century. By the early twenty-first century there were over six times as many African Americans in Congress as there had been in 1965, as well as thousands of black men and women serving in state and municipal offices. Almost all were Democrats. Despite the substantial presence of black Democrats in office (and some Republicans at the highest levels of office, notably Secretary of State Condoleezza Rice), most African Americans remained politically marginalized and poor—as the world witnessed in the wake of Hurricane Katrina in Louisiana in 2005. One-third of African Americans had incomes below the poverty line. On the whole, African Americans have also had markedly higher infant mortality rates, disproportionately higher levels of incarceration and unemployment, and lower life expectancy than the rest of the U.S. population.

Even though the black middle class may have more than tripled since the 1960s, the vast majority of African Americans simply did not reap all the benefits resulting from the modern civil rights movement, including better educational opportunities, jobs, and health care. The default strategy coming out of the Gary convention—increasing the number of black elected officials via the Democratic Party—fell short of the vision of creating a more empowered black electorate.

Partisanship largely prevailed over policies that could be of value to the black community. Consequently, as black elected officials prioritized their partisan allegiances, a dealignment of African Americans from the Democratic Party followed. Extreme partisan allegiances among black elected leaders for instance were made manifest in 2004 by the Congressional Black Caucus (CBC). That year, the CBC took undemocratic measures against the possible defection of black voters in favor of independent presidential candidate Ralph Nader by attempting to have him withdraw from the race. Meanwhile, at the instigation of the Democratic National Committee, Nader petitioners and petition-signers were subjected to various degrees of harassment, accompanied by a coordinated effort to remove his name from the ballots in more than a dozen states.

While most African Americans self-identify and vote as Democrats, with a small percentage Republican, nearly 30 percent of African Americans identify themselves as politically independent—an identification that has steadily grown over the past fifteen years (Pew Research Center for the People and the Press, 2005). According to the Joint Center for Political and Economic Studies, the youngest generation of eligible black voters are least tied to the two major parties; black voters, like all other voters, increasingly reject partisan identification altogether.

A significant challenge to partisan-driven politics came in 2008 when Illinois Senator Barack Obama, an insurgent Democratic candidate, was elected the first African American president of the United States. His major party nomination—the first of a black person—was propelled by a "black and independent alliance," which saw 90 percent African American and majority white independent support for his candidacy in the primaries and caucuses. Breaking partisan convention by reaching out to Republicans and independents, in addition to rank-and-file Democrats, Obama not only defeated the Democratic Party's establishment choice, New York Senator Hillary Clinton, but helped to ignite a movement for change that won him the presidency in the general election. For African Americans, the election of the nation's first black president signaled a new beginning while opening up new possibilities for all Americans.

[*See also* Black Panther Party; Black Power Movement; Black Radical Congress; *Brown v. Board of Education*; Civil Rights Movement; Congress, African Americans in; Congressional Black Caucus; Conservatism and Conservatives, Black; Democratic Party; National Association for the Advancement of Colored People; Political Participation; Political Parties and Civil Rights; Politics and Politicians; Populist Party; Republican Party; Southern Politics and Race; Universal Negro Improvement Association; *and biographical entries on figures mentioned in this article*.]

Bibliography

Adam, Anthony J., and Gerald H. Gaither. *Black Populism in the United States*. Westport, Conn.: Praeger, 2004. A valuable resource for further studies on black populism.

Ali, Omar H. *In the Balance of Power: Independent Black Politics and Third Party Movements in the United States*. Athens: Ohio University Press, 2008. Details the history of black independents and their role in advancing civil and political rights.

Ayers, Edward L. *The Promise of the New South: Life after Reconstruction*. New York: Oxford University Press, 1990. Chapters 9–14 are valuable in understanding the context of black politics in the decades following Reconstruction.

Bositis, David A. *Diverging Generations: The Transformation of African American Policy Views*. Washington, D.C.: Joint Center for Political and Economic Studies, 2001. Traces national political trends among African Americans.

Breitman, George, ed. *Malcolm X Speaks: Selected Speeches and Statements*. New York: Merit Publishers, 1965. The "Ballot or the Bullet" speech was delivered in Ohio on 4 April 1964.

Dawson, Michael C. *Behind the Mule: Race, Class and African American Politics*. Princeton, N.J.: Princeton University Press, 1994. Issues of race and class in the 1980s and an explanation of political cohesion among African Americans from different socioeconomic backgrounds.

Du Bois, W. E. B. *The Souls of Black Folk*. Edited by David Blight and Robert Gooding-Williams. Boston: Bedford/St. Martin's, 1997. Includes a helpful introduction to the Du Bois classic.

Hacker, Andrew. *Two Nations: Black and White, Separate, Hostile, Unequal*. Rev. ed. New York: Ballantine, 1995. Valuable analysis and political and economic statistical information on African Americans in the late twentieth century.

James, Winston. *Holding Aloft the Banner of Ethiopia: Caribbean Radicalism in Early Twentieth-Century America*. London: Verso, 1998. Chapters 5 and 6 are helpful in understanding the significance of the African Blood Brotherhood, Garvey, and UNIA.

Kelley, Robin D. G. *Hammer and Hoe: Alabama Communists during the Great Depression*. Chapel Hill: University of North Carolina Press, 1990.

Lewis, David Levering. *W. E. B. Du Bois: The Fight for Equality and the American Century, 1919–1963*. New York: Henry Holt, 2000.

Marable, Manning. *Race, Reform, and Rebellion: The Second Reconstruction in Black America, 1945–1990*. Jackson: University Press of Mississippi, 1991. An overview of black politics from the mid-twentieth century through the 1990s.

Naison, Mark. *Communists in Harlem during the Depression*. New York: Grove, 1984. A valuable work on black communism in the North and the electoral tactics of African Americans during the era.

Pew Research Center for the People and the Press. Washington, D.C., 2005. October 6–10, 2005 national survey conducted by Schulman, Ronca and Bucuvalas Inc.

Ransby, Barbara. *Ella Baker and the Black Freedom Movement: A Radical Democratic Vision*. Chapel Hill: University of North Carolina Press, 2003. This biography provides a helpful way of understanding the decades prior to the modern civil rights movement.

Sitkoff, Harvard. *A New Deal for Blacks: The Emergence of Civil Rights as a National Issue: The Depression Decade*. New York: Oxford University Press, 1978.

Walton, Hanes, Jr. *African American Power and Politics*. New York: Columbia University Press, 1997. Examines the larger context of black politics from the 1980s through the mid-1990s.

—OMAR H. ALI

BLACK POWER MOVEMENT. In 1849 Frederick Douglass noted in "No Progress without Struggle" that "Power concedes nothing without a demand." Black Power itself was such a demand, a demand from blacks to the white power structure. Considered a twentieth-century phenomenon, philosophically the rhetoric of Black Power actually finds its origins in the "freedom" discourse of the Declaration of Independence and the discourse on the respect for personhood of the U.S. Constitution. Ironically, this same constitution defined blacks as equaling three-fifths of a human being, and voting rights were conferred to the slave owner. Ideologically, Black Power finds its antecedents in the antislavery rhetoric of the early eighteenth century that fought to change the material reality of enslaved and free blacks.

Black Power was expressed culturally in the early writings of African Americans. The critical discourse of Black Power is seen in the abolitionist writings and speeches of David Walker (*Walker's Appeal*, 1829), Henry Highland Garnet ("Call to Rebellion" speech, 1843), Martin Delany (*Condition, Elevation, Emigration, and Destiny of the Colored People of the United States*, 1852), James T. Holly (*A Vindication of the Capacity of the Negro Race for Self-Government and Civilized Progress*, 1857), and Alexander Crummell ("The Relations and Duties of Free Colored Men in America to Africa," 1860, and the "Future of Africa," 1862): together they show the germinations of a Pan-African consciousness tied to the ideology of self-reliance and self-determinism. Also, the slave narratives of Harriet Jacobs, Frederick Douglass, and Henry Bibby argued for Black Power in the abolition of slavery.

After the Civil War and the passage of the Thirteenth, Fourteenth, and Fifteenth amendments, black advances in the political arena led to early realizations of Black Power. In many places blacks numerically outnumbered whites, but through the grandfather clause, the poll tax, literacy tests, and gerrymandering, whites successfully diminished and neutralized the black electorate. The failed promise of Reconstruction, which ended in 1877, left blacks wondering what good "freedom" was without the means to shape its reality or secure its perpetuity by participating in the political process. It took another hundred years after Reconstruction before Black Power would achieve a similar level of success.

Nevertheless, blacks fought on. Oddly enough, though seen as accommodationists, Booker T. Washington and T. Thomas Fortune were early proponents of Black Power ideology in that they supported separate black institutions, but it was W. E. B. Du Bois who broadened the ideology by arguing for the coalition of blacks worldwide in the fight against white domination. Up through the mid-twentieth century, African American missionary efforts to Africa, Ethiopianism, and Marcus Garvey's Universal Negro Improvement Association—with its back-to-Africa movement—all contained aspects of Black Power. The writers Richard Wright, John Oliver Killens, and James Baldwin argued for Black Power in their creative and critical writings. Also, the Nation of Islam and Malcolm X pushed many facets of Black Power in their teachings, and resistance movements across the African continent became independence celebrations that added fuel to the ascendancy of Black Power in the United States.

The historical desire for Black Power is evidenced in the countless riots and rebellions of the early part of the twentieth century, which were physical expressions of the powerless attempting to exercise power. Malcolm X, the Deacons for Defense and Justice, and eventually the Black Panthers reflect this physical nature of Black Power: they believed in blacks' arming themselves to defend themselves and fellow blacks from white violence.

Finally, Black Power and the black church had a love-hate relationship. Christianity played a pivotal role in the measured response of many blacks to their oppression. Part of blacks' accommodating attitude was a function of Christianity's pivotal role in the development of black leaders. Their actions were dictated by their faith in God and the idea that "long suffering" was a virtue. For the most part, blacks cut their political teeth in the church, because in the absence of decent schools, church was the place to learn to read and write and to hone leadership skills; however, the black church was a double-edged sword in the campaign against white rule. In some respects the black church hindered black militancy, but some black theology became a prodigious agitator against the status quo, fostering the revolutionary fervor that gave birth to Black Power.

The 1960s. Dismantling racially separatist practices led to ideological movements—antislavery, emigration, Pan-Africanism, and black nationalism—each of which was a signification of the self-defining impulse articulated by marginalized blacks. Unfortunately, by the mid-1960s, black leaders had not suggested new paradigms for addressing the real problems that blacks faced.

During the 1960s, assassinations, war, and the struggle for equality took center stage. As the civil rights movement gained steam in the early 1960s, young blacks were visible during the sit-ins, Freedom Rides, voter registration drives, and other demonstrations. Chapters of youth-led organizations like the Congress of Racial Equality (CORE), the Student Nonviolent Coordinating Committee (SNCC), and the Council of Federated Organizations (COFO) began to sprout across the United States. These grassroots, direct-action, nonviolent resistance organizations, along with the Southern Christian Leadership Conference (SCLC), shared similar ideas. Although each desired what could be termed "Black Power," they differed on the means by which it would be achieved.

Many whites, particularly in the South, defended white supremacy with massive resistance to civil rights workers.

The teachings of Malcolm X—that blacks should defend themselves and not be nonviolent to those who were violent to them—spurred an active response from blacks and contributed to the growing impatience and hostility of many blacks. During a protest march in Mississippi in June 1966 and with the prompting of Willie Ricks, the SNCC leader Stokely Carmichael took the stage and called for "Black Power:"

> "The only way we gonna stop them white men from whuppin' us is to take over. We been saying freedom for six years and we ain't got nothin'. What we gonna start saying now is Black Power!"
>
> The crowd was right with him. They picked up his thoughts immediately.
>
> "Black Power!" They roared in unison. (Carmichael and Thelwell, p. 507)

No longer looking for handouts and tired of petitioning whites for redress, many black youths responded enthusiastically to the call for Black Power. Black Power was not about acceptance from whites; instead Black Power advocated blacks defining blackness. Black Power insisted on blacks making the decisions about the tactics, programs, and ideology that would impact their general welfare. It was not that whites were not appreciated or allowed to participate, it was just that blacks came to realize that freedom through negotiation was not the goal. The ultimate goal was liberation.

What was Black Power? Black Power was an organized effort to secure the rights and privileges afforded all citizens through active participation in the political process. Black Power was about deciding who would represent the interests of the black community, which included the redistribution of desperately needed resources. Black Power advocated blacks running for political office on every level and in every facet of government, at the judicial, county, school, and every other level. Nevertheless, what Black Power meant often depended upon who was being asked.

The discourse of Black Power was based on the need for a renewed consciousness along with the simultaneous drive for economic, social, and political self-determination. The discourse of blackness espoused in Black Power was about black pride and raising the consciousness of blacks from the psychological shackles of deference, dependence, and inferiority. Respect, dignity, and the struggle for civil rights were aspects of Black Power. Although focusing on the plight of African Americans, leaders of the civil rights movement included all citizens of the United States in the scope of their demands. As a discourse seeking liberation, Black Power sought to empower the full range of human experiences lumped together under the label "black."

Black Power Activists. Stokely Carmichael, LeRoi Jones, and H. Rap Brown in Michaux's Bookstore in Harlem, 1967. Photograph by James E. Hinton. Prints and Photographs Division, Library of Congress

James Boggs's Marxist analysis saw Black Power as an inevitable response to white supremacy. Likewise, James Cone, the father of black liberation theology, saw Black Power as a logical response to the "absurdity" of the very real lived experience of black folks whose opportunities were limited and genius confiscated because of the color of their skin. Ontologically speaking, blackness was considered antithetical to personhood, and that so-called reality afforded no other response than the call for Black Power and the right to self-definition. Though Carmichael's declaration gave voice to the yearnings of black America, it also created a number of problems for the leadership of the civil rights movement.

Criticisms. Attacked by the NAACP leadership and some members of the SCLC and other civil rights organizations, Black Power was portrayed by the 1960s media as creating a rift between the young and old guards of the civil rights movement. Granted, there were some members of the SCLC and the NAACP who openly attacked the demand for "Black Power." In reality, no aspect of the civil rights movement could sustain itself without the financial support of liberal whites, who, although sympathetic to the plight of blacks, often advocated patience. Also, whites, and many blacks, found the tenor of Black Power rhetoric unsettling.

The Reverend Martin Luther King Jr. was often represented as taken aback by the rhetoric of Black Power; although he held to his position of nonviolence, one can see in his speeches after Carmichael's June 1966 remarks—for instance, in King's speeches on the Vietnam War and on the glacial pace of change in the United States—a shift that understood the need for power to improve the lot of blacks across the nation. King and civil rights proponents wanted blacks to gain the right to vote and participate in the democratic process, thereby choosing representation that reflected the needs of blacks. In short, King did not find Black Power problematic objectively, nor did he publicly denounce Black Power; instead he found "Black Power" as a slogan proffered by the media to be conducive to oversimplification of the real and complex issues confronting the black community.

Despite criticisms that it was a just a fad, Black Power had been the basis of SNCC programming in Alabama and Mississippi and had been articulated long before that day in 1966 in Mississippi when the press latched onto the idea and vilified its proponents. SNCC was instrumental in organizing the Mississippi Freedom Democratic Party in 1964 and the Lowndes County Freedom Organization in Lowndes County, Alabama, in 1965.

Media distortion prompted Carmichael and other SNCC organizers to produce written clarifications on the subject of Black Power. The first such compilation was the position paper entitled "Toward Black Liberation," by Carmichael and Michael Thelwell, published by the *Massachusetts Review* in autumn 1966. Critics of Black Power took issue with what they considered to be the lack of critical discourse about liberation. In their 1967 book *Black Power*, Carmichael and Charles Hamilton saw liberation for the many, as opposed to for the token few, as the basis for black Americans' claims for power: "In the first place, black people have not suffered as individuals, but as members of a group; therefore, liberation lies in group action" (p. 54). In short, Carmichael and Hamilton showed that integration was possible only between groups of equal or commensurate power.

The virulence of many whites' response to blacks' demands for power reflected the efficacy of blacks' demands. After the advent of Black Power, blacks and whites castigated proponents of Black Power as racist and "anti-white." Further, black women raised charges of sexism against the Black Power leaders, all of whom were male.

Eventually the shouts of "Black Power" that fanned the flames of black unrest and galvanized black youth faded. Carmichael and SNCC organizers understood that mass action lacking the associated consciousness for change was not the formula for liberation. Another, outside criticism of Black Power was that although it galvanized black youth, it created, as the longtime civil rights worker Ella Baker noted, an equally devastating problem for the civil rights movement: "But this [Black Power] began to be taken up, you see, by youngsters who had not gone through any experiences or any steps of thinking and it did become a slogan, much more of a slogan, and the rhetoric was far in advance of the organization for achieving that which you say you're out to achieve" (quoted in Payne, pp. 379–380). Baker's analysis proved prophetic.

Blacks involved in the sit-ins and other demonstrations became disillusioned when little progress seemed to result, and other blacks took to the streets to express their pent-up frustrations over the deaths of such black activists as Medgar Evers in June 1963, Malcolm X in February 1965, and King in April 1968; they particularly did so in the mayhem, death, and destruction of the so-called hot summer of '68. Unfortunately for blacks, no answers were found in the streets or in the Christian-based pleadings of their leaders.

Impact. Black Power had an immediate and longstanding impact on the history and culture of African Americans and U.S. society. Carmichael's call for Black Power reverberated internationally, too, in South Africa's Black-Consciousness Movement. Like Black Power, Black Consciousness was an inward-looking process that proved ineffective without the means of changing the material condition of blacks. In the United States, Black Power

Black Power Overseas. Black U.S. Marine artillerymen greet each other with clenched fists, the symbol of Black Power, at the large U.S. military base at Con Thien, Vietnam, 1968. Photograph by Johner. AP IMAGES

spawned the Black Arts Movement, the "black is beautiful" cultural movement, and the black aesthetic literary movement, as well as other forms of political, cultural, and social consciousness.

Black Power gave substance to a number of organizations that forwarded black pride and uplift, the most notable being the Black Panther Party for Self-Defense, founded by Huey P. Newton and Bobby Seale in Oakland, California, in 1966. Though mainly known for their stance on bearing arms in defense of the black community, the Black Panthers started out monitoring police activities and providing free breakfasts and drug and health education in Chicago and Oakland. The impact of the Black Panthers and Black Power resonated at the 1968 Olympics in Mexico City when two black American sprinters, Tommie Smith and John Carlos, winners of the gold and bronze medals, raised black gloved fists—the so-called Black Power salute—during the playing of the "Star-Spangled Banner."

Black and African American studies programs and departments began to sprout up on the campuses of many universities as a direct response to Black Power, and even without a department or specific program, course offerings and faculty focusing on the contributions of African Americans were increased. Eventually Temple University launched the first PhD program in African American studies in 1988. The inclusion of African American studies in the curricula of higher education led to Afrocentric curricula filtering down into the elementary and high schools.

In terms of social consciousness, blacks embraced the idea that "black is beautiful." According to William L. Van Deburg, Black Power fostered "soulful folk expressions" in fashion, speech, and other forms of expressive culture. The number of movies and television shows depicting blacks increased, and the ascendancy of the Motown, Chicago, Philly, and Memphis sounds helped to fashion the musical stylings of Curtis Mayfield, Marvin Gaye, Aretha Franklin, the Last Poets, Gil Scott-Heron, and the many other artists of the 1960s and 1970s who used music to articulate the new "black is beautiful" consciousness.

Across the country, community organizations—including day camps, after-school art programs, and black theater and dance companies—helped develop and uplift black youth. The writer and activist Amiri Baraka (born Everett LeRoi Jones) began the Black Arts Movement as an artistic offshoot of Black Power. Poets and writers such as Gwendolyn Brooks, Jayne Cortez, Nikki Giovanni, Woodie King, Haki Madhubuti (born Don L. Lee), Ron Milner, Larry Neal, Sonia Sanchez, and Ntozake Shange all participated in the Black Arts Movement.

[*See also* Black Nationalism; Black Panther Party; Black Studies; Civil Rights Movement; Liberation Theology; Pan-Africanism; Radicalism; Student Nonviolent

Coordinating Committee; *and biographical entries on figures mentioned in this article.*]

BIBLIOGRAPHY

Barbour, Floyd B., ed. *Black Power Revolt: A Collection of Essays*. Boston: P. Sargent, 1968.

Boggs, James. *Racism and the Class Struggle: Further Notes from a Black Worker's Notebook*. New York: Monthly Review Press, 1970.

Carmichael, Stokely, and Charles V. Hamilton. *Black Power: The Politics of Liberation in America*. New York: Vintage, 1967.

Carmichael, Stokely, with Ekwueme Michael Thelwell. *Ready for Revolution: The Life and Struggles of Stokely Carmichael (Kwame Ture)*. New York: Scribner, 2003.

Payne, Charles M. *I've Got the Light of Freedom: The Organizing Tradition and the Mississippi Freedom Struggle*. Berkeley: University of California Press, 1995.

Van Deburg, William L. *New Day in Babylon: The Black Power Movement and American Culture, 1965–1975*. Chicago: University of Chicago Press, 1992.

—LLOREN A. FOSTER

BLACK PRESS. By the end of the nineteenth century a number of black journalists had learned enough from their predecessors to be able to keep normally short-lived black newspapers running. Among these pioneers were W. Calvin Chase of the *Washington Bee*, T. Thomas Fortune of the *New York Age*, John Mitchell of the Richmond *Planet*, Chris Perry of the Philadelphia *Tribune*, and John H. Murphy Sr. of the *Baltimore Afro-American*. As of this writing, two of these papers, the *Tribune* and the *Afro-American*, are still in existence.

Late Nineteenth and Early Twentieth Centuries. Black newspapers at the end of the nineteenth century represented the outlook of the black elite, which though tiny in number still strove to speak for and to the race. Like the first black newspaper, *Freedom's Journal*, newspapers such as the *Bee*, the *Planet*, and the *Afro-American* had a dual mission to protest racial oppression and also to encourage their readers to uplift themselves socially, morally, and intellectually. This second mission intersected with the goals and activities of the most powerful and important African American of the time, Booker T. Washington.

Washington's policies of accommodation to the nation's subordination of African Americans made him the favorite of the white establishments of the North and South. For example, northern white philanthropists approved of Washington's ideology, and their support—important for the survival of many black educational and social welfare enterprises—flowed through his hands. President Theodore Roosevelt favored Washington as well, putting him in charge of federal patronage for blacks and southern whites. Washington founded the National Negro Business League for the support of black businessmen, and during Washington's heyday it was difficult for any African American professional to advance without his support.

Augmenting Washington's power base in the white community was his popularity in the black community. Most of the black elite, as well as the masses, approved of his advocacy of black advancement through the creation of socially and economically self-sufficient black communities. Nevertheless, Washington's public acceptance of the South's denial of civil and political rights to blacks alienated significant segments of black opinion, an alienation expressed by certain black newspapers.

The black newspaper most critical of Washington was the *Guardian*, founded in 1901 by Monroe Trotter, a combative Boston realtor. Although the *Guardian* performed the services of a traditional newspaper, its main reason for being was to lead the opposition to Booker T. Washington. As Washington's power waned in the 1910s so did the *Guardian*, and it shut down in 1913. Chicago was another center of anti-Bookerite activity. Ida B. Wells, the leading black female journalist of her time, and her husband, Ferdinand Barnett, published the Chicago *Conservator*. Wells had published the Memphis *Free Speech* in the 1890s and in that capacity had crusaded against lynching—one of the few southern black leaders to do so. For her advocacy Wells was herself nearly lynched when a Memphis mob destroyed her newspaper offices and printing plant. Wells then moved to Chicago, where she married Barnett, who was publishing the *Conservator*. Her background made her a natural enemy to Washington, whose public statements on lynching were always cryptic and tactful. Other black newspapers critical of Washington were the Cleveland *Gazette*, the Richmond *Planet*, and, initially, the *Washington Bee*.

Except for the Richmond *Planet*, southern black newspapers supported Washington, and some northern black newspapers—such as the *Indianapolis Freeman* and the *New York Age*, edited by the preeminent black journalist of the era, T. Thomas Fortune—did so, too. Washington gained the support of most of the black press through his "Tuskegee machine," an organization of educators, politicians, businessmen, journalists, ministers, civic leaders, and other stalwarts of the black bourgeoisie beholden to him and his white allies. Many southern black newspaper publishers depended on paid press releases and advertising from the Tuskegee Institute and from black businesses and churches favored by Washington. Washington's political power was vital in ensuring the safety of black newspaper offices and printing plants. Also, Booker T. Washington was a covert investor in at least two major black newspapers: T. Thomas Fortune's *New York Age* and the *Washington Bee*. Washington purchased the *Age* through his associate Fred Moore in 1907. The *Age* was the most influential black newspaper of the era, and Fortune was called the "dean of black journalism." Under Washington's control, the *Age* became an even stronger advocate of his policies. Washington also in 1907 became a silent partner in the *Washington Bee* and ensured its support for him. Of all the black newspapers in the South, only John Mitchell's Richmond *Planet* stood up to the Tuskegee machine.

Meanwhile the *Baltimore Afro-American* saw no contradiction in the approaches to the race question taken by Booker T. Washington on the one hand and his critics—now gathered into the Niagara Movement—on the other. The *Afro-American* was established in 1892 by a consortium of black preachers and small businessmen and then was taken over in 1896 by John H. Murphy Sr. The *Afro-American* explained that Washington's approach of forming economically and socially self-sufficient and prosperous black communities within a framework of accommodation to southern racial mores was best suited to conditions in the South. Meanwhile, as the *Afro-American* explained, the approach advocated by W. E. B. Du Bois and his associates in the Niagara Movement was generated by and consistent with conditions in the North. The Niagara Movement's approach was one of agitation through publicity, litigation, and political action for the civil, social, and political rights denied blacks in the South and elsewhere. The approaches of Washington and of the Niagara Movement were complementary, not contradictory. The *Afro-American* constantly emphasized this complementarity in its treatment of the Washington–Niagara Movement struggle during the latter half of the 1900s.

The *Afro-American* was not alone in its judicious treatment of the controversy between Booker T. Washington and the Niagara Movement. Until 1907 the *Washington Bee* supported both sides, as did the *Indianapolis Freeman*. The location of these two newspapers in the borderlands between the North and the South helps account for their fence straddling. Yet it is likely that these papers also expressed mainstream black opinion, which, though not happy with blacks' subordination, still found hope in Washington's philosophies of self-help and racial uplift. The clash between Washington and his critics may have been based more on frustration with Washington's dictatorial powers over black institutions than on a deep ideological cleavage.

In the first two decades of the twentieth century the black press, despite the almost complete suppression of its audience by racism, operated on a much firmer basis than ever before. Newspapers such as the *Baltimore Afro-American*, the *New York Age*, the *Richmond Planet*, the *Washington Bee*, and the *Philadelphia Tribune* were financially stable, and some of them lasted throughout the twentieth century and into the twenty-first. In the early twentieth century, the black press with few exceptions turned away from Washingtonian accommodation to racial oppression and turned toward W. E. B. Du Bois's and the NAACP's crusades to end racism.

As time went by, the black press intensified its protest against racial oppression. In the first two decades of the twentieth century, racial segregation was codified in the South and imposed informally everywhere else. Black newspapers in Chicago, Pittsburgh, New York, and elsewhere in the North, as well as in Baltimore and Washington, vigorously crusaded against racism north and south. Not only did they protest racial oppression through news stories, columns, and editorials but they also provided financial aid, office space, and employment to civil rights organizations and leaders. Black newspapers also provided these leaders with media platforms. W. E. B. Du Bois, James Weldon Johnson, Ida B. Wells, Kelly Miller, Walter White, and Marcus Garvey all had columns in black newspapers or, in the case of Wells and Garvey, published their own newspapers. Black newspapers were among the most successful businesses in the black community, with many of the newspapers lasting fifty to a hundred years and with some of them still in existence. This was quite unlike the nineteenth-century black press and was a testament both to the critical mass of black journalists and publishers who could establish a newspaper and also to the critical mass of a black readership that now could sustain a newspaper in black communities north and south. Along with the black church, the black press provided media coverage, outlets, and material sustenance for black protest and advancement organizations.

Black newspapers and magazines were open to all within the black community who had something to say. Since aspiring black journalists were barred from most if not all journalism schools in the early twentieth century, black newspapers had to train their own reporters, columnists, and critics, and in doing so, they tapped the rich, developing source of black literary talent. Black publishers were for the most part highly literate and educated people who wanted to showcase black literary and artistic talent to the world.

Enter the *Chicago Defender*. One of the most important black newspapers, the *Chicago Defender*, made its first appearance in 1905. Its publisher and editor was Robert S. Abbott. Born on Saint Simons Island, Georgia, in 1868, Abbott grew up in Savannah and was raised by his mother and his stepfather, John Sengstacke. Abbott attended Hampton Institute, where he was trained as a printer. Printing jobs were hard to find, however, so he studied law. Despite completing a law course, Abbott was not admitted to the Georgia bar, so he turned to journalism.

Newsroom. *Washington Tribune* newsroom, c. 1935. Photograph by Addison Scurlock. Scurlock Studio Records, Archives Center, National Museum of American History, Smithsonian Institution

In 1905 Abbott decided to start his own newspaper; he chose to base it in Chicago, a city whose black population was 40,000 and growing. Abbott called his newspaper the *Defender*. From an initial press run of 300 copies in 1905, the *Defender* grew to a circulation of more than 200,000 during World War I. The newspaper was distributed throughout the Midwest and as far as the Deep South. It constantly publicized and crusaded against racism, especially in the South. To combat southern Jim Crow, the *Defender* urged its southern readers to migrate north, preferably to Chicago. As a result of this campaign Chicago's black population increased 144 percent to 110,000 between 1910 and 1920; most of the blacks were migrants from the South. The newspaper's circulation, wealth, and influence increased when many of these newcomers became *Defender* readers.

From the 1920s on, the *Chicago Defender* was the most widely read black newspaper in the country, with a circulation approaching 250,000. The *Defender* became a sensationalist newspaper, appealing to all segments of the black community. Not only did the *Defender* crusade against local and national racism but it also provided comprehensive coverage of the day-to-day life of Chicago's black community. The *Defender* was divided into sections covering local, national, and international news; sports, entertainment, and society; and editorials and opinion—as well as a features section that spotlighted black writers and artists. The *Defender*'s layout was imitated throughout the rest of the black press, and by the late 1920s most black newspapers had adopted its sensationalist comprehensive format. Politically, the *Defender* differed little from its contemporaries in the black press; it generally supported the Republican Party both locally and nationally. Befitting his status as a successful entrepreneur, Robert Abbott was moderate to conservative on most issues besides race.

Abbott and the *Defender* fell on hard times during the Depression. The newspaper's circulation dropped by 75 percent, and Abbott was forced to dip into his personal assets to keep the paper afloat. Then his health began to fail in the late 1930s. In 1939 Abbott turned over control of the *Defender* to his nephew John Sengstacke. Shortly thereafter, in February 1940, Abbott died. Under Sengstacke's leadership the *Defender* revived itself during World War II, reaching new heights in circulation and influence because of its extensive coverage of and advocacy for equitable black participation in the war.

Pittsburgh Courier. The *Pittsburgh Courier* was established in 1910 by a consortium of black businessmen. Robert L. Vann, one of the few black attorneys in

Pittsburgh, organized their legal affairs. When they were unable to keep the newspaper going, Vann took it over and in ten years built it to equal the *Defender* in circulation and influence. The *Courier*'s layout followed that of the *Defender*, except that the *Courier* was less sensational. The *Courier*'s columnists and writers also tended to be of higher quality than those of the *Defender*.

The *Courier* was an activist newspaper. It crusaded for racial equality in Pittsburgh, in Pennsylvania, and nationwide. It was one of the few black newspapers that supported the labor movement, giving news coverage and editorial support to A. Philip Randolph's effort to organize Pullman porters into the Brotherhood of Sleeping Car Workers. From the 1920s on the *Courier*, though not the most widely read black newspaper (the *Defender* had higher circulation), was perhaps the most influential, because of its excellent leadership and staff.

The Depression damaged the *Courier*, as it did other black newspapers. But by the late 1930s the *Courier*'s health had improved. The newspaper's coverage of the impending World War II and its tireless advocacy of full black participation in the war effort restored the *Courier* to national prominence. It led the black community's "Double V" campaign for victory over racism at home and over Fascism abroad. Sadly, Robert Vann did not live long enough to see this revival. He died of cancer in 1940.

Baltimore Afro-American. Founded in 1892 the *Baltimore Afro-American* predated both the *Defender* and the *Courier*. The *Afro-American* grew to dominate the black media markets along the Eastern Seaboard, and it joined the *Defender* and the *Courier* as one of the "big three" of the black press.

Throughout its history the *Afro-American* continuously crusaded for racial justice and advancement in Baltimore, in Maryland, and nationwide. Among the movements led by the newspaper were the efforts to equalize teacher salary in Baltimore, the efforts to maintain and increase black membership in the Baltimore city council, the struggles for black representation on the local school board and the police department, and crusades against lynching. Nationwide the *Afro-American* supported antilynching legislation and called for increased federal patronage for black Republicans.

The *Afro-American* was progressive for its time, supporting leftist views and politicians. For example in 1924 it endorsed the third-party candidate Robert La Follette for president. In 1928 the *Afro-American* supported the Democratic Party candidate Alfred E. Smith over the Republican Herbert Hoover. Then in the 1930s the newspaper gave covert endorsements of Communist and Socialist Party candidates for local, state, and national offices. The *Afro-American* also had a wide range of quality columnists and feature writers. Walter White, head of the NAACP, Kelly Miller, dean of Howard University, James Weldon Johnson, and others all had columns in the newspaper.

Unlike its competitors the *Defender* and the *Courier*, the *Afro-American* expanded and prospered during the Depression. It established branch offices and editions in Washington, Philadelphia, Richmond, and Newark. The *Afro-American* reached unprecedented highs in circulation, income, and influence during World War II, becoming a million-dollar company in 1945. It remained at that level for many years afterward.

Negro World. In 1918 Marcus Garvey established the *Negro World* to publicize the activities of the Universal Negro Improvement Association (UNIA). For a time the *Negro World* was the most important black newspaper in Harlem. At its peak its circulation approached 200,000. T. Thomas Fortune, who had published the *New York Age* and was considered to be the most important black journalist at the turn of the century, edited the *Negro World*. Along with hard news, the *Negro World* promoted Garvey's Black Nationalism in its editorials and featured serialized fictional stories of Africans overthrowing white colonialists. As did other black newspapers of the era, the *Negro World* published poems, essays, and short stories, by authors like Alain Locke, Claude McKay, and Zora Neale Hurston. Over time the *Negro World* became solely a propaganda organ for the UNIA. The *Negro World* flourished as long as Marcus Garvey did. When Garvey was imprisoned for mail fraud in 1925, however, and was deported to Jamaica in 1927, the UNIA faded away. So did the *Negro World*. Still, during its heyday it was the strongest voice for black nationalism.

Norfolk Journal and Guide, Richmond Planet,* and *Kansas City Call. The *Baltimore Afro-American*, *Chicago Defender*, and *Pittsburgh Courier* were national in circulation and influence. But there were other black newspapers in the first half of the twentieth century that, though not as widely influential, were still important in their respective regions. One of the most noteworthy of these was the *Norfolk Journal and Guide*. Founded by P. B. Young, the *Journal and Guide* was especially influential in tidewater Virginia. The newspaper was more conservative than its peers in the black press, preferring a conciliatory approach toward racial problems. Nonetheless, when black interests were threatened locally or nationally, the *Journal* protested loudly. In the 1920s the newspaper campaigned against lynching and called for better schools, improved housing, and jobs for its readers. It also took a strong stand on crime reduction within the black community.

The *Norfolk Journal and Guide*'s main rival for journalistic dominance in Virginia was the *Richmond Planet*. The *Planet* was run by John Mitchell from 1884 until his death in 1929. From its beginnings the *Planet* crusaded against the disfranchisement of black voters in the South and led boycotts of streetcar companies that segregated black riders. It took a far more militant stance on racial matters than the *Journal and Guide* did and represented the more militant "New Negro" of Du Bois and his followers. The Norfolk paper harked back to the accommodationist ways of Booker T. Washington. After John Mitchell died, the *Richmond Planet* declined. The newspaper was taken over by the *Baltimore Afro-American* in 1938. Renamed the *Richmond Afro-American and Planet*, it followed the parent *Baltimore Afro-American* in layout, but its news coverage and editorials focused on Richmond.

An important Midwest black newspaper was the *Kansas City Call*, started by Chester A. Franklin in 1919. After a difficult beginning, by the mid-1920s the *Call* had attained a firm financial and journalistic footing. Like other black newspapers of the time, it campaigned for racial equality locally and nationally. It led crusades against lynching, the Ku Klux Klan, and police brutality. It also campaigned for desegregated education and housing and for increased job opportunities for blacks. The *Call* constantly presented the local and national black community in the most positive light, emphasizing news about black religious, social, and cultural activity. The *Call* also employed a distinguished roster of reporters and columnists. The most important of these was Roy Wilkins, later the head of the NAACP, who started his career as a reporter columnist for the *Call* in the late 1920s.

Civil Rights Movement. Along with the black church, the black press provided an important institutional base for the civil rights movement. By providing intensive news coverage, editorial support, and sometimes financial and material assistance to civil rights groups, the black press justifiably can claim some of the credit for the successes of the civil rights movement.

It can be said that the civil rights movement began with World War II. That conflict brought momentous changes to American life and was a catalyst for the early civil rights movement. Generations of racism, plus the tradition of racial exclusion and segregation in the armed forces, caused the black community to be apathetic toward the American war effort. Apathy turned to anger over the exclusion, segregation, and mistreatment of African Americans in the military and the grudging inclusion of blacks in the war production effort.

Black newspaper publishers, who for the most part were optimistic about the war's effect on race relations, recognized this anger and tried to channel it into nonviolent protests of domestic racism. This strategy was called the Double V campaign. First popularized by the *Pittsburgh Courier* in 1942, the strategy's goal was to convince the black community that World War II was a struggle against racism and tyranny at home as well as abroad. The newspapers hoped to accomplish this through intensive coverage of the exploits of black servicemen and the relentless exposure of the racial abuse heaped upon those soldiers. Through these tactics black organizations enlisted their readers in an effort that they believed would lead to the end of racial discrimination in the postwar era.

The black press's intense coverage of racial abuse in the armed forces worried government agencies such as the Office of War Information, the FBI, and the Justice Department. They were concerned that such coverage would weaken the black community's support for the war. This concern reached the White House, and President Roosevelt in 1942 asked Walter White of the NAACP to use that organization to muzzle the black press. White then called a meeting of black newspaper publishers to convey the president's sentiments and warn the publishers against going too far in their criticism of racism in the war effort. There even was talk in high government circles about charging some black newspapers, particularly the *Baltimore Afro-American*, with sedition. The attorney general, Francis Biddle, however, a strong supporter of free speech, squelched such talk. Nevertheless the *Afro-American*, *Pittsburgh Courier*, *Detroit Tribune*, *Chicago Defender*, *Philadelphia Herald*, and other black newspapers were the subjects of intense surveillance from the FBI and the Post Office. These newspapers' exposure of racism in the armed forces prompted the FBI to spy on them throughout World War II. No seditious material was found, though J. Edgar Hoover, if he had his way, would have closed the *Afro-American* and other black newspapers.

In any event, black newspapers were not deflected from their coverage and criticism of racism in the armed forces. Black newspapers such as the *Afro-American*, *Journal and Guide*, *Courier*, *Defender*, and *Atlanta Daily World* covered the reluctance of the army to use black soldiers in combat roles in France, the mistreatment of black officers at Freeman Field, Indiana, and racial abuse of black soldiers in southern army camps, among other racial wrongs.

As a result of the black press's exposure of racism in the armed forces, the army decided to cooperate with black newspapers in efforts to boost black morale. The army set up pooling arrangements for black newspapers so that war correspondents from these papers could cover wider areas. Resulting from this cooperation was an endless stream of stories in black newspapers stressing the heroism of black soldiers. The *Afro-American*'s pages were particularly filled with this kind of news, since the newspaper sent six of its reporters overseas as war correspondents—more than any other black newspaper. Among other black newspapers, the *Journal and Guide* also sent reporters overseas and filled its pages with stories of blacks in combat. Such stories fulfilled the Double V mission.

The Double V campaign, plus the intense hunger of blacks for news about their brethren overseas and a black community prosperous as never before, brought the black press heretofore-unseen wealth and influence. The big three of the black press—the *Chicago Defender*, the *Pittsburgh Courier*, and the *Baltimore Afro-American*—all averaged 300,000 in circulation during the war. By 1945 the *Afro-American*, having become a newspaper chain with branches in Baltimore, Washington, Philadelphia, Newark, and Richmond, grossed more than 1.1 million dollars.

The prosperity of the black press continued in the postwar era. By 1947 the total circulation of black newspapers had risen to 2,120,000. Of this circulation, 38 percent (812,000) could be attributed to just four newspapers: the *Courier* (277,900), the *Afro-American*, (235,600), the *Defender* (193,900), and the *Amsterdam News* in New York City (105,300). Other black newspapers prospered proportionately during World War II and in the years immediately following.

In the immediate postwar period black newspapers were more powerful than ever. For example the black sports journalists Wendell Smith of the *Pittsburgh Courier* and Sam Lacy of the *Baltimore Afro-American* were significant factors in the desegregation of Major League Baseball, leading the media coverage of Jackie Robinson's joining the Brooklyn Dodgers in 1947. The *Afro-American* sent Sam Lacy to the Dodgers' spring training camp in Havana, Cuba, in March 1947 to cover Robinson's activities. The *Afro-American* and other black newspapers intensely covered Jackie Robinson during his first season and covered subsequent black baseball pioneers in the late 1940s and early 1950s, such as Larry Doby, Roy Campanella, Don Newcombe, and Willie Mays.

By 1950 the black press was exponentially stronger than it had been a century earlier. Two important new black newspapers were the *Atlanta Daily World*, established in 1928 by William Alexander Scott II and later published by his descendants (even as of this writing), and the *Amsterdam News* in New York, founded in 1909 but greatly overshadowed by T. Thomas Fortune's *New York Age*, which was the main black media outlet in New York. But by the late 1930s the *Age* was no more, and the *Amsterdam News*, now owned by C. B. Powell and Philip Savory, was the leading black newspaper in New York.

By then black newspapers had their own wire service, the Associated Negro Press (ANP). Founded by Claude Barnett in 1919 the ANP proved vital to rural and small-market black newspapers by providing them with national and international black news stories that they could obtain nowhere else. The Associated Press (AP) and other white services ignored black newspapers, so Barnett's ANP filled that vacuum. And in 1940 the leading black newspaper publishers formed their first trade association, the Negro (later National) Newspaper Publishers Association. This group spoke for the interest of black newspapers as a whole and coordinated many of their activities.

In their support for the civil rights movement, black newspapers in some instances were civil rights organizations themselves, bringing lawsuits challenging Jim Crow or using their reporters and employees to test racial segregation laws and policies. These tactics sometimes took place long before the 1950s and 1960s, the popularly accepted dates for the civil rights era. For example, as far back as 1929 the *Baltimore Afro-American* used its reporters to test the segregated seating on Baltimore's buses. After the *Afro-American* brought unwelcome publicity and boycotts to the bus company, the company changed its policies and desegregated. In 1943 two reporters from the same newspaper attempted to travel in whites-only railroad cars in Virginia. When they were removed from the train, they sued, and a federal court ruled that racial segregation was unconstitutional on intrastate railroads. In the early 1960s the *Afro-American* dressed up some of its reporters as African diplomats to see whether they would be served in diners and motels along U.S. Route 1, the main highway between Washington, D.C., and New York. Some African diplomats had been refused service along that highway by motel and restaurant owners. The *Afro-American* wanted to shed light on these practices, and the resulting diplomatic crisis helped generate support for the Civil Rights Act of 1964 that prohibited racial discrimination in public accommodations.

Other black newspapers were just as vigorous in their coverage of and support for the civil rights movement. The other two members of the black press big three, the *Chicago Defender* and the *Pittsburgh Courier*, closely covered the civil rights movement in the South, where they had branch newspapers, and in the North, where there were local antiracist movements. The *Defender*, especially, covered Martin Luther King's civil rights activities in Chicago and conducted a poll there to determine the extent of his popularity. It found that 76 percent of the respondents considered Dr. King the preeminent leader of his people. Midwestern black newspapers such as the *Kansas City Call* and the *St. Louis Argus* also strongly supported the civil rights movement and King, as did black newspapers on the West Coast.

The record of southern black newspapers in the civil rights era is mixed. Many southern black newspaper publishers were conservatives, still following Booker T. Washington's policy of conciliation and accommodation with the southern racial order. In some instances their newspapers were dependent on local white businessmen for advertising, supplies, and credit. Finally, the youthful, radical nature of the movement, especially as expressed by groups such as the Student Nonviolent Coordinating Committee (SNCC), grated on the sensibilities of these "old school" black publishers. For example the publisher of the *Advocate* in Jackson, Mississippi, Percy Greene, was openly critical of the Montgomery bus boycott, the *Brown* decision, and the sit-in movement. This made his newspaper unpopular in black Mississippi. Not helpful were revelations that Greene received subsidies from the Mississippi state sovereignty commission, a state agency dedicated to preserving racial segregation in Mississippi.

A similar story was told in South Carolina, where one of the leading black newspapers, the *Orangeburg Herald*, actually filed suit against the local NAACP to cripple its activities. This newspaper and others in South Carolina were heavily dependent on covert subsidies from white businessmen, which accounts for their reactionary stances. Even in the birthplace of the sit-in movement, Greensboro, North Carolina, the black newspaper, the *Greensboro Herald*, gave little or no coverage to the demonstrators or to the civil rights movement in general. The Deep South's most powerful black newspaper, the *Atlanta Daily World*, though generally supportive of the goals of the civil rights movement, deplored some of its more radical tactics, like sit-ins. The *Norfolk Journal and Guide* took a similar stance.

Nevertheless, some southern black newspapers strongly supported the civil rights movement at all costs. Throughout the 1950s the *Birmingham World* urged its readers to register to vote and staged voter registration drives, and in 1963 the *World* was firmly behind the civil rights demonstrations in Birmingham. The *World* supported the demonstrators so strongly that Eugene "Bull" Connor, Birmingham's notorious police chief, threatened to exile its editor, Emory Jackson. Texas's two leading black newspapers, the *Houston Informer* and the *Dallas Express*, both run by Carter Wesley, also closely covered and supported the civil rights movement. In fact Heman Sweatt, whose NAACP-conducted lawsuit opened the University of Texas law school to black students, was the circulation manager for the *Houston Informer* and was urged by that newspaper to bring forth the lawsuit.

Contemporary Black Press. The 1960s and the years following saw immense changes in the nature and organization of the black press. For the first time, black alternative media in the form of alternative newspapers such as *The Black Panther*, *Muhammad Speaks*, and *The Final Call*, magazines such as *Jet*, *Ebony*, and *Essence*, and Internet Web sites such as Africana.com and BlackVoices.com made their appearances. Meanwhile, traditional black newspapers faced unprecedented challenges. These challenges stemmed from the changes in the American racial order generated by the civil rights and Black Power movements, and from the creation of a black community considerably different from the one that existed before.

Rise of an Alternative Black Press. One little-remarked result of the 1960s was the appearance of alternative black newspapers. Not only did these publications oppose the white power structure but they also set themselves in opposition to the black establishment for whom the black press spoke. The two most important of these newspapers were the organ of the Black Panther Party, *The Black Panther*, and that of the Nation of Islam, *Muhammad Speaks*.

The Black Panther Party was founded in 1966 in Oakland, California, by Huey P. Newton and Bobby Seale, two militant and articulate students at Oakland's Merritt Junior College. They wanted to start a movement that would end local, national, and international racial and economic repression. Consequently, they organized their local black community around political education classes, free food programs—especially breakfasts for children—and free health counseling clinics. Their chief organizing tool was their campaign against police brutality, then rampant in Oakland. The armed Panther membership paraded around Oakland's ghetto with their weapons in full view (which was legal at that time) to defend its residents from out-of-control police. This was more theatrical bluff than anything else, but it did inspire the black community. The Black Panthers attracted the unwanted attention of the Oakland white power structure and the police, who viewed the Panthers as a threat to their control of the city.

The newspaper the *Black Panther* was generated by the police killing of a black man in Richmond, California, in early April 1967. The refusal of the white press or of mainstream black newspapers to give much coverage to the incident prompted the Black Panthers to set up their own newspaper to publicize this and other incidents of police brutality. The first issues of the *Black Panther* were mimeographed sheets stapled together. Soon the *Black Panther* was published as a tabloid newspaper selling for 24 cents a copy. True to its anticapitalist ideology, the Black Panther Party newspaper would not carry business advertising; it depended instead on circulation, with each member of the party having to sell a certain number of newspapers each week.

From its beginnings the *Black Panther* harshly criticized American capitalism and racism, seeing these phenomena as inextricably linked. It prominently displayed the Black Panther ten-point platform on its front page. Among other things, this platform called for full employment for all, for the black community to control its own institutions, for decent housing and education for all, for an end to police brutality, for the release of all black prisoners, and for reparations for slavery. According to the newspaper, this platform was to be accomplished through the violent overthrow of the U.S. political and economic system and its replacement by a democratic socialist state. The *Black Panther*'s news coverage concentrated on local and nationwide incidents of racial injustice and police brutality. The newspaper was vividly designed, with drawings and silhouettes of machine guns and rifles; with heroic pictures of Huey Newton, Bobby Seale, and other leaders; and with cartoons of bloodthirsty police officers depicted as pigs assaulting innocent blacks.

The *Black Panther* was first edited by Eldridge Cleaver, the minister of information of the party. Huey Newton, Bobby Seale, and David Hilliard had prominent roles in the newspaper, with numerous signed columns and editorials. The newspaper frequently accepted outside columns from such sympathizers and fellow travelers as Angela Davis. Although the leadership of the Black Panthers was predominantly male, women members of the party kept the newspaper going, doing the typing and layout, as well as writing many of the articles.

The *Black Panther* captured the spirit of the times. It had a large circulation in the late 1960s—estimates ran from 100,000 to 200,000—and the newspaper was sold everywhere there was a Black Panther chapter. The newspaper's strong stance against the Vietnam War made it popular with radical young whites, who were a significant part of its readership. The *Black Panther* spread the word of the Black Panthers both nationwide and internationally. It inspired the creation of chapters everywhere, and these chapters in turn helped the paper to build its circulation.

Sadly, the *Black Panther* lasted only as long as the party did, and that was not very long. Illegal FBI and local police surveillance and harassment had fatally weakened the Black Panthers by the early 1970s. These actions caused the party's membership to dwindle both in numbers and in morale. As a result the *Black Panther* came out less frequently, going from a weekly to a biweekly in the late 1970s, then finally to a monthly in 1980, just before it shut down. But though the *Black Panther* is gone, it is not forgotten. As of this writing, a version of it is still published in Oakland.

The other major alternative black newspaper of recent times was *Muhammad Speaks*, known as of 2008 as the *Final Call*. This newspaper was published in Chicago by the Nation of Islam. The Nation of Islam was founded in the depths of the Depression in Detroit by W. D. Fard and was carried on by his disciple Elijah Muhammad after Fard's mysterious disappearance. Fard and Muhammad preached a version of Islam that claimed that blacks were the lost nation of Islam, that they were the original humans, and that whites were "devils" who had denied blacks their rightful place as rulers of the world. Muhammad preached that on judgment day, Allah would restore blacks to their primary place in the world. This theology was attractive to those downtrodden blacks who needed a reason to believe in themselves.

The Nation of Islam might have remained an insignificant cult within the black community had it not been for Malcolm X. Born Malcolm Little in 1925, Malcolm X joined the Nation of Islam while imprisoned. Once freed he turned his back on his previous life of petty crime and became a minister and missionary for Elijah Muhammad. In doing so Malcolm X transformed the Nation of Islam from a small cult group centered in the Midwest to a social and religious organization with nationwide membership, influence, and notoriety. He organized temples in New York, Boston, Philadelphia, Los Angeles, and elsewhere, bringing in thousands of converts to the Nation of Islam. In 1960 the Nation of Islam burst upon the public as the result of televised documentaries, newspaper articles, and books. Malcolm X, charismatic and witty, put forth the Nation of Islam as the militant black nationalist alternative to the civil rights movement.

Aiding Malcolm X in his efforts to make the Nation of Islam a powerful national presence was the organization's newspaper *Muhammad Speaks*. Professionally designed and laid out, *Muhammad Speaks* covered local, national, and international black news as comprehensively as did the more established black newspapers. However, it was primarily the house organ for the Nation of Islam. It extensively covered Nation of Islam rallies, as well as Elijah Muhammad's speeches. The newspaper prominently featured Nation of Islam theology in its editorials and published a manifesto that resembled that of the Black Panthers in that it called for reparations for slavery by carving land out of the United States to create a black nation.

Yet *Muhammad Speaks* was hardly as radical as the *Black Panther*. The Nation of Islam's millennial theology precluded its members from taking radical action in the here and now to change the system. Members of the Nation were to live law-abiding, abstemious lives, built around the local temple. Malcolm X, the most radical of the Nation's hierarchy, chafed at its reluctance to immerse itself in the black liberation movements of the era. After Malcolm was forced out, the Nation of Islam lost its most militant voice and remained quiet for the rest of the 1960s and 1970s.

Still, *Muhammad Speaks* seemed a successful operation. Like the *Black Panther*, *Muhammad Speaks* was sold by the members of the parent organization, each of whom had to sell a quota of newspapers every week. Unlike the *Black Panther*, *Muhammad Speaks* carried advertising, mostly from local black businesses. During the 1960s the Nation of Islam claimed a circulation of 600,000 for *Muhammad Speaks*. If that figure is accurate then *Muhammad Speaks* was the most widely circulated, if not read, black newspaper of all time. Even if, as seems likely, the figure is exaggerated, *Muhammad Speaks* was a fixture in many black urban communities; almost daily, one saw immaculately dressed Black Muslims selling the newspaper.

Warith Deen Muhammad took over the Nation of Islam in 1975 upon the death of his father and turned it into a mainstream Islamic sect, dropping the theology that made the Nation of Islam unique. To symbolize the break with the past, *Muhammad Speaks* was changed to the *Bilalian News*, Bilal being one of the prophet Muhammad's black lieutenants. That this change was unpopular with its readers is demonstrated by the fact that the newspaper disappeared a few years later.

One of Elijah Muhammad's lieutenants, Louis Farrakhan, displeased at the direction that Muhammad's son was taking the organization, broke away to form a new group that continued the theology and legacy of Elijah Muhammad. Called the Nation of Islam after its predecessor, Farrakhan's group put out its own newspaper, the *Final Call*, and this is the real successor to *Muhammad Speaks* in that it follows its predecessor's layout, format, and ideology. While not as widespread in black communities as *Muhammad Speaks* was, the *Final Call* remained a popular if controversial source of news and opinion not found in the white press or mainstream black newspapers. As the main media outlet for Louis Farrakhan and his Nation of Islam, the *Final Call* had (and as of this writing continues to have) considerable influence in contemporary black communities.

Black Magazines. Black magazines have existed almost from the beginnings of the black press. In fact black newspapers in the nineteenth and early twentieth centuries more resembled magazines than newspapers in their weekly distribution, layout, and news coverage. In the 1910s and 1920s black literary magazines made their appearance, most notably *The Crisis* and *Opportunity*. Although these magazines were officially the house organs of the NAACP and Urban League, respectively, under the editorship of W. E. B. Du Bois and Charles S. Johnson, *The Crisis* and *Opportunity* served as media outlets for the essayists, poets, and novelists of the Harlem Renaissance. When the Harlem Renaissance collapsed, both magazines reverted back to being house organs for their respective organizations. There were also black radical journals during this era, most notably the *Messenger* published by A. Philip Randolph and Chandler Owen. During its heyday from 1917 to 1928 the *Messenger* was a major source of socialist thought in the black community.

Black periodical publishing took off in the 1940s when John H. Johnson created *Negro Digest*, *Ebony*, and *Jet* magazines. An insurance salesman, Johnson used a $500 loan from his mother to start *Negro Digest* in 1942. This magazine, similar to *Reader's Digest* in that it published reprinted articles—in this instance articles covering black topics—became an instant success and provided Johnson with the resources to create *Ebony* and *Jet* magazines. From the beginning Johnson wanted his periodicals to reflect the most positive aspects of African American life. This was particularly true of *Ebony*, which had a format and layout similar to *Life* magazine. When not portraying them in a negative light, white magazines such as *Life*, *Look*, and *Reader's Digest* ignored African Americans. These white magazines had a national reach and influence unimaginable today, so there was tremendous need for glossy magazines for the black community that would counteract the white magazines' racist coverage. *Ebony* in particular filled that need and still does as of 2008; it and *Jet* remain integral parts of the black community. *Life* and *Look* are no more, but *Ebony*, created to serve an audience overlooked by these two white magazines, stands alone as a mass-circulation, general-news picture magazine. As it did during the 1940s, 1950s, and 1960s, *Ebony* emphasizes black achievement and prosperity. For that the magazine was criticized during the 1960s by militant blacks, who claimed that it painted too rosy a picture of black life. Yet *Ebony* survives and flourishes even as of this writing, while more militant magazines have faded away. John H. Johnson's publishing company was for years the largest and most profitable black business in the nation, and Johnson himself wound up on the Forbes list of the 400 richest Americans. The Johnson Publishing Company is one of the most successful black media enterprises of all time.

One of the more important periodical voices of the black liberation movement was *Black World*. It was published by Johnson Publications and was originally the *Negro Digest*. That magazine, the first of the Johnson stable, was ended in 1951 only to be brought back in 1961 to serve as an outlet for black writers connected to and with the civil rights movement. Under the editorship of Hoyt Fuller, during the 1960s the *Negro Digest* and *Black World* published articles from such writers as LeRoi Jones (later Amiri Baraka), Langston Hughes, Audre Lorde, Julian Mayfield, Nathan Hare, Wole

Soyinka, and John A. Williams. Through his magazine, Hoyt Fuller helped bring about the Black Arts Movement of the 1960s and beyond. To reflect his cultural nationalist outlook Fuller changed the name of *Negro Digest* to *Black World* in 1970. Unfortunately the magazine did not last long into the 1970s. Johnson, never comfortable with the magazine's radical black nationalism and disliking Fuller, shut the magazine down because of its low circulation and consistent losses. Its demise created a vacuum that has not been completely filled.

Black magazines came and went during the 1980s and 1990s, but two that stood out were *Emerge* and *Essence*. *Emerge* appeared in the early 1990s as a black-oriented news magazine along the lines of *Time* and *Newsweek*. Under the editorship of George Curry, *Emerge* was highly regarded, but it was shut down by its publisher, the black cable-king Robert Johnson, for much the same reason that John Johnson had earlier shut down *Negro World*. Out of *Emerge*'s ashes came *Savoy*, which attempted to be a black version of *GQ* magazine in catering to an upscale black urban market, but it shut down, too.

One contemporary black magazine that found lasting success is *Essence*. Founded in the 1970s to cater to college-educated black women, *Essence* was quite political in its outlook, promoting the ideals of black feminism. It was not just a political magazine, though. If it had been it would not have lasted as long as it has. From its beginnings *Essence* covered the fashion, beauty, health, relationship, and family concerns of black women, and in so doing filled a historic vacuum, since white women's magazines routinely ignored black women. The concerns of black women were also shortchanged by mainstream black magazines and alternative media. The only magazine that caters exclusively to black women, *Essence* has enjoyed enduring success. Today *Essence* is not as explicitly political as it was in its earlier years, now more resembling a black women's version of *Cosmopolitan* magazine.

Decline of the Traditional Black Press. Since the civil rights era, the mainstream black press has lost circulation, prosperity, and influence. It is instructive to look at the fates of the big three of the black press, the *Chicago Defender*, the *Pittsburgh Courier*, and the *Baltimore Afro-American*. The *Chicago Defender*, taken over by Robert Abbott's nephew John Sengstacke on Abbott's death in 1940, became a daily newspaper in 1956. It continued to prosper under Sengstacke's leadership into the 1960s, becoming the major black newspaper chain in the Midwest, acquiring the *Pittsburgh Courier*, Memphis's *Tri-State Defender*, and Detroit's *Michigan Chronicle*. The *Chicago Defender*'s circulation was less as a daily than it had been as a weekly, however, and even that circulation began dropping after the 1970s. Sengstacke kept control of the paper for a long time, relinquishing control only upon his death at age eighty-four in 1997. By then the *Defender* and its chain newspapers were close to extinction. A five-year dispute among Sengstacke's descendants over the terms of his will further crippled the *Defender*, as well as the *Courier*. The confusion was finally resolved when Thomas Picou, a nephew of Sengstacke's, and Kurt Cherry purchased the Sengstacke properties to form Real Times Media. As of 2008 the *Defender* was still publishing daily, while the *Courier*, renamed the *New Pittsburgh Courier*, published twice a week. But neither newspaper is as influential as it once was. As of this writing, the *Baltimore Afro-American* is still going strong, though its chain of newspapers has been greatly reduced. Since the late 1980s declining circulation forced it to close its Philadelphia, Newark, and Richmond branches. The last closing was particularly painful because the *Richmond Afro-American* had originally been the *Planet*, so its closing ended that paper as well. Financial reverses in the early 1990s almost killed the *Afro-American*, but through closing unprofitable branches, moving to a more economical office building, and other economies, the *Afro-American* survived and remained the main black newspaper for Baltimore and Washington, D.C. While the *Defender*, the *Courier*, and the *Afro-American* survive, though in an attenuated form, many other black newspapers have shut downed since the 1960s.

There are many reasons for this. First, the rise of television and the Internet has imperiled all print media, regardless of race. Many mainstream white newspapers and magazines have shut down since the 1960s. For example, at one time New York City had more than seven major daily newspapers, but as of 2008 it had just three. Few major urban areas have more than one major daily today. Black newspapers could not be immune from these trends, and those that survived did so by adapting, by revamping their formats and developing Web sites.

Another reason for the decline of the traditional black press was publishers' inability to attract or retain new talent. Family-owned enterprises for the most part, black newspapers did not bring in enough nonfamily talent, so they became inbred and stagnant. Aggravating this was the competition for black journalists now coming from the white media. Newspapers such as the *New York Times*, the Washington *Post*, and the Chicago *Tribune* offer higher pay, better working conditions, and more prestige than do their black counterparts. Though the number of black journalists in white newsrooms is still disproportionately small, it is enough to drain black newspapers of their talented journalists, greatly diminishing their quality. Many traditional black newspapers—still run in some instances by publishers and editors from before the civil rights era—did not keep up with the social and demographic changes in the black community. They were the victims of their own successful crusades for civil rights and racial integration. As the black elite for whom back newspapers spoke moved more and more into white institutions and even into neighborhoods, they felt less and less need for the black newspapers that helped them to get there. Today newspapers like the *Afro-American* are distributed and read primarily in inner-city black communities.

Future of the African American Press. Despite the decline and fall of many traditional black newspapers, the black press is far from dead. There are still more than 300 black newspapers. The NNPA provides Web sites to twenty-six black newspapers through its black press network, and all told, sixty-seven black newspapers have Web sites. Thanks to low start-up costs, it is easy to start a small community-based newspaper, and many of these exist and flourish in the early twenty-first century. One example is the Baltimore *Times*, established in the 1980s. It publishes weekly and, since it subsists on advertising income, is free to its readers. The *Times* has become a credible competitor to the *Afro-American*. With low overheads and volunteer staffs, these small-scale community newspapers are the best hope for keeping the black press alive, since they fill a niche ignored by white or traditional black newspapers. For the black press to have a future, it may have to return to its roots in the small-scale black newspapers of the nineteenth century. But so long as there is a black community, there will be a black press.

[*See also Amsterdam News*; Associated Negro Press; *Atlanta World*; *Baltimore Afro-American*; Black Panther Party; *Boston Guardian*; Broadcast Industry, African Americans in; *Chicago Defender*; Civil Rights and the Media; *Colored American Magazine; Ebony; Horizon, The; Houston Informer*; *Indianapolis Freeman*; *Jet*; Johnson Publishing Company; Journalism, Print and Broadcast; Literature; *Moon Illustrated Weekly*; National Newspaper Publishers Association; *Negro World; New York Age*; *Pittsburgh Courier*; Radio and Television Stations, African American; *Southern Workman*; *Washington Bee*; *and biographical entries on figures mentioned in this article*.]

BIBLIOGRAPHY

The Afro American Newspaper. http://www.afro.com/. This Web site for the *Baltimore Afro-American* is one of the best of its kind.

Alexander, Ann Field. *Race Man: The Rise and Fall of the "Fighting Editor," John Mitchell Jr.* Charlottesville: University Press of Virginia, 2002.

BlackPressUSA.com: Your Independent Source of News for the African American Community. http://www.blackpressusa.com/. This Web site of the National Newspaper Publishers Association is excellent evidence that the black press is still alive.

Buni, Andrew. *Robert L. Vann of the "Pittsburgh Courier": Politics and Black Journalism*. Pittsburgh, Pa: University of Pittsburgh Press, 1974. Still the standard biography of this significant black publisher and political kingmaker.

Dann, Martin E., ed. *The Black Press, 1827–1890: The Quest for National Identity*. New York: G. P. Putnam, 1971. Exhaustive and comprehensive, this collection of articles from black newspapers paints a vivid picture of the ideologies put forth by nineteenth-century black journalists.

Dates, Jannette, and William Barlow, eds. *Split Image: African Americans in the Mass Media*. Washington, D.C.: Howard University Press, 1990. A contemporary account of the mass media's effect on African Americans.

Farrar, Hayward. *The "Baltimore Afro-American," 1892–1950*. Westport, Conn.: Greenwood, 1998. The definitive study of the first fifty years of one of America's most important black newspapers.

Finkle, Lee H. *Forum for Protest: The Black Press during World War II*. Rutherford, N.J.: Fairleigh Dickinson University Press, 1975. Still the best account of the black press during World War II.

Gatewood, Willard B. *Aristocrats of Color: The Black Elite, 1880–1920*. Bloomington: Indiana University Press, 1990. The standard account of upper-class blacks, whom the black press spoke for and to.

Harlan, Louis R. *Booker T. Washington: The Wizard of Tuskegee, 1901–1915*. New York: Oxford University Press, 1983. The Pulitzer Prize–winning biography.

Hogan, Lawrence D. *A Black National News Service: The Associated Negro Press and Claude Barnett, 1919–1945*. Rutherford, N.J.: Fairleigh Dickinson Press, 1984.

"Making an Impact in Real Time: Real Times Inc. Assumes Ownership of Chicago Defender." http://www.leadingedgealliance.com/issues old2003/spring/realtimes/. This article gives the latest information on the *Chicago Defender* and the *Pittsburgh Courier*.

Meier, August. *Negro Thought in America, 1880–1915*. Ann Arbor: University of Michigan Press, 1963. Still the best black intellectual history of that era.

Ottley, Roi. *The Lonely Warrior: The Life and Times of Robert S. Abbott*. Chicago: H. Regnery, 1955.

Pride, Armistead S., and Clint C. Wilson II. *A History of the Black Press*. Washington, D.C.: Howard University Press, 1997. This comprehensive survey of the black press from its beginnings emphasizes the publishers of black newspapers and their activities on behalf of black advancement and uplift.

Suggs, Henry Lewis. *P. B. Young, Newspaperman: Race, Politics, and Journalism in the New South, 1910–1962*. Charlottesville: University Press of Virginia, 1988.

Suggs, Henry Lewis, ed. *The Black Press in the Middle West, 1865–1985*. Westport, Conn.: Greenwood, 1996.

Suggs, Henry Lewis, ed. *The Black Press in the South, 1865–1979*. Westport, Conn.: Greenwood, 1983.

Thompson, Julius E. *The Black Press in Mississippi, 1865–1985*. Gainesville: University Press of Florida, 1993. An extensive listing and account of the black press in Mississippi.

Thornbrough, Emma Lou. *T. Thomas Fortune: Militant Journalist*. Chicago: University of Chicago Press, 1972. The standard biography of the most renowned black journalist in the era of Booker T. Washington.

Vogel, Todd, ed. *The Black Press: New Literary and Historical Essays*. New Brunswick, N.J.: Rutgers University Press, 2001. Particularly good in its essays on alternative newspapers and black magazines.

Wolseley, Roland E. *The Black Press, U.S.A.* 2d ed. Ames: Iowa State University Press, 1990. The only definitive account of the contemporary black press.

—HAYWARD "WOODY" FARRAR

BLACK RADICAL CONGRESS. In March 1998 several African American political and social activists called on progressive and radical black individuals and organizations to renew the struggle to end racial inequality and attain full civil and human rights for people of African descent in the United States and around the world. Organizers, including the labor unionist Bill Fletcher, the anthropologist Leith Mullings, the philosopher Angela Davis, the poet Sonia Sanchez, the sociologist Abdul Alkalimat and the historians Barbara Ransby, Robin D. G. Kelley, and Manning Marable, envisioned a congress to reinvigorate black freedom and liberation movements. In June 1998 in Chicago, Illinois, at least two thousand African American community activists, intellectuals, labor union members, students, and others involved in grassroots activities, campaigns, and politics participated in the founding of the Black Radical Congress (BRC, pronounced "brick"). An expanding organization and movement, the BRC has established local committees in New York City; Washington, D.C.; St. Louis; and other locales. It promotes dialogue among politically left-of-center African Americans; hosts conferences with annual themes, forums, and educational seminars and discussion groups; issues publications; maintains Internet Web sites; supports black organizers from labor unions, community groups, and student groups; and builds alliances with other progressive political, social, and cultural formations. BRC members and supporters acknowledge the need for a progressive black radical movement for the twenty-first century to improve the quality of life for black people and attain social justice.

BRC sees its activism and mission squarely in the historical tradition of black people fighting for freedom, and equality. As the Black Radical Congress works toward black people's political, social, cultural, and economic advancement, it draws lessons from numerous black movement and united front organizations, including the National Negro Convention Movement (1830s), National Afro-American League (1890s), National Negro Congress (1930s), Black Power Conferences (1960s), National Black Political Convention (1970s), and National African American Leadership Summit (1990s). BRC opposes warfare, militarism, racism, sexism, heterosexism, social hierarchies, class exploitation, and capitalism, which BRC claims has birthed or maintained inequality, injustice, poverty, institutionalized white supremacy, police brutality, pervasive racial and gender discrimination, inadequate social services, and high levels of underemployment, unemployment, and incarceration that weigh disproportionately heavily on black working people.

The Black Radical Congress blends revolutionary black nationalism, radical feminism, "new Afrikan," socialism, and Marxism as it forges new analyses and theories. It seeks radical and democratic solutions to political, social, and economic problems as it works primarily with working-class African Americans on local, national, and international issues that affect black communities. Based on its freedom agenda, issued in April 1999, the BRC pledges to fight for the human rights of black people and all people, a clean and healthy environment, political democracy, free public education, reparations for African Americans, and a noncapitalist society; to eliminate the superexploitation of southern workers, police brutality, unwarranted incarceration, the death penalty, and state terrorism; to secure gender equality and human rights for heterosexual women and lesbian, gay, bisexual, and transgendered people; to build multicultural solidarity and alliances among people of color; and to advance beyond capitalism that fails to address basic human needs.

[*See also* Radicalism.]

BIBLIOGRAPHY

McCarthy, Timothy Patrick, and John McMillian, eds. *The Radical Reader: A Documentary History of the American Radical Tradition*. New York: New Press, 2003. Contains segment on the Black Radical Congress.

Marable, Manning, and Leith Mullings, eds. *Let Nobody Turn Us Around: Voices of Resistance, Reform, and Renewal; An African American Anthology*. Lanham, Md.: Rowman and Littlefield, 2000. Contains three documents, including "Principles of Unity," issued by the Black Radical Congress.

—CHARLES L. LUMPKINS

BLACK STAR LINE. Founded by the black leader Marcus Garvey, the Black Star Line was projected to be a group of transatlantic ocean liners that would help achieve Garvey's dream of repatriating blacks to Africa. Garvey conceived the company as a complement to the British White Star Line of luxurious cruise ships. The Black Star Line's first ship, *Yarmouth*, was active between 1919 and 1922.

Born in Jamaica in 1887, Garvey was a labor organizer when he was in his teens. He left Jamaica in 1910 and traveled throughout Central America and Europe, eventually forming the Universal Negro Improvement Association (UNIA), which called for blacks throughout the world to return to Africa. Garvey moved to the United States in 1916, settling in Harlem, New York, where he founded a string of businesses, including the successful newspaper the *Negro World*.

In 1919 Garvey began calling for blacks to invest financially in purchasing a fleet of ocean liners to run between the United States and Africa. Though he was criticized by admirers and detractors alike for imagining too grandiose a scheme, Garvey persevered, asking for donations at all meetings of the UNIA. In May 1919 Garvey incorporated the Black Star Line Steamship Company and began selling stock in the company for five dollars per share. In September the company bought its first ship, *Yarmouth*, for $165,000. The ship was thirty years old and had been used as a freighter during World War I.

Yarmouth was launched on 31 October 1919, sailing from New York City. Though the initial voyage was successful, the ship was plagued by problems. It was in need of expensive repairs, and crew members, accused of holding varying loyalties, were suspected of sabotaging the ship. Additionally, *Yarmouth*'s captain Joshua Cockburn—who had been involved in negotiating the vessel's selling price—was accused of inflating its costs for his own financial gain. Nevertheless, *Yarmouth* sailed for several months between Cuba and New York transporting liquor in the final days before Prohibition.

In 1922 Garvey purchased two more ships, SS *Shadyside* and SS *Kanawha*. In January of that year Garvey was arrested on charges of federal mail fraud for selling stock in *Orion*, a ship that he had not yet purchased and that some claimed did not exist. The arrest and succeeding trial were spearheaded by J. Edgar Hoover, the head of the Federal Bureau of Investigation and one of Garvey's most fervent enemies. The charges ultimately marked the end of the Black Star Line, which had already been plagued by high costs, corruption, and sabotage. The legacy of the Black Star Line stands as having defied many of its detractors by getting as far as it did and becoming one of the earliest black-owned companies.

[*See also* Africa, Idea of; Entrepreneurship; Garvey, Marcus; Pan-Africanism; *and* Universal Negro Improvement Association.]

BIBLIOGRAPHY

Grant, Colin. *Negro with a Hat: The Rise and Fall of Marcus Garvey*. New York: Oxford University Press, 2008.

Martin, Tony. *The Pan-African Connection: From Slavery to Garvey and Beyond*. Dover, Mass.: Majority Press, 1983.

Stein, Judith. *The World of Marcus Garvey: Race and Class in Modern Society*. Baton Rouge: Louisiana State University Press, 1986.

Vincent, Theodore G. *Black Power and the Garvey Movement* (1970). Baltimore: Black Classic Press, 2006.

—RONALD ENICLERICO

BLACK STUDIES. Black studies and its variants, African American studies, Afro-American studies, African and African American studies, Africana studies, Pan-African studies, diaspora studies, or the more recent Africology, Africa New World studies, and black women diaspora studies, have emerged since the 1960s as full-fledged academic departments in colleges and universities in the United States and abroad. Black studies is the systematic study of the knowledge, thoughts, and modes of being of African people in both their current and historical manifestations. It intersects various methodologies and perspectives; its unit of analysis is the black world, but it also engages white hegemonic powers and their history of exclusion and dominance. Reviewed here are its historical lineages and stages of development as well as the directions and trends of contemporary scholarship.

Historical Lineages. Black studies, defined very broadly as the study of black people, can be traced to the early empires of ancient Egypt, Mali, and Songhai and their intellectual traditions. As a university-based discipline, it is the result of the critical thinking of scholars who explore the cultural, economic, political, and intellectual practices and experiences of people of African descent in Africa, the Americas, and throughout the African diaspora and of the larger sociohistorical contexts from which they evolve. It is part of a historical movement that endeavors to refute and contest pervasive theories of the inferiority of blacks, scholarly omissions about the past heritage and culture of blacks, deeply rooted misrepresentations, legally sanctioned injustices, and a systemic climate of noninclusion and discrimination. It is ultimately the study of and commitment to black advancement.

Black studies, seen as part of the historical freedom movements that started with nineteenth-century black radical traditions, had produced reinterpretations of black histories and cultural life as early as 1882 through the work of George Washington Williams, with his *History of the Negro Race in America from 1619 to 1880: Negroes as Slaves, as Soldiers, and as Citizens*, published in that year. This was followed shortly by that of William T. Alexander, with his *History of the Colored Race in America*, published in 1887. These pioneering works were followed by groundbreaking reexaminations of black history and culture by the eminent historian and sociologist W. E. B. Du Bois, who wrote *The Philadelphia Negro: A Social Study*, completed in 1899, followed by *The Souls of Black Folk*, the subject of great acclaim, published in 1903. Further foundational work was accomplished by Harold M. Tarver, who published *The Negro in the History of the United States from the Beginning of English Settlements in America, 1607, to the Present Time* in 1905; Benjamin Brawley, with *A Short History of the American Negro* in 1913; and Willis D. Weatherford, with *The Negro from Africa to America* in 1924. Du Bois's *Black Reconstruction in America: An Essay toward a History of the Part Which Black Folk Played in the Attempt to Reconstruct Democracy in America, 1860–1880*, published in 1935, later served as the road map for the discipline.

The Atlanta University Project, an important development within the black intellectual tradition, was started in 1897 by Du Bois, who organized yearly conferences at

Atlanta until 1910 on aspects of the African American experience linked to practical concerns of black life in the United States and globally. This was a major contribution to black studies and antiracist scholarship. So was the work of Carter G. Woodson, the noted scholar and visionary who, in 1915 in Washington, D.C., founded the Association for the Study of Negro Life and History, an organization that published the *Journal of Negro History* and served as an academic society that celebrated black life and culture. Woodson also established Negro History Week, now Black History Month, and was involved in publishing the *Negro History Bulletin*. Other scholars who contributed to what was then called Negro history at historically black colleges and universities (HBCUs) include the sociologist Charles S. Johnson at Fisk University, who surveyed race relations in seven U.S. cities; the distinguished historian Benjamin Quarles at Morgan State University, who later headed the Maryland Commission on Negro History and Culture; the sociologist Monroe N. Work at Tuskegee Institute; the scholars E. Franklin Frazier and Ralph Johnson Bunche at Howard University; the social anthropologist Allison Davis; and the writers Horace Mann Bond and Alain Locke. Later, the work of Harold Wright Cruse, Rayford W. Logan, St. Clair Drake, and John Hope Franklin was also foundational. Contemporary scholars seek to claim rather than reject the earlier efforts of the HBCUs that laid the groundwork for the current discipline. In the early 1920s, for example, there were as many as eighteen courses at nine HBCUs that examined exclusively black life and culture. In the 1960s the Institute of the Black World (IBW) was established as part of the Martin Luther King Jr. Center for Nonviolent Social Change, the research center established in Atlanta as part of the national historic site in King's name that includes his birthplace and the Ebenezer Church; we note the work of the theologian and historian Vincent Harding there.

Unfortunately, in the 1970s and 1980s many top black faculty from HBCUs left for white institutions that offered better funding and research programs. Ironically, the successes of desegregation hurt the very institutions that formed generations of black intellectuals and professionals while nurturing the black intellectual movement over the course of the past century. However, during segregation, traditionally white institutions did start their own black studies departments. Noteworthy contributions during this early period by progressive white scholars include critical work by Melville Herskovits and Herbert Aptheker, who offered reassessments of the historical contributions of blacks in their great works, *The Myth of the Negro Past*, published in 1941, and *To Be Free: Studies in American Negro History*, published in 1948, respectively. At about this time a few programs in African studies emerged, such as the one started at Northwestern University in 1948.

Forty Years of Growth and Development: The 1960s to the Early Twenty-first Century. The climate of protest following the decision in *Brown v. Board of Education of Topeka, Kansas* of 1954 facilitated educational changes, including black students having, for the first time, greater access to institutions of higher learning. In 1950 and 1960, 75,000 and 200,000 black students respectively were engaged in postsecondary education; by the mid 1970s, the number reached a million, and in 1980 it exceeded 1.1 million. Black students not only were admitted into these institutions but also demanded that the institutions change. Campuses across the nation were forced to address issues of exclusion, marginalization, and the oppression of people of color within and outside the academy. Demands mirrored larger political crises for civil rights, the rejection of assimilation, and the desire for cultural autonomy. Specifically, black studies departments and programs emerged out of the context of the critical expression of black faculty and students who demanded inclusion and fair representation in the academy. Additionally, the civil rights movement itself, the Black Power movement, liberation movements, the anti–Vietnam War protest, feminism, demonstrations against the treatment of the poor, the rise of affirmative action, gay rights activism, and social support for the liberation of Third World nations all inspired the creation of black studies programs. Demands were made, strategies were formulated, protests and strikes were held, and eventually programs were created and curricula were developed.

The first initiative toward the establishment of a black studies program, at Merritt Junior College in Oakland, California, in 1963, failed but led to the creation of the Soul Students' Advisory Council, a precursor of the Black Student Union that initiated the first black studies program in 1967–1968 at San Francisco State University; the following year it became the first autonomous black studies department in the country. On 14 October 1968 at the University of California at Santa Barbara, a student takeover of the university's main computer installation led to the launching of that school's black studies department, the Center for Black Studies, and a black studies library in 1969.

By the late 1960s, black studies was established in more than one hundred colleges and universities. Within ten years, the number of programs reached five hundred. In the 1980s the number declined to around four hundred, but other gains emerged. The departments of black studies at Ohio State University and Temple University, for example, have each had over sixteen full-time faculty members at one time and were the first to offer graduate programs in the field.

As of March 2007, the comprehensive Web site of the sociologist Abdul Alkalimat, eblackstudies.org, reported a substantial decrease in black studies departments, with only 311 degree-granting black studies programs, of which 185 (59 percent) are at public institutions. They are spread throughout the East, Midwest, South, and West. Interestingly, the two regions with states having the smallest black populations, the East and the West, have the largest number of institutions offering black studies; this is because New York and California have the greatest number of programs, 58 and 60 respectively; between the two of them, their institutions of higher learning offer over a third of the total. Of the 311 schools, 258 have a name directly associated with black studies: African American or Afro American (100), Africana (63), African and African American (45), black (37), Pan-African (7), African (5), and Africology (1). Africology is a name adopted solely by the University of Wisconsin, Milwaukee. The other 53 fall within those with the more general appellations of diasporic, multicultural, or interethnic studies. Among them, 100 are departments, 168 are programs, 15 are centers or institutes, and 28 are "others." These programs grant mostly undergraduate degrees: 158 grant a bachelor of arts degree with black studies as a major; 88 grant a black studies minor within a bachelor of arts degree; and 10 grant an associate of arts degree. Master of arts degrees are granted at 21 institutions, while only 9 schools offer doctor of philosophy degrees. They are Harvard University, Michigan State University, Morgan State, Northwestern University, Temple, the University of California at Berkeley, the University of California at San Diego, the University of Massachusetts at Amherst, and the University of Southern California. Alkalimat points out, "Black studies as a labor market deserves more attention . . . [since] . . . the founding generation will be retiring . . . [and] . . . creating a 20 to 30 percent faculty turnover in the next ten years." This situation cannot be solely remedied by the ten doctorates granted, on average, per year.

Deep ideological divisions about what black studies should be have caused considerable controversy since the 1960s: the inclusionists in the 1970s (at Yale University, for example) coexisted amicably with other departments while the nationalists, generally not viewed favorably by administrations, sought the power to hire and grant tenure to their own faculty and to control curricula. The legacy of Du Bois and the historians and political activists Paul Robeson, C. L. R. James, and Walter Rodney led others to tackle the capitalist political economy and served as a precursor of transnationalism and diasporic studies. A Marxist black radicalism program was created by Alkalimat at Fisk in the 1970s. By the 1980s, the nationalist model was increasingly characterized by the ideological concept of Afrocentricity developed by the scholar Molefi Kete Asante, and was prevalent in many programs, namely at Temple and at most HBCUs. Conflicts, controversies, and polemics remain part of the black studies narrative today.

Contemporary Scholarship. Black studies programs suffered severe repression in the 1980s with the backlash of the Reagan era. Financial aid for students, minority scholarship programs, and admission were stalled by fierce attack from the Right and by assaults on affirmative action. Some even suggest urban nihilism and organized genocide against black people and the poor were at work. At the same time, however, some foundations took an interest in diversity and minority education. The Ford Foundation, for example, underwrote the W. E. B. Du Bois Institute for Afro-American Research (now the W. E. B. Du Bois Institute for African and African American Research) at Harvard starting in the 1980s; financed the Huggins Harvard-based report of 1985, *Afro-American Studies*, on the state of minority education; and awarded Darlene Clark Hine at Michigan State in 1991 for her Comparative Black History PhD Degree Program.

What was in the 1960s and 1970s the driving polemic between black nationalism and Marxism seems now to be between Afrocentrism and elite public intellectual debate. Scholars shaping new directions for black studies in the contemporary period include Manning Marable, Cornel West, Henry Louis Gates Jr., Asante, Hine, Alkalimat, Angela Y. Davis, Gerald Horne, William Julius Wilson, George Lipsitz, Johnnetta Cole, and Stuart Hall; and in the next generation, Eddie S. Glaude Jr., Tricia Rose, and Robin D. G. Kelley. Now in its third phase, black studies is being shaped by new conversations about gender and sexuality, violence, corporate greed and influences on culture, environmental racism, urban geographies, colorblind and postracial ideologies, whiteness studies, cross-racial exchanges, foreign media, diaspora studies, and new global paradigms. Also, new technologies are to be reckoned with in the production, distribution, and consumption of forms of knowledge that some would say are more egalitarian because they are no longer bound by the walls of the academy. Alkalimat, in particular, has advocated for information freedom on the Internet as a means to communicate with the poor and offer a new paradigm for black liberation.

Today black studies continues to present research findings to recover and reconstruct the various histories of blacks in America as well as those in the African diaspora and to credit their contributions in the making of U.S. and global societies. Black studies also perseveres in its efforts to create alternative visions and institutions. It goes beyond the critique of the assumptions of the dominant culture to engage in improving the lives of aggrieved communities and to fulfill the distinctly public mission that it has always had. Ultimately, as black scholars maintain a strong intellectual presence on college campuses nationwide, they also preserve their community ties and commitments. More than ever, black studies continues to play its role in closing the gap between impoverished communities and the academy as well as in reshaping the current cultural, political, educational, and economic landscape. The impact of black studies on the body politic of the twenty-first century is real, as is the underlying significance of this body of work for the American citizenry as a whole.

[*See also* Historically Black Colleges and Universities; *Journal of Negro History*; Schomburg Center for Research in Black Culture; *Souls of Black Folk, The*; *and biographical entries on figures mentioned in this article*.]

BIBLIOGRAPHY

Alkalimat, Abdul. *Africana Studies in the US*. Eblackstudies.org, March 2007. The most comprehensive study to date of African studies programs in the country.

Carmichael, Stokely, and Charles V. Hamilton. *Black Power: The Politics of Liberation in America*. New York: Random House, 1967. First serious scholarly analysis of the concept of Black Power and the movement.

Cruse, Harold. *Crisis of the Negro Intellectual*. New York: William Morrow, 1967. Criticism of the role that black intellectuals played in the twentieth century.

Drake, St. Clair, and Horace R. Cayton. *Black Metropolis: A Study of Negro Life in a Northern City*. New York: Harcourt, Brace, 1945. Most thorough study of an urban African American community c. 1940.

Du Bois, W. E. B. *Black Reconstruction: An Essay toward a History of the Part Which Black Folk Played in the Attempt to Reconstruct Democracy in America, 1860–1880*. New York: Harcourt, Brace, 1935. Overturned misinterpretations about Reconstruction as a period of Negro decadence and recast it as a period of growth and democratic promises.

Du Bois, W. E. B. *The Souls of Black Folk: Essays and Sketches*. Chicago: A. C. McClurg, 1903. Considered one of the most influential books of the century. Essays on race, economic problems, and black history.

Franklin, John Hope. *From Slavery to Freedom: A History of American Negroes* New York: Alfred A. Knopf, 1947. Standard and oldest comprehensive text on African American history.

Herskovits, Melville. *Myth of the Negro Past*. New York and London: Harper & Brothers, 1941. Validates African heritage and the foundation of African American culture.

Hurston, Zora Neale. *Mules and Men*. Philadelphia: J. B. Lippincott, 1935. Pioneer work in the field of black folklore, anthropology, and feminism.

Marable, Manning, ed. *Dispatches from the Ebony Tower: Intellectuals Confront the African American Experience*. New York: Columbia University Press, 2000. A critical assessment of the field of black studies after three decades of scholarship and teaching.

Rodney, Walter. *How Europe Underdeveloped Africa*. London: Bogle-L'Ouverture Publications, 1972. Explanation of how specific economic policies led to the economic enrichment and empowerment of Europe and the underdevelopment of Africa.

Thompson, Robert Farris. *Flash of the Spirit*. New York: Random House, 1983. The movement of African culture—sculptures, textiles, architecture, and religion—into the New World.

Van Sertima, Ivan. *They Came Before Columbus*. New York: Random House, 1976. Suggests the discovery of the New World and African settlements on several occasions before Columbus's voyages.

—CLAUDINE MICHEL

BLACK TOWNS. For three centuries, Americans of African descent have at times sought to establish communities where they could live in partial or complete isolation from the dominant culture. Settlements of formerly enslaved African Americans existed on the East Coast after the Revolutionary War. All-black settlements also developed among the Seminole Nation in Florida as early as the eighteenth century. As the nation industrialized, segregated company towns also were built in various locations.

The phrase "all-black towns" usually refers to the period of self-segregation and town-building that began after Reconstruction and continued into the early twentieth century. Historians estimate that at least seventy-five to one hundred all-black towns were founded during this time, mainly in the South and the West.

The Origins of Black Towns. The black town-building period coincided with the demise of the Republican Party in the post-Reconstruction South, a period in which African Americans faced increasing violence, economic repression, and disfranchisement. Violence and terrorism against would-be voters from 1876 to 1890 was intolerably high, especially in Louisiana. This period marked the completion of the Democratic takeover of the southern political system.

In the years leading up to this turning point, a small percentage of black citizens and leaders in the former Confederate states weighed options for physically leaving the South. Colonization of Liberia was considered. However, relocation to another continent was not economically feasible for most southern blacks, as indeed it was not for most Americans. In addition, the majority of African Americans had been born in the United States and identified as Americans.

Some historians have pointed out the influence of Booker T. Washington's philosophies on the black town movement, while others have downplayed the racial elements and argued that the towns developed like

Eatonville, Florida. The city council and jail in Eatonville, Florida, from *The Negro in Business* (1907) by Booker T. Washington. General Research & Reference Division, Schomburg Center for Research in Black Culture, The New York Public Library, Astor, Lenox and Tilden Foundations

any other agricultural communities in the West and the South—as money-making devices for developers. Although the profit motive has been well documented, it is also clear that a certain number of African Americans had come to accept conditions in the South as hopeless and were willing to try their luck elsewhere.

Many of the black towns were short-lived in terms of economic viability. This was largely because they were farming towns founded at a time when rural America was losing ground to urbanization. However, they played an important role socially and politically for their residents even when their populations declined. With the exception of Nicodemus, Kansas, the towns described below have all persisted as viable communities.

Many of the black towns were located in the former Confederate states of the South. The best known was Mound Bayou, Mississippi, founded in 1887 by Isaiah T. Montgomery. Montgomery was born into slavery and later amassed a fortune in land and property. When the Louisiana, New Orleans, and Texas Railroad planned to build a rail stop in Bolivar County, Mississippi, it recruited Montgomery to attract black settlers and establish a community at a location of his choosing. The town's site was situated in near-wilderness considered uninhabitable by many whites, but in which a number of black sharecroppers or small landowners already lived.

During Reconstruction, Bolivar County had produced several black public officials, including Blanche Kelso Bruce and Joseph E. Ousley. Ousley was a former slave who served as county clerk. By 1900, however, most black males had been disfranchised in county, state, and federal elections. In 1900 the town was formally incorporated and self-governing. Montgomery was mayor; he governed along with three aldermen.

Mound Bayou's early success was greatly aided by its location on the railroad. The town depended on cotton farming in the surrounding district and supported many black-owned businesses, including four cotton gins and three sawmills. Thanks largely to Montgomery's promotional abilities, Mound Bayou also attracted the attention of Booker T. Washington, who took a personal interest in its success and provided support for a local bank as well as training for farmers through the Tuskegee Institute. Montgomery's personal fortune was another key to the town's economic viability.

In the early twentieth century, as racial persecution in Mississippi intensified, Mound Bayou's population increased. On the eve of World War I the town had about one thousand residents and seven thousand to eight thousand farmers living in the surrounding area. The town prospered for twenty-five years. By the early 1920s, however, its leaders were dead, and a depression in the cotton industry weakened the town's economy. Many families joined the exodus of southern blacks to northern cities. The community continued to serve as a political foundation for the Mississippi Delta, however, and in 2008 Mound Bayou persisted as a small black community with a rich historical legacy.

Spread of Black Towns. Other southern blacks looked to the western territories for homesteading opportunities. During the 1870s and 1880s, twenty-five thousand African Americans settled in Kansas, long remembered for its abolitionist past and strong Republican political tradition. This movement included about six thousand "Exodusters" from Louisiana, Mississippi, and Texas who moved during 1879 alone.

The best-known black town in Kansas was Nicodemus, settled initially in 1877–1878. Farming conditions were difficult; but most settlers learned to make the land yield corn and wheat. For about a decade, Nicodemus received national attention and drew new residents from around the country. But the town's initial promise did not last. Harsh weather in 1885 ruined so much wheat that many farmers moved out. In 1887 the town leaders failed in their attempt to attract three separate railroads to Nicodemus, a crucial loss for any farming community. By 1888 many residents had moved out, and promoters stopped boosting the town.

During Nicodemus's peak, the Kansas political structure was still favorably inclined toward black autonomy. Edward P. McCabe was attracted to Nicodemus and became Kansas's most accomplished black politician. Born in Troy, New York, McCabe was experienced in local politics when he set himself up as a land agent in Nicodemus in 1878. Within two years McCabe had convinced Governor John St. John to appoint him clerk of Graham County, and in 1882 McCabe was elected state auditor. McCabe's election and reelection caused great controversy among white leaders, however, and his attempt at a third term was unsuccessful. When the territorial governor of Oklahoma offered him a post as deputy auditor for Logan County, Oklahoma Territory, he accepted.

Eventually Oklahoma would contain the greatest number of black towns in the nation. Some of the earliest of these developed after the Civil War, as settlements of black former slaves of Native Americans. Then, in the 1880s the federal government reduced the size of Indian reservations in the Oklahoma and Indian territories and opened the "surplus lands" to homesteaders, resulting in the famous land run of 1889. In 1892, thousands of African Americans raced for the opening of the Cheyenne-Arapaho lands and, the next year, for Cherokee lands.

McCabe jumped at the opportunity and in 1890 began to develop the all-black town of Langston. Settlers poured in from the southern states. Langston was incorporated in 1891 and became a guidepost for dozens of other black towns in Oklahoma. Eventually a population of viable small communities supported by black farmers emerged on the Oklahoma prairie, and Oklahoma's black population soon outnumbered that of Kansas.

Settlers initially lived in dugouts to protect themselves from tornadoes; they grew vegetables, hunted, and raised poultry. Over time there were enough of them to support about thirty towns with black-owned businesses, banks, cotton gins, restaurants, grocery stores, and necessary professionals such as doctors, lawyers, and dentists.

Some of the best-documented towns were Clearview, Lima, Redbird, Rentiesville, Taft, Tullahassee, and Vernon. But Oklahoma's most successful black town was Boley. It was founded in 1903 by a white attorney, a white railroad manager, and a black farmer and entrepreneur. With the double advantages of good farmland and a rail line, Boley took off quickly, and within a few years a thousand people lived in the township with another two thousand black farmers surrounding it. Boley had all the businesses, services, and institutions of a well-established community. In time the town's leaders diversified its economy by winning contracts to host the state's principal black fraternal lodge, a black tuberculosis hospital, and the State Training School for Negro Boys. Washington praised Boley and its residents, and the town became a well-known symbol of black independence and self-governance.

White Oklahomans reacted with fear to the rapid in-migration of blacks during this time. McCabe's ambitious promotion of Langston frightened many, and sensationalized accounts of his ideas led to the claim that McCabe wanted to establish an all-black state. This fueled an already tense racial situation that would culminate in 1907 when Oklahoma became a state and passed its own Jim Crow legislation. Boley was somewhat insulated from the impacts of segregation, but most blacks were disfranchised when a grandfather clause was enacted in 1910.

Like Mound Bayou, Boley and the other Oklahoma towns were hard hit by the cotton depression of the early 1920s. By this time, the Great Migration of African Americans to northern cities was well under way, and many residents moved out. As of 2008 Boley's population remains mostly black and includes many descendants of the town's original settlers.

Though most of the black towns were located in the South and West, some were farther east. One of these was Whitesboro, New Jersey. The unincorporated hamlet was founded in 1901 by a group of black investors led by the former North Carolina congressman George Henry White. White was the last former slave to serve in Congress, and in 1896 he was the highest ranking black public official in the nation. He lived through the intense racial violence in North Carolina that culminated in the 1898 Wilmington race riots and the ensuing disfranchisement legislation in 1900.

After his retirement from Congress, White and his partners purchased seventeen hundred acres on a plantation in Cape May County, New Jersey. They envisioned the settlement as a refuge for North Carolina blacks. Within a few years several hundred families were supporting themselves by farming, fishing, and running a sawmill. White also founded a bank in Philadelphia and used it to help families purchase their own homes. During the mid-twentieth century, Whitesboro was an all–African American community in the middle of an affluent resort region. It persists as an integrated, unincorporated community.

The early residents of the black towns fully embraced political life, and they voted at a higher frequency than white Americans—usually at least two-thirds of the population turned out to vote. The towns were usually organized with a mayor–council form of government typical of working-class towns in the country. The case of McCabe illustrates that African American settlers participated in politics enthusiastically as far as territorial or state laws would allow. In general, however, by the early twentieth century voters were legally restricted to political participation within town limits.

Political and Social Roles. Even under these circumstances, black town dwellers continued to find ways to influence government and politics. For instance, as Melissa Stuckey has written, blacks in Boley helped to organize a statewide, and eventually national, fight to invalidate laws that used grandfather clauses to disfranchise blacks. Victory in this effort was finally achieved through U.S. Supreme Court decisions in 1915 (*Guinn v. United States*) and 1939 (*Lane v. Wilson*). In 1915, the Court ruled in *Guinn v. United States* that Oklahoma's grandfather clause was unconstitutional; this clause was the means by which illiterate men in Oklahoma could vote by proving their grandfathers could vote. The language was intended to enfranchise illiterate white men while disallowing illiterate African American men to vote. After *Guinn v. United States*, the Oklahoma legislature passed another law in 1916 which included another form of grandfather clause, and it was this law that the Supreme Court found unconstitutional in *Lane v. Wilson* (1939).

Mound Bayou has also been a springboard for national political influence. Isaiah Montgomery's eldest daughter was a Republican National Committeewoman for the state in 1937. The activist Medgar Evers became involved with the Regional Council of Negro Leadership there after graduating from college, and the council held its annual conferences in Mound Bayou from 1952 to 1954. Today, leaders in fields from business to the arts credit their early lives in black towns with influencing their later successes.

America's black towns were thus unique in the social and political roles they played for African Americans. From within them came many strong and effective voices disproving racial prejudices in white society and helping to tear down legal restrictions on black autonomy. They were also an integral part of the nation's homesteading movement and expansion into the western territories. Historians have pointed out that, practically speaking, the towns were unremarkable compared with others in the South and West. Most were developed with a strong profit motive, and they declined economically for the same reasons as did more diverse communities.

[*See also* Agriculture and Agricultural Labor; American Colonization Society; Black Capitalism; Black Migration; Civil Rights; Civil Rights, State Actions; Democratic Party; Disfranchisement of African Americans; Economic Life; Evers, Medgar Wylie; Florida; Grandfather Clause; Great Migration; Jim Crow Laws; Judges and the Judiciary; Kansas; Laws and Legislation; Liberia; Louisiana; Mississippi; New Jersey; Oklahoma; Political Participation; Political Parties and Civil Rights; Republican Party; Segregation; Texas; Tuskegee Institute; Urbanization; Violence against African Americans; Voting Rights; *and* Washington, Booker T.]

BIBLIOGRAPHY

Crockett, Norman L. *The Black Towns*. Lawrence: Regents Press of Kansas, 1979. Arranged by analytical topic rather than town; contains useful chapters on economies and politics in the black towns.

Hamilton, Kenneth Marvin. *Black Towns and Profit: Promotion and Development in the Trans-Appalachian West, 1877–1915*. Urbana: University of Illinois Press, 1991. Focuses on the promoters who developed black towns in the West, with chapters on Nicodemus, Kansas; Mound Bayou, Mississippi; North Carolina; Langston City, Oklahoma; Boley, Oklahoma; and Allensworth, California. Includes selected bibliography.

Painter, Nell Irvin. *Exodusters: Black Migration to Kansas after Reconstruction*. New York: Alfred A. Knopf, 1977. Detailed analysis of political, social, and economic conditions in the post-Reconstruction South leading up to the "Exodus" of 1879.

Stuckey, Melissa. "Boley, Oklahoma (1903–)." http://www.blackpast.org/?q=aaw/boley-oklahoma-1903.

Taylor, Quintard. *In Search of the Racial Frontier: African Americans in the American West, 1528–1990*. New York: W. W. Norton, 1998. The chapter on "Migration and Settlement 1875–1920" is a good overview of black settlement in the West from 1875 to 1920. Extensive bibliography.

Turner, Morris III. *America's Black Towns and Settlements*. Rohnert Park, Calif.: Missing Pages Productions, 1998. A short survey of black towns for general audiences. Useful because it includes settlements in all regions of the country; however, "town" is loosely defined.

Woodson, Carter G. *A Century of Negro Migration*. Washington, D.C.: Association for the Study of Negro Life and History, 1918. Available as free e-book by Project Gutenberg. Short, detailed study of black colonization from the eighteenth century to World War I. Information on the black towns built from 1875 to 1915 is only general; however, valuable description of antebellum period. Woodson is known as the "father of black history" and was founding editor of the *Journal of African American History*. www.blackpast.org. An online reference center housed at the University of Washington, Seattle. Materials include an online encyclopedia of over a thousand entries, bibliographies, timelines, and links to fifty digital archive collections, museums, and other international resources.

—Barbara C. Behan

BLACK WORKERS CONGRESS. Founded in 1971, the Black Workers Congress (BWC), an African American organization of primarily industrial workers, called on working people, especially black and other nonwhite workers, to solve their shop-floor issues by taking matters into their own hands rather than waiting for union officials and managers to make decisions. The BWC aimed to steer black workers and the labor movement in a militant and radical direction. The congress, which also had Hispanic American, Asian American, and Native American affiliates, announced its long-term mission to achieve workers' control of factories, offices, and other worksites; an end to workplace exploitation; and the establishment of a society that values human rights above property rights.

The BWC had its roots in the revolutionary union movements (RUMs), centering on black auto workers in late-1960s Detroit, Michigan. Some of the founders and early leaders of the BWC, including John Watson and General Gordon Baker Jr., numbered among the many working-class black Detroiters who became politically radicalized during the civil rights and the Black Power movements, the 1967 Detroit urban rebellion, and the heady activism of the Black Panther Party and other radical left black groups. In May 1968 black workers at the Dodge Main plant in Hamtramck, Michigan, organized an interracial wildcat strike largely because the United Automobile Workers (UAW) union failed to address plant safety, racism, exploitation, and other workplace issues. After the strike, the company fired most of the strikers, a disproportionate number of them black workers. Watson, Baker, and other fired workers who had founded or allied with a local black Marxist-Leninist newspaper, *Inner City Voice*, established the Dodge Revolutionary Union Movement (DRUM) at Dodge Main and in June led a wildcat strike that shut down the factory for three days. Within a year, black workers founded the Ford Revolutionary Union Movement (FRUM) at Ford's massive River Rouge complex, the Eldon Avenue Revolutionary Union Movement (ELRUM) at Chrysler's Eldon Avenue Gear and Axle plant, and more than eight other RUMs, including a few at nonautomobile workplaces. In June 1969 RUM members created the League of Revolutionary Black Workers (LRBW) to coordinate the RUMs and assist black workers forming RUMs in automobile factories in Fremont, California; Mahwah, New Jersey; and Baltimore, Maryland; and in steel mills in Birmingham, Alabama, and elsewhere.

The BWC, created by the RUMs and the league to function as an independent formation, failed to make headway, although around five hundred persons attended its founding convention in 1971. The organization was immediately burdened by ideological discord between Baker's faction, which charged that the BWC moved away from maintaining a political base among black factory workers, and Watson's faction, which argued for the BWC—then headed by James Forman, former leader of the Student Nonviolent Coordinating Committee—to recruit members and build alliances that differed from that of the league. The Black Workers Congress did not survive the disputes and within a year ceased to be a viable entity.

[*See also* Organized Labor *and* Radicalism.]

Bibliography

Elbaum, Max. *Revolution in the Air: Sixties Radicals Turn to Lenin, Mao, and Che*. New York: Verso, 2002. Places the Black Workers Congress and other post-1968 self-identified Marxist organizations within the context of achieving justice and equality for nonwhite people and others through revolutionary movements.

Georgakas, Dan, and Marvin Surkin. *Detroit: I Do Mind Dying*. Cambridge, Mass.: South End Press, 1998. First published 1975 by St. Martin's Press as *Detroit: I Do Mind Dying: A Study in Urban Revolution*. Focuses on the Dodge Revolutionary Union Movement, the League of Revolutionary Black Workers, and the Black Workers Congress and their impact on labor struggles and the black liberation movement.

—Charles L. Lumpkins

BLACK WORKERS FOR JUSTICE. Black Workers for Justice (BWFJ), founded in 1981 and located mainly in North Carolina, engages in community activism and trade unionism. It organized the first statewide public workers' union affiliated with the United Electrical, Radio and Machine Workers of America (Local 150), and formed the African American/Latino Alliance to strengthen relations between the two groups, comprising primarily low-wage workers. BWFJ has a monthly newspaper, *Justice Speaks*; operates workplace committee schools and a workers' center; sponsors a women's commission that it established in 1987 to promote women's issues; and works with Transnational Information Exchange, an international workers' network in Europe and developing nations to foster labor solidarity and empower workers to resist globalization. BWFJ seeks to nurture leadership within the rank-and-file in order to build trade unions and a culture of labor organizing in the black community.

BWFJ emerged from a labor dispute that began in 1981 when African American women Kmart employees in Rocky Mount, North Carolina, launched an antidiscrimination fight after management unjustly fired six of their colleagues. After failing to obtain support from many leaders of community and local civil rights groups, Naeema Muhammed and the other Kmart women decided to pursue their own campaign after contacting black worker activists, including the political leftist Abner W. Berry. They and black workers from ten counties convened a workers' rights conference in Fremont, North Carolina, and formed Black Workers for Justice. Though the Kmart women failed to get the fired workers reinstated, they built a movement with the aim to empower working people of all colors.

Black Workers for Justice has an uphill struggle to win even modest objectives because the South has been a historical bastion of antiunionism, often encoded in "right to work" laws. For decades southern working people, particularly African American wage earners, have confronted employers and local and state government officials determined to suppress workers' rights in order to attract industry to a low-wage, low-tax region. Since the early 1980s, BWFJ and southern workers also watched textile and other manufacturing jobs move overseas, where wages and taxes have been lower than in the South.

BWFJ argues that black workers need to construct movements that combine union organizing and community activism and that advocate radical social change if they want effective, successful struggles against racism, sexism, and workplace exploitation. It supports gender and sexual equality and the rights of immigrants. The organization states that African American workers must take the lead to form trade unions and community groups to end oppressive conditions in the workplace and community; that real black power lies with black workers' organization and control over major economic, social, and political institutions; that interracial working-class unity against racism and white supremacy must be encouraged; that the government owes reparations to African Americans; and that American workers must forge international labor solidarity. BWFJ considers its main task assisting black workers in organizing a conscious, radical, independent mass base, leading the African American liberation movement, and making black workplace actions key issues for the African American community.

[*See also* Organized Labor.]

BIBLIOGRAPHY

As of this writing, easily accessible books about Black Workers for Justice have not been published. At present, the most easily available sources of information on BWFJ are on the Internet.

Black Workers for Justice. "About Black Workers for Justice." http://www.bwfj.org/about/. Briefly presents the program of Black Workers for Justice.

Muhammad, Saladin. "Twenty Years of Black Workers for Justice." *Freedom Road Magazine* 1 (Spring 2001). http://www.hartford-hwp.com/archives/45a/577.html. A short histor highlighting the origin and activities of Black Workers for Justice.

—CHARLES L. LUMPKINS

BLAKE, EUBIE (b. 7 February 1887; d. 12 February 1983), composer and pianist. Born James Hubert Blake in Baltimore, Maryland, Blake was the only surviving child of eleven born to John Sumner Blake, a stevedore, and Emily Johnston Blake, a laundress, both of whom were freed slaves. Though the year of Blake's birth is traditionally considered to have been 1883, recent research suggests that it was 1887. His early enthusiasm for music convinced his parents to buy him an organ. He took lessons from a local church organist but soon became obsessed with popular ragtime music. Around the turn of the century, in his teens, he got a job as a pianist at Aggie Shelton's bordello.

After an apprenticeship in piano and dancing jobs in New York and Baltimore, from 1910 to 1915 Blake played the piano during the summer in Atlantic City, New Jersey. In 1910 he married his former schoolmate Avis Lee. In 1914 his ragtime compositions "Chevy Chase" and "Fizz Water" were published. A year later, working for Joe Porter's Serenaders, he met the singer and lyricist Noble Sissle. They formed a partnership, performing at local functions. Their first sale of a song, to the vaudeville legend Sophie Tucker, encouraged them to join vaudeville as the Dixie Duo, immaculately dressed and without the blackface makeup conventional at the time. In 1916 they joined James Reese Europe's Society Orchestra. They separated when Europe and Sissle enlisted to serve in World War I.

In 1918 Blake played vaudeville with a partner called Broadway Jones. On Sissle's return, Blake reunited with him, and in 1920 they teamed with the comedians Flournoy Miller and Aubrey Lyles to produce the show *Shuffle Along* (1921). It became a Broadway sensation, made its authors famous, and launched a new era in black show business. It ran on Broadway and toured for more than three years. In 1923 Sissle and Blake contributed music for a white show, *Elsie*, and made a short sound film, *Snappy Songs*.

When the partnership with Miller and Lyles ended, Sissle and Blake's next show, *Chocolate Dandies* (1924), included Josephine Baker but did not match the success of *Shuffle Along*. In 1925 they toured England successfully, but on their return to America they split up. Blake found a new lyricist, Henry Creamer. They staged *Shuffle Along Jr.* on the Orpheum vaudeville circuit with modest success during 1928 and 1929. Blake then formed a partnership with the lyricist Andy Razaf for Lew Leslie's *Blackbirds of 1930*. Despite including some of his best songs, including "Memories of You," it was a box-office flop. The Great Depression was biting on Broadway.

In 1933 Sissle, Blake, and Miller reunited for a failed attempt to repeat their earlier success with *Shuffle Along of 1933*. The 1930s were difficult for Blake, though his talents were undimmed. In 1939 he was devastated by the death of his adored wife, Avis. A collaboration with Razaf, *Tan Manhattan*, never got a major production despite including some first-class songs. Blake worked on USO (United Service Organizations) shows during World War II. In 1945 he married Marion Gant Tyler, who had been in *Shuffle Along*. Her devoted management turned his life around, including obtaining improved rates for ASCAP (American Society of Composers, Authors, and Publishers) royalties. In 1948 the campaign of the presidential candidate Harry S. Truman adopted the song "I'm Just Wild about Harry" from *Shuffle Along*, bringing Blake renewed fame and more royalties. Blake undertook formal music study at New York University with the composer and conductor Rudolf Schramm, graduating with a music degree in 1950. Reuniting with Sissle for *Shuffle Along of 1952* proved another disappointment, but Blake's star was about to rise again.

The 1950 book *They All Played Ragtime*, by Rudi Blesh and Harriet Janis, stimulated new interest in ragtime. Blake was in demand for recordings, interviews, and television. He became a guru for young musicians such as his protégé Terry Waldo. There were honors such as a 1965 ASCAP event honoring Blake and Sissle at New York's Town Hall. In 1969 Columbia Records released a double album of Blake's music, *The Eighty-Six Years of Eubie Blake*. As the ragtime craze grew, fueled by the 1973 movie *The Sting*, Blake was in demand for jazz festivals, visiting Denmark, Germany, Norway, and France. His ninetieth birthday celebration brought greetings from the U.S. president and an official "Salute Eubie Blake" day in Baltimore. He received numerous honorary doctorates. In 1978 a successful Broadway show, *Eubie*, commemorated his career and greatest songs.

On 28 June 1982 Blake's devoted wife, Marion, died. The following February a concert featuring many ragtime pianists was held to honor what was thought to be his hundredth birthday. Ill with pneumonia, Blake watched via closed-circuit television. He died five days later. He is remembered as a major figure of black entertainment and the Harlem Renaissance, for *Shuffle Along* and for many great songs, especially "Memories of You" and "I'm Just Wild about Harry." He is also an important figure in jazz and was a unique stylist—primarily in ragtime but also in stride piano. His longevity and fame late in life ensured that his legacy is well documented.

[*See also* Composers; Entertainment Industry and African Americans; Jazz; Minstrel Tradition; Music; Music Industry; Musical Theater; Ragtime; Television; Vaudeville, African Americans in; *and biographical entries on figures mentioned in this article*.]

BIBLIOGRAPHY

Hanley, Peter. "Eubie Blake: 'Everybody's just wild about Eubie.'" http://www.doctorjazz.co.uk/portlater.html#eblake. Provides evidence to support a birth year of 1887; also has useful postscript information for Rose's book.

Kimball, Robert, and William Bolcom. *Reminiscing with Sissle and Blake*. New York: Viking, 1973. Lavishly illustrated, comprehensive survey of the partners' careers up to 1972, compiled with their collaboration.

Rose, Al. *Eubie Blake*. New York: Schirmer Books, 1979. Blake's official biography, written largely in his own words, with many anecdotes plus the author's own memories.

—BILL EGAN

BLAKEY, ART (b. 11 October 1919; d. 16 October 1990), jazz musician. Arthur William Blakey was born in Pittsburgh, Pennsylvania, and was raised by relatives and a family friend. His father, Bertram, a barber, had left the family when Blakey was an infant, and his mother died when he was twenty-one months old. By age fourteen he was working as a pianist in a Pittsburgh nightclub. He switched to drums, learning to play a hard swinging style by listening to recordings of Chick Webb and Sid Catlett.

After a stint in the Mary Lou Williams combo in 1942, Blakey traveled with Fletcher Henderson's orchestra in 1943–1944. From 1944 to 1947 he played in Billy Eckstine's orchestra, a group that included the influential musicians John Birks "Dizzy" Gillespie, Charlie "Bird" Parker, and Miles Davis. Blakey formed his own group, the Seventeen Messengers, in 1947, making the first recordings under his name for the Blue Note label later that year. On his return from a trip to Africa in 1948 he converted to Islam and changed his name to Abdullah Ibn Buhaina, but he ceased practicing the faith in 1956.

With the pianist Horace Silver, Blakey assembled a quintet in 1953 that became the Jazz Messengers. The band played a hard bop style of the 1950s, typified by a driving, primal, bluesy sound that stressed a rhythmic foundation. Silver left the Jazz Messengers in 1956, and Blakey became the leader and led the band until his death.

Aside from his powerful skills as an instrumentalist, Blakey was an excellent scout, mentor, and trainer of new talent. His sidemen included Wayne Shorter, Wynton Marsalis, and Branford Marsalis. His band became a university of jazz, where he encouraged the musicians to compose their own music and go on to start their own bands.

[*See also* Jazz; Music; *and biographical entries on figures mentioned in this article*.]

BIBLIOGRAPHY

Gourse, Leslie. *Art Blakey: Jazz Messenger*. New York: Schirmer, 2002.

—TIMOTHY J. O'BRIEN

BLAXPLOITATION FILMS. Between 1970 and 1975, Hollywood released over one hundred movies, mostly over-the-top action films, aimed primarily at African American filmgoers. These films have come to be known collectively as blaxploitation cinema. The term was coined in 1972 by Junius Griffin of the Beverly Hills/Hollywood NAACP in response to *Superfly*. Griffin and others felt that the film, the story of a cocaine dealer named Priest trying to make one final drug deal before leaving the business, exploited African American audiences' desire to see African American stories portrayed onscreen by "taking our money [and] feeding us a forced diet of violence, murder, drugs, and rape." Despite protests that black audiences were not being exploited, the term persisted and offers important insight into why these films were created and why they were so intensely popular during the first half of the 1970s.

Black Power and Black Film. As the 1960s drew to a close, many young African Americans embraced Black Power ideology. After the tumult of the 1960s and the assassination of Martin Luther King Jr., racial reconciliation seemed to be an unattainable fantasy. Consequently, black culture generally shifted in the direction of black nationalism. This tendency created a new black cultural renaissance and aesthetic in which "black [was] beautiful." Particular interest was placed on redeeming black masculinity. Black studies programs sprang up throughout the country. "Afro" hairstyles and traditional African clothing became fashionable. This new trend, often characterized as separatism, created new sounds in African American soul music and transformed African American literature and arts with the Black Arts Movement.

The new cultural frankness concerning racial issues manifested itself in a series of films in 1970. Perhaps the most important of these was Ossie Davis's *Cotton Comes to Harlem*. *Cotton* was not a great film; however, it offered three things that would come to define early 1970s films aimed at black audiences. First, *Cotton* is a crime story with strong male leads, "Grave Digger" Jones and "Coffin" Ed Johnson. Second, the story is set in Harlem, harking back to the classic "race" films of the 1930s and reflecting 1970s black cinema's tendency to produce films set in the nation's urban ghettos. Third, it was profitable. *Cotton* was produced for $2.2 million. It grossed just over $15 million. This was wonderful box office at a time when many major Hollywood films were losing a great deal of money. Its success, coupled with the success of Melvin Van Peebles's *Watermelon Man*, a farce in which a white bigot awakens to find himself black, got Hollywood's attention.

Melvin Van Peebles and *Sweet Sweetback's Baadasssss Song*. The explicit sexual and political content of Melvin Van Peebles's 1971 cult classic *Sweet Sweetback's Baadasssss Song* made it one of the decade's most controversial films. Produced for $150,000, *Sweetback* grossed over $15 million domestically. Sweetback, a sex worker, kills two white police officers to save a black nationalist.

Shaft. Richard Roundtree in *Shaft's Big Score!*, directed by Gordon Parks, 1972. MGM/PHOTOFEST

Sweetback then runs for the Mexican border, evading the pursuing police. The film was overtly political. In perhaps its most effective sequence, Sweetback stumbles through the desert after having been shot by the police. As he runs to freedom, a Greek chorus sings behind him, "He bled your mama! He bled your papa!" The voice of Van Peebles comes in over the chorus to say, "But he wont bleed me!" This theme of black nationalism is all the more prominent in the closing title: "Watch Out! A Baadasssss Nigger Is Coming Back to Collect Some Dues!" Since Van Peebles clearly intended *Sweetback* to be a political statement, it is ironic that most critics agree that it spawned blaxploitation cinema.

***Shaft, Superfly,* and Beyond.** Gordon Parks Sr.'s *Shaft* was also released in 1971. As Shaft, Richard Roundtree embodied African American cool and sexuality. As the theme song says, he is "the black private dick who's a sex machine to all the chicks." He was also a black nationalist hero. Shaft is coolly dismissive of the police and their overtures for his help until he realizes that a gang war could break out in Harlem without his intervention. He literally "sticks his neck out for his brother man." *Shaft* became the most financially successful of the blaxploitation films, earning over $23 million.

Shaft's "cool" explains the movie's popularity. *Shaft* also foreshadowed two other major draws in blaxploitation cinema: music and sexuality. Following Van Peebles's use of Earth, Wind and Fire on the *Sweetback* soundtrack, Parks had approached Isaac Hayes of Memphis's Stax Records to score *Shaft*. The score won an Oscar. After Hayes's score came scores by the 1970s soul legends Curtis Mayfield (*Superfly*), James Brown (*Black Caesar*, 1973), and Marvin Gaye (*Trouble Man*, 1972). *Shaft's* sexuality, particularly as expressed in Shaft's sexual encounters with white women, would become a hallmark of blaxploitation.

The next year, Gordon Parks Jr. released *Superfly*, the first of the 1970s pimp films and the movie that launched the antiblaxploitation effort. As that movement continued, protesters had more ammunition. In 1973 Pam Grier, the undisputed queen of blaxploitation, appeared in her first lead in *Coffy*, the story of a nurse who avenges her heroin-addicted sister's drug-induced coma with equal parts of sex and violence.

The End of Blaxploitation. Protests about black images were not enough to stop blaxploitation cinema. Ultimately, the movies were undone by their poor quality and the same market forces that spawned them. Production values were generally poor even on the best of them. Boom microphones, the large microphones used to record dialogue, appeared onscreen with alarming frequency (in fact, a boom mike and the sound man holding it are visible in one sequence in the 1975 cult classic *Dolemite*), and continuity gaffes abounded. In *TNT Jackson*, for example, Jeannie Bell's underwear changes color in the middle of a fight sequence and then abruptly shifts back. Scripts were usually clichéd by-the-numbers revenge tales set in the urban ghettos of New York or Los Angeles. Direction was problematic. The actors were often amateurs, black athletes, and celebrities with little, if any, formal training trying to make the transition to the screen.

Foxy Brown. Pam Grier in the title role, 1974. AIP/PHOTOFEST

By 1975 the heady thrill of seeing Shaft, Priest, or Coffy sticking it to "the Man" had lost much of its luster, especially since most of the films were stunningly bad. Audiences wanted something new and found it in the summer of 1975 when *Jaws* introduced the summer blockbuster. With the runaway success of *Jaws* and then the phenomenon of *Star Wars* in 1977, Hollywood no longer needed to grind out low-budget black crime dramas to generate profits. Once the profit incentive was gone, it was simply time for the "next big thing."

[*See also* Black Arts Movement; Black Nationalism; Black Power Movement; Black Studies; Film and Filmmakers; Film and Television Depictions of African

Americans; Harlem; King, Martin Luther, Jr., Assassination of; Music; Sexuality; Soul Music; Stereotypes of African Americans; *and biographical entries on figures mentioned in this article*.]

BIBLIOGRAPHY

Bogle, Donald. *Toms, Coons, Mulattoes, Mammies, and Bucks: An Interpretive History of Blacks in American Films*. 4th ed. New York: Continuum, 2001. Informative and provocative; the best one-volume history of African American film in print.

Martinez, Gerald, Diana Martinez, and Andres Chavez. *What It Is . . . What It Was!: The Black Film Explosion of the '70s in Words and Pictures*. New York: Miramax, 1998. Its most important contribution is its collection of several blaxploitation-era film posters.

Schulman, Bruce J. *The Seventies: The Great Shift in American Culture, Society, and Politics*. Cambridge, Mass.: Da Capo Press, 2002. The second chapter has an excellent introduction to the racial politics of the decade and their impact on the media.

Van Deburg, William L. *New Day in Babylon: The Black Power Movement and American Culture, 1965–1975*. Chicago: University of Chicago Press, 1992. A first-rate history of the impact of Black Power on African American culture and fashion.

—DWAIN C. PRUITT

BLIGE, MARY J. (b. 11 January 1971), groundbreaking singer and performing artist. Mary Jane Blige was born in the Bronx, New York; she grew up in Yonkers in the Schlobohm Housing Project. She faced the harsh conditions many poor urban teenagers deal with—crime-ridden neighborhoods, extreme peer pressure, and premature exposure to adult responsibility. Blige was one of four children. Her mother was a single parent who worked long hours. Blige's father left the family around 1975 and moved to Michigan; this made Blige tough and street savvy with a bad attitude about life and a hardened heart. While her street credibility would later enable her to become the most influential African American female vocalist of the past two decades, when she was growing up Blige could have had no idea she would reign as the Queen of Hip-Hop Soul for fifteen years.

Much like the legends Aretha Franklin and Whitney Houston, Blige began singing in a church choir. There, she sharpened her vocal skills, and her love of music grew. During her visits to Michigan, her father taught her harmonization. She loved to sing, but she never thought of singing as a career. After she recorded a karaoke demo tape at the mall, her mother found the tape and gave it to her boyfriend. It landed in the hands of the record executive Andre Harrell, who immediately signed Blige to Uptown Records.

Blige has won four Grammy Awards—in 1995, 2002, 2003, and 2006—and a great many other honors. However, these accolades alone do not give her legendary status. It is the love of her fans, particularly the African American female community, that has made her an icon. Through the fusion of hip hop and rhythm and blues, Blige has been able to tell the story of women who have been voiceless. Blige's soulful lyrics express the hardship and lack of love that many black women experience. Partially because of male homicides and imprisonment, many black women are single mothers who regularly deal with many problems, including infidelity and domestic abuse. Because Blige was a product of her environment and experienced similar pain, she sings songs that speak to these women. With songs like "Not Gon' Cry" and "Be Happy," Blige went on a journey with her fans in search of love and acceptance. But for Blige that journey was one filled with self-hatred and substance abuse. She realized she was on a path to self-destruction and that she had to change.

Now there is a new Blige. She made many changes and found happiness, and in 2003 she married. Her husband, Kendu Isaacs, has helped her heal the wounds of her past and finally learn to love herself. She focuses on being a positive role model for her fans to show them that they, too, can overcome obstacles and love themselves. Unfortunately, this change has caused Blige to lose some of her fan base: some fans still recognize only misery and pain. But Blige has made a vow to remain positive. She knows the only way to be free is to go through the pain and break through.

[*See also* Music.]

BIBLIOGRAPHY

Mayo, Kierna. "Mary J.: Finding Peace and Celebrating 15 Years of Making Hits." *Essence* (June 2007): 136–145.

Smith, Jessie Carnie, ed. "Mary J. Blige." *Notable Black American Women*, Book 3. Detroit, Mich.: Gale Group, 2002. (Reproduced in *Biography Resource Center*. Farmington Hills, Mich.: Gale, 2008.)

—JAWANA O. SOUTHERLAND

BLUES. The term "blues" may be restricted to songs that use a repetitive sequence of twelve-bar chords with tonal variations known as "blue notes" (the flattened third and seventh notes of the major scale), a description that encompasses thousands of loosely related tunes. Because blues music is a product intended for mass sales, the definition of "blues music" is affected by its commercial appeal. In today's market, the label "blues music" encompasses the range of music lumped together as African American that was created before 1950 and that is not classified as jazz, classical, or gospel. Such titles might include barroom, work, double entendre, and ragtime music. After 1950 the label "blues music" can include any form of black popular music that did not cross over or appeal to white audiences. Paradoxically, in the early twenty-first century, blues enthusiasts are largely white and middle class, whereas African Americans generally eschew the form in favor of such descendants as rhythm and blues and rap.

Blues music has attracted schools of thought that jealously guard its historical meaning. To many, blues was the rural folk music of African Americans in the South in the first part of the twentieth century. Although female "blues queens" were highly popular in the 1920s during the congealing of the music's appeal through recordings, blues is now remembered as a masculine musicology. Regardless of gender or content, blues music evokes a worldly wisdom or a sadness gained from great loss and experience; conversely it also includes party songs that have earthy, sexual gusto. Fundamentally, blues is the secular music of a folk at work and play.

Roots. Blues has its roots in slavery and in Africa. Nathaniel Uring, a European visiting Angola in 1701, observed young men and women who "often meet together in small companies by moon-light and Sing and Dance most part of the night, which they choose for coolness. . . . This custom of dancing is kept up in all our American plantations" (quoted in Hodges). As Uring also observed, blacks gathered together on feast days and on Sundays. Among the most popular entertainers were griots, or "good talkers," who earned good pay and esteem but who were also feared for allegedly consorting with evil spirits or for composing insult songs. Even so, African music was communal and participatory, using call-and-response.

Such traditions traveled with enforced slave migrants to the New World. There slaves conjoined with white sailors, servants, and other members of the motley crew who populated the lower orders of colonial society. Enslaved blacks gathered in taverns and at the homes of free blacks in port cities along the Atlantic Coast during the colonial era. Authorities warned Domingo Angola, a free black man in New York City in the 1670s, to stop entertaining slaves. Blacks in New York gathered for parties in the fields of Brooklyn in the early eighteenth century. Pinkster or Pentecost, a mid-Atlantic holiday, had a distinctly secular cast and featured music. One commentator observed the house servant "tuning his Banger (banjo)." Asked what his intention was, the enslaved man responded that it was a holiday and advised his questioner to follow and "see Ninegar play Banger for true; dance too" (quoted in Hodges). Similar good times occurred in taverns in tidewater Virginia and Charleston, South Carolina. Conspirators in the failed Negro insurrection in New York City in 1741 mixed music, dancing, and drinking with sworn oaths to a conspiracy to overthrow the white government. Later, during the American Revolution, blacks and English officers met at Ethiopian balls where black orchestras played the hurdy-gurdy. Combined spiritual and secular chants called ring shouts were common in both the South and the North.

There is ample evidence of a blues culture after the American Revolution. Charles Dickens was but one of many white tourists who visited interracial bars in the Five Points of New York City to listen to music. Walt Whitman, who attended these regularly as a journalist in the 1840s, prophesied that the sounds of the Five Points "presaged a grand American opera" (quoted in Hodges). Outside in the butcher markets, blacks would "pat juba" using tap-dance methods to suggest drumming. By the mid-nineteenth century, black music was absorbed into white minstrelsy, a format that combined exaggerated, humorous racial characterizations and vaudeville.

Farther south, enslaved blacks created tunes that were termed "the sounds of slavery." As late as the 1860s, travelers in North Carolina saw black dancers in costumes that included horned headdresses and cow tails while musicians played "gumbo boxes," which allowed for a percussive beat. By the 1890s, the cultural historian Cecil Brown argues, blacks in Saint Louis constructed the Frankie and Johnny myth about gamblers in blues dens who fought over perceived violations of honor. By the onset of the twentieth century, blacks north and south, east and west, were well acquainted with a vocal vocabulary and blues sensibility characterized by pursuits of pleasure and sexual prowess leavened by an existential understanding of individual limits and memories of past failures at love. As Elijah Wald cogently demonstrates, if much of this music used the twelve-bar chord progression, it also incorporated minstrelsy, cowboy, gospel, and other contemporary music formats.

The archaeologist Charles Peabody, during an excavation of ancient Indian mounds in Coahoma County, Mississippi, in 1901–1902, listened to his black workmen utter rhythmic song lines during a fifteen-mile trek back to the main camp. One strong-voiced man took the lead, improvising short lines that touched on the day's events, female types and girlfriends, and biblical themes, while the others responded with repetitive lines. On other occasions, Peabody heard the men accompany themselves with guitars and with repertoires borrowed from minstrel shows, white country music, and ragtime. Other songs were less derivative and included songs about hard luck, troubles with women, even legal problems. The melancholic laments that Peabody eventually described in his 1904 report on the excavation were the latest in the genealogy of blues songs dating back to the earliest colonial days and were examples of contemporary fusions that blacks fashioned to keep themselves amused and to get through hard work days and lonely nights. Black cotton workers in the South often re-created African whooping or yodeling along with vocal masking or verbal alternations.

W. C. Handy, often called the father of the blues, first encountered this music in 1903. By that time he was a famous orchestra leader traveling by train through the South. During one train delay he heard a black man in ragged clothes play a guitar, pressing a knife against the string to get from the instrument a slurred, moaning sound akin to the human voice. All the while the singer repeated lyrics about "Goin' where the Southern cross the Dog," referring to spots where two famous train lines intersected, as he drew responses out of his guitar. Peabody and Handy were hearing the same kinds of field hollers, work songs, spirituals, country string-bands, and fife-and-drum songs that were precursors of blues music.

Commercial Blues. Commercial blues music appeared in the fall of 1912 when "Dallas Blues," "Baby Seal Blues," and "Memphis Blues (Mr. Crump)" became sheet-music hits. W. C. Handy used the melody he had heard on the train to create a campaign song for E. H. Crump, a mayoral candidate in Memphis, Tennessee, where Handy lived. Handy followed this composition with the "St. Louis Blues," which Wald describes as his most enduring composition. Soon, every dance or vaudeville orchestra had to include the moaning styles of the blues in its repertoire.

In 1914 the Victory Military Band issued on record a version of Handy's "Memphis Blues"; the composer followed up with his own side the following year. Morton Harvey sang the first blues on record, Handy's "Memphis Blues," also in 1914. White ethnic impersonators followed suit, combining blues music with Irish and Jewish lyrics. Some of this descended from minstrelsy, but the new twelve-bar format, replete with moans and doleful lyrics, quickly became popular. White and black artists and writers worked together to promote the blues.

Takeoff of the new music came in 1920 when Mamie Smith's "Crazy Blues" sold more than a million copies in six months, largely to an emerging "race" or African American market. Soon other blues queens, including Ethel Waters, Alberta Hunter, Sara Martin, Ma Rainey, and, the most famous, Bessie Smith, cut hundreds of blues songs. Bessie Smith employed a distinctive blues style but also incorporated vaudeville and Tin Pan Alley songs; like Rainey and Hunter, Smith filled large theaters north and south. Blues queens dressed in elaborate outfits that stimulated their audiences' fantasies, though they never lost contact with their southern roots. Blues queens regularly drew more interest than their male counterparts did, although that original interest is hardly represented in today's reissues, which are decidedly tilted toward male blues artists.

Papa Charlie Jackson, a veteran minstrel and medicine show artist, became the first big male blues singer, hitting in 1924 with "Salty Dog Blues," a comic ragtime piece that could easily have fit into the country-and-western venues. Similarly, Albert "Lonnie" Johnson, a major influence on the later blues legend B. B. King, used a suave delivery and was adept at blues and jazz, regularly recording with Duke Ellington. Johnson is cited as being a deeply influential guitarist. Though he was considered a blues singer, Johnson was also comfortable in a cabaret setting.

Closer to the prototype that historians and blues enthusiasts have created of blues musicians was the powerful Blind Lemon Jefferson, a rough-hewn, powerfully intense artist akin to blind musical beggars who appear globally in every rural society. Jefferson's style was, however, no more "authentic" than that of any of the other popular, more urban blues musicians. Jefferson was a professional performer who worked easily with vaudevillians and performed in a number of styles. Other bluesmen such as Charlie Patton, Blind Blake, and Barbecue Bob had more localized appeal and were products of the juke-joint circuit.

Two other performers, Tampa Red and Leroy Carr, had long-lasting influences. Carr was an influential blues singer whose casually assured style and accompaniment by a piano affected the development of Nat King Cole, Sam Cooke, Otis Redding, David Ruffin of the Temptations, and Jerry Butler, thus extending a method lasting from the late 1920s into the 1970s. The guitarist Tampa Red recorded with the pianist Georgia Tom using a trademark risqué style called "hokum." The lyrics from their giant hit "It's Tight Like That," in a call-and-response between Red and the female impersonator Frankie "Half-Pint" Jaxon, include:

> Red: "Woman, you reading the Lady's Home Journal?"
> Jaxon (in falsetto): "Yes, Daddy, but I want that Saturday Evening Post."

Such double entendres were staples of blues lyrics into the 1980s and beyond and can easily be heard in any rap duet today.

The effect of the Great Depression on blues music was paradoxical. Piano-and-guitar duets, often enlarged by a bass, harmonica, kazoo, or washboard and often recorded by a small group of seasoned professionals, were common. Yet despite the homogeneity of the sound and the perilous economic conditions, blues music, after a brief falter in 1930, sold widely and regained 1920s boom conditions by the middle of the 1930s. Popular appetites for the blues were doubtless conditioned by the hard times. During this era Tampa Red dominated recording, with more than 250 sides, not including his religious songs. Big Bill Broonzy, who often used repetitive methods, was next, followed by such familiar names as Lonnie Johnson, Peetie "the Devil's Son-in-Law" Wheatstraw, and Bessie Smith, who recorded 160 sides before her death in 1933. Memphis Minnie was the other prominent female stylist, with more than 158 songs issued between 1928 and 1941, although her career extended beyond that.

Unrecorded Folk Singers. Beyond these and other popular singers were often unrecorded folk singers whose broad styles and skills ranged across a number of genres. Descended from songsters of the colonial period, who were expected to know any number of popular melodies for audiences that were often mixed race, such artists of the 1930s played older instruments such as the banjo and fiddle and played in minstrel and other shows that many modern critics consider demeaning.

Other noncommercial music had great long-term effect. John and Alan Lomax, two white musicologists, traveled throughout the South in the 1930s, accompanied on at least one occasion by the black folklorist and novelist Zora Neale Hurston. The Lomaxes specialized in field hollers and work and prison songs. Their great discovery was Huddie Ledbetter, known as Leadbelly, who was incarcerated in Angola State Penitentiary, the infamous Louisiana prison. Ledbetter was adept at blues and at children's rhymes sung as field hollers and work songs. The Lomaxes brought him to New York, where he appeared at Carnegie Hall in a memorable concert in 1935. The blues world knew nothing about Leadbelly, but he soon became an icon for the white, liberal intelligentsia. The white blues cult, composed of record collectors, connoisseurs, jazz fans, and the beats, had strict standards of excellence, regarded themselves as marginal as blues singers, and felt a virtuous respect for and solidarity with the downtrodden.

One figure notably important among white blues aficionados but little known to his contemporaries is Robert Johnson, elevated to "King of the Blues" when his small catalog of songs was reissued in the early 1960s. Johnson was born near Hazlehurst or Robbinsville in Copiah County, Mississippi, in 1911 and had a short, troubled life. He married, lost his wife in childbirth, and then abandoned a second wife for a life on the road. He was deeply inspired by the country-music minstrels Charley Patton, Son House, and Willie Brown. A wanderer and a ladies' man, Johnson drank and smoked excessively and shaped his songs out of his adventures. Initially an inexperienced and crude guitarist, he returned from one trip with exceptional new skills, leading his acquaintances to believe that he had made a contract with the devil. According to an abiding myth—one that proved immensely popular among later American and British rockers—Johnson met Papa Legba, the darkest spirit, at the crossroads at midnight and allowed him to tune his guitar in exchange for his soul. Johnson sang of this experience in his song "Crossroads Blues," later popularized by the English blues and rock star Eric Clapton.

Johnson had but two recording sessions, one in San Antonio on 23–26 November 1936 and then another in a Dallas warehouse the following June. Shortly after that, a jealous boyfriend poisoned Johnson with strychnine-laced whiskey after the bluesman had flirted with the man's girlfriend. Johnson was dead at age twenty-seven. Johnson's extraordinary intensity, his tortured lyrics, and his verbal gymnastics have fascinated the world ever since. His compositions are now treated as poetry, and his guitar-playing methods, adopted by Clapton, Keith Richards of the Rolling Stones, Jimmie Page of Led Zeppelin, and Jimi Hendrix, have given Johnson global fame. Among African American bluesmen, Johnson influenced Muddy Waters, Elmore James, Johnny Shines, and Robert Junior Lockwood, the master's apprentice.

Later Impacts. The African American migration to the city, the modernization of American society, and World War II all had powerful impacts on blues music. As millions of American blacks left the southern states with hopes of jobs and better lives in northern cities, they adapted blues music to electrical amplification. As World War II brought fuller employment, blacks had more money to spend and made larger demands on society for equality. Yet blues music became a sound track for the disappointed dreams of millions whose migration earned only a temporary prosperity, while city life produced racial conflict and anomie or rootlessness. Lil Green's masterly World War II blues "Why Don't You Do Right" featured Green sharply reminding her lover of his failures and telling him to "get out of here and bring me some money, too!" Peggy Lee later made Green's hit a standard. As female vocalists moved into jazz- or gospel-influenced pop music, there were fewer female blues singers, though Willie Mae "Big Mama" Thornton became renowned for her hit "Hound Dog," later covered by Elvis Presley. Perhaps the best female blues singers were such jazz musicians as Sarah Vaughan and Diana Washington. Blues-inflected rhythms inspired some of the 1950s jazz classics such as Miles Davis's *Kind of Blue* and the duet of Johnny Hartman and John Coltrane.

Urban life, a bit more cash, and electric amplification produced startlingly brilliant blues showmen who combined recollection of their rural roots with an urbane toughness. Muddy Waters, Howlin' Wolf, Jimmy Reed, and the incomparable B. B. King combined ferocious guitar lines with strong, booming voices that fronted full-blues orchestras and superb lyrics first to enchant a generation of black nightclub fans, then to enchant a generation of English rockers, and then, in King's case, to become deified. Still active in the early twenty-first century, King has even received a presidential medal, and his persona is widely admired. An ambassador for

Blues Group. The Blues Fuse playing at Smiley's Schooner Saloon north of San Francisco, c. 2001. Berisford "Shep" Shepherd (*front left*) on both trombone and percussion, Arthur Lee Harris on the Hammond B-3 organ, and Robert Labbe on drums. Photograph by Ilka Hartmann. © ILKA HARTMANN

the blues, King is largely responsible for its place in the canon of American arts.

King and other urban bluesmen worked consistently through the 1950s and 1960s, even as white enthusiasts were arguing over the purity of Robert Johnson and other long-dead performers. The rock revolution of the 1960s brought notoriety if not income to veteran bluesmen. Hendrix was only the most visible of the guitar-driven bandleaders of the 1960s, many of whom laced their lyrics with allusions to drugs. Such psychedelic was often blues-based, as in the example of Canned Heat, the Paul Butterfield Blues Band (itself a terrific example of a mixed-race urban blues group), and the English groups the Yardbirds, Cream, and the Rolling Stones.

Among blacks the rise of soul music seemed to doom traditional blues, although Howard Tate's critically acclaimed, if little-known, album *Get It While You Can* (1967) showed the power of fusion of the two elements. Similarly, James Brown's *Papa's Got a Brand New Bag*, which seemed to announce a new style of horn-dominated, orchestral black music, was itself based upon twelve-bar blues. Hokum music made an undeniable reappearance later in the 1970s in George Clinton's Parliament Funkadelic Bands that satirized minstrelsy, blues, and white psychedelic. The internationally famous Jimi Hendrix Trio relied heavily on blues. Younger bluesmen, especially Buddy Guy, Z. Z. Hill, Little Milton, and Latimore, emphasized their urbanity more than the rural roots of the blues. As with audiences who had grown more middle class, the older blues forms favored by white purists were reminders of slavery days and southern oppression, which most of them hoped soon to forget.

By the early twenty-first century, although B. B. King made appearances at the White House and in European capitals, blues music was more a museum piece than a live musicology. Rap musicians may echo hokum songs with their emphasis on high living and rough, criminal personae, but the melancholic quality of blues has largely been sublimated into mainstream music. As with the work of the earliest practitioners who combined blues with other popular styles in their repertoires, blues in the twenty-first century is so completely absorbed into American standards as to become indistinguishable. During times of economic downturns and personal troubles, blues has become virtually an American poetry.

[*See also* Gospel Music; Jazz; Minstrel Tradition; Music; Oratory and Verbal Arts; Ragtime; Soul Music; Spirituals; Vaudeville, African Americans in; *and biographical entries on figures mentioned in this article*.]

BIBLIOGRAPHY

Brown, Cecil. *Stagolee Shot Billy*. Cambridge, Mass.: Harvard University Press, 2003.

Dicaire, David. *Blues Singers: Biographies of 50 Legendary Artists of the Early 20th Century*. Jefferson, N.C.: McFarland, 1999.

Hodges, Graham Russell. *Root and Branch: African Americans in New York and East Jersey, 1613–1863*. Chapel Hill: University of North Carolina Press, 1999.

Keil, Charles. *Urban Blues*. Chicago: University of Chicago Press, 1966.

Palmer, Robert. *Deep Blues*. New York: Viking Press, 1981.

Wald, Elijah. *Escaping the Delta: Robert Johnson and the Invention of the Blues*. New York: Amistad, 2004.

—GRAHAM RUSSELL GAO HODGES

BOAS, FRANZ (b. 9 July 1858; d. 21 December 1941), pioneer in discrediting the racist concepts that characterized early twentieth-century anthropology and other social sciences. Franz Boas was born in Minden, Germany. He received his PhD in physics from the University of Kiel in 1881, but he soon shifted interest into the field of human geography. In 1883 he conducted his first fieldwork, among the Inuit people of Baffin Island. In 1887 he began research among the Indians of the Pacific Northwest. In 1899 he became the first professor of anthropology at Columbia University. When Boas began his anthropological work, anthropology was far from being a scientific field. It was infested with racist practitioners and amateurs. Boas held that too often people developed theories and then sought to gather information to prove their theories.

The 1906 Atlanta Address. Boas developed a methodology that focused on gathering hard evidence first and delaying the development of grand theories until serious research had been conducted, research that itself remained open to further examination. This open-mindedness characterized his examination of race and its relationship to culture. In a seminal address to the commencement class of Atlanta University in 1906, he famously laid out criticisms of scientific racism that became crucial in the development of American anthropology.

Stating that anthropology has a "broad view of races and cultures," Boas presented arguments that not only put African achievements in the broader context of history but demonstrated the African foundation of modern achievements. He cited examples of African innovations such as iron smelting and agriculture, described the sophistication of African kingdoms such as the Zulu Empire as well as the great empires of Ghana, Malay, and Songhai, explained the indigenization of Arabic influences such as markets, money, judicial proceedings, and art, and pointed to the volume and splendor of the great art of Africa. He also observed that there was no place in the United States where the triumphs of African culture are publicly displayed and honored but that collections in the world capitals of Paris, London, and Berlin pay tribute to these works.

The evidence from cultural anthropology, Boas argued, is thus stacked against those who argue for racial inferiority. Both anthropology and history suggest the logic of improving the status of African Americans and aiding them to find appropriate work in American life. Meanwhile, Boas indicated, the situation of African Americans is best understood in the comparative aspect of other colonized peoples.

Legacy. In subsequent decades of the twentieth century, Boas formed close alliances with black leaders such as W. E. B. Du Bois and E. Franklin Frazier in their efforts to bring the evidence of social science to bear in the fight against racism. Boas's research as well as that of his students found its way into legal briefs against segregation, including the famous *Brown v. Board of Education* in 1954.

Boas fought his battles against racism using every subdiscipline in American anthropology—physical anthropology, linguistics, archeology, cultural anthropology, and even a field that had not yet emerged, applied anthropology. For Boas, anthropology was not simply an abstract, objective "scientific" discipline disengaged from the everyday world. Rather it was a means of implementing liberal objectives—such as ending the evils of racism and colonialism—while aiding their victims. In Boas's hands, "science" became a weapon against social Darwinists and others who sought to use pseudoscience to oppress those at a power disadvantage.

With the ascendancy of the virulent racism of fascism at the onset of World War II, Boas became more open about the politics behind his research. He pressed the argument that humans are similar in their physical makeup and that environmental influences are the paramount factor in shaping any differences within and between groups. He attacked not only racial prejudice but the very notion of race, plainly stating in an article for the Kansas *Plain Dealer* on 1 August 1941 that there is no "pure race among humans" and that "the greatest inbreeding cannot produce a race of people that are all alike. Even in families, the individual differences between brothers and sisters, including identical twins, remain very great."

Boas argued that all the small truths of his research and that of his student Melville Herskovits led to one great truth: that one cannot justifiably apply psychological terms to an entire population. Boas demonstrated that all human populations are fundamentally similar and that consequently any inferiority observable among Negroes as contrasted to white populations in the United States was due to environmental conditions, including lack of opportunity—that is, culture exerts a greater force on behavior than heredity. His dying words were, "I have proved a point about race."

Boas's students, Margaret Mead, Melville Herskovits, and others, furthered his work on the priority of culture over biology, an essential tool in the fight against racism. The detailed fieldwork of those who came after him is a further testimony to his impact on the discipline of cultural anthropology and its use as a tool against racism.

[*See also* Du Bois, W. E. B., *subentry* Life and Career; Eugenics Movement; Frazier, E. Franklin; *and* Science and Scientists.]

BIBLIOGRAPHY

Boas, Franz. *A Franz Boas Reader: The Shaping of American Anthropology, 1883–1911*. Edited by George W. Stocking Jr. Chicago: University of Chicago Press, 1989.

Boas, Franz. *Race and Democratic Society*. New York: J. J. Augustin, 1945.

Boas, Franz. *Race, Language, and Culture*. New York: Macmillan, 1940.

Cole, Douglas. *Franz Boas: The Early Years, 1858–1906*. Seattle: University of Washington Press, 1999.

Williams, Vernon J., Jr. *Rethinking Race: Franz Boas and His Contemporaries*. Lexington: University Press of Kentucky, 1996.

—FRANK A. SALAMONE

BO DIDDLEY (b. 30 December 1928; d. 6 June 2008), blues guitarist, singer, and songwriter. The blues performer known as Bo Diddley was born Ellas Otha Bates in McComb, Mississippi, to Eugene Bates, a father whom he never knew, and Ethel Wilson, a teenage mother. He was raised by his mother's first cousin Gussie McDaniel, and when his adoptive father, Robert McDaniel, died in 1934, Gussie moved the family to Chicago.

Diddley first studied music as a child under Professor O. W. Fredrick while attending Ebenezer Missionary Baptist Church in Chicago. While attending Foster Vocational High School in Chicago, he studied various instruments, including the guitar, harmonica, and trombone. His sister bought his first guitar for him when he was twelve. During his high school years, he also formed a band, the Hipsters, later called the Langley Avenue Jive Cats. In the late 1940s Diddley tried his hand at a number of pursuits, including semipro boxing, and he also performed with a washboard trio. In 1951 he began to perform in Chicago clubs as a singer and guitarist, with a repertoire influenced by the likes of John Lee Hooker and Muddy Waters. Around this time he also adopted the stage name Bo Diddley, a nickname by which he was addressed as a youth. The phrase is southern black slang with the meaning "nothing at all," and it also refers to a one-stringed African instrument.

In 1955 Diddley signed a recording contract with the Checkers label, a subsidiary of Chess Records. His debut recording on 2 March 1955 was a dual-sided disc, "Bo Diddley" and "I'm a Man." The single "Bo Diddley" went to number one on the rhythm-and-blues chart, and Diddley became known for his signature beat, a distinctive, African-based 5/4 rhythm that has been imitated by numerous artists. Diddley's lyrics reflect his African American working-class background, a combination of the Deep South of Mississippi and the streets of Chicago. His style, which walks a line between rhythm and blues and rock and roll, is indebted, lyrically, to the traditions of the dozens and signifying—boastfully and cleverly talking negatively about someone else. The rhythmic beat that Diddley originated is reminiscent of the hambone beat of black folk music.

Diddley's influence on other musicians is well known, and his songs have been recorded by numerous other artists, including Buddy Holly, the Rolling Stones, the Animals, and the Kinks. He has recorded with other blues musicians, including Chuck Berry (*Two Great Guitars*, 1964) and Muddy Waters and Howlin' Wolf (*Super Super Blues Band*, 1967). In 1966 he released *The Originator*, an album whose title reflects Diddley's claim that he is a rock-and-roll pioneer. Some of Diddley's other hits include "Road Runner" (1960) and "You Can't Judge a Book by the Cover" (*Bo Diddley*, 1962). In recent years Diddley has received numerous awards and accolades in recognition of his career, and on 21 January 1987 he was inducted into the Rock and Roll Hall of Fame. At the time of his death in 2008 Diddley resided in Archer, Florida, with his family.

[*See also* Music *and* Rhythm and Blues.]

BIBLIOGRAPHY

Collis, John. *The Story of Chess Records*. New York: Bloomsbury, 1998.

White, George. *Bo Diddley: Living Legend*. London: Sanctuary, 1998.

—FRANK E. DOBSON JR.

BOND, HORACE MANN (b. 8 November 1904; d. 21 December 1972), educator and scholar. The grandson of slaves, Horace Mann Bond was born in Nashville, Tennessee, to two graduates of Oberlin College, Jane Alice Browne, a schoolteacher, and James Bond, a minister. Named after the abolitionist and educator Horace Mann, Bond was an academic prodigy, graduating from high school at the age of fourteen. He attended Lincoln University in Pennsylvania and was something of a mascot to his older classmates. Labeled the "class baby" by some, Bond proved himself a leader, becoming involved in a number of activities, including the school newspaper, debate, and a social fraternity. Bond graduated from Lincoln with honors in 1923, at the age of eighteen.

Following graduation Bond was offered a teaching post at Lincoln; in preparation he took graduate courses at Pennsylvania State College. While at Penn State, Bond excelled academically, but he encountered racism from a white professor who refused to seat him next to a white female in the class. Bond returned to Lincoln in the fall of 1923 as an instructor and prefect in one of the dormitories. However, he was dismissed for not ending a gambling ring in the dormitory he was in charge of.

Following his dismissal from Lincoln, Bond moved to Chicago, where he enrolled as a graduate student at the University of Chicago. He completed both his master's (1926) and PhD (1936) degrees at Chicago, where he studied education and sociology in a department that pioneered research on the impact of environment and society on individual personality. In 1929 Bond married Julia Agnes Washington; the couple had three children, including Horace Julian (b. 1940), known as Julian, who became a prominent civil rights activist.

Bond's academic career—which began before he finished his graduate work—was spent conducting research while also carrying out various jobs as an administrator and faculty member at historically black colleges. Between 1924 and 1939 he taught and served as an administrator at Langston University in Langston, Oklahoma; Alabama State Normal School in Montgomery, Alabama; Fisk University in Nashville; and Dillard University in New Orleans. In 1939 Bond became the president of Fort Valley State College in Fort Valley, Georgia, a position that he held until 1945. Then from 1945 to 1957 he served as president—the first African American president—of his alma mater, Lincoln.

As president of Lincoln, Bond was something of an activist, making vocal his support of Pan-Africanism, university programs in African studies, and desegregation of public schools. He also worked to expand Lincoln and increase its number of black professors. His activism aroused opposition to his presidency, and in 1957 he resigned after a dispute with the board of trustees. He became dean of the School of Education at Atlanta University, where he remained until his retirement in 1971.

Throughout his career Bond also made important contributions as a scholar, particularly in the areas of educational testing, educational history, and educational sociology. An early critic of intelligence testing, Bond assailed its cultural bias and ignorance of environmental factors in education. In his first book, *The Education of the Negro in the American Social Order* (1934), he offered a history of blacks in education from the antebellum era to the 1930s. His second book, *Negro Education in Alabama: A Study in Cotton and Steel* (1939), an interpretation of Reconstruction in Alabama, was based on his doctoral dissertation. In it Bond attacks the views of the southern historian Walter L. Fleming by suggesting that white capitalists, not black politicians, saddled the state of Alabama with massive debts. In the 1950s, following his departure from Lincoln, Bond took a lectureship at Harvard University, which resulted in another book, *The Search for Talent* (1959). Bond also wrote *Black American Scholars: A Study of Their Beginnings* (1972) and *Education for Freedom: A History of Lincoln University*, published posthumously in 1976. During his last years much of Bond's energy was focused on helping the civil rights activities and political career of his son Julian. Horace Mann Bond died in December 1972 in Atlanta, Georgia.

[*See also* Bond, Julian; Education; Educators and Academics; Historically Black Colleges and Universities; *and* Lincoln University (Pennsylvania).]

BIBLIOGRAPHY

Urban, Wayne J. *Black Scholar: Horace Mann Bond, 1904–1972.* Athens, Ga.: University of Georgia Press, 1992. Focuses on his academic career and writings.

Williams, Roger M. *The Bonds: An American Family*. New York: Atheneum, 1971.

—FRANK E. DOBSON JR.

BOND, JULIAN (b. 14 January 1940), civil rights activist, politician, and television host. The son of the prominent educator Horace Mann Bond, Horace Julian Bond spent his early years in Philadelphia, where his father was the president of Lincoln University. In 1957 the family relocated to Atlanta, where Horace Mann Bond accepted a faculty position at Atlanta University. Julian Bond attended a Quaker preparatory high school and then enrolled at Morehouse College. Although his family hoped that he would follow in his father's footsteps and become a scholar, Julian was far more interested in political protest than in his academic coursework. In 1961 he dropped out of school to work full-time in the civil rights movement, not completing his BA in English at Morehouse until 1971.

Eager to fight for desegregation in Atlanta, Bond cofounded the Committee on Appeal for Human Rights (COHAR). On 15 March 1960 he was arrested after he led a group of students in an attempt to integrate the cafeteria at the Atlanta City Hall. That same year COHAR merged with the newly formed radical civil rights organization the Student Nonviolent Coordinating Committee (SNCC). Bond became SNCC's director of communications, a position he held until 1965 when he decided to run for elective office. He also edited the SNCC newspaper, the *Student Voice*.

In 1965 Bond was elected to the Georgia house of representatives, but the legislature barred him from taking his seat because of his outspoken views against the war in Vietnam. In 1966 the Supreme Court ruled that the Georgia legislature had violated Bond's First Amendment rights. On 9 January 1967 he was allowed to assume his elected position, serving in that capacity until 1974 when he was elected to the state senate. While a member of the Georgia legislature, Bond sponsored a number of bills aimed at fighting poverty and promoting equal treatment for the state's black citizens.

In 1968 Bond led a group of rival delegates to the Democratic National Convention to challenge the regular delegates, who did not accurately represent the racial mixture in Georgia. Remarkably, Bond and the other delegates were successful in working out a compromise and gaining recognition at the convention. Bond was nominated for vice president, becoming the first African American to be selected for that office. He withdrew his name because at twenty-eight he was too young to hold the position. The Constitution stipulates that vice presidents be at least thirty-five. However, Bond's achievements showed Democrats that African American voters could not be ignored.

After completing his sixth term in the state senate, Bond decided to run for a seat in the U.S. Congress in 1986. He narrowly lost the Democratic primary to his former SNCC colleague and longtime friend John Lewis. Throughout the campaign Lewis repeatedly demanded that Bond submit to a drug test. The rumors that Bond used drugs were given new life in 1987 when his wife of twenty-six years publicly accused Bond and other prominent local blacks of using cocaine. Shortly thereafter Bond's reputed mistress was arrested on drug charges. Bond, known for his charisma, his sense of humor, and his youthful good looks, soon recovered from the scandal, revived his flagging reputation, and changed directions.

Some observers had already begun to suspect that Bond's enthusiasm for politics was waning. His opponents charged him with being ineffective and with frequent absenteeism. In 1976 Bond had turned down an opportunity to work for the newly elected president Jimmy Carter, a decision that seemed to indicate that he had less interest in politics.

In 1998 Bond achieved a longtime goal when he was elected chairman of the board of the National Association for the Advancement of Colored People (NAACP). In that capacity he oversaw an aggressive fund-raising campaign and sought to revitalize the venerable organization by attracting new members and increasing its influence. Much as his father initially hoped, Bond also entered academia. Awarded twenty-five honorary degrees, he has taught at a number of universities, including Harvard, Drexel, American, and Virginia.

In addition to his civil rights and political activities, Bond wrote *A Time to Speak, a Time to Act: The Movement in Politics* (1972) and contributed articles and poems to numerous periodicals and anthologies. He narrated *Eyes on the Prize* (1987–1990), the acclaimed PBS documentary about the civil rights movement, as well as the Academy Award–winning documentary *A Time for Justice* (1994). From 1980 to 1997 he hosted the syndicated television program *America's Black Forum*.

[*See also* Bond, Horace Mann; Georgia; Politics and Politicians; *and* Student Nonviolent Coordinating Committee.]

BIBLIOGRAPHY

Neary, John. *Julian Bond: Black Rebel*. New York: William Morrow, 1971.

Williams, Roger M. *The Bonds: An American Family*. New York: Atheneum, 1971.

—JENNIFER JENSEN WALLACH

BONDS, BARRY (b. 24 July 1964), record-setting Major League Baseball player. Barry Bonds has set many records in Major League Baseball, but he has also been accused of involvement in a major drug scandal.

Barry Lamar Bonds was born into a baseball family in Riverside, California. His father, Bobby Bonds, and his godfather, Willie Mays, both had outstanding careers in baseball. Barry Bonds attended Arizona State University, playing baseball there from 1983 to 1985, and began his professional career in 1985 when he was drafted by the Pittsburgh Pirates. He spent seven consecutive seasons with the Pirates, from 1986 through 1992. In 1990 Bonds earned his first Gold Glove (for fielding excellence) and Silver Slugger (for batting) awards and was voted the National League's most valuable player (MVP). Bonds, a left fielder, won another MVP award in 1992.

Bonds began playing for the San Francisco Giants in 1993. He grew up in the San Francisco area, and both his father and his godfather began their careers playing for the Giants (when Mays started, the Giants were in New York City). Bonds's contract made him baseball's highest-paid player at that time, and in his first season in San Francisco, Bonds again won the league's MVP award. During the next five years Bonds continued to perform well, and in 1996 he became the fourth baseball player in history to join the "300-300" club, having hit at least 300 home runs and stolen at least 300 bases over the course of his career. Two of the three men who preceded Bonds to the 300-300 mark were his father and his godfather. Barry Bonds is the only player in history to have surpassed 500 home runs and 500 steals.

Bonds's performance during the period from 1990 to 1998 alone probably would have earned him a berth in the Baseball Hall of Fame. After an injury-plagued season in 1999, however, Bonds showed dramatic improvements in his power-hitting abilities in 2000, hitting more home runs (forty-nine) and recording a higher slugging average (.688) than in any prior season in his career. In 2001 Bonds hit seventy-three home runs and recorded a .863 slugging average, breaking both the single-season home run record of Mark McGwire and Babe Ruth's single-season slugging record. Bonds won his fourth MVP award, and he received three more MVPs—more than any previous player—with power performances during the 2002, 2003, and 2004 seasons. During the 2007 season Bonds broke one of his sport's most hallowed records, exceeding the career home run total of Henry Aaron.

Bonds was accused of involvement in a steroid scandal in 2003. His personal trainer Greg Anderson served jail time for distributing steroids, a performance-enhancing drug, the use of which was by then viewed as improper. Bonds admitted using two performance-enhancing substances given to him by Anderson but maintained that he did not know that the substances were illegal. Allegations about performance-enhancing drugs have persisted and dogged Bonds's career, and he was not re-signed by the Giants for the 2008 baseball season. Bonds has two children by Susann Margreth Branco: Nikolai Lamar Bonds (b. 1989) and Shikari Bonds (b. 1991). He has one daughter, Aisha Lynn Bonds (b. 1999), with Liz Watson.

[*See also* Baseball; Mays, Willie Howard; *and* Sports.]

BIBLIOGRAPHY

Fainaru-Wada, Mark, and Lance Williams. *Game of Shadows: Barry Bonds, BALCO, and the Steroids Scandal That Rocked Professional Sports*. New York: Gotham Books, 2006.

"Major League Baseball Player Files." http://www.mlb.com. Major League Baseball maintains a Web site with extensive player performance records, including on-base and slugging percentages by season.

—JEFFREY WOMACK

BONTEMPS, ARNA (b. 13 October 1902; d. 4 June 1973), poet, anthologist, and librarian during the Harlem Renaissance. Born in Alexandria, Louisiana, from age three Arna Wendell Bontemps grew up in the Watts neighborhood of Los Angeles. After attending public schools there, he attended Pacific Union College in Angwin, California, graduating in 1923.

After college Bontemps, who had already begun writing, moved to New York City and became a teacher in Harlem. Like his contemporary Arthur A. Schomburg, Bontemps excavated the rich cultural heritage of the African American community and won recognition quite early. *Opportunity* magazine awarded Bontemps its Alexander Pushkin poetry prize twice: in 1926 for the poem "Golgotha Is a Mountain" and in 1927 for "The Return." Also in 1927 his poem "Nocturne at Bethesda" won *The Crisis* magazine's first-ever poetry contest. In 1926 he married Alberta Johnson; they had six children.

Bontemps's first published novel for adults, *God Sends Sunday* (1931), is the story of the struggles and adventures of the black jockey Little Augie—based on Bontemps's favorite uncle, Buddy—as he confronts overt and covert racism. Later, in 1946, Bontemps collaborated with Countée Cullen to create a musical, *St. Louis Woman*, based on this novel. In 1931 Bontemps and his family moved to Huntsville, Alabama, where he became a teacher at Oakwood Junior College. In 1932 his short story "A Summer Tragedy"—a moving account of the struggles and hopeless finality of the fate of a sharecropping couple in the Old South—won *Opportunity*'s short-story prize. Bontemps also began writing for children. With Langston Hughes he produced a colorful travel book, *Popo and Fifina: Children of Haiti*, in 1932; Bontemps self-published *You Can't Pet a Possum* in 1934 and *Golden Slippers: An Anthology of Negro Poetry for Young Readers* in 1941. *The Story of the Negro* (1948), a history book also written for children, was a Newbery Honor Book for 1949 and also won the Jane Addams Book Award in 1956.

Meanwhile in 1934 Bontemps was dismissed from Oakwood for his nonconformist political views and for his personal book collection, part of which the school forced him to destroy. He began writing *Black Thunder: Gabriel's Revolt: Virginia, 1800*—about the life and rebellion of an actual slave whose resistance failed because of the deceit of a human being and the inclement weather—in 1932 but had to finish it while living in his father's house in Los Angeles after leaving Oakwood. The novel was published in 1936 and was a critical success. Now living in Chicago, Bontemps wrote a third novel, *Sad-Faced Boy* (1937), funded by a grant from the Julian Rosenwald Fund. The positive reception of *Sad-Faced Boy* paved the way for two more fellowships, facilitating Bontemps's pursuit of a master's degree in library science, which he received in 1943 from the University of Chicago.

Soon after receiving his degree Bontemps became a librarian at Fisk University, where he stayed until his retirement in 1965. In 1966 he was briefly a professor at the University of Illinois before becoming the curator of the James Weldon Johnson Memorial Collection of Negro Arts and Letters at Yale University. Through all this time Bontemps continued to be a prolific writer. Bontemps diligently engaged the print mode to excavate the forgotten, neglected, and unclaimed blueprints of black heritage, transforming them into documented archives of African American history and culture. If the "New Negro" is emblematic of the spirit of the Harlem Renaissance, then Arna Bontemps was truly a New Negro and truly a renaissance man, always excavating, collecting, anthologizing, and chronicling, always creating

Arna Bontemps with Other Poets, 1945. At the Jackson State College festival, Mississippi. Back row, left to right: Arna Bontemps, Melvin Tolson, Jacob Reddix, Queen Dodson, and Robert Hayden. Front row: Sterling Brown, unidentified, Margaret Walker, and Langston Hughes. Melvin B. Tolson Papers, Prints and Photographs Division, Library of Congress

legacies for the future generations of African Americans through his work as a librarian, poet, short-story writer, historian, and anthologist.

For example, Bontemps wrote *100 Years of Negro Freedom* (1961), selected and introduced slaves' memoirs in *Great Slave Narratives* (1969), and wrote *The Harlem Renaissance Remembered: Essays, Edited, with a Memoir* (1972), an insightful retrospective on the movement and its time, place, and artists. Aware of the treasures of folk culture, Bontemps edited *The Book of Negro Folklore* (with Langston Hughes, 1958) and *American Negro Poetry* (1963). Bontemps also edited the biography of W. C. Handy, *Father of the Blues*, in 1941, proving the undeniable connection among music, Harlem, and the resurgence of the African American identity.

As a writer-in-residence at Fisk University in 1973, Bontemps further lived his commitment as an interactive artist of the community. He died there in Nashville, Tennessee, in 1973. The Arna Bontemps African American Museum and Cultural Arts Center in Alexandria, Louisiana, his birthplace, is a fitting tribute to the tireless energies of a man actively engaged in reclaiming and reviving African American culture.

[*See also* Harlem Renaissance; Hughes, Langston; *and* Literature.]

Bibliography

Fleming, Robert E. *James Weldon Johnson and Arna Wendell Bontemps: A Reference Guide*. Boston: G. K. Hall, 1978. Compares the important themes and issues in the lives and visions of Johnson and Bontemps.

Jones, Kirkland C. *Renaissance Man from Louisiana: A Biography of Arna Wendell Bontemps*. Westport, Conn.: Greenwood Press, 1992. Places Bontemps within the cultural context of the Harlem Renaissance.

Nichols, Charles H., ed. *Arna Bontemps–Langston Hughes Letters, 1925–1967*. New York: Dodd, Mead, 1980. An excellent and engrossing compilation.

—Navneet Sethi

BOONDOCKS. *See* McGruder, Aaron and *Boondocks*.

BOSTON. Boston has long described itself as "The Cradle of Liberty." But in the late nineteenth century and into the twentieth, pressures of national events, immigration, and the migration of African Americans from the rural South forced Boston to make adjustments to no longer being America's most important urban center and to deal with becoming less a cradle than a hotbed of racial and ethnic conflict.

Before 1895, most of Boston's black population lived in the West End, the area now called the North Slope of Beacon Hill. The first arrivals in 1638 were slaves, by the end of the Revolutionary War outnumbered by free blacks. The first federal census in 1790 showed Massachusetts as the only state with no slaves. After 1895, large numbers of African Americans began moving to the South End. By 1900, 30 percent of the black population lived there, and by 1914, 40 percent. Between 1880 and 1920, the total African American population in Boston went from 5,873, to 16,350, increased in part by migration from the South, especially Georgia and Alabama; and after World War I, by immigration from the West Indies.

For a time, from the 1890s to the death of the educator Booker T. Washington in 1915, Boston was at the center of the national debates over race. This was in part because Washington had strong connections to Boston, and he identified with the lifestyles of the upper-class whites, many of whom were descendents of Civil War–era abolitionists. The admiration was mutual—after his Atlanta Exposition Address in 1895, Harvard University awarded Washington a degree.

Boston's position at the center of the debates was due also to one from the upper crust of African American families in Boston. But William Monroe Trotter, a Harvard graduate, was a rebel to his proper class, willing to pick a fight anywhere for a cause, and he chose the cause of equal civil rights for all African Americans. He also had ample money from real estate holdings to found and maintain for three decades a voice for his radical thought in the newspaper called the *Boston Guardian*.

The keystone event in the conflict became known as the "Boston Riot" of 1903. Washington spoke in Boston on a sweltering July day. Trotter shouted questions at him, got thrown in jail, and wrote editorials from there, ending "Yours jailed but not extinguished." Thus Trotter's voice was for a time heard above all others as questioning accommodation to segregation, decreasing funding for schools, and decreasing political power. (Decrease was felt in Boston: from 1876 to 1895 a black person from the West End—then Ward 9—regularly filled a seat on the Boston Common Council. Then Democrats redistricted the old Republican neighborhood and blacks lost this representation.) Though he tried to join with others who also began to question Washington's stranglehold on black issues, such as the scholar W. E. B. Du Bois (also a Harvard graduate), Trotter was a loner, standing apart from the organization that emerged from the Washington opposition, the NAACP.

The culmination of Boston's and Trotter's central position in race issues came with opposition to D. W. Griffith's powerful and racist feature film, *Birth of a Nation*, in 1915. Others, including two African American women, became prominent in this fight and in the battle for universal suffrage. Josephine St. Pierre Ruffin (1842–1924), whose husband was a Harvard Law School graduate and a Boston judge, was a friend and associate of the fiery activist Ida B. Wells-Barnett. Ruffin and Maria L. Baldwin managed to organize eight hundred clubwomen to demonstrate against the showing of Griffith's film.

Between 1910 and 1970, 6.5 million African Americans were pushed from their homes in the rural South by discrimination and job loss and pulled to job opportunities in northern industrial centers. For Boston, the greatest influx occurred after the invention of the mechanical cotton picker in 1944 and the opportunities in World War II industries. There were some 23,000 African Americans in Boston in 1940; by 1950, there were 40,000, almost twice as many. Roxbury, which contained many of the neighborhoods where African Americans settled, was bulging at the seams and putting pressure on immigrant neighborhoods.

This rapid growth and ethnic/racial mix set the scene for the conflicted period of 1954 and the *Brown v. Board of Education* school desegregation decision to the 1980s, as the ramifications of that decision played themselves out through the courts and on the streets of Boston. African Americans in Boston were inspired to look at their own situation by the model of Martin Luther King Jr., by the Civil Rights Act of 1964 and the Voting Rights Act of 1965, and with a push for power and coalition-building begun with the election of Kevin Hagan White as mayor in 1967. His first term represented an advance in communication with and programs for the black community.

But after 1972, when the Boston branch of the NAACP filed a school suit in U.S. District Court (*Morgan et al. v. Hennigan et al.*), and 1974, when the federal judge W. Arthur Garrity ordered busing to achieve racial balance, White withdrew from the pressure of black demands and white fears and concentrated on downtown businesses and what was called the "New Boston."

By 1983 White retired, setting the stage for the election of Raymond L. Flynn, who became Boston's forty-sixth mayor and the first who was African American, on 2 January 1984. In September 1985, Dr. Laval Wilson became Boston's first African American superintendent of schools; following his appointment, Garrity returned control of Boston's schools from the court to the city's school committee. And in 1986, Bruce C. Bolling became the first African American elected as president of the City Council—the previous year he had signed a petition for a referendum on Roxbury seceding from Boston, called the Mandela Referendum.

Over the period of the busing conflict, the picture of African Americans and other minorities in Boston and its schools changed enormously. By 1985, out of 59,895 students in the system, 28,551 were black; 10,760 Hispanic; 4,742 Asian; and only 15,842 white, down from 45,000 ten years earlier. And out of all this conflict and change, the positive has been rewarded. In 2006, after four years as a finalist, the Boston school system won the Broad Prize for Urban Education, the largest prize in public education, granted by the Broad Foundation.

During his time in office, Flynn responded to many African American community needs—low-cost housing, cleaner streets, and more parks and recreational facilities. He created the Mayor's Office of Neighborhood Services and the Mayor's Hunger Commission and the Linked Deposit program with banks, in which banks holding city funds were obliged to invest in minority neighborhoods. He was reelected in 1987 with 67 percent of the vote. His national visibility led him to hope for a cabinet position when Bill Clinton was elected president in 1992, but he was instead offered the position of ambassador to the Vatican. This he accepted, and on his resignation as mayor he was succeeded by the City Council head Thomas Menino, Boston's first Italian American mayor.

Boston has been able to get over another hurdle, the crime rate following the arrival of crack cocaine in the inner city in 1988, with homicides at 152 in 1990, and the terrible relations with the police and the black community after the Charles and Carol Stuart murder case in 1989, when the man who turned out to have murdered his pregnant wife was easily able to convince officers at the scene that a black man had done it. Especially through cooperation between the police and black clergy, since then "the Boston Plan" of crime prevention and control has become a model for other cities. Over a six-year period from 1990 to 1996 Boston's homicide rate dropped 58.7 percent. There are other ways to look at Boston's progress through the race conflicts and achievements of the twentieth century. In the sports world, the African American baseball player Jackie Robinson was rejected by the Boston Red Sox in a tryout in 1945. The Red Sox, long owned by the Yawkee family, were the last major league team to be integrated, and that not until 1959, when Pumpsie Green, a utility infielder, was signed. By the period of 1979 to 1984, the team had only two black players; and well into the 1980s, when the exclusive Elks Club entertained the team, only the white players were allowed to attend.

And on the other, positive, side, the heroic who struggle to make a difference, there is the example of Elma Lewis, born in 1921, raised in Boston, who in 1950 founded the Elma Lewis School of Fine Arts in her six-room Roxbury apartment. By 1968, her school had grown into an umbrella institution called the National Center of Afro-American Artists, sheltering jazz and classical orchestras, a dance company, and a museum. By 1973 the school had its own building and over five hundred pupils, ages 4 to 75, and a large staff of choreographers, artists, costume designers, and music and drama teachers. Students paid a fifteen-dollar monthly tuition fee, but most of the support came from Lewis's perpetual fund-raising. In 1983 she was awarded a well-deserved Presidential Medal and Citation for the Arts.

At the end of the twentieth century, African Americans were the largest minority group, 140,305 in a city with a population of 589,141 and a majority of minorities. Fifty thousand new immigrants had arrived in Boston in the previous decade. Maybe a sign of the times and the future, interestingly, is the fact that over 18,000 Bostonians took the opportunity first introduced on the 2000 census to indicate that they belonged to more than one race.

[*See also Boston Guardian*; Boston Riot; Massachusetts; *and* Trotter, William Monroe.]

BIBLIOGRAPHY

Bryant, Howard. *Shut Out: A Story of Race and Baseball in Boston*. New York: Routledge, 2002. Perhaps enduring, this devastating look at racism as a kind of penance enabled the Red Sox to do better following its publication. Bryant is a Boston native.

Cromwell, Adelaide M. *The Other Brahmins: Boston's Black Upper Class, 1750–1950*. Fayetteville: University of Arkansas Press, 1994. This revised version of Cromwell's considerably earlier dissertation still includes a lot of valuable information covering a two-hundred-year period. She is a sociologist, and she writes with a mixture of history and sociology that can at times be very revealing.

Formisano, Ronald P. *Boston against Busing: Race, Class, and Ethnicity in the 1960s and 1970s*. Chapel Hill: University of North Carolina Press, 1991. Formisano focuses on the white antibusing people, looking for the social and economic roots of what he calls "reactionary populism."

Nelson, Adam R. *The Elusive Ideal: Equal Educational Opportunity and the Federal Role in Boston's Public Schools, 1950–1985*. Chicago: University of Chicago Press, 2005. This covers over thirty years of legal battles and tax strategies, with considerable relevance to urban schools. The failure of educational policy at all levels is put under a powerful microscope.

Schneider, Mark Robert. *Boston Confronts Jim Crow, 1890–1920*. Boston: Northeastern University Press, 1997. Especially good in looking at magazines, newspapers, and difficulties of the power elite in the Du Bois–Booker T. Washington controversy.

Sollors, Werner. *Blacks at Harvard: A Documentary History of African-American Experience*. New York: New York University Press, 1993. A collection including two hundred years of scholarly writings, poems, short stories, speeches, newspaper articles, letters, and other material.

—CAROLYN WEDIN

BOSTON GUARDIAN. The *Boston Guardian* weekly newspaper was initiated and financed in 1901 by the successful mortgage broker, member of the black elite, and Harvard graduate William Monroe Trotter (1872–1934), with the technical help of George W. Forbes of the Boston Public Library. Until Trotter's death in 1934, the paper would be synonymous with his outspoken speeches, articles, and editorials, though it also included national news, social notes, church items, sports, fashion, and even fiction. It would be continued after his death by his sister and her husband, finally expiring by 1960.

The *Guardian*'s and Trotter's most influential years were during the newspaper's first decade, particularly in protesting Booker T. Washington. An index of the first two years of the paper indicates the high number of anti-Washington pieces published. While W. E. B. Du Bois was still hesitant about attacking the "Wizard of Tuskegee," Trotter's *Guardian* editorials held nothing back—on 20 December 1902, in "Why Be Silent?" Washington was denounced as a traitor to the race. The attacks could be distressingly personal, such as Trotter's description of Washington's "harsh" features, "vast leonine jaws," "mastiff-like rows of teeth . . . clinched together like a vice," a "great cone" of a forehead, eyes "dull and absolutely characterless." Because of its vehemence—even with a circulation by 1904 only of about twenty-five hundred copies a week, peaking just over that by 1910—the *Boston Guardian* during its early years had an impact far disproportionate to its size and status as one of two hundred black papers in the United States.

Its impact was enhanced by events such as the Boston Riot in July 1903. Questions at a raucous, sweltering Washington speech in Boston got Trotter thrown in jail as, the *Guardian* said, a first martyr "in the cause for redemption from Booker Washington." The editor wrote from prison, signing letters, "Yours jailed but not extinguished," and friends got the paper out.

Since jail didn't work, Washington tried to defang the *Guardian* by financing competing papers and funding a libel lawsuit by a young Yale orator, William Pickens, later of the NAACP. The *Guardian* called Pickens "a little black freak" with "a monkey grin co-extensive with his ears," who had emasculated his manhood with a speech on Haiti suggesting it might be better run by white men.

Battle between the camps created increasing financial difficulties for the *Guardian*, but it also nudged Du Bois closer to Trotter, and in 1905 they cooperated in the Niagara Movement, with the *Guardian* as publicity outlet. But Trotter had difficulty working with anyone except immediate family members. His wife, Geraldine Louise ("Deenie") Pindell Trotter, became his greatest supporter and coworker on the *Guardian* after Forbes left in 1904 because of threats to his library employment and the paper's financial difficulties. Eschewing "help" from whites in the crusades he undertook for black rights over the following years, Trotter became increasingly independent in principle and language, but he was dependent to keep the paper going—both in its influence and financial support—on a further series of variously publicized battles.

The first of these was with Woodrow Wilson, who had inspired the *Guardian*'s support as a candidate for president but who moved precipitously to segregate federal offices after his inauguration in 1913. The second fight, 1915, was against the powerful, racist D. W. Griffith film *Birth of a Nation*. Trotter and the *Guardian* had been instrumental earlier in forcing its theatrical predecessor, *The Clansman*, from a Boston stage; now the editor flirted with group protest to fight the film version.

During World War I, military intelligence looked into "Negro subversion." Trotter—described as a "radical colored man"—announced a national convention for blacks, and the War Department, after failed attempts to intimidate and entice him, scheduled an alternative convention in advance of the Bostonian's "Colored Liberty Congress." Trotter alone of the many heads of black papers did not attend the government's sessions.

As the war was ending, Trotter's wife, who by that time was coeditor of the *Guardian*, died in the 1918 influenza epidemic. Trotter's work continued, however: he first attempted to get a large black delegation to the peace conference at Versailles, and when all were denied visas, he hung around the New York shipping docks for six weeks until he finally got a job as a cook on a boat to France. He arrived abroad too late to do any good on the peace settlement, but he worked to educate the French as to the status of the Negro in America.

Amazingly, even through the 1920s (when for several years the paper carried Deenie's picture and her widower's dedication: "To My Fallen Comrade . . . I dedicate the best that is in me till I die"), the *Guardian* missed only two weekly deadlines in Trotter's lifetime—once when he was sick and once when he was in Europe. The paper had no polish, no appealing journalistic touches. There were also no profits, in part because Trotter conscientiously refused ads for liquor or tobacco, and subscriptions were haphazardly collected, in part because of the relatively small Boston market. Once owner by inheritance of many Boston properties, Trotter mortgaged and then lost them all in support of his cause, his paper. But the *Guardian* held fast to unwavering principles of black independence, societal integration, and equal rights, and so it opposed, for example, both the establishment of separate training for Negro officers in World War I and Marcus Garvey's separatist back-to-Africa movement.

In his last years, Trotter's tongue lost some of its early sharpness, but even with softer words, his criticisms rang clear, castigating his people for superficiality ("all tinsel and no metal") and apathy. By the time of Trotter's death in 1934, on his sixty-second birthday, most probably by suicide, both he and his writing had become increasingly overworked and hectic. Trotter had deliberately placed the *Guardian* offices in the building of the abolitionist William Lloyd Garrison's *Liberator*. Two of a kind, committed to uncompromising protest and unchanging principles, they were desperately needed for a time and then seemingly not needed so much, as history swept by. But pendulums swing, and the stock in Trotter's unwavering protest has risen since the 1960s. The *Guardian* itself, however, became insignificant after Trotter's death, when it was continued primarily as a society paper by his sister and her husband, Maude Trotter Steward and Charles Steward (a dentist), until just after Maude's death in 1957.

[*See also* Black Press; Boston Riot (1903); Niagara Movement; *and biographical entries on figures mentioned in this article*.]

BIBLIOGRAPHY

Ellis, Mark. *Race, War, and Surveillance: African Americans and the United States Government during World War I*. Bloomington: Indiana University Press, 2001.

Fox, Stephen R. *The Guardian of Boston: William Monroe Trotter*. New York: Atheneum, 1970. The standard, authoritative biography of Trotter, putting the *Boston Guardian* into his life context.

Gatewood, Willard B. *Aristocrats of Color: The Black Elite, 1880–1920*. Bloomington and Indianapolis: Indiana University Press, 1990. Provides the Boston societal context for the *Guardian* and the Trotter family.

Pride, Armistead Scott, and Clint C. Wilson II. *A History of the Black Press*. Washington, D.C.: Howard University Press, 1997.

Smith, Jessie Carney. "William Monroe Trotter." In *Black Heroes*, edited by Jessie Carney Smith, pp. 605–610. Detroit, Mich.: Visible Ink Press, 2001. A readable story of Trotter and the *Guardian*.

West, Dorothy. *The Living Is Easy*. Boston: Houghton Mifflin, 1948. Presents a fictionalized version of the Boston political scene. The character of Simeon Binney and his paper, the *Clarion*, is based on Trotter and the *Guardian*.

—CAROLYN WEDIN

BOSTON RIOT. On 30 July 1903, two thousand people waited to hear Booker T. Washington speak at the African Methodist Episcopal Zion Church in Boston. Washington, the founding principal of the Tuskegee Institute in Alabama, was the most famous African American of his generation. He urged blacks to focus on industrial education, the pursuit of property, and the accumulation of wealth and to deemphasize demands for political rights until a firm economic base was attained in the black community.

Although "Bookerites," as supporters of Washington were called, had arrived in force, they were not alone. A group of "anti-Bookerites," led by Monroe Trotter, were scattered throughout the crowd. Trotter had come to confront Washington's political influence and refute his philosophy that black leaders who demanded immediate political and civil rights for blacks were extremists. A sense of foreboding filled the crowded hall.

The anti-Bookerites, or "Trotterites," hissed at the speaker, T. Thomas Fortune, when he praised Washington during the introduction. Fortune provoked the anti-Bookerite audience, prompting Granville Martin, an anti-Bookerite, to rush the podium, at which time several policemen removed him. Amid the confusion, someone sprinkled cayenne pepper over the platform. When Fortune resumed speaking he began to cough, while others on the platform began to sneeze. Fortune reached for the water pitcher only to find that it was empty. While Fortune caught his breath, Martin burst back into the meeting and began bellowing, hissing, and stomping his feet. Martin was arrested as Fortune continued his speech.

When William H. Lewis introduced Washington, shouts of opposition rang from the crowd, and brawling broke out throughout the hall. Encouraged, Monroe Trotter stood on a chair and heckled Washington. The police led Martin, Bernard Charles (one of the fighters), Trotter, and Trotter's sister Maude away. The men were arrested, but Maude was released.

When order returned to the hall, Washington gave a speech about his philosophy of thrift, the dignity of labor, the mastery of skilled trades, and the importance of building an economic base within the black community. Despite Washington's efforts to downplay it, the incident made national news.

While a case was being prepared against Trotter, W. E. B. Du Bois, a friend and former classmate of Trotter's, sided with the anti-Bookerites. Du Bois, a Harvard-trained PhD, used the publicity caused by the riot to advocate for the education of an intellectual elite—the Talented Tenth—and to demand full political, civil, and social rights for African Americans.

Despite having once been friends, Du Bois and Washington would not yield their positions. Though they complimented and respected each other, their philosophies had grown in different directions—probably the result of their backgrounds. Du Bois grew up in the North, attended integrated schools, had his undergraduate education funded by whites, and supported protest and studious pride. Washington had grown up as a slave in the South and favored humility and thrift.

For more than fifty years these two men symbolized the African American plight. The Boston Riot marked a divergence between the philosophy of economic and moral uplift and the philosophy of organized aggressive action to attain equal rights.

[*See also* Du Bois, W. E. B.; Fortune, Timothy Thomas; Talented Tenth; Trotter, William Monroe; Washington, Booker T.; *and* Washington–Du Bois Conflict]

BIBLIOGRAPHY

Norrell, Robert J. *Reaping the Whirlwind: The Civil Rights Movement in Tuskegee*. New York: Alfred A. Knopf, 1985.

Wolters, Raymond. *Du Bois and His Rivals*. Columbia: University of Missouri Press, 2002.

—PAULA COCHRAN

BOXING. Perhaps no sport has influenced African American culture and society more than boxing. Long before the sport was formalized, slaves worked as prize-fighters, sometimes gaining their freedom if they earned their masters enough money and prestige through their exploits in the ring. The first American to compete for the world heavyweight championship was Bill Richmond, a black man and former slave, who took on and lost to England's Tom Cribb in 1805. The former slave Tom Molineaux, who gained his emancipation through pugilism, also challenged Cribb for the crown, losing bouts in 1810 and 1811. Long before their official participation in other professional sports, African Americans were making their mark in the prize ring.

Although boxing was the most popular spectator sport in the United States from the late 1840s until the Civil War, blacks were excluded from the big-money contests that captured the public's attention. Although bouts between slaves were commonplace throughout the South, slave masters were reluctant to hold interracial contests because victories by African Americans in such bouts would help destroy the ideas of white supremacy that slavery depended upon for ideological sustenance. As a result, most black fighters toiled in obscurity, with little to gain other than small favors and privileges from their masters and prestige among their fellow slaves.

Following the Civil War, boxing standardized its rules and gained a degree of respectability it had previously lacked, although an unfortunate part of that respectability was dependent upon a strict prohibition against interracial fights, especially those involving African Americans. Nevertheless, black fighters, especially those who were born abroad, began to make major gains in the sport during the last decade of the nineteenth century. In fact, the first three black fighters to become either the world champion or widely accepted as the best fighter in his weight class were Anglo-Africans who competed in America.

They were George Dixon, the champion bantamweight (1890) and featherweight (1891) fighter who was born in Canada; Joe Walcott, the welterweight champion born in Barbados who won the title in 1901; and Peter Jackson from Saint Croix, West Indies, who held both the Australian and the British Commonwealth heavyweight titles in 1886 but was at first barred from fighting for the world heavyweight championship when the Americans John L. Sullivan and James J. Corbett refused to fight a black man—and risk their titles against him. In 1891, a year before he took the crown from Sullivan, Corbett fought to a draw with Jackson.

First African American World Champions. Always capable of competing at the sport's highest levels, African Americans finally began to win world championships near the turn of the twentieth century. The first African American to win a world title was Joe Gans, who in 1902 won the lightweight crown in a bout in Ontario. Gans also won the world welterweight championship in 1906. Despite Gans's excellence, some of his bouts and their aftermaths indicated the troubles that African American boxers faced. In his first try at the title, a 1900 match against the champion Frank Erne in New York, Gans quit during the twelfth round, ostensibly because of a cut. Later that year, probably in order to get another shot at the championship, Gans threw a match in Chicago against Terry McGovern, which caused the city council to ban the sport for the next twenty-six years. When he fought a rematch against Erne in Canada in 1902, Gans took the title by first-round knockout, which indicated to many that he had deliberately lost their initial bout.

Throughout the era, black fighters were forced to lose. Many times they were promised advancement within the sport if they lost, but often they were threatened with death unless they lost. Another indicator of the hostility surrounding black fighters was Gans's 1906 lightweight title fight in Nevada against the Danish boxer Oscar "Battling" Nelson. Following Gans's victory, there were outbursts of racial violence across the country. African Americans in a number of cities were attacked by whites who were angered by the result of the fight.

The second African American to win a world championship was Aaron Brown, but in a controversial bout. Brown defeated Walcott for the welterweight title in San Francisco in 1904 when the referee disqualified Walcott for no apparent reason. It was later discovered that the referee had wagered on Brown. As a result, Brown abdicated the throne, and it was returned to Walcott.

Because it was so difficult for blacks to get fights against whites, especially in the United States, and because most of the world championships were held by white Americans, African Americans were usually forced to fight each other. Some fighters were recognized as "colored champions," and there were often quasi-title bouts to determine who among black fighters was the best. One such man was the Canadian-born Sam Langford. One of the greatest boxers in the history of the sport, Langford never contested for a world championship. However, he took on almost all of his era's toughest fighters, including world champions who would meet him only in nontitle matches. Langford fought anywhere between 150 and 190 pounds and was a veteran of more than three hundred professional bouts from 1902 to 1926. Sadly, like so many of his peers, Langford suffered from poor health, was rendered blind from his years in the ring, and died penniless.

Although African Americans and other black fighters had become contenders and champions in almost all of boxing's weight divisions during the first decade of the twentieth century, they were still barred from fighting for the heavyweight championship. Although white supremacists were angered when blacks won titles, especially in bouts against whites, they took comfort from the maintenance of the color line in the heavyweight division. Then and now, the heavyweight championship is the most important title in boxing. Not only is it the most lucrative position in the sport, but it is also generally presumed that the heavyweight champion is the world's best fighter, capable of beating anyone else. For the huge number of Americans who believed that blacks were physically and mentally inferior to whites, even when confronted with evidence to the contrary in the lower weight divisions, the heavyweight title provided reinforcement for their worldview.

Like their predecessors Sullivan and Corbett, the next two white heavyweight champions, Bob Fitzsimmons and Jim Jeffries, also drew the color line. Jeffries, who won the title in 1899, was a particularly popular titleholder who held the crown until 1904, when he became the first heavyweight champion to retire undefeated. The next year, a fighter named Marvin Hart won a bout designated to determine Jeffries's successor. In 1906, however, Hart dropped a decision to the Canadian boxer Tommy Burns. Although Burns initially refused to defend his championship against a black fighter, he eventually yielded to public pressure and the promise of a huge payday to meet the African American contender Jack Johnson.

Jack Johnson Becomes Heavyweight Champion. As indicated by his becoming the first African American of the modern era to get a shot at the world heavyweight title, Jack Johnson was no ordinary man. In fact, it was Johnson's unique ability to promote himself—the very ability that soon made him perhaps the most hated person in America—that helped him break the color line. Johnson was a wonderful fighter who was recognized as the "colored" heavyweight champion. He had beaten many of the era's greats, including Sam Langford. But what really set Johnson apart from his peers was his creativity and personality. Johnson did everything in his power to convince people that Tommy Burns was afraid to fight him. Although the sporting public usually presumed that the world heavyweight champion was a standard bearer of white male supremacy, Johnson's relentless promotional campaign cast doubt in many people's minds about Burns's fitness for that role.

Johnson followed Burns around the world, calling his ability into question whenever he had the chance. If Burns was scheduled to go abroad for a title defense, Johnson would arrive there ahead of time. Johnson's antics, combined with his extraordinary ring record, made people want to see a heavyweight championship match between Johnson and Burns. Newspapers began calling for a Burns–Johnson fight. And when promoters offered Burns a very large purse to meet the black challenger, he had finally run out of excuses. The 1908 bout was held in Sydney, Australia. Perhaps the best indicator of the era's irrational racial ideologies was Burns's being a three-to-two betting favorite—in retrospect, remarkable odds considering that Burns is known as one of history's least capable heavyweight champions, while boxing experts consider Johnson one of the best.

Johnson demolished Burns, taunting him throughout the fight before finishing him off in the fourteenth round. Thus began what would become perhaps the most controversial championship reign in the history of boxing. Although Johnson could have defended his title against one of the many capable black fighters of the period, he refused to do so until his fifth year as champion, and did so only once. Furthermore, Johnson had been openly dating and eventually married a white woman, which broke one of the era's strictest taboos and inflamed the already tense racial climate that emerged following his title victory. As a result, African Americans were ambivalent about Johnson. Though the black public respected Johnson's initiative and his right to do what he pleased, many also felt that he brought undue scrutiny and pressure onto a people who already suffered vicious repression.

If blacks were unsure of the meaning of Johnson's title victory, whites were certain that it was dangerous. Almost immediately after the Burns–Johnson match the white press and public began its search for a "Great White Hope" to regain the crown from Johnson. The obvious choice was Jim Jeffries, even though he had retired undefeated in 1904.

In the history of boxing, there was probably never a bigger event than the 4 July 1910 championship match between Jack Johnson and Jim Jeffries in Reno, Nevada. Both fighters made huge money. The press churned out article after article about the tiniest details surrounding the fight. As in his title victory against Burns, Johnson dominated his opponent, taunting and slowly dismantling him before winning in the fifteenth round. Although the fight itself was important—shattering once and for all

Boxing Match. Jack Johnson in the ring with James J. Jeffries in Reno, Nevada, 4 July 1910. PRINTS AND PHOTOGRAPHS DIVISION, LIBRARY OF CONGRESS

the notion of innate white physical superiority—it was the contest's aftermath that truly indicated its social significance.

Blacks around the country were ecstatic about the fight's outcome, and their displays of joy incensed angry whites. That night, the Fourth of July, the United States was gripped by race riots that went unmatched in number and volume until the assassination of Martin Luther King Jr. nearly sixty years later. From Houston to Little Rock to Pueblo, Colorado, to New York City to Los Angeles, bands of whites assaulted, murdered, and lynched blacks who dared to celebrate Johnson's victory. In order to prevent people from seeing the fight, the U.S. Congress passed a law banning the interstate commerce of fight films. Various city councils passed similar laws barring movies of the bout from being shown. Whites became obsessed with stopping Jack Johnson.

Johnson's defiance of white authority figures and unwillingness to conform to the standards of humility demanded of blacks, along with the movement by whites to crush him, only intensified following his title victory. He purchased a black-and-tan club in Chicago, married a white woman and then another when the first committed suicide, drove fancy cars, dressed exquisitely, and traveled the world. Local and federal authorities realized that Johnson could not be stopped in the ring, so they used the law to punish him. They stripped his tavern of its liquor license. He was the first person indicted for violating the Mann Act (7 November 1912) by sending his white girlfriend a train ticket to go from Pittsburgh to Chicago (the act was meant to stop the interstate movement of prostitutes); he was convicted and sentenced to a year in prison.

But Johnson proved unstoppable. Not yet incarcerated, he fled to Europe and remained in exile for nearly seven years. While abroad he defended the title, acted, and fought a slew of exhibitions. Time and fast living eventually caught up with Johnson, and in 1915 he lost the title to Jess Willard, a white. In 1920 he surrendered to U.S. authorities and finally served his prison sentence. Johnson died in a car accident in 1946 while driving to New York to see a title defense by the second black heavyweight champion, Joe Louis.

Following Johnson's defeat, white heavyweight titleholders once again drew the color line. Black fighters in other divisions, including the Senegalese light heavyweight Battling Siki and the African American middleweight Tiger Flowers, won championships during the 1920s. But black heavyweight contenders like Harry Wills were barred from fighting for the title.

Amateur boxing during this era proved to be far more egalitarian than the prize ring. In 1923 the Golden Gloves debuted in Chicago as part of a plan to resurrect a sport that had been moribund in the city since the disgraceful Gans–McGovern match twenty years earlier. Other major cities around the country followed the Chicago model and began hosting tournaments to determine the best amateur fighters. From the beginning, African Americans faced few restrictions and were welcomed into Golden Gloves tournaments. One boxer who emerged from these contests was Joe Louis, who became the first black fighter to receive a heavyweight title shot since Johnson was deposed.

Joe Louis: The Second Black Heavyweight Champion. Just as it took a person with the audacity of Jack Johnson to break boxing's color line, it took someone equally special to undo the legacy that Johnson and the whites who hated him had left behind. Joe Louis was that person. After a successful amateur career, Louis turned professional in 1934. Louis's backers knew that it would be an uphill struggle for a black heavyweight, and they insisted that he follow certain rules of conduct that would make him acceptable enough to white fans and boxing officials that he could one day get a shot at the title. They instructed Louis never to taunt his opponents or smile after he defeated them, as Johnson had. They instructed him never to be photographed with a white woman, or to go into a nightclub alone, as Johnson had. They instructed him never to badmouth an opponent, as Johnson had. Additionally, they refused to allow Louis to throw fights, as so many blacks had been forced to do. Louis and his backers wanted him to be perceived as having a sterling character, and they did what was necessary to counter the biases that faced the era's black heavyweights.

Louis's rise to the top was rapid. He reeled off twenty-two consecutive victories in less than a year before being matched with the former champion Primo Carnera. The bout was significant not only because it marked Louis's debut in New York, then boxing's capital, but also because of the political symbolism that some people invested in the match. Carnera was Italian, and his 1935 bout with Louis occurred while the fascist dictator Benito Mussolini was preparing to invade Ethiopia. Louis destroyed Carnera and became a hero to many African Americans. He then reeled off four more wins against top opposition, including the former champion Max Baer, before being knocked out in 1936 by the former champion Max Schmeling who was a huge underdog in the match. The loss to Schmeling was only a temporary setback, however: Louis quickly returned to the ring and earned a championship match against Jim Braddock in 1937, thus becoming the first African American to fight for the heavyweight title since Johnson had lost the crown over twenty years earlier. Louis dominated the match, gaining the championship by knockout and electrifying black America, which celebrated his victory. Unlike after Johnson's fight against Jeffries, however, whites did not respond violently. They accepted the new champion, which testified to the care that had gone into crafting Louis's public image.

Louis's 1938 rematch with Schmeling, a German, was the most important of his career and one of the most politically charged matches in boxing history. Following his victory over Louis, Schmeling had become a symbol of white racial superiority to the Nazis, who had begun to commit atrocities against Jews and were threatening to take over Europe. At a meeting with Franklin D. Roosevelt, the president told Louis that he hoped he would defeat Schmeling. Louis did not disappoint. With incredible fury he demolished Schmeling in the first round to retain his heavyweight title.

Most of the press and American public celebrated Louis as a national hero, a defender of American values, and a representative of democracy and freedom. African Americans were especially elated because it seemed for the first time that the rest of America began to realize what they already knew, that the country would grow only stronger as blacks fully participated in its institutions.

Louis's standing as a beloved figure was intensified when he voluntarily enlisted in the U.S. Army during World War II. He temporarily halted his career, instead fighting a series of charity matches that benefited the armed forces and staging exhibitions for troops stationed in Europe. Although never again a great fighter following his tour of duty, Louis held the championship until 1948. He finally retired in 1951. Louis's twenty-five title defenses over eleven years made him both the longest reigning and the most active heavyweight champion in the sport's history. He died in 1981.

Greats of the 1930s, 1940s, and 1950s: Armstrong, Robinson, and Moore. Although Louis dominated the headlines during the 1930s and 1940s, several other African American fighters emerged during the era whose greatness made them into boxing legends and heroes beyond the ring. Henry Armstrong made his professional debut in 1931. Over a fourteen-year career, fighting incredibly tough competition, he amassed 151 wins against 21 losses and 10 draws. During the late 1930s Armstrong went on an unprecedented run that, as of 2008, was still unmatched in boxing history. He won the world featherweight championship in 1937, defeating Petey Sarron by knockout. Six months later he won a unanimous decision against the great Barney Ross to claim the world welterweight championship, which he went on to defend sixteen times. In his next fight, he took a split decision from the world lightweight champion Lou Ambers, thus becoming the first and only man simultaneously to hold world championships in three divisions.

As great as Armstrong was, most boxing experts agree that the best pound-for-pound fighter in history was Sugar Ray Robinson, who campaigned from 1940 to 1965 and had a record of 175 wins, 19 losses, and 6 draws, with the great majority of the losses coming at the end of his career. From 1940 to 1951, Robinson was virtually unbeatable, at one point holding a record of 128 wins, 1 loss, and 2 draws, with the only loss being to the hall-of-fame middleweight Jake LaMotta, who outweighed Robinson by fifteen pounds. In 1946, Robinson won the world welterweight championship. In 1951 he knocked out LaMotta to take the world middleweight championship. In 1952 he nearly won the world light-heavyweight championship, but he collapsed from heat exhaustion at the end of the thirteenth round of a fight that he was winning easily against the champion Joey Maxim.

Although things had gotten better for black fighters during the 1930s and 1940s, the career of Archie Moore proved that they still had to overcome obstacles that their white counterparts did not. For five years during the late 1940s and early 1950s, Moore was the number one light-heavyweight contender. Yet Moore was continually passed over by champions who knew that they would lose the title if they took him on. Finally, in 1952, Maxim granted the thirty-nine-year-old Moore a title shot, but only under outrageous terms: of the $100,000 purse, Moore received only an $800 share.

This was the price that black fighters sometimes had to pay in order to advance in the sport. Such considerations were not unique to Moore. For example, in order for Joe Louis to receive his 1937 title shot, he had to agree to give up to the champion 10 percent of his net earnings over the next ten years of his career. Moore never lost the light-heavyweight title in the ring, holding it for approximately ten years before being stripped of it for failing to defend the crown. Moore retired in 1963 with an amazing record of 187 wins, 23 losses, and 11 draws, and, as of 2008, he held the all-time mark for knockouts with 132.

The Civil Rights Era: The Political Significance of the Heavyweight Title. One of the most anticipated heavyweight title fights in history took place in 1962 between two African Americans, the champion Floyd Patterson and the number one contender Sonny Liston. With the civil rights movement gaining momentum and spreading throughout the country, fights involving African Americans took on heightened importance as people nationwide sought to make sense of the political activity that seemed to be making headlines daily. The Patterson–Liston fight vividly brought into focus the feelings engendered by the era. Many who were threatened by the intensity of the civil rights movement took comfort from the title reign of the humble Patterson, whom they considered to be a proper black representative. Liston, on the other hand, who had a criminal past, an intimidating manner, and a devastating knockout record, was feared by those same people. Such feelings spread all the way to the White House: President John F. Kennedy, in a meeting with Patterson, told him that he hoped he would beat Liston. Nonetheless, the seemingly invincible Liston knocked out Patterson in the first round to become champion.

Boxing fans were shocked in 1964 when Liston lost the championship to a brash young fighter named Cassius Clay. Although an Olympic gold medalist and undefeated in nineteen fights, Clay was a substantial underdog to defeat the champion. But Clay dominated the bout and won when Liston did not answer the bell for the seventh round.

Although many people had disliked Clay because of his flamboyance, it was his actions after winning the championship that turned much of the American public against him. Following the bout he announced that he was a member of the Nation of Islam, a racial separatist group that professed its desire to live independently from whites. Such a position directly countered the mainstream civil rights philosophy of integration. Clay was then given a new name, Muhammad Ali, by the Nation of Islam leader Elijah Muhammad. Although most of the public refused to acknowledge the name change, it symbolized that the champion was no longer willing to accept the social and political conventions demanded of him by many whites and blacks.

While Ali continued to defend his title and prove himself to be a great fighter, public animosity toward him intensified when in 1966 he declared his opposition to the Vietnam War and refused to be drafted into military service. Following his indictment for draft evasion in 1967, even though he had not yet been tried, state boxing commissions nationwide stripped Ali of his boxing license. He was convicted and given the maximum sentence, five years in jail and a fine of $10,000.

Although Ali remained out of prison while appealing the conviction on the grounds that he was a religious minister who should be exempt from military service, his inability to get a boxing license prevented him from fighting in the United States. Furthermore, because his passport was taken away when he was convicted, he could not fight abroad. For three and a half years Ali was barred from professional boxing at what would have been the peak of his fighting abilities, since he was twenty-five years old in 1967.

Ali's legal team sued to regain his boxing license, and he returned to the ring in 1970, winning a pair of tune-up bouts before taking on Joe Frazier—who meanwhile had emerged as Ali's successor—the following year. In one of the most anticipated bouts in boxing history, which pitted two undefeated champions against each other, Frazier won a fifteen-round decision. Despite the loss, however, 1971 proved to be joyous for Ali when the Supreme Court overturned his conviction. Furthermore, as public opinion began to turn against the Vietnam War, many of Ali's former detractors began to realize the valor of his stand.

Reinvigorated and free to box both in the United States and abroad, Ali began his quest to regain the championship and defeated a series of contenders. In 1973, however, the thirty-one-year-old Ali lost a decision to the upstart Ken Norton, who broke the former champion's jaw. Many people felt that Ali was finished as a serious challenger for the heavyweight title, which Frazier had lost by a devastating knockout to the fearsome George Foreman. Ali avenged his losses to Norton and Frazier, however, and became the logical choice to face Foreman. But Ali was a substantial underdog against the younger man, who had dismantled each of the two fighters, Norton and Frazier, who had defeated Ali.

The fight between Foreman and Ali took place in 1974 in Zaire; it was the first heavyweight title fight ever held in Africa, which lent it political and social significance. To the shock and delight of fans around the world, Ali stopped Foreman in the eighth round to regain the championship. Following the title victory, President Gerald Ford invited Ali to be honored at the White House, and the champion accepted. In less than ten years he had gone from one of the country's most reviled public figures to one of its most beloved. The Zaire fight was also significant because it was promoted by Don King, who became the first African American to promote a heavyweight championship fight. Since the 1970s King has been one of the sport's leading promoters. Ali held the crown until 1978 and retired in 1981.

Boxing after Ali. Although no fighters since the 1970s have achieved the kind of social significance that Jack Johnson, Joe Louis, and Muhammad Ali did, several African Americans have captured the public's attention with their boxing skill and charisma. Most of the best fighters of the 1980s were black, including Ray Leonard, Thomas Hearns, Aaron Pryor, Marvin Hagler, and Larry Holmes. Leonard deserves special attention because he helped fill the void that was left following Ali's retirement, becoming the sport's biggest draw and a mainstream cultural hero who captured the hearts even of people who were not boxing fans.

Following his gold medal performance in the 1976 Olympics, Leonard made his professional debut in a nationally televised fight against Luis Vega that generated great interest, and he quickly became a star. "Sugar Ray" won the welterweight crown in 1979, beating Wilfred Benitez by a fifteenth-round technical knockout, but he lost the belt the following year to the former lightweight champion Roberto Duran. Leonard avenged his defeat in November 1980, completely outclassing Duran and making him quit during the eighth round in what is known as the "No Mas" ("no more") fight.

Leonard proved his greatness by defeating Hearns in 1981, but he retired shortly thereafter because of a detached retina. The lure of the sport proved too great, however, and Leonard alternated between ring activity and retirement over the next fifteen years. In a hugely anticipated 1987 fight he won a narrow decision over the middleweight champion and three-to-one favorite Hagler, cementing his legendary status. Leonard's ascent following Ali's retirement was significant because he gave fans a noncontroversial African American figure to celebrate in the wake of the politically charged civil rights era.

As Leonard's career wound down, the spotlight again shone upon the heavyweights as an electrifying young fighter named Mike Tyson demolished all of the division's contenders en route to winning the championship in 1986. He held the title for three and a half years before losing it to James "Buster" Douglas in what is widely believed to be the biggest upset in boxing's history. The loss was early evidence of what became a decades-long downward spiral for Tyson.

Tyson was in prison between 1992 and 1995 after being convicted of rape. He returned to the ring following his parole and again rose to the top of the heavyweight division, but he lost the title to Evander Holyfield in 1996. Their rematch the following year degenerated into controversy when Tyson, frustrated by his inability to dominate Holyfield, was disqualified after biting off a portion of Holyfield's ear. Tyson continued to fight until 2005 but had become a shell of his former self, serving as cannon fodder for lesser boxers who once would not have lasted three rounds with him. Tyson's tumultuous personal life has continued to get the better of him, as evidenced by public battles with drug addiction, mental illness, and bankruptcy.

George Foreman's story is as uplifting as Tyson's is depressing. Foreman, who retired from the sport in 1977, became a born-again Christian following what he perceived to be a near-death experience. After working as an ordained minister over the next decade, he returned to the ring in 1987 to pursue what most observers felt was a foolish crusade to regain the crown. Foreman reeled off a series of victories against weak opposition, and in 1991, at the age of forty-two, fought valiantly in a title bout against Evander Holyfield before losing a unanimous decision.

Foreman pressed on over the next two years, but it appeared that the Holyfield bout had sapped him; he was unable to recapture the vitality he had shown in that contest. Although the overwhelming opinion was that Foreman should retire, he was granted a 1994 title bout against Michael Moorer, who had defeated Holyfield for the crown. Most observers believed that Moorer would have an easy time with the faded Foreman, and for nine rounds they were correct. But in the tenth round, in a stunning turn of events, Foreman knocked Moorer out with a single punch. At forty-five years old, twenty years after losing the title to Ali, Foreman became the oldest fighter to capture the world heavyweight championship. It was his final magic moment in the ring, and a number of grueling bouts over the next few years convinced him to retire permanently in 1998.

George Foreman's wonderful story, however, was not finished. He became a corporate pitchman, and during the late 1990s a kitchen product called the George Foreman Lean Mean Fat-Reducing Grilling Machine became a worldwide sensation. In 1999, Foreman received one of the largest promotional deals ever given to a professional athlete when Salton Inc. purchased the rights to the indoor grill and to Foreman's endorsement for $127.5 million. He continued working as a motivational speaker.

[*See also* Sports *and biographical entries on figures mentioned in this article*.]

BIBLIOGRAPHY

Ashe, Arthur R., Jr. *A Hard Road to Glory, Boxing: The African-American Athlete in Boxing*. New York: Amistad, 1993. A comprehensive overview of the experiences of African American prizefighters.

Boyd, Herb, with Ray Robinson II. *Pound for Pound: A Biography of Sugar Ray Robinson*. New York: Amistad, 2005. A detailed life story of Sugar Ray Robinson.

Cottrell, John. *Muhammad Ali, Who Once Was Cassius Clay*. New York: Funk & Wagnalls, 1967. An in-depth study of the early part of Muhammad Ali's life and boxing career.

Early, Gerald, ed. *The Culture of Bruising: Essays on Prizefighting, Literature, and Modern American Culture*. Hopewell, N.J.: Ecco Press, 1994. A collection of well-written essays that connect boxing with other areas of American society and culture.

Erenberg, Lewis A. *The Greatest Fight of Our Generation: Louis vs. Schmeling*. New York: Oxford University Press, 2006. A detailed social history of Joe Louis's rematch with Max Schmeling.

Gilmore, Al-Tony. *Bad Nigger! The National Impact of Jack Johnson*. Port Washington, N.Y.: Kennikat Press, 1975. A summary and analysis of contemporary newspaper reactions to Jack Johnson.

Gorn, Elliott J., ed. *Muhammad Ali: The People's Champ*. Urbana: University of Illinois Press, 1995. A collection of scholarly essays that analyze Ali's historical and social impact.

Hauser, Thomas. *Muhammad Ali: His Life and Times*. New York: Simon & Schuster, 1991. An oral history covering Ali's life and career that serves as the definitive Ali biography.

Marqusee, Mike. *Redemption Song: Muhammad Ali and the Spirit of the Sixties*. London: Verso, 1999. A scholarly work that positions Ali in relation to the political climate of the civil rights era and the Black Power movement.

Mead, Chris. *Champion: Joe Louis, Black Hero in White America*. New York: Scribner's, 1985. A survey and analysis of contemporary newspaper and periodical coverage of Joe Louis.

Newfield, Jack. *Only in America: The Life and Crimes of Don King*. New York: William Morrow, 1995. A critical look at the first African American to become a major boxing promoter.

Olsen, Jack. *Black Is Best: The Riddle of Cassius Clay*. New York: G. P. Putnam, 1967. A psychological study of Muhammad Ali and his role in American society.

Roberts, Randy. *Papa Jack: Jack Johnson and the Era of White Hopes*. New York: Free Press, 1983. A study of the social and psychological impact of Jack Johnson's boxing career.

Sammons, Jeffrey T. *Beyond the Ring: The Role of Boxing in American Society*. Urbana: University of Illinois Press, 1988. A historical overview of the racial and social dimensions of professional boxing in American life.

Ward, Geoffrey C. *Unforgivable Blackness: The Rise and Fall of Jack Johnson*. New York: Alfred A. Knopf, 2004. A detailed chronicle of the life and career of Jack Johnson.

—MICHAEL EZRA

BRADLEY, ED (b. 22 June 1941; d. 9 November 2006), broadcast journalist and news correspondent. Edward Rudolph Bradley Jr. was born and raised in Philadelphia, Pennsylvania. He was raised by his mother Gladys Bradley, who taught him the value of hard work. He spent part of each summer in Detroit, Michigan, with his father Edward Bradley Sr., who owned a restaurant. Bradley graduated from Cheyney State College (now Cheyney University of Pennsylvania) in 1964 with a degree in education. During his senior year Bradley was introduced to radio by Georgie Woods, a popular radio DJ, who gave a talk to his class about using community resources to reach out to children. After his graduation, Bradley began teaching and worked for free at Philadelphia's WDAS radio station in the evenings. He offered to cover the riots in 1965 and used a pay phone to call the radio station to report on the event by interviewing community leaders. When Bradley returned to the station, his supervisors sent him out with a tape recorder. The radio station was impressed with his work and hired him for $1.50 an hour. While at WDAS, Bradley reported on other riots and protests in the city and covered one of the speeches given by Martin Luther King Jr.

Bradley realized that teaching was not for him. He would not be able to obtain an administrative position without a master's degree. However, he could not work two jobs and go to graduate school. Consequently he gave up his career as a teacher and focused on getting a job in broadcasting.

In 1967 WCBS, the CBS-owned New York radio station, hired Bradley. He later quit this job and moved to Paris, where he joined CBS News as a stringer in September 1971; he was transferred to the Saigon bureau a year later. In April 1973 Bradley was named a CBS News correspondent, and he was wounded while on assignment in Cambodia. He was assigned to the CBS News Washington bureau in June 1974. In March 1975 he returned to Indochina to report on the fall of Cambodia and Vietnam. In 1976 he returned to Washington and covered Jimmy

Carter's successful campaign for U.S. president. Bradley became CBS's first black White House correspondent when he followed Carter to the White House.

During his tenure Bradley held several positions at CBS News. He anchored the *CBS Sunday Night News* and the news magazine *Street Stories*. He served as a principal correspondent for *CBS Reports*.

In 1981 Bradley married Priscilla Coolidge; they divorced in 1984. Bradley joined the *60 Minutes* broadcast as a correspondent during the 1981–1982 season. His duties also included anchoring and reporting hour-long specials. His work was recognized with numerous awards, including the Robert F. Kennedy Journalism Award, the Lifetime Achievement Award from the National Association of Black Journalists, the George Peabody Award, and the Alfred I. DuPont–Columbia University Award. He won a total of nineteen Emmy Awards, including one for a segment about the reopening of the investigation into the murder of Emmett Till fifty years after Till's death and another for an interview with Lena Horne. Bradley died of leukemia at Mount Sinai Hospital in New York, survived by his wife, Patricia Blanchet.

[*See also* Journalism, Print and Broadcast.]

BIBLIOGRAPHY

CBS News. "Ed Bradley, 1941–2006." 60 Minutes: Bios. http://www.cbsnews.com/stories/1998/07/08/60minutes/bios/main13501.shtml.

McCoy, Machala. "Bradley, Ed(ward) (R.)." Revised by Alan Jalowitz. Pennsylvania Center for the Book, Pennsylvania State University. http://www.pabook.libraries.psu.edu/LitMap/bios/Bradley__Ed.html.

Public Broadcasting Service. "Modern Journalists: Ed Bradley." http://www.pbs.org/blackpress/modern_journalist/bradley.html.

—SHANTEL AGNEW

BRADLEY, TOM (b. 29 December 1917; d. 29 September 1998), lawyer, activist, and first African American mayor of Los Angeles. Thomas J. Bradley was born to Lee and Crenner Bradley in Calvert, Texas. The Bradleys moved to Los Angeles in 1924; there his father worked as a porter on the railroad and his mother worked as a maid. His father abandoned the family shortly after they all moved out West.

Bradley excelled in athletics at Polytechnic High School in Los Angeles, serving as captain of the track team and making the all-city football team. Bradley graduated in 1937 and attended the University of California at Los Angeles on a track scholarship. He dropped out during his junior year to join the Los Angeles Police Department (LAPD) in 1940 as a lieutenant; at the time he was the highest-ranking African American police officer in Los Angeles. In 1941 he married his childhood sweetheart, Ethel Mae Arnold. The Bradleys eventually had three daughters, Lorraine, Phyllis, and another who died in infancy. In 1956, having gone to night school, Bradley graduated from Southwestern University Law School.

In the 1950s Bradley was actively involved in the Crenshaw Democratic Club, a reformist group that was part of the California Democratic Council and had ties to the presidential candidate Adlai Stevenson. The club's members were mostly white and Jewish, which put Bradley at odds with the African American community and its leaders. Bradley was elected to the Los Angeles City Council in 1963, representing the predominantly white Tenth District. During his time on the council he criticized both racial politics in the LAPD and also its handling of the 1965 Watts Riot.

In 1969, Bradley ran for mayor against the incumbent Sam Yorty. Bradley led throughout the campaign but lost after being portrayed by Yorty as a dangerous radical. He ran again in 1973 with the widespread support of African American and white liberals and moderates. He won, thus becoming the first African American mayor of Los Angeles during a time when the African American population there was 15 percent.

During Bradley's five terms as mayor—from 1973 to 1993—Los Angeles International Airport was renovated, the Port of Angeles became the biggest and busiest in the country, and the city's major businesses were revitalized. Los Angeles hosted the 1984 Summer Olympic Games and passed Chicago to become the country's second most populous city. Bradley was offered a cabinet post by President Jimmy Carter but refused it. Then Walter Mondale, the Democratic nominee for president in 1984, seriously considered Bradley for vice president before choosing Geraldine Ferraro.

Bradley ran unsuccessfully for governor of California in 1982 and 1986, both times against the Republican George Deukmejian. The 1982 election was close, with Bradley the projected winner; he lost the election by less than 1 percent of the 7.5 million votes cast. The false projections gave rise to the term "Bradley effect," which refers to the tendency of white voters to tell pollsters that they are undecided or are likely to vote for a black candidate but then actually vote for his white opponent.

In 1992 the city erupted in three days of riots following the acquittal of four white police officers who had been caught on videotape beating a black motorist, Rodney King. The riots cost more than fifty lives and $1 billion in damages. Deeply affected by the riots, Bradley announced that he would not seek a sixth term as mayor. After leaving office Bradley joined the law firm Brobeck, Phleger and Harrison, specializing in international trade. In 1998, at age eighty, Bradley died of a heart attack.

[*See also* Los Angeles; Rodney King Riots; *and* Watts Riot.]

Bibliography

Pearson, Richard. "Tom Bradley Dies at 80." *Washington Post*, 30 September 1998.

Riordan, Richard. "The Man Who Got Things Done: Mayor Tom Bradley, 1917– 1998." *Newsweek*, 12 October 1998.

—Jamal Donaldson Briggs

BRAITHWAITE, WILLIAM STANLEY (b. 6 December 1878; d. 8 June 1962), poet, anthologist, and literary critic. The second of five children, Braithwaite was born into a genteel upper-middle-class Boston family. His father, William Smith Braithwaite, was a member of a prominent and wealthy British Guiana family, while his mother, Emma DeWolfe, was the descendant of North Carolina slaves. During his early childhood Braithwaite enjoyed a life of comfort and privilege. However, following his father's death in 1886, the family quickly sank into poverty. Emma Braithwaite was forced to take menial jobs, while young William had to leave school at the age of twelve to seek employment. He took a typesetting job with a Boston publishing house, which introduced him to the world of literature. Braithwaite was especially attracted to the work of British Romantic poets like John Keats, William Wordsworth, and Robert Burns. Largely self-educated, Braithwaite read widely, and with great determination pursued a career as a poet. Publishing initially in Boston area newspapers, in 1904 he brought out his first book of poems, *Lyrics of Life and Love*. Two years later he became a literary writer for the *Boston Evening Transcript*.

Although as a poet Braithwaite had limited talent, in the early twentieth century he became an influential scholar and critic of poetry as well as a publisher of poetry and literary works. Through his literary column, he reviewed and commented on most emerging poets, black and white, in the early twentieth century. Shortly after launching his column, he brought out his first of three anthologies of poetry, *The Book of Elizabethan Verse* (1906). These collections established his reputation as a literary scholar. More significantly, between 1913 and 1929 he edited an annual collection of new poetry, the *Anthology of Magazine Verse*. Inclusion in Braithwaite's annual anthology was a mark of distinction for young poets. Among those who received Braithwaite's stamp of approval were Robert Frost and Amy Lowell; through this venue he also brought black poets like Langston Hughes, Countée Cullen, and James Weldon Johnson to the attention of the white literary establishment.

Braithwaite was somewhat of an anomaly among African American literary figures in the early twentieth century. As a poet he took his literary inspiration from Keats and avoided racial themes and anything that would label him as a black poet. He also situated much of his career in white institutions and gained his reputation as a literary critic and promoter of poetry, not as an African American scholar. This does not mean that he separated himself from African Americans. On the contrary, he was a significant figure in the Harlem Renaissance and offered young black writers advice, assistance, and often a place to publish (although his publishing operations often required subvention, or financial support, from the author). Also, his poetic aesthetic and critical values did not conform to those of most of the participants in the Harlem Renaissance. In writing of Claude McKay and the other poets of the emerging movement, he observed "Negro poetic expression hovers for the moment, pardonably perhaps, over the race problem, but its higher allegiance is to Poetry—it must be so." (*The Crisis*, September 1924). For Braithwaite the highest accomplishments in poetry came from the expression of aesthetic beauty, not political polemic or even racial identity.

In 1935 Braithwaite accepted a position as a professor of creative literature at Atlanta University. In 1946 he left the university and retired in Harlem. He spent the rest of his life working on his autobiography and other book projects. He died in Harlem in June 1962. In addition to his reputation as a literary scholar, in 1918 the NAACP bestowed on him its highest honor, the Spingarn Medal, which recognized African Americans for distinguished merit and achievement.

[*See also* Harlem Renaissance *and* Literature.]

Bibliography

Braithwaite, William Stanley. "The House under Arcturus." *Phylon* 2 (1941): 9–26, 121–136, 250–259; and *Phylon* 3 (1942): 31–44, 183–194. Incomplete autobiography.

Braithwaite, William Stanley. "The Negro in American Literature." *The Crisis* (September 1924). This piece outlines Braithwaite's views on the way in which African Americans are depicted in literature and discusses the work on black writers including those of the Harlem Renaissance. It appears in a number of anthologies, including Sondra Kathryn Wilson, editor, *The Crisis Reader: Stories, Poetry, and Essays from the N.A.A.C.P.'s* Crisis Magazine (New York: The Modern Library, 1999).

Braithwaite, William Stanley. *The William Stanley Braithwaite Reader*. Edited by Philip Butcher. Ann Arbor: University of Michigan Press, 1972. This contains a collection of Braithwaite's major work.

Hutchinson, George. *The Harlem Renaissance in Black and White*. Cambridge, Mass.: Belknap Press of Harvard University Press, 1995. See pages 350–360. Hutchinson provides a detailed discussion of Braithwaite's role as a anthologist and a publisher, and assesses the impact he had on both black and white poets.

Wintz, Cary D. *Black Culture and the Harlem Renaissance*. College Station: Texas A&M University Press, 1996. First published 1988 by Rice University Press. See pages 130–135. This work discusses Braithwaite primarily in terms of his role as a literary critic and his impact on writers of the Harlem Renaissance.

—Cary D. Wintz

BRANTON, WILEY (b. 13 December 1923; d. 15 December 1988), lawyer and civil rights activist. Wiley Austin Branton was born in Pine Bluff, Arkansas. His father, Leo Branton, owned and operated a prosperous taxicab business, and his mother, Pauline Wiley, was a schoolteacher and a graduate from the Tuskegee Institute. Branton's education at the Arkansas Agricultural, Mechanical, and Normal College (now the University of Arkansas at Pine Bluff) was interrupted in 1943, when he was drafted into the U.S. Army and fought in World War II, working in intelligence and bridge construction.

Branton returned to Pine Bluff to inherit his father's business. Horrified by the discrimination he had witnessed in the segregated army, Branton became active in civil rights, joining the Arkansas State Conference of NAACP Branches. His efforts to instruct local African Americans how to mark election ballots during a 1948 voter registration drive resulted in a misdemeanor conviction for "teaching the mechanics of voting."

Branton married Lucille McKee in 1948. The couple had six children. Branton had resumed his undergraduate studies after the war, and graduated with a degree in business administration in 1950. In the same year, he entered the University of Arkansas School of Law, in part to protest the Arkansas governor Ben Laney's plans to found another graduate school for African American students rather than allow them to register at the University of Arkansas.

Branton received his degree in 1952, the third African American student to graduate from the School of Law. He then opened a law office in Pine Bluff and practiced privately. In 1956, working with the NAACP's Legal Defense and Educational Fund, Branton filed suit against the Little Rock, Arkansas, school board for failing to integrate the public schools after the U.S. Supreme Court's *Brown v. Board of Education* decision. Branton's suit was heard by the Supreme Court as *Cooper v. Aaron* in 1958, and ultimately led to the desegregation of Central High School in Little Rock. During the case, Branton and his family received repeated death threats, and crosses were burned on his lawn.

Branton's national prominence after the suit led to his appointment in 1962 as the first executive director of the Southern Regional Council's Voter Education Project. The project registered over six hundred thousand African American voters in southern states. In the early 1960s Branton also continued his private practice, representing freedom riders and other voter registration activists throughout the South.

In 1965 Branton was appointed the executive secretary to President Lyndon B. Johnson's Council on Equal Opportunity. He was charged with coordinating implementation of the Civil Rights Act of 1964. The council was dissolved in 1965, and President Johnson asked Branton to serve as his representative in the Department of Justice as a special consultant to the attorney general.

In 1967 Branton left the Department of Justice to be the executive director of the United Planning Organization, which provided social services programs in Washington, D.C. Branton moved to the Alliance for Labor Action in 1969 in order to create social service programs across the country. Branton returned to private legal practice in 1971, founding a law firm in Washington, D.C. There, he successfully obtained a court order protecting FBI surveillance files on the Reverend Martin Luther King Jr. from destruction.

Branton was dean of Howard University School of Law from 1977 to 1983, then returning to private practice until his death.

[*See also* Legal Profession *and* NAACP Legal Defense and Educational Fund.]

BIBLIOGRAPHY

Kilpatrick, Judith. *There When We Needed Him: Wiley Austin Branton, Civil Rights Warrior*. Fayetteville: University of Arkansas Press, 2007.

—ERIN L. THOMPSON

BRAUN, CAROL MOSELEY. *See* Moseley Braun, Carol.

BRAWLEY, BENJAMIN (b. 22 April 1882; d. 1 February 1939), educator, social historian, and literary critic. The son of a prominent Baptist minister, Benjamin Griffith Brawley demonstrated a precocious zeal for formal learning and had already studied Greek, Latin, Victor Hugo, and Shakespeare when he entered Atlanta Baptist College (subsequently Morehouse College) at the age of thirteen. After a brief stint teaching in a one-room schoolhouse in Florida, Brawley returned to Morehouse as an English instructor and simultaneously pursued further academic training in white universities, as did many early-twentieth-century African American intellectuals. He earned a second bachelor's degree from the University of Chicago (1906) and a master's degree from Harvard University (1908). Brawley held significant academic positions at Morehouse College (1902–1910, 1912–1920), Shaw University (1923–1931), and Howard University (1910–1912, 1931–1939). He wrote prolifically about African American history and artistic and literary accomplishments from the colonial era to his own time. Brawley's long academic career was interrupted only once, in 1920–1922, when he traveled to Liberia to examine and report on that country's society and then lived briefly in Boston, where he was ordained a Baptist minister.

As a narrator of the historical past, Brawley focused on the triumphs of the African American over the violent humiliations of slavery and the degradations of the Jim Crow era; he described universally praiseworthy accomplishments of African American heroes and heroines. Writing for a white audience in 1918, Brawley asserted in *Your Negro Neighbor*, "The Negro daily suffers indignities as make the very words Liberty and Democracy a travesty," and concluded, "We call upon our country for a new consecration—to law, to order, to justice" (n.p.). His *A Social History of the American Negro* (1921) and *The Negro in Literature and Art in the United States* (1918) presented accounts of African American gifts and achievements designed to be inspiring to whites and African Americans alike. Strongly influenced by W. E. B. Du Bois's notion of the Talented Tenth and impressed by the standards and mores of the black intellectual elite of which he became a part by his early twenties, Brawley reiterated his understanding of the New Negro's opportunities and responsibilities in many books and articles; his fundamental views did not change even as younger African American critics and writers began to reject them.

Adhering to increasingly outdated anthropological notions of race character, Brawley identified the particular gifts of African Americans as lying in the creative arts. He exhorted poets and novelists to reveal the nobility of the Negro race by striving to achieve the beauty and elegance of Dante, Shakespeare, and Milton. Brawley decried the development of experimental free verse and the exploration of themes and stories of the urban lower classes.

By the late 1920s Brawley was increasingly perceived by innovative writers and intellectuals of the Harlem Renaissance as trenchantly conservative. "Brawleyism" came to stand for rigidly genteel pedantry. Brawley, in turn disturbed by the works of the "new realists," excoriated their pernicious low literary standards and coarse sensationalism. In addition he lamented the culturally skewed focus on Harlem that celebrated lurid jazz and gin parties and elevated the life of the cabaret to a "fetish" while ignoring the steady and productive lives of other African Americans in other places.

Brawley's difficult estrangement from intellectual leaders of the Harlem Renaissance was clear in his 1928 refusal to accept the second place Harmon Award for excellence in education. Believing that most previous winners had produced only mediocre work, he chose not to be associated with the prize.

Though contentiousness characterized Brawley's dealings with many Harlem writers in the last fifteen years of his life, respect for his academic leadership and scholarship in the African American educational community was deep. With John Hope and Samuel Howard Archer, Brawley oversaw the development and expansion of a rigorous classical humanist education at Morehouse College. Academic colleagues and students appraised his teaching career positively and noted that in all situations he conducted himself according to principles of Christian idealism and justice. Brawley's career sheds useful light on the tensions between the generation of African American intellectuals trained primarily in the late-nineteenth-century southern historically black colleges and universities, on the one hand, and the younger generation of artists, writers, and activists working in the rapidly changing urban environment of Harlem between the world wars, on the other.

[*See also* Education; Historians; *and* Literature.]

BIBLIOGRAPHY

Brawley, Benjamin Griffith. *The Negro in Literature and Art in the United States*. New York: Duffield, 1930. A survey of African American historical literary and artistic achievements and an appraisal of contemporary writers and artists in light of the historical survey.

Brawley, Benjamin Griffith. *A Social History of the American Negro, Being a History of the Negro Problem in the United States, Including a History and Study of the Republic of Liberia*. New York: Macmillan, 1921. An overview of Brawley's understanding of African American social, economic, and political history.

Brawley, Benjamin Griffith. *Your Negro Neighbor*. New York: Macmillan, 1918. Valuable as a direct appeal to white readers to understand the impact of World War I on race relations in the United States.

Parker, John W. "Benjamin Brawley: Teacher and Scholar." *Phylon* 10, no. 1 (First Quarter 1949): 15–24. A balanced mid-twentieth-century survey of Brawley's career.

—JEAN BALLARD TEREPKA

BRIGGS, CYRIL (b. 28 May 1888; d. 18 October 1966), one of the earliest black members of the Communist Party and the editor of several key radical periodicals. He was also the founder of the African Blood Brotherhood (ABB), a secret paramilitary group that advocated militant black self-defense against oppression.

Cyril Valentine Briggs was born on the Caribbean island of Nevis. A child of mixed race, he was fair-skinned enough that he would later describe himself as the "angry, blond Negro." Briggs immigrated to the United States in 1905, and soon he became involved in radical politics. Although he had a severe speech impediment that prevented him from speaking on behalf of his causes, he compensated by sharpening his skills as an author. He began working with the *Amsterdam News* in 1912. While with the newspaper, he wrote increasingly militant articles arguing against American involvement in World War I and for establishing an autonomous black nation within the United States.

Interest in "race patriotism" led Briggs to establish the *Crusader* magazine in 1918. Particularly after the Red Summer of 1919, in which a series of deadly race riots occurred, the periodical began to espouse a policy mixing militant black nationalism with socialism. At that time, the journal also became the organ for the ABB. The group consisted almost entirely of West Indians, including the writer Claude McKay from Jamaica; W. A. Domingo from Jamaica; and Richard Moore from Barbados.

Briggs's militancy increased after the Tulsa riot of 1921 when more than 150 blacks were killed. Accusations against Briggs made in the *New York Times* were never proven (and never denied by Briggs), but the publicity provided proved to be a short-term boon to the organization, increasing their numbers to perhaps as many as three thousand. Ultimately, however, the organization was unable to sustain itself. The *Crusader* folded in 1922 as a result of growing government pressure and diminishing financial sources. The ABB itself was dissolved in 1925, with most of its members already having joined the Communist (Worker's) Party.

Despite the demise of the ABB, Briggs continued his radical activities. He headed the Crusader News Agency, which disseminated radical news items to more than two hundred newspapers. He also published articles in various Marxist periodicals including the *Daily Worker* and the *Communist*. In addition, he edited the *Negro Champion*, the voice of the Communist-supported American Negro Labor Congress, and the *Negro Liberator*. Briggs was also at the forefront of the controversial movement toward establishing an independent black homeland within the United States as advocated by the Comintern (the international arm of Soviet Russia's Socialist Party) in 1928.

Briggs's continued support of black nationalism caused him to clash with the communists, who maintained that black inequality would be eliminated only when class divisions ended. Briggs's differing perspectives led to his expulsion from the party in 1939. He moved to Los Angeles in 1942 and was reinstated in the party in 1948. While living in California, Briggs worked as an editor with the *Los Angeles Herald-Dispatch*, the *People's World*, and the *California Eagle*. He continued his lifelong dedication toward gaining equality for blacks until his death from a heart attack in 1966.

[*See also* African Blood Brotherhood; Communism and African Americans; McKay, Claude; Moore, Richard; *and* Tulsa Riot.]

Bibliography

Hill, Robert A., ed. *The Crusader*. 3 vols. New York: Garland, 1987.

James, Winston. *Holding Aloft the Banner of Ethiopia: Caribbean Radicalism in Early Twentieth-Century America*. New York: Verso, 1998.

Solomon, Mark I. *The Cry Was Unity: Communists and African Americans, 1917–1936*. Jackson: University Press of Mississippi, 1998.

Turner, Joyce Moore. *Caribbean Crusaders and the Harlem Renaissance*. Urbana: University of Illinois Press, 2005.

—Louis J. Parascandola

BRIMMER, ANDREW F. (b. 13 September 1926), economist and educator. Some individuals are important because they exemplify the historical past, while others are important because they embody generational change toward social progress. As the first African American governor of the U.S. Federal Reserve Board (1966–1974), Andrew Felton Brimmer is both the former and the latter.

The life story of this extraordinary leader began on 13 September 1926 in Newellton, Louisiana. The son of Andrew Brimmer Sr., a sharecropper, and Vellar Davis Brimmer, a warehouse worker, Brimmer picked cotton as a child in rural northeastern Louisiana while attending segregated public schools. Rather than allowing the hardships of poverty and racial injustice to discourage him, Brimmer used these experiences as a motivating force. Early on he was determined to earn a college degree so that he could serve in positions where he could help others.

Brimmer graduated from high school in 1944 and joined the U.S. Army, eventually becoming a staff sergeant. After his discharge in 1946, a federal education grant for military personnel provided him with the opportunity to enroll at the University of Washington. There Brimmer earned both a BA and an MA in economics. With a growing interest in foreign economies, he studied in India on a Fulbright fellowship and drafted several scholarly articles on the Indian economy. In 1957 he earned his doctorate in economics from Harvard University. Shortly thereafter he served as a professor at Michigan State University. During his five-year tenure there he published his first book, *Life Insurance Companies in the Capital Market* (1962).

Later Brimmer taught economics at the University of Pennsylvania. He also became an assistant secretary for economic affairs with the U.S. Department of Commerce. His governmental service reached its pinnacle when in 1966 President Lyndon B. Johnson appointed him to fill a vacancy on the distinguished seven-member board of governors of the Federal Reserve System. The Federal Reserve is widely considered the nation's bank, and the board of governors its bankers.

Much of Brimmer's government life and by extension his public service was focused on improving unemployment rates and addressing historical patterns of racial discrimination—namely, discrimination against African American–owned businesses and hiring practices that discriminated against minorities. More broadly, while a visiting professor in the graduate school of business administration at Harvard University in 1974, Brimmer suggested an income-tax reduction plan to President Gerald R. Ford to stimulate the economy and to help end the 1973–1975 recession. After modest modification, Congress enacted the provision, which accounted for $8.1 billion of the $22.8 billion tax reduction passed early in 1975.

For more than forty years Brimmer served as an economic resource for Americans in general and African Americans in particular. He served on the board of economists of *Black Enterprise*, a monthly magazine geared toward African American financial matters. In this capacity he shared his experiences, perspectives, and economic knowledge, especially as they related to the African American business community. Through his economic consulting firm, moreover, Brimmer not only worked effectively with clients on investments, public relations, and crisis management but also continued to be a leading spokesperson for the African American economic community, proposing solutions to monetary challenges, championing prosperity, and emphasizing his personal credo: never be bound by the limits of convention.

[*See also* Economic Life *and* Education.]

BIBLIOGRAPHY

Brimmer, Andrew F. "Economic Cost of Discrimination against Black Americans." In *Economic Perspectives on Affirmative Action*, edited by Margaret C. Simms. Washington, D.C.: Joint Center for Political and Economic Studies, 1995.

Brimmer, Andrew F. *The World Banking System: Outlook in a Context of Crisis*. New York: New York University Press, 1985.

Quartey, Kojo A. *A Critical Analysis of the Contributions of Notable Black Economists*. Burlington, Vt.: Ashgate, 2003. This solid interdisciplinary work reviews the foremost African American economists of the twentieth century, highlighting the contributions of such leaders as W. E. B. Du Bois, Thomas Sowell, and Brimmer (chapter 10), to name a few.

—DARIUS V. ECHEVERRÍA

BROADCAST INDUSTRY, AFRICAN AMERICANS IN THE. The broadcast industry in the United States was born in the early 1920s as a result of the mass production of radios. It expanded significantly in the 1950s with the addition of television and has since become a constant presence in American life. From the birth of broadcasting, African Americans have played a vital part in the industry as performers, executives, and consumers.

In the 1920s recorded music found its first widespread audience through airplay on the earliest radio stations. Although jazz music, which was pioneered and usually performed by blacks, was popular at the time, angry whites quickly denounced what they considered to be the decadence and lewdness inherent in the music. As a result, black jazz musicians found themselves receiving less airplay than their white counterparts did—even though these counterparts often performed the same material. Still, African American musicians like Fletcher Henderson, Louis Armstrong, and Duke Ellington received significant exposure from radio stations like WHN in New York, which aired live broadcasts from jazz nightclubs like the Cotton Club in Harlem in the late 1920s.

Censorship in early radio was common. NBC radio featured Sunday morning gospel broadcasts that, in addition to music, featured sermons from guest speakers each week. These were carefully monitored by the network, which would "blue-pencil" out any remarks that were deemed at all controversial. According to William Barlow's *Voice Over*, when Arthur Barnett Spingarn, a white lawyer who was the president of the NAACP from 1940 to 1965, departed significantly from a prewritten speech during a 1938 broadcast by criticizing policies of racial discrimination, the network quickly dropped the speech segment from the program.

In 1929 Jack Cooper, a black vaudeville performer, launched his comedy show, the *All-Negro Hour*, on WSBC in Chicago. The show featured a variety of black entertainers and led to a series of comedy serials. In 1932 the program's piano player quit shortly before a broadcast; Cooper put a record player next to his microphone and played recorded music instead, marking one of the earliest performances of prerecorded music on the radio. Cooper began frequently playing records on the show, defining the modern concept of the disc jockey (DJ), playing records and talking between songs.

The African American singer Paul Robeson was another pioneer in radio history. A 1939 CBS broadcast of his performance of the song "Ballad for Americans," which criticized racism and segregation as un-American, was such a success that it was turned into one of the first-ever live albums. Robeson was popular throughout World War II, though his progressive politics and public calls for peace with the Soviet Union after the war led to his being ostracized by the show-business community.

In the later 1940s a new market of radio emerged, broadcasting African American rhythm-and-blues (R&B) music on white-owned stations that catered to black audiences. Black DJs like Jesse "Spider" Burke from KXLW in Saint Louis and Ramon Bruce from WHAT in Philadelphia popularized the new style of music and won loyal followings.

Though R&B music eventually crossed over to teenage white audiences—who accepted the music and especially its musical descendant rock and roll—black DJs were less fortunate. Only blacks who were able to sound "white" were allowed to work on mainstream radio, and they were usually fired if major sponsors were alerted to their true ethnicity.

Amos 'n' Andy. *Amos 'n' Andy* was a serialized radio comedy that became a national phenomenon throughout the United States, running in various formats from 1928 until the 1960s. The title characters were performed by the white actors Freeman Gosden and Charles Correll, and the two also wrote the scripts. *Amos 'n' Andy* was rooted in the racist tradition of minstrel shows, which in the late nineteenth century showcased white men in blackface paint rendering stereotyped and unflattering portraits of blacks.

The show began as *Sam 'n' Henry*, debuting on WGN in Chicago in January 1926. The program was popular locally, prompting Gosden and Correll to propose the idea of recording each episode of the show and then selling to radio stations throughout the United States the rights to rebroadcast them—essentially originating the concept of syndication. WGN was wary of sharing the rights to the program, so Gosden and Correll left that station and were hired by Chicago's WMAQ, which accepted the idea. Having lost the rights to *Sam 'n' Henry* in the process, the duo reimagined the program as *Amos 'n' Andy*. The show, now heard nationwide, was an immediate sensation from its first broadcast in March 1928. Protests began several weeks after the show's debut because of its portrayal of blacks as lazy and unintelligent. In the early 1930s the NAACP issued a statement saying, "The sooner they are off the air the better it will be for the Negro. Radio points to one side of the Negro, the worst side, most frequently" (quoted in Andrews and Julliard).

Despite such protests, *Amos 'n' Andy* was popular with prominent American figures, including Will Rogers, Charles Lindbergh, and President Herbert Hoover. The show's popularity continued through the Great Depression and World War II, and in 1951 *Amos 'n' Andy* was adapted into one of the first televised sitcoms.

On CBS television the show's protagonists—Amos, Andy, and their friend George "Kingfish" Stevens—were performed by the African American actors Alvin Childress, Spencer Williams, and Tim Moore, respectively. The televised version of *Amos 'n' Andy* was perceived by many, including the NAACP, as giving an even more unflattering portrayal of blacks than the radio show. *Amos 'n' Andy* ran for two seasons on TV before it was canceled, at the height of its popularity, because of continuing protests. The seventy-eight filmed episodes of the series were shown in syndication until 1966 but have seldom been broadcast since.

Television and the Rise of BET. For many years *Amos 'n' Andy* was emblematic of the portrayal of blacks on television. In the 1960s things began to change with live newscasts of the civil rights movement. By the 1980s blacks had become some of the most popular and powerful personalities on television, with performers like Bill Cosby and Oprah Winfrey drawing millions of viewers to their programs.

In 1965 Cosby, a successful standup comedian, became the first African American to star in a television drama when he was cast in the program *I Spy*. His sitcom *The Cosby Show*, which debuted in 1984 on NBC, was one of the first sitcoms to be about a stable, middle-class black family. A hit, the show ran until 1992.

Oprah Winfrey started her career at the age of nineteen as a news anchor for WLAC (now WTVF) in Nashville, Tennessee. In 1984 she moved to Chicago, where she hosted the program *AM Chicago*—which soon, because of its host's rapid rise in popularity, changed its name to *The Oprah Winfrey Show*. The program became nationally syndicated in 1986 and has since been one of the highest-rated shows on television. Winfrey is famous for her influence over her audience; books showcased on the program routinely sell millions of copies thanks to Winfrey's endorsements alone.

Blacks also found success in public media. In 1980 Jennifer Lawson joined the Public Broadcasting System (PBS) as a liaison between the network and filmmakers it hired. In 1989 she became the executive vice president of PBS, prompting a profile of Lawson in the *New York Times* (20 October 1989) to cite her as the most powerful executive in public television.

In 1979 Robert L. Johnson, a former congressional aide and lobbyist for the National Cable Television Association trade group, announced the formation of Black Entertainment Television, a cable network that would run for two hours each week on the USA cable television network. BET launched in January 1980 with a broadcast of the film *A Visit to a Chief's Son* (1974). The network found a warm reception with black audiences and by 1984 had expanded to feature twenty-four-hour programming. By 1991 BET was reaching millions of cable subscribers. In November of that year Johnson took the company public on the New York Stock Exchange.

In 1981, because the first cable music channel, MTV, did not often broadcast videos by black performers, BET launched *Video Soul*, which showcased promotional music videos from black artists. Exposure from BET helped launch the careers of many early hip-hop artists,

Television Writer. Shonda Rhimes, creator and writer of the television series *Grey's Anatomy*, poses with the cast member Sandra Oh after the series won the Golden Globe for best drama series, 2007. Photograph by Fred Prouser. REUTERS

including Kurtis Blow and Run-DMC, as well as the careers of future R&B superstars like Mary J. Blige and Boyz II Men.

By the mid-1990s BET was broadcasting gangsta-rap videos, which often displayed images of violence and drug use. Such videos became the predominant fare on the channel and drew criticism from many blacks, including members of the NAACP and the network's own talk show host Tavis Smiley. A particularly harsh critic was the cartoonist Aaron McGruder, author of the comic strip *The Boondocks*. His strips frequently lampooned BET and criticized its lack of morals in its attempts to sell advertising time.

In the late 1990s, as a result of the deregulation of laws governing the ownership of broadcasting companies, a series of large mergers took place that minimized the numbers of black-owned television and radio stations. In 2000 BET was purchased for $3 billion by Viacom, which also owned the cable networks MTV and Nickelodeon. As a result of the deal, Robert Johnson joined Oprah Winfrey as one of the few African American billionaires. Despite smaller numbers of black-owned broadcasting networks, increasing numbers of African Americans continue to thrive as executives and artists.

[*See also Amos 'n' Andy*; Black Entertainment Television; Film and Television Depictions of African Americans; Journalism, Print and Broadcast; Radio; Radio and Television Stations, African American; Stereotypes of African Americans; Television; *and biographical entries on figures mentioned in this article*.]

BIBLIOGRAPHY

Andrews, Bart, and Ahrgus Juilliard. *Holy Mackerel! The Amos 'n' Andy Story*. New York: E. P. Dutton, 1986.

Barlow, William. *Voice Over: The Making of Black Radio*. Philadelphia: Temple University Press, 1999.

Pulley, Brett. *The Billion Dollar BET: Robert Johnson and the Inside Story of Black Entertainment Television*. Hoboken, N.J.: John Wiley & Sons, 2004.

—RONALD ENICLERICO

BROOKE, EDWARD (b. 26 October 1919), lawyer, politician, and writer. Born and raised in Woodrow Wilson's Washington, D.C., Edward William Brooke III proved to be a trailblazer who built a legal and political career that exceeded the socially imposed limits on blacks in America. At the height of his career, Brooke represented a social justice wing of the Republican Party that has disappeared. Even in his retirement he continues to be a pioneer as an advocate for cancer detection in men.

Brooke grew up in a middle-class household; his father was a lawyer for the Veterans Administration. Brooke attended the segregated public schools of Washington, graduating from Dunbar High School in 1936 and from Howard University in 1941. Shortly thereafter the U.S. Army drafted Brooke. During his tenure in the military he served with the 366th Combat Infantry Regiment and defended enlisted men in military court cases. Following the deployment of his unit to Italy, Brooke was promoted to captain and received the Bronze Star and Distinguished Service Award.

After his discharge from the army, Brooke enrolled in Boston University Law School. He became editor of the *Boston University Law Review* and earned both an LLB and an LLM by 1949. Subsequently Brooke practiced law in the Roxbury section of Boston and became active in such civic organizations as the Greater Boston Urban League, the Boston chapter of the NAACP, and the American Veterans of World War II.

Although his initial foray into politics was unsuccessful, by 1961 he became chair of the City of Boston's Finance Committee. In the following year Brooke won election as Massachusetts attorney general. As the state's top lawyer he targeted government corruption, housing discrimination, and organized crime, among other things. He garnered significant publicity as he conducted the investigation that apprehended the serial killer known as the "Boston Strangler." Despite his popularity among the electorate, Brooke faced criticism on a number of fronts. Some leaders within the state Republican Party, all of whom were white, chided Brooke for his ambition when he announced that he would run for a seat in the U.S. Senate. On the other hand, local civil rights activists criticized Brooke for his relative conservatism, perhaps the thing that made him a viable political candidate in the first place.

In the face of resistance from within his own political party, Brooke won election to the Senate in 1966, becoming the first African American to serve in Congress since Reconstruction. He was reelected in a landslide victory in 1972. Brooke's career in the Senate was shaped by his intelligence, generally liberal sensibilities, and ability to cross partisan lines in a period when the overwhelming majority of African Americans had abandoned the Republican Party.

Brooke helped shape the 1968 Civil Rights Act and was an opponent of the escalation of the Vietnam War. Following a fact-finding trip to Asia, Brooke advocated an end to the bombing campaign and a cessation of the use of napalm. He later called on the United States to end trade with South Africa because of its apartheid policies. Brooke also challenged the expansion of nuclear arsenals and worked to improve relations between the United States and the People's Republic of China. Although a faithful Republican, Brooke advocated for low-income housing, the development of mass-transit systems, and an increased minimum wage. In addition he fought President Richard Nixon's nomination of two anti–civil rights judges to the U.S. Supreme Court and was the first senator to call on Nixon to resign in the wake of the Watergate scandal.

Later a well-publicized, contentious divorce and charges of financial impropriety blemished Brooke's image, and he lost his reelection bid in 1978. Since his departure from public life Brooke has worked with nonprofit organizations including the National Low-Income Housing Coalition and the Alpha Phi Alpha fraternity's World Policy Council. In 2002 Brooke was diagnosed with breast cancer and underwent a radical mastectomy. Since that time he has become a spokesperson for the early diagnosis and treatment of male breast cancer. In the early twenty-first century Brooke resided in Warrenton, Virginia, a suburb of Washington.

[*See also* Boston; Congress, African Americans in; Massachusetts; *and* Republican Party.]

BIBLIOGRAPHY

Brooke, Edward W. *Bridging the Divide: My Life*. New Brunswick, N.J.: Rutgers University Press, 2007.

Brooke, Edward W. *The Challenge of Change: Crisis in Our Two-Party System*. Boston: Little, Brown, 1966.

—GEORGE WHITE JR.

BROOKINS, H. HARTFORD (b. 1933), prominent African Methodist Episcopal (AME) bishop and political counselor. Hamel Hartford Brookins spent the latter half of the twentieth century attempting to integrate American politics and spur international black economic development. Born the son of sharecroppers in Yazoo, Mississippi, Brookins found early institutional success and spiritual support from the AME Church through his education in Ohio at Wilberforce University and Payne Theological Seminary. While attending graduate school in Wichita, Kansas, Brookins led an interracial ministerial alliance that defused the violence following the Supreme Court's school-desegregation mandate in 1954 with *Brown v. Board of Education*. This mediating prowess led to Brookins's appointment to the First AME Church of Los Angeles, where he remained for more than ten years.

During his time in Los Angeles, Brookins cultivated his pastoral skills while developing his political interests, establishing First AME as the symbolic center of black Los Angeles. From the multimillion-dollar church complex he developed, Brookins worked to quell the Watts riot in 1965, led antiwar protests throughout the 1960s, and spoke out against the growth of police brutality. Brookins also used his position to encourage and endorse major African American political candidates, including Tom Bradley, the three-term mayor of Los Angeles, Congressman Floyd H. Flake from Queens, New York, and the presidential candidate Jesse Jackson. For these men's campaigns Brookins not only supplied financial support but also served as campaign chairman and personal adviser. Although Jackson's 1984 presidential bid was unsuccessful, his impressive showing in the polls demonstrated Brookins's deft management skills and paved the way for other black candidacies.

While Brookins continued to labor on behalf of individual black politicians, he also continued to ascend the ranks of the AME Church. After being named their ninety-first bishop in 1972, Brookins headed a number of prominent districts within the church, including the Seventeenth Episcopal District, which ultimately incorporated five countries in central Africa. Brookins's support of the black freedom fighters in Zimbabwe increased his international profile and cemented his position as an arbiter for justice and black political independence. Throughout the 1970s and 1980s he increased the American and African membership ranks of the AME Church while cultivating the church's social programming, including setting up the People's Trust Fund, which raised millions to provide loans to black entrepreneurs, scholarships to seminary students, and emergency funds for the elderly.

In 1985, Brookins was appointed Presiding Prelate of the Second Episcopal District, a region that includes the District of Columbia, North Carolina, Maryland, and Virginia. Brookins labored to improve the schools in his district that had majority-black enrollment, but he also found himself embroiled in controversy. In 1993, Bishop Brookins was asked to resign from his post after alleged financial mismanagement. He was transferred to a churchwide position, where he continued to fight for black political enfranchisement through his involvement with Jackson's Operation PUSH, for Third World liberation through his board membership with TransAfrica (an influential lobbying group in Washington, organized by African Americans), and for business enterprise as director of the South Los Angeles Development Corporation. In 2002, Brookins was honored by Jesse Jackson and former president Bill Clinton for "his vision and ability to see beyond what appears to be impossible" (quoted in McRae).

[*See also* AME Church *and biographical entries on figures mentioned in this article*.]

Bibliography

Goodstein, Laurie. "AME Council Replaces Washington's Bishop after Questions about Finances." *Washington Post*, 2 November 1993, p. A10.

McRae, F. Finley. "Brookins Tribute Draws Hundreds." *Los Angeles Sentinel*, 16 May 2002, p. A1.

—Kathryn Lofton

BROOKS, GWENDOLYN (b. 7 June 1917; d. 3 December 2000), poet and community activist. Gwendolyn Brooks was born in Topeka, Kansas, to David Anderson Brooks, a janitor, and Keziah Wims Brooks, a former schoolteacher. The house in Kansas belonged to Brooks's grandmother, and soon the family moved to their home in Chicago, Illinois, where Gwendolyn grew up in the city's South Side with her parents and younger brother, Raymond. For most of her life she remained associated with the South Side. Brooks attended Forrestville Elementary School, and it was during these earliest years of her education that her mother began to encourage in her an interest in poetry and verse recital.

Brooks attended Hyde Park High School for a time but later transferred from that mostly white school first to an all-black school and later to an integrated one. Though her home life afforded her some stability and happiness, Brooks was keenly aware of the social and racial divisions that threaded through even the African American community. She was, it seemed, too dark-skinned and her hair not straight enough to mingle fully and comfortably with those who formed the higher strata of the city's black community.

Spurred on, Brooks continued to write, and she was prolific. By the time that she was in her mid-teens she had produced scores of poems, many of which drew upon the people and places most familiar to her. Largely through her mother's urging, she came to meet the great Harlem Renaissance writers James Weldon Johnson and Langston Hughes, the latter of whom she found especially encouraging and with whom she struck up an enduring correspondence and friendship. Soon she was publishing her work in a number of publications, including the *Chicago Defender*, one of the country's most noteworthy black newspapers, though she ultimately failed to procure the full-time staff positions she sought. By the time she left the *Defender* to attend college, she had seen some one hundred of her poems in print.

In 1936 Brooks graduated from Woodrow Wilson Junior College (later renamed Kennedy-King College following the assassinations of Robert Kennedy and Martin Luther King Jr.). Two years of higher learning, however, did not lead to financial or professional security, and Brooks found herself moving from job to job. She worked as a domestic for a short time and as a typist. Meanwhile she

Gwendolyn Brooks. The 1968 Illinois poet laureate Gwendolyn Brooks sits in the Poet Room at the Library of Congress, where she served as poetry consultant from 1985 to 1986, March 1986. AP IMAGES

became active in the local NAACP branch, and through that work in 1939 she met and married Henry Blakely, also a poet. The couple had two children, Henry Jr. and Nora.

Brooks took part in a number of writers' workshops, and her body of work continued to grow and evolve. It was a fortuitous moment. The South Side's literary scene proved to be fertile ground for the young poet. Mingling among its luminaries she met Richard Wright and Arna Bontemps. Soon her work began to find publication in increasingly more important poetry and literary journals and to win prizes, all of which brought Brooks to the attention of a wider national audience. In 1943 the Midwestern Writers' Conference awarded her its prestigious poetry award. Two years later Harper and Brothers published her first collection, *A Street in Bronzeville*, its title a reference to one of the South Side's more famous nicknames. Brooks's *Bronzeville* is densely populated with the ordinary people that she had lived among since her earliest childhood: street people and domestics, business owners and ministers. The book was an immediate critical success and did much to cement her reputation as an important new poetic voice and a daring one.

Bronzeville did not shy away from potential controversy or from honest and revealing appraisals of the lives of its citizenry. Among its most famous pieces, "The Mother" opens:

> Abortions will not let you forget.
> You remember the children you got that you did not get,
> The damp small pulps with a little or with no hair,
> The singers and workers that never handled the air.
> You will never neglect or beat
> Them, or silence or buy with a sweet.
> You will never wind up the sucking-thumb
> Or scuttle off ghosts that come.

The poem closes with the plaintive, heartrending lines, "Believe me, I loved you all. / Believe me, I knew you, though faintly, and I loved, I loved you / All."

Not long after the appearance of *A Street in Bronzeville*, Brooks was awarded a Guggenheim Fellowship, her first, and the magazine *Mademoiselle* named her one of its Ten Young Women of the Year.

Four years later, in 1949, Brooks published her second collection, *Annie Allen*, a series of connected poems that included the long poem "The Anniad." For this book she was awarded the 1950 Pulitzer Prize in poetry, the first African American so honored. Her reputation as an honest and innovative chronicler of the African American experience in the United States was cemented. In 1953—and in no small part as an attempt to earn enough money to remove her family to better housing—Brooks published her first novel, the autobiographical *Maud Martha*. Her third collection of poems, *The Bean Eaters*, appeared in 1960. The book continued Brooks's examination of black urban life, now adding just a hint of the political as well. It also contained what is her most enduring, most popular, and best-known poem, "We Real Cool," instantly famous for its evocative, insouciant, jazzy swagger:

> *The Pool Players.*
> *Seven at the Golden Shovel.*
> We real cool. We
> Left school. We
>
> Lurk late. We
> Strike straight. We Sing sin. We
> Thin gin. We
>
> Jazz June. We
> Die soon.

By 1962 Brooks's reputation as a leading poetic light was such that President John F. Kennedy invited her to read at a poetry festival at the Library of Congress. A year later she procured a teaching position at Columbia College in Chicago, the first of many throughout her long career. In 1967 Brooks's work and politics took a turn when she attended a workshop at Fisk University, the historically black college in Nashville, Tennessee, during which she came face-to-face with the Black Arts Movement. She came away with a renewed dedication to the idea of herself as a voice for positive change within the African American community. Following this transition, Brooks's work became more explicitly political. She began to publish her collections and other writings through smaller publishing houses, organized workshops and poetry seminars for residents of the South Side, and taught writing to members of the Blackstone Rangers street gang.

In 1968 Brooks was named poet laureate of Illinois, following Carl Sandburg. That same year *In the Mecca*, a collection of poems having largely to do with life in the urban ghetto, made its appearance to much critical acclaim and a National Book Award nomination. Among Brooks's many awards and positions, in 1985 she served as poetry consultant to the Library of Congress, and she was inducted into the National Women's Hall of Fame three years later. She was the recipient of dozens of honorary degrees and remained until the time of her death one of America's most active and recognizable public artists. Brooks died of cancer in Chicago's South Side.

[*See also* Black Arts Movement; Chicago; *and* Literature.]

BIBLIOGRAPHY

Kent, George E. *A Life of Gwendolyn Brooks*. Lexington: University Press of Kentucky, 1990.

Madhubuti, Haki R., ed. *Say That the River Turns: The Impact of Gwendolyn Brooks*. Chicago: Third World, 1987.

Melhem, D. H. *Gwendolyn Brooks: Poetry and the Heroic Voice*. Lexington: University Press of Kentucky, 1987.

Mootry, Maria K., and Gary Smith, eds. *A Life Distilled: Gwendolyn Brooks, Her Poetry and Fiction*. Urbana: University of Illinois Press, 1987.

Wright, Stephen Caldwell, ed. *On Gwendolyn Brooks: Reliant Contemplation*. Ann Arbor: University of Michigan Press, 2001.

—JASON MILLER

BROTHERHOOD OF SLEEPING CAR PORTERS.

Organized in New York in 1925, the Brotherhood of Sleeping Car Porters (BSCP) was the largest and most effective predominantly African American union in the years before the civil rights movement. Led by A. Philip Randolph and Milton P. Webster, the BSCP succeeded in becoming the first African American–led union to gain American Federation of Labor (AFL) recognition in 1935 and succeeded in negotiating its first contract in 1937. Through its organizing, the BCSP vaulted many working-class African Americans into relative financial security for the first time and launched the career of Randolph, perhaps the most important civil rights leader between W. E. B. Du Bois and the rise of the Southern Freedom movement, as well as countless other civil rights leaders and organizers.

Pullman Porters. Immediately after the Civil War, George Pullman consolidated his luxury sleeping car business into the Pullman Palace Car Company. Pullman himself envisioned the porters on these high-end cars to be emancipated slaves, reflecting both his personal vision of post–Civil War racial uplift and the larger cultural division of African Americans as people who served and whites as the people to be served. Indeed Pullman sought out African Americans as porters precisely because of their economic and cultural identity as people who served whites. Despite some of the relative material advantages of working as a Pullman porter for African American men, this status division was further culturally ensconced by the key component of the porter's wage—the tip. Tipping as a practice forced African Americans to evince the ideal of subordinate servitude that their white passengers and patrons desired from them and thus, in the minds of many porters, replicated the social relations of slavery.

Besides porters' financial dependence on the often degrading practice of tipping, working conditions were notoriously tough. In order to be paid a full salary, porters were required to work either four hundred hours or eleven thousand miles a month. Conditions were even worse for the hundreds of African American women who worked as maids aboard Pullman cars. These women catered to the needs of white female passengers and were paid and tipped decidedly less than men. Thus the racialized and gendered division of work, wages, and conditions on Pullman cars reflected the broader economic and cultural logic of racial and gender discrimination. African American men were hired solely as tip-based porters, African American women provided personal services to white women, and white men worked in the more prestigious and better paid job of salaried conductor. It was not until the late 1960s in fact that African Americans were hired as conductors on Pullman cars.

The Pullman Company itself practiced a brand of corporate paternalism toward its workers and the larger African American community. Pullman and his successors, including Robert Todd Lincoln, the son of former president Abraham Lincoln, strongly believed in a form of conservative racial uplift that envisioned Pullman porters strengthening the employment status of African Americans across the nation. Pullman donated money to African American churches and uplift organizations, and many porters achieved at least the material trappings of a middle-class identity. Pullman's financial support for institutions such as the desegregated Provident Hospital on Chicago's South Side earned the company tremendous goodwill among African Americans. At the same time the company was notoriously antiunion and regularly spied on its workers and fired anyone deemed guilty of union activity. Yet by the end of the nineteenth century Pullman porters—despite their relatively low pay in comparison to white conductors and the intermittence of their tip-based wages—represented a burgeoning African American labor aristocracy.

Porters were often among the most highly educated African Americans. Despite no possibility of advancement within the company, many men used the relatively high combination of their tips and wages to fund their educations, the opening of small businesses, and the purchase of property. Indeed important African American leaders, such as the Morehouse College president and educator Benjamin E. Mays and the Chicago-based banker Jesse Binga, financed their educations and early business ventures by working as Pullman porters.

By the middle of the 1920s the Pullman Company was the nation's largest employer of African Americans with a peak of more than twenty thousand. Porters were concentrated in industrialized cities, such as New York, Pittsburgh, and Chicago, the home to the largest number of Pullman porters. After World War I such African American cultural centers as New York's Harlem and Chicago's Bronzeville, exploding in population as a result of the Great Migration, were also centers of growing African American political, social, and economic assertiveness. It was out of such a cultural and historical milieu that the Brotherhood of Sleeping Car Porters was formed in Harlem in the summer of 1925. Despite decades of attempts by porters to form a union and initiate large-scale organizing, the relative goodwill Pullman generated in the African American community through its paternalism had continually rebuffed rank-and-file attempts at organizing.

Organization of the Union. This changed in 1925, as more than five hundred porters met in New York and chose Randolph, a prominent African American socialist and radical, as its leader. Randolph was the publisher of the Harlem-based periodical *The Messenger*, the leading African American socialist newspaper of the era. During the height of the post–World War I red scare, Attorney General Mitchell Palmer called Randolph "the most dangerous Negro in America," as high a compliment as a radical labor or African American leader could hope to receive at the time. The choice of Randolph to lead the union was a momentous one for the future of the brotherhood. In picking Randolph, the brotherhood chose a leader with strong connections to both African American activism and the labor movement. Equally important, Randolph, unlike rank-and-file leaders, was unencumbered by the paternalism of the Pullman Company and was not dependent on its largesse for his livelihood.

The brotherhood, Randolph, and Webster, Randolph's chief organizer in Chicago, faced two significant problems in attempting to organize what became the nation's first large-scale African American union. Besides Pullman's vociferous antiunion intransigence, the company, through its financial support of leading African American churches, newspapers, and hospitals, had generated tremendous support and goodwill in northern African American communities. Nowhere was this support more apparent than in Chicago, home to Pullman and more porters than any other city in the United States. Overcoming community support for Pullman proved to be one of the brotherhood's toughest challenges. In the long run the brotherhood succeeded in this regard by linking its organizing to a broader African American political and cultural impulse demanding independence from white control.

By 1928 the brotherhood had made strong inroads against Pullman's community and had enlisted over six thousand members, but it remained unrecognized by Pullman. That April, by an overwhelming margin of 6,053 to 17, the brotherhood voted to strike. The strike was called off though before it had a chance to even get underway, as Pullman hired strikebreakers, beefed up its company union the Pullman Porters and Maids Protective Association, and was aided by a sympathetic and antiunion federal government that did not recognize the validity of the brotherhood's grievances.

Following the failed strike attempt, the brotherhood witnessed a period of decline that lasted through the early years of the Great Depression. In 1935, however, the union won two important victories that paved the way for its collective bargaining success. Congress amended the Railway Labor Act that governed railroad workers in 1934 and in 1935 passed the Wagner Act. The net result was a federal government sympathetic to the claims of organized labor and the establishment of a national right to collective bargaining. In this climate the brotherhood won both certification from the federal government as the legitimate representative of Pullman porters and AFL recognition, becoming the first African American union to achieve such successes. Buoyed by the support of the federal government and the AFL, the union signed its first contract with Pullman in 1937.

Long-Term Impact. The legacy of the Brotherhood of Sleeping Car Porters for African American politics and social life was tremendous. As the nation's largest African

Eleventh-Anniversary Parade. The New York division of the Brotherhood of Sleeping Car Porters holds its eleventh-anniversary parade, 1936. Photograph by Brown Brothers. PRINTS AND PHOTOGRAPHS DIVISION, LIBRARY OF CONGRESS

American union, it increased the wages and bettered the working conditions of thousands of African Americans. It provided a conduit to the nation's growing labor movement, as Randolph and Webster became important national labor leaders. Randolph himself used his power as the brotherhood's president to become one of the most important and effective civil rights leaders in mid-twentieth-century America, as he led the charge to push the Franklin D. Roosevelt administration to establish the Fair Employment Practices Commission in 1941 and seven years later was instrumental in convincing President Harry S. Truman to desegregate the military.

The brotherhood was involved in early southern civil rights organizing as well. Porters provided a physical link to the relative openness of the North and helped spread important African American publications, like the *Chicago Defender*, across southern states that had banned such publications. Finally, the brotherhood helped launch the careers of civil rights leaders, ranging from Edgar Daniel Nixon to Bayard Rustin, and provided social and political organizing experience for men and women who contested inequality and segregation in postwar America.

By the mid-1950s railway travel was on a sharp decline, as passenger airlines became more popular and affordable. Such changes led to a sharp decrease in the number of porters and in the brotherhood's membership. In 1978, with few members remaining, the brotherhood merged with the Brotherhood of Airway, Railroad, and Steamship Clerks.

[*See also* Organized Labor *and* Randolph, A. Philip.]

BIBLIOGRAPHY

Arnesen Eric. *Brotherhoods of Color: Black Railroad Workers and the Struggle for Equality*. Cambridge, Mass.: Harvard University Press, 2001. Places the BSCP in the larger context of postbellum African American railroad work.

Bates, Beth Tompkins. *Pullman Porters and the Rise of Protest Politics in Black America, 1925–1945*. Chapel Hill: University of North Carolina Press, 2001. A detailed history that places the BSCP in the broader history of twentieth-century civil rights.

Harris, William H. *Keeping the Faith: A. Philip Randolph, Milton P. Webster, and the Brotherhood of Sleeping Car Porters, 1925–37*. Urbana: University of Illinois Press, 1977. An analytical history of the brotherhood's leadership and the Pullman organizing campaigns.

Pfeffer, Paula F. *A. Philip Randolph: Pioneer of the Civil Rights Movement*. Baton Rouge: Louisiana State University Press, 1990. The most complete political biography of Randolph; argues for his overwhelming importance in developing the strategies of the civil rights movement.

—THOMAS JESSEN ADAMS

BROWN, CHARLOTTE HAWKINS (b. 11 June 1883; d. 11 January 1961), educator. Born in Henderson, North Carolina, to Caroline Frances Hawkins, an unwed mother of sixteen, at age six "Lottie" moved to Cambridge,

Massachusetts, with her mother, with her mother's new husband, Nelson Willis, with her brother Mingo, and with several cousins and aunts. Brown excelled at the Allston Grammar School and Cambridge English High School. The whole family worked, from doing laundry to taking in boarders. Pushing a baby carriage with one hand and reading her Latin book in the other, Brown encountered Alice Freeman Palmer, president of Wellesley College, and with Palmer's assistance she ended up attending the State Normal School in Salem. Another chance encounter led to a job offer from the American Missionary Association (AMA); she accepted a teaching position at Bethany Institute, a small school in Sedalia, outside Greensboro, North Carolina.

Within a year the AMA closed the school, and the parents of Brown's fifty students offered her fifteen acres and an old building if she would stay. She was nineteen. She accepted the offer and, after learning of the death of her

Dr. Charlotte Brown Group. Mary McLeod Bethune (*left*) stands with Charlotte Hawkins Brown (*right*) and an unidentified woman (*center*), 1942. Scurlock Studio Records, Archives Center, National Museum of American History, Smithsonian Institution

benefactress, named her school Palmer Memorial Institute, an all-grades boarding school. The older students renovated an old blacksmith building to provide the first housing. Brown's first priority was fund-raising. She solicited support on trips back to Boston, then from white New Yorkers who hunted in the North Carolina woods, and ultimately from people in the Greensboro area as well. She kept the school going, and by 1905 she had raised enough for her first building, Memorial Hall, which was destroyed by fire just after the 1922 dedication of the $150,000 Alice Freeman Palmer Building. Fire was a repeated problem; by 1916 there were four main campus buildings, which burned in 1917, 1922, 1924, and 1932.

If necessary, Brown emphasized industrial education to donors to get and keep their support. But she went her own way, easing the education offered at Palmer beyond the basic survival skills needed by her first students to add ever more liberal arts and arts subjects. She increased the level of offerings into first the high school, accredited in 1922, and then the teacher-training junior college, begun in 1932. Student performers in music and theater also added funds to the school with their campus and touring presentations. In 1947 Palmer was featured in *Ebony* magazine as the premier finishing school for black children from wealthy families, and by 1950 one thousand students were applying annually for thirty vacancies.

Brown married twice, first to Edward S. Brown from Boston, considerably her senior. He taught at Sedalia for a year before leaving, and they divorced in 1916. In 1923 she married John W. Moses, a charming Palmer teacher considerably her junior. In less than a year their marriage was annulled. Her personal life was not without nurturing, however, for she raised several of her nieces and nephews, and in 1927 she was able to move into her own house on the campus, Canary Cottage.

Brown's activity and visibility beyond the campus and the fund-raising for Palmer was considerable. A founder of the North Carolina Federation of Women's Clubs, she became president in 1911 and remained so for two decades. She wowed the audience of mostly white women at the Memphis meeting of the Commission on Interracial Cooperation in 1920 by using the segregation that she had suffered on the train getting there as material for part of her speech. She was one of seven educators honored at the Philadelphia sesquicentennial celebration of American independence in 1926. She lectured at Wellesley and received honorary doctorates from Wilberforce University, Howard University, Lincoln University of Pennsylvania, and the Tuskegee Institute. She served as president of the North Carolina Teachers Association.

Palmer never did achieve financial independence, perhaps because, as her board often claimed, Brown was ready to borrow money and use it before there were sure ways to repay. Between 1926 and 1934 financial support was taken over by the AMA, but Brown insisted on being in control, and it did not last. Even after she was forced to relinquish her duties as president in October 1952, she insisted on interfering with matters, including classes. She died in 1961 at L. Richardson Memorial Hospital in Greensboro. Ten years later Palmer was closed; its campus passed through other hands before the state of North Carolina acquired it in 1987. The Charlotte Hawkins Brown Memorial State Historic Site was dedicated on 7 November 1987.

[*See also* Educators and Academics *and* Women's Clubs.]

BIBLIOGRAPHY

Brown, Charlotte Hawkins. *Mammy: An Appeal to the Heart of the South; and, The Correct Thing to Do—to Say—to Wear*. Introduction by Carolyn C. Denard. New York: G. K. Hall; London: Prentice Hall International, 1995. The two short essays by Brown demonstrate her talent and influence, both as a writer and as an early-twentieth-century "Miss Manners," dispensing advice and rules of behavior to young women and also to men and boys.

Marteena, Constance Hill. *The Lengthening Shadow of a Woman: A Biography of Charlotte Hawkins Brown*. Hicksville, N.Y.: Exposition, 1977. This study, targeted for young adults, is useful, if not exciting, tending toward the factual rather than the interpretive.

Wadelington, Charles W., and Richard F. Knapp. *Charlotte Hawkins Brown and Palmer Memorial Institute: What One Young African American Woman Could Do*. Chapel Hill: University of North Carolina Press, 1999. An outstanding biography, sympathetic and objective.

Wilds, Mary. "Charlotte Hawkins Brown." In *I Dare Not Fail: Notable African American Women Educators*, pp. 40–56. Greensboro, N.C.: Avisson, 2004. In the Avisson Young Adult Series, this book also includes essays on other African American women educators.

—CAROLYN WEDIN

BROWN, CLARENCE. (b. 18 April 1924; d. 10 September 2005), musician, performer, songwriter, and southern musical legend. Clarence "Gatemouth" Brown—"Gatemouth" because of his deep voice—emerged as a musical legend in the South for more than fifty years. Brown was heavily influenced by the music of Texas and Louisiana, and his range of styles included the blues, rhythm and blues (R&B), country, swing, jazz, and Cajun. A virtuoso on guitar, violin, mandolin, viola, harmonica, and drums, Brown influenced and was influenced by performers as diverse as Albert Collins, Eric Clapton, Frank Zappa, Lonnie Brooks, Guitar Slim, and Joe Louis Walker. Throughout his career he recorded more than thirty albums. Those who have been featured on his albums include Eric Clapton, Ry Cooder, Amos Garrett, Jim Keltner, Maria Muldaur, and Leon Russell.

Born on 18 April 1924 in Vinton, Louisiana, Brown was raised in Orange, Texas. While growing up he learned how to play the guitar and fiddle from his father, who introduced to his son the music of the region—including traditional French songs and German polkas. Brown began his professional career as a drummer in San Antonio, Texas, during World War II. After serving in the army he made his debut as a guitarist in 1947 at Don Robey's popular Bronze Peacock club in Houston when in the middle of a set he picked up the guitar of an ailing T-Bone Walker and finished the show. His performance captivated the crowd and caught the attention of Robey, who had him front a twenty-three-piece swing band orchestra on a tour across the South and Southwest. Brown's music blended together the swing of Texas country with the R&B and themes of life in Louisiana.

Throughout his career in the United States, Brown remained popular in the South but could never break onto the national scene. In the early 1960s Brown began recording country music when he lived for a brief time in Nashville to participate in the R&B television show *The Beat*. Brown made other appearances on music and variety television shows such as *Hee Haw* and *Austin City Limits*. By the 1970s Brown had toured and gained audiences in Europe, New Zealand, Australia, Central America, East Africa, and the Soviet Union, eventually touring as a musical ambassador for the United States State Department. Known in the United States as a regional performer, Brown won his only Grammy, in the traditional blues category, in 1982 for his album *Alright Again!* In 1999 Brown was inducted into the Blues Foundation Hall of Fame, and he won the W. C. Handy Award, the blues equivalent to the Grammy, eight times. In 1997 he also received the prestigious Pioneer Award from the Rhythm & Blues Foundation.

Clarence "Gatemouth" Brown, 1997. Photograph by Michael Wilderman. © MICHAEL WILDERMAN/JAZZVISIONSPHOTOS.COM

Except for a brief time in the late 1960s when he moved to New Mexico and became a deputy sheriff, Brown performed and recorded music until doctors diagnosed him with lung cancer in September 2004. After being evacuated from his home in Slidell, Louisiana, before Hurricane Katrina in August 2005, Brown returned to his hometown of Orange, Texas, to live with his brother. He died there soon after, on 10 September 2005. Brown's career spanned fifty years, and his music, as diverse as the population, left its mark on the South.

[*See also* Blues *and* Rhythm and Blues.]

BIBLIOGRAPHY

Barkley, Roy R., ed. *The Handbook of Texas Music*. College Station: Texas A&M University Press, 2003.

Wood, Roger. *Down in Houston: Bayou City Blues*. Austin: University of Texas Press, 2003.

—CHARLES D. GREAR

BROWN, H. RAP (b. 4 October 1943), civil rights activist and religious leader. Hubert Gerold "H. Rap" Brown was born in Baton Rouge, Louisiana, in 1943. He attended Southern University in Baton Rouge, studying sociology from 1960 to 1964. He then relocated to Washington, D.C., where he became chairman of the Nonviolent Action Group (NAG), a civil rights organization. During his brief tenure with the NAG, Brown attended a high-profile meeting with President Lyndon B. Johnson. Much to the chagrin of more moderate black leaders, Brown refused to show deference to the president, instead rebuking him for the state of American race relations.

In 1966 Brown joined the Student Nonviolent Coordinating Committee (SNCC), becoming director of the Alabama Project. In 1967 at the age of twenty-three he was elected chairman of the organization. Brown led SNCC in a transition away from the nonviolent philosophy of the early days of the civil rights movement. He believed that African Americans had the right to arm themselves in their struggle for equal rights, famously declaring that "violence is as American as cherry pie." After resigning from SNCC, Brown became minister of justice of the radical Black Panther Party (BPP) in 1968.

Because of Brown's high-profile position within the BPP, he was under constant surveillance by the FBI's counterintelligence program (COINTELPRO) and by various local authorities who arrested him on a series of charges, many of dubious merit. In April 1970 he failed to appear in court on the charges of inciting a riot in Cambridge, Maryland. He remained at large for seventeen months, during which he appeared on the FBI's Ten Most Wanted list. In 1971 he was found at the scene of a shooting at a Manhattan bar; he was arrested, charged with armed robbery, and incarcerated for five years. While in prison in Upstate New York he converted to orthodox Islam and changed his name to Jamil Abdullah Al-Amin.

After his release in 1976 Al-Amin moved to Atlanta, where he opened a small grocery store and founded a mosque. He devoted himself to the revitalization of Atlanta's poverty-stricken black neighborhoods and to religious study, becoming a well-respected imam (spiritual leader) in his community. He articulated his beliefs on living a Muslim life in *Revolution by the Book* (1993).

Even after his conversion Al-Amin remained under police surveillance. He was interrogated after the 1993 bombing of the World Trade Center even though no evidence linked him to the crime. He was also arrested on charges of shooting an Atlanta man in 1995, but he was released when the victim claimed that police forced him to identify Al-Amin as the assailant. In 2002 Al-Amin was sentenced to life in prison for the 2000 murder of an Atlanta police officer. The prosecution claimed that Al-Amin shot the officer while the officer was attempting to serve him with an arrest warrant on charges of driving a stolen car and impersonating a police officer. Al-Amin has steadfastly denied these charges but remains in prison.

[*See also* Black Panther Party; Civil Rights Movement; COINTELPRO; *and* Student Nonviolent Coordinating Committee.]

BIBLIOGRAPHY

Al-Amin, Jamil Abdullah [H. Rap Brown]. *Die, Nigger, Die!* (1969) Chicago: Lawrence Hill, 2002. This reprint of Brown's political biography also contains an update by Ekwueme Michael Thelwell that includes information about Brown/Al-Amin's religious conversion and legal troubles.

Carmichael, Stokely, and Ekwueme Michael Thelwell. *Ready for Revolution: The Life and Struggles of Stokely Carmichael (Kwame Ture)*. New York: Scribner, 2003.

—JENNIFER JENSEN WALLACH

BROWN, JAMES (b. 3 May 1933; d. 25 December 2006), singer, songwriter, and bandleader. Born in Barnwell, South Carolina, to Joe Brown (né Gardner), a turpentine worker, and Susan Behlings, James Brown experienced extreme poverty in early childhood. His mother left the family when Brown was four. When he was six, he was sent to Augusta, Georgia, to live with an aunt who ran a brothel. In addition to picking cotton and shining shoes, the young Brown earned money by tap-dancing for World War II troops and by singing in talent contests.

As a teenager Brown broke into a car to steal a coat and was sentenced to eight to sixteen years in prison. He served three years and was released in 1953. He then sang in a doo-wop and gospel ensemble headed by Bobby Byrd. Brown soon emerged as the lead singer, and the band, the Fabulous Flames, wowed audiences with their dancing, theatrics, and flawless performances. Brown maintained martial-style control over his bands throughout his career.

Brown's first success in recorded music was "Please, Please, Please" in 1956, and the band signed a contract with the Federal label of King Records. Syd Nathan, the owner of King, was skeptical about Brown's music but was consistently proven wrong. Brown's stage theatrics grew wilder and wilder. When Brown appeared close to collapse, an accompanist would cover him with a cape, an inspiration from the flamboyant wrestler Gorgeous George. Known widely as the "hardest-working man in show business," Brown cared deeply about his audiences. "Try Me" in 1958 was his first genuine hit. Lacking support from King Records, he paid for and oversaw the recording of *Live at the Apollo*. Released in 1963, it became one of the first albums by an African American to cross over and sell appreciably well to white audiences, and Brown experienced success performing before desegregated audiences.

Turning a new musical corner in 1965, the year of Malcolm X's assassination and the Watts Riot, Brown virtually invented what came to be known as "funk." The revolutionary song "Papa's Got a Brand New Bag" had almost no chord changes, and the instruments and vocals focused entirely on rhythm. Brown employed grunts, moans, and screeches. The downbeat was on the first note ("on the one") to increase tension with other elements, such as scratchy guitar riffs. The hits of 1965 catapulted Brown to stardom.

In the evolution of Brown's political awareness, 1966 was a watershed year. He went public with his concerns for civil rights and came to be perceived as a leader in the black community. That year Brown welcomed Roy O. Wilkins of the NAACP onstage at the Apollo in Harlem. Brown visited the civil rights activist James Meredith after Meredith was attacked and performed a show for Meredith's supporters, including Martin Luther King Jr.

James Brown. R&B singer James Brown in performance. PHOTOFEST

and Stokely Carmichael of the Student Nonviolent Coordinating Committee (SNCC).

Ultimately, however, tensions arose between the moderates and the radicals in the civil rights movement, and Brown fell into the moderate camp. He was a black entrepreneur who owned a production company and three black-oriented radio stations. The following year he met with the radical H. Rap Brown, then head of SNCC. The two men could not see eye to eye. Nevertheless in 1968 James Brown publicly contributed to H. Rap Brown's defense fund. Brown's music became increasingly socially relevant. "Don't Be a Drop Out" highlighted a stay-in-school campaign that won Brown kudos from Vice President Hubert Humphrey.

On 4 April 1968, King was assassinated. The following day, on live television, Brown went onstage with the Boston mayor Kevin White to urge nonviolence. Brown then went to Washington, D.C., to quell rioting and was invited to the White House in appreciation. In June 1968, Brown toured Vietnam and wrote "America Is My Home," a patriotic song. Under pressure to take a more radical stand, Brown was accused of being an Uncle Tom. Yet in the same year he released "Say It Loud, I'm Black and I'm Proud," which has been described as an anthem for the Black Power movement and represented a radical shift in Brown's lyrics. In 1969 the title of an article in *Look* magazine asked, "Is This the Most Important Black Man in America?" Although "Say It Loud" gave Brown even greater importance in the black community, this bitter song may have cost him his white audience. He did not have another Top Ten hit until 1986.

Brown took several trips to Africa. In 1970 he met the Nigerian musician Fela Kuti. Brown had influenced Fela, who in turn influenced Brown's drummer Clyde Stubblefield and his bassist Bootsy Collins. Collins and other members of Brown's band achieved great success in the funk ensemble Parliament Funkadelic. Brown could not, however, consciously identify how African music became embedded in his own music.

Brown released "Get on the Good Foot" in 1972. The hip-hop pioneer Afrika Bambaataa contends that this was the first song that people break-danced to. The same year Brown endorsed Richard Nixon, whom Brown perceived as pro–black business, for president. Brown continued to have a string of hits from the late 1960s through the mid-1970s, including "Get Up (I Feel like Being a) Sex Machine" (1970) and "Hot Pants" (1971), but he did not have another hit until "Living in America," from the movie *Rocky IV*, in 1986. His career, in other words, hardly recovered from the Nixon endorsement, and he had run-ins with the law, including a three-year term in jail.

Brown's performance style and dancing influenced Michael Jackson, Prince, and Mick Jagger. Sly and the Family Stone, the Temptations, and other soul groups incorporated funk, as did Miles Davis in fusion jazz. Hip hop and rap endlessly sampled Brown, and Kool Herc, widely considered the inventor of hip hop, credits Brown with providing the genre's foundation. "Funky Drummer" (1970) may be the most widely sampled beat in hip hop.

After Brown's son Teddy died in 1973, he took on the Reverend Al Sharpton as a protégé. When Brown died on Christmas Day 2006, Sharpton officiated at public and private memorial services, which celebrities and thousands of fans attended. Sharpton described Brown as an enigmatic figure. Driven by his ambitions, Brown saw himself as a "solo man," independent of others and uncompromising in his control of his image and his career.

[*See also* Hip Hop; Music; Rhythm and Blues; Soul Music; *and biographical entries on figures mentioned in this article*.]

BIBLIOGRAPHY

Brown, James, with Bruce Tucker. *James Brown: The Godfather of Soul*. New York: Thunder's Mouth Press, 2002. One of three memoirs by Brown; the other two repeat much of the same narrative.

George, Nelson. *The Death of Rhythm and Blues*. New York: E. P. Dutton, 1989. A definitive text on the history of the black music industry.

Guralnick, Peter. *Sweet Soul Music: Rhythm and Blues and the Southern Dream of Freedom*. New York: Harper and Row, 1986. This book was reissued in 1999 and is considered a core text on the topic, connecting history to music; includes extensive bibliographic references.

Hirshey, Gerri. "Funk's Founding Father." *Rolling Stone*, 25 January 2007, pp. 40–44. A heartfelt obituary by a music journalist who knew Brown well.

Ramsey, Guthrie P., Jr. *Race Music: Black Cultures from Bebop to Hip-Hop*. Music of the African Diaspora, vol. 7. Berkeley: University of California Press, 2003. An excellent book on the social history of black music. Ramsey offers many fresh insights and includes extensive bibliographic notes.

Vincent, Rickey. *Funk: The Music, the People, and the Rhythm of the One*. New York: St. Martin's Griffin, 1996. Focusing chiefly on music, rather than on African American history, Vincent writes in detail about how Brown was the creator of funk; includes extensive bibliographic references.

—MONICA BERGER

BROWN, JIM (b. 17 February 1936), athlete, actor, civic activist. Jim Brown is generally recognized as the greatest football player and the greatest lacrosse player of all time. At 6 feet 2 inches tall, weighing 228 pounds, and with a 32-inch waist, Brown combined great speed with a powerful running style and fearsome stiff-arm to terrorize National Football League (NFL) defenders for nine years. The only person in history voted into three halls of fame (college football, college lacrosse, and the NFL), Brown is arguably the greatest athlete of the twentieth century.

James Nathaniel Brown was born on Saint Simons Island, Georgia, to Swinton "Sweet Sue" and Theresa Brown. Swinton Brown left his family barely two weeks after his son was born, and they rarely heard from him afterward. When Jim was two, his mother left him in the care of his great-grandmother and moved to Great Neck, Long Island, where she worked as a domestic. Brown joined his mother when he was eight.

Upon arrival in Great Neck, Brown earned a reputation as an aggressive and hard-nosed kid with spectacular athletic ability. Though Brown did not have a father to raise him, he received male guidance from his high school football coach, Ed Walsh, and a local attorney, Kenneth Molloy. At nearby Manhasset High School, Brown earned thirteen varsity letters in his three years of eligibility (freshmen did not play varsity sports in high school or college) in football, basketball, baseball, track, and lacrosse.

As a senior in 1952, Brown averaged 14.9 yards per carry in football and more than 38 points per game in basketball. His talents on the football field were such that he received more than forty scholarship offers including one from Ohio State University. Molloy and other local businessmen with ties to Syracuse University, however, steered Brown to that school and paid for his tuition until he earned a football scholarship his junior year. Brown did not find out that he was not a four-year scholarship athlete until after he graduated.

Midway through his sophomore year Brown became the starting running back at Syracuse and won All-American honors. Averaging more than six yards per carry as a senior, Jim Brown led the Orangemen to a 7–1 record and a berth in the 1957 Cotton Bowl against Texas Christian University. Though Syracuse lost, Brown was exceptional, scoring 21 of his team's 27 points. Jim Brown also ran track and played lacrosse at Syracuse, earning All-American honors in each sport.

The Cleveland Browns drafted Jim Brown with the fifth overall pick in the 1957 draft, and he rewarded the team by earning Rookie of the Year honors. He went on to play nine years in the NFL and set literally every rushing and scoring record in the team and league's history. Brown's combination of power, speed, intelligence, and determination made him the only running back in NFL history whom defensive players physically feared. It was rare for even two men to tackle Brown, and though the Browns did not use him much as a pass receiver, his skills in that area may be unparalleled.

Before retiring from the Browns after the 1965 season, Jim Brown appeared on several television shows and was cast in the movie epic, *The Dirty Dozen*, released in 1967. Brown went on to star in several other feature films including*100 Rifles* (1969) with Raquel Welch, and *Ice Station Zebra* (1968). Brown was one of the first black leading men in cinematic history and paved the way for later black actors.

Jim Brown's commitment to helping black Americans has been exceptional. While still a member of the Browns, he founded what became the Black Economic Union, an organization dedicated to helping black women and men gain funding to begin their own businesses. Moreover, Brown has worked tirelessly over the years to rid Southern California and other communities of gangs, working with members encouraging them to find gainful employment and become useful members of society. Almost single-handedly, he has dramatically reduced the numbers of gang members and gang conflicts in greater Los Angeles. In 1988, Brown founded the Amer-I-Can Program, dedicated to helping prisoners prepare for life on the outside by restructuring personal habits and attitudes toward themselves, family, the community, and careers; since then he has worked with thousands of prisoners to help them stay clear of trouble after their release. In 2002, Brown himself spent six months in prison after being

Jim Brown. Cleveland Browns fullback Jim Brown, c. 1960.
PHOTOFEST

sentenced for attacking his wife, an accusation Brown vehemently denies. He had been arrested on charges of domestic abuse on several other occasions.

Jim Brown remains the most popular athlete ever to wear a Cleveland uniform. Though he lives in Los Angeles, he has maintained ties with the Cleveland Browns, regularly attends their games, and, at times, acts as an unofficial consultant to the team. Though his rushing and touchdown records are falling by the wayside, Jim Brown remains the most dominant offensive force in the game's history.

[*See also* Football.]

BIBLIOGRAPHY

Brown, Jim, and Delsohn, Steve. *Out of Bounds*. New York: Kensington Publishers, 1989. Jim Brown's autobiography with an emphasis on his relationships with teammates, opponents, friends, and the women in his life.

Freeman, Michael. *Jim Brown: The Fierce Life of an American Hero*. New York: William Morris, 2006. An excellent biography of Jim Brown.

Isaacs, Stan. *Jim Brown: The Golden Year, 1964*. Englewood, N.J.: Prentice-Hall, 1970. A look at Jim Brown and his leadership during the Cleveland Browns' run to the NFL championship.

—JULIAN C. MADISON

BROWN, LEE (b. 4 October 1937), law enforcement officer, mayor, cabinet secretary, and professor. Lee Brown is best known as a high-profile law enforcement officer who held the position of chief of police or its equivalent in four major U.S. cities, served in President Bill Clinton's cabinet as drug czar, and was the first black mayor of Houston, Texas.

Lee Patrick Brown was born in Wewoka, Oklahoma, on 4 October 1937 to Andrew and Zelma Brown, who worked as farm laborers. When Brown was five the family moved to Fowler, California, about ten miles south of Fresno. As a child Brown often joined his parents in the fields, picking crops. But he also stayed in school, and he attended Fresno State University on a football scholarship, studying sociology and criminology.

In 1960, one semester before graduation, Brown left college and took a job as a patrolman with the San Jose Police Department. While working as a policeman Brown continued his education, graduating from Fresno State with a BS degree in criminology in 1961 and earning his master's degree in sociology from San Jose State in 1964. He continued graduate work at the University of California at Berkeley, where he received a second master's degree, this one in criminology, in 1968, and then in 1970 a doctorate in criminology. Brown was the first African American to receive a doctorate in this field.

In 1968 Brown took a faculty position at Portland State University in Oregon, where he was the founding chair of the Department of Administration of Justice; in 1972 he moved to Howard University, where he established a program in criminal justice. After two years at Howard, Brown returned to Portland to serve as the sheriff of Multnomah County, and in 1976 he became director of the Department of Justice Services there. Over the next twenty years Brown headed a series of law enforcement agencies.

From 1978 to 1982 Brown served as the director of public safety in Atlanta, Georgia, a job that involved supervision of the police and fire departments, correctional facilities, and civil defense operations. During his tenure in Atlanta he handled a high-profile case involving a serial killer who targeted African American children. Between July 1979 and May 1981 an estimated twenty-nine black youths were murdered in Atlanta. The case grabbed national headlines, the FBI was called in, and President Ronald Reagan committed federal resources to the case. The arrest, trial, and conviction of an African American man did not end all speculation that there were several serial killers, many more victims, or even involvement by the Ku Klux Klan. However, subsequent investigations failed to substantiate any of these rumors, and Brown, who headed the task force that solved the case, emerged as a national figure in law enforcement. He was credited with holding the community together during those difficult days.

In 1982 the newly elected mayor of Houston, Kathy Whitmire, hired Brown to become chief of the city's troubled police department. The Houston Police Department had a national reputation for racial bigotry and brutality, especially when dealing with the city's large black and Hispanic populations. Brown worked quickly to change the culture of the department. He implemented a requirement that police cadets have at least two years of college, and he recruited more minorities into the department and into positions of leadership. In addition he instilled a set of values in the department, perhaps the most important of which was that the job of a policeman was not only to enforce the law but also to protect the constitutional rights of the people. Finally, Houston became a laboratory for Brown's concept of community policing, which placed a permanent police presence within neighborhoods, especially in areas with high numbers of crimes. Brown did not solve all the problems with the police force, but his reforms were successful enough that the department ceased being a major political issue. He is recognized throughout the law enforcement community as the father of community policing.

In 1990 the New York City mayor David Dinkins recruited Brown to become the police commissioner of New York City. New York suffered from a high level of violent crime, much of which was linked to drugs and drug gangs and to an understaffed police force. Brown implemented his concept of community policing, as well as a "safe city, safe streets" program that involved the recruitment of an additional nine thousand police officers. Within one year violent crime had begun to decline, and it continued its decrease during the administration of Dinkins's successor Rudolph W. "Rudy" Giuliani.

While Brown was New York City police commissioner, the ethnically divided Crown Heights section of Brooklyn was the scene of an August 1991 race riot between the African American and African Caribbean majority and the Jewish, mostly Lubavitch, minority. Even though the New York police contained the disorder, Mayor Dinkins was criticized for not responding adequately, and he was defeated by Giuliani's law-and-order campaign in the next election, in 1993. Brown had resigned in 1992 and returned to Houston to be with his wife, Yvonne Streets Brown, who was terminally ill.

In 1993 President Clinton appointed Brown to the cabinet-level position of director of the Office of National Drug Control Policy. As the so-called drug czar Brown shifted the focus of the office from interdicting drug shipments to decreasing demand for drugs through education, treatment, and prevention. In December 1995, after nearly three years as drug czar, Brown was convinced by Houston political leaders to return to the city and run for mayor. Brown took a position on the faculty at Rice University and organized his political campaign. In November 1997 Brown became the first African American to be elected mayor of Houston. His victory was especially impressive because blacks made up less than a quarter of the city's population.

Brown served three two-year terms as mayor of Houston, the most allowed by the city's term-limit ordinance. Though his administration generated significant opposition, especially among white Republicans, he retained the support of the downtown business interests, as well as of the large majority of black and Hispanic voters. Brown's greatest accomplishment as mayor was the implementation of a large number of infrastructure projects that his predecessors had failed to get started. He attributed his success to his lack of ambition for higher office, which made him not worry about the political consequences of pushing controversial projects.

Consequently, Brown completed the first phase of a light-rail system that had been debated for a generation, and he gained voter approval for a comprehensive thirty-year transit expansion plan. He also built a city-financed convention hotel and doubled the size of the convention center, implemented a massive and highly criticized reconstruction of all downtown city streets and underground utility systems, enlarged the airport, built three new sports stadiums, and developed a new water plant. In addition he expanded the city's international trade initiatives and upgraded the city's affirmative action program by using minority firms as prime contractors rather than as subcontractors. Less successful were his initiatives to revitalize historically neglected poor neighborhoods.

Brown left the mayor's office in January 2004 and spent the next year as a visiting scholar at Rice University's School of Social Sciences. In 2005 he became chairman and CEO of Brown Group International, a consulting group specializing in public safety issues. Projects that Brown has worked on include a management study of the post–Hurricane Katrina New Orleans Police Department and the development of a training program for the Nigerian police. Brown lives in Houston with his second wife, Frances Young-Brown, an educator with the Houston Independent School District.

[*See also* Clinton, Bill, Administration of; Drugs; *and* Houston.]

Bibliography

Dulaney, W. Marvin. *Black Police in America*. Bloomington: Indiana University Press, 1996. Discusses Brown's years in law enforcement within the context of the history of black police officers.

Headley, Bernard. *The Atlanta Youth Murders and the Politics of Race*. Carbondale: Southern Illinois University Press, 1998. Provides

a detailed analysis of the Atlanta murders, including Brown's involvement in the case.
Watson, Dwight. *Race and the Houston Police Department, 1930–1990: A Change Did Come*. College Station: Texas A&M University Press, 2005. Devotes a chapter to Brown's years as Houston's police chief.

—CARY D. WINTZ

BROWN, RON (b. 1 August 1941; d. 3 April 1996), the first African American secretary of commerce and the first African American chairman of a national political party. Ron Brown was born in Washington, D.C., on 1 August 1941 and was raised in the Harlem section of New York City. He attended Middlebury College, where he was the first African American member of Sigma Phi Epsilon, a national men's collegiate fraternity that for a long time had accepted only white Christians. Upon graduation from Middlebury, Brown joined the U.S. Army in 1962 and served with distinction in Europe and South Korea. After being honorably discharged in 1967, he joined the National Urban League, one of the premier groups in the United States espousing equality. He also earned a law degree from St. John's University in 1970.

Because of his organizational and oratorical skills, Brown was appointed deputy campaign manager for Senator Edward M. Kennedy of Massachusetts, who sought the Democratic Party's presidential nomination in 1980. Eight years later, in 1988, Brown was named by the Reverend Jesse L. Jackson to head Jackson's convention team at the Democratic National Convention in Atlanta.

Brown understood the significance of the change in American politics that was manifested in the 1989 off-year election. That year, for the first time, a black Democratic governor was elected in Virginia and a black Democratic mayor was elected in New York City. Democrats also picked up four congressional seats, including a seat in the conservative bastion of Indiana—a seat once held by Vice President Dan Quayle.

In 1992, while President George H. W. Bush was earning high marks for the nation's victory in the Persian Gulf War, Brown was deeply involved in the nitty-gritty of electoral politics, as he sought to reenergize the Democratic Party's base. He helped to transform the image of the Democratic Party from that of "tax and spend" to a party of inclusion that could accommodate fiscally conservative economic policies along with middle-class values of mainstream America. As the chairman of the Democratic National Convention in July 1992, he was instrumental in naming Bill Clinton as the party's presidential nominee. Upon Clinton's assuming the presidency in January 1993, Brown was named secretary of commerce—the nation's first African American secretary of commerce. In spite of controversies related to Brown's previous background as a lobbyist in the Washington lobbying firm of Patton, Boggs, and Blow in 1968–1969, he made tangible efforts in promoting American business interests worldwide.

On 3 April 1996, while on an official trade mission to Croatia, the plane carrying Brown and thirty-four other people crashed, killing everyone on board. In honor of Brown, President Clinton established the Ron Brown Award for Corporate Leadership. The U.S. Department of Commerce also gives out the annual Ronald H. Brown American Innovator Award in his honor.

[*See also* Clinton, Bill, Administration of *and* Democratic Party.]

BIBLIOGRAPHY

Brown, Tracey L. *The Life and Times of Ron Brown: A Memoir*. New York: William Morrow, 1998. Provides glimpses into Brown's multifaceted personality.
Clinton, Bill. *My Life*. New York: Alfred A. Knopf, 2004. Contains rich tributes to Brown.
Holmes, Steven A. *Ron Brown: An Uncommon Life*. New York: John Wiley and Sons, 2000. Contains useful information about Brown's rise from being Edward Kennedy's campaign manager to his chairing the Democratic National Convention in 1992.

—MOHAMMED BADRUL ALAM

BROWN, STERLING (b. 1 May 1901; d. 13 January 1989), English professor, poet, essayist, and anthologist. Sterling Allen Brown was born in Washington, D.C., into the middle-class family of Sterling Nelson Brown, an esteemed minister and theologian, and Adelaide Allen Brown. He graduated from Dunbar High School in 1918 as class valedictorian, and in the fall of that year he enrolled at Williams College on a minority scholarship. Brown excelled at Williams, studying French and English literature and winning the Graves Prize for an essay titled "The Comic Spirit in Shakespeare and Molière." He was elected to Phi Beta Kappa in his junior year and graduated from Williams in 1922 as the only student awarded final honors in English. Brown accepted a Clark Fellowship for graduate studies in English at Harvard University, where he studied with, among others, George Lyman Kittredge, whose work with the vernacular of the British Isles influenced Brown to take on critical and creative projects involving African American folk speech. Brown completed his MA in English in 1923, then headed south to teach at Virginia Seminary and College in Lynchburg, Virginia. He subsequently taught for a short time at Lincoln University in Missouri and at Fisk University in Tennessee before beginning his forty-year career at Howard University in 1929.

During his three years in Lynchburg, Brown immersed himself in folktales, history, music, and idioms of rural black life. "I was first attracted by certain qualities that

I thought the speech of the people had," he said, "and I wanted to get for my own writing a flavor, a color, a pungency of speech. Then later, I came to something more important—I wanted to get an understanding of people, to acquire an accuracy in the portrayal of their lives" (Brown, "Remarks at a Conference," p. 506). Brown sought to use folk material and the African American idiom just as Robert Frost, E. A. Robinson, Edgar Lee Masters, and especially Carl Sandburg had used the white American idiom to highlight the extraordinary, and sometimes heroic, within the lives of ordinary citizens. He also wanted to challenge black audiences to be receptive to an array of representations of black people.

In his 1930 essay "Our Literary Audience," first published in *Opportunity* magazine, Brown shifts the emphasis of black art from the artist (where it had sat squarely since Langston Hughes's landmark 1926 essay, "The Negro Artist and the Racial Mountain") to the audience. In an effort to illustrate what he sees as the problem with black audiences, Brown details in the essay "fallacies" within black society as of 1930: "We look upon Negro books regardless of the author's intention, as representative of all Negroes, i.e. as sociological documents. We insist that Negro books must be idealistic, optimistic tracts for race advertisement. We are afraid of truth telling, of satire. We criticize from the point of view of bourgeois America, of racial apologists" (p. 46). He argues that the aforementioned generalizations, fears, narrow tastes, and faulty logic are a product of African Americans being "not a reading folk." He acknowledges that "there are reasons, of course" (alluding to obvious societal and economic difficulties) but asserts that "even with those considered, it remains true that we do not read nearly as much as we should." Brown found success in his professional life around the time he arrived at Howard. In the 1920s he began to publish poems as well as a column titled "The Literary Scene: Chronicle and Comment" in *Opportunity*. His early poems were reprinted in several influential anthologies, including Countée Cullen's *Caroling Dusk* (1927) and James Weldon Johnson's *The Book of American Negro Poetry* (1922). Brown's first book of poems, *Southern Road*, was released in 1932. Brown served as the editor on Negro affairs for the Federal Writers' Project from 1936 to 1939, and in 1937 he was awarded a Guggenheim Fellowship, which provided him with the time and resources to finish *The Negro in American Fiction* and *Negro Poetry and Drama*, both published in 1937. Next he edited, with Ulysses Lee and Arthur P. Davis, the landmark anthology *The Negro Caravan*, which was released in 1941. The text brings together songs, speeches, essays, letters, and literature and remains a touchstone in African American studies.

Brown also remained active as a poet, placing poems with magazines such as *The Crisis*, the *New Republic*, and the *Nation* and completing a second poetry manuscript, "No Hiding Place." To his great disappointment, however, he could not find a publisher for the book. As a result throughout the 1940s, 1950s, and 1960s he focused less on poetry and more on teaching courses on African American culture and writing groundbreaking essays, such as "The Blues," "Negro Folk Expression: Spirituals, Seculars, Ballads, and Work Songs," and "The New Negro in Literature (1925–1955)." In the latter essay he argued that the Harlem Renaissance should be called instead the New Negro Renaissance, since many major artists of the period, including himself, Johnson, Georgia Douglas Johnson, and Jean Toomer, lived and wrote about life outside of Harlem.

During the final two decades of his life, Brown was rediscovered as a poet and was celebrated as a pioneering teacher in the field known then as Afro-American studies. *Southern Road* was republished in 1974; a volume of ballad poems, *The Last Ride of Wild Bill and Eleven Narrative Poems*, followed in 1975; and *The Collected Poems of Sterling A. Brown*, which included the poems originally intended for "No Hiding Place," was edited by Michael S. Harper and released in 1980. Brown was named poet laureate of the District of Columbia in 1984, five years before he died in Takoma Park, Maryland, at the age of eighty-seven.

[*See also* Howard University; Johnson, James Weldon; Literature; *and* New Negro.]

Bibliography

Brown, Fahamisha Patricia. "And I Owe It All to Sterling Brown: The Theories and Practice of Black Literary Studies." *African-American Review* 31 (Autumn 1997): 449–453.

Brown, Sterling A. *The Collected Poems of Sterling A. Brown*. Edited by Michael S. Harper. 1st ed. New York: Harper and Row, 1980.

Brown, Sterling A. "Our Literary Audience." *Opportunity* 8, No. 2. (February 1930): 46.

Brown, Sterling A. "Remarks at a Conference on the Character and State of Studies in Folklore." *Journal of American Folklore* 59 (October 1946): 506.

Gabbin, Joanne V. *Sterling A. Brown: Building the Black Aesthetic*. Westport, Conn.: Greenwood, 1985.

Rowell, Charles H. "'Let Me Be with Ole Jazzbo': An Interview with Sterling A. Brown." *Callaloo* 14.4 (1991): 795–815.

Stepto, Robert. "Sterling A. Brown: Outsider in the Harlem Renaissance?" In *The Harlem Renaissance: Revaluations*, edited by Amritjit Singh, William S. Shiver, and Stanley Brodwin, pp. 73–81. New York: Garland, 1989.

Stepto, Robert. "'When de Saints Go Ma'chin Home': Sterling Brown's Blueprint for a New Negro Poetry." *Callaloo* 21.4 (1998): 940–949.

—Daniel Donaghy

BROWN, TONY (b. 11 April 1933), academician, businessperson, author, talk-show host, and journalist. The fifth son of Royal Brown and Katherine Davis Brown, William Anthony Brown was born in Charleston, West Virginia. The marriage of his parents broke down in the racist environment of Charleston. His father was a light-skinned person, whereas his mother was of dark color. For several years he was raised by a foster family, Elizabeth Sanford and Mabel Holmes, before he was reunited with his mother and three siblings. Brown had a turbulent childhood, but by sheer determination, perseverance, and hard work along with the support of his foster parents and several school teachers, he rose in life—primarily through education. After high school he attended Wayne State University in Detroit, where he earned a BA in sociology (1959) and an MSW in psychiatric social work (1961).

After graduation Brown obtained a job working at Detroit's PBS station, where he produced a television program that targeted African Americans—*Colored People's Times*. While in Detroit he also became involved in civil rights and joined a march organized by Martin Luther King Jr. This experience, which included his first encounter with a hostile police officer, raised his political and racial consciousness. Brown also pursued a career in education, serving as a faculty member at Central Washington University and Federal City College. In 1971 he became the founding dean of Howard University's School of Communications.

Brown is best known for his work on radio and television. In 1970 he became the executive of *Black Journal* (renamed *Tony Brown's Journal* in 1977). *Black Journal* exposed the social and economic problems of African Americans and brought Brown both fame and controversy. His aggressive style as well as his candid discussion about the prevalence of racism in broadcasting created enemies within the industry. The political and racial positions he championed, especially his criticism of affirmative action and his argument that blacks should focus more on economic advancement than civil rights, caused many African Americans to compare him with Booker T. Washington's conservative views. Brown in response linked his views to those of black nationalists who championed self-sufficiency rather than dependence on the welfare system. In 1990 Brown further surprised many of his followers when he joined the Republican Party.

In spite of the controversy surrounding some of his political views, Brown's broadcasting career continued to expand. In 1995 he launched a radio talk show, *Tony Brown*, and a year later a Web site, Tony Brown Online; of course he developed his own blog. His original show, *Tony Brown's Journal*, aired continuously after its founding in 1970, making it the longest-running PBS series in the early twenty-first century. This success brought Brown a number of honors. He was the first recipient of the National Directors' Legacy Award for Journalism from the U.S. Department of Commerce's Minority Business Development Agency, and he was inducted into the National Academy of Television Arts and Sciences' prestigious Silver Circle, a distinction he shared with Walter Cronkite. The NAACP nominated his television series for the 1991 NAACP Image Award for Outstanding News, Talk, or Information Series/Special.

Brown's broadcasting career did not end his interest in higher education. In 1982 he launched his Black College Day initiative in an effort to showcase African American institutions of higher education and the importance of a college education for black youth. Brown also became outspoken in his support for historically black colleges and universities and their survival in the challenging times they faced at the end of the twentieth century. To this end he became the honorary chairperson of the National Organization of Black College Alumni. In 2004 he again assumed a position in academia when he accepted appointment at the first dean of the Scripps Howard School of Journalism at Hampton University. His Council for the Economic Development of Black Americans established in 1985 exhorted African Americans to patronize stores owned by other blacks.

Apart from broadcasting Brown used other media to spread his ideals. He produced and directed a film, *The White Girl* (1990), depicting the evils of drug addiction and self-hate. Although the film was panned by the critics, he arranged screenings in black communities for a year and half. Brown also authored several books. His first, *Black Lies, White Lies: The Truth according to Tony Brown* (1995), suggesting ways and means for solving racism, was appreciated by many throughout United States. He criticized some who were enjoying power in high places in his second book, *Empower the People: A Seven-Step Plan to Overthrow the Conspiracy That Is Stealing Your Money* (1998). Brown's courage, determination, and struggle in adverse circumstances were delineated in the autobiographical work *What Mama Taught Me: The Seven Core Values of Life* (2003). In 2001 Brown again stirred up controversy when he voiced "anti-Hindu" remarks on his talk show. After strong protest by the Indian Hindu community, he was forced to apologize.

Brown became a member of the Harvard Foundation for Intercultural and Race Relations and the Association for the Study of African American Life and History. In the early twenty-first century he continued to host his radio program and *Tony Brown's Journal* while serving as dean at Hampton University. He also continued to receive numerous speaking engagements and honors and awards. He remained controversial, consistent in his advocacy of self-reliance but somewhat out of step with most African American leaders.

[*See also* Journalism, Print and Broadcast; Radio; *and* Television.]

BIBLIOGRAPHY

Bigelow, Barbara C. *Contemporary Black Biography: Profiles from the International Black Community*. Vol. 2. Detroit: Gale Research, 1992.

Brown, Tony. *Black Lies, White Lies: The Truth according to Tony Brown*. New York: W. Morrow, 1995.

LaBlanc, Michael L. *Contemporary Black Biography: Profiles from the International Black Community*. Vol. 1. Detroit: Gale Research, 1992.

—PATIT PABAN MISHRA

BROWN, WILLIE (b. 20 March 1934), activist, lawyer, politician, talk show host, and actor. Willie Lewis Brown Jr. was born in the East Texas town of Mineola to Minnie Collins Boyd and Willie Lewis Brown Sr. during the grinding poverty of the Great Depression. His grandmother Anna Lee Collins primarily raised Brown, his brother, and his three sisters. Racial oppression and extreme violence created even greater dangers and hardships for Brown's family as for many black families during the era. Affectionately called "Brookie" during his childhood, Brown performed such menial labor as picking cotton and shining shoes, yet his family's ingenuity helped overcome much of the abject poverty that most experienced. His enterprising family, including bootleggers and gamblers, greatly influenced him, particularly his strong people skills.

As a teenager Brown was gregarious and outspoken. His grandmother feared for his life, so hostile were whites to any kind of black self-assertion. In 1951 he graduated from Mineola Colored High School, then moved to San Francisco to live with his flamboyant uncle Itsie Collins, a casino owner who applied the skills he obviously honed during his gambling days in Mineola.

Brown graduated in 1955 from San Francisco State University with a degree in political science. In 1958 he graduated from Hastings College of the Law, University of California, in San Francisco. In 1957 he married Blanche Vitero; they had two daughters and one son. They separated but never divorced.

Brown's NAACP activism propelled him into the public eye. Older and wilier politicians, including Phillip Burton, an invaluable white mentor, and the Reverend Hamilton Boswell, an African American civil rights leader, began grooming him. Dianne Feinstein, who later served as the mayor of San Francisco then a U.S. senator from California, was also an ally. In 1962 Brown ran for the California state assembly but was narrowly defeated by six hundred votes. He ran again in 1964 and won, becoming the first African American legislator to represent San Francisco. He remained in office until 1995, winning reelection fifteen consecutive times. From 1980 to 1995 he served as speaker of the California House, the first African American to hold this position and the longest serving speaker in the history of California to that time. His amassing of political power finally gave way to legislation establishing term limits that forced him out of office.

Not ready to retire from politics, Brown challenged San Francisco's mayor Frank Jordan and defeated him handily, becoming the first black mayor of San Francisco. A visionary and a risk taker, Brown brought that boldness to city government, appointing a record number of women, people of color, and young professionals to fill upper-level positions and commissions. He served two terms, from 1996 to 2004, and again was restricted by term limits from running a third term.

A consummate politician, Brown's rise from modest beginnings to extraordinary power and influence was considered phenomenal. He continued to be a formidable political force nationally and statewide. His fame and success led the people of Mineola, including whites, to give him a rousing welcome home. His unique style of dress and leadership distinguished him in politics and on the big screen, where he typically played himself. His small role in *Godfather III* (1990) was his most renowned. Brown also cohosted a morning radio show with the comedian Will Durst on a local San Francisco Air America Radio affiliate and a TV news show.

[*See also* California.]

BIBLIOGRAPHY

Academy of Achievement. "Willie L. Brown, Jr." http://www.achievement.org/autodoc/page/bro0bio-1.

Richardson, James. *Willie Brown: A Biography*. Berkeley: University of California Press, 1996. http://ark.cdlib.org/ark:/13030/ft0m3nb07q/.

—MALAIKA B. HORNE

BROWNIES' BOOK, THE. *The Brownies' Book* was a children's magazine published by the National Association for the Advancement of Colored People (NAACP) and its monthly journal, *The Crisis*, for a brief period from January 1920 until December 1921. The magazine was the brainchild of W. E. B. Du Bois, managing editor of *The Crisis*, and his literary editor, Jessie Redmon Fauset, who became the most prolific contributor to and managing editor of the new publication. She was ably assisted by Augustus Granville Dill, the business manager of *The Crisis*. Du Bois had a long-standing interest in childhood education and literature, evidenced in part by his willingness to devote one *Crisis* issue each year, the

"Children's Number," to the education and acculturation of black children. The new magazine was first advertised in the pages of *The Crisis* in October 1919 and promised to "teach Universal love and Brotherhood for all little folk—black and brown and yellow and white"; it would be "designed for all children, but especially for ours," a group that Du Bois was fond of calling "the children of the sun." Subscription rates were to be one dollar a year; individual copies could be had for ten cents each. The first issue appeared in January 1920.

Editor Fauset attracted an impressive number of talented contributors to each monthly edition. Du Bois himself wrote for the magazine, and the rest of the contributors included several luminaries. The graphic artist Laura Wheeling Waring designed many of the illustrations for all twenty-four editions, and the playwright Willis Richardson published his first children's play, *The King's Dilemma*, in the pages of *The Brownies' Book*. The young Langston Hughes, who later became the unofficial poet laureate of the Harlem Renaissance, published five poems, a short play, and several other pieces under Fauset's editorship. Regular monthly features included "The Jury," in which young readers could voice their opinions; "The Judge," in which Fauset handed out advice of all kinds; and "As the Crow Flies," (authored by Du Bois himself), which brought world events to the attention of young readers.

The education of African American children was an important component of Du Bois's thinking on education generally. Perhaps deriving in part from his firsthand, and sometimes frustrating, experience with his daughter's schooling, he was determined that black children learn about their own uniqueness and their own potential instead of treading water in a white-dominated educational system. Fauset's dedicatory poem reflected this kind of thinking:

> To Children, who with eager look
> Scanned vainly library shelf and nook
> For History or Song and Story
> That told of Colored Peoples' glory—
> We dedicate *The Brownies' Book*

A precipitous decline in *The Crisis* subscribers from a high of 100,000 in 1919 to less than half that number two years later and a similar decline in *Brownies' Book* readers signaled the doom of the *Brownies'* experiment. Du Bois tried in vain to shore up financial support with an increase in the subscription rate, but by late 1921 diminishing revenues forced him to cancel *The Brownies' Book*, one of his favorite projects.

[*See also biographical entries on figures mentioned in this article*.]

BIBLIOGRAPHY

Johnson-Feelings, Diane, ed. *The Best of "The Brownies' Book."* New York: Oxford University Press: New York, 1996. Provides reproductions of many of the issues of *The Brownies' Book* as well as biographical sketches of many of its authors.

Lewis, David Levering. *W. E. B. Du Bois: The Fight for Equality and the American Century, 1919–1963*. New York: Henry Holt, 2000. The classic interpretation of Du Bois's career, which contains some insightful comments about his ideas concerning the education of African American children.

Smith, Katharine Capshaw. *Children's Literature of the Harlem Renaissance*. Bloomington: Indiana University Press, 2006. Contains an interesting account of Du Bois's motivation for separating *The Brownies' Book* from the main pages of *The Crisis*.

—CHARLES ORSON COOK

BROWNSVILLE RAID. An acrimonious civilian-military conflict reached into the halls of Congress and the White House when residents of Brownsville, Texas, accused the all-black First Battalion, Twenty-fifth Infantry, of attacking the town from Fort Brown around midnight on 12 August 1906, claiming the life of one townsman and injuring two others.

The disputed episode took place against the background of deteriorating racial relations in the state and region, an enhanced self-confidence of black soldiers following their heroic achievements in the Spanish-American War and the Philippine insurrection, and the economic decline of Brownsville, a southern Texas town bordering the Rio Grande. Texas, like other southern states, was tightening segregation at the turn of the century. Brownsville, bypassed when rail joined San Antonio to Laredo, Texas, in the late nineteenth century, failed to recover its Civil War–inspired prosperity.

Companies B, C, and D, previously stationed at Fort Niobrara, Nebraska, drew the wrath of some Brownsvillians even before their arrival on 28 July, when they replaced the white Twenty-sixth Infantry. As happened in other Texas garrison towns, complainants wired Washington of their disapproval of black troops. Expressed hostility had led to physical confrontations at Laredo, Rio Grande City, and El Paso from 1899. Threats from white Texas National Guardsmen prompted the military command to cancel the participation of the Twenty-fifth in maneuvers at Camp Mabry, Austin. Federal officials, ironically, exacerbated matters. The inspector of customs Fred Tate pistol-whipped Private James W. Newton for supposedly jostling Tate's wife and another white woman on a sidewalk. Another customs officer, A. Y. Baker, pushed Private Oscar W. Reed, whom he accused of drunkenness and boisterous behavior, into the river. Soldiers complained of racial insults directed at them in the streets.

On the evening of 12 August, Mrs. Lon Evans stated that a uniformed black man had thrown her to the ground before he fled into the darkness. Mayor Frederick J. Combe met with the post commander, Major Charles W. Penrose, to defuse the potentially explosive situation. Penrose imposed an eight o'clock curfew on his men, which seemed to be successful until shots rang out at about midnight near the wall separating the fort from the town. Various residents testified to having seen a shadowy group of from nine to twenty persons charging through an alley toward town, firing several hundred shots indiscriminately or into lighted areas. Evidently dividing into two sections, the raiders mortally wounded the bartender Frank Natus and shot the horse from under the police lieutenant Joe Dominguez, shattering the man's arm and leading to its being amputated. A bullet grazed the bookbinder Paulino Preciado, barely missing other bystanders. Witnesses insisted that the raiders were soldiers, some claiming to have seen them and others describing the shots as reports from military rifles. Townsmen were unable to identify any culprits individually.

Conversely, the soldiers maintained their innocence. Private Joseph Howard, guarding the area closest to the wall, and Matias Tamayo, post scavenger, assumed that there was an attack on the garrison, a belief shared by Major Penrose until confronted by Mayor Combe. A roll call of troops found all present or accounted for and an inspection of weapons and ammunition noted none missing. A search of the fort uncovered no spent shells, discarded cartridge belts, or any indication of firing from the post. However, the morning visit of the Brownsville mayor, who displayed empty cartridges that had been found in the city streets, reversed Penrose's belief in his command's innocence.

Many outside the fort and town shared the post commander's new view of the soldiers' culpability. Beneath sensational headlines, Texas newspapers reported the story with an assumption that the soldiers were guilty. Editors, seconded by Texas officeholders ranging from congressmen to Governor S. W. T. Lanham, demanded the withdrawal of all African American troops from the state.

President Theodore Roosevelt dispatched Major Augustus P. Blocksom, assistant inspector-general of the Southwestern Division, to Brownsville only days after the raid. After eleven days of inquiry, the major submitted a report to the White House concurring in the guilt of members of the garrison. Deciding that both sides had exaggerated the facts, Blocksom judged that Tate had probably overreacted in his whipping of Private Newton and that some of the citizenry were obviously racially prejudiced. Nevertheless, asserting that black soldiers had adopted a more aggressive stance on social equality, the major outlined a scenario of troop culpability. He conjectured that some soldiers began firing between the barracks and the wall, that others fired into the air to create an alarm, and that from nine to fifteen men jumped the wall and rushed through an alley into the streets. The shooters subsequently returned to camp to clean and reassemble their weapons, duping their officers.

Acknowledging that witnesses had failed to identify specific culprits, that some bars had served enlisted men, and that the victim Natus had never quarreled with troops, Blocksom nevertheless held the testimony of the townspeople superior to that of the soldiers and based his judgment squarely on that testimony. In this manner he discounted the revelation that the discovered cartridges did not fit the recently assigned Springfield rifles. Blocksom recommended the discharge of all the enlisted men of the battalion, without option to reenlist in any military branch, if they refused to identify the guilty by a date determined by the War Department. Heeding the demands of Texans, Roosevelt ordered the First Battalion to Fort Reno, Oklahoma.

Penrose, along with the Texas Ranger captain William J. "Bill" McDonald, a formidable critic of black garrisons, set curious guidelines in selecting a dozen suspects. The list included the sentinel, the scavenger, the two victims of physical abuse, and an eyewitness to one of the latter incidents. The Cameron County grand jury grudgingly abstained from entering any indictments, and the War Department scheduled Fort Brown for temporary closure.

Determined to uncover the guilty, Roosevelt sent General Ernest A. Garlington, inspector-general at Washington, to Fort Reno and Fort Sam Houston, at San Antonio, where the unindicted suspects remained. The president instructed Garlington to threaten the battalion with dismissal without honor, as Blocksom had suggested, if uncooperative. When even the specter of dismissal could elicit no information, the general urged the president to issue the order. Roosevelt complied on 4 November, thus widening the controversy from Texas to the nation.

The postelection edict caused particular criticism from the African American community. The *Richmond Planet* and the *Atlanta Independent* accused Roosevelt of waiting until after the congressional elections to ensure the black vote in key northern states. Black ministers entered the fray, and the rising activist W. E. B. Du Bois urged his followers to vote Democratic in the 1908 elections. Booker T. Washington, the widely publicized White House guest and the administration's envoy to the African American constituency, stood with Roosevelt, sharing the criticism directed at both Roosevelt and his heir apparent, Secretary of War William Howard Taft.

An interracial organization, the Constitution League, first raised the argument of the troops' innocence.

Director John Milholland, a white Progressive, assailed racism, haste, and inconsistencies in the reports of Blocksom and Garlington. The criticism stung Roosevelt, who had cultivated a reputation for racial fairness since his military service alongside black troops in the Spanish-American War. From the outcry, the Republican senator Joseph B. Foraker took up the cause of the cashiered battalion.

Whether acting from principle, from old grudges against Roosevelt, or in pursuit of presidential ambitions, the Ohio conservative Foraker became the soldiers' most celebrated advocate. His efforts produced a Senate investigation of the raid and a summons to the War Department for all evidence leading to its decision. Roosevelt countered with a message defending the summary dismissals. The Senate Committee on Military Affairs held hearings between February 1907 and March 1908, during which Foraker attacked the absence of trials and suggested that outside forces had raided the town. Foraker's campaign for the soldiers failed in tandem with his presidential candidacy. Voting 9 to 4, the committee sustained the administration's action, and Foraker mustered only 16 delegate votes at the Republican National Convention against 702 for Taft. By November most blacks had drifted back to the Republican Party and contributed to Taft's victory. Roosevelt made only two concessions before leaving office, enabling the debarred soldiers to reapply for military service and lifting the ban on their employment in the civil service. Inexplicably, in 1910 the War Department allowed fourteen of the troops to reenlist, never stating its criteria for the selections. Courts-martial of Major Penrose and officer of the day Captain Edgar Macklin, for dereliction, produced no convictions, though Macklin suffered gunshot wounds from an unidentified assailant after his transfer to Fort Reno.

No subsequent evidence came to light, but in 1972, President Richard Nixon, acting on a proposal by Representative August Hawkins, a Democrat of California, granted honorable discharges and a pension of $25,000 to each of the unredeemed 153 men of the First Battalion, without placing blame for the raid. The decision followed the publication in 1970 of a history of the incident, *The Brownsville Raid*, by John D. Weaver, who blamed outside raiders or townsmen. Only one survivor, former private Dorsey Wills, benefited from the measure. He maintained the innocence of the battalion until his death five years later.

[*See also* Military; Roosevelt, Theodore, Administration of; *and* Texas.]

BIBLIOGRAPHY

Christian, Garna L. *Black Soldiers in Jim Crow Texas 1899–1917*. College Station: Texas A&M University Press, 1995. Offers a concise view of the raid and controversy and the first description of the unsolved shooting of Captain Macklin at Fort Reno.

Lane, Ann J. *The Brownsville Affair: National Crisis and Black Reaction*. Port Washington, N.Y.: Kennikat Press, 1971. Examines the raid and aftermath in detail. Like Christian, Lane does not assess guilt, but she criticizes Roosevelt for denying the soldiers due process.

Tinsley, James A. "Roosevelt, Foraker, and the Brownsville Affray." *Journal of Negro History* 41 (January 1956): 43–65. Revives the controversy in a scholarly forum after decades of neglect. The author doubts a conspiracy of silence on the part of the soldiers but concentrates on Roosevelt's motivations for denying trials.

Weaver, John D. *The Brownsville Raid*. New York: W. W. Norton and Company, 1970. The first book-length study and the most influential writing on the subject, this book led directly to the belated honorable discharges of the debarred servicemen.

—GARNA L. CHRISTIAN

BROWN V. BOARD OF EDUCATION. In *Brown v. Board of Education of Topeka*, 347 U.S. 483 (1954), the U.S. Supreme Court held that legally mandated racial segregation in the public schools was unconstitutional. Decided on the last day of the Supreme Court's term in May 1954, the Court found that segregation denied African American children the "equal protection of laws" in violation of the Fourteenth Amendment to the Constitution. Speaking for a unanimous Supreme Court, Chief Justice Earl Warren explained that "in the field of public education, the doctrine of 'separate but equal' has no place. Separate educational facilities are inherently unequal."

Brown is unquestionably the most important legal case affecting African Americans in the twentieth century and one of the most important Supreme Court decisions in American constitutional history. The case technically involved only segregation in the public schools. Chief Justice Warren carefully limited the scope his decision to schools, asserting that the decision did not overturn *Plessy v. Ferguson* (1896), which had upheld the right of the states to require racial segregation in public transportation. However, the implications of *Brown* were clearly applicable to all forms of segregation, and thus the case provided the legal underpinning for the civil rights revolution of the 1950s and 1960s and the dismantling of all forms of statutory segregation.

In the decade and a half before *Brown* the Court had almost always sided with blacks in civil rights cases, but the Court never struck down major aspects of state segregation. Thus in a series of cases from Missouri, Oklahoma, and Texas the Court required all-white state universities to admit blacks to graduate and professional programs because the states failed to provide a "separate but equal" alternative. In *Sweatt v. Painter* (1950) the Court had required the integration of the University of Texas's law school, even though the state had just created a law school for blacks at Texas Southern University (ironically now called the Thurgood Marshall School of Law). In *Sweatt* the Court accepted the arguments of NAACP lawyers for the NAACP Legal Defense and Educational Fund, Inc. (known as the "Inc. Fund"), led by Thurgood Marshall, that the hastily created law school for blacks was not "equal" to the famous University of Texas School of Law, which included among its alumni one of the members of the Court, Justice Tom C. Clark. However, that case, like all the other cases about graduate and professional programs, had not challenged the segregation per se, but only its implementation.

Similarly, in *Morgan v. Commonwealth of Virginia* (1946) the Court had struck down laws requiring segregation in interstate transportation on grounds that such laws violated the Constitution's commerce clause—and federal statutes passed in Congress—because only Congress could regulate interstate transportation. That case also did not challenge the constitutionality of segregation per se. *Brown*, however, signaled that any state segregation laws might be successfully challenged.

In addition to declaring that segregation was unconstitutional in all public schools, *Brown* undermined segregation in three other ways. First, it signaled to civil rights advocates that one branch of the national government was unanimously supportive of their cause and goals. This was a reaffirmation of cases like *Sweatt v. Painter*, but the language in *Brown* was appreciably more forceful and direct, declaring that segregation could be "inherently unequal." Knowing that the Court was on their side would embolden civil rights activists to take greater risks in directly challenging segregation.

Second, *Brown* ultimately forced the nation's executive branch to take a stand on the issue of segregation. When southern states resisted *Brown*, the Dwight D. Eisenhower administration had no choice but to enforce court orders, most dramatically by sending federal troops to Little Rock, Arkansas, in 1957.

Finally, Chief Justice Warren's opinion in *Brown*, along with the national media coverage that followed it, served as a valuable tool in educating the general public on the need for integration and racial equality. In this way Warren's opinion is in the tradition of the great opinions of Chief Justice John Marshall, such as *McCulloch v. Maryland* (1819) and *Cohens v. Virginia* (1821), in being designed to persuade politicians and citizens of the correctness of the outcome.

Background of the Case. *Brown* combined separate cases from Kansas, South Carolina, Virginia, and Delaware that turned on the meaning of the Fourteenth Amendment's requirement that states not deny their citizens "equal protection of the law." The Court also heard a similar case from Washington, D.C., *Bolling v. Sharpe*, which involved the meaning of Fifth Amendment's due process clause.

In 1954 laws in eighteen states plus the District of Columbia mandated segregated schools, and other states allowed school districts to maintain separate schools if they wanted to do so. Although theoretically guaranteeing blacks "separate but equal" education, segregated schools were never equal for blacks. Linda Brown, whose father sued the Topeka school system on her behalf, had to travel an hour and twenty minutes to school each way. If her bus was on time she was dropped off at her school half an hour before it opened. Her bus stop was six blocks from her home, across a hazardous railroad yard; her school was twenty-one blocks from her home. The neighborhood school that her white playmates attended was only seven blocks from her home and required neither bus nor hazardous crossings to reach.

The *Brown* companion cases presented segregation at its worst. Statistics from Clarendon, South Carolina, illustrate the inequality of separate but equal. In 1949–1950 the average expenditures for white students was $179, but for blacks it was a paltry $43. The county's 6,531 black students attended school in 61 buildings valued at $194,575. Many of the black schools lacked indoor plumbing or heating. The 2,375 white students in the county attended school in 12 buildings valued at $673,850 and having far superior facilities. Teachers in the black schools received, on average, salaries that were one-third less than those that the teachers in the white schools received. Finally, Clarendon provided school buses for white students in this rural county but refused to provide them for blacks. These conditions led parents to sue for equalization of the schools in *Briggs v. Elliott*, as well as for a declaration that segregated schools were themselves unconstitutional.

The plaintiffs could easily have won orders requiring state officials to equalize the black schools on the grounds that education was separate but not equal. Since the 1930s the Court had been chipping away at segregation in higher education, interstate transportation, housing, and voting. Indeed, the U.S. District Court judge who heard *Briggs v. Elliott* told lawyers for the NAACP Legal Defense Fund that he would order such equalization immediately, but he also indicated that once equalization was ordered, the plaintiffs could not then also sue to have segregated schools themselves be declared unconstitutional. In the cases that were combined with *Brown*, the Inc. Fund, led by Thurgood Marshall, decided to challenge directly the whole idea of segregation in schools.

Marshall and other lawyers at the Inc. Fund had been planning for such a challenge since the 1930s. The *Briggs*

Linda Brown. At age nine in 1952. Brown was a third grader in 1951 when her father started the class-action suit *Brown v. Board of Education*, which led to the U.S. Supreme Court's landmark 1954 decision against school segregation. AP IMAGES

case provided such an opportunity, as did the cases in Delaware and Virginia. However, the Supreme Court strategically held off on hearing these cases until *Brown* was ready for appeal. The Court often combines cases of a similar nature for reasons of efficiency. Here, however, there was another motive: the Court did not want the case to appear to be wholly an attack on the South. By promoting the *Brown* case, which was from Kansas, to the lead case, the Court was able to stress that racial equality was a national problem.

The Jurisprudence of Race. Marshall's bold challenge of segregation per se led the Court to reconsider older cases, especially *Plessy v. Ferguson* (1896), which had upheld segregation. In that case the Court had upheld the right of Louisiana to require segregation in railroad cars. In other cases the Court had upheld state laws requiring segregation in specific instances. Thus in *Gong Lum v. Rice* (1927) the Court allowed Mississippi to classify Chinese Americans with blacks for purposes of public education, but no one in *Gong Lum* questioned whether segregation itself might be unconstitutional. However, since *Plessy* no case had ever asked the Court to decide if segregation was inherently unconstitutional.

By directly challenging the idea of segregation the Inc. Fund compelled the Court to consider the meaning of the Fourteenth Amendment, which had been written at a time when most states allowed some forms of segregation and when public education was undeveloped in the South. The states defending segregation in *Brown* noted that the same Congress that passed the Fourteenth Amendment, and sent it on to the states for ratification, had also established a segregated school system in Washington, D.C. Thus they argued that the Fourteenth Amendment, as understood by its authors, was not meant to prohibit segregation in the public schools.

The Court heard arguments on some of these issues in its 1952–1953 term but then ordered attorneys for both sides to present briefs and rearguments on these historical matters in the following term. Over the summer of 1953 a number of scholars, including the historians John Hope Franklin and Alfred Kelly, worked with Thurgood Marshall's team to create a historical brief that would blunt the "originalist" claims of the segregating states. The Court heard oral arguments on these issues in December 1953 and announced its opinion in May 1954. In the end the Court found the historical argument to be:

> At best...inconclusive. The most avid proponents of the post-War Amendments undoubtedly intended them to remove all legal distinctions among 'all persons born or naturalized in the United States.' Their opponents, just as certainly, were antagonistic to both the letter and the spirit of the Amendments.... What others in Congress and the state legislatures had in mind cannot be determined with any degree of certainty.

After reviewing the histories of the Fourteenth Amendment, public education, and segregation, Chief Justice Earl Warren, speaking for the unanimous Court, concluded, "In approaching this problem, we cannot turn the clock back to 1868, when the Amendment was adopted, or even to 1896, when *Plessy v. Ferguson* was written. We must consider public education in the light of its full development and its present place in American life throughout the Nation." Warren found that "in the field of public education, the doctrine of 'separate but equal' has no place. Separate educational facilities are inherently unequal."

Brown did not technically overturn *Plessy*—which involved seating on railroads—or the doctrine of separate but equal. But that technicality was unimportant. *Brown* signaled an end to the legality of segregation. Within a dozen years the Supreme Court would strike down all vestiges of legalized segregation.

Brown did not lead to an immediate end to segregated education. The Court understood that it was mandating a social revolution and that it would take some time to accomplish this. Furthermore, the justices understood that different circumstances in different states might lead to slower or faster implementation of the decision. To sort all this out, the Court ordered new arguments for the next year to determine how to begin the difficult social process of desegregating schools. In a second case, known as *Brown II* (1955), the Court ordered that integration be supervised by the district courts in all of the segregating states. In an unfortunate use of terminology, the Court ordered that its mandate be implemented with "all deliberate speed." Southern opponents of integration focused on the term "deliberate" and used whatever tactics they could to avoid desegregation. Thus the process of ending segregation turned out to be extraordinarily slow. Linda Brown, for example, did not attend integrated schools until junior high; none of the plaintiff children in the Clarendon County case ever attended integrated schools.

In a few places integration was accepted and was at least somewhat successful. Tulsa, Oklahoma, for example, turned its previously all-black Booker T. Washington High School into a magnet school that was half white and half black. Public schools in some Upper South cities were immediately integrated, as were private Catholic schools throughout the South. But integration in much of the South, especially in most of the former Confederate states, was delayed and undermined by both public and private decision makers. Southern public school systems developed a variety of tactics to avoid integration. Freedom-of-choice plans declared that all schools were open to all children and that children were free to attend whatever school they wanted. But social and economic pressure was then placed on black families to send their children to the previously segregated black schools, while white children went to what had been the white schools.

When courts struck down these plans, school districts came up with new ones that drew school boundaries along racial lines or that provided for certain classes—such as advanced foreign languages or sciences—to be offered in only the white schools, and then allowed students to transfer for educational purposes. Some school districts, including that of Prince Edward County, Virginia, simply shut down their public schools to avoid integration and stopped collecting school taxes. White families then created segregated private academies. The courts struck down these schemes as well. But courts could not compel parents to send their children to public schools, and in many places private, segregated schools flourished more than half a century after *Brown*, with almost all the white children attending those schools and blacks attending the technically integrated but almost entirely all-black public schools.

Segregation had existed in the North in a few districts—mostly in Illinois, Kansas, and New Jersey—despite state laws prohibiting such segregation. These practices disappeared almost immediately after *Brown*, but integrated schooling did not become the rule for most northern blacks. In metropolitan areas schools were segregated by neighborhoods, housing patterns, and suburban town lines. Much of this segregation had been created by private actors or by public policy surrounding housing, urban renewal, and highway construction. Residential segregation was exacerbated by the steady movement throughout the nation of people to suburbs and by so-called white flight in some places when integration seemed likely to occur. Half a century after *Brown*, most urban and suburban whites attended schools with some black and Hispanic students. But in inner cities in the North and the South, as well as in much of the rural South, vast numbers of minority children—black and Hispanic—attended schools that were segregated in fact—what is called de facto segregation—even though the schools are, legally, integrated.

Legacy. The legacy of *Brown* is mixed. *Brown* offered great hope, and the decision shattered the idea that segregation can be legal or constitutional. The civil rights movement that followed—with demonstrations, marches, and boycotts—relied on the logic of *Brown* and the promise of a friendly Supreme Court that almost always sided with integration and civil rights demonstrators. By 1961 the Court had struck down almost all forms of state-sponsored segregation and had formally overturned the doctrine of *Plessy* for all aspects of American life. With the Civil Rights Act of 1964, Congress made almost all forms of private discrimination illegal, and in 1965 it passed legislation to protect the right of blacks to vote. The Court upheld all these laws, often relying explicitly—and always implicitly—on the logic and doctrine of *Brown*. Ironically, the one area where the logic of *Brown* has been least successful in integrating society has been in the public schools. Still, half a century after *Brown* significant numbers of children did attend schools with members of other groups, and Americans under the age of about twenty-five were generally much more racially tolerant than their parents and grandparents were.

[*See also* Desegregation and Integration, *subentry* Public Education; Jim Crow Laws; Laws and Legislation; Marshall, Thurgood; NAACP Legal Defense and Educational Fund; Segregation; *and* Supreme Court.]

BIBLIOGRAPHY

Finkelman, Paul. "Civil Rights in Historical Context: In Defense of *Brown*." *Harvard Law Review* 118 (2005): 973–1027.

Klarman, Michael J. *From Jim Crow to Civil Rights: The Supreme Court and the Struggle for Racial Equality*. New York: Oxford University Press, 2004.

Kluger, Richard. *Simple Justice: The History of "Brown v. Board of Education" and Black America's Struggle for Equality*. New York: Alfred A. Knopf, 1975.

Tushnet, Mark V. *The NAACP's Legal Strategy against Segregated Education, 1925–1950*. Chapel Hill: University of North Carolina Press, 1987.

—PAUL FINKELMAN

BROYARD, ANATOLE (b. 16 July 1920; d. 11 October 1990), literary critic. Anatole Broyard was born in New Orleans, the son of Paul Broyard, a carpenter, and Edna Miller. Young Anatole was the second of three children. His older sister, Lorraine, was fair complexioned and his younger sister, Shirley, was brown complexioned. Anatole was pale to olive skinned as a boy. This color distinction is important, because that issue defined the future writer's life.

Anatole's family moved to Brooklyn's Bedford-Stuyvesant in the 1920s. Anatole's father arrived in town as a master carpenter, but he learned that the carpenters' union barred applicants of color. Paul Broyard decided to identify himself as white in order to work. The rest of the family did not overtly pass for white; they muted their racial identity, and that worked in multiethnic Brooklyn.

Young Anatole meanwhile picked up the nickname "Buddy," according to the historian Henry Louis Gates Jr. In the 1930s the teenager graduated from Boys High School in Bedford-Stuyvesant, then enrolled at Brooklyn College. Broyard cultivated a passion for modern culture, mostly European literature and cinema.

During World War II, Broyard married and started a family. He wed a Puerto Rican of African descent, and they produced a daughter. Passing as white, Broyard entered the U.S. Army and served as captain of an all-black stevedore battalion. When Broyard returned home from the war, he began his writing career. Broyard and his wife parted ways in 1946; she and their daughter moved to California, and he moved into a Greenwich Village apartment with Sherri Donatti, a painter. Broyard enrolled in the New School for Social Research with other aspiring postwar writers and artists. Broyard and his friends lived bohemian lifestyles filled with literary discussions and debates about fine and performing arts.

Broyard self-identified as white; he is thus believed to be among at least 150,000 African Americans in the 1940s who "passed" as white in an American society that was legally segregated in the South and socially segregated in the North. Broyard was committed to becoming a writer, and he did not want to be defined as a Negro writer or live as a second-class citizen.

Through the 1950s, Broyard lived the writing and bohemian life in New York City. In 1961, at age forty, he met Alexandra "Sandy" Nelson, twenty-three, a white dancer. They married and two years later moved to Connecticut before the arrival of their first of two children. For seven years in the 1960s Broyard worked full-time as a copywriter for a Manhattan advertising agency. In the late 1960s he wrote some front-page pieces that were published in the *New York Times Book Review*, and the newspaper hired him as a daily book reviewer in 1971. He wrote for the *New York Times* through the late 1980s, and then left while suffering from prostate cancer.

Broyard was a reliably brutal book reviewer. Philip Roth was one of his favored few writers, according to the *New York Times* journalist Brent Staples. Staples said that after Broyard was exposed as an American of African descent by Gates in a 1996 *New Yorker* article, he became the inspiration for Coleman Silk, the lead character in Roth's 2000 novel *The Human Stain*, which became a movie starring Anthony Hopkins.

[*See also* Gates, Henry Louis, Jr.; *and* Passing.]

BIBLIOGRAPHY

Broyard, Anatole. *Kafka Was the Rage: A Greenwich Village Memoir*. New York: C. Southern Books, 1993.

Broyard, Bliss. *One Drop: My Father's Hidden Life—A Story of Race and Family Secrets*. Boston: Little, Brown, 2007.

Gates, Henry Louis, Jr. "The Passing of Anatole Broyard." In *Thirteen Ways of Looking at a Black Man*, pp. 180–214. New York: Random House, 1997.

—WAYNE DAWKINS

BRYANT, KOBE (b. 23 August 1978), basketball player. After an extraordinary career at Lower Merion High School in suburban Philadelphia, in 1996, at age seventeen, Kobe Bean Bryant became the youngest guard to be drafted in the history of the National Basketball Association (NBA). Drafted by the Charlotte Hornets with the thirteenth pick, Bryant was subsequently traded to the Los Angeles Lakers for Vlade Divac. Bryant blossomed into an NBA superstar within his first three years and went on to lead the Lakers to three consecutive championships from 2000 to 2002. His eighty-one-point performance against the Toronto Raptors on 22 January 2006 is second only to Wilt Chamberlain's one-hundred-point performance forty-four years prior. Bryant's decision to go straight to the NBA influenced several high school players to forgo college, until the NBA imposed an age minimum of nineteen years in 2006.

Kobe Bryant. Los Angeles Lakers star player Kobe Bryant scores on a steal and pass by his teammate Eddie Jones during a game against the Charlotte Hornets at The Forum, Inglewood, California, 16 February 1999. Photograph by Sam Mircovich. REUTERS

In 2003 Katelyn Faber, a white, seventeen-year-old hotel employee, accused Bryant of rape during his stay in Colorado for knee treatment. Bryant, who had married Vanessa Laine in 2001, contended that the sexual encounter was consensual. Although charges in the criminal trial were dropped and the civil case dismissed, Bryant's image suffered considerably. He consequently lost several endorsement deals and remained under the critical scrutiny of fans and the news media. Despite this, Bryant remains one of the most popular figures in the NBA and around the world.

Kobe Bean Bryant is the son of the former NBA player Joe "Jellybean" Bryant and Pam Bryant. Named after Japan's famous "Kobe" beef, Bryant spent seven years of his childhood in Italy and speaks fluent Italian. He and his wife have two daughters, Natalia Diamante, born in 2003, and Gianna Maria-Onore, born in 2006.

[*See also* Basketball *and* O'Neal, Shaquille.]

BIBLIOGRAPHY

Shapiro, Jeffrey Scott, and Jennifer Stevens. *Kobe Bryant: The Game of His Life*. New York: Revolution, 2004.

—JASON HENDRICKSON

BUCHANAN V. WARLEY. In 1910 Baltimore passed a residential segregation ordinance. Baltimore's counterparts followed its example: Richmond and Norfolk in Virginia, Atlanta, New Orleans, St. Louis, Louisville in Kentucky, and other southern cities and towns soon passed their own segregation ordinances. Louisville became a test case. It designated city blocks with a majority of African Americans "black blocks" and those with a majority of whites "white blocks." Blacks were not allowed to move into white blocks, and whites were not allowed to move into black blocks. These ordinances were drafted to look fair and equal so that they could pass muster under the Fourteenth Amendment, but as the historian T. J. Woofter Jr. explained in 1928:

> Although theoretically the law is supposed to apply to white and colored alike, in practice it never does. The colored people do not protest against white invasion, while the white people in mixed blocks do not hesitate to protest. Altogether about 50 cases have been made against Negroes under the New Orleans ordinance, and there has not been a single case against a white person. (p. 71)

In 1917 in *Buchanan v. Warley* the U.S. Supreme Court held the Louisville ordinance unconstitutional. Moorfield Storey argued the case for the NAACP. In 1917 no plea for black rights would have been likely to prevail; some scholars argue that Storey won because a white right was also at stake: the right of a white seller to sell his house to the highest bidder, even if that person happened to be black. However, in the larger legal landscape, this decision was consistent with other court decisions upholding property rights. A different decision might have undermined many aspects of property law.

The Court held that the Louisville ordinance "destroyed the right of the individual to acquire, enjoy, and dispose of his property," violating the due process clause of the Fourteenth Amendment. Consistent with this analysis is the 1926 decision in *Corrigan v. Buckley*. In this case the Supreme Court unanimously upheld the right of private individuals to agree to restrictive covenants that prohibited property owners from selling their houses to blacks, Asians, Jews, and other minorities. Here the Court upheld the property rights of the owners of all the houses in the neighborhood, who had collectively agreed to act as private homeowners. The Court upheld this right because these were agreements between private citizens. Following precedent dating from the 1870s, the Court made a distinction between constitutionally permissible private actions and inequality created by "state action," which is what the Fourteenth Amendment prohibited.

Covenants were not really private, though, because many suburban governments would not approve new developments without them. Many communities proceeded to encumber every square inch of their residential land with restrictive covenants, thus remaining all white. However, in *Hansberry v. Lee* (1940) the Court unanimously struck down a restrictive covenant on the grounds that it had technically never been properly signed and agreed to by the homeowners. This was a case that marked, along with others, the beginning of the Court's support for black equality. This case involved the parents of the playwright Lorraine Hansberry, and her famous play *A Raisin in the Sun* (1959) was in part influenced by these events.

Many southern and border states cities simply ignored *Buchanan* and continued to enact residential segregation ordinances for decades. Indianapolis passed one in 1926. Attempts to enforce them in the courts were still made as late as the 1950s. Not only towns ignored *Buchanan*. During the Depression the federal government acted as if *Buchanan* did not exist when it set up at least seven towns that explicitly kept out African Americans. The Federal Housing Administration required restrictive covenants before ensuring housing loans. If the United States government, charged with enforcing *Buchanan*, could exclude African Americans, obviously any community could.

In 1968 the federal government finally switched sides. Sympathetic reaction to the assassination of Dr. Martin Luther King Jr. gave Congress the political will to pass Title VIII of the Civil Rights Act of 1968. Often called the Fair Housing Act, this law prohibits racial discrimination in the sale, rental, and financing of housing. The Supreme Court followed in *Jones v. Alfred H. Mayer Co.* (1968).

[*See also* Fair Housing Act; Laws and Legislation; Restrictive Covenants; *and* Storey, Moorfield.]

BIBLIOGRAPHY

Hixson, William B., Jr. *Moorfield Storey and the Abolitionist Tradition*. New York: Oxford University Press, 1972.

Loewen, James W. *Sundown Towns: A Hidden Dimension of American Racism*. New York: New Press, 2005.

Woofter, T. J., Jr. *Negro Problems in Cities* (1928). New York: Harper & Row, 1969.

—JAMES W. LOEWEN

BULLINS, ED (b. 2 July 1935), playwright. Bullins, an American dramatist of the black theater movement, was born in Philadelphia to Edward Dawson Bullins and Bertha Marie Queen Bullins. He lived with his mother, a power machine operator, and attended integrated schools. He dropped out of high school and joined the U.S. Navy in 1952. While in the navy, Bullins competed as a pugilist, using the skills that he had learned and needed on the tough streets of North Philadelphia.

Out of the navy in 1955, Bullins attended two college-prep high schools. Three years later, without a diploma and apparently financially hoodwinked by a female classmate, he left Philadelphia for California. Bullins earned his GED and then continued at Los Angeles City College, publishing his short stories, essays, and poetry in the literary magazine *Citadel*, which he founded with an instructor, Isabelle Ziegler.

Bullins the playwright emerged during the vortex of the civil rights and Black Power movements. In 1964, Bullins relocated to San Francisco, where he saw and was inspired by *Dutchman* (1964) by Amiri Baraka (LeRoi Jones), a forerunner in the Black Arts Movement (1965–1976). In 1965 the Firehouse Repertory Theater in San Francisco presented Bullins's first play, *How Do You Do?*, and two others after local black theaters rejected his nontraditional staging, street language, and characters who reveal intimacies of black life previously hidden from American audiences.

Soon after, Bullins and others formed Black Arts/West, a cultural and political organization. He also collaborated with Eldridge Cleaver, author of *Soul on Ice* (1968), to form the Black House Theater. The building housing the theater would also function later as the headquarters for the Black Panther Party. Bullins served as cultural director of Black House until 1967 when artistic members dissented over alliances with white activists. He also served as minister of culture of the Black Panthers.

Bullins moved to New York in 1967 at the invitation of Robert Macbeth, director of the New Lafayette Theatre in Harlem. He began his ambitious Twentieth-Century Cycle of twenty plays intended to depict the lives of African Americans. Inaugurated by *In the Wine Time* (1968), the cycle's plays have interlocking themes and have characters who are related by blood, marriage, and community. Bullins received an Obie award for the second in the series, *In New England Winter* (1971). Set in locales from California to New York, many of the plays suggest some of the same experiences and predicaments that Bullins himself had.

Bullins and his work were not without controversy. He lambasted the 1972 Lincoln Center production of his play *The Duplex* (1970), accusing the directors of making it a "coon show." The theater critic Erika Munk called Bullins's *Jo Anne!!!* (1976) a hypocritical depiction of the real 1974 trial of Joan Little. Using a pseudonym, Bullins penned *We Righteous Bombers* (1969), a cynical look at the motives of revolutionaries in the Black Power movement.

Author of more than a hundred works, Bullins has received many accolades, including the New York Drama Critics Award for *The Taking of Miss Janie* (1975) and two Guggenheim Fellowships. He earned his MFA from San Francisco State University in 1994 and in 1995 became a professor of theater at Northeastern University in Boston.

[*See also* Black Panther Party; Literature; *and* Theater.]

BIBLIOGRAPHY

Bullins, Ed. *The Theme Is Blackness: "The Corner" and Other Plays*. New York: William Morrow, 1972. The introduction by Bullins is a rare view of his perspective on black theater.

Hay, Samuel A. *Ed Bullins: A Literary Biography*. Detroit, Mich.: Wayne State University Press, 1997. A revealing account, complete with photographs, documenting the playwright's life through examination of his work.

—KISSETTE BUNDY

BUMSTEAD, HORACE (b. 29 September 1841; d. 14 October 1919), white soldier, minister, educator, and administrator. Horace Bumstead was a pivotal figure in the education of African Americans at the turn of the twentieth century. Born in Boston to well-to-do parents, Bumstead was educated at Boston Latin School and Yale, from which he graduated in 1863. He was commissioned as a major during the Civil War and commanded black troops serving in the Richmond and Petersburg campaigns in 1864 and 1865. After the war Bumstead graduated from Andover (Massachusetts) Theological Seminary in 1870, studied in Europe, married in 1872, and served a Congregationalist church in Minneapolis. In 1875 he joined his Yale classmate Edmond Asa Ware at Atlanta University to teach natural science and Latin; he was named interim president in 1886 and president in 1888.

Bumstead—an advocate of industrial instruction as well as of traditional higher education for blacks—inherited a tenuous financial situation in 1888. Founded in 1865 by the American Missionary Association (AMA) and supported financially by the Freedmen's Bureau, Atlanta University was the nation's oldest black institution for higher education and trained many of the region's African American teachers and librarians. Beginning in 1874, Atlanta University had received an annual appropriation of $8,000 from Georgia's Landscrip Fund. In 1887, visiting state commissioners observed white students (children of white missionaries) in classes with blacks; as a result the state legislature eliminated the annual appropriation, offering to restore it if and when only blacks were being educated at the university. Bumstead stood firm against this pressure; as a result the institution's debt increased dramatically. After five years Atlanta University was $21,000 in debt. Bumstead and the trustees turned to the AMA, which agreed to an annual appropriation of $3,000 for five years with the stipulation that the association would nominate six trustees.

Bumstead raised money and recruited new supporters and faculty—among them W. E. B. Du Bois from the University of Pennsylvania. It was under Bumstead that Atlanta University initiated the Atlanta Conference for the Study of the Negro Problems, an annual conference now associated with Du Bois.

Bumstead was instrumental in attracting Carnegie funds for a library (1904) at the university, as well as for other campus buildings. A university press was established. A student publication was begun in 1895, and football was introduced in 1896. In 1906 Atlanta University escaped damage during a race riot in which white mobs killed and injured dozens of blacks—twenty-seven people died and another seventy were injured as a result of three days of death and destruction. Bumstead, a white administrator of black students, can be credited with much of his university's success. Du Bois spoke well of him, and Francis J. Garrison—son of the great abolitionist William Lloyd Garrison—greatly admired Bumstead, calling him the leading advocate for black education of his era.

Bumstead retired to his native Massachusetts in 1907 and died in 1919 in New Hampshire.

[*See also* Atlanta University *and* Du Bois, W. E. B.]

BIBLIOGRAPHY

Adams, Myron W. *A History of Atlanta University*. Atlanta: Atlanta University Press, 1930.

Lewis, David L. *W. E. B. Du Bois: Biography of a Race, 1868–1919*. New York: Holt, Rinehart, and Winston, 1993.

—BOYD CHILDRESS

BUNCHE, RALPH JOHNSON (b. 7 August 1903; d. 9 December 1971), scholar, university professor, diplomat, UN administrator, and Nobel Peace Prize recipient. In the 1950s and 1960s Bunche was the most visible African American on the world stage. But his accomplishments were far in the future when he was born in modest circumstances in Detroit, Michigan, the son of Fred Bunche, a barber, and Olive Bunche. His parents, however, were constantly in poor health, and after their early deaths Bunche was raised by his grandmother, Lucy Johnson, in Los Angeles.

His grandmother's diligence and inspiration guided and shaped Bunche's youth, and he compiled a record of stellar achievement both in athletics—he later was a guard on the basketball team of the University of California at Los Angeles (UCLA)—and in academics. This he did while holding numerous jobs, from delivering newspapers to laying carpets on merchant ships. His early years also brought a discovery of discrimination. African Americans were barred from public swimming facilities, and he was deliberately excluded from a citywide honor society on account of his race. But this did little to deflect Bunche from success. At UCLA he was one of the best students in political science, and he pursued graduate study at Harvard University, thanks to funds raised in the local African American community.

Academic Career. Outstanding achievement as a student served as preparation for Bunche's subsequent career as a university professor. While still a graduate student at Harvard, he was asked to join the faculty of Howard University, where he was a founding member of the Department of Political Science. Bunche's work in political science was characterized by subtlety and nuance. His study of British and French colonial policies in Africa, where he traveled extensively in 1932–1933 and 1937–1938, reveals keen insight and political psychology, especially his idea that the colonial powers and their subjects were not separate and opposed entities but together formed a new society. This new Africa was characterized by social and economic transformation, the withering of traditional African culture and customs, and the emergence of a Western-educated African elite dedicated to nationalist politics in part because it found itself cast adrift in a changing world. The academic expertise that produced such a portrayal was rare in the United States at this time. Bunche's scholarship was the reason he was recruited, following U.S. entry into World War II in December 1941, into the Office of Special Services (OSS), the newly created intelligence and research agency.

Bunche's accomplishments in the 1930s and 1940s were not limited to Africa. Much of his scholarship concerned the place of African Americans in the New Deal, the initiative launched by the administration of President Franklin D. Roosevelt for overcoming the effects of the Great Depression. Here again Bunche's academic work was characterized by sophistication and complexity. While some programs, such as those for cotton farmers sponsored by the Agricultural Adjustment Act (AAA), increased the involvement of African Americans in the economy, others, particularly subsidy programs and the economic reorganization favored by the National Recovery Administration (NRA), had the unintended consequence of inhibiting necessary economic change.

Spingarn Medal. Ralph Bunche arrives at the convention in Los Angeles where he received the 1949 Spingarn Medal, the NAACP's highest honor. NATIONAL ASSOCIATION FOR THE ADVANCEMENT OF COLORED PEOPLE RECORDS, LIBRARY OF CONGRESS

In response Bunche consistently advocated an integrationist strategy—participation by the African American community within a broad political coalition emphasizing economic redistribution and the spread of labor unions—that offered greater social and economic benefit than a policy of separatism. The weakness of the latter, he argued, was that it led to the isolation of the African American community and left it bereft of the political allies and resources needed to overcome the plight of the ordinary African American, who was often mired in poverty at the bottom of American society.

This continuing belief informed not only Bunche's activity with public organizations, such as the National Negro Congress, but also his academic work with the Carnegie Corporation's celebrated project on race relations in the United States led by the Swedish economist Gunnar Myrdal. The latter also led to Bunche's most lasting academic work, later published as *The Political Status of the Negro in the Age of FDR* (1973), which contains a detailed analysis of the societal position of the African American and, as befitting a political scientist, a thorough examination of those political mechanisms, such as political corruption and deliberately obstructive voting laws and procedures in the American South, that retarded the advance of the African American and undermined fundamental American political principles. One of the most studied texts in American political science, it contributed in no small part to his selection as president of the American Political Science Association for the 1953–1954 term. He was the first African American to hold this position.

The United Nations. Bunche always maintained that American political principles were rooted in liberalism, progress, and self-determination. Their relevance was not limited to the United States; indeed they were deserving of international application, and the establishment of these principles in the international sphere formed a major endeavor in Bunche's life. His student involvement in supporting the League of Nations foreshadowed his work in the development of the United Nations (UN). During World War II, Bunche was transferred from the OSS to the State Department, where he was responsible for the planning and organization of the new international body that became the United Nations. He was an official American delegate at its beginning at the San Francisco Conference in the spring of 1945, and demonstrating his commitment, he resigned from the State Department (though in 1948 President Harry Truman tried to encourage him to return with the offer of assistant secretary of state) to become one of the first officials of the United Nations. Bunche helped establish and headed the UN Trusteeship Council. This body played a significant part in the process of African decolonization throughout the 1950s and 1960s; simply put, without it the independence of many African countries would have been considerably delayed.

More pressing concerns, however, soon dominated Bunche's service at the United Nations. The establishment of Israel and the passing of French and British decolonization throughout the region led to turmoil in the Middle East. As the assistant to Count Folke Bernadotte, the UN mediator whom Bunche later succeeded, Bunche's natural diplomatic discretion, patience, and confidence-building skills were deployed to full effect. Bunche arranged a cease-fire between the warring parties during the course of arduous negotiations on the island of Rhodes in the early months of 1949. This achievement was not limited to securing personal agreement among the various leaders and statesmen. Subsequent to establishing the truce, Bunche played a vital part in laying the foundations through the deployment of international monitors and the inauguration of a reconciliation commission to ensure that war did not erupt again. This was then a novel practice in international relations, and from this moment the United Nations had the capacity to actively prevent conflict through its peacekeeping operations. For bringing about this change in world politics, Bunche was awarded the Nobel Peace Prize in 1950.

Peacekeeping concerns continued to preoccupy Bunche's work at the United Nations throughout the 1950s, but the collapse of the Congo into chaos following a hasty Belgian decolonization effort posed altogether new challenges to the UN peacekeeping office Bunche headed as undersecretary general. The issue was not so much to separate combatants but to bring about the acceptance of a framework for a national government and the creation of political order where none existed. Along with Secretary-General Dag Hammarskjöld, who died in an airplane crash in the Congo on 17 September 1961, Bunche spent many anxious months in the Congo.

From the moment of his arrival in the Congo, just a few days after the country's independence on 25 June 1960, Bunche was confronted with the prospect that a unified and peaceful Congo was unlikely given the dismal state of affairs in the country. With college graduates in single figures, a territory of massive size without even rudimentary roads and infrastructure, and countless ethnic rivalries and animosities, it was easy to understand why no stable government was in place following the official Belgian withdrawal. The country's first prime minister, Patrice Lumumba, was a charismatic but controversial figure. Bunche found his dealings with Lumumba difficult not so much because of Lumumba's behavior, which was perceived as erratic—Bunche, after all, had long experience dealing with similar politicians and world leaders—as because he found Lumumba's plans for restoring order to the Congo contradictory and unrealistic. The Congolese government simply lacked the resources to implement Lumumba's designs for sweeping changes and political centralization. Indeed Lumumba's own army later proved unreliable, and after Lumumba discarded the protection of the United Nations, the military was complicit in his kidnapping and assassination. Lumumba's frustration often led to actions Bunche considered rash, including sanctioning the military attack on the people of Kasai, suddenly seeking Soviet military assistance, and public attacks on the credibility of the UN mission in the Congo.

Lumumba was not the only problem facing Bunche. The UN operation in the Congo was the largest yet undertaken by the organization, and Bunche was charged with coordinating not only the swelling numbers of peacekeepers but also their diversity. Contingents from such far-flung places as Morocco, Ireland, and Fiji had to be integrated within a UN command system. But the main obstacle was Katanga, a secessionist breakaway province in the country's southeast. Led by Moise Tshombe, a bitter personal enemy of Lumumba, Katanga was largely organized by recalcitrant Belgians who wished to maintain not only their resource holdings in the region owned by the mining conglomerate Union Minière du Haut Katanga but also to continue their influence in the politics of central Africa.

Even after relative political calm was achieved in the main part of the Congo in 1962, the tension between that area and Katanga threatened to again embroil the country in confusion and disorder. That this dire possibility did not unfold was due in no small part to the personal diplomacy of Bunche. Displaying considerable personal courage in the face of danger, including when his UN airplane was nearly shot down by Katangese troops, he tirelessly traveled between the national capital Léopoldville and the seat of the Katangese government in Elizabethville. After months of stressful bargaining, he secured the Kitona agreement, whose eight-point declaration was drafted primarily by Bunche, between Cyrille Adoula, the prime minister of the Congo, and Tshombe that ended the conflict and enabled Katanga to rejoin the Congo. This was a landmark achievement, and thanks to Bunche's efforts the United Nations stood at the height of its prestige and effectiveness, a force for peacemaking as well as peacekeeping.

Civil Rights. While matters at the United Nations understandably dominated Bunche's professional life, his status as a Nobel Peace Prize winner ensured that his remarks and policy interventions at home received wide notice. In the 1950s he delivered the prestigious Walgreen Lectures at the University of Chicago, where his emphasis on the need for government to guarantee economic security for its citizens demonstrated that he was both aware of and engaged with the trends affecting American society.

The need to advance civil rights, too, commanded Bunche's attention. As early as 1936 he picketed the National Theatre in Washington, D.C., over its refusal to admit African Americans. During the 1950s, a time often fraught with dangers, he spoke at venues and forums throughout the American South in support of civil rights. He was a participant in the major civil rights events of the 1960s. Bunche spoke immediately preceding Martin Luther King Jr. when the latter delivered his famous "I have a dream" speech at the Lincoln Memorial on 28 August 1963, and he was in the front row of the 1965 civil rights march from Selma to Montgomery, which he completed despite suffering painfully from the effects of diabetes and phlebitis. Not all of Bunche's civil rights work was conducted in the public eye. His leadership resulted in the Rockefeller Foundation establishing programs in December 1967 directed at ameliorating conditions inside the African American ghettos of major cities, and he ensured that the National Association for the Advancement of Colored People (NAACP) remained open to citizens of all races and ethnic groups.

Bunche never retired from public service. When he died in a New York City hospital, he was still working at the United Nations with Secretary-General U Thant's efforts to broker a cease-fire in the Vietnamese conflict. Like so many quiet, modest, and hardworking persons, Bunche's accomplishments and life were perhaps not given the notice they deserved in his time, but a longer perspective yields a true picture and understanding. In this light his achievement and success continue to gain both appreciation and admiration.

[*See also* Afrocentrism; Civil Rights Movement; *and* Civil Rights, International.]

BIBLIOGRAPHY

Bunche, Ralph J. *The Political Status of the Negro in the Age of FDR.* Chicago: University of Chicago Press, 1973. Bunche's most important academic work.

Henry, Charles P. *Ralph Bunche: Model Negro or American Other?* New York: New York University Press, 1999. An accessible biography of Bunche that also draws upon Bunche's papers and interviews with family members and associates.

Holloway, Jonathan Scott. *Confronting the Veil: Abram Harris Jr., E. Franklin Frazier, and Ralph Bunche, 1919–1941.* Chapel Hill: University of North Carolina Press, 2002. A thorough treatment of Bunche's early academic work and its context in American intellectual life.

Keppel, Ben. *The Work of Democracy: Ralph Bunche, Kenneth B. Clark, Lorraine Hansberry, and the Cultural Politics of Race.* Cambridge, Mass.: Harvard University Press, 1995. A consideration of Bunche's evolving thought and concern with American racial issues.

Mann, Peggy. *Ralph Bunche: UN Peacemaker*. New York: Coward, McCann, and Geoghegan, 1975. A thorough and detailed accounting of Bunche's career with the United Nations.

Urquhart, Brian. *Ralph Bunche: An American Life*. New York: W. W. Norton, 1993. A comprehensive biography of Bunche that benefits from the fact the author served with Bunche at the United Nations.

—JOSEPH C. HEIM

BURNHAM, LOUIS (b. 29 September 1915; d. 12 February 1960), civil rights activist and journalist. Louis Everett Burnham was born in Barbados and raised in Harlem, New York. His parents, Charles, a building superintendent, and Louise, a hairdresser, were Barbadian immigrants who moved to Harlem for better opportunities for themselves and for their children.

Graduating in 1932 from Townsend High School, Burnham enrolled in the City College of New York, where he became a proponent of racial justice. He served as president of the Frederick Douglass Society and aided in organizing the American Student Union.

Burnham's quest for racial justice did not end upon graduating from City College in 1936. Instead it accelerated, and Burnham's work in the South in the 1940s led him into dangerous predicaments. In Birmingham, Alabama, Burnham worked to end the discrimination and segregation of the Jim Crow era. In the fight for desegregation of public accommodations, Burnham helped to organize sit-ins at lunch counters. As a journalist, he wrote articles depicting the injustices of Jim Crow.

Burnham also worked to realize voting rights for all blacks. Although blacks' voting rights were protected by the Fifteenth Amendment, in southern states, legal barriers such as the poll tax and reading or writing tests had been implemented to prevent blacks from voting. As the organizational secretary for the Southern Negro Youth Congress (SNYC) in Alabama, Burnham helped to organize voter registration campaigns and nonviolent marches. And he worked on the 1948 presidential campaign of Henry A. Wallace, the Progressive Party candidate, who believed in racial equality.

Upon returning to Harlem in the 1950s, Burnham cofounded the newspaper *Freedom*. Using his pen as a weapon to fight against racial injustice, Burnham wrote articles on a variety of subjects, such as the murder of Emmett Till. Louis Burnham dedicated his life to fighting against racial injustice. He died in 1960, but remnants of his life's work live on. We must remember that he, along with others, paid the price for future generations.

[*See also* Desegregation and Integration, *subentry* Overview; Jim Crow Laws; Journalism, Print and Broadcast; Poll Taxes; Sit-ins; Till, Emmett, Lynching of; *and* Voting Rights.]

BIBLIOGRAPHY

New York Times. "Louis Burnham, 44, Editor on Weekly," 14 February 1960, 84. The obituary of Louis Burnham.

—MARTHA J. ROSS-RODGERS

BURNS, HAYWOOD (b. 15 June 1940; d. 2 April 1996), a central figure in the civil rights and human rights movement in the United States as an activist, attorney, and scholar. Born in New York City in 1940, William Haywood Burns helped integrate the swimming pool in Peekskill, New York, at fifteen years of age and was a leader in the struggle for human rights and civil rights over the next four decades. He graduated from Harvard College in 1962. As a law student at Yale University, he participated in the 1964 Freedom Summer in Mississippi. He already had authored *The Voices of Negro Protest* (1963), which critiqued the leadership and mass character of the civil rights movement, and throughout his career he contributed chapters to other books. He was assistant counsel to the NAACP Legal Defense and Educational Fund in the late 1960s. Later he served as general counsel to Martin Luther King Jr.'s Poor People's Campaign in 1968.

Burns cofounded the National Conference of Black Lawyers in 1967, serving as executive director for the first decade of the organization's existence. During that time he pioneered a progressive legal career and strategic template that included creative representation in key cases such as the aftermath of the Attica prison rebellion in New York State in 1971; he also represented the militant Communist Party activist Angela Davis in the face of criminal charges. During the 1970s Burns worked at the City College of New York, where he served as the director of the Max E. and Filomen M. Greenberg Center for Legal Education and Urban Policy and was chair of the Urban Legal Studies Program. During the 1980s Burns played a leading role in dozens of civil rights and human rights organizations and was president of the National Lawyers Guild, the largest organization of progressive lawyers in the United States.

In 1987 Burns was appointed dean of the City University of New York Law School at Queens College, thus becoming the first African American to serve as dean of a law school in New York State. He held that position until 1994. During his tenure CUNY Law School developed its identity and reputation as a public-interest law school, educating a generation of lawyers committed to working on behalf of people in need instead of pursuing careers for self-interest.

Burns then went into private practice with Robert van Lierop, focusing on international law and human rights work. In April 1996, while attending a conference of the International Association of Democratic Lawyers in South Africa, Burns died from injuries sustained in a car accident. He was memorialized around the world, and he left a legacy of legal activism and scholarship as a model for future generations of civil rights and human rights advocates. The corner where his New York City law office was located, 143d Street and Convent Avenue, was renamed W. Haywood Burns Corner in 2000.

[*See also* Legal Profession; Mississippi Freedom Summer; National Conference of Black Lawyers; *and* Poor People's Campaign.]

—Joseph Wilson
—David Addams

BURRELL COMMUNICATIONS. A full-service advertising agency with a focus on public relations, event marketing, and consumer promotions, Burrell Communications Group has been the nation's leading advertising agency specializing in African American, urban, and youth markets. Some of the services include brand consulting, account planning, public relations, event marketing, research, and creative ad work.

The brain behind Burrell Communications Group (also known as the Group) is the founder Thomas Burrell. The Group opened in Chicago, Illinois, in 1971, and a branch opened in Atlanta, Georgia, in 1972. As a result of a deal brokered in 1999 the French ad giant Publicis Groupe owns 49 percent of the Burrell Group, which has served some very large clients and brands, such as the Art Institute of Chicago, Polaroid Corporation, Crest, Sears, Tide, Toyota, and Olay. The Group has garnered numerous awards, including the Association of American Advertising Agencies award for Multicultural Agency of the Year, the Association of National Advertisers Multicultural Excellence Award, and the BE (Black Enterprise) Advertising Agency of the Year award. In the early twenty-first century, the Burrell Communications Group billed close to $200 million annually.

The Group is corporate America's source for developing specialized advertising and marketing campaigns targeting African Americans, youths, and the urban market. In the early twenty-first century McDonald's restaurants remained Burrell's oldest and largest client, with about twenty-seven thousand restaurants in 119 countries. Verizon's African American–targeted advertising is handled by Burrell Communications with a newer focus on Verizon's products and customer service commitment. The firm remained strong despite challenges posed by a struggling economy, with increased billings and the addition of major clients including General Mills, Hewlett-Packard, and Toyota in 2001.

When the Group opened its doors in 1971 it "had no secretary, one telephone, and three old desks which we painted red, green, and orange," Burrell asserted in an interview with *Black Enterprise*'s Monique Brown. That mind-set helped the firm stay afloat then and subsequently helped it focus on business. With employees numbering about 135 and increased billing annually, Burrell has proven that it pays to portray African Americans realistically. Burrell continued:

> We depicted them as families that had lives, loves, passions, and emotions. We showed people doing things such as going to church. The response was enormous, simply because we had not seen ourselves in a positive setting. It gave people a wonderful feeling about the products being advertised as well as an affection for the companies delivering those messages.

[*See also* Stereotypes of African Americans.]

Bibliography

Brown, Monique R. "Born to Transform: The Burrell Communications Group Bursts Out of the Ad Agency Box to Become Bigger, Better, and Bolder." *Black Enterprise*, 1 June 2002.

Edwards, Eddie K. "Profiles of Progress: Thomas J. Burrell." *Michigan Chronicle*, February 1994.

McGeehan, Pat. "The Burrell Style: Building a Solid Base on Michigan Avenue." *Advertising Age*, 19 December 1985.

—OluwaTosin Adegbola

BUSH, GEORGE H. W., ADMINISTRATION OF. The George H. W. Bush administration, from 1989 to 1993, promised to be less oppressive for blacks after eight years of Reaganism, arguably the most racist presidency since the Jim Crow era. Bush, a conservative and Ronald Reagan's vice president, promised a "kinder, gentler" style of governing that suggested a retreat from the mean-spirited rhetoric and policies of 1981–1989. Bush had a track record as a supporter of the United Negro College Fund since his student days at Yale University. As a congressman from Texas from 1967 to 1971, Bush supported the antidiscriminatory Fair Housing Act (Title VIII of the Civil Rights Act) of 1968 and at that time angered many of his white constituents.

Yet Bush's 1988 campaign for president was accused of making racist appeals. Bush campaign advertisements displayed images of the convicted rapist-murderer Willie Horton, a black man released on parole by Massachusetts. That commonwealth's governor, Michael Dukakis, was Bush's Democratic opponent, and Bush was elected handily. In 1990, shortly before his death from brain cancer, Bush's campaign manager Lee Atwater apologized for the racially inflammatory advertisements.

Bush chose Louis Sullivan of the historically black Morehouse College for the Health and Human Services cabinet post. Months later in 1989, General Colin Powell was promoted to commander of the Joint Chiefs of Staff, a first for an African American. A number of blacks filled meaningful subcabinet posts, including Michael Williams at the Department of Education. By 1991, Condoleezza Rice appeared on Americans' radar: this African American woman was Bush's expert on the Soviet Union and nuclear arms control.

Bush's rhetoric and gestures were less hostile than Reagan's had been, but he still pushed policies that a number of black leaders said were harmful. A civil rights bill promoting affirmative action was debated in Congress. Bush scornfully called the legislation a "quota bill" even though the bill forbade the use of fixed numbers or percentages for hiring. Congress passed the bill, but Bush vetoed it in October 1990. A Senate override failed by one vote. In 1992, Bush signed a compromise civil rights bill. In 1990, Bush unsuccessfully attempted to place the black conservative William Lucas as assistant attorney general for civil rights in the Justice Department.

Bush's most lasting decision was his nomination of Clarence Thomas in July 1991 to fill the U.S. Supreme Court vacancy created by the retirement of Thurgood Marshall, the first and at the time only black on the high court. Thomas was presented as a poor black boy from Georgia who overcame poverty and discrimination to excel in America. Thomas was an undistinguished federal judge—appointed by Bush to the Court of Appeals in 1990—and former head of the Equal Employment Opportunity Commission (EEOC). Thomas's nomination appeared secure until Anita Hill, a former EEOC employee, charged that Thomas sexually harassed her and that he was therefore unfit for the lifetime appointment. After bruising Senate confirmation hearings, Thomas was nevertheless elevated to the high court.

Black support in the old-line civil rights community was deeply divided over Thomas. One side appealed for the addition of a black, any black, to the bench to replace the only one—Marshall—who had now departed. The other side argued that color was not good enough if the person's ideas were harmful. Ever since his appointment, Thomas has been regarded as an ultraconservative, anti–civil rights justice.

Thanksgiving in Saudi Arabia. President George H. W. Bush celebrates Thanksgiving with members of the U.S. Army's 197th Infantry Brigade in Saudi Arabia during the Gulf War, 1990. George Bush Library, National Archives and Records Administration

Regarding foreign policy, Powell, Bush's joint chief of the four military branches, was a confident and resolute leader, whether he was extracting the strongman Manuel Noriega from Panama in Central America or punishing Saddam Hussein after the Iraqi leader invaded Kuwait in late 1990 and allied forces retaliated in 1991. That war with Iraq lasted less than two months and resulted in minimal U.S. casualties.

Sullivan, Bush's Health and Human Services secretary, campaigned successfully to ban Uptown cigarettes, R. J. Reynolds Tobacco Company's high-nicotine tobacco targeted to urban African American consumers. In education, Michael Williams was flag bearer of the proposal to end so-called race-based scholarships that aided black and other minority recipients. Williams argued that the programs were discriminatory; critics countered that other special-interest groups were allowed to offer restricted scholarships. Bush rejected Williams's proposal.

One of Bush's last major challenges was managing the boatlift of thousands of Haitian refugees to South Florida. The Caribbean blacks were intercepted by authorities and imprisoned at Guantánamo Bay, the U.S. naval base in Cuba. The Haitians said that they sought asylum from a murderous regime; the Bush administration insisted that the "illegal" immigrants were economic refugees. The Democrat Bill Clinton, Bush's successor, inherited the problem and initially followed Bush's policy.

[*See also* Clinton, Bill, Administration of; Reagan, Ronald, Administration of; *and biographical entries on figures mentioned in this article*.]

BIBLIOGRAPHY

Bennett, Lerone, Jr. *Before the* Mayflower: *A History of Black America*. 8th ed. Chicago: Johnson, 2007.

Dawkins, Wayne. *Rugged Waters: Black Journalists Swim the Mainstream*. Newport News, Va.: August Press, 2003.

Lockman, Norman, ed. *Black Voices in Commentary*. Wilmington, Del.: News-Journal, 1995.

McAndrews, Lawrence J. "Beyond Busing: George H. W. Bush and School Desegregation." *Educational Foundations* 15, no. 4 (2001): 41–56.

—WAYNE DAWKINS

BUSH, GEORGE W., ADMINISTRATION OF.

Though he began his first term as president in 2001, George W. Bush declined to speak at the NAACP's annual convention until 2006; after the 2000 election the NAACP had led a legal challenge against what it considered the purging of black voters from the registration rolls in Florida, and as a result the relationship between Bush and the NAACP had been cold. In this first address to the NAACP, Bush commented, "I consider it a tragedy that the party of Abraham Lincoln let go of its historic ties with the African American community. For too long my party wrote off the African American vote, and many wrote off the Republican Party." In 2000 George W. Bush received only 8 percent of the African American vote, the weakest support that a Republican nominee had received since Barry Goldwater in 1964 and a stark contrast to Bush's own 1998 reelection as the governor of Texas, when he won 30 percent of the African American vote.

Following the 2000 election, along with the NAACP, many African Americans contended that George W. Bush had stolen the election from Al Gore. However, polling data at the time reported that most African Americans did not feel angry about the result of the election, and most were willing to accept Bush as the legitimately elected president. Paradoxically, his appointment of Colin Powell as secretary of state and Condoleezza Rice as national security adviser—making the pair the highest-ranking African American government officials ever—lowered African Americans' confidence in the Bush administration.

Compassionate Conservative. As president-elect, Bush convened a meeting to discuss his so-called compassionate-conservative policy agenda. He pledged to create a $700 million Compassion Capital Fund to help launch what he called his "faith-based initiative," seemingly tailored to inner-city, predominantly African American churches. The fund was created in 2002. Despite opposition from liberals and conservatives the president won the support of African American clergy. Bush's strategy of featuring politically sympathetic African American clergy seemed to confirm that the leadership of minority groups is often out of step with most of the members of the groups themselves.

Speaking to the National Urban League in 2004, Bush asked African Americans to "take a look at my agenda," highlighting his faith-based initiative, government support for home ownership and small businesses, education reforms and voucher programs, and support for the traditional family. And indeed in 2004, 11 percent of African Americans voted for Bush, compared with 8 percent in 2000. Bush's expansion of African American support is attributed to his southern, religious personality, coupled with his overwhelming opposition to same-sex marriage and civil unions, views that made him more popular among African American conservative Christians.

The Bush administration's efforts of increasing minority homeownership were thwarted by the predatory subprime lending in African American communities. Further, although small-business loans to African Americans were up by 75 percent in one year, Bush's administration consistently targeted for elimination the Small Business Administration's venture-capital, microlending, and loan-guarantee programs for women, minorities, and underserved populations.

Critics have asserted that the $1.6 trillion, ten-year tax cut, the hallmark of Bush's fiscal policy, widened the racial and ethnic wealth and income divide by rewarding with lower taxes those who have investment income and penalizing with higher taxes those with wage income. Some assert that Bush's tax-cut plan caused a rise in the number of adults and children living in poverty, with a disproportionate number of African Americans affected. In 2005 the poverty rate for blacks was 24.7 percent, three times the poverty rate for whites. In 2004 the unemployment rate for blacks was more than double that for whites: 10.8 percent for blacks and 4.7 percent for whites. Studies show that this gap has continued to widen.

Policies. President Bush has received sharp criticism for nominating certain people to federal judgeships that some fear will turn the clock back on civil rights enforcement, laws protecting women's reproductive choice, and access to justice for the poor. Another point of contention is the overall number of black nominations to the federal bench. Of Bush's two hundred judicial appointments overall, only fifteen, or 7.5 percent, were African American—four on circuit courts and eleven on district courts. This contrasts sharply with his predecessor, Bill Clinton, who named sixty-one African Americans to federal judgeships among his 373 appointments. Bush's record on African American judicial appointments is worse in the South, where most African Americans live.

The Bush administration has aggressively fought affirmative action policies in higher education. Notably Bush announced his decision to oppose two affirmative action programs at the University of Michigan on Martin Luther King Jr.'s birthday in 2003.

Hurricane Katrina of 29 August 2005 took thousands of lives and caused hundreds of billions of dollars in property damage along the Gulf Coast. The Congressional Research Service (CRS) estimated that of the people most likely to have been displaced by the hurricane, about half lived in New Orleans. Because of the city's social and economic composition, the storm impacted the poor and African Americans most heavily. The CRS estimated that one-fifth of those displaced by the storm were likely to have been poor, and 30 percent had incomes that were well below the poverty line. African Americans were estimated to have accounted for approximately 44 percent of the storm victims.

The president's response to Hurricane Katrina was seen by many African Americans as inadequate and as evidence that he did not care about them. The rapper Kanye West caused controversy just days after Hurricane Katrina struck when he said on live television, "George Bush doesn't care about black people." Bush's actions after Katrina persuaded African Americans that he was a president who was totally insensitive to their concerns and their needs: for several days after the storm, the president continued his vacation at his ranch in Crawford, Texas.

According to a Gallup poll taken in May 2007, 85 percent of African Americans say that initiating the war in Iraq was a mistake, compared to 53 percent of white Americans. The enrollment of African Americans in the military may be at its lowest point since the creation of the all-volunteer military in 1973. In 2000, 23.5 percent of U.S. Army recruits were African American. By 2005 the percentage was 13.9 percent. The drop in African American enrollment in the military may be as powerful a collective political statement about Iraq as when Muhammad Ali refused to be drafted during the Vietnam War.

Ironically, the Bush administration has gained some praise for its commitment to providing aid to Africa—the administration has done more than the Clinton administration did. Bush's legacy includes labeling atrocities in Darfur as genocide, increasing funding to combat the HIV/AIDS pandemic, creating the Millennium Challenge Corporation (MCC) that provides grants to developing countries, and increasing development assistance by 54 percent.

[*See also* Hurricane Katrina; Iraq War; *and* No Child Left Behind.]

BIBLIOGRAPHY

Jones, Joyce A. "Bush Administration Not Making the Grade: What Has the Government Done for African Americans Lately?" *Black Enterprise*, 1 February 2006.

"President Bush Addresses NAACP Annual Convention." Office of the Press Secretary, 20 July 2006. http://www.whitehouse.gov/news/releases/2006/07/20060720.html.

Stevenson, Richard W. "The 2004 Campaign, the President: Bush Urges Blacks to Reconsider Allegiance to Democratic Party." *New York Times*, 24 July 2004.

—JAMAL DONALDSON BRIGGS

BUSINESS. *See* Entrepreneurship.

BUTLER, OCTAVIA (b. 22 June 1947; d. 24 February 2006), award-winning science fiction author. Octavia Estelle Butler was born in Pasadena, California, to Laurice Butler, a shoeshine man who died when she was an infant, and Octavia Margaret Butler, a domestic. She was raised in a multicultural neighborhood in Pasadena by her mother and grandmother. Butler wrote her first science fiction story at the age of ten after viewing a television program and deciding that she could write a better story. She attended Pasadena City College and graduated in 1968.

Butler did not receive formal training in science fiction writing until she attended the 1970 Clarion Science Fiction Writer's Workshop. One of her short stories produced as a part of this workshop was published in the 1971 Clarion anthology, and after that her work began to be more widely admired and published. Over the years she was a winner of Hugo awards (given by science fiction writers) and Nebula awards (given by science fiction fans), and in 1995 she received a MacArthur Foundation fellowship (the "genius grant").

Butler's novels and short stories pointedly expose various sexual, racial, and cultural chauvinisms. Her fiction is enriched by a historical consciousness that allows her to explore imaginary pasts and futures paralleling contemporary human existence. Butler frequently uses African American women as her protagonists, although characters who are white or male or both are also an essential part of her novels. The diversity of her characters allows Butler to explore relationships along various racial and gender lines, whether black and white or human and alien.

[*See also* Literature.]

BIBLIOGRAPHY

Benbow-Pfalzgraf, Taryn, ed. *American Women Writers, a Critical Reference Guide: From Colonial Times to the Present*. Detroit, Mich.: St. James Press, 2000.

Butler, Octavia E. *Kindred*. Boston: Beacon Press, 2003.

Hine, Darlene Clark, ed. *Black Women in America: An Historical Encyclopedia*. 2d ed. Oxford: Oxford University Press, 2005.

Page, Yolanda Williams, ed. *Encyclopedia of African American Women Writers*. Westport, Conn.: Greenwood Press, 2007.

—COURTNEY L. YOUNG

BUTTS, CALVIN (b. 19 July 1949), pastor of the historic Abyssinian Baptist Church in Harlem, New York, and president of the State University of New York College at Old Westbury. From the pastoral post long held by Congressman Adam Clayton Powell Jr. (1908–1972), Calvin Otis Butts III developed a model of financial revitalization mirrored by other late-twentieth-century black churches struggling to sustain their communities and retain political influence in the post–civil rights era.

Born in New York City and educated at Morehouse College, Union Theological Seminary, and Drew University, Butts began his career in 1972 as associate pastor of Abyssinian. Upon being named head pastor in 1989, Butts consolidated the economic interests of his church into the Abyssinian Development Corporation (ADC), which has managed more than $300 million in housing and commercial development in Harlem, as well as several social-service operations, including a transitional shelter, a family-services program, and a tenant cooperative. Butts's support of commercial expansion in Harlem has been met with mixed reviews by resident blacks, many of whom take issue with his endorsement of prominent Republican politicians and collusion with corporate contractors.

Despite his detractors, Butts has achieved considerable political sway in New York City and abroad, serving as president of the Council of Churches of the City of New York, chairman of the National Affiliate Development Initiative of the National Black Leadership Commission on AIDS (BLCA), and president of Africare, an organization dedicated to the improvement of the quality of life in rural Africa. After teaching at City College, New York, and Fordham University, Butts was appointed president of the SUNY College at Old Westbury on Long Island in 1999.

[*See also* Abyssinian Baptist Church.]

BIBLIOGRAPHY

Lambert, Bruce. "From a Pulpit to a College Presidency." *New York Times*, 19 September 1999.

—KATHRYN LOFTON

C

CALIFORNIA. The history of African Americans in California since 1890 has been characterized by explosive population growth, impressive political achievements, and persistent employment and housing discrimination.

African Americans arrived in California in small numbers in the mid-nineteenth century. The state's white residents discriminated against African Americans, but they expressed even more hostility toward Native Americans, residents of Mexican ancestry, and Chinese immigrants. African Americans who came to California in the 1850s and 1860s organized and fought to gain the right to vote and the right to testify in court cases involving white people. These efforts did not succeed, and African Americans in the state gained the right to vote only when the Fifteenth Amendment to the Constitution was ratified. In 1880 the California legislature revised the state's school law so that it did not allow separate schools for different racial groups. (The state later sanctioned separate schools for Asian Americans and American Indians; it did not completely ban segregation until 1947.)

The 1890 census counted only 11,322 African Americans in California. This small number of African Americans faced discrimination in housing, employment, and access to hotels, restaurants, and theaters. African American leaders in Bakersfield, Fresno, Los Angeles, Marysville, Monrovia, Oakland, Pasadena, Riverside, Sacramento, San Francisco, San Jose, and Stockton established branches of the Afro-American League (later the Afro-American Council) in the 1890s to fight discrimination. Women's clubs, many affiliated with the California Association of Colored Women's Clubs, also worked to end discrimination against African Americans. In the 1890s the legislature passed laws that outlawed discrimination in public accommodations. These laws, however, did not effectively end such discrimination.

The state's African American population actually declined during the 1890s, but after that decade the African American population nearly doubled every ten years until the period covered by the 1940 census. In 1910 about 20,000 African Americans lived in California. The population growth facilitated the emergence of new civil rights organizations. The attorney E. Burton Ceruti and the dentist John Alexander Somerville led the effort that established a branch of the National Association for the Advancement of Colored People (NAACP) in Los Angeles in 1914. An NAACP branch was established in the San Francisco Bay area in the following year.

Until the early twentieth century, the number of African Americans in most California communities was too small to constitute a powerful political constituency. By the end of the second decade of the century, however, the number of African Americans in one district had grown large enough to facilitate the election of an African American candidate to the assembly, the lower house of the state legislature. In the 1918 primary election, many white voters in the 74th District split their votes among four white candidates. This split allowed the African American undertaker and newspaper publisher Frederick Roberts to win the Republican nomination. His success in the primary assured him of victory in the general election in this heavily Republican district. Once in office, Roberts introduced legislation to strengthen California's civil rights law by providing heavier penalties for business owners found guilty of racial discrimination.

In 1920 nearly 40,000 African Americans lived in California. In the early 1920s Marcus Garvey's Universal Negro Improvement Association (UNIA) attracted some of the state's most prominent African American leaders, including the *California Eagle* publishers Joseph and Charlotta Bass, the journalist and realtor Noah D. Thompson, and the attorney Hugh Macbeth. All but one hundred of the one thousand UNIA members in Los Angeles, however, abandoned the organization late in 1921, when Thompson reported on the national convention in New York. The convention convinced Thompson that Garvey and his top lieutenants were mismanaging one of the organization's businesses, the Black Star Line. A Los Angeles branch of the National Urban League was established in the early 1920s. A Bay Area branch of the Urban League was not organized until after World War II.

Most African Americans who came to California found jobs in already established and growing industries. Some, however, possessed an entrepreneurial spirit and established their own businesses. In 1925 William Nickerson Jr., Norman O. Houston, and George A. Beavers Jr. established the Golden State Mutual Life Insurance Company in Los Angeles. This firm quickly grew to become one of the largest black-owned insurance companies.

Residential segregation in Southern California led to the emergence of a vibrant cultural life. Discrimination forced a large percentage of African Americans to live in a narrow strip that straddled Central Avenue south of downtown Los Angeles. Because of this concentration, a number of businesses that catered to African Americans were established on Central Avenue. African American musicians from around the country attracted diverse audiences, including local residents and Hollywood stars, to Central Avenue nightclubs in the years between 1920 and the 1950s.

During the 1930s the growth rate of the African American population slowed, affected by the Great Depression. In 1930 about 80,000 African Americans lived in California. The 1940 census counted nearly 125,000 African Americans in the state. In addition to slowing the growth rate, the Depression led to a dramatic shift in African American politics. Roberts had consistently won reelection to the state assembly since his election in 1918. In 1934, however, shifting party affiliations allowed the Democrat Augustus Hawkins, also an African American, to unseat him. By this time the district boundaries had been redrawn so that African Americans constituted a greater percentage of the voters in the district. By 1940, 60 percent of the residents of this district were African Americans. For fourteen years Hawkins was the only African American in the state legislature. Like his Republican predecessor, Hawkins worked to address discrimination in California, but he found little support from European American lawmakers.

Although few African Americans were able to take advantage of higher education, California's colleges and universities did not exclude them. In the period before World War II, a number of African Americans who had studied at the University of California emerged as important public officials and athletes. Walter Gordon earned a bachelor's degree and a law degree at the Berkeley campus. As an attorney and NAACP leader in Alameda County, Gordon came to know the district attorney Earl Warren, who later was elected governor of California and then appointed chief justice of the U.S. Supreme Court. President Dwight D. Eisenhower appointed Gordon governor of the U.S. Virgin Islands in 1955. Ralph Bunche graduated summa cum laude from the Los Angeles campus (UCLA) in 1927. He earned his doctorate in political science at Harvard University. Bunche worked for the U.S. government and the United Nations during and after World War II. He negotiated armistice agreements between Arabs and Jews in Palestine, for which he was awarded the NAACP's Spingarn Medal in 1949 and the Nobel Peace Prize in 1950. A building on the UCLA campus is named for him. Kenny Washington and Woody Strode, who desegregated professional football in 1946, and Jackie Robinson, who desegregated major league baseball in 1947, all studied at UCLA.

World War II. World War II led to an unprecedented and transformative migration of African Americans to California. During the war the African American population of Los Angeles doubled, from under 65,000 to more than 133,000. Oakland's African American population increased by more than 360 percent (from 8,000 to more than 37,000), and San Francisco's African American population increased by more than 500 percent (from fewer than 5,000 to nearly 32,000). The most spectacular population growth occurred in Richmond, a small city twenty miles north of Oakland. Richmond's African American population grew from 270 in 1940 to more than 5,000 in 1943—an increase of 1,750 percent. Over the course of the 1940s the state's African American population increased by more than 270 percent. The 1950 census counted 462,172 African Americans in California.

The promise of jobs in the state's booming shipyards and aircraft factories drew many of the African Americans who moved to California during the war. In the first year after Pearl Harbor, however, many employers continued to refuse to hire African Americans. By 1943 a persistent shortage of workers led many employers to hire African Americans. A change in hiring policies did not signal the end of employment discrimination. Many employers hired African Americans only for the dirtiest and most dangerous jobs, and most refused to promote their African American employees. Some unions refused to represent the interests of African American workers.

Although many African Americans found jobs in wartime California, far fewer found adequate housing. Military use took priority over civilian use of building materials; few new houses and apartment buildings were constructed during the war. Discrimination prevented many African Americans from obtaining new or well-maintained houses. Several families shared single-family dwellings, and some families ended up renting garages and sheds.

After the war many African Americans continued to struggle against employment discrimination. The unemployment rate for African Americans in the state was usually significantly higher than the unemployment rate for European Americans. The end of wartime restrictions on construction materials, however, allowed many African Americans to move into better housing. As European Americans moved into new housing developments, many African American neighborhoods expanded. Some developers also built communities from which African Americans were not excluded.

The movement of large numbers of African Americans to California that began before World War II did not abate until the 1990s. The 1960 census counted nearly 900,000 African Americans in California. By 1970 more than 1.4 million African Americans lived in the state. This number increased to 1.8 million in 1980 and 2.2 million in 1990. The wartime and postwar growth of the African American population set the stage for dramatic changes in California politics. In 1948 the Berkeley pharmacist William Byron Rumford joined Hawkins in the assembly. Rumford represented a district that included parts of Oakland and Berkeley.

In 1962, after twenty-eight years in the assembly, Hawkins successfully sought election to the U.S. House of Representatives, where he also served for twenty-eight years before retiring in 1990. The growth of the African American population in Los Angeles also led to the election of two African Americans, Mervyn M. Dymally and F. Douglas Ferrell, to the assembly in 1962. In 1964 Willie L. Brown Jr. of San Francisco was elected to the assembly. Brown won election as the speaker of the assembly in 1981; he retained that position until 1995, when the Democrats lost their majority in the house. In 1995 Brown left the assembly and was elected mayor of San Francisco. He served two terms as mayor, leaving office in January 2004.

African Americans also began to win election to local offices in the early 1960s. Gilbert Lindsay was appointed to fill a vacancy on the Los Angeles City Council in 1962. A coalition of African Americans and liberal European American Democrats, many of them Jewish, elected the retired police officer Tom Bradley to a seat on the council in 1963. Billy Mills won a third seat on the council later that year.

The presence of growing numbers of African Americans in the legislature contributed to the passage of groundbreaking legislation. In 1963, for example, the legislature passed the Rumford Fair Housing Act, which outlawed discrimination in the sale or rental of homes. The passage of the fair housing act, however, did not reflect a dramatic shift in European American attitudes. The act enraged real estate brokers and developers, who succeeded in repealing the legislation when California voters approved Proposition 14 on the 1964 ballot. The success of Proposition 14 left many African Americans disenchanted. Many African Americans also found it difficult to find good jobs. Many employers moved offices and factories from the central city to suburban areas. Inadequate public transportation made it impossible for people without cars to commute to these jobs, and housing discrimination made it difficult for African Americans to move closer to these jobs. Moreover, conflicts between African Americans and the police intensified in the early 1960s. Frustration erupted in rioting in Los Angeles in August 1965. By the time the National Guard had restored order in the southern part of the city, known as Watts, thirty-four people, most of them African Americans, had died.

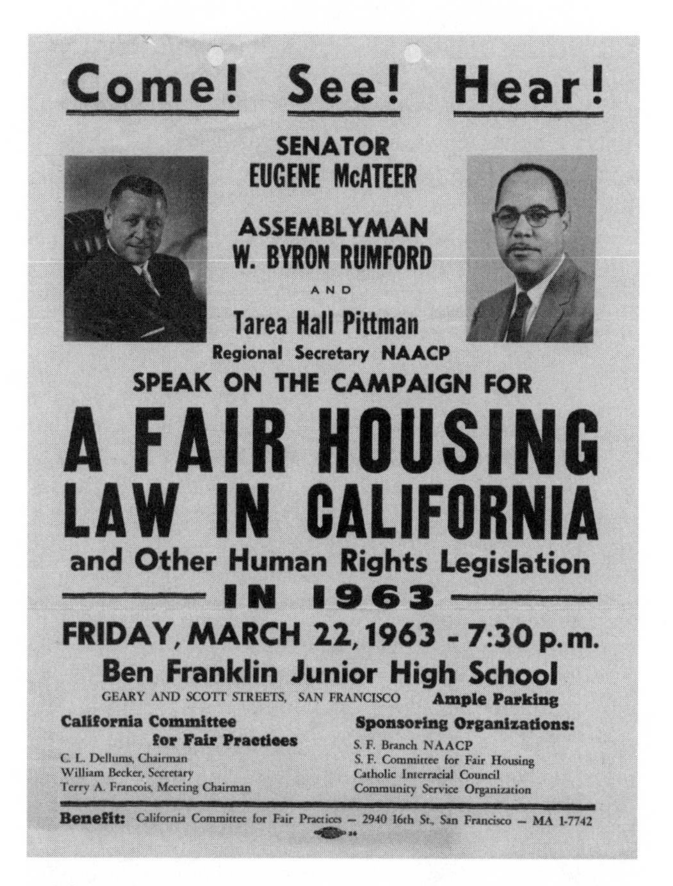

California Fair Housing Law. A flyer advertises a Fair Housing Law campaign event with Senator Eugene McAteer, Assemblyman W. Byron Rumford, and Tarea Hall Pittman, 1963. BANCROFT LIBRARY, UNIVERSITY OF CALIFORNIA, BERKELEY

The Watts Riots. The Watts uprising of 1965 prompted some local, state, and federal officials to take action to address the problems facing African Americans in California. After the riots a hospital was built in Watts, and programs were implemented to address poverty among African Americans. These programs, however, had limited success. African Americans continued to face rising unemployment as the heavy industries that had employed many black men moved their operations overseas. Inferior schools in many neighborhoods left many African Americans unable to pursue higher education or obtain jobs in expanding high technology fields. And many police officers continued to treat all African Americans as criminals.

In the Bay Area some African Americans responded to police mistreatment not by rebelling but by creating a new kind of organization. Huey P. Newton and Bobby Seale established the Black Panther Party for Self-Defense in Oakland in 1966. The party called for full employment and self-determination for African Americans. It distributed groceries to poor residents of the community and provided breakfast to thousands of schoolchildren. The party's emphasis on armed self-defense attracted pressure from law enforcement officials, and internal dissension limited the party's ability to attract and retain supporters. Nonetheless, by the 1970s the party had moved into electoral politics, and its efforts helped to lead to the election of Lionel Wilson as Oakland's first African American mayor in 1977.

The rebellion in Los Angeles in 1965 did not prevent African American politicians from continuing to make gains. In 1966 Yvonne Brathwaite Burke, Bill Green, and Leon Ralph won election to the assembly from Los Angeles, and John Miller won election to the assembly from Berkeley. In the same year, Dymally became the first African American to win election to the state senate. Dymally served two terms in the senate, and in 1974 he was elected lieutenant governor. After he failed to win reelection to that office in 1978, Dymally was elected to the U.S. House of Representatives in 1980. Ronald Dellums of Berkeley joined Hawkins in the U.S. House of Representatives in 1970. Burke was elected to the U.S. House in 1972. She gave up her seat to run for attorney general in 1978, but she was not elected. In 1992 Burke became the first African American to win election to the Los Angeles County Board of Supervisors, the five-member governing body of the nation's most populous county.

Perhaps the most impressive political achievement by an African American was Bradley's election as mayor of Los Angeles. Although the 1965 riots damaged their electoral coalition, Bradley and his allies were able to repair that damage. They were assisted by the fact that Mayor Sam Yorty moved increasingly to the right, alienating not only African Americans but also many liberal and moderate Democrats. Bradley failed to unseat Yorty in 1969, but he succeeded in ousting the incumbent in 1973. When Bradley was elected, African Americans constituted only about 18 percent of the city's population. Bradley was reelected four times. Bradley presided over the city when population growth made Los Angeles the nation's second-largest city, when it hosted the 1984 Olympic games, and when corporate investors rebuilt the city's downtown business district.

These African American elected officials continued to work to end discrimination and to address the effects of past discrimination. Their efforts, however, were hampered by a 1978 U.S. Supreme Court ruling. A European American named Alan Bakke was denied admission to the medical school at the University of California, Davis, in 1973 and 1974. He filed suit, arguing that the university's affirmative action program constituted discrimination against him because he was white. A state court ruled in his favor, but the university appealed the case to the U.S. Supreme Court. The Supreme Court declared that affirmative action programs could not rely upon racial quotas.

The Rodney King Riots. Despite Bradley's liberal political orientation and his background as a Los Angeles Police Department officer, he was not able to solve the economic problems that continued to plague the city's African Americans nor to improve relations between the police department and African American residents. In 1991 a resident of the Lake View Terrace section of Los Angeles captured on videotape four Los Angeles Police Department officers' brutal beating of Rodney King, an African American recently paroled from prison who had attempted to elude law enforcement officers. The tape was played nationwide; for many African Americans in Southern California it provided proof of continuing police brutality. When the four officers who had beaten King were acquitted on charges of use of excessive force in April 1992, rioting erupted in Los Angeles. Unlike the riots in 1965, the 1992 riots were not isolated to predominantly black neighborhoods. Violence occurred in many different neighborhoods, and Latinos as well as African Americans participated in the uprising. By the time the National Guard, the army, and the Marines restored order after four days of rioting, more than fifty people were dead. The riots marred Bradley's fifth and final term as mayor and raised doubts about the successful efforts of local and state officials to address long-term problems related to racial inequality.

The 1992 riots led some officials to renew their efforts to address the effects of discrimination. At the same time, however, many Californians continued to oppose such efforts, particularly affirmative action. A few African Americans, most notably the Sacramento consultant Ward Connerly, joined European Americans and Asian Americans who mounted a campaign against affirmative action. Connerly argued that such programs stigmatized all African Americans by suggesting that they could not compete on an equal basis with any other Americans. In 1996, following a campaign spearheaded by Connerly, California voters passed Proposition 209, which eliminated affirmative action programs in the state.

Persistent poverty, strained police–community relations, and statewide hostility toward affirmative action finally led to a decline in African American migration to California in the 1990s. The state's African American population increased by fewer than 60,000 between 1990 and 2000, although a change in census categories and procedures may have obscured a greater population growth. The state no longer attracted African Americans as it once had, but twentieth-century migrations had made African Americans politically important in California in the early twenty-first century.

[*See also* Latinos and Black Latinos; Los Angeles; Rodney King Riots; San Francisco; Simpson, O. J., Trial of; Watts Riot; Women's Clubs; *and biographical entries on figures mentioned in this article.*]

BIBLIOGRAPHY

Broussard, Albert S. *Black San Francisco: The Struggle for Racial Equality in the West, 1900–1954*. Lawrence: University Press of Kansas, 1993. A careful examination of the economic and political history of African Americans in San Francisco.

Cox, Bette Yarbrough. *Central Avenue—Its Rise and Fall, 1890–c. 1955: Including the Musical Renaissance of Black Los Angeles*. Los Angeles: BEEM Publications, 1996. The first third of this book describes the musical history of African American Los Angeles, and the remainder consists of transcripts of oral histories of important musicians.

Daniels, Douglas Henry. *Pioneer Urbanites: A Social and Cultural History of Black San Francisco*. Philadelphia: Temple University Press, 1980. This study of the African Americans who moved to San Francisco before the 1940s emphasizes the differences between these migrants and those who moved to northern cities.

de Graaf, Lawrence B., Kevin Mulroy, and Quintard Taylor, eds. *Seeking El Dorado: African Americans in California*. Los Angeles: Autry Museum of Western Heritage; Seattle: University of Washington Press, 2001. A collection of essays by leading scholars; most deal with the experiences of African Americans in the twentieth century.

Flamming, Douglas. *Bound for Freedom: Black Los Angeles in Jim Crow America*. Berkeley: University of California Press, 2005. A thorough examination of African American culture and politics in southern California before World War II.

Horne, Gerald. *Fire This Time: The Watts Uprising and the 1960s*. Charlottesville: University Press of Virginia, 1995. A provocative book that connects the suppression of the left in the 1940s and 1950s with the unrest in Los Angeles in 1965.

Lemke-Santangelo, Gretchen. *Abiding Courage: African American Migrant Women and the East Bay Community*. Chapel Hill: University of North Carolina Press, 1996. Notable for its reliance on fifty oral interviews, this study explores the efforts of African American women to establish community institutions.

Moore, Shirley Ann Wilson. *To Place Our Deeds: The African American Community in Richmond, California, 1910–1963*. Berkeley: University of California Press, 2000. This study of Richmond focuses largely on the wartime migration of African Americans and the effects of demobilization on the community.

Self, Robert O. *American Babylon: Race and the Struggle for Postwar Oakland*. Princeton, N.J.: Princeton University Press, 2003. A bold reinterpretation of the "white flight" hypothesis that explains both the concentration of poor African Americans in Oakland and the rise of the Black Panther Party for Self-Defense.

Sides, Josh. *L.A. City Limits: African American Los Angeles from the Great Depression to the Present*. Berkeley: University of California Press, 2003. A highly readable survey of the history of African Americans in Los Angeles, with an emphasis on the 1940s and 1950s.

Sonenshein, Raphael. *Politics in Black and White: Race and Power in Los Angeles*. Princeton, N.J.: Princeton University Press, 1993. The definitive study of the emergence of Tom Bradley's electoral coalition by the leading scholar of Los Angeles politics.

—KEVIN ALLEN LEONARD

CAMPANELLA, ROY (b. 19 November 1921; d. 26 June 1993), baseball catcher who helped break baseball's color line. Campanella was also known for his courage and determination off the field as an automobile accident in 1958 left him a quadriplegic and permanently in a wheelchair.

Campanella was born and raised in Philadelphia. His father, John Campanella, was a first-generation American of Italian descent, and his mother Ida Mercer Campanella was African American. As a child he developed an interest in sports, with baseball becoming his first love. He took up the position of catcher as nobody else in the integrated neighborhood wanted to play baseball's most grinding position.

At the age of fifteen Campanella started playing Negro League ball for the Washington Elite Giants, and he continued with the team when it moved to Baltimore the next season. With his parents' permission, he quit school at age sixteen to pursue professional baseball. He proved to be a workhorse, often playing both games in a doubleheader and most years playing winter ball in Puerto Rico, Venezuela, Cuba, or Mexico.

In the 1940s the Brooklyn Dodgers considered signing Campanella to a contract. They held talks with Jackie Robinson, Campanella, Don Newcombe, and several other players in 1945. The college-educated Robinson became the Dodgers' first choice to break the color line when the general manager Branch Rickey signed him in 1945. In March 1946 Rickey signed Campanella and Newcombe, who along with Robinson became pioneers in breaking baseball's color line. While Robinson played the 1946 season with the Dodgers' top farm team in Montreal, Canada, Campanella and Newcombe starred for class B Nashua (New Hampshire). With the exception of a few African American players in the late nineteenth century, Campanella and Newcombe became the first black players for a U.S.-based major league farm club team. In 1947, as Robinson was called to the majors for his historic breaking of the Major League color barrier, Campanella played for Montreal. In 1948, at the age of twenty-six, Campanella became the second African American to wear a Dodger uniform. He did not play a full season because Rickey asked "Campy," as he was called, to do a two-month stint in Saint Paul, Minnesota, as the first to integrate the American Association League. The next year was Campanella's first full season with the Dodgers as the "boys of summer" began a run in which they played in five World Series in an eight-year span against the crosstown rival New York Yankees.

Along with Yogi Berra, Campanella was the best catcher of his generation and one of the best of all time. He was the National League's most valuable player in 1951, 1953, and 1955. The 1953 season was his best statistically as he

Roy Campanella. Baseball legends Jackie Robinson (*left*) and Roy Campanella (*right*), the Dodgers' first two African American stars. AP IMAGES

became the first catcher to hit more than forty home runs, with forty-one. His 1955 numbers were impressive, but even more special was that he helped the Dodgers win their first-ever World Series when they defeated the Yankees in seven games.

By the 1957 season Campanella was slowing down as he only caught in 100 games out of 142; however, he was preparing to accompany the Dodgers in their move from Brooklyn to Los Angeles. During the off-season in January 1958, Campanella was in an automobile accident that severely injured his spinal cord and broke his neck, leaving him almost completely paralyzed from the shoulders down. He had a small amount of movement in his hands.

Campanella's struggle with paralysis is well documented in his 1959 autobiography *It's Good to Be Alive*. After the accident, doctors thought Campanella would live possibly another ten to twenty years, but he proved them wrong, overcoming numerous illnesses, including pneumonia and diabetes, to live a productive thirty-five years. In retirement Campanella was one of baseball's best ambassadors, working in the community relations department for the Dodgers and as an instructional coach during spring training. He also performed numerous engagements at hospitals to bring words of encouragement to other disabled people. In 1969 the baseball writers selected Campanella to the Hall of Fame, and the Dodgers great became a regular at the yearly ceremonies in Cooperstown, New York.

Campanella was married three times and had five children from his first two marriages. His son Roy Campanella Jr. became a successful television director.

[*See also* Baseball.]

BIBLIOGRAPHY

Campanella, Roy. *It's Good to Be Alive*. Lincoln: University of Nebraska Press, 1995. The inspirational book traces Campanella's life from childhood to just after the auto accident. The 1995 edition contains an excellent introduction by Jules Tygiel, who summarizes the last thirty-three years of Campanella's life.

Kahn, Roger. *The Boys of Summer*. New York: HarperPerennial, 1998. Kahn's classic book on the Brooklyn Dodgers was originally published in 1971 and contains a full chapter on Campanella, "Manchild at Fifty." Campanella's role with the Dodgers is discussed throughout the book.

Tygiel, Jules. *Baseball's Great Experiment: Jackie Robinson and His Legacy*. New York: Oxford University Press, 1997. Campanella's days as a Negro League player and his role in breaking the color line are discussed, showing that Robinson did not do it alone.

—ROBERT M. O'BRIEN

CARIBBEAN, THE. "The Caribbean" refers to the island nations located in the Caribbean Sea that contain numerous African-derived populations who are often in the majority. Caribbean nations with significantly large Afro-Carib populations include the Bahamas, Cuba, Jamaica, Haiti, the Dominican Republic, Puerto Rico, Saint Kitts and Nevis, Martinique, Antigua and Barbuda, Barbados, Grenada, and Trinidad and Tobago. All of these islands have seen migrations of Afro-Carib populations to the United States, and their peoples have contributed significantly to African American culture in the twentieth and twenty-first centuries. Among Afro-Caribbeans, Jamaicans have had a disproportionately large influence on African American history, but the people of other nations have had their effect as well.

Most Caribbean island nations began the twentieth century in colonial servitude to European powers, Great Britain in particular. Those that did not—Haiti, the Dominican Republic, and Cuba—were subject to U.S. invasion and occupation under the provisions of the Roosevelt Corollary to the Monroe Doctrine. Such military interventions were carried out ostensibly in service to democratic reform, but in reality they were usually intended to stem the tide of socialism and to protect U.S.

manufacturing and financial interests. It was in direct response to his perception of the colonial and military exploitation of Afro-Carib and African peoples that the Jamaican Marcus Garvey founded the Universal Negro Improvement Association, which brought him to Harlem in 1916. Thus, the conditions in which Afro-Caribbeans lived were a direct source for the foundations of the twentieth-century African American civil rights movement. Garvey's establishment of the *Negro World* newspaper in Harlem provided an outlet for the energies of the writers of the Harlem Renaissance. His influence in the United States also spread his name back home in the Caribbean: a 1919 dockworkers' strike in Trinidad drew inspiration from the *Negro World* and Garvey's politics, and this strike was perceived to be a root of black nationalism in the United Kingdom and the British Commonwealth.

After World War II, many of Britain's Caribbean colonies—by then, poor and long neglected by the metropole—gained independence. At first, the British Colonial Office, long in charge of maintaining the empire's colonies, tried to unite the soon-to-be independent nations of Jamaica, Barbados, and Trinidad and Tobago in a West Indies federation, but within months of the actual independence of the three islands in 1962, the federation had collapsed because of economic differences. Instead of federalizing, their populations joined the rest of the Caribbean's poor independent nations in the struggle to attract industry and finance outside of tourism. One of the heroes of that struggle was Michael Manley, a prominent member of Jamaica's parliament and occasionally the prime minister, who criticized American economic policies in the Caribbean as neocolonialism and openly courted the friendship of Fidel Castro's Cuba.

Most of the Caribbean influence on African Americans stemmed more from cultural than political sources, however. Rastafarianism, the modern religious movement, had its roots in Jamaica, and it regards Garvey as a prophet. The Rasta fashion for dreadlocks and the Rasta emphasis on the colors of the Ethiopian flag—red, gold, and green—have permeated African American life deeply.

Rastafarianism's most overt impact in the United States has been in music. Jamaican-derived ska, or bluebeat, first traveled on immigrant ships to Britain, where the practice of "toasting," or speaking rhymes over the beat of the music, originated. Toasting is often taken to be a direct ancestor of African American rap and hip hop. Ska's hurried three-quarters time on the beat was slowed down in the later 1960s by Jamaican bands to create reggae, whose most prominent exponent was the Rastafarian and black nationalist Bob Marley, a hero throughout the African-derived world.

Afro-Caribbeans have been prominent in the history of baseball since the 1950s. The Cuban Orestes "Minnie" Minoso of the Cleveland Indians came from the Negro Leagues and was one of the pioneering black players in the American League. Felipe Alou debuted in 1958 with the San Francisco Giants as one of the first of nearly five hundred baseball players from the Dominican Republic, and the Puerto Rican Roberto Clemente—one of the best hitters ever—became a hero as a Pittsburgh Pirate for his social activism and humanitarian work.

The greatest impact of Afro-Caribbeans has come from migration. Millions of Afro-Caribbeans have moved to the United States seeking a better life, and some of them have also later returned to their island homes to retire. In between, they have become integrated into the African American community, mainly in urban areas. Statistically, the most popular destination is New York, which has the largest communities of Barbadians, Dominicans, Jamaicans, and Trinidadians; if one includes New Jersey and Connecticut, nearly three-quarters of the Caribbean population in the United States is living in the New York City metropolitan area. Florida has high populations of Cubans. Haitians migrate to both New York and Florida; smaller populations from all of the Caribbean islands migrate to California and Massachusetts.

[*See also* African Diaspora; Black Migration; Haiti; Immigration to the United States, Black; *and* Pan-Africanism.]

BIBLIOGRAPHY

Bandon, Alexandra. *West Indian Americans*. New York: Maxwell Macmillan International, 1994.

Halliburton, Warren J. *The West Indian–American Experience*. Brookfield, Conn.: Millbrook Press, 1994.

Henke, Holger. *The West Indian Americans*. Westport, Conn.: Greenwood Press, 2001.

Knight, Franklin W., and Colin A. Palmer, eds. *The Modern Caribbean*. Chapel Hill: University of North Carolina Press, 1989.

—DAVID SIMONELLI

CARMICHAEL, STOKELY (b. 29 June 1941; d. 15 November 1998), activist and writer who popularized the "Black Power" slogan in the 1960s. A native of Trinidad, Carmichael, later known as Kwame Ture, immigrated to the United States at the age of eleven to join his parents, who had migrated several years earlier. Even as a child he demonstrated an interest in politics, and the socialist activist Bayard Rustin was one of his earliest role models.

A gifted student, Carmichael attended the Bronx High School of Science, graduating in 1960. Although he was offered admission to a number of colleges and universities, his growing racial consciousness led him to the historically black Howard University in Washington, D.C. He received his bachelor's degree in philosophy in 1964.

While a student, he became involved in the civil rights movement, participating initially in demonstrations organized by the Nonviolent Action Group (NAG), an organization devoted to challenging segregation in the vicinity of Washington, D.C. He also volunteered to be one of the first freedom riders, traveling through the South on integrated buses to challenge local segregation customs. While riding through the South in the spring of 1961, he was arrested on the first of many occasions and was forced to spend forty-nine days in the notorious Parchman Penitentiary. During his career as a civil rights activist, Carmichael was arrested at least thirty-two times.

After graduating from Howard, Carmichael began to work for the civil rights movement full time as a field organizer for the radical civil rights organization the Student Nonviolent Coordinating Committee (SNCC). In that capacity he organized an extensive voter registration project in Alabama. While in Alabama, he helped organize the Lowndes County Freedom Organization, a political party that adopted the black panther as its symbol. Because neither local Republicans nor local Democrats welcomed black voters, Carmichael and his supporters reasoned that blacks should form their own political party.

In 1966 Carmichael was elected SNCC chairman, replacing the beloved civil rights veteran John Lewis. Carmichael's election reflected an ideological shift in the civil rights movement at large, revealing tensions in SNCC in particular. Under his leadership, the organization moved away from its integrationist origins, ousting white members. Although Carmichael was personally ambivalent about asking whites who had made numerous sacrifices for the sake of the movement to leave the organization, he was also sympathetic to the changing mood within SNCC. Tired of being beaten, many members of SNCC began to openly challenge the principles of nonviolent resistance that had guided the early years of the civil rights struggle. Many also began to question the desirability of achieving integration, a cherished goal of leaders like Martin Luther King Jr. and SNCC's own Lewis.

Stokely Carmichael, 1966. New York World–Telegram and the Sun Newspaper Photograph Collection, Prints and Photographs Division, Library of Congress

At a rally in Mississippi in 1966, Carmichael publicly articulated his advocacy of "Black Power," a phrase he used to describe the belief that black people should seize their own destinies and work together to achieve economic and political goals. At Carmichael's speaking engagements, crowds enthusiastically chanted the "Black Power" mantra, a phrase that some black activists found enthralling and others frightening. Both King of the Southern Christian Leadership Conference (SCLC) and Roy Wilkins of the National Association for the Advancement of Colored People (NAACP) were fearful that the rallying cry would damage the black freedom struggle and be interpreted by whites as reverse racism. Undaunted, Carmichael continued to agitate for Black Power, elaborating on this philosophy in *Black Power: The Politics of Liberation in America* (1967), which he coauthored with Charles Hamilton.

In 1967 Carmichael decided not to run for reelection to the SNCC chairmanship, embarking on a world tour instead. He visited Cuba, Vietnam, and several African countries, where he gave speeches denouncing the Vietnam War and American racism. Upon his return, his passport was revoked for ten months. In 1968 the Black Panther Party (BPP), which had borrowed its symbol from the Lowndes County Freedom Organization, elected Carmichael honorary prime minister. However, he broke all ties with the BPP in 1969 due to the organization's willingness to cooperate with white radical groups in its quest for black empowerment.

In 1968 Carmichael married the famous South African singer Miriam Makeba; they had one child. The following year Carmichael and Makeba went into voluntary exile in West Africa. Kwame Nkrumah of Ghana and Ahmed Sékou Touré of Guinea became Carmichael's mentors, instructing him in Pan-Africanism and the linkage between the freedom struggles in the United States and those in Africa. To honor them, Carmichael adopted their first and last names, becoming in 1978 Kwame Ture. Makeba and Carmichael divorced in 1978, and Carmichael married the Guinean physician Marlyatou Barry. That relationship also produced one child and later ended in divorce.

Though he is now best known as a proponent of black nationalism, Carmichael continued to fight for a unified socialist Africa even as the political situation in many African countries, newly freed from colonial rule, began to deteriorate. One of the founders of the Marxist-oriented All-African People's Revolutionary Party, he spent the rest of his life working for the organization while continuing to write and lecture on socialism and fight against racism and American imperialism.

In 1996 Carmichael was diagnosed with prostate cancer. He received cancer treatment in Cuba and financial support from the Nation of Islam leader Louis Farrakhan. After his diagnosis, Carmichael began writing his memoir with the assistance of Ekwueme Michael Thelwell, his former SNCC colleague and longtime friend. *Ready for Revolution: The Life and Struggles of Stokely Carmichael (Kwame Ture)* appeared posthumously in 2003. Although he spent time in the United States while writing his book, Carmichael was determined to die on African soil. He returned to the African continent in August 1998 and died in Guinea later that year.

[*See also* Black Panther Party; Black Power Movement; Civil Rights Movement; *and* Student Nonviolent Coordinating Committee.]

BIBLIOGRAPHY

Carmichael, Stokely, and Ekwueme Michael Thelwell. *Ready for Revolution: The Life and Struggles of Stokely Carmichael (Kwame Ture)*. New York: Scribner, 2003.

Carson, Clayborne. *In Struggle: SNCC and the Black Awakening of the 1960s*. Cambridge, Mass.: Harvard University Press, 1995. History of SNCC, including Carmichael's involvement with the organization.

—JENNIFER JENSEN WALLACH

CARNEGIE CORPORATION. Founded in 1911 by Andrew Carnegie (1835–1919), the Carnegie Corporation of New York was created, according to its Web site, to promote "the advancement and diffusion of knowledge and understanding" by supporting institutions of higher learning, libraries, research, and reports. Initially endowed with $125 million, its grants largely benefit the people of the United States, with 7.4 percent going to the rest of the English-speaking world (in the early twenty-first century, mainly Africa).

In his *Miscellaneous Writings* (1904), the Scottish-born, self-educated Carnegie also discussed "White and Black in the South." While he supported "racial uplift," he considered it to be a southern problem. Since 1898, white leaders had discussed black education and coordinated their grant policies. They often favored Booker T. Washington's more practical approach to "Negro education" over W. E. B. Du Bois's push for educating the Talented Tenth. Carnegie was no exception. He contributed to both the Hampton and Tuskegee institutes.

Nonetheless, it is difficult to trace the corporation's impact on African Americans. For example, while conceding to "the extent and severity of the Negro problem," Emerson Andrew's 1956 *Philanthropic Foundations* merely observed that even though "substantial foundation funds have been appropriated, but in a changing climate of opinion," only a relatively small number of foundations included programs for "Negroes."

The Carnegie Corporation invested more than $1.7 million in "Negro education" between 1911 and 1932. In the 1930s, some people in the corporation wondered whether to assist liberal arts colleges for African Americans. In this climate, Alain Locke of Howard University became acquainted with the corporation's president, Frederick Paul Keppel. They freely discussed ideas, which was unusual for that time. As a result, between 1931 and 1934, Locke was involved in the corporation's adult education projects at public libraries in Harlem and Atlanta. But even though Keppel agreed that it was a success, he did not develop Locke's concepts further.

Instead, the corporation asked Gunnar Myrdal to write what would become a pathbreaking study on the "Negro problem" published in 1944. Myrdal was from Sweden; a European was thus called to examine a central "problem" of U.S. culture. The study was intended to explore "black education" and to compare it with "white education." Yet it turned out to unravel African Americans' isolation within U.S. society. As it was cited in the 1954 *Brown v. Board of Education* decision, the Myrdal report came to influence public-policy making directly, while also having a more indirect impact on public opinion.

The corporation did not build on Myrdal's study until the 1960s, which insiders perceived by 1975 as "perhaps the greatest missed opportunity in history, one that can be regretted now with hindsight." The corporation itself diversified only in the 1970s during the presidency of Alan Pifer. In 1974 and 1976 the corporation sponsored evaluation reports such as *Programs to Increase Black Lawyers in the South* between 1969 and 1973 and *Black Elite: The New Market for Highly Educated Black Americans*. More recent references to the corporation's activities with regard to African Americans are scarce.

[*See also American Dilemma, An*; *and* Philanthropy.]

BIBLIOGRAPHY

Lagemann, Ellen Condliffe. *The Politics of Knowledge: The Carnegie Corporation, Philanthropy, and Public Policy*. Middletown, Conn.: Wesleyan University Press, 1989. A history of the Carnegie Corporation that discusses the Myrdal study and takes up the question of African Americans after the civil rights movement.

Myrdal, Gunnar, Arnold Rose, and Richard Sterner. *An American Dilemma; The Negro Problem and Modern Democracy*. New York and London: Harper & Brothers, 1944. An influential study commissioned by the Carnegie Corporation that would influence the civil rights movement but did not immediately or profoundly change the ways of the Carnegie Corporation in allocating grants for the benefit of American Americans.

—Anja Becker

CARNEGIE HALL CONFERENCE. The educator and founder and president of Tuskegee Institute, Booker T. Washington, proposed to convene a conference in 1904 at Carnegie Hall in New York City to discuss ways that elite black leaders could guide African Americans to improve their conditions and status. A powerful machine politician of black America, Washington needed a venue to reaffirm his position as the premier spokesperson of African Americans as he faced an expanding black opposition to his policy of accommodation to white supremacy, that is, to disfranchisement and legalized segregation of and discrimination against millions of black southerners. Washington invited the intellectual social activist W. E. B. Du Bois, one of the leading figures associated with the growing black anti-Washington faction, to participate in the conference, help set the conference agenda, and issue invitations. Washington oversaw the preconference plans and the list of possible attendees; he and Du Bois did not invite William Monroe Trotter and other black activists who were vehemently critical of Washington and who refused to enter into a working relationship with the "Wizard of Tuskegee." Washington hoped the conference would convince African Americans and his white supporters that he still maintained his political influence within the white and black communities, and he hoped to heal the breach with Du Bois that had surfaced following the confrontation with Trotter at the "Boston Riot" in the summer of 1903. Both Washington's allies and Du Bois's moderately militant friends gathered at the conference to forge a compromise between the Washingtonian and Du Boisian factions. The academician Kelly Miller; attorneys Clement G. Morgan, Archibald Henry Grimké, and Frederick L. McGhee; and twenty-four other African American men discussed an array of topics, including education, voting rights, and legal defense.

The Carnegie Hall Conference of 6–8 January 1904 provided an opportunity for black participants, in an atmosphere that ranged from tense to congenial, to chart their leadership role for African Americans who had endured a decade of unprecedented, heightened racism and relentless assaults on their property, persons, and rights of citizenship. The meeting also included the industrialist Andrew Carnegie, who funded the conference; the railroad tycoon William H. Baldwin Jr.; the Congregationalist minister Lyman Abbott; the journalist Oswald Garrison Villard; and twenty other white attendees—all Washington's supporters who made brief appearances and gave speeches reminding their black listeners that African Americans needed white guidance before they could regain their civil rights. Washington agreed with Du Bois about the need for higher education for the African American elite and greater access to public accommodations. He convinced the Du Boisians to accept his outlook that the vast majority of black southerners must continue to reside in the South and that industrial education remained the best, if not the sole, path for social advancement for most young African American men and women. The conference represented a victory engineered by Washington, who won accolades for his leadership style and program even from Du Bois's friends, Grimké and Miller.

Washington emerged from the Carnegie Hall Conference thinking that he had secured his status as the acknowledged leader with a viable, meaningful strategy for black men and women to advance socially and economically by concentrating their energy and resources on building a black-owned economic infrastructure and attaining an industrial education. Washington hoped that, with black leaders endorsing his program, African Americans would return to the public sphere as equals to white Americans and that white northern philanthropists would continue to fund his projects and the Tuskegee machine. He thought that his victory over the Du Boisian faction had routed his radical critics, forcing them into submission and to the margins of African American political life. Washington succeeded in obtaining Du Bois's agreement to work on the newly constituted Committee of Twelve, charged with continuing the work of the conference.

The Carnegie Hall Conference had immediate historical significance as a pivotal moment in the Washington–Du Bois debate and the black struggle for civil rights. The conference became the battleground between Washington's conservative program with its stress on moral and economic uplift and Du Bois's advocacy of political agitation for full equality. The event ostensibly blended conservatives' and militant radicals' principles, but it actually boosted Washington's political prestige and failed to become a platform for Du Bois and other moderate radicals to advance the cause of full racial equality. Du Bois withdrew from the Committee of Twelve within a few months.

The Carnegie Hall Conference marked the high point of Washington's interest in sustaining black allegiance for his policies and the beginnings of Du Bois's earnest endeavor to institutionalize a movement—which he and militant radicals did in 1905 by founding the Niagara

Movement—for civil rights and equality, independent of the Washington machine.

[*See also* Committee of Twelve; Du Bois, W. E. B.; Trotter, William Monroe; Washington, Booker T.; *and* Washington–Du Bois Conflict.]

BIBLIOGRAPHY

Harlan, Louis R. *Booker T. Washington: The Wizard of Tuskegee, 1901–1915*. New York: Oxford University Press, 1983. Narrates Washington's interest in the Carnegie Hall Conference.

Lewis, David Levering. *W. E. B. Du Bois: Biography of a Race, 1868–1919*. New York: H. Holt, 1993. Describes Du Bois's involvement in the Carnegie Hall Conference.

Marable, Manning. *W. E. B. Du Bois: Black Radical Democrat*. Boston: Twayne, 1986. Discusses the Carnegie Hall Conference in the context of Du Bois's radicalism.

—CHARLES L. LUMPKINS

CARROLL, DIAHANN (b. 17 July 1935), singer and actress. Carol Diahann Johnson was born in the Bronx, New York. As a teenager she performed as a nightclub singer and a model while attending the famous New York High School of Music and Art. She made her film debut in 1954 in *Carmen Jones*, working with Harry Belafonte and Dorothy Dandridge. Paired again with Dandridge, Carroll had a role in *Porgy and Bess* (1959). Film and television appearances continued, including an Emmy nomination in 1963 for her work in the crime drama *Naked City*.

In 1968 Carroll made television history by becoming the first black actress to star in her own series. NBC's *Julia* received both popular praise and critical acclaim, and Carroll received an Emmy nomination in its first year. Generations of African American performers remember Carroll's *Julia* as a turning point, providing inspiration that roles for black actors could go beyond servants and other stereotypes to represent true-to-life, multidimensional characters. Yet some African Americans criticized the show for not moving beyond situation comedy to explore racial tension or discrimination. After three years Carroll asked to be released from her contract, citing the controversies as her reason for leaving the series. While the scripts for *Julia* may not have delved into racial issues, its mere presence (and its success) helped pave the way for future sitcoms that portrayed a wide variety of African American families and experiences.

In 1974 Carroll again broke ground by starring in *Claudine*, a film about a single mother raising six children in Harlem. She was nominated for a Golden Globe and an Academy Award for her role.

Diahann Carroll. A still from the 1961 film *Paris Blues* with Paul Newman, Diahann Carroll, and Sidney Poitier. UNITED ARTISTS/PHOTOFEST

By the 1980s Carroll had come to represent glamour by starring in the prime-time soap operas *Dynasty* and *The Colbys* as Dominique Devereaux. She received another Emmy nomination in 1989 for her recurring guest role as Marion Gilbert on *A Different World*. Subsequently she made guest appearances on television shows, continued to appear in films, and lent her voice to animated work as well. In April 2006 she returned to Broadway, opening her own cabaret show.

Carroll was diagnosed with breast cancer in 1998. As a survivor and an activist, she became a spokesperson for the National Women's Cancer Research Alliance and helped launch a national education program aimed at African American women. The two-pronged campaign focuses on early detection and tumor marker tests for those living with the disease.

Besides Carroll's philanthropic work and her continued devotion to stage and screen, she also created her own line of wigs, clothes, and eyewear. She became a fashion icon as much as an entertainer.

[*See also* Actors and Actresses.]

BIBLIOGRAPHY

Carroll, Diahann, with Ross Firestone. *Diahann: An Autobiography*. Boston: Little, Brown, 1986.

"Diahann Carroll: Gorgeous at 70, She's Still in a Class of Her Own." *Ebony*, March 2006, 26–27.

"Diahann Carroll Helps Launch 'Test Your Tumor Campaign.'" *New York Amsterdam News*, 11 May 2000.

—COURTNEY Q. SHAH

CARSON, BENJAMIN (b. 18 September 1951), neurosurgeon. Carson was born into relative poverty in Detroit, Michigan. When he turned eight, his parents divorced, and his mother, who had married at the age of thirteen and who had only a third grade education, struggled to raise Benjamin and his older brother Curtis on her own. This personal upheaval left Carson a troubled youth with a ferocious temper and little confidence in school. By the fifth grade, his failing grades and frequent altercations so concerned his mother that she forced her son to improve his grades and develop his reading skills. The new regime quickly created success in school, and by the sixth grade Carson's grades had dramatically improved along with his personal confidence and ambition. Buoyed by the support he found at home and at church, he devoted himself to academic excellence, and by his senior year he had secured a scholarship to Yale University.

Carson's studies at Yale ultimately led him to pursue neurosurgery. Upon graduating from the University of Michigan School of Medicine in 1977, he served as a resident in neurological surgery at the Johns Hopkins Hospital in Baltimore, Maryland. After a short tenure at Queen Elizabeth II Medical Center in Western Australia, he returned to Johns Hopkins in 1984 to become the chief of pediatric neurosurgery.

Carson entered medicine in the generation after hospitals and medical schools had been desegregated, and consequently he was able to take advantage of the opportunity forged by others. While he infrequently encountered outright racial discrimination—some white patients did request he be taken off their cases—the general presumption against a black doctor meant that he was commonly mistaken for an orderly by fellow hospital staff and generally assumed by black and white patients to be anything but the chief physician on the case. These incidents of bias notwithstanding, Carson rose to national prominence at Johns Hopkins.

Carson's first celebrated case came in 1985, when he removed one hemisphere of a toddler's brain (a cerebral hemispherectomy) to stop the child's intractable seizures (prior to the surgery she had suffered over one hundred seizures per day). Subsequent studies revealed that between 78 and 86 percent of hemispherectomy patients at Johns Hopkins Children's Center between 1975 and 2001 reported a total or near-total cessation of the seizures. In 1986 Carson followed his first success with an equally acclaimed but much more controversial intrauterine surgery on a fetal twin with a pregnancy-threatening case of hydrocephalus. The surgery was announced after the fact and generated a good deal of controversy. Carson's renown was secured the following year, when he and a team of surgeons separated a set of German brothers joined at the back of the head (occipital craniopagus twins). Prior to Carson's successful operation, efforts to separate occipital craniopagus twins had resulted in the death of at least one of the pair. Carson's team succeeded in preserving the lives of both boys, although the two did suffer severe disabilities thereafter. Finally, Carson added to his list of accomplishments in 1997, when he led a team of African surgeons in a successful separation of twins joined at the top of the head (type-2 vertical craniopagus twins). Remarkably, this was the first time twins joined in this fashion were separated with no consequent neurological abnormalities.

Carson's prestigious career earned him numerous awards and honorary degrees, and he sits on the board of directors of the Kellogg Company, the governing body of Yale University, and the board of America's Promise. Though he battled prostate cancer in 2002, Carson accepted President George W. Bush's appointment to the President's Council on Bioethics in 2004.

Along with Carson's leadership in his field of academic medicine, he and his wife launched the Carson Scholars Fund in 1994. The fund provides college scholarships to students who excel in academic performance and community involvement, and it is part of Carson's larger vision to encourage black academic achievement in the biosciences. Carson has also worked to interweave the practice of academic medicine with his Christian faith.

[*See also* Medical Profession.]

BIBLIOGRAPHY

Carson, Ben, with Gregg Lewis. *The Big Picture: Getting Perspective on What's Really Important in Life*. Grand Rapids, Mich.: Zondervan Press, 1999.

Carson, Ben, with Cecil Murphey. *Gifted Hands: The Ben Carson Story*. Grand Rapids, Mich.: Zondervan Press, 1996.

O'Connor, Clint. "Success Surpasses Fame, Renowned Doctor Recounts." *Plain Dealer*, 17 October 1997.

—STEPHEN INRIG

CARTER, BENNY (b. 8 August 1907; d. 12 July 2003), jazz musician, composer, and arranger. Bennett Lester "Benny" Carter was one of the most remarkable musicians ever to grace the American music scene. A multi-instrumentalist, he was truly brilliant on the alto saxophone, near-brilliant on the trumpet and clarinet, and proficient on the trombone and piano. Carter and the other leading saxophonist Johnny Hodges crafted an elegant alto saxophone voice for the swing band that set the standard for playing the instrument before the appearance of Charles "Charlie" Parker. Carter was an equally talented composer and arranger, and at times in his life each skill overshadowed the other.

Carter was born in New York City on 8 August 1907. His parents were musicians, and he began playing the piano at an early age and also attempted to play the trumpet. He settled on the saxophone after finding the trumpet difficult to master. By the early 1920s he was competent enough to find employment as a professional musician with local bands in Harlem. Carter's playing improved rapidly, and he learned how to arrange music, a talent that would serve him well. Carter polished his skills playing with the Fletcher Henderson and Chick Webb bands, became the musical director of McKinney's Cotton Pickers in 1931, and was the leader of the Chocolate Dandies, a band created from Henderson's big-band personnel.

Although he was only twenty-eight years old, Carter was already a seasoned musician with a glowing reputation as an arranger and composer when he moved to Europe in 1935. The move proved to be a wise career choice, and he spent three productive years in Europe. He recorded with the great tenor saxophonist Coleman Hawkins and the guitarist Django Reinhardt, the first European musician to have a significant impact on jazz. He also led an international, interracial band on tours through Holland, arranged music for the British Broadcasting Corporation's Dance Orchestra, and recorded in France. In 1938, as a bellicose Germany threatened to engulf Europe in war, Carter left England. He returned to New York and quickly formed a house band that worked at the famous Savoy Ballroom in Harlem for two years. In addition he continued to make arrangements for other bandleaders including Count Basie, Benny Goodman, and Edward Kennedy "Duke" Ellington.

In 1942 Carter recorded his novelty song "Cow Cow Boogie." With this pop hit on his résumé, he went west in 1943 and formed a West Coast orchestra in Los Angeles that at times included such jazz luminaries as the trombonist J. J. Johnson, the tenor saxophonists Dexter Gordon and Lucky Thompson, the drummer Max Roach, and the trumpeter Miles Davis. Carter also composed and arranged music and performed with all-star groups that included such greats as the clarinetist Benny Goodman and the tenor saxophonist Coleman Hawkins.

During 1943 Carter also worked as a studio musician in Hollywood, becoming the first African American to arrange and compose music for motion pictures. For his first studio project he arranged and composed the music for the all-black film *Stormy Weather*, starring the singer Lena Horne, the dancer Bill "Bojangles" Robinson, and the pianist-composer Thomas "Fats" Waller. The music score added immensely to the success of the film, and Carter's precedent-setting studio work opened doors for other talented black composers and arrangers in movies and television, including the pianist John Lewis and Quincy Jones.

Carter broke up his last band in the late 1940s but continued to work at a frenetic pace. He toured with Norman Granz's Jazz at the Philharmonic, recorded some excellent albums for Granz's record label, and in 1952 joined his fellow alto greats Johnny Hodges and Charlie Parker in a studio recording session. Always in demand by vocalists, Carter often took time off from touring and recording to write arrangements for Billy Eckstine, Ella Fitzgerald, Peggy Lee, Sarah Vaughan, Ray Charles, Billie Holiday, and many others. Afterward, however, he always resurfaced to tour and record.

During the 1960s and 1970s Carter performed in various foreign venues from Toronto, Ontario, to Japan, and in 1975 he visited the Middle East on a U.S. State Department tour. Some of his most remarkable work occurred when he was over eighty years old. He recorded a number of extended compositions including *Central City Sketches*, "Good Vibes," "Tales of the Rising Sun," and the acclaimed "Harlem Renaissance," for which he received a Grammy nomination in 1992 in the "Best Large Jazz Ensemble Performance" category. In 1996 Carter performed with the trumpeter Wynton Marsalis and the Lincoln Center Jazz Orchestra in a celebration of Carter's music. The evening concluded with the premier of Carter's new suite, "Echoes of San Juan Hill."

Carter received many accolades and awards during his lifetime, but he never seemed to allow the limelight to affect his quiet, soft-spoken, self-effacing, elegant personality. The tributes confirmed what music lovers already knew, that whatever the yardstick—brilliance, longevity, productivity—Carter possessed them all and was indeed a seminal figure in the history of jazz for more then seventy years. Benny Carter died on 12 July 2003.

[*See also* Jazz *and biographical entries on figures mentioned in this article.*]

BIBLIOGRAPHY

Berger, Morroe, Edward Berger, and James Patrick. *Benny Carter: A Life in American Music*. Metuchen, N.J.: Scarecrow, 1982. The definitive biography of Carter; contains ponderous amounts of material.

Yanow, Scott. *Bebop*. San Francisco: Miller Freeman, 2000. A short profile of Carter is on pages 210–211.

—DONALD ROE

CARTER, BETTY (b. 16 May 1929; d. 26 September 1998), also known as Lorene Carter, Lorraine Carter, and Betty Bebop, jazz vocalist, arranger, composer, and musician. Betty Carter was born Lillie Mae Jones in Flint, Michigan, to James Jones II and Bertha Jones. Her father worked as a press operator for the Ford Motor Company, making the family middle class.

Carter's musical influences were varied. She sang in her church's choir, which her father led. Her parents forbade listening to secular music and did not own a record player, but Carter listened to her brother-in-law's jazz albums, particularly those of Duke Ellington, and to radio jazz programs. She cut school to listen to bebop, a type of jazz that uses fast tempos and improvisation, on local jukeboxes; at the time—the 1940s—bebop was the latest musical craze. As a teenager Carter took piano lessons at the Detroit Conservatory. She sang pop music for school events and after school, but her niche was bebop.

Whenever famous jazz musicians performed in Detroit, Carter attended. Still in her teens, she performed with Charlie Parker and Dizzy Gillespie, and in June 1948 she joined Lionel Hampton's band as lead vocalist, using the name Lorraine or Lorene Carter. Hampton soon replaced both names and called her Betty Bebop, a name she disliked. Carter became particularly known for her scat singing.

Carter left Hampton's band in 1951 and moved to New York City to be a soloist, using the name Betty Carter. She performed at local venues. These led to tours, album recordings, and various collaborative projects. Carter understood the importance of satisfying three audiences: herself, her band, and her patrons. She permitted her band members to play for thirty minutes prior to her performance. Instead of singing to the melody, Carter allowed her voice to accompany her band members' instruments. The melody remained, yet each musician's style was emphasized. Carter's first solo album, *Out There with Betty Carter*, was released in 1958.

In 1960 Carter met her common-law husband, James Redding, a bartender. Their first child, Myles Kevin James, was born in March 1961, shortly before Carter recorded the album *Ray Charles and Betty Carter*. This album's song "Baby It's Cold Outside" topped the rhythm-and-blues charts. Carter's second son, Kagle, was born in February 1965.

After bad experiences with record companies and their keeping ownership of her albums, in 1970 Carter founded her own record company, Bet-Car. She released a number of albums on this label, starting with *Betty Carter* in 1970. In 1987 Carter signed an agreement with Verve Records that made Bet-Car one of its imprints but allowed Carter to retain full creative control over her work.

Betty Carter's impact on jazz can hardly be overstated. Many of her former musicians became successful jazz performers and credited her for helping them. In 1993 she began the Betty Carter's Jazz Ahead program at Kennedy Center. This musical residency program allows upcoming jazz artists to study under professionals. In 1997 the Grammy-winning Carter—who also composed and arranged songs, including her signature "Open the Door"—received a National Medal of Arts award from President Bill Clinton. Carter's career earned its due recognition only later in her life. She was diagnosed with pancreatic cancer in August 1998 and died a month later.

[*See also* Jazz *and* Music Industry.]

BIBLIOGRAPHY

Bauer, William R. *Open the Door: The Life and Music of Betty Carter*. Ann Arbor: University of Michigan Press, 2002.

—HOPE W. JACKSON

CARTER, JIMMY, ADMINISTRATION OF. Liberal Democrats distrusted the presidential candidate and former Georgia governor Jimmy Carter not only because he was not in the "old-boy network" but also because he was a southerner—and thus potentially a closet conservative. Liberals were skeptical because Carter seemed friendly to the diehard segregationists Lester Maddox and George Wallace and failed to speak out against segregated academies.

Supporters of Carter pointed to his gubernatorial record of appointing blacks at every level of government. Carter also established a state mediation service and deputized Georgia's high school principals as voting registrars to implement the Voting Rights Act of 1965. He overhauled the state's jails, in which blacks were overrepresented. He even attended black functions and made appropriate gestures toward the memory of Martin Luther King Jr. Carter was strong on civil rights but was against so-called forced busing, preferring voluntary busing if busing had to be used at all to implement desegregation.

With this gubernatorial record, Carter had the endorsement of the black Georgia congressman Andrew Young and the bulk of the old civil rights leadership in the presidential campaign of 1976. Carter campaigned effectively and proved appealing to black and white, poor and rich, conservative and liberal. He won 19 of 31 primaries, beat Gerald Ford in the general election, and became president in 1977.

Carter's civil rights accomplishments as president were many. He included a significant number of minorities and women among his 265 appointments to the federal judiciary. Carter appointed 37 black federal judges; by contrast, all previous presidents plus Carter's successor Ronald Reagan combined appointed 34 black judges, and 11 of these were appointed by Lyndon Johnson. George H. W. Bush appointed 13. Only Bill Clinton matched Carter's total. Seven of Carter's appointees were black women. Before Bill Clinton, the total number of black women appointed by all presidents was 19. Carter also appointed 14 Hispanics.

In its first year the Carter administration filed an amicus brief in *Regents of the University of California v. Bakke*, thereby affirming the federal commitment to affirmative action in college admissions. Then Carter applied the ban on discrimination set out by Title VII of the 1964 Civil Rights Act to the White House office. His administration filed the first federal suit to force police and fire departments in fifty-four cities and parishes in Louisiana to hire blacks. For minority businesses, it put $100 million of federal deposits in minority-owned banks, set aside 10 percent of the $4 billion 1977–1978 public works appropriation for minorities, set aside 15 percent of the Northeast Corridor railroad project for minorities, and ordered federal agencies to double their purchases from minority firms to $2 billion in two years. The administration also appointed blacks and other minorities to high-level positions.

Louis E. Martin served as special assistant for black affairs between 1978 and 1981. Carter established or expanded programs such as the Summer Youth Employment Program and Jobs for Youth that by May 1980 had created more than 2 million jobs for Hispanics and blacks. Carter increased minority procurement, established minority business grants in the Commerce Department, and promoted increasing the assets of minority-owned banks.

President Carter in the South Bronx. Jimmy Carter greets residents of the South Bronx, New York, 1977. JIMMY CARTER LIBRARY, NATIONAL ARCHIVES

Carter tried but failed against a filibuster to enact new fair-housing legislation. His Black College Initiative increased federal involvement with historically black colleges and universities. The Carter administration also maintained contacts with the leadership of traditional black organizations such as churches.

Carter said that if he could bypass the Senate he would appoint 12 percent black, 3 percent Hispanic, and 40 percent women to the bench. The record shows that his appointees to circuit courts were 16 percent black and 3.6 percent Hispanic. His judicial nominating commissions that screened candidates were 87 percent Democrat, as were 79 percent of the candidates they recommended. A report showed that in October 1980, 97.8 percent of Carter's selectees were Democrats. Carter vetted his candidates through not only the traditional American Bar Association but also the predominantly black National Bar Association and the Federation of Women Lawyers.

Following the pattern set by John F. Kennedy and Lyndon B. Johnson, Carter appointed blacks to ambassadorships in non-African nations such as Finland, Luxembourg, Syria, Spain, East Germany, Romania, Malaysia, and Algeria. Carter appointed Andrew Young as the first black ambassador to the United Nations and Patricia Roberts Harris as the first black cabinet secretary. Harris had earlier been the first black female ambassador, to Luxembourg, being appointed by Lyndon Johnson after seconding his nomination in 1964.

Recent administrations have reverted to stereotyping in appointing African Americans mostly to embassies only in Africa or the nations of the diaspora. Critics of the Carter administration acknowledge its accomplishments but argue that most of them are more show than substance. The biggest failing of the Carter administration is that, beset by economic woes, it proved unable to improve the overall economic condition of African Americans.

[*See also* Affirmative Action *and* Judges and the Judiciary.]

BIBLIOGRAPHY

Bourne, Peter G. *Jimmy Carter: A Comprehensive Biography from Plains to Post-Presidency*. New York: Scribner, 1997.

"The Higher Education of the Nation's Black Women Judges." *Journal of Blacks in Higher Education* 16 (Summer 1997): 108–111.

Kaufman, Burton I., and Scott Kaufman. *The Presidency of James Earl Carter, Jr.* 2d ed. Lawrence: University Press of Kansas, 2006.

—JOHN HERSCHEL BARNHILL

CARTER, ROBERT (b. 11 March 1917), lawyer, jurist, and ardent civil rights activist who has worked for equal rights since high school. Carter was born in Careyville, Florida, but his family moved to Newark, New Jersey, soon after his birth. When Carter was one year old, his father died, leaving his mother (who worked as a domestic) to raise eight children. As a senior at East Orange High School, Carter successfully ended segregation of the school's swimming pool (a hollow victory as the school closed the pool rather than integrate). Although encounters with racism did not discourage the youthful Carter, he admitted that he was delusional to think that race was irrelevant. Graduating from historically black Lincoln University in 1937 and Howard Law School in 1940, Carter earned a master's degree in law from Columbia (1941). At Howard, Carter met Dean William Hastie, who was a mentor to Carter later in life. After completing his education, Carter entered the army and served three years in the U.S. Army Air Corps as a second lieutenant—three years that polarized his views on race and equality and launched what became a lifelong struggle against racial injustice.

In 1941 the segregated U.S. Army proved a hostile environment for black servicemen, turning many against the armed forces and the nation. Carter's experience was no exception. After initial training at Fort Dix, New Jersey, Carter was assigned to Fort Gordon, an air base in Augusta, Georgia, where his all-black group included several college graduates. Their assigned officer minced no words, saying he did not believe in education for blacks and would not tolerate their "uppity" attitude. He promised trouble, and Carter found it. Carter insisted the army provide its black officers the same privileges, pay, and housing as whites—actions which resulted in an administrative discharge. With Hastie's intercession, Carter left the armed services with an honorable discharge, but the exposure to rampant racism led Carter and many other African American men to distrust white authority and to fight for civil rights.

Hastie recommended Carter for the position of assistant special counsel for the National Association for the Advancement of Colored People (NAACP) Legal Defense Fund, where he served directly under the future Supreme Court Justice Thurgood Marshall. For over a decade Bob Carter worked in the shadow of Marshall, despite the fact that he won twenty-one of twenty-two cases before the U.S. Supreme Court involving civil rights in universities, labor unions, housing, and employment. The first was *McLaurin v. Oklahoma State Regents* (1950), in which the Court overruled a decision limiting graduate education for blacks. Yet the star in his legal crown was the landmark *Brown v. Board of Education* case decided in 1954. The cases centered on the "separate but equal" principle stemming from the Court's ruling in *Plessy v. Ferguson* (1896). Carter utilized the research of the social scientist Kenneth B. Clark, a Howard University faculty member, in a South Carolina federal district case in 1951, and at his insistence the NAACP agreed to use Clark's study in the *Brown* arguments. In the Court's written ruling in favor of the NAACP, Chief Justice Earl Warren cited Carter's use of Clark's behavioral science research as a major factor in the Court's decision. Although they were never close friends, Marshall relied heavily on Carter's judgment in the *Brown* decision; preferring to work in the background, Carter never received the credit—Marshall did. In 1956, Marshall moved on to the judiciary and Carter was named general counsel for the NAACP, only to resign in 1968 when he protested the firing of an NAACP lawyer who penned an article critical of the Supreme Court's retreat from aggressive civil rights adjudication.

After three years in private practice in New York, Carter was appointed by President Richard Nixon to the federal bench for the Southern District of New York. Before accepting senior status in 1988, Judge Carter ruled on numerous important cases including a 1980 decision stating that the New York Police Department used discriminatory written tests in hiring. Although Carter had his critics and a high rate of reversal, many saw him as pro-government yet fair.

Carter won numerous awards, garnered various honors, and received several honorary degrees throughout his career. Cofounder (with Floyd McKissick) of the National Conference of Black Lawyers in 1972, he is a widower with two sons, one of whom is a judge. In 1965, Carter had an experience that shaped the course of his remaining years; he joined a small group of civil rights activists in testing the integration of public facilities in Mississippi. Carter admitted his fear upon exiting one establishment, yet he persisted in the face of that fear, as he continued to do so throughout his life. Largely unheralded in the civil rights movement, Bob Carter's career in the movement is best defined by the title of his autobiography, *Matter of Law* (2005).

[See also *Brown v. Board of Education*; Legal Profession; Marshall, Thurgood; National Association for the Advancement of Colored People; *and* Supreme Court.]

BIBLIOGRAPHY

Carter, Robert L. *Matter of Law: A Memoir of Struggle in the Cause of Equal Rights*. New York: New Press, 2005.

Greenberg, Jack. *Crusaders in the Courts: How a Dedicated Band of Lawyers Fought for the Civil Rights Revolution*. New York: Basic Books, 1994.

—BOYD CHILDRESS

CARTER, RON (b. 4 May 1937), jazz bassist. Ronald Levin Carter was born in Ferndale, Michigan, and started playing the cello when he was ten years old. In 1951 his family moved to Detroit, where he realized that the opportunities in classical music were limited because of racial prejudice. After a switch to the double bass he acquired an interest in jazz. He attended the Eastman School of Music (where the Ron Carter Audio Archives were established in 2001) in Rochester, New York, on scholarship and graduated with a bachelor's degree in 1959. Continuing his studies at the Manhattan School of Music, he received his master's degree in 1961.

Although he played with many top-rate jazz artists, Carter is renowned for his work in the acclaimed Miles Davis Quintet from 1963 to 1968. His playing on more than twenty-five hundred albums resulted in a well-deserved reputation as one of the most influential jazz bassists of all time. He is known for being an unselfish player who pushes other musicians to bring out their best.

Aside from his work in jazz as a collaborator and a leader of his own groups, Carter has recorded with classical and hip-hop artists. He has also composed the scores for several films and shows for PBS and has written two books: one an instructional manual on bass playing and another that includes 140 of his compositions. Among his awards are two Grammys. For nineteen years Carter taught at the City College of New York, retiring in 2002 as a distinguished professor emeritus. He was awarded honorary doctorate degrees from the Manhattan School of Music and the New England Conservatory of Music.

[*See also* Davis, Miles; *and* Jazz.]

BIBLIOGRAPHY

Stryker, Mark. "Ace of Bass: Everybody Wants to Work with Ferndale Native Ron Carter, Whose Influential Style Has Entered the DNA of Modern Jazz." *Detroit Free Press*, 24 August 2003. A comprehensive overview of Carter's career.

—TIMOTHY J. O'BRIEN

CARTOONISTS. Early African American creators of cartoons skirted the issue of their race to publish their works in a segregated society. George Herriman (1880–1944), the African American creator of the *Krazy Kat* comic strip, regarded as a twentieth-century classic, created the strip in 1913; published through King Features Syndicate—a major national distributor of comic strips to majority newspapers in large cities and owned by the newspaper magnate William Randolph Hearst—the strip ended only with Herriman's death in 1944. Herriman found public acceptance by letting people think that he was Greek; in fact he was a mulatto Creole whose family moved from New Orleans, Louisiana, to California when Herriman was young.

During the 1930s, 1940s, and 1950s, Elmer Simms Campbell (1906–1971), the first openly African American cartoonist to be published in national mainstream magazines, drew only white characters. In some circles—even among some African Americans—he faced criticism for his drawings of sexy white redheads called "Cuties." Others recognized that economic forces limited Campbell's character selection. Campbell's work appeared often in *Esquire* magazine: in fact, Campbell created the magazine's mascot, Esky.

Scholars continue to research the history of black cartoons before and during World War II. Early creators of black cartoons—frequently limited to black newspapers and publishers—faced economic pressure, censorship, and obscurity. Black newspapers traditionally lacked a comic-strip page, but they did carry comics ranging from humor centered on black themes to protest about racial inequalities.

Jackie Ormes, born Zelda Mavin Jackson (1911–1985) and recognized as the first African American female cartoonist, produced the strip *Dixie to Harlem* for the *Pittsburgh Courier* from 1937 to 1938. Starring Torchy Brown, *Dixie to Harlem* was a black-oriented humorous comic strip about a young African American woman who migrates to Harlem from the South and achieves fame as a performer at the Cotton Club. Ormes created a number of other strips for other black newspapers, and in 1950 when the *Courier* began a comics insert, she reinvented Torchy for *Torchy and the Heartbeats*.

Oliver "Ollie" Harrington (1912–1995), recognized as the first African American editorial cartoonist, created *Dark Laughter* for the *Amsterdam News* in 1935. This strip starred what became Harrington's best-known character, the heavyset fun-loving African American gentleman Bootsie. Harrington's cartoons addressed racism and lynching and were also published in the *Chicago Defender* and the *Pittsburgh Courier*.

In 1947, Orrin C. Evans (1902–1971) created *All Negro Comics*, the first comic book by an African American cartoonist to present an African American hero. *All Negro Comics* had a short run, and mainly reached only the Philadelphia area because majority publishers refused to sell it.

Black cartoonists who used cartoons for social protest faced open hostility from an unsympathetic white public. In the late 1940s, for example, Harrington's editorial cartoons came under the scrutiny of the Federal Bureau of Investigation and the House Committee on Un-American Activities, prompting his immigration to France in 1951. The works of many early black cartoonists appeared without bylines in black newspapers. Researchers have yet to uncover the identities of many pioneering African American cartoonists.

The civil rights era opened the door to syndication of black cartoons in majority newspapers. Yet one African American cartoonist per syndicate was the trend. In 1965 Morrie Turner (b. 1923), an African American cartoonist, introduced *Wee Pals*, which had a multiethnic cast of characters and was published in King Features Syndicate. *Wee Pals* is considered the first syndicated strip with a multiethnic cast, as well as the first such strip to be published in both majority and minority newspapers.

Black cartoonists have promoted health awareness through the use of their characters in public-service announcements about AIDS, diabetes, organ donorship, and teenage pregnancy. The struggles of black cartoonists have ranged from how to gain initial recognition to paying the bills. The limited number of majority newspapers carrying black comic strips continued to be a challenge into the twenty-first century.

Profile of a Contemporary Cartoonist. Bill Murray, an African American syndicated cartoonist, spent his childhood in Chicago drawing. Murray attended the Chicago Institute of Art and published some artwork freelance with the *Saturday Evening Post*. Typically, of twenty or so drawings he sent, one would be accepted. He got his first professional breakthrough at the Chicago-based Johnson Publishing Company. Herbert Temple, a Johnson Publishing artist who drew cartoons for Johnson's *Ebony* magazine, made Murray an art apprentice. Then in the mid-1970s he did editorial cartoons for the *Pittsburgh Courier*, the *Chicago Defender*, and others.

The comic strip *Those Browns*, which Murray based upon his real-life family, ran from 1976 to 1981, distributed by Sammy Davis Jr. Enterprises. After numerous unsuccessful phone calls, Murray had impersonated a close friend of Sammy Davis Jr. to reach the performer. Because *Those Browns* had an all-black cast, Murray had had trouble finding a distributor.

Since 1981 Murray has drawn the strip *SonnyBoy* for Real Times Media, the largest African American–owned and operated newspaper chain in the country and the publisher of newspapers such as the *Chicago Defender* and the *New Pittsburgh Courier*. By the early twenty-first century Murray also regularly produced editorial cartoons for a number of major magazines and newspapers. Murray's comic strips *Jet News*, whose syndicated political satire features a character named Archie Bumper, a black version of Archie Bunker, and *The Golden Years* appear in more than eleven hundred papers worldwide.

Bill Murray was one of about ten black cartoonists to participate in a collective protest organized by syndicated African American artists held in February 2008. The protest was in direct response to majority newspapers editors' perceived views of black cartoonists' work as esoteric and easily replaced. If a majority newspaper carried a minority strip, usually they carried just one. There are cities with African American mayors that do not have a black comic strip in their majority newspapers. The difficulty of selling comic strips with a majority-black cast remains, even as those with multiethnic casts are more prevalent. One strip with a black cast that achieved fame at the turn of the twenty-first century was Aaron McGruder's *The Boondocks*; the Universal Press Syndicate distributed the strip from April 1999 through March 2006. The success of the strip was such that McGruder was even able to sell the television and film rights to Sony Pictures Entertainment.

Black Age of Comics. Since the early 1990s the Black Age of Comics Convention has offered cartoonists opportunities for networking, professional development, and youth mentoring. In 1993 Turtel Onli, an independent Chicago African American cartoonist, first organized the Black Age of Comics Convention, which promoted an eclectic African American art aesthetic. Cartoon workshops, drawing scholarship contests, and business management presentations fostered the development of comics with African American settings, characters, or themes.

Beginning in 2002 the East Coast Black Age of Comics Convention, a spin-off of the Black Age of Comic Convention, was developed by Turtel Onli with the comic book historian William H. Foster III and Jerry Craft, creator of the black comic strip *Mama's Boyz* (syndicated by King Features since 1995). The East Coast Black Age of Comics Convention, held annually in May, has brought together creators and fans. The convention has become a place to attract new talent and mentor youth.

The East Coast Black Age of Comics Convention has recognized current talent and black cartoon pioneers. The convention awards the Glyph Comics Award, named in honor of the cartoon reviewer Rich Watson's blog "Glyphs: The Language of the Black Comics Community," launched in 2005 to promote discourse about black-themed comics. The Glyph Comics Awards committee, made up of cartoon historians, journalists, and Rich Watson, selected the best black comics and creators in nine categories based upon material submitted from the prior year. A tenth and final award was a people's choice, selected by fans. The Pioneer Awards recognized those early illustrators and writers in the field for their struggles. The struggle of black cartoonists has a long-standing history, if partially obscured, and continues.

[*See also* Black Press; McGruder, Aaron, and *Boondocks*; *and* Visual Arts.]

BIBLIOGRAPHY

Burma, John H. "An Analysis of the Present Negro Press." *Social Forces* 26, no. 2 (December 1947): 172–180.

Early, Gerald. "The 1960s, African Americans, and the American Comic Book." In *Strips, Toons, and Bluesies: Essays in Comics and Culture*, edited by D. B. Dowd and Todd Hignite. New York: Princeton Architectural Press; Saint Louis, Mo.: Washington University, 2006.

Goldstein, Nancy. *Jackie Ormes: The First African American Woman Cartoonist*. Ann Arbor: University of Michigan Press, 2008.

Strömberg, Fredrik. *Black Images in the Comics: A Visual History*. Seattle, Wash.: Fantagraphics, 2003.

—ROLAND BARKSDALE-HALL

CARVER, GEORGE WASHINGTON (b. July 1864?; d. 5 January 1943), naturalist, agricultural chemurgist, and educator. With arguably the most recognized name among black people in American history, George Washington Carver's image is due in part to his exceptional character, mission, and achievements; in part to the story he wanted told; and in part to the innumerable books, articles, hagiographies, exhibits, trade fairs, memorials, plays, and musicals that have made him a symbol of rags-to-riches American enterprise. His image has been used for postage stamps, his name has been inscribed on bridges and a nuclear submarine, and he even has his own day (5 January), designated by the United States Congress in 1946.

Thanks in large part to Linda O. McMurry's 1981 book, *George Washington Carver: Scientist and Symbol*, it is now possible to separate legend from fact and discover the remarkable child, youth, and man behind the peanut. McMurry concludes that Carver was a person out of step with his era—an exceedingly gifted black man in a time of white supremacy, a man of conservation and ecology in an age of exploitation. Carver was born to a slave woman, Mary, most likely in July 1864; his father was a slave on a neighboring farm and was killed in an accident before Carver was born. Susan and Moses Carver were the owners of the southwest Missouri homestead (near Diamond Grove) and of Mary and George. When bushwackers—vigilantes under the control of neither the Union nor the Confederate forces—kidnapped the mother and child, the Carvers were able to get the baby back, but Mary was not recovered.

Because the small child (now an orphan but no longer a slave) was so sickly, he spent his time helping Susan around the house, acquiring the skills of cooking, sewing, and cleaning that he would later use to pay his tuition for school and college, where he often took on such tasks as doing laundry for other students. Impressive to all around him was the youngster's affinity for plants and his ability to cultivate and nurture them. When he was old enough, he made his way to school, in Neosho, and from there, at age thirteen, to a series of high schools and various employment in Kansas, graduating in Minneapolis, Kansas. He went on to Simpson College in Indianola, Iowa, in 1890, and from there to the State Agricultural College at Ames, Iowa, in 1891. As a student, he found himself torn between his love for art and music and his more marketable skill with plants.

Carver's botanical talents, especially in mycology (the study of fungi), at Iowa State College, where he earned his Bachelor of Agriculture degree in 1894, led to his appointment to the faculty while he studied for his master's degree (awarded in 1896). At this point his life and career took a dramatic and defining turn; Booker T. Washington recruited him to come to Tuskegee Normal and Industrial Institute in rural Alabama.

Transforming Tuskegee. Carter's success during his forty-year tenure at Tuskegee can be credited to his persistence, hard work, inspiration, dedication, and inventiveness—the other faculty looked down on him for his dark skin and resented the fact that their principal had brought in a northern-educated scientist. Their hostility was exacerbated by Carver's special privileges; his salary was twice theirs, and he enjoyed two rooms in the dormitory (most faculty were assigned only one). Carver's consistent carelessness with his dress furthered their scorn, and Booker T. Washington, busy creating an impressive campus for his northern philanthropic visitors, was troubled by Carver's failure to look the part of the noble black educator. From Carver's perspective as the new director of agricultural research, Tuskegee was woefully underequipped, unable to provide adequately for a research scientist. He had expected to have time for his work with fungi, but instead he was kept busy with administrative work, for which he had neither interest or skill, and teaching duties that (while rewarding once he got beyond the students' disrespect) were also incredibly time-consuming. The farmers surrounding Tuskegee whom he was supposed to help were shockingly poor and busily engaged in wearing out the already deficient soil with cotton production. They could not afford fertilizer, and soil erosion took such a bitter toll on the fertility of their fields that subsistence farming was prevalent.

Fortunately George Washington Carver was not a man to despair or to give up easily. He created laboratory equipment from junk picked up on his countryside wanderings. He put his mind to work on possibilities for food crops and set his hopes on two that could restore nutrients to the soil and bring much-needed nourishment to the diets of farm families: the peanut and the sweet potato. He then came up with hundreds of ways those crops could be used and marketed, from glues and paints to medicinal oils and cosmetics. Carver created a mobile school, the Jesup Wagon, which allowed him to reach the farmers

Tuskegee Institute. George Washington Carver (*first row, center*) with his staff at the Tuskegee Institute, c. 1902. Photograph by Frances Benjamin Johnston. BOOKER T. WASHINGTON COLLECTION, LIBRARY OF CONGRESS

with his products and recommendations (such as crop rotation and contour plowing). Little by little, he patiently transformed southern agriculture.

None of this pleased Booker T. Washington; Carver's neglect of his administrative duties got him demoted. Happily, this left him with more time for his labs and his students. Carver corresponded with people he had known and impressed in Missouri, in Kansas, and in Iowa as well as with many he met during their visits to Tuskegee. Most of them were white, as he was more comfortable with white people than with blacks. As he became more widely known, outside recognition came his way, culminating in his election to Fellow of the Royal Society for the Encouragement of Arts in London in 1916. Washington died in late 1915 and was replaced by the more congenial Robert Moton, who saw Carver's work as an asset to fund-raising. In 1921, Carver was allotted ten minutes to make a presentation before the Committee on Ways and Means of the U.S. House of Representatives in favor of a tariff on peanuts. The legislators, initially restive, kept him talking for the next two hours.

Other honors fell Carver's way in the 1920s and 1930s. He received the Spingarn Medal from the National Association for the Advancement of Colored People in 1923 for distinguished service to science and an honorary doctor of science degree in 1928 from Simpson College. He was appointed as collaborator to the Mycology and Plant Disease Survey, Bureau of Plant Industry, U.S. Department of Agriculture in 1935. A bronze bust was dedicated to Tuskegee in 1937, a gift from friends across the country, and a feature film, *Life of George Washington Carver*, was made in 1938. The George Washington Carver Museum opened in 1938, and Carver later received the Roosevelt Medal for Outstanding Contribution to Southern Agriculture and an honorary membership in the American Inventors Society in 1939. Henry Ford Sr. dedicated the Museum at Tuskegee in 1941, and in 1942 Greenfield Village at Dearborn, Michigan, erected the George Washington Carver Cabin.

Carver died in 1943 at Tuskegee amid the droning aircraft sounds of the planes of the Tuskegee Airmen—in another age, during another war. His entire estate of more than $60,000 went to the George Washington Carver Foundation at Tuskegee. The George Washington Carver National Monument in Diamond Grove, Missouri, was established by the Seventy-eighth Congress in 1943 with Harry S. Truman as one of its sponsors, and numerous other recognitions and honors have followed over the decades, including science buildings at Iowa State and Simpson College that bear his name. Scientist, chemist, naturalist, entrepreneur, artist, musician—no single term can encompass Carver's talents and the gifts he exercised on behalf of his fellow human beings.

[*See also* Agriculture and Agricultural Labor; Educators and Academics; Entrepreneurship; Moton, Robert Russa; Science and Scientists; Tuskegee Institute; *and* Washington, Booker T.]

Bibliography

Adler, David A. *A Picture Book of George Washington Carver* (Picture Book Biography Series). Illustrated by Dan Brown. New York: Holiday House, 2000. An example of a children's book currently in print. One could argue that the misleading cover illustration, which depicts a very light-skinned black man in a white lab coat and blue tie does not resemble Carver very closely.

Carver, George Washington. *George Washington Carver in His Own Words*. Edited by Gary R. Kremer. Columbia: University of Missouri Press, 1987. A refreshing look at Carver through selected letters and other materials (such as his testimony before the House Ways and Means Committee). Each section is in the form of a narrative with lengthy quotes from Carver's writing.

Holt, Rackham. *George Washington Carver: An American Biography*. New York: Doubleday, 1963. First Published in 1943. Holt spent a great deal of time meeting with George Washington Carver before his death and had access to his scrapbooks. The book has a lively style and excellent photographs.

McMurry, Linda O. *George Washington Carver: Scientist and Symbol*. New York: Oxford University Press, 1981. Solidly researched and documented, fair and honest, this biography is also a good read.

Means, Florence Crannell. *Carvers' George, A Biography of George Washington Carver*. Illustrated by Harve Stein. Boston: Houghton Mifflin, 1952. Biography written for children. Means visited Carver at Tuskegee and conducted numerous interviews. A short, age-appropriate bibliography.

Nelson, Marilyn. *Carver: A Life in Poems*. Asheville, N.C.: Front Street, 2001. An unusual but highly effective approach to Carver's life and character, containing fifty-nine poems plus historical photographs and notes.

—Carolyn Wedin

CATLETT, ELIZABETH (b. 15 April 1915), sculptor and printmaker. Catlett was born six months after her father died of tuberculosis. The Washington, D.C., native was the daughter of two educators. Her father was a teacher at Tuskegee Institute and in the Washington, D.C., public schools, and her mother was trained at the Scotia Seminary in North Carolina as a teacher. Upon Elizabeth's father's death, her mother immediately sought a job, eventually working as a truant officer in the Washington, D.C., public school system. Catlett's mother always strongly emphasized education for her three children. The granddaughter of freed slaves, Catlett credited her resolve in sculpture to her family's commitment to education, noting that her profession has traditionally been reserved for white men.

Catlett identified with four underserved groups: women, blacks, Mexicans, and poor people. She did not see herself as exceptional, rather she saw herself as exceptionally fortunate. A precocious student, she skipped two grades and had to adjust to working with much older students.

After being rejected by the Carnegie Institute in Pittsburgh because of her race, she attended Howard University and studied with the artist and art historian James Porter, who was a constant supporter throughout her career. After graduating, Catlett taught for some time in the segregated school system in Durham, North Carolina, but she left when she was unable to achieve equal pay for black and white teachers. She enrolled at the University of Iowa, where she studied with the regionalist painter Grant Wood, from whom she received solid technical instruction. Wood's rigorous program and his open, nonracist, and nonconforming personality made Catlett's experience at Iowa extremely positive. Wood encouraged her to explore working with wood and to become a sculptor rather than a painter. Catlett began to work with stone too and earned the first MFA in sculpture from Iowa in 1940.

Catlett worked at the historically black Dillard University in New Orleans, where she was considered controversial for using nudes in drawing classes and taking her students to the Delgado Museum of Art (now the New Orleans Museum of Art), which was located in the segregated City Park. Catlett studied at the Chicago Art Institute, where she met the painter and printmaker Charles White. The two married and moved to New York City. There Catlett became part of a strong arts community that included the visual artists Aaron Douglas, Jacob Lawrence, Romare Bearden, and Hale Woodruff as well as literary artists such as Langston Hughes and Gwendolyn Bennett.

In 1942–1943 Catlett received further training in sculpture from the white cubist sculptor Ossip Zadkine. She began to experiment with solids and voids. Her training continued with six months at Hampton Institute under the direction of Viktor Lowenfeld, then in 1944 she studied printmaking at the Art Students League in midtown Manhattan. Her work in a Harlem high school, where she taught in the evenings, reinforced her interest in art for ordinary people. Catlett won a Rosenwald grant in 1946 that enabled her to focus more on her printmaking; in 1947 she traveled to Mexico to study at the state school. Divorced from White in 1947, she shortly thereafter married the Mexican Indian artist Francisco Mora. At this time Catlett created a series of prints on *The Black Woman*, which harked back to the realism of Wood but with a simpler, sharper stylistic edge. In the series she evoked the struggles and courage of black women. Her sculptures of this period also focus on black women; while they are classical and recall some of the simple lines of the sculptor Henry Moore, they are also influenced by art deco sculpture and cubism.

Catlett and Mora often worked together in Mexico. Their life was a struggle, with three young sons and limited funds, and their artist friends, including Diego Rivera and Frida Kahlo, provided inspiration and collaboration. With all three sons in school, Catlett returned to her own studies, working with Jose L. Ruiz and experimenting with mahogany and cedar for her images of black women and children. Her loving, strong, muscular women and children evoke independence and warmth.

Catlett's sculpture of the 1970s became more abstract and more cubist in nature. Her *Mother and Child* of 1970 is much more angular with very little detail. In this period she showed her interest not only in cubism and abstraction but also in African sculpture. During the 1960s and 1970s Catlett's work sensitively expressed the struggle of the civil rights era in sculptures such as *Black Unity* (1968). During this period she became even more determined to show the struggle and tragedies for equality and civil rights.

Catlett's style is direct and immediate. She received numerous public commissions, including the ten-foot bronze statue *Louis Armstrong* for New Orleans in 1976. Her expansive career includes woodcuts, linocuts, and sculptures of various media. She is represented in major collections and museums worldwide, including the Instituto of Fine Arts and the Museum of Modern Art in Mexico; the Schomburg Collection, the Metropolitan Museum of Art, and the Museum of Modern Art in New York City; the Library of Congress in Washington, D.C.; the Barnett-Aden Collection in Tampa, Florida; the High Museum in Atlanta, Georgia; the National Museum of Prague; the New Orleans Museum of Art; the State University of Iowa; Howard University; Fisk University; and Atlanta University. Making her home in Mexico, Catlett remained committed to expressing the life and struggles of women, blacks, Mexicans, and the poor. Her twenty-first century works include a 2003 sculpture paying homage to the writer Ralph Ellison that stands in Harlem, New York.

[*See also* Visual Arts.]

BIBLIOGRAPHY

Gouma-Peterson, Thalia. "Elizabeth Catlett: The Power of Human Feeling and of Art." *Woman's Art Journal* 4.1 (Spring–Summer 1983): 48–56.

Herzog, Melanie Anne. *Elizabeth Catlett: An American Artist in Mexico*. Seattle: University of Washington Press, 2000.

—AMY HELENE KIRSCHKE

CHAMBERLAIN, WILT (b. 21 August 1936; d. 12 October 1999), basketball player. A legendary basketball player, Wilt Chamberlain was a gifted offensive shooter who scored and rebounded prolifically. In the 1961–1962 season, averaging 50 points a game, he became the first and only National Basketball Association (NBA) athlete ever to score 4,000 points in a season. Through his fourteen-year playing career Chamberlain—a center who was seven feet one inch tall—set NBA single-game records for the most points (100), the most consecutive field goals, and the most rebounds. Not only was he the NBA scoring leader for seven years in a row, but he also was the league's top rebounder in 11 out of his 14 seasons. Ultimately Chamberlain scored 31,419 points in his career.

Born in Philadelphia, Wilton Norman Chamberlain was one of nine children born to and raised by William, a welder and a janitor, and Olivia, a domestic worker. Although at first Chamberlain was interested in track and field, his extraordinary height made him a natural for basketball in high school. In three varsity seasons at Philadelphia's Overbrook High, the six-foot eleven-inch Chamberlain led the team to two Philadelphia city championships and himself broke the high school record for the most points in a season, scoring more than two thousand. When Chamberlain continued to make sports headlines, a Philadelphia reporter gave him the nickname "the Stilt," yet Chamberlain hated this name and others, such as "Goliath." Because his friends saw him dip his head when he walked underneath doorways, they nicknamed him "Dippy" or the "Big Dipper," and he accepted these titles with good humor.

After more than a hundred colleges recruited him, Chamberlain decided to attend the University of Kansas in 1955. At the time NCAA (National Collegiate Athletic Association) rules prevented freshmen from joining the varsity squad, so Chamberlain played on the freshman squad. In December 1956 he made his varsity debut and was a starting player in a game against Northwestern, where he set a school record by scoring 52 points. Later in the season, in the 1957 NCAA title against North Carolina, Chamberlain led his team in a very close game, and although North Carolina beat Kansas by one point in triple overtime—largely because Chamberlain was constantly defended by three North Carolina players—tournament officials named Chamberlain the Most Outstanding Player of the Final Four.

Unwilling to abandon his love of track and field, in 1958 Chamberlain won a NCAA high-jump competition with an impressive clearance of six feet six inches. In May 1958, before his senior year in college, Chamberlain left Kansas and turned professional. Because of an NBA guideline that prohibited collegiate athletes from playing until after their intended graduation date, he spent a transitional year playing for the Harlem Globetrotters.

In 1959 the Philadelphia Warriors selected Chamberlain in the draft. During his first game he scored 43 points and had 28 rebounds against the New York Knicks, and at the end of the season he won both the NBA Rookie of the Year and the NBA Most Valuable Player (MVP) awards. Chamberlain's scoring power enabled the Warriors to rise from last place to second place, and when the team competed against the Boston Celtics in the 1960 NBA playoffs Chamberlain faced Bill Russell, the man who became his greatest rival. From 1960 until Russell retired at the end of the 1968–1969 season, Chamberlain and Russell competed in the playoffs eight times, yet Chamberlain overcame Russell only once, in the 1967 playoffs.

During his first season Chamberlain had been battered by aggressive, intentional physical hits from opposing players, and he shocked the sports world when he contemplated retirement. Instead he improved his physical conditioning in order to withstand his opponents' shoving and elbowing. On 2 March 1962, Chamberlain scored a

Wilt Chamberlain. The Philadelphia 76ers' Wilt Chamberlain scores over the Boston Celtics' Bill Russell during the Eastern Conference finals at the Boston Garden, 3 April 1967. AP IMAGES

record-making 100 points in a game against the Knicks. Even though Chamberlain had reportedly stayed out late the night before the game, he also made 28 of 32 free throws—remarkable because he was notoriously unskilled at making free throws.

When the Warriors moved to San Francisco in 1962, Chamberlain followed, and there he led the league in scoring for two seasons. In 1965 he was traded to the Philadelphia 76ers, who were not a winning team before Chamberlain joined; the following season Philadelphia had the best record in the league, and in 1967 they were the NBA champions. Chamberlain was again selected league MVP in 1966, 1967, and 1968. In 1968 Chamberlain was traded to the Los Angeles Lakers, and from 1968 to 1973 his skills enabled the Lakers to advance to the NBA finals four times. His 1971–1972 Lakers set an NBA record by winning 33 games in a row.

After retiring from the NBA in 1973, Chamberlain spent a year as the player-coach of the San Diego Conquistadors of the American Basketball Association (ABA). In 1984 he worked with another famous athlete, Arnold Schwarzenegger, when they appeared together in the movie *Conan the Destroyer*. After his professional basketball career Chamberlain also occupied himself with playing competitive volleyball, tennis, and marathon running. Once he even challenged the boxer Muhammad Ali to fight.

Even when he was in his fifties several NBA teams approached Chamberlain about returning. Instead, he read, wrote several books, maintained his status as a bachelor, and gave motivational speeches. He shocked readers in his 1991 memoir *A View from Above* when he claimed to have slept with twenty thousand women. This claim brought serious scrutiny from fans, women's groups, and critics, including the African American tennis star Arthur Ashe, who faulted Chamberlain for reinforcing negative stereotypes about the sexual behavior of African American men.

In 1978 Chamberlain was elected to the Naismith Memorial Basketball Hall of Fame, and in 1996 for the NBA's fiftieth anniversary he was named one of the fifty greatest players in NBA history. On 12 October 1999, Chamberlain died of heart failure at his Southern California home, named Ursa Major for the constellation widely known, like himself, as the Big Dipper.

[*See also* Basketball; Harlem Globetrotters; *and* Russell, Bill.]

BIBLIOGRAPHY

Chamberlain, Wilt, with David Shaw. *Wilt: Just like Any Other 7-foot Black Millionaire Who Lives Next Door*. New York: Macmillan, 1973.

Cherry, Robert Allen. *Wilt: Larger than Life*. Chicago: Triumph Books, 2004.

Lynch, Wayne. *Season of the 76ers: The Story of Wilt Chamberlain and the 1967 NBA Champion Philadelphia 76ers*. New York: Thomas Dunne Books, 2002.

Pomerantz, Gary M. *Wilt, 1962: The Night of 100 Points and the Dawn of a New Era*. New York: Crown, 2005.

Taylor, John. *The Rivalry: Bill Russell, Wilt Chamberlain, and the Golden Age of Basketball*. New York: Random House, 2005.

—RACHELLE GOLD

CHAMBERS, JULIUS (b. 6 October 1936), civil rights attorney and university administrator. Julius LeVonne Chambers was born in Mount Gilead, North Carolina, where his father ran a service station. Chambers decided to pursue a career in law after his father was unable to find an attorney to help him collect a debt from a white customer. He went on to earn a law degree from the University of North Carolina at Chapel Hill, where he was the first African American editor in chief of the university law review and the top-ranked student in his class. After graduating law school in 1962, Chambers earned his master of laws degree at Columbia University in 1963 and interned on the staff of the NAACP Legal Defense and Educational Fund. In 1964 he opened a law office in Charlotte, North Carolina.

Chambers is best known for his role as the lead attorney in the 1971 Supreme Court case *Swann v. Charlotte-Mecklenburg Board of Education*, the landmark busing case. In *Swann* the Court unanimously held that the Constitution does not permit a school board to assign children to neighborhood schools if the pupil-assignment plan preserves a segregated school system. To desegregate the Charlotte schools, the Supreme Court approved a controversial plan that proposed the massive busing of white children to schools in black neighborhoods and black children to schools in white neighborhoods. By extending the rule of the 1954 decision in *Brown v. Board of Education*, which prohibits the assignment of pupils based on race, *Swann* confirmed that school boards have an affirmative duty to abolish segregated schools.

From 1984 to 1993 Chambers led the NAACP Legal Defense Fund in New York. In 1993 he returned to North Carolina to become chancellor of North Carolina Central University, his alma mater. In 2001 Chambers retired from the university and returned to his legal practice in Charlotte. A year later he was named director of the University of North Carolina Center for Civil Rights.

[*See also* Desegregation and Integration, *subentry* Public Education.]

BIBLIOGRAPHY

Douglas, Davison M. *Reading, Writing, and Race: The Desegregation of the Charlotte Schools*. Chapel Hill: University of North Carolina Press, 1995.

Schwartz, Bernard. *Swann's Way: The School Busing Case and the Supreme Court*. New York: Oxford University Press, 1986.

—MARC SENNEWALD

CHARITABLE INSTITUTIONS, AFRICAN AMERICAN. In the nineteenth century, African Americans had comparatively little cash surplus to give to philanthropic and charitable causes. Yet the black community made a disproportionately large effort to help its unfortunate and underprivileged. In the early twenty-first century, African Americans gave more than any other group in American society, donating 25 percent more of their discretionary income to charities than whites did. On average, black households gave $1,614 to their favorite causes, and additionally many black families contributed 10 percent of their incomes to the church. In 2004, African Americans gave $11.4 billion to charitable causes; $7.2 billion went to churches and faith-based organizations, and $4.2 billion went to charities, education, politics, and other causes.

Roots of African American Charity. From the Underground Railroad to orphanages, homes for the aged and the blind, hospitals, and sanitariums, many charitable causes of the nineteenth century were funded openly or covertly by black dollars. Institutionalized black philanthropy was expressed primarily through black churches, which were also among the earliest institutions to raise funds for schools and scholarships. After the Civil War, African Americans established numerous charitable institutions to take care of the social, educational, and

Atlanta Tuberculosis Association, 1945. African American women were active participants and leaders in this organization from its founding in 1907. SPECIAL COLLECTIONS AND ARCHIVES, GEORGIA STATE UNIVERSITY LIBRARY

economic needs of the black community, both in the North and in the South. Many of these institutions, like the Tennessee Orphanage and Industrial School in Nashville, the Carrie Steele Orphanage in Atlanta, the Pickford Sanitarium of Southern Pines in North Carolina, or the Louisiana Association for the Benefit of Colored Orphans, were prinicipally or exclusively funded and maintained by blacks. Mutual benefit societies also provided much-needed charitable work in a society that excluded African Americans from many public agencies and charitable institutions, following the motto of the Atlanta Colored Benevolent Society: "We assist the needy; we receive our sick; we bury our dead."

Although black charities addressed universal needs, pervasive racism and segregation in American society often meant the creation of a separate network of social services. At a time when African Americans were frequently denied access to the institutions of the emerging American welfare state, they had to find their own solutions to the needs of their communities. Lay workers and professionals like teachers, doctors, nurses, and librarians volunteered their services to charitable institutions concerned with health care, education, and housing. Yet their numbers remained relatively small and their resources limited.

Black charitable institutions received a boost after the emergence of the black women's club movement in the last decade of the nineteenth century. Although black women's clubs considered education the most important area of their work, their members also supported and reinforced the charitable work of black churches, fraternal orders, and mutual benefit societies. Black women established and maintained kindergartens, homes for the aged, and hospitals, and they participated in the settlement house movement. Their working girls' homes provided lodging, employment information, and job training. Fund-raising efforts constituted a large part of this charity work, and seemingly frivolous activities like balls, card games, and whist clubs made important economic contributions to the black community. Thus women's club work served as an important link between private charity and professional career work, and, like white charity work, it influenced the formation of the American welfare state.

The Progressive Era and the New Deal. The nature of black charities changed tremendously with the migration waves of African Americans that started to reach northern cities in the second decade of the twentieth century and reached its height in the 1920s. In 1911 a group of conservative African Americans, white philanthropists, and social workers allied with Booker T. Washington founded the National Urban League as the chief black social welfare agency. It counseled black migrants, placed them in jobs, assisted them in finding housing, and conducted research on the problems that black migrants faced in an urban environment. Although traditional charitable institutions remained, new multiservice institutions were now established, often in collaboration with black women's clubs, that offered travelers' aid, lodging, job placement, night classes, and training for industrial workers, black nurses, and social workers.

Yet for all the general reform activities and social advances that gave the Progressive Era its name, their effect on African Americans was minimal because the benefits of charity work applied chiefly to immigrant but not to black ghettos and applied to industries that employed comparatively few blacks. Safe, clean, and sanitary housing in particular remained a tremendous problem in the ghettos of northern cities, a problem that black charities were unable to address as business interests, inexpensive mass transit, and pervasive racism reshaped American cities.

The small accomplishments of black charitable institutions in the first three decades of the twentieth century were wiped out by the Great Depression of the 1930s. With the programs of Franklin D. Roosevelt's New Deal, public welfare increasingly substituted for private charity. However, even though blacks had the highest unemployment rates, their share of public jobs and relief was disproportionately small, and they did not profit from the social security legislation to the same extent that whites did. Charitable institutions, both black and white, were hard pressed in the 1930s: they were overwhelmed with relief requests while their funds dwindled dramatically. Black churches, along with the National Urban League, remained the most important black charitable agencies, assisting black families in need and helping to place hundreds of thousands of unemployed blacks in jobs. In addition, public health emerged as an important issue for black charitable institutions. Across the country Africans Americans started to establish free clinics and lobbied local governments and private organizations to include blacks in existing programs.

Post–World War II Developments. Since World War II, American charities have undergone tremendous changes. Their number rose from fifty thousand in 1950 to more than nine hundred thousand by 2007. Black charities multiplied as well, and new issues emerged in the African American community along with new charitable institutions. With unemployment and poverty still endemic among blacks in the 1950s, charities continued to address these issues. In addition African American health became the focus of many local philanthropic efforts, as many hospitals and other medical services remained segregated.

Elite female philanthropists founded organizations like Jack and Jill of America (1938) and The Links (1946) to provide social service programs to children and support cultural and civic activities. In 1955 the United Negro Appeal was founded, an institution that, similar to the United Way, served as an agency to collect and provide funds for local black charities, coordinated relief services, and counseled and referred clients to cooperating agencies. It derived its name from the United Jewish Appeal. Black neighborhood centers with programs for children, youth, and adults multiplied, as did black veteran organizations.

In the 1960s the funds of black churches and charities, along with the financial support from the NAACP and the federal government, became instrumental for the success of the civil rights movement. In addition, many nonprofit organizations were created specifically to support the goals of the movement. Staffed mostly by volunteers, they not only raised funds but also provided meals for freedom riders, took in the children of those who marched or were imprisoned, and thus acted as important facilitators for social change.

In the last two decades of the twentieth century, black charities formed local associations in order to raise funds and coordinate services more efficiently. For example, the member agencies of the Associated Black Charities of New York City, founded in 1982, provide such diverse services as emergency food and shelter, clothing distribution, rent assistance, pregnancy prevention, medical and mental health care, family counseling, and rehabilitation for drug users, but also run day-care and senior-care centers and offer school tutoring, job training, and career counseling.

In 1999 the National Center for Black Philanthropy was incorporated in Washington, D.C., "to promote and strengthen African American participation in philanthropy." The specific goals of the center are to increase giving and volunteering in the black community, educate the public, and support African American philanthropic projects as well as research into the contributions of black philanthropy. The biannual National Conference on Black Philanthropy has developed into the most important forum to discuss and plan African American philanthropic endeavors.

As a new generation of African Americans seizes power in the business world and particularly in the music and film industry, its members without doubt accumulate wealth on a scale unprecedented in the black community. The Baby Boom generation and the Silent Generation have traditionally given to black colleges and universities, to civil rights organizations, and to black churches, but the philanthropic causes of the black post–civil rights generation remain somewhat undefined. Yet for the first time in American history African Americans possess the means substantially to finance charitable institutions that serve their communities and all Americans.

[*See also* Black Church; Fraternal Organizations, African American; Jack and Jill of America, Inc.; National Urban League; Philanthropy; Public Assistance; *and* Women's Clubs.]

Bibliography

Clegg, Claude A. "Philanthropy, the Civil Rights Movement, and the Politics of Racial Reform." In *Charity, Philanthropy, and Civility in American History*, edited by Lawrence J. Friedman and Mark D. McGarvie, pp. 341–361. New York: Cambridge University Press, 2003. Assesses the idealistic motives, economic interests, and social visions of the supporters of the civil rights movement.

Franklin, John Hope, and Alfred A. Moss Jr. *From Slavery to Freedom: A History of African Americans*. 8th ed. New York: Alfred A. Knopf, 2000. Chapter 16, "Philanthropy and Self-Help," provides the historical context for the emergence of black charitable institutions.

Salem, Dorothy. *To Better Our World: Black Women in Organized Reform, 1890–1920*. Brooklyn, N.Y.: Carlson, 1990. One of the most comprehensive assessments of black women's charitable and reform work.

Weiss, Nancy. *The National Urban League, 1910–1940*. New York: Oxford University Press, 1974. Looks at the first three decades of the community work of the National Urban League.

—Anja Schüler

CHARLES, RAY (b. 23 September 1930; d. 10 June 2004), singer, pianist, composer, and bandleader. Among the characters that the comedian Clerow "Flip" Wilson portrayed on his television variety show in the early 1970s was the sassy, "get you straight" Geraldine Jones, who routinely declared her love and devotion for Ray Charles. The fictional Geraldine, like legions of fans black and white, young and old, admired Charles not only for his considerable musical talent but also for his tenacity in overcoming blindness to become an American music icon.

Ray Charles Robinson was born in Albany, Georgia, the son of Bailey Robinson, a married railroad track worker, and the teenager Aretha Williams, a field hand and laundress. Unwed and facing an uncertain future, Williams moved with her son to Greenville, Florida, shortly after his birth. Although his family was poor, the young Ray lived a relatively happy and normal childhood until one terrible day in 1936 when he watched helplessly as his four-year-old half brother George drowned in a large washtub. The incident left an indelible impression on the young boy. Ray's personal tragedies continued as he gradually lost his eyesight, becoming totally blind by about age seven. His mother realized that she could not properly care for her son and placed him in the segregated Colored Department of the Florida School for the Deaf and Blind in Saint Augustine, Florida.

Ray Charles. At the Chicago Blues Festival, 1998. Photograph by Michael Jackson. © MICHAEL JACKSON

The school was a godsend for Ray. He learned to read Braille and how to live without sight. He also received instruction in playing musical instruments. He dabbled in playing the saxophone and the clarinet but favored the piano. He preferred boogie-woogie-style piano playing and had shown an interest in this genre of music as a youngster in Greenville. In fact, he first learned the rudiments of piano playing under the tutelage of Wiley Pitman, a local stride and boogie-woogie pianist who held court at the Red Wing Café.

Ray decided by age fifteen that he wanted to be a professional musician and singer. After the death of his mother in 1945, Ray Charles Robinson—who later shortened his name to Ray Charles to distinguish himself from the prominent boxer Sugar Ray Robinson—went out on his own. He toured throughout Florida, playing the piano and singing in small bands. He preferred the small band format with vocalist, particularly as exemplified by the Nat King Cole Trio and the Three Blazers with Charles Brown. Charles made his way to Seattle, Washington, in 1948 and performed in local bands. Coincidentally, he met and mentored a young Quincy Jones in the art of writing and arranging music. Charles became something of a local celebrity in Seattle, and after a mostly successful two-year run he relocated to Los Angeles seeking wider recognition.

In a career that spanned more than fifty productive years after his arrival in Los Angeles, Charles, more than any of his contemporaries, redefined the boundaries of pop, jazz, blues, and country-and-western music. During the early 1950s he recorded with Swing Time Records and toured nationally with the guitarist Lowell Fulson's small fusion band. In 1952 Charles signed a contract with Atlantic Records, and Ahmet Ertegün, one of Atlantic's owners, encouraged his independence in writing and recording. Consequently Charles defined and refined his own musical style, which included fusing secular blues, jazz, and rhythm-and-blues music with the religious music he learned as a child. Many of his hit recordings—such as "I Got a Woman" (1955), "Drown in My Own Tears" (1956), "The Night Time (Is the Right Time)" (1959), and "What I Say" (1959)—not only resulted in significant crossover popularity but also helped to define a musical genre that came to be known as soul music.

Although Ray Charles is best known for his rhythm-and-blues and soul music, his foray into country-and-western music—despite confusing and dismaying many loyal fans—produced two highly popular albums of soul-infused country-and-western music: *Modern Sounds in Country and Western Music* (1962) and *Modern Sounds in Country and Western Music, Vol. 2* (1962). One song, "I Can't Stop Loving You," from the first album was a megahit. Moreover, Charles never lost his love for jazz and continued to record and sing jazz music throughout his career. He recorded a classic duet cover of "Baby, It's Cold Outside" with the jazz singer Betty Carter in 1962 and made a show-stopping appearance at the 1958 Newport Jazz Festival.

He also had a lifelong association with the jazz greats David "Fathead" Newman, Hank Crawford, Jeff Willis, and Marcus Belgrave.

Charles received many honors during his lifetime, including having his soulful rendition of Hoagy Carmichael's "Georgia on My Mind" proclaimed the official state song of Georgia. He was the recipient of numerous Grammy awards and received a star on the Hollywood Walk of Fame. In addition, he was inducted into the Rock and Roll Hall of Fame, the Jazz Hall of Fame, the Songwriters Hall of Fame, and the Rhythm and Blues Foundation. He recorded a duets CD shortly before his death that crossed various music genres, and he was an adviser for the film *Ray* based on his life. Unfortunately, he died before the 2004 film was released and never saw the extraordinary, Oscar-winning performance of Jamie Foxx, who portrayed him in the film. Charles, who married twice and fathered twelve children by nine different women in and out of wedlock, died in Los Angeles of liver disease on 10 June 2004.

[*See also* Blues; Jazz; Music; Rhythm and Blues; *and* Soul Music.]

BIBLIOGRAPHY

Charles, Ray, and David Ritz. *Brother Ray: Ray Charles' Own Story*. 3d ed. New York: Da Capo Press, 2004. Provides insightful anecdotes and personal observations but lacks significant historical context.

Lydon, Michael. *Ray Charles: Man and Music*. Rev. ed. New York: Routledge, 2004. An interesting chronological study and memoir.

—DONALD ROE

CHARLESTON, OSCAR (b. 14 October 1896; d. 5 October 1954), Negro Leagues superstar and manager, with a career in professional baseball that spanned almost forty years and more than a dozen teams. Oscar Charleston was born in Indianapolis, Indiana, on 14 October 1896, and as a lad he was the batboy for the local Indianapolis ABCs, a Negro team. In 1910 he left home to join the army, at the age of fourteen. He was stationed in the Philippines, where he played baseball and ran track as a sprinter. Charleston was mustered out of the service and returned to his hometown in 1915; there he joined the ABCs, where he established himself as a left-handed power hitter and a southpaw outfielder of extraordinary speed and agility. From his center-field position, Charleston claimed to be able to cover the entire outfield; one unconfirmed account has it that his outfield teammates covered only foul territory, allowing him to cover the rest of the field. He also demonstrated a mercurial temper, which occasionally erupted against opposing players and even umpires, leading him to become known as the "black Ty Cobb." Many suggest, however, that he was a better fielder than Cobb, a faster base runner, and, at six feet and 190 pounds, a slimmer, but equally powerful, version of Babe Ruth. Some baseball historians, in fact, have claimed that he was the best all-round player in the history of the Negro Leagues. In 1916, Charleston and the ABCs defeated the Chicago American Giants to win the Black World Series. In 1921, he led the new Negro National Leagues in batting, home runs, and stolen bases during their fifty-game season. By 1923, Charleston was one of the highest-paid athletes in the Negro Leagues at $325 a month, and at his peak he may have been the most popular black player in the game.

Charleston's career as a player-manager began with the Harrisburg Giants of the Eastern Colored League in 1922, and he led that league with a .445 batting average in 1925. After short stays with two teams, he joined the legendary Homestead (Pennsylvania) Grays in 1930, where he played with such luminaries as Smokey Joe Williams and Josh Gibson. That same year he helped the Grays win a championship series with the Lincoln Giants. In 1932, Charleston moved to the independent Pittsburgh Crawfords as a player-manager whose team included five future Hall of Famers. In his first year, he finished second on the Crawfords in hitting (.363) to the famous Josh Gibson for 135 games. In each of the next three seasons, he played in the East-West All-Star game. After 1941, Charleston gave up playing and concentrated on managing full-time with several teams. In 1954 he was the skipper of the Indianapolis Clowns. It was his last year of baseball: on 6 October of that year he suffered a stroke and died a few days later in Philadelphia. With a lifetime batting average of .344 and his blazing speed and powerful throwing arm, Charleston was a consensus choice for posthumous election to the Major League Baseball Hall of Fame in 1976.

[*See also* Baseball, *subentry* Negro League.]

BIBLIOGRAPHY

Hogan, Lawrence. *Shades of Glory: The Negro Leagues and the Story of African American Baseball*. Washington, D.C.: National Geographic Society, 2006. Places the Negro Leagues in historical perspective.

Lanctot, Neil. *Negro League Baseball: The Rise and Ruin of a Black Institution*. Philadelphia: University of Pennsylvania Press, 2004. A scholarly study of the Negro Leagues, with an extensive bibliography.

Peterson, Robert. *Only the Ball Was White: A History of Legendary Black Players and All-Black Professional Teams*. New York: McGraw-Hill, 1984. A readable overview of the Negro Leagues; contains useful information on Charleston and other African American baseball players.

—CHARLES ORSON COOK

CHASE, W. CALVIN (b. 2 February 1854; d. 3 January 1921), editor and publisher of the *Washington Bee* and prominent member of the Republican Party. William Calvin Chase was born in 1854, probably at home, 1109 I Street NW in Washington, D.C., to William Chase, a blacksmith who had migrated to the District from Maryland as a free man in 1835, and Lucinda Seaton, a daughter of one of "the best and purest families in the Commonwealth of Virginia" (Gatewood, p. 57). After her husband died from a reported accidental gunshot in 1863, she instilled her extraordinary sense of family pride, her commanding presence, and her studied dignity in her only son and five daughters—to such an extent that three of her daughters lived at home their entire lives, and in the same home, Calvin Chase always maintained the office of his influential newspaper, the *Washington Bee*. The publication's motto, "Honey for Friends, Stings for Enemies," defined the man, his paper, and his career as a journalist, lawyer, and politician; his life was a blend of pride and protest until his sudden death of a heart attack sitting in his editorial chair in 1921.

Because of his relatively privileged socioeconomic status, Calvin grew up in the Fifteenth Street Presbyterian Church, a pillar of the free black community, and attended John F. Cook's elementary school in the church basement, where he learned the abolitionist tradition that Cook had experienced at Oberlin College. Chase gained his secondary education in the Preparatory Department of Howard University, where he later attended law school classes before being admitted to the bar in Virginia and the District of Columbia. Despite this extraordinary formal education, Chase was not a scholar but rather a practical man who preferred facts to theories. Physically, Chase was tall and thin, perhaps standing six feet, seven inches tall like his equally dark-complexioned maternal uncle, John A. Seaton, who, like Chase, was very involved in Republican Party politics. Also like his uncle, Chase added to his presence by dressing very well.

Chase established and maintained the *Bee* in his urban hometown, the capital of black and white America. For forty years the paper's four and eight pages heralded the achievements of African Americans in Washington, D.C., and the nation; it is the most complete record of African American news and opinion during the rise of the Jim Crow system of segregation, disfranchisement, and lynching following Reconstruction. Week in and week out, Chase independently shelled the citadel of racial prejudice rather than become involved in the organized efforts of the Afro-American League and Council, the Niagara Movement, or the NAACP. Nor did Chase become a cog in the so-called Tuskegee Machine. In fact, from his initial denunciation of Booker T. Washington's 1895 Atlanta Address as an "apology" to the time of "the Wizard's" death in 1915, Chase was largely critical of Washington. He was no follower of Du Bois either, apparently because of his disdain for Du Bois's scholarly aloofness and certainly because of the competition between *The Crisis* and the *Bee* as a national voice for African Americans. Yet, Chase and Du Bois had in common that they were both relentless foes of discrimination, disfranchisement, lynching, and white mob attacks. In articles, editorials, and front-page cartoons after 1900, Chase railed passionately against white racism, and the level of his passion seemed to rise as he grew older.

One of the constants in his life was his allegiance to the Republican Party. He was fond of publishing Frederick Douglass's famous quote, "It [the Republican Party] is the ship, all else the sea." He did flirt with "independence" (support for the Democratic Party) during Grover Cleveland's first term, and he supported the Socialist Party in 1904 and 1919. But the Republican Party was his political home, and he was a delegate to the national party conventions in 1900 and 1912. His birth family was the other constant in his life. Although he married Arabella V. McCabe and had two children with her (Beatriz and William Calvin Jr.), he lived apart from his wife after the children were grown. In sum, William Calvin Chase was an independent individual whose legacy is the "stings and honey" in the pages of the *Washington Bee* rather than any notable personal bonds with family and friends.

[*See also* Black Press; *Washington Bee*; *and biographical entries on figures mentioned in this article*.]

BIBLIOGRAPHY

The primary source for this essay was the doctoral dissertation of Hal S. Chase, "'Honey for Friends, Stings for Enemies': W. Calvin Chase and the *Washington Bee*, 1882–1921" (University of Pennsylvania, 1973). The most in-depth publication is Hal S. Chase, "'Shelling the Citadel of Race Prejudice': William Calvin Chase and the *Washington Bee*, 1882–1921," *Records of the Columbia Historical Society* 49 (1973–1974): 371–391. Also see Willard B. Gatewood, *Aristocrats of Color: The Black Elite, 1880–1920*. Fayetteville: University of Arkansas Press, 2000.

—HAL S. CHASE

CHASE-RIBOUD, BARBARA (b. 26 June 1939), sculptor, poet, and novelist. Barbara Chase-Riboud was born and raised in Philadelphia, Pennsylvania, and received a BFA from Temple University in 1957 and an MFA from Yale University in 1960. In 1957 she received a John Hay Whitney Foundation fellowship, which allowed her to study in Rome and Egypt. In 1961 she married the French photojournalist Marc Riboud and moved to Paris permanently.

Chase-Riboud's sculpture is characterized by bronze shapes combined with silk and wool fabrics, and it exhibits African and Asian influences. Her sculpture is housed among the permanent collections of the Centre Georges Pompidou in Paris and the Metropolitan Museum of Art and the Museum of Modern Art in New York City.

Chase-Riboud is a poet and a novelist as well as a sculptor. In 1974 she published her first volume of poetry, *From Memphis to Peking*, which was edited by Toni Morrison. In 1979 she published her best-known novel, *Sally Hemings*. A work of historical fiction, the novel explores an affair between Thomas Jefferson and a slave mistress—a relationship that Chase-Riboud presents as a loving one. Written at a time when the American historical community denied that the relationship between Jefferson and Hemings had taken place, the book was criticized by many historians as an irresponsible representation of real historical figures. However, in other quarters it was well received, winning the Janet Heidinger Kafka Prize for excellence in fiction by an American woman. In 1994 Chase-Riboud continued the saga of Jefferson and Hemings with *The President's Daughter*, which is written from the perspective of Sally's daughter Harriet.

[*See also* Literature *and* Visual Arts.]

BIBLIOGRAPHY

Janson, Anthony F., and Peter Howard Selz. *Barbara Chase-Riboud, Sculptor*. New York: Harry N. Abrams, 1999. This critical assessment of Chase-Riboud's sculpture contains one hundred photographs of her work.

—JENNIFER JENSEN WALLACH

CHAVIS-MUHAMMAD, BENJAMIN (b. 22 January 1948), minister and civil rights activist. Benjamin Franklin Chavis Jr. was born in segregated Oxford, North Carolina, to a family that had an impressive legacy within the African American community: the family patriarch, John Chavis (1763–1838), was a Revolutionary war hero, landowner, and the first black ordained preacher of the Presbyterian Church. Chavis extended that legacy with his own education at the University of North Carolina, Duke University Divinity School, and Howard University, as well as with his involvement with the Southern Christian Leadership Conference (SCLC) as statewide youth coordinator in North Carolina from 1965 to 1969.

In 1969, Chavis was sent to Wilmington, North Carolina, as the newly appointed Southern Regional Program Director of the United Church of Christ Commission on Racial Justice (UCC-CRJ). There he joined an interracial coalition of ministers attempting to quell the escalating violence surrounding school desegregation. Several black activists, including Chavis, were arrested and charged with arson. After spending almost five years in prison (1976–1980), Chavis and the "Wilmington Ten" were cleared of all charges. Following his imprisonment, Chavis returned to his work with the United Church of Christ, working as executive director and, ultimately, as vice president of the National Council of Churches USA.

In 1993, Chavis became the youngest person ever named executive director and CEO of the National Association for the Advancement of Colored People (NAACP). While executive director, Chavis focused on the endemic effects of environmental racism, a concept that he had helped define with other civil rights activists during the 1980s. With renewed vigor and political emphasis, the NAACP swelled in membership during Chavis's brief sixteen-month tenure. However, in 1994 the NAACP board of directors fired Chavis after they discovered that he had committed $332,000 in association funds to settle a sexual harassment and discrimination claim against him.

From his post at the NAACP, Chavis became executive director and CEO of the National African American Leadership Summit (NAALS), an organization that sought to create operational unity within the civil rights movement. It was during his affiliation with the NAALS that Chavis deepened his ties with Louis Farrakhan, leader of the Nation of Islam. Together they organized the 1995 Million Man March in Washington, D.C. Increasingly disaffected by what he perceived as the conciliatory work of the mainstream civil rights movement, Chavis developed an affinity for Farrakhan's aggressive economic proposals and the social asceticism of the Nation. In 1997, Chavis converted to Islam, added "Muhammad" to his name, and was appointed by Farrakhan to be East Coast Regional Minister of the Nation of Islam. "The God of Judaism and the God of Christianity and the God of Islam is the same one God," explained Chavis-Muhammad (quoted in *Jet*, p. 8). However, for many African American Christians involved in civil rights efforts, Chavis-Muhammad's conversion signaled a shift away from interracial collaboration. In 2000, Chavis-Muhammad joined with the hip-hop music producer Russell Simmons to found the Hip-Hop Summit Action Network (HSAN), the largest and broadest national coalition of hip-hop artists, recording-industry executives, youth activists, and civil rights leaders.

[*See also* National Association for the Advancement of Colored People *and* Nation of Islam.]

BIBLIOGRAPHY

Mercadante, Linda A. "Questioning Chavis Muhammad." *Christian Century*, 4 June 1997, pp. 548–550.
"United Church of Christ Says Chavis Can No Longer Be a Minister in Its Denomination." *Jet*, 12 May 1997, p. 8.

—KATHRYN LOFTON

CHENAULT, KENNETH (b. 2 June 1951), lawyer, businessman, and one of the first African American chief executive officers (CEO) of a Fortune 500 company. Chenault was born on Long Island, New York. His father,

Hortenius Chenault, was a dentist, and his mother, Anne Chenault, was a dental hygienist. Kenneth Chenault graduated with numerous honors from Waldorf High School, a private school in Garden City, New York. He completed one year at Springfield College before transferring to Bowdoin College in Brunswick, Maine. There he earned a bachelor's degree in history in 1973. He earned a JD from Harvard Law School in 1976.

After he graduated from Harvard, Chenault was hired as an associate by the law firm Rogers and Wells in New York City. In 1979 he worked as a management consultant for Bain and Company despite not having a master's degree in business administration. Chenault passed the Massachusetts bar exam in 1981. That same year he was recruited by American Express to become a director of strategic planning in travel related services. In 1983 he joined the company's merchandise services unit, where the division's sales skyrocketed under his leadership. In 1989 Chenault became president of the American Express Consumer Card Group. This period was challenging because the U.S. economy was experiencing a recession. Chenault played an instrumental role in turning around the charge-card business. Some of his accomplishments included signing on gas stations, discounters, and supermarkets as acceptors of the card; establishing the membership rewards loyalty program; broadening the customer base past the affluent who paid their balances monthly; and striking partnerships with companies that allowed American Express to expand its lending business through the issuing of co-branded cards that permitted customers to carry balances.

In 1993 Chenault was appointed head of U.S. travel related services. He helped restructure the company, and the number of cards issued continued to increase. He was named vice chairman in 1995, and two years later he was named president and chief operating officer. In January 2001, after the retirement of Harvey Golub, Chenault became chairman and CEO of American Express. This made him one of the first African American CEOs of a Fortune 500 company. As CEO, chairman of the board, and director of American Express, he made choices that kept his company in the forefront, namely the decision to keep the American Express corporate headquarters in Lower Manhattan's World Financial Center after the attacks of 11 September 2001.

Chenault is on the board of directors of IBM, American Express Company, and New York University Medical Center–New York University School of Medicine. He is a member of the American Bar Association and a fellow of the American Academy of Arts and Sciences. He has frequently been named one of the 100 Most Influential Black Americans by *Ebony* magazine and has received numerous honorary degrees. Chenault married Kathryn Cassell on 20 August 1977; they have two sons, Kenneth Jr. and Kevin.

[*See also* Legal Profession.]

BIBLIOGRAPHY

CNN.com. "Kenneth Chenault: Corporate CEO." Black History Month. http://www.cnn.com/SPECIALS/2002/black.history/stories/08.chenault/index.html.

Halpern, Tim. "Kenneth I. Chenault, 1951–." Reference for Business, Business Biography. http://www.referenceforbusiness.com/biography/A-E/Chenault-Kenneth-I-1951.html.

—SHANTEL AGNEW

CHESNUTT, CHARLES W. (b. 20 June 1858; d. 15 November 1932), writer. Charles Waddell Chesnutt was born in Cleveland, Ohio, to free parents, Ann Maria Sampson Chesnutt and Andrew Jackson Chesnutt, who in 1856 had fled the slave-holding South for better opportunities in the North. Chesnutt, the oldest of his father's eleven children from two marriages, became the first black author that the American literary establishment took seriously. Greatly influenced by his intellectual mother—a teacher who shortly after Chesnutt's birth moved her family from Cleveland to Oberlin, Ohio, because of the educational opportunities that Oberlin College might provide—and his abolitionist father, the blue-eyed and white-looking Chesnutt from the age of eight grew up black in Fayetteville, North Carolina (the Patesville of his fiction), where his family resettled at the end of the Civil War.

In *The Journals of Charles W. Chesnutt*, published posthumously in 1993, Chesnutt documents how he read voraciously to nourish a "mind . . . so constituted that it cannot remain idle" (p. 136), received some private tutoring from local whites, and attended the segregated Howard School in Fayetteville, which was underwritten by concerned community residents and Reconstruction agencies. To prevent the precocious fourteen-year-old from dropping out of school to supplement the family income, Robert Harris, principal of the Howard School (soon renamed the State Normal School of Fayetteville and now Fayetteville State University), offered Chesnutt a position as pupil-teacher and also sent him to Charlotte, North Carolina, for three years to assist his younger brother Cicero Harris, principal of the local Peabody School. After Robert Harris's untimely death, Chesnutt became the second principal of the State Normal School of Fayetteville.

In 1878 at age twenty he married Susan Perry, a teaching colleague. They had two daughters, and in 1883 Chesnutt decided to migrate north. After working for six months as a reporter for the Dow-Jones Company in New York and

Charles W. Chesnutt. Print Collection, Miriam and Ira D. Wallach Division of Art, Prints and Photographs, The New York Public Library, Astor, Lenox and Tilden Foundations

writing a daily Wall Street gossip column for the *New York Mail and Express*, he settled permanently in Cleveland, where he worked for the Nickel Plate Railroad and in 1885 began reading law in the office of Judge Samuel E. Williamson. Although Chesnutt passed the Ohio bar examination with the highest grade, he never practiced law. He established a stenographic business that supported his family's upper-middle-class lifestyle and began a literary career that aimed to expose the nation's elaborate racial fictions, often masked behind hypocritical declarations of democracy.

In 1899 Chesnutt closed his stenographic business to give full attention to his fiction, which addressed slavery and the Jim Crow laws. Having expressed in a 29 May 1880 journal entry his desire to "write for ... a high, holy purpose," adding that "the object of my writings would be not so much the elevation of the colored people as the elevation of the whites," Chesnutt unequivocally targeted those who introduced "the unjust spirit of caste which is so insidious as to pervade a whole nation" (*Journals*, p. 139). As a pacifist who would not "appeal to force," he preferred a "moral revolution" that would surreptitiously mine America's racist garrison until "we [blacks] find ourselves in their [the mainstream's] midst before they think it" (*Journals*, p. 140).

Nevertheless, like his friend and fellow educator Booker T. Washington, Chesnutt also shared in the Gilded Age's aspiration for material success and regularly avoided projects that might compromise his ability to generate income. For example, in 1890 he turned down the novelist George Washington Cable's invitation to serve as secretary of the Open Letter Club, organized as a public forum for discussion of southern racial politics. Chesnutt also refused in 1893 to support Judge Albion Tourgée's *National Era* magazine, which used slightly different methods to achieve similar social ends, because he feared that the magazine could not attract a strong enough subscription base.

In April 1905 Chesnutt replaced W. E. B. Du Bois, a prominent leader who soon founded the National Association for the Advancement of Colored People (NAACP), on Washington's Committee of Twelve. When Du Bois asked him to sign the essay "Race Relations in the United States," which appeared in the 12 November 1910 edition of the *Cleveland Gazette* and criticized Washington's rosy picture of American racial relations, Chesnutt explained that he had a personally beneficial relationship with the Tuskegee Institute founder.

Chesnutt's writings show keenly sly insights into American society. His first published book, *The Conjure Woman* (1899), a collection of short stories, features the former-slave narrator Uncle Julius, a character parody inspired by Joel Chandler Harris's romanticized Uncle Remus and used by Chesnutt to satirize John, the character who symbolizes America's smugly predatory capitalist elite. A second collection of short stories, *The Wife of His Youth and Other Stories of the Color Line* (1899); the Beacon biography *Frederick Douglass* (1899); and three novels, *The House behind the Cedars* (1900), *The Marrow of Tradition* (1901), and *The Colonel's Dream* (1905), all appeared during Chesnutt's lifetime. Collections of his many short stories, essays, and letters and five novels—*Mandy Oxendine* (1997), *The Quarry* (1999), *Paul Marchand, F.M.C.* (1998), *A Business Career* (2005), and *Evelyn's Husband* (2005)—were published posthumously. These texts display an American romantic aesthetic ironically undermined by the author's signifying moral realism. *The Wife of His Youth*, *Mandy Oxendine*, *The House behind the Cedars*, *The Quarry*, and *Paul Marchand, F.M.C.*, for instance, weigh the difficulties of sex and "passing" across racial lines against the likelihood of economic and social advantage.

Although *The Colonel's Dream*, *A Business Career*, and *Evelyn's Husband* focus mainly on the lives of white characters, Chesnutt portrays them as haunted by the nation's moral and racial hypocrisy. Expressing outrage in *The Marrow of Tradition* at the riot in Wilmington, North Carolina, in 1898 that led to the first overthrow in the United States of a legitimately elected government and exploring in *The Colonel's Dream* the impact of the Civil War on a supposedly recuperative South, Chesnutt misjudged the effect of his literary realism on predominantly white readers. Not surprisingly that audience bemoaned his thematic focus on "race." Yet some scholars with a deeper understanding of Chesnutt, like Eric J. Sundquist in *To Wake the Nations: Race in the Making of American Literature* (1993), note that at the time "it was nearly impossible for the minority writer to do otherwise" (p. 12). Significantly, in 1905 Chesnutt—certainly for financial and perhaps for literary and political reasons as well—reopened his stenography business, but he remained an occasional public advocate for black rights. For example, in March 1928 he testified before a U.S. Senate committee against the Shipstead anti-injunction bill, which he feared would strengthen the ability of predominantly white unions to discriminate further against black workers. His essay "The Negro in Cleveland" (1930) is one of the best sociological studies of that city for its time.

After long misjudging Chesnutt's signifying narrative techniques and calling him an accommodator of American racism, literary commentators have increasingly come to understand and appreciate the sophistication and profundity of Chesnutt's realism. For instance, he was among the first African American authors to examine seriously the racial implications of evolutionary theory, largely reaffirmed by modern DNA evidence. In such essays as "What Is a White Man?" (*Independent*, 30 May 1889) and "Race Prejudice: Its Causes and Its Cure" (*Alexander's Magazine*, 1 July 1905) and in his three "Future American" articles (*Boston Evening Transcript*, 18 August 1900–1 September 1900) he argues that white America's problem is not so much a superiority as an inferiority complex, rooted in nature's not choosing whites as the models for the human race.

Likewise, in the first "Future American" essay, subtitled "What the Race Is Likely to Become in the Process of Time," Chesnutt cites the anthropologist William Z. Ripley's assertion in *The Races of Europe: A Sociological Study* (1899) that "the European races, as a whole show signs of a secondary or derived origin" (*Selected Writings*, p. 48), a scientific assertion that establishes black and not white chronological and genetic primacy in human evolution. Caucasians display this inferiority when they revel in the conquest of colored people, whom they then transform into worthy foes and even ennoble precisely because these victims can make melanin, the skin-coloring ingredient denied whites by nature. Indeed, economic and emotional oppression of African Americans enable Euro-Americans to create a "superior" self that exacts a vicarious revenge on nature.

Awarded the NAACP's Spingarn Medal in 1928, Chesnutt remained unapologetic for making the color line his major fictional domain. His acceptance speech echoed the first "Future American" essay's bold argument that Americans should amalgamate and facilitate the natural formation of a future American ethnic type "of people who look substantially alike, and are moulded by the same culture and . . . ideals" (*Selected Writings*, p. 49), a result that would eliminate racial difference and thus racial strife altogether. In a 1915 essay entitled "The Disfranchisement of the Negro," he graphically describes how biological dissimilarity caused whites to leave colored people "absolutely without representation, direct or indirect, in any law-making body in any court of justice, in any branch of government" (*Selected Writings*, pp. 68–69).

But as if to warn of the futility in defying human nature through such terrorism, Dr. William Miller, Chesnutt's protagonist in *The Marrow of Tradition*, evokes evolutionary history: "The negro was here before the Anglo-Saxon evolved, and his thick lips and heavy-lidded eyes looked out from the inscrutable face of the Sphinx across sands of Egypt while yet the ancestors of those who now oppress him were living in caves, practicing human sacrifice, and painting themselves with woad—and the negro is still here."

Chesnutt used literature to promote the benefits of a nascent evolutionary biology that he proposed could unify diverse genes, increase human longevity, and, most significantly, offer amalgamated blacks a chance to achieve the American Dream unmolested. Thus he kills off Rena Walden, the heroine of *The House behind the Cedars*, because she refuses to marry the white racist George Tryon and values love over material gains, unlike her brother John, who "passes" and inherits the riches of his unknowing white wife. Chesnutt promoted racial uniformity through genetic diversity until he died, still perhaps naively hoping that removing physical differences through miscegenation would finally eliminate racial distress from the United States.

[*See also* Literature; Passing; Race, Theories of; *and* Racism.]

Bibliography

Chesnutt, Charles W. *Charles W. Chesnutt: Essays and Speeches*. Edited by Joseph R. McElrath Jr., Robert C. Leitz III, and Jesse S. Crisler. Stanford, Calif.: Stanford University Press, 1999.

Chesnutt, Charles W. *An Exemplary Citizen: Letters of Charles W. Chesnutt, 1906–1932*. Edited by Jesse S. Crisler, Robert C. Leitz

III, and Joseph R. McElrath Jr. Stanford, Calif.: Stanford University Press, 2002.

Chesnutt, Charles W. *The Journals of Charles W. Chesnutt*. Edited by Richard Brodhead. Durham, N.C.: Duke University Press, 1993.

Chesnutt, Charles W. *Selected Writings: Charles W. Chesnutt*. Edited by SallyAnn H. Ferguson. Boston: Houghton Mifflin, 2001. Reprints both *The Conjure Woman* and *The Wife of His Youth and Other Stories* and includes generous selections of Chesnutt's most important essays, as well as some of the most incisive criticism about the writer.

Simmons, Ryan. *Chesnutt and Realism: A Study of the Novels*. Tuscaloosa: University of Alabama Press, 2006. An examination and update of Chesnutt's African American realism.

Sundquist, Eric J. *To Wake the Nations: Race in the Making of American Literature*. Cambridge, Mass.: Harvard University Press, 1993. Chapter 4, "Charles Chesnutt's Cakewalk," provides a riveting examination of Chesnutt's literary signifying.

—SallyAnn H. Ferguson

CHEYNEY UNIVERSITY OF PENNSYLVANIA. Cheyney University of Pennsylvania was founded as the African Institute in 1837 by the Quaker abolitionist Richard Humphreys, who left $10,000 in his will to establish the school. Humphreys was a native of a West Indies slave plantation who had migrated to Philadelphia in 1764, where he became a silversmith. Moved by the plight of impoverished free blacks in Philadelphia, Humphreys emended his will in 1829 to include the school appropriation. He died in 1832, and the school was founded five years later. Within weeks of the school's founding, however, its name was changed to the Institute for Colored Youth, providing a free education for qualified black students in Philadelphia. The institution was governed by a Quaker board of managers.

The school continued as an urban institution throughout the nineteenth century, but in 1902 it moved twenty-five miles west of the city, to a farm sold to the university by George Cheyney, whose family had held the property since the early 1700s. Upon the school's move, the steel magnate and philanthropist Andrew Carnegie donated $10,000, matched by the school's board of governors, to build a library at the new location. His gift formed the cornerstone of the university's quadrangle and provided an anchor for the newly constructed institution. It opened in 1909.

In 1913 the poet and educator Leslie Pinckney Hill took over the administration of the school. Hill was a two-time graduate of Harvard who began his teaching career at Booker T. Washington's Tuskegee Institute. Hill argued that education was the key to racial progress, and to that end he developed an educational model that emphasized "the human family." Black students would find success by learning to cooperate with each other while keeping in mind their commonalities with the white population that surrounded them. Hill published two volumes of poetry in the 1920s and remained at the helm of the university for thirty-eight years. In 1962 the school renamed the Carnegie Library in his honor.

In July 1914, the year after Hill's arrival, the university was renamed the Cheyney Training School for Teachers. Six years later, in September 1920, the Pennsylvania state government certified the institution as a state normal school, with graduates receiving certification to teach in state public schools. It was only a small step from state certification to operating under state auspices, and in 1921 the state senator Albert McDade sponsored a bill that authorized the purchase of the school property, to be run by the State Board of Education. The $75,000 expenditure made Cheyney a state university on 1 January 1922 (although Quaker involvement with the school did not completely cease, and as of the early 2000s the Quaker community still participates in school activities). The takeover also provided the school with the rudiments of a varsity athletics program. By the early 1930s, the university was issuing its first bachelor of science (in education) degrees.

In 1951 the school's name changed again, to Cheyney State Teachers College, and it was accredited by the Middle States Association of Colleges and Secondary Schools. It became Cheyney State College in 1959, and in 1968 the university launched its first graduate degree program. In 1983 Pennsylvania consolidated control of state universities, creating the State System of Higher Education. Cheyney was included and again underwent a name change, becoming Cheyney University of Pennsylvania.

After Cheyney's takeover by the state of Pennsylvania in the early 1920s, the school began to admit a modicum of white students, causing controversy over the effects of integration on both white and black youths. The normal school was creating teachers, and those teachers would eventually filter into the state public school system, with influence over the minds of all of Pennsylvania's youth. At the time, the idea of such potential integration was highly contested. The legacy of that contest was revived more than seventy years later. In 1991 Eugene Jones, chair of the Cheyney Sciences Department, argued that he would not hire any white professors to fill departmental vacancies. When two white professors protested the hiring freeze, Jones responded by encouraging students to harass them and charge them with racism. The resulting lawsuit, *Gentner v. Cheyney University of Pennsylvania* (1999) awarded the former professors almost $2 million in damages.

The racial animosity of the late twentieth century has abated, however, and in the early twenty-first century Cheyney University annually trains more than a thousand undergraduates and almost two hundred graduate students of many races and nationalities, offering a broad curriculum and twenty-eight bachelor's degrees, as well as master's degrees in education. It is the oldest surviving historically black college in the nation.

[*See also* Higher Education *and* Historically Black Colleges and Universities.]

BIBLIOGRAPHY

Conyers, Charline Howard. "A Living Legend: The History of Cheyney University, 1837–1951." Unpublished manuscript in the Archives of Leslie Pinckney Hill Library, Cheyney University of Pennsylvania.

Hill, Leslie Pinkney. "The State Teachers' College at Cheyney and Its Relation to Segregation in the North." *Journal of Negro Education* 1 (October 1932): 408–413.

James, Milton M. "Leslie Pinkney Hill." *Negro History Bulletin* 24 (March 1937): 135–137.

—THOMAS AIELLO

CHICAGO. Standing today at the corner of Michigan Avenue and Wacker Drive, it is hard to imagine the frontier wilderness that lay before Jean Baptiste Point du Sable, Chicago's first longtime resident of the city. Of African and French descent, du Sable arrived sometime in the 1770s and established a fur trading post on the Chicago River, near Lake Michigan. Du Sable's entrepreneurial spirit and intimate ties to what was, even then, a multicultural population, may have offered a glimpse—in retrospect—of Chicago's future. But it would take more than a century for the city to take full advantage of its location astride major transportation routes and for the town's leadership to display the ingenuity of its first settler. Nor was it until the late nineteenth century that more than just a handful of African Americans could seek out the possibilities envisioned by du Sable. Though it developed much later and for different reasons than the black communities in Philadelphia, Boston, and New York, perhaps no population is as illustrative of the national and global transformations experienced by twentieth-century cities as is Chicago's African Americans.

While the city was never without African American residents in the nineteenth century—despite Illinois black laws that attempted to keep free blacks from migrating to the state during the antebellum era—it was not until after the Civil War that the black population began to achieve some stability and presence within Chicago. Many who arrived in Chicago during the late nineteenth century belonged to what W. E. B. Du Bois called the Talented Tenth, a group of African Americans who generally came from more privileged and educated backgrounds than later migrants. Even though it constituted less than 2 percent (roughly 23,000) of Chicago's overall population in 1896, a recognizable black community had already coalesced around a network of fraternal orders, churches—Quinn Chapel AME most prominent among them—social clubs, and activist organizations such as the National Colored Men's Protective Association. The latter originated in 1891 and, along with the national Afro-American League—the brainchild of T. Thomas Fortune—worked to combat the violence and discrimination directed towards blacks in the South. The community was small enough that interracial alliances—organizational, marital, and sporting (primarily baseball)—could be forged. Despite the Illinois Civil Rights Act of 1885, however, blacks were often discriminated against in hotels, restaurants, and theaters. While a small group of intellectual elites provided the point of contact between blacks and whites and assumed a leadership role in the city's African American community, the majority of black residents belonged to the working or lower classes. Most of these individuals worked in domestic and personal service, as the meatpacking and steel industries were generally dominated by European immigrants.

The revolutions in transportation and mechanization that transformed the United States in the latter part of the nineteenth century held particular importance for Chicago. As a railroad hub and growing industrial powerhouse, the lakefront city saw many of the commodities and perishables traversing the country go through it—or originate in it. Once a mere regional outpost, Chicago quickly assumed a position of importance second only to New York City in a nation that was, by the late nineteenth century, the most formidable global economy. To announce and celebrate these two developments, plans were made to hold the 1893 World's Columbian Exposition in Chicago. In combination with the rising tide of violence and oppression in the southern states, this event helped to spur future migrations of African Americans to Chicago—though this result was not immediately evident to citizens of Chicago or blacks in the South.

The fair was a veritable crazy quilt of displays and exhibitions, ranging from the manufacturing halls heralding the country's growing technological prowess to companies such as Quaker Oats capturing fairgoers with its visible product placement to the human zoo depicting Filipinos, Eskimos, and members of other "exotic" nationalities in their "native habitats." African Americans were noticeably absent from the fair's proceedings, as they seemed to fit uneasily in the narrative of progress that the famed African American leader Frederick Douglass had denounced as racist. Fair leaders scrambled to organize a "Negro Day," which prompted other notable African Americans to join their voices to that of the former abolitionist leader in objecting to a special day that segregated black accomplishments and did not fully acknowledge their American citizenship. Two individuals, in particular, took center stage: the Chicago resident Fannie Barrier Williams, who decried the racism of white women at the fair, and Ida B. Wells, who had fled the South and would eventually settle in Chicago after repeatedly pointing the finger at southern leaders and lynch mobs who perpetuated the myth of black rapists. Nor did Wells endear herself to southerners by advocating gun ownership and self-defense for African Americans threatened with violence. Wells would later marry Ferdinand Barnett, already a respected race leader in Chicago. More quietly, a young man and future Chicagoan, Robert Abbott, performed with a New Orleans jazz troupe at the Columbian celebration and took in the sights, sounds, and energy of Chicago, black and white.

Northward Migration. As the laws and practices targeting southern African Americans for segregation, disfranchisement, and violence further constricted their lives in the 1890s, more blacks shifted their attention to the North for the economic, political, and educational opportunities increasingly denied them in the South. From roughly 1890 to 1910 about 200,000 African Americans migrated to northern cities. Many of these people came from states in the Upper South and did not differ radically from longtime northern residents. In Chicago, newer settlers pushed the boundaries of the existing black residential district farther south beyond its nine blocks reaching from 22nd to 31st streets. The numbers within existing European communities on the South Side of the city, clustered around the Armour and Swift packinghouse complex where most of the European immigrants worked, were further swelled by ongoing immigration. Though the African American and European communities lived very close to one another, there was virtually no contact between them because the Illinois Central Railroad tracks created a geographical barrier. Blacks were virtually shut out of work at the packinghouse and steel industry in Chicago and only employed as a means to break the occasional strike that erupted between workers and employers.

Situations such as these contributed to escalating racial tension within the city. Though the African American population hovered around only 35,000 in 1910, black assertiveness, accomplishments, and institutions—locally and nationally—became more visible by the early 1900s. As professional baseball moved to ban African Americans from its league in 1898, Rube Foster, who had migrated to Chicago to play baseball, bought the hometown Leland Giants and renamed them the Chicago American Giants, becoming one of the first black owners of teams that comprised an early edition of the Negro Leagues. By 1920 Foster successfully organized other black teams into the Negro National League, effectively professionalizing and guiding a business that remained financially viable until 1930, when it collapsed because of the Depression. Negro League teams were vital to their home communities and also helped to create a wider sense of racial pride as they played exhibition games throughout the county.

Chicago was also, by 1910, the home of Jack Johnson, the first black heavyweight boxing champion in the United States. Johnson inspired African Americans throughout the nation with his exploits in the ring and his dashing, uncompromising lifestyle outside it—though his desire to live as freely as any white person ultimately led to his demise. Oscar De Priest, originally a house painter after he migrated to Chicago in the late nineteenth century, was in 1915 the first black alderman elected in Chicago and symbolized to many African Americans the political opportunities that were virtually nonexistent in southern locales. He later served as a congressman in the U.S. House of Representatives. Black institutions such as the Overton Hygienic Manufacturing Company, the well-known maker of cosmetics for African American women, relocated to Chicago in 1911. Perhaps most important, Robert Abbott—the musician who performed at the 1893 World's Fair—launched the *Chicago Defender* in May 1905. The *Defender* almost immediately became one of the most widely circulated black newspapers in the country, and it played a pivotal role in the first mass migration of African Americans out of the South.

The Great Migration. It was not until the outbreak of World War I in 1914 that African Americans had a real alternative to the economic and social oppression they faced in the South. As immigration to the United States came to a standstill with the conflict in Europe, a labor shortage in northern industrial cities led employers to recruit a heretofore untapped source: African Americans. Between 1916 and 1919, roughly 500,000 blacks migrated north seeking work, schooling for their children, a less suffocating racial environment, and generally all the perquisites associated with citizenship and freedom in the United States. Seventy thousand of those migrants settled in Chicago, enticed by the *Defender* stories they pored over in southern barbershops discussing job opportunities, integrated schooling, various black institutions, Chicago nightlife, and the accomplishments of Foster's Giants. While those who migrated found conditions in Chicago far from idyllic, few regretted the move despite the hardships they encountered.

As the African American community ballooned in size, conflicts emerged between those "Old Settlers" who had arrived in Chicago well before World War I and recent migrants, who differed from previous generations in their overwhelmingly working-class, Deep South roots. Old Settlers feared that the newer migrants—more rural, less educated, and employed in menial and/or industrial positions—would reflect badly on the more polished and accomplished "respectable" classes. While greater class differentiation emerged within the growing black community, what older generations feared could be seen in growing white concerns of a "black belt" or "black ghetto" that was residentially and perceptually distinct from other communities. As soldiers returned from World War I, including black soldiers from the Eighth Illinois Regiment, racial tensions flared throughout the country. Chicago witnessed one of the worst racial conflicts of this era when on 27 July 1919 seventeen-year-old Eugene Williams swam across the invisible line in Lake Michigan that demarcated black and white territories. A group of young white youths belonging to the Ragen Colts gang attacked and killed Williams. The battle spilled into the neighborhoods for several days, resulting in the deaths of 23 blacks and 15 whites. An additional 537 residents were injured in the rioting. Though future struggles over space would not be so deadly, the riot of 1919 was only the first of what would be many racial contests over residential and public space.

The migration years were also the beginning of the thriving Black Metropolis on the South Side of Chicago. As racial tension and discrimination accelerated in these years, African Americans continued to build institutions within their community that served their needs. Other institutions provided a respite from daily living. In the late teens and throughout the 1920s, the first notable collection of blues and jazz musicians brought their distinctive sounds to Chicago nightclubs and recording studios. These included Louis Armstrong, Joe Oliver, and Blind Lemon Jefferson, among others, launching Chicago's reputation as home to the blues. Owing to the productions of locally based Paramount Studios and the development of national "race records" companies such as Black Swan and Okeh Records, the music of local musicians traveled the country and reaffirmed the kinship and migratory ties between Chicago and the Deep South, particularly Mississippi.

The Great Depression, World War II, and the Postwar Years. Each of these trends—migration to Chicago and further cultivation of blues artists in Chicago—continued throughout the Depression, peaking again as the United States entered World War II. A turn toward the spiritual sound of gospel during the lean years of the 1930s was best embodied by the Chicagoan Mahalia Jackson, who moved to Chicago as part of the Great Migration of the World War I era. The Chicago Housing Authority (CHA), created in 1937 to help furnish affordable public housing, was charged with creating low-cost apartments for a variety of residents. The initial projects consisted of low-rise buildings of from two to four stories; three of these were located on the North, West, and South sides of Chicago in predominantly white neighborhoods. The fourth development, the Ida B. Wells Homes, was located in—and intended for—the surrounding black neighborhood.

While the construction of these early housing units was consistent with federal policy stating that the occupants of a public housing facility reflect the population of the neighborhood in which the building was located, World War II and the ensuing black population increases transformed the nature and look of public housing in Chicago. Between 1940 and roughly 1960, the number of African Americans residing in Chicago grew by more than 500,000. While the percentage shift of the earlier Great Migration was larger than this second migratory stream, the absolute numbers were incomparable to those of the later generation of migrants. Many African Americans, in Chicago and other major cities such as Detroit and New York, entered war-related work and industries, solidifying the foothold they established twenty years before.

This population shift stretched the boundaries of the black community on the South Side of Chicago and strained the capacity of the CHA, which continued to erect public housing for migrants and war-related workers. While these complexes were not necessarily racially segregated, one project—Altgeld Gardens, on the outskirts of the city—was built solely for black workers. Following the war, city and federal housing plans dovetailed to initiate an era that witnessed the racial segregation of Chicago's poor and low-income black population. As white aldermen refused to build public housing developments in their neighborhoods, the CHA took the path of least resistance and began to construct housing projects on the South and West sides—read black areas—of the city, or near existing public developments. In the fifteen years following the end of World War II, most of these projects took the cookie-cutter form of high-rise complexes between fifteen and twenty stories spanning a width of about a quarter mile—and a length of several miles—on State Street. What had once been the proud and vibrant center of Chicago's Bronzeville neighborhood was now filled with stark, lifeless towers devoid of architectural beauty. The notorious Cabrini Green projects on the near North Side, a mere stone's throw from the wealthy Gold Coast residences on State Street, grew slowly from a cluster of low-rise buildings to a collection of high-rise complexes so rife with gang violence that in 1981, the mayor, Jane Byrne, moved into an apartment there for several weeks, hoping to slow the crime rate.

As African American residents continued to take advantage of low-cost housing and moved beyond the traditional boundaries of the black ghetto into historically white neighborhoods, racial conflicts over space and housing became Chicago's version of the civil rights movement then unfolding in the South. Several riots drew national attention in what was generally a volatile period within Chicago's history. The Cicero riot of 1951, in which several thousand whites (estimated at between two thousand and five thousand) gathered to protest the presence of a single black family in one apartment building (ultimately burned and looted by the white mob) composed of twenty units, garnered international attention. In the white neighborhood of South Deering on the city's far South Side, a residential housing project that was unintentionally "integrated" by a light-skinned woman—Betty Howard—and her husband ignited weeks of rioting against the couple. The police made few interventions, and while Trumbull Park was later integrated by several more black families as a means of supporting the Howards, racial tension continued to flare for another decade. Throughout this period, African Americans were continually harassed, beaten, or obstructed in their attempts to gain access to public parks, beaches, and pools in all parts of the city.

Though the racial struggles in the South were qualitatively different from those of the North, the murder of the fourteen-year-old Chicagoan Emmett Till in August 1955 during a visit to his uncle in Money, Mississippi, engendered one of the most poignant and pivotal media moments in the civil rights struggle. Declaring that she wanted "the whole world to see" what had been done to her child, Till's mother brought her son's body back to Chicago, where an open-casket wake was held. Images of Till's grotesquely swollen and disfigured face circulated throughout the country. *Jet* magazine's coverage of the wake, the subsequent trial of the two white suspected murderers, and Mamie Till-Bradley's dignified handling of both amplified the kinship ties between African Americans in Mississippi and Chicago, as well as the racial struggles shared by northern and southern blacks. *Jet*, a spinoff of *Ebony* magazine, further enhanced the national reputation and standing of the Chicago businessman John H. Johnson, who founded them both and whose corporate headquarters were located downtown on South Michigan Street. As with the local blues, gospel, and soul musicians who increasingly produced for a national market after World War II, Johnson geared his publications toward a national market and the broader African American community—which the publications also helped to fashion.

By the 1960s, it has been estimated that nearly 20,000 of the 27,000 African Americans who lived in public housing developments were children. Whereas blacks represented only 4 percent of Chicago's population in 1920, by the 1960s they comprised 30 percent. As the campaign for adequate housing in Chicago continued, Martin Luther King Jr. traveled north in order to apply his nonviolent tactics in one of the city's most segregated neighborhoods. King and his followers undertook a series of marches in the white areas that ringed heavily black neighborhoods. On one of these marches, he and his supporters were driven back by a hail of rocks, one of which struck King. As he convened with Mayor Richard J. Daley, and local citizens continued their campaign with lawsuits targeting the CHA with discrimination and segregation, it became clear that the increasing separation of black and white was becoming an intractable problem with no easy solution.

Shift in Economic Base. Making matters worse, the primary reason that many southerners had turned to Chicago in earlier years was disappearing, as manufacturing industries left for the suburbs or other regions on the trail of cheaper labor and production costs. As information technologies and the employers associated with them assumed a more integral position in the national economy, many lower-skilled African Americans were left with few options. As more blacks nationally began to acquire the education to enter white-collar and professional fields, they moved out from the inner city as well; in Chicago, this meant that most of those African Americans who continued to live within the city limits fell on the lower end of the wage scale, if not beneath it among the unemployed.

These economic transformations had an impact on most northern industrial cities, but their impact seemed most glaring in cities such as Detroit and Chicago. King's assassination in 1968 provoked more than a hundred riots in many of these cities, further destroying once-viable urban enclaves. The generation of children who came of age in the 1980s found fewer opportunities in urban areas; crime, violence, and gang activity mushroomed in Chicago, and the city itself seemed to be careering toward the fate of Detroit. It was within this context that Harold Washington, Chicago's first black mayor, was elected in 1983. Washington campaigned on a platform seeking to revitalize the business district, end police brutality, create broad economic programs and opportunities, and continue to enhance the tourist industry of Chicago. While he was acutely aware of the problems facing African Americans in Chicago, he continually articulated a philosophy that embraced issues broader than race-specific problems. Despite the hostility he encountered from resistant and skeptical whites—including prominent journalists—with entrenched racial views, Washington succeeded well enough to win reelection in 1987, only to die unexpectedly later that year.

Nationally, the former civil rights activist Jesse Jackson—who was based in Chicago and had founded Operation Push in the Kenwood area just north of the racially integrated

Chicago Mayor. Harold Washington with his fiancée, Mary Smith, after becoming the first black elected mayor of Chicago, 13 April 1983. Photograph by Charles Knoblock. AP IMAGES

island of Hyde Park, home of the University of Chicago—ran for the Democratic nomination in the presidential races of 1984 and 1988. Somewhat like Washington, Jackson ran on a broad economic platform emphasizing the common struggles encountered by women, minorities, migrants, and the aged in an era of global transformation. Though unsuccessful in his bid for the presidency, Jackson's address at the 1984 Democratic Convention remains one of the most electrifying and inspiring speeches ever delivered. Though African Americans were gradually entering higher positions in business, politics, and law throughout the country, racial problems persisted in a variety of forms. Not long after the Rodney King riots in Los Angeles in 1992, the relatively inexperienced and politically conservative Clarence Thomas was nominated by President George H. W. Bush to fill the retiring Thurgood Marshall's position on the U.S. Supreme Court. Blacks were divided on Thomas based on his race and his Republican affiliation. When a former law clerk, the Oklahoma law professor Anita Hill, brought sexual harassment charges against him during the judicial confirmation process, a firestorm of debate over racial and gender politics ensued, riveting the nation. Though Thomas was ultimately confirmed, the backlash from voters resulted in the ouster of many senators who had voted to confirm Thomas's nomination. In Illinois, this meant that the Chicagoan Carol Moseley Braun became only the second African American—and first African American woman—to win a seat in the U.S. Senate since the end of Reconstruction. Barack Obama, also a Chicagoan, was elected in 2004.

The process of globalization in all its forms—economic, technological, and informational—that has transformed the nation has made it more difficult to find local solutions to persistent problems such as poverty, medical care, and education, all of which continue to trouble young African Americans. Recent studies suggest that only three out of every one hundred black or Latino public high school students will earn a bachelor's degree by the age of twenty-five. Though homicides within Chicago dropped during the first years of the twenty-first century, they remain higher than in cities such as New York and Los Angeles. A Guggenheim study cites the lack of affordable housing—a persistent Chicago problem—as a key factor in this statistic. It has also made the success of iconic figures such as Michael Jordan, who spent the majority of his basketball career with the Chicago Bulls, less representative of the fate of the city's—and nation's—African Americans. The city of Chicago became more prominent through Jordan's exploits; blacks did not. And, while the blues culture that emerged in Chicago has been succeeded by the sounds of rap favorites such as Common, Kanye West (a Chicago State University dropout), Twista, and Lupe Fiasco—Chicagoans all—each must struggle to remain relevant to both his home community and to his artistic integrity in the commercialized world of hip-hop culture. Perhaps, then, Barack Obama's win of the presidency in 2008 bodes well for the future of Chicago's—and the nation's—African Americans.

[*See also* *Chicago Defender*; Chicago Riot; Great Migration; Great Migration, Second; Illinois; Johnson Publishing Company; *and biographical entries on figures mentioned in this article.*]

BIBLIOGRAPHY

Drake, St. Clair, and Horace R. Cayton. *Black Metropolis: A Study of Negro Life in a Northern City*. Chicago: University of Chicago Press, 1993. First published in 1945. Classic ethnography of black life and culture in mid-twentieth-century Chicago.

Green, Adam. *Selling the Race: Culture, Community, and Black Chicago, 1940–1955*. Chicago: University of Chicago Press, 2007. Examines black life and culture within the city and black Chicago's relationship to national issues and racial formation in the United States. Blues musicians and recording studios, *Jet* and *Ebony* magazines, and the national response to Emmett Till's murder anchor Green's argument.

Grossman, James R. *Land of Hope: Chicago, Black Southerners, and the Great Migration*. Chicago: University of Chicago Press, 1989. A comprehensive treatment of black migration from the South to Chicago from 1916 to the early 1920s. Particular attention is paid to reasons for migrating, work experiences, black institutions, and race relations in Chicago.

Grossman, James R., Ann Durkin Keating, and Janice L. Reiff, eds. *The Encyclopedia of Chicago*. Chicago: University of Chicago Press, 2004. Broad coverage and detailed entries on various aspects of Chicago from its founding.

Hirsch, Arnold R. *Making the Second Ghetto: Race and Housing in Chicago, 1940–1960*. New York: Cambridge University Press, 1983. An excellent analysis of public housing in Chicago, with particular emphasis on how certain developments were racially contested and/or segregated.

Knupfer, Anne Meis. *The Chicago Black Renaissance and Women's Activism*. Urbana: University of Illinois Press, 2006. An examination of black women's activism in Chicago from roughly 1930 to 1960. The author explores the paths of artists, writers, club leaders, organizations, teachers, and public housing advocates in creating Chicago's vibrant community life.

McClain, Leanita. *A Foot in Each World: Essays and Articles*. Evanston, Ill.: Northwestern University Press, 1986. A collection of pieces on identity, politics, and social issues in Chicago by the South Side native Leanita McClain, a columnist and the first African American member of the editorial board of the *Chicago Tribune*. Her essays on Harold Washington's aspirations and the changing Chicago political scene are especially notable.

Reed, Christopher Robert. *Black Chicago's First Century*. Columbia: University of Missouri Press, 2005. A very detailed overview of the founding of Chicago's black community during the antebellum era through the Spanish American War. Of particular importance are the chapters discussing black Chicago's leaders and movements in the late nineteenth century and the Chicago World's Fair of 1893.

Venkatesh, Sudhir Alladi. *Off the Books: The Underground Economy of the Urban Poor*. Cambridge, Mass.: Harvard University Press, 2006. A sociological study of a community on the South Side of Chicago in the 1990s through the early twenty-first century.

Wilson, William Julius. *The Truly Disadvantaged: The Inner City, the Underclass, and Public Policy*. Chicago: University of Chicago Press, 1987. A sociological study of the economic transformations and public policy decisions affecting African American life in Chicago's inner city from the 1960s to the early 1980s.

—JILL DUPONT

CHICAGO DEFENDER. The *Chicago Defender*, a leading African American newspaper, was founded in 1905 by Robert Sengstacke Abbott (1868–1940). The St. Simon's Island, Georgia, native learned printing at Hampton Institute. He first saw Chicago when he traveled there as a tenor in the Hampton Quartet. Chicago's black population reached forty thousand in 1905, and with three black newspapers there already, Abbott's nascent weekly almost failed. However, several idealistic black writers contributed free columns; among them was the freelancer W. Allison Sweeney, who skewered antiblack politicians. Pullman porters distributed the *Defender* nationwide to black sellers. African American actors sold copies to theater patrons. Abbott's church chorale helped with story ideas and sales until the *Defender* appeared on newsstands in the 1910s.

The *Defender*'s Powerful Moral Suasion. Abbott built the *Defender*'s reputation by positively reporting African Americans' achievements. The *Defender* mostly referred to blacks as the "Race" to foster pride. The *Defender* frequently reported African Americans' military heroism. Major Charles Young corresponded with adventures of the U.S. Tenth Cavalry's pursuit of Pancho Villa in Mexico. The paper trumpeted black combat units' valor during World War I, focusing on Harlem's Old Fifteenth Regiment and the Old Eighth Illinois. Because the *Defender* reported inconsistencies between war aims and racism at home (such as the thirteen black soldiers' executions after a violent confrontation with whites in Houston in 1916), the War Department investigated the paper for disloyalty. However, Attorney General A. Mitchell Palmer, who vigorously prosecuted radicals, concluded that the *Defender*'s complaints were not groundless.

The *Defender* successfully confronted moral issues in "yellow" journalistic style. As Roi Ottley discusses in *The Lonely Warrior: The Life and Times of Robert S. Abbott* (p. 106), headlines of the 1910s, crafted by the *Defender*'s sensationalizing managing editor J. Hockley Smiley, such as "100 Negroes Murdered Weekly by White Americans" and "Jim Crow Cars Running Out of Chicago Depot," boosted race consciousness and sales. In 1919, the *Defender*'s sensationalism exacerbated Chicago's race riot by manufacturing a story of whites' killing of a black mother and infant. Abbott promised greater responsibility, and circulation grew to 230,000 by 1920. By then the *Defender* featured sports, theater, and society sections and had adopted the slogan "World's Greatest Weekly." Aiding the *Defender*'s publicity were whites' attempts to hinder its circulation. The Arkansas governor Charles Brough, attempting to remove the *Defender* from the mail, charged that the paper fomented the 1919 racial violence in Elaine. A lawsuit by William Randolph Hearst, who claimed the *Defender*'s masthead copied his papers' designs, also attracted attention.

In response to the virulence of southern racism, Abbott inaugurated in 1917 the *Defender*'s "Great Northern Drive," inviting blacks north so they could "live like men." Chicago's African American population soon reached 150,000. The lure of wartime industrial jobs helped this "Great Migration." The *Defender*'s encouragements were powerful, as represented in this stanza in the poem "Bound for the Promised Land" (reprinted in Ottley, p. 159):

> Why should I remain longer South
> To be kicked and dogged around?
> Crackers to knock me in the mouth
> And shoot my brother down.

After the Chicago riot, Abbott adopted a gradualist approach for change. The riot revealed dangerous dependence on unionized white printers, who would not go to the riot-plagued Union Stockyard area to print the *Defender* on the leased press of the *Drovers Journal*. Racism in unions had limited blacks' opportunities to learn skilled trades. So, in 1921, Abbott purchased a press on the South Side and hired black apprentices to train under white mechanics. The *Defender* still promoted blacks' achievements, such as Carter Woodson's columns on African American history and Joe Louis's boxing victories. The *Defender* criticized Marcus Garvey's black nationalist movement as counterproductive to racial unity. In 1923, Abbott started a "Bud Billiken" column and club for African American children. In 1929, the children's club had one million members, and the first Bud Billiken Parade was held to benefit underprivileged children. One thousand people paraded with honored guests Freeman Gordon and Charles Cornell of the *Amos 'n' Andy* radio show. Over the years, the parade grew as Joe Louis, Tom Mix, Roy Rogers, and Lena Horne were later honored guests, and the event remained a Chicago tradition into the early 2000s.

Abbott could still agitate, however. He supported A. Philip Randolph's organization of Pullman porters in 1925, and he rejected the Republican Herbert Hoover for president in 1928, criticizing his "Lilly-White Party," but he later also challenged Democrats in "Is This the New Deal?" when the congressional restaurant barred two blacks in 1934 (Ottley, pp. 343, 347). Abbott's crusading brought results; Chicago had 27,700 black employees and more black firemen than any other major city by 1932.

Surviving the Great Depression, a World War, and the Cold War. The Great Depression nearly bankrupted the *Defender*. Circulation dropped to sixty thousand by 1932. Abbott used $261,000 of personal funds to sustain his creation. Abbott brought freshness to the *Defender* by appointing his nephew John H. H. Sengstacke as general manager in 1934. After Abbott's death in 1940, Sengstacke led the *Defender* toward financial recovery and the political left. The *Defender* voiced antiwar sentiment before the 1941 attack on Pearl Harbor and demanded federal legislation against lynching and poll taxes. Suspecting the paper of Communist influence, the Office of War Intelligence (OWI) monitored the *Defender*. However, the *Defender* promoted the "Double V" campaign against fascism abroad and racism domestically. Joining the *Defender* in 1942 was Langston Hughes, who contrasted war aims with segregation's pervasiveness. In one 1946 article republished in Christopher De Santis's 1995 volume *Langston Hughes and the Chicago Defender* (p. 57), Hughes describes how a waitress in the Kansas City train station tried to seat him at inconspicuous tables. Hughes protested, "My relatives fought and died in this war ... and colored people are tired of being put in corners." A Communist until the 1940s, Hughes undoubtedly raised suspicion about the *Defender*'s politics when he reflected in 1943, "Stalin represents ALL of his citizens ... there are ... no frightful regions like Mississippi where Ku Klux Klans ... run wild" (quoted in De Santis, p. 127).

By the 1950s the *Defender* had moderated politically. According to Bill Mullen in *Popular Fronts* (pp. 71–72), the *Defender* denounced its former contributor W. E. B. Du Bois as a "turncoat to Americanism" in 1951, and the OWI gave the *Defender* full press privileges at the White House.

During the civil rights movement's peak in the decades following World War II, the *Chicago Defender* championed direct action campaigns that would fight discrimination and inequality in the city. When Dr. Martin Luther King Jr. and his Southern Christian Leadership Conference decided to join the local Coordinating Council of Community Organizations (CCCO) in a "Freedom Movement" to crusade against housing discrimination around Chicago in 1966, the *Defender*'s Bill Van Alstine characterized the movement as a "juggernaut" determined to win its fight against realtors and municipal public housing authorities, and his fellow reporter Betty Washington reported the power of the movement when a march on the white neighborhood Gage Park "scared" whites (20–26 August 1966).

The paper was not opposed to the militancy of younger African American activists and groups who challenged King's nonviolence. James Forman was a reporter for the *Defender* in 1960 and from there was inspired to join the Congress of Racial Equality (CORE) to help African American sharecroppers he had heard about in West Tennessee who were evicted by white landlords for registering to vote. The next year he became a leader of the Student Nonviolent Coordinating Committee. In 1969, the *Defender* gave positive coverage to local gangs such as the Conservative Vice Lords, the Blackstone Rangers, and the Black Gangster Disciples, who all joined the greater Coalition for United Community Action (CUCA) to protest discrimination in building trades unions who were employed to construct the University of Illinois at Chicago. The *Defender* noted in its 4 December 1969 issue that the Black Gangster Disciples raised $1,400 with a raffle for helping needy persons at Christmas and for building a community center in Englewood.

Sengstacke led the *Defender* until his death in 1997. Estate taxes threatened the paper's existence, but in 2000 Realtimes, a company led by Sengstacke's nephew Thomas Picou, purchased the paper and started a financial turnaround.

[*See also* Black Press; Chicago; Great Migration; *and* Riots and Rebellions, *subentry* Riots of 1919.]

BIBLIOGRAPHY

De Santis, Christopher C., ed. *Langston Hughes and the Chicago Defender: Essays on Race, Politics, and Culture, 1942–62*. Urbana: University of Illinois Press, 1995. This book is a comprehensive collection of Hughes's writings, as he skewered segregationist whites and repeatedly showed the inconsistency between World War II's democratic aims and segregation at home.

Marcus, Robert D., David Burner, and Anthony Marcus. *America Firsthand*. 7th ed. 2 vols. Boston: Bedford/St. Martin's, 2007. This reader of primary documents from post–Civil War U.S. history features in part 3 of Volume 2 letters by African Americans asking the *Chicago Defender* for information about the North during the *Defender*'s "Great Northern Drive."

Mullen, Bill. *Popular Fronts: Chicago and African-American Cultural Politics, 1935–1946*. Urbana: University of Illinois Press, 1999. This work addresses the *Defender*'s turn to the left and the limited extent of Communist influence on its staff in the 1930s. Mullen also discusses how the *Defender* survived government surveillance and moderated politically after World War II.

Ottley, Roi. *The Lonely Warrior: The Life and Times of Robert S. Abbott*. Chicago: Henry Regnery, 1955. Ottley effectively recounts how Abbott reconciled his acceptance of Booker T. Washington's philosophy of advancement with Abbott's own penchant for agitation via the pages of the *Defender*. Ottley shows how Abbott's confrontational side grew more intense after he saw better race relations in Europe and South America in his travels of the 1920s.

—WESLEY BORUCKI

CHICAGO RIOT. On the heels of the Allied victory in World War I, renewed prosperity and greater economic opportunity awaited workers in American cities. Chicago was especially such a city. It attracted job seekers of all ethnicities and races. The popular *Chicago Defender* newspaper appealed to blacks in the South to migrate north and take advantage of the offerings of the sprawling city. As a result, from 1900 to 1920 the city's black population swelled by seventy-nine thousand. But opposition accompanied those opportunities. With the flood of new citizens into Chicago came competition with the city's white residents for work, housing, and turf. Antagonisms festered, leading to one of the worst riots in 1919, a year that witnessed many racial conflicts.

Upon arriving in Chicago, blacks scrambled for whatever jobs opened to them. In the early summer months of 1919, blacks often served as replacements for striking white workers in several meatpacking companies. This fostered resentment from whites striking for better pay and working conditions while blacks assumed their jobs. The black workers experienced threats and taunts entering the workplace. In addition blacks were confined to living in a greatly congested eight-square-mile area on the South Side called the Black Belt and were systematically excluded from better housing in nearby neighborhoods even if they could afford it. Whites threatened retaliation if blacks dared permeate the invisible boundaries into white areas. In June 1919 blacks roaming into white neighborhoods triggered sporadic violence, bombing, and assaults, stirring concern among city leaders of an imminent riot. Ida B. Wells-Barnett warned the city to stand up and take notice of the outbreaks. She implored Chicago to immediately confront the challenges of racial injustice before the city would be disgraced by bloody experiences, as East Saint Louis had been a few years earlier. The city did little to heed these warnings. On 26 July 1919 black troops marched down the city streets in a welcome home parade for its returning World War I soldiers, surely expecting equality and rights after they had fought for a guarantee of those rights in Europe. Blacks, especially younger blacks, were determined not to retreat from equality they felt they justly deserved and were not content to endure humiliation. However, events one day following this parade would prove that whites were equally resolved not to allow blacks to encroach on their neighborhoods and their jobs.

On Sunday, 27 July, seventeen-year-old Eugene Williams was swimming in a section of Lake Michigan that whites had claimed for themselves. According to accounts, upon noticing the black youth, a nearby young white man pelted Williams with rocks, and when other bathers attempted to rescue Williams, other whites joined in the rock throwing until Williams let go of the raft he was on and drowned. Witnesses identified the assailants, but when police refused to arrest the whites responsible—arresting an indignant black bystander instead—blacks retaliated by attacking the assailants and then turned on the police. Whites jumped in, and an all-out riot followed. Police sent out a call for reinforcements, and until the reinforcements arrived, the surrounding areas were simmering caldrons. Rumors spread across the neighborhood offering different versions of what really happened at the beach. The flurry of accounts prompted anger and violence, fueled by the summer heat. Armed with clubs and revolvers, gangs were caught up in the waves of random shootings and beatings, and incidents began for numerous blocks, especially in the Black Belt. Cars were stopped in these sections, and innocent occupants of varying races were pulled from vehicles and beaten. Clashes broke out from the South Side into the Cottage Grove section, then into Chicago's business district, the Loop. At day's end the South Side was enveloped in constant turmoil. By nightfall, with the police unable to regain control, the city was catapulted into a full-scale race war.

By Monday morning the violence had abated. Citizens hoped that any intention to renew violence had also dissipated and that tensions had been spent in the action. But by mid-afternoon on Monday, the riot had renewed with vigor. The ferocity was uninterrupted on Tuesday, with all the indications of a full-scale race war. Over the course of the next few days, continual and horrific violence enveloped Chicago. Whites ravaged city streets, yanking blacks at random from the trolleys and from sidewalks, often beating them severely with iron bars, bats, and stones. Whites in some areas armed themselves with billy clubs and guns awaiting any approaching blacks. Blacks fought back, torching and destroying both white and black neighborhoods. When approximately fifty whites took refuge in a grocery store, blacks smoked them out. Police roamed neighborhoods, often randomly beating black pedestrians, and on one occasion an army of over a thousand black residents cornered and confronted roughly a hundred police officers. Blacks frustrated many attempts by the police to arrest rioters and haul them away. Reports circulated that more blacks at the beaches were victimized with rock throwing and that whites were assaulting black women at the stockyards. Blacks retaliated by beating any whites—including police—who responded to the call. Hospitals, especially in the black neighborhoods, overflowed with patients. Some victims died before medical attention could be given them. The situation became so intense that schools, drugstores, and private houses were converted to makeshift hospitals. Trucks, drays, and hearses were used for ambulances. Firemen had to simply abandon raging fires because they could not fight the flurry of fires endlessly appearing everywhere. In the course of the week, hundreds of blacks escaped the riot by train, heading for Milwaukee and other cities. Blacks armed themselves with hand grenades in defiance of imminent attacks. Policemen were given orders to shoot to kill any person, black or white, who initiated riot action.

So widespread were the burning, looting, and killing that by Wednesday the Illinois governor called out the National Guard, trained for riot duty. By week's end, the military presence, cooler temperatures, and downpours of rain muted the outdoor activity. Fifteen whites and twenty-three blacks were killed, and more than five hundred people were injured. More than a thousand families, largely black, were left homeless.

Blacks and whites both were appalled at the rioting in Chicago, though the Windy City was not alone in the national spectacle of racial conflict. In 1919 alone more than twenty-five riots flared, prompting the poet James Weldon Johnson to pen it as "The Red Summer" in which the blood flowed on sidewalks from the violence.

Many squared the Chicago violence on the shoulders of both races, emphasizing the need for greater communication and cooperation. George Hall, a black doctor in Chicago, condemned the city police for instituting and enforcing lines of segregation on the beaches and elsewhere. However, Hall equally criticized black city aldermen, whom he accused of representing the wishes of the white police rather than their constituents. Hall charged that black residents were being sold out by their black leaders. The *Chicago Defender* relayed the desperation in the city, not blasting either side but condemning the reign of terror as an orgy of hate. In the wake of the Chicago outbreak, twice the number of blacks than whites were accused, and further discrimination was charged in the handling of legal actions against rioters. African American organizations in Chicago combined forces to form the Joint Committee to Secure Equal Justice for Colored Riot Defenders to defend indicted blacks. Several who were acquitted would not have been without that key support.

Aware of the antagonism from both sides, an interracial Chicago Commission on Race Relations was formed to examine the causes of the riot. *The Negro in Chicago*, a seven-hundred-page report, followed. The report's author, the Urban League official Charles Johnson, interviewed over two hundred families and documented the histories of southern migrants to Chicago, inquiring why they came, what their family lives were like, what the housing experience held for them, and their sentiments on the community and race relations. The findings demonstrated that extreme disparity existed between the white and black Chicago residents, manifesting itself in the form of segregation, natural antagonism, and the need to escape those limitations on the part of blacks. W. E. B. Du Bois's

The Crisis likewise published a response to the riot titled "Chicago and Its Eight Reasons." The assistant executive secretary of the NAACP, Walter White, authored the article, speculating on rationales such as race prejudice, competition, housing, police inefficiency and unpunished victimization of blacks, media manipulation of riot coverage, and the sense of independence gained from the recent war experience. White concluded that these factors energized blacks to retaliate against the system. Like Hall, however, White criticized city leaders, both black and white, for their lack of foresight in stemming racial problems and in allowing segregation.

In a 2 August 1919 editorial the *Chicago Defender* condemned lawlessness on all sides but unashamedly admitted that the publication had been humiliated by the pressure of the prejudice of whites. Summing up the Chicago riot, the editorial continued that in Chicago the riot was a reaction to the imaginary spheres blacks were supposed to recognize—spheres that neither were sanctioned by law nor followed common sense. Blacks naturally resisted those assumptions, and hence riots had flared.

[*See also* Chicago; *Chicago Defender*; Civil Rights, White Responses and Resistance to; Du Bois, W. E. B.; *and* Riots and Rebellions.]

BIBLIOGRAPHY

For day-to-day newspaper accounts of riot activity, see the *Chicago Daily News* (28 July 1919), *Chicago Daily Tribune* (28 July–4 August 1919), and *Chicago Defender* (2 August 1919). Articles list names and exact locations of much of the rioting.

Chicago Commission on Race Relations. *The Negro in Chicago*. Chicago: University of Chicago Press, 1922. The exhaustive study commissioned by the city of Chicago and headed by the Urban League examined why the riot occurred, which concluded what most already knew.

Drake, St. Clair, and Horace R. Cayton. *Black Metropolis: A Study of Negro Life in a Northern City*. Chicago: University of Chicago Press, 1993. A comprehensive exploration of the problems blacks faced in urban sectors of the nation.

Lewis, David Levering. *W. E. B. Du Bois: Biography of a Race, 1868–1918*. New York: Henry Holt, 1993. A weaving of the life of Du Bois and the racism in the United States at the time.

Tuttle, William M., Jr. *Race Riot: Chicago in the Red Summer of 1919*. New York: Atheneum Press, 1970. Highlighting Chicago as the worst of the many riots in that explosive year.

—RON KELLER

CHILDHOOD. Childhood is the time when identity is formed. In the modern sense, childhood has not always existed. The invention of childhood entailed the creation of a protracted period in which the child would ideally be protected from the difficulties and responsibilities of daily life—including the need to work. In this respect, slave and working-class children did not have much of a childhood since they were obliged to work and did not have years to devote to play and study. By the 1890s, the end of slavery and the growth of an African American middle class created the opportunity for African American children to engage in the activities that define childhood in modern America.

The history of how African Americans experienced childhood in the nineteenth and early twentieth centuries cannot be separated from the legacy of slavery. While the children were not slaves, they had parents and grandparents with life views that had been shaped by slavery. The end of the Civil War brought the end of slavery as Reconstruction governments in the South began to establish systems for public education for both black and white children.

Early Childhood Education. Former slaves wanted education for their children as a symbol of liberty as well as a tool for social and economic advancement. They knew that education was power, but so did whites. Most of the Reconstruction governments made no real effort to integrate the public schools and, while they adopted policies of equal financial support, a dual system quickly emerged that gave preference to white-only schools. This system continued until the *Brown v. Board of Education* Supreme Court decision in 1954 declared separate but equal public schools to be illegal.

Early childhood education programs, not generally accepted as an integral part of education until the 1930s, often were operated separately from the public school system. An idea imported from Germany in the mid-nineteenth century, the kindergarten movement remained in its infancy in the 1890s as both white and black educators worked to promote the concept. For blacks, the National Association of Colored Women (NACW), organized in 1896, spearheaded the African American kindergarten movement. As president of the NACW, the educator Mary Church Terrell established a kindergarten department within the association and helped advance the idea of kindergarten in the South. By 1901, the Deep South still had no public kindergartens for African American children, but the NACW cooperated with private citizens and denominational schools to establish them.

The creation of preschools, combined with the establishment of mothers' clubs to educate the mothers of the pupils, was designed to "uplift the race" by getting to the root of the problem of elevation—the children. Nursery schools, which emerged in the United States in the 1920s as another European educational import, began as a way to provide a favorable environment for a child's physical, mental, and social needs while offering expert guidance for parents. Nursery schools provided clean and safe

Children in Indiana. Newspaper carriers for the *Indianapolis Recorder* participate in a kite-flying contest. INDIANAPOLIS RECORDER COLLECTION, INDIANA HISTORICAL SOCIETY

places for children to get nutritious food, receive health inspections, and engage in planned activities. African Americans' nursery schools were often sponsored by historically black colleges and universities as an important aspect of the overall education of African Americans. Among the institutions that created nursery schools in the 1930s were the Hampton Institute in Virginia, the Alabama State Teachers College in Montgomery, and Spelman College in Atlanta. The Spelman nursery school began in 1930 at the same time as the Alabama State Teachers nursery school. Both emphasized that they were not in the business of babysitting. The schools aimed to provide an environment for the maximum development of children two to five years of age, an opportunity for parents to observe practical work with young children, and training for college students in home economics. The Hampton nursery school, opened in 1932, did not act as a laboratory school and focused on supervised play.

Head Start, a federal child development program that formed part of President Lyndon B. Johnson's War on Poverty, built on the successes of preschools and kindergartens and on a successful League of United Latin American Citizens program designed to prepare Mexican American children for the public schools. Head Start serves low-income, preschool children from the ages of three to five years in a center-based, half-day preschool setting. The overall position of black families toward the bottom of the economic ladder means that many African Americans, especially those in inner cities, are served by Head Start. Education, health, parental involvement, and social services are the four major components of the program, which aims to eliminate the possible limits of a disadvantaged home environment on children by providing opportunities for socialization and learning in an enriching environment. Longitudinal studies have shown that children who participate in early intervention programs, such as Head Start, are less likely to be placed in special education classes, are more able to graduate from high school, and have higher levels of self-esteem. The Early Head Start program, established in 1994, extends the benefits of Head Start to low-income families with children under three years of age and to pregnant women.

Public School Education. In 1954, when the Supreme Court issued the *Brown* decision it essentially stated that racial integration was so beneficial to American society that it would be pursued even in the face of significant southern resistance. Furthermore, children would be at the center of the movement for racial equality. Civil rights activists, especially members of the NAACP, supported children who wanted to fight against segregation. The next years brought searing images of black children running gauntlets of hostile whites in North Carolina, Louisiana, and, most famously, Little Rock, Arkansas, in order to integrate public schools. The effects of integration remain a topic of considerable debate.

When the *Brown* decision was handed down, the doors to well-equipped and well-maintained public schools gradually opened to blacks. At the same time, many African American teachers who had served as role models for black children were unable to compete with white teachers who had been able to earn qualifications from better teacher preparatory programs. Many black children were also bused to distant white schools to help those schools achieve court-mandated racial balance. Busing made it difficult for black children to participate in after-school programs since transportation home was not always readily available. Integrated public schools did not necessarily help black children.

As the number of single-parent African American families increased after 1960, after-school care became increasingly necessary. In urban and low-income neighborhoods, after-school programs have been put into place to help African American children. These programs typically counteract the effects of limited opportunities and resources by providing opportunities for privacy to complete homework, assistance with homework or self-help skill development, physical activities, and nutritious meals and snacks. While some of these programs are operated by government agencies, others are run by Boys' and Girls' Clubs, the Young Men's Christian Association, and the Young Women's Christian Association.

Play. African American families joined immigrant working-class families at the start of the twentieth century in rejecting white, middle-class attitudes toward recreation and leisure. Instead of looking upon sports that required only a ball and field with contempt, black children took up baseball with enthusiasm. In time, basketball joined baseball in popularity as both were easy-to-play games that did not require much expense in the way of equipment. Black families placed a high value on play, spontaneity, reciprocity, and conviviality. By the 1920s, most modern families placed less emphasis on self-control and more on self-fulfillment than did their predecessors.

While technology determined the forms of white family leisure, black children have been far less likely to get in the car to drive to drive-in restaurants, drive-in movies, and weekend or summer vacations. They have, however, participated in the post–World War II trend of devoting a greater percentage of time to leisure. These activities have increasingly moved out of public places and into the

Children at Play. A group of children outside the Ida B. Wells home in Chicago, Illinois, 1973. Photograph by John H. White. NATIONAL ARCHIVES AND RECORDS ADMINISTRATION

home, as black children spend less time at the movies and on the basketball court and more time in front of the television. Part of the shift is attributable to safety concerns, as parents worry about preadolescents spending large amounts of their spare time in unorganized and unsupervised activities. Demographic shifts have reduced the numbers of family members available to supervise black children at play.

Black Migration. The African American population shifted dramatically in the 1890s and early twentieth century from predominantly rural and southern to increasingly urban and national. Migration altered the structure of African American families and the configuration of black households. Leaving the South was a family decision since it required emotional and material support, often meant periods of long separation, and could possibly result in the migration of other family members. Most migrants were poor or working class and had few resources. Men usually worked their way north and then sent for their families to join them. Women made a single trip, generally either accompanied by a relative or with kin or friends waiting to receive them.

Many migrants created surrogate families to cushion their adjustment to urban life. Urban households were more likely than rural households to include friends and boarders. Households headed by women were likely to be the result of death, divorce, or desertion. Boarders, employers, coworkers, church or club members, and neighbors acted as unofficial parents or godparents, siblings, aunts, or uncles. For some urban black migrants, surrogate family members provided the emotional and economic support important for large extended families. These families often included younger or older female relatives who came to assist with child care or young children who were also sent north to be educated. In these families, some children began working at very young ages as they ran errands, polished shoes, sold newspapers, or delivered messages. Although children's labor was important to the economic well-being of migrant families, African American parents frequently took extra jobs so that their children could stay in school.

Many migrants maintained ties to families in the South by sending their children for summer visits, making trips home, or bringing family members for visits. One of the most famous northern children who went south for a summer was Emmett Till. Sent from Chicago to Mississippi by his Mississippi-born mother in 1955 to spend time with his grandfather and cousins, Till became one of the most famous victims of lynching. For apparently whistling at a white woman grocery store clerk, Till was dragged out of bed, beaten to death, and thrown into a creek. Till's mother, Mamie, insisted upon an open casket so that all the world could see what had been done to her boy. The photograph of an almost-unrecognizable Till shocked and galvanized a generation of civil rights activists.

Many women left their children with relatives in the South when they moved north. Absentee mothering made adjustment to urban life into a long, drawn-out, and often incomplete process. Women who left children in the South maintained emotional ties to their families through correspondence and frequent visits. Despite the pressures of migration and adjustment to new urban lifestyles, however, most migrant families were intact, two-parent households.

Economic Pressures. The southern labor system shifted after emancipation from legal slavery to semi-slavery as African American families became trapped in the sharecropping system. This system lasted until the 1930s. Sharecropping began because most black families lacked the financial wherewithal to purchase land, and the U.S. government did not distribute confiscated Confederate lands to former slaves, as many had once expected. The South became a place where whites had land but not the labor to farm and blacks had labor but no land to farm. Sharecropping proved an alternative to wage labor that allowed black families to work together on sections of farmland for a share of the profits. Sharecropping also recognized the authority of black men to make economic decisions for their families as fathers negotiated contracts that obligated children to labor for a particular landowner. Black mothers typically withdrew from the labor force to concentrate on household and child-care responsibilities. African American children, therefore, remained an important element of the family labor unit.

African American families suffered more in the upheaval of the Great Depression than whites and received comparatively less government assistance. Some landowners cut back on supplies to sharecroppers while others threw sharecroppers off the land to take advantage of New Deal Agricultural Adjustment Act programs that took farmland out of production. In the 1930s, many African Americans continued to depend on kinship and community-based institutions for help. Black women cared for each other's children while families shared bathroom facilities, household utensils, and other goods. Children helped by aiding with gardens, canning fruits and vegetables, fishing, and hunting. The Civilian Conservation Corps (CCC) accepted boys aged sixteen to twenty-one, but only about 5 percent of the slots went to African Americans. The youths enrolled in the CCC were required to send part of the paychecks home to help support their families.

Collapse of the Black Family. Until the 1960s, 75 percent of African American families were headed by both a mother and a father. Economic restructuring during the 1960s created havoc for black families in the form of high unemployment rates for African American men that contributed to high divorce rates and fewer marriages. Daniel Patrick Moynihan described these trends and blamed the problems of black children on black mothers in his controversial 1965 study, *The Negro Family: The Case of National Action*. In the succeeding decades, the crisis facing black inner city families and black inner city children has continued to grow. By the early 1980s, 40 percent of black families with related children under eighteen years of age were headed by women.

The changes wrought by economic restructuring produced a population of African American families who lived in depleted and violent inner-city neighborhoods. In such families, mothers watched their sons seek shelter in gang involvement while their daughters sought significance in motherhood. At one time, black mothers could rely on their extended families as a resource when faced with a crisis. However, in this new economic climate, many of these extended families were too poor to offer assistance.

For these young black males, childhood became fraught with risk and was often marked by time spent in prison. Gang membership has been described by scholars as a way to establish a sense of belonging and a sense of pride. By the early twenty-first century, increasing numbers of girls were joining their brothers in gangs and committing crimes alongside the boys.

Studies of African American teenage mothers living in inner city areas show that these girls did not believe that they had much of a future and became pregnant as a way to feel good about themselves. They felt they did not have other options, but they could still be mothers. Like other children, teenage mothers wanted to be cared for by their own mothers. However, researchers have reported that the older women expressed anger that their unemployed daughters became pregnant outside of marriage and without the means to live independently. They did not want to raise another child. The clash reflects a struggle over issues of independence and identity that typically marks the adolescent years.

[*See also* Education; Family; Head Start; No Child Left Behind; *and* Single-Parent Households.]

BIBLIOGRAPHY

Beatty, Barbara, Emily D. Cahan, and Julia Grant, eds. *When Science Encounters the Child: Education, Parenting, and Child Welfare in 20th-Century America*. New York: Teachers College Press, 2006.

Billingsley, Andrew. *Climbing Jacob's Ladder: The Enduring Legacy of African-American Families*. New York: Simon & Schuster, 1992.

Kaplan, Elaine Bell. "Black Teenage Mothers and Their Mothers: The Impact of Adolescent Childbearing on Daughters' Relations with Mothers." *Social Problems* 43.4 (1996): 427–443.

Lascarides, V. Celia, and Blythe F. Hinitz. *History of Early Childhood Education*. New York: Falmer Press, 2000.

Levander, Caroline F., and Carol J. Singley, eds. *The American Child: A Cultural Studies Reader*. New Brunswick, N.J.: Rutgers University Press, 2003.

Polakow, Valerie. *Lives on the Edge: Single Mothers and Their Children in the Other America*. Chicago: University of Chicago Press, 1993.

—CARYN E. NEUMANN

CHILDRESS, ALICE (b. 12 October 1916; d. 14 August 1994), activist, actor, and author of plays, essays, screenplays, and fiction. Alice Herndon Childress was born in Charleston, South Carolina, in 1916. When she was five, her parents separated. They sent Childress to Harlem, New York, to live with her maternal grandmother, Eliza Campbell White. From her grandmother, she gained a love of education, books, writing, and theater. Her formal education ended in her second year of high school, when her grandmother died. In the years that followed, Childress explored theater and writing while working multiple jobs. She gave birth to one daughter, Jean R. Childress, in 1935.

In 1941, she began her theatrical career, acting and working behind the scenes with the famed American Negro Theatre (ANT) in Harlem. Her apprenticeship with ANT lasted until 1952. During this time, she performed in numerous productions, including Theodore Brown's *Natural Man* (written in 1937 and produced in 1941) and Abram Hill's *On Striver's Row* (written in 1939 and produced in 1940). When Childress published her first play, *Florence* (1949), ANT produced it. Over subsequent years, Childress received numerous awards and honors, many of which had never before been granted to an African American or to a woman. When she appeared as Blanche in the Broadway production of *Anna Lucasta* in 1944, her performance drew a Tony Award nomination. Her piece *Gold through the Trees* (1952) was among the earliest plays written by an African American woman to be professionally produced in the United States. In 1956, *Trouble in Mind* (1954), her first play produced outside of Harlem, won an Obie Award for best original Off-Broadway play. She was the first woman to receive this prestigious award.

However much acclaim followed Childress throughout her career, fame eluded her. She was a prolific playwright, penning almost twenty plays; nonetheless, Broadway productions of her work never materialized. Producers and financiers considered the politicized nature of her plays too risky to be profitable. Childress rejected the components of racial uplift or integrationist literature. Her subject matter focused singularly on the black American experience, and she refused to conflate her gender and racial identities. Furthermore, Childress explored the complexity of black womanhood with assertiveness and conviction, while encouraging the audience to interrogate attitudes that perpetuated or accepted the concept of racial inferiority.

Offstage, her work also sparked controversy. Some local affiliates refused to televise a version of her play *Wedding Band: A Love/Hate Story in Black and White* (1972), which ABC aired in 1973. Soon after, a campaign ensued to ban her adolescent novel *A Hero Ain't Nothing but a Sandwich* (1973) because of what some considered to be "edgy" subject matter. Set in an impoverished New York City neighborhood in the early 1970s, the novel examines complex questions of self-image, racial identity, and personal commitment versus communal responsibility while telling the story of one boy's struggle against drug addiction. Several public libraries in the South removed the book. Throughout her career, Childress remained invested in the value of recognizing and understanding the unique subtleties of individual life experiences. Despite snubs from Broadway and critics, her plays were professionally produced from 1949 until the 1990s. She remains the only African American woman playwright whose career has experienced such longevity.

[*See also* Literature *and* Theater.]

BIBLIOGRAPHY

Jennings, LaVinia Delois. *Alice Childress*. New York: Twayne, 1995. The only scholarly biography covering Childress's literary production.

Jordan, Shirley M. *Broken Silences: Interviews with Black and White Women Writers*. New Brunswick, N.J.: Rutgers University Press, 1993. Includes a lengthy interview in which Childress discusses race relations and recurrent themes in her work.

—AISHA FRANCIS

CHILDRESS, ALVIN (b. 10 September 1907; d. 19 April 1986), actor and comedian. Alvin Childress, best known for his portrayal of Amos Jones in the controversial television version of the *Amos 'n' Andy Show*, stumbled into acting almost accidentally. Born in Meridian, Mississippi, Childress was the youngest of three children. His mother taught school and his father was a dentist. Childress graduated in 1931 from Rust College in Holly Springs, Mississippi, having taken numerous premedical science courses. Childress had also taken an active interest in campus theater productions that Venzalla Jones directed. Jones thought that Childress showed enough potential to become an actor on stage.

Alvin's mother, Beatrice Childress, in addition to teaching, was also a home demonstration agent for Coahoma County, Mississippi. After Alvin graduated from college, she encouraged him to become an agent as well. However, Jones, who had gone to New York to join the cast of a play called *Wharf Nigger*, recommended Alvin for a role in the play, and Childress left Mississippi to pursue a career as a thespian. Although the play was canceled, Jones got him a part in *Savage Rhythm*. During the 1930s Childress also worked under the auspices of the Works Progress Administration at Columbia University as a writer and drama coach. He was also actively involved in American Negro Theatre (ANT) projects. He played Noah in the 1944 ANT production of Philip Yordan's hit play *Anna Lucasta* and directed one of the road companies of the play.

In 1949, after hearing that Charles Correll and Freeman Gosden were bringing the *Amos 'n' Andy Show* to CBS television, Childress contacted Gosden and arranged an audition. Although Childress was concerned that his skin was too light for a role in the show, the audition went well and he landed the role of Amos Jones, owner of the Fresh Air Taxi Company. The Amos Jones role was the least stereotyped of all the characters. Apparently, Childress was the first person chosen for the series and actually went on the road to audition other prospective actors for the cast. Among those he auditioned for the role of the Kingfish were the noted band leaders Cab Calloway and Lucky Millinder. The part ultimately went to Tim Moore.

The completed cast of the major characters included Childress (Amos Jones), Spencer Williams (Andrew Hogg Brown), Moore (George "Kingfish" Stevens), Ernestine Wade (Sapphire Stevens), Johnny Lee (Algonquin J. Calhoun), Nicodemus Steward (Lightnin'), Amanda Randolph (Mama), and Lillian Randolph (Madam Queen). Amos narrates each episode but usually appears only to dispense words of wisdom, settle disputes, and offer solutions to the brothers in that great fraternity the Mystic Knights of the Sea—namely, Andy and the Kingfish. The plots usually concern the schemes and shenanigans of the Kingfish in swindling the lovable, woman-crazy, but intellectually challenged Andy Brown.

In some ways Childress's Amos is the most difficult character to define in the controversial series. Existing in the shadows, neither a full-scale positive depiction of an African American nor an outrageous stereotype, Amos was a cabdriver who worked diligently every day to support his upwardly mobile family. Their English, while black dialect–tinged, was free of offensive malapropisms and heavy, southern drawls. The Amos character somewhat mimicked Childress's real-life experiences and family values. He grew up in an upwardly mobile African American family in the Deep South, but had only a slight southern accent, having lost most of it through formal education and his training as an actor on stage.

Amos 'n' Andy did not bring Childress and the other cast members the positive recognition and monetary rewards that they envisioned, consistent with having a hit television program. The series lasted a mere two years from 1951 to 1953, but CBS continued the show in syndication until 1966, finally agreeing to withdraw the program from circulation as a result of the NAACP's continuing protests and legal actions and the moral imperative of the civil rights movement, which objected to the negative stereotypes of the leading characters. Nonetheless, Childress and Wade continued to argue that at the time *Amos 'n' Andy* was the only television program that depicted blacks in tangential though important roles as judges, lawyers, doctors, businessmen, policemen, and other professionals and, as such, set a positive precedent.

After the demise of *Amos 'n' Andy*, Childress never had another opportunity to star in a hit television series. However, he continued to make guest appearances on such television series as *Good Times*, *Sanford and Son*, *Perry Mason*, and others. In addition, he appeared in several movies and occasionally returned to the stage. An intelligent, quiet, and dignified man, Childress was married briefly to the playwright and actress Alice Childress and fathered a daughter when they were both active in the American Negro Theatre in the 1930s. Alvin Childress died of Parkinson's disease and diabetes in Inglewood, California, on 19 April 1986 at the age of seventy-nine.

[*See also* Actors and Actresses; *Amos 'n' Andy*; Comedians; Film and Television Depictions of African Americans; *and* Television.]

BIBLIOGRAPHY

Andrews, Bart, and Ahrgus Julliard. *Holy Mackerel! The Amos 'n' Andy Story*. New York: E. P. Dutton, 1986. An interesting volume overall that includes information on Childress but lacks notes *and* source information.

Ely, Melvin Patrick. *The Adventures of Amos 'n' Andy: A Social History of an American Phenomenon*. New York: Free Press, 1991. A well-researched, -analyzed, and -documented volume that includes information about Childress.

—DONALD ROE

CHINA. African American identification with China stemmed from black perceptions of international politics and from a shared sense of misery in American society. Adherents of W. E. B. Du Bois melded African and Asian resistance to European imperialism with African American internationalism toward Asia. Following Reconstruction, American blacks faced violent terrorism and legal repression, and Americans of Chinese descent also faced bullying mobs. In 1882 the infamous Chinese Exclusion Act dramatically limited Chinese immigration.

Such mutual suffering persuaded Du Bois to regard China sympathetically as an ally behind what he called the color line. By 1933 Du Bois called, naively, for Japan and China to unite to drive Europe out of Asia. In 1937, as war expanded between the two nations, Du Bois visited Shanghai. There he argued that Japanese imperialism against China was a lesser evil than European colonialism with its attendant racism. Ultimately, Japanese depredations against the Chinese forced Du Bois to admit the contradictions of his earlier support, though he blamed Japanese aggression on Japan's borrowing the methods of Western imperialism.

Du Bois was not the only African American invested in the war in Asia. Encouraged by the novelist Pearl Buck, the black press in America began publishing positive articles about China. Buck and Paul Robeson appeared on radio programs and at public rallies extolling black support for China and appealing for help to repeal the Chinese Exclusion Act. Liu Liang-Mo, a spokesman for United China Relief, exhorted students at Lincoln University in Pennsylvania to help China; his articles appeared between 1942 and 1945 in the *Pittsburgh Courier*. One article praised Robeson's recording of Chinese folk songs as "a strong token of the solidarity between the Chinese and Negro people."

Buck, Liu, and Lin Yu Tang assured readers of the *Survey Graphic* that the Chinese were not racists. Roi Ottley pointed out how securely integrated were Chinese residents of Harlem. The black press covered Madame Chiang Kai-shek's visit to the United States but became deeply frustrated by her refusal to meet with African American supporters. Rayford Logan edited the book *What the Negro Wants* (1944), in which the contributors Sterling Brown, Mary McLeod Bethune, and Roy Wilkins, among others, agreed that black Americans and Chinese were united in opposing racism.

After World War II, African Americans divided over support for Chiang Kai-shek and his Nationalist Party. Du Bois was critical, whereas the NAACP leader Walter White was sympathetic to Chiang. Matters worsened when military orders surfaced signed by Chiang and the American general Albert Wedemeyer that restricted the entry of black GIs into China. When the story hit the black press in America, the alliance between American blacks and the Chinese Nationalists collapsed. The victory of the Chinese Communist Party (CCP) over the Nationalists in 1949 obviated such concerns.

Clarence Adams, an African American prisoner of war, chose to remain in China after the Korean War. Captured on 30 November 1950 by Chinese soldiers, Adams was interned at a prisoner-of-war camp near the Yalu River. Convinced by the Chinese that he was not the exploiter but the exploited, Adams felt equality among the Chinese. He earned a college diploma from Wuhan University in 1961. He married Liu Lin Feng in 1957; their daughter Della was born in 1958, and a son, Louis, was born in 1964. Adams worked at the Foreign Languages Press in Beijing and made an antiwar broadcast to American troops in Vietnam in 1965. Adams returned to the United States in 1966, where he was subpoenaed to appear before the House Un-American Activities Committee to face charges of "disrupting the morale of American fighting forces in Vietnam and inciting revolution in the United States." After these charges were dropped, he and his family struggled to survive economically. Eventually, through sheer perseverance, they were able to fulfill at least part of the American dream; by the time he died in 1999, the family owned and operated eight successful Chinese restaurants in his native Memphis.

In 1959 Adams met Du Bois in Beijing. While he was in Beijing, Du Bois celebrated his ninety-first birthday in a speech declaring that China had finally risen to its feet and leaped forward. Du Bois published a lengthy poem, "I Sing to China," as a salute to the CCP. The speech and poem were both published in China.

Du Bois was not the only leftist African American to admire the CCP. Robert F. Williams, author of *Negroes with Guns* (1962), fled to China in 1965, and leaders welcomed him there as if he were a visiting head of state. The CCP produced a documentary film about him. Williams joined Chairman Mao Zedong at the 1 October National Day and made a speech to the throngs at Tiananmen Square. Williams later advised Mao and the Americans about reconciliation and was able to broker his own return to the United States.

The CCP and the Cultural Revolution (1966–1976) also inspired the Black Power movement. Stokely Carmichael, prime minister of the Panthers, visited Beijing. The Black Arts Movement in Detroit and Chicago emulated the militant stance of the CCP.

After Mao's death in 1976, black admiration of the Chinese Communists waned. As China's political economy shifted into state capitalism, basketball represented black America in Chinese eyes. The first National Basketball Association (NBA) game played in China occurred in 1979. During the 1990s millions of young Chinese men adopted the English name "Michael" in honor of the Chicago Bulls superstar Michael Jordan. As basketball came to rival soccer in popularity in China, as of 2007, more than thirty African Americans played the game for China's professional teams.

The NBA has capitalized on the game's popularity in China. Kobe Bryant's jersey sells the most among fashionable Chinese youth; Yao Ming, the seven-foot six-inch Chinese-born player for the Houston Rockets, is the only nonblack among the top-ten jersey sellers in China. Music is a second outlet for black American culture in China. Hip-hop music is heard in many clubs there, though most listeners prefer the sweeter melodies of Stevie Wonder or Whitney Houston. The 2008 Olympics in Beijing advanced Chinese familiarity with African American athletes and entertainers.

[*See also* Basketball; Communism and African Americans; Japan; *and biographical entries on figures mentioned in this article*.]

BIBLIOGRAPHY

Adams, Clarence. *An American Dream: The Life of an African American Soldier and POW Who Spent Twelve Years in Communist China*. Edited by Della Adams and Lewis H. Carlson. Amherst: University of Massachusetts Press, 2007.

Gallicchio, Marc. *The African American Encounter with Japan and China: Black Internationalism in Asia, 1895–1945*. Chapel Hill: University of North Carolina Press, 2000.

Mullen, Bill V. *Afro-Orientalism*. Minneapolis: University of Minnesota Press, 2004.

Mullen, Bill V., and Cathryn Watson, eds. *W. E. B. Du Bois on Asia: Crossing the World Color Line*. Jackson: University Press of Mississippi, 2005.

—GAO YUNXIANG

CHISHOLM, SHIRLEY (b. 30 November 1924; d. 1 January 2005), politician, women's rights advocate, and educator. Chisholm was born Shirley Anita St. Hill in Brooklyn, New York, to Charles St. Hill and Ruby Seale, immigrants from the Caribbean island of Barbados. During the Depression, Chisholm and her two younger sisters were sent to live with their grandmother in Barbados. They stayed there for seven years. Chisholm claimed that her sense of pride in herself and her race came largely from her father, an ardent follower of Marcus Garvey.

Chisholm attended Brooklyn College from 1942 to 1946, where she developed her oratorical skills in the Debate Society. At the same time, her membership in the Harriet Tubman Society and the Political Science Society stimulated her racial and political consciousness. Her leadership skills attracted attention, and one of her professors suggested that she consider entering politics.

Chisholm's career in early childhood education spanned nearly two decades. Between 1946 and 1964, she rose from a position as a teacher's aide to a consultant to the New York City Division of Day Care, where she supervised ten day care centers. She also attained a master's degree in early childhood education from Columbia University.

Chisholm's political career started in 1953 at the local level, where she participated in efforts to gain resources for the Bedford-Stuyvesant community in Brooklyn.

Shirley Chisholm. Congresswoman Shirley Chisholm delivers a speech at one of the first pro-choice rallies in New York City, 1972. Photograph by Bettye Lane. © BETTYE LANE

In 1961, she was part of an insurgent group, the Unity Democratic Club (UDC), which did a significant amount of grassroots political education and organizing. In 1964, Chisholm ran successfully for the New York State Assembly with the support of the UDC. In the state assembly, Chisholm was an active legislator, fighting, among other things, for affordable public housing and for a program called SEEK, which enabled men and women from disadvantaged backgrounds to go to college.

In 1968 Chisholm made history as the first black woman to be elected to Congress. She ran successfully against the prominent civil rights leader James Farmer. In Congress, she fought for the rights of the poor and unemployed, African Americans, women, children, and the elderly.

In 1972, Chisholm ran for the United States presidency. She entered the Democratic primaries and secured enough delegates to participate in the party's convention in Miami, Florida. During her campaign, she tried to bring national attention to the issues she had been fighting for in Congress. After her defeat, she returned to Congress, where she served her district until 1982, winning every election with over 80 percent of the vote.

Chisholm was also an activist for women's rights. In the late 1960s, she was an officer in the National Organization for Women (NOW), the honorary president of the National Association for the Repeal of Abortion Laws (NARAL), and a member of the Women's Equity Action League (WEAL). In 1971 she was a cofounder of the National Women's Political Caucus and, in 1984, a cofounder of the National Political Congress of Black Women.

After her retirement from Congress, Chisholm taught at Mount Holyoke College and was a visiting scholar at Spelman College. In 1993, President Bill Clinton nominated Chisholm as ambassador to Jamaica, but she declined the position because of health issues.

[*See also* Black Politics; Congress, African Americans in; *and* Politics and Politicians.]

BIBLIOGRAPHY

Brownmiller, Susan. *Shirley Chisholm: A Biography*. Garden City, N.Y.: Doubleday, 1970.

Chisholm, Shirley. *The Good Fight*. New York: Harper & Row, 1973.

Chisholm, Shirley. *Unbought and Unbossed*. Boston: Houghton Mifflin, 1970.

Diamonstein, Barbaralee. *Open Secrets: Ninety-four Women in Touch with Our Time*. New York: Viking, 1972.

Haskins, James. *Fighting Shirley Chisholm*. New York: Dial, 1975.

Pollack, Jill S. *Shirley Chisholm*. New York: Franklin Watts, 1994.

—JULIE GALLAGHER

CHITLIN CIRCUIT. If African American performers in the first half of the twentieth century had relied solely on work that could be gained through white theaters, then most black entertainers would never have worked at all. This problem created the birth of venues throughout the United States commonly known as the Chitlin Circuit. The term "chitlin" is the common vernacular of the word "chitterlings," the small intestines of a pig, prepared as "soul food," a phrase describing a cuisine that is popular in the African American community. Though many of these venues were in small towns, well-known theaters like the Apollo in Harlem, the Regal in Chicago, and the Royal in Baltimore were also considered to be venues on the Chitlin Circuit. During times of racial segregation and racist violence, these clubs and theaters were relatively safe and acceptable locations in which African American musicians, comedians, and theater troupes could perform.

The ability to perform or tour at the venues that made up the Chitlin Circuit was left up to the Theater Owners' Booking Association, more commonly called TOBA, TOBY, or Toby Time. TOBA was sardonically said to be an acronym for "tough on black acts" or "tough on black asses"—a reference to the barriers that African Americans found in trying to perform at mainstream venues. TOBA began in 1909 and flourished in the 1920s, disappearing during the Great Depression. The association is more often thought of as related to black theater or vaudeville, while the Chitlin Circuit is usually thought of as a home to music and musical artists.

Though the development of TOBA created a smoother road to work for African American talent, the experience was far from easy. Unless you were a headliner the pay was lower than that in white booking organizations, and because of segregation laws travel was by a second-class train. Few acts could afford a band to accompany them, so once performance time arrived the act had to rely on locally available musicians as support. Many of the circuit venues were in very small towns, so talent, sets, and costumes were often at a bare minimum.

During this time the best that many black performers could hope for in mainstream entertainment was performing in minstrel shows or possibly being the "black act" for majority-white audiences, so the variety of entertainment available to audiences on the circuit was wide. It was possible to see comedians, ventriloquists, magicians, acrobats, and dancers in addition to actual theatrical performances such as one-act plays. The most common and best-known acts were singers and musicians—many of which eventually crossed over into widespread popular recognition. Singers such as Ma Rainey, Bessie Smith, Billie Holiday, and Lena Horne all found their beginnings on the Chitlin Circuit. Renowned comedians and social satirists like Moms Mabley and Dick Gregory both began their legends working at various circuit venues. Before the dancer Bill "Bojangles" Robinson and the actress Ethel Waters entertained the whole nation, they were entertaining African Americans through TOBA.

The actual Theater Owners' Booking Association has a fairly specific life span, whereas "Chitlin Circuit" is a more casual term for the locations of performances. Thus artists well into the middle of the twentieth century were said to have come out of the Chitlin Circuit. Muddy Waters and B. B. King are two blues singers and musicians who began at the venues of the Chitlin Circuit. Even more modern groups like The Jackson Five, Gladys Knight and the Pips, and Ike and Tina Turner were considered to have worked the Chitlin Circuit before crossing over into mainstream entertainment.

Over time a few African American artists began to make their way to the stage before white audiences—Paul Robeson and Duke Ellington are two examples. As the civil rights movement made integration commonplace and persevering talents like Lorraine Hansberry (*A Raisin in the Sun*, 1959) wrote hit plays for Broadway that made African American talent more desirable to white audiences, the need for the Chitlin Circuit did not seem so great. Though many artists still work in smaller venues, since the days of integration African American artists can be found performing in a variety of venues all across the country. In the genre of music in the twentieth century the Chitlin Circuit is, for the most part, a thing of the past. It was a necessity for presenting and developing black artists at a time when they were not given access to audience and stage.

In the early twenty-first century, the term "Chitlin Circuit" may be used with a negative connotation to refer to black urban theater, and often instead of "Chitlin Circuit" the term "urban theater circuit" may be used. Urban theater now consists primarily of black musical-comedy plays that provide an inspirational message. Some think that this circuit is an important aspect of black entertainment because the plays are often written, produced, and directed by African Americans, use primarily African American actors, and are frequented by African American audiences. Critics of these plays say that the comedy and minstrel-like characters are an embarrassment to the African American community and that they should not be considered legitimate theater.

Despite current opinions of the Chitlin Circuit, it and its overlapping relationship with the Theater Owners' Booking Association were the birth of organized touring for African American performers in the twentieth century. Without its inception and continued existence, performers now considered to be legendary and groundbreaking would not have been known.

[*See also* Vaudeville, African Americans in.]

Bibliography

Hughes, Langston. "The Negro and American Entertainment." In *The American Negro Reference Book*, edited by John P. Davis, pp. 826–849. Englewood Cliffs, N.J.: Prentice-Hall, 1966.

Gates, Henry Louis, Jr. "The Chitlin Circuit." *New Yorker*, 3 February 1997, pp. 44–55. Explores the black theater—its operations, its audiences, and the people involved in the production of its shows.

—Niambi Lee-Kong

CHOREOGRAPHERS. African American choreography cannot be reduced to or defined by a single "black" style; many dancers and choreographers question the meaning of such terms as "black dance" or "black choreography." Acknowledging the many contributions made by and social barriers particular to African American artists, experienced voices within the dance community nevertheless express concern that to talk of "black" or "African American" dance or choreography is to create a lesser subset of American dance, of ballet, of modern dance, and of dance overall.

Variety of forms, inspiration from the streets or the church, and the range and engagement with music resonate throughout the work of all black choreographers. Several prominent choreographers—such as Arthur Mitchell and Pearl Primus—draw equally from European classical ballet and traditional African dance. Black choreographers find inspiration in church spirituals, the written and spoken word, and the urban "ghetto" and hip hop.

Yet within this multigenerational heterogeneous group of choreographers there are several constants in their life experiences that unite them, including the desire to bring dance to the underprivileged and the necessity to fight for civil rights for all African Americans. To achieve their artistic goals in the highly competitive world of dance they had to disprove the low expectations that many whites had for black dancers. They also had to face and overcome the policies and attitudes of Jim Crow segregation that, for example, limited Katherine Dunham to performing only before white, segregated audiences or that prevented the televising of a ballet with a black male lead paired with a white female partner. Pernicious beliefs that the black body and mind were incapable of performing ballet resulted in potential choreographers being denied entrance to dance academies. For an African American to make it in the world of dance, he or she had to become, in the words of Mitchell, "a political activist through dance."

Pioneers: Dunham, Ailey, and Mitchell. Katherine Dunham (1909–2006), both a dancer and a choreographer, was among the first black artists to form a ballet troupe and to receive acclaim for the modern dances she created; her choreography was both for Broadway and for film. In 1963 with her choreography of *Aida*, Dunham became the first black choreographer to work for the Metropolitan Opera in New York City. Her Dunham School of Dance and Theater, founded in Manhattan in 1945, trained black artists both in ballet and in African and Caribbean dance forms. Dunham earned a master's degree in cultural anthropology, studying for her thesis the dances of the slave descendants in the Caribbean, South America, and the American South—looking for cultural remnants of Africa that were thought to be lost.

Dunham stated, "I had the classical training, but it was the idea of the body as an instrument that appealed to me. My real effort was to free the body from restriction." (Bernstein 2006). Dunham's choreography emphasized a flexible torso and spine, a sharp and articulated pelvis, limbs acting in isolation, and polyrhythmic stages of movement.

The great choreographer Alvin Ailey (1931–1989) experienced more than most the racial and social battles for artistic opportunity and expression. Under Ailey's direction, modern dance became a popular art form, and theater seats were filled with racially and economically mixed audiences. In the late 1950s Ailey founded the Alvin Ailey American Dance Company, known for its physical daring and for the choreographer's humanistic visions; the company toured internationally and always met with great enthusiasm. In the troupe's signature celebrated pieces Ailey drew from memories of church

Katherine Dunham. In costume for *Bamboche!* (1962). Dunham was the Metropolitan Opera's first black choreographer in 1963, choreographing *Aida*. New York World–Telegram and the Sun Newspaper Photograph Collection, Prints and Photographs Division, Library of Congress

services, spirituals, and forbidden dances from his childhood in his all-black neighborhood of Rogers, Texas.

As a teen and young man Ailey trained in Los Angeles, ultimately directing the Horton Dance Troupe when its founder, Lester Horton, died in 1953. After several years choreographing for Broadway, Ailey became inspired by the blues. In 1958 Ailey created *Blues Suite*, which included his most powerful and remarkable piece "Revelations," with men and women scrambling from the golden heavens to amend their sins. The ultimate release comes at the end when God's children are spiritually released to the sounds of "Rocka My Soul in the Bosom of Abraham." "Revelations" became Ailey's signature piece and one of the highest achievements in dance during the twentieth century. Working with the dancer (and later choreographer) Judith Jamison, Ailey created *Cry* for her in 1971, and she made it one of the best-known pieces of American dance. Ailey used the motions of Jamison's body to depict the struggles and joys of black women everywhere.

Despite his gift and talent, Ailey struggled with the financial burdens of maintaining a dance troupe and being a role model. In the 1980s he suffered a mental breakdown, was HIV positive, and became worn down by the social ills that he had sought to eradicate. When Ailey died in 1989, thousands of people mourned at his funeral and celebrated his talent and life.

The dancer, choreographer, and creative director of both the Dance Theatre of Harlem (his troupe) and its related dance academy, Arthur Mitchell (b. 1934) had a lasting impact on American dance that cannot be overvalued. Acknowledging that his life was saved through education, in the late 1960s Mitchell established the Dance Theatre of Harlem as a teaching academy and performing dance troupe. After high school Mitchell won a scholarship to the School of American Ballet, and in 1955 he joined George Balanchine's New York City Ballet. In 1959 he became the first African American principal danseur in a major white ballet company. Many critics and dance historians consider Mitchell's interpretation of Puck—a role that Balanchine choreographed just for Mitchell—in *A Midsummer Night's Dream* to be his finest. Mitchell was often partnered with white ballerinas at a time when this was highly unusual and controversial.

The 1968 assassination of Dr. Martin Luther King Jr. prompted Mitchell to return to Harlem. With his teacher and mentor Karel Shook (1920–1985), Mitchell established his troupe and a teaching academy. Mitchell's Dance Theatre of Harlem School began in a church basement with three hundred neighborhood children; by the early twenty-first century it had more than five hundred students a year. As a choreographer, Mitchell's signature pieces include *Rhythmetron* (1968) and *Ode to Otis* (1969), a posthumous tribute to Otis Redding (1941–1967). Mitchell's choreography shows musical and artistic inspirations that range from the townships of Soweto, South Africa, to European classical composers, and the soul singing of Aretha Franklin and James Brown.

Other Prominent Choreographers. Judith Jamison (b. 1943) trained mainly in classical ballet. The famed choreographer Agnes de Mille learned of this young, beautiful talent and recruited her for the American Ballet Theater in 1964. One year later Jamison joined the Alvin Ailey American Dance Theater, where she was the principal ballerina and the choreographers Ailey, Geoffrey Holder, and others tailored works to highlight her ability to convey emotion and her lean, graceful body. (Jamison was five feet ten inches tall.)

Jamison and Ailey collaborated closely on dances for her to perform, such as her acclaimed solo *Masakela Language* in 1969. When Ailey died in 1989, Jamison, by then a choreographer in her own right, became his company's artistic director.

Born in Trinidad, Geoffrey Holder (b. 1930) first caught the attention of Agnes de Mille in London and sold paintings in order pay his passage to New York. Unfortunately de Mille could not offer him a position. Instead Holder taught classes at the Katherine Dunham School to support himself. His powerful stature (six feet six inches tall) and formal attire at a dance recital attracted the attention of Broadway producers. During 1955 and 1956 Holder was a principal dancer with the Metropolitan Opera Ballet in New York. He also appeared with his troupe, Geoffrey Holder and Company, through 1960. Holder has choreographed pieces for the leading black dance troupes, both modern and ballet. For instance, Holder created *Prodigal Prince* (1967), based on the life of a Haitian folk painter, for the Alvin Ailey American Dance Theater. The Dance Theatre of Harlem includes in its repertoire Holder's 1957 piece *Bele*, which like most of his work combines African and European elements.

From age fourteen Talley Beatty (1923–1995) studied and worked with Katherine Dunham: he was a member of her troupe from 1937 to 1943. When he made his professional debut in 1937, dance critics felt that his style was more balletlike than that of the other company members. In 1952 with a program called *Tropicana*—featuring a fusion of African and Latin American influences—Beatty formed his own dance company and toured the United States and Europe. Beatty's choreographing included dancing for both solos and groups, interspersed with drum solos and vocal interludes. In 1959 he choreographed *The Road of the Phoebe Snow*, about life on the Lackawanna Railroad and accompanied by the music of Duke Ellington and Billy Strayhorn. This work entered the repertoire of the Alvin Ailey American Dance Theater in

1964 and has become one of Beatty's greatest and most lasting works. Beatty and Ellington worked together often during the 1950s and 1960s; Beatty choreographed several of Ellington's extended works, including *A Drum Is a Woman* (1957) and *My People* (1963).

Born in Cartagena, Colombia, Eleo Pomare (b. 1937) moved to Harlem at age ten and attended the High School of Performing Arts in New York City. Trained in dance by José Limón and other luminaries, by 1958 Pomare was directing his own company. After studying in West Germany and Holland in 1962–1964, he organized a second company that was well received around Europe. In 1965 Pomare returned to the United States and sought to connect his dance with American culture. In 1967 he founded the Dancemobile, which brought free professional dances to the streets of New York. His Eleo Pomare Dance Company performed throughout the United States and the world. Pomare's style is characterized by unexpected shapes that twist, bend, fall, and lean in continuous movement.

Pomare often creates dances inspired by visual and literary works or sociopolitical issues. In the late 1980s he participated in the American Dance Festival's three-year project entitled The Black Tradition in American Modern Dance, a project meant to preserve the work of African American choreographers. Over the years Pomare received a Guggenheim Fellowship (1972) and several awards from the National Endowment of the Arts.

Alfred "Pepsi" Bethel (1918–2002) began his career in New York City choreographing and performing popular jazz dance; he often preformed on the Broadway stage. A teacher to many, in 1960 Bethel formed his own troupe, the Pepsi Bethel Authentic Jazz Dance Theater. He had performed previously at the Savoy, making his mark with his own renditions of the Lindy Hop and the cakewalk. Bethel was the consulting choreographer for many Broadway musicals and movies.

Tap dance flourished from 1900 to the 1950s, but then it came to be seen as a lesser novelty act. By the end of the twentieth century the young phenomenon Savion Glover (b. 1973), a choreographer and tap dancer, had brought new attention and vibrancy to a long artistic heritage that includes Fayard and Harold Nicholas of the Nicholas Brothers, Bill "Bojangles" Robinson, and Gregory and Maurice Hines of Hines, Hines, and Dad. Glover won a Tony Award in 1996 for *Bring in 'da Noise, Bring in 'da Funk* on Broadway. With his regular appearances on television's *Sesame Street* from 1990 to 1995, Glover introduced the world of dance to younger generations.

[*See also* Alvin Ailey American Dance Theater; Blues; Dance; Dance Theatre of Harlem; *and biographical entries on figures mentioned in this article*.]

Bibliography

Aschenbrenner, Joyce. *Katherine Dunham: Dancing a Life*. Urbana: University of Illinois, 2002.

Bernstein, Adam. "Dancer Katherine Dunham; Formed Black Ballet Troupe." *Washington Post*, 23 May 2006.

Dunning, Jennifer. *Alvin Ailey: A Life in Dance*. Reading, Mass.: Addison-Wesley, 1996.

Dunning, Jennifer. "DANCE: Defining Black Dance, in Its Dizzying Variety." *New York Times*, 6 February 2000.

Dunning, Jennifer. *Geoffrey Holder: A Life in Theater, Dance, and Art*. New York: Harry N. Abrams, 2001.

Glass, Barbara S. *African American Dance: An Illustrated History*. Jefferson, N.C.: McFarland, 2007.

Gottschild, Brenda Dixon. *The Black Dancing Body: A Geography from Coon to Cool*. New York: Palgrave Macmillan, 2003.

Long, Richard A. *The Black Tradition in American Dance*. London: Prion, 1989.

—Diana L. Linden

CHURCH, ROBERT R. (b. 18 June 1839; d. 29 August 1912), banker, real estate magnate, activist, and philanthropist, considered the first southern African American millionaire. Robert Reed "Bob" Church was born in 1839 in Holly Springs, Mississippi, to an enslaved mother, Emmeline, and a white steamboat captain, Charles B. Church. His mother, a seamstress, died when Robert was twelve years old, and he spent much of his childhood on the Mississippi River with his father. Because of his closeness to his father, Robert enjoyed privileges not generally associated with slavery. While working on a steamboat during the Civil War, however, Union troops captured him, and he soon settled as a freedman in Memphis, Tennessee.

Church entered into business in postwar Memphis, but success did not shield him from the violence of Reconstruction. During the 1866 Memphis riot in which white mobs attacked freedmen, vigilantes ransacked Church's saloon and shot him. Church survived and remained in the city, even in the wake of an epidemic of yellow fever in 1878. After Memphis was classified as only a taxing district, Church bought the first $1,000 bond to return it to city status, and he invested in real estate when most residents fled the city and its epidemic.

In the post-Reconstruction period, which saw the entrenchment of Jim Crow segregation, Church catered to black consumers, opening saloons, gambling houses, and a hotel in downtown Memphis. A millionaire by the late 1880s, he opened the Church Park and Auditorium in 1899. There W. C. Handy, the "Father of the Blues," conducted the orchestra, and notables including Booker T. Washington and Theodore Roosevelt made appearances. The site also functioned as a meeting site for black Republicans, and in 1900 Church, a staunch Republican activist, served as Memphis's delegate to that party's national convention.

A life member of Washington's National Negro Business League, Church valued black entrepreneurship, opening Beale Street's Solvent Savings Bank and Trust Company in 1906, making him the first black to own and operate a Memphis bank. His enormous wealth and political clout earned Church the moniker "Boss of Beale Street," Beale Street being the part of town that became infamous in the 1920s for its blues music and nightlife. Church was an associate of other accomplished blacks of his era, including Frederick Douglass, Blanche K. Bruce, P. B. S. Pinchback, John Mercer Langston, and Booker T. Washington. Church and his children were close associates of Washington, but their emphasis on both economic uplift and political engagement occasionally placed them at odds with the "Wizard of Tuskegee."

Church married Louisa Ayers while they were both enslaved, and the couple had two children: Thomas Church, an attorney and author, and Mary Church Terrell, founder of the National Association for Colored Women and charter member of the NAACP at W. E. B. Du Bois's personal request. Following a divorce Church married Anna Wright and fathered Robert Jr., a prominent Memphis Republican, and Annette, a charter member of the Memphis NAACP. Church died in 1912 and was buried in Memphis. Church Park became part of the Beale Street National Historic Landmark historic district in 1994.

[*See also* Entrepreneurship; Memphis; *and biographical entries on figures mentioned in this article*.]

BIBLIOGRAPHY

Church, Annette E., and Roberta Church. *The Robert R. Churches of Memphis: A Father and Son Who Achieved in Spite of Race*. Memphis, Tenn.: A. E. Church, 1974. An intimate portrait of Church and his son Robert Jr., authored by family members.

Gatewood, Willard B. *Aristocrats of Color: The Black Elite, 1880–1920*. Bloomington: Indiana University Press, 1990. Describes the origins and actions of the black social, economic, and intellectual elite at the turn of the twentieth century.

—RASHAUNA R. JOHNSON

CHURCH, BLACK. *See* Black Church.

CHURCH OF GOD IN CHRIST. The Church of God in Christ is a predominantly African American Christian denomination practicing a Holiness Pentecostal faith. Founded in the late nineteenth century by Charles Harrison Mason and Charles Price Jones, the Church of God in Christ combines traditional African worship styles and theological attitudes with a Holiness doctrine.

Founding. Born in Tennessee in 1866, Charles Harrison Mason admired the religious conviction and practices of his freedmen parents, Jerry and Eliza Mason. Having already been licensed to preach by a Baptist church in Arkansas, Mason entered the historically black Arkansas Baptist College in November 1893, but he did not stay long. The college was teaching new biblical interpretations and theological methods of which Mason was suspicious: he viewed these teachings as contributing to the loss of the traditional religion of the slaves. In January 1894, Mason left Arkansas Baptist College and set out in the full-time ministry. A year later he met Charles Price Jones, then a Baptist preacher in Jackson, Mississippi, and the two became fast friends and partners in the ministry.

Jones had graduated from Arkansas Baptist College in 1891. A talented preacher and writer, he held various offices in the Arkansas Baptist Convention. His reputation crossed state lines and led to his being called to pastor in Alabama and then in Mississippi, where he began to preach the doctrine of Holiness, or perfectionism, and Sanctification, or spiritual separation from the sinful world.

After being expelled from the Baptist convention for preaching contrary doctrine, Jones, Mason, and a few other brothers started their own denomination and searched for a while for a name. Mason recounted that in 1897 while walking in Little Rock, Arkansas, God gave him the name "Church of God in Christ," based on I Thessalonians 2:14. Ten years later Jones and Mason disputed over glossolalia, or speaking in tongues. Mason was fresh from his Holy Ghost experience at the Azusa Street Revival, a Pentecostal revival led by the African American preacher William Joseph Seymour that took place in Los Angeles beginning in 1906; Jones had sent Mason and two other brothers to investigate the revival. Mason maintained, like Seymour, that glossolalia is the initial proof of the baptism of the Holy Ghost. The dispute between Mason and Jones led to a split in 1907. Mason retained the name and became the undisputed leader of the newly organized Church of God in Christ.

Growth during the Twentieth Century. From 1907 onward the Church of God in Christ has held an annual convocation in Memphis, Tennessee, at which the unity of the group was refreshed and the weary souls were revived. Though the leadership was always African American, the Church of God in Christ was interracial in its early history. The Memphis authorities persecuted whites for violating the Jim Crow laws. In 1913 most white members of the Church of God in Christ left to form the Assemblies of God, which is still regarded as a sister denomination.

Members of mainline African American churches openly criticized and persecuted members of the Church of God in Christ, who were largely poor and uneducated. Holiness and sanctification was referred to as "that mess" and was widely seen as the fruit of ignorance. Thus the annual convocation was a spiritual and psychologically relieving necessity that gave a renewed impetus to cope with persecution and spread the gospel. Despite their disdain for the ecstatic worship styles and extreme doctrine of Church of God in Christ members, African Americans of other denominations usually respected the "saints," as they were called, and often came for prayer and divine healing—which often resulted in the conversion of detractors.

Convocations and other church gatherings involve the collection of large sums of cash, giving church leaders unprecedented access to money. Church leaders invested in the education of members' children and in small businesses, providing jobs. The result was the eventual change of church demographics: increasingly the church's members were educated and middle class. During World War II, Mason and his followers also built a temple that at the time was the largest structure owned by African Americans. The temple was named for Mason and is where his remains are entombed. Today the structure still stands, a symbol of the unity and financial strength of the Church of God in Christ.

Mason developed an episcopal government with "overseers" or bishops appointed over specific geographic areas. Originally Mason appointed three overseers, one each to Tennessee, Arkansas, and Mississippi. As the church grew in a short time he appointed three additional overseers to Texas, Missouri, and California, and added the position of field secretary. A corresponding female leader organized and led the women's work in the same area. In 1911 Mason named Lizzie Woods Roberson as the first supervisor of women. Roberson's personality and leadership style helped to shape the early church. She traveled around the country, establishing the women's work in the churches and building the women's departments in the jurisdictions. Harnessing the dual-sex system of authority and work inherited from their West African cultural ancestry, Mason and Roberson managed the church. Mason established jurisdictions and appointed overseers, and Roberson appointed overseers of women's work.

Historically women established Church of God in Christ churches and then deferred to male leadership, allowing a male pastor to be appointed. By the twenty-first century women continued to begin new congregations but in many cases were left to pastor the churches. Women were also the first missionaries abroad, though men led the resulting churches. The Church of God in Christ is noteworthy in that it created a licensure for women, known as evangelist-missionary licenses. In order for a woman to hold a position, she must possess the license. This gave African American women an opportunity to develop leadership qualities. When Mason established the licensure system he was being progressive, but by the twenty-first century there was division over the ordination of women within the Church of God in Christ. Some bishops ordain women in violation of church regulations, but the church has not taken action against them.

By the time of Mason's death in 1961, the church had experienced rapid growth that necessitated reorganization. Five more bishops were elected, expanding the existing board of bishops to twelve, and Bishop O. T. Jones Sr., the last surviving of the first five bishops that Mason consecrated, took the helm of the church as senior bishop. This was a controversial time because the position of senior bishop had not been clearly delineated, and in 1964 a dispute arose over the powers of the senior bishop. In 1968 a constitutional convention was called to reorganize the church. The senior-bishop structure was abandoned in favor of a system of a presiding bishop and a general board of eleven bishops serving as an executive branch.

Mason's son-in-law, James Oglethorpe Patterson Sr., was elected presiding bishop and led the church until his death in 1989. Patterson led the church into a new era of prestige and wider acceptance. Patterson's nephew, G. E. Patterson, an internationally known evangelist, served as the fourth presiding bishop from 2000 until his death in 2007. Under his leadership All Saints Bible College was founded in Memphis. In 2007, Charles E. Blake succeeded Patterson. Blake, a well-known theologian and preacher, pastored the West Angeles Church of God in Christ, the largest Church of God in Christ congregation, with well over twenty-two thousand members.

The Church of God in Christ continued to experience explosive growth. From 1972 to 1997, the church's membership grew from 3 million to 5.4 million. The growth continued into the twenty-first century: it had more than 6 million members and was the largest predominantly African American denomination and one of the largest denominations in the United States. The church has competition from other African American Pentecostal bodies, however, most of which are splinter groups from the Church of God in Christ. Nondenominational charismatic churches also pose a challenge to the growth of the Church of God in Christ. However, stable structural organization and a respected name continue to give the church an edge.

[*See also* Black Church *and* Religion.]

BIBLIOGRAPHY

Butler, Anthea. *Women in the Church of God in Christ: Making a Sanctified World.* Chapel Hill: University of North Carolina Press, 2007.

Church of God in Christ. *Official Manual with the Doctrines and Discipline of the Church of God in Christ.* Memphis, Tenn.: Publishing Board of the Church of God in Christ, 1973.

Clemmons, Ithiel C. *Bishop C. H. Mason and the Roots of the Church of God in Christ.* Bakersfield, Calif.: Pneuma Life, 1996.

Pleas, Charles. *Fifty Years Achievement from 1906–1956: A Period in History of the Church of God in Christ.* Memphis, Tenn.: Church of God in Christ Public Relations, 1991.

—DOUGLAS THOMAS

CIVIL DISOBEDIENCE. Prior to 1955, civil rights activists relied heavily on lobbying and litigation as the primary means of advancing their agenda of social change. Such efforts eventually led to the Supreme Court decision in 1954 in *Brown v. Board of Education*, which held that the "separate but equal" doctrine from the *Plessy v. Ferguson* decision of 1896 was unconstitutional. The *Brown* decision implied that African Americans were entitled to equal access not only in education but also in other areas of public life. In response to this ruling, however, the most racist and virulently violent elements of the South gained influence on the wave of a massive backlash. Membership increased dramatically in organizations such as the Ku Klux Klan and White Citizens' Councils, and state and local governments, law-enforcement agencies, and business communities joined forces to mobilize the white population around the segregated way of life that had been the status quo since the end of Reconstruction, if not since the end of the Civil War in 1865 or even since the beginnings of slavery. Their main strategy combined the use of violence, voter suppression, and economic apartheid. The *Brown* decision made segregation illegal, yet initially it was little enforced.

Civil disobedience emerged as the principal strategy for combating racist violence and advancing the civil rights of African Americans. Combining nonviolent resistance with direct action, practitioners of civil disobedience helped bring the issues of desegregation to the forefront of national attention, creating crisis situations that made the nation aware of the violence being carried out by local and state governments and vigilantes throughout the South. Through Freedom Rides, sit-ins, boycotts, and marches, the civil rights movement was able to topple Jim Crow and segregation throughout the United States. Above all, civil disobedience meant that demonstrators freely and openly violated laws that they deemed to be unjust—for example, eating at racially segregated lunch counters—and accepted the consequences of their actions.

The philosophy of civil disobedience is part of both biblical and classical tradition, but in the modern world its most notable philosophical exponent is Henry David Thoreau, an author and philosopher born in Concord, Massachusetts, in the antebellum era. Thoreau argues in his essay "On the Duty of Civil Disobedience" (1849) that it is the obligation of the individual not to cooperate with unjust laws. This and others of Thoreau's writings had a significant impact on the Indian independence leader Mohandas K. Gandhi. Gandhi first employed Thoreau's techniques to fight for Indian rights in South Africa and later combined civil disobedience with Indian nationalism to create the concept of satyagraha, or holding to truth. Gandhi's use of satyagraha played a decisive role in ending Britain's colonial rule in India, bringing about one of the few successful nonviolent revolutions of the first half of the twentieth century.

Gandhi had a tremendous impact on a variety of African American activists and organizations during the period leading up to the civil rights movement, most notably Howard Thurman, Benjamin Mays, and Bayard Rustin. Nevertheless, one of the twentieth century's best-known practitioners of nonviolence and civil disobedience was Dr. Martin Luther King Jr., founder of the Southern Christian Leadership Conference (SCLC). King first learned of the concept as a freshman at Morehouse College, a historically black university in Atlanta, Georgia. King read Thoreau's essay on civil disobedience and also studied Thurman and Gandhi. King's Christian faith and keen understanding of both Thoreau and Gandhi led him eventually to view civil disobedience as the most practical and moral means of achieving the goals of the civil rights movement. King's extraordinary oratorical style was rooted both in the black church and in liberal Protestant theology, allowing him to craft an eloquent message that appealed to a wide cross section of American society. He was the central figure of the civil rights movement during the period 1955–1968, and by the twenty-first century his name was often used synonymously with the terms "nonviolence" and "civil disobedience."

There was a lesser-known constellation of intellectuals, activists, and organizations that also embodied Thoreau's views on civil disobedience. One of the first organizations to attack segregation through the use of nonviolence and civil disobedience was the Congress of Racial Equality (CORE), an interracial and pacifist organization of young people founded in 1942. One of CORE's first successful targets was a skating rink in Chicago, Illinois, that was illegally practicing discrimination against African American customers. Later, in 1947, the group embarked on the Journey of Reconciliation, a trip that included sixteen men—eight white and eight black—challenging segregation in transportation facilities in the South. This trip was an inspiration for the Freedom Rides that later played a pivotal part in desegregating transportation facilities in the Deep South. CORE's first leader, James Farmer, played an integral role in organizing many of the Freedom Rides of the 1960s. The freedom riders—not only black and white men but also women—journeyed through the Deep South on buses to test whether bus terminals and seating were desegregated. They were often met by angry and violent mobs. The activists, well trained in the techniques of civil disobedience, faced not only violence but also imprisonment, often within the notoriously cruel and harsh confines of the Parchman penitentiary, located in the Mississippi Delta.

Sit-ins were another form of civil disobedience implemented by students. During the period 1960–1961, students in Greensboro, North Carolina, Atlanta, and Nashville, Tennessee, targeted the segregated lunch counters of local stores. Well dressed and well behaved, the demonstrators would enter the stores, shop and make some purchases, and then sit down at every other stool at the lunch counters. They hoped not only to provoke the authorities but also to gain white sympathizers. Most often they encountered violent responses from police, as well as from rogue elements recruited for the sole purpose of attacking them. As the authorities violently removed one group from the stores, another group of students would sit-in. The demonstrators had pledged not to retaliate physically and, once jailed, not to post bail, creating a financial burden for the local authorities. Many of the students who formed the Student Nonviolent Coordinating Committee (SNCC) in 1960 were veterans of these sit-ins. SNCC focused more on voter registration but also employed civil disobedience. SNCC's leadership included such civil rights icons as Stokely Carmichael, Ella Baker, and John Lewis.

On 7 March 1965 the SCLC and SNCC together organized a nonviolent march of six hundred people to highlight voter suppression in Alabama. They intended to march from Selma to Montgomery, Alabama, but as they crossed the Edmund Pettus Bridge they were violently confronted by state troopers and local police. Numerous marchers were gassed and beaten, and more than thirty were severely injured, including the SNCC leader Lewis, who later became a congressman. Millions viewed the national media's images of state troopers, many on horseback, beating and gassing nonviolent marchers. President Lyndon Baines Johnson spoke in support of the marchers and signed the Voting Rights Act of 1965 a few months later. This epochal legislation capped the triumphant rise of civil disobedience in the United States.

[*See also* Civil Rights Movement; Congress of Racial Equality; Freedom Rides; Jim Crow Laws; King, Martin Luther, Jr., Philosophy of; Massive Resistance; Quakers; Rustin, Bayard; Sit-ins; Southern Christian Leadership Conference; Student Nonviolent Coordinating Committee; *and* Violence against African Americans.]

BIBLIOGRAPHY

Ackerman, Peter, and Jack Duvall. *A Force More Powerful: A Century of Nonviolent Conflict*. New York: St. Martin's Press, 2000.

Branch, Taylor. *Parting the Waters: America in the King Years, 1954–63*. New York: Simon & Schuster, 1988.

Carmichael, Stokely, with Michael E. Thelwell. *Ready for Revolution: The Life and Struggles of Stokely Carmichael (Kwame Ture)*. New York: Scribner, 2003.

Garrow, David. *Bearing the Cross: Martin Luther King, Jr., and the Southern Christian Leadership Conference*. New York: Quill, 1999.

Zinn, Howard, ed. *The Power of Nonviolence: Writings by Advocates of Peace*. Boston: Beacon, 2002.

—LARVESTER GAITHER

CIVIL RIGHTS. "Civil rights" is not a term precisely defined, even by lawyers. A legal dictionary equates civil rights with personal, natural rights protected by the U.S. Constitution, but the leading casebook in the field insists that civil rights include statutory as well as constitutional guarantees. Nor is it clear to whose rights the term refers. One "Civil Rights Reader" discusses the poor, people with disabilities, and categories of gender and sexuality, as well as race. In U.S. history, however, the term most often refers to the legal rights of racial minorities, especially African Americans. Those rights deteriorated markedly during the last years of the nineteenth century, improved somewhat during the Progressive Era and the interwar period, and were transformed by a "Civil Rights Revolution" triggered by World War II. A period of accelerating progress climaxed with Supreme Court decisions and landmark federal legislation in the 1960s. Since the mid-1970s, with issues changing and white support for measures African Americans consider important declining, forward movement has stalled. Civil rights remain however more extensive and better protected than throughout most of American history.

***Plessy* Era.** Securing equal rights for African Americans was one of the major objectives, and appeared to be one of the most important achievements, of the Reconstruction that followed the Civil War. Many of the Radical Republicans in Congress believed that by prohibiting slavery the Thirteenth Amendment, adopted in 1865, by implication required that all citizens, black and white, be treated equally. The doubts of others about whether this was really so, along with the obvious unwillingness of white southerners to treat blacks equally, drove Congress to supplement the Thirteenth Amendment with a Fourteenth, ratified in 1868. This prohibited states from making or enforcing any laws that abridged the privileges or immunities of citizenship, depriving anyone of life, liberty, or property without due process of law, or denying to any persons the equal protection of the laws. In 1870 Republicans supplemented these guarantees with a Fifteenth Amendment, which forbade depriving any citizen of the right to vote because of race, color, or previous condition of servitude. Southern resistance to these amendments, highlighted by the violent outrages of the Ku Klux Klan, inspired the enactment in 1866, 1870, and 1871 of federal statutes designed to enforce them. Those laws and the constitutional amendments they were intended to implement remained, when Reconstruction ended in 1877 and for nearly a century thereafter, the principal legal guarantees of African American civil rights.

During what the historian Michael Klarman, referring to *Plessy v. Ferguson* (1896), calls the "*Plessy* Era," African Americans lost most of what these laws promised. Because the Fifteenth Amendment did not actually guarantee anyone the right to vote, but only prohibited taking it away for specified racial reasons, it was possible to deprive African Americans of the franchise using racially neutral devices that had a hugely disproportionate impact on the impoverished and largely illiterate black electorate. That is what states in the South did, beginning with Florida and Tennessee in 1889 and Mississippi in 1890, accelerating after the demise of southern populism in the late 1890s, and concluding with Georgia in 1908. Eleven of the states adopted the poll tax, a small but often cumulative levy that had to be paid in order to vote. Seven states coupled this with a literacy test, and seven initiated the secret paper ballot, which served as a de facto literacy test, since those who could not read it could not vote.

Such measures might have disfranchised thousands of poor and uneducated whites too, but in order to broaden support for them, conservative Democrats in five states created loopholes whites could slip through. These included exemptions from literacy tests for owners of small amounts of property and for those who could explain a passage from the state constitution when it was read to them (a requirement easily administered in a racially discriminatory manner). In a half dozen states grandfather clauses waived literacy tests for lineal descendants of persons who had been qualified to vote before African Americans first gained the right to do so in 1867. Using such legal gimmicks and informal pressure, whites had by 1900 virtually eliminated the black electorate, except for a few hundred voters in large cities. In *Williams v. Mississippi* (1898), however, the Supreme Court, while conceding that the poll tax and the literacy test were designed to disfranchise African Americans, concluded that since they did not deprive anyone of the right to vote on the basis of race they were not violations of the Fifteenth Amendment.

The Court's opinion, written by a Republican from California, suggests how pervasive racism was in America at the end of the nineteenth century. For more than a decade after Reconstruction ended, state legislatures in the North continued to pass laws prohibiting various kinds of racial discrimination, including school segregation. These statutes were often enacted by hypocritical politicians really more interested in black votes than in civil rights, but when African Americans sued under them, courts do generally seem to have enforced them. Where blacks did not litigate, however, they were often blatantly ignored. Toward the end of the century white attitudes hardened, as *Plessy v. Ferguson* illustrates. The issue in that case was whether a state law requiring railroads to provide separate cars for white and colored passengers violated the Fourteenth Amendment's guarantee of equal protection of the laws. The Supreme Court held that it did not. It ignored the fact that the principal reason for the adoption of a growing number of state statutes and local ordinances making mandatory a racial separation that had earlier been voluntary was the increasing unwillingness of African Americans (most of whom had grown up since slavery ended) to defer to whites. The Court myopically rejected as fallacious "the assumption that the enforced separation of the two races stamps the colored race with a badge of inferiority." So long as the facilities provided the two races were equal, it declared, there was no violation of the Equal Protection Clause. *Plessy*'s conclusion seemed so obvious to most people in 1896 that the 8–1 opinion, written by Henry Billings Brown, a Michigan Republican, passed virtually unnoticed by the popular press.

The reason was that in 1896 almost all whites considered African Americans intellectually and morally inferior. Although the Supreme Court did reaffirm earlier decisions holding that excluding them from juries violated the Fourteenth Amendment, other rulings made such discrimination almost impossible to prove. For the first three decades of the twentieth century, virtually no African Americans sat on southern juries.

Their exclusion enhanced the bias of a criminal justice system that afforded African Americans virtually no protection from lynching. During the *Plessy* era extralegal executions were the ultimate bulwark of white supremacy. Once common in frontier areas throughout the country, lynching, which peaked in 1892, had become primarily a southern phenomenon, targeting mostly African Americans. Although the victims were generally accused of some crime (often of raping a white woman), the real purpose, as the barbaric character of many of these killings demonstrated, was to cow all blacks. Lynching was murder, but despite the fact that the identity of the perpetrators was generally widely known, lynchers were seldom arrested or indicted and almost never convicted or punished. As of 1933 only four southern states had recorded even one conviction for lynching.

African Americans were not the only victims of this violent method of enforcing racial subordination. In the Southwest lynching was also employed by whites against Mexican Americans. Like African Americans, Latinos suffered from state-sanctioned segregation. In addition devices such as the poll tax and the all-white Democratic primary were used to exclude Mexican Americans, as well as blacks, from the political process. The treatment of both groups was part of a widespread denial of civil rights to members of racial minorities that also affected Asians on the Pacific Coast. Even after the Fourteenth Amendment made African Americans citizens, Asians remained ineligible for citizenship. In 1882 Congress passed the Chinese Exclusion Act, the first of a series of laws designed to block members of that ethnic group from immigrating into America. Seven years later the Supreme Court upheld the constitutionality of this exclusion legislation. Japanese were the particular targets of the San Francisco school board when in 1906 it adopted a policy of segregating Asians into separate schools. In 1913 California became the first of thirteen states to adopt an Alien Land Law, prohibiting the ownership of real estate by "aliens ineligible for citizenship" (namely, Japanese and other Asians).

Progressive Era. As the enactment of that law demonstrates, discrimination against nonwhites continued during the Progressive Era. Indeed throughout the country racial attitudes actually deteriorated between 1900 and 1920. Lynching did decline 66 percent between 1900 and 1917, but it more than doubled in 1919, swollen by an increase in racial tensions following World War I. As African American migration to the North increased in the first decade of the twentieth century and exploded in the second, black-white tensions escalated. Northerners embraced more and more southern racial attitudes and practices. In many places streetcars and public schools became legally segregated, and the Wilson administration even segregated the federal civil service.

Yet during the 1910s, ironically, African Americans won some civil rights victories in the Supreme Court. In *Guinn v. United States* (1915) the Court invalidated Oklahoma's grandfather clause, holding that it violated the Fifteenth Amendment. The Court also ruled that two Alabama statutes transgressed the Thirteenth Amendment and an 1867 federal statute prohibiting peonage. It thought the one it struck down in *Bailey v. Alabama* (1911) had the effect of criminalizing breach of a labor contract, something even southern courts considered impermissible. *Alabama v. Reynolds* (1914) invalidated a criminal-surety statute that authorized the state to hire out petty offenders to private parties who paid their fines and court costs. Since breach of a surety contract was itself a crime, these minor lawbreakers often wound up working years for white planters, providing them with a cheap labor supply. In *McCabe v. Atchison, Topeka and Santa Fe Railway Company* (1914) the Court expressed the opinion that an Oklahoma statute that permitted railroads to provide luxury accommodations, such as dining and sleeping cars, for white passengers but not for black ones was unconstitutional, rejecting the argument that railroads should not have to comply fully with "separate but equal" if African American demand for a particular service was so low that making them do so would be unreasonable. At least in a quantitative sense, equal meant equal. African Americans also triumphed in *Buchanan v. Warley* (1917), in which the Court invalidated a Louisville, Kentucky, housing ordinance requiring segregation of residential lots into white and black blocks. The Court considered it an interference with the property rights protected by the Due Process Clause of the Fourteenth Amendment.

Why it decided these cases in favor of African American civil rights during an era of rising racism and expanding segregation is a question that has long confounded scholars. No one factor explains all of these rulings. Among those that seem to have played a role were the particularly blatant nature of some of the constitutional violations involved, rejection of the challenged practices by progressive southerners, and the contemporary veneration of property rights. In none of these cases did the Court really challenge the racist assumptions that had restricted civil rights since at least 1890. Collectively however, they constituted a small step forward for African Americans.

Interwar Period. These Progressive Era rulings were precursors to much more meaningful legal victories during the period between 1920 and American entry into World War II. In one respect this was a frustrating period for proponents of African American rights. Beginning in 1918 the NAACP campaigned tirelessly but in futility for the enactment of federal legislation against lynching. Antilynching bills passed the House three times between 1922 and 1940, but southern opposition always kept the Senate from acting on them.

Although the South controlled Congress, demographic and political change was undermining its domination of national civil rights policy. As a result of the Great Migration, beginning around 1914, hundreds of thousands of African Americans moved to the North. In the short run, their coming heightened racial tensions; but in the long run, because they could vote there, it heightened black political power. The New Deal inspired African Americans to cast their ballots for the Democratic Party because, although often administered in a racist manner, its programs benefited the poor, and blacks were the poorest of the poor. Eventually, these developments helped make them part of a politically dominant liberal coalition that promoted civil rights.

During the interwar period, however, racial equality was not yet part of the liberal Democratic agenda. Consequently, African Americans made their greatest gains in the Supreme Court. The Court repeatedly broke with recent precedent to allow federal intervention (through habeas corpus proceedings) in patently unjust state criminal cases. In *Moore v. Dempsy* (1923) it overturned convictions of African American defendants obtained in trials that had been dominated by a mob. *Powell v. Alabama* (1932) and *Norris v. Alabama* (1935) arose out of the infamous Scottsboro Incident, in which a group of African American boys and young men had been convicted for a rape of two white prostitutes that almost certainly never happened. In *Brown v. Mississippi* (1936) the Court overturned death sentences against three black sharecroppers that were based on confessions extracted through torture. These decisions required the creation of new constitutional law that expanded the jurisdiction of the federal judiciary, something the justices seem to have been willing to do simply because they found the blatant unfairness of the state proceedings intolerable.

The Court also proved willing to expand slightly on prior understandings of the constitutional limitations on state authority in order to counter the white primary. After the 1890s Democrats dominated politics in all southern states; the winner of their primary always won the general election. By 1930 whites had managed to exclude African Americans from participation in these crucial contests. Generally this was done by custom or party rule, but in 1923 Texas passed a law requiring it. In *Nixon v. Herndon* (1927) the Supreme Court invalidated that statute as a violation of the Equal Protection Clause. The Texas legislature then empowered the Democratic executive committee to set qualifications for party membership. As expected it barred nonwhites. Although a blatant effort to evade Herndon, what it had done was not obviously unconstitutional, for the Fourteenth and Fifteenth Amendments restrict only state action, and the Democratic Party was at least nominally private. Arguably all the 1923 statute did was allow this private group to go on excluding African Americans and Mexicans, as it had done ever since 1903. Nevertheless in *Nixon v. Condon* (1932) the Supreme Court by a 5–4 vote held it unconstitutional. The Democrats, without any legal authorization, then adopted at their annual convention a resolution excluding nonwhites. Holding that this time there had been no state action, the Court in *Grovey v. Townsend* (1935) ruled unanimously in their favor.

The public-private distinction that preserved the white primary also limited how far the Court was willing to go in combating residential segregation. It summarily struck down ordinances requiring it; in *Corrigan v. Buckley* (1926) however a unanimous Court rejected a constitutional challenge to one of the restrictive covenants by which white property owners contracted among themselves not to sell to nonwhites.

Although more concerned about property rights than civil rights, the Court did strike at the inequality that characterized supposedly separate-but-equal education. Although the border state of Missouri operated a law school for whites, all it provided African Americans was tuition for a limited number to attend integrated institutions in neighboring states. Chief Justice Hughes declared in *Missouri ex rel. Gaines v. Canada* (1938) that this policy violated the Equal Protection Clause. By demonstrating that the Court took seriously the "equal" half of separate but equal, *Gaines* spurred southerners to spend somewhat more on their pathetically underfunded black schools. Since most southern states proceeded after the decision to adopt the very sort of out-of-state scholarship laws *Gaines* had prohibited, however, its impact was limited.

So was the impact of most African American legal successes during the interwar period. While the civil rights of African Americans were not expanding very much, however, at least they were not, like those of Asian Americans, shrinking rapidly. In 1920 California voters adopted by initiative a new and more stringent Alien Land Law, designed to plug loopholes that had rendered the 1913 one ineffective. Two years later the Supreme Court ruled that prohibiting aliens from owning land did not violate the Fourteenth Amendment. That same year it interpreted the naturalization laws as making someone born in Japan ineligible for citizenship. In *Gung Lum v. Rice* (1927) the Court effectively condemned Asians to share the legal discrimination visited on African Americans, announcing that a Mississippi school district might, without violating the Equal Protection Clause, exclude a girl of Chinese ancestry from its white school, as long as it provided a separate "colored" one for black, brown, and yellow children.

World War II and After. Legal discrimination against Asians on the West Coast reached its height during World War II when approximately 112,000 persons of Japanese ancestry (over 70,000 of them U.S. citizens) were subjected to a curfew, then banned from coastal areas and required to report to collection centers for transportation to concentration camps in the interior. The Supreme Court avoided passing on the legality of the concentration camps, but in *Hirabayashi v. United States* (1943) and *Korematsu v. United States* (1944) it affirmed the constitutionality of the curfew and the exclusion order, respectively. *Korematsu* eventually became the legal authority for the proposition that all classifications based on race are inherently suspect, and therefore constitutional only if they serve some compelling governmental interest. At the time however, these Japanese American cases were, as the Yale Law School Professor Eugene Rostow astutely observed, a "disaster."

African Americans' rights, on the other hand, benefited from World War II. Fighting a racist regime in Germany forced whites to confront the similarities between Nazi racial policies and their own. For blacks, defending freedom by serving in a segregated military was unacceptable; men of military age especially became increasingly militant in demanding their rights. A. Philip Randolph of the Brotherhood of Sleeping Car Porters even threatened to lead blacks in a massive march on Washington. Because the war opened up economic opportunities for African Americans and spurred increased migration to the North and West, it increased black political leverage, a new reality President Roosevelt acknowledged by banning racial discrimination in the federal government and defense industries and setting up a Fair Employment Practices Commission. By the end of the war some small steps had even been taken toward integration of the once rigidly segregated armed forces. African American veterans returned from the war determined to fight for equality at home. So did Mexican American veterans, who organized the militant American GI Forum.

The veterans' return home was also followed by the development of the Cold War. As the United States plunged into competition with the Soviet Union for power and influence around the world, racial discrimination became a foreign policy liability, something communist propagandists could use to discredit America. The Cold War created an imperative for racial change that African American leaders exploited, and to which government officials responded. Among those who did so was President Truman, who among other things issued an executive order desegregating the armed forces. Truman's surprise reelection victory in 1948, despite the defection of many Southern Democrats, confirmed the growing political power of African Americans and their allies.

African Americans were not the only minority that benefited from the egalitarian thrust generated by World War II and the Cold War. In 1946 a federal district court in California declared segregation of Mexican American students in an Orange County school district unconstitutional; two years later a Texas court held illegal the practice of designating separate school buildings for Mexican Americans. In 1946 the California legislature repealed the statute authorizing segregation of Asians in the state's public schools.

The Supreme Court had already enlisted in what became a multifaceted attack on racial discrimination. Its decision in *Smith v. Allwright* (1944) had advanced the interests of both African Americans and Mexican Americans by overruling *Grovey v. Townsend* and striking down Texas's white primary. The ruling was facilitated by one in a 1941 nonracial case holding that because primaries were part of the machinery used to choose state officials, they were state action. This meant, the Court now decided, that they had to comply with the Fifteenth Amendment, no matter who ran them.

The Supreme Court also handed down a series of rulings against racial discrimination in interstate transportation, based on the Interstate Commerce Act (ICA) and the Commerce Clause of the Constitution. In *Mitchell v. United States* (1941), at the urging of the U.S. Department of Justice, the Supreme Court ruled that a railroad had violated the ICA when it prevented an African American congressman from using a Pullman sleeping car available to whites. In *Morgan v. Virginia* (1946) it found the application to an interstate bus passenger of a state law requiring segregation on common carriers a violation of the Commerce Clause. Highlighting where its biases now lay, the Court, using reasoning seemingly contradictory to that underlying *Morgan*, held two years later that Michigan had not infringed on the federal commerce power when it prohibited an excursion boat company from discriminating against African Americans in service between Detroit and a Canadian island. Finally, in *Henderson v. United States* (1950) it held restricting black passengers to a screened-off portion of dining cars, a common practice of southern railroads, to be a violation of the ICA.

The Court was by now willing to resort to quite innovative legal reasoning to rule against segregation. *Shelley v. Kraemer* (1948, from the border state of Missouri) and *Barrows v. Jackson* (1953, from California), both of which involved restrictive covenants, demonstrated this. The Court did not reverse its earlier decision that these were lawful. Instead, encouraged by the Justice Department, it ruled that although restrictive covenants were private agreements, judicial enforcement of them would be state action violating the Equal Protection Clause. In Barrows it decided that while a white seller who had been sued for damages for breaking such a covenant had suffered no constitutional wrong himself, he could assert as a defense the equal protection rights of the African American purchaser.

Although less significant nationally than restrictive covenants, the segregation of public education was far more important in the South, where it was viewed as one of the pillars of white supremacy. After two 1950 Supreme Court decisions, that pillar was clearly crumbling. For both tactical and financial reasons, the NAACP decided to move away from seeking equalization of black and white schools within the separate-but-equal framework and toward challenging segregation itself. In *Sweatt v. Painter* (1950) it attacked the policies of the University of Texas Law School, which would not admit African Americans. After the NAACP filed suit on behalf of black applicant Herman Sweatt, the state legislature appropriated some money to build a separate law school. Until it was ready Sweatt could attend a three-room school near the state capitol, staffed by three part-time professors and lacking either an adequate library or a law review. The Court held Texas had not met the demands of the Equal Protection Clause. Besides the obvious physical differences between the two institutions, it noted that "the University of Texas Law School possesses to a far greater degree those qualities which are incapable of objective measurement but which make for greatness in a law school." Among the factors it cited were prestige, influence of alumni, and opportunities for interaction with the white majority with whom practicing lawyers had to deal. In *McLaurin v. Oklahoma State Regents* (1950) the Court relied even more on intangible differences. Oklahoma had admitted G. W. McLaurin to its education doctoral program, but segregated him within it, requiring him to use a desk located in an anteroom of the classroom and to sit at special tables in the library and cafeteria. Although McLaurin was receiving an education in all tangible ways exactly like what white students were getting, he had been denied the equal protection of the laws, the Court ruled, because he could not engage in the sort of discussion and exchange of ideas with them that was essential to learning his profession. The Court's new emphasis on intangibles evinced commitment to a conception of equality that made providing a separate but equal education impossible.

McLaurin and *Sweatt* emboldened the NAACP to ask the Court for complete repudiation of the separate-but-equal rule in cases challenging school segregation in South Carolina, Virginia, Delaware, Kansas, and Washington, D.C. These were argued in 1952 and reargued in 1953. Reargument did not change the outcome of *Brown v. Board of Education* (1954); it was a tactic intended to provide time to unify the Court. It meant however that because a national election intervened, the justices heard arguments by both the outgoing Truman (Democratic) and incoming Eisenhower (Republican) administrations. Both took the position that school segregation was unconstitutional, thus seemingly establishing that there was broad support, outside the South, for that proposition. The delay also meant that by the time *Brown* was decided Chief Justice Fred Vinson, who favored retaining the separate-but-equal standard, had died. His replacement, Earl Warren, not only voted the other way but also used his considerable political skills to unite all of the justices behind a single opinion. This bluntly announced that in the field of public education the doctrine of separate but equal had no place: "Separate educational facilities are inherently unequal."

Yet *Brown* did not completely repudiate the separate-but-equal doctrine. Indeed Warren relied on the uniqueness of public education to justify the result. The Court however quickly began to declare the segregation of a wide range of public facilities unconstitutional, using one-sentence opinions that cited only *Brown* or no authority at all. Although narrowly written Warren's opinion was quickly broadened into the most important judicial endorsement ever of the principle of equality.

Civil Rights Revolution. What *Brown* did not do was eliminate school segregation. Washington, D.C., and the border states abandoned it rather quickly, but the Deep South resorted to massive resistance, which sometimes turned violent. In *Cooper v. Aaron* (1958) the Supreme Court dramatically announced that it would not accept violence as an excuse for delaying implementation of a desegregation plan, but officials simply closed their schools rather than obey orders to integrate. Eventually, under pressure from parents and business groups to reopen them, authorities opted for token compliance, achieved through complicated pupil placement schemes, grade-a-year plans, and, increasingly after 1963, freedom of choice. These devices eliminated legal barriers to black children attending white schools, but did not produce integration. As late as the 1963–1964 academic year, only 1.2 percent of African American students in eleven southern states were attending school with whites.

What actually integrated southern schools was not *Brown* but federal legislation. The increasing political power of African Americans and northern liberals engendered the enactment in 1957 and 1960 of the first new civil rights laws since Reconstruction. Modest measures, they provided some additional protection for voting rights. The 1957 law also fixed qualifications for federal jurors, and the 1960 act made arson and bombing federal crimes if the perpetrators crossed state lines.

The *Brown* decision had triggered a flurry of these crimes, along with beatings and riots, in the South. This violence escalated in response to the direct-action tactics a burgeoning civil rights movement employed with increasing frequency following lunch counter sit-ins in Greensboro, North Carolina, in February 1960. Defenders of the racial status quo countered sit-ins, Freedom Rides, marches, and voter registration drives with cross burnings, beatings, bombings, and murder. A political reaction against *Brown* had thrust into office in the South public officials who not only tolerated but also encouraged and even assisted the perpetrators of this violence. Police attacked peaceful protesters with clubs, dogs, and fire hoses. The media attention this orgy of anti–civil rights violence received, especially on national television, aroused a previously apathetic northern public to demand more meaningful legislation.

The result was the Civil Rights Act of 1964. Proposed by President John Kennedy and actually enacted in the administration of Lyndon Johnson after Kennedy's assassination, this was the most important and comprehensive civil rights law in American history. Its most controversial provision, Title II, forbade discrimination in places of public accommodation on the basis of race, color, religion, or national origin. This title was strikingly similar to an 1875 statute the Supreme Court had invalidated in 1883 because it regulated private conduct rather than state action. Congress sought to get around that ruling by basing the new legislation on the Commerce Clause, rather than the Fourteenth Amendment. Accepting this somewhat disingenuous approach, the Court upheld Title II in *Heart of Atlanta Motel, Inc. v. United States* (1964). In *Katzenbach v. McClung* (1964) the justices approved its use against a neighborhood restaurant whose only connection with interstate commerce was buying out of state about half the meat it sold.

March on Washington. A National Broadcasting Company television crew at the March on Washington, 28 August 1963. US Information Agency, Press and Publications Service, National Archives

Less controversial in 1964 than Title II but a far greater source of controversy and litigation later was Title VII, which prohibited discrimination in employment on the basis of sex as well as race. Other important provisions authorized the attorney general to initiate school desegregation suits (Title IV) and the Civil Rights Commission to investigate racially and religiously motivated denials of equal protection (Title V). Title VI prohibited discrimination on the basis of race, religion, or national origin in programs receiving federal financial assistance. This meant that southern school districts wanting their share of a huge federal aid-to-education appropriation passed by Congress in 1965 would have to comply with *Brown*. Charged with implementing Title VI, the Department of Health, Education, and Welfare (HEW) in 1966 issued guidelines requiring districts to demonstrate actual progress toward eliminating segregation and setting forth goals and timetables they must meet. The U.S. Court of Appeals for the Fifth Circuit adopted HEW's approach in *United States v. Jefferson County Board of Education* (1966), announcing that district courts in that circuit must follow it in writing decrees in school desegregation cases. The Fifth Circuit emphasized that the only remedy for a system-wide policy of segregation was "a system wide policy of integration." Earlier, Chief Judge John Parker of the Fourth Circuit had declared that all *Brown* required was an end to segregation (governmentally enforced separation of the races), not the actual mixing of white and black students in schools; but the Supreme Court disagreed. In *Green v. County School Board of New Kent County* (1969), confronting an obvious attempt to avoid eliminating segregation by a district with only two schools that adopted a freedom of choice plan, rather than simply splitting itself into two attendance zones, it ruled that the school board bore the burden of demonstrating it was dismantling its old dual system. Only numerical proof of actual integration would now constitute compliance with *Brown*. By the 1972–1973 school year 91.3 percent of African American elementary and secondary students in the South (exclusive of Tennessee and Texas) were attending school with whites.

The increase in African American political participation was equally dramatic. Title I of the 1964 Civil Rights Act included provisions intended to provide effective enforcement of the right to vote. Rampant franchise discrimination continued, however, and in early 1965

Martin Luther King Jr. staged a series of demonstrations against it in Selma, Alabama. Sheriffs' deputies and state troopers brutally attacked the demonstrators, and 25,000 northern liberals then poured into Alabama to join King on a march from Selma to the state capitol in Montgomery. Selma spurred enactment of the Voting Rights Act of 1965, a tough law filled with provisions designed to combat tactics whites had long employed to keep African Americans from voting. It suspended the use of devices such as literacy tests in states and parts of states where less than half those of voting age had registered or voted in the 1964 presidential election. It also authorized the appointment of federal examiners in states with a history of violating the Fifteenth Amendment, and empowered them to prepare their own registration lists. To prevent creative southerners from simply devising new gimmicks to keep African Americans from voting, Congress required states and localities covered by the act to obtain advance approval from the Justice Department or from a federal district court in Washington for any new voting requirements or procedures. Although southerners claimed it went beyond what the Fifteenth Amendment empowered Congress to do, the Supreme Court upheld the constitutionality of the Voting Rights Act in *South Carolina v. Katzenbach* (1966). It also found valid a northern-directed section banning an English-language literacy requirement that New York had adopted to keep Puerto Ricans from voting.

The impact of the Voting Rights Act on the South was dramatic. Between 1964 and 1969 African American registration rose from 36 to 65 percent. By 1968 at least 120 African Americans had won elective office in the states where federal inspectors had been utilized. In 1970 Congress extended the law's preclearance requirement for five years, and in 1975 it added seven more. In 1982 it extended the law's life an additional twenty-five years, while also amending it to prohibit existing electoral laws and practices that although not originally adopted for discriminatory purposes now had the effect of keeping African Americans from winning as many offices as their population warranted.

Along with the Voting Rights Act and the Civil Rights Act of 1964, the egalitarian ferment of the 1960s also inspired enactment of the Civil Rights Act of 1968. This prohibited discrimination in the sale or rental of most housing and criminalized interference by violence or intimidation with the enjoyment of a variety of benefits and activities provided for by the Constitution and federal legislation. Six titles guaranteed Native Americans living under tribal rule most of the rights enumerated in the Bill of Rights and the Fourteenth Amendment.

Congress also struck at the poll tax by amending the Constitution. On 27 August 1962 it passed the Twenty-fourth Amendment, which forbade states and the federal government to deny or abridge the right of a citizen to vote in a presidential or congressional election because of failure to pay such a tax. By early 1964 the amendment had won ratification and was part of the Constitution. Two years later in *Harper v. Virginia Board of Elections* (1966), the Supreme Court held that the assessment of a poll tax for the privilege of voting in a state election violated the Equal Protection Clause.

In recent years historians and political scientists have stressed the role of Congress in expanding civil rights during the 1960s and denigrated the accomplishments of the Supreme Court, but the contributions the Court made under the leadership (1953–1968) of Chief Justice Earl Warren were substantial. It consistently upheld as constitutional legislation that stretched previous conceptions of the scope of congressional authority. It also consistently overturned, on a variety of grounds, state convictions of participants in the direct-action campaign against segregation. These rulings, often inconsistent with preexisting legal doctrine, created complications later in several areas of the law, but they ensured eventual appellate reversal of almost all the convictions of civil rights demonstrators in southern courts.

Finally, the Court rendered decisions enlarging the civil rights to which Congress was extending protection. In *Jones v. Alfred H. Mayer Co.* (1968), for example, it interpreted the Civil Rights Act of 1866 as creating a prohibition on discrimination in the sale or rental of housing broader than the one Congress had just included, two months earlier, in the Civil Rights Act of 1968. Earlier, in *Burton v. Wilmington Parking Authority* (1961), the Court had held that when a private restaurant rented space from a municipal parking garage, its conduct became state action and the Equal Protection Clause prohibited it from discriminating on the basis of race.

The Supreme Court in this period championed equal rights not only for African Americans but also for Mexican Americans. Indeed, two weeks before rendering its historic decision in *Brown v. Board of Education*, it had acknowledged Hispanics' historic subordination in *Hernandez v. Texas* (1954). Rejecting the contention that "there are only two classes—White and Negro—within the contemplation of the Fourteenth Amendment," the Court had ruled that systematically excluding Mexican Americans from Texas juries violated the Fourteenth Amendment. Thus fortified by the Equal Protection Clause, an increasingly assertive Mexican American population shared in many of the civil rights gains of African Americans during the 1960s. Yet legal recognition of their discrete status was important. In 1970 a federal district judge in South Texas held that because they were an identifiable ethnic group, it was a subterfuge to combine Mexican

Americans with African Americans to meet school integration requirements.

Progress Halted. Only three years later, however, *San Antonio Independent School District v. Rodriguez* held that Texas had not violated the Equal Protection Clause by relying primarily on local property taxes to fund public education. This was so even though that system resulted in huge disparities in per-pupil expenditures between predominantly white and predominantly Mexican American districts in the same metropolitan area. *Rodriguez* was only one of many indications that the augmentation of minority civil rights had stalled, victim of a white backlash, which began after 1965 rioting in Watts (a black section of Los Angeles) and grew as civil disturbances swept the African American ghettos of dozens of other cities over the next three years. In part spurring this reaction was the Black Power movement, spearheaded by the Black Panther Party, whose violent antiwhite rhetoric far outran the violence of its deeds. By 1966 the political coalition that had secured enactment of the Civil Rights Act of 1964 and the Voting Rights Act was starting to disintegrate. In 1968 Republican Richard Nixon captured the presidency, in part by openly wooing southern white voters. Over the next four decades his party would control the White House for all but twelve years, its reign interrupted only by the administrations of two moderate Democrats from the South, Jimmy Carter and Bill Clinton. Some Republican presidents, such as George W. Bush, made a greater effort to appeal to African Americans than did others, such as Nixon and Ronald Reagan, but the country was now governed by a coalition that reflected the values of the segment of the country least sympathetic to civil rights.

Fueling this anti–civil rights reaction was busing. In *Swann v. Charlotte-Mecklenburg County Board of Education* (1971) the Supreme Court held that ordering the transportation of students from one school to another was a method federal judges could employ to achieve integration. Two years later, in *Keyes v. School District No. 1, Denver Colorado*, the Court held that busing could be mandated even in districts where segregation had never been required by law, but existed primarily because of segregated housing patterns—provided there had been some actions by school officials that contributed to the situation. Since housing segregation was a nationwide problem, busing became a nationwide phenomenon. Parental resistance, notable especially in virulent rioting in Boston, was at least as strong in the border states and in the North as in the Deep South. The Supreme Court responded to the antibusing furor with *Milliken v. Bradley* (1974), holding that judges could not combine primarily white suburban with heavily black central-city school districts in order to achieve the integration of large urban areas. Without that, real integration was impossible. In 1991 the Court held that once a school system had attained "unitary" status, further action was not required to preserve integration, if demographic change upset the racial balance. In the 1990s, after decades of progress toward integration, southern schools began to grow more segregated.

Even in fields where past achievements were not being lost, little was being done to build on them. The Supreme Court's ruling in *Washington v. Davis* (1976) was typical. That decision, holding that a facially neutral qualification exam that resulted in far fewer blacks than whites being hired would not violate the Equal Protection Clause unless it could be shown to have been adopted for a discriminatory purpose, made it more difficult for African Americans to obtain public employment. *McKleskey v. Kemp* (1987) came to a similar conclusion with respect to the Georgia death penalty, saying that even though it produced hugely disproportionate numbers of executions of African Americans, it was constitutional because there was no proof it had been either adopted or applied for racially discriminatory reasons. Likewise, in *City of Mobile v. Bolden* (1980), the Supreme Court held that only electoral practices shown to have been instituted or maintained for discriminatory reasons violated the Fifteenth Amendment.

Congress and the Supreme Court were no longer the champions of civil rights they had once been, but the nature of the issues confronting them was changing, too. As the twentieth century gave way to the twenty-first, Americans were fighting their most bitter civil rights battles over affirmative action. Rather than discrimination against African Americans, these fights concerned efforts to make up for the effects of discriminatory treatment they had received in the past; alienated whites excoriated these efforts as "reverse discrimination." In *Regents of the University of California v. Bakke* (1978) the Supreme Court, in a confusingly fragmented group of opinions, had appeared to say that racial quotas for purposes of affirmative action were unlawful but that it was permissible to consider race along with other factors in deciding whom to admit to graduate programs. As the years passed the Court grew increasingly disaffected with affirmative action, especially in the employment context. In *Adarand Constructors, Inc. v. Pena* (1995) it announced that even racial classifications designed to help minorities were unconstitutional "unless they are narrowly tailored measures that further compelling governmental interests." Many predicted the imminent demise of affirmative action. In *Grutter v. Bollinger* (2003), however, despite applying its new "compelling governmental interest" test in a law school admissions case, the Court, urged by the military

Arrest at a Protest. A demonstrator is arrested at New York's City Hall during a rally for greater civil rights for gays and lesbians, 1973. Although the connection is disputed by some, many consider the gay rights movement, especially the struggle for marriage rights, to be a continuation of the civil rights movement. Photograph by Bettye Lane. © BETTYE LANE

and many business leaders, reiterated by a narrow 5–4 margin essentially the position it had taken in *Bakke*.

Affirmative action, clearly the most controversial civil rights development of the late twentieth century remained constitutional—at least in some contexts. The revolution that had transformed the place of African Americans in society and law after World War II was obviously over. It was equally clear however that there would be no return to the blatant denials of civil rights that had disgraced the Jim Crow era.

[*See also* Affirmative Action; Black Panther Party; Black Power Movement; Black Radical Congress; *Brown v. Board of Education*; Civil Rights, International; Civil Rights, State Actions; Civil Rights, White Responses and Resistance to; Civil Rights Act of 1957; Civil Rights Act of 1960; Civil Rights Act of 1964; Civil Rights and the Media; Civil Rights Movement; Congress, African Americans in; Congressional Black Caucus; Congress of Racial Equality; Constitution, U.S.; Desegregation and Integration; Discrimination; Equal Employment Opportunity Commission; Fair Employment Practices Commission; Fair Housing Act (1968); Federal Bureau of Investigation; Jim Crow Laws; Laws and Legislation; Martyrdom and Civil Rights; *Missouri ex rel. Gaines v. Canada*; *Plessy v. Ferguson* and Segregation; Segregation; Segregation in Federal Government; *Smith v. Allwright*; Social Sciences and Civil Rights; Supreme Court; Voting Rights; Voting Rights Act; *and biographical entries on figures mentioned in this article*.]

BIBLIOGRAPHY

Barnes, Catherine. *Journey from Jim Crow: The Desegregation of Southern Transit*. New York: Columbia University Press, 1983. Excellent on transportation cases.

Belknap, Michal R. *Federal Law and Southern Order: Racial Violence and Constitutional Conflict in the Post-Brown South*. Athens: University of Georgia Press, 1987. A history of the fight against anti–civil rights violence in the 1950s and 1960s.

Belknap, Michal R., ed. *Civil Rights, the White House and the Justice Department 1945–1968*. 18 vols. New York: Garland, 1991. A huge collection of documents from various federal agencies, including the extremely valuable A. B. Caldwell Papers, otherwise available only at the University of Arkansas.

Bender, Leslie, and Daan Braveman. *Power, Privilege and Law: A Civil Rights Reader*. St. Paul, Minn.: West Publishing, 1995. A collection of cases and essays designed primarily, but not exclusively, for lawyers.

Cortner, Richard. *Civil Rights and Public Accommodations: The Heart of "Atlanta Motel" and "McClung" Cases*. Lawrence: University Press of Kansas, 2001. Although written by a political scientist, a very thoroughly researched historical monograph.

Douglas, Davison M. *Jim Crow Moves North: The Battle over Northern School Segregation, 1865–1954*. New York: Cambridge University Press, 2005. An insightful study that provides understanding of the complex legal relationships between white and black students in northern schools.

Dudziak, Mary L. *Cold War Civil Rights: Race and the Image of American Democracy*. Princeton, N.J.: Princeton University Press, 2000. Makes a persuasive argument for the influence of foreign policy considerations on civil rights.

Finkelman, Paul. "Civil Rights in Historical Context: In Defense of *Brown*." *Harvard Law Review* 118 (January 2005): 973–1029. A critical review of Klarman's *From Jim Crow to Civil Rights*, which it faults on several grounds.

Graham, Hugh Davis. *The Civil Rights Era: Origins and Development of National Policy, 1960–1972*. New York: Oxford University Press, 1989. A massive and extremely detailed study that focuses on civil rights legislation.

Halpern, Stephen C. *On the Limits of the Law: The Ironic Legacy of Title VI of the 1964 Civil Rights Act*. Baltimore: Johns Hopkins University Press, 1995. Interesting analysis by a political scientist.

Hine, Darlene Clark. *Black Victory: The Rise and Fall of the White Primary in Texas*. Millwood, N.J.: KTO Press, 1979; Columbia: University of Missouri Press, 2003. Good study of the crucial voting rights cases from the 1930s and 1940s.

Irons, Peter. *Jim Crow's Children: The Broken Promise of the "Brown" Decision*. New York: Viking, 2002. An extremely readable study by a lawyer–political scientist that is particularly valuable because it traces historical developments almost to the present.

Kim, Hyung-chan. *A Legal History of Asian Americans, 1790–1990*. Westport, Conn.: Greenwood Press, 1994. A good short survey.

Klarman, Michael J. *From Jim Crow to Civil Rights: The Supreme Court and the Struggle for Racial Equality*. New York: Oxford University Press, 2004. Massive and brilliant study of the Jim Crow era that ends with the reaction to *Brown v. Board of Education*. Advances a controversial argument about the relationship between *Brown v. Board of Education* and the success of the civil rights movement.

Klarman, Michael J. "How *Brown* Changed Race Relations: The Backlash Thesis." 81 *Journal of American History* (June 1994): 81–118.

Kluger, Richard. *Simple Justice: The History of* Brown v. Board of Education *and Black America's Struggle for Equality*. 2d ed.; New York: Alfred A. Knopf, 2004. Still the most moving account of the events along the long road to *Brown*.

Landsberg, Brian K. *Enforcing Civil Rights: Race Discrimination and the Department of Justice*. Lawrence: University Press of Kansas, 1997. Account of how civil rights are enforced, by a government lawyer involved in doing it for over twenty years.

Lawson, Steven F. *Black Ballot: Voting Rights in the South, 1944–1969*. New York: Columbia University Press, 1976. Excellent study spanning a crucial period.

Morin, Jose Luis. *Latino/a Rights and Justice in the United States*. Durham, N.C.: Carolina Academic Press, 2005. A good introduction for those seeking a basic knowledge of the subject.

Nieman, Donald G. *Promises to Keep: African-Americans and the Constitutional Order, 1776 to the Present*. New York: Oxford University Press, 1991. A wonderful short summary that is now, unfortunately, becoming somewhat dated.

Patterson, James T. *"Brown v. Board of Education": A Civil Rights Milestone and Its Troubled Legacy*. New York: Oxford University Press, 2001. Discusses the case and its effects.

Tushnet, Mark V. *Making Civil Rights Law: Thurgood Marshall and the Supreme Court, 1936–1961*. New York: Oxford University Press, 1994. The best source there is on the man who was for many years the NAACP's leading litigator, and many of the cases he tried as a lawyer.

Tushnet, Mark V. *The NAACP's Legal Strategy against Segregated Education, 1925–1950*. Chapel Hill: University of North Carolina Press, 1987. Makes a strong case for the extreme significance of *Sweatt v. Painter* and *McLaurin v. Oklahoma State Regents*.

Wilkinson, J. Harvie. *From "Brown" to "Bakke": The Supreme Court and School Integration: 1954–1978*. New York: Oxford University Press, 1979. A thoughtful and readable analysis by a lawyer who was sometimes mentioned as a possible George W. Bush Supreme Court nominee.

—MICHAL BELKNAP

CIVIL RIGHTS, INTERNATIONAL. Most of the history written about the African American civil rights movement has focused on the topic from a domestic perspective. However, domestic policy merged with international policy as the Cold War and the civil rights movement converged.

Civil Rights and National Security. When the civil rights movement commenced during the 1950s, it was already deeply entwined with the international Cold War and anticolonialist politics. After America's military helped defeat Nazism in World War II, U.S. foreign policy shifted to an emphasis on the Cold War. Its former World War II ally, the Communist Soviet Union, was now the principal rival of the United States in the quest for influence around the world, including in Africa, South America, and the Caribbean, and the Soviet Union held up the mistreatment of black Americans as a sign of the failure of democracy and of the hypocrisy of the U.S. government.

International condemnation regarding issues such as lynching, Jim Crow, and racism was nearly always an important factor in civil rights decisions made by the U.S. government. For example, the international media coverage of angry mobs of white people gathered in front of Central High School in Little Rock, Arkansas, preventing the entrance of African American children caused near irreparable harm to America's reputation as a nation with liberty and justice for all. Thus when President Dwight D. Eisenhower enforced the *Brown v. Board of Education* (1954) decision in Little Rock in 1957 with an executive order directing the use of federal troops, he was acting in the interest of national security. As he addressed the nation, Eisenhower made note of the harm that was being done to the prestige, influence, and safety of the United States throughout the world.

During the summer of 1963 when Sheriff Eugene "Bull" Connor ordered the fire-hosing of nonviolent demonstrators—mostly children—in Birmingham, Alabama, the foreign press's coverage proved highly damaging to the U.S. reputation abroad. Scenes of police dogs being unleashed on children, as well as of fire hoses set at dangerous levels being sprayed on people, forced the John F. Kennedy administration to intervene more aggressively in the negotiations between the Southern Christian Leadership Conference and the white business community. Later in the summer Kennedy even sent troops to the University of Alabama so that two African American students could be enrolled, forcing the staunch segregationist Governor George Wallace to step aside. After giving a historic speech on civil rights the same night, 11 June 1963, Kennedy submitted his civil rights bill to Congress a week later.

In 1963 when Secretary of State Dean Rusk made an appearance before the Senate Commerce Committee to testify on behalf of the public accommodations bill—an earlier version of the Civil Rights Act of 1964—he argued that its passage was essential to winning the Cold War, pointing out that the segregation faced by African and Asian diplomats undermined national security. President Lyndon B. Johnson eventually also signed the Voting Rights Act of 1965 into law, yet it was widely believed that massive resentment from white southerners would lead to the Democratic Party's forfeiting its hold on the South in future elections. With each successive civil rights victory, white southerners became even more convinced of a vast, worldwide Communist conspiracy, yet the State Department still preferred that its image abroad be closely aligned with that of the integrationist civil rights movement. Such interventions by the federal government in the face of fierce anticommunist hysteria testify to the primacy given to foreign relations during the civil rights period.

African Americans as Agents of Change. It would be historically inaccurate, however, to view the trajectory of the civil rights movement as one solely manipulated by the State Department, or to minimize the Pan-African and transnational agency of African Americans themselves in advancing the aims and goals of the civil rights movement. Individuals such as Paul Robeson; Ferdinand Smith, the Jamaican cofounder of the influential National Maritime Union; Cyril Lionel Robert James, a Marxist Trotskyite theoretician; Amy Jacques Garvey, coleader of Universal Negro Improvement Association and coeditor of *Negro World*; Claudia Jones, an influential activist in the Communist Party; George Padmore, the head of the Negro Bureau of the Communist International of Labor Unions; James Baldwin, an influential author; Bayard Rustin, a civil rights activist and principal organizer of the March on Washington in 1963; Alphaeus Hunton, an activist and philosopher; Shirley Graham and W. E. B. Du Bois; and Mabel and Robert F. Williams, NAACP leaders in Monroe, North Carolina—just to name a handful—were instrumental in linking the domestic and international struggles of African peoples transnationally and laying the groundwork for the civil rights movement's sustained international engagement. Such individuals and organizations like Marcus Garvey's Universal Negro Improvement Association, Elijah Muhammad's Nation of Islam, the Council on African Affairs, and the International African Services Bureau stood in a long tradition of Pan-African and international agency extending back to the eighteenth century.

Nevertheless it was the involvement of African American soldiers in battle during the two world wars that sowed the seeds of massive protests against segregation. For a brief spell, during the period leading up to President Harry S. Truman's 1948 executive order to desegregate the military's armed forces, mainstream African American leadership primarily defined the progress of the race in domestic terms. Not merely coincidental, this was a direct consequence of a fierce campaign by the Federal Bureau of Investigation (FBI) alongside other law enforcement agencies to undermine organizations and leadership aligned with Soviet policies or politics that interfered with its Cold War initiatives.

By 1947 the leading civil rights organization, the NAACP, had aligned itself with the administration's Cold War politics and purged radicals from its organization in the face of the government's Red Scare repression. Du Bois, the NAACP's most prominent member, remained highly critical of U.S. foreign policy, and he was dismissed from the NAACP in 1948. However, it was not until 1951 when he was indicted under the Foreign Agents Registration Act of 1938 that he was effectively isolated from the civil rights leadership establishment. Although he was acquitted in 1952, the State Department refused to renew his passport until 1958.

In 1950 when the influential human rights activist and artist Paul Robeson refused to stop speaking out against injustice, he was denied a passport to travel abroad and was thus relegated to the sidelines during the most critical period of the civil rights movement. The longtime influential political organizer and Communist Party member Claudia Jones was repeatedly arrested and eventually served a year in prison before being deported to Great Britain in 1955, as was the radical Marxist theoretician Cyril Lionel Robert James in 1957; both were Trinidadians. Thus activists such as Du Bois were marginalized or, as in the case of Robert F. Williams, exiled at the height of the civil rights movement as a result of governmental repression.

Nonetheless, the internationalization of the African American civil rights struggle was sustained in other ways. As thousands of African Americans fought for their nation yet returned home to face worse prejudices than did the German prisoners of war they stood guard over, the slowly unfolding irony of racism at home and abroad gained traction. In addition more than 2 million African Americans left the South in search of jobs in the defense industry, which had also been desegregated, weakening the white southerners' stranglehold on black labor and political mobility. There were also a significant number of artists, writers, and musicians, like James Baldwin, Richard Wright, and Josephine Baker, who were part of a vibrant expatriate community in Paris and who played a critical role in building ties with the European Left.

Pan-Africanism. Perhaps an even more important factor in strengthening the bonds of international solidarity during the civil rights movement was the fact that by 1960 seventeen African nations had achieved independence, making racism an important issue in the United Nations. After the Cuban Revolution in 1959, its leaders sought to link its struggle with those of newly independent African nations, as well as with the more radical segment of the civil rights movement. Thus the U.S. government had to contend not only with international pressures from its archenemy the Soviet Union but also with the emergence of a third force in the Caribbean and Africa.

Although Ghana's president Kwame Nkrumah emphasized African continental unity, he also adhered to the vision of Pan-African internationalism put forth by his mentors Padmore and Du Bois, which meant the inclusion of the African diaspora in his conception of African unity. Padmore became a citizen of Ghana, as did Du Bois before his death in 1963. Malcolm X spent a considerable amount of time in Accra, Ghana, lobbying African leaders there to put pressure on the U.S. government through the United Nations, and he seriously contemplated citizenship in this African nation. Lesser-known yet equally influential individuals like the activist and writer Julian Mayfield, editor of *African Review* and cofounder of Ghana's branch of the Organization of Afro-American Unity, took up residence in Ghana. The Student Nonviolent Coordinating Committee leader Stokely Carmichael (Kwame Ture) settled in Guinea.

[*See also* Anticommunism and Civil Rights; Cold War; Communism and African Americans; Foreign Policy; Pan-Africanism; Peace Movements, International; *and biographical entries on figures mentioned in this article*.]

BIBLIOGRAPHY

Anderson, Carol. *Eyes off the Prize: The United Nations and the African American Struggle for Human Rights, 1944–1955*. New York: Cambridge University Press, 2003.

Dudziak, Mary L. *Cold War and Civil Rights: Race and the Image of American Democracy*. Princeton, N.J.: Princeton University Press, 2002.

Joseph, Peniel. *Waiting til the Midnight Hour: A Narrative History of Black Power in America*. New York: Henry Holt, 2006.

Kornweibel, Theodore. *Seeing Red: Federal Campaigns against Black Militancy, 1919–1925*. Bloomington: Indiana University Press, 1999.

Plummer, Brenda G. *Rising Wind: Black Americans and U.S. Foreign Affairs, 1935–1960*. Chapel Hill: University of North Carolina Press, 1996.

Von Eschen, Penny M. *Race against Empire: Black Americans and Anticolonialism, 1937–1957*. Ithaca, N.Y.: Cornell University Press, 1997.

Woods, Jeff. *Black Struggle, Red Scare: Segregation and Anti-Communism in the South, 1948–1968*. Baton Rouge: Louisiana State University Press, 2003.

—LARVESTER GAITHER

CIVIL RIGHTS, STATE ACTIONS AND. Most modern Americans see protection of civil rights as the obligation of the national government. During the Civil War, Congress passed laws to end slavery in the District of Columbia and the federal territories, to allow the army not only to liberate slaves but also to provide them with food and other necessities, and to prohibit racial discrimination in newly chartered streetcars in the District of Columbia. Most important, late in the war Congress sent to the states the Thirteenth Amendment, which when ratified at the end of 1865 forever prohibited slavery in the United States.

In the first years after the war, Congress expanded civil rights through the Freedmen's Bureau, the Civil Rights Act of 1866, and the Fourteenth Amendment, which when ratified in July 1868 made blacks citizens of the United States with all the rights that other Americans had. In February 1870 the states ratified the Fifteenth Amendment, prohibiting discrimination in voting on the basis of race or previous status as a slave, and then Congress went on to pass a series of laws to protect black voters and suppress the Ku Klux Klan. Finally, in the Civil Rights Act of 1875, Congress prohibited racial discrimination on public transportation and in restaurants, hotels, theaters, and other places of public accommodation.

This early commitment to civil rights was undermined by a series of Supreme Court decisions. Most important, in the *Civil Rights Cases* (1883) the Court held that the Fourteenth Amendment limited only actions by the state, not by private individuals or businesses, and that Congress had no power to regulate most private behavior. Thus the provisions of the Civil Rights Act of 1875 could not be enforced against individual owners of businesses, such as restaurants or theaters. Such private discrimination could be regulated only by the states. The southern states, where most blacks lived, did not pass such legislation, and in fact under the doctrine of "separate but equal"—which the Court approved in *Plessy v. Ferguson* (1896)—the former slave states, along with West Virginia and later Oklahoma, passed laws allowing or requiring segregation. In the same term that it struck down the

Civil Rights Act of 1875, the Court in *Pace v. Alabama* (1883) also upheld an Alabama law that made interracial marriage a criminal offense.

State Laws in the North. While the South, with the acquiescence of the Supreme Court, moved toward discrimination, the North moved in the opposite direction. From the early 1880s until World War II the states outside the South—in the North, the Midwest, and the far West—passed legislation to protect the civil rights of African Americans and other minorities. The courts in most of these states usually upheld these statutes, although enforcement was generally less strong in the earlier period than it was later on. A number of states responded to the 1883 Supreme Court decisions with laws that provided state protections where federal law no longer did.

New Jersey's Civil Rights Act of 1884 provided for substantial fines, ranging from $500 to $1,000, for acts of discrimination. This was equivalent to the buying power in the year 2000 of between $9,000 and $18,000. This law also provided the right of the complaining witness to pursue a private action of debt for $500. The law further provided for the possibility of jailing offenders for up to one year. In addition to civil rights, the law protected the right to serve on a jury and provided a fine of up to $5,000 for any official who refused to call a black person for jury service. In 1912 in *Miller v. Stampul* the New Jersey Supreme Court upheld the application of the state's 1884 civil rights law, along with a $500 fine, against a theater owner who refused to admit blacks on the same basis as whites.

Minnesota's act of 1885 prohibited hotels, restaurants, common carriers, and other businesses from denying blacks equal access. Penalties under the law included fines from $25 to $100 and jail time of thirty to ninety days. The law also allowed for civil damages of $25 to $500. Pennsylvania's law of 1887 provided a fine of $50 to $100 for denying equal access to public transportation, theaters, hotels, restaurants, concerts, "or place[s] of entertainment or amusement."

In 1884 Ohio adopted a civil rights law declaring that all its citizens were "equal before the law" and that such a status was "essential to just government." The statute prohibited private businesses from discriminating and specifically prohibited discrimination in all "inns, public conveyances on land or water, theaters and other places of public amusement." A second act, passed later the same year, amended this law to also cover "restaurants, eating-houses, barber-shops ... and all other places of public accommodation and amusement." Three years later Ohio repealed its last remaining black laws with the passage of the "Arnett bill," a law sponsored by Benjamin Arnett, a black state legislator who represented predominantly white Greene County. In 1894 Ohio strengthened its laws, raising the maximum fines for violation of the civil rights laws from $100 to $500, raising the maximum jail time from thirty days to ninety days, and, most important, providing for the first time a statutory minimum for violators of $50 or thirty days in jail. In 1896, the same year that the Court decided *Plessy*, Ohio passed a tough antilynching law.

In 1885 Nebraska passed a law entitled "An act to provide that all citizens shall be entitled to the same civil rights, and to punish all persons for violations of its provisions." In *Messenger v. State* (1889), the Nebraska Supreme Court upheld this law against a white barber who refused to shave a black man. The court declared:

> The statute will not permit him to say to one: "You were a slave or a son of a slave; therefore I will not shave you." Such prejudices are unworthy of our better manhood, and are clearly prohibited by the statute. In this state a colored man may sit upon a jury, cast his ballot at any general or special election where he is entitled to vote, and his vote will be counted, and he has the right to travel upon any public conveyance the same as if he were white. The authority of the state to prohibit discriminations on account of color in places of public resort, as a barber-shop, is undoubted, and the proprietors of such shops can adopt and enforce no rules which will not apply to white and colored alike.

In 1905 the Iowa Supreme Court upheld a judgment against a restaurant that refused to serve a black man. Similarly, in 1902 an Ohio court upheld the right of a black man to sue under a state civil rights statute after he was denied the right to use a bowling alley at a public resort.

In 1883 Michigan repealed its ban on interracial marriages and retroactively legitimized all interracial marriages that had already taken place in the state. What had once been the most volatile issue regarding race and law had suddenly and without much fanfare disappeared in Michigan. This law was adopted the same year that the U.S. Supreme Court upheld Alabama's law making such marriages illegal. In 1899 Michigan passed a new marriage law, reaffirming that interracial marriages were legal in that state.

In 1885 the Michigan legislature passed "An Act to protect all citizens in their civil rights." The law declared that all persons "within the jurisdiction" of Michigan were "entitled to the full and equal accommodations, advantages, facilities, and privileges of inns, restaurants, eating-houses, barber shops, public conveyances on land and water, theaters, and all other places of public accommodation and amusement." Penalties for violating the law included fines of up to $100 and up to a month in jail. In *Ferguson v. Gies* (1890) the Michigan Supreme Court upheld this law against a restaurant owner who refused to serve blacks in his main dining room. Speaking for the Michigan Supreme Court, Judge Allan B. Morse, a Civil War veteran who had lost an arm in combat, wrote

> in Michigan there must be and is an absolute, unconditional equality of white and colored men before the law. The white man can have no rights or privileges under the law that is denied to the black man. Socially people may do as they please within the law, and whites may associate together, as may blacks, and exclude whom they please from their dwellings and private grounds; but there can be no separation in public places between people on account of their color alone which the law will sanction.

Perhaps reflecting on why he had lost his arm, Judge Morse wrote: "The humane and enlightened judgment of our people has decided—although it cost blood and treasure to do so—that the negro is a man; a freeman; a citizen; and entitled to equal rights before the law with the white man. This decision was a just one." In 1893 Michigan banned differential life insurance rates for blacks and whites. By 1950 six other northern states had passed similar laws.

The Twentieth Century. In the twentieth century most northern states continued to pass new and stronger civil rights acts. New York passed its Civil Rights Act in 1885, and it was strengthened and amended in 1918, 1935, 1937, and four times more between 1942 and 1945. In 1945 New York passed the nation's first fair employment practices act, the Ives-Quinn Act. By 1949 New Jersey, Massachusetts, Connecticut, Oregon, Rhode Island, New Mexico, and Washington had passed similar laws. In 1950 New York prohibited discrimination in any housing that was built with public money. In 1947 the President's Committee on Civil Rights reported that "New York State, in particular, has an impressive variety of civil rights laws on its statute books."

Other states continued to pass similar laws. Michigan, for example, passed a new civil rights law in 1937 that strengthened the existing Civil Rights Act, making it applicable to

> inns, hotels, restaurants, eating houses, barber shops, billiard parlors, stores, public conveyances on land and water, theaters, motion picture houses, public educational institutions, in elevators, on escalators, in all methods of air transportation and all other places of public accommodation, amusement, and recreation, where refreshments are or may hereafter be served.

This law was sponsored by a black state senator, Charles C. Diggs. After the passage of this law there were some arrests and prosecutions for refusing blacks service. An act of 1941 prohibited discrimination in civil-service hiring, and in 1955 the state passed a full Fair Employment Practices Act. The Michigan experience, like that in New York, was copied in many other northern states. In 1947 the President's Committee on Civil Rights reported that New York and "a few other states" had made important steps toward greater civil rights, "especially in the fair employment practice field." By the time Congress passed the 1964 Civil Rights Act, twenty-two states had passed a Fair Employment Practices Act. These acts were implemented by state agencies and state courts upheld them. Twenty-one of these states were outside the South, but in 1961 Missouri also passed such a law.

By the eve of the 1954 *Brown v. Board of Education* decision, most of the states outside the South had prohibited almost all formal, de jure segregation. A few school districts in the North were formally segregated, although this segregation was in violation of state law. Many states had elaborate laws that banned discrimination in all aspects of public life. The one area where the states had failed to support civil rights, however, was in housing discrimination. The real estate industry freely and openly discriminated, with almost no state interference so long as the houses were privately owned and not built with state money.

The numerous state civil rights statutes did not create full equality in the North. But they did provide for far greater opportunity than existed in the South and for far less discrimination. Almost every northern state university was integrated before World War II, and many had been integrated since the late nineteenth century. Though not completely overcoming discrimination, these state laws provided a model that allowed Congress in the 1960s to undermine—if not completely eliminate—discrimination in most businesses and institutions that were open to the general public. The state civil rights laws passed from the 1880s through the 1950s provided the model for the Civil Rights Act of 1964, the Voting Rights Act of 1965, and Title VIII of the Civil Rights Act of 1968 (the Fair Housing Act).

[*See also* Jim Crow Laws; Laws and Legislation; Miscegenation Laws; *and entries on U.S. states*.]

BIBLIOGRAPHY

Benedict, Michael Les, and John F. Winkler, eds. *The History of Ohio Law*. Athens: Ohio University Press, 2004.

Finkelman, Paul. "Civil Rights in Historical Context: In Defense of *Brown*." *Harvard Law Review* 118 (2005): 973–1027.

Finkelman, Paul, and Martin J. Hershock, eds. *The History of Michigan Law*. Athens: Ohio University Press, 2006.

Mangum, Charles S., Jr. *The Legal Status of the Negro*. Chapel Hill: University of North Carolina Press, 1940.

Murray, Pauli, ed. *States' Laws on Race and Color* (1951). Athens: University of Georgia Press, 1997.

—PAUL FINKELMAN

CIVIL RIGHTS, WHITE RESPONSES AND RESISTANCE TO. Shattered windows, bombed-out churches, white mobs jeering at black schoolchildren, southern governors defiantly proclaiming that their states would never integrate—these are, with good reason, the images of the white response to civil rights that remain seared into American public memory. Violence always underpinned the South's system of Jim Crow segregation and black disfranchisement, and a significant number of whites were prepared to suppress violently any African American challenge to the prevailing racial hierarchy. Yet the acts of terrorism against civil rights workers and the bombast of white-supremacist politicians, though important, do not capture the full spectrum of the white response to the African American freedom struggle of the late 1940s, 1950s, and 1960s.

The term commonly used to describe white opposition to the civil rights movement, "massive resistance," implies a unified, synchronized counterattack. As leaders of the organized resistance discovered, however, strategic unanimity eluded segregationists from the start. Some whites favored an unconditional, any-means-necessary fight to preserve Jim Crow; others had no stomach for extralegal violence. Some made bald appeals to the crudest forms of racism; others fretted about respectability and spoke the more innocuous language of states' rights. And although an overwhelming majority of southern whites opposed racial integration, only a vocal minority mobilized to defend white supremacy openly. Hard-line segregationist leaders tried to coerce conformity, but white unity was always more veneer than reality.

Over time, most advocates of segregation adapted their strategies and retooled their political messages, so that by the mid-1960s brazen defiance largely had been replaced with subtler—but arguably more enduring—tactics to obstruct, delay, or undo progress toward genuine racial equality. White flight supplanted angry white mobs, and white southern voters helped lead the nation's drift toward political conservatism, giving birth to a new set of challenges for the post–civil rights era.

The Early Phases of White Resistance, 1946–1960. As African American servicemen returned home from World War II, having spent long months or even years overseas fighting for the principles of democracy, the first substantial cracks appeared in the South's repressive racial hierarchy. Emboldened by the Supreme Court ruling in *Smith v. Allwright* (1944), which outlawed the whites-only primary, African Americans mounted widespread voter registration campaigns. White southerners served notice that this invigorated black activism would face fierce resistance. In early July 1946, Medgar Evers, a soon-to-be field secretary for the NAACP, led a group of African American veterans to the county courthouse in Decatur, Mississippi, to cast ballots in the Democratic primary. There they encountered more than a dozen white men, armed and determined physically to prevent black voting—a scene replayed across the region. The postwar peace also was marred by a rash of grisly murders of African Americans, many of them veterans who had registered or voted.

Responding in part to the wave of racially motivated crimes, Harry S. Truman established the President's Committee on Civil Rights (PCCR) in late 1946. Truman's endorsement of federal civil rights legislation, however tentative, precipitated a southern political bolt from the national Democratic Party, an early expression of organized white resistance. After the Democrats added a civil rights plank to their 1948 platform, a small band of southern delegates formed the States' Rights Party—commonly referred to as the "Dixiecrats"—and nominated the South Carolina senator Strom Thurmond for president. Thurmond went on to a poorer-than-expected showing, winning only four states, all of them in the Deep South; still, southern whites delivered an unmistakable message to the national Democratic leadership.

The fear of alienating southern voters, the tense political climate of the early Cold War years, and the Republican takeover of Congress in the 1946 midterm elections combined to shelve the PCCR's legislative recommendations. Meanwhile the NAACP's legal assault on segregation continued to advance through the court system. On 17 May 1954 the Court handed down its landmark ruling in *Brown v. Board of Education*.

Many white southerners had begun to marshal the forces of resistance well before *Brown*, but the decision gave civil rights opponents a specific target and a dramatically heightened sense of urgency.

For the briefest moment following the *Brown* announcement, calm and reason prevailed in white southern communities. But the storm gathered quickly, and by the late part of 1954 the strident defenders of white supremacy had launched their counterattack. For the remainder of the decade a chorus of ardent segregationists largely drowned out—or, more accurately, snuffed out—the voices of moderate and liberal whites, and hard-line segregationists exercised a disproportionate influence over the southern political landscape.

The early phases of white resistance urged open defiance of *Brown*. In 1954 and 1955 southern lawmakers passed a dizzying array of state measures designed to uphold segregation. Several states even authorized their governors to close schools before allowing black and white children to attend class together. A handful of segregationist leaders championed "interposition," an updated version of the nineteenth-century nullification doctrine, and claimed that southern states could simply reject the validity of the Supreme Court ruling. Virginia, Alabama, Georgia, South Carolina, Mississippi, Louisiana, and North Carolina all adopted resolutions advocating some variant of interposition.

Out of this fray emerged the most concerted thrust of white political resistance: the Declaration of Constitutional Principles, better known as the "Southern Manifesto," issued 12 March 1956. Nineteen of the South's twenty-two senators and nearly three-quarters of its representatives signed the manifesto, which called *Brown* a "clear abuse of judicial power" and promised to "use all lawful means to bring about a reversal of this decision." More symbol than substance, the document nevertheless signaled that southern congressmen were ready to contest *Brown*'s enforcement.

Grassroots segregationist organizations also sprang up across the South in 1954 and 1955. Of the countless small groups that developed—many choosing names designed to drape the segregationist South with a patriotic mantle, such as the Federation for Constitutional Government—the White Citizens' Councils emerged as the most powerful. The first council formed on 11 July 1954 in the Mississippi Delta town of Indianola, under the leadership of the plantation manager and onetime Mississippi State University football star Robert B. Patterson. At its peak the councils' membership across the South may have been as high as a quarter of a million, and frequently the organization had cozy relationships with local mayors, police chiefs, state representatives, and governors.

Styling itself as a lawful, respectable alternative to the Ku Klux Klan, the Citizens' Councils nominally eschewed violence. Instead, members freely deployed other forms of intimidation to deter African American activism. Many members were bank presidents, attorneys, and other prominent professionals, and they wielded their substantial economic and social power to prevent African Americans from obtaining jobs, housing, loans, insurance, or health care. In Yazoo City, Mississippi, in 1955, fifty-three black parents signed a petition urging local compliance with *Brown*'s desegregation orders. To retaliate, the Citizens' Council purchased an advertisement in the local newspaper that contained the name and address of each signer. Virtually all of the parents suffered—their jobs lost, their businesses sabotaged, or their families threatened. Whites who ran afoul of Citizens' Council objectives also had to withstand harassment. The councils' tactics were so crippling that some historians have referred to an "economic lynch law."

Members of the organized white resistance also worked systematically to expunge African Americans from voter registration rolls. In Louisiana's Ouachita Parish, local Citizens' Council members invoked an arcane anticorruption law, intended to prevent fraudulent voting, to challenge the validity of certain registrations. More than three thousand African Americans—two-thirds of the parish's registered blacks—faced challenges, whereas only twenty-three whites did. Defenders of an all-white electorate pressured registrars to enforce constitutional interpretation or literacy tests, and often council members had sufficiently entrenched power to force out uncooperative registrars.

Alarmed by the organizational effectiveness of the NAACP and fearful that they were being outflanked, the Citizens' Councils initiated a relentless campaign to hobble that civil rights organization. The segregationist organization blanketed the South with scathing propaganda that smeared the NAACP as directed by Communists. Here the councils enjoyed support from southern state legislatures. Under the guise that the NAACP had improperly registered with the state, for example, Alabama officials tried to coerce the NAACP into surrendering lists of every member's name. When NAACP leaders refused to comply, the state barred the NAACP from operating. By the close of the 1950s, NAACP membership in the South had declined precipitously, and nearly 250 local branches had been forced to fold.

Although the officers of Citizens' Councils publicly avowed their opposition to vigilantism, in fact the organization often tacitly condoned violence against civil rights workers. Extralegal and legal means of resistance could work symbiotically: the incendiary rhetoric of council leaders created a climate of fear and implicitly promoted extremism. Even if unwilling to carry out violent acts of their own, many whites gave their unspoken consent to violence when they allowed crimes to go uninvestigated and unpunished.

The various school crises of the late 1950s revealed the intricate web of different tactics that whites used to block integration. A few communities, including Norfolk, Virginia, and Little Rock, Arkansas, closed public schools entirely for some duration. But only a fraction of white voters favored such drastic action. So-called pupil-placement plans became a popular alternative. Scrubbed free of the words "Negro," "white," or "race," these state laws permitted school districts to assign students based on factors such as academic preparation or ill-defined "character" qualities. Other state legislatures adopted freedom-of-choice laws, which put the onus on individual black parents to request transfers from segregated schools. Black parents, therefore, had not only to navigate a maze of bureaucratic procedures but also to subject their families to inevitable harassment from hostile whites. Under both types of plans school boards could summarily reject black transfer applications. To challenge the statutes, civil rights attorneys had to initiate separate lawsuits against individual districts, an impossible task. As a result school integration proceeded glacially or essentially stalled.

Grassroots protests and occasional vigilantism supplemented the political maneuvers. The most uncompromising segregationists despised pupil-placement plans, which, at least in theory, permitted black enrollment at white schools. Instead they encouraged white parents to take their own stand. A seething mob of more than twelve hundred whites gathered to stop Autherine Lucy from entering the University of Alabama in February 1956. Crowds hurled eggs and rocks and shouted vicious epithets—some held signs calling Lucy a "nigger whore." Citing safety concerns, university officials suspended Lucy three days later. In Little Rock, Arkansas, a group of white women formed the Mothers' League of Central High and contributed prominently to the lawlessness and frenzied protests that eventually prompted a reluctant President Dwight D. Eisenhower to send federal troops to Little Rock. And in New Orleans's 1960 school crisis, white mothers known as the "cheerleaders" thronged outside the schools targeted for integration, taunting, screaming, pounding on cars, and verbally assaulting the parents—white and black—escorting their small children inside.

Direct Action and Direct Counteraction, 1960–1964. The battles over school integration had reached something of a stalemate by the close of the 1950s, but the mass civil rights protests of the early 1960s brought a fresh surge of brutality against African Americans. Sit-ins and other forms of direct action exposed black protesters to new physical dangers. Anne Moody, a participant in the sit-in movement in Jackson, Mississippi, endured unflagging abuse. She later recounted being grabbed by her hair and dragged bodily off her lunch-counter stool, and she described enraged whites throwing ketchup, sugar, or anything within reach. One of her fellow demonstrators had the word "nigger" spray-painted on his shirt.

Small groups of determined white resisters also terrorized the interracial Freedom Rides, led by the Congress of Racial Equality (CORE) in the spring and summer of 1961. Knowingly risking their own safety, CORE volunteers flouted segregation strictures by sitting together on buses and using terminal cafeterias and waiting rooms without respect to race. Upon arrival at Anniston, Alabama, one bus confronted a belligerent phalanx: roughly fifty cars and pickups began pursuit, slashing tires, smashing windows, and ultimately throwing a firebomb onto the bus, forcing the freedom riders to disembark and face the awaiting mob. Ku Klux Klansmen greeted the second bus in Birmingham, Alabama, and brutally beat several of the riders. Undeterred, the riders pressed on, eventually securing federal protection.

Participants in the 1963–1964 Mississippi Delta campaigns organized by the Student Nonviolent Coordinating Committee (SNCC) faced an unparalleled degree of terror. Klan membership spiked, and new white-supremacist groups formed as black and white volunteers descended on the state. SNCC workers had to cease their first voter-registration drive in the Delta; the SNCC leader Robert P. Moses, himself the victim of a gruesome beating, made the difficult choice after Herbert Lee, a local farmer, was murdered in 1961. When later registration campaigns began in the Delta, civil rights workers were threatened, stalked, arrested, and fired on, sometimes fatally. Many SNCC volunteers kept weapons in their vehicles for protection.

One of the best-remembered victims, Medgar Evers, tolerated near-constant harassment over the two years that he worked to enroll James Meredith at the University of Mississippi. He installed bulletproof blinds on the windows at his home in Jackson, and Evers's three small children knew to stay away from the windows at night and to drop to the floor if they heard a loud crack. In the early hours of 12 June 1963, Evers pulled into his driveway, and as he stepped out of his car a high-powered-rifle shot ripped through the night and struck him. His murderer did stand trial but was released after a hung jury.

A year later, on the day after Congress passed the Civil Rights Act, 21 June 1964, the civil rights workers James Chaney, Andrew Goodman, and Michael Schwerner—one black, two white—went to Neshoba County, Mississippi, to investigate a church fire. They never returned. Their bodies were discovered buried under a dam, victims of white vigilante justice.

Whites in Birmingham, Alabama, committed equally appalling acts of violence to curb the rising power of African American protest. As early as the late 1940s when African Americans tried to purchase homes in traditionally all-white neighborhoods, vigilante whites introduced the resistance tactic that earned the city the nickname "Bombingham." In spring 1963 the city's notorious public-safety commissioner Eugene "Bull" Connor unflinchingly released police dogs and fires hoses on crowds of protesters that included thousands of black children and teens. That summer a court mandated the enrollment of black children at a previously all-white school. Stoking the already tense atmosphere, the National States' Rights Party—a militant, venomously racist organization—called for a white boycott of the targeted school. On the morning of Sunday, 15 September 1963, a bomb ripped through the Sixteenth Street Baptist Church, the unofficial headquarters for Birmingham's mass movement. Four black girls died in the blast. As crowds of mourners gathered, young white men drove past, lofting signs that read, "Negroes Go Back to Africa."

Resistance to Civil Rights. Protesters and a States' Rights Party member (*right*) outside Graymont Elementary School, Birmingham, Alabama, 1963. BIRMINGHAM NEWS/POLARIS

Resistance Redefined. The shocking deaths of the four Birmingham girls, Evers, and the Mississippi civil rights workers turned some whites against the excesses of resistance. More important, the murders sparked long-overdue federal action on civil rights. As a result, naked white resistance to integration and African American voting rights dwindled by the middle part of the 1960s. In its place emerged new methods to preserve white political, economic, and social power.

Rather than insisting on legal segregation for all public facilities, masses of white southerners opted simply to leave urban centers and withdraw from tax-funded, public spaces. Many embraced ostensibly race-free philosophies that emphasized individual freedoms: the rights of home owners to select buyers for their properties, of business owners to operate without undue regulation, and of parents to choose schools for their children, free of government intervention. Less visible but equally damaging to the cause of genuine racial equality, these ideologies fueled the rise of a new conservative coalition in American politics—a movement that flatly rejected federal attempts to remake social relations, including race relations.

As white southerners moved to suburbs and adopted a language of community control and individual rights, racial mores in Dixie came to resemble more closely those in other parts of the United States. The Mississippi Delta and Birmingham are emblazoned in public memory as the focal points of white resistance to civil rights, but cities like Chicago, Detroit, Boston, and Los Angeles were all roiled by hate-filled confrontations over residential desegregation, fair-housing plans, and integration through busing. The legislative victories won by African American protest were unassailable, but the protean character of white resistance meant that new obstacles cropped up as soon as old barriers were hewn.

[*See also* Ku Klux Klan; Lynching and Mob Violence; Violence against African Americans; White Citizens' Council; White Supremacy; *and biographical entries on figures mentioned in this article*.]

BIBLIOGRAPHY

Bartley, Numan V. *The Rise of Massive Resistance: Race and Politics in the South during the 1950s*. Baton Rouge: Louisiana State University Press, 1969.

Carter, Dan T. *The Politics of Rage: George Wallace, the Origins of the New Conservatism, and the Transformation of American Politics*. New York: Simon & Schuster, 1995.

Chappell, David L. *A Stone of Hope: Prophetic Religion and the Death of Jim Crow*. Chapel Hill: University of North Carolina Press, 2004. See in particular pp. 105–190.

Crespino, Joseph. *In Search of Another Country: Mississippi and the Conservative Counterrevolution*. Princeton, N.J.: Princeton University Press, 2007.

Eskew, Glenn T. *But for Birmingham: The Local and National Movements in the Civil Rights Struggle*. Chapel Hill: University of North Carolina Press, 1997.

Fairclough, Adam. *Race and Democracy: The Civil Rights Struggle in Louisiana, 1915–1972*. Athens: University of Georgia Press, 1995.
Kruse, Kevin M. *White Flight: Atlanta and the Making of Modern Conservatism*. Princeton, N.J.: Princeton University Press, 2005.
Lewis, George. *Massive Resistance: The White Response to the Civil Rights Movement*. London: Hodder Arnold, 2006.
Payne, Charles M. *I've Got the Light of Freedom: The Organizing Tradition and the Mississippi Freedom Struggle*. Berkeley: University of California Press, 1995.
Sokol, Jason. *There Goes My Everything: White Southerners in the Age of Civil Rights, 1945–1975*. New York: Alfred A. Knopf, 2006.
Webb, Clive, ed. *Massive Resistance: Southern Opposition to the Second Reconstruction*. New York: Oxford University Press, 2005.

—ANN ZIKER

CIVIL RIGHTS ACT OF 1957. The Civil Rights Act of 1957 was the first law protecting African American rights passed by the U.S. Congress since Reconstruction. It grew out of the desire of the Eisenhower administration to shore up its image among black voters prior to the 1956 presidential elections. Eisenhower's attorney general Herbert Brownell drafted a bill that included the establishment of both a federal Civil Rights Commission and a Civil Rights Division within the U.S. Department of Justice. Furthermore, Brownell proposed to strengthen the federal government's authority to take court action against violations of voting rights in the states. The bill was passed by the House of Representatives in April 1956 but met with massive resistance in the Senate from southern white supremacists, who in the past had killed all civil rights legislation by filibustering. In particular, the southerners complained that the bill did not provide for a jury trial if state officials were held in contempt of court. Obviously, such a provision would have rendered the law toothless because no southern official who defied a federal court order to enforce black civil rights had to fear conviction by an all-white jury of his peers. Nevertheless, after Eisenhower's reelection the administration and the Senate majority leader, Lyndon Johnson of Texas, engineered a compromise that included a jury trial and persuaded the southerners to let the bill pass without a filibuster.

The civil rights community, however, was sharply divided over the compromise bill. The National Association for the Advancement of Colored People (NAACP), the largest civil rights group, had strictly opposed the jury trial amendment and vowed to fight all lawmakers who voted in favor of it. But when the Senate passed the diluted bill in August 1957, the NAACP leaders Roy Wilkins and Clarence Mitchell suddenly changed course and argued in favor of supporting the bill even with the invidious amendment. Their action provoked much criticism from within the NAACP and the black community at large. Wilkins and Mitchell, however, insisted that a stronger law simply had not been attainable and that the advocates of civil rights could not afford to publicly oppose the first civil rights legislation of the twentieth century. A start had been made, and the law might prove to be useful after all.

To make the law effective, the NAACP began showering the Department of Justice with reports about the discrimination and harassment black voters and civil rights activists faced in the South. For the time being, however, the federal government remained on the sidelines. In the two years following the passage of the 1957 Civil Rights Act the attorney general brought a mere four lawsuits against local registrars for denying blacks the right to register and vote. By holding public hearings and publishing detailed reports, the Civil Rights Commission, on the other hand, began to assume an important role in educating the American people about the realities of southern racism and the need for political action. The 1957 Civil Rights Act surely was not a breakthrough and looked disappointing at the time. Yet from the vantage point of history it marks the beginning of the civil rights reforms that profoundly changed American race relations.

[*See also* Civil Rights Act of 1960; Civil Rights Act of 1964; *and* Eisenhower, Dwight D., Administration of.]

BIBLIOGRAPHY

Berg, Manfred. *The Ticket to Freedom: The NAACP and the Struggle for Black Political Integration*. Gainesville: University Press of Florida, 2005. A comprehensive political history of the NAACP focusing on the period from 1909 to 1970.
Burk, Robert F. *The Eisenhower Administration and Black Civil Rights*. Knoxville: University of Tennessee Press, 1984. A detailed analysis of Eisenhower's civil rights policies, including the Civil Rights Act of 1957.

—MANFRED BERG

CIVIL RIGHTS ACT OF 1960. Following the passage of the rather weak Civil Rights Act of 1957, African American lobbyists, led by the NAACP, pressed the administration of Dwight D. Eisenhower and Congress for more effective legislation to protect southern blacks claiming their civil and political rights. In the election year of 1960 these efforts dovetailed with the desire of both the Democratic and the Republican parties to improve their civil rights record without alienating white voters. The intention of both parties was to keep the thorny issue of civil rights and desegregation out of the election campaign. Thus in April 1960, Congress passed a bill that contained two major items.

First, it introduced several new criminal offenses under federal law. For example, Congress made it illegal to flee from prosecution for exploding bombs in an assassination attempt and to interfere with court orders mandating school desegregation. These stipulations were purely fictitious and resulted in no federal prosecutions whatsoever.

The second item was a plan for the better protection of black voting rights. If federal judges detected a "pattern of discrimination" in a particular jurisdiction, they were authorized to appoint so-called referees, who would then review the registration papers of a rejected applicant and report back to the judges. If the court found in favor of the applicant, it could add him or her to the registration list. However, even after a pattern of discrimination had been established by the federal court, individual black voters still had to present themselves to the local registrars and go through all the motions before the court could finally appoint a referee. The procedure prescribed by the law was mind-boggling and tedious and had virtually no practical significance. As a matter of fact, segregationist southern lawmakers openly hailed it as a victory, while liberal supporters of civil rights such as Senator Paul Douglas of Illinois decried it as meaningless tokenism.

The black civil rights community had been fully aware that the civil rights bill was little more than window dressing by the parties and had kept largely aloof from the congressional negotiations. The NAACP leader Roy O. Wilkins aptly characterized the act as requiring black voters to pass more checkpoints and examinations than if they wanted to get to the U.S. gold reserves in Fort Knox, Kentucky. The NAACP, which had experienced serious internal friction after its controversial support for the Civil Rights Act of 1957, had no intention to associate itself with legislation that it rightly considered almost useless. On the other hand, the hopes of the bill's drafters that for the time being it might give lawmakers a break on the civil rights front proved to be spectacularly mistaken. Over the next five years the nonviolent direct action and voter registration campaigns of the civil rights movement triggered a political momentum that resulted in the landmark legislation of the 1964 Civil Rights Act and the 1965 Voting Rights Act. Compared to these major achievements, the 1960 law is of minor significance.

[*See also* Civil Rights *and* Eisenhower, Dwight D., Administration of.]

BIBLIOGRAPHY

Berg, Manfred. *The Ticket to Freedom: The NAACP and the Struggle for Black Political Integration*. Gainesville: University Press of Florida, 2005. A comprehensive political history of the NAACP focusing on the period from 1909 to 1970.

Burk, Robert F. *The Eisenhower Administration and Black Civil Rights*. Knoxville: University of Tennessee Press, 1984. A detailed analysis of Eisenhower's civil rights policies, including the Civil Rights Act of 1957.

—MANFRED BERG

CIVIL RIGHTS ACT OF 1964. The Civil Rights Act of 1964 is one of the most significant pieces of civil rights legislation adopted since Reconstruction (1865–1877). This legislation was comprehensive: it prohibited discrimination in public facilities, government, and employment. By making it illegal to compel segregation of the races in schools, housing, or hiring, it challenged and ultimately abolished the Jim Crow laws in the South. Its guarantees of equal voting rights (Title I); its prohibition of segregation or discrimination in places of public accommodation (Title II); its ban on discrimination, including sex-based discrimination, by trade unions, schools, or employers that are involved in interstate commerce or that do business with the federal government (Title VII); its desegregation of public schools (Title IV); and its insistence on nondiscrimination in the distribution of funds under federally assisted programs (Title VI) were all historic.

The death knell that the act served on Jim Crow and racial segregation demonstrated the impact Congress could have on revolutionizing social conditions in America. Moreover, the history of the act's lineage—rooted in the hopes and failures of the Civil War and Reconstruction—and of its place as a cornerstone of the rebirth of the civil rights movement in the mid-twentieth century is a telling story of America and the nation's continuing struggle with race and racism.

Origins: Déjà Vu. The most striking feature of the 1964 act is its source. It was rooted in the post–Civil War era and the Civil Rights Act of 1875, which attempted to guarantee that

> all persons [in the United States] shall be entitled to the full and equal enjoyment of the accommodations, advantages, facilities, and privileges of inns, public conveyances on land or water, theaters, and other places of public amusement ... and applicable alike to citizens of every race and color, regardless of any previous condition of servitude.

There is certainly a feeling of déjà vu when comparing the 1875 act with 1964 act's guarantee, "All persons shall be entitled to the full and equal enjoyment of the goods, services, facilities, privileges, advantages, and accommodations of any place of public accommodation." The protection against discrimination and segregation afforded by Title II of the 1964 act is no more than a repetition of that guaranteed by the 1875 legislation. Thus, the origins of the 1964 act extend back almost one hundred years in a modern attempt to achieve the same protections that the post–Civil War Congress had sought.

The failure of the 1875 act to accomplish these ends can be traced to the U.S. Supreme Court. In 1883, in several cases joined together as the *Civil Rights Cases*, 109 U.S. 3 (1883), the Court declared the public accommodations provision of the 1875 legislation unconstitutional. The Court held that the Fourteenth Amendment, and therefore the legislation, could not reach racial discrimination that was private in character because it limited the reach of the amendment to "state action." The effect of this decision was to place the very idea of civil rights legislation into a "Constitutional limbo" for three quarters of a century.

Adoption: The 1964 Act. Almost ninety years later, pressed on by the civil rights movement and the leadership provided in the Supreme Court's landmark school desegregation decision in *Brown v. Board of Education*, the nation once more turned its attention to the practice of segregation in the South. Congressional action, however, was limited by a monolithic block of southern Democrats in the Congress (particularly in the Senate) who sought to preserve apartheid and Jim Crow by flexing their political muscle to apply procedural techniques that would permanently delay any legislation. In 1957, bowing to rising political pressure, Congress adopted the first major civil rights legislation since Reconstruction: the Civil Rights Act of 1957. The new law, however, was significant in name only, as southern Democrats in the Senate applied procedural tools that limited the scope of the act so that it had little or no effect on racial segregation. A 1960 civil rights act proved equally ineffectual for similar reasons.

Kennedy and the civil rights movement. Against this background and the rising tide of the civil rights movement, the Massachusetts Democrat John F. Kennedy was elected president along with a Democratic majority in Congress. During the first two years of his presidency, Kennedy failed to put forward any civil rights legislation. Though criticized by civil rights leaders, Kennedy felt he could not overcome southern legislative roadblocks and that any such attempt might jeopardize both his domestic and his foreign agenda. To the African American leadership this was simply another American president bowing to political pressure and forsaking a meaningful civil rights bill, a bill that could end segregation and racial oppression in the South.

On 28 February 1963, Kennedy sent Congress a strong message on the immediate need for civil rights legislation:

> The Negro baby born in America today . . . has about one-half as much chance of completing high school as a white baby born in the same place on the same day, one-third as much chance of completing college, one-third as much chance of becoming a professional man, twice as much chance of becoming unemployed . . . a life expectancy which is seven years less, and the prospects of earning only half as much. (Kennedy, "Radio and Television Report," 11 June 1963.)

Yet, and much to the dismay of African Americans, the legislation he ultimately proposed echoed the civil rights legislation of 1957 and 1960: it was symbolic in character but deficient in substance. In the end, to Kennedy, a strong civil rights bill, one that would really end racial segregation and racial oppression in the southern United States, was simply not politically achievable, necessitating a battle not worth the cost to his political will and political strength. To the leadership of the civil rights movement, Kennedy had yielded on civil rights legislation to achieve other political ends. Soon after the bill's release, a meeting of the leaders of more than seventy civil rights organizations was called. The group, including a list of notable African Americans, adopted the name the Leadership Conference on Civil Rights. The group felt it was clear that Kennedy had given up before the fighting had even begun, and therefore the proposed bill was hardly worth their efforts.

Martin Luther King Jr. and Birmingham. A response to these political problems, one that changed the entire political landscape, came from a most unexpected source. In May of 1963, Martin Luther King Jr. and his Southern Christian Leadership Conference began a series of nonviolent demonstrations to protest the harm that the legislation sought to remedy, the segregation of public facilities in Birmingham, Alabama. King, as he sought to hang out the "dirty underwear" of apartheid for the world to see, was aided by tactics employed by the Birmingham city police chief, T. Eugene ("Bull") Connor, an avowed segregationist. Connor brought out police dogs, fire hoses, and electric cattle prods to face the protestors. The reports of the ensuing violent tactics perpetrated by Connor flooded the nation's newspapers and television; they included a particularly vivid picture of a helpless demonstrator being attacked by one of Connor's dogs. The nation and the world saw firsthand the oppression faced by African Americans in the South. Many cite the events in Birmingham as having changed American public opinion on civil rights. The streets had provided the energy where politics had failed; and civil rights leaders had their answer. Demands for action began pouring into the White House and Congress from across the country.

Birmingham thus played a central role in the evolution of civil rights legislation. It forced Kennedy to change his tentative position on civil rights. Admitting as much at a White House strategy meeting with civil rights leaders called in response to Birmingham, Kennedy stated, "Bull Connor has done more for civil rights than anyone in this room." He said, "The civil rights movement should thank God for Bull Connor. He's helped it as much as Abraham Lincoln."

Suddenly prospects for civil rights legislation advanced. The Leadership Conference, and even the Democratic congressional leadership, urged the president to send a strong bill to Capitol Hill. Kennedy responded by instructing the attorney general, his brother Robert Kennedy, to draft the most sweeping civil rights proposal that any president had ever presented to Congress.

On 17 June 1963, Kennedy forwarded legislation to Congress. It was much like the 1875 statute; it included provisions to ban discrimination in public accommodations in order to provide "the kind of equality of treatment which we would want for ourselves." (Kennedy, "Radio and Television Report," 11 June 1963) Though this legislation, spurred by the post-Birmingham public outcry, would culminate in the Civil Rights Act of 1964, it would still face a most arduous path. Southern representatives in Congress blocked the bill in committee as they continued to apply procedural tactics to try to defeat any civil rights legislation.

The March on Washington. With the legislation caught in the southern political quagmire, civil rights protest once again took center stage: African American leaders hoped for another event as dramatic as Birmingham. In August, more than 250,000 Americans of all races celebrated the centennial of the Emancipation Proclamation by participating in a march on Washington. The event was led by key civil rights figures such as A. Philip Randolph, Roy Wilkins, Bayard Rustin, and Whitney Young. But the most memorable moment came when King delivered his "I Have a Dream" speech. With a nation now galvanized by King's most famous oration, the comprehensive civil rights bill finally cleared several hurdles placed by the southern Democrats, and by the fall of 1964 it received the endorsement of several House and Senate Republican leaders.

The bill was reported out of the House Judiciary Committee in late November 1963. It immediately went to the House Rules Committee, where the chairman, Howard Smith, still asserting southern resistance through procedural tactics, claimed he would bottle up the bill forever. With the nation in turmoil over civil rights and poised for this climactic battle, Kennedy boarded Air Force One to fly to Dallas. On November 22, Kennedy was assassinated. The assassin's bullet that killed Kennedy changed America forever, but not in any way quite as much as in the future of civil rights and the 1964 legislation.

LBJ: A civil rights bill in memory of John Kennedy. The act was still in committee when Lyndon B. Johnson assumed the presidency. The new president, a southerner from Texas who would need to run for reelection as soon as 1964, knew he must convince northern and western liberals that he was an acceptable leader for the national Democratic Party. To Johnson, the civil rights bill appeared to be a perfect vehicle to accomplish this. Five days after Kennedy's assassination, he told a joint session of the House and Senate: "We have talked long enough in this country about equal rights.... It is time now to write the next chapter, and to write it in the books of law."

Johnson sought adoption of the bill in memory of his slain predecessor, thereby stirring strong emotions. Johnson "spoke with black groups and with individual leaders of the black community and told them that John Kennedy's dream of equality had not died with him. I assured them that I was going to press for the civil rights bill with every ounce of energy I possessed" (*The Vantage Point*, p. 29).

Exerting every ounce of his plentiful political muscle he had garnered in his days as the powerful Senate majority leader prior to the 1960 election, Johnson exhibited a breathtaking political acuity in pursuit of his goal. Johnson twisted arms and sought the aid of his political opponents. Johnson felt that Everett Dirksen, the Republican Senate minority leader, was the key to getting the civil rights bill out of the Senate. He gave him the opportunity to be a "hero in history," urging him and his Republican colleagues to forget partisan politics and get the legislative machinery of the United States moving forward.

Once Dirksen and Johnson, through the Senate majority whip Hubert Humphrey, successfully negotiated an amended bill, the procedural tactics of cloture and filibuster fell aside in deference to the rising spirit of the nation in memory of its slain leader. On 10 June 1964, for the first time in its history, the Senate voted cloture on a civil rights bill. Soon afterward the Senate adopted the Dirksen-Humphrey amendments, and then the final bill as amended. The House quickly agreed to the Senate amendments, and on 2 July 1964, before an audience of more than one hundred senators, representatives, cabinet members, and civil rights leaders, Johnson, a southerner who was now a civil rights hero, signed the Civil Rights Act of 1964 into law.

Judicial Review. The new legislation faced one more hurdle before it could be relied on for enforcement: judicial review by the Supreme Court. This was significant because the legislation's public accommodations provisions, the heart of its strike against Jim Crow, had previously been held unconstitutional when the Court found that similar protections in the Civil Rights Act of 1875 lacked the requisite "state action" in the *Civil Rights Cases* in 1883. Both Kennedy and Johnson, as well as congressional supporters, were aware of this when the legislation was drafted.

Though the state action limitation had been broadened somewhat by 1964, it had nonetheless remained a prerequisite for application of the Fourteenth Amendment and its guarantee of "equal protection of the law." Supporters, however, embraced the more expansive authority the Court had allowed under Congress's Article I power to

Civil Rights Act. President Lyndon B. Johnson signs the 1964 Civil Rights Act in the East Room of the White House, 2 July 1964. Photograph by Cecil Stoughton. LYNDON B. JOHNSON LIBRARY, NATIONAL ARCHIVES

"regulate interstate commerce." Burke Marshall, the assistant attorney general in the civil rights division, and Attorney General Robert Kennedy both so argued, worrying about an unconstitutional finding if the legislation were based solely on the Fourteenth Amendment and urging Congress to support the legislation by both the commerce clause and the Fourteenth Amendment. The attorney general pleaded, "We need to obtain a remedy. The commerce clause will obtain a remedy and there won't be a problem about the constitutionality." (Levy, *Minority Rights*, p. 212)

The bill, when adopted, laid a clear predicate for application of the commerce clause, though it was based upon both constitutional provisions. The Court, then at the height of the relatively liberal and activist Warren era, quickly docketed two cases to review the constitutionality of the act during the 1964 term. In *Heart of Atlanta Motel v. United States* (1964), where an interstate motel located on an interstate highway in Atlanta discriminated against African Americans, and in *Katzenbach v. McClung* (1964), where Ollie's Barbecue, a local establishment with almost no "interstate" connection, discriminated on the same basis, the Court upheld the constructional validity of the public accommodation provisions, finding that this activity could be reached under the federal commerce power because this discrimination, when viewed as a class of all such establishments across the county, substantially affected interstate commerce. To those African Americans who needed to find lodging and food before they could attempt any travel in the South, this had long been obvious. Thus, with the support of the very institution that had limited this protection some seventy-five years earlier, the Civil Rights Act of 1964 was now deemed constitutional and was ready for enforcement—ready to make a historic impact and create a legacy.

Significance and Legacy. The first provision of the act to have immediate and revolutionary impact was Title II's revival of the 1875 legislation's attempt to establish the "illegality of discrimination in places of public accommodation." This took down Jim Crow. Backed by enforcement in the federal courts, this provision became one of the greatest examples of social engineering in the nation's history. It exemplified the power of law and of Congress to set a national moral tone and to revolutionize American culture.

Close behind and arguably just as meaningful in America today was Title VI's guarantee of "nondiscrimination in federally assisted programs." With the growth and increasing reach of the federal government in the second half of the twentieth century, federal spending involved itself in almost every nook and cranny of American life. Local and state governments came to rely on these funds for their everyday operation, and therefore the force of the dollar mandated compliance with the act's nondiscrimination provisions.

Perhaps no other federal statute has affected the American landscape more than Title VII's guarantee of "equal employment opportunity," as it outlawed employment discrimination based on race, color, religion, sex, or national origin (see 42 U.S.C. § 2000e-2) and created the Equal Employment Opportunity Commission (EEOC) to enforce this provision. (42 U.S.C. § 2000e-4). This, because it was constitutionally based upon the expansive contemporary commerce clause, reached private employers. Title VII would have enormous social and economic impact. A 1972 amendment to this legislation, the Equal Employment Opportunity Act, extended Title VII's coverage to employees of state and local governments, increased the authority of the EEOC, and for the first time explicitly protected women. The original legislation had planted the seed for this impact, and this amendment led to widespread administrative and judicial enforcement. The Court played a major role when it held that sexual harassment was sexual discrimination and thus prohibited under the act. Title VII had become one of the most significant pieces of legislation ever adopted by Congress.

Several other provisions were meaningful as well. With the turmoil that existed in the 1960s social environment, Title V's "Commission on Civil Rights" found the commission serving as a significant political vehicle to help nudge America away from its history of racial segregation and oppression. Title I's "voting rights" was the first modern legislation to speak to the southern denial of the African American right to vote. Though the 1964 act's provisions spoke to unequal voter registration and literacy tests, it did not abolish or provide a basis for significant action. Much like Title VII, however, it was most significant in that it laid a predicate for the adoption of the all-encompassing and successful Voting Rights Act of 1965. Title IV spoke to "desegregation of public education" and allowed the attorney general to file suit to enforce the mandate of *Brown* to desegregate public schools.

The Civil Rights Act of 1964 certainly revealed that Congress can change social conditions in the United States if it truly wishes to do so. It showed that despite all obstacles, even political consequences, both the president and Congress, with the nation rallied behind them, can accomplish what appears politically unthinkable. Most significant, the tenacious and deeply ingrained practice of enforcing the Jim Crow laws that dominated southern racial coexistence and oppression was struck a just and fatal blow. With the blood of slain martyrs and protestors as a memorial, justice was finally served.

[*See also* Civil Rights; Constitution, U.S.; Jim Crow Laws; Johnson, Lyndon B., Administration of; Kennedy, John F., Administration of; Laws and Legislation; Supreme Court; *and biographical entries on figures mentioned in this article.*]

Bibliography

Blaustein, Albert, and Robert L. Zangrando. *Civil Rights and the American Negro*. New York: Trident Press, 1968.

Brauer, Carl M. "Women Activists, Southern Conservatives, and the Prohibition of Sex Discrimination in Title VII of the 1964 Civil Rights Act." *Journal of Southern History* 49 (February 1983).

Dallek, Robert. *Flawed Giant: Lyndon Johnson and His Times, 1961–1973*. New York: Oxford University Press, 1998.

Garfinkel, Herbert. *When Negroes March: The March on Washington Movement in the Organizational Movement for FEPC*. Glencoe, Ill.: Free Press, 1959.

Graham, Hugh Davis. *The Civil Rights Era: Origins and Development of National Policy, 1960–1972*. New York: Oxford University Press, 1990.

Johnson, Lyndon B. *The Vantage Point: Perspectives of the Presidency, 1963–1969*. New York: Holt, Rinehart, and Winston, 1971.

Kennedy, John. F. "Radio and Television Report to the American People on Civil Rights." Boston: John F. Kennedy Library and Museum, 2002.

Kluger, Richard. *Simple Justice: The History of* Brown v. Board of Education *and Black America's Struggle for Equality*. New York: Alfred A. Knopf, 1976.

Kotz, Nick. *Judgment Days: Lyndon Baines Johnson, Martin Luther King Jr., and the Laws that Changed America*. Boston: Houghton Mifflin, 2005.

Levy, Martin L. "The Supreme Court, Minority Rights and Principled Adjudication." *Texas Southern Law Review* 2, no. 208 (1972).

Loevy, Robert D., ed. *The Civil Rights Act of 1964: The Passage of the Law That Ended Racial Segregation*. Albany: State University of New York Press, 1997.

Loevy, Robert D. *To End All Segregation: The Politics of the Passage of the Civil Rights Act of 1964*. Lanham, Md.: University Press of America, 1990.

Oates, Stephen B. *Let the Trumpet Sound: The Life of Martin Luther King Jr.* New York: Harper and Row, 1982.

Public Papers of the Presidents of the United States: Lyndon B. Johnson, 1963–64. Washington, D.C.: United States Government Printing Office, 1970.

Rauh, Joseph. Unpublished manuscript on the role of the Leadership Conference on Civil Rights in the civil rights struggle of 1963–1964. Washington, D.C.: Leadership Conference on Civil Rights, 1964.

Rodriguez, Daniel B., and Barry R. Weingast. "The Positive Political Theory of Legislative History: New Perspectives on the 1964 Civil Rights Act and Its Interpretation." *University of Pennsylvania Law Review* 151 (2003).

—Martin L. Levy

CIVIL RIGHTS AND THE MEDIA. Throughout the twentieth century, African Americans promoted in newspapers, in newsmagazines, and on radio and television their quest for civil rights, including eliminating segregation, discrimination, and racial barriers to social, political, and economic advancement. Through such media black people counteracted racist ideologies and dehumanizing characterizations that supported the view that African Americans did not deserve full rights of citizenship. Whenever feasible, black men and women founded their own media to voice the civil rights message that white media regularly ignored, trivialized, blocked, denounced, or sought to channel within limits acceptable to majority-white audiences. But neither the black nor the white media was monolithic; each had factions that advanced their own definition, scope, and extent of civil rights.

Early Twentieth Century. Many African American journalists championed racial equality as post-Reconstruction assaults—including the U.S. Supreme Court ruling in *Plessy v. Ferguson* (1896), which made segregation constitutional—eroded black people's civil rights. During the 1890s when white newspapers publicized lynchings, encouraged antiblack mass violence, and approved white supremacy, the investigative journalist Ida B. Wells-Barnett continued the tradition of militancy in the black press that began with black abolitionists during the antebellum era. Following in this tradition, the newspaper publisher of the *Boston Guardian*, William Monroe Trotter, met with criticism from the white press for opposing the policy of accommodation to white supremacy advocated by the African American leader and educator Booker T. Washington.

African American journalists debated the strategies and tactics that best advanced the civil rights struggle, particularly after the U.S. entry into World War I in April 1917. Black journalists condemned the military's racist treatment of black servicemen and the government's indifference to white people's attacks on black people. Many agreed with an editorial in the black-owned Virginia newspaper the *Richmond Planet* that patriotism would win for African Americans "the rights and privileges to which they are entitled as citizens" (Jordan, p. 36). Others, like the socialist owners of *The Messenger*, A. Philip Randolph and Chandler Owen, argued that racism was the reason that African Americans must oppose the war.

But regardless of their position on the war, African American editors were silenced by government threats that severely limited freedom of the press and advocacy of civil rights. In addition, wartime black patriotism failed to convince the government and the white press of the worthiness of the African American struggle for civil rights. The black press reached an impasse with its white counterpart over the limits of coverage of civil rights, laying the foundation for future treatment of civil rights in the media.

Radio, which emerged in the 1920s, became a cultural arena where debates raged over whether black people deserved equal rights. Radio productions appropriated black cultural expressions of music, humor, and language popular with disaffected white youth for entertainment that reached millions of black and white homes. The medium adapted minstrelsy, which had appealed to generations of white audiences, and aired blackface programs like *Amos 'n' Andy*, which caricatured African American life and culture, reinforced antiblack stereotypes, and conveyed the idea that black people were not ready for civil rights. Producers ignored the *Pittsburgh Courier* and other black-press organs that demanded the cessation of such programs. Radio operated in a consumer-driven economy in which corporate advertisers catered to far larger white audiences that remained indifferent or hostile to civil rights and racial equality.

During World War II, African Americans enjoyed somewhat sympathetic coverage of civil rights in white-owned newspapers and newsmagazines and on radio. Black media generally committed itself to supporting the federal government's war policy and publicized African American grievances and demands for civil rights without inviting government repression. Black journalists connected African American patriotism to civil rights. The *Pittsburgh Courier* in February 1942 initiated the "Double V" campaign—"V" for victory for democracy overseas and "V" for victory for democracy at home—which black newspapers across the nation promoted.

Even major white-owned newspapers, newsmagazines, and radio linked racism to fascism and advanced the message of interracial democracy as a necessary war aim. During the war the federal government incorporated radio into the war effort, producing such programs as *Freedom's People*, which documented African American participation in past wars. White media outlets hired African American journalists like Earl Brown, who wrote articles pertaining to racial issues for *Life*, *Look*, and *Harper's*. The War Department, in need of black manpower and in order to counteract fascist propaganda, sponsored radio programs that presented the black perspective on civil rights and included black people in Armed Forces Radio Service shows. But the war had scarcely ended when white civilian and military radio began canceling programs that featured discussion of civil rights issues and African American social and economic advancement.

Post–World War II Media Environment. The immediate post–World War II media environment remained somewhat receptive to civil rights as white Americans increasingly realized that segregation and discrimination contradicted American democracy. Additionally, the white media in its desire to tap into an expanding black consumer market began to pay attention to African

American campaigns for civil rights. Radio networks aired programs that appealed to black people and sometimes devoted their entire schedules to programs designed for African Americans.

In 1949 black-owned radio stations first appeared, increasing the popularity of radio among African Americans. Television, which became commercially available in the late 1940s, frequently broadcast programs featuring African American performing artists. Popular television figures, among them the talk-show host Steve Allen, the variety-show emcee Ed Sullivan, and the news journalist Edward R. Murrow, advocated fair treatment for African Americans. Meanwhile, black newspapers and newsmagazines, like *Ebony* and *Jet*, publicized the news of civil rights and black achievements.

Like white-owned newspapers and radio during the 1950s and 1960s, television presented material that ran the gamut from blatant hostility to indifference to guarded support for racial equality. Some stations, especially in the South, would neither air civil rights protests nor strike a balance by presenting civil rights activists' point of view. They received moral support from some major white media outlets; for example, *U.S. News and World Report*, a national newsmagazine, stated in 1963 that the black civil rights leader Martin Luther King Jr.'s Southern Christian Leadership Conference demonstration—that is, the Children's Crusade, in Birmingham, Alabama—was "evidence of a conspiracy on the part of the Federal government to usurp the authority of the Southern States" (Larson, p. 172).

Amos 'n' Andy, which migrated in 1951 from radio to television, and similar shows presented African Americans in ways that reinforced antiblack prejudice. But television stations that voiced editorial support for civil rights filtered the movement's message through a variety of perspectives that calmed the fears of white audiences. Networks imposed limits on what they regarded as permissible to broadcast about civil rights, as when they banned the radical social commentator Paul Robeson, a friend of the Communist Party of the United States, from the air. In general, television avoided in-depth analyses of civil rights and race relations because the networks and corporate advertisers feared alienating their largest consumer market, white Americans.

Civil rights activists needed print and broadcast media to publicize their cause, and the media welcomed, for a variety of reasons, primarily financial, the chance to report on the movement. Civil rights workers and leaders applauded the media's coverage of their protests, which reached into millions of households. They noted the extensive coverage that the media gave to major events, including the 1962 white riot that accompanied the desegregation of the University of Mississippi and the 1963 March on Washington. Of all the media, television found civil rights demonstrations irresistibly good copy: tailor-made for broadcasting in brief news segments, particularly when such actions became dramatic, as when local authorities or thugs attacked demonstrators.

The media split in several ways when covering civil rights. Black-owned and black-oriented media often displayed concern, sometimes exerting effort to analyze the movement. The Philadelphia radio disc jockey Georgie Woods, for one, gave King airtime when the famous civil rights leader came to town. Indeed, black radio personalities like Woods made radio the medium of choice for most African Americans. The white-owned media, on the other hand, kept its coverage of movement events within parameters that framed racism in subtle ways to negate a critique of the repression, violence, and discrimination that African Americans, especially southerners, experienced on a daily basis.

The white media reinforced stereotypes that valued white life over black when it devoted more coverage to white than to black victims of white brutality. When mounted police beat black demonstrators during the 1963 Birmingham demonstrations, *U.S. News and World Report* described the police actions as "justified" because "the blacks were one step removed from savagery" (Barlow, pp. 204–206). Major white-owned newsmagazines such as *Time* and *Newsweek* initially hesitated to cover movement activities, with *Newsweek* disapproving King's tactic of having marchers in the streets. In an effort to make racism a southern problem, *Time* carefully distinguished Selma, where in 1965 state troopers had brutally repressed black demonstrators, from the rest of the nation.

Though the media published a few articles or ran a few programs on civil rights and racism, it did not go into any depth on the reasons for the demonstrations or the central issues of the civil rights struggle. For example, in 1965 the *New York Times* devoted almost an entire front page and all of an inside page to the Selma-to-Montgomery march to encourage black people to vote, yet it never mentioned that only 10 percent of eligible black voters in Alabama were registered or the horrible violence meted out to those who attempted to register.

During the 1960s, print and broadcast media's record on civil rights was at best ambivalent. It generally supported the enactment of civil rights legislation, including the Civil Rights Act of 1964, the Voting Rights Act of 1965, and the Fair Housing Act of 1968. The media also began hiring more African American professionals. Television networks featured black news journalists, actors, and actresses more frequently in their programming.

Meet the Press. Civil rights leaders discuss the role of black soldiers in the Vietnam War on the 21 August 1966 civil rights special of the television show *Meet the Press*. From left, Edwin Newman of NBC News, host Lawrence Spivak, Roy Wilkins of the NAACP, Whitney Young of the National Urban League, Floyd B. McKissick of CORE, Stokely Carmichael of SNCC, and the civil rights activist James H. Meredith. LAWRENCE E. SPIVAK COLLECTION, LIBRARY OF CONGRESS

The media praised, however grudgingly, civil rights demonstrators and King for their commitment to nonviolence, although some journalists quipped that they provoked their opponents to violence. Pro–civil rights media outlets ignored or played down stories of black violence in response to white aggression during or after various civil rights demonstrations. But the white media eagerly covered urban disturbances or riots occurring after 1964 to dramatize the idea that some black people remained dissatisfied after the government enacted the Civil Rights Act of 1964.

More important, the media continued to limit the civil rights message to a range of concerns that did not include addressing economic inequities. For example, the media paid less attention to King in 1967 when he announced his opposition to the Vietnam War, promoted plans for the Poor People's Campaign to address issues of maldistribution of income and wealth, and argued in favor of what later became known as affirmative action. In the meantime the media fanned fears and a backlash among many white Americans.

From the 1970s to the end of the twentieth century, in a situation that suggested the glass half empty or half full, the African American quest for civil rights received ambivalent treatment in the media. On one hand, black people increasingly occupied positions of responsibility working for white-owned newspapers, newsmagazines, radio, and television. Celebrities like the talk-show host Oprah Winfrey and the comedian Bill Cosby, in their shows that appealed to both black and white audiences, attracted millions of viewers. On the other hand, African Americans either as media subjects or as professionals were often shunted to stereotypical roles that black people had been allowed to perform for decades. White media gave serious attention to *The Bell Curve: Intelligence and Class Structure in American Life* (1994) by the political scientist Charles Murray and the psychologist Richard Herrnstein. *Newsweek* in a twenty-eight-hundred-word defense of the book theorized that black people were genetically inferior to white people.

Most important, the white media, with its overwhelming resources and interests in serving corporate sponsors, succeeded in popularizing the notion that African Americans had won their civil rights completely and decisively. Black-owned media, which historically functioned as assertive promoters of racial equality, became a less effective opposition to the white media in part because of Federal Communications Commission regulations in the 1990s that led to a reduction of black-owned media outlets and in part because the black media, too, became concerned about meeting the needs of corporate sponsors. As the twentieth century drew to a close, the media continued in a pattern established a hundred years earlier, split over the issue of civil rights.

[*See also* Black Press; Journalism, Print and Broadcast; Radio; Radio and Television Stations, African American; Television; *and entries on newspapers and magazines mentioned in this article*.]

BIBLIOGRAPHY

Barlow, William. *Voice Over: The Making of Black Radio*. Philadelphia: Temple University Press, 1999. Argues that black radio has played a tremendous role in shaping black urban and white popular cultures; includes bibliographical notes.

Dates, Jannette L., and William Barlow, eds. *Split Image: African Americans in the Mass Media*. Washington, D.C: Howard University Press, 1990. A collection of essays discussing the bifurcation of black images in American culture along racial lines; includes a short bibliographical essay and bibliographical notes.

Jordan, William G. *Black Newspapers and America's War for Democracy, 1914–1920*. Chapel Hill: University of North Carolina Press, 2001. Looks at the effectiveness of words as weapons during World War I; includes an extensive bibliography.

Larson, Stephanie Greco. *Media and Minorities: The Politics of Race in News and Entertainment*. Lanham, Md.: Rowman & Littlefield, 2006. Challenges widely held assumptions and shows how the media helps maintain the racial status quo; uses numerous sources from various disciplines.

MacDonald, J. Fred. *Blacks and White TV: African Americans in Television since 1948*. 2d ed. Chicago: Nelson-Hall, 1992. Narrates a history of television's contradiction of showcasing black talent and perpetuating stereotypical caricatures; includes a bibliography and notes.

Martindale, Carolyn. *The White Press and Black America*. New York: Greenwood, 1986. Discusses the white news media and their problems, and suggests ways for the media to resolve such problems; includes a bibliography and bibliographical notes.

Newkirk, Pamela. *Within the Veil: Black Journalists, White Media*. New York: New York University Press, 2000. Argues that late twentieth-century portrayals of African Americans rivaled the worst of those of the nineteenth century; includes bibliographical notes.

Simmons, Charles A. *The African American Press: A History of News Coverage during National Crisis, with Special Reference to Four Black Newspapers, 1827–1965*. Jefferson, N.C.: McFarland and Company, 1998. Shows the changing ways in which black and other Americans thought about racial identity; includes a bibliography and bibliographical notes.

Tinney, James S., and Justine J. Rector, eds. *Issues and Trends in Afro-American Journalism*. Lanham, Md.: University Press of America, 1980. A collection of essays tracing the history of the black American press; includes bibliographical notes.

Torres, Sasha. *Black, White, and in Color: Television and Black Civil Rights*. Princeton, N.J: Princeton University Press, 2003. Explores how racial politics and American television have nurtured, relied on, and exploited each other; includes bibliography and bibliographical notes.

Ward, Brian, ed. *Media, Culture, and the Modern African American Freedom Struggle*. Gainesville: University Press of Florida, 2001. A collection of essays arguing that African American art, music, and other cultural expressions played an active role in defining the goals and methods of the civil rights movement; includes bibliographical notes.

—CHARLES L. LUMPKINS

CIVIL RIGHTS LAWS. *See* Laws and Legislation.

CIVIL RIGHTS MOVEMENT. "Civil rights movement" is an umbrella term that refers to the various efforts of African American activists to gain full citizenship rights and to end racial discrimination in American society. Sustained civil rights organizing began in the early twentieth century, matured in the 1940s and 1950s, and culminated in the mass nonviolent protests of the 1960s. After securing civil rights legislation in the mid-1960s, the movement became more radical, increasingly rejecting nonviolent protest and advocating more fundamental change. Though the movement lost momentum in the late 1960s, militant Black Power activism and political organizing continued until the mid-1970s.

The Roots of the Movement. After the Civil War, the Thirteenth, Fourteenth, and Fifteenth Amendments abolished slavery, made African Americans citizens of the United States, and accorded black men full voting rights. But blacks soon lost these rights and the political power they had gained during Reconstruction (1865–1877). Beginning in the early 1880s, southern authorities enacted legislation that mandated racial segregation in public life and disfranchised black men. In 1896 the U.S. Supreme Court's *Plessy v. Ferguson* decision affirmed the constitutionality of what came to be known as Jim Crow. White southerners used intimidation and violence, particularly lynching, to enforce the region's racial hierarchy. Although most northern blacks could vote, they, too, faced discrimination, segregation, and racist violence.

African Americans used various strategies to resist their subordination. Between 1900 and 1906 black middle-class activists staged unsuccessful boycotts against segregated streetcars in more than twenty-five cities in every state of the former Confederacy. By contrast, the black leader Booker T. Washington argued that southern blacks ought to accept segregation and disfranchisement and focus their energies on self-help and vocational education to advance the race. Black intellectuals such as W. E. B. Du Bois and William Monroe Trotter condemned Washington's approach and called for an immediate end to all forms of racial discrimination. In 1905 Du Bois organized the short-lived Niagara Movement, bringing together a number of prominent black leaders and intellectuals who seconded his demands. The founding of the National Association for the Advancement of Colored People (NAACP) in 1909 marked the beginning of sustained efforts to gain civil rights for African Americans. Founded by an interracial group of social activists, among them Du Bois and Ida B. Wells-Barnett, the NAACP sought to secure blacks' constitutional rights by challenging in the courts segregation and disfranchisement. In addition, the organization widely publicized lynchings and other instances of racial injustice to confront American society with the violent consequences of white racism.

World War I and the Great Migration of African Americans from the rural South to northern cities in the second decade of the twentieth century had a significant impact on race relations and black activism. Between 1910 and 1930 more than a million blacks left the South, hoping to escape racial oppression and to find both better living conditions and better jobs. The National Urban League, a black social welfare organization that was founded in 1910, tried to help these migrants adjust to the conditions they encountered in northern cities. As a result of the migration, northern black communities grew tremendously, which led to frictions with white city residents. On several occasions racial tensions exploded into violent race riots. In some of these clashes black World War I veterans defended their communities against white attackers. In the 1920s the black nationalist Marcus Garvey and his enormously popular Universal Negro Improvement Association exemplified and nurtured such militancy, which found cultural expression in the Harlem Renaissance.

The 1930s proved an important phase for civil rights organizing, despite the economic hardship brought about by the Great Depression. Some white activists attempted to forge alliances with African Americans to work for social change. In 1932 the seminary-trained Myles Horton cofounded the Highlander Folk School, a Tennessee-based institution that aimed to bring together black and white labor activists. Two years later the socialist Henry L. Mitchell founded the Southern Tenant Farmers' Union (STFU), an interracial organization that sought to improve the pitiable plight of black sharecroppers in Arkansas, Oklahoma, and Missouri. The American Communist Party also supported the struggles of civil rights activists and black workers.

Throughout the decade African Americans began to use more overt forms of protest. In 1936 the newly founded National Negro Congress (NNC), an umbrella organization that sought to unite various civil rights groups, advocated boycotts and picketing. In thirty-five cities across the nation African Americans used such tactics to protest against racial discrimination in retail employment. In the North some blacks also staged small demonstrations against segregation in public accommodations and schools or participated in rent strikes and anti-eviction protests. The NAACP's legal strategy continued to yield the most tangible results. Under the leadership of Charles Hamilton Houston and Thurgood Marshall, NAACP lawyers successfully challenged the exclusion of blacks from professional and graduate schools, an approach that was intended to prepare the ground for challenging the constitutionality of segregated education.

The 1940s and 1950s. World War II initiated and accelerated social and political developments that would facilitate future civil rights organizing. The booming war industry provided jobs for thousands of black southerners who streamed into northern and western cities. Black communities' growing resources led to the creation of larger black churches and colleges, independent black newspapers, and powerful political organizations, all of which strengthened social networks that civil rights activists could draw on. Outside the Deep South, moreover, African Americans became an important voting bloc in national politics, frequently providing the winning margin in presidential elections. Foreign policy concerns, coupled with blacks' increasing political weight, forced the federal government to pay more attention to black demands. America's proclaimed mission to fight for genuine democracy abroad clashed with racist realities at home and embarrassed the U.S. government in the fight against Nazi Germany.

During the war a few civil rights activists experimented with nonviolent protest. In 1941 the black labor leader A. Philip Randolph warned President Franklin D. Roosevelt that he would bring one hundred thousand African Americans to Washington, D.C., to protest against blatant discrimination in the defense industry. Exploiting the embarrassing international implications of Jim Crow, Randolph's threatened March on Washington campaign compelled Roosevelt to issue Executive Order 8802, which ended discrimination in the defense industry and established the Fair Employment Practices Commission.

Shortly after this success Randolph founded the March on Washington Movement (MOWM) to sustain pressure on white authorities. Like Randolph the members of the Congress of Racial Equality (CORE), a small interracial group of pacifists that was founded in Chicago in 1942, believed in the power of nonviolence as articulated by the Indian activist Mohandas Gandhi. Between 1942 and 1943, CORE chapters staged numerous successful "sit-down" campaigns in northern cities, forcing restaurants and public accommodations to end their policy of de facto segregation. In 1947 CORE launched it first national project, the Journey of Reconciliation, which tested a U.S. Supreme Court decision that had declared segregation in interstate travel unconstitutional.

The NAACP's tremendous wartime growth, coupled with important legal victories, further prepared the ground for future activism. By 1946 the association's membership had soared tenfold to five hundred thousand in more than one thousand chapters across the country. Two years earlier the NAACP had won a crucial victory in the struggle for voting rights. In *Smith v. Allwright* the U.S. Supreme Court outlawed the white primary, a tool designed by Southern Democrats to disfranchise African

Americans. The *Smith* decision reenfranchised black voters in Florida, Tennessee, and Texas, and it helped NAACP chapters and other local groups to register several hundred thousand African American voters. In this task they received support from numerous black World War II veterans, whose military service had become a catalyst for civil rights activism. In the North the NAACP focused on protesting against job and housing discrimination.

In the 1940s and early 1950s the advent of the Cold War proved both beneficial and detrimental to the civil rights cause. On the one hand, the implications of racial discrimination for America's ideological struggle with the Soviet Union provided black activists with powerful political leverage. After World War II the NNC and the NAACP used the United Nations as an international forum to accuse the United States of genocide. Concerns about the damaging effect of such public embarrassments, combined with blacks' growing political influence and Randolph's continued threats of civil disobedience, compelled President Harry S. Truman to issue directives that abolished discriminatory hiring practices in federal government employment and initiated the desegregation of the armed forces. On the other hand, domestic anticommunism led to the destruction of left-wing civil rights organizations such as the NNC and seriously impeded the activities of CORE, the NAACP, and other like-minded groups, which were hard-pressed to disprove allegations that they were infiltrated by Communists.

After surviving the initial anticommunist onslaught, the NAACP achieved one of its greatest victories. On 17 May 1954, in *Brown v. Board of Education of Topeka*, the U.S. Supreme Court declared school segregation unconstitutional, rescinding its "separate but equal" ruling of 1896. Yet while border states such as Maryland, Kentucky, and Missouri initiated school desegregation soon after *Brown*, whites in the Deep South devised various strategies to prevent racial integration. In July 1954, white middle-class Mississippians organized the White Citizens' Council, which used threats and economic pressure to stop racial integration.

Another Supreme Court decision, known as *Brown II*, in May 1955 failed to set a timetable for the implementation of school desegregation, thus encouraging southern white supremacists to step up the region's massive resistance. In the following months White Citizens' Councils spread quickly across the South and boasted a membership of almost a quarter of a million by 1956. Southern politicians also vowed to defend white supremacy. In March 1956 ninety-six U.S. congressmen from the region signed a "Southern Manifesto," in which they expressed their determination to uphold Jim Crow. Meanwhile southern authorities attempted to destroy the NAACP, again charging that it was linked to Communism. Several states banned the organization, which cost the NAACP almost fifty thousand southern members. Segregationists also used violence to stop the black freedom movement. Killings such as the murder of the NAACP activist George W. Lee and the lynching of the black teenager Emmett Till in 1955 frightened many but also inspired others to become involved in the struggle.

Amid the furor created by the *Brown* decision, blacks in Montgomery, Alabama, staged a successful boycott to end segregation on the city's bus lines. Local activists, among them Edgar Daniel Nixon and Jo Ann Robinson, had long considered civil disobedience to challenge Jim Crow. When on 1 December 1955 the black activist Rosa Parks violated Alabama's segregation laws by refusing to vacate her seat for a white man, Nixon, Robinson, and others initiated the boycott and used her conviction as a legal test case to challenge bus segregation in federal court. The young Baptist minister Martin Luther King Jr. agreed to lead the local struggle, which lasted 381 days. In November 1956 the U.S. Supreme Court finally declared Alabama's segregation laws unconstitutional.

The success of the Montgomery boycott inspired a number of similar campaigns in the South and made King the black freedom movement's most visible spokesman. It also resolved King and other activists to establish the Southern Christian Leadership Conference (SCLC) in 1957 to encourage and coordinate civil rights protest in the region. Advocating nonviolence, the SCLC demanded full citizenship rights for African Americans and their integration into American society. Until the end of the 1950s, however, the SCLC accomplished little, primarily because it lacked funds and an organizational program.

After the Montgomery bus boycott, white southerners' continuing efforts to stop school desegregation dominated the headlines. The most violent incident took place in Little Rock, Arkansas, where Governor Orval Faubus ordered national guardsmen to prevent nine black students from attending the city's all-white Central High School. Spurred on by Faubus's defiance of federal law, a white mob later besieged the school and harassed some of the students. The governor's rebelliousness infuriated President Dwight D. Eisenhower, who was far from being a champion of racial equality but brooked no insubordination. In an action unprecedented since Reconstruction, the president dispatched federal troops to Little Rock to quell the disorder and to protect the black students. Ultimately, however, the Little Rock crisis did little to speed up school integration. Although massive resistance subsided by the end of the 1950s, many southern authorities successfully prevented desegregation by adopting discriminatory pupil-placement laws, by giving tuition grants to white students to attend private schools, or by simply closing those schools that were ordered to enroll black students.

The civil rights movement's attempts to increase the number of southern black voters in the second half of the 1950s were more successful but had a similarly negligible impact on the racial status quo. New civil rights legislation failed to help activists overcome the obstacles they confronted. Neither the Civil Rights Act of 1957 nor the Civil Rights Act of 1960 provided federal authorities or the Justice Department with sufficient power to enforce school integration or to prosecute cases of voter discrimination and racist violence on a widespread basis. Confronted with strong southern resistance and reluctant federal authorities, the civil rights movement appeared to be stalled.

Mass Protest and Voter Registration. In February 1960 a student-led sit-in movement against segregated lunch counters revived the stagnating civil rights movement. By April almost fifty thousand students had staged sit-ins in seventy-eight cities in nine southern states. Lunch counters in border states quickly desegregated as a result of the demonstrations, but the Deep South remained a bulwark of Jim Crow. When student activists pondered joining the established civil rights organizations during a conference in Raleigh, North Carolina, in April 1960, the veteran activist Ella Baker convinced them to form their own group: the Student Nonviolent Coordinating Committee (SNCC). In the Freedom Ride of 1961, which was organized by CORE, SNCC activists had a chance to continue the nonviolent direct-action techniques they had used during the sit-ins. Modeled on the Journey of Reconciliation, the Freedom Ride was designed to test the U.S. Supreme Court's *Boynton v. Virginia* decision, which had extended desegregation to all terminal facilities in interstate travel.

On 4 May 1961 two interracial teams of activists set off for the Deep South from Washington, D.C. White mob violence in Anniston and Birmingham, Alabama, served CORE's goal of focusing national and international attention on southern injustice. Because of the crises the Freedom Ride created, President John F. Kennedy dispatched federal troops to the South to protect the activists. In Jackson, Mississippi, the journey was finally stopped when local authorities arrested the freedom riders for violating local segregation laws, but similar campaigns spread quickly in the following months. In September 1961 the Interstate Commerce Commission finally desegregated all interstate travel facilities.

After the Freedom Ride the SCLC staged two ambitious nonviolent demonstrations in southern cities. In Albany, Georgia, however, where SNCC activists had helped to organize a local movement, black activists' efforts in 1962 to provoke extensive media coverage and federal

March to Register Voters. Thousands of marchers walk fifty-four miles from Selma to Montgomery to promote awareness of the low number of registered black voters in the South, March 1965. Photograph by Jack Hopper. BIRMINGHAM NEWS/POLARIS

intervention by staging peaceful demonstrations soon collapsed. The SCLC's campaign in Birmingham, Alabama, in May 1963 reflected the lessons that activists had learned in Albany. Thoroughly planned, the project concentrated on local white merchants' discriminatory practices. More important, activists expected Birmingham's racist public safety commissioner Eugene "Bull" Connor to react with violence to their peaceful demonstrations, which they hoped would trigger the media coverage that had eluded the Albany movement.

In early May, Connor fulfilled the SCLC's expectations, ordering his deputies and local firemen to attack protesting black children with clubs, dogs, and high-pressure water hoses. The violence shocked national and international audiences and compelled the administration of President Kennedy to intervene as a mediator. Although not all of the SCLC's demands were met, Birmingham was considered a major success for the civil rights movement. It triggered a wave of similar demonstrations across the South and contributed to the decision of President Kennedy to propose civil rights legislation in a televised address to the nation. In June 1963 almost a quarter of a million people descended on Washington, D.C., in a peaceful March on Washington to lobby for the new bill. After the assassination of President Kennedy in November 1963, his successor, Lyndon B. Johnson, managed to secure the passage of the landmark Civil Rights Act of 1964, which banned racial discrimination in public life and employment.

Although the media concentrated on civil rights activism in the Deep South, the black freedom struggle of the 1960s did not remain confined to the former Confederacy. In midwestern and northern cities such as New York, Philadelphia, Cleveland, Milwaukee, and Wichita, Kansas, black activists and their white allies also used nonviolent demonstrations, boycotts, and legal action to protest de facto school segregation and discrimination in employment and housing. Sometimes these efforts proved successful, but many activists quickly learned that breaking racist customs in the North frequently proved just as hard and as dangerous as trying to topple legalized white supremacy in the South. In Cambridge, Maryland, for instance, the black civil rights leader Gloria Richardson and her followers had to rely on armed guards to protect themselves against white mobs that invaded the black community.

Following the passage of the Civil Rights Act of 1964, the southern movement tested white compliance with the new law and focused on securing black southerners' right to vote. SNCC and CORE had been attempting to launch voter registration campaigns in the Deep South since 1961. In subsequent organizing efforts, local black women became the backbone of the movement, participating in civil rights meetings, voter registration drives, and demonstrations far more often than did men. But white violence seriously hampered civil rights activism. Especially in Mississippi, the Ku Klux Klan and other terrorist groups intimidated black supporters and murdered veteran civil rights leaders such as Medgar Wylie Evers with impunity. SNCC's 1964 Freedom Summer project, which brought hundreds of white northern volunteers to Mississippi to conduct voter registration drives and to teach black children in so-called Freedom Schools, was intended to focus national attention on the state and to force the federal government to protect SNCC's activities. Even though the brutal murder of three activists brought the attention that SNCC sought, President Johnson did nothing to ensure the safety of black and white civil rights organizers.

Confronted with racist terrorism and a procrastinating White House, a number of southern black activists established self-defense groups to protect themselves and their white allies. As early as 1957 the NAACP leader Robert F. Williams formed a protective unit in Monroe, North Carolina. In the 1960s more sophisticated defense organizations emerged in the Deep South, among them the Deacons for Defense and Justice in Jonesboro, Louisiana, and a protective squad in Tuscaloosa, Alabama. In Mississippi similar groups protected white and black activists during SNCC's Freedom Summer project. Such defensive efforts helped local freedom movements survive in the face of racist violence, frequently bolstered the morale of nonviolent protesters, and instilled pride in many black protectors, but they also triggered heated debates over the legitimacy of self-defense within SNCC and CORE. Ultimately, many activists came to accept armed resistance as an integral part of civil rights organizing in the South.

In 1965 the civil rights movement finally secured legislation that ended the disfranchisement of African Americans in the Deep South. Despite the grassroots organizing of CORE and SNCC, white resistance had prevented any considerable increase in the number of black voters. SNCC's effort to challenge the legitimacy of Mississippi's racist Democratic Party by establishing the Mississippi Freedom Democratic Party (MFDP) also failed to convince federal authorities of the need for voting rights legislation or the inclusion of blacks in the Democratic Party.

To lobby for a new voting rights bill, the SCLC launched a protest campaign in Selma, Alabama, in January 1965. When the SCLC led a protest march from Selma to the state capital Montgomery in March, Alabama state troopers responded with clubs and tear gas. The unprovoked attack on peaceful protesters triggered a national outcry of indignation and stimulated a broad consensus in favor of federal legislation. In August 1965, President Johnson

Bloody Sunday. The Selma Movement leader Amelia Boynton is aided after being gassed and clubbed to the ground by police upon her attempt to cross the Edmund Pettus Bridge with other marchers in the Selma-to-Montgomery March in Alabama, 7 March 1965. Photograph by Spider Martin.

signed the Voting Rights Act of 1965 into law. Banning tests designed to disqualify black applicants and enabling the attorney general to send federal voting registrars to states that were suspected of discriminating against its voters, the new law led to a tremendous upsurge of African Americans on the voter rolls.

Radicalization and Demise. After the Selma campaign the radicalization of SNCC and CORE pushed the movement in a more militant direction. In large part this radicalization was a consequence of activists' experience in the South. During their long struggle, activists had become increasingly distrustful of the federal government and traditional party politics. Many became convinced that blacks would have to organize outside mainstream politics to gain power. In addition the dominant role of white volunteers in civil rights projects and the patronizing attitude of white liberal supporters had led activists to the conclusion that the movement ought to concentrate on forming independent all-black organizations and institutions. Their support for nonviolent tactics had also been eroded by years of racist terrorism.

Other factors that contributed to the growing militancy of SNCC and CORE were the influence of the black Muslim minister Malcolm X, race riots in northern and western cities that testified to the limited impact of civil rights legislation outside the South, and the escalation of the Vietnam War. During the 1966 James Meredith March against Fear, the SNCC leader Stokely Carmichael first voiced the slogan "Black Power," which was the crystallization of these various tactical and ideological reconsiderations and became synonymous with the movement's radicalization in the following years.

But not only the southern activists contributed to the emergence of Black Power in the second half of the 1960s. Outside the South, black militants had long argued for alternative strategies to tackle poverty, unemployment, discrimination, and police brutality in urban black communities. In Detroit activists such as Albert Cleage Jr., Richard and Milton Henry, and James and Grace Lee Boggs became part of a vital network of black militants. Cleage's Group on Advanced Leadership (GOAL), founded in 1961, advocated independent black political activism and forged alliances with black nationalist groups such as the Nation of Islam (NOI). The NOI's leader Elijah Muhammad denounced white people as "devils" and advocated black pride, moral uplift, and economic self-reliance.

In the late 1950s and early 1960s, Malcolm X, a hustler-turned-Muslim-minister, became the NOI's most famous spokesman, lambasting King's nonviolent philosophy and recruiting thousands of new followers. Malcolm's advocacy of black pride and self-defense influenced many black militants. Among his followers were Maxwell Stanford and Donald Freeman, who in 1962 founded the Revolutionary Action Movement, an organization that sought to use mass action and armed resistance to foster a revolutionary black movement. The revival of black nationalism in the late 1950s and early 1960s was also fueled by the Cuban revolution and the process of decolonization in Africa. In such publications as the *Liberator*, *Soulbook*, and *Muhammad Speaks*, black nationalists from across the nation discussed the meaning of these revolutionary events, as well as their political and cultural programs.

Throughout the late 1960s and 1970s, Black Power remained an ambiguous term, and the vital movement that the slogan inspired was multilayered and had many different agendas. Common themes that could be found in most Black Power programs were black pride, black political and economic power, community control of black institutions, radical internationalism, and armed self-defense. The various strands of the Black Power movement, however, advocated different strategies to accomplish these goals. Revolutionary nationalists such as the Black Panther Party for Self-Defense (later the Black Panther Party, or BPP), which was founded in Oakland, California, in 1966, ultimately sought to establish global socialism by overthrowing U.S. capitalism and imperialism. Cultural nationalists such as Maulana Ron Karenga, who founded US Organization (or Organization US) in Los Angeles in 1965, argued that a reaffirmation of the uniqueness and beauty of African American and African culture had to predate any revolutionary action.

For activists like Karenga, the Black Arts Movement became one of the major vehicles to link cultural nationalism and political struggle. Territorial nationalists such as Milton Henry and his group Republic of New Africa, on the other hand, called for an independent black nation within the United States, claiming five Deep South states and some black enclaves in northern cities as the new nation's territory. On hundreds of college campuses, meanwhile, African American student activists pressed white authorities to establish African American studies programs and institutional changes that were grounded in Black Power principles. And in numerous urban communities across the nation, African American activists struggled to implement Black Power principles at the local level.

In part because of its ambiguity, Black Power encountered strong opposition from both black civil rights leaders and white Americans. The NAACP's executive secretary Roy O. Wilkins initially denounced Black Power as a violent form of reverse racism. King, though acknowledging the frustrations that fueled the movement's radicalization, also argued that it contained dangerous connotations of separatism and violence. Many black militants, in turn, ridiculed King's insistence that nonviolent protest would help end poverty and unemployment in northern black communities.

King's assassination on 4 April 1968 suggested to many that the era of nonviolence was over. White liberals, on the other hand, felt betrayed by the Black Power stance adopted by SNCC and CORE in 1966 and stopped supporting these two organizations. Federal authorities and the Federal Bureau of Investigation (FBI) were even more concerned, considering Black Power a threat to national security. The FBI regarded the martial rhetoric of black nationalist organizations and the hundreds of race riots that rocked northern and western cities between 1964 and 1968 as a justification for government repression. Black Power groups were considerably weakened by COINTELPRO, a highly sophisticated domestic counterintelligence program that the FBI used to disrupt and destroy black militant organizations.

Despite the demise of nonviolent protest in the late 1960s and the opposition that Black Power groups encountered, black activism continued across the nation until the mid-1970s. In the South, African Americans used voter registration and litigation to implement the new civil rights laws and also fought for economic justice and political power. The national NAACP and its local chapters remained at the forefront of this struggle. In terms of political representation, these efforts yielded impressive results. By 1970 more than seven hundred African Americans had won political offices in the states of the former Confederacy—compared to twenty-four elected officials in 1964. However, since many of these politicians held minor offices and needed the support of white allies, they rarely managed to bring about significant social change in their communities.

Outside the South an increasing number of Black Power activists sought to combine cultural nationalism, institution building, and political organizing, gradually abandoning earlier plans to use revolutionary violence to transform American society. On the East Coast the black nationalist Amiri Baraka helped organize a series of black conventions that brought together various Black Power groups to discuss the future of the black community and to support black political candidates. The 1972 National Black Political Convention in Gary, Indiana, marked the zenith of Baraka's efforts to unite the Black Power movement, bringing together thousands of activists and elected officials.

Although the black convention movement lost momentum in the following years, black political representation in northern and western cities increased considerably. By 1974 more than fifteen hundred elected African Americans officials served on various levels outside the South. Six years later there were almost twenty-five hundred. In the 1970s and 1980s a number of black politicians became mayors of large cities, among them Coleman Young in Detroit and Harold Washington in Chicago. In the 1980s the former SCLC activist Jesse Jackson emerged as one of the most visible black politicians, becoming the second African American (after Shirley Chisholm in 1972) to seek the presidential nomination of the Democratic Party.

But the civil rights movement also faced a serious white backlash that sought to delay or prevent social change. Whereas school integration was finally implemented in the South in the early 1970s, for instance, the desegregation of northern schools encountered severe resistance. In 1974 white parents in Boston began a three-year campaign to prevent the busing of black children to formerly all-white schools. That same year the U.S. Supreme Court ruled in *Milliken v. Bradley* that white children from suburban neighborhoods could not be forced to be bused to inner-city schools to achieve racial integration. In part because of this court decision, an increasing number of urban schools abandoned desegregation in the following two decades.

The backlash could also be seen in national politics. In the 1968 presidential election the segregationist third-party candidate George Wallace enjoyed considerable support from white voters across the nation. The election of the Republican Richard Nixon reflected an increasingly conservative political climate that was less supportive of civil rights. In the 1980s President Ronald Reagan's opposition to affirmative action and his decision to cut funding for welfare programs represented a further blow to the movement for racial justice. Though the powerful coalition of conservative Republicans that came to be known as the New Right could not completely undo the changes brought about by the civil rights movement, it continued to wage political and legal assaults on laws that benefited African Americans.

Impact and Legacy. The civil rights movement had an enormous impact on American society. Because of the increased educational and employment opportunities that desegregation and affirmative action programs provided, a growing proportion of African Americans were able to enter the middle class. African Americans' political representation also grew tremendously in the decades that followed the civil rights struggle. By 2001 there were more than 9,000 black elected officials in the nation, compared to 103 in 1964. In addition, the activism of civil rights organizations and Black Power groups helped reinterpret African American identity and left a significant cultural and intellectual legacy that continues to shape American society in the twenty-first century. The prominence of black intellectuals such as Henry Louis Gates Jr., Toni Morrison, Nell Irvin Painter, and Cornel West, as well as the controversial Million Man March in 1995, the Million Woman March in 1997, and similar protests, testify to the power of this legacy. Finally, the black freedom struggle became a catalyst for other movements for equal rights, among them the women's movement and the protest movements of Mexican Americans and Native Americans.

Not all African Americans benefited from the movement's victories, however. Many blacks continue to struggle with economic problems. In 2004, 24.7 percent of African Americans lived below the poverty line, compared to 8.6 percent of non-Hispanic whites. In many poor urban communities, crime, gang warfare, family breakdowns, and drugs thwart African Americans' efforts to share in the wealth of American society. The Civil Rights Act of 1968, passed in reaction to the wave of civil disorders in the 1960s and forbidding housing discrimination on the basis of race, failed to integrate or improve rundown inner-city neighborhoods. In urban communities across the United States, patterns of residential segregation remain unchanged.

Police brutality and racial profiling, which civil rights and Black Power groups had criticized in the 1960s, also continued largely unabated in many parts of the nation. In 1992 the frustration over this injustice once more exploded into violence when blacks in South Central Los Angeles rioted in reaction to a court verdict that acquitted four white police officers who had brutally beaten a black man named Rodney King. In light of such instances of injustice, many black politicians and activists argue that full racial equality is a goal yet to be achieved.

[*See also* Anticommunism and Civil Rights; Birmingham Campaign; Black Nationalism; Black Panther Party; Black Power Movement; Civil Disobedience; Communism and African Americans; Congress of Racial Equality; Desegregation and Integration; Disfranchisement of African Americans; Freedom Rides; Highlander Folk School; Jim Crow Laws; Journey of Reconciliation; Laws and Legislation; Marches on Washington, D.C.; Martyrdom and Civil Rights; Massive Resistance; Mississippi Freedom Summer; Montgomery Bus Boycott; Legal Defense and Educational Fund; National Association for the Advancement of Colored People; National Negro Congress; National Urban League; Niagara Movement; Political Parties and Civil Rights; Poor People's Campaign; Riots and Rebellions, *subentry* Riots and Rebellions of the 1960s; Segregation; Sit-ins; Social Sciences and Civil Rights; Southern Christian Leadership Conference; Student Nonviolent Coordinating Committee; Voting Rights; *and biographical entries on figures mentioned in this article*.]

Bibliography

Berg, Manfred. *The Ticket to Freedom: The NAACP and the Struggle for Black Political Integration*. Gainesville: University Press of Florida, 2005. The first full-scale study of the oldest civil rights organization in the United States.

Carson, Clayborne. *In Struggle: SNCC and the Black Awakening of the 1960s*. Cambridge, Mass.: Harvard University Press, 1981.

Dittmer, John. *Local People: The Struggle for Civil Rights in Mississippi*. Urbana: University of Illinois Press, 1994. An essential read for students interested in the contribution of local black activists to the black freedom struggle in the Magnolia State.

Dudziak, Mary L. *Cold War Civil Rights: Race and the Image of American Democracy*. Princeton, N.J.: Princeton University Press, 2000. A meticulously researched account of the connections between civil rights activism and American foreign policy.

Fairclough, Adam. *Better Day Coming: Blacks and Equality, 1890–2000*. New York: Viking, 2001. One of the best general introductions to civil rights activism in the twentieth century.

Fairclough, Adam. *Race and Democracy: The Civil Rights Struggle in Louisiana, 1915–1972*. Athens: University of Georgia Press, 1995. A detailed study of civil rights organizing in the Pelican State that demonstrates the historical continuities of civil rights activism before and after World War II.

Garrow, David J. *Bearing the Cross: Martin Luther King, Jr., and the Southern Christian Leadership Conference*. New York: William Morrow, 1986.

Johnson, Ollie A., and Karin L. Stanford. *Black Political Organizations in the Post–Civil Rights Era*. New Brunswick, N.J.: Rutgers University Press, 2002.

Joseph, Peniel E. *Waiting 'til the Midnight Hour: A Narrative History of Black Power in America*. New York: Henry Holt, 2006. The most recent introduction to the Black Power movement, stressing continuities between black activism in the 1950s and Black Power militancy in the 1960s and 1970s.

Joseph, Peniel E., ed. *The Black Power Movement: Rethinking the Civil Rights–Black Power Era*. New York: Routledge, 2006. A collection of essays that provides fresh perspectives on black radicalism in the 1960s and 1970s.

Lawson, Steven F. *Running for Freedom: Civil Rights and Black Politics in America since 1941*. 2d ed. New York: McGraw-Hill, 1997. A detailed study of black activists' efforts to end black disfranchisement and the impact of the black vote on American society.

Massey, Douglas S., and Nancy A. Denton. *American Apartheid: Segregation and the Making of the Underclass*. Cambridge, Mass.: Harvard University Press, 1993. A sociological study of the persistence of residential segregation and its impact on African Americans in the post–civil rights era.

Meier, August, and Elliot Rudwick. *CORE: A Study in the Civil Rights Movement, 1942–1968*. Urbana: University of Illinois Press, 1975.

Payne, Charles. *I've Got the Light of Freedom: The Organizing Tradition and the Mississippi Freedom Struggle*. Berkeley: University of California Press, 1995. A pathbreaking study of traditions of civil rights organizing in post–World War II Mississippi.

Perry, Bruce. *Malcolm: The Life of a Man Who Changed Black America*. Barrytown, N.Y.: Station Hill, 1991. A controversial yet meticulously researched biography of the militant black activist who has influenced generations of African Americans.

Stern, Mark. *Calculating Visions: Kennedy, Johnson, and Civil Rights*. New Brunswick, N.J.: Rutgers University Press, 1992. A comprehensive account of the federal government's reaction to the civil rights movement.

Theoharis, Jeanne F., and Komozi Woodward, eds. *Freedom North: Black Freedom Struggles outside the South, 1940–1980*. New York: Palgrave Macmillan, 2003.

Tyson, Timothy B. *Radio Free Dixie: Robert F. Williams and the Roots of Black Power*. Chapel Hill: University of North Carolina Press, 1999. A gracefully written biography that sheds light on armed resistance and the international implications of civil rights activism in the 1950s and 1960s.

Van Deburg, William L. *New Day in Babylon: The Black Power Movement and American Culture, 1965–1975*. Chicago: University of Chicago Press, 1992. A detailed and analytical introduction to the Black Power movement and its cultural dimension.

Webb, Clive, ed. *Massive Resistance: Southern Opposition to the Second Reconstruction*. New York: Oxford University Press, 2005. Provides examples of the most recent scholarship on the southern white reaction to the civil rights movement.

Wendt, Simon. *The Spirit and the Shotgun: Armed Resistance and the Struggle for Civil Rights*. Gainesville: University Press of Florida, 2007. A comprehensive study of the role of armed self-defense in the black freedom movement.

—Simon Wendt

CLANSMAN, THE. Published in 1905, Thomas Dixon Jr.'s novel *The Clansman: An Historical Romance of the Ku Klux Klan* was the second in a series of three novels known as his *Reconstruction Trilogy*. The first in the trilogy, *The Leopard's Spots*, appeared in 1903, and the series was completed in 1907 with the publication of *The Traitor*. All three books celebrated the lost cause of the South and detailed the tragedy of racial equality imposed on the South during Reconstruction. Beginning at the close of the Civil War, *The Clansman* explores the war, Reconstruction, and especially race relations through the lives of the Stoneman and Cameron families. In 1915 the novel was adapted for the screen and released as D. W. Griffith's major motion picture *The Birth of a Nation*.

The novel's character Austin Stoneman, a Radical Republican statesman from the North, is openly modeled on the Pennsylvania senator Thaddeus Stevens. The patriarch of the southern family, Dr. Richard Cameron, is modeled on Dr. J. Rufus Bratton, a South Carolina physician active in the Ku Klux Klan during Reconstruction. The sons of these two men, Phil Stoneman and Ben Cameron—who had been friends before the so-called War of Northern Aggression—reunite following Civil War service for their respective regions, and the Stonemans travel south for a reunion of sorts.

Set in South Carolina, one of two southern states to have an African American–majority legislature during Reconstruction, *The Clansman* details the "catastrophe" of racial equality as imposed by northerners such as Stoneman. *The Clansman* depicts the wanton black legislators, the insouciant former slaves, and others who are incapable of running the state government, all the while demanding equal treatment from whites. The climax of the plot revolves around the rape of Marion Lenoir, a young southern woman, by the former slave Gus and "four black brutes" who burst in on Marion and her mother, Mrs. Lenoir. Marion and Mrs. Lenoir make a suicide pact to hide their shame, jumping from a cliff to their deaths.

Despite their attempt to hide the truth, Dr. Cameron sees the "bestial figure of a negro" while examining their bodies: it is Gus, his image captured in the dead eyes of Mrs. Lenoir. Ben Cameron and the Ku Klux Klan rally to avenge the honor of these southern ladies. Following widespread violence against black southerners, the novel ends with the triumph of white supremacy when Ben Cameron proclaims that "I am a successful revolutionist—that Civilization has been saved, and the South redeemed from shame."

Among the general public *The Clansman* was a popular success; Dixon adapted it for the stage in the fall of 1905. The play made a profitable tour of the South—and was also performed in northern areas sympathetic to southern attitudes—but was generally criticized in the press as liable to stir racial unrest and violence. Indeed, many historians tie its adaptation for the screen in *The Birth of a Nation* to the resurgence of the Ku Klux Klan in the 1920s.

Both Booker T. Washington and W. E. B. Du Bois held little respect for Dixon and his writings, but as a southerner Washington received more attention from the author. In early 1906 Dixon wrote Washington, pledging $10,000 of the profits from *The Clansman* to the Tuskegee Institute. Dixon also challenged Washington to a debate on the question of the "Future of the Negro in America." Washington politely declined, remarking, "I cannot feel that any good can be accomplished at this time by taking up the subjects in the manner your communications suggest" (Harlan and Smock, pp. 508 and 510).

[*See also Birth of a Nation, The*; Dixon, Thomas, Jr.; Ku Klux Klan; *and* White Supremacy.]

BIBLIOGRAPHY

Harlan, Louis R., and Raymond W. Smock, eds. *The Booker T. Washington Papers*. Vol. 8: *1904–6*. Urbana: University of Illinois Press, 1979.

Slide, Anthony. *American Racist: The Life and Films of Thomas Dixon*. Lexington: University Press of Kentucky, 2004. Offers literary criticism of Dixon's main novels, plays, and film adaptations.

—L. DIANE BARNES

CLARK, MAMIE PHIPPS AND KENNETH, educational psychologists. Kenneth Bancroft Clark (b. 24 July 1914; d. 1 May 2005) and Mamie Katherine Phipps Clark (b. 18 April 1917; d. 11 August 1983) were husband-and-wife collaborators who studied the relationship between racial identity and children's self-esteem and development.

Kenneth Clark was born in 1914 in the Panama Canal Zone, where his father, Arthur, worked for the United Fruit Company. In 1919 his mother, Miriam, decided to move to America, so she separated from her husband and moved to Harlem with Kenneth and his younger sister. When Kenneth was in junior high school, a career counselor recommended that he prepare for a vocational trade, but his mother, who was earning a very low wage as a seamstress, insisted that he transfer to a school where he would have a rigorous course of study. He went on to earn his bachelor's and master's degrees at Howard University and then, in 1940, his PhD in psychology at Columbia University—the first African American to do so there. In 1942 he became a professor at the City College of New York, where he taught until 1975 and was the first black tenured professor. Clark's many books include *Prejudice and Your Child* (1955), *Dark Ghetto: Dilemmas of Social Power* (1965), and *Crisis in Urban Education* (1971).

When he was a master's student at Howard, Clark met Mamie Phipps. Phipps was born in 1917 in Hot Springs, Arkansas, where her father, Harold, a native of the British West Indies, was a doctor; her mother, Kate, assisted him with procedures. Her father's medical practice allowed the family middle-class status, but Mamie's education was still segregated. In 1934 she graduated from high school and, having won a scholarship, attended Howard University intending to study math and physics. After she met Kenneth, he suggested that she pursue instead his field, psychology, because then she could explore her interest in children.

In 1937 Mamie and Kenneth eloped, in part because her parents disapproved of her marrying before graduation. In 1938 Mamie graduated magna cum laude from Howard, and she was offered a graduate fellowship so that she could pursue her master's degree at Howard. She began working with children in an all-black nursery school, studying their self-identification. Mamie's research involved two psychological tests: a coloring test and a test with dolls. In 1939 she completed her master's thesis, "The Development of Consciousness of Self in Negro Pre-School Children." She and Kenneth proposed further research on self-perception in black children, and they updated her versions of the coloring and doll tests. Their proposal was awarded a Rosenwald Fellowship in 1939, renewed twice.

The fellowship enabled Mamie to pursue her PhD in psychology at Columbia, which she earned in 1943—the first African American woman and the second African American, after Kenneth, to do so there. Kenneth and Mamie Clark conducted many studies on racism's effect on child development and found that segregation was psychologically damaging and emotionally harmful to both black and white children. In one famous study—subsequently criticized by some scholars—black children stated that they preferred white dolls to black dolls. The Clarks interpreted the responses to mean that the children saw themselves as inferior to their white peers, and they published their research and findings.

Facing racism and sexism from employers, from 1944 to 1946 Mamie Clark held two jobs that she was overqualified for, analyzing data for the American Public Health Association and researching for the U.S. Armed Forces Institute. In 1946 she became a testing psychologist at the Riverdale Home for Children, working with black girls, and while there she became aware of the lack of psychological services for Harlem's children, many of whom were simply labeled "mentally retarded." The Clarks petitioned existing service agencies to offer mental-health support for black and other minority children; when they met resistance they created their own agency.

Thus in March 1946 the Clarks opened the Northside Testing and Consultation Center, later called the Northside Center for Child Development, and offered psychiatric and psychological services to children and families in Harlem. Because of the stigma of mental illness, Harlem residents were initially afraid to use the center, but soon the center's intelligence testing services made it popular. Many parents wanted their children who had been labeled mentally retarded by the state schools to be tested independently because they doubted the diagnosis. The center staff determined that most of the children had IQs exceeding mental retardation, thus revealing the schools' illegal practice of misidentifying children based on their race.

Kenneth Clark's Center for Child Development. Dr. Kenneth Clark, New York psychologist, educator, and founder of the Northside Center for Child Development, attends a staff meeting at the center, 1965. AP IMAGES

In order to compensate for a lack of educational support for minority children, in 1947 the Clarks instituted remedial math and reading programs at Northside. Mamie Clark served as Northside's executive director from its founding until 1979. In addition to advising the national Head Start planning committee, she served on the boards of, among others, the New York Public Library, Teachers College of Columbia University, the Phelps-Stokes Fund, and the Museum of Modern Art.

Meanwhile, in 1953 Kenneth Clark worked with other social scientists to compose a brief report showing the results of the Clarks' study on black children's self-perception, and the report was presented to NAACP lawyers. Subsequently the Clarks' work was cited in the landmark 1954 Supreme Court school-desegregation decision in *Brown v. Board of Education*, which acknowledged the psychological harm of segregation on children as one reason that separate schools were inherently unequal. Kenneth Clark often spoke before the New York school system in the 1950s and 1960s and advocated for fully integrated classrooms, reduced class sizes, more advanced curriculum for all children regardless of race, and higher-quality school buildings.

In 1961 Kenneth Clark received the Spingarn Medal, the NAACP's highest award. Clark was the first African American to be elected to the New York Board of Regents, where he served for twenty years from 1966. In 1971 Clark became the first African American to be elected president of his profession's premier organization, the American Psychological Association.

The Clarks had a daughter, Kate, in 1940 and a son, Hilton, in 1943. Mamie and Kenneth Clark were married forty-five years before Mamie died in 1983. Kenneth died at his home in Hastings-on-Hudson, New York, in 2005.

[*See also Brown v. Board of Education and* Social Sciences and Civil Rights.]

BIBLIOGRAPHY

Clark, Kenneth B. "An Architect of Social Change: Kenneth B. Clark." In *Against the Odds: Scholars Who Challenged Racism in the Twentieth Century*, edited by Benjamin P. Bowser and Louis Kushnick with Paul Grant, pp. 14–157. Amherst: University of Massachusetts Press, 2002. A personal account.

Clark, Mamie Phipps. "Mamie Phipps Clark." In *Models of Achievement: Reflections of Eminent Women in Psychology*, edited by Agnes N. O'Connell and Nancy Felipe Russo, pp. 266–277. New York: Columbia University Press, 1983. A personal account.

Markowitz, Gerald E., and David Rosner. *Children, Race, and Power: Kenneth and Mamie Clark's Northside Center*. Charlottesville: University Press of Virginia, 1996.

Philogène, Gina, ed. *Racial Identity in Context: The Legacy of Kenneth B. Clark*. Washington, D.C.: American Psychological Association, 2004.

—RACHELLE GOLD

CLARK, SEPTIMA (b. 3 May 1898; d. 15 December 1987), educator, community organizer, and civil rights activist. Septima Poinsette Clark was born in 1898 in Charleston, South Carolina, to Peter Poinsette, a former slave, and Victoria Warren Anderson Poinsette, a native Charlestonian who had spent her childhood in Haiti. Clark had a distinguished sixty-year career as a pioneering educator and civil rights activist, earning the sobriquet "Queen Mother of the Civil Rights Movement." In 1916 she graduated from the Avery Institute and began teaching at the Promised Land School on John's Island, South Carolina. In 1919, she moved back to Charleston to teach at the Avery Institute; there she joined the National Association for the Advancement of Colored People (NAACP) and worked to overturn the law that barred black teachers from Charleston public schools. Septima Poinsette married Neils Clark in 1920 and bore two children, only one of whom survived, before she and her husband separated. She returned to Johns Island from 1926 to 1929 before she settled in Columbia, South Carolina, as an elementary school teacher.

Clark finished her BA degree in 1942 at Benedict College and completed an MA at Hampton Institute shortly after World War II. While living in Columbia she assisted the NAACP in preparing its 1945 case for equalizing salaries of black and white teachers in South Carolina; in that same year a South Carolina federal district court ruled in favor of the class action suit on behalf of black Charleston teachers. In Columbia she also became involved in adult education by teaching illiterate black soldiers how to read and write. Teaching adult literacy would form an integral part of her career for the better part of two decades. Indeed, as a beginning teacher on John's Island in 1919, she had successfully experimented with teaching adults basic literacy skills, but in Columbia she got a chance to see the potential of a long-term program for adult education.

Clark moved back to Charleston in 1947 to care for her ailing mother and continued her community involvement with the local chapter of the NAACP. In 1956, the South Carolina legislature made it illegal for public employees—including teachers—to be affiliated with any civil rights organization. Clark was fired when she refused to conceal her NAACP activities. But her background in adult education had put her in touch with the crusading white liberal Myles Horton, whose Highlander Folk School in Monteagle, Tennessee, sought to break down racial barriers and to promote a variety of social justice causes. Clark became the director of Highlander's adult education program and immediately began organizing citizenship schools in South Carolina. The Highlander connection also put her in touch with many of the most effective and determined civil rights advocates in the South, including Ella Baker, Rosa Parks, and Martin Luther King Jr.

When Tennessee authorities closed Highlander in 1961 (it would reopen the next year under another name), Clark accepted the invitation of Martin Luther King Jr. to move her work to the Southern Christian Leadership Conference (SCLC) as director of the Citizen Education Project. In that role she traveled throughout the eleven states of the Deep South giving adult workshops on topics ranging from how to make out a bank check to strategies for voter registration. Clark established more than eight hundred SCLC Citizenship Schools, which graduated more than one hundred thousand adult African American students, many of whom became community organizers for civil rights. Throughout her career, Clark remained steadfast in her belief that community organization was essential for racial progress, and she remained skeptical of the effectiveness of national leadership. In that way she joined other civil rights advocates like Ella Baker and Jo Ann Robinson, who discovered the necessity of local organizing to achieve meaningful gains. In her later years, she also became an outspoken supporter of gender equality. She addressed the National Organization for Women at its first annual convention on the key role of women in civil rights, and on several occasions she expressed criticism of male dominance, including that of Martin Luther King Jr., in the civil rights movement.

Clark retired from the SCLC in 1971, but she continued to be active in community development. Among her most satisfying accomplishments was her election to the Charleston school board in 1975, the very organization that had fired her almost twenty years earlier. In 1979 she received the Living Legacy Award from President Jimmy Carter for her work in behalf of black empowerment. Just before her death on 15 December 1987, Septima Clark was given an American Book Award for her second autobiography, *Ready from Within: Septima Clark and Civil Rights*.

[*See also* Civil Rights Movement; Highlander Folk School; Southern Christian Leadership Conference; *and biographical entries on figures mentioned in this article*.]

BIBLIOGRAPHY

Clark, Septima. "Citizenship and Gospel." *Journal of Black Studies* 90 (June 1980): 461–466. A brief, though useful, reminiscence by Clark of her dedication to adult education.

Clark, Septima, with LeGette Blythe. *Echo in My Soul*. E. P. Dutton: New York, 1962. The standard edition of Clark's recollections and reminiscences.

Clark, Septima, and Cynthia Stokes Brown. *Ready from Within: Septima Clark and the Civil Rights Movement*. Navarro, Calif.: Wild Trees Press: 1986. A brief memoir of Clark's participation in the civil rights movement.

Crawford, Vicki L., Jacqueline Anne Rouse, and Barbara Woods. *Women in the Civil Rights Movement: Trailblazers and Torchbearers, 1941–1965*. Bloomington: Indiana University Press, 1993. One chapter of this volume contains perhaps the most readable short account of Clark's career.

—CHARLES ORSON COOK

CLARK ATLANTA UNIVERSITY. Clark Atlanta University (CAU), established in 1988, is a historically black university in Atlanta, Georgia, enrolling more than five thousand students. Its parent institutions are Clark College (founded in 1869), which was a four-year liberal arts college, and Atlanta University (founded in 1865), which offered only graduate and professional degrees. From their inception in the late nineteenth century, these institutions were committed to achieving racial equality and social justice. Their alumni were active participants in various political movements, especially the civil rights movement of the 1960s. In April 1988, the board of directors of Clark College and Atlanta University ratified a consolidation agreement that dissolved the former institutions and created Clark Atlanta University. On 1 July 1988, CAU was founded under the leadership of its first president, Thomas Winston Cole, who remained at the helm until 2002. On 1 August 2002, Walter Broadnax began his tenure as CAU's second president. CAU has dual mottoes: "I'll Find a Way or Make One" and "Culture for Service." The university offers a broad range of bachelor's, professional, and graduate degrees, and is dedicated to teaching, research, and service. CAU continues to honor its heritage of social consciousness and community activism on local, national, and global levels. The institution boasts the largest enrollment in the Atlanta University Center, Inc., a unique consortium of six historically black colleges and universities (Clark Atlanta University, Morehouse College, Morehouse School of Medicine, Morris Brown College, Spelman College, and the Interdenominational Theological Center) located within a five-mile radius.

[*See also* Higher Education *and entries on other institutions of higher education mentioned in this article*.]

BIBLIOGRAPHY

Bacote, Clarence. *The Story of Atlanta University: A Century of Service (1865–1965)*. Atlanta: Atlanta University, 1969. A comprehensive history of Atlanta University.

Brawley, James P. *The Clark College Legacy: An Interpretive History of Relevant Education (1869–1975)*. Atlanta: Clark College,1977. A definitive account of the origins of Clark College.

—AISHA X. L. FRANCIS

CLARKE, JOHN HENRIK (b. 1 January 1915; d. 16 July 1998), educator, nationalist, Pan-Africanist, writer, historian, and poet. Born John Henry Clark to Willie Ella Mays and John Clark, a sharecropper, Clarke changed his name, legalizing Henry to Henrik and adding an "e" to Clark, thereby cementing his admiration of the Scandinavian playwright Henrik Ibsen. The Clark family moved from Union Springs, Alabama, to Columbus, Georgia, when Clarke was four years old. Clarke's mother, a laundrywoman, died of pellagra, a diet deficiency, when Clarke was still very young. With his mother's illness and subsequent death, the Clark family began to feel the effects of poverty.

Though he clearly demonstrated academic ability, along with a strong desire to learn and excel, Clarke's academic goals encountered much resistance. As a teenager Clarke held a number of menial jobs; he was a part-time student and a part-time farmer and worker. As a result he attended school only up to the first half of the seventh grade. In his youth Clarke taught junior class at Sunday school and began a search for African people in the Bible. His quest led him to question the color of Christ, Moses, and the angels. Curious about his own people and culture, Clarke asked a white attorney, whom he worked for and borrowed books from, for a book on African history. The attorney informed Clarke that Clarke came from a people with no history. Clarke later marked this incident as the point in his life when he began a systematic search for Africans and their role in history. In Columbus, blacks were not allowed to use the segregated public library, so Clarke, an avid reader, forged a letter from a white person granting himself the access to the books he wanted.

In 1932 at age seventeen Clarke took a freight train to New York, wanting to pursue a career as a writer. He was aware of the literary and cultural gains of the Harlem Renaissance and wanted to participate. Clarke settled in Harlem, supported himself by working at a number of low-paying jobs, and focused on securing his own education. He enjoyed success with the publication of a number of his short stories and poems. Still wanting to learn all that he could about African history, Clarke went to the Harlem branch of the New York Public Library (now the Schomburg Center for Research in Black Culture) to meet Arthur A. Schomburg. Clarke had read Schomburg's essay "The Negro Digs Up His Past" in *The New Negro*, edited by Alain Locke; the book was Clarke's first encounter with the notion that black people had a solid history worthy of study. Schomburg suggested that Clarke first examine the history of Europe for a full understanding of Africa's stolen history and guided Clarke's reading until Schomburg's unexpected death in 1938. Clarke later credited Schomburg with shaping his life as well as his interest in the field of African history and the history of black people all over the world.

Clarke surrounded himself and studied with many other literary greats. He joined the Harlem History Workshop and Willis N. Huggins's Harlem History Club, which was renamed the Blyden Society in 1937. J. A. Rogers, Nnamdi Azikiwe, Kwame Nkrumah, Will Marion Cook, and many others attended Blyden Society meetings. William Leo Hansberry, John O. Killens, Huggins, and John G. Jackson mentored Clarke in a fashion similar to Schomburg. Unfortunately, in 1941 with the onset of World War II and the mysterious death of its leader, Huggins, the Blyden Society dissolved and Clarke was drafted by the military. Stationed in San Antonio, Texas, Clarke attained the rank of master sergeant in the Army Air Corps. After the war Clarke returned to Harlem to continue his research, his writing, and his cultural and political activism.

Clarke took classes in history and world literature at New York University, Columbia University, and the New School for Social Research. His continuing quest for knowledge made him an international traveler; Clarke made numerous trips to Africa after being invited by Kwame Nkrumah, who was then president of Ghana. Clarke also traveled to the Caribbean, Asia, and Europe as he continued to do research on Africa's history. The body of knowledge that he acquired was put to use in his writing as well as in his teachings. During the 1940s Clarke began teaching African and African American history in a number of Harlem community centers. From 1956 to 1958 Clark taught at the New School for Social Research in New York and earned a license to teach African and African American history in New York from People's College in Malverne, Long Island.

In 1964 Clarke became the director of the Heritage Teaching Program for Harlem Youth Opportunities Unlimited (Haryou-Act), and in 1969—without a degree—he managed to secure a teaching position at Hunter College, City University of New York. Clarke played a major role in the development of the black studies program there and retired with the title of professor emeritus of African and world history. Clarke founded a number of organizations, including the Harlem Writers Guild, Présence Africaine, the African Heritage Studies Association, the Association for the Study of Negro Life and History, the National Council of Black Studies, and the Association for the Study of Classical African Civilizations.

In addition to lecturing, Clarke wrote more than fifty short stories, with "The Boy Who Painted Christ Black" (1940) being his best known; this story has been translated into more than a dozen languages. Clarke's articles and conference papers on African and African American history and culture have been published in leading journals internationally. Clarke wrote six books and edited or contributed to at least seventeen others. His major book of poetry, *Rebellion in Rhyme*, was published in 1948. Clarke's other publications include edited books, major essays, and book introductions; his nationalist, Pan-Africanist, and Afrocentric views are reflected in his works.

Clarke was a cofounder of the Black Academy of Arts and Letters and associate editor of *Freedomways* magazine. He was also the recipient of honorary degrees from the University of Denver, the University of the District of Columbia, and the Medgar Evers College of the City University of New York. In 1986 a library at Cornell University in Ithaca, New York, was renamed the John Henrik Clarke Africana Library. Clarke, a professor in the Africana Studies and Research Center, helped to found the black studies program at Cornell. In 1993 the Clark University Woodruff Library Center in Atlanta dedicated a wing of the library in Clarke's honor. In 1995 Clarke earned his doctoral degree from Pacific Western University in California.

Clarke married one of his students in 1962, fathering a daughter, Nzingha Marie Clarke, and a son, Sonni Kojo Clarke; the marriage ended after thirty years. In 1997 Clarke married his best friend, Sybil Williams. On 16 July 1998, Clarke died of a heart attack at the age of eighty-three.

[*See also* Afrocentrism; Black Studies; Educators and Academics; *and* Pan-Africanism.]

BIBLIOGRAPHY

Adams, Adjua Barbara. "Elder Scholars: John Henrik Clarke." In *Encyclopedia of Black Studies*, edited by Molefi Kete Asante and Ama Mazama. Thousand Oaks, Calif.: Sage, 2005.

Adams, Barbara Eleanor. *John Henrik Clarke: Master Teacher*. Brooklyn, N.Y.: A & B Publishers Group, 2000.

Crowe, Larry, F. *Reflections on the Life of Dr. John Henrik Clarke, January 1, 1915 to July 16, 1998*. Chicago: Kemetic Institute, 1998.
Golus, Carrie. "John Henrik Clarke." In *Contemporary Black Biography Profiles from the International Black Community*, vol. 20, edited by Shirelle Phelps. Detroit, Mich.: Gale Research, 1999.

—ROCHELL ISAAC

CLASS. Class as a factor in the lives of African Americans in the twentieth century created mixed reactions. In a society that in some ways generally regards itself as classless, many Americans regard economic inequality as a social problem that needs fixing—through government programs or, preferably, individual initiative. For African Americans, the massive impact of race and racism seemed to render all blacks victims of white prejudice. W. E. B. Du Bois's dictum that the color line would be the major problem of the twentieth century had the effect of underscoring that African Americans were behind a racial veil apart from white Americans: material conditions made this analysis convincing. Until the late twentieth century, few African Americans could be described as wealthy, and fewer owned the means of production.

By the early twenty-first century, for the first time, there were significant numbers of blacks with money and power. In addition to wealthy and conspicuous athletes and entertainers, in 2007 three African Americans were chief operating officers of Fortune 500 companies, and several African Americans, including the former basketball star Earvin "Magic" Johnson, owned companies worth hundreds of millions of dollars. From 2003 to 2007, Stanley O'Neal, the grandson of a slave, served as chairman of the board, chief executive officer, and president of Merrill Lynch, the world's largest investment firm. Even during the two administrations of George W. Bush, a conservative Republican president, the African Americans Colin Powell and Condoleezza Rice each held the prominent post of secretary of state. Rice was widely considered a future presidential candidate, and after only partially completing his first term in the Senate, Barack Obama was elected the first African-American President: such political ascension suggests the relative rise of African Americans generally.

Such well-known blacks are only the most visible beneficiaries of improved racial mores. In the aftermath of the civil rights movement of the 1950s and 1960s, many blacks have now moved solidly into the middle class.

Class. Strivers' Row, a section of late-nineteenth-century townhouses in Harlem, New York City, 1973. Strivers' Row is known for the upper-middle-class black professionals, performers, and artists who live there. Famous African Americans who have lived on Strivers' Row include the musicians Eubie Blake, Fletcher Henderson, and W. C. Handy; the performers Stepin Fetchit and Bill "Bojangles" Robinson; and the congressman Adam Clayton Powell Jr. Photograph by Chester Higgins. © CHESTER HIGGINS JR.

As the United States has at least superficially distanced itself from historic legal and social discrimination, by the twenty-first century blacks were found routinely in local, state, and federal bureaucracies, as elected officials, in the professions, and in businesses. In literature and the arts, blacks are an important presence.

Class as a Marker. Despite these gains, class has become an even greater marker in black America than ever before. The sociologist William Julius Wilson has argued that there are now two classes within black America: the middle class and an impoverished class. He points out that the biggest class of African Americans is the middle class, and that the percentage of black children living at or beneath the poverty line is almost the same in the early twenty-first century as it was on the day in 1968 when Martin Luther King Jr. was killed. It may be argued that in fact there are four classes: an elite, the middle class, the lower-middle or working class, and a sizable class that is severely economically disadvantaged and is often stigmatized by felony convictions.

The black intellectual leadership is at odds on the causes and solutions of African American social inequality. Wilson contends that access to higher-paying jobs is increasingly based upon education and that relations between racial groups are based more on the character of economic relations than on race. Now that the United States has opened social mobility to educated and well-placed blacks, those with the requisite skills can advance, while those without them are stuck far behind. Criticizing this view are scholars who point to the immense differences that still exist between white and black Americans in educational, economic, and political power; these scholars maintain that race remains, a century after Du Bois, the unifying factor for African Americans.

There are major disagreements about how to improve the lot of the poorest, least privileged blacks. The entertainer Bill Cosby and scholars such as Manning Marable differ on the importance of class among black Americans. Cosby tends to blame African Americans at the bottom of the steep American socioeconomic pyramid for their own troubles. Disadvantaged blacks must work harder; be smarter about acquiring the skills, education, habits, and values of accomplished blacks and whites; and avoid outwardly self-indulgent fascinations with drugs, sports, and "street" music. Marable, in contrast, sees class as a bold interpretive and political framework that identifies interrelated structures of inequality and prejudice, and he calls for a massive restructuring of dominant American institutions. The roots of the disagreement between these two perspectives lie far back in African American conceptions of class.

Historically, black Americans did not use material conditions to create ranks. Before the civil rights movement, other, more subtle measures differentiated elite blacks from poorer ones. One reason is that there were very few blacks with economic independence. In the early twentieth century, most African Americans were agricultural workers. Across the American South, where the bulk of African Americans lived, more than 90 percent of African Americans were farmers or farm managers, while slightly less than 5 percent were farm and general laborers. The vast majority were sharecroppers who worked small plots of land for a few years, then moved to another piece of land nearby. That mobility did not translate into prosperity but rather into debt peonage. Within that semi-servitude, the church and local taverns served as cultural centers. Consumer acquisitions might, with great effort, include radios, phonograph players, and records, and, with substantial savings, a car. Telephones were common only by 1950, and even by then, electricity was not a given.

Early in the Great Migration to cities blacks unintentionally encountered class conflict. Knowing little about unionization and strikes and suspicious of white workers, some African Americans were used as strikebreakers, a tactic that bolstered racial enmity. In New York, Chicago, and Philadelphia, as well as in smaller cities such as Milwaukee, employers actively recruited African Americans as strikebreakers. Occasionally such replacement workers continued to hold jobs after the strike ended, but in Milwaukee, for example, strikebreakers in the steel industry all lost employment in the city's blast furnaces and rolling mills within a short time. Many within the black leadership also counseled strikebreakers to keep separate from white workers. Later, as black workers became more aware of their misuse, they, too, formed unions and attempted to collaborate with whites going on strike. At the same time the National Urban League, a black business-oriented organization, helped recruit black strikebreakers into the 1920s to disrupt white work actions. The league showed a similar dislike, however, of black efforts at unionization.

Unhappy with their lives, African Americans migrated from rural regions to southern and northern cities in search of better economic opportunity, protection from white terrorism, and stronger communities. Between 1920 and 1930 the black population of Chicago doubled as nearly sixty thousand newcomers arrived from the South. Houston, Texas, experienced a similar gain, as did Detroit, New York City, and Newark, New Jersey. In the South, blacks moved into Atlanta, Baltimore, Memphis, and New Orleans in sizable numbers. Only Charleston, South Carolina, saw a decline in its black population. These patterns were amplified by the mid-twentieth century.

Blacks accounted for more than 40 percent of the populations of Montgomery and Birmingham, Alabama, by 1950.

Blacks living and working in the cities were ultimately successful in quashing the more noxious types of segregation. Through the inspired efforts of Martin Luther King Jr. and such organizations as the NAACP, the Congress of Racial Equality (CORE), the Student Nonviolent Coordinating Committee (SNCC), and others, and with the valiant contributions of ordinary black and white people, the United States slowly swept away denigrating racial prohibitions in transportation, hotels, public buildings, and streets. Perhaps most important, the vote and educational systems were regained and reopened to all.

Social and political opportunity did not translate into economic opportunity. As blacks became the most urbanized of Americans, they remained disproportionately working class or poorer. Most of the job opportunities arose in areas such as the service industry, an area that had historically been open to them. Scholars have contended that in fact blacks who migrated in the later twentieth century arrived in urban promised lands barren of opportunities: industrial and white-collar jobs moved into the suburbs by the 1960s, moved into the white-dominated intermountain western states, and then moved overseas in the 1990s and early twenty-first century. As visible signs of racism declined, economic opportunity also declined. An example in the early twenty-first century is the decision by General Motors and other automobile companies to close several U.S. plants, disproportionately affecting black union workers. As a result, these industrial workers lost the trappings of the middle class that they had hoped to pass along to their children, and they lost mobility accordingly.

The black middle class in the South. In the early twentieth century the black middle class in the South was very small. Middle-class blacks in Birmingham formed social clubs, fraternal orders, and churches in an effort to build community and separate themselves from their poorer brethren. But in the segregated South, to maintain total separation was economically unfeasible. Black businessmen who faced competition for African American customers from white entrepreneurs espoused the rhetoric of economic nationalism to encourage race loyalty among potential black clients. Most middle-class blacks adhered to Booker T. Washington's philosophies of self-help, economic independence, and racial solidarity. Washington nurtured close relationships with black leaders in Birmingham and other southern cities. These elite blacks named their businesses after him, met regularly in the evenings to discuss his work and writings, and flocked to hear him speak at local churches.

Membership in Birmingham's black middle class translated into leadership positions. A combination of ego gratification and civic enhancement inspired members of the black middle class to work on improving race relations, particularly with paternalistic and somewhat liberal whites. Whites' financial support was critical for black personal advancement and to the growth of black economic and social institutions. Ties with rich whites, along with the constant threat of terrorism from whites, created a subdued, quiescent black middle class. Rather than rail against racial injustice or violence, they concentrated on the elements of Washington's philosophy. Although whites and blacks working together at times helped ameliorate the worst conditions, in the early decades of the twentieth century there were few if any real attempts to change the system of segregation.

The black elite in Washington, D.C. Despite the fierce legal and social limitations for blacks in an America defined by the harsh Jim Crow restrictions, a tiny black elite clung tenuously to its position. Washington, D.C., was regarded as the center for the black elite. Washington's so-called Black 400 were in fact a few hundred of the 75,000 blacks living in the nation's capital. Many of this upper crust were several generations removed from slavery and came to Washington from other major cities and from rural areas. Given the prospect of white-collar jobs and government sinecures, educational possibilities, and the existence of a black social group that shared the same values, tastes, and self-conceptions, leading blacks from New York, Boston, Philadelphia, Charleston, and New Orleans gravitated to the city. Intermarriage between families of the Black 400 gave the city a nationwide network of social and blood relations.

The John F. Cook family was perhaps the most distinguished in black Washington, D.C. Cook established private schools for blacks in the mid-nineteenth century. His son George F. T. Cook was the superintendent of the Washington black public schools for a quarter of a century after 1883. Another son, John F. Cook Jr., was a trustee of Howard University for thirty-five years and served as the tax collector for Washington. With an estate derived from his real estate interests, the younger John F. Cook was the wealthiest black in Washington. George W. Cook was registrar of Howard University for ten years and worked for the university for four decades. Other members of the Cook family served on the Washington boards of education and trade and held prominent positions as lawyers, physicians, and teachers.

Other Washington black elites could trace their ancestry back to the abolitionist movement. The Grimké family, known for its efforts in racial uplift, included Archibald, an author and lecturer, and his brother, Francis J., a minister. Charlotte Forten Grimké was Francis's wife and the granddaughter of the famed sailmaker James Forten of Philadelphia. Archibald's daughter, Angelina Weld Grimké, was named after her white great-aunt, Angelina Grimké, who married the abolitionist Theodore Weld.

Prominent black Washington families had distinguished members in each generation. Mary Ann Shadd was the most visible member of a well-known family dating back several generations. Shadd worked as a teacher in Pennsylvania and New York and then spent a period living in Canada, where she founded the *Provincial Freeman*, the first newspaper edited by a black woman in North America. Later she moved back to Washington and taught at the Lincoln Industrial School and in 1883 earned a law degree from Howard University.

Black Washingtonians were prominent in politics. Frederick Douglass was of course the most famous, and his home in Anacostia attracted many of the city's elite. His sons by his first marriage, Lewis and Charles, were deeply involved in the local gentry. P. B. S. Pinchback was formerly the acting governor of Louisiana; after his move to Washington in 1893 he became part of this gentry, along with his daughter, Nina. Her son, the famed novelist Jean Toomer, portrayed the local elite in his novel *Cane* (1923). Blanche K. Bruce of Mississippi, the first black U.S. senator to complete a full term, stayed in Washington after the end of Reconstruction and married well, to a society woman named Josephine Wilson. Their son, Roscoe Conkling Bruce—named after the senator who escorted Bruce to his seat in the Senate—went to Harvard and then became an assistant superintendent of "colored" schools. Another family, the Syphaxes, claimed descent from Martha Washington's grandson and were active in education.

Membership in prominent institutions anchored upper-class black Washington. Education was important to the Washington black elite. Most people in this group sent their children to either the black Preparatory High School or, later, to Spingarn High School. Then the children went on to historically black universities such as Howard, which educated large swaths of the black elite of Washington and other cities. Other favored historically black universities were Fisk, Atlanta, and Wilberforce. Many students in this black elite chose to go to receptive white colleges such as Dartmouth, Cornell, Harvard, Oberlin, and Yale.

Church membership was considered critical. Most upper-class blacks chose Saint Luke's Episcopal Church, which had become more progressive under the leadership of the famed abolitionist and intellectual Alexander Crummell. The more conservative blacks attended Union Bethel African Methodist Episcopal Church, where John W. Stevenson held a controversial position after 1880. His fund-raising and emphasis on ostentatious architecture irritated some members, who shifted to the Plymouth Congregational Church. Plymouth was led by Sterling N. Brown, father of the poet of the same name. Another favorite congregation of the elite was the Nineteenth Street Baptist Church.

Social settings were important. The black elite formed a Grand Lodge of the Free Masons in 1848, and innumerable prominent figures were officers. In time, Washington blacks contributed to a black YMCA, and they were frequent participants in other clubs. They gave money to the Freedman's Hospital and used its medical staff extensively. As was the case among elite blacks across the nation, college alumni often continued their undergraduate memberships in such black fraternities as Alpha Phi Alpha, Kappa Alpha Psi, and Omega Psi Phi. The major black sorority was Alpha Kappa Alpha.

For black elites from the 1880s to the present, time spent at the right summer place has also been critical. There have been geographically accessible favorites such as Harpers Ferry, West Virginia, and Colton, Maryland, for Washington elites; but Martha's Vineyard and Nantucket, Massachusetts, have also been the top attractions for wealthy blacks from across the nation.

Elite blacks in Washington were deeply interested in their history. In addition to valorizing free-black ancestry and deifying historically significant blacks such as Douglass and Crummell, they created, under Crummell's leadership, the American Negro Academy, an early forerunner of the Washington-based Association for the Study of Negro Life and History (now the Association for the Study of African American Life and History) headed by Carter G. Woodson. History was an important component of the racial uplift movement; through history, elite blacks could show their allegiance with poorer blacks while maintaining a social distance from them.

A few blacks, most notably the Cook family, had holdings in the hundreds of thousands of dollars. Because the Jim Crow laws insisted on separate institutions for blacks and whites, there were black members of virtually every field of work: blacks had to provide for themselves doctors, lawyers, shops, and everything else. Being an undertaker became a popular occupation, as did photography.

The black elite elsewhere. As Washington, D.C., led, so elite black society elsewhere followed, but there were significant variations. Elite blacks in Charleston, South Carolina, had a reputation for being excessively snobby and color conscious. Often descendants of antebellum free blacks, elite Charleston people of color lived in a world of their own in the late nineteenth century. They lived closeted in such institutions as Saint Mark's Episcopal Church, Avery Normal Institution, the Brown Fellowship, and the Friendly Moralist Society. Charleston also exported elite blacks to Milwaukee, Brooklyn, Washington, and Boston. Wherever they went, however, these scions of black Charleston revered their origins and nearly always returned to the city to find a spouse.

New Orleans rivaled Charleston in the free-black origins of its black elite, but its blacks had the additional benefit of ancient bloodlines from free white French and Spanish people and were termed Creoles. Such Creoles regarded themselves as more French than African American and distanced themselves from their poorer black brethren; they included some slave masters who had fought for the South during the Civil War. In post-Reconstruction New Orleans, racism caused whites to equate the Creoles with darker-skinned blacks; still, Creoles' French origins allowed for a defensive distinction. As in Washington, the New Orleans black elite prized education and sent their children to private and even public schools that discriminated against anyone seen as too dark. Jim Crow pushed Creoles in New Orleans into political action, though their efforts invariably failed. As a result, some in the New Orleans black elite lapsed into an apparently pleasure-based way of life, which to some seemed to mask an economic dynamic that lagged behind that of other southern cities.

In the North, urban black elites could trace their lineages back over a century. In Philadelphia the descendants of James Forten automatically qualified as elite. More recent arrivals from Santo Domingo and Haiti included such families as the de Baptists, the Le Counts, and the Augustins. Others included émigrés from southern cities and, later, well-educated arrivals such as Dr. Edwin Clarence Howard, a Harvard-trained physician, and his wife, Joan Imogene, a graduate of New York University. One family, the Bustills, came from nearby New Jersey and could claim multigenerational achievements back to 1732.

Elite blacks in Philadelphia, with the possible exception of the Forten family, were hampered by racial discrimination in the trades. Many earned their fortunes through catering or in professional but lower-paying jobs as ministers and teachers. As Du Bois noted in 1899 in his classic study *The Philadelphia Negro*, education and breeding had to count more than money. At the same time, the Philadelphia black gentry were more interested in fellow gentry in New York and Boston than they were in local lower-class blacks.

As in Philadelphia, high-ranking New Yorkers could trace their families far back into national history. Members of the New York African Society of Mutual Relief and Saint Philip's Episcopal Church, along with those who had ties with the Dutch families, were considered elite. Elite black New Yorkers seemed to forget that slavery had existed in their city and even avoided celebrating Emancipation Day. Additional elite New Yorkers were more recent arrivals who had come from the South and from Santo Domingo. But in a city where capitalism and ostentatious wealth were common, few black New Yorkers had much money at all, though a little was more than most local blacks had. Following the example of Washington, D.C., most elite black New Yorkers preferred private, isolated, and refined ceremonies and events. After the Draft Riots of 1863, Brooklyn emerged as a home for elite blacks.

Scholars of the black elites of America's major cities generally emphasize the elites' aloofness and distaste for mingling with lower-class blacks. In general, superior airs were based more on style than substance. The elites' combined wealth in 1901 of around $700 million was less than that of the nation's first billion-dollar corporation, U.S. Steel, organized in 1901 with very few if any black workers.

The black elite and capitalism. As Booker T. Washington and Du Bois engaged in their famous feud over the development of a black citizenry and black enterprise in a society divided by race, it was Washington's portrait that could be found in the homes and businesses of black America. Washington's creation of the National Negro Business League in 1900 charted the road to success through industrial development for and by blacks. Du Bois—who, along with many northern blacks, disliked Washington's politics of accommodation to white racism—generally agreed with the economic approach. But unlike Washington, Du Bois insisted upon the need for a liberal education. The philosophies of Washington and Du Bois met in the creation of black banks and insurance companies that became the focal point for creating a series of black-controlled businesses in a racially divided society. Soon, in transportation and leisure enterprises, in real estate and construction, in the extractive industries, in manufacturing, and in health care and beauty aids, blacks were able to create solid businesses that catered to a black clientele. Outside of a few nightclubs in Harlem, no black business would think of excluding ordinary blacks from their customer bases.

With the development of a black capitalism, the African American elite began to change dramatically. In New York City the black elite was joined by the arrival of thousands of newcomer African Americans in the 1910s and 1920s. What occurred in New York during the blossoming of black cultural expression in the Harlem Renaissance of the 1920s and 1930s reflected changes elsewhere. Although the historic elite remained, upstarts from the worlds of real estate, entertainment, the arts, and later sports gradually supplanted them. As white New Yorkers traveled uptown to "slum," musicians such as Duke Ellington became famous and wealthy. The boxer Sugar

Ray Robinson and later the baseball player Jackie Robinson gained elite status through their fame and instant wealth. As New York liberalized in the post–World War II era, the actors Harry Belafonte and Sidney Poitier paved the way for other famed blacks. The civil rights movement spawned significant black New Yorkers such as Kenneth Clark, while the novelist Ralph Ellison gained instant acceptance from his novel *Invisible Man*, published in 1952, and his genteel, cosmopolitan behavior.

The Turn of the Twenty-first Century. Black Hollywood stars were few at first, and only in the 1990s were the leading men Denzel Washington and Morgan Freeman able to command top salaries. Even more impressive, of course, were black entertainers who could maximize their talents in myriad ways. Here Oprah Winfrey and Bill Cosby are illustrative. By the 1990s black athletes competed equally with whites for enormous annual salaries. Notable among highly paid black athletes were the basketball star Michael Jordan, the baseball players Barry Bonds and Derek Jeter, and the golfer Tiger Woods. Few were able to sustain their incomes after their playing careers ended, though the example of Dave Bing, a basketball star who founded a large steel company, is instructive. This democratization of fame created a national elite black society. To such famous names as Jordan, Winfrey, and Denzel Washington can be added the names of the internationally famous novelist Toni Morrison and the historian Henry Louis Gates Jr.

Still, as in the past, black capitalism and its corresponding elite relied on racial solidarity. Major black capitalists including S. B. Fuller, Arthur G. Gaston, John H. Johnson, and Berry Gordy Jr. all became multimillionaires selling products to a largely black audience. Such men had varying political philosophies, but it is unlikely that they felt disaffection from the black masses. They had little choice. Integration did not affect all elite blacks, and many retained membership in their own elite organizations.

Older social organizations have grown even larger. By 2000, Alpha Phi Alpha, the oldest black fraternity, boasted more than 150,000 members in more than 750 chapters. On its roster of members from the past century were such names as the Supreme Court justice Thurgood Marshall; Martin Luther King Jr.; the Atlanta mayors Andrew Young and Maynard Jackson; Du Bois; the Olympic gold medalist Jesse Owens; the *Ebony* magazine founder and publishing magnate John H. Johnson; the National Urban League presidents Hugh Price, Lester Granger, and Whitney Young; the congressman Adam Clayton Powell Jr.; and the New York City mayor David Dinkins.

Elite blacks around the country have maintained their status through interlocking children's groups such as Jack and Jill of America; through women's groups such as the Links and the Smart Set; and through summers at Sag Harbor on Long Island and at Oak Bluffs on Martha's Vineyard. Men joined the Boulé, the Guardsmen, or local branches of 100 Black Men.

The black middle and lower classes. The contours of the black middle class have been part assimilationist and part nationalist. Many blacks have shared with many whites an appetite for the bourgeois joys of suburban homes, large televisions and cars, and a devotion to sports. They have shared with elite blacks and whites strong support for education, church, and community. After the United States removed its obnoxious racial laws, blacks and whites still kept social distances outside work. African American neighborhoods and suburbs abounded. Not unlike newer immigrant groups, blacks have displayed a powerful devotion to memories of the ancestral homeland. If they do not actually visit Africa, they recall it in rituals, clothing, and names.

What was sometimes referred to as black "underclass" culture did not emphasize education, the pursuit of which was sometimes derisively regarded as "acting white." Sports became the principal public method of social mobility, even though its triumphs are typically rare and fleeting. For some young people, gang membership replaced fraternal orders and self-help groups.

Black music. Black popular music, which in the 1960s and 1970s produced some of the best American music with a romantic theme, changed in the 1990s to a tougher rendition of the blues mixed with a kind of street poetry known as the "dozens," in which competing chanters strive to outwit their opponents with taunts, threats, and superior rhymes. Throughout the 1990s rap and hip hop often glorified gangster behavior to the extent that jail terms sometimes seemed to become almost requisite parts of a musician's résumé. Assassination even seemed to bolster careers, according to some critics. Such music could not disguise the tragedy of sacrificed lives.

Blacks and imprisonment. As a result of the growth of prisons as an industry, harsher patterns of sentencing, racism, and the merciless war on drugs, blacks are disproportionably represented in prisons. In Alabama, blacks are 26 percent of the population but 62 percent of prison inmates. In New York State, blacks are 16 percent of the population but 55 percent of its inmates. In Maryland, blacks are 28 percent of the population but 73 percent of inmates. The effects of this reach far beyond time in jail. The poorest class of African Americans includes many men and women who are stigmatized by felony convictions that incarcerate them for decades or push them far behind other Americans in political, social, and economic potentials. Sizable numbers of black men in southern states cannot vote because of felony convictions. Legal problems hinder many more from finding secure employment.

Black Attitudes toward Class and Race. According to the theory that class is more important than race, middle-class blacks should feel separate from poorer blacks and more akin to middle-class whites. Recent studies conclude, however, that both lower- and middle-class blacks have greater race consciousness than they do class consciousness. Most blacks still feel that race is a very significant factor in determining their life chances and opportunities. Despite widespread claims that the United States no longer allows prejudice, middle-class blacks find themselves confronted with racial discrimination, racial barriers, and blocked opportunities. Lower-class blacks face similar if higher barriers but are more likely to place emphasis on protests, social pressures, and social actions to eliminate racial discrimination. Middle- and lower-class blacks continue to see racial discrimination as a genuine obstacle and believe that blacks with the most education and economic means should help less fortunate blacks.

For lower-class blacks there is a high likelihood that rage, violence, and criminal behavior will be met with harsh punishments. The lack of real discussion about reforming of sentencing laws for small-scale drug sales and use even in a liberal state such as New York is indicative of how punitively American society responds to its economically less privileged black members.

As the optimistic era of racial integration faded in a conservative political climate, racial solidarity and the support networks that blacks have built among themselves appear to be more important than the often solitary gains that highly visible blacks in politics, entertainment, and business have made for themselves. In an era in which significant numbers of young black men and women are stigmatized by the judicial system, it is unlikely that even the wealthy, prosperous black elite can remain aloof and distance themselves through class.

[*See also* Black Capitalism; Criminal Justice; Entrepreneurship; Hip Hop; Middle Class; Peonage; Poverty, Culture of; Racial Profiling; Talented Tenth; *and biographical entries on figures mentioned in this article*.]

Bibliography

Feldman, Lynne B. *A Sense of Place: Birmingham's Black Middle-Class Community, 1890–1930*. Tuscaloosa: University of Alabama Press, 1999.

Gatewood, Willard B. *Aristocrats of Color: The Black Elite, 1880–1920*. Bloomington: Indiana University Press, 1990.

Graham, Lawrence Otis. *Our Kind of People: Inside America's Black Upper Class*. New York: HarperCollins, 1999.

Hurt, R. Douglas, ed. *African American Life in the Rural South, 1900–1950*. Columbia: University of Missouri Press, 2003.

Hwang, Sean-Shong, Kevin M. Fitzpatrick, and David Helms. "Class Differences in Racial Attitudes: A Divided Black America?" *Sociological Perspectives* 41, no. 2 (1998): 367–380.

Lewis, Earl. *In Their Own Interests: Race, Class, and Power in Twentieth-Century Norfolk, Virginia*. Berkeley: University of California Press, 1991.

Moore, Jacqueline M. *Leading the Race: The Transformation of the Black Elite in the Nation's Capital, 1880–1920*. Charlottesville: University Press of Virginia, 1999.

Trotter, Joe William, Jr. *Black Milwaukee: The Making of an Industrial Proletariat, 1915–1945*. Urbana: University of Illinois Press, 1985.

Walker, Juliet E. K. *The History of Black Business in America: Capitalism, Race, Entrepreneurship*. New York: Macmillan Library Reference, 1998.

—Graham Russell Gao Hodges

CLAY, WILLIAM, SR. (b. 30 April 1931), politician, community activist, and sixteen-term United States congressman. William Clay Sr. was one of Missouri's most successful champions of civil rights in the twentieth century. Born one of seven children to Luella Hyatt and Irving Clay in Saint Louis, Missouri, young Clay attended Roman Catholic schools, where he was academically successful despite the disadvantages inherent in a segregated education. After high school, he enrolled in Saint Louis University and graduated with a bachelor's degree in political science in 1953. Clay completed a two-year tour of duty with the U.S. Army in 1955. After a brief flirtation with a career in business, he became a labor organizer, a community activist, and ultimately a congressman from Missouri's First Congressional District for thirty-two years. Clay has spoken of the racial injustices he encountered early in life. He recalled initiating a movement of black servicemen to desegregate the base swimming pool, and by the late 1950s, his local chapter of the NAACP Youth Council had its charter revoked because its members were thought to be too militant. Many of these young activists, including Clay, drifted into the more radical Congress of Racial Equality (CORE). In 1959, he successfully campaigned for a seat on the Saint Louis Board of Aldermen from the predominantly black Twenty-Sixth Ward in a bitter contest with a white opponent—he relied mostly on grass-roots support from neighborhood voters. His six years as alderman earned him a reputation as an enthusiastic voice for equal rights and community development.

Perhaps the most dramatic episode of his early commitment to civil rights was his part in a 1963 demonstration staged against a neighborhood bank that had dismissed its black employees when it moved into a white area; the demonstration soon spread to other businesses with discriminatory hiring practices. Known locally as the Jefferson Bank Boycott, the protest lasted several months and has been described by many as the most dramatic single civil rights event in the history of Saint Louis. For his role, Alderman Clay was arrested and spent more than a hundred days in jail, but he gained a local reputation as a champion of the African American community. A few years later, in 1968, a statewide redistricting initiative created a predominantly black First Congressional District and Clay was the popular choice to represent it in Congress.

William Clay Sr. served a total of sixteen consecutive terms in the House of Representatives from 1969 until 2001. At retirement, he was the third most senior member of the House, and, as a founding member of the Congressional Black Caucus, he was the second–longest-serving African American in Congress. Over a span of more than three decades, he compiled an enviable record as an advocate for a wide range of labor and social welfare issues, and as a ranking member of several committees, he was a remarkably effective legislator. He took great pride in his efforts to win passage of the Medical and Family Leave Act of 1993. He was however, frequently at odds with the local press in Missouri, and his congressional career was sometimes tainted by controversy. He was, for instance, accused in the 1970s of falsifying travel vouchers, and in 1993 he was one of several congressmen caught up in the so-called House banking scandal, accused of writing hundreds of overdrafts. But to many in Missouri's First Congressional District, he remained a hero and a legend.

William Clay Sr. retired from public service in 2001 and continued to live in Saint Louis with his wife of more than a half century, Carol Ann Johnson. His son, William Lacy Clay Jr., succeeded his father in Congress as the representative from Missouri's First Congressional District.

[*See also* Congress, African Americans in; *and* Politics and Politicians]

BIBLIOGRAPHY

Clay, William Lacy, Sr. *Bill Clay: A Political Voice at the Grass Roots*. Saint Louis: Missouri Historical Society Press, 2004. A useful autobiographical perspective from the congressman's point of view.

—CHARLES ORSON COOK

CLEAGE, ALBERT (b. 13 June 1911; d. 20 February 2000), clergyman, **AND PEARL** (b. 7 December 1948), author, journalist, and playwright. Albert Buford Cleage was born in Indianapolis, Indiana, and grew up in Detroit, Michigan, where his father was a distinguished physician. Despite his upper-class origins, young Cleage gravitated toward issues of social justice and civil rights. At the age of thirty-one he received his BA from Wayne State University in Detroit and a divinity degree from Oberlin Graduate School of Theology a year later. Initially Cleage was committed to integration. In 1943 he was ordained in the Congregational Church and soon after became interim pastor at the integrated San Francisco Church for the Fellowship of All Peoples, a congregation cofounded by the renowned African American theologian Howard Thurman (1900–1981). But he became disillusioned by the social inequality within the congregation, particularly toward the church's Japanese American members, who had been removed from their homes against their will and imprisoned in internment camps during World War II.

After moving to serve as pastor of Saint John's Congregational Church in Springfield, Massachusetts, Cleage returned to Detroit's inner city to serve as pastor of Saint Mark's United Presbyterian mission. There he quickly came into conflict with the church's white suburban establishment, and in 1953 he led a group of dissidents out of the church. In 1956, he founded the Central Congregational Church of Christ (CCCC). This religious body focused on community programs for the poor in Detroit, organized against police brutality, campaigned for political offices, and called for control of public schools. Cleage became increasingly involved in politics, and in 1962 he ran unsuccessfully for governor of Michigan on the Freedom Ticket. His political action committee, the Black Slate, Inc., played a primary role in the election of Coleman A. Young, Detroit's first African American mayor. In 1967 he launched the Black Christian National Movement, urging black churches to reexamine Jesus as a revolutionary black leader seeking to establish a black nation, and CCCC was renamed the Shrine of the Black Madonna on Easter Sunday of that same year.

In 1968, following a year of racial ferment in Detroit, Cleage published *The Black Messiah* (1968) and changed his name to Jaramogi Abebe Agyeman, meaning "liberator, holy man, savior of the nation" in Swahili. In 1972 he published a second book, *Black Christian Nationalism*, and changed the name of the Black Christian Nationalist Movement to the Pan African Orthodox Christian Church (PAOCC). PAOCC churches were established in Detroit, Michigan; Atlanta, Georgia; and Houston, Texas. Agyeman died on the church's thirty-six-hundred-acre farm in Beulahland, Abbeville County, South Carolina, on 20 February 2000.

Agyeman's daughter, Pearl Michelle Cleage, was born in Springfield, Massachusetts, in 1948. She has achieved critical acclaim as a playwright, and her first novel, *What Looks Like Crazy on an Ordinary Day* (1998), was a New *York Times* best seller, an Oprah's Book Club selection, and a Black Caucus of the American Library Association

Literary Award winner. Her controversial book *Mad at Miles* (1990) offered harsh criticism of the American jazz icon Miles Davis and sparked considerable debate within the African American community around the issue of domestic violence. Her literary work has focused on women's issues, sex, and race.

[*See also* Black Nationalism; Literature; *and* Religion.]

BIBLIOGRAPHY

Cleage, Albert, Jr. *The Black Messiah*. Trenton, N.J.: Africa World Press, 1989. For Cleage's views on black nationalism and Christianity.

Dillard, Angela D. "Social Justice in the City: The Reverend Albert B. Cleage Jr. and the Rise of Black Nationalist Coalition in Detroit." In *Freedom North: Black Freedom Struggles outside the South, 1940–1980*, edited by Jeanne Theoharis and Komozi Woodard, chapter 6. New York: Palgrave Macmillan, 2003. Excellent historical analysis of Cleage's organization and political activities in Detroit.

Peterson, Bernard L. *Contemporary Black American Playwrights and Their Plays*. Westport, Conn.: Greenwood Press, 1988. For a comprehensive list of Pearl Cleage's plays and bibliography.

—LARVESTER GAITHER

CLEAVER, ELDRIDGE (b. 1 August 1935; d. 1 May 1998), author, writer, essayist, and political activist. Leroy Eldridge Cleaver was the eldest son of Leroy Cleaver and Thelma Hattie Robinson Cleaver. He was born in Little Rock, Arkansas, where his father waited tables at a hotel and played piano in a nightclub. Cleaver's relatively happy childhood was shattered when his father began beating his mother. In his unpublished autobiography, Cleaver described the abuse his mother suffered each weekend and the frustration he felt due to his inability to stop it. The deterioration of his family, particularly his father's violent assaults on his mother, profoundly affected Cleaver. Thelma Cleaver and her children moved in with her in-laws on their farm in Wabbaseka, Arkansas. Later they moved to the Rose Hill section of Los Angeles, and the Cleavers divorced.

Cleaver defined this move to California as the event that changed his life. By the time he was sentenced to Soledad Prison in 1954 on possession of marijuana, he had been in the California juvenile corrections system since 1947. At Soledad a fellow inmate gave Cleaver a copy of Karl Marx's *Communist Manifesto*, a document that helped shape his revolutionary perspective on the liberation of African Americans.

Between 1954 and 1966 Cleaver was imprisoned in both Soledad and San Quentin prisons. He was paroled from Soledad in 1957. Consumed by rage, he became a rapist. In his essay "On Becoming," published in *Soul on Ice* (1967), Cleaver described rape as an act of insurrection. By his own admission, had he not been caught he would have become a murderer. Once again incarcerated, Cleaver began taking stock of his life and found that his own behavior repulsed him. He sought to rid himself of the religious teachings of his childhood. His goal was to become a true revolutionary, and his role model was Che Guevara. He and another future member of the Black Panther Party, Alprentice "Bunchy" Carter, spent hours planning how to achieve liberation for African Americans through the Organization of Afro-American Unity, the entity created by Malcolm X.

Cleaver and the Black Panthers. Cleaver was paroled in late 1966 and attended his first Black Panther meeting in February 1967. He described his encounter with them as love at first sight. On that February night Cleaver met Huey P. Newton, Bobby Seale, Bobby Hutton, and Sherwin Forte. He was impressed by their appearance

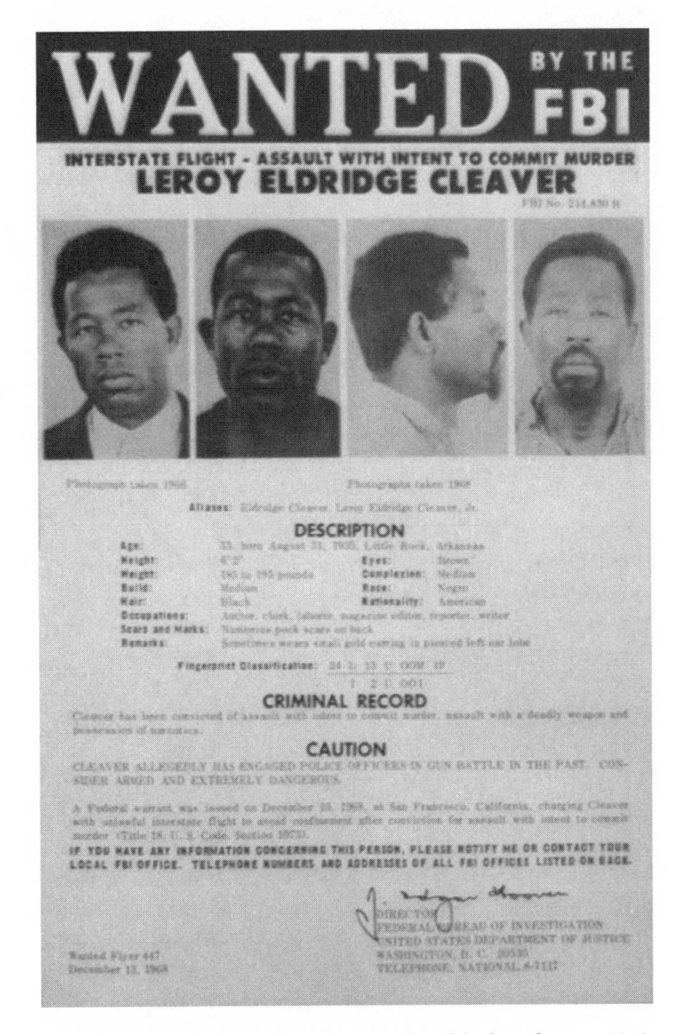

Eldridge Cleaver. FBI Wanted poster for Eldridge Cleaver, 1968. YANKEE POSTER COLLECTION, PRINTS AND PHOTOGRAPHS DIVISION, LIBRARY OF CONGRESS

and most especially the fact that each man carried a gun. Shortly thereafter Cleaver joined the Panthers. He was appointed minister of information and editor of their newspaper, the *Black Panther*.

Cleaver was also a writer for *Ramparts* magazine, a radical left-wing publication in San Francisco. His prison writings first appeared in *Ramparts*, and the magazine's publisher was instrumental in securing his release from prison. One of his first assignments was an article on Stokely Carmichael, then the chairman of the Student Nonviolent Coordinating Committee (SNCC). Carmichael is generally given credit for coining the phrase "Black Power" in a speech he gave in Mississippi shortly before leaving the SNCC to join the Black Panther Party.

Cleaver and Carmichael had an adversarial relationship. Carmichael, who was named prime minister of the Black Panther Party, was adamantly against forming coalitions with whites, while Cleaver, who ran for president on the Peace and Freedom Party's 1968 ticket, believed that coalitions of like-minded people were essential to achieving the goal of liberation for African Americans and American society.

On the evening of 27 October 1967 several Panthers engaged in a shoot-out with the Oakland Police Department. Officer John Frey was killed, and Newton was seriously injured. Newton was subsequently arrested and charged with the policeman's death. Cleaver, a parolee, quickly began to mobilize support to free Newton. As a result, his parole officer sought to have Cleaver's parole revoked. Cleaver petitioned the court in response, and the Solano County Superior Court judge Raymond Sherwin ruled in his favor. Cleaver was released on $50,000 bond. The case was appealed to the California Court of Appeals, where Cleaver did not prevail. Thus he was ordered to surrender to prison authorities on 27 November 1968. Determined not to be incarcerated again, Cleaver disappeared.

Cleaver in Exile. From late 1968 until November 1975 Cleaver lived in exile in Cuba, Algeria, and France. He escaped to Havana with the expectation of establishing a revolutionary training center for the Black Panthers. Although he was warmly received initially in Cuba, Cleaver soon realized that his presence was not welcomed universally. When his presence there was disclosed to the international press, Cleaver was forced to flee. He traveled to Algiers, where he and his former wife, Kathleen Cleaver, were reunited. Ultimately, the Algerian government announced that Cleaver was legally in the country to participate in the first Pan-African Cultural Festival.

Cleaver and his family lived in Algeria for four years, and during that time they visited the Soviet Union, Czechoslovakia, East Germany, the People's Republic of China, North Vietnam, and North Korea. Eventually, however, Cleaver disavowed communism as the vehicle for achieving black liberation.

While Cleaver was in exile, FBI counterintelligence efforts effectively split the Black Panthers. Newton expelled Cleaver from the party in 1971, further solidifying the rupture. Cleaver, now truly on his own, lived as a fugitive expatriate with his family in France. His writings reveal a desperately lonely and homesick man. He was saddened to discover that old acquaintances in the United States, among them such elected officials as Mervyn Dymally and Ronald Dellums, were either unwilling or unable to assist him in his efforts to return home.

Despondent, Cleaver decided to commit suicide at his apartment in Cannes. While summoning the courage to kill himself, he experienced a religious conversion that led him to surrender to U.S. authorities. Cleaver returned to the United States in November 1975. His sentence was commuted to approximately two thousand hours of community service. He became a born-again Christian and political conservative, though toward the end of his life he seemed to be evolving away from this philosophy. He died in Pomona, California.

Cleaver was an often brilliant thinker, a gifted writer, a revolutionary of sorts, and a notable raconteur. His writings are frequently lucid, provocative, and insightful. His life is best understood when interpreted through his voice.

[*See also* Black Nationalism; Black Panther Party; Black Power Movement; Black Press; Carmichael, Stokely; *and* Newton, Huey P.]

BIBLIOGRAPHY

Cleaver, Eldridge. *Eldridge Cleaver: Post-Prison Writings and Speeches*. New York: Random House, 1969.

Cleaver, Eldridge. *Soul on Fire*. Waco, Tex.: Word Books, 1978.

Cleaver, Eldridge. *Soul on Ice*. New York: McGraw-Hill, 1967.

Cleaver, Eldridge. *Target Zero: A Life in Writing*. Edited by Kathleen Cleaver. New York: Palgrave Macmillan, 2006.

—THERESA W. BENNETT-WILKES

CLEAVER, KATHLEEN NEAL (b. 13 May 1945), attorney and political activist. Born in Dallas, Texas, Kathleen Neal Cleaver was the first child of Ernest Neal and Juette Johnson Neal. Her father was in the foreign service and the family lived in India, Liberia, Sierra Leone, and the Philippines. When Cleaver returned to the United States, she enrolled in a boarding school near Philadelphia, Pennsylvania. She attended Oberlin College in Ohio and later transferred to Barnard College in New York.

In 1966 Cleaver left college to work for the Student Nonviolent Coordinating Committee (SNCC). At a SNCC

Rally Speaker. Kathleen Cleaver of the Black Panther Party attends the "No Extradition" rally in support of the American Indian Movement's Dennis Banks, San Francisco, 1975. Photograph by Ilka Hartmann. © ILKA HARTMANN

conference at Fisk University in Tennessee, she met Eldridge Cleaver, the minister of information for the Black Panther Party (BPP). Attracted by the party's radical approach to social change, she left SNCC and joined the Black Panthers. She married Eldridge Cleaver on 27 December 1967.

As the national communications secretary for the BPP, Kathleen Cleaver became the first female member of the party's decision-making body, the Central Committee. In 1968 she organized a national campaign to free the party's jailed minister of defense, Huey P. Newton, and ran unsuccessfully for the California state assembly.

When Eldridge Cleaver was involved in a conflict between several Panthers and the San Francisco police, the couple, unwilling to face prison, fled the country. Between 1968 and 1975 they lived in hiding, traveling from Cuba to Algeria, North Korea, and France. When the two returned to the United States in late 1975, Eldridge was immediately jailed.

Shortly after her husband's legal situation was settled, Kathleen Cleaver moved with her two children to New Haven, Connecticut, where she attended Yale University. She graduated in 1983, summa cum laude and Phi Beta Kappa, with a bachelor of arts degree in history. A year after divorcing Eldridge in 1987, Kathleen received a law degree from Yale. In 1992 Kathleen Cleaver joined the faculty of Emory University in Atlanta, Georgia, where she taught law and was in wide demand as a lecturer and journalist.

[*See also* Black Panther Party; Cleaver, Eldridge; Newton, Huey P.; *and* Student Nonviolent Coordinating Committee.]

BIBLIOGRAPHY

Bray, Rosemary L. "A Black Panther's Long Journey." *New York Times Magazine*, 31 January 1993.

—CANDACE CARDWELL

CLEMENTE, ROBERTO (b. 18 August 1934; d. 31 December 1972), Major League Baseball player. Roberto Clemente Walker was born in Barrio San Anton in Carolina, Puerto Rico, the youngest of the seven children of Melchor Clemente and Luisa Walker. His father was a foreman on a sugarcane plantation, and his mother ran a grocery store for plantation workers. As an adolescent, Clemente excelled in sports such as track and field and played amateur baseball with the Juncos double-A club and with the Santurce Crabbers in what was known as the Puerto Rican Winter League. Because he was fast, had a great throwing arm, and was also a strong hitter, scouts from big league teams watched him play in high school.

When Clemente graduated in 1953, the scout Al Campanis signed him with the Brooklyn Dodgers with a $10,000 bonus. The following season, however, the Dodgers assigned Clemente to play for their top affiliate in the minors, the Montreal Royals, at the risk of losing him at the end of the year. According to Charles Mercer, Clemente did not play well with the Dodgers at first because he did not know English and also because of the segregation laws in the United States that prevented him from staying with the white team members in some cities. Apparently Clemente felt homesick for Puerto Rico, where he had rarely experienced racial discrimination.

In 1955 Clemente joined the Pittsburgh Pirates, where he played for his entire major league career, eighteen years. "In a way I was born twice," Clemente said on 25 July 1970 in a special ceremony at Three Rivers Stadium. "I was born in 1934 and again in 1955, when I came to Pittsburgh."

The first of Clemente's many stellar seasons was in 1960. After winning the National League pennant, the Pirates faced the New York Yankees in the World Series and prevailed. The most famous home run in Clemente's life came in 1971 when the Pirates faced the Baltimore Orioles in the World Series. After the Orioles won the first two games, the Pirates won three straight, and Clemente had nine hits. In the fourth inning of the final game, when Clemente went to bat he swung and missed. One observer noted that when he swung again the crack of the bat was heard all over the stadium, the ball flew far over the center field wall, and Clemente trotted around the bases.

In 1964 Clemente married Vera Cristina Zabala, a secretary from Carolina, Puerto Rico. They had three boys. Always proud of his native soil, Clemente insisted that all three children be born in Puerto Rico. At the time of Clemente's death Vera was only thirty-two, and the boys were seven, five, and four.

Clemente stood 5 feet 11 inches and weighed 175 pounds. The Pirates retired his uniform number, 21, shortly after his death. His playing record included 2,433 games, 9,454 at bats, 3,000 hits, 2,154 singles, 440 doubles, 166 triples, 240 home runs, 1,416 runs, and 1,305 RBIs. A 12-time National League all-star, Clemente batted .311 or higher in 13 seasons and won 4 National League batting titles. Additionally he was the 1966 National League most valuable player (MVP), the 1971 World Series MVP, and the eleventh major league player to record three thousand hits.

After Clemente's death the Baseball Hall of Fame's board of directors voted to waive the customary five-year waiting period for induction and thus opened the door for a special election on Clemente's behalf. On 5 August 1973 he became the first Hispanic player inducted into the Hall of Fame. Twenty-two years later, in 1995, he was inducted into the World Sports Humanitarian Hall of Fame for his charitable work.

Roberto Clemente. Looking at the New York Mets coach Yogi Berra's lineup before an exhibition game in Saint Petersburg, Florida, 1972. AP IMAGES

Clemente died the way he lived, helping others. On 23 December 1972, Managua, Nicaragua, was nearly leveled by an earthquake. When Clemente discovered that food, medicine, and supplies from abroad were going into the hands of profiteers and not reaching the victims, he started a relief effort in Puerto Rico and insisted on taking the supplies he had collected to Nicaragua himself to make sure that they reached the neediest people. Tragically, his plane crashed.

Unfortunately, the selfless final chapter of Clemente's life often deflects attention away from his contributions to Hispanic and black pride, as well as away from his other humanitarian and philanthropic efforts. Moreover, the tragedy of his death at times obscures the determination that characterized his life. When he arrived in the United States, Clemente could not speak English; he was a black Latino in Jim Crow America. Neither success nor the subsequent abolition of the segregation laws changed these experiences or Clemente's memory of them. To the end Clemente remained proud of his homeland and ancestry. Clemente is often quoted as saying: "I am from the poor people. I represent the poor people. I like workers. I like people that suffer because these people have a different approach to life from the people that have everything" (O'Brien).

Clemente died without seeing the completion of his project Sports City in his hometown of Carolina. Incorporated in 1973, Sports City, a sports complex on 304 acres, is the result of Clemente's mission to enrich the lives of the young children of Puerto Rico and reinforce their self-esteem by teaching them to become better citizens through sports and educational programs. Sports City, which includes six baseball fields, batting cages with ten pitching machines, four tennis courts, a swimming pool, a running track, volleyball and basketball facilities, and fields for soccer and football, commemorates Clemente's life as an athlete and a humanitarian. Host to more than two hundred thousand youths yearly, it is a living memorial to one of Puerto Rico's finest sons.

[*See also* Baseball, *subentry* Integrated Professional Baseball; Latinos and Black Latinos; *and* Sports, *subentry* Professional Sports.]

BIBLIOGRAPHY

Maraniss, David. *Clemente: The Passion and Grace of Baseball's Last Hero*. New York: Simon & Schuster, 2006. An excellent biography.

Markusen, Bruce. *The Team That Changed Baseball: Roberto Clemente and the 1971 Pittsburgh Pirates*. Yardley, Pa.: Westholme, 2006.

Mercer, Charles. *Roberto Clemente*. New York: G. P. Putnam, 1974.

O'Brien, Jim. *Remember Roberto*. Pittsburgh, Pa.: James P. O'Brien, 1994.

Regalado, Samuel O. "The Latin Quarter and the Major Leagues: Adjustment and Achievement." In *The American Game: Baseball and Ethnicity*, edited by Lawrence Baldassaro and Richard A. Johnson, pp. 162–176. Carbondale: Southern Illinois University Press, 2002.

Sabin, Lewis. *Roberto Clemente*. New York: Troll Communications, 1992.

Walker, Paul Robert. *Pride of Puerto Rico: The Life of Roberto Clemente*. New York: Harcourt Brace Jovanovich, 1991.

—BEATRIZ RIVERA-BARNES

CLEVELAND. Cleveland, Ohio, celebrated its centenary in 1896, the year in which the U.S. Supreme Court upheld segregation laws in its decision in the *Plessy v. Ferguson* case. Twenty years later Cleveland was one of several destination cities for African American migrants fleeing the hostile racial climate and economic oppression of the South. Compared to the rural Jim Crow South, Cleveland offered a wider variety of employment opportunities in its burgeoning industrial sector, and African Americans joined native whites and European immigrants in making their way to the urban North. Over time, segregation ordinances, racial intimidation, economic conditions, and individual choice combined with other factors to consolidate a predominantly African American community in the area around Central and Cedar avenues on the east side of Cleveland's Cuyahoga River. Although some African Americans shared in the city's prosperity at the turn of the twentieth century, evidence also suggests that the segregation and poverty that plagued many of Cleveland's neighborhoods in the first decade of the twenty-first century resulted, in part, from policies and practices rooted in an earlier period in the history of the city and the state.

Ohio's African American population remained relatively small through the end of the nineteenth century. The same was true for the city of Cleveland, where African Americans numbered only 799 in 1860. During the first half of the twentieth century, however, Cleveland experienced phenomenal growth and diversification of its population. In 1900 the city's African American population was just under 6,000, or approximately 1.6 percent of the total population. By 1940 the number had increased to almost 85,000, roughly 10 percent of the city's population.

In describing the shifting demographics of African Americans during the interwar period, the historian Horace Mann Bond suggested that there was a direct relationship between migration, industrialization, and urbanization on the one hand and the urgent need for social reforms, including in the public schools, on the other. Through activities associated with numerous social clubs, civic organizations, churches, and fraternal and benevolent groups, African Americans struggled to enjoy a greater measure of control over their own lives.

In the religious community, the members of the Mount Zion Congregational Church were very active in nineteenth-century reform efforts, but the Methodist and Baptist congregations had by far the largest and most influential churches in the city. Saint John's African Methodist Episcopal Church, established in 1830, is the oldest of all the African American congregations in Cleveland. Shiloh Baptist Church, established in 1849, is Cleveland's oldest African American Baptist church. Before the end of the nineteenth century, Antioch Baptist Church, Saint James African Methodist Episcopal Church, Triedstone Baptist Church, and others had thriving congregations. In the twentieth century the largest of these churches frequently worked in tandem with local government agencies to provide social services and economic relief.

The smaller so-called storefront churches also served as important cultural institutions for recent African American migrants because they tended to preserve the folk spirituals and quartet singing styles that were so popular in the South. During the 1930s members of these small churches helped fuel the movement to make Thomas Andrew Dorsey's gospel music a mainstay in worship services.

Early Activism. By 1931 when Depression-era unemployment rates were in excess of 60 percent for residents in Cleveland's Central Avenue community, economic challenges combined with the poor treatment given African Americans in restaurants, hotels, parks, and schools as the catalysts for change. Political activism proved to be an important weapon in the battle to achieve racial uplift and social and economic justice. Leadership from the ranks of the Republican Party continued to be significant in Cleveland, even in the face of national shifts in party affiliation as African Americans began to support the Depression-era programs of the Democratic president Franklin D. Roosevelt. Among the local African American Republicans who were able to galvanize voters after Roosevelt's second successful presidential campaign in 1936 was William O. Walker, the longtime publisher of the *Call and Post*, one of Cleveland's African American weekly newspapers.

Through organizations such as the Future Outlook League, African Americans in Cleveland were also able to capture the spirit of the "don't buy where you can't work" movement led by John O. Holly, founder of the Future Outlook League in 1935. Holly's confrontational leadership style stood in stark contrast to the civil deportment of many middle-class African Americans, including the native Clevelander, Spingarn Medal recipient, author, and businessman Charles W. Chesnutt.

Chesnutt worked with African Americans and whites to improve opportunities for African Americans, including those associated with what is considered the oldest African American theater in the United States, Karamu House. From the inception in 1915 of the Karamu Settlement House—originally called the Playhouse Settlement—its directors planned and implemented programs in the arts for young people in the African American community. The organization was the outgrowth of committee work conducted by the Men's Club of the white Second Presbyterian Church in 1914. In 1927 the Karamu Theater was founded in a building adjacent to the original complex.

Even more than the arts, schools were targeted by African American reformers in Cleveland. According to the 1920 census, Cleveland led the nation in the percentage of African Americans ages seven to fifteen who were actually enrolled in school. Enrollment of African Americans in Cleveland's public schools increased steadily throughout the 1920s, and the NAACP campaigned for and, in 1929, won the election of the first African American to the Cleveland Board of Education, Mary Brown Martin. In the 1930s the NAACP also challenged—with little success—board practices of labeling African American students "retarded" and placing them in remedial classes and industrial-type schools. The conditions facing students in Cleveland's inner city provided ongoing challenges for community leaders and school officials throughout the remainder of the twentieth century.

After World War II. African American migration to Cleveland continued unabated through World War II, but the African American population increase was not always accompanied by an increase in the number of economic and housing opportunities. In 1950 the city's population peaked at 914,808, and then Cleveland began to experience major population and job loss. The coincident success in the civil rights arena helped fuel a rising tide of expectations in communities across the country, but unmet expectations sometimes gave rise to growing frustration among African Americans. By 1960, 251,000 African Americans lived in Cleveland, and many of them joined others across the nation in calling for improved social and economic conditions at home and, by 1968, for an end to the Vietnam War.

Like other urban areas, Cleveland experienced its share of social unrest in the 1960s, including the Hough riot of 1966 and the Glenville riot of 1968. Increased political activism in the 1960s helped Carl B. Stokes become the first African American mayor of a major American city in 1968, when African Americans made up approximately one-third of the city's population. During his tenure

Stokes succeeded in creating a more inclusive city government and strengthening ties between City Hall and grassroots leadership, including African American pastors. In addition, nationally known religious and civil rights leaders, including the Reverend Martin Luther King Jr. and Malcolm X, forged important ties with pastors and social-justice groups, including the Congress of Racial Equality, in Cleveland during the 1960s. Both King and Malcolm X spoke at the city's Cory United Methodist Church in the historic Glenville community, and King worked closely with both Stokes and the Reverend Odie M. Hoover of Cleveland's Olivet Institutional Baptist Church.

While serving as mayor, Stokes increased opportunities for African Americans to do business with and work for the city, even as his detractors complained of his administration's mismanagement of funds for community-based programs. Stokes's second term as mayor ended in 1971, but he later returned to public life and served as a municipal judge in Cleveland from 1983 to 1994. The city elected its second African American mayor, Michael R. White, in 1989; he served as mayor through 2002, becoming Cleveland's longest-serving mayor.

Louis Stokes, the elder brother of Carl B. Stokes, also rose to power during the 1960s. Louis Stokes was elected to the U.S. House of Representatives from the newly created Twenty-first Congressional District, encompassing Cleveland's east side, in 1968. He served fifteen consecutive terms, retiring in 1999 as one of the most influential members of the Congressional Black Caucus. The attorney, former judge, and county prosecutor Stephanie Tubbs Jones was elected to be Stokes's successor. Tubbs Jones is the first African American woman from Ohio to serve in the House of Representatives.

Throughout the second half of the twentieth century the NAACP continued to focus on the role of the public schools as perpetuators of inequality and racial discrimination in Cleveland. In 1976 the NAACP won a major victory in the local school desegregation case *Reed v. Rhodes*, in which the courts determined that Cleveland's schools were guilty of deliberately creating and maintaining a racially segregated public school system. Although peacefully implemented, busing for desegregation faced resistance from both African Americans and whites. The shrinking real estate property tax base and tax abatement for corporations added fiscal challenges to the list of woes for school administrators in the closing decades of the twentieth century.

In 1998, George W. White, an African American judge, ended the school-desegregation effort when he ruled that the schools had done everything possible to comply with the remedial order in the case. In that same year Mayor Michael R. White, with the approval of Ohio's state legislature, took over Cleveland's troubled school system, ending a period of state oversight and the direct election of school board members. Under Mayor White's leadership, Barbara Byrd Bennett, an African American educator from New York, was hired to serve as the Cleveland Metropolitan School District's first chief executive officer.

According to the 2000 census, African Americans accounted for 243,939 of the city's total population of 477,459. At 51 percent of the population, this number represented the highest percentage ever of African Americans in Cleveland's population. In 2005 the city elected its third African American mayor, Frank G. Jackson. Although African American sports figures, including Lebron James of the Cleveland Cavaliers professional basketball team, were attracting crowds and generating income for downtown arenas and other businesses, in the early twenty-first century poor and working-class Africa Americans continued to grapple with many of the same issues that troubled members of the race a century earlier. In the 2006–2007 academic year, 67 percent of the school district's approximately fifty-six thousand students were African American.

Eugene Sanders, an African American school administrator from Toledo, Ohio, became the district's second chief executive officer in 2006. The state of Ohio described the schools as being in a state of "continuous improvement." In the early twenty-first century, Cleveland remained at or near the top of the nation's list of the poorest and most segregated cities. In response to these and other social ills, groups such as the Cleveland Foundation, one of the nation's oldest and largest community foundations, have partnered with African American churches, county officials, and the federal government to enhance school, community, and employment programs.

[*See also* Desegregation and Integration, *subentry* Public Education; Industrialization and Deindustrialization; Mayors; Ohio; *and biographical entries on figures mentioned in this article*.]

BIBLIOGRAPHY

Davis, Russell H. *Black Americans in Cleveland from George Peake to Carl B. Stokes, 1796–1969*. Washington, D.C.: Associated Publishers, 1972.

Kusmer, Kenneth L. *A Ghetto Takes Shape: Black Cleveland, 1870–1930*. Urbana: University of Illinois Press, 1976.

Miller, Carol Poh, and Robert A. Wheeler. *Cleveland: A Concise History, 1796–1996*. 2d ed. Bloomington: Indiana University Press, 1997.

Phillips, Kimberley I. *AlabamaNorth: African-American Migrants, Community, and Working-Class Activism in Cleveland, 1915–1945*. Urbana: University of Illinois Press, 1999.

—REGENNIA N. WILLIAMS

CLEVELAND, GROVER, ADMINISTRATION OF. Grover Cleveland, the twenty-second and twenty-fourth president of the United States, was born on 18 March 1837 at Caldwell, New Jersey, to the Presbyterian minister Richard Falley Cleveland and Ann Neal. He is the only U.S. president to serve two nonconsecutive terms. Cleveland was educated at local schools in New York State, then read law at the Buffalo firm of Rogers, Bowen, and Rogers. After being admitted to the bar in 1859 he practiced with his mentor until attaining a position as an assistant district attorney in 1863. He avoided service in the Civil War by hiring a substitute when called for the military draft. Cleveland gained prominence in the New York Democratic Party following the Civil War and was elected as Buffalo's mayor in 1881. The following year he was elected governor of New York, making state civil service reform a priority. In 1884 Cleveland received the presidential nomination of the Democratic Party on the convention's second ballot, then captured the White House by a slim majority of the electoral college. He received only 48.5 percent of the popular vote and won in his own state of New York by just over one thousand votes.

As the first Democratic administration to occupy the White House since before the Civil War, Cleveland's presidency was lauded by Democrats in all regions of the nation but was especially appealing to southern conservatives. He appointed two prominent southern conservatives to his cabinet, suggesting that his administration would take a new political turn from recent Republican tactics. A definite Washington outsider, Cleveland gained a reformer's reputation. He corrected mismanagement in the Navy Department, oversaw the creation of the Interstate Commerce Commission in 1887, and elevated the Department of Agriculture to a cabinet position. He also reversed the tradition of appointing prominent African Americans to minor federal positions. However, Cleveland did allow Frederick Douglass to retain his position as recorder of deeds for the District of Columbia, and he appointed blacks to a handful of minor posts. Those were the only efforts he made during his first term to assist African Americans.

Cleveland lost his reelection bid in 1888 to the Republican Benjamin Harrison, but he regained the presidency for a nonconsecutive second term in 1892. His return to Washington was followed by the panic of 1893, which marked the onset of one of the worst economic depressions to strike the United States. Cleveland defended the federal use of the gold standard as the basis for the nation's currency, sparking a revolt within the Democratic Party from advocates of silver and those opposing the president's plan for borrowing to replenish the federal gold reserve. In 1894, Cleveland lost any support he had from labor when he authorized federal intervention in the Chicago-based Pullman strike. That same year he earned criticism of the business community for his mishandling of tariff reform. The handling of race relations was similarly dismal during Cleveland's second term.

African Americans continued to face discrimination in government hiring practices. The president believed that southern blacks should look to their former masters, not the federal government, for guidance and economic assistance. He believed that education was an important stepping-stone for African Americans, once remarking, "If our colored boys are to exercise in their mature years the right of citizenship, they should be fitted to perform their duties intelligently and thoroughly" (quoted in Welch, pp. 67–68). This mentality certainly must have tainted Cleveland's interactions with Booker T. Washington in 1895. That fall, the president read the text of Washington's address at the opening of the Atlanta Exposition and was much impressed. He agreed with Washington's advocacy of manual education and believed it wise to downplay the possibility of social equality between the races. On 23 October 1895, Cleveland visited the Atlanta Exposition, spending an hour shaking hands and singing autographs in the Negro Building.

Despite his willingness to make a personal appearance in Atlanta, as a Democratic president, Cleveland preferred to leave the issue of black rights to the southern states. He did little to curb the passage of Jim Crow laws in the South, and in 1896 he actually applauded the Supreme Court's decision in *Plessy v. Ferguson*, which codified the separate-but-equal premise that spurred racial segregation. Grover Cleveland's most revealing statement on race came after his presidency, in a speech delivered before the Southern Educational Association meeting in New York in 1903. The former president told those assembled, "I believe that neither the decree which made the slaves free, nor the enactment that suddenly invested them with the rights of citizenship, any more cured them of their racial and slavery-bred imperfections and deficiencies than it changed the color of their skin" (quoted in "Grover Cleveland: A Powerful Advocate of White Supremacy," p. 54). Cleveland died on 24 June 1908.

[*See also* Atlanta Exposition Address (Atlanta Compromise); Democratic Party; Jim Crow Laws; *Plessy v. Ferguson* and Segregation; Segregation in Federal Government; *and* Washington, Booker T.]

BIBLIOGRAPHY

"Grover Cleveland: A Powerful Advocate of White Supremacy." *Journal of Blacks in Higher Education* 31 (Spring 2001): 53–54.

Harlan, Louis, Stuart B. Kaufman, Barbara S. Kraft, and Raymond W. Smock, eds. *The Booker T. Washington Papers*. Vol. 4, *1895–1898*.

Urbana: University of Illinois Press. Available online, http://www.historycooperative.org/btw/index.html.
Welch, Richard E. *The Presidencies of Grover Cleveland*. Lawrence: University Press of Kansas, 1988.

—L. DIANE BARNES

CLIFTON, LUCILLE (b. 27 June 1936), poet and author of children's books. Clifton was born Thelma Lucille Sayles in Depew, New York, the daughter of Samuel Louis Sayles Sr., a steelworker, and Thelma Moore Sayles, a laundress. The family moved to Buffalo, where Clifton grew up. Her extended family included grandparents and several uncles. Lucille's mother wrote poetry for personal enjoyment and encouraged her daughter's interest in writing.

Early Writing Experiences. Clifton entered Howard University in 1953 on a scholarship provided by her church. There she met Sterling Brown; A. B. Spellman; Amiri Baraka, formerly known as LeRoi Jones; and Chloe Wofford, now known as Toni Morrison, and studied under Owen Dodson. Clifton starred in the inaugural performance of James Baldwin's play *The Amen Corner*. She left Howard in 1955 due to a lack of money and transferred to the State University of New York at Fredonia (known at that time as Fredonia State University).

At Fredonia, Clifton read and performed plays with a group of students that included Ishmael Reed and her future husband Fred James Clifton, a philosophy instructor at the University of Buffalo. Lucille Clifton also began writing poetry, which she shared with Reed. He showed her poems to Langston Hughes, who published them in his anthology *The Poetry of the Negro, 1746–1949*.

Clifton did not graduate from college. She said that her formal education took place at Howard and her informal education has been ongoing. She is the recipient of numerous honorary doctorates from colleges and universities that include the State University of New York, Colby College, Dartmouth University, Washington College, and the University of Maryland.

Clifton married in 1958 and bore six children over seven years. She continued to write poetry while rearing her family and working. In 1969 she sent some of her poems to Robert Hayden, who entered them in a competition for unknown writers sponsored by the Young Women's–Young Men's Hebrew Association Poetry Center. She won their Discovery Award for her first collection, *Good Times*. It was published by Random House and named one of the ten best books of 1969 by the *New York Times*. In 1970 she received her first creative writing fellowship from the National Endowment for the Arts.

Clifton wrote her first children's books in 1970, *The Black BCs* and *Some of the Days of Everett Anderson*. She was employed as a literature assistant by the U.S. Department of Education from 1969 to 1971. Part of her job involved finding books for schools. Dismayed by the lack of literature on African Americans, she created Everett Anderson, a little boy living in a fictional inner city. *Everett Anderson's Goodbye*, published in 1983, won the Coretta Scott King Book Award in 1984. Clifton has written more than twenty children's books.

Clifton's Writing Style. The beauty of Clifton's work lies in her willingness to tell terrible stories of the past, according to her longtime friend and colleague Michael S. Glaser, professor of English at Saint Mary's College of Maryland. Acceptance enables her to embrace these stories with love and forgiveness, transforming them into gifts of inclusion and humanness. Her language and content have an integrity and an honesty that speak of genuine courage in reporting out, as clearly as she can, the stories she has to tell.

Clifton has an unerring sense of her own aesthetic. She works with the poetic line and uses unpretentious language intensified by its precision and accuracy. She possesses an uncanny feel for the cadence and rhythm of sounds, which are particularly noticeable when she reads her creations aloud. Her language is honed to the essentials, devoid of adornment and without a single unnecessary breath or period. Much of her work celebrates her African and African American heritage.

Clifton was named poet laureate of Maryland in 1974 and was inducted into the Maryland Women's Hall of Fame in 1993. She was inducted into the Literary Hall of Fame for Writers of African Descent in 1998. *Two-Headed Woman* (1980), *Good Woman: Poems and a Memoir* (1987), and *Quilting Poems: 1987–1990* (1991) were each nominated for the Pulitzer Prize.

In 1989 Clifton became the first Visiting Distinguished Professor of Humanities at Saint Mary's College of Maryland. In 1990 she joined the faculty permanently as a tenured Distinguished Professor of Humanities. In 1991 she was awarded the Hilda C. Landers Endowed Chair in the Liberal Arts. She retired in the spring of 2005 and became professor emerita and friend of the college.

[*See also* Literature.]

BIBLIOGRAPHY

Andrews, William L., Frances Smith Foster, and Trudier Harris, eds. *Oxford Companion to African American Literature*. New York: Oxford University Press, 1997. Biographical entry and assessment of Clifton's work.
Coleman, Jeffrey. "Lucille Clifton: A Legacy of Words and Deeds." *River Gazette* 6, no. 3 (2006): 8.
Ostrom, Hans, and J. David Macey Jr. *The Greenwood Encyclopedia of African American Literature*. Vol. 1. Westport, Conn.: Greenwood,

2005. Informally written biographical sketch of Clifton that contains a detailed list of her work.

Regents of the University of Minnesota. "Lucille Clifton, b. 1936." Voices from the Gaps: Women Artists and Writers of Color. http://voices.cla.umn.edu/vg/Bios/entries/clifton_lucille.html. Biographical information and criticism on Clifton, selected bibliography of her works, works about Clifton, non-English works, and related links.

—THERESA W. BENNETT-WILKES

CLINTON, BILL, ADMINISTRATION OF. William Jefferson Clinton was elected in 1992 as the forty-second president of the United States. Within his administration he undertook extensive reform of welfare, balanced the federal budget, created the initiative called "One America in the Twenty-first Century" (1997), and attempted to reconcile some of the social and cultural injustices that certain Americans face. The U.S. economy also boomed during Clinton's tenure. His administration was marked both with political and personal success and also with scandal, as when he faced ouster in 1998 for his conduct involving a White House intern and for his subsequent lying about that conduct. He was impeached by the House of Representatives but was found not guilty by the Senate, and he enjoyed the highest approval ratings of his presidency, 72 percent, shortly thereafter.

One of the most sweeping reforms ever of the social welfare system began during the administration of President Bill Clinton. August 1996 saw the establishment of the Personal Responsibility and Work Opportunity Reconciliation Act, which created amendments to the existing welfare system. Among the changes were term limits of no more than five years over the course of a lifetime for all beneficiaries, whether consecutive or nonconsecutive and transferring the funding of welfare services to a block-grant format. Block grants allowed states to receive a "block" of funds to be distributed at the discretion of the state; the funds could support subsidized day care and transportation programs that would assist recipients in transitioning to employment. As a result of the reforms, welfare recipient rosters decreased by 57 percent—though some claimed that this decrease was the result of the boom in the economy at the time. Critics also charged that the measures were exceedingly punitive and harmful to the poorest citizens.

President Clinton maintained a strong focus on race relations throughout his presidency. Clinton's race initiative, called "One America in the Twenty-first Century" and announced on 14 June 1997, was a yearlong conversation designed to create a unified country that was free of the cultural inequities that had always plagued the United States. The goal of this initiative was to improve race relations, while establishing a multicultural democracy that reflected the country's changing demography. The Clinton administration took on the challenge of addressing race issues at a time when there were no major social upheavals, a luxury not enjoyed by many of his predecessors. Clinton created an advisory committee of seven Americans to engage the public in a dialogue about the causes of race-related tension in the United States and potential solutions for defusing those tensions. The committee consisted of John Hope Franklin, Linda Chavez-Thompson, Suzan D. Johnson Cook, Thomas H. Kean, Angela E. Oh, Robert J. Thomas, and William F. Winter. The committee was composed of politicians, academics, theologians, legal experts, and executives, all of which were renowned in their respective fields.

The work of the committee culminated with a report that outlined current policies in need of change and created a reference used to address social change. The report, titled *One America in the 21st Century: Forging A New Future,* can be accessed via the National Archives and Records Administration online.

In addition to creating a dialogue about the status of race relations in America, President Clinton increased the representation of women and minorities in government. More than half of the people he appointed to federal positions were minorities or women, and 63 percent of the people he appointed to federal judgeships were African American. More African Americans held appointed positions during the Clinton administration than in any other presidency in history.

Clinton also made history with his 1994 crime bill. In conjunction with the 1993 Brady Bill, which mandated a five-day waiting period for handgun purchases, the crime bill banned the sale of automatic weapons with the exception of slightly more than six hundred types of hunting rifles. Additionally, the crime bill expanded the number of offenses that were punishable by death. In an effort to reduce crime and reclaim neighborhoods, the crime bill created grant funding that would place one hundred thousand new police officers across the country. Critics charged, however, that these crime initiatives did little or nothing to halt the growing incarceration of African Americans and may have exacerbated this trend.

Clinton's call to action for education in the twenty-first century drew attention to the needs of children from diverse economic and cultural backgrounds. The Clinton administration also improved educational opportunities for minorities by creating accountability structures and allowing for school choice in areas where schools were underperforming, while increasing funding for programs like Head Start. Additionally, President Clinton tackled tax reform by creating lower rates for taxable income, per child credits, and decreased penalties for low-income Americans, which directly benefited the 22.1 percent of

Clinton Homage to the Equal Pay Act. President Clinton displays a photograph of President Kennedy signing the Equal Pay Act; Dorothy Height, the woman beside Clinton, appears in the photo. Clinton used this occasion to support a bill that allows women to sue for compensatory and punitive damages should they suffer wage discrimination. Photograph by Mark Wilson. REUTERS

African Americans living below the poverty level in 2000. This was the lowest level since the U.S. Census Bureau began collecting poverty statistics in 1966.

[*See also* Affirmative Action; Arkansas; Discrimination; Poverty, Culture of; *and* Public Assistance.]

BIBLIOGRAPHY

Bovard, James. *Feeling Your Pain: The Explosion and Abuse of Government Power in the Clinton-Gore Years*. New York: St. Martin's Press, 2000.

Clinton, William J. *My Life*. New York: Random House, 2004.

Clinton, William J. *Giving: How Each of Us Can Change The World*. New York: Alfred A. Knopf, 2007.

Cronin, Thomas E., and Michael A. Genovese. "President Clinton and Character Questions." *Presidential Studies Quarterly* 28, 1998.

Edwards; George C. "Bill Clinton and His Crisis of Governance." *Presidential Studies Quarterly*, 28, 1998.

Kim, C. J. "Clinton's Race Initiative: Recasting the American Dilemma." *Polity* 33, no. 2 (2001): 175–198. A discussion of the ideology behind the formation of the Race Commission and potential implications.

O'Connor, Brendon. "Policies, Principles, and Polls: Bill Clinton's Third Way Welfare Politics 1992–1996." *The Australian Journal of Politics and History*, 48, 2002

Wattier, Mark J. "The Clinton Factor: The Effects of Clinton's Personal Image in 2000 Presidential Primaries and in the General Election." *White House Studies*, 4, 2004.

Wickham, DeWayne. *Bill Clinton and Black America*. New York: Ballantine Books, 2002.

—CARLY WOMACK WYNNE

CME CHURCH. The Christian Methodist Episcopal Church was formed out of the Methodist Episcopal Church, South, which had separated in 1844 from the Methodist Episcopal Church in America, primarily over the issue of slavery. During the antebellum and Civil War periods, the Methodist Episcopal Church, South, included a large number of slaves, who were cared for by slave preachers. In the wake of the Civil War and the emancipation of the slaves, the newly freed slaves under the leadership of their former slave preachers separated from the Methodist Episcopal Church, South (ME Church, South), and established the Colored Methodist Episcopal Church (the CME Church), which was later renamed the Christian Methodist Episcopal Church.

Origins. During the antebellum period and the Civil War, many slaves formed a relationship with the ME Church, South, because of the services of their slave preachers. After the Civil War, many former slaves and slave preachers developed a sense of religious freedom and a separate religious identity that was fostered in part by their slave experience. On the other hand, many of those same slaves and their slave preachers were both suspicious of and put off by the arrogance and self-righteousness that they perceived in the missionaries from the African Methodist Episcopal (AME) Church and the African Methodist Episcopal Zion (AME Zion) Church who poured into the South after the Civil War. The solution for these former slaves was to establish their own church. In 1866 these former slaves and their slave preachers, who were members of the ME Church, South, petitioned the bishops of the ME Church, South, to authorize the establishment of their own congregation.

In December 1870 the ME Church, South, at an Organizing General Conference, established the Colored Methodist Episcopal Church in America. This was the former slaves' church, and its early leaders included former slave preachers, such as William Henry Miles and Richard H. Vanderhorst, who were the church's first two bishops. Bishop Miles was born a slave in Kentucky in 1828. He obtained his freedom in 1864 and migrated to Ohio but later returned to Kentucky, where he became a pastor and leader in the AME Zion Church. He later resigned from the AME Zion and joined the newly organized Kentucky Colored Conference of the ME Church, South, in 1868. He rose to the rank of presiding elder and pastor. At the December 1870 organizing conference he was very influential and was elected the first bishop of the CME. He served in this capacity until his death in 1892. Bishop Vanderhorst, the second bishop of the CME, was born in Georgetown, South Carolina, in 1813. He joined the ME Church, South, in 1833 and became a preacher but was never ordained. Vanderhorst joined the AME in 1865 in Charleston but broke with it in 1868 to join the Georgia Conference of the ME Church, South. He, too, rose to presiding elder and was a very active and persuasive participant at the organizing conference. He died in 1872.

Although the CME maintained a good relationship with the ME Church, South—despite the latter's somewhat paternalistic attitude—the CME had numerous disputes with both the AME and the AME Zion churches. These early disputes arose over the title to church property. Often the property had previously been owned by ME Church congregations, but in the years after the Civil War, many in a congregation had converted to either AME or AME Zion, and the succeeding congregation claimed title to the property. In some instances the ME Church assisted the CME in establishing its right to the property, as the successor to the ME Church, South.

Since the CME was for the most part a church composed of former slaves, its membership was originally centered in the southern states, ranging from Tennessee to the Carolinas and from Virginia to Florida. Its membership, however, grew quickly. In 1873 it numbered 67,889; this grew to more than 200,000 by 1902 and to more than 350,000 by 1922. This growing membership now included congregations in Cleveland, Saint Louis, and Arizona.

Educational Efforts. As with the African Methodist Episcopal churches, the CME viewed education as an important element in its mission. The church established several educational institutions, the most important of which were Paine College, in Augusta, Georgia, and Lane College, in Jackson, Tennessee. Paine College was established in 1882 with the cooperation and support of the ME, South. The trustees came from both churches, and the first president was the Reverend George W. Walker, a white presiding elder of the ME, South. The presidency of the college was held by a white until 1971 when Lucius Henry Pitt became the first African American CME president of Paine College. The ME, South, Church provided scholarships for CME young men to attend the college, and after the ME, South, merged into the United Methodist Church in the twentieth century, the United Methodists continued this support.

Lane College was also founded in 1882 but did not receive its present name until 1896. The college was named for Bishop Isaac Lane, who was a patron of the school. Lane College was also a combined effort of the CME and ME, South. Its first president was the Reverend T. F. Saunders, a white minister of the ME, South, who served until 1902. In that year he was succeeded by James A. Bray, a graduate of Lane, who became the first African American president of the school. The announced purpose of the college was to provide African American students with a classical education.

The CME's efforts in education declined somewhat after 1933. This is often attributed to the growth of other philanthropic efforts in this area and the limited resources of the CME. Much of the funding dedicated to education before 1933 was used for both elementary and high school. After 1933 the funds were redirected to the collegiate institutions.

The Modern Church. After World War I a major change in African American demographics occurred when African Americans started moving in large numbers from southern rural areas to northern urban areas. This change was reflected in the CME. First, membership in the southern areas declined, while membership increased in the North. Second, a middle-class African American population developed, and they demanded a role in their church. In the CME this issue came to a head in the form of a constitutional debate over the authority of the General Conference (which was composed in part of lay members) to recommend the appointment of bishops to the various districts of the church. The bishops argued that this action was unconstitutional. The process of establishing a constitution that would require the College of Bishops to share its authority with the laity was quite protracted. In 1950 the Constitution of the Judiciary Court was first adopted and began to function. Finally, in 1974 the full constitution of the CME was put in place.

It was during the 1950s that the name of the church became a point of debate. In the mid-1800s "colored" was the most common term used by African Americans to refer to themselves. As the civil rights movement developed and "colored" was seen as having negative connotations, the church began to reconsider its name. Therefore, at the General Conference of the church held in May 1954, the church officially changed its name to the Christian Methodist Episcopal Church.

In the shadow of Jim Crow, the early CME believed that it was important for the church to maintain friendly relations with the dominant white society. As a corollary to this idea, the CME believed that it was important for the church to avoid all political involvement. Therefore, during its history the church eschewed political involvement as an institution. Nevertheless, in the late 1930s and 1950s the church did protest the lynching of African Americans and other discriminatory actions. It also supported the activities of such civil rights organizations as the National Association for the Advancement of Colored People (NAACP) and the National Urban League. Furthermore, individual ministers, such as the Reverends J. W. Bonner, Henry C. Burton, and R. B. Shorts, became prominent leaders in the 1960s civil rights movement. Bonner, the pastor of the First CME Church of Montgomery, Alabama, served as a member of the Montgomery Improvement Association, which later became the Southern Christian Leadership Conference (SCLC). Burton was also an active member of the SCLC board of directors. Shorts, the pastor of the West Mitchell CME Church in Atlanta, led the boycott against Coca-Cola until that company hired African Americans. He also helped place the first African Americans on the Atlanta police force.

As early as 1898 the CME showed interest in establishing missions in Africa, but it did not have the resources; by the 1950s the church reconsidered. At its 1958 General Conference, the members voted to establish CME missions in Africa, first in Ghana and then in Nigeria. In the 1970s the CME expanded its missionary activities to include the Caribbean. This action resulted in the establishment of a Jamaica conference in 1982.

As the twentieth century came to an end, the CME became more outspoken and sought to streamline its organization. In celebrating its centennial in 1970, the church announced that it was rededicating itself to the principles of human dignity, black identity, and liberation—a restatement of the principles of the civil rights movement. In the 1980s the CME hired consultants to study the structure of its internal government, and in 1986 the church was restructured to improve efficiency and reduce the number of departments and officers.

[*See also* AME Church; AME Zion Church; Black Church; Religion; *and* Religious Communities and Practices.]

Bibliography

Lakey, Othal Hawthorne. *The History of the CME Church*. Memphis, Tenn.: CME Publishing House, 1996. The official history of the CME Church, emphasizing the politics of the appointment of its bishops.

Lane, Isaac. *Autobiography of Bishop Isaac Lane, LL.D., with a Short History of the C.M.E. Church in America and of Methodism*. Nashville, Tenn.: Publishing House of the M.E. Church, South, 1916. An early look at the church by one of its leading bishops.

Lincoln, C. Eric, and Lawrence H. Mamiya. *The Black Church in the African American Experience*. Durham, N.C.: Duke University Press, 1990. A composite review of black churches that includes a short but excellent entry on the CME Church.

—Thomas E. Carney

COALITION OF BLACK TRADE UNIONISTS. The Coalition of Black Trade Unionists (CBTU) has provided an independent voice for African Americans and other underrepresented workers within the house of labor and in the political arena since the 1970s. After the executive council of the American Federation of Labor and Congress of Industrial Organizations (AFL-CIO) refused to oppose the reelection of President Richard Nixon in 1972, the black labor leaders William Lucy (international secretary-treasurer of the American Federation of State, County, and Municipal Employees), Nelson "Jack" Edwards (vice president of the United Auto Workers), William Simons (president of the Washington Teachers Union, Local 6), Charles Hayes (vice president of the United Food and Commercial Workers Union), and Cleveland Robinson (president of the Distributive Workers of America, District 65) called together over twelve hundred black workers from a variety of unions to form the CBTU. The organization was formed not as a civil rights or separatist group but rather to improve the image of the labor movement within minority communities, increase black and minority participation within unions and their leadership structures, and ensure that the rectification of issues regarding race and discrimination are central to organized labor's agenda. It has greatly contributed to the diversification of the labor movement, and it played a central role in the defeat the AFL-CIO's old-guard leadership during the 1990s. Politically, the CBTU has mobilized black voters to influence policy and elections both nationally and internationally. Led by a thirty-member executive council, a seven-member executive committee, and its longtime president and executive treasurer, William Lucy, as of 2008 the CBTU had fifty-five active chapters in the United States and Canada, representing workers from more than fifty different international unions. Public sector workers, however, play a disproportionate role, representing both the limitations of the organization as well as the importance of Lucy to the organization's size, strength, and continued existence.

[*See also* Organized Labor.]

BIBLIOGRAPHY

Marable, Manning. *Race, Reform, and Rebellion: The Second Reconstruction and Beyond in Black America, 1945–2006*. 3d ed. Jackson: University Press of Mississippi, 2007.

—DAVID A. GOLDBERG

COBB, CHARLES, SR. (b. 28 September 1916; d. 28 December 1998), religious civil rights leader, and **CHARLES COBB JR.** (b. 23 June 1943), civil rights activist and journalist. The Reverend Dr. Charles Earl Cobb Sr. was born in Durham, N.C., in 1916 and graduated from North Carolina College. He received his bachelor of divinity degree from Howard University, a master's in theology from Boston University, and a doctor of divinity degree from Huston-Tillotson College in Austin, Texas. In 1966, Cobb became the first executive director of the United Church of Christ's Commission for Racial Justice. The defining moment in his tenure as the executive director was brought about by his advocacy for the Wilmington Ten. In 1971, ten civil rights activists were charged with arson and conspiracy in Wilmington, North Carolina. Cobb was instrumental in getting his denomination to support the Wilmington Ten, and the convictions were eventually overturned.

Understanding the need for collaboration, Cobb founded the National Conference of Black Christians, the first ecumenical organization of religious civil rights leaders. He was a founding board member of TransAfrica and the Interreligious Foundation for Community Organization (IFCO). Known for walking the picket lines, Cobb was arrested for demonstrating against the apartheid South African government. In 1982, under his leadership, demonstrators gathered in Warren County, North Carolina, to protest the dumping of toxic waste in a predominantly African American and low-income community. Several years of national investigation ensued. As a result, in February 1994 President Bill Clinton issued Executive Order no. 12,898, Federal Actions to Address Environmental Justice in Minority Populations and Low-Income Populations, which was the first executive order of its kind. After his retirement from the UCC commission, Cobb remained active in the struggle for civil and human rights until his health began to fail. Cobb Sr. died in 1998 at Georgetown University Hospital in Washington, D.C. He was eighty-two.

Cobb and his wife, Martha Cobb, had a son, Charles Cobb Jr., born in 1943 in Washington, D.C. In 1961, while a student at Howard University, Charlie Cobb Jr. joined the Nonviolent Action Group (NAG), an affiliate of the Student Nonviolent Coordinating Committee (SNCC), and participated in sit-ins in the District of Columbia, Maryland, and Virginia. In the summer of 1962, Charlie Cobb became a SNCC field secretary, in Ruleville, Mississippi. In 1964, SNCC, along with the Congress of Racial Equality (CORE) and the NAACP, organized its Freedom Summer campaign. The Freedom Summer project drew national attention to racial oppression in Mississippi and especially the state's denial of voting rights to black Mississippians. Charlie Cobb was instrumental in the creation of the Mississippi Freedom Schools during the 1964 Freedom Summer project. Cobb was convinced that any summer project designed to change Mississippi must also include a school program to deal with the problems faced by black children. After Freedom Summer, Cobb lived in Tanzania for two years and was actively involved in the decolonization battles in Africa. In the late 1960s, Charlie Cobb worked as a press reporter in Atlanta, Georgia. His career as a journalist later evolved, and he became a freelance writer for several publications. In 1985, Cobb joined the staff of *National Geographic*. In 1995, Cobb received the National Association of Black Journalists award and a Harry Chapin Media Award from World Hunger Year for a National Public Radio documentary on Eritrea. Like his father, Charlie Cobb has given his life to the pursuit of civil rights. In 2001, Charlie Cobb, along with fellow SNCC alum Bob Moses, authored *Radical Equations*, a book that connects the voting and civil rights of the late 1960s with the current struggle to redefine pedagogy. As of 2008, Charlie Cobb was a senior diplomatic correspondent with the news distributor allAfrica.com.

[*See also* Congress of Racial Equality; North Carolina; *and* Student Nonviolent Coordinating Committee.]

BIBLIOGRAPHY

Winslow, William C. "Racial Justice Advocate, Charles Cobb, Dies." *World Faith News Archives*, 30 December 1998. http://www.wfn.org/1999/01/msg00025.html.

—CASSANDRA MCKAY

COCHRAN, JOHNNIE (b. 2 October 1937; d. 29 March 2005), lawyer. Johnnie L. Cochran Jr. was born in Shreveport, Louisiana, to Johnnie L. Cochran, an insurance company executive, and Hattie Cochran. The great-grandson of a slave, Cochran grew up in an affluent and loving family that moved to California when his father accepted a position at Golden State Mutual Life Insurance Company. Cochran was an exceptional student in high school as well as at the University of California at Los Angeles, where he earned a bachelor's degree in 1959. While an undergraduate, he sold insurance policies for his father's company to support himself.

In 1963 Cochran graduated from Loyola Marymount University Law School and passed the California bar exam. He took his first job as a lawyer that year as a deputy city criminal prosecutor for the city of Los Angeles. After two years he joined the private practice of a criminal attorney named Gerald Lenoir before he started his own firm, Cochran, Atkins, and Evans. Cochran's first famous case came in May 1966, when in a civil suit he represented the family of Leonard Deadwyler, a young black man killed by police as he rushed his pregnant wife to the hospital. Cochran claimed that the Los Angeles Police Department used excessive force, but his argument proved unsuccessful as he and his firm lost the case. The experience taught him how volatile the issue of police brutality was within the African American community and led him to become increasingly interested in matters of racial justice.

A few years later, in the early 1970s, Cochran defended the Black Panther Party leader Geronimo Pratt in a murder trial in Santa Monica, California. He lost that case too, but it caused him to become more outspoken about what police officers represent to white Americans as opposed to African Americans. Cochran worked on Pratt's case on and off for more than twenty years, finally getting the conviction overturned in 1997 and successfully representing Pratt in a $4.5 million wrongful imprisonment lawsuit against California.

By the mid-1970s Cochran was handling numerous civil suits against law enforcement agencies. In 1978, however, in an effort to reshape his image and expand his political influence, he accepted a position with the Los Angeles County district attorney's office, where he remained until 1983, when he returned to private practice. One of his first cases after leaving the district attorney's office and one of his first major victories as a defense attorney was his defense of the family of Ron Settles, a college football player who died in a jail cell after being booked for speeding. Police reports claimed that Settles hanged himself, but after Cochran demanded that Settles's body be exhumed, a coroner found that he had been strangled. In the first of many damage awards that went in favor of Cochran's clients, Settles's family was awarded $760,000. Cochran followed that case by representing a teenage girl who had been sexually assaulted by an off-duty police officer who threatened the girl with physical harm if she told anyone about the incident. Cochran rejected an out-of-court settlement offer and took the case to court, eventually winning for the girl a settlement $4.6 million.

As Cochran's fame and reputation grew, he began to take on more celebrity clients, including Michael Jackson, whom he successfully defended against child molestation charges, and the *Diff'rent Strokes* television star Todd Bridges, who had been charged with attempted murder. Cochran took on his most famous client, perhaps the most famous and infamous defendant in the nation's legal history, O. J. Simpson, in 1994 after Simpson was charged with the murders of his ex-wife Nicole Brown Simpson and her friend Ron Goldman. Cochran helped put together what became known as the Simpson "Dream Team" of defense attorneys, which included Robert Shapiro and F. Lee Bailey. Cochran warned the jury not to rush to a judgment and systematically picked apart the prosecutors' charges against Simpson. He was especially effective in discrediting one of the case's investigating officers, Mark Fuhrman, whom Cochran argued was a racist. In his closing remarks to the jury at the end of a trial swirling with controversy and racial tensions, Cochran urged it to find his client not guilty and, in doing so, make a statement that such behavior from law enforcement is unacceptable. The predominantly black jury deliberated just four hours before finding Simpson not guilty on all counts.

As a result of the Simpson criminal case, Cochran became the most famous and most sought-after criminal defense attorney in the United States. He was not spared negative publicity, however, as many accused him of playing the "race card" to sway the Simpson verdict. In addition he was confronted with serious challenges in his personal life. During the Simpson trial his first wife, Barbara Berry Cochran, published a memoir in which she claimed Cochran abused her and was unfaithful to her. In 1996 Cochran tried to shape his image once again in his own memoir *Journey to Justice*, in which he traced his rise as a lawyer and his passion for civil rights activism up to and including his work on the Simpson case. In 1998 Cochran suffered a personal tragedy when his brother RaLonzo Phlectron Cochran was found shot to death in

Los Angeles. At the same time, Cochran and his attorneys worked through a laborious libel lawsuit against the *New York Post*. Still Cochran kept working. In addition to his work on the Pratt case, he defended four men shot by police during a traffic stop in what he saw as an egregious example of racial profiling. In 2001 he took on another high-profile celebrity case, successfully convincing a jury that Sean "P. Diddy" Combs was not guilty of gun possession and witness tampering.

Cochran died in his Los Angeles home from a brain tumor. He had battled illness for over a year and had been out of the public spotlight since surgery in April 2004. Many former clients and numerous friends attended his funeral, including Jackson, Combs, Simpson, Stevie Wonder, Magic Johnson, Gloria Allred, Abner Louima, the Reverend Jesse Jackson, and the Reverend Al Sharpton. On 24 January 2006 Los Angeles Unified School District officials approved the renaming of Mount Vernon Middle School, which Cochran had attended, to Johnnie L. Cochran Jr. Middle School. The mixed reactions that the honor received bring into the light Cochran's complicated legacy as well as the racial tensions that his work made clear still exist in the United States.

[*See also* Combs, Sean; Jackson, Michael; Legal Profession; Pratt, Geronimo; *and* Simpson, O. J., Trial of.]

BIBLIOGRAPHY

Cochran, Johnnie, and David Fisher. *A Lawyer's Life*. New York: St. Martin's Press, 2002.

Cochran, Johnnie, and Tim Rutten. *Journey to Justice*. New York: Ballantine Books, 1996.

Schiller, Lawrence, and James Willwerth. *American Tragedy: The Uncensored Story of the Simpson Defense*. New York: Random House, 1996.

—DANIEL DONAGHY

COINTELPRO. The reach of the FBI's Counter Intelligence Program, or COINTELPRO, extended to all so-called dissident groups, including the American Indian Movement (AIM), the Communist Party, the Socialist Workers Party, and all those considered part of the New Left. But it was the black nationalist groups, particularly the Black Panther Party, that suffered most from COINTELPRO. Indeed, COINTELPRO set very specific goals with regard to African Americans:

> For maximum effectiveness of the Counterintelligence Program, and to prevent wasted effort, long-range goals are being set. . . . 1. Prevent the coalition of militant black nationalist groups. . . . 2. Prevent the rise of a "messiah" who could unify, and electrify, the militant black nationalist movement. . . . 3. Prevent violence on the part of black nationalist groups. . . . 4. Prevent militant black nationalist groups and leaders from gaining respectability, by discrediting them. . . . 5. A final goal should be to prevent the long-range growth of militant black nationalist organizations among youth. (quoted in Churchill and Vander Wall, pp. 110–111)

Though the program's specific origins remain unclear, the general period of operation is roughly from 1956 to 1976. Few who study the history of black activism in the United States discount the role played by COINTELPRO in inhibiting black liberation movements. The program targeted black leaders whose diversity of approach was seen as uniform in their potential threat to established order and policy. Leaders ranging from Malcolm X to Martin Luther King Jr., Elijah Muhammad, Stokely Carmichael (Kwame Ture), and Huey P. Newton were all targets of COINTELPRO activities.

The particular focus on black America and the Black Panther Party specifically followed a statement from the FBI's director J. Edgar Hoover that these groups posed the greatest threat to national security. To neutralize such threats, the FBI implemented tactics drawn from international espionage. These included false letter-writing and phone-call campaigns designed to create and foment intragroup dissension, wiretapping and video surveillance, the installation of informants, and ultimately assassination.

The complete tale of COINTELPRO remains undisclosed in part because of its secrecy but also because of the FBI's retention of most files. The files exposed by the early twenty-first century were internal memos meant strictly for FBI viewing only. Many of these files remained undisclosed until March 1971 when the Citizen's Committee to Investigate the FBI removed them from an office in Media, Pennsylvania, and turned them over to the press. Subsequent documents were obtained through the Freedom of Information Act (FOIA) during the years following the Vietnam War.

The 1975 establishment of the U.S. Select Committee to Study Governmental Operations with Respect to Intelligence Activities, otherwise known as the Church Committee after its chair Frank Church, helped to publicize some of the abuses carried out under COINTELPRO. However, the committee only required the FBI to turn over cleansed documents, and its contribution to sanitizing the FBI's past, present, and future activities has made the committee's role in shedding light on and ending such programs a disputed one. Much of the work conducted under the auspices of COINTELPRO was never put in print, and operatives remain legally bound to secrecy. This makes the work of uncovering the details a formidable challenge. But what has been unearthed leaves plenty on which to formulate an analysis of the goals and impacts on targeted groups and individuals.

COINTELPRO has been implicated in fomenting the dispute between Malcolm X and the Nation of Islam, leading to the assassination of Malcolm X. It engaged in similar campaigns to exploit factions within the Black Panther Party, which led to several killings, including that of the Black Panther newspaperman Sam Napier. More directly, however, COINTELPRO has been implicated in the assassinations of the Black Panther members Fred Hampton and Mark Clark, as well as in the disputed charges against and convictions of Assata Shakur, Geronimo Ji Jaga Pratt, Mutulu Shakur, and Dhoruba Bin Wahad, among others. Suspension of the use of the term "COINTELPRO" by the FBI in the twenty-first century frustrates attempts to track such activities. However, as evidenced by the varied experts who have gathered at Congressional Black Caucus panels convened on the subject by Cynthia McKinney, a Democrat from Georgia in the House of Representatives, in 2002, 2005, and 2006, there are apparent continuities between COINTELPRO and contemporary legislation, such as the Patriot and Military Commission acts.

[*See also* Black Panther Party; Civil Rights Movement; Federal Bureau of Investigation; Nation of Islam; Radicalism; *and biographical entries on figures mentioned in this article*.]

BIBLIOGRAPHY

Carson, Clayborne. *Malcolm X: The FBI File*. Edited by David Gallen. New York: Carroll and Graff, 1991. Offers analysis of and a direct look at the actual files that the FBI kept on Malcolm X.

Churchill, Ward, and Jim Vander Wall. *The COINTELPRO Papers: Documents from the FBI's Secret Wars against Dissent in the United States*. Cambridge, Mass.: South End, 1990. Offers analysis and primary-source views of the actual FBI COINTELPRO documents.

Evanzz, Karl. *The Judas Factor: The Plot to Kill Malcolm X*. New York: Thunder's Mouth, 1992. An expert analysis of primary documents, as well as of the context into which COINTELPRO inserted itself.

The Murder of Fred Hampton (1971). DVD. Directed by Howard Alk. Produced by Mike Gray. Chicago: Facets Multimedia, 2007. A documentary made of the fallen Black Panther Party leader, examining his assassination at the hands of the Chicago police, themselves working at the behest of the FBI.

Newton, Huey P. *The Huey P. Newton Reader*. Edited by David Hilliard and Donald Weise. New York: Seven Stories, 2002. A collection of writings by Huey P. Newton in which he describes COINTELPRO from the perspective of the targeted.

Shakur, Assata. *Assata: An Autobiography*. Westport, Conn.: L. Hill, 1987. Among the more popular and powerful supplemental resources, providing further insight into the impact of such efforts as those implemented through COINTELPRO.

—JARED BALL

COLD WAR. The Cold War (1917–1991), the popular name given to the political, economic, and military struggle between the United States and the Soviet Union, had its origins in 1917 with the success of the Bolshevik Revolution in Russia and concluded with the dissolution of the Soviet nation in 1991. Although most Cold War battles were fought on the international front, America's fight against Communism often had marked domestic repercussions as well. In both the international and domestic conflicts related to the Cold War, African Americans were not passive observers but active (if sometimes unwilling) participants.

Early Stages. In the initial stages of the conflict between the United States and the Soviet Union (before it came to be known as the Cold War in the post–World War II period), the impact on the African American population was relatively negligible. A small number of black Americans were drawn to the Communist movement in the United States, and the Communist Party USA (CPUSA) cooperated with groups such as the African Blood Brotherhood (formed in 1918) in arguing for civil rights for African Americans. Perhaps the best-known example of the CPUSA's alliance with black Americans in the civil rights struggle was the party's vocal and active participation in the defense of the Scottsboro Boys—nine young African American males accused of raping a white woman in 1931.

Even before World War II and the intensification of both the Cold War and African American interest in international relations, however, black Communists were making connections between the status of African Americans in the United States and the colonized people of the world. The American Negro Labor Congress, founded in 1925 and basically supplanting the earlier African Blood Brotherhood, constantly compared the struggles of black workers in Africa and the Caribbean to those faced by African Americans. At the center of the oppression endured by all people of color, the organization declared, was capitalism and imperialism. In 1928, James W. Ford (who later became the vice-presidential candidate of the CPUSA) chided his Communist comrades in the Soviet Union for failing to recognize sufficiently that the combined forces of racism and imperialism in Africa, the Caribbean, and the American South were creating inviting fields for Communist workers. He passionately declared that black workers around the world would eagerly embrace the struggle for the "overthrow of capitalism and the downfall of imperialism." In the 1930s, African American Communists joined other black groups to condemn both the Italian invasion of Ethiopia and the tepid United States response to Italy's aggression against one of the only two independent black nations in Africa.

After World War II. In the years following World War II the tensions between the United States and the Soviet Union quickly escalated, resulting in what came to be known as the "Cold War." The connections between this global struggle of East and West and African Americans also increased rapidly during the postwar period. At the center of the complex interconnections between African Americans and the Cold War was the dramatic rise of the civil rights movement in the United States. World War II greatly accelerated African American interest in international relations, and this continued into the Cold War years. This interest, however, was no longer confined to groups and individuals that had in the prewar period been labeled radical or even communist. Groups such as the NAACP began to involve themselves more intensely in foreign affairs, most notably by highlighting the similarities between the black struggle for civil rights at home and the anticolonial struggles for freedom occurring around the world. Racism and civil rights were no longer purely domestic issues, as the declarations made by representatives of many nonaligned nations at the Bandung Conference of 1955 dramatically illustrated. African American newspapers and journals and individuals such as Walter White, A. Philip Randolph, and W. E. B. Du Bois were often scathing in their denunciation of colonialism, as well as of U.S. policies that seemed to support the colonialists. In addition, they were unrelenting in their attacks on the apartheid regime in South Africa and consistently pressed the United States and the United Nations to enact sanctions against that odious government.

African Americans were also among the first in the United States to note the deleterious impact that American racism was having on its image around the world, thus playing into the hands of Communist propagandists. How, they asked, could a nation that purported to be the leader of the free world deny basic civil and human rights to millions of its own citizens? It was preposterous, they argued, to criticize the Soviet Union for orchestrating sham elections in Poland and elsewhere when thousands of African Americans were barred from voting in Mississippi and South Carolina. Polls conducted overseas by the U.S. government supported this position. In nearly every poll the one area in which the United States was most criticized was its treatment of its black population. And, as African Americans suggested, the Communist bloc proved more than ready to play up any incident of racial violence in America.

Demonstrating the power of racist notions in America, the U.S. government's response to the issue was tepid, at best. Answers to the international critiques of America's race problem ranged from angry denials that such problems existed or righteous indignation at Communist propaganda that "exaggerated" the problems. When these approaches proved to be ineffective, however, a narrow avenue of participation in America's diplomacy opened for African Americans. Black artists, writers, and intellectuals were recruited by the U.S. Department of State (and, after 1953, the United States Information Agency) to act as unofficial diplomats for the American way of life. Jazz musicians such as John Birks "Dizzy" Gillespie and Louis "Satchmo" Armstrong (who initially refused to participate), athletes such as the Harlem Globetrotters, the singer Marian Anderson, black theatrical troupes performing *Porgy and Bess*, and the journalist Carl T. Rowan all embarked on world tours set up and sponsored by the U.S. government.

More significant (but still quite limited) opportunities for African Americans occurred in the foreign policy making bureaucracy of the United States. Blacks had been virtually invisible in the Department of State and Foreign Service before World War II. Suddenly faced with international condemnation of America's treatment of African Americans, however, the U.S. government responded by naming more blacks to high-profile positions. Edward R. Dudley was named the first African American ambassador in the nation's history in 1949, appointed to that position in Liberia. (It should be noted that Ralph Johnson Bunche, who won the Nobel Peace Prize in 1950, consistently refused to work for the Department of State because he would have had to live in segregated Washington, D.C., to do so.) In 1961, Clifton Wharton Sr. was named U.S. ambassador to Norway, becoming the first black to serve as ambassador outside of Africa. Terence Todman served as U.S. ambassador to six different nations from the 1960s through the 1990s and was named assistant secretary for Latin American affairs during the presidency of Jimmy Carter. Despite these successes, the African American presence in the Department of State remained small throughout the Cold War, and well over 80 percent of black U.S. ambassadors were named to nations with significant black populations in Africa and the Caribbean.

African Americans who were considered too troublesome or critical of American policies during the Cold War often found themselves the object of intense scrutiny and sometimes persecution by the U.S. government. Du Bois was indicted by the federal government in 1951 and charged with failure to register as a "foreign agent" because of his participation in groups critical of atomic weapons. His passport was also seized. The U.S. government also hounded the actor, singer, and activist Paul Robeson and had his passport taken away. Even the expatriate singer-dancer-actress Josephine Baker found herself shadowed by U.S. officials and the FBI during her international tours, and any remarks she made critical of the American government were duly noted and cataloged.

Vietnam War. The Vietnam War most starkly revealed the intersections between African Americans and U.S. Cold War policies. From the onset of direct U.S. military involvement in Vietnam in 1965, a number of African American individuals and groups began to raise some disquieting questions. When it was revealed that black soldiers accounted for nearly 25 percent of all U.S. combat deaths in 1965, an outcry arose from civil rights leaders such as Martin Luther King Jr. The criticisms had some impact, although by 1968 African Americans still made up nearly 14 percent of U.S. killed in action in Vietnam, despite comprising just over 10 percent of the total American population. Black veterans of the war complained about unfair treatment from their white peers and lack of promotions, and they noted that they left one battlefield in Vietnam simply to return to the race riots engulfing major American cities during the mid- and late-1960s. African American soldiers at the Long Binh Jail rose up in 1968 to protest their treatment at the hands of white military police.

As the war progressed, African American opinion on the war began to diverge fairly sharply from many other Americans. In 1967, a much higher percentage of black Americans wanted to quickly disengage from Vietnam. By 1969, over 50 percent of African Americans felt the war was immoral; barely a third of white Americans felt the same way. Notable African Americans began to take very public stands against the war. Muhammad Ali refused induction, famously declaring that, "No Vietcong ever called me nigger." King, who initially supported President Lyndon B. Johnson because of the civil rights legislation passed in 1965 and 1966, came to conclude that the war was a "cruel manipulation of the poor."

During the 1970s and 1980s many African Americans continued to question U.S. Cold War policies. In particular, U.S. support for the viciously apartheid government of South Africa drew constant and intense condemnation from black leaders such as the Reverend Jesse Jackson. The Congressional Black Caucus, formed in 1969, also spearheaded attacks on South Africa and any U.S. policies that supported that government. The United States invasion of Grenada, a small black Caribbean nation, in 1983 also inspired the ire of a number of African Americans, who criticized the administration of President Ronald Reagan for so quickly resorting to crushing military power against the small black Caribbean nation purportedly to rescue endangered U.S. medical students on the island—most of whom, it was noted, were white.

For African Americans, the Cold War was always a difficult and complex issue. On the one hand, they wished to prove their loyalty to their nation. On the other, the contradictions between U.S. policy abroad with its rhetoric of freedom, justice, and democracy, and the oppressive reality of a segregated American society at home became blatantly apparent not only to black Americans but also to the wider world audience. American defense of colonial powers in the 1950s, its constant support of the racially oppressive South African government, and a merciless war against another people of color in Vietnam often forced African Americans to question the values and goals of their government. When the Berlin Wall was dismantled in 1989, signaling the coming end of the Cold War, more than one African American observer wondered what might have been if the United States had put the same amount of resources, time, and national effort into destroying the walls of bigotry and discrimination in America.

[*See also* Civil Rights, International; Communism and African Americans; *and* Military, Racism in the.]

BIBLIOGRAPHY

Foner, Philip S., and James S. Allen. *American Communism and Black Americans: A Documentary History, 1919–1929*. Philadelphia: Temple University Press, 1987.

Harris, Joseph E. *African American Reactions to War in Ethiopia, 1936–1941*. Baton Rouge: Louisiana State University Press, 1994.

Horne, Gerald. *Black and Red: W. E. B. Du Bois and the Afro-American Response to the Cold War, 1944–1963*. Albany: State University of New York Press, 1986.

Krenn, Michael L. *Black Diplomacy: African Americans and the State Department, 1945–1969*. Armonk, N.Y.: M. E. Sharpe, 1999.

Levy, Peter B. "Blacks and the Vietnam War." In *The Legacy: The Vietnam War in the American Imagination*, edited by D. Michael Shafer. Boston: Beacon, 1990.

Plummer, Brenda Gayle. *Rising Wind: Black Americans and U.S. Foreign Affairs, 1935–1960*. Chapel Hill: University of North Carolina Press, 1996.

Solomon, Mark. *The Cry Was Unity: Communists and African Americans, 1917–36*. Jackson: University Press of Mississippi, 1998.

Von Eschen, Penny M. *Race against Empire: Black Americans and Anticolonialism, 1937–1957*. Ithaca, N.Y.: Cornell University Press, 1997.

—MICHAEL L. KRENN

COLE, BOB (b. 1 July 1868; d. 2 August 1911), actor, director, producer, lyricist, librettist, composer. Bob Cole was, arguably, the most versatile theater talent of his day, black or white. His array of skills, his ambition and energy, and his showbiz pragmatism permeated the first era of black musical theater. Indeed, the era began when, in 1897, he wrote, directed, and starred in the first full-length black musical comedy. He had hit songs, hit shows, vaudeville and stage stardom, and international triumphs as songwriter and entertainer. If Bert Williams was the face of black Broadway, Cole was its muscle, a multitasking dynamo who could do everything that needed doing to make shows.

Robert Allen Cole Jr. was born in Athens, Georgia, to parents who had been slaves. His father, Robert Cole, was a carpenter who was occasionally active in local politics, and his mother, Isabella Thomas Cole, was a housewife. The elder Coles had not had much education themselves, and they were determined that Bob and his sisters would go to school. Bob spent a few years in Athens public schools and received informal, but thorough, musical training from his mother. In his mid-teens he was sent to Atlanta University's prep school and, from there, to a year or so at the university itself. He left before graduating, first drifting to Jacksonville, then to New York City, taking menial jobs along the way. By age twenty-two, he was in Chicago, still working at lowly jobs but also beginning to sing in neighborhood saloons and, probably, to feel the tug of show business.

Cole's first professional break came in 1890, when he was hired for Sam T. Jack's original *Creole Show* company, which was based in Chicago. Besides his acting duties, Cole served as Jack's stage manager. Cole (who seemed to need professional partnerships) worked with several partners in attempts to make a song-and-dance act. First there was Lew Henry, then Pete Staples, then Stella Wiley (whom he had met in *The Creole Show* and who later became his wife). Cole and Wiley were hired for the *Creole*'s 1894 edition, and Cole wrote several songs for the show. A few of these were published in Chicago, the first songs on Cole's long list, which would eventually total nearly 120 publications. In 1896, while working in the original company of Black Patti's Troubadours, he formed a writer-performer partnership with Billy Johnson, and it was the first partnership that clicked for Cole. Cole and Billy Johnson wrote a one-act musical farce, *At Jolly Coon-ey Island*, for the Troubadours, and their songs from this show brought Cole more publications. The team's short play was the hit of the Troubadours' evening, winning acclaim for their writing as well as for their comic performances.

The season-long success of *Coon-ey Island* prompted Cole—as the play's author, composer, director, and star—to approach the company's management, in June 1897, and demand a raise in salary. When he was refused a raise, he took his script and score and left the show. In the arbitration that followed the dispute, the Troubadours company was given ownership of the play but was required to pay Cole for the use of his songs in the performance of it.

Johnson also quit the Troubadours, choosing to work with Cole rather than to stay with the prestigious touring show. They had taken a step toward nonminstrel musical theater with their short *Coon-ey Island* play, and they had seen its effect on audiences, black and white. They determined to write (and to star in) a full-length, narrative musical for a black company, and to produce it themselves. By September 1897 it was ready. Their show was called *A Trip to Coontown*, and it was the first evening-long book musical to be written, produced, and performed by blacks. The musical began its life in a small theater in South Amboy, New Jersey. It was hard to secure bookings (theater owners had never heard of anything like it), but the *Coontown* company was a hit everywhere it went. In its second season on the road, it played in bigger and better theaters than in its first. Several of the *Coontown* songs were published, and Cole and Billy Johnson sailed into a third season of touring.

As the play's title suggests (and as its song lyrics confirm), its writers were riding the wave of Tin Pan Alley's hottest fad, the coon song. Beginning in the mid-1890s, the dim-witted rural stereotypes of minstrel song lyrics had given way to the urban stereotypes of riotous, razor-toting, gin-guzzling blacks. No professional songwriter who wanted hits could dismiss the genre out of hand. Coon songs were titillating, naughty, and up-to-the-minute. Audiences and amateur performers perked up at the sound of them. They signified hipness in 1900. Practically every songwriter of the time dabbled in coon songs, and several songwriters, black and white, took them as a specialty. The fad would last about ten years, ending around 1906, but, at its high tide, Cole abandoned it. He wanted to go further than the coon song could take him.

The strain of producing and touring *A Trip to Coontown* took its toll on the partners. During a hiatus in New York City, in 1899, Cole met two brothers from Jacksonville, Florida, who had come to town to peddle a comic opera they called *Toloso*. They were J. Rosamond Johnson (1873–1954), the composer, and James Weldon Johnson (1871–1938), the lyricist. Neither had Cole's showbiz savvy, but Rosamond was a classically trained pianist, and James Weldon was an intellectual with literary ambitions. They were not interested in making coon songs either; they had something more serious in mind. The Johnsons immediately liked Cole, and his fraying partnership with Billy Johnson snapped.

Cole and the brothers began to write together, and (for fifty dollars) they sold performing rights to "Louisiana Lize," their first song, to May Irwin. The sale to Irwin, a popular (white) stage singer who championed black writers, got them a hearing at Joseph W. Stern and Company, a publisher whose success was built on songs by blacks. Stern later offered them a three-year contract. With a stage star and a major publisher behind them, Cole and the Johnson Brothers were on their way.

Irwin came through for them right away, by singing three of their songs in her next Broadway show, *The Belle of Bridgeport* (1900). Over the next five years, they would place dozens of songs in more than twenty Broadway shows. They had stage hits ("Under the Bamboo Tree," "The Maiden with the Dreamy Eyes," "My Castle on the Nile," "Congo Love Song") and pop hits ("Oh, Didn't He Ramble," "Lazy Moon"). They wrote most of the songs for *Humpty Dumpty* and for *In Newport*, two Broadway shows of 1904. By 1902 Cole and Rosamond were renowned enough to do a "greatest hits" double act in first-class vaudeville houses. Like their songs, their act was classy and highly polished. The team played the great variety houses of London in 1905–1906.

In 1906 Cole and Rosamond wrote, produced, and starred in their first all-black show, *The Shoo-Fly Regiment*. (James Weldon had left the team to serve as the U.S. consul in Venezuela.) The show's story follows a small-town black regiment from enlistment to service in the Spanish-American War, and it reaches the musical heights of operetta in its (mostly) serious plot. *Shoo-Fly* toured first, came to Broadway in 1907, then toured again.

Their second (and last) show, *The Red Moon* (1908), followed the same pattern, arriving in New York City in 1909. Though its book (about the kidnapping of an Indian maiden) was thinner than that of *Shoo-Fly*, *The Red Moon*'s score—with its sweeping ballads, Indian motifs, and lightly syncopated comic numbers—is their best, and one of the best of its time. Perhaps because of their relative seriousness—not ordinary subjects for black musicals—the Cole and Johnson shows barely broke even. The strain of producing exhausted the team. They vowed to take a season off from theater after *Red Moon* and went back to performing in vaudeville in October 1910. On the closing night of their first engagement, Cole collapsed onstage. He spent several months in Bellevue Hospital, then went for rest and recuperation in the mountains. He drowned in a lake in the Catskills in the summer of 1911, probably a suicide.

Bob Cole could (and did) replace his partners, but he himself was irreplaceable. There was not another black musical on Broadway for ten years after his death.

[*See also* Johnson, J. Rosamond; Johnson, James Weldon; *and* Musical Theater.]

BIBLIOGRAPHY

Jasen, David A., and Gene Jones. *Spreadin' Rhythm Around: Black Popular Songwriters, 1880–1930*. New York: Routledge, 2005.

Johnson, James Weldon. *Along This Way*. New York: Penguin Books, 1990. First published in 1933.

Morath, Max, ed. *Max Morath's Songs of the Early 20th Century Entertainer*. New York: E. B. Marks Music Corporation, 1976. Eighteen songs from the first black Broadway era, five of them by Bob Cole. Excellent photos of black musical theater pioneers.

Riis, Thomas L. *Just before Jazz: Black Musical Theater in New York, 1890–1915*. Washington, D.C.: Smithsonian Institution Press, 1989.

Sampson, Henry T. *The Ghost Walks: A Chronological History of Blacks in Show Business, 1865–1910*. Metuchen, N.J.: Scarecrow Press, 1988.

—GENE JONES

COLE, JOHNNETTA (b. 19 October 1936), educator and college president. Johnnetta Betsch was born in Jacksonville, Florida, into a middle-class family. A precocious learner, she entered Fisk University at the age of fifteen, transferred to Oberlin College the next year, and earned a degree in anthropology in 1957. Continuing her study of anthropology, she then attended Northwestern University, earning an MA in 1959 and a PhD in 1967. In 1960 Betsch married Robert Cole, a white economist whom she met at Northwestern; they had three sons and divorced in 1982. In 1988 she married Arthur J. Robinson Jr.

Cole held teaching positions at Washington State University, at the University of California at Los Angeles, and at the University of Massachusetts at Amherst, where she remained for thirteen years, 1970 to 1983, both as a professor and later as an associate provost. She also taught at Hunter College of the City University of New York from 1983 to 1987.

In 1987 she became the first African American woman to serve as president of Spelman College, a historically black college for women in Atlanta. Shortly after Cole's inauguration, Bill and Camille Cosby presented the school with a $20 million donation. During her tenure at Spelman, Cole raised $113.8 million in the most successful capital campaign ever conducted by a historically black college or university. Cole also worked to enhance the college's already strong academic reputation. In 1992 the magazine *U.S. News and World Report* rated the college number one in its annual "Best College Buys" rankings. In 2002 Cole accepted the position of president at another historically black women's college, Bennett College, in Greensboro, North Carolina.

Cole has received forty-seven honorary degrees. She is the author of several books and edited *All American Women: Lines That Divide, Ties That Bind* (1986). She has also received numerous awards including the Radcliffe Medal in 1999 and the Alexis de Tocqueville Award for Community Service in 2001.

[*See also* Higher Education *and* Historically Black Colleges and Universities.]

BIBLIOGRAPHY

Bobo, Jacqueline, Cynthia Hudley, and Claudine Michel, eds. *The Black Studies Reader*. New York: Routledge, 2004.

Cole, Johnnetta B. *Conversations: Straight Talk with America's Sister President*. New York: Doubleday, 1993. Contains a brief autobiographical sketch and Cole's thoughts on issues including race, education, and leadership.

—Jennifer Jensen Wallach

COLE, NAT KING (b. 17 March 1919; d. 15 February 1965), singer and pianist. An influential jazz pianist, Nat King Cole transformed himself into a popular balladeer and one of the most successful entertainers of the 1950s and early 1960s. Although he was criticized for his supposed commercialism and accommodation of segregation, Cole's appeal endured until his death from lung cancer in 1965.

Born in Montgomery, Alabama, at age four Nathaniel Adams Coles moved to Chicago with his parents, part of the Great Migration of southern African Americans seeking a better life in northern cities. His father, Edward James Coles, ministered to a Baptist congregation, and his mother, Perlina Coles, directed the church choir and encouraged her six children to study and perform music. Cole—he adopted his stage name in the late 1930s—sang and played organ in his father's church from age twelve and played piano for several bands in Chicago during and after high school. His evolving keyboard technique owed an acknowledged debt to Earl Hines, combining "trumpet style" right-hand runs with concise, swinging accompaniment from the left hand.

After leaving town with the touring show *Shuffle Along* in 1936—the same year he married the dancer Nadine Robinson—Cole settled in Los Angeles, where he soon organized the King Cole Trio with the guitarist Oscar Moore and the bassist Wesley Prince. The group's unusual instrumentation inspired the pianists Art Tatum, Oscar Peterson, and Ahmad Jamal to adopt a similar format, and Cole kept the trio—with some personnel changes—until 1951. The group's first hit, "Straighten Up and Fly Right" (1943), echoed a sermon by the Reverend Edward Coles and featured Nat King Cole's urbane singing.

During the next decade Cole increasingly showcased his vocals in front of an expanding orchestra at the expense of his piano playing and small-group work. "The Christmas Song" (1946) was his first solo vocal record accompanied by a small string section, and the number one song "Nature Boy" (1948) used a full orchestra. Maria Ellington, who became Cole's wife in 1948—his first marriage had ended in divorce—encouraged Cole's emergence as a featured celebrity. The phenomenal success of "Mona Lisa," an orchestrated arrangement that stayed at number one for eight weeks in 1950, confirmed this shift in direction.

During the 1950s Cole solidified his position as the most accomplished black entertainer of his era with a series of popular hits, including the ballads "Unforgettable" (1951), "Answer Me, My Love" (1953), and "Smile" (1954). His intimate, husky, yet clearly articulated vocal delivery generated enormous crossover appeal, enabling Cole to expand his presence into a variety of media. He was the first African American artist to host a weekly radio program (1948–1949) and the first African American entertainer to sustain a network television series (1956–1957). He appeared in several films, most notably portraying W. C. Handy in *St. Louis Blues* (1958).

Yet Cole's prominence highlighted the constraints placed upon even the most successful African American professionals. In 1948 he faced objections from white neighbors when he purchased a house in the Los Angeles suburb of Hancock Park, and in 1948 and 1949 he sued hotels in Pennsylvania and Illinois for denying him service. In 1956 white supremacists affiliated with the North Alabama Citizens' Council attacked Cole onstage in Birmingham, slightly injuring his back. Part of a campaign against popular music, which the council considered a symbol of miscegenation and generational independence, the incident drew attention to Cole's cautious attempts to negotiate the color line. During a time of growing grassroots activism, Cole faced criticism from civil rights advocates for rejoining a tour that played to segregated audiences. Cole's stated unwillingness to take a stand proved costly. The head of the Associated Negro Press, Claude Barnett, called Cole a traitor, and Thurgood Marshall, chief counsel of the NAACP, called him an Uncle Tom. As black listeners smashed Cole's records in the streets of Harlem, Cole hastily joined the NAACP, but he never visited Alabama again.

Cole extended the stylistic innovations of Hines, modeled the drumless piano trio format, and performed with some of the leading swing-era musicians. As he made the transition from sit-down pianist to stand-up singer, his visibility drew unprecedented rewards and sometimes unwelcome scrutiny of his racial politics. His music continued to win accolades after his death in Santa Monica, California, at age forty-five. In 1989 the National Academy of Recording Arts and Sciences awarded him a Lifetime Achievement Grammy. In the early 1990s his daughter Natalie Cole won her own Grammy for a duet of "Unforgettable" that featured his dubbed vocal.

[*See also* Music.]

Bibliography

Cole, Maria, with Louie Robinson. *Nat King Cole: An Intimate Biography*. New York: William Morrow, 1971. An affectionate, anecdotal remembrance by Cole's widow.

Epstein, Daniel Mark. *Nat King Cole*. New York: Farrar, Straus and Giroux, 1999. An extensively researched, sympathetic biography.
Gourse, Leslie. *Unforgettable: The Life and Mystique of Nat King Cole*. New York: St. Martin's, 1991. Contains a survey discography.

—Iain Anderson

COLLECTIBLES, BLACK. The term "black collectibles" refers to any artifact documenting or depicting the African American experience, excluding high art. Many different types of items fit into this category, such as books, photographs, prints, posters, film, folk art, textiles, paper ephemera, and sports and music memorabilia. Critics of high culture insist that there are two major subcategories of black collectibles; the first group, "black Americana," encompasses straightforward relics of African American culture and history, emanating from actual events and the lives of real people. These items are highly valued because they demonstrate exactly how black history looked and felt to previous generations of African Americans, affording their collectors a rare look at the historical black experience. The second subcategory, "black memorabilia," includes objects that typically depict blacks in a derogatory fashion; many of these were created during the age of segregation for consumption by whites, and reflect the cultural biases and social sensibilities of their intended owners. Many collectors are attracted to black memorabilia because these artifacts reveal much about the darkest recesses of the American psyche during one of the nation's ugliest eras.

Black Americana, the material record of African American history and culture, is the primary focus of individuals and institutions striving to preserve and interpret the African diasporic experience. Long before African American museums became a fixture of the American landscape, and certainly before major museums exhibited African American works of art and history, lay historians, bibliophiles, and historically black colleges and universities collected and preserved artifacts documenting the black experience. Many African Americans who came of age prior to the civil rights movement remember those curios seen in black homes and institutions that contained the proof of black survival and resistance. These homespun exhibits of black history attempted to prove that African Americans had made significant contributions to American society, and that material proof and positive imagery of them making those contributions existed. Early collectors of black artifacts constitute an important (if unheralded) aspect of the Negro History movement begun by Carter G. Woodson in 1926. That movement cultivated an appreciation for African American history within the general Negro population, and a resultant interest in the collection of black Americana. Many of these archives, assembled with care and sensitivity by their collectors, were scattered to the four winds by heedless family members and estate administrators. Nonetheless, a high regard for black history (and the resulting tendency to collect anything demonstrating its legitimacy) motivated many collectors of black Americana then, as it does today.

Other collectors acquire black Americana out of an interest in its role in the ongoing development of African American works of history, literature, and the visual arts. In this way, certain individuals amassed significant collections of artifacts relating to the African diaspora that fed the creative impulses of Harlem Renaissance artists and the work of other prominent African American intellectuals in the twentieth century. Arthur Schomburg, an Afro-Puerto Rican who migrated to New York in 1891, collected numerous books, manuscripts, historical artifacts, and works of art in the late nineteenth and twentieth centuries that were purchased by the Carnegie Corporation in 1926 and donated to the Harlem branch of the New York Public Library. That collection became the basis for the current holdings of the Schomburg Center for Research in Black Culture, considered to be the most distinguished collection of research materials on the African diasporic experience to date. Similarly, Dorothy Porter Wesley's collection of black Americana served as the foundation for Howard University's famed Moorland-Spingarn Collection, another important research archive for scholars investigating the black experience. Today, the two collections serve as a touchstone for serious collectors of black Americana, who also wish to preserve the black experience.

Black memorabilia, on the other hand, includes a plethora of manufactured items, handicrafts, and vintage advertising relics that romanticize the Old South, belittle the African American, and denigrate the African past. Modern-day reproductions of these items sell for handsome prices, but the original versions were created and produced during the high tide of Jim Crowism. Because black memorabilia was produced during a period in which blacks lacked the political and economic power to oppose its sale and distribution, it contains some of the most demeaning exaggerations of the African physiognomy. It reflects many of the racial stereotypes dominant in American literature and popular discourse during the period of its creation, which accounts for the numerous representations of black mammies, happy-go-lucky Sambos, dancing jig-a-boos, brute Negroes, sexualized black females, and primitive African Zulus. In addition to slandering the character and dignity of African Americans, black memorabilia objects show blacks with grossly exaggerated physical features: bulging eyes and widely grinning lips, hair that was visibly nappy or covered with a bandanna in the case of female figures. Last but not least, jet-black skin was common in such figures because it helped to sell shoe polish, whitening creams, soap powders, and other products intended to blacken articles or clean them up until they were squeaky clean—and white. A subtext of such imagery is that it also highlighted the physical distinctions between their subject matter and their intended owners.

Black Response to Memorabilia. Many attribute the conception and development of black memorabilia to the rise of mass consumerism and modern advertising in the United States. In the late nineteenth century, revolutionary changes in manufacturing and transportation facilitated the flow of consumer goods to the nation's ever-expanding markets. Convenience foods, household furnishings, decorative pieces, toys, and entertainment devices were among the many choices Americans had for improving their quality of life. It is unfortunate that, at least in the case of black memorabilia, the imagery that accompanied these new consumer products came at the expense of the most vulnerable segment of this country's population. All too often, advertisers hawked goods by playing upon racist sentiments embedded in the fabric of American culture.

Progressive elements within the black community denounced the use of Negro caricature for the promotion and sale of consumer products from the start. African Americans understood that they were not the intended consumers of racist ephemera—they were located predominantly in the rural South in the late nineteenth century and still suffering from the debilitating effects of the sharecropping and crop lien systems. The small-but-growing segment of middle-class blacks who could afford convenience items rejected them because they had been educated in missionary schools and vocational institutions in the postbellum South, trained to embrace a more sophisticated black aesthetic than was evident in contemporary advertising. In fact, leaders of the race such as Frederick Douglass, Booker T. Washington, and W. E. B. Du Bois cautioned African Americans to maintain certain standards for self-representation and their creation of black imagery. In 1914, the National Association of Colored Women challenged the manufacturers of the Gold Dust Twins soap powder to stop using stereotypical images of blacks on the labels of their products.

In the early twenty-first century, middle- and upper-class blacks are some of black memorabilia's most enthusiastic consumers. Many are baby boomers who came of age during segregation and the civil rights movement, and they know intimately the visual discourse of racial antipathy and discrimination. Some collectors maintain that every piece of black memorabilia they purchase takes one more piece out of circulation. Others say their possession of it symbolizes the fact that with the passage of time and the rise of a new race consciousness, such forms of racial castration have been rendered impotent. Still, they acquire memorabilia so that future generations will know of its existence and the social conditions that spawned it. Despite unflattering portrayals of African Americans, some memorabilia can be graphically interesting and intellectually provocative, and is sometimes used for scholarly instruction, art creation, and home decorating purposes.

Black collectibles have grown steadily more popular in the black community since the 1980s. African Americans have more disposable income now to spend on leisure activities and collecting habits. At the same time, museums of African American history and culture have introduced a new generation to the creative display of black collectibles and the pleasure that can be derived from viewing them. High-profile entertainers and sports figures like Oprah Winfrey, Bill Cosby, and Grant Hill are among the avant-garde who rendered such objects more desirable by showcasing their personal collections through various media, such as television and coffee table books. Following the trend, serious collectors will go to extraordinary lengths to acquire rare items in order to inflate their reputations with American repositories and among other collectors. Those who acquire black collectibles do so because of the emotional connection they feel toward black history, recognition gained from other collectors, and, increasingly, the financial benefits derived from the commercial use of their collections.

[*See also* African Diaspora; Harlem Renaissance; Schomburg, Arthur A.; Schomburg Center for Research in Black Culture; *and* Stereotypes of African Americans.]

BIBLIOGRAPHY

Buster, Larry Vincent. *The Art and History of Black Memorabilia*. New York: Clarkson Potter, 2000. Examines the history of and issues surrounding the imagery of black memorabilia objects.

Goings, Kenneth W. *Mammy and Uncle Mose: Black Collectibles and American Stereotyping*. Bloomington: Indiana University Press, 1994. Examines the historical use of racial stereotypes in the production of black memorabilia.

Montgomery, Elvin, Jr. *Collecting African American History*. New York: Stewart, Tabori & Chang, 2001. Explores the reasons for the current popularity of collecting black Americana.

Pieterse, Jan Nederveen. *White on Black: Images of Africa and Blacks in Western Popular Culture*. New Haven, Conn.: Yale University Press, 1992. Contextualizes the imagery of blacks in the Western hemisphere from ancient times to the present.

Taha, Halima. *Collecting African American Art: Works on Paper and Canvas*. New York: Crown, 1988. A basic introduction to collecting African American art.

—YOLLETTE TRIGG JONES

COLLINS, CARDISS (b. 24 September 1931), U.S. congresswoman. Cardiss Collins distinguished herself as the longest-serving African American woman in the U.S. Congress: at the time of her retirement in 1996 she had served twenty-three years (twelve terms) in office. A Democrat representing Illinois's Seventh Congressional District, Collins was the first African American woman elected from Illinois to serve in Congress. In 1973 she filled the post vacated by her late husband George W. Collins, who died in an airplane crash.

Cardiss Collins was born Cardiss Robertson in Saint Louis, Missouri, the only child of Finley Robertson, a laborer, and Rosia Mae Cardiss Robertson, a nurse. When Cardiss was ten the family moved to Detroit, Michigan, where she attended Bishop and Lincoln elementary schools and graduated from Detroit's High School of Commerce. She subsequently moved to Chicago, where at first she found a job at a mattress factory. She then secured a position as a stenographer with the Illinois Department of Labor. She was promoted to secretary with the Illinois Department of Revenue, then to accountant, and she eventually moved into the position of revenue auditor. She attended night school at Northwestern University and earned a certificate of accountancy. While at Northwestern she met George Collins, and they married in 1958. George Collins was elected to the U.S. Congress in 1970.

Cardiss Collins was encouraged to run in a special election to fill the seat left vacant by her husband and was elected on 5 June 1973 with 93 percent of the vote. Thus began her long and distinguished career in the U.S. Congress. Her legacy of firsts as a woman and an African American established her as a trailblazer in Congress. Collins was the first African American woman to represent a congressional district in the Midwest, and she became Democratic whip at large, chair of the House Government Operations Subcommittee on Manpower and Housing, and chair of the Subcommittee on Commerce. She also served as a member of the Energy and Commerce Subcommittee on Oversight and Investigations and was the ranking Democratic member of the Government Operations Committee.

In 1979 Collins became the second woman to chair the Congressional Black Caucus. She helped unify the seventeen African American members of Congress and encouraged them collectively to challenge legislation that would reverse the gains of the civil rights movement. Her leadership efforts in the Congressional Black Caucus gave national attention to issues affecting African Americans. The caucus defeated an antibusing amendment to the Constitution, monitored the 1980 census to protect African Americans from being undercounted, and pushed for antiapartheid sanctions in South Africa.

Collins's other efforts in Congress included introducing the first successful bill to make mammographies payable by Medicare. Other health measures included legislation to allow Medicaid payments for screening of breast and uterine cancers. On issues of affirmative action, Collins pushed for hiring and employment equality in the communications and airline industries. She was one of the first representatives to introduce gun-control legislation. In 1996 Collins announced that she would not seek reelection. Her career had been one of a tireless crusader for African Americans and women, with a record of service to causes important to the black community and its leaders in Congress.

[*See also* Congress, African Americans in; *and* Congressional Black Caucus.]

BIBLIOGRAPHY

Gill, LaVerne McCain. *African American Women in Congress: Forming and Transforming History*. New Brunswick, N.J.: Rutgers University Press, 1997.

Hine, Darlene Clark, ed. *Facts on File Encyclopedia of Black Women in America*. Vol. 9: *Law and Government*. New York: Facts on File, 1997.

—LAVERNE GRAY

COLORADO. In 1900, Colorado had a total population of 539,700 approximately 2 percent of which was African American, living mostly in Denver but with smaller numbers in Colorado Springs, Pueblo, and several other communities. At the end of the twentieth century in 2000, the state's total population had grown to 4,301,261, with about 3.8 percent (roughly 163,448) of its inhabitants being black, over 90 percent of whom lived in the Denver metropolitan area.

One thing that characterizes the history of blacks in Colorado during the first half of the twentieth century in particular was the way that black population growth occurred mainly because of natural increase rather than because of immigration from some other place, as had been the case throughout the nineteenth century. World War II—because of increased military expenditures, including the construction of new military bases east of Denver and in the Colorado Springs area, and the construction and expansion of war plants along the Front Range of the Rocky Mountains—brought additional economic opportunities to Colorado and consequent population growth, including many people who remained after the war, adding to their communities new values and attitudes. In Denver, as a case in point, the black population rose from 7,800 in 1940 to 15,400 in 1950, a change that was instrumental in the transformation of the city's old "Five Points" neighborhood, which had once been the center of black activity in Denver; as new groups moved in, African Americans relocated throughout the northeastern quadrant of the city and beyond, mainly into Adams and Arapahoe counties.

White racial prejudice and discriminatory practices persisted in Colorado throughout the twentieth century, as was the case elsewhere in the United States where black populations were relatively small, black islands in a white sea. Within these communities, there were the fortunate few—professionals, business owners—and the larger body that fleshed out the ranks of servants, porters, domestics, and common laborers. All, however, experienced a kind of inequity that allowed some well-placed persons to realize significant gains whereas most struggled to survive. Antidiscrimination statutes that had appeared as early as 1885 were updated in 1917; they were essentially toothless, however, when it came to certain of their provisions being enforced. This is best seen in events like the hanging of Washington Wallace in La Junta in 1902 and the particularly heinous public burning at the stake of John Preston Porter Jr., who was alleged to have killed an eleven-year-old white girl in the town of Limon just east of Denver. The Ku Klux Klan appeared as a significant political force in Colorado in the early 1920s. The lengthy de facto segregation case of *Keyes v. Denver School District No. 1* (1973), with roots that traced back to the 1950s, lasted until court supervision was ended in 1995. And the city of Pueblo was still looking for its first black firefighter in 1999.

At the same time, however, African American successes included V. B. Spratlin, an 1892 graduate of the University of Denver's medical college who became the city's chief medical inspector. Justina Ford, Colorado's first woman physician of color, began her practice in 1902 at a time when black people were not allowed to use Denver hospitals. Fifty years later when she retired, she had delivered an estimated seven thousand babies of all races, classes, and ethnicities, mostly in the homes of her patients, to which she was driven. Her home on California Street in Denver is now the site of the Black American West Museum.

In 1910, O. T. Jackson founded the African American agricultural colony of Dearfield, thirty miles southeast of Greeley, which lasted until the middle of the Depression; in 1911, the State Federation of Colored Women's Clubs was formed by Elizabeth Ensley, a former Howard University professor; and in 1915, Clarence Holmes, a student in the dental school at Howard, founded the first of several branches of the National Association for the Advancement of Colored People (NAACP) in the state in Denver. The 1920s and 1930s saw the beginnings of the struggle to end discrimination in public accommodations in Colorado. And in 1944, after several earlier attempts, Lieutenant Earl W. Mann was elected to his first term in the state legislature. In 1956 the University of Colorado informed all of its fraternities and sororities that they were to be desegregated by 1962. And in 1957 the state's prohibition against interracial marriage was lifted. A small Black Panther chapter was formed in Denver during the 1960s; however, the city's black middle-class conservatism did not provide the most hospitable environment for the group and it was not terribly effective. George Brown, a black state senator, was elected lieutenant governor in 1974, the same year Penfield Tate II was chosen by his colleagues on the city council to become the first black mayor of Boulder. And in 1991, Wellington Edward Webb was elected to the first of three terms as mayor of the City of Denver.

[*See also* Black Panther Party; Ku Klux Klan; Lynching and Mob Violence; Monuments, Museums, and Public Markers; National Association for the Advancement of Colored People; *and* Women's Clubs.]

Bibliography

Abbot, Carl, Stephen J. Leonard, and Thomas J. Noel. *Colorado: A History of the Centennial State*. Boulder: University Press of Colorado, 2005.

Leonard, Stephen J., and Thomas J. Noel. *Denver: Mining Camp to Metropolis*. Niwot: University Press of Colorado, 1990.

Taylor, Qunitard. *In Search of the Racial Frontier: African Americans in the American West, 1528–1990*. New York: W. W. Norton, 1998.

—William M. King

COLORED AMERICAN MAGAZINE. Founded in 1900 in Boston, the *Colored American Magazine* primarily appealed to a middle-class and educated black audience with a blend of fiction and contemporary commentary. Pauline Hopkins, for example, published the first black mystery novel in its pages, and the famous war correspondent Ralph Waldo Tyler wrote a regular column on Washington politics. Much of the magazine was devoted to the popular self-improvement philosophy popularized by Booker T. Washington, and at one time its publisher claimed as many as fifteen thousand subscribers. The *Colored American Magazine* was an important pro-"Bookerite" organ in the turn-of-the-century propaganda wars over leadership of the African American community. One early editorial contained a vigorous attack on Booker T. Washington, but subsequent issues were increasingly friendly to the "Sage of Tuskegee." Pauline Hopkins was the journal's intellectual soul and literary editor in the early years. Three of her novels were serialized in its pages, and she wrote scores of other pieces, ranging from short stories to a series of brief biographical sketches of prominent African Americans. But she had significant assistance from a small group of expatriate Virginia intellectuals that included Walter Wallace, Jesse Watkins, and Harper Fortune. In 1904 the publication fell on hard times, and Booker T. Washington used his influence and finances to rescue the magazine. Washington, who may have virtually owned the *Colored American Magazine* for a time, publicly denied any connection to the publication, but clearly he was successful in appointing a new editor, Fred Moore, and moving the headquarters to New York. Moore kept the magazine afloat for another few years, but he eventually resigned and publication ceased altogether in 1909.

The editorial policy of *Colored American Magazine* was largely pro-Washington in its endorsement of economic self-help and the growth of a Negro bourgeoisie, but it frequently took independent, and sometimes strident, positions on several issues about which Washington was reluctant to speak out. Foremost among those was lynching, which the magazine attacked much more vociferously than did Washington himself. It did stop short of calling for a federal antilynching law and never endorsed the antilynching campaign of the African American journalist Ida Wells, but its tone was obviously more strident than that of Washington himself.

The magazine was equally outspoken on the issue of black disfranchisement. In his public pronouncements, Washington appeared to accept new disfranchisement legislation passed by various southern state legislatures. To be sure, he did promote legal challenges to the legislation in Alabama and Louisiana, but Washington deliberately kept his role discreetly quiet. In the pages of the *Colored American Magazine*, however, Moorefield Storey and others minced few words defending the historical efficacy of Negro suffrage and the Fifteenth Amendment.

Despite the fact that the journal frequently took more advanced and vocal positions than those taken by Booker T. Washington, it usually remained well within the "Bookerite" universe while exercising a modicum of editorial independence. In fact, it may well have been that Washington was willing to allow the *Colored American* editors considerable latitude in editorial policy as long as they did not directly support his enemies.

[*See also biographical entries on figures mentioned in this article*.]

BIBLIOGRAPHY

Meier, August. "Booker T. Washington and the Negro Press: With Special Reference to the *Colored American Magazine*." *Journal of Negro History* 38 (January 1953): 67–90. A dated but classic summary of the magazine's history.

Schneider, Mark R. "*The Colored American and Alexander*'s: Boston's Pro-Civil Rights Bookerites." *Journal of Negro History* 80 (August 1995): 157–169. Provides valuable insight into the extent of the Bookerite journalistic influence.

—CHARLES ORSON COOK

COLTRANE, JOHN (b. 23 September 1926; d. 17 July 1967), tenor saxophonist, composer, and bandleader. John Coltrane, often called Trane, is considered one of the most influential musicians in the history of jazz, both for his technical influence and for the spiritual nature of his music.

John William Coltrane was born in Hamlet, North Carolina, and when he was two months old his parents, John Sr. and Alice, moved to High Point, North Carolina. There Coltrane lived in the home of his maternal grandparents. His grandfather, the Reverend William Wilson Blair, was a prominent member of the African Methodist Episcopal Zion Church. Coltrane's father played several musical instruments, and at age twelve John joined the band of the Boy Scout troop of the church, first playing E-flat alto horn and then clarinet.

While in high school Coltrane began to play the alto saxophone. He considered the alto saxophonist Johnny Hodges, a member of the Duke Ellington Orchestra, his first musical influence. In 1939 Coltrane's father, grandparents, and uncle died, and his mother, aunt, and cousin were left to assume the responsibilities of the family. Joining millions of black families that migrated to northern cities during World War II, they moved to New Jersey. When he graduated from high school in 1943, Coltrane moved to Philadelphia, where he was joined by his family.

In Philadelphia he enrolled in the Ornstein School of Music, where he studied alto saxophone with Mike Guerra. During this period, Coltrane befriended such Philadelphia jazz musicians as Jimmy Heath, Benny Golson, and Ray Bryant, performing with them in small groups around the city. Coltrane was inducted into the navy in 1945, was first stationed in California, and then spent a tour of duty on Oahu, Hawaii. He performed on clarinet and alto saxophone in the dance band the Melody Masters while in the navy. His first recording session was with a small group of navy musicians in 1946. After returning to Philadelphia he continued his musical education at the Granoff Studios.

In 1947 Coltrane spent three months in the band of the trumpeter King Kolax and then worked around Philadelphia with Heath's big band. In 1948 he began to work as a tenor saxophonist with Eddie "Cleanhead" Vinson. Coltrane toured with Vinson until the summer of 1949 when he joined John Birks "Dizzy" Gillespie's big band. In 1950 he joined Gillespie's small ensemble as the tenor saxophonist in a band that included Milt Jackson on vibes, Percy Heath on bass, and Specs Wright on drums. In March 1951, Coltrane recorded with Jackson and the guitarist Kenny Burrell on the Dee Gee label.

In April 1952 he toured with the alto saxophonist Earl Bostic, and in 1954 he joined Hodges's band. During 1955 Coltrane worked in Philadelphia with Jimmy Smith. When

Sonny Rollins left the Miles Davis band in 1955, Coltrane was asked to join the ensemble. With Davis he recorded on the classic Prestige albums *Cookin'*, *Relaxin'*, *Workin'*, and *Steamin'*. Coltrane appeared on Davis's first solo Columbia album, *'Round about Midnight*. In 1955 he married Juanita Grubbs (Naima) and moved to New York City. He returned to Philadelphia in 1957 because of his heroin addiction, which he overcame during this period.

In the summer of 1957 Coltrane worked at the New York club The Five Spot with Thelonious Monk, along with the bassist Wilbur Ware and the drummer Shadow Wilson. Recordings of his work with Monk were released in 1993 on Blue Note Records as *Live at the Five Spot/Discovery!*, and in 2005 a live recording of the Thelonious Monk Quartet at Carnegie Hall in November 1957 was discovered at the Library of Congress and subsequently released on Blue Note Records to enormously positive critical response.

In May 1957, Coltrane recorded his first album, *Coltrane*, for Prestige Records. During 1957 he also recorded the album *Blue Train*, considered one of the modern jazz classics of all time, for Blue Note Records. Coltrane wrote, "During the year 1957, I experienced by the grace of God, a spiritual awakening which led me to a richer, fuller more productive life. . . . All Praise to God" (from the liner notes to *A Love Supreme*, Impulse, 1964). In 1958 Coltrane rejoined the Miles Davis group, which included the alto saxophonist Julian "Cannonball" Adderley, with whom he recorded the album *Milestones*. He recorded with Davis again on the classic album *Kind of Blue* (1959).

In Concert. John Coltrane performs at Randall's Island, New York, 1959. Photograph by Bettye Lane. © Bettye Lane

With the recording of the album *Giant Steps* in 1959 (Prestige), Coltrane's original compositions "Giant Steps" and "Countdown" expanded the harmonic vocabulary of the jazz repertoire and marked a pivotal transition in the development of jazz. In 1960 Coltrane formed his own groups and after several personnel changes chose the pianist McCoy Tyner, the bassist Steve Davis, and the drummer Elvin Jones. In 1961 Jimmy Garrison replaced Davis; Garrison remained with the group until Coltrane's death in 1967. In October 1960 the group recorded *My Favorite Things* (Impulse), on which Coltrane plays the title tune on soprano saxophone. This recording initiated Coltrane's use of modality as the primary harmonic basis for the majority of his compositions and performances. In 1961 he recorded *Africa/Brass* with an eighteen-piece orchestra playing arrangements by Eric Dolphy.

One of Coltrane's most enduring compositions, "Alabama"—which was used as the theme for the Spike Lee documentary on the bombing of Sixteenth Street Baptist Church in Birmingham, Alabama (*Four Little Girls*, 1997)—was recorded in November 1963 and released on the album *Live at Birdland* (Impulse). In December 1964, Coltrane recorded the four-section suite *A Love Supreme*, which became *Down Beat* magazine's album of the year and was Coltrane's best-selling album. In 1965 he recorded *Ascension* (Prestige), a forty-minute performance with six additional instrumentalists, which initiated a departure from his prior uses of tonality, melody, and rhythm into an exploration of freer forms, atonality, and ideas based on the music of various indigenous cultures.

In September 1965 the tenor saxophonist Ferrell "Pharaoh" Sanders joined Coltrane's group. Tyner left the band and was replaced by the pianist and harpist Alice McCleod from Detroit, who became Coltrane's second wife in 1966. For a short period Coltrane added the drummer Rashied Ali to the group and used two drummers. Garrison was the only member of the original quartet to remain with Coltrane.

Since Coltrane's death in 1967 there have been many reissues of his work, and numerous live recordings have been released. His popularity in terms of recording sales and as a symbol of an artist with a spiritual goal has grown worldwide, and the John Coltrane Foundation was established to provide scholarships for outstanding young jazz musicians.

[*See also* Jazz; Music; *and biographical entries on figures mentioned in this article*.]

BIBLIOGRAPHY

Cole, Bill. *John Coltrane* (1976). New York: Da Capo, 1993.

Fujioka, Yasuhiro, with Lewis Porter and Yoh-ichi Hamada. *John Coltrane: A Discography and Musical Biography*. Metuchen, N.J.: Scarecrow; Newark, N.J.: Institute of Jazz Studies, Rutgers University, 1995.

Porter, Lewis. *John Coltrane: His Life and Music*. Ann Arbor: University of Michigan Press, 1998.

Thomas, J. C. *Chasin' the Trane: The Music and Mystique of John Coltrane*. Garden City, N.Y.: Doubleday, 1975.

—MAXINE GORDON

COMBS, SEAN (b. 4 November 1969), singer, hip-hop impresario, and songwriter. Combs has also been known as Puff, Puffy, Sean John, Puff Daddy, and Diddy. Sean John Combs spent part of his childhood in Mount Vernon, New York, until in 1972 his father was murdered on his way home from a party. After the tragedy the Combs family moved to the Bronx, where Sean attended a Catholic school before going to Howard University in Washington, D.C. Dropping out of Howard, Combs became an intern for Uptown Records, and he later became a top executive until he was fired in 1992.

During his tenure at Uptown Records, Combs produced successful albums with artists such as Mary J. Blige, Father MC, and Jodeci. After his departure he worked as a remixer and created Bad Boy Entertainment, which soon became a multimillion-dollar business. Bad Boy signed two hit artists, Craig Mack and the Notorious B.I.G.

In 1994 Craig Mack's remix "Flava in Ya Ear" became a Top Ten hit, and in 1995 the Notorious B.I.G.'s "Big Poppa" reached number six on the pop charts. This meant two platinum records for Bad Boy. Later that year Bad Boy signed Faith Evans, 112, and Total and produced three additional platinum sellers.

In 1996 Combs was responsible for more than $100 million in total record sales and was named the American Society of Composers, Authors, and Publishers songwriter of the year. Then one of Combs's and Bad Boy's rivals, the rap artist Tupac Shakur of Death Row Records, was murdered. In March 1997, in apparent retaliation for Shakur's murder, B.I.G. was murdered in the same way that Shakur had been. Out of grief Combs stopped working for several months, only to return with a vengeance with the singles "Can't Nobody Hold Me Down" and "I'll Be Missing You," and the album *No Way Out* made 1997 his best year to that date. In 1998 *No Way Out* won the Grammy Award for Best Rap Album, and "I'll Be Missing You"—a song in memory of B.I.G.—won the Grammy Award for Best Rap Performance.

On 15 April 1999, Combs was accused of assaulting Steve Route of Interscope Records. In December of that year Combs was arrested at Club New York along with his fellow rapper Shyne for weapons violations. Combs was later indicted on bribery charges. This incident and the subsequent trial contributed to his breakup with his girlfriend Jennifer Lopez, the actor and singer, on Valentine's Day 2001.

Acquitted of all the charges stemming from the Club New York incident, Combs changed his name to P. Diddy and took a new direction by recording a gospel album. In the summer of 2001 Combs produced his biggest hit in years, "Bad Boy for Life." In 2002 Arista stopped distributing Bad Boy records, and *We Invented the Remix* was Combs's last album for Arista. He then signed with Universal and released *Bad Boy's 10th Anniversary: The Hits* in 2004. In 2006 the successes of Yung Joc's "It's Going Down" and Cassie's "Me & U" followed. Amid this activity Combs embarked on an acting career, appearing on both stage and screen.

Combs has been criticized for overly commercializing hip hop and for claiming that he invented the remix. Nonetheless he created what has been estimated to be a $346 million empire.

[*See also* Hip Hop; Music Industry; *and biographical entries on figures mentioned in this article*.]

BIBLIOGRAPHY

Cable, Andrew. *A Family Affair: The Unauthorized Sean "Puffy" Combs Story*. New York: Ballantine Books, 1998.

Ro, Ronin. *Bad Boy: The Influence of Sean "Puffy" Combs on the Music Industry*. New York: Pocket Books, 2001.

Wittmann, Kelly. *Sean "Diddy" Combs*. Bloomall, Pa.: Mason Crest, 2007.

Wolny, Philip. *Sean Combs*. Rosen, 2006.

—BEATRIZ RIVERA-BARNES

COMEDIANS. In the late nineteenth century, black comedy was about to burst out of the shadows of minstrelsy that it had been forced into by whites. Born in Africa via folktales and verbal contests and raised in America, eighteenth- and nineteenth-century African American humor was created by several tensions: the relationship between the master and the slave, the folktales stressing trickery and mental skill, the stories that showed the superiority of the slave over the master, and the parodies of slave life. The creation of the minstrel shows had resulted in a struggle between whites attempting to control black humor and black minstrels attempting to subvert the degrading black stereotype, performing instead a pantomime that mocked the white audience by playing exaggeratedly to its expectations while at the same time injecting a strain of human dignity into the parts they played.

Bert Williams, who appeared in the *Ziegfeld Follies* on Broadway in the early years of the twentieth century, mastered this technique, giving his portrayal of the down-on-his-luck vagrant—the straight man of "The Two Real Coons" team of Williams and George Walker—a noble quality that transcended the caricatures popularized by D. W. Griffith's 1915 racist film classic, *The Birth of a Nation*. Williams was dressed like a coon character, in blackface, in a full suit, singing. However, he turned the stereotype around, showing the dignity and pathos of the African American experience.

The development of mass media (film, radio, and television) during the twentieth century created many new opportunities for humor to be created, captured, and transmitted throughout the United States and the world. For African Americans the roles were again adopted from the template of minstrelsy—the shiftless, lazy slave, the mammy, and the coon, among others. In the old and new forums these characters were objects of humor as well as humorists themselves. In the hands of gifted comics like Lincoln Perry ("Stepin Fetchit") and Hattie McDaniel, however, such Sambo and Mammy film roles, respectively, became dominant personalities within their small scenes, with the joke being on the white characters around them. Perry (as Sambo) skillfully avoids work that, it can be assumed, he is being paid little if anything to complete; McDaniel's performance in *Gone with the Wind* (1939) easily overshadows—and overpowers—Vivien Leigh's Scarlett O'Hara. Mammy is in control not only of the household in general but of Scarlett in particular; she knows what buttons to push to get Scarlett to do what Mammy wants done. McDaniel's performance won her an Academy Award for Best Supporting Actress, making her the first African American to win an Oscar.

Comedic Pair. Bert Williams (*right*) and George Walker (*left*) in street clothes. YALE COLLECTION OF AMERICAN LITERATURE, BEINECKE RARE BOOK AND MANUSCRIPT LIBRARY, YALE UNIVERSITY

The two most popular African American comedians in the United States were, ironically, not African Americans at all: they were white men updating minstrelsy on the radio. *Amos 'n' Andy*, a program about the misadventures and get-rich-quick schemes of northern, urban African Americans, was a huge hit for the NBC radio network in the 1920s and 1930s. But perhaps the best African American humor of the period was found not on the radio, but in print. The "Simple" stories, told in the *Chicago Defender* op-ed columns by Langston Hughes, were tales of urban humor, parody, irony, and anger about white racism relayed in short, intelligent bursts: Hughes's black comedy provided an honest, intelligence picture of the African American experience that stood in stark contrast to the popular racist narrative of *Amos 'n' Andy*.

The Underground and the Mainstream. As the twentieth century progressed, the creation of urban black enclaves gave black comedians more and better options for developing their style of humor and for the audience to which they would cater. Jackie "Moms" Mabley was a mainstay of the Chitlin Circuit—the informal collection of segregated nightclubs, theaters, and movie houses around the nation that black performers toured. Moms was a master of combining working-class storytelling, wit, and wordplay with slight raunchiness: in one routine she destroyed the Mammy caricature, saying that it could not apply to her. "No dam Mammy, Mobs. I don't know nothin' 'bout no log cabin; I ain't never seen no log cabin: . . . split level in the suburbs, baby!" Her talks about romantic and sexual relationships were respectful but frank for a female comic.

With the coming of the LP (long-playing) record, black comedians like Mabley and Dewey "Pigmeat" Markham now had routines that could be owned and enjoyed by the entire public, freeing black comedy from the constraints of geography and time. "Race records," as black LP performances were called, also served as showcases for black humor. Markham, for instance, became famous for his "Here Come de Judge" routine, in which he played a sharp-tongued jurist.

As the 1960s approached, however, some black comics wanted to leave or bypass the Chitlin Circuit altogether, and to go out into the lucrative white mainstream. A young comic from Philadelphia named Bill Cosby represented colorless humor without any political or sexual innuendo. He was a breakthrough comic artist for both the burgeoning television age and the civil rights movement. Cosby appeared on national television, eventually guest-hosting NBC's *The Tonight Show Starring Johnny Carson*, where he had his national television debut in 1963. Cosby's first album, *Bill Cosby Is a Very Funny Fellow . . . Right*, told stories of growing up in Philadelphia with his brother Russell. Another black comic, Dick Gregory, performed political satire in the 1960s; he was as pointed as Cosby was purposely bland. (When President Lyndon B. Johnson first made his speech in Congress denouncing the evil of John F. Kennedy's assassination, twinning it with the evil of Jim Crow, Gregory quipped that "twenty million of us unpacked.")

A third comic, Redd Foxx, decided to take Mabley's tone one or two steps further; his act was raunchy, intraracial, and filled with the profane language of both the urban street and the backwoods shack. There was one comic who initially wanted to follow in Cosby's tradition, changed paths, became a superstar, and helped to change the art of stand-up forever: his name was Richard Pryor.

Richard Pryor: Comedy, Drama, and Tragedy. Pryor was a stand-up comic who in the mid-1970s wrote occasional episodes of *Sanford and Son* (Foxx's 1970s television sitcom) and cowrote the film *Blazing Saddles*, a biting parody of the Western and modern race relations, with the comedian Mel Brooks. Pryor had immersed himself in both comedy and the social and political countercultures of the late 1960s and early 1970s in California, and it began to show in his groundbreaking performances. His albums—including *That Nigger's Crazy*, *Richard Pryor in Concert . . . Is It Something I Said?* and *Richard Pryor: Live on the Sunset Strip*, two of which, *Concert* and *Live*, were filmed and shown in theaters—established Pryor as one of the most creative American comics since Mark Twain.

Pryor, who had a short-lived comedy skit show on NBC in the mid-1970s that mixed humor with black-oriented social commentary, was always deft at merging the social and the political with the absurd. Pryor's poignant stage character, Mudbone—who typically got a section of Pryor's routine to himself—turned his act into true art. These albums were like the comedic cousin of the spoken-word recordings of the political musicians Gil Scott-Heron and the Last Poets—artists who also used comedy as a way to engage. The comic Whoopi Goldberg used some of Pryor's attitude and his template for creating meaningful but funny characters in her one-woman show in the 1980s.

Other Mainstream Successes. The 1970s brought new network television opportunities for black performers. Flip Wilson, a black comic who, like Cosby, played to mainstream white audiences, became the first black with his own variety show since Nat King Cole. His characters—the hustler Reverend Leroy of the Church of What's Happening Now! and Geraldine, his sassy but modern black woman—had black roots but also resonated with audiences who grew up with Milton Berle in a dress.

Wilson, whose show lasted from 1970 to 1974 on NBC, used the style of black comedy without most of its political and social undercurrent. He took intraracial slapstick, humor, and wordplay and mainstreamed it for a white audience. Other comics had televised success with this formula; also during the 1970s, Nipsey Russell began to be popular as panelist on television game shows because of his ability to improvise jokes in rhyme, not unlike the way the boxer Muhammad Ali (né Cassius Clay) had done a decade before or the way recorded hip-hop music would do a decade later.

Modern Days. Opportunities for black comics expanded with the channel spectrum created by the coming of cable television. Eddie Murphy, the biggest black movie star of the 1980s, had a hit 1983 HBO special, *Delirious*, that was also on record. Robert Townsend—who wrote, directed, and starred in *Hollywood Shuffle*, a movie about a black actor having to deal with racism in Hollywood—did several HBO specials with his writing partner, Keenan Ivory Wayans. These *Robert Townsend and His Partners in Crime* specials—airing years before Wayans produced FOX-TV's *In Living Color*, a sketch show with a musical guest—gave many comedians, such as Robin Harris, their first national exposure.

By 1989 the comic Arsenio Hall had his own late-night talk show, and a new generation of comics—Sinbad, Martin Lawrence, and Steve Harvey—were on their way to having their own sitcoms by the middle of the following decade. Wayans and Sinbad, in particular, tried to imitate Hall by building a multicultural following with late-night talk programs.

Free for All. At the turn of the millennium, comedians were free to mix satire and silliness. With his HBO specials and his 1997–2000 HBO show, Chris Rock made himself into a modern-day Will Rogers, while Chris Tucker, Eddie Griffin, and Tommy Davidson demonstrated the ability to mix raunch, satire, and parody. D. L. Hughley was able for the most part to keep it clean on network television in his

Film Comedy. The cast of *Harlem Nights*, directed by Eddie Murphy (*center*), with Redd Foxx (*left*) and Richard Pryor (*right*), 1989. Photograph by Bruce Talamon. Paramont Pictures/Photofest

ABC (and later UPN) sitcom *The Hughleys*, as well as to be raunchy on stage on Black Entertainment Television's *Comic Scene* or in other venues.

The breakout star of the first decade of the new century, however, gave himself complete freedom, including the freedom to walk away from a third season and millions of dollars. Dave Chappelle's Comedy Central show *Chappelle's Show* could be brutally wicked with its satire, as in a sketch presenting a mock documentary on a blind southern black man who believes he is white and holds racist views of blacks. Chappelle's program—seen by some as a fulfillment of Pryor's aborted 1970s NBC show—was a huge success for the cable network during its two full seasons beginning in 2003.

In 2007 the playwright Tyler Perry enjoyed stage, film, and book success with his character Medea. Not unlike Flip Wilson's Geraldine character, Medea is a sort of homage to black women characters and caricature. She is tough and blunt, like Moms Mabley, using wordplay and the quick ability to evaluate the state of affairs to survive, not unlike Brer Rabbit of the folktales. Characters like Perry's Medea suggest that traces of African-inspired humor will continue well into the future.

[*See also Amos 'n' Andy*; Black Entertainment Television; Chitlin Circuit; Entertainment Industry and African Americans; Film and Television Depictions of African Americans; Folklore; Minstrel Tradition; Stereotypes of African Americans; Vaudeville, African Americans in; *and biographical entries on figures mentioned in this article*.]

BIBLIOGRAPHY

Schechter, William. *The History of Negro Humor in America*. New York: Fleet Press Corporation, 1970.

Watkins, Mel. *On the Real Side: A History of African American Comedy*. 2d ed. Chicago: Lawrence Hill Books, 1999.

Williams, Elsie. *The Humor of Jackie Moms Mabley: An African American Comedic Tradition*. New York: Routledge, 1995.

—TODD STEVEN BURROUGHS

COMER, JAMES (b. 25 September 1934), psychiatrist, educational reformer, and author. Born to working-class parents during the Great Depression, James Pierpont Comer became a world-renowned child psychiatrist. He spent his childhood in East Chicago, Indiana, but then traveled to the East Coast and did work at some of America's most prestigious academic institutions. By the early twenty-first century he stood as an intellectual pioneer and an advocate for disadvantaged children.

Comer's parents lacked extensive formal education, and both worked outside the home—his father as a laborer at a steel mill and his mother as a domestic. Yet they created an environment that cultivated self-esteem, confidence, and high academic achievement for James and his siblings. After completing high school in 1952, Comer attended and graduated from Indiana University, but his negative experiences in Bloomington encouraged him to attend medical school elsewhere. He earned his MD in 1960 from Howard University and a master of public health degree from the University of Michigan in 1964. He eventually did postdoctoral work at Yale and continued his education during his internship at Saint Catherine's Hospital in East Chicago, followed by volunteer work at Hospitality House in Washington, D.C. It was there that Comer began to develop his interest in psychiatry and child development.

In 1968 Comer developed a school intervention program that came to be known as the "Comer Process." He also created the School Development Program (SDP) as the organization to implement the Comer Process in school communities. The Comer Process stresses healthy child development as the cornerstone of academic achievement and life success. Comer maintains that pouring information into the heads of children will not create academic achievement. Indeed, the Comer Process emphasizes the retraining of teachers and administrators. To that end the Comer Process attempts to engender an atmosphere in which parents, teachers, administrators, and support staff begin to trust one another and work in concert to meet the developmental and behavioral needs of students.

The SDP first implemented the Comer Process in two elementary schools in New Haven, Connecticut. In the 1980s the New Haven School Board introduced the Comer Process to all of its schools. Thereafter many school districts across the nation began using Comer's reform approach in their schools. In 1990 the Rockefeller Foundation announced its plans to use the Comer Process in ten elementary schools in Washington, D.C.

Comer is a prolific writer: he has nine books and hundreds of articles in scholarly and popular publications to his credit. Among these is the powerful and personal *Maggie's American Dream: The Life and Times of a Black Family* (1988), which tells the story of Comer's mother and recounts his own childhood. Comer has served as a consultant to the Children's Television Workshop, producers of the *Sesame Street* show. The intellectual rigor and real-world success of the Comer Process has garnered its inventor numerous prestigious honors, such as the John P. McGovern Behavioral Science Award from the Smithsonian. Comer is the Maurice Falk Professor of Child Psychiatry at the Child Study Center of Yale University's School of Medicine.

[*See also* Connecticut; Education; *and* Educators and Academics.]

BIBLIOGRAPHY

Comer, James P. *Waiting for a Miracle: Why Schools Can't Solve Our Problems—and How We Can*. New York: Dutton, 1997.

"Comer School Development Program." http://info.med.yale.edu/comer.

—GEORGE WHITE JR.

COMMISSION ON INTERRACIAL COOPERATION. The Commission on Interracial Cooperation was begun during the so-called Red Summer of 1919 as the Interracial Commission. During this summer, racial tensions—rooted in unequal treatment for blacks, including for soldiers returning from World War I, and white fear of black militancy and job competition—flared up in riots and lynchings across the country. In what Gunnar Myrdal in his *An American Dilemma* (1944) called a courageous new start, several white men met in Atlanta, Georgia, self-described as a group without constituency or money, with only a driving sense of responsibility for what needed to be done.

The prime mover was a Methodist minister, Will Alexander, who had worked with black and white soldiers in Europe during World War I. He had secured funding from the Young Men's Christian Association's war funds to staff offices for two men, one white and one black, for each southern state. Renaming itself the Commission on Interracial Cooperation, or CIC, in the early 1920s, the group gradually involved ministers, college and university educators, and business leaders from across the South—whites and blacks who were "sympathetic and intelligent regarding the race situation." Alexander became the first executive director, with John J. Egan as the first president. The earliest blacks involved were Robert Russa Moton, head of Tuskegee Institute; John Hope, president of Morehouse College; and Robert E. Jones, a Methodist clergyman.

From the beginning there were women involved, too, mostly working through church organizations. One such group of Methodist women sponsored a conference in Memphis, Tennessee, in October 1920 from which emerged the Woman's Committee of the Commission on Interracial Cooperation. Black women involved from early on in this committee were Mary McLeod Bethune, principal of the Daytona Normal and Industrial School for Negro Girls, and Charlotte Hawkins Brown, founder and principal of the Palmer Memorial Institute.

From the beginning the CIC worked with a decentralized model of autonomous state and local interracial committees that were affiliated with, but not controlled by, the CIC office in Atlanta. Funding came from private foundations and church organizations. As the state groups became organized—by the late 1920s there were some eight hundred local interracial committees affiliated with the commission—the central office emphasized more research, publicity, and education, advocating better schools, health facilities, and living conditions, a legal aid program, abolition of lynching, and study of segregation. For twenty years, under Robert B. Eleazer, educational and publicity director, a massive number of pamphlets, reports, periodicals, magazine articles, books, and press releases supported the commission's positions and mobilized local support.

From fieldwork and local impetus many programs emerged, and some, such as the Association of Southern Women for the Prevention of Lynching (ASWPL), became separate entities for a time. A Texas white woman, Jessie Daniel Ames, had in 1929 become the third director of women's work at the CIC. Ames is described by her biographer as brilliant and compelling to her fans, abrasive and domineering to her critics—not the ladylike hostess that the commission's men expected. With the support of Bethune and others, Ames organized and ran the single-issue ASWPL for the next twelve years, first convincing Alexander to underwrite a meeting in November 1930 and then getting him to give her $2,000 a year from the $100,000 CIC budget, with full control. "The men," Ames said, "were out making studies and ... so the women had to get busy and do what they could to stop lynchings!"

In 1929 the commission began a fund-raising campaign with the intent of broadening its program, and that year it was also incorporated, with permanent officers, an executive committee, and a board of directors. Its mission was reaffirmed as bettering race relations and advancing educational and social welfare. When the Great Depression intervened the plans had to be scaled down again, and the outcome was more concentration on research. Conferences also remained part of the program, and out of several of them came the Southern Regional Council, not confined to race in dealing with development issues. The CIC merged with the Southern Regional Council on 16 February 1944.

Some have pointed out that the CIC for the most part stayed away from the issues of disfranchisement and segregation, and others have suggested that "interracial cooperation" just became the new catchphrase to replace "racial accommodation." Although it is hard to gauge the full impact of the CIC, it is certain that hundreds of thousands of individual interactions and activities were enhanced by the Commission on Interracial Cooperation during its lifetime.

[*See also* Antilynching Campaign; Southern Regional Council; *and biographical entries on figures mentioned in this article*.]

Bibliography

Commission on Interracial Cooperation and Federal Council of the Churches of Christ in America, Department of Race Relations. *Toward Interracial Cooperation: What Was Said and Done at the First National Interracial Conference, Held under the Auspices of the Commission on the Church and Race Relations of the Federal Council of the Churches and the Commission on Inter-racial Cooperation, Cincinnati, Ohio, March 25–27, 1925*. New York: Negro Universities Press, 1969. Each section of this book begins with questions that had been provided to the participants ahead of time, followed by comments by various people, making for surprisingly interesting reading.

Dykeman, Wilma, and James Stokely. *Seeds of Southern Change: The Life of Will Alexander*. Chicago: University of Chicago Press, 1962. Shows Alexander's developing beliefs in grassroots activity and decentralized organization, his suspicion of big bureaucracies and organization, and his first encounters with issues of poverty and race, all of which led to the formation and the particular makeup of the CIC.

Hall, Jacquelyn Dowd. *Revolt against Chivalry: Jessie Daniel Ames and the Women's Campaign against Lynching*. Rev. ed. New York: Columbia University Press, 1993.

—Carolyn Wedin

COMMITTEE OF TWELVE. The Committee of Twelve grew out of the Carnegie Hall Conference held 6–8 January 1904 in New York City. The conference was an effort to mend the ideological rift between Booker T. Washington and W. E. B. Du Bois. In 1904 Washington was the principal of the Tuskegee Institute and the most influential African American in the country. The "Wizard of Tuskegee" seemed to control everything, from education to politics to the press. He emphasized economic advancement and industrial education for the African American masses and eschewed political rights and social equality; his opponents, led by Du Bois, demanded immediate social equality and full civil rights as well as access to higher education.

Du Bois was reluctant to participate in the conference because he believed it would not lead to a rapprochement with Washington. Most of the fifty white and black men in attendance were in Washington's camp. Du Bois's key allies, William Monroe Trotter, the fiery editor of the *Boston Guardian*, and his associate William Ferris, had not been invited. Du Bois secured an invitation for his friend Kelly Miller, a Howard University sociologist, but he was clearly outnumbered. The meeting began on a positive note, as the two sides agreed on several key resolutions. All forms of education were essential to the progress of the race, higher education for the elite and elementary and industrial education for the black majority in the South. Washington publicly agreed that universal suffrage was critical to racial progress and that segregation ought to be challenged in court. The attendees condemned lynching, mob violence, and rape while favoring cooperation with whites of goodwill.

Conferees selected twelve men to gather important information on racial matters from across the country. They were to keep members informed of ongoing developments; promote understanding, communication, and unity among the racial uplift organizations; and litigate against racial discrimination in public accommodations.

These men constituted the Committee of Twelve. On 8 January 1904 the conference ended with Washington and Du Bois agreeing to share leadership of the committee.

Du Bois could not trust Washington or get beyond their ideological differences, and he resigned during the summer of 1904. Washington was elected chairman, Archibald Grimké treasurer, and Miller secretary. Du Bois, however, declined to participate in any of the committee's meetings as he distanced himself from Washington. The Committee of Twelve never achieved its goals because of a lack of funding and the ideological differences between its members; it disbanded in 1908. The committee chairmanship confirmed Washington's power over African American affairs and widened the divide between him and Du Bois. Du Bois and his allies created the Niagara Movement in 1905 and the National Association for the Advancement of Colored People (NAACP) in 1909. The committee provided Du Bois with the opportunity to draft a platform for what would become the NAACP and inspired Washington to challenge Jim Crow segregation in southern courts.

[*See also* Carnegie Hall Conference; National Association for the Advancement of Colored People; Niagara Movement; Washington–Du Bois Conflict; *and biographical entries on figures mentioned in this article*.]

BIBLIOGRAPHY

Harlan, Louis R. *Booker T. Washington: The Wizard of Tuskegee, 1901–1915*. New York and London: Oxford University Press, 1983.

Lewis, David Levering. *W. E. B. Du Bois: The Fight for Equality and the American Century, 1919–1963*. New York: Henry Holt, 2000.

Wolters, Raymond. *Du Bois and His Rivals*. Columbia: University Press of Missouri, 2002.

—SYLVIE COULIBALY

COMMUNISM AND AFRICAN AMERICANS. The Communist Party USA (CPUSA) emerged out of the Socialist Party, the Industrial Workers of the World (IWW), and various labor unions during and immediately after World War I. Though always advocating an ultimate proletariat revolution, from the beginning the party was focused on two shorter-term goals: improving the conditions of working-class and lower-class Americans and garnering support for the Soviet Union. Very quickly the American party came under the control of the Soviet party, always supporting whatever position the Soviet party and the Soviet Union dictated. American Communists who opposed the twists and turns were either expelled from the American party or left the party to form their own organizations—such as the Socialist Workers Party, founded in 1938, which followed the doctrines and philosophy of Leon Trotsky.

Most early Communists were from white labor backgrounds or were recent immigrants from Europe. Early on, however, the American party recruited blacks and sought to integrate them into the party hierarchy. Communist affinity for African Americans was tied to a number of party doctrines and policies. Vladimir I. Lenin, the first leader of the Soviet party and the Soviet Union, placed great emphasis on support for liberation movements in the European colonial empires. He denounced as "social chauvinists" those in European working-class and socialist movements who accepted imperial domination of so-called inferior races by their own nations. Thus fighting racism in the United States dovetailed with general Communist opposition to colonialism. Because blacks were the poorest and most politically oppressed people in the United States, they seemed, from a Communist perspective, ideal recruits for the party.

Because racism, along with the segregation it led to, was the most obvious flaw of American capitalism, Communists also saw that denouncing the oppression of blacks was a way of denouncing the United States and its liberal capitalistic political structure. The party reasoned that by focusing on the oppression of blacks it could recruit not only blacks but also whites who opposed segregation. Finally, during the Cold War an antiracist policy for the American party supported the Soviet Union's worldwide struggle against the West by helping to convince leaders of newly emerging nations in Africa and Asia that the Soviet Union was their best friend in the world and that Communism was the economic and political ideology best suited to their needs.

This resonated with some African Americans, while also making the so-called Negro question a touchstone of orthodoxy within the American Communist Party. Communist opposition to segregation led a few prominent and widely respected African Americans to conclude that Communism offered the only way, or the most potent weapon, for ending white supremacy. Most African Americans saw Communism as a distraction or a poison—as something that would doom their efforts to build a place for blacks within American culture and politics. Religion also played a role in the black rejection of Communism. Communist ideology considered religions to be the "opiate of the masses," and both the American party and the Soviet Union were officially atheist. In contrast, the most important social force in black communities from the 1920s through at least the 1970s was the black church. African American leaders, many of whom were either ordained ministers or deeply connected to religious organizations, opposed Communism in part because the Communists were hostile to people of faith and to churches.

White opposition to Communism also undermined the recruitment of blacks to the party. From 1918 through the 1960s, die-hard advocates of racial segregation routinely charged that any civil rights movement, whatever its origins, was "Communist subversion." Sincere white supremacists firmly believed that "our Negroes" were perfectly content with their subordinate, second-class, disfranchised status. The intervention of "Communist agitators" appeared to be a logical explanation for any evidence of aspiration to equality and freedom. More cynical white supremacists were equally quick to press the same charges as a convenient defense of the profitable and politically advantageous racial prejudices upon which their domination rested.

Thus even where blacks found allies within the Communist Party, they were often reluctant to work with Communists for very pragmatic reasons. As Roy Wilkins, the NAACP executive from 1955 to 1977, recalled in his autobiography *Standing Fast* (1982), "God knows it was hard enough being black, we certainly didn't need to be red too" (p. 210). He had made the same point many times in previous decades. Other African Americans, though not won over to Communism, agreed with the black newspaper the *Chicago Defender* that the Communist Party was the one organization in white America that practiced complete political, economic, and social equality.

Before the Cold War. The first Comintern document on American race problems, issued in 1922 at the Fourth Comintern Congress, focused on Negroes assisting African nations to gain liberation from colonial empires. Founded in 1925, an organization called the American Negro Labor Congress, which existed mostly just on paper, was hailed by party leaders as an "unprecedented mass organization," but it drifted into oblivion by 1930.

The Sixth Comintern Congress, meeting in 1928, formed a Negro Commission that had seven Americans among its thirty-two members and formulated the definition of American Negroes as an oppressed nation within a nation, consisting of a "Black Belt" of counties with an African American majority stretching across the southern states. This led to Communist Party demands for the creation of autonomous states in the Deep South to be in effect run by African Americans. The party called this the Black Belt program. The program mirrored the creation of national or ethnic republics within the Soviet Union but made little sense in the American context. Almost no American blacks endorsed the program. The party, again following the lead of Moscow, believed that blacks would flock to such a program, in part because African Americans were one of the lowest-paid segments of the working class, oppressed by overt discrimination, and thus, according to Communist theory, a natural constituency to be approached by any party with revolutionary intentions.

Although the theory of the Black Belt attracted few blacks to the party, the economic and social crisis of the Great Depression did bring some blacks into the party because they saw it as an active ally of impoverished blacks. The party also gained enormous fame and credibility with blacks during the Scottsboro case. In March 1931 nine black youths between ages twelve and nineteen were accused—falsely, as it turned out—of raping two white girls on a train near Scottsboro, Alabama. Within five days of their arrest they were tried, convicted, and sentenced to death in proceedings that lacked any semblance of due process.

At this point the International Labor Defense (ILD) intervened on behalf of the so-called Scottsboro Boys. The ILD was affiliated with the Communist Party, although not technically controlled or run by the party. The NAACP tried to gain the right to represent the Scottsboro Boys, but the ILD, built and staffed by well-known Communists, including the African American William L. Patterson, fought a protracted battle with the NAACP for influence, credit, and control in defense of the Scottsboro Boys. Both the ILD and the NAACP claimed to have been the first to recognize the importance of the case and mobilize support. A tug-of-war developed in which defendants and their families took sides and sometimes changed sides. Both organizations brought legal teams in for various rounds of the trials and appeals. Both wanted the defendants acquitted and released, but both wanted credit for that accomplishment.

Carl Murphy—the editor of the *Baltimore Afro-American*, who had insisted that the Communists were "the only party going our way"—bluntly observed in 1931 that "the Communists have the National Association of the Advancement of Colored People licked" because the ILD had the backing of the parents and of most of the defendants. At least some of the parents, including Mrs. Janie Patterson, found the NAACP condescending and the ILD kind and respectful. Walter White, the NAACP executive secretary from 1931 to 1955, invited the famed white defense attorney Clarence Darrow into the case as a wedge for NAACP influence. White's successor Roy Wilkins later observed, "Communists wanted to score propaganda points; Negroes wanted the boys to go free." Ultimately Darrow and the NAACP withdrew from the case on 4 January 1932. Darrow defined the differences in strategy by asserting that "you can't mix politics with law": the cases would have to be won in Alabama, "not in Russia or New York."

In the end the ILD had mixed success. The Scottsboro cases went to the U.S. Supreme Court twice, and retrials led to guilty verdicts but not death sentences. By the mid-1930s almost everyone in the world knew of the Scottsboro case—it was an international cause célèbre, with the

Communist parties all over the world using the case as a way to denounce the United States, capitalism, and racism. Although no rapes had taken place and all of the Scottsboro Boys were innocent of all charges, they were nevertheless convicted in a number of trials and retrials, and many spent years in prison. The party and the ILD may have saved their lives, but a less political defense—one not tainted by Communism, which the NAACP would have offered—might well have led to a better outcome for the unfortunate young men arrested at Scottsboro. While the party was able to proclaim its role in fighting racism, the Scottsboro boys languished in Alabama prisons.

In 1932 authorities in Georgia arrested Angelo Herndon, a black Communist trying to organize unemployed people in Atlanta. He was charged with sedition and sentenced to eighteen to twenty years on the Georgia chain gang, which was tantamount to a slow death. The party used the Herndon case to raise money, publicize race discrimination in the South, and appeal to blacks to join the party. The ILD twice took Herndon's case to the Supreme Court, and in *Herndon v. Lowry* (1937) the Court overturned his conviction on First Amendment grounds. The case gained some adherents to the party. The future historian Herbert Aptheker said that he first became interested in the party through agitation over the Herndon case.

In addition to providing lawyers to defend Herndon, in 1932 the ILD hired a young black lawyer in Atlanta, Benjamin J. "Ben" Davis Jr. Davis had attended Amherst College and Harvard Law School, and by the end of the Herndon case he had decided to become a Communist. Davis spent the rest of his life as a party organizer, becoming one of the two most prominent blacks in the party, along with William L. Patterson. Davis moved to New York City, where he served two terms on the city council and became known as the "Communist Councilman from Harlem." He was later convicted under the Smith Act and spent five years in prison.

Despite the massive unemployment of the Depression, the Communist Party recruited relatively few Americans and even fewer blacks. The Scottsboro case, the Herndon case, and persistent Communist organizing in Harlem and other black neighborhoods in the North gave the party a clear presence in the black community, but these things did not lead to massive support or huge membership. However, some blacks did join and become career Communists.

African Americans in the Communist Party. Among the prominent African Americans who joined CPUSA and remained loyal to the party all their lives was Henry Winston, who joined the Young Communist League in 1930 at age nineteen and served as the party's national chair from 1966 until his death twenty years later. William L. Patterson, who served as executive secretary of the International Labor Defense and the Civil Rights Congress, later chaired the party's National Negro Commission. Benjamin J. Davis Jr. served as the party's national secretary from 1959 to 1964.

From 1948 to 1954 Pettis Perry was executive secretary for the party's National Negro Commission. Charlene Mitchell ran as the Communist candidate for president of the United States in 1968, and Jarvis Tyner ran for vice president in 1976 and later served as the party's executive vice chair. W. E. B. Du Bois concluded a life of scholarship and civil rights activism by joining the CPUSA in 1961, two years before he died.

Revels Cayton, the grandson of the Reconstruction-era U.S. senator from Mississippi, Hiram Revels, joined the Communist Party in 1934 and left it in 1952. In a 1982 interview Cayton recalled, "I found a new world . . . a kind of equality with whites, within the Party, that I'd never known before. And it was attractive." Hosea Hudson, who joined the party in 1931, expressed similar sentiments.

Communist parties that formed to the left of the CPUSA in the post–World War II years included a few prominent African American Communists. For instance, Nelson Peery and Admiral Kilpatrick were leading members of the Communist Labor Party, a party that took the name of the short-lived party formed by John Reed in 1919. Peery was a home-grown American Communist who recounted his youth and World War II military service in *Black Fire*. Motivated by both racial and political solidarity he was drawn to the Young Communist League in the late 1930s.

Writers and Artists. Many African American writers featured American Communism in their work, including Richard Wright, notably in his novel *Native Son* (1940), and Ralph Ellison. Wright formally joined the Communist Party in 1933 after attending meetings of the John Reed Club, a Communist-inspired literary group. He served as the Harlem editor of the *Daily Worker* beginning in 1937 but left the party in 1944, publishing an article in *Atlantic Monthly* called "The God That Failed"—a title that was used again in 1949 for an influential anticommunist anthology edited by Richard Crossman. "I wanted to be a communist," Wright said, "but my kind of communist."

Ellison wrote extensively for left-wing publications, some of them organized by Communist Party members, including *New Challenge*, *New Masses*, *Direction*, *Tomorrow*, *Negro Quarterly*, and *Negro Story*. Although the organization known in Ellison's novel *Invisible Man* (1952) as "The Brotherhood" is routinely assumed to be the Communist Party, Ellison observed that it was not, because it represented political patterns "which still exist and of which our two major political parties are guilty in their relationships to Negro Americans" (Gray-Rosendale and Rosendale, p. 33). Although never a party member, Ellison asserted that he could write a "very revealing account" of the "swings and twitches of the U.S. Communist line during the thirties and forties" (Ellison, p. 296), but would not do so in fiction.

Paul Robeson is perhaps the best-known artist who was closely associated with the Communist Party, as well as being a welcome guest in the Soviet Union and the German Democratic Republic (East Germany). In late 1942, FBI agents assigned to keep the world-renowned actor and singer under surveillance reported, "It would be difficult to establish membership in his case but his activities in behalf of the Communist Party are too numerous to be recorded." Asked during a 1948 hearing before the Senate Judiciary Committee what American Communists stood for, Robeson responded, "For complete equality of the Negro people," adding that he had "many dear friends who are Communists" who "have done a magnificent job" (Duberman, pp. 328–329).

Nelson Peery's recollection of his response when the Nazi Wehrmacht invaded the Soviet Union was shared by not a few blacks aware of international events: "Russia is all we got. If Russia is defeated, there is nothing to defend us. They'd have already hanged the Scottsboro boys if it wasn't for Russia telling the whole world about it. They'll drive us back to slavery— or worse." Hearing his elders discuss the Spanish Civil War in the late 1930s, the teen-aged Peery concluded "It's the same all over the world—people like the Klan [Franco's nationalists] fighting people like us." In neighborhoods like Peery's in Minneapolis, there were a few high school students whose parents were known Communists as well as women who came around selling the *Daily Worker*.

Communism and Black Nationalism. The Black Belt theory committed the party, on paper, to the creation of a distinct nation for African Americans, with its own territory carved out of the South. But meanwhile, black majorities were vanishing from southern counties, as well as from the states of South Carolina and Mississippi, because of massive northward migrations by blacks. Although formal nationhood never became a popular cause among African Americans, individuals who favored the idea were attracted to the Communist Party and were ultimately disappointed that the party did not follow through on the idea. Harry Haywood, who joined the CPUSA after returning from military service in World War I, was expelled in 1957 for his insistence on pressing "the national question." Ben Davis, a more orthodox party leader, rejected Haywood's "petit-bourgeois nationalism," as well as that of the maverick Revels Cayton.

Experienced in maritime unions on the West Coast and having served as the Seattle organizer of the League of Struggle for Negro Rights in 1934, Cayton argued in 1946 for black caucuses within industrial unions in order to open more job opportunities for black workers. Party leadership had never resolved how to expand its influence among white workers while pushing to open opportunities for black workers. Many unions in the American Federation of Labor still had whites-only policies, while the rank and file of many unions in the Congress of Industrial Organizations were not interested in black issues. Cayton looked to working-class unity as the path to liberation, but he told Davis that the white working class was "not doing a goddamn thing for blacks. . . . Our folks are really moving, and if I have to decide between the two, I'm going to go with my people" (Duberman, p. 310).

The demise of the National Negro Congress (NNC), an organization created with Communist support and participation, marked a failure of Popular Front activity by the party. Formed in 1935, the NNC first met in Chicago in 1936, where more than eight hundred delegates representing more than five hundred organizations with more than 3 million constituents gathered. The NNC elected A. Philip Randolph as its first president, but Randolph left the organization in 1940 when numerically dominant Communist delegates pushed through resolutions in line with the then-current Communist line that the United States should stay out of the "imperialist war" in Europe. Revels Cayton was asked in 1945 to serve as executive secretary of the NNC, which fell apart by 1947. Cayton candidly remarked, "We didn't have a base, we didn't have any credentials in the black community" (Duberman, p. 311).

Civil Rights Congress and Growing Irrelevance. One of the last Communist-initiated organizations with a mass membership, significant community support, and a record of accomplishment for African Americans was the Civil Rights Congress (CRC). Prominently listed on the Attorney General's List of Subversive Organizations, the CRC was formed in 1946 by Communist Party leaders and sympathizers from the National Federation for Constitutional Liberties and what remained of the International Labor Defense. Party members were indeed assigned to the CRC. Non-Communists from churches, neighborhoods, and trade unions were also promoted into leadership roles. A good part of the CRC's local chapters existed only on paper. The CRC did, however, organize the presentation to the United Nations in 1951 of the antilynching petition "We Charge Genocide," endorsed by the AME Zion bishop W. J. Walls, W. E. B. Du Bois, and Mary Church Terrell, as well as by Paul Robeson, William L. Patterson, and Ben Davis. Local chapters of the CRC were effective in combating police brutality and

Benjamin J. Davis Jr. Leaving the federal courthouse while on trial for being a leader of the Communist Party. Davis served two terms on the New York City Council and was known as the "Communist councilman from Harlem." Photograph by C. M. Stieglitz. NEW YORK WORLD–TELEGRAM AND THE SUN NEWSPAPER PHOTOGRAPH COLLECTION, PRINTS AND PHOTOGRAPHS DIVISION, LIBRARY OF CONGRESS

mobilizing hundreds of people to defend the right of black veterans to purchase and occupy houses in newly built developments where a portion of white neighbors objected.

The CRC's unsuccessful 1951 campaign for the exoneration of Willie McGee in Mississippi, charged with raping a white woman who had blackmailed him into carrying on a seven-year sexual affair with her, resulted in a postmortem in the press that actually blamed McGee's conviction and execution on the CRC's support. *Time* wrote that the sentence might never have been carried out, but "as the Communists moved in, such groups as the NAACP drew back." The *Nation* wrote that after the CRC "took up the fight, people seemed no longer to care about any evidence." In fact the CRC won two appeals, only to see a local jury reconvict McGee, and the CRC shocked the Mississippi legal establishment by organizing both black and white individuals from several states to protest the execution.

Shortly after World War II, American Communists came under enormous pressure as the Cold War pitted the United States against the Soviet Union. At the same time a growing demand for equality among blacks led to a dynamic and growing civil rights movement. Communist Party members were sympathetic to the movement and wanted to offer their organizing skills and experience. Generally, however, they were ignored or rejected. Black leaders such as A. Philip Randolph, Bayard Rustin,

Thurgood Marshall, and Martin Luther King Jr. realized that any taint of Communism could, in the Red Scare and McCarthyist atmosphere of the United States, undermine or even destroy the civil rights movement. Internationally, Communist parties attacked colonialism and supported national liberation movements in Africa, Asia, and Latin America. But in the United States the mainstream civil rights organizations rejected offers of help from known Communists and assiduously avoided any ties to what remained of the Communist Party.

Meanwhile, prosecutions of Communist leaders, the revelations of the atrocities of Joseph Stalin, and overall lack of interest in the movement led to the rapid decline of the party. A few blacks, such as Paul Robeson and the aging W. E. B. Du Bois, continued to defend Communism and support the party, but most black Americans, just like most white Americans, rejected Communism and the party. Black and white radicals in the 1960s and 1970s turned to newer, less rigidly ideological organizations that were not tied to the party or to the Soviet Union. For both blacks and whites the Communist Party had become an irrelevant artifact of an earlier age.

[*See also* American Negro Labor Congress; Anticommunism and Civil Rights; China; Cold War; Herndon, Angelo, Case of; National Negro Congress; Political Parties and Civil Rights; Scottsboro Incident; Union of Soviet Socialist Republics; *and biographical entries on figures mentioned in this article*.]

BIBLIOGRAPHY

Carter, Dan T. *Scottsboro: A Tragedy of the American South*. Rev. ed. Baton Rouge: Louisiana State University Press, 2007.

Duberman, Martin B. *Paul Robeson*. New York: Alfred A. Knopf, 1988.

Ellison, Ralph. *Going to the Territory*. New York: Random House, 1986,

Foley, Barbara. "Ralph Ellison as Proletarian Journalist." *Science and Society* 62 (Winter 1998–1999): 537–556.

Gray-Rosendale, Laura, and Steven Rosendale. *Radical Relevance: Toward a Scholarship of the Whole Left*. Albany: State University of New York Press, 2005.

Herndon, Angelo. *Let Me Live* (1937). Ann Arbor: University of Michigan Press, 2007.

Horne, Gerald. *Black Liberation/Red Scare: Ben Davis and the Communist Party*. Newark: University of Delaware Press, 1993.

Horne, Gerald. *Communist Front? The Civil Rights Congress, 1946–1956*. Rutherford, N.J.: Fairleigh Dickinson University Press, 1988.

Mitford, Jessica. *A Fine Old Conflict*. New York: Alfred A. Knopf, 1977.

Naison, Mark. *Communists in Harlem during the Depression*. Urbana: University of Illinois Press, 1983.

Peery, Nelson. *Black Fire: The Making of an American Revolutionary*. New York: New Press, 1994.

Record, Wilson. *Race and Radicalism: The NAACP and the Communist Party in Conflict*. Ithaca, N.Y.: Cornell University Press, 1964.

Soloman, Mark. *The Cry Was Unity: Communists and African Americans, 1917–36*. Jackson: University Press of Mississippi, 1998.

—CHARLES ROSENBERG
—PAUL FINKELMAN

COMPOSERS. When most listeners think of African American music, jazz, blues, gospel, rhythm and blues, and other popular musical genres come to mind. However, many creative black musicians pursued the path of classical composition, producing fully notated musical scores for orchestra, wind band, choir, string quartet, and other vocal and instrumental combinations. The origins of both popular and classical African American music reflect several basic characteristics of African music including cross-rhythms, percussive sounds from all instruments (including the human voice), the close relationship between vocal music and tonal languages, antiphonal practices, and the association of music with ritual.

During the post–Civil War era, African American composers drew on work songs, spirituals, and other vernacular folk elements. A few had the opportunity to study at American conservatories and learned classical composition practices from the white European composers teaching at these institutions. Most publishers did not accept works from black composers in the late nineteenth and early twentieth centuries. Consequently, many relied on teaching and performance as their primary careers.

Early Twentieth Century. Harry T. Burleigh (1866–1949) was the first African American composer to achieve widespread recognition for writing art songs based on Negro spirituals. Burleigh, who composed nearly three hundred musical works, studied with Antonin Dvořák at the National Conservatory of Music of America in New York. Some of Burleigh's best-known works are *Six Plantation Melodies* (1901) and *Southland Sketches* (1916). Both works were written for violin and piano. Burleigh's contemporary Will Marion Cook (1869–1944) studied violin at the Oberlin Conservatory beginning at age fifteen and wrote several musical theater pieces, among them a Broadway musical entitled *The Southerners* (1904).

Although African American composers faced many social and professional obstacles, they nevertheless enjoyed the advantage of having been acquainted with Negro spirituals all their lives, rather than having to make the effort to familiarize themselves with them as did white composers who drew on black traditions. Robert Nathaniel Dett (1882–1943) remarked that he wrote classical compositions based on spirituals and other black folk melodies as a means of preserving black musical traditions for posterity. Secular black folk melodies and dance rhythms were combined with symmetrical European phrase structure and harmony in a style known as "classic ragtime." Scott Joplin (1868–1917) was the most widely recognized ragtime composer. His "Maple Leaf Rag," the best-known work in this idiom, was published in 1899. Joplin also composed an opera titled *Treemonisha* in 1905, but it did not receive its premiere until 1972. Other prominent

Composer. The British composer Samuel Coleridge-Taylor, described by New York orchestral players as the "black Mahler," at the piano, c. 1910. The works and writings of Paul Laurence Dunbar, Frederick Douglass, W. E. B. Du Bois, Booker T. Washington, and the Fisk Jubilee Singers were among Coleridge-Taylor's greatest inspirations, and his compositions in turn influenced American music and culture. The Coleridge-Taylor Choral Society, which he visited twice, was founded by black singers in Washington, D.C., in 1901. Photograph by Addison Scurlock. SCURLOCK STUDIO RECORDS, ARCHIVES CENTER, NATIONAL MUSEUM OF AMERICAN HISTORY, SMITHSONIAN INSTITUTION

ragtime composers included Thomas Million Turpin (1873–1922) and James Sylvester Scott (1886–1938).

The music of African American composers was not often accepted for performance by the music directors of white orchestras at the turn of the twentieth century. However, several black orchestras such as the Clef Club Symphony Orchestra scheduled all-black composer programs in beginning in 1912. Burleigh and Cook were among the composers active in the National Association of Negro Musicians. Founded in 1919, this organization provided unprecedented opportunities for performances of works by African American composers. By the 1920s and 1930s however, major performance companies also began to program their works. The Rodman Wanamaker Contest, established in New York City in 1927, also provided recognition for outstanding African American composers. Most, however, remained marginalized and continued to depend on the black churches and colleges for performance venues.

John Wesley Work III (1901–1968) was a scholar of black folksong as well as a composer. He also published articles on black folklore. William Dawson (1899–1990) established the music program at Tuskegee University and served on its faculty from 1931 to 1956. His *Negro Folk Symphony* was premiered in 1934 by the Philadelphia Orchestra under the baton of Leopold Stokowski.

William Grant Still (1895–1978) was known to his colleagues as the "Dean of African American composers." He studied with Edgard Varèse, a pioneer in experimental and electro-acoustic music, and was influenced by the European avant-garde, jazz, blues, and the musical traditions of Native American, African, and Latin American cultures. Still was the most successful of black composers in having works performed by mainstream ensembles. His *Afro-American Symphony* was premiered by the Rochester Philharmonic (New York) in 1931 under the direction of Howard Hanson. This was the first time a major U.S. orchestra had performed a work by a black composer.

Mid-to-Late Twentieth Century. By the middle of the twentieth century, African American composers were becoming more eclectic than their predecessors, and not as strongly tied to black folk traditions. For example, art songs composed by African American composers during this period were more likely to be based on texts of contemporary black or white poets than on spirituals or folk songs. Leslie Adams (b. 1932) composed "For You There Is No Song" on a text by Edna St. Vincent Millay, and George Walker (b. 1922) set Robert Burns's "A Red Red Rose." Robert Owens (b. 1925) set many Langston Hughes poems including "Faithful One" and "Genius Child."

In 1968 the Society of Black Composers was formed in New York City by approximately twenty-five black jazz and classical composers. The society was crucial in securing grants from organizations such as the Ford, Fulbright, Guggenheim, and Whitney foundations. Members included Alvin Singleton (b. 1940), who served as composer in residence with the Atlanta Symphony Orchestra from 1985 to 1988; Adolphus Hailstork (b. 1941), who was commissioned by a consortium of five orchestras to compose a piano concerto, which was premiered by Leon Bates in 1992; and Olly Wilson (b. 1937), elected to the American Academy of Arts and Letters in 1995.

Ulysses Kay (1917–1995) incorporated modern techniques as well as neo-Romantic influences into his compositions for symphony orchestra, band, voice, chamber ensembles, and solo instruments, and an opera entitled

Jubilee (1976) composed for the U.S. Bicentennial. George Walker (b. 1922) was also one of the first African American composers to combine black folk elements with the European avant-garde. An accomplished pianist as well as a composer, he wrote many solo piano works. Other well-known works include *Address for Orchestra* (1959), *Music for Brass—Sacred and Profane* (1976), and Concerto for Cello and Orchestra (1981).

The African American composer best known for the use of the serial or twelve-tone method of composition, developed by the Viennese composer Arnold Schoenberg, is Hale Smith (b. 1925). Smith also worked as a film composer and jazz arranger, and his works are characterized by a combination of twentieth-century serial techniques, jazz improvisation, and other African American influences. His compositions include *Ritual and Incantations* (1974) for orchestra and *Meditations in Passage* (1980) for soprano, tenor, and piano. In addition to serialism and atonality, some African American composers included elements of chance in their compositions. Known as indeterminacy, this procedure was largely attributed to the white American composer John Cage. For example, T. J. Anderson (b. 1928) used a technique he calls "orbiting" in which each performer plays independently from the others in *Intermezzi* (1983), for clarinet, alto saxophone, and piano.

Women Composers. The challenges faced by black women composers were similar to those faced by their male counterparts The first black female composer to gain widespread international recognition was Florence Price (1888–1953), a graduate of the New England Conservatory of Music. Price composed art songs and arrangements of spirituals, chamber pieces, and orchestral works. Her "Songs to the Dark Virgin," published in 1941, was performed by Marian Anderson. Price's Symphony in E Minor was performed by the Chicago Symphony Orchestra at the 1933 World's Fair. Margaret Bonds (1913–1972), a student of Price, composed a piano and voice setting of "The Negro Speaks of Rivers" (1942), a poem by Langston Hughes. Bonds's "Ballad of the Brown King" was based on the story of Balthazar, one of the three kings who brought gifts to the infant Jesus. It was originally scored for orchestra, chorus, and soloists, but the orchestral parts were reduced to piano when released by Fox Publishing Company in 1961. Julia Perry (1924–1979), the most modernistic of the black female composers, studied in Paris with Nadia Boulanger. Two of her best-known works are *Stabat Mater* (1951), a liturgical work for contralto and string orchestra, and *Homunculus C. F.* (1960) for percussion, harp, and piano.

In the late twentieth century, many black classical composers were influenced more by jazz musicians like John Coltrane and Miles Davis than by spirituals or black folklore. Political events and social issues inspired composers like Anthony Davis, who wrote the 1985 opera *X, The Life and Times of Malcolm X*. African American composers born after 1950 include Julius Williams (b. 1954), Harvey Stokes (b.1957), and John Cornelius (b. 1966). Though many are affiliated with historically black educational institutions, others have cultivated successful careers at majority institutions.

The evolution of African American concert music, though distinctive in many ways, exists in a parallel relationship with that of European-derived twentieth-century classical music, reflecting its modernism, diverse influences, and stylistic plurality. Following the turn of the twenty-first century, African American composers continue to draw on varied musical styles while nevertheless maintaining strong ties with their cultural traditions.

[*See also* Gospel Music; Music; *and* Musical Theater.]

Bibliography

"AfriClassical.com: African Heritage in Classical Music." http://chevalierdesaintgeorges.homestead.com/Smith.html.

de Lerma, Dominique-René, ed. *Black Music in Our Culture: Curricular Ideas on the Subjects, Materials, and Problems*. Kent, Ohio: Kent State University Press, 1970.

Floyd, Samuel A., Jr. *The Power of Black Music: Interpreting Its History from Africa to the United States*. New York: Oxford University Press, 1995.

Green, Mildred Denby. *Black Women Composers: A Genesis*. Boston: Twayne, 1983.

Haas, Robert Bartlett. *William Grant Still and the Fusion of Cultures in American Music*. Los Angeles: Black Sparrow, 1972.

Rockwell, John. *All American Music: Composition in the Late Twentieth Century*. New York: Alfred A. Knopf, 1983.

Schwartz, Elliott, and Daniel Godfrey. *Music since 1945: Issues, Materials, and Literature*. New York: Schirmer, 1993.

Southern, Eileen. *The Music of Black Americans: A History*. 2d ed. New York: W.W. Norton, 1983.

—Daniel Adams

CONDUCTORS AND BANDLEADERS. Over the centuries the African American contribution to American music has been vast and varied. In terms of stylistic innovation, influence, and musical form these contributions have defined fundamental aspects of American culture. For instance, African Americans were essential to the flowering of that most iconic of American art forms, jazz. Given the enormity of these influences, any musical assessment will undoubtedly exclude important and noteworthy musicians.

Beginnings. This rich musical legacy began many years before such legendary figures as the ragtime innovator Scott Joplin (1868–1917) and the father of the blues, W. C. Handy (1873–1958), appeared on the musical scene. As an early example of musical pioneers, Francis Johnson (1792–1844) from Philadelphia stands out. His success is more remarkable given the level of racism of the era and the general lack of steady work for professional musicians.

Johnson mastered numerous instruments, including the bugle and violin, and he composed more than three hundred musical pieces. In addition he was a successful bandleader. His triumphs, though, were not without incident. Often white bands refused to perform with him, and violence could accompany performances. Such incidents occurred during tours of Saint Louis and Pittsburgh.

Johnson's first published composition appeared in 1818, and he later wrote much of the music for the 1824 state visit of France's Marie du Motier de Lafayette to Philadelphia. He took his band to Europe in 1837 and upon returning introduced the European promenade concert tradition to America. Johnson's success against great adversity made him the first major African American bandleader of outstanding stature.

The Twentieth Century. William Grant Still (1895–1978), born in Woodville, Mississippi, was an African American classical composer of distinction who wrote more than 150 compositions and became the first African American conductor of a major symphony orchestra. His Symphony No. 1 (*Afro-American Symphony*) was played by the Rochester Philharmonic Orchestra in 1931, and in 1936 he conducted the Los Angeles Philharmonic. In addition his opera *Troubled Island* was performed by the New York City Opera Company in 1949.

In 1955 Still conducted the New Orleans Philharmonic Orchestra—a first for an African American in the Deep South. Still's music was performed by many orchestras abroad, and the quality of his career was reflected in the award of two Guggenheim fellowships. He eventually settled in Los Angeles and established a successful career composing and arranging for films.

Edward Kennedy Ellington (1899–1974), better known as Duke Ellington, stands out as perhaps the most important composer and bandleader of the jazz and big band era. His impact on American music is still being felt, as the sales of his recordings indicate. Born in Washington, D.C., Ellington demonstrated musical talents early and dedicated himself to improving his abilities. As a teenager he wrote his first composition, "Soda Fountain Rag," in 1913.

Ellington formed his first band, the Serenaders, in 1917, and early success encouraged him to move to New York City in 1923. There during the Prohibition era he performed at all the top nightclubs, including Harlem's famous Cotton Club. During the 1920s the ever-increasing popularity of radio broadcasts gave Ellington's music a much wider audience, and he and his band became famous in the process. Hit albums followed, as well as national and international tours. The Ellington band shifted seamlessly from the 1920s jazz era to the swing styles of the 1930s, even defining the age with their recording, "It Don't Mean a Thing (If It Ain't Got That Swing)."

Other important and now classic compositions include "Satin Doll," "Mood Indigo," and "Come Sunday." Ellington also composed symphonic pieces—such as *The River*; *Black, Brown, and Beige*; and *Harlem*—that are still performed by orchestras the world over. He remained active as a performer and bandleader throughout his life. From 1965 until 1973 he wrote three extensive and ambitious *Sacred Concerts*, which reflected his own spiritualism and combined many of the varied musical styles, such as jazz, classical, choral, and gospel, that had shaped his creativity and his incomparable virtuosity.

William "Count" Basie (1904–1984), an Ellington contemporary, was a performer, bandleader, and composer of the highest rank. Born in Red Bank, New Jersey, Basie by his teens was an accomplished piano player, and through lessons with Thomas "Fats" Waller in Harlem he also became a polished organist. By his twenties he was touring the country, eventually settling in Kansas City, where he joined Walter Page's Blue Devils and then the Bennie Moten Band, thus serving his jazz apprenticeship with some of the best musicians of the day. Following the death of Moten in 1935, Basie formed his own band, the Barons of Rhythm, made up of many former Moten musicians, and this group evolved into the Count Basie Orchestra.

Chicago beckoned, and it was there that Count Basie in 1936 began his successful recording career. His "One O'Clock Jump" (1937) and "Jumpin' at the Woodside" (1938) became big Decca hits. During the 1930s the band's popularity drew them to New York City, which became their operational base until 1950, when changing styles and rising costs led Basie to reconstitute his band. In 1952, as the swing and big band era faded, the Basie band reorganized as a sixteen-piece orchestra. This smaller unit preserved the jumping beat associated with Basie's distinct sound. Since the 1930s Basie's musicianship had attracted some of the best singers of the age to his band. Blues singers of distinction such as Billie Holiday, Big Joe Turner, and Joe Williams, among many others, performed and recorded with the "Count."

This tradition continued through the 1950s when albums such as *One O'Clock Jump* and his live album *Count Basie at Newport* ensured Basie and his orchestra's continuing fame. In the 1960s and 1970s important black and white artists such as Ella Fitzgerald, Frank Sinatra, Tony Bennett, and the arranger Quincy Jones worked with Basie. These collaborations led to some of their most successful recordings such as *Ella and Basie*, *Sinatra at the Sands*, and Bennett's *Strike Up the Band*.

Count Basie helped define jazz and swing in the twentieth century, and his influence was felt nationally and internationally. His special place in musical history was acknowledged with Kennedy Center Honors in 1981 and with a posthumous Grammy Lifetime Achievement Award in 2002.

Quincy Delightt Jones (b. 1933) is another striking musical figure. An accomplished trumpeter, conductor, composer, arranger, and producer, Jones is not a classic bandleader in the old sense—although he was at one time the musical director of Dizzy Gillespie's band. Nevertheless, as a producer at Mercury Records, and as a composer of more than thirty film scores, Jones has for more than five decades been at the heart of America's most successful films and popular music recordings.

New generations of bandleaders and composers of distinction have also appeared, such as Calvin E. Simmons (1950–1982), who became director of a major philharmonic orchestra, the Oakland Philharmonic. Simmons also conducted many of the best orchestras in the world and was a contributor to numerous major opera productions at New York City's Metropolitan Opera and elsewhere. His career at the forefront of American music unfortunately was cut short by a fatal accident when he was at the threshold of greatness.

African American musical contributions have been central to the development of American music. As innovators, stylists, and composers, African Americans have influenced musical tastes and careers as divergent as those of George Gershwin and Leonard Bernstein.

[*See also* Composers; Gospel Music; Jazz; Music; Musical Theater; *and biographical entries on figures mentioned in this article*.]

BIBLIOGRAPHY

Burnim, Mellonee V., and Portia K. Maultsby, eds. *African-American Music: An Introduction*. New York: Routledge, 2006. A valuable overview of African American musical contributions.

Gates, Henry Louis, Jr., and Cornel West. *The African American Century: How Black Americans Have Shaped Our Country*. New York: Free Press, 2000. A contextual exploration of the African American legacy through a series of artistic portraits.

Hasse, John Edward. *Beyond Category: The Life and Genius of Duke Ellington*. New York: Simon & Schuster, 1993. An important contribution that outlines Ellington's achievements and success.

Kernfeld, Barry, ed. *The New Grove Dictionary of Jazz*. Vol. 1. 2d ed. London: Macmillan, 2002. A valuable guide to the many fundamental African American contributions to the development of jazz.

Peress, Maurice. *Dvořák to Duke Ellington: A Conductor Explores America's Music and Its African American Roots*. New York: Oxford University Press, 2004.

Tate, Eleanora E., and James Haskins. *African American Musicians*. New York: Wiley, 2000. An important academic investigation of the African American musical experience.

—THEODORE W. EVERSOLE

CONGRESS, AFRICAN AMERICANS IN. The formal end of Reconstruction in 1877 curtailed, but did not fully erode, black participation in American politics. Violence, intimidation, and fraud kept many African Americans from the polls and certainly ensured that no black candidates were elected at the state level or to the U.S. Senate, even in majority-black states such as Louisiana, South Carolina, or Mississippi. But as late as 1890, three black Republicans sat in the U.S. House of Representatives, and African Americans maintained a presence in several state legislatures, even in Mississippi, where so-called Redemption of the state from black Republican rule had been bloodiest. After George H. White from North Carolina's Second Congressional District, the "Black Second," retired from Congress in 1901, however, no African American was elected to Congress until 1928, when the Illinois Republican Oscar De Priest was elected to the House. The principal reason for the disappearance of African Americans from Congress was a series of disfranchisement campaigns that began in Mississippi in 1890 and spread throughout the former states of the Confederacy in the decade that followed.

Two factors prompted southern white conservatives to pursue disfranchisement of blacks in the 1890s. First was a fear of the tentative efforts of African American Republicans to make common cause with the economically strapped whites in Farmers Alliances and in the Greenback and Populist parties. Second was a concern over legislation passed by the Republican-dominated U.S. House in 1890—but filibustered in the Senate by southern Democrats—that would have required the use of federal supervisors to monitor elections. The 1890 Mississippi state constitutional convention established new criteria for voting that required the payment of a poll tax and included an "understanding clause" that required voters to interpret a passage of the state constitution. In theory the clause might have been used to disfranchise illiterate white as well as illiterate black voters, but the discretion given to state election officials—all of whom were white—to interpret a voter's understanding meant that in practice only African Americans were disfranchised.

The consequences of the Mississippi convention became evident in the elections of 1892 when the number of African Americans registered to vote in the state fell to 8,615, from 190,000 in 1890. Other southern states followed suit, imposing literacy requirements, poll taxes, party primaries closed to black voters, and, in Louisiana, a "grandfather clause" that limited voting rights to citizens eligible to vote, or descended from eligible citizens, in 1867. These constitutional amendments had the net effect of excluding all but a small number of property-owning blacks from the right to vote in those states.

Blacks Return to Congress. African Americans continued to exercise their franchise in northern states that did not impose race-based restrictions on voting, and following the Great Migration of southern blacks to the northern cities that began in World War I, they played an increasing role in northern politics. Success at the local level foreshadowed the return of blacks to Congress. Oscar Stanton De Priest, elected to the U.S. House from Illinois in 1928, began his political career as a South Side Chicago alderman in 1915. De Priest served in Congress for three terms but lost in 1934 to another African American, Arthur Mitchell, a Democrat. Mitchell owed his margin of victory to whites in the First Congressional District, but African Americans would soon flock to the Democratic Party of Franklin Delano Roosevelt and the New Deal. For the next fifty-eight years, all blacks elected to the House would be Democrats, though even in 1954, the year of the Supreme Court's landmark *Brown v. Board of Education* decision, there were only two African Americans in the House: William Dawson, who replaced Mitchell in 1942, and Harlem's Adam Clayton Powell Jr., who joined him in 1944.

The growing black populations of Philadelphia, Detroit, and Los Angeles yielded three additional black members of the House from those cities by 1964. Although all generally supported the liberal agenda of their party, the cautious party loyalist Dawson stood in sharp contrast to the flamboyant maverick Powell, who flirted with supporting the Republican president Dwight Eisenhower. Seniority did, however, allow black congressmen gradually to take on leadership roles in the House, and Dawson became the first African American to chair a congressional committee (the Committee on Expenditures in the Executive Departments) in 1949. Powell first chaired the much more important House Education and Labor Committee in 1961 and was a central figure in securing passage of President John Kennedy's New Frontier and President Lyndon Johnson's Great Society legislation.

The passage of the 1965 Voting Rights Act and the growing black consciousness movement of the late 1960s dramatically changed the black delegation in Congress in the 1970s. In addition to Edward Brooke, a Massachusetts Republican who entered the Senate in 1966, nine black members of the House formed the first Congressional Black Caucus (CBC) in 1970–1971, with Charles Diggs of Michigan as its first chair. By the time of the Ninety-fifth Congress in 1979, the CBC boasted fifteen members, including the first African American woman in the House, Shirley Chisholm of New York, and the first southern black representatives since George White: Barbara Jordan of Texas and Andrew Young of Georgia.

Like most northern and western members of the CBC, Jordan and Young represented urban constituencies. On social and economic matters and in foreign affairs, the CBC provided a fairly coherent and consistent liberal voice within the Democratic majority in Congress, although some members—notably John Conyers of Michigan and Ron Dellums of California—were more liberal than others like Robert Nix of Pennsylvania. The CBC gained some early attention for its boycott of President Richard Nixon's 1971 State of the Union address, to protest Nixon's nomination of federal judges hostile to civil rights, but had few concrete achievements at the end of the 1970s. President Jimmy Carter credited the CBC for its role in the passage of the 1978 Full Employment and Balanced Growth Act, commonly known as the Humphrey-Hawkins Act after its leading sponsors, Senator Hubert Humphrey and the CBC member Gus Hawkins of California. The Humphrey-Hawkins Act established the federal government's responsibility to ensure full employment, long a demand of blacks in Congress.

The election of the conservative Republican Ronald Reagan as president in 1980 rendered Humphrey-Hawkins toothless, however, leaving the members of the CBC isolated standard-bearers of Keynesian intervention in the economy in the face of massive cuts in social and welfare spending. Black members of Congress were unanimous in their opposition to sharp increases in military spending at the same time that federal aid for education and housing was being slashed.

Despite the mutual antipathy between the Reagan administration and blacks in Congress on foreign and domestic policy, in the early 1980s the CBC secured President Reagan's support for two major pieces of legislation: the passage of a federal Martin Luther King Jr. holiday—first proposed by Conyers in 1968—and the extension and strengthening of the Voting Rights Act. Blacks in Congress also played a central role in the passage of the 1986 Comprehensive Anti-Apartheid Act—overturning Reagan's veto of the legislation—which was first proposed by Dellums in 1972. The act, which imposed sanctions on South Africa's apartheid regime and called for the release of Nelson Mandela and other political prisoners, proved an important catalyst for ending white-minority rule in South Africa.

Though the role of African Americans in Congress was somewhat overshadowed by the election of black mayors in Chicago, Philadelphia, and New York City in the 1980s and early 1990s, blacks also moved into the front line of the House Democratic leadership. The Philadelphia congressman Bill Gray became chair of the House Budget Committee in 1985 and served as Democratic majority whip from 1989 to 1991.

Growth and Fragmentation. The elections of 1992 brought a dramatic increase in the number of African Americans in Congress. That year witnessed the election of the first black female and first black Democratic member of the Senate, Carol Moseley Braun of Illinois, as well as an increase in the number of African American members of the House from twenty-five to thirty-nine. The immediate cause of the increase was the decennial reapportionment of Congress in 1990, which resulted in the creation of a number of black-majority congressional districts in the rural South. North Carolina, for example, elected two African Americans to Congress that year—Melvin Watt, representing an urban Piedmont district that snaked from Charlotte to Greensboro, and Eva Clayton, representing much of the rural eastern part of the state that had elected George White in the 1890s.

Though these majority-minority districts were challenged in the federal courts in the 1990s for allegedly discriminating against white voters, they persisted into the twenty-first century and were largely unaltered by the 2000 reapportionment. The number of African Americans elected to Congress since 1992, however, remained virtually static. As of 2008 there were forty voting black members of the House and one black senator, Barack Obama of Illinois. During that period only two black members of the House were Republicans: Gary Franks of Connecticut, who joined the CBC, and J. C. Watts of Oklahoma, who did not, but who did serve as the fourth-highest ranking member of the Republican-controlled Congress in 1998 as chair of the House Republican Conference.

The unprecedented influence of African Americans within the House Democratic Party coincided with a period of Republican control of the House, beginning with the so-called Gingrich Revolution in 1994. This greatly diminished the influence of the CBC, whose members proved to be among the most loyal supporters of Bill Clinton's presidency and were among the fiercest critics of the administration of George W. Bush. Some commentators noted a fragmentation of the black delegation during the Bush years, with a few younger southern and border-state members such as Harold Ford Jr. of Tennessee and Albert Wynn of Maryland willing to buck the CBC's traditional liberal policy agenda on social issues and foreign policy. Ford and Wynn were among four black lawmakers who supported the Bush administration's decision to invade Iraq in 2003, and they also were among a larger group of CBC moderates who supported the Bush administration on energy policy and taxes.

The Democratic recapture of the House in 2006 propelled a number of veteran African American liberals to leadership positions. Among these were Charles Rangel of New York, chair of the Budget Committee; John Conyers of Michigan, chair of the Judiciary Committee; and Jim Clyburn of South Carolina, majority whip. The move away from traditional liberal politics seemed to have come to an end, a striking example of which could be seen in the defeat during a 2008 Democratic primary of Maryland's Wynn by a liberal opponent who criticized Wynn's support of the Iraq War and the broader Bush agenda. African American members of Congress wielded more political clout during the 110th Congress (2007–2009) than at any other time in the nation's history. The 2008 Democratic presidential primary made clear that the black congressional delegation was far from monolithic. Members of the black caucus initially divided their support evenly between Senator Hillary Clinton of New York and the CBC member Barack Obama, although several black caucus members later switched support from Clinton to Obama.

[*See also* Congressional Black Caucus; Democratic Party; Disfranchisement of African Americans; Laws and Legislation; Politics and Politicians; Republican Party; Voting Rights; Voting Rights Act; *and biographical entries on figures mentioned in this article*.]

BIBLIOGRAPHY

Christopher, Maurice. *Black Americans in Congress*. New York: Crowell, 1976. A comprehensive survey of the careers and political philosophies of the forty-five African Americans who served in the U.S. Congress from Reconstruction through the early 1970s.

Freedman, Eric, and Stephen A. Jones. *African Americans in Congress: A Documentary History*. Washington, D.C.: Congressional Quarterly Press, 2007. An authoritative, thorough, and accessible history of African Americans in Congress from Reconstruction to 2006.

Hahn, Steven. *A Nation under Our Feet: Black Political Struggles in the Rural South from Slavery to the Great Migration*. Cambridge, Mass.: Harvard University Press, 2003. A pioneering synthesis of African American politics.

Lusane, Clarence. "Unity and Struggle: The Political Behavior of African American Members of Congress." *Black Scholar* 24, no. 4 (Fall 1994): 16–27. Analyzes sources of division within the Congressional Black Caucus, notably in relation to black nationalism.

—STEVEN J. NIVEN

CONGRESSIONAL BLACK CAUCUS. The Congressional Black Caucus (CBC) is an association within the U.S. Congress that is committed to the welfare of African Americans and other underrepresented communities in the United States. The founding members of the CBC stated that their goal was "to promote the public welfare through legislation designed to meet the needs of millions of neglected citizens." One of the CBC's core missions has been to reduce—and, ultimately, to eliminate—disparities that exist between African Americans and white Americans in every aspect of life. The CBC asserts that continuing and troubling disparities make it more difficult, and often impossible, for African Americans to reach their full potential.

Toward the middle of the twentieth century the number of African Americans in the U.S. Congress slowly began to increase. In 1969 there were nine black members of Congress. Though this was a gain—there had been only four members in 1959, for example—their voices were isolated and relatively powerless. Charles Diggs, an African American representative from Michigan, believed that if the African American members of Congress worked with a unified voice and vote that they would be more likely to effect change. He developed the Democratic Select Committee in January 1969, and during its three years of existence the committee investigated the murders of several Chicago Black Panther Party members and helped to defeat the nomination of the conservative judge Clement Haynsworth to the Supreme Court.

In 1971 the committee had increased from nine to thirteen members and was reorganized and renamed the Congressional Black Caucus on the motion of Charles B. Rangel of New York. Representative Diggs became the first chair of the Congressional Black Caucus in this, the Ninety-second Congress. The founding members included the representatives Shirley Chisholm, William Clay, George Collins, John Conyers, Ronald Dellums, Charles Diggs, Augustus Hawkins, Ralph Metcalfe, Parren Mitchell, Robert Nix, Charles Rangel, and Louis Stokes, and the District of Columbia delegate Walter Fauntroy. Several of the founders later served as chair of the CBC.

The newly christened caucus received its first national recognition when its members met with President Richard Nixon in March 1971 and presented him with a list of sixty recommendations for government action on issues both foreign and domestic.

In March 1972 the CBC was one of the sponsors of the National Black Political Convention, a gathering of several thousand African Americans in Gary, Indiana, to take action on such issues as a guaranteed minimum wage and a national health-care system. The convention pulled together a cross section of people representing a wide range of political philosophies and parties. In 1976 the caucus established the Congressional Black Caucus Foundation, Inc., a nonpartisan, nonprofit public policy, research, and educational institute.

A major accomplishment of the CBC was its help in getting the U.S. government to impose sanctions on apartheid South Africa, through what became known as the Comprehensive Anti-apartheid Act (1986). Like many of the CBC's initiatives, this campaign was buoyed by a highly energized African American community outraged by human rights violations perpetrated by a white-minority regime. Though opposed by President Ronald Reagan, the CBC was able to mobilize sufficiently to get this legislation passed—a landmark in the CBC's history.

The caucus is officially nonpartisan, but it is and has been primarily composed of Democrats, and it tends to function as a lobbying group within the wider congressional Democratic Party. Indeed, the CBC is probably the most liberal bloc in Washington. Since the CBC's inception an increasing number of African Americans have been elected to Congress; in 2005 the caucus had forty-three members.

Priorities of the caucus include closing the achievement and opportunity gaps in education, providing quality health care for all Americans, increasing employment and economic security, building wealth and developing businesses, ensuring justice for all, guaranteeing retirement security for all Americans, and promoting equity in foreign policy. The CBC also asserts priorities that focus more closely on African American concerns. These include building stronger African American families, improving the welfare of children, and increasing African American political representation. Reducing inequities and improving opportunities for African Americans to advance in the military, documenting and preserving African American history by ensuring that financing and construction of the National African American History Museum in Washington, D.C., move forward, and eliminating waste, fraud, abuse, and disparities in every area of government are also concerns and goals of the caucus. The CBC's mission statement makes clear that the CBC has never sought to limit the benefits of its endeavors to African Americans and that it firmly believes that its priorities will benefit all Americans and will make the country better for all people.

In the 1970s—on the heels of the civil rights struggles and during the adolescence of integration in the United States—the need for and the development of the Congressional Black Caucus was recognized and positively received by African American politicians. However, as the twentieth century closed and a new century opened, questions of the relevance and effectiveness of the CBC made their way into political discussion. Members do not always feel that it is necessary to speak or act as a unit.

[*See also* Congress, African Americans in; Laws and Legislation; *and biographical entries on figures mentioned in this article.*]

BIBLIOGRAPHY

Perry, Huey L., and Wayne Parent, eds. *Blacks and the American Political System*. Gainesville: University Press of Florida, 1995.

Singh, Robert. *The Congressional Black Caucus: Racial Politics in the U.S. Congress*. Thousand Oaks, Calif.: Sage, 1998.

—NIAMBI LEE-KONG

CONGRESS OF AFRICAN PEOPLE. In 1970 in Atlanta, Georgia, the Congress of African People (CAP) established itself as a united-front organization of black nationalists, Pan-Africanists, and civil rights activists determined to construct black political unity. Amiri Baraka, formerly LeRoi Jones, of the Committee for a United Newark (New Jersey); Louis Farrakhan (Louis X) of the Nation of Islam; Jesse Jackson of People United to Save Humanity; Whitney Young of the National Urban League; Coretta Scott King and Betty Shabazz, who were carrying on the work of their assassinated husbands, Martin Luther King Jr. and Malcolm X, respectively; Mayor Richard Hatcher of Gary, Indiana; the Georgia state legislator Julian Bond; and other black elected officials and representatives of several political and cultural black nationalist groups were among the three thousand attendees at the founding convention.

CAP was tasked with promoting the economic and political development of black communities and coordinating coalition work among black nationalists and civil rights workers in twenty-five American cities with sizable African American populations. To Baraka and other cultural nationalists, CAP symbolized "nation time," when African Americans would forge black political networks, black-owned economic institutions, and a black nation.

Black cultural nationalism formed the core of CAP's vision, mission, and activities. The ideology stressed among other things the notion that African Americans have the right of self-determination to form their own nation where they could experience the full, unimpeded unfolding of black culture. Cultural nationalism had rapidly spread among African Americans during the 1960s when black urban rebellions against police brutality and other injustices occurred in Newark and other cities across the nation. This ideology and its institutional major national vehicle, the annual national Black Power conferences held from 1966 to 1968, enabled the playwright, poet, and political activist Baraka to become prominent among black cultural nationalists and thus to become the leader of CAP.

CAP focused on themes of nation building within the United States. It promoted Pan-Africanism, organized African Liberation Day and the African Liberation Support Committee, and insisted that only through revolutionary struggle would black Americans attain psychological and national liberation from white Americans. CAP engaged in voter registration campaigns, politicized the black community, supported African American and Puerto Rican candidates for elective office, and formed alliances with radical nonwhite organizations in the United States and various Third World nations. Guided by Baraka's theories of core black cultural nationalist concepts, CAP viewed its activities as laying the foundation for black nation-building, liberation, and self-determination.

By 1974, CAP entered a period of internal political turmoil as Baraka jettisoned cultural nationalism and elevated revolutionary Marxism, specifically Maoism, as the guiding set of principles toward achieving African American self-determination. Intense debates between nationalists and Marxists ensued, with Baraka arguing that black liberation must undergo a social transformation that would usher in some form of socialism. CAP collapsed and ceased to exist in 1976 after Baraka established the Revolutionary Communist League. But by the time of its demise, the Congress of African People had achieved historical significance for its development, dominance, and leadership of black cultural nationalism.

[*See also* African Liberation Support Committee; Baraka, Amiri; Black Nationalism; Black Power Movement; *and* Pan-Africanism.]

BIBLIOGRAPHY

Joseph, Peniel E., ed. *The Black Power Movement: Rethinking the Civil Rights–Black Power Era*. New York: Routledge, 2006. Includes a section on the Congress of African People by Amiri Baraka in the context of the book's overall thesis that Black Power ideas existed before the 1965 black uprising in Watts, Los Angeles.

Woodard, Komozi. *A Nation within a Nation: Amiri Baraka (LeRoi Jones) and Black Power Politics*. Chapel Hill: University of North Carolina Press, 1999. Sections of the book discuss Amiri Baraka's role in Black Power politics before, during, and after his sojourn in the Congress of African People.

—CHARLES L. LUMPKINS

CONGRESS OF RACIAL EQUALITY. The Congress of Racial Equality (CORE) was founded in 1942 as the Committee of Racial Equality by an interracial group of students in Chicago. The group changed its name to the Congress of Racial Equality in 1943. In the late 1930s and early 1940s World War II was heralded as the war for freedom and democracy, yet in America black soldiers who had experienced first-class citizenship abroad were treated as second-class citizens at home.

American students, influenced by the Christian student movement of the 1930s, were aware of this contradiction. They formed a small band of dedicated young pacifists, initially called the Fellowship of Reconciliation (FOR). FOR members were deeply committed to applying Mahatma Gandhi's teachings of nonviolent resistance to everyday life. One cell group of FOR, established at the University of Chicago in October 1941, was intensely committed to applying Gandhian principles to racial problems. From the work of this cell group emerged the first CORE group, the Chicago Committee of Racial Equality. Six individuals founded the organization. Two were African American and four were white. Bernice Fisher and Homer Jack were white divinity students at the University of Chicago; Joe Guinn, an African American from Chicago, and James R. Robinson, a white from upstate New York, were liberal arts students at the University of Chicago; James Farmer, an African American FOR fieldworker, earned a bachelor of divinity degree from Howard University; and George Houser was a white part-time FOR fieldworker and conscientious objector to World War II. Houser had served a prison term before his matriculation as a University of Chicago divinity student. Both Farmer and Houser had been prominent in Methodist student circles in the 1930s, and their Methodism influenced their early leadership of CORE.

In 1942, CORE began protests against segregation of public accommodations. One of the first direct actions taken by the cell group was the establishment of Fellowship House, an interracial men's cooperative, to challenge discriminatory housing practices around the University of Chicago campus. Continued interest grew in combating racial discrimination in the area, attracting a diverse number of young people. CORE was primarily funded by voluntary contributions from its members. Members were required to be well-versed in the principles of nonviolent philosophy and to attend general and committee meetings regularly. Committee or action units investigated and planned projects against discrimination in schools, hospitals, housing, and places of public accommodation. The Chicago CORE chapter attacked acts of racist discrimination at the University of Chicago's hospital and medical school. Off-campus and downtown restaurants were also challenged for their discriminatory practices against blacks. CORE held interracial sit-ins demanding services to all people and petitioned patrons to protest as they paid their bills.

Nationally, James Farmer and Bayard Rustin, a pacifist and former FOR youth secretary, were instrumental in CORE's fight against racial discrimination. The New York City chapter targeted the unfair employment practices of the Woolworth Company. The CORE chapter of Syracuse, New York, tackled housing discrimination, as well as the city's largest hotel, which banned accommodations to blacks. The Denver, Colorado, chapter tested the local theaters' and restaurants' federal compliance for nondiscriminatory accommodations of blacks. As a result of the chapter's direct action, some restaurants began to serve blacks for the first time.

Although there was increased national interest in the fight against racial discrimination, CORE's relationships with other national organizations were tentative at best. In the early days of CORE the organization opposed all racial chauvinism and aimed to break down barriers of segregation, even break down black nationalism. CORE viewed the work of A. Philip Randolph, planner of the March on Washington Movement (MOWM) of 1941, as nationalistic. The Vanguard League of Baltimore, Maryland, was considered separatist and nonpacifist. The work of the NAACP and the Urban League was seen as only peripheral to the nation's racial problem. CORE members emphasized interracial and nonviolent direct action because they believed that such action was key to solving the problem of racial discrimination.

The first national convention was held in 1943. James Farmer became the first national chairman and Bernice Fisher was elected secretary-treasurer. The established constitution reiterated the purpose of CORE: to form multiracial groups that would work to abolish the color line through direct acts of nonviolence. This constitution did not however establish a national organization structure. National CORE had the power to affiliate new chapters and suspend inactive ones, but no other centralized structure was instituted. Decentralization was seen as a way to respect the freedom of individual chapters to work on behalf of their local concerns rather than the concerns of a national organization. Unfortunately, as a result of this decentralization, the national organization lacked membership lists of chapter affiliates, funding for salaries, and a national office space.

At the 1944 convention a new constitution was adopted. James Farmer and Bernice Fisher were reelected as chairman and secretary-treasurer, respectively. In addition three vice chairmen were added. Still, this new arrangement proved to be ineffectual, with officers failing to carry out their responsibilities.

In 1945 the constitution was modified to reflect a more conventional organizational structure. The executive committee now consisted of one chairman, one vice chairman, one treasurer, one executive secretary, and one recording secretary. A council was also established consisting of the executive committee and two representatives from each CORE chapter. The creation of the executive secretary position allowed for a centralized structure, yet the establishment of the council allowed CORE leaders to be more responsive to affiliates. The council met semiannually and made major decisions. The council also had the power to affiliate new chapters. The executive committee met more frequently, but was empowered to make only emergency decisions. James Farmer stepped down as national chairman and was succeeded by Frank Shearer of the Vanguard League. George Houser became the first executive secretary.

As executive secretary, Houser envisioned a yearlong leadership-training project in preparation for a large-scale multiracial nonviolent movement. Recognizing the need for more experienced leadership, Houser reluctantly enlisted the help of A. Philip Randolph of MOWM, as well as of Roy Wilkins, assistant secretary to the NAACP. Unfortunately, all involved parties doubted the feasibility of the project and the vision died, not to be revived again until the civil rights movement of the 1960s.

The Age of Martin Luther King Jr. In the late 1940s CORE was now a national organization, but its budget was nevertheless practically nonexistent; therefore the members of the council were unpaid. Houser, as executive secretary, reluctantly pushed for chapter members' dues to be divided among national and local offices. Local chapters did not comply, and the national budget remained minuscule. Despite the inadequate budget, a national project, the Journey of Reconciliation, was implemented. In April 1947 CORE sent eight white men and eight black men into the upper southern states in order to test compliance with the 1946 Supreme Court decision against segregation in interstate travel. This Journey of Reconciliation was to be a two-week pilgrimage through Virginia, North Carolina, Tennessee, and Kentucky. But instead, riders of the Journey of Reconciliation team were threatened with violence and were arrested several times, and three of the riders were forced to work on a chain gang. Arrested riders confronted North Carolina citizens, police, and judges who had no knowledge of the 1946 Supreme Court decision. Subsequently, charges were dropped in most of the team's cases. The direct action of the Journey did not lead to compliance with transportation desegregation but it did achieve a great deal of publicity for CORE. Still, affiliates were reluctant to support financially the hiring of staff to continue CORE's momentum as a force for civil rights.

During President Truman's administration, civil rights for blacks greatly increased with the desegregation of the armed forces and the appointment of the first black circuit court judge. Yet during this time, CORE—being more radical than other civil rights organizations—lost members because of the McCarthy anticommunist hysteria. On the national level CORE had to rally local chapters together in order to provide a more directed and singular focus for civil rights. It could no longer function as a fractured group of autonomous affiliates. In December 1955 the charismatic civil rights leader Martin Luther King Jr. successfully led the Montgomery bus boycott. The use of nonviolent direct action was attributed to CORE, whose philosophy had laid the foundation for such action.

In 1961 James Farmer was elected as the first national director of CORE. His leadership and the improved national climate for racial equality resulted in a revival of CORE's popularity. During that same year CORE, along with the Student Nonviolent Coordinating Committee (SNCC) and the Southern Christian Leadership Conference (SCLC), reinstated the Journey of Reconciliation rides, later naming them the Freedom Rides. The direct action of the Freedom Rides resulted in the Interstate Commerce Commission (ICC) finally enforcing the 1946 decision and also in the 1960 Supreme Court ruling against segregated interstate carriers and terminal stations. The law became effective on 1 November 1961.

The Freedom Rides placed a tremendous financial burden on CORE. It was only by the generous donations of the NAACP Legal Defense and Education Fund that CORE was able to post bail and pay arraignment fees for arrested riders. In 1963 CORE helped to organize the March on Washington. On 28 August of that year more than 200,000 people marched peacefully to the Lincoln Memorial to demand equal justice for all citizens. In the mid-1960s CORE boasted 80,000 members. CORE's paid staff had grown from 7 to 137, and there were now 140 full-fledged chapters.

The civil rights movement's turning point was 1964. The Civil Rights Act of 1964 was passed. Also, three major civil rights organizations, CORE, the SNCC, and the NAACP, organized their Freedom Summer campaign. Freedom Summer's main objective was to empower African Americans in the Deep South politically, via voter registration and so-called Freedom Schools. Yet even as progress was being made in the fight for civil rights, delegates of the Mississippi Freedom Democratic Party were denied a voting seat at the 1964 Democratic Convention. As a result civil rights organizations began to split into moderate and radical factions. The more radical blacks embraced Black Power. The assassination of Malcolm X in 1965 also sparked more militancy among blacks. Presiding members of CORE followed this trend and changed its emphasis from integration to a more nationalist agenda. This sentiment influenced the election of Floyd McKissick as national director in 1966, replacing James Farmer. Because of this revised agenda, many moderates left the organization.

Behind CORE's stance of black separatism, there was little successful program development. CORE continued to struggle financially, losing many of its financial backers of the past. New initiatives to empower black political leadership and increase job training failed from lack of financial support and suspected mismanagement of funds. In 1968 Floyd McKissick announced his retirement and Roy Innis replaced him as the national director. That same year Martin Luther King Jr. was assassinated. Dr. King had been a member of CORE's advisory committee and was even offered the national directorship before James Farmer was elected to the position. CORE had already made a shift to black nationalism, yet the assassination of King still rattled CORE members' commitment to nonviolence. There was a surge of discontent with the effectiveness of nonviolence, when violence seemed to permeate the country. In its fight for civil rights CORE continued to adopt a more radical stance than other civil rights organizations did. The notion of Black Power would move the organization away from its initial mission of racial integration and nonviolence to one of racial separatism and self-preservation.

Contemporary America. Since CORE's inception in 1942 there have been three national directors: James Farmer (1961–1966), Floyd McKissick (1966–1968), and Roy Innis, who has been the national director since 1968. Innis's first acts as national director were to deny whites active membership in CORE and to convert the organization into a small centralized body, restricting the autonomy of local chapters. In the press Innis declared that CORE had finally become a black nationalist organization emphasizing separatism, so that blacks could control their own destiny. He demanded that the American Constitution be revised to recognize blacks as a separate nation.

To further this cause Innis supported the 1968 presidential bid of the Republican Richard Nixon. Innis felt that Nixon's support of school decentralization and community control were better strategies for black advancement than the welfare programs supported by the Democrats. In the South, Innis pushed for separate school districts that would be completely controlled by blacks. He rejected any population programs and birth-control policies formulated by whites. He felt that such plans were inherently genocidal. Focusing on political leverage Innis actually favored a heavy urban population of blacks, hoping to maintain an increase in their political representation.

Over the years Innis has been admired and despised as an opportunist. In the 1970s Innis toured seven African countries, seeking to enhance and build on the black pride movement of the previous decade. Yet Innis is also known to have befriended Idi Amin, the tyrannical president of Uganda. He later recanted his association because of the brutality of Amin's regime. In 1978 Innis was charged by New York State officials with mismanagement of charitable funds, but he later settled out of court.

In 1993 Innis made an unsuccessful bid for mayor of New York City. He challenged the incumbent David Dinkins, the first black person to hold the that office. With little capital Innis still won 26 percent of the vote at the Democratic primary. Continuing his relations with Africa, Innis led a team of delegates to Nigeria in 1996—at the time Nigeria was transitioning from military to civilian rule—in order to monitor the first elections. A nationally known advocate of Second Amendment rights, Innis has tried to help the National Rifle Association overturn a Maryland ban against cheap handguns. Innis joined the Libertarian Party in 1998 and advocates the idea that the most fundamental freedom for all people is the right to govern themselves.

Contrary to his former separatist stance, Innis has embraced the conservative Republican Party. In 2002 he suggested to the Bush administration that new Nation of Islam converts, particularly African American inmates and college students, should be watched carefully because of their alleged potential involvement in terrorist acts against the United States. In that same year the Republican Senator Trent Lott called upon Innis in hopes of mending relations with black citizens after Lott voiced support for the 1948 presidential campaign of the segregationist Strom Thurmond. Roy Innis has held membership on the board of several conservative organizations, including the Hudson Institute, a right-wing think tank, the National Rifle Association, and the Landmark Legal Foundation, one of the more vocal critics of former president Bill Clinton. CORE maintains its headquarters in New York City.

[*See also* Civil Disobedience; Civil Rights Movement; Freedom Rides; Mississippi Freedom Democratic Party; National Association for the Advancement of Colored People; Student Nonviolent Coordinating Committee; *and biographical entries on figures mentioned in this article*.]

Bibliography

Farmer, James. *Freedom—When?* New York: Random House, 1965.

Farmer, James. *Lay Bare the Heart: An Autobiography of the Civil Rights Movement*. New York: Arbor House, 1985.

Meier, August, and Elliot Rudwick. *CORE: A Study in the Civil Rights Movement, 1942–1968*. Urbana: University of Illinois Press, 1975. An excellent source regarding the intricacies of the civil rights movement.

"Roy Innis: From Left-wing Radical to Right-wing Extremist." *The Journal of Blacks in Higher Education* 39 (30 April 2003): 69.

—Cassandra L. McKay

CONNECTICUT. According to U.S. Census Bureau reports, African Americans accounted for 12,302 of 746,258 Connecticut residents in 1890, representing less than 2 percent of the state's population. This number increased steadily during the first half of the twentieth century as cities became more industrialized and as the state exhibited progress in matters of civil rights. Despite the prevalence of lynching throughout the nation, Connecticut had no lynchings of record after 1890. Blacks were among the graduates of state colleges and universities in the first decades of the twentieth century, and the 1930s and 1940s saw legislation that secured rights and provided protection from discrimination, including a unique ruling against pricing discrimination (*Ross v. Schade*, 1940).

While war industries fueled the job market, African Americans were limited primarily to service and agricultural jobs, and an interracial committee was formed in 1943—two years after the implementation of its federal counterpart—to advocate for the elimination of discrimination in the workplace. This committee, now known as the Connecticut Commission on Human Rights and Opportunities, was allowed to hear employment-related discrimination complaints after the Fair Employment Practices Act was passed in 1947, but the committee was not given the power to resolve such issues until more than a decade had passed. Similarly, housing discrimination, prohibited in the public realm in 1949, remained an issue until laws were extended to private housing in 1963.

As the agricultural industry declined and as tension increased over civil rights issues in the late 1960s, race riots erupted in several Connecticut cities, including New Haven, a city that had been nicknamed the Model City for its prominent role in urban renewal—a controversial federal response to poverty, unemployment, and civic decay. Governor John Dempsey held a conference in 1967 to encourage unity and implementation of the teachings of Martin Luther King Jr., but rioting continued, heightened by King's assassination in 1968.

Despite such turbulence, the state's African American population nearly doubled between 1960 and 1970, although a trend of migration to suburbs became apparent. In the decades that followed, the black population continued to grow amid developments such as assistance for small African American–owned businesses, statewide affirmative action, and the election in Hartford of Thurman Milner and Carrie Saxon Perry, the first male and first female African American mayor of a New England city. However, the rate of population growth tapered off considerably.

The 2000 U.S. Census indicated that approximately 10 percent of Connecticut's population was African American, with numbers in excess of 300,000. Although Connecticut continued to move forward with reform efforts, encouraging recognition of those people and sites associated with the struggle for freedom, some long-standing issues lingered. Though Connecticut was one of only a few states in the late 1940s without laws allowing segregation, de facto segregation in schools remained a problem. Long after the 1996 Connecticut Supreme Court ruling that de facto segregation violated the state constitution (*Scheff v. O'Neill*), as of 2008 legislators were still working to address this controversial issue.

[*See also* Agriculture and Agricultural Labor; Civil Rights; Civil Rights Movement; Desegregation and Integration; Discrimination; King, Martin Luther, Jr., Assassination of; Mayors; *and* Riots and Rebellions, *subentry* Riots and Rebellions of the 1960s.]

BIBLIOGRAPHY

Connecticut Commission on Human Rights and Opportunities. "Historical Overview." http://www.ct.gov/chro/cwp/view.asp?a=2523&Q=315814. A brief but thorough history of the commission that includes a review of civil rights progress in the state.

Moret, Marta. *A Brief History of the Connecticut Labor Movement*. Storrs: University of Connecticut Labor Education Center, 1982. An overview of the state labor movement from colonial to contemporary times. Though the African American population is not referenced frequently, this volume touches on corresponding civil rights matters and provides insight into the dynamics behind population trends.

Rae, Douglas W. *City: Urbanism and Its End*. New Haven, Conn., and London: Yale University Press, 2003. An insightful volume on the decline of American cities and the impact of urban reform that uses New Haven, Connecticut, as its model.

—JENNIFER BANACH PALLADINO

CONNERLY, WARD (b. 15 June 1939), successful entrepreneur and political activist. Connerly is nationally known for his controversial campaign to prohibit the use of affirmative action in state agencies, employment, and public education.

Wardell Connerly was born in Leesville, Louisiana, and was primarily raised by his grandmother after his mother died when he was five. Connerly describes his racial ancestry as one-quarter French Canadian, three-eighths Irish, one-quarter African, and one-eighth Choctaw. However, he rejects racial categories and prefers to identify himself as simply American.

Connerly graduated from Sacramento State College with a BA in political science in 1962. He was the first black student to become the student body president and the first and only black member of Delta Phi Omega fraternity. Upon graduating from college Connerly worked for the Redevelopment Agency of the City and County of Sacramento, which spawned his interest in housing and real estate. In 1966, Connerly became the community development coordinator for the California Department of Housing and Community Development and later served as its chief deputy director. By 1973 Connerly and his wife, Ilene, started a consulting firm, Connerly and Associates, Inc. Over the years Connerly became a successful entrepreneur. His longtime friend California governor Pete Wilson appointed Connerly to the University of California Board of Regents in 1993 as a part of a mandate to make the board more diverse.

Connerly's campaign against affirmative action was ignited by the empathy that he felt for white applicants who were rejected from the University of California schools. Connerly maintained that these students' life chances were severely diminished because they were of the wrong race. As a regent, Connerly convinced Governor Wilson that affirmative action was racial preference in disguise and that it discriminated against whites and Asians. In 1995 the Board of Regents proposed a ban on the use of race in admissions despite heated debates and protests by students and pro–affirmative action groups such as By Any Means Necessary (BAMN). African American enrollment has since plummeted at the University of California's flagship schools, UCLA and Berkeley.

In 1995, Connerly became the chairman of the California Civil Rights Initiative, also known as Proposition 209, founded by Glynn Custred and Thomas Wood. Custred and Wood developed their arguments against affirmative action by adopting a strict reading of Title VII of the Civil Rights Act of 1964 and the Fourteenth Amendment of the U.S. Constitution in order to protect whites rather than African Americans, the original target group. Part of Connerly's strategy was to call affirmative action programs "racial preferences," which have historically been objectionable even to those who support affirmative action or diversity. In his autobiography *Creating Equal: My Fight against Race Preferences*, Connerly defines "preference" as a "commitment to put a certain number of black and ethnic students into the university, even if their admission meant discriminating against those who were better qualified."

Connerly became a frequent guest on radio and television programs as a champion of civil and equal rights in order to push his anti–affirmative action agenda. In 1996, Proposition 209 passed with a 54 percent vote, prohibiting discrimination and preferential treatment in state and local governments and other public entities. Opponents accused Connerly of manipulating the image and language of the civil rights movement in order to mislead voters. After the passage of Proposition 209, the controversy continued when some voters claimed that they did not realize the measure would end affirmative action.

The following year in 1997, Connerly founded the American Civil Rights Institute and American Civil Rights Coalition to expand his anti–affirmative action campaign on a national level. He helped to fund and organize the Washington Initiative 200 (I-200) in 1998 and the Michigan Civil Rights Initiative (Michigan Proposal 2) in 2004, both of which were successful in abolishing affirmative action, referred to as race and gender preferences.

Connerly continued his campaign in 2003 when he placed Proposition 54 on the California ballot to prohibit the state from classifying individuals according to race, ethnicity, or national origin. Critics opposed Proposition 54, also called the Racial Privacy Initiative, based on the difficulties it would impose on the collection of data regarding health and medicine, as well as on the tracking of racism in the areas of housing and racial profiling. Californians did not pass Proposition 54.

Connerly's efforts to change public policy have garnered the support of the Republican Party and the financial backing of neoconservative foundations and think tanks such as the Lynde and Harry Bradley, John M. Olin, and Heritage foundations.

[*See also* Affirmative Action *and* Conservatism and Conservatives, Black.]

BIBLIOGRAPHY

Chávez, Lydia. *The Color Bind: California's Battle to End Affirmative Action*. Berkeley: University of California Press, 1998. Details the relationship between Ward Connerly and the California Civil Rights Initiative.

Connerly, Ward. *Creating Equal: My Fight against Race Preferences*. San Francisco: Encounter Books, 2000. Connerly's own narrative about his upbringing and his views on race.

—LA TASHA B. LEVY

CONSERVATISM AND CONSERVATIVES, BLACK. Black conservatism is a political ideology that presents an alternative to the traditional liberalism of African American political culture. Although African Americans are usually considered to be social conservatives, their politics—characterized by an ongoing struggle for freedom and racial equality—have traditionally fallen on the left side of the political spectrum.

The rise of black conservatives in the post–civil rights era is directly connected with the election of the Republican Ronald Reagan in 1980. Reagan's presidency represented the triumph of the New Right, a radical resurgence of conservative politics that advanced an anti–civil rights platform that sought to erode civil rights legislation and delegitimize the quest for racial justice and equality. Despite the racism that was associated with Ronald Reagan's presidential campaign, he attracted a small margin of black supporters who were disillusioned with the unfulfilled promises of the Democratic Party. Reagan reached out to black conservatives in order to cultivate what he hoped would be a new black leadership to challenge traditional civil rights leaders. Prior to Reagan, President Richard Nixon also attempted to court a new black leadership in the 1970s, particularly among Black Power advocates. However, Reagan was more successful, partly because of the Fairmont Conference, which helped to facilitate the Republican Party's outreach to conservative blacks. In the twenty-first century, the Republican Party turned to black ministers and megachurches to garner support among African Americans by making socially conservative issues, such as gay marriage, central in the political debate.

The Fairmont Conference. In 1980 the Institute for Contemporary Studies convened the Black Alternatives Conference at the Fairmont Hotel in San Francisco, California. Commonly referred to as the "Fairmont Conference," this event laid the foundation for an oppositional movement among conservative African Americans of the far right. Supported by Edwin Meese III, a white conservative, who resigned as the director of the Institute for Contemporary Studies to join Ronald Reagan's administration, the conference represented a shift from moderate black Republicanism to a brand that was more extreme in its opposition to the civil rights legacy. Henry Lucas Jr., Meese's successor as the director of the institute, and Thomas Sowell, a senior fellow of the conservative Hoover Institution, invited a diverse group of African Americans who were interested in formulating alternative solutions to the crises among the black, urban poor, a group whose conditions were deteriorating alongside the growth of a black middle class.

Conference participants included the economist Walter Williams, Martin Kilson, Tony Brown, Clarence Pendleton Jr., and the lawyer Clarence Thomas. Although Kilson made a presentation at the Fairmont Conference, he later became an ardent critic of black conservatives. Other participants included liberals with alternative ideas such as Percy Sutton and Charles V. Hamilton. Henry Lucas Jr. implored President Reagan to look to this group for new strategies. In fact, Reagan ultimately appointed Walter Williams, Clarence Pendleton Jr., and Clarence Thomas to key positions in his new administration. The conference participants were diverse, but they all shared a belief in the alleged failure of civil rights legislation and social programs, such as the War on Poverty, to address the crisis among the black poor. Many of the participants believed that social programs and the expansion of the welfare state actually created or exacerbated the crisis.

Participants of the Fairmont Conference were optimistic that Reagan's economic agenda and his opposition to the welfare state would benefit African Americans and break what they believed was a cycle of dependency. The conference papers proposed free-market approaches, entrepreneurship, community control, individual choice, school vouchers, and diverse party affiliation as alternative solutions. The participants believed that the focus should be "opportunity" rather than "equality." Once African Americans have equal opportunity, the participants asserted, which is guaranteed by the United States Constitution, they must rely on their own individual efforts to achieve equality. The participants did not offer a critique of capitalism or institutional practices of racism.

The Fairmont Conference was a historic event that propelled a network of black conservatives, prompting the creation of conservative organizations, journals, and scores of articles and books. Black conservative organizations include the Lincoln Institute for Research and Education, Project 21, the Center for New Black Leadership, and the Black Political Action Committee. Among the most popular black conservative magazines are the *Lincoln Review* and *Headway*, formerly known as *National Minority Politics*. Although the conference began as a dialogue on alternative solutions to the conditions of the black poor, over time many of the contributors abandoned this position in favor of color blindness and rugged individualism. Black conservatives assume that these policies will force African Americans to fend for themselves and prove that they are equal to whites.

The Rise of "New" Black Conservatives. The Fairmont Conference set the parameters that gave rise to a cadre of "new" black conservatives. Through the support of Ronald Reagan and the funding of conservative think tanks and foundations like the Hoover Institution, the American Enterprise Institute, the Manhattan Institute, the Heritage Foundation, the John M. Olin Foundation, and the Lynde and Harry Bradley Foundation, black conservatives have become central voices in the racial discourse.

Since the 1980s black conservatives have split into two groups. The first group is composed of traditional black conservatives who have gained visibility in the Republican Party. Most notable is George W. Bush's administration, which included Colin Powell as secretary of state and Condoleezza Rice, first as national security adviser and then as secretary of state. This group of black conservatives prefers minimal government regulation, yet they typically acknowledge the significance of racism and generally support affirmative action. The second group is more extreme and is often referred to as representing "black neoconservatism." Black neoconservatives have gained popularity in the media because they often defame civil rights leaders and ridicule black culture and politics. Black neoconservatives downplay charges of white racism and often accuse African Americans of perpetuating "reverse racism." Although there is a spectrum of black conservatism that ranges from moderate to extreme, the terms "black conservative" and "black neoconservative" are often used interchangeably to refer to the emergence of "new" black conservatives as a visible collective in the public domain.

In the post–civil rights era, black conservatives can also be divided into four categories: (1) public intellectuals, such as Thomas Sowell, Shelby Steele, Carol M. Swain, and John McWhorter; (2) media commentators or cultural critics, such as Armstrong Williams, Larry Elder, and Stanley Crouch; (3) civic activists, such as Ward Connerly, Star Parker, Robert Woodson, and Jay A. Parker; and

(4) government officials, such as the Supreme Court justice Clarence Thomas.

Major Tenets. Though black conservatives sometimes hold divergent stances, there are at least ten identifiable tenets that characterize black conservative ideology:

1. rugged individualism
2. free-market economics and entrepreneurship
3. color blindness and rejection both of race consciousness and oftentimes of racial identity
4. hostility toward government intervention, particularly affirmative action and welfare; such intervention is seen as central to the promotion of dependency and victimization
5. contempt for traditional black leadership, especially civil rights leaders such as Jesse Jackson, Congresswoman Maxine Waters, and the Congressional Black Caucus
6. antipathy for the black poor and their allegedly debased culture and lack of values
7. the belief that racism is no longer responsible for the stifling economic, political, and social conditions among African Americans
8. the belief that the post–civil rights era is one of unlimited opportunities and of congenial racial attitudes among whites
9. the belief that self-help and personal responsibility are the only solutions to the nation's racial disparities
10. the belief that a victim-oriented identity, often referred to as "victimhood" and "victimology," exaggerates racism and masks low self-esteem and fear of competing with whites

These premises and political positions are consistent themes in the black conservative books that have been popularized in the post–civil rights era. In addition to promoting these tenets, popular books among black conservatives are heavily dependent on autobiographical sketches. They use their personal stories to unveil what they claim is the truth regarding black cultural deficiencies, immorality, anti-intellectualism, and forced racial conformity. These personal stories also legitimize anti-black rhetoric and political stances.

Black conservatives are important participants in the ideological war that has been waged in popular media, universities, and think tanks regarding racism and the validity of African American claims to justice and equality. Unlike the conservative individuals of the past, black conservatives have organized as a collective. They often cite each other's work, they receive fellowships from the same core of conservative think tanks and foundations, and they have initiated numerous publications and organizations to espouse their beliefs. Though they have a limited following among the vast majority of African Americans, black conservatives claim to speak for the "silent majority." Nevertheless, the success of black conservatives rests in their relationship with white conservative patrons.

[*See also* Bush, George W., Administration of; Reagan, Ronald, Administration of; Republican Party; *and biographical entries on figures mentioned in this article*.]

Bibliography

Anderson, Bernard E., et al. *The Fairmont Papers: Black Alternatives Conference, San Francisco, December 1980*. San Francisco: Institute for Contemporary Studies, 1981. A compilation of papers presented at the historic Fairmont Conference.

Bonilla-Silva, Eduardo. *White Supremacy and Racism in the Post–Civil Rights Era*. Boulder, Colo.: Lynne Rienner, 2001. Provides a valuable analysis of the various definitions of racism and the role and function of color blindness.

Conti, Joseph G., and Brad Stetson. *Challenging the Civil Rights Establishment: Profiles of a New Black Vanguard*. Westport, Conn.: Praeger, 1993. One of the few monographs on black conservative ideology by conservatives.

Faryna, Stan, Brad Stetson, and Joseph G. Conti, eds. *Black and Right: The Bold New Voice of Black Conservatives in America*. Westport, Conn.: Praeger, 1997. A collection of essays by black conservatives describing their beliefs and experiences; includes an essay by the Supreme Court justice Clarence Thomas and an interview with the journalist Larry Elder.

Reed, Adolph, Jr., ed. *Without Justice for All: The New Liberalism and Our Retreat from Racial Equality*. Boulder, Colo.: Westview Press, 1999. A collection of essays documenting the new political terrain of neoliberalism and racial inequality.

Tate, Gayle T., and Lewis A. Randolph, eds. *Dimensions of Black Conservatism in the United States: Made in America*. New York: Palgrave, 2002. An overview of black conservatism in America from the late nineteenth century on.

Walters, Ronald W. *White Nationalism, Black Interests: Conservative Public Policy and the Black Community*. Detroit, Mich.: Wayne State University Press, 2003. Public policy in the post–civil rights era and white resistance to the civil rights legacy; chapter 9 is a discussion of black conservatives.

—La TaSha B. Levy

CONSTITUTION, U.S. The U.S. Constitution has been both a curse and a blessing to African Americans. Numerous clauses in the original Constitution directly affect blacks; although four amendments were added to protect black rights, they also protected the rights of other Americans. The specific language of these many constitutional provisions has been interpreted and implemented by the courts, the Congress, the executive branch, and the states. The original Constitution contained a series of clauses to protect the interest of masters in their slaves and prevent states from emancipating fugitive slaves. Although the proslavery Constitution of the antebellum period did not specifically regulate race relations, the overwhelming majority—95 percent in 1860— of all blacks in the nation were held as slaves. Moreover, in *Dred Scott v. Sandford* (1857) the Supreme Court held that free blacks had no rights under the Constitution, could not ever be considered citizens of the United States, and could not use the courts of the United States to vindicate their rights.

The Civil War led to three new amendments to the Constitution—the Thirteenth (1865), Fourteenth (1868), and Fifteenth (1870)—that permanently altered the status of African Americans, freeing them from slavery, guaranteeing them citizenship and equality, and giving them the right to vote on the same basis as whites. From 1865 to the mid-1870s Congress and the executive branch helped implement these amendments, as blacks began to participate in politics at the local, state, and national levels, while many accumulated property and hundreds of thousands gained access to literacy. Starting in the mid-1870s blacks in the South—where some 95 percent of all blacks still lived—began to see their rights taken away by an aggressive white majority. The Supreme Court usually supported these efforts. Republican presidents tried, with mixed enthusiasm and little success, to protect black rights, but as northern Republicans lost control of Congress it became impossible to vindicate the rights promised in the new amendments. In the 1880s and 1890s northern states passed civil rights laws that at least on paper protected black rights, but these laws offered no protection to the overwhelming majority of African Americans, who lived in the South.

From *Plessy* to World War I. In 1896 the Supreme Court gave its blessing to the emerging regime of segregation, upholding Louisiana's railroad segregation law in *Plessy v. Ferguson*. Reading this decision as a green light to eviscerate black rights, the southern states effectively segregated, isolated, and disfranchised almost all blacks. Generally denied access to education, capital, political power, the jury box, and higher-paying jobs, southern blacks were increasingly forced into poverty, with few rights and little political power.

The Fourteenth Amendment presumably prohibited segregation with language declaring that "No state shall ... deny to any person within its jurisdiction the equal protection of the laws." At first glance it would seem that segregated facilities represented a denial of this equal protection. In *Plessy*, however, the Court found that "equal protection" could be satisfied if separate facilities were "equal." Thus, in the case of Homer Plessy, state-mandated segregation in railroad cars was permissible if the railroad cars for blacks were substantially the same as those for whites.

Similarly, although the Fifteenth Amendment prohibited denial of the vote "on account of race, color, or previous condition of servitude," the Supreme Court interpreted the Constitution to allow states to deny many blacks the right to vote on other grounds. States could not boldly declare that blacks or the descendants of slaves could not vote. Nor could states predicate the right to vote on circumstances that were unavailable to blacks because of their race or their heritage of being slaves. Thus, in *Guinn v. United States* (1915) the U.S. Supreme Court struck down an Oklahoma law that exempted from a required literacy test all voters who would have been able to vote had they been adults in 1867 or any adult men who were the legal descendants of people who could vote in 1867. This grandfather clause enfranchised all white men without requiring them to take a literacy test, while denying the vote to blacks unless they could pass such a test. The Supreme Court unanimously struck down the law on the ground that it violated the Fifteenth Amendment because it in effect denied blacks an equal right to vote on the basis of their race and the previous condition of servitude of their fathers and grandfathers.

The Oklahoma statute was so blatantly directed at blacks that the Court easily overturned it. But the emerging interpretation of the Constitution allowed numerous other restrictions on voting that were not, on their face, directed at blacks. The Court narrowly construed the Fifteenth Amendment to prohibit blatant discrimination in voting on the basis of race, but not to prohibit laws that had the effect of preventing blacks from voting. Thus, courts approved literacy tests, complicated residency and registration requirements, poll taxes, and felony disfranchisement. The result was that by the beginning of World War I black voting was insignificant in the seventeen southern states. Similarly, those states segregated blacks in schools and all other public facilities on the basis of the Equal Protection Clause and also either allowed or required all private institutions and businesses to practice segregation.

Illustrative of this trend was the Supreme Court's decision in *Berea College v. Kentucky* (1908). Berea was a private college with an integrated student body. A 1904 Kentucky law prohibited integrated education, even in private settings. The Court upheld Kentucky's right to regulate colleges in this manner as a legitimate "police power" of the state.

On the eve of World War I the rights of African Americans under the Constitution had become limited and constrained. The separate-but-equal doctrine seemed like an amendment to the Fourteenth Amendment, virtually annulling the meaning of the phrase "equal protection of the laws." On top of this, Congress and the executive branch increasingly accepted the constitutional theory of states' rights. This was not the antebellum notion that the states could overrule federal law (although the South would revive this argument in the 1950s and 1960s). Rather, it was an understanding that the states had the right to regulate their social and political institutions as long as they did not blatantly contradict the Constitution. One illustration of this is the regulation of voting. Although the Fifteenth Amendment empowered Congress to pass laws to protect black voting rights, supporters of civil rights were never able to muster a majority in both houses of Congress to accomplish this. Thus the regulation of voting remained entirely in the hands of the states, except when state laws blatantly discriminated against voters solely on the basis of their race.

From World War I to World War II. World War I and the Great Depression profoundly altered American race relations. During this period millions of blacks moved out of the South and into the Northeast and Midwest, doubling the percentage of blacks in those areas. In 1910 the Midwest had a black population of about 540,000, but by 1940 this figure had grown to 1.4 million; in the Northeast the black population increased from about 480,000 to more than 1.3 million. In the South the percentage of blacks decreased while the actual number of blacks barely rose. Blacks headed north for the promise of better jobs, greater educational opportunity, and the chance to escape segregation, racial oppression, and lynching. The North was hardly perfect, but there was some respect for constitutional rights. Throughout the North blacks could vote without harassment or intimidation. In a number of cities they held public office, and in 1928 Oscar De Priest of Chicago became the first African American elected to Congress from the North. Most of the northern states had civil rights laws that guaranteed equal access to schools, restaurants, hotels, theaters, and other places of public accommodation. Enforcement of these laws varied, and was imperfect at best. But in many ways the northern states recognized and implemented their constitutional obligations through the adoption of these state civil rights laws.

The growing political power of blacks in the North slightly altered the constitutional politics of the era. These changes were also tied to the emergence of the NAACP as a force for lobbying and litigation. In the 1930s Congressman De Priest proposed legislation to allow black defendants to remove their trials to other states if they felt they could not get a fair trial where they were. This bill, which struck directly at the notion of states rights, never got out of committee. But it was the beginning of a movement to provide for federal enforcement to protect fundamental constitutional rights. De Priest proposed a federal antilynching bill, which also was buried in committee. Similar bills would fail throughout the decade, as southerners in Congress contended that regulation of criminal acts—such as lynching—was purely a state matter but also argued that lynching was a popular and almost legitimate response to black crime.

The Court in this period slowly began to alter its understanding of the constitutional rights of blacks. In *Buchanan v. Warley* (1917) it struck down a local ordinance from Louisville, Kentucky, that had prohibited blacks from buying property on blocks where there was a white majority or whites buying property where there was a black majority. The goal of the statute was to create wholly segregated neighborhoods. This was as much a property case as one involving civil rights, but the Court's ruling indicated that it was ready to take a new look at the constitutional rights of blacks. However, the Court's understanding of the nature of law and race remained limited. In *Corrigan v. Buckley* (1926) it upheld the right of private parties to refuse to sell land to blacks. The Court insisted that private discrimination did not violate the Constitution, because the Fourteenth Amendment only limited state action.

In *Moore v. Dempsey* (1923) the Supreme Court overturned the convictions of a number of blacks after proceedings that could barely be called trials. The defendants had been victims of a race riot in which many blacks, and one white, died. Not only was no one charged for attacking the blacks but the victims themselves were also tried and convicted by all-white juries after witnesses had been whipped and otherwise intimidated into testifying against the defendants. During the trials mobs surrounded the courthouse and threatened to kill jurors who voted for acquittal. The appointed counsel for all the defendants called no witnesses and did not ask for a change of venue. The first trial lasted only forty-five minutes and it took the jury five minutes to convict all the defendants. In *Powell v. Alabama* (1932) the Court overturned the convictions of the Scottsboro Boys, a group of black youths accused (unfairly as it turned out) of raping two white girls. The Court found that the trials, like those in Moore, lacked minimal fairness. Similarly, in *Brown v. Mississippi* (1936) the Court overturned convictions of black tenant farmers because the defendants had been brutally beaten and whipped until they confessed to crimes they did not commit. In *Norris v. Alabama* (1935) and *Smith v. Texas* (1940) it overturned convictions because blacks were systematically excluded from both petit and grand juries. In *Chambers v. Florida* (1940) the Court overturned another set of convictions based on coerced convictions.

These cases showed an emerging understanding of the Constitution that local law and states' rights were limited by notions of due process. In *Chambers* the state of Florida argued that the U.S. courts had no jurisdiction over the state's criminal jurisprudence and that if a state court approved the police procedures, including the "third-degree" questioning of witnesses and defendants, the federal courts could not interfere. The Supreme Court emphatically rejected this analysis. During this period the Court did not reject all claims of states' rights. Moreover, it did not directly confront southern segregation. But in cases involving torture of prisoners, the utter lack of due process, segregated juries, and the lack of effective counsel the Court began to see the Constitution in a new light.

The meaning of the Fifteenth Amendment remained uncertain in this period. Federal law and the Supreme Court generally allowed the states to set their own rules for running elections. Throughout the South blacks were kept from the polls through various restrictions on voter registration that were not directly related to race. Literacy tests, for example, were ostensibly racially neutral, but given the poor state of black education in the South far more blacks than whites could not read. Even where blacks could vote, their ballots in the general election were often meaningless because in the one-party South of the period the real election was in the Democratic primary. Thus, to make sure that the few blacks who could vote had no political influence, states passed laws preventing blacks from voting in the primaries. In *Nixon v. Herndon* (1927) the Court ruled that a state could not prohibit blacks from voting in the primaries any more than they could for the general election. In response to this decision a new Texas statute provided that the parties would be free to set their own membership. The Texas Democratic Party then declared that only whites could be members of the party, and thus only whites could vote in the primary. In *Nixon v. Condon* (1932) the Court ruled that this too violated the Constitution. The state could not delegate to a political party what the Constitution prohibited the state from doing directly. This did not end the problem, however. The Texas legislature then passed an act that completely divorced the state from all regulation of primary elections. The parties were now completely private organizations, and their primaries were nothing more than the election of officers in a private club. In *Grovey v. Townsend* (1935) the Court found that this arrangement did not violate the Constitution because no state action was involved. Blacks in Texas were once again prevented from voting in the primaries. In *United States v. Classic* (1941), a case involving vote fraud in Louisiana, the Court held that citizens had a fundamental right to vote, even in primaries. *Classic* did not involve race or race discrimination, but it set the stage for a rethinking of what the Constitution meant. Finally, in *Smith v. Allwright* (1944) the Court held that even if the Texas Democratic Party was a private organization it could not prohibit blacks from voting in the primary, because this violated the Fifteenth Amendment.

The decision in *Smith v. Allwright* set the stage for ending the white primary in the South. More important, it led to a new understanding of the meaning of the Constitution. The case considerably narrowed the line between private and public action. Moreover, the Court found that the Fifteenth Amendment's language was broad enough to be read as requiring that any election be open to all people without regard to race. The amendment provided that the right to vote could not be "abridged by the United States or by any State on account of race, color, or previous condition of servitude." In *Grovey v. Townsend* the Court had concluded that this language could not regulate a private organization, such as the Democratic Party. But a decade later the Court had a new understanding of what it meant to vote. Essentially, the Court now understood that the state could not abdicate its responsibility to maintain fair and racially neutral elections by withdrawing from the process of running primaries.

From the beginning of World War I to the end of World War II segregation remained fully legal. The states had the right to regulate race as they chose. In *Gong Lum v. Rice* (1927), for example, the Court sustained a Mississippi law that assigned Chinese American children to attend school with blacks. The Constitution—as interpreted by the Courts, supported by the Congress, and generally understood by most Americans—allowed the states to regulate race, separate the races, and segregate society, as long as the fiction of "separate but equal" was maintained. However, there was an important caveat in this understanding: where Congress had specific power it could override state segregation. In *Mitchell v. United States* (1941) the Court held that the states could not segregate passengers on interstate trains because the power to regulate interstate commerce was an entirely national power and Congress had never authorized segregation of railroad cars. Significantly, this civil rights victory was rooted not in the Civil War amendments to the Constitution but in the Commerce Clause, which gave Congress exclusive power to regulate all interstate commerce.

The Postwar Period to the Age of Equality. World War II altered the way Americans thought about race and civil rights. The war against Nazi and Japanese racism forced Americans to rethink their own racial ideology. The stench of Buchenwald and the bloody streets after the Rape of Nanking taught most Americans that racism could lead to places that were too horrible to contemplate. The Cold War also led Americans to reconsider their own racial views. The United States could hardly compete with Communist ideology and Soviet propaganda if the colored peoples of the world were constantly seeing images of racism, segregation, and lynching. The war also altered how Americans understood the Constitution and the powers of Congress. A strong national government had been necessary to combat the Great Depression and German and Japanese militarism. States' rights had been undermined by the exigencies of economic collapse in the 1930s and war in the 1940s. Americans now saw their

Constitution in a new light, as giving the federal government the power to regulate race relations, just as it could regulate the economy and mobilize the nation to win a world war. Equally important, African Americans were empowered as millions of black men and women returned home from military service. The war years also saw an accelerated movement of blacks out of the South and to the urban North, where they gained new political power and influence. Between 1940 and 1950 the black population of the South grew by only 300,000, while the combined growth of blacks in the rest of the nation was nearly 2 million. This was due to vast out-migration, as the percentage of blacks decreased in the South while it rose throughout the rest of the nation. Changing demographics, shifts in political power, and the importance of black veterans all affected how American understood their Constitution. Spearheading these changes in constitutional thought was the NAACP Legal Defense and Educational Fund, which began to challenge segregation and the prevailing interpretation of the Constitution.

During the war the Supreme Court heard a series of cases involving the internment of American citizens of Japanese ancestry. In *Hirabayashi v. United States* (1943) the Court upheld curfew for Japanese Americans, with sharp language from some of the judges condemning the race discrimination. In a concurrence that read more like a dissent, Justice Frank Murphy noted that this was "the first time" the Court had ever "sustained a substantial restriction of the personal liberty of citizens of the United States based on the accident of race or ancestry" and that such a policy went to the "very brink of constitutional power." In *Korematsu v. United States* (1944) the Court upheld the constitutionality of the internment, but Justice Hugo Black declared that "all legal restrictions which curtail the civil rights of a single racial group are immediately suspect" and that such restrictions should face "the most rigid scrutiny."

The Japanese-internment cases, which did not involve blacks, set the stage for the dismantling of segregation. In these decisions the Court said that race discrimination was constitutionally permissible only under the most dire circumstances, when issues of war, peace, or national security were at issue. Racial segregation of blacks could never meet this standard or survive the test of "rigid scrutiny."

Even before World War II the understanding of constitutional rights had begun to change, as the Court chipped away at segregation in cases involving railroads and criminal due process. In *Missouri ex rel. Gaines v. Canada* (1938) the Court had also taken a first tentative step toward putting teeth into the "equal" element of the separate-but-equal doctrine. Lloyd Gaines, a black resident of Missouri, had been denied admission to the University of Missouri School of Law solely because he was black. Missouri offered to pay for Gaines to attend a law school in a neighboring state that allowed integrated education, but this was not constitutionally sufficient. The Court did not reject the idea of segregation in *Gaines*, but created a precedent that, when expanded a decade later, would force the southern states to integrate their graduate and professional schools.

In the decade immediately after the war the Court began a move toward a revolution in constitutional thought. By 1950 segregation would be under assault from a series of court decisions brought about by aggressive NAACP-sponsored litigation and aided by a southern president—Harry S. Truman—who had little tolerance for race discrimination. Following on the *Gaines* decision the Court held that the "equal" prong actually had a substantive constitutional meaning. In *Sweatt v. Painter* (1950) it held that a recently created law school for blacks was not "equal" to the famous and well-funded University of Texas School of Law, which was therefore required to accept blacks because they could never get an "equal" education at a segregated institution. In other cases the Court forced the integration of the law school and the graduate school of education of the University of Oklahoma.

The higher-education cases put a new spin on the meaning of "equal protection" under the Fourteenth Amendment by requiring the separate-but-equal facilities to be actually equal, and if the state could not make them equal (as in the Texas law school case) then they could not be separate. An equally significant change occurred in the Court's interpretation of the Commerce Clause. In *Morgan v. Virginia* (1946) the Court overturned a Virginia law that required segregated seating in interstate buses on the grounds that this violated Congress's power to regulate interstate commerce. In a similar decision, *Bob-Lo Excursion Co. v. Michigan* (1948), the Court refused to interfere with a Michigan state court's decision banning segregation on a ferry that went from Detroit to Canada. The ferry owners argued that the Michigan law was an unconstitutional interference with Congress's power over commerce, just as Virginia's law requiring segregation on buses interfered with interstate commerce. However, the Court did not accept this argument, demonstrating that a new constitutional understanding was now in place. The default position in constitutional law now favored equality and clearly disfavored segregation and discrimination. Thus, under the Commerce Clause a state was free to require equality, as Michigan had, but was not free to require segregation, as Virginia had. Presumably, Congress could have passed laws either allowing or mandating segregation in interstate transportation, but it did not do so and there was no possibility that it would do so. The final step in this process was taken in *Henderson v. United States* (1950), in which the Court held that the Interstate Commerce Commission must provide black railroad passengers with the same opportunity to eat in dining cars that white passengers had. Railroads could not have, as the Southern Railway had, only a limited number of tables for black passengers and more tables for whites. Under this ruling all dining facilities had to be open to all passengers on a first-come, first-served basis.

The cases involving interstate transportation fundamentally altered the meaning of the Constitution. In *Hall v. DeCuir* (1878) the Court struck down a Reconstruction-era Louisiana law that had required integration on all trains in the state. The Court said this interfered with interstate commerce because it meant that trains passing through states that required segregation (such as Mississippi) would have to segregate passengers when the trains left Louisiana. In reaching this result the Court had made segregation the default position under the Constitution.

A Revolution in Constitutional Thought. On the last day of its 1953–1954 term, in May, the Supreme Court decided *Brown v. Board of Education*, holding that "in the field of public education the doctrine of 'separate-but-equal' has no place. Separate educational facilities are inherently unequal." This decision did not technically overturn the separate-but-equal doctrine in all areas of law. But it set the stage for a revolution in how the Constitution was understood. After 1954 the Supreme Court never again upheld any segregation statute. The Court now read the provision in the Fourteenth Amendment requiring "equal protection of the laws" to mean that law could not be used to discriminate against racial minorities. In the next ten years the Court would strike down scores of statutes designed to segregate. It would also overturn the convictions of civil rights demonstrators who challenged public and private segregation.

The *Brown* decision did not lead to an immediate end to segregation, and ultimately some southern states would delay integration for more than a decade through pupil-placement schemes, "freedom of choice" programs that allowed parents to choose which schools their children would attend, and in parts of Virginia simply closing down the public school systems. The aftermath of the case illustrates the limits of the Constitution to change society. The irony of *Brown* is that, although it led to a wholesale reconception of the meaning of the Constitution and an end to formal segregation everywhere in the country, it did not lead to school integration in much of the country. Throughout the South politicians and white civic leaders denounced the decision as a violation of states' rights and constitutional principles. But such claims had little support in the rest of the nation, and even in the South some whites were beginning to realize that segregation must somehow come to an end.

The Court was not the only institution of government that focused on constitutional change. In 1957 Congress passed a civil rights act with limited power. In August 1962 Congress approved what would become the Twenty-fourth Amendment, which was ratified by the states in January 1964. It prohibited the collection of poll taxes for voting in federal elections. The fact that the amendment applied only to federal elections showed the tentative nature of Congress's movement toward equality and its continued deference to states' rights.

In the summer of 1964, in the wake of the assassination of President John F. Kennedy and after years of demonstrations in the South and violence against demonstrators, Congress passed a sweeping civil rights act that prohibited private discrimination in public accommodations, such as restaurants, hotels, and theaters. Congress had attempted to do this nearly a century earlier, with the Civil Rights Act of 1875. However, in *Civil Rights Cases* (1883) the Court struck down this law, asserting that the Fourteenth Amendment did not allow Congress to regulate "private" behavior. In dissent Justice John Marshall Harlan argued that, because restaurants, hotels, theaters, and other public facilities were regulated by the state, segregation in them—even if practiced by private parties—violated the Fourteenth Amendment. The Court, however, rejected this theory, arguing that the Fourteenth Amendment only limited "state action."

In the 1964 Civil Rights Act Congress effectively avoided the state-action doctrine by asserting that it was prohibiting most private discrimination under the Commerce Clause because restaurants, hotels, and other public accommodations engaged in interstate commerce and thus could be regulated by Congress. The Court upheld this theory of the Constitution in *Katzenbach v. McClung* (1964) and *Heart of Atlanta Motel v. United States* (1964). A year later Congress used its enforcement power under the Fifteenth Amendment to pass the Voting Rights Act of 1965, which the Court upheld in *South Carolina v. Katzenbach* (1966). That year the Court also held, in *Harper v. Virginia State Board of Elections* (1966), that poll taxes in state elections were unconstitutional because they violated the equal-protection clause of the Fourteenth Amendment. In *Loving v. Virginia* (1967) the Court applied this clause to the last remaining area of legal race discrimination, striking down a Virginia law that banned interracial marriage. A year later, following the assassination of Martin Luther King Jr., Congress passed the Open Housing Act of 1968, to eliminate discrimination in housing.

Beyond the Civil Rights Movement. Between 1870 and 1970 there was only one formal amendment to the Constitution that was designed to protect black civil rights: the Twenty-fourth Amendment, which banned poll taxes in federal elections. There was, however, a revolution in how the Courts, Congress, the executive branch, and the public understood the Constitution. The words of the document had not changed, but its interpretation had. This change resulted partly from factors that had little to do with race. The revolution in Commerce-Clause jurisprudence that took place during the Great Depression led to a huge increase in the ability of Congress to regulate not only the economy but also the larger society. Thus, Congress relied on its commerce powers, as well as the Fourteenth Amendment, to pass the 1964 Civil Rights Act.

Since 1970 the Courts and Congress have focused on numerous areas of civil rights, including affirmative action, minority set-asides, and the creation of congressional districts with black majorities. These issues have led to complex interpretations of equal protection and due process. Sometimes supporters of these programs have won, sometimes they have not. Whatever the outcome of these cases and legislative issues, they have all been fought under the post-*Brown* Constitution, which recognizes that race discrimination has no place in the U.S. Constitution. Supporters or opponents of affirmative action, for example, all agree that race discrimination is unconstitutional. They disagree on the nature of specific programs—specifically, whether affirmative action ends discrimination or results in reverse discrimination. Although courts often decide these issues on narrow and technical grounds, all the debates are predicated on the assumption that the U.S. Constitution does not support or protect race discrimination. In this sense the nation witnessed a constitutional revolution in the third quarter of the twentieth century, and that constitutional revolution remains very much in place.

[*See also Brown v. Board of Education*; *Buchanan v. Warley*; Civil Rights; Jim Crow Laws; Judges and the Judiciary; Laws and Legislation; *Loving v. Virginia; Missouri ex rel. Gaines v. Canada*; *Plessy v. Ferguson* and Segregation; *Smith v. Allwright*; Supreme Court; *Sweatt v. Painter; and* Voting Rights.]

BIBLIOGRAPHY

Bass, Jack. *Unlikely Heroes: The Dramatic Story of the Southern Judges of the Fifth Circuit Who Translated the Supreme Court's Brown Decision into a Revolution for Equality*. Tuscaloosa: University of Alabama Press, 1981.

Belknap, Michal R. *Federal Law and Southern Order: Racial Violence and Constitutional Conflict in the Post-"Brown" South*. Athens: University of Georgia Press, 1987.

Belsky, Martin H., ed. *The Rehnquist Court: A Retrospective*. New York: Oxford University Press, 2002.

Chin, Gabriel J., ed. *Affirmative Action and the Constitution*. 3 vols. New York: Garland, 1998.

Cottrol, Robert J., Raymond T. Diamond, and Leland B. Ware. *"Brown v. Board of Education": Caste, Culture, and the Constitution*. Lawrence: University Press of Kansas, 2003.

Douglas, Davison M. *Jim Crow Moves North: The Battle over Northern School Segregation, 1865–1954*. New York: Cambridge University Press, 2005.

Finkelman, Paul. "Civil Rights in Historical Context: Why *Brown* Really Was Correct." *Harvard Law Review* 118 (2005): 973–1027.

Horwitz, Morton J. *The Warren Court and the Pursuit of Justice: A Critical Issue*. New York: Hill and Wang, 1998.

Klarman, Michael J. *From Jim Crow to Civil Rights: The Supreme Court and the Struggle for Racial Equality*. New York: Oxford University Press, 2004.

Kluger, Richard. *Simple Justice: The History of "Brown v. Board of Education" and Black America's Struggle for Equality*. New York: Alfred A. Knopf, 1976.

Tushnet, Mark V. *Making Civil Rights Law: Thurgood Marshall and the Supreme Court, 1936–1961*. New York: Oxford University Press, 1994.

Tushnet, Mark V. *The NAACP's Legal Struggle against Segregated Education, 1925–1950*. Chapel Hill: University of North Carolina Press, 1987.

Urofsky, Melvin I., and Paul Finkelman. *A March of Liberty: A Constitutional History of the United States*. 2d ed. 2 vols. New York: Oxford University Press, 2002.

—PAUL FINKELMAN

CONYERS, JOHN (b. 16 May 1929), U.S. congressman since 1965 who has been distinguished during his long career as a leading advocate for human rights and civil rights in the United States. Born and raised in Detroit, Michigan, John Conyers Jr. graduated from Northwestern High School in Detroit and then served in the Michigan National Guard (1948–1950) and the U.S. Army (1950–1954). During his time in the army he served in Korea as an officer in the U.S. Army Corps of Engineers. Back in Michigan he acquired his BA in 1957 and his law degree in 1958, both from Wayne State University in Detroit. Before winning office in 1964 as a representative from Michigan, Conyers, a Democrat, worked as an assistant for the Democratic Michigan congressman John Dingell. As of 2008 Conyers and Dingell were the two longest-serving members of the U.S. House of Representatives.

During his tenure Conyers rose to the status of highest-ranking Democrat on the House Judiciary Committee and was the first African American to chair the committee. He was also a founding and leading member of the Congressional Black Caucus. Rosa Parks, one of the preeminent figures of the civil rights movement, served on his staff for more than twenty years. Conyers's importance as a legislator was ratified when President Richard Nixon included him on his "enemies list."

As a strong advocate for the African American community, the labor movement, and an array of other human rights and civil rights causes in the United States, Conyers is widely considered to be the most progressive member of Congress. He has consistently opposed U.S. military intervention around the world, including the U.S. occupation of Iraq in 2003. He was a strong advocate for the anti-apartheid movement, opposing U.S. government and corporate support for the racist white government of the Republic of South Africa during the 1970s and 1980s. He also opposed the U.S. military intervention in 1983 in the tiny Caribbean island of Grenada.

Conyers's legislative record includes his leadership and sponsorship on key civil rights measures, including the National Voter Registration Act, the Racial Justice Act, the Police Accountability Act, and the Hate Crime Statistics Act. In the 1980s he held national hearings on police brutality and put the New York mayor Edward I. Koch in the spotlight at a time when questions about relations between the police and the community were leading the African American and Latino communities in New York City to call for more civilian control of the police; the scrutiny played a role in the election of the city's first African American mayor, David Dinkins, in 1989.

Conyers highlighted problems with the election and reelection of President George W. Bush in 2000 and 2004—defects with voting machines, intimidation of minority voters, the controversial U.S. Supreme Court decision in *Bush v. Gore*, and the like—and has been a strenuous critic of President Bush's expansive views of the president's powers under the U.S. Constitution in fighting the so-called war on terror. Conyers is also the leading congressional advocate for the recognition and preservation of the legacy of jazz as the indigenous classical music of the United States. In what may be his most controversial—and, perhaps, most important—legislative initiative, Congressman Conyers has repeatedly introduced a bill calling for a commission to study the question of reparations to the descendants of formerly enslaved African Americans.

[*See also* Congress, African Americans in; Congressional Black Caucus; *and* Reparations.]

BIBLIOGRAPHY

Herek, Gregory M., and Kevin T. Berrill, eds. *Hate Crimes: Confronting Violence against Lesbians and Gay Men*. With a foreword by John Conyers. Newbury Park, Calif.: Sage, 1991.

Miller, Anita, ed. *George W. Bush versus the U.S. Constitution: The Downing Street Memos and Deception, Manipulation, Torture, Retribution, Coverups in the Iraq War, and Illegal Domestic Spying*. With an introduction by Joseph C. Wilson and a foreword by John Conyers. Chicago: Academy Chicago Publishers, 2006.

Miller, Anita, ed. *What Went Wrong in Ohio: The Conyers Report on the 2004 Presidential Elections*. With an introduction by Gore Vidal. Chicago: Academy Chicago Publishers, 2005.

—JOSEPH WILSON

COOK, WILL MARION (b. 27 January 1869; d. 19 July 1944), musician and composer. Born Will Mercer Cook in Washington, D.C., Cook adopted the middle name Marion during his college years. His father was John Cook, the first dean of Howard University Law School, and his mother was Belle Lewis Cook, a graduate of Oberlin College. After his father's death, Cook was partly raised by his grandparents in Chattanooga, Tennessee, where he first heard traditional black music. Around 1886 he went to the Oberlin Conservatory to study violin, and he won a scholarship at the Berlin Music Academy in 1888–1889. In 1894–1895 he studied at the National Conservatory of Music under Antonín Dvořák and John White, gaining advanced skills in harmony.

A man of fiery temperament, Cook found that a black person seeking a concert career faced discrimination. He had a passionate belief in the ability of his race and the unique value of its musical heritage, so he abandoned classical music for ragtime-based black popular music. The first fruit of his new direction was *Clorindy, the Origin of the Cakewalk* (1898). Though featuring stereotyped "coon" songs, the musical was nevertheless an important break from minstrelsy. It established Cook as a major figure in black musical theater. For the next fifteen years he was a pervasive influence as a composer, conductor, orchestrator, and musical director for the shows of Bert Williams and George Walker; for his own collaborations with the poet Paul Laurence Dunbar; for incidental music for many white shows on Broadway, including the *Ziegfeld Follies*; and for black groups like Black Patti's Troubadours, Miller and Lyles, and Harlem's Negro Players.

Following *Clorindy*, Cook married its young star Abbie Mitchell. The marriage ended in 1912, but they maintained a professional association for many years. Despite his difficult temperament and uncompromising attitude toward discrimination, Cook was respected for his musical ability. He was a generous mentor to aspiring young musicians like Eubie Blake, Edward Kennedy "Duke" Ellington, and Harold Arlen, as well as, in the classical field, Clarence Cameron White and Eva Jessye. At the beginning of the twentieth century Cook's songs were among the most popular in Tin Pan Alley, including "Red, Red Rose" (*Bandanna Land*) and "Swing Along" (*In Dahomey*). He published many in *A Collection of Negro Songs* (1912).

In 1903 Cook went to England as the orchestra leader for Williams and Walker's *In Dahomey*, which included a command performance at Buckingham Palace. In 1905 he was a driving force behind the Gotham (later Gotham-Attucks) Music Company, which provided publishing opportunities for black composers. When black musical theater declined around 1911, Cook continued freelance orchestral work. In 1919 he established his Southern Syncopated Orchestra, which toured the United States and Europe to acclaim.

Although the Southern Syncopated Orchestra foreshadowed big band jazz, Cook did not regard the new jazz as serious black music. On his return to the United States in 1922, he continued freelancing as an orchestrator and chorus leader, though with a lower profile. Nevertheless "I'm Coming Virginia," featured by Ethel Waters in *Africana* (1927), is his most recorded composition. Cook died of cancer. In the early twenty-first century there were signs of new interest in his music and a reevaluation of his significance through books and recordings.

[*See also* Jazz; Music; Musical Theater; Ragtime; *and biographies of people mentioned in this article*.]

BIBLIOGRAPHY

Brown, Willie, Will Marion Cook, and Ann Sears. *Swing Along: The Songs of Will Marion Cook*. TROY839-40. Albany, N.Y.: Albany Records, 2006. William Brown (tenor) and Ann Sears (piano) re-create Cook's best-known songs.

Riis, Thomas L. *Just before Jazz: Black Musical Theater in New York, 1890–1915*. Washington, D.C.: Smithsonian Institution Press, 1989. In the absence of a full biography, this gives useful biographical background, detailed technical analysis of some of Cook's music, and a bibliography that points to unpublished biographical material.

—BILL EGAN

COOKE, SAM (b. 22 January 1931; d. 11 December 1964), gospel and pop musician, pioneer black record-company owner, and civil rights activist. Samuel Cook [*sic*] was born in Clarksdale, Mississippi, to the Reverend Charley Cook and Annie Mae Cook. The musical aspects of his father's preaching deeply influenced Cooke's formative years. According to Mahalia Jackson, a popular gospel singer, the church had a special rhythm retained "from slavery days" (Wolff, p. 21). Clarksdale also was home to Delta blues artists such as Robert Johnson and Skip James. The milieu in which Cooke grew up was musically oriented and deeply religious.

At the age of sixteen Cooke joined the fledgling gospel quartet the Highway QCs, which catalyzed his later initiation into the more widely recognized group the Soul Stirrers. In 1951, with Cooke singing lead, the Soul Stirrers recorded the hit single "Jesus Gave Me Water." Between 1951 and 1957, the year Cooke left the band, the Soul Stirrers recorded a number of singles, while also regularly playing gigs.

Perhaps his penchant for women and money, his keen knowledge of the music industry, or his stylistic growth influenced Cooke's crossover into the historically white world of pop. With hits like "Twistin' the Night Away," which was later covered by the British musician Rod Stewart, Cooke straddled two worlds, black and white. Forsaking his longtime producer Art Rupe and gospel music itself, Cooke unflinchingly moved into the world of pop, reshaping it with his original vocal styling. "You Send Me," a B-side single, was a hit among black and white audiences, reflecting Cooke's ability to transcend what was then a segregated world. He also wrote the hits "Summertime" and "Chain Gang."

Cooke's 1958 appearance on the *Ed Sullivan Show* jump-started his success, popularity, and wealth. That same year he and two friends started what became one of the first black-owned record labels. In *Dream Boogie: The Triumph of Sam Cooke*, Peter Guralnick notes that Cooke started SAR Records to cut a record for his old band the Soul Stirrers. The label later became a way for Cooke to record black artists whom he deemed worthy of recognition.

In the early 1960s Cooke became involved in the burgeoning civil rights movement. Daniel Wolff notes in *You Send Me: The Life and Times of Sam Cooke* that Cooke was concerned with African American history and black musicians, read works by W. E. B. Du Bois, and was friends with Malcolm X and Muhammad Ali. The bombing in 1963 of Birmingham's Sixteenth Street Church, a renowned meeting place for civil rights activists, including Dr. Martin Luther King Jr., reinforced Cooke's devotion to the cause. In 1964 he recorded "A Change Is Gonna Come," which became synonymous with the civil rights movement. Like his own life, the song crossed barriers. It was both a gospel and a blues song and contained elements of both the protest song and the spiritual ballad. It was an attempt to unite Cooke's diverse audience.

In December 1964, Cooke was shot to death in a motel in South Central Los Angeles. He was with a known prostitute, and the circumstances surrounding his death remain contested. Although he was wealthy and famous, it was not unlike him to associate with society's lower and upper echelons. As did his music, Cooke existed in two worlds, crossing boundaries of race and class. His context was change, and as represented in his song "A Change Is Gonna Come," his music symbolized hope in the movement toward a better world.

[*See also* Gospel Music; Music; *and* Music Industry.]

BIBLIOGRAPHY

Guralnick, Peter. *Dream Boogie: The Triumph of Sam Cooke*. New York: Little, Brown, 2005.

Wolff, Daniel, with S. R. Crain, Clifton White, and G. David Tenenbaum. *You Send Me: The Life and Times of Sam Cooke*. New York: Morrow, 1995.

—CHRISTOPHER IAN FOSTER

COOLIDGE, CALVIN, ADMINISTRATION OF. John Calvin Coolidge Jr. (b. 4 July 1872; d. 5 January 1933), described as a country lawyer who revered the law and political office, served as thirtieth president of the United States during the racially intolerant 1920s. Born in Plymouth, Vermont, the first child of John Calvin Coolidge and Victoria Coolidge, he grew up in a small rural community. His father farmed, ran a general store, and served in public office. Coolidge admired his father's dedication to public service and developed a great respect for the law. He entered Amherst College in Amherst, Massachusetts, and studied history, politics, and oratory. Known for his excellent speeches, Coolidge graduated cum laude in 1895.

Law was his passion, but Coolidge chose not to attend law school; instead he studied with two attorneys in Northampton, Massachusetts. He passed the bar in 1897 but soon ran for public office. Running as a Republican, between 1898 and 1920 Coolidge won local and state offices including city council member, Northampton mayor, state legislator, Massachusetts lieutenant governor, and Massachusetts governor. As governor, Coolidge was fiscally conservative but pushed for progressive issues. Coolidge believed that his performance as governor and during the Boston police strike of 1919 captured the attention of the Republican Party and propelled him into national politics. In 1920 he and Warren Harding, the Republican nominees, won the national presidential election. Coolidge served as vice president for two years before tragedy struck: in August 1923, Harding died. Coolidge became president.

Nicknamed "Silent Cal," Coolidge did not let his true ideas and beliefs become public knowledge. As president, he was in a unique position to provide support and leadership to the civil rights movement and support to the work of civil rights leaders such as W. E. B. Du Bois. Considering Coolidge's upbringing and the culture of the region from which he came, African Americans might have assumed that he would support their positions on issues concerning race. Vermont was the first state to abolish slavery, and Coolidge portrayed himself as an egalitarian. In 1923 he outlined the need for antilynching legislation, he called for the creation of a biracial federal commission to investigate the social and economic conditions of African Americans, he encouraged African Americans to run for office, and he proposed federally funded scholarships for African Americans to attend medical schools. He appointed a few African Americans to overseas positions such as the U.S. ambassador to Liberia, and he commuted the sentence of the back-to-Africa leader Marcus Garvey and, in an action based on federal law, deported Garvey to his home country of Jamaica.

Coolidge Praises Rescuer. President Calvin Coolidge thanks Tom Lee for rescuing thirty-two people after their boat capsized in the Mississippi River near Memphis, 1925. PRINTS AND PHOTOGRAPHS DIVISION, LIBRARY OF CONGRESS

On the surface Coolidge seemed to support civil rights, but he was not sincere. The antilynching legislation failed in the Senate because Coolidge did not encourage passage of the actual bill. To attract southern voters, Coolidge suggested that the Republican Party replace southern black delegates with white delegates, and he refused to speak out against the newly revitalized Ku Klux Klan.

During the election of 1924, Coolidge's Democratic Party opponent, John W. Davis, denounced the Klan and encouraged Coolidge to do the same. Coolidge refused to comment publicly on the issue. In the face of criticism that Coolidge actually supported the Klan, his presidential secretary, C. Bascom Slemp, issued a statement that Coolidge was not a supporter nor a member of the Klan. Despite this rebuttal and his eventual denouncement of the Klan, the Republican Party continued to attract Klan supporters as Coolidge backed anti-immigration laws and Prohibition, issues favored by the Klan.

By 1924, Du Bois expressed disappointment with the Republican Party and with Coolidge. In the 1920s the majority of African Americans who voted supported Republican candidates, but Coolidge's lack of support for his African American constituents divided them. Disgusted with both political parties, Du Bois argued that neither party was to be trusted. Du Bois's final disappointment with Coolidge centered on his handling of the great Mississippi flood of 1927. The flood affected seven states and 700,000 people, mostly African Americans, and by the most conservative estimates it killed 246 people, although some historians place the death toll closer to 500. Congress and Coolidge were divided on how to handle the disaster. Coolidge believed that the people, not the government, were responsible for the cleanup and rebuilding. Without government assistance, many families, especially African Americans, could not rebuild and instead relocated to northern cities and politically shifted from the Republican to the Democratic Party.

Coolidge's actions as president demonstrated his deep misunderstanding of the important issues facing African Americans. At a time when change was possible, he remained silent, and organizations such as the Ku Klux Klan interpreted his silence as support. Coolidge declined to run for the presidency in 1928 and retired from public life. He resumed private law practice in Northampton; served on several boards, such as that of Amherst College; and wrote his autobiography. He died of a heart attack at the age of sixty.

[*See also* Du Bois, W. E. B.; Garvey, Marcus; Ku Klux Klan; *and* Republican Party.]

BIBLIOGRAPHY

Coolidge, Calvin. *The Autobiography of Calvin Coolidge*. New York: Cosmopolitan Book Corporation, 1929. An extensional interpretation of Coolidge's role as president; provides a limited view of his policies and actions.

Ferrell, Robert H. *The Presidency of Calvin Coolidge*. Lawrence: University Press of Kansas, 1998. Provides insight into Coolidge's presidential policies and his stance on race relations.

Greenberg, David. *Calvin Coolidge*. New York: Times Books, 2006. Attempts to provide a balanced view of Coolidge's presidency and the reasons for his decisions.

Gross, Norman, ed. *America's Lawyer-Presidents: From Law Office to Oval Office*. Evanston, Ill.: Northwestern University Press, 2004. An overview of several presidents who began their careers as lawyers; provides an understanding of how the practice of law influenced Coolidge's presidency.

—SANDRA D. HARVEY

COOPER, ANNA J. (b. 10 August 1858; d. 27 February 1964), educator and humanitarian. Cooper was born Anna Julia Haywood in Raleigh, North Carolina, to Hannah Stanley Haywood and purportedly her master, George Washington Haywood. Cooper was a noted scholar at a young age. In 1868 she received a scholarship to attend Saint Augustine's Normal School and Collegiate Institute, founded to provide education to former slaves and their families. Cooper spent fourteen years at the institute, both as a pupil and as a teacher. She excelled at the humanities, as well as at math and science, and she fought for her right to take "men's" courses, such as Greek. On 21 June 1877 she married the Reverend George A. C. Cooper, her teacher in the Greek theological class. Her marriage barred her from teaching at Saint Augustine's. Her husband died two years later, and she never married again.

In 1880 Cooper won a scholarship to Oberlin College in Ohio, and in 1881 she entered the school as a sophomore. She tutored her classmates in advanced algebra. She earned a BA in mathematics in 1884 and earned her master's degree in mathematics in 1887. Soon afterward she started teaching at Washington High School (which later became the famed M Street High School) in Washington, D.C. She proved to be a dedicated and challenging teacher and was appointed the principal in 1901. Under her headship the standards of education were equal to those of any other school, and several students received valuable scholarships to Ivy League colleges. This came to the notice of the white members of the Washington school board, who tried to force Cooper to lower her academic standards, which she refused to do. In spite of protests from the patrons of the school, she was not reinstated as principal, but she continued as an instructor for another forty years.

In 1914 Cooper took courses for her doctoral degree at Columbia University in New York City. Later she transferred those credits to the University of Paris–Sorbonne and completed her coursework in ten years. The highlight of her educational career was when she was granted her PhD at the age of sixty-five in the presence of the African American scholar Alain Locke.

Cooper left M Street High School in 1930 and took on the headship of Frelinghuysen University, also in Washington, D.C., which had been founded in 1906 by a former had been slave. She struggled over the next twelve years to get funding and maintain the accreditation of the

Anna J. Cooper. In the parlor of the registrar's office at Frelinghuysen University, c. 1930. Photograph by Addison Scurlock. Scurlock Studio Records, Archives Center, National Museum of American History, Smithsonian Institution

university. After retiring in 1942, she continued to write about the evils of slavery and the necessity of education until her death.

In addition to her active teaching career and her dedication to ensuring the future of her students, Cooper cared for the orphaned children of her deceased brother and found the time and enthusiasm to engage actively in the educations of newly freed African American men and women. She lectured in 1892 in Hampton, Virginia, at a forum with Booker T. Washington and received some acceptance from the all-male American Negro Academy. She attacked social problems by forming several organizations, including the first black settlement house in the nation's capital and the first black YWCA. Cooper also participated in the launch of the first national organization of black women, the National Association of Colored Women's Clubs, in 1896.

Cooper's major work, *A Voice from the South* (1892), is a collection of her speeches and thoughts on the importance of the education of women and expresses sadness at the blindness of African American men to the necessity of viewing women as equal partners in the struggle for racial improvement and uplift. Cooper wrote metaphorically and often included her personal experiences, examples, and opinions to emphasize the urgency of her message. Her writing shows her acute awareness of the hostility and indifference of her audience, black or white, and her endeavor to be seen foremost as an educated black woman. She fought to dissipate the image of women as helpless creatures with limited abilities waiting to be nurtured or rescued by their men.

Though Cooper was an incipient feminist, her position as a highly educated (middle-class and self-educated) African American woman and her perspective on the black intellectual's role in the future of the black race make her seem distant and condescending at times. Her stance was largely theoretical, and her polemic was directed toward other intellectuals, mostly men, who felt that the destiny of African Americans lay in their own hands and who suggested compromise and mediocrity in education, work, or business instead of ambition. She joined Washington in siding with big business against unrest among black laborers, mainly to maintain public peace and decorum. Though she was in agreement with Washington on industrial education for the black urban poor, she supported many students with aspirations for higher education. She also spoke strongly against the sexual demonizing of black women, a subject that most black intellectuals did not address adequately. Her actions as a reformer, educator, and humanitarian and her enormous social contributions speak for themselves. Sadly, Cooper's work and her writing were mostly ignored by her male peers, whose validation she often sought.

[*See also* Education; Educators and Academics; National Association of Colored Women; Pan-African Conference, London; *and* Washington, Booker T.]

BIBLIOGRAPHY

Cooper, Anna Julia. *Slavery and the French Revolutionists (1788–1805)*. Translated by Frances Richardson Keller. Lewiston, N.Y.: Edwin Mellen Press, 1988.

Gaines, Kevin K. "The Woman and Labor Questions in Racial Uplift Ideology: Anna Julia Cooper's Voices from the South." In his *Uplifting the Race: Black Leadership, Politics, and Culture in the Twentieth Century*, pp. 128–151. Chapel Hill: University North Carolina Press, 1996.

Lemert, Charles, and Esme Bhan, eds. *The Voice of Ann Julia Cooper: Including "A Voice from the South" and Other Important Essays, Papers, and Letters*. Lanham, Md.: Rowman and Littlefield, 1998.

Logan, Shirley Wilson. " 'What Are We Worth': Anna Julia Cooper Defines Black Women's Work at the Dawn of the Twentieth Century." In *Sister Circle: Black Women and Work*, edited by Sharon Harley and the Black Women and Work Collective, pp. 146–163. New Brunswick, N.J.: Rutgers University Press, 2002.

—Abha Sood Patel

CORE. *See* Congress of Racial Equality.

CORTEZ, JAYNE (b. 10 May 1936), poet, performance artist, and visual artist. Jayne Cortez was born in Fort Huachuca, Arizona. In her formative years she was greatly inspired by the jazz musicians Charlie Parker, Billie Holiday, Thelonious Monk, and others, whom she cites as artists who helped her to explore her creative possibilities as a musician and a writer. Her successful literary and artistic career, which spans more than three decades, conveys her genuine respect for her predecessors as well as her affinity for individuals who comment about the diaspora, utilizing interdisciplinary methods to examine the world and its dynamics via Pan-Africanist perspectives.

After moving to California with her family, Cortez attended Manual Arts High School, an art and music high school, and Compton Junior College. It was in the Watts section of Los Angeles that she sought to become dexterous in the visual and literary arts, studying drama at Ebony Showcase in Watts and becoming more adept in drawing and painting. In 1954 Cortez married the jazz musician Ornette Coleman; she gave birth in 1956 to their son Denardo, who would become an accomplished drummer for Cortez's band the Firespitters. Cortez and Coleman divorced in 1964; that same year she cofounded the Watts Repertory Theater Company, where she remained artistic director until 1970. Her activism in the civil rights movement and an assortment of factory jobs, paired with her formalized training in creative writing workshops, provided inspirations that would greatly affect the tone, mood, and subject matter of her poetry and music.

Subsequently, Cortez moved to New York City and published two volumes of poetry, *Pissstained Stairs and the Money Man's Wares* (1969) and *Festivals and Funerals* (1971). Her written and performance-based literary style has been regarded as urban, musical, controversial, sarcastic, and candid in reflections that narrate experiences common to blacks worldwide. In 1972 she founded Bola Press ("Bola" means successful in Yoruba), and in 1973 she celebrated the publication of *Scarifications*, her third volume of poetry. She released the sound recording *Celebrations and Solitudes: The Poetry of Jayne Cortez* (Strata East Records) in 1974, and a year later she married the sculptor Melvin Edwards. From 1977 to 1983 she was a writer in residence and a professor of literature at Livingston College of Rutgers University and gave countless lectures at colleges and universities. Cortez has continued publishing, performing, traveling internationally, and garnering awards. In addition to numerous publications in journals, she has produced *Coagulations: New and Selected Poems* (1984), *Poetic Magnetic* (1991), *Somewhere in Advance of Nowhere* (1997), and *A Jazz Fan Looks Back* (2002). Her sound recordings include *Maintain Control* (1986), *Cheerful & Optimistic* (1994) with the band the Firespitters, and *Borders of Disorderly Time* (2003). Cortez resides in New York City.

[*See also* Music *and* Visual Arts.]

BIBLIOGRAPHY

Brown, Kimberly N. "Of Poststructuralist Fallout, Scarification, and Blood Poems: The Revolutionary Ideology behind the Poetry of Jayne Cortez." *Modern American Poetry*. www.english.uiuc.edu/maps/poets/a_f/cortez/poetry.htm, 1998?

Ostrom, Hans, and J. David Macey Jr., eds. *The Greenwood Encyclopedia of African American Literature*. Westport, Conn.: Greenwood Press, 2005.

Wilkinson, Michelle J. "Cortez, Jayne." In *The Oxford Companion to African American Literature*, edited by William L. Andrews, Frances Smith Foster, and Trudier Harris. New York: Oxford University Press, 1997.

—VAN G. GARRETT

COSBY, BILL (b. 12 July 1937), comedian, actor, philanthropist. When Bill Cosby, the wealthy, well-educated, mild-mannered comedian, goes on stage and begins a monologue of funny stories relating to his poverty-stricken background, the stories are most likely true. William Henry Cosby Jr. was born in Germantown, Pennsylvania, to William Henry Cosby Sr. and Anna Cosby in 1937. Known by its inhabitants as the "Jungle," the Richard Allen housing projects, where Cosby grew up, were depressing, stylized, beige-colored, concrete housing, seemingly designed to prevent poor people from "contaminating" the rest of society.

When an IQ test confirmed that Cosby was highly intelligent, his mother enrolled him in Central High School—a school for gifted children. However, Cosby found it difficult to adjust there and transferred to Germantown High School. There, athletics provided a positive outlet for Cosby, but his academic performance declined. When school officials required him to repeat the tenth grade, he dropped out of high school in 1956 to join the U.S. Navy.

Cosby's years in the navy exposed him to the wider world and gave him time to examine his life in a different context. He found time to earn his high school equivalency diploma. After leaving the navy in 1960, Cosby accepted an athletic scholarship to attend Temple University. He played fullback on Temple's football team and performed in several track and field events. Because the scholarship was insufficient to cover his expenses he found employment as a bartender.

Early Career. Cosby had a knack for storytelling and enjoyed doing comedy routines around Philadelphia, where he became a favorite in several local clubs. In 1962 Cosby appeared at the Gaslight Café in Greenwich Village for the summer. Cosby practiced clean comedy; unlike Redd Foxx, Richard Pryor, Dick Gregory, and a few other noted contemporary black comedians, he avoided biting political commentary, prurient sexual references, and the "N" word. In deference to the Village crowd of bohemians, hipsters, and white middle-class nightclub hoppers, Cosby sometimes punctuated his storytelling routines with racial and political humor, but this was merely a distraction from his usual routine. His reviews were generally favorable, and soon Cosby was getting so much work he dropped out of Temple University to become a full-time comedian.

Cosby's big break in the world of entertainment occurred in 1963, when his agent, Roy Silver, arranged for him to audition for NBC's *Tonight Show*, a late-night talk show that starred Johnny Carson. Actually, Carson was on a one-week sabbatical and Allan Sherman, his guest host for the week, auditioned Cosby and brought him on the show. Cosby's appearance was a huge success and led to offers of well-paid jobs at such well-known nightclubs as Mr. Kelly's in Chicago and the Hungry i in San Francisco. In addition, he appeared at the Flamingo Hotel and Casino in Las Vegas and Harrah's Hotel and Casino in Reno. In 1964 Cosby recorded a comedy album—*Bill Cosby Is a Very Funny Fellow, Right!*—the first of a number of comedy albums he recorded that were Grammy Award winners.

Bill Cosby. At a rally for the voting rights of displaced New Orleans residents, 2006. Photograph by Lee Celano. REUTERS

Although a follow-up comedy album to *Funny Fellow* was not a commercial success, 1964 was a special year for Cosby. During that year, he married Camille Hanks, and his comedy, particularly a karate routine, caught the attention of the television producer Sheldon Leonard. Leonard contacted Cosby and broached the idea of his costarring in a television series about two undercover American spies. The mere suggestion that a white man and a black man appear in a television series as equals in the mid-1960s was radical. However, Leonard was persistent, and NBC and a number of sponsors finally agreed to support the project.

I Spy premiered in 1965 with Cosby and Robert Culp portraying two undercover CIA spies—Alexander Scott and Kelly Robinson, respectively—who traveled around the world as a tennis player (Culp) and his trainer (Cosby) while working for "Uncle Sam." The series was a milestone for African Americans in many ways. It was the first television program to feature an African American in a dramatic role and the first to portray blacks and whites as equals. Moreover, the image projected by Scott—a Rhodes scholar who spoke several languages—was light years away from the stereotyped black characters in *Amos 'n' Andy, Beulah, The Jack Benny Program,* and others. Beautiful black women including Nancy Wilson, Barbara McNair, and Eartha Kitt appeared in episodes in nontraditional roles and provided romantic possibilities for Scott. One 1967 episode featured tender, intimate moments between Scott and an enemy spy portrayed by Janet MacLachlan; the portrayal of this type of romantic feeling between a black male and female was unprecedented in media representations of African Americans before *I Spy*.

I Spy, which used Cosby's offbeat, comedic wit to great effect, was popular among a broad range of television viewers, and only four southern stations boycotted the series. However, there were some African Americans who believed the show was unrealistic and danced around depicting life as it really was for blacks in the United States. Critics faulted Cosby for portraying a character that was "irrelevant" to black aspirations and the struggle for equal rights. Cosby faced similar criticism for his stand-up comedy and comedic recordings. Nonetheless, many blacks saw the series as a step forward and felt a great deal of pride when Cosby won three Emmy Awards in the "best actor in a dramatic series" category for his portrayal of Scott.

Later Career. The success of *I Spy* made it financially possible for Cosby to take his career in any direction he desired. During the period from 1969 to 1980 he had several shows on television. *The Bill Cosby Show* (NBC, 1969), in which he portrayed a physical education teacher, was marginally successful, but his cartoon series for children, *Fat Albert and the Cosby Kids* (CBS, 1973) was popular and enduring. Cosby's other television series during this period—*The New Bill Cosby Show* (CBS, 1972) and *Cos* (ABC, 1976), a comedy-variety show and a sitcom—were flops. However, the 1970s were not unproductive years for Cosby. He returned to Temple University and completed the requirements for his bachelor's degree in sociology and then earned masters and doctoral degrees in education from the University of Massachusetts. He also made a trilogy of films with Sidney Poitier that collectively were a critical and commercial success—*Uptown Saturday Night* (1974), *Let's Do It Again* (1975), and *A Piece of the Action* (1977).

In 1984 Cosby redeemed his television bona fides with the premier of what became one of the most popular and commercially successful television shows ever—*The Cosby Show*, a family sitcom about the trials and tribulations of an upwardly mobile, professional black couple and their five children. The splendid cast included Phylicia Rashad, Lisa Bonet, Malcolm-Jamal Warner, Tempestt Bledsoe, Keshia Knight Pulliam, and Raven-Symone. While the sitcom centered on a relatively wealthy black family, it had an "everyman" feel to it that made the show immensely popular across race, age, and gender boundaries. Nonetheless, some critics, both black and white, excoriated the show for presenting an unrealistic and fanciful portrayal of black urban life. The show, however, remained very popular in syndication and reportedly earned Cosby several hundred million dollars.

In the 1980s and 1990s Cosby authored several books and remained influential in the world of entertainment. However, controversy surrounded his criticism of poorer African Americans for accepting anti-intellectualism, the decline of morals, drug use, single motherhood, and the high crime rate in many black urban neighborhoods. His comments about self-respect, self-improvement, and social and parental responsibilities elicited blistering criticism in some quarters. While one may disagree with what Cosby has said or the forum in which he has said it, he has brought to the public arena issues worthy of discussion throughout the black community. Moreover, he and his wife, Camille Cosby, have been ardent advocates for education, and their donation of millions of dollars to historically black colleges and universities demonstrates their commitment to the African American community.

[*See also* Actors and Actresses; Comedians; *and* Entertainment Industry and African Americans.]

Bibliography

MacDonald, J. Fred. *Blacks and White TV: Afro-Americans in Television since 1948*. Chicago: Nelson-Hall, 1983. Provides a thoughtful and scholarly analysis of the history of African Americans in television, with pertinent information on Cosby.

Smith, Ronald L. *Cosby: The Life of a Comedy Legend*. Amherst, N.Y.: Prometheus, 1997. A readable and informative biography, but lacks bibliography, source notes, and index.

—Donald Roe

COTTON CLUB. The Cotton Club opened in 1923 at 142d Street and Lenox Avenue, in the heart of New York City's Harlem. It was a lavishly refurbished version of the Club Deluxe previously run by the former heavyweight boxing champion Jack Johnson. Ironically, although Johnson had pioneered the "black and tan" integrated clubs of Chicago's South Side in 1912, the Cotton Club was segregated from the beginning. The new owner was Owney Madden, a quiet but ruthless gang boss who controlled a major part of the illegal liquor trade. Madden kept a low profile, with his partner "Frenchy" De Mange as the front man.

The Cotton Club served as a respectable front for the mobster's illegal activities. It attracted the cream of white society, lured by the thrill of slumming uptown in Harlem, where they could safely observe "exotic" black people without actually mixing with them. In addition to fancy decor and lavish food and drink, there was high-class entertainment delivered by top black musicians and entertainers and arranged by the Broadway producer Lew Leslie and the veteran songwriter Jimmy McHugh. Fast-moving revues featured a chorus line of attractive and lavishly gowned—or scantily clad—young light-skinned black women and athletic black male dancers supported by a jazz band and comedians, and the club staged a new show every six months.

The club succeeded from the start. England's nightclubbing Lady Mountbatten dubbed it "the aristocrat of Harlem." In 1925 the Cotton Club was closed for a time on suspicion of violating Prohibition laws. For the rest of the club's life, Herman Stark took over as stage manager. Leslie's replacement, a talented young performer named Dan Healy, brought new snappiness to the floor shows.

In 1927 the rising Duke Ellington and his band replaced the original Andy Preer band. This was the era of Ellington's "jungle music," with many of his great early compositions such as "Creole Love Call." The lyricist Dorothy Fields teamed with Jimmy McHugh to write hit songs like "I Cant Give You Anything but Love." For wealthy socialites, the Cotton Club became the place to be seen. Regular radio broadcasts from the club brought fame to Ellington. In 1931 when Ellington was away, Cab Calloway, with his "hi-de-ho" vocals and jive talk, became the backup house band.

From 1930 the songwriters Harold Arlen and Ted Koehler contributed many memorable tunes, including "I've Got the World on a String" and "Stormy Weather." Throughout the 1930s the entertainment was a Who's Who of black entertainment: Ethel Waters, Bill "Bojangles" Robinson, Lena Horne, Louis "Satchmo" Armstrong, and the Nicholas Brothers all were among the performers at the Cotton Club. The production team was almost entirely white, with some use of the lyricist Andy Razaf and the choreographer Clarence Robinson. Playing for gangsters did not worry the entertainers: the gangsters wanted a respectable front and paid generously. However, the gangsters did not hesitate to use muscle when contractual difficulties arose. They strong-armed Robinson to release Ellington from a Philadelphia contract, destroyed the rival Plantation Club before Calloway could start there, and blocked Horne from leaving the club, among other notable incidents.

In 1933 Madden retired after a brief sojourn in Sing Sing prison for parole violations, and Congress repealed Prohibition. The club continued to thrive, with Waters a big hit. In 1934 Jimmie Lunceford's orchestra took over as the house band. However, the Depression hit Harlem hard. When serious riots occurred in Harlem in 1935, the Cotton Club moved downtown to 48th Street and Broadway. The new venue featured the same lavish floor shows and top talent, but times and tastes were changing. By 1940 Stark and the club management were in trouble over tax evasion. On 10 June 1940 the downtown Cotton Club finally closed its doors.

Though the Cotton Club has been portrayed as a symbol of the Harlem Renaissance, its segregation policy led many to view it as reflecting the phony nature of some aspects of the renaissance. Its patrons were shielded from real contact with the mass of Harlem's African American population. However, though barred from the club, the residents of Harlem found reflected glory in the high status of the club's performers. The club's emphasis on jungle music and scantily clad dancers was seen as pandering to the image of the primitive, exotic Negro. Though the club may have been part of a phony fringe of the Harlem Renaissance, it was also a center of excellence for jazz music and popular songwriting. It gave employment to many important bandleaders, musicians, singers, dancers, songwriters, and comedians, allowing them to showcase their talents to a world of potential promoters. Significantly, the Cotton Club's demeaning context failed to diminish the dignity of a Duke Ellington, an Ethel Waters, or a Lena Horne.

[*See also* Conductors and Bandleaders; Dance; Great Depression; Harlem; Harlem Renaissance; Harlem Riots, *subentry* Harlem Riots of 1935; Music; *and biographical entries on figures mentioned in this article*.]

BIBLIOGRAPHY

Calloway, Cab, and Bryant Rollins. *Of Minnie the Moocher and Me*. New York: Crowell, 1976. Tells of the Cotton Club years from Calloway's own point of view.

Haskins, James. *The Cotton Club*. New York: Random House, 1977. A generously illustrated history of the club.

Hasse, John Edward. *Beyond Category: The Life and Genius of Duke Ellington*. New York: Simon & Schuster, 1993. Covers Ellington's Cotton Club years comprehensively.

—BILL EGAN

COUNCIL ON AFRICAN AFFAIRS. Initially founded in 1937 as the International Committee on African Affairs (ICAA), the Council on African Affairs (CAA) proved to be the most significant anti-imperialist organization established by African Americans in support of African independence. The cofounders of the CAA were Paul Robeson and Max Yergan. They had met in 1931 through their work on Africa. Born in Princeton, New Jersey, in 1898, Robeson, the son of a former slave, was arguably one of the most internationally acclaimed African Americans. Along with earning a law degree from Columbia University, he was a graduate of Rutgers, where in addition to achieving accolades for his performance in sports—Robeson was the third African American to receive All-American honors in football—he excelled academically and was inducted into Phi Beta Kappa. Moreover Robeson was a talented and gifted musician and actor, and his performances included traveling to Europe and especially Great Britain. Robeson's interest in Africa blossomed during his residence in England, and he acquired knowledge of several African languages.

Born in Raleigh, North Carolina, in 1892, Max Yergan graduated from Shaw University and later served as a representative for the segregated YMCA. One of the first African Americans to travel internationally on behalf of the YMCA, Yergan spent time in India and later in South Africa. In South Africa he established ties with the African National Congress, as well as with the South African Communist Party, and he even made a trip to the Soviet Union in 1934.

Given their commonality with regard to progressive politics and an interest in Africa, Robeson and Yergan joined together to form the ICAA in 1937. Given Yergan's South African connections and Robeson's links to African students in London, the ICAA made considerable headway in networking with emerging African leaders in various organizations. That number included A. B. Xuma and D. T. T. Javabu of South Africa, Wallace Johnston of Sierra Leone, and Jomo Kenyatta of Kenya. The task of supporting the educational efforts of African students was one of the early objectives of the ICAA.

In its formative years the ICAA was primarily an educational organization with supporting members from groups of various political and ideological persuasions. With the emergence of the National Negro Congress (NNC), the leftward ideology of Yergan became more prominent when he eventually served as the NNC president. The political relationship between liberals and more radical left-leaning supporters of the ICAA over time became strained and even antagonistic.

During the period of World War II, the alliance formed between the Soviet Union and the United States allowed for some level of flexibility with regard to the ideological differences among liberals and the political Left. This was extremely important for the CAA, which wanted to expand its structure to include a grassroots and mass orientation on the one hand and, on the other, to deepen the political understanding of its grassroots constituency by introducing ideas about the dangers of imperialism and its foundation in capitalism. It was possible, during a short time, for the CAA to forge an alliance with liberals and to persuade them to join its membership; this included strong efforts to enlist their support for the anti-imperialist cause as it related to Africa. Nevertheless the organization was reorganized in 1942 with the idea of establishing more consistent programmatic efforts at mass organization, protests, and publicity campaigns and a stronger leftward perspective on the struggle for African independence.

With the restructuring of the CAA and as the newly established educational director, Alphaeus Hunton assumed the bulk of the daily administration of the group. After the termination of World War II and the acceleration of the Cold War, the dynamics of the CAA increasingly pointed to an ideological struggle regarding the political direction of the organization. Although Yergan was a member of the Communist Party, at the beginning of the Cold War he reversed his political position and became a staunch anticommunist. At this juncture an intense struggle took place over the control of the CAA, and ultimately Robeson and Hunton prevailed over Yergan. Upon his departure from the NAACP, W. E. B. Du Bois joined forces with Hunton and Robeson in the vanguard of the CAA. Du Bois's commitment to the cause of African liberation was long recognized through the series of Pan-African conferences that he started as early as 1919.

To a great degree Du Bois's break from the NAACP centered on that organization's lack of an anti-imperialist conception regarding U.S. foreign policy. In particular Africa was not considered in the framework of an anti-imperialist struggle, and the Truman Doctrine and other Cold War policies were not understood as detrimental to the cause of African independence. Consequently when Du Bois joined the CAA, he was right in step with the progressive leftward position of Robeson and Hunton. Du Bois's collaboration with the CAA brought an additional arsenal of intellectual power and scholarly understanding of contemporary African conditions. Under pressure from the State Department, the CAA closed its doors in 1955.

[*See also* Communism and African Americans; Du Bois, W. E. B.; Hunton, Alphaeus; National Negro Congress; Pan-Africanism; *and* Robeson, Paul.]

BIBLIOGRAPHY

Lynch, Hollis R. *Black American Radicals and the Liberation of Africa: The Council on African Affairs, 1937–1955*. Ithaca, N.Y.: Africana Studies and Research Center, Cornell University, 1978. One of the first comprehensive examinations of the Council on African Affairs.

Von Eschen, Penny M. *Race against Empire*. Ithaca, N.Y.: Cornell University Press, 1997. Provides considerable information on the Council on African Affairs, especially from the point of its reorganization in 1943 to its demise in 1955.

—JOHN H. MCCLENDON III

CRAFT, JUANITA (b. 9 February 1902; d. 6 August 1985), civil rights activist and councilwoman. Juanita Craft, a grassroots leader involved in the local civil rights movement in Dallas, Texas, stated in her autobiography that she accepted the challenge to fight for the rights of her people in the battle against segregation. She was born Juanita Jewel Shanks in Round Rock, a small town north of Austin, Texas, to David Shanks, a principal, and Eliza Balfour Shanks, a seamstress and a teacher. Her parents, each a descendant of slaves, had no other children, and they instilled in Juanita the value of hard work and being able to take care of herself. During her early childhood years, Juanita spent her days sewing, gardening, and taking music lessons. She said to an interviewer once that her childhood days were interesting because she did not have time to get lonely.

Craft was introduced to the horrors of racism and segregation during her youth. As a teenager, she attended Anderson High School in Austin, but would graduate from a high school in Columbus, Texas, after her mother's death. In 1918, when Craft was sixteen years old, her mother died after being denied treatment for tuberculosis.

Shanks had been diagnosed with tuberculosis, and her physician suggested that she relocate to a dry climate for treatment. Craft and Shanks traveled to San Angelo, Texas, where a state facility for tuberculosis patients was available, but Shanks was denied admission to the hospital because of her race. After observing the horrendous lack of treatment offered to her mother by the hospital officials in San Angelo, Craft pledged to fight against segregation.

In 1919 Craft enrolled in Prairie View State Normal and Industrial College (now Prairie View A&M University), which her father had attended and graduated from as valedictorian in 1895. She hoped to attend the University of Texas at Austin but could not because of her race. Craft despised being forced to attend a university designated for Negro students by the Texas State Education Board because she knew that she would not receive an education comparable to that of her white peers attending the University of Texas. She graduated from Prairie View in May 1921 with a certificate in dressmaking and millinery.

Juanita Craft, 1944. National Association for the Advancement of Colored People Records, Library of Congress

During the summer of 1921, she enrolled in Samuel Houston College and attended "summer normals," a teacher training program, earning a teaching certificate to teach elementary education.

Craft worked briefly as a second-grade teacher before she became a bell maid at the prestigious Adolphus Hotel in Dallas, Texas, in 1925. As an employee of the hotel she provided services to visiting dignitaries including Louis Armstrong, Eleanor Roosevelt, and Charles Lindbergh. She earned a respectable salary that was supplemented with generous tips from the hotel patrons. Her employment was criticized by her father, who believed that the hotel was inundated with alcohol and promiscuous women. Craft assured her father that she did not demean herself with the vagrancies, nor did she condone the hotel's discriminatory practice of not allowing African Americans to enter through the front door of the hotel.

Formal civil rights activism for Craft began in 1935, when she joined the Dallas branch of the National Association for the Advancement of Colored People (NAACP). She initially worked as a field organizer, traveling across the state encouraging African Americans to pay their dues and to continue their support of the Progressive Movement's civil rights organization. Many African Americans in Dallas shied away from membership in the years prior to 1935 because of the reemergence of the Ku Klux Klan in the state, so membership campaigns by Craft and others provided what some observers called blood transfusions to a flailing organization.

Craft, who was promoted to Youth Council adviser of the Dallas NAACP in 1946, began to challenge segregation in education and public accommodations. In 1946 the Houston postal carrier Heman Marion Sweatt applied for admission to the University of Texas Law School and was denied admission because of his race. Craft and Youth Council members mobilized, raised money, and protested the university's denial of a first-class education. Their efforts contributed to public reaction and the Supreme Court ruling in *Sweatt v. Painter* (1950) that would lead to future education desegregation decisions, including *Brown v. Board of Education* (1954).

In 1955 Craft and Dallas Youth Council members challenged the political oligarchy in the city and a landmark entertainment institution, the State Fair. Tired of being allowed to attend the State Fair only on Negro Achievement Day, the NAACP members picketed the Fair, distributing handbills to prospective patrons about the protest. The protest received national recognition and would influence white leaders in Dallas to integrate the Fair in the mid-1960s.

Juanita Craft lived a promise to end segregation and establish an egalitarian society. She believed that she and other African Americans had a right to everything in this country and that a person's rights should not be denied because of the color of one's skin. Her work as an NAACP field organizer and Youth Council adviser demonstrated her commitment to dismantling the inherently unequal policy for one of equality.

[*See also Brown v. Board of Education*; Dallas; Discrimination; National Association for the Advancement of Colored People; *and Sweatt v. Painter*.]

BIBLIOGRAPHY

Craft, Juanita Jewel. "Interview with Juanita Jewel Craft." Interview by Dorothy R. Robinson (20 January 1977). *The Black Women Oral History Project*. Westport, Conn.: Meckler and the Schlesinger Library, Radcliffe College, 1991. Oral history project containing the memoirs of African American women who participated in public and civil service.

Gillette, Michael L. "The Rise of the NAACP in Texas." *Southwestern Historical Quarterly* 81 (April 1978): 393-416. One of the best known articles providing a detailed history of the organization on the state level.

Vaughan, Chandler, ed. *A Child, the Earth, and a Tree of Many Seasons: The Voice of Juanita Craft*. Dallas, Tex.: Halifax Publishing, 1982. An oral biography of Juanita Craft.

—YVONNE DAVIS FREAR

CRIMINAL JUSTICE. The history of the criminal justice system has been closely linked to the African American experience in the twentieth century. In the wake of emancipation, southern states turned to the criminal justice system to perform social control functions previously served by slavery. After the civil rights movement of the mid-twentieth century, politicians used the language of crime control to signify lingering racial animosities. In the meantime blacks were arrested, convicted, and incarcerated in numbers far greater than would be predicted based on their representation in the total population. In 1940 the *Uniform Crime Reports* compiled by the Federal Bureau of Investigation reported that the arrest rate for serious felonies was 17 per thousand for blacks compared to 6 per thousand for whites. By 1978 those rates had climbed to 100 per thousand for blacks and 35 per thousand for whites. In 1923 blacks constituted about 10 percent of the total general population but 21 percent of the prison population; in 1995 half the nation's prisoners were black, though they accounted for only 12 percent of the population.

Critics of the American criminal justice system cite these historical trends as evidence that the ideal of equal justice has not been met in the United States. It is important to remember, however, that disparity does not necessarily translate into discrimination. Racially unbalanced arrest rates, for instance, may reflect different rates of offending among racial groups, and disparities in sentences may be explained by legally relevant factors such as the severity of the offense or a defendant's prior criminal record. Most criminologists agree that, even when accounting for the effects of selective enforcement and institutional bias, blacks commit a disproportionate share of violent crimes.

Additionally, many times it is difficult to ascertain the motivation behind a policy that has a disparate impact on racial groups. For example, the decision by a police department to patrol black neighborhoods more intensively than white neighborhoods could reflect either a rational choice to focus resources on high-crime areas or a discriminatory policy to target minority populations. In either case the effect of the policy produces greater surveillance and control of racial minorities. Perhaps most important, crime tends to be intraracial; approximately 80 percent of violent crimes involve offenders who are of the same race as their victims. Arguably, because high rates of black criminality primarily endanger the safety and stability of black communities, aggressive enforcement of the criminal law produces greater safety for law-abiding black citizens.

At the same time black criminal behavior must be understood as the result not of innate racial characteristics but of social institutions and public policies that have limited the opportunities of minorities. The legacy of Jim Crow—particularly residential segregation, employment discrimination, and inadequate education—fostered a criminogenic environment of poverty and social disorganization. The professionals charged with enforcing the law in these areas were not immune from the racial prejudice that afflicted other Americans. Even after most overt discrimination was weeded out from the system, the effects of race-neutral policies seemed to weigh more heavily on minorities. Thus a central challenge of the criminal justice system has been to balance the sometimes competing demands for pubic safety and social justice.

The Shadow of Slavery. In many ways the criminal justice systems of the southern states replaced slavery as the preeminent device for racial and labor control. The Fourteenth Amendment, ratified in 1868, negated the penal measures of the notorious black codes passed after the end of the Civil War, codes that had explicitly prescribed more severe punishments for blacks than for whites. Whatever else the phrase "equal protection of the laws" meant—and courts would define it narrowly for several decades—it clearly prohibited states from defining criminal acts or meting out punishments solely on the basis of race. Nevertheless, southern legislatures imaginatively devised statutes that were racially neutral as written but that clearly applied to behavior, such as sharecropping, that was correlated to race or that could be enforced in a discriminatory manner.

Among the most odious of these devices were contract enforcement laws, which made it a crime for a worker, tenant, or sharecropper who received an advance on future wages to quit his job before the end of his employment contract. By providing a small salary advance, unscrupulous employers could bind their workers to the company. If a worker left, an employer could rely on local courts either to fine the worker—which the employer would pay, thus creating a new debt—or to sentence him to gang labor, which might be leased from the state. In essence these laws thwarted workers' economic mobility by making breach of contract a criminal offense, although the states maintained that their goal was to prevent fraud, not restrict freedom of contract.

These laws ostensibly applied to workers of all races, but in practice African Americans were more likely to be required to accept long-term contracts rather than employment at will for daily or weekly wages. Although the U.S. Supreme Court and several state courts held that these practices constituted unlawful debt peonage and violated the Thirteenth Amendment's ban on "involuntary servitude" (*Bailey v. Alabama*, 1911), the practice continued in some states until the 1940s because it provided an effective way to perpetuate the benefits of slavery: obtaining black labor though coercion, tying black laborers to an owner and his land, and preventing blacks from maximizing the value of their labor by leaving an employer for a more lucrative opportunity, particularly when labor was scarce.

Vagrancy laws, supported by formal and informal criminal surety systems, operated in a similar fashion. Between 1893 and 1909 ten southern states broadened their vagrancy statutes to encompass behavior such as "wandering or strolling in idleness" or leading an "immoral, profligate life" and increased the severity of penalties. These statutes, though written without explicit mention of race, nevertheless permitted police to round up African American workers and press them into service when their labor was needed by private employers, such as during harvest time, or for public works. In 1937, for example, the city of Miami, Florida, arrested more than fifty African Americans as vagrants and put them to work as garbage collectors.

Often private employers would pay the fines and court costs or post bail for a prisoner accused of vagrancy or another petty crime, creating a debt that would ensure service from the prisoner until his expenses were paid. Breaches of these surety contracts were criminal offenses that would lead to even longer terms of service, binding petty offenders in seemingly perpetual servitude. The Supreme Court condemned criminal surety as debt peonage in 1914 in *U.S. v. Reynolds*, but the practice continued into the 1940s because fear of retaliation and the persistent threat of the chain gang discouraged victims of peonage from pressing charges. Even when prosecutions were brought, southern juries consistently proved reluctant to condemn a practice that functioned both as a source of cheap labor and as a system of racial discipline.

The threat of being sentenced to convict labor powerfully reinforced these systems of coercion. As onerous as the contract enforcement and criminal surety regimes were, defendants favored submitting to them rather than working on a chain gang. During the postbellum period, the leasing of convicts to private enterprises dominated the southern penal system. Convicts picked cotton, laid railroad track, felled timber, and mined coal, iron, and phosphate. During the Progressive Era, convict leasing of state inmates disappeared—although leasing of county prisoners continued to a degree—partly in response to humanitarian reform efforts but also because states sought a cheap and reliable source of labor for improvements to the infrastructure that would benefit the public at large rather than a few extractive industries.

Mississippi and Tennessee abolished convict leasing in the 1890s; the practice lingered until the 1920s in Florida and Alabama, where the turpentine and mining industries relied heavily on convict labor. Most chain gangs built and repaired roads; in Louisiana they constructed and maintained the levees. The vast majority of these workers—75 to 95 percent, depending on the county—were black, some of them hardened criminals but most convicted of petty offenses. The work was treacherous, the conditions brutal, and discipline harsh. Prisoners were shackled at the ankles around the clock. Their food and bedding was infested with vermin. Rifles, whips, straps, bloodhounds, and the sweat box were all used to maintain discipline. Conditions like these, and the highly visible presence of the chain gangs throughout the South, provided a strong incentive to accept the penurious terms of employment offered under the contract enforcement and criminal surety systems.

Jury Discrimination. Other features of the southern criminal justice system, in particular the exclusion of blacks from service on grand and petit juries, reinforced the political disfranchisement of African Americans after Reconstruction. In the late nineteenth and early twentieth centuries, jury service was regarded in many areas of the country as an important form of political office holding. Therefore excluding blacks not only denied black defendants of their right to a jury of their peers but also prevented African Americans from democratic participation in the judicial process as prospective jurors.

Although in *Strauder v. West Virginia* (1880) and *Neal v. Delaware* (1881) the Supreme Court had declared overt measures to exclude blacks from jury service, such as statutory prohibitions or discriminatory exercise of discretion by public officials, to be unconstitutional, states still managed to keep blacks out of the jury box, either by linking jury eligibility to voting qualifications or by imposing vague character or intelligence tests. Blacks who managed to be impaneled frequently suffered harassment, intimidation, and violence. Assuming that they could afford a lawyer, black defendants found it difficult to find defense counsel willing to challenge exclusionary practices, and when they did, judges proved unwilling to enforce *Strauder* and *Neal*.

Some states employed the "key man" system of jury selection, in which prominent members of the community submitted names of prospective jurors, invariably white, to county jury commissioners. Louisiana exempted "all daily wage earners," which included most working-class blacks, from grand jury service. As a result, according to one legal historian, "For the first three decades of the twentieth century, essentially no blacks sat on southern juries" (Klarman, p. 40).

Lynchings and "Legal Lynchings." Another aspect of postbellum social control that continued into the twentieth century was lynching. Before 1900 lynching had been a broad phenomenon, found in the West as well as in the South, and as likely to victimize whites as blacks. After 1900 lynching became almost entirely a southern phenomenon, and the lynching of whites nearly disappeared. The pace of this racial and regional concentration was dramatic. Arthur F. Raper's *Tragedy of Lynching*, a study of the history of lynching published in 1933, found that in 1899, 46 percent of reported lynching victims were white; five years later, less than 5 percent were white. The black victims of lynching were usually accused of murdering or, less frequently, raping a white person, and the public spectacle of lynchings, often accompanied by the torture and mutilation of the victim, clearly conveyed the price of transgressing racial boundaries.

No state officially permitted lynching, but authorities did little to deter or punish the incidents. In 1933 James Chadbourn, a white southern-born law professor, estimated that less than 1 percent of all lynchings committed since 1900 resulted in a conviction. The failure of police to arrest, prosecutors to charge, and judges and juries to convict those responsible for lynching demonstrates how inaction by the state could be as harmful as selectively targeting blacks for prosecution.

The incidence of reported lynching declined dramatically after 1920. This occurred for several reasons, including increased national scrutiny of Jim Crow practices, vigorous resistance by armed African Americans, the stabilization of race relations, and growing moral repugnance against the practice among white southerners themselves. A prolonged campaign by the NAACP, the Association of Southern Women for the Prevention of Lynching, and other civil rights organizations to enact a federal antilynching bill, even though the campaign failed in its stated goal, drew widespread attention to and criticism of the phenomenon. Ultimately legislators, prosecutors, and judges promoted the criminal justice system as a more efficient and legitimate means to accomplish the goals of mob rule. During the 1920s some southern states, including Alabama, Virginia, and Kentucky, passed antilynching laws and speedy trial statutes that met the demands both of reformers and of conservatives who promoted modern law enforcement as the most effective method of preserving white supremacy within the rule of law.

For African Americans accused of crimes, the difference was barely perceptible. After all, in the eyes of the white establishment the purpose of this new regime was simply to reduce the prevalence of lynching, not to improve the quality of justice for black defendants. Critics accused local governments of replacing mob violence with "legal lynchings," in which black defendants were swiftly tried, convicted, and sentenced to death by all-white juries in kangaroo courts without the benefit of counsel or other due-process protections. Mobs still surrounded courthouses to remind jurors of their racial obligations, ready to terrorize defendants who were lucky enough to be acquitted.

The cause célèbre of this phenomenon was the Scottsboro case beginning in Alabama in 1931, in which nine black youths were convicted for the rape of two white women and all but the youngest one were sentenced to die. To most observers, introduced to the case by an intensive publicity campaign by the Communist-affiliated International Labor Defense, Scottsboro bore all of the hallmarks of a classic "legal lynching." Fundamental due-process protections were ignored, and blacks were systematically excluded from the jury pool. A mob atmosphere surrounded the trials. Even though the convictions were overturned several times on appeal, and one of the alleged victims recanted her testimony, local juries continued to convict the defendants on retrial. Over the next three decades similar "little Scottsboros" across the South seemed to confirm the region's propensity for this peculiar brand of justice.

The prevalence of the stereotypical "legal lynching" is probably exaggerated in the popular imagination. Depending on the circumstances, not all black defendants were regarded as equally dangerous, nor were all white victims deemed equally deserving of the full measure of the law's protection. In Virginia, for example, of 271 African Americans charged with raping a white woman between 1900 and 1960, fifty (18 percent) were executed, forty-eight (18 percent) received the maximum prison sentence, eighty-one (30 percent) received sentences of between five years and the maximum, fifty-two (19 percent) were sentenced to five years or less, and thirty-five (13 percent) were acquitted or had the charges dismissed. Nevertheless, enough examples of atrocious treatment drew scrutiny from the press, appellate courts, and civil rights organizations to demonstrate that the administration of justice to blacks in the South was far from perfect.

The Rights of Black Defendants. As cases such as Scottsboro demonstrated, just because the laws on the books were formally color-blind did not mean that justice was meted out equally. Criminal laws were selectively enforced based on the identities of the perpetrators and victims. Serious assaults among blacks were dismissed as "normal" behavior for their kind, whereas petty theft from a white victim by a black person might result in a lengthy prison sentence. It was considered pointless to prosecute blacks for morals violations, such as bigamy, unless a white woman's virtue was brought into question. These choices muted the faith that African Americans could place in the legal process and—at least indirectly—encouraged black criminals to victimize their own communities.

Black criminal defendants frequently encountered lax procedural and evidentiary standards. Coerced confessions were routinely admitted. Black defense attorneys were rare in the South, and white attorneys were either unavailable to black clients or unwilling to challenge the practices of Jim Crow courtrooms by requesting a change of venue, for instance, or by subpoenaing witnesses for the defense.

In an effort to stave off lynch mobs, the right to speedy trial assumed farcical proportions. In Mississippi during the first three decades of the twentieth century, for example, contested trials—that is, those in which the accused asserted his innocence—typically lasted less than six hours, including the time for jury selection and deliberation. Men on trial for murder and rape who managed to avoid the death penalty were reluctant to appeal their verdicts, even if the evidence of innocence or due-process violation was strong, because they were afraid that they would receive a harsher sentence on retrial. Appeals of state court rulings to the federal judiciary were rare; when they occurred, federal judges usually affirmed the state courts' rulings, reflecting a commitment to both formalism—refusing to recognize discriminatory practices unless they were explicitly authorized by legislation—and federalism, holding that the Constitution endowed state courts with the authority and obligation to monitor the practices of local criminal justice systems.

Coerced Confession. Police arrested and beat W. D. Lyons (*center*) until he confessed to killing a couple and their child in Hugo, Oklahoma, in 1941, but the murders had been committed by a convict on temporary leave from a state prison. The jury found Lyons guilty but imposed a life sentence instead of the death penalty. Lyons's defense attorney, Thurgood Marshall, who had been sent to Oklahoma to represent him by the NAACP, took the case to the Supreme Court, where the conviction was upheld. The men surrounding Lyons are the police and attorneys who made the case against him. Prints and Photographs Division, Library of Congress

Before 1920 the U.S. Supreme Court had overturned state court convictions only four times, all of them cases involving racial discrimination in jury selection. Over the next two decades, however, the Court revolutionized constitutional criminal procedure in a series of cases, all involving southern black defendants, that invalidated fundamental practices of southern law enforcement. In *Moore v. Dempsey* (1923) the Court held for the first time that mob-dominated criminal proceedings violated the due process clause of the Fourteenth Amendment and that, upon petition for a writ of habeas corpus, federal courts were obligated to release state court defendants who could prove that mob action influenced their convictions.

Two decisions arose from the Scottsboro proceedings. In *Powell v. Alabama* (1932) the Court held that the due process clause required states to appoint counsel for indigent defendants accused of capital crimes and that fair-trial standards required a reasonable time for attorneys to prepare their case. In *Norris v. Alabama* (1935) the Court reversed the convictions on the grounds that African Americans had been systematically excluded from the grand jury and the trial jury. *Norris* reinvigorated earlier rulings because it averred that federal courts were independently to assess whether discrimination had occurred, rather than defer to state court findings, and that courts could infer discrimination from long patterns of absence of blacks from jury service, even without proof of intentional exclusion.

The Court also tackled the problem of coerced confessions. In 1934 three black Mississippi farm hands were arrested for murdering a white farmer and convicted on the basis of confessions that had been obtained by whipping the defendants with metal-tipped straps. One of the men had been repeatedly hanged from a tree limb, leaving a mark on his neck that remained during his trial. Under cross-examination a deputy sheriff admitted that he had beaten one of the suspects, but "not too much for a Negro." In *Brown v. Mississippi* (1936) a unanimous Supreme Court held that physical coercion of testimony amounted to torture that violated due process. Four years later the Court expanded *Brown* to prohibit confessions obtained while holding suspects incommunicado, depriving them of sleep, and interrogating them at length for more than a week, even in the absence of more active physical torture.

Decisions such as these revolutionized constitutional law, establishing that state criminal proceedings were now subject to federal judicial review. Given the flagrant abuses of process revealed by these cases, as well as the likely innocence of the defendants, the Court had little choice but to depart from its long-standing reluctance to interfere with the local administration of justice. This doctrinal revolution did not necessarily translate into improved justice for blacks, however. Despite winning their appeals and avoiding the electric chair, five of the Scottsboro Boys and all of the defendants in *Brown v. Mississippi* served prison sentences. Most black defendants did not have access to attorneys who would press their constitutional rights, and appeals were expensive and risky. As the Court continued to hear cases involving jury exclusion and coerced confessions, it became clear that state courts were allowing police and prosecutors to circumvent these new constitutional rules, especially in the Lower South and in rural, presumably less professionalized, jurisdictions.

Policing Urban America. The racial caste system of the South, accompanied by the need for workers in northern industries, particularly during World War I, generated what is often called the Great Migration of blacks to northern and midwestern cities. Between 1890 and 1920 more than a million African Americans left the South, seeking a better life. By 1960 the typical African American experience was in the urban North, not the rural South, and the intersection of race and criminal justice could no longer be considered a distinctly southern phenomenon.

Although conditions were generally better in the North than in the South, blacks still encountered discrimination, residential segregation, and racial violence. Between 1917 and 1921 dozens of race riots erupted in cities including East Saint Louis, Illinois; Tulsa, Oklahoma; and Omaha, Nebraska. More than twenty riots occurred in the summer of 1919 alone. The worst incident, in Chicago, had to be quelled by the state militia and left thirty-eight people dead (twenty-three of them black), five hundred injured, and more than a thousand homeless. A study by the Chicago Commission on Race Relations conducted in the wake of the riots placed much of the blame on the police department, both for its inaction in allowing whites to attack African Americans and for its discriminatory enforcement of the law. Even though most of the violence could be attributed to whites, the commission noted, two-thirds of those arrested during the riots were black.

Though the spate of rioting subsided, tensions between police and African Americans persisted. Black citizens' complaints of mistreatment by police grew louder, especially in large cities such as New York, Miami, and Washington, D.C. These complaints were not limited to the problem of coerced confessions or so-called third-degree tactics, but encompassed broad patterns of violence, intimidation, and indignity that African Americans routinely experienced at the hands of law enforcement. Police harassment was not the dirty secret of interrogation chambers; it was an overt threat that guided the conduct of blacks' everyday lives, from racial slurs and rude treatment from police officers to lethal encounters. Gunnar Myrdal in his monumental study of American race relations, *An American Dilemma* (1944), asserted that with the decline of mob violence, police brutality had become the primary mechanism for asserting white supremacy. In 1947 the President's Committee on Civil Rights identified police brutality as a threat to the safety and security of African Americans on a par with lynching.

During the 1930s and 1940s civil rights attorneys in the Department of Justice and the NAACP received complaints of police brutality from across the country. The NAACP received far more appeals for assistance than it could answer, but it achieved limited victories before departmental disciplinary boards and in civil lawsuits against police officers and departments, though damage awards were usually small and rarely paid. The Civil Rights Section of the Justice Department brought federal prosecutions against law enforcement officers who had harassed blacks, Jehovah's Witnesses, and other minorities.

In *Screws v. United States* (1945), however, the U.S. Supreme Court severely restricted the circumstances in which federal civil rights actions could be brought in police brutality cases. The court overturned the conviction of a Georgia sheriff who had beaten a black suspect to death with a heavy iron bar during an interrogation because the government had not proved that the sheriff specifically intended to deprive the victim of his constitutional rights, as required by the civil rights act. The appropriate remedy was to prosecute the sheriff for homicide in state court. Even when the Justice Department prosecuted cases that met this restrictive standard, it usually encountered juries that were reluctant to convict police officers. Sheriff Screws himself was acquitted in his retrial and was later elected a state legislator.

Urban unrest reemerged in 1943 with destructive riots in Detroit, Harlem, and Los Angeles. In all three instances whites had instigated violence against racial minorities—blacks in Detroit and Harlem, Hispanics in the so-called zoot-suit riot in Los Angeles. Again police were blamed for inaction and discriminatory enforcement, but because the violence threatened vital defense industries, modest calls for changes in the relations between police and community were heeded. Several departments solicited sociologists and psychologists to design training programs to reduce racial prejudice among police officers.

Immediately after World War II, complaints about police brutality increased. Often these incidents involved black veterans who felt entitled to assert new freedoms after fighting in the cause of democracy. In February 1946, for example, Isaac Woodard, a black soldier who had just been honorably discharged from the U.S. Army, was ejected from a bus for mouthing off to the driver and was beaten unconscious by a South Carolina police chief, leaving Woodard permanently blind. Woodard subsequently engaged in a national speaking tour sponsored by the NAACP, becoming a symbol of the country's double standard of combating tyranny abroad while tolerating it at home. Most incidents were not as horrific but involved lesser incidents of intimidation "as a means of reestablishing the patterns of deference that had been upset by the war" (Fairclough, p. 110). Blacks who seemed to violate boundaries of class or status—by conspicuously driving a new car, for instance—were especially targeted.

Increasingly, reformers insisted that the recruitment of black police officers held the greatest promise for ensuring the impartial enforcement of the law. By 1950 every large city, even in the South, had hired black police officers in token numbers. Too often, however, racial customs were replicated within police organizations. Black officers were assigned to segregated units, were forbidden from wearing uniforms (a badge of authority), and were restricted to patrolling only black neighborhoods or relegated to undesirable assignments. Promotion to higher rank was difficult, and command positions were unthinkable.

Capital Punishment Sentencing. After World War II the most egregious violations of black defendants' procedural rights subsided. Professionalized police, prosecutors, and judges recognized that adherence to minimal due-process requirements immunized them from appellate review and granted them wide latitude to control crime and enforce order. As a result allegations of racial bias in the criminal justice system shifted from complaints about process to complaints about result, particularly racial inequality in sentencing. Nowhere was this more evident than in attacks on capital punishment.

From the 1940s onward, criminologists such as Harold Garfinkel, Thorsten Sellin, and Marvin Wolfgang identified pronounced racial disparities in capital punishment sentencing in the South. Between 1930 and 1972 slightly more than half of the persons legally executed in the United States were black, far outstripping their representation in the total population or in the population of those convicted of capital offenses. In southern states between 1930 and 1972 that figure was 72 percent. Ninety percent of the executions for rape—a penalty for rape used only in the South—involved black convicts. Six jurisdictions that authorized the death penalty for rape—Louisiana, Mississippi, Oklahoma, Virginia, West Virginia, and the District of Columbia—had never executed a white man for the offense. In Florida all but one of the thirty-four prisoners executed for rape between 1925 and 1957 were African American.

Before long, criminal defense lawyers began invoking figures like these on behalf of their clients. In 1950 attorneys for the so-called Martinsville Seven, convicted and sentenced to death in Virginia for the gang rape of a white woman, pioneered the use of statistical evidence to prove systematic discrimination against African Americans in capital cases. Evidence of their clients' guilt was strong, so lawyers from the Richmond, Virginia, branch of the NAACP used information culled from penitentiary records to challenge the death sentences of their clients, arguing that the application of the death penalty in Virginia violated the equal protection clause of the U.S. Constitution. Similar arguments soon found their way into state and federal courtrooms in Mississippi, Louisiana, Florida, and Arkansas.

In the early 1960s the NAACP Legal Defense and Educational Fund, Inc. (LDF) mounted a national campaign to abolish the death penalty for rape, focusing on the sentencing-disparity argument that had been developed by local black lawyers during the preceding decade. Despite these efforts, such equal protection arguments uniformly failed in court because judges were wary of statistical evidence, were unwilling to second-guess juries and legislatures, and were distressed that the only remedies for the disparities appeared to be abolishing the death penalty for rape or suspending executions of African Americans until a proportionate number of whites had been executed. When the U.S. Supreme Court finally declared the death penalty for rape unconstitutional in *Coker v. Georgia* (1977), its decision did not mention race or sentencing disparity at all.

In *McClesky v. Kemp* (1987) the Supreme Court directly addressed for the first time the issue of racial disparity in capital sentencing. LDF lawyers presented evidence drawn from an extensive multivariate analysis of homicide sentencing in Georgia conducted by David Baldus and his colleagues. Controlling for more than two hundred variables, the Baldus study found no significant link between capital sentencing and the race of the defendant, but it discovered that murderers of whites were 4.3 times as likely as murderers of nonwhites to be sentenced to death. The researchers also found that the race of the victim affected prosecutors' decisions to charge suspects with capital crimes.

Conceding merely that the study "indicates a discrepancy that appears to correlate with race," the Court held that the condemned person had to prove overt bias by the prosecutor or jury in deciding his particular case, an almost impossible standard to meet because of the nonpublic nature of charging decisions and jury deliberations. The Court betrayed skepticism about the role of statistical methods in legal analysis, emphasized the primacy of state legislatures in formulating death-penalty policy, and placed great faith in jurors' abilities to render unbiased decisions. After *McClesky*, efforts to end racial discrimination in capital sentencing shifted to the legislative arena, but elected representatives in Congress and the states proved as reluctant as judges to limit the discretionary powers of prosecutors and juries.

Rights, Rebellion, and Reaction in the 1960s. In the 1960s the civil rights movement that had been brewing for decades gained powerful momentum. Responding to an organized protest movement that brought attention to the abuses of Jim Crow, Congress and the Supreme Court mandated reforms intended to guarantee voting rights, equal employment opportunity, full access to public accommodations, and an end to de jure segregation. Civil rights activism also generated claims for fair treatment in the justice system and reform of institutions that adversely affected the poor: prisons, bail, and juvenile justice. In an address to Congress in 1966, President Lyndon B. Johnson insisted that "effective law enforcement and social justice must be pursued together, as the foundation of our efforts against crime" (quoted in Walker, *Popular Justice*, p. 195).

Demands for civil rights sparked a violent reaction among white supremacists, who terrorized African Americans and white civil rights workers with shootings, beatings, arson, and bombings. In June 1963, Medgar Evers, the Mississippi field secretary for the NAACP, was gunned down in his driveway. His accused killer, Byron De La Beckwith, was tried twice in state court for murder, but both trials ended in hung juries. (He was finally convicted by a predominantly black jury in 1994.) Once again a legitimate but cramped fealty to the principle of federalism left victims without protection from the federal government when local district attorneys failed to prosecute the assailants. Even when federal prosecutors managed to bring charges for civil rights violations, they found themselves stymied by juries who shared the defendants' segregationist views and refused to convict. It was considered a surprising victory when an all-white federal jury in Mississippi convicted seven of the fourteen Klansmen suspected of abducting, torturing, and murdering the black Mississippian James Chaney and two white Jewish civil rights volunteers from New York, Andrew Goodman and Michael Schwerner, during the 1964 Mississippi Freedom Summer.

Of course, civil rights demonstrators intentionally broke the law themselves, practicing civil disobedience to challenge the unjust laws that undergirded segregation and disfranchisement. Segregationists consequently equated rights activism with the decline of law and order, branding demonstrators as hoodlums, criticizing federal officials for coddling lawbreakers, and using police power to quash dissent. At the federal level the FBI director J. Edgar Hoover, convinced that the civil rights movement was aligned with Communist subversives, authorized the FBI illegally to wiretap Martin Luther King Jr. Such wiretapping escalated in 1966 when the FBI and state and local police forces targeted black radicals after the Black Panthers compared the police to an army of occupation and engaged the police in armed confrontations.

The use of the criminal justice system to quell civil rights activism called into question not only the legitimacy of Jim Crow laws but also the legal system itself. After all, black activists noted, the same legal authority that had made it a crime for their grandparents to marry, worship, or learn to read now branded them as criminals for asserting their constitutional rights. In 1966 James Baldwin asserted that "to respect the law in the context in which the Negro finds himself is simply to surrender ... self-respect," and two years later Eldridge Cleaver more sweepingly declared in *Soul on Ice* that all black inmates were by definition political prisoners (quoted in Kennedy, p. 399 n. 74) . This particular legal consciousness, perfectly comprehensible in the context of civil rights abuses, engendered a broader distrust of the rule of law among African Americans that persisted through the rest of the twentieth century.

Inside America's prisons, black militancy was fueled by the Nation of Islam, or black Muslims, who found ready converts in the growing minority prison population. Black Muslims were vocal about the discrimination they felt at the hands of predominantly white guards drawn from the rural populations where most prisons were located. Initially focused on issues of religious freedom, they ultimately developed a broad critique of modern penology and prison management that spawned the successful prisoners' rights litigation of the 1970s.

During this period economic and demographic transformations contributed to an increase in urban crime, a development that disproportionately affected African Americans. Contrasting markedly with the general prosperity of the postwar period, economic opportunities in urban areas, particularly entry-level positions, declined as white residents moved to the suburbs and factory jobs disappeared. Consequently, the unemployment rate of young blacks was double that of young whites at the same time that the first cohorts of baby-boom males began to age into the crime-prone years of fourteen to twenty-two years old. A number of factors peculiar to aging cities—including rampant poverty, the prevalence of illicit drugs, inadequate education and health care, high rates of teenage pregnancy, and federal housing policies that replaced established neighborhoods with high-rise urban renewal projects—fostered the marginalization of urban blacks and bred habits of behavior that made social integration difficult.

From 1964 to 1968 a wave of riots plagued American cities, including New York, Philadelphia, Newark, Detroit, Cleveland, San Francisco, and the Watts community of Los Angeles. In 1967 alone, rioting in fifty-six cities caused eighty-four deaths, thirty-four hundred injuries, and hundreds of millions of dollars of property damage. In Wilmington, Delaware, national guardsmen patrolled the city for ten months after rioting erupted in the wake of Martin Luther King's assassination. The Kerner Commission, appointed by President Lyndon Johnson to investigate the causes and suggest ways to prevent urban disorder, blamed toxic relationships between police and inner-city residents as the primary cause of the riots. Most of the disturbances had been sparked by police encounters with black suspects, in settings such as traffic stops, raids, or fatal shootings.

Complaints about police brutality and use of lethal force haunted urban police departments during the 1960s, although it is difficult to ascertain whether that reflects a true resurgence or a raised awareness of a vexing social problem. What is most striking is that the complaints typically centered not on extreme actions by rogue officers but on the routine performance of officers acting as they had been trained. The aggressive crime-prevention tactics and exercise of street-level discretion that were part of the so-called new police professionalism exacerbated the resentment of African Americans whose communities were patrolled by predominantly white police forces.

In the wake of the urban riots, few white Americans questioned the legitimacy of using overwhelming force to protect persons or property. Training in race relations had become routine, at least in the largest departments, but officers still possessed virtually unbridled discretion to arrest or use physical or deadly force. Data on police shootings showed that seven blacks were killed by police for every white who was killed. Between 1967 and 1972 black students were shot to death by police on the campuses of four historically black colleges. During the 1970s police departments developed new rules that authorized officers to fire their weapons only in the defense of life, producing a marked decline in fatal shootings by police and correlating with a decline in the number of officers killed in the line of duty. By the 1990s the majority of police forces had established citizen or external boards to review allegations of brutality or excessive force.

One reaction to the Kerner Commission's findings was the increase of the representation of minorities in criminal justice professions, especially police departments. In 1972, Title VII of the Civil Rights Act of 1964 was amended to prohibit employment discrimination by state and local governments. Black officers took advantage of this legislation to sue their employers, and the resulting consent decrees established affirmative action plans for recruitment and promotion that dramatically boosted the numbers of minority police officers. From 1960 to 1990 the percentage of sworn officers nationally who were African American grew from 3.6 to 10.2; the share of other minorities, especially Hispanics, also increased. In 1990, 130 American cities had black police chiefs. In 1992 whites constituted less than half of the police forces in Detroit, Miami, and Washington, D.C.

The War on Drugs. In October 1982, in partial fulfillment of his campaign promise to use federal resources to target violent street crime, President Ronald Reagan announced his administration's "war on drugs." Congress passed several mandatory minimum laws for drug possession and trafficking, culminating in the Anti–Drug Abuse Act of 1986, and appropriated millions of dollars to agencies charged with criminal prosecution of drug offenses, such as the Drug Enforcement Administration and the Customs Service, while cutting the budgets of treatment and prevention programs. State sanctions became more punitive as well; in 1978, for example, Michigan enacted a law mandating life imprisonment without parole for possession of 650 grams or more of cocaine. The effect of these laws fell disproportionately on minorities. In 1990 a study by the Sentencing Project, a liberal reform group, revealed that although African Americans constituted 13 percent of drug users in the United States (as measured by reliable social surveys), they accounted for 35 percent of drug arrests, 55 percent of drug convictions, and 74 percent of prison sentences for drug offenses. Much of this was attributable to policy decisions by police departments to police aggressively minority communities, where they assumed drug activity was heaviest.

One of the most dramatic examples of sentencing disparity, frequently cited by critics of the war on drugs, is the disparity in sentencing for different forms of cocaine. In 1986 Congress reacted both to the death of the college basketball star Len Bias of a cocaine overdose and also to a perceived epidemic in crack-cocaine abuse by passing the Anti–Drug Abuse Act. African American legislators, especially Representative Charles Rangel, a Democrat from New York, were among the bill's most vocal champions. The statute authorized penalties differentiated between crack and powder at a 100:1 ratio based on weight. For example, a first offender convicted of selling 5 grams of crack cocaine and another one convicted of selling 500 grams of powder cocaine would both trigger the same mandatory prison sentence of five years. Supporters of the bill justified this difference on the grounds that crack cocaine was significantly more potent and addictive than powder cocaine and was more closely associated with gangs and other criminal activity. However, because blacks are more likely than whites to use crack, nearly 90 percent of those prosecuted for crack offenses are African American.

In 1996 the U.S. Sentencing Commission, finding that the relative dangers of crack cocaine had been overstated and that crack-cocaine sentences were the most significant factor contributing to racial disparity in federal sentencing, recommended narrowing the disparity to 2:1 by raising the amount of crack required to trigger the mandatory sentence; the Bill Clinton administration countered with a proposal to reduce the disparity to 10:1 by lowering the trigger amount for powder. Congress declined to enact either proposal.

The Beginning of the Twenty-first Century. By the 1980s the intersection of race and crime had become a defining trope of American politics and culture. Tom Wolfe in his best-selling novel *The Bonfire of the Vanities* (1987) depicted the criminal courts of New York City as riven by racial, ethnic, and class antagonisms, beholden to minority community activists steeped in a culture of victimhood, and burdened with processing an endless clientele of black, brown, and poor. In 1988 Republican strategists created an advertisement that criticized the Democratic presidential candidate Michael Dukakis, then governor of Massachusetts, for releasing Willie Horton, a convicted murderer who committed a rape and armed robbery while on furlough from prison. Horton was black, and the ad was widely interpreted as intending to depict Dukakis not only as "soft on crime" but also as someone who would not protect Americans from dangerous types.

Meanwhile, African Americans displayed widespread distrust in the fairness of the criminal justice system. Many blacks continued to support the cause of Tawana Brawley, a black teenager from Upstate New York who in 1987 accused six white men, including police officers, of brutally raping her, even after her story was revealed as unfounded. A 1990 *New York Times* poll concluded that one-quarter of black respondents believed that the government deliberately aided the distribution of drugs in poor neighborhoods as a means to harm the black population.

Two media-saturated events in the early 1990s encapsulated the racially polarized perceptions of the criminal justice system. In March 1991 a passerby videotaped four white Los Angeles police officers pulling a black driver from his car and beating him after a lengthy pursuit. Televised repeatedly on national and local news broadcasts, the tape showed the driver, Rodney King, prone on the ground while the police kicked him and beat him with their batons. The officers claimed that the use of force was necessary because King was high on PCP and was belligerently resisting arrest, but to most viewers who saw excerpts of the videotape it looked like a textbook case of police brutality. A year later when a jury containing no blacks acquitted the four officers of charges of use of

Police-Community Relations. A woman protests the killing of Amadou Diallo by the police, New York City, c. 1999. Photograph by Salimah Ali. © SALIMAH ALI

excessive force, deadly riots erupted in the heavily black neighborhoods of South Central Los Angeles.

By contrast, in October 1995 when a Los Angeles jury consisting of nine blacks, two Hispanics, and one white found O. J. Simpson not guilty of murdering his former wife and her companion, television networks replayed scenes of blacks cheering the acquittal. Most whites, convinced by the prosecutor's forensic and circumstantial evidence, were incredulous. Blacks were more likely to believe that the evidence had been fabricated and planted by the Los Angeles Police Department to frame Simpson. Polls taken at the time revealed the racial divide: 75 percent of white respondents expressed their belief that Simpson was guilty; an equal percentage of blacks believed that he was innocent.

Several other racially tinged issues received attention in the 1980s and 1990s. For a long time prosecutors had been evading rules against jury discrimination by using their peremptory challenges to exclude black jurors. Peremptory challenges allow counsel to strike a limited number of prospective jurors without showing cause. In *Batson v. Kentucky* (1986) the Supreme Court held that prosecutors could not exercise race-based peremptory challenges because they violated the defendant's right to a jury trial; six years later defense attorneys were held to the same standard. Statistics showing that 73 percent of the cars stopped and searched along Interstate 95 in Maryland were driven by African Americans revealed the extent of racial profiling, and the American Civil Liberties Union won lawsuits curbing the practice in Maryland, New Jersey, and Florida. Several states and the federal government passed legislation against hate crimes, which authorized enhanced penalties for crimes motivated by racial, ethnic, or gender animus.

The burden of the new mass-incarceration policies of the federal and state governments, which swelled the nation's total prison and jail population from 326,000 in 1972 to more than 2 million in 2003, fell particularly hard on African Americans. From 1980 to 1995 the number of blacks in prison tripled, and the percentage of prisoners who were black grew from 40 to 55. Most of this was because of mandatory drug sentences. In 1995 one in three African American males, or more than 2 million, were in jail or prison, on probation, or on parole—more than were attending college. It is estimated that 32 percent of black males born in 2001 will spend some portion of their lives behind bars.

[*See also American Dilemma, An*; Antilynching Campaign; Civil Disobedience; Civil Rights; Drugs; Kerner

Commission Report; Laws and Legislation; Lynching and Mob Violence; NAACP Legal Defense and Educational Fund; Peonage; Prisoners' Rights and Reform Movements; Racial Profiling; Riots and Rebellions; Rodney King Riots; Scottsboro Incident; Simpson, O. J., Trial of; Supreme Court; *and* Voting Rights.]

Bibliography

Baldus, David C., George Woodworth, and Charles A. Pulaski Jr. *Equal Justice and the Death Penalty: A Legal and Empirical Analysis*. Boston: Northeastern University Press, 1990.

Belknap, Michal R. *Federal Law and Southern Order: Racial Violence and Constitutional Conflict in the Post-"Brown" South*. Athens: University of Georgia Press, 1987. Especially useful in explaining how principles of federalism delayed the federal government's legal response to racial violence during the civil rights movement.

Carter, Dan T. *Scottsboro: A Tragedy of the American South*. Baton Rouge: Louisiana State University Press, 1969. The classic account of the Scottsboro case; effectively recounts the legal proceedings.

Cohen, William. "Negro Involuntary Servitude in the South, 1865–1940: A Preliminary Analysis." *Journal of Southern History* 42 (February 1976): 31–60. The seminal analysis of coerced labor practices in the South after Reconstruction.

Cole, David. *No Equal Justice: Race and Class in the American Criminal Justice System*. New York: New Press, 1999. An accessible example of the idea that the criminal justice system affirmatively depends on inequality.

Cortner, Richard C. *A "Scottsboro" Case in Mississippi: The Supreme Court and "Brown v. Mississippi."* Jackson: University of Mississippi Press, 1986.

Dorr, Lisa Lindquist. *White Women, Rape, and the Power of Race in Virginia, 1900–1960*. Chapel Hill: University of North Carolina Press, 2004. A compelling challenge to traditional interpretations of "legal lynchings," arguing that myriad racial, class, and gender assumptions affected the punishments meted out to blacks accused of rape.

Dulaney, W. Marvin. *Black Police in America*. Bloomington: University of Indiana Press, 1996.

Fairclough, Adam. *Race and Democracy: The Civil Rights Struggle in Louisiana, 1915–1972*. Athens: University of Georgia Press, 1995.

Kennedy, Randall. *Race, Crime, and the Law*. New York: Pantheon Books, 1997. A historically informed critique that argues that meaningful reform of the criminal justice system is thwarted both by liberals who deny that substantial progress has been made in eliminating racially discriminatory practices and by conservatives who deny that significant vestiges of racism, particularly in police surveillance and capital sentencing, remain.

Klarman, Michael J. *From Jim Crow to Civil Rights: The Supreme Court and the Struggle for Racial Equality*. New York and Oxford: Oxford University Press, 2004. In this magisterial analysis of civil rights litigation, Klarman argues that judicial review of cases involving southern black defendants revolutionized the constitutional doctrine of criminal procedure but had little effect on the actual administration of justice in the South.

Lichtenstein, Alex. *Twice the Work of Free Labor: The Political Economy of Convict Labor in the New South*. London and New York: Verso, 1996.

McMillen, Neil R. *Dark Journey: Black Mississippians in the Age of Jim Crow*. Urbana and Chicago: University of Illinois Press, 1989. A meticulously researched study of the African American experience under Jim Crow in the Deep South; see especially part 4.

Oshinsky, David M. *"Worse than Slavery": Parchman Farm and the Ordeal of Jim Crow Justice*. New York: Free Press, 1996.

Rise, Eric W. *The Martinsville Seven: Race, Rape, and Capital Punishment*. Charlottesville: University Press of Virginia, 1995.

Walker, Samuel. *Popular Justice: A History of American Criminal Justice*. 2d ed. New York and Oxford: Oxford University Press, 1998. Very good at relating issues of race and class to the development of the American criminal justice system.

Walker, Samuel, Cassia Spohn, and Miriam DeLone. *The Color of Justice: Race, Ethnicity, and Crime in America*. 3d ed. Belmont, Calif.: Wadsworth, 2004. An excellent synthesis of current research on race and criminal justice.

Wilbanks, William. *The Myth of a Racist Criminal Justice System*. Monterey, Calif.: Brooks/Cole, 1987. A controversial scholarly expression of the thesis that racial disparities in arrests, convictions, and incarceration do not prove systematic discrimination in the administration of justice.

Wright, George C. *Racial Violence in Kentucky, 1865–1940: Lynchings, Mob Rule, and "Legal Lynchings."* Baton Rouge: Louisiana State University Press, 1990.

—Eric W. Rise

CRISIS, THE: A RECORD OF THE DARKER RACES. *The Crisis: A Record of the Darker Races* was first published on 1 November 1910 as the official magazine of the National Association for the Advancement of Colored People (NAACP), which itself began in 1909. *The Crisis*'s founding editor W. E. B. Du Bois—the leading black intellectual in the United States, who had already published two classic works, *The Philadelphia Negro* in 1899 and *The Souls of Black Folk* in 1903—stated the magazine's purpose in an editorial in its first issue. *The Crisis* would, Du Bois wrote, "show the danger of race prejudice, particularly as manifested today toward colored people. It takes its name from the fact that the editors believe that this is a critical time in the history of the advancement of men." The world stood at a crossroads: it could either "make the world-old dream of human brotherhood approach realization," or else "bigotry and prejudice, emphasized race consciousness and force can repeat the awful history of the contact of nations and groups in the past"; *The Crisis* would encourage brotherhood. Du Bois continued that *The Crisis* would "first and foremost be a newspaper," reporting on events and movements that "bear on the great problem of inter-racial relations"; second, it would review literature dealing with racial questions and respond to opinions on race relations offered in other publications; and finally, in what soon proved to be a great understatement, "it will publish a few short articles." The editorial page "will stand for the right of men, irrespective of color or race, for the highest ideals of American democracy, and for reasonable but earnest and persistent attempts to gain these rights and realize these ideals."

National leaders in the movement for black and civil rights, both African Americans such as Du Bois, J. Max Barber—founding editor of the *Voice of the Negro* magazine in Atlanta who was forced to relocate to Chicago because of threats to his life—the author James Weldon Johnson, and Dean Kelly Miller of Howard University and whites such as Oswald Garrison Villard, publisher of *The Nation*, and the civil rights activist and NAACP cofounder Mary White Ovington were among *The Crisis*'s founders. In a 1914 article Ovington claimed that she inspired the magazine's name when she stated at a board meeting that she was moved more by the 1844 poem "The Present Crisis" by the abolitionist James Russell Lowell than by any other; the board recognized at once the appropriateness of the term.

Early Success. Headquartered at 20 Vesey Street in downtown Manhattan, *The Crisis* was a financial success, selling 16,000 copies a year as early as 1912 and reaching a circulation of 100,000 by 1919, more than either *The Nation* or *The New Republic*, the nation's longest-circulating and most popular left-of-center magazines. From the first, Du Bois published special issues: one a year was devoted to education, and another to children. Every issue contained at least a page of poetry by an African American author. But *The Crisis* gave special attention to race riots and lynchings, of which more than six hundred were reported in the 1910s. From the time that he joined the NAACP in 1918, the NAACP sent Walter White—an African American who had blond hair and blue eyes and sometimes passed as white—to do research in the South and to visit the sites of lynchings and race riots, where he obtained photographs and firsthand accounts that he published in *The Crisis* in articles containing graphic if not gruesome descriptions of what Du Bois termed, in an editorial, "the lynching industry."

The Crisis also recruited some of the most important authors and intellectuals in the United States. The quality of the articles, the importance of the topics, and Du Bois's uncompromisingly radical editorials made *The Crisis* the magazine of choice for the American Left. In one article, Franz Boas, a Columbia professor and one of the founders of modern anthropology, criticized racial stereotypes from a scientific perspective. James Weldon Johnson

Newsroom of *The Crisis*. W. E. B. Du Bois and the publication staff of *The Crisis*, c. 1910s. PHOTOGRAPHS AND PRINTS DIVISION, SCHOMBURG CENTER FOR RESEARCH IN BLACK CULTURE, THE NEW YORK PUBLIC LIBRARY, ASTOR, LENOX AND TILDEN FOUNDATIONS

first published "Lift Ev'ry Voice and Sing" (1899)—called the "Negro National Anthem"—in its pages. The critic H. L. Mencken in 1929 warned of the complacency of the black middle class and another time encouraged black artists to satirize whites. The black sociologist E. Franklin Frazier spoke out against economic, educational, and housing discrimination as the causes of black poverty.

Despite these distinguished writers, Du Bois dominated the magazine and, especially, its editorials and political stance during his twenty-four years of service. He later praised the patience of the NAACP for allowing him such a free hand, but he claimed that without this free hand an editorial consensus would have been impossible to achieve, and the magazine would not have had a distinctive focus. In numerous powerful editorials Du Bois kept urging his fellow contributors not to cater to conservative opinion. He insisted that without upsetting people there was no way that a controversy could arise that would encourage them to work for change. *The Crisis*—that is, Du Bois—criticized black colleges, whose faculties were inferior and often chosen because of family connections. Meanwhile the black newspapers, Du Bois sarcastically noted, in addition to exhibiting appalling writing skills, failed to address social issues other than local marriages and murders. "Join the NATIONAL ASSOCIATION FOR THE ADVANCEMENT OF COLORED PEOPLE or be strangled to a slow and awful death by growing prejudice," Du Bois inveighed in an editorial in January 1914. The NAACP implicitly rebuked Du Bois's comments about black newspapers by unanimously praising the nation's black press at its 1914 convention.

But Du Bois had plenty of other causes: he supported women's rights, African nationhood and Pan-Africanism at the conclusion of World War I, racial intermarriage, and the rights of labor, and he pointed out the political and cultural achievements of "the darker races" from ancient Africa to the present day. A "Men of the Month" column—including some women—gave African Americans contemporary role models to inspire their struggle. Du Bois did not mince words, as in his April 1915 editorial "Immediate Program of the American Negro":

> The Negro must have power; the power of men, the right to do, to know, to feel and express that knowledge, action and spiritual gift. He must not simply be free from the political tyranny of white folk, he must have the right to vote and rule over the citizens, white and black, to the extent of his proven foresight and ability.

Harlem Renaissance. In the Roaring Twenties *The Crisis* partially conformed to the national mood, which had moved away from concern with foreign affairs and progressive reform in the 1910s to domestic and cultural concerns. Though not abandoning its political radicalism, *The Crisis* became equally noted for its literary contributions. In 1919 Jessie Redmon Fauset became the literary editor. She published and gave initial public exposure to many of the young writers of what became the Harlem Renaissance, including Arna Bontemps, Langston Hughes, Countée Cullen, Zora Neale Hurston, and Jean Toomer. Financial support for creative writers came as well through the form of literary prizes. Photographs and works of art by leading black artists—some as stunning covers for the magazine—appeared as well. When Fauset left *The Crisis* in 1926, however, this river of literary genius mostly dried up, and Du Bois's political concerns again became dominant. Yet this wealth of literary material was apparently not good for business: the magazine's circulation declined during the 1920s—perhaps partly because the price rose in 1919 from $1.00 to $1.50 per issue, and then because of the onset of the Great Depression—until it reached ten thousand by the early 1930s.

Du Bois's increasingly militant commitment to socialism and to what later would be called Black Power once the Great Depression began may have been yet another reason for the decline in circulation. He clashed with the other editorial board members, and in 1933 the NAACP made itself and *The Crisis* separate legal entities, partly to protect the association from any trouble caused by Du Bois's editorial decisions and partly so that the magazine could be a for-profit enterprise. Roy O. Wilkins, the NAACP's assistant executive secretary and a former editor of the *Kansas City (Mo.) Call*, ran the publishing entity, though Du Bois was still editor. Troubles continued when Du Bois began to write columns endorsing segregation. Believing that New Deal programs discriminated against African Americans—especially in the South, where local officials controlled who received jobs, relief, and subsidies for farms—Du Bois urged the creation of parallel black businesses, institutions, and political organizations. Only through independent actions and institutions, he believed, could emancipation and equality be achieved. The last straw came when southern congressmen gleefully publicized Du Bois's arguments. Du Bois resigned from the NAACP and from *The Crisis* in 1934.

Roy Wilkins took Du Bois's place, serving as editor in chief until 1949. Instead of radicalism and artistic innovation, *The Crisis* during Wilkins's tenure stressed progress within the system and scholarly materials. Unlike Du Bois, Wilkins supported Roosevelt and the New Deal and believed that persuasion of political officials, legal action, and education were the best means of obtaining equality and integration. Articles in *The Crisis* stressed the gains that blacks were in fact making—which became more pronounced in the 1940s—and were written by people such as the lawyer and future Supreme Court justice

Thurgood Marshall who were involved in practical legal and political struggles.

The most notable new feature added while Wilkins was editor was an annual bibliography compiled by Arthur Barnett Spingarn—begun in 1937 and published until Spingarn retired at the age of ninety in 1968—of scholarly books and articles on black studies. This was, and still is, an invaluable tool for researchers during the era before historical journals (now the Internet) compiled such materials. By the 1940s *The Crisis* had ceased to report news, given the proliferation of black newspapers, radio, and later television: instead, articles, editorials, and news of black publications, events, and so on have since filled far more space.

After the Civil Rights Era. The managing editor James W. Ivy replaced Wilkins in 1949 as editor in chief when Wilkins became the acting head of the NAACP, and Ivy retained this post until his retirement in 1966. Ivy was a multilingual scholar who gave *The Crisis* a greater global emphasis. He translated articles from and about the "darker races" overseas, in keeping with a general greater interest in world affairs during the postwar era. The general emphasis, however, was on the need for economic aid, better education, and freedom from political interference by the great powers in the affairs of developing nations. He was replaced by Henry L. Moon in 1966. Since 2007 Jabori Asim has been editor.

Issues of *The Crisis* since 2000 reflect the continuity in its policies from the 1960s. For instance, the January/February 2000 issue published the scholar Stanley Fish's argument that affirmative action has turned into reverse discrimination; another issue presented both sides of an argument over whether extreme racism is a form of mental illness. Special issues have featured environmental concerns, education (frequently), urban renewal, and elections. The NAACP's civil rights ratings for candidates are published, which amount to endorsements of those who score high. Articles on prominent blacks include Sarah Vaughan, Malcolm X, and Ella Baker. Articles frequently criticize U.S. foreign policy in Iraq and discrimination against women and homosexuals, although articles on homosexuality, which is controversial in the black community, have been rare.

From 1997 to 2003 the magazine tried to increase its appeal by changing its title to *The New Crisis: The Magazine of Opportunities and Ideas*, but then once again it became *The Crisis*. The magazine is published once every two months. Circulation rose to 59,000 by the end of World War II, to about 100,000 in the 1960s, to about 250,000 in the early twenty-first century. But circulation in the early twenty-first century was only about half the membership of the NAACP itself. That the magazine has retained a scholarly, high-brow approach and has not published many articles on the lives of film stars and athletes or articles taking extreme positions (except from a critical perspective) may be the reason that it has not flourished as other popular magazines have. Further, many more national outlets now exist for people who wish to discuss the issues of race and civil rights in a reasonable, restrained, and fair manner.

[*See also* Black Press; Journalism, Print and Broadcast; National Association for the Advancement of Colored People; *and biographical entries on figures mentioned in this article*.]

BIBLIOGRAPHY

Du Bois, W. E. B. *The Autobiography of W. E. B. Du Bois: A Soliloquy on Viewing My Life from the Last Decade of Its First Century*. New York: International Publishers, 1968.

Lewis, David Levering. "Du Bois and the Challenge of the Black Press." *The Crisis*, July 1997. http://www.thecrisismagazine.com/his_dlewis.htm.

Moon, Henry Lee. "History of *The Crisis*." *The Crisis*, November 1970. http://www.thecrisismagazine.com/his_hmoon.htm.

Wilkins, Roy, with Tom Mathews. *Standing Fast: The Autobiography of Roy Wilkins*. New York: Viking, 1982.

Wilson, Sondra Kathryn, ed. *The "Crisis" Reader: Stories, Poetry, and Essays from the N.A.A.C.P.'s "Crisis" Magazine*. New York: Modern Library, 1999.

—WILLIAM PENCAK

CROCKER, FRANKIE (b. 18 December 1937; d. 21 October 2000), radio DJ and programmer. A central figure in the mainstreaming of African American culture on radio, Crocker appealed to both black and white audiences without compromising any of his cultural identity. Born in Buffalo, New York, he got his start in radio at WUFO when he was studying pre-law at the University of Buffalo. During the 1960s he was the most popular DJ on the soul and rhythm and blues station WWRL in New York City. In 1969 Crocker moved to the top 40 New York station WMCA, becoming the first black member of that station's popular "Good Guys." In doing so Crocker broke new ground for African Americans in the number one radio market in the United States.

As music listeners migrated from AM to FM in the early 1970s, so did Crocker, moving to WBLS as DJ and program director. There Crocker created the urban contemporary format. Centered on African American music, the format featured a fairly wide playlist of rhythm and blues, soul, disco, and some white pop music. Crocker crafted a sound that attracted black and white listeners. WBLS was the number one station in New York on and off throughout the 1970s. He instituted the format when he programmed KUTE in Los Angeles in the late 1970s. His success on both coasts helped establish the urban contemporary format for decades and inspired black radio programmers across the nation.

Crocker had a unique on-air presence, combining sophisticated and cool sounds that connected directly with his listeners. This, with his beautiful baritone voice, influenced a generation of black radio announcers, including Tim Reid's character Venus Flytrap on television's *WKRP in Cincinnati*. Crocker was one of the legendary DJs who could paint pictures for his listeners. He sometimes hosted an "evening bath," complete with the sound of water and soothing and sexy music. Crocker's on-air patter included Jocko Henderson–influenced rhyme and good-natured braggadocio. His nicknames included "Chief Rocker" and "Hollywood," the latter gained during the 1970s disco era, when Crocker made high-profile nightclub appearances in his flamboyant clothes.

At the height of his 1970s radio popularity, Crocker appeared in five films, including *Cleopatra Jones* (1973), *Five on the Black Hand Side* (1973), and *Darktown Strutters* (1975). He was one of the first VJs on VH-1 in 1985 and hosted episodes of *Friday Night Videos*, NBC's early 1980s answer to MTV.

Crocker was a musical tastemaker. Among the records he is credited with breaking is "Soul Makossa" (1972) by Cameroon's Manu Dibango and Donna Summers's disco opus "Love to Love You, Baby" (1975). His music mix included creative picks, something unusual as commercial radio playlists tightened from the 1970s on. He always ended his show with King Pleasure's version of "Moody's Mood for Love" (1952). In the mid-1970s Crocker was convicted of charges of making false statements in a federal investigation of payola—that is, being paid to play the music of specific artists—a conviction that was later overturned. He left WBLS under that cloud but returned twice over the next two decades, helping to propel the station to ratings success.

[*See also* Music *and* Radio.]

Bibliography

Barlow, William. "Commercial and Noncommercial Radio." In *Split Image: African Americans in the Mass Media*, edited by Jannette L. Dates and William Barlow, pp. 189–264. Washington, D.C.: Howard University Press, 1993. An excellent overview of African American radio.

Doane, Rex. "Frankie Crocker and the Legends of Black Radio." *On the Media*, National Public Radio, 12 November 2000. http://www.onthemedia.org/yore/doane112300.html. Transcript of an NPR radio segment discussing of the impact of Crocker.

Jackson, Hal, with James Haskins. *The House That Jack Built*. New York: Amistad, 2001. Autobiography of the New York African American DJ and co-owner of Inner City Broadcasting.

—Gregory Adamo

CROCKETT, GEORGE (10 August 1909–7 September 1997), a leading African American attorney, judge, and congressman from Detroit, Michigan. Born and raised in Jacksonville, Florida, George Crockett graduated from Morehouse College and the University of Michigan Law School. Subsequently he started a law practice and later was a cofounder of the National Lawyers Guild, the nation's first racially integrated lawyers' organization which he then served as vice president. In 1939, Crockett became the first African American attorney in the United States Department of Labor and, later, in the Federal Employment Practices Commission. In 1943, he directed the United Auto Workers' Fair Practices Commission, which sought to prevent white workers from engaging in "hate" strikes designed to bar black workers from working in auto plants.

In 1946 in Detroit, he helped form the country's first integrated law firm (Goodman, Eden, Crockett and Robb) and served as a partner until 1966. In 1949, Crockett was sentenced to four months in federal prison for contempt while forcefully defending a member of the Communist Party who was being prosecuted under the Smith Act, in events that set the stage for the initiation of what came to be called the "Red Scare." During the anticommunist hysteria of this era, he represented the future Detroit mayor Coleman Young and also the Reverend Charles Hill before the 1952 House Un-American Activities Committee's hearings.

In 1964 Crockett recruited National Lawyers Guild lawyers to participate in "Freedom Summer," which pioneered in registering African American voters in the Deep South in the face of fierce opposition, and to this end he opened the Jackson, Mississippi, office of the guild. After the notorious arrest and disappearance of three civil rights workers (James Chaney, Andrew Goodman, and Michael Schwerner) in a nearby county known as Ku Klux Klan territory, Crockett dispatched guild attorneys to join him in searching for the young men, at risk of their own safety. The three civil rights workers were found murdered several days later.

In 1967 Crockett was elected a criminal court judge in Detroit, and in this role he was criticized sharply by the (mostly white) police force and much of the local press for enforcing the due process rights of predominantly black criminal defendants, that is, granting them bail, not imposing draconian sentences, and the like. Shortly after his election, Crockett was in the middle of a controversy resulting from the mass arrest of people in the African American New Bethel Baptist church. A police officer had been shot outside of the church, which led to officers storming the religious establishment. Crockett released those arrested, which included juveniles, and this ignited a firestorm of criticism.

In 1979, Crockett became acting corporation counsel for Detroit's mayor, Coleman Young. In 1980, he was elected as a Democratic congressman in a special election to fill the vacancy caused by the forced resignation of Congressman Charles C. Diggs Jr. In Congress, Crockett used his seat on the Foreign Affairs Committee to oppose United States relations with the apartheid government of South Africa, and he became known as an eloquent voice of opposition to this outlaw regime. Congressman Crockett has been memorialized with the naming of two schools after him.

BIBLIOGRAPHY

Crockett, George W., Jr. "A Black Judge Speaks" Judicature, 1970, Vol. 53 (9), pp 360–365.

Washington, Linn. *Black Judges on Justice*. New York: The New Press, 1994.

—JOSEPH WILSON

CROTHERS, SCATMAN (b. 23 May 1910; d. 22 November 1986), actor, singer, and musician. Born Benjamin Sherman Crothers in Terre Haute, Indiana, Crothers began his musical career as a teenage drummer in a local speakeasy and performed in music, film, and television venues until his death. He adopted the nickname "Scat Man" during a radio audition in 1932 as a nod to his abilities at scat singing, a form of vocal improvisation found in jazz, bop, and ragtime most often using syllables, rather than words, to sing improvised melodies similar to those found in instrumental solos. His nickname was later condensed to a single word, "Scatman," and stood as Crothers's professional identity for the rest of his extensive career.

Starting out in show business as a musician in the 1930s, Crothers toured with Montague's Kentucky Serenaders. His experiences of racism while touring the South ultimately led him to leave the group and relocate in Dayton, Ohio, where he performed as a solo musician and later formed his own band. In 1937 he met and married his lifelong partner, Helen Sullivan. Until 1945 Crothers continued as a regular on the Midwest music scene, occasionally playing with Dizzie Gillespie and Charlie Parker. After relocating to the West Coast, Crothers continued his music career with the Slim Gallard Trio and received acclaim as a songwriter for popular melodies like "Chattanooga Shoeshine Boy" (written with Phil Harris), "On the Sunny Side of the Street," and "Dead Man's Blues."

While Crothers's film career began in 1935 with an uncredited role opposite Billie Holliday in the Duke Ellington short *Symphony in Black*, his feature-length film debut was not until *Meet Me at the Fair* (1953). His filmography in the 1950s and 1960s includes *Between Heaven and Hell* (1956), *Three on a Couch* (1966), and *Hello Dolly!* (1969). Crothers won a Saturn Award for best supporting actor for his role as Dick Hallorann in the 1980 thriller *The Shining*, in which he appeared with his longtime friend Jack Nicholson. Crothers and Nicholson also paired in three earlier films, *The King of Marvin Gardens* (1972), *The Fortune* (1975), and *One Flew over the Cuckoo's Nest* (1975). Crothers's numerous other film credits include *The Great White Hope* (1970), *Silver Streak* (1976), *Bronco Billy* (1980), and *Twilight Zone: The Movie* (1983).

A familiar face on television as well, Crothers was the first African American actor on a regular television series (*The Dixie Showboat*, 1949). The actor appeared in supporting and cameo roles in countless series of the 1960s through the 1980s, such as *Hill Street Blues*, *The Paper Chase*, *Chico and the Man*, *Dragnet*, *The Love Boat*, and *Laverne and Shirley*. While often typecast in stereotypical African American roles, such as porters, attendants, shoe shiners, and garbagemen, Crothers also performed as the voice of the Autobot Jazz in the 1980s series *The Transformers* and appeared as himself on *The Colgate Comedy Hour*; *The Tonight Show, Starring Johnny Carson*; *The Fifth Annual Black Achievement Awards*; and *This Is Your Life: Scatman Crothers*. Crothers's lifetime of contributions to the television industry was honored with a star on the Hollywood Walk of Fame at 6712 Hollywood Boulevard.

In 1985 Crothers developed a malignant tumor in his left lung. The lung cancer spread to his esophagus, and in 1986 his condition was complicated by pneumonia. He died in Van Nuys, California, at the age of seventy-six.

[*See also* Actors and Actresses *and* Music.]

BIBLIOGRAPHY

Feather, Leonard, and Ira Gitler, eds. *The Biographical Encyclopedia of Jazz*. New York: Oxford University Press, 2007. A solid overview of Crothers's musical career; also provides good context for his career among his contemporaries.

Haskins, James, with Helen Crothers. *Scatman: An Authorized Biography of Scatman Crothers*. New York: William Morrow, 1991. Written in collaboration with Crothers's wife of forty-nine years.

—CYNTHIA J. MILLER

CROUCH, STANLEY. *See* Conservatism and Conservatives, Black.

CROWN HEIGHTS RIOT. In 1991, the flames of racial discord engulfed a Brooklyn neighborhood. On 19 August of that year, a station wagon driven by a Hasidic man, Yosef Lifsh, swerved onto a sidewalk killing a seven-year-old black child, Gavin Cato, and injuring his cousin Angela Cato. Three hours later, a Jewish scholar, Yankel

Rosenbaum, surrounded by a group of black youth, was robbed and stabbed four times. Following the attack, officers nabbed several suspects and brought them to the victim, who lay dying on the hood of a car. Rosenbaum was able to identify Lemrick Nelson Jr. as one of his attackers. Nelson was arrested and taken to the 71st precinct, where, according to the testimonies of detectives, he confessed to stabbing Rosenbaum.

Following the two deaths, the neighborhood of Crown Heights, Brooklyn, experienced four days of rioting, firebombings, and mass demonstrations. Vehicles were smashed, burned, and turned over on their roofs. Throughout the three days and four nights of rioting in August 1991, the Crown Heights community was divided along ethnic lines. Black community leaders were calling for justice on behalf of the Cato children, while leaders of the Jewish community called for the arrests of those involved in Rosenbaum's death. Rosenbaum would later die from his stab wounds. Jewish residents complained that the city failed to protect them and that the rioters were allowed to rampage unchecked. Black rioters, they argued, hurled rocks and bottles at Hasidic residents while Brooklyn police stood between the two groups holding the line but doing nothing to stem the attack.

Although people on both sides had been angered by the deaths of the Cato child and Yankel Rosenbaum, the riot was the result of ethnic tensions that had been brewing in Crown Heights for nearly twenty years. Constituting only 10 percent of the total Crown Heights population, the Jewish community there had been growing in numbers and strength and had become viewed as an economic and cultural threat to the dominant African and Caribbean American community. The hatred was so deep-seated that it was common to hear blacks shouting anti-Semitic taunts at Jews on the streets of the neighborhood. The response by the Hasidic community was relatively passive, but Crown Heights Jews tended to be openly critical of blacks as well. In fact, their criticisms often also smacked of bigotry.

Almost one year later, on 29 October 1992, a Brooklyn jury acquitted seventeen-year-old Lemrick Nelson Jr. on all counts for the murder of Yankel Rosenbaum, despite the fact that the police had found a bloody knife and three bloody dollar bills in one of his pockets. The Brooklyn neighborhood was again split into half following the Nelson decision. Following the acquittal, angry Hasidic Jews poured out of the courthouses and onto the streets and demonstrated on the steps of City Hall in protest of what they felt was an unjust ruling. Anna Deavere Smith's 1993 drama *Fires in the Mirror* is a complex exploration of the Crown Heights riots that presents the events from various points of view; it was adapted as a television movie for American Playhouse.

[*See also* Black-Jewish Relations *and* Riots and Rebellions.]

BIBLIOGRAPHY

Daughtry, Herbert D. *No Monopoly on Suffering: Blacks and Jews in Crown Heights (and Elsewhere)*. Trenton, N.J.: Africa World Press, 1997.

Gourevitch, Philip. "The Crown Heights Riot and Its Aftermath." *Commentary*, January 1993, pp. 29–34.

Horowitz, Craig. "Brooklyn Burning." *New York*, 31 March 2003. http://nymag.com/nymetro/news/anniversary/35th/n_8555/

Lerner, Michael, and Cornel West. *Jews and Blacks: Let the Healing Begin*. New York: G. P. Putnam's Sons, 1995.

—JESSE J. ESPARZA

CRUMMELL, ALEXANDER (b. 3 March 1819; d. 10 September 1898), pioneering scholar, religious thinker, and black nationalist leader. Alexander Crummell was born in 1819 in New York City to Boston Crummell, a former slave, and Charity Hicks Crummell, a freeborn black woman. Crummell's father was taken from Sierra Leone at age thirteen and sold into slavery in America. Crummell's parents were members of a group known as "Free Africans," and they were activists in the movement to abolish slavery, as well as in other social-uplift efforts for blacks. John Russwurm and Samuel Cornish, the editors of the first black newspaper, *Freedom's Journal* (1827), were associates of Boston Crummell and met regularly within the Crummell home. Alexander Crummell was educated at the African Free School—alumni of which included Henry Highland Garnet and Ira Aldridge—and at the Canal Street High School run by Peter Williams, a black clergyman and abolitionist who became a mentor to Crummell. After graduating, Crummell, along with Garnet and one other young black, attended the Noyes Academy in Hampshire. The school, however, was destroyed by a racist mob that ran off Crummell and his two friends. Subsequently Crummell enrolled in the Oneida Institute in Whitesboro, New York, from which he graduated in 1839.

While studying at Oneida, Crummell decided to become a priest in the Episcopal Church, and in 1839 he applied for admission to the General Theological Seminary in New York City but was denied on the basis of his race. Following this, Crummell petitioned the seminary's trustees and was again rejected. As a result Crummell studied privately with leading clergymen in Boston and in Providence, Rhode Island, and thus went on to receive holy orders, being ordained in 1842. After unsuccessfully attempting to establish a mission church among blacks in Providence, Crummell moved to Philadelphia.

In 1847 Crummell traveled to England to raise money for his congregation at the Church of the Messiah. While there, Crummell preached and spoke about the abolition of slavery in the United States and raised funds for his congregation. He also enrolled at Queens' College, Cambridge, and received his AB in theology in 1853.

That same year Crummell arrived in Liberia as a missionary of the Episcopal Church of the United States. There he hoped to establish a black Christian republic, and he actively enjoined black Americans to join him in the African nation. Crummell's years in Liberia were marked by contention and controversy, from both blacks and whites. Within Liberia opposition came from black American Liberians (mulattoes) who opposed "pure Negroes" (native Africans and Crummell) with respect to educational opportunities for natives and governance of the new nation. Outside Liberia, Crummell was involved in an ongoing series of disputes with the Episcopal Board of Trustees back in America.

Crummell also published his first collection of sermons and essays, *The Future of Africa* (1862), during his time in Liberia. In it he espoused his philosophy of black nationalism and self-determinism. Essays such as "Hope for Africa" and "The Negro Race Not under a Curse" speak of his sense of a divine calling for those of African heritage.

In 1873 Crummell returned to the United States. Once back on American soil he took on the task of running Saint Mary's Episcopal Mission. In 1882 Crummell published *The Greatness of Christ*, a collection of sermons more religious in scope than his earlier more political tracts. In *Jubilate: The Shades and Lights of a Fifty Years' Ministry* (1894) Crummell discusses his years in Liberia. He spent the last years of his life establishing the American Negro Academy, which opened in 1897, the first African American scholarly society in the United States. The academy was yet another attempt by Crummell to direct and influence black destiny, by formulating a strong intellectual leadership, one that would not pander to white influence—as Crummell believed leaders such as Booker T. Washington did.

Crummell was ever the black nationalist, devoted to the moral, intellectual, and spiritual development of people of African descent and leaving behind an impressive body of work. By the time of his death in 1898 in Point Pleasant, New Jersey, Crummell had become a revered statesman among the black intelligentsia, a sentiment articulated by W. E. B. Du Bois in a memorable essay about Crummell in Du Bois's *The Souls of Black Folk* (1903).

[*See also* American Negro Academy; Black Nationalism; Intellectuals; *and* Liberia.]

BIBLIOGRAPHY

Franklin, V. P. "Alexander Crummell: Defining Matters of Principle." In his *Living Our Stories, Telling Our Truths: Autobiography and the Making of African American Intellectual Tradition*, pp. 21–58. New York: Scribner, 1995. Discusses Crummell as a forerunner of black nationalist thought.

Moses, Jeremiah Wilson. *Alexander Crummell: A Study of Civilization and Discontent*. New York: Oxford University Press, 1989. A solid and thorough general discussion of Crummell's life and work.

—FRANK E. DOBSON JR.

CRUSE, HAROLD WRIGHT (b. 8 March 1916; d. 30 March 2005), writer, editor, educator, artist, and intellectual, best known as a social critic. Cruse defined the relationships between African Americans and American society. His 1967 book *The Crisis of the Negro Intellectual: A Historical Analysis of the Failure of Black Leadership* energized activists intellectually, both within the United States and in a few black nations, and thus contributed to the roots of the so-called black revolution.

Harold Wright Cruse was born in Petersburg, Virginia; his father was a railroad porter. During Cruse's childhood his father and his stepmother divorced, and he was taken to New York to live with his father's sister in Queens. Before graduating from high school, Cruse was introduced to what remained of the Harlem Renaissance, to the country's radicalism of the 1930s, and to a lecture given by the scholar W. E. B. Du Bois, all of which provoked his thinking about blacks in America. He became enthusiastic about the black arts and about the social concerns of black Americans. After graduating from high school, Cruse held a variety of jobs before completing a term of service in the U.S. Army during World War II. Wishing to complete college, Cruse attended the City College of New York, but he was sidetracked by many artistic projects and never received a degree. Eventually he joined the Communist Party in 1947, as did many black intellectuals who wanted the freedom from racism that the party offered them. He also wrote for the socialist *Daily Worker* until he quit the party in 1952.

Cruse was largely self-educated. There were times when he spent hours in the library absorbed in reading and learning. As a consequence he became an avid thinker. Although he continually professed that his first love was the theater, and for years he harbored the lingering hope of becoming a playwright, he eventually became more fascinated with the issues that he saw as resulting in the sabotaging of black political leadership. Accordingly Cruse developed a revolutionary mentality that was strengthened by his experiences as a black in America and by a 1960 visit to Cuba with a group of African American intellectuals that included the poet and playwright Leroi Jones (later Amiri Baraka) and other leaders of the Black Arts Movement.

When the civil rights movement waned, several African American groups began serious discussions about the direction of the "black crusade." Most of these discussions were conducted by groups of African Americans who were younger and more aggressive than their activist predecessors. They rejected integration and were tired of pandering to whites. *The Crisis of the Negro Intellectual* provided an analysis of African American cultural history that was used to help gauge the notion of Black Power. Cruse was against consolidation of the races. He suggested that African Americans should form their own political, economic, and cultural base. Almost immediately after its publication the book was considered a must-read, and Cruse was given credit for developing the intellectual underpinnings of and rendering a plan for what became the Black Power movement.

After the success of his first book, Cruse began to deliver a series of lectures throughout the country and at the University of Michigan, where he became a professor of African American studies in 1968. He taught there until his retirement in 1988.

In addition to *The Crisis of the Negro Intellectual*, Cruse wrote a collection of essays, *Rebellion or Revolution?* (1968); together with George Breitman and Clifton DeBerry, wrote *Marxism and the Negro Struggle: Articles* (1972); and wrote *Plural but Equal: A Critical Study of Blacks and Minorities and America's Plural Society*. In 2002 William Jelani Cobb edited *The Essential Harold Cruse: A Reader*.

[*See also* Black Arts Movement; Black Power Movement; Communism and African Americans; *and* Intellectuals.]

Bibliography

Cruse, Harold. *The Crisis of the Negro Intellectual: A Historic Analysis of the Failure of Black Leadership* (1967). New York: New York Review Books, 2005.

Watts, Jerry G., ed. *Harold Cruse's "The Crisis of the Negro Intellectual" Reconsidered*. New York: Routledge, 2004.

—Fred Lindsey

CRUZ, CELIA (b. 21 October 1925; d. 16 July 2003), Afro-Cuban musician. Cruz was born Úrsula Hilaria Celia Caridad Cruz Alfonso in a neighborhood known as Santos Suárez in Havana, Cuba. In her autobiography she describes Santos Suárez as the poorer section of a working-class neighborhood of different races and ethnicities. As to the date of her birth, she always said that anyone wishing to know her age would have to wait until the funeral home made the date public.

Early on, Cruz's father insisted that each of his children must have a profession, so she decided to become a schoolteacher. In 1947, however, while she was a student at Havana's teacher's college, one of her cousins signed her up to compete in an amateur singing contest at a local radio station, the first of many contests she won. Though she became well known at several radio stations owing to her singing prowess, she only entered contests that did not conflict with her schedule at school, and with her winnings she put herself through college. She remained committed to becoming a teacher until Marta Rainieri, her favorite teacher, told her to stop wasting her time trying to become a teacher and pursue a singing career. In her autobiography Cruz quotes her teacher as saying, "You'll be able to make in one day what it takes me one month to make" (Cruz, p. 38). From then on Cruz recorded in radio stations, and she made her first recording in 1948 in Venezuela.

In 1950 Cruz debuted live with the Sonora Matancera Orchestra, and by the mid-1950s she branched out and recorded her performances at concerts. Her big-screen debut was in 1955 in the Cuban film *A Spanish Woman in Havana*. During the rest of the decade she appeared in more movies and in television specials while she continued to tour the island with Sonora Matancera.

On 15 July 1960 Cruz boarded a plane to Mexico City, choosing self-imposed exile in the wake of the Cuban Revolution led by Fidel Castro in 1959. At her Mexico City debut on 22 July 1960 at La Terraza Cassino nightclub, the crowd was so large that the management placed tables and chairs on the sidewalk to accommodate the overflow crowd. The following year Cruz and her band traveled to the United States to perform at the Los Angeles Palladium.

During the 1960s Cruz and Tito Puente recorded eight albums, but they were not as successful as expected. In 1974 an album Cruz recorded with Johnny Pacheco attained enormous success. In 1990 Cruz and Ray Baretto won a Grammy Award for Best Tropical Latin Performance.

Cruz had sworn that she would never marry a musician because she thought they were too promiscuous. Nevertheless, in 1962 she married her lead trumpeter Pedro Knight, whom she had known for twelve years before they started dating. Eventually Knight became her manager, and their marriage lasted until Cruz's death.

On 5 December 2002 Cruz entered New York Presbyterian Hospital to have a cancerous tumor in her brain surgically removed. In July of the following year she died in her penthouse in Fort Lee, New Jersey. After her death her body was taken on a tour of U.S. cities. In 1990, while on a visit to Guantanamo Bay to sing to the Cuban refugees held there, Cruz had put her hand through the barbed wire border fence and collected Cuban soil that was later placed in her casket.

Cruz's album *Regalo del Alma* was released after her death and won a posthumous award as the best salsa release of the year. This final award was suggestive of the growing popularity of her music, which was characterized by pulsating rhythms and driving percussion emblematic of music derived from Africa. Moreover, her increased record sales at the end of her career were also indicative of the growth of the Spanish-speaking population in the United States that was deeply appreciative of her strong and distinctive voice crooning songs of love and devotion.

[*See also* Latinos and Black Latinos *and* Music.]

BIBLIOGRAPHY

Cruz, Celia, with Ana Cristina Reymundo. *Celia: My Life*. New York: Rayo, 2004.

Marceles, Eduardo. *Azúcar! The Biography of Celia Cruz*. New York: Reed, 2004.

Rodriguez-Duarte, Alexis. *Presenting Celia Cruz*. New York: Clarkson Potter, 2004.

—BEATRIZ RIVERA-BARNES

CULLEN, COUNTÉE (b. 30 May 1903; d. 9 January 1946), poet, scholar, teacher, editor, playwright, and novelist. Cullen was born Countée Leroy Porter most likely in Louisville, Kentucky. Exactly where he was born remains a mystery since there is no extant birth certificate and Cullen himself claimed two cities as his birthplace at different points in his life. On his application to New York University, he wrote that he was born in Louisville. Cullen's second wife, Ida Mae Roberson, and his friends Langston Hughes and Harold Jackman each said that Cullen also told them he was born there. After Cullen gained a reputation as one of the most respected writers of the Harlem Renaissance, however, he claimed on several occasions that he was born in New York City. Another mystery surrounding Cullen's early years is his relationship with Amanda Porter, who raised him from his infancy, moving with him to New York City when he was nine and caring for him until she died in October 1917. Most scholars believe she was his grandmother, although how the two were related has not been confirmed.

Cullen was taken in by Frederick Asbury Cullen, minister of the twenty-five-hundred-member Salem Methodist Episcopal Church in New York City, and his wife, Carolyn Belle Mitchell Cullen, after Porter's passing. The Reverend and Mrs. Cullen were impressed by the teenager's intelligence and good manners, and they set up a room for him in the church's fourteen-room residence. While no records show that he was ever officially adopted, Countée Leroy Porter changed his name to Countée Porter Cullen around 1921. (He dropped his middle name in 1925.) He and the Reverend Cullen grew very close, sharing a deep love for books and literature.

Cullen was an outstanding student at DeWitt Clinton High School, which he attended from 1918 to 1922. He was elected to the school's honor society Arista, he edited the school's newspaper the *Clinton News*, he helped edit

Countée Cullen. Signed photograph. PHOTOGRAPHS AND PRINTS DIVISION, SCHOMBURG CENTER FOR RESEARCH IN BLACK CULTURE, THE NEW YORK PUBLIC LIBRARY, ASTOR, LENOX AND TILDEN FOUNDATIONS

the school's literary magazine *Magpie*, and as a freshman he started writing poems. His poem "Song of the Poets," first published in *Magpie* in 1918, celebrates the great English poets he loved, such as Lord Byron, John Keats, and Alfred Tennyson, as well as Paul Laurence Dunbar, who at the time was by far the most popular African American poet in the country's history. Cullen's "I Have a Rendezvous with Life," written in response to Alan Seeger's poem "I Have a Rendezvous with Death," won first prize in a New York City poetry contest sponsored by the Empire Federation of Women's Clubs. After graduating from high school, Cullen accepted a State Regents Scholarship and enrolled in New York University. There, in addition to taking courses in Greek, Latin, French, English, math, philosophy, and the sciences, he wrote most of the poems that were in his first three published collections. He won second prize in the 1923 and 1924 Poetry Society of America's Witter Bynner undergraduate poetry contests and won first prize in 1925. In addition he placed poems in such influential journals as *Opportunity*, *The Crisis*, *American Mercury*, *Poetry*, *Scribner's*, *Harper's*, and *Vanity Fair*. Cullen's first book, *Color*, was released in

1925, the same year he graduated Phi Beta Kappa from New York University.

Color is divided into three sections and contains seventy-four poems, one-third of which (including "Incident," "Yet Do I Marvel," and "Heritage") address racial issues. Most of the poems in *Color* are written in the forms—particularly the sonnet and ballad forms—frequently used by the British Romantic poets he so greatly admired. Unlike other Harlem Renaissance poets, such as Hughes and later Sterling Brown, Cullen did not integrate African American dialect and the rhythms of jazz and the blues into his work. Doing so, Cullen believed, would put more emphasis on his identity as an African American than as a writer. As he wrote in the *Brooklyn Eagle* on 10 February 1924, he wanted to

> be POET and not NEGRO POET. . . . This is what has hindered the development of artists among us. Their one note has been the concern with their race. That is all very well, none of us can get away from it. I cannot at times. You will see it in my verse. The consciousness of this is too poignant at times. I cannot escape it. But what I mean is this: I shall not write of negro subjects for the purpose of propaganda. That is not what a poet is concerned with. Of course, when the emotion rising out of the fact that I am a negro is strong, I express it. But that is another matter.

Furthermore Cullen said elsewhere that he did not believe that such material fit within the realm of poetry. In a review published in the January 1926 issue of *Opportunity* magazine, Alain Locke called Cullen a "genius!" He went on to proclaim that *Color* "transcends all of the limiting qualifications that might be brought forward if it were merely a work of talent" (Locke, p. 14). Praised by white and black critics because of its display of technical mastery and emotional power, *Color* won the prestigious Harmon Foundation Literary Award.

Cullen earned more major literary awards than any other black writer of the 1920s. He received a Guggenheim Fellowship, *Poetry*'s John Reed Memorial Prize, and *The Crisis* magazine's Amy Spingarn Award. By the time he completed his master's degree in English and French at Harvard in 1926, he was one of the most popular African American writers. He took a job as an assistant editor for the Urban League's *Opportunity*, for which he wrote a column entitled "The Dark Tower." In his column Cullen critiqued the state of contemporary African American literature by way of book and theater reviews, commentaries, and critical essays, articulating what he saw as the need for African American artists to represent their race in all of its complexities without being confined to examining only race issues. During this time Cullen also prepared three book manuscripts for publication, *Caroling Dusk* (1927), an anthology of thirty-eight African American poets ranging from Dunbar in the late nineteenth century to the poets of the late 1920s, and two collections of poems, *Copper Sun* (1927) and *The Ballad of the Brown Girl* (1927). *Caroling Dusk*, which he edited, was hailed as an important contribution to African American letters, and the two volumes of poetry were generally well received. Neither poetry volume was seen, however, as an equal to *Color*. In a 1938 interview with *Magpie*, Cullen admitted that he too liked *Color* more than his other poetry collections. In the same interview he deemed "Heritage" his best poem.

To cap off what was perhaps the busiest time of his personal and professional lives, Cullen married Nina Yolande Du Bois, the only child of the NAACP founder W. E. B. Du Bois, on 9 April 1928. The elaborate ceremony—called by many the social event of the decade in Harlem—was conducted by the Reverend Cullen in Salem Methodist Church. Du Bois welcomed Cullen's interest in his daughter, whom Cullen had met in the summer of 1923. Despite Yolande being considered by some to be of modest intelligence, and despite her being quite open about her infatuation with the jazz bandleader Jimmie Lunceford, Cullen went through with the ceremony, even asking Hughes and Arna Bontemps to serve as ushers. Two months after the wedding, Cullen left for Paris on a Guggenheim Fellowship for creative writing with his father and Jackman. Yolande visited him in Paris in July, and during her visit the two agreed to end their marriage.

Cullen spent two very satisfying years in Paris. He studied at the Sorbonne, met frequently with a group of African American artists that included the sculptor Augusta Savage and the writer Eric Walrond (to whom Cullen had dedicated "Incident"), and completed his fourth poetry collection, *The Black Christ and Other Poems*, which was published in 1929 to lukewarm reviews. Most critics saw the book as uneven and lacking the focus and intensity of Cullen's earlier work. He admitted in a later interview to being often distracted while in France both by the disintegration of his marriage and by the many experiences available on the streets of Paris.

While Cullen worked hard to be seen as a poet, rather than a black poet, he also worked to present himself as a straight poet, rather than a homosexual or a bisexual one. While he did not publicly disclose his homosexuality, Cullen had several affairs with men in both Harlem and Paris. A close reading of his work, particularly poems such as "For a Poet," "Fruit of the Flower," "The Shroud of Color," "Spring Reminiscence," and "Tableau," reveals Cullen's use of figurative language to address some of the frustrations he felt about not being able to express or fully embrace that integral part of his identity. Cullen returned to the United States in 1930, when he officially filed for divorce from his wife and began work on his only novel,

One Way to Heaven. Published in 1932, the book tells the story of Sam Lucas, a con artist, and Mattie Johnson, a maid for a wealthy black family in Harlem. Despite no longer receiving unconditionally glowing reviews of his work, Cullen remained popular on the lecture and speaking circuits. For example, in 1931 he read from his work in seventeen states and in Canada. Cullen turned down positions at several colleges to remain in New York City. He worked at first as a substitute teacher, then beginning in 1934 as a French teacher at Frederick Douglass Junior High School, where he taught until his death. Among his many hundreds of students was the famous African American writer James Baldwin.

Cullen enjoyed teaching, although it slowed his writing productivity. He completed *The Medea and Some Poems*, published in 1935, which consisted of eighteen new poems and his translation of Euripides' play. His was the first translation of a major play by a twentieth-century African American writer. In 1940 he married Ida Mae Roberson. Cullen published two more books, *The Lost Zoo* (1940), a children's book subtitled *A Rhyme for the Young, but Not Too Young*, and *My Lives and How I Lost Them* (1942). Both books detail the adventures of his cat Christopher, whom Cullen claimed helped write the stories. In fact *My Lives and How I Lost Them* is credited to two authors: Christopher Cat and Countée Cullen.

At the time of his death from high blood pressure in 1946, Cullen was on the verge of completing, with Bontemps, the script for a Broadway musical, *St. Louis Woman*, based on Bontemps's novel *God Sends Sunday*. The show opened on 30 March 1946 and ran for four months. Although he had largely turned his attention away from poetry, Cullen had prepared the manuscript for *On These I Stand*, a collection of, in Cullen's opinion, his best poems. Published posthumously in 1947, the book helped secure Cullen's place among the most talented writers of the Harlem Renaissance.

[*See also* Harlem Renaissance *and* Literature.]

BIBLIOGRAPHY

Baker, Houston A., Jr. "A Many-Colored Coat of Dreams: The Poetry of Countee Cullen." In *Afro-American Poetics: Revisions of Harlem and the Black Aesthetic*, pp. 45–87. Madison: University of Wisconsin Press, 1988.

Bontemps, Arna, ed. *The Harlem Renaissance Remembered*. New York: Dodd, Mead, 1972.

Collier, Eugenia W. "I Do Not Marvel, Countee Cullen." In *Modern Black Poets*, edited by Donald B. Gibson, pp. 69–83. Englewood Cliffs, N.J.: Prentice-Hall, 1973.

Cullen, Countee. *On These I Stand: An Anthology of the Best Poems of Countee Cullen*. New York: Harper & Bros., 1947.

Davis, Arthur P. *From the Dark Tower: Afro-American Writers, 1900 to 1960*. Washington, D.C.: Howard University Press, 1974.

Early, Gerald, ed. *My Soul's High Song: The Collected Writings of Countée Cullen, Voice of the Harlem Renaissance*. New York: Doubleday, 1991.

Ferguson, Blanche E. *Countee Cullen and the Negro Renaissance*. New York: Dodd, Mead, 1966.

Locke, Alain. "*Color*: A Review." *Opportunity* 4 (January 1926): 14.

Lomax, Michael L. "Countee Cullen: From the Dark Tower." PhD diss., Emory University, 1984.

Perry, Margaret. *A Bio-Bibliography of Countée P. Cullen, 1903–1946*. Westport, Conn.: Greenwood, 1966.

Shucard, Alan R. *Countee Cullen*. Boston: Twayne, 1984.

—DANIEL DONAGHY